HOW TO STUDY EFFECTIVELY & EFFICIENTLY

In Your Room...
- Good lighting
- Study in a comfortable environment

At the Library...
- Study in groups
- Eliminate distractions

In Class...
- Be prepared to jot down key facts and concepts!
- Print out your professor's notes & PowerPoints!
- Bring textbook to class!

On the Go...
- Create your own flashcards
- Take notes on a PDA
- eBook online (to learn more visit www.coursesmart.com)

Created by
Diana Chen, New York University
Rosellen Flete, SUNY New Paltz
2007 Student Interns

TO HELP YOU STUDY, WE ASKED INSTRUCTORS, "WHICH OF THE FOLLOWING ASSIGNMENTS CONTRIBUTE TO THE STUDENTS' LETTER GRADE IN YOUR COURSE?"

Reading of text chapters	71%	680 responses
Research study analysis/mini-paper	52%	495 responses
Individual research paper or project	52%	500 responses
Self-assessments	27%	256 responses
Group projects	26%	245 responses
Other	25%	243 responses
Homework from the publisher's Web site or CD, or the homework management system	23%	216 responses

If you're always on the go like me, print or download your notes from the Online Learning Center and study wherever you go.
—Janicky

Flashcards are the best way for me to study. I write down the key terms, how the terminology is used, and I even include a real life example to help me remember!
—Veronica

What's up with the orange?
The orange captures Laura King's objective to present PSYCHOLOGY as an integrated field in which the whole is greater than the sum of the parts, but the parts are essential to the whole.

PSYCHOLOGY

THE SCIENCE OF

AN APPRECIATIVE VIEW

PSYCHOLOGY

THE SCIENCE OF

AN APPRECIATIVE VIEW

STUDY EDITION

Laura A. King

University of Missouri, Columbia

McGraw-Hill
Higher Education

Boston   Burr Ridge, IL   Dubuque, IA   New York   San Francisco   St. Louis
Bangkok   Bogotá   Caracas   Kuala Lumpur   Lisbon   London   Madrid   Mexico City
Milan   Montreal   New Delhi   Santiago   Seoul   Singapore   Sydney   Taipei   Toronto

Published by McGraw-Hill, an imprint of The McGraw-Hill Companies, Inc., 1221 Avenue of the Americas, New York, NY 10020. Copyright © 2009. All rights reserved. No part of this publication may be reproduced or distributed in any form or by any means, or stored in a database or retrieval system, without the prior written consent of The McGraw-Hill Companies, Inc., including, but not limited to, in any network or other electronic storage or transmission, or broadcast for distance learning.

This book is printed on acid-free paper.

1 2 3 4 5 6 7 8 9 0 DOW/DOW 0 9 8

ISBN: 978-0-07-353214-1
MHID: 0-07-353214-2

Editor in Chief: *Mike Ryan*
Publisher: *Beth Mejia*
Executive Editor: *Mike Sugarman*
Executive Marketing Manager: *James Headley*
Executive Market Development Manager: *Sheryl Adams*
Director of Development: *Dawn Groundwater*
Developmental Editor: *Cara Labell, Sylvia Mallory*
Supplements Editor: *Meghan Campbell*
Editorial Coordinator: *Jillian Allison*
Marketing Specialist: *Rebecca Saidlower*
Production Editor: *Christina Gimlin*
Manuscript Editor: *Jennifer Gordon*
Art Director: *Jeanne Schreiber*
Design Manager and Cover Designer: *Preston Thomas*
Interior Designer: *Pam Verros, Kim Menning*
Art Editor: *Robin Mouat*
Production Supervisor: *Tandra Jorgensen*
Illustrators: *John Waller, Judy Waller, and Arthur Mount*
Transparency inserts illustrators: *John and Judy Waller*
Student Interns: *Diana Chen, Rosellen Flete*
Composition: *10/12 Times Roman, Aptara York*
Printing: *45# Influence Gloss Plus, R. R. Donnelley and Sons/Willard, OH*

Cover: Front and back cover images: © Stockbyte/Getty Images

Credits: The credits section for this book begins on page C1 and is considered an extension of the copyright page.

Library of Congress Cataloging-in-Publication Data

King, Laura.
    The science of psychology : an appreciative view study edition / Laura King. — 1st ed.
        p. cm.
    "With study questions added throughout and at the end of the chapters"
    Includes bibliographical references and index.
    ISBN-13: 978-0-07-353214-1 (alk. paper)
    ISBN-10: 0-07-353214-2 (alk. paper)
    1. Psychology—Textbooks.   I. Title.
BF77.K53 2010
150—dc22

                        2008041747

The Internet addresses listed in the text were accurate at the time of publication. The inclusion of a Web site does not indicate an endorsement by the authors or McGraw-Hill, and McGraw-Hill does not guarantee the accuracy of the information presented at these sites.

www.mhhe.com

Laura A. King Laura King did her undergraduate work at Kenyon College, where, an English major, she declared a second major in psychology during the second semester of her junior year. She completed her A.B. in English with high honors and distinction and in psychology with distinction in 1986. Laura then did graduate work at Michigan State University and the University of California, Davis, receiving her Ph.D. in personality psychology in 1991.

Laura began her career at Southern Methodist University in Dallas, moving to the University of Missouri, Columbia, in 2001, where she is now a professor. In addition to seminars in the development of character, social psychology, and personality psychology, she has taught undergraduate lecture courses in introductory psychology, introduction to personality psychology, and social psychology. At SMU, she received six different teaching awards, including the "M" award for "sustained excellence" in 1999. At the University of Missouri, she received the Chancellor's Award for Outstanding Research and Creative Activity in 2004.

Her research, which has been funded by the National Institutes for Mental Health, has focused on a variety of topics relevant to the question of what it is that makes for a good life. She has studied goals, life stories, happiness, well-being, and meaning in life. In general, her work reflects an enduring interest in studying what is good and healthy in people. In 2001, her research accomplishments were recognized by a Templeton Prize in positive psychology. Laura's research (often in collaboration with undergraduate and graduate students) has been published in the *Journal of Personality and Social Psychology, Personality and Social Psychology Bulletin, Cognition and Emotion,* the *Journal of Personality,* and other publications. A new paper on the place of regrets in maturity is forthcoming in the *American Psychologist.*

Currently editor-in-chief of the *Journal of Research in Personality,* Laura has also served as associate editor of *Personality and Social Psychology Bulletin* and the *Journal of Personality and Social Psychology,* as well as on numerous grant panels. She has edited or co-edited special sections of the *Journal of Personality and the American Psychologist.* In "real life," Laura is an accomplished cook and enjoys listening to music (mostly jazz vocalists and singer-songwriters), gardening, and chasing Sam, her 3-year-old son.

To see a preview of *The Science of Psychology: An Appreciative View,* please go to **www.mhhe. com/kingpreview.**

For Sam

Brief Contents

Contents

CHAPTER 3

CHAPTER 4

CHAPTER 5

CHAPTER 10

CHAPTER 11

CHAPTER 14

CHAPTER 15

HEALTH PSYCHOLOGY 606

PREFACE

The Science of Psychology: *An Appreciative View*

I taught introductory psychology for the first time several years ago. About 2 months into the semester, I was confidently sailing through the fascinating worlds of research methods, biological foundations, and sensation and perception when a young woman approached me after class with a question: "Dr. King, when are we going to get to psychology?"

Startled, I had no idea what she meant. "We've been talking about psychology for the entire semester," I replied cheerily. Her face told me I might just as well have been speaking Greek.

"No," she responded, "I mean, when are we going to get to *psychology?* So far this has all just been *science!*" I could literally hear the italics in her voice. Like many people, she thought psychology meant clinical psychology or psychopathology. Together, we turned to her notebook, and sure enough, there it was in her notes for the very first lecture: "Psychology is the scientific study of human behavior, broadly defined." It was clear that, despite my best efforts, "psychology" to her meant, essentially, abnormal psychology. What did this mind-set mean for her ability to appreciate what psychology is really about: her behavior, her mind and body, her thoughts, feelings, and relationships—in short, her life? This dilemma has inspired my work in this book.

Watchology and Psychology

In the opening chapter, I invite students to think about creating a fictional science of "watchology." I ask them to imagine two watches that have had the unfortunate trauma of being left in the pocket of a pair of jeans as the jeans went through the laundry. One watch no longer tells time. The other has emerged from the event still ticking. Which watch, I ask readers, would you use to develop the new science of watchology? Clearly, the working watch would help them understand watches better than the broken one.

What does watchology have to do with psychology? Quite simply, in psychology as in watchology, it makes sense to start with what works: to gain a general understanding of human behavior and then to apply that knowledge to those who have emerged from life's experiences in dysfunction. As an instructor and now as a textbook author, my goal has been to demonstrate that the science of psychology as a broad field of human behavior and functioning is just as interesting, as a whole, as that segment of our field that is occupied with mental illness. Even when things are working, the science of psychology has important knowledge to share.

The Science of Psychology: An Appreciative View grew out of my initial intention to join John Santrock as a co-author on his successful introductory psychology textbook. Due to those roots, it should come as no surprise that this new, first-edition text carries on the foundations of John Santrock's work—a strong and current research foundation, breadth of coverage, and clear and accessible writing.

> "*In psychology as in watchology, it makes sense to start with what works: to gain a general understanding of human behavior and then to apply that knowledge to those who have emerged from life's experiences in dysfunction.*"

Appreciating Why Things Go Right

One of the challenges instructors face in focusing on function first is going against the grain of human nature. Research in psychology itself tells us that the negative captures our attention more readily than the positive. Indeed, that student who approached me after class might have felt some disbelief at the notion that psychology is really about her and her everyday life. After all, what is interesting about a person who is functioning well, who is going about life and navigating the big and little bumps in the road along the way? Could she (and the majority of people in the world) possibly be as interesting as this year's latest serial killer?

There is no question that bad news makes the headlines. We live in a challenging world. Global terrorism, global warming, global economic competition, and soaring global population growth are but a few of the myriad daunting "globals" confronting us in the twenty-first century. Close to home, in our daily lives, we juggle the demands of education, work, family, finances, and more. We strive and struggle to find balance and to sculpt a happy life.

Everyday problems and frustrations, however, need not be viewed as pathology or as exceptions to the rule in an otherwise "perfect" life. Rather, good times and bad times exist together in human life. Our journey through our time in the world offers a bounty of options for negotiating life's challenges. The science of psychology has much to offer in terms of helping us to understand the choices we make and the implications of these choices for our quality of life and that of people throughout the world.

But what is not inherently interesting about happiness, love, gratitude, altruism, and the experience of meaning in life? The science of psychology offers important clues about these positive aspects of human existence. As teaching psychologists, by exploring with our students the implications of psychological discoveries for people everywhere, we have an opportunity to instill in them an enduring interest in our field. Applying science to such topics does not devalue their mystery. Indeed, the more we know about these "goods" in life, the richer our understanding of them and the deeper our appreciation for human thriving. The appreciative view that I underscore in the title of this book is just that: seeing human behavior, broadly defined, with the curious, open, and enthusiastic eyes and mind of a scientist. So, rather than focusing on why things go wrong, *The Science of Psychology: An Appreciative View* focuses on why things go right.

What constitutes an "appreciative" science of general human function (not simply dysfunction)? How does a writer or an instructor emphasize a positive perspective and yet maintain student interest and motivation? What is left pedagogically after we set aside the serial killers and psychopaths who have become, at the very least, a reliable source of interest? I believe that the greatest secret of psychology is the sheer wonder and delight that psychologists take in understanding the most complex, fascinating, and, to be sure, at times troubling subject of our science: human beings. From the newborn who enters the world full of possibility to the aged retiree reflecting on life during the twilight years; from the firing of a single neuron in the brain to the complex biological and mental experience of a blue sky—the human experience fascinates us, just as stars intrigue the astronomer and the atom captivates the physicist. There is no need to cash in on our knowledge of the power of the negative over the positive to engage students if we admit that there is not a single thing about human beings that has not fascinated someone in our field.

This fascination is not an idiosyncrasy of psychologists. People are keenly interested in learning about themselves and relish the opportunity for self-discovery. How else can we explain the compulsion to take quizzes in magazines or online, or to consult one's horoscope or Chinese astrological sign? Introducing students to psychology is an opportunity to allow them to learn about themselves as a scientist would come to know them.

In bringing this grateful spirit to the book as a whole, I have sought to communicate the nature and breadth of psychology and its value as a science with an appreciative

Why do things go right?

perspective. My goal is to help students think like psychological scientists, which means asking questions about their own lives and experiences (both positive and negative). Throughout the text, I have tried to nurture students' curiosity through interesting and timely examples. I have also made an effort to reconnect psychology to people—particularly students—by focusing on what it all means for ordinary people and especially for their health and wellness.

Appreciating Psychology as an Integrated Whole

The exquisite image of an orange on the cover of this book elegantly captures my objective to present psychology as an integrated field in which the whole is greater than the sum of the parts but the parts are essential to the whole. The whole orange (or tangerine), with its many segments, is an analogy for the science of psychology. Each segment is important and contributes to making up the whole orange. Similarly, psychology is made up of many important segments or fields that make up the whole of psychology.

In support of this integrative approach, I have illustrated many areas where specialized subfields overlap and where research findings in one subfield support important studies and exciting discoveries in another. Students often have difficulty seeing the relationships among these various areas. They ask, how can the neurosciences have anything to do with social psychology? *The Science of Psychology: An Appreciative View* develops an understanding of such interconnections and an awareness of how one discovery can build on another. In these ways the text reveals to readers the potency of psychology in action.

By integrating topics, research approaches, and the findings of various subfields across chapters, the text sharpens readers' sense of the whole that is the powerful field of psychology. I have paid close attention to making concrete cross-chapter links to help students appreciate the connections among the various subfields. Both the chapter narrative and the feature called Intersection illuminate these connections. Intersections in particular showcase research that stands at the crossroads of two areas or that shows the influence of one area of psychology on another. For example, in the neuroscience section of Chapter 3 (Biological Foundations of Behavior), I present research on the neural correlates of happiness; in the cognitive section of Chapter 8 (Memory), I discuss links between sensation and memory by looking at studies on the influence of smell on remembering; and in Chapter 12 (Social Psychology), I use longitudinal developmental research on the relationship between self-esteem and aggression to highlight the usefulness of this work in helping us to make sense of the social psychology of aggression.

Appreciating Psychology's Role in Health and Wellness

By the beginning of the twenty-first century, growing numbers of psychologists were calling for a new emphasis on the scientific understanding of human strengths and capacities. Today, there is enough accumulated research and theory to make possible, and compelling, the integration of a positive psychological perspective in each chapter of this book, providing a more balanced view of the discipline. The integration of this new dimension richly accents the text's appreciative emphasis.

One of the central goals of positive psychology, and the one that I personally value most highly, is to develop awareness of the importance of psychology to people everywhere. *The Science of Psychology: An Appreciative View* illustrates the relevance of psychology to students by focusing on the implications of the material covered for their own health and wellness. Many of the different subfields of psychology have examined the importance of psychosocial variables to physical health and psychological well-being. Thus, I often use the topics of health and wellness throughout the text to answer the question, "Why does this matter to me and my psychological well-being and health?"

Indeed, in each chapter I have taken an appreciative view and woven health and wellness strands into the narrative fabric while keeping this material in appropriate balance with other contemporary perspectives, as well as traditional coverage. I have provided plentiful discussion and examples related to human strengths and capacities, health, and wellness to cultivate students' appreciation for the practical, applied nature of psychology and to help guide them through life. For example, Chapter 4 (Human Development) examines the key role of positive parenting in human development; Chapter 9 (Thinking, Intelligence, and Language) explores the benefits of creative-thinking ability for finding unconventional solutions to life's challenges; and Chapter 10 (Motivation and Emotion) looks at how gay men's and lesbians' acceptance of their sexual orientation is important in promoting their psychological well-being.

Beyond the text narrative, the following two features further magnify the focus on positive psychology, health, and wellness:

- **Experiencing Psychology chapter-opening stories:** Each chapter opens with a high-interest introduction spotlighting real people—the book's readers and others—and the very real hurdles and roadblocks life can impose. The situations and solutions described in these Experiencing Psychology vignettes illustrate the unique and constructive ways in which people deal with and triumph over some of life's continuous challenges. For example, Chapter 6's vignette profiles the experience of Terry Wallis, the survivor of a near-fatal truck accident, who emerged from a state of minimal consciousness after almost 20 years through a remarkable process of neural rewiring deep within his brain. Chapter 13's vignette looks at the success of two individuals, Moe Armstrong and Frederick Frese, in overcoming their schizophrenia to lead satisfying, productive lives.

- **Chapter-concluding ". . . and Health and Wellness" sections:** Each chapter closes with a major text section tying the chapter's main topic to the themes of health and wellness. These analyses highlight both influential recent research and practical, positive strategies for navigating life's challenges. For example, Chapter 3's closing discussion probes into research on the role of the biological foundations of human psychology in the body's stress response and outlines a technique by which readers can monitor their self-talk to deal positively with stressful life events. The concluding section of Chapter 6 looks at the pioneering work of Jon Kabat-Zinn on meditation in medical settings and provides a how-to on the application of research findings on meditation to daily life.

Appreciating Function to Understand Dysfunction

To help students appreciate that psychology as a whole is concerned more with function than dysfunction, I have placed chapters that focus on "normal" individuals ahead of chapters on abnormal psychology. Thus, the chapter on social psychology (12) precedes the chapters on psychological disorders (13) and therapies (14). In addition, I have placed the treatment of health psychology at the end of the book. As Chapter 15, it serves as a capstone discussion drawing together in one place the text's collective unifying themes.

Chapter 15 delves in depth into major topics that are specific to health psychology. Less central coverage of health topics is incorporated in chapters dedicated to other content areas (for example, I discuss the Type A behavior pattern in Chapter 11, Personality). Thus, Chapter 15 provides the scaffolding for making a compelling concluding argument for the appreciation of the important place of psychology in the lives of healthy, normal people.

Appreciating the Visual Power of Biological Art

Of all the material in the introductory psychology course, students struggle the most with biology. Many are surprised that they have to know some basics of human biology—the brain, the nervous system, the senses—in order to understand psychology. To help students meet this challenge head-on, I am proud to introduce "Touring the Brain and Nervous System" and "Touring the Senses": two transparency overlay inserts located, respectively, in Chapter 3, Biological Foundations of Behavior, and Chapter 5, Sensation and Perception. Developed with the help of introductory psychology instructors and neuroscientists, these transparency overlays offer an active and visually enhanced presentation of key biological structures and processes that are essential to student understanding of psychology. Each piece of art is accompanied by learning objectives and assessment questions, with answers at the end.

Appreciating Psychology "at Work": Online Chapter: Industrial and Organizational Psychology

The Online Chapter: Industrial and Organizational Psychology examines the role of psychology in the workplace, the environment where most of us spend (or will spend) the majority of our waking hours each week. I/O psychology presents a context where psychology can be shown to have important lessons for "just plain folks." For example, although most people on the job are likely to say they would rather be doing something else, there is considerable evidence that work is the prime setting for the experience of flow, an optimal state where the person loses track of time and self-consciousness and experiences being completely immersed and engaged in an activity. The inclusion of this chapter became essential for communicating the relevance of the workplace milieu to life satisfaction, sense of meaning, financial security, and friendships and for introducing students to the full range of topics psychologists study.

Appreciating a Contemporary Perspective

The text's attention to function before dysfunction, up-to-date coverage, and broad scope reflect the field of psychology *today*. These qualities not only provide students with a survey of the field as state of the art but also underscore psychology's vital and ongoing role in advancing knowledge about ourselves and others and our interactions in the world. Psychology is a vigorous young science, and knowledge changes quickly. In the main text of each chapter, I have interwoven the most current research with classic findings to give students a sense of this vitality. For instance, in Chapter 3, I have paid particular attention to fMRI, perhaps the most exciting development in the science of psychology because it allows us literally to see what is happening in the brain in real time, while it is working. In Chapter 4, classic approaches to moral development are supplemented and updated with current research on prosocial behavior. In Chapter 10, a new section on the moral emotion of gratitude helps to expand students' understanding of the breadth of emotion research. In Chapter 11, I have added a discussion of the compelling life story approach to personality.

Making room for new material has necessitated compression in some other chapters. To guide difficult decision making about coverage, I have relied on my own experience as an instructor and a researcher. For example, I have combined the topic of intelligence with thinking and language and offered a streamlined treatment of personality that reflects the field today.

> "I like the focus on presenting an integrated view showing how areas overlap and are connected as students do often see it made up of discrete sections." *Anre Venter, University of Notre Dame*

In conjunction with creating a book whose overall focus is current and contemporary, I have included citations that bring the most important recent and ongoing research into the text. Updated references give students and instructors alike the very latest that psychology has to offer on each topic. For example, of the 181 references to research in Chapter 3, 151 (or 83 percent) are for studies published in 2000 or later, including fully 117 (or 65 percent) from 2006 and later.

"New" by itself is not necessarily better or best, of course; a very current research citation that bears small relevance to students is little more than window dressing. I have therefore tried to tie recent research to current events in creative ways. For instance, in Chapter 1, I present new research on the psychology of forgiveness in the context of the tragic shooting of Amish schoolgirls in 2006. In Chapter 3, I discuss recent stem cell research in the context of the contemporary debate on that issue. In Chapter 12 on social psychology, new research on face perception is tied in with the congressional election results from 2000, 2002, and 2004.

A contemporary perspective also means appreciating disagreements in the field. Each chapter contains a Critical Controversy feature highlighting current psychological debates and posing thought-provoking questions that encourage students to examine the evidence on both sides. For example, Chapter 12 includes a Critical Controversy titled "Do Violent Video Games Lead to Violence?"; the Critical Controversy in Chapter 9 is titled "Is Bilingual Education a Good Thing?"

Finally, a contemporary perspective means appreciating psychology's value in everyday life. Each chapter includes a Psychology and Life feature that invites students to apply what they have learned to their own lives. For example, Chapter 10 includes a Psychology and Life looking at the subject of "How Goal-Directed Are You?"

Pedagogy for Success

The Science of Psychology: An Appreciative View, Study Edition provides important study tools to help students learn about psychology. An integrated learning system is built around the print and media components of *The Science of Psychology: An Appreciative View*. Using it will help students to master the material with ease. The chapter outline at the beginning of each chapter previews the chapter's major topics of focus as revealed in its main headings. Within the text narrative, each main heading is followed by the section's key learning goal. Then, at the end of each major section, the student comes to Review, Assess, and Sharpen Your Thinking. The bulleted items in this section-review ask the reader to recap each of the main subtopics in the section. A short multiple choice quiz then allows students to confirm understanding of key concepts before moving on. At the end of the chapter comes a Summary organized by the main chapter headings. The Summary restates the learning goals and reviews the key take-away information section by section. This information matches up in a one-to-one fashion with the bulleted statements in each of the chapter's section reviews. One learning strategy is for the student to look at a bulleted item in Review, Assess, and Sharpen Your Thinking within a chapter, try to answer the item, and then turn to the corresponding bullet in the summary at the end of the chapter to see if the answer is on track. Next, the Assess Your Knowledge section provides a chapter quiz. The chapter concludes with Apply Your Knowledge activities that help students review and apply core concepts.

Tools for Success

The Tools for Success accompanying *The Science of Psychology: An Appreciative View* is an integrated program offering invaluable support to instructors teaching and students studying introductory psychology. The award-winning instructors who make up the author team explore the issues of culture and diversity that are critical to an introductory psychology course. In addition, my own experience and teaching methods are reflected throughout the program, from the scaffolding approach to assessment to the techniques by which the Student Study Guide develops students' study skills. The Tools for Success program creates a pedagogical safety net designed to facilitate course instruction and to help students get the most out of introductory psychology.

For Instructors

All of the instructor ancillaries described below can be found on the text's Online Learning Center at **www.mhhe.com/king1.**

PrepCenter for Introductory Psychology   The PrepCenter for Introductory Psychology is a comprehensive online media library that allows instructors to search for individual media assets the way they want to search—by chapter, concept, or media type. This site features instructor materials, videos, and images to enhance lectures—and ultimately, students' learning experiences. New to PrepCenter are McGraw-Hill's Dynamic PowerPoints. Our research showed that, while PowerPoints are very important lecture components, instructors found themselves spending significant time editing them to reflect their own course priorities. Therefore, we've taken a fresh approach by focusing our Dynamic PowerPoints on concepts rather than chapters. Through our We Listen campaign, we identified 80 concepts as the most important in the introductory psychology course. For each, we've developed highly artistic, engaging, and flexible mini-presentations that instructors can easily drop into the Lecture Points that accompany this text, their own course PowerPoints, or use as is. Carefully designed and thoroughly reviewed, these slides will allow instructors to spend time developing their course rather than typing or editing chapter outlines. To access PrepCenter, go to **http://prepcenter.mhhe.com/prepcenter.**

Instructor's Manual by Nina Tarner, Sacred Heart University   The Instructor's Manual provides a wide variety of tools and resources for presenting the course, including learning objectives, ideas for lectures and discussions, and handouts. The Connections section serves as a roadmap outlining all the other ancillaries for that chapter and points out all the unique and interesting features available.

Test Bank by Edna Ross, University of Louisville, Nina Tarner, Sacred Heart University   The Test Bank includes more than 100 questions per chapter. The items test factual, applied, and conceptual understanding and build on the skills students gain through use of the Student Study Guide and online quizzes. The Test Bank is compatible with EZTest Online, McGraw-Hill's Computerized Test Bank software. Any instructor who uses EZ Test Online can now create and deliver multiple-choice and true/false quiz questions to students' iPod™s using Apple™'s new iQuiz™ application. Once students download the quiz into their iPod, they can take the interactive iQuiz, self-assess, and receive quiz scores instantly. Instructors can learn more about EZ Test Online by visiting www.eztestonline.com.

PowerPoint Presentations by Chris Randall, Kennesaw State University   The PowerPoint Presentations cover the key points of each chapter and include charts and graphs from the text. The presentations serve as an organizational and a navigational tool integrated with examples and activities from an expert teacher. The slides can be used as is or modified to meet the needs of the individual instructor.

Classroom Performance System (CPS) by Mary Anne Taylor, Clemson University   The Classroom Performance System's mix of factual and opinion questions allows instructors

The Tools for Success author team met in Washington, D.C. to meet each other and Laura King to exchange ideas and devise a collaborative plan for this program. Pictured from left to right: Mary Anne Taylor, Clemson University; Chris Randall, Kennesaw State University; Edna Ross, University of Louisville; Chad Burton, University of Missouri, Columbia; Laura King, University of Missouri, Columbia; Nathan Smith, Texas Woman's University; and Nina Tarner, Sacred Heart University.

to know what concepts their students are variously mastering and those with which students are having difficulty. CPS, a "clicker" system, is a great way to give interactive quizzes, maximize student participation in class discussions, and take attendance.

Image Gallery The Image Gallery features the complete set of figures and tables from the text. These images are available for download and can be easily embedded into instructors' PowerPoint slides.

For Students

eBook MHHE eBooks offer students new choices in the format of their textbook content and considerable savings—about half the price of a traditional printed book! Enhanced MHHE eBook features make reading interactive as you search, highlight, bookmark, annotate, and print. MHHE's eBooks can be viewed online on any computer with an Internet connection or downloaded to an individual's computer.

Interested in an online eBook? Then visit www.coursesmart.com. Want your eBook downloaded to your computer? Then try http://textbooks.vitalsource.com/. CourseSmart is a new way to find and buy Textbooks. At CourseSmart you can save up to 50% off the cost of a print textbook, redue your impact on the environment, and gain access to powerful webtools for learning. CourseSmart has the largest selection of eTextbooks available anywhere, offering thousands of the most commonly adopted textbooks from a wide variety of higher education publishers. CourseSmart eTextbooks are available in one standard online reader with full text search, notes and highlighting, and email tools for sharing notes between classmates.

The Study Edition Practice Questions by Nathan Smith, Texas Woman's University The Study Edition includes multiple choice quiz questions in the Review, Assess, and Sharpen Your Thinking section after each main topic; a full chapter quiz at the end of each chapter; practice mid-term (covering Chapters 1–7) and final exams in Appendix A. Answers to the section Assess questions are printed on the back endpapers. Answers and feedback to the remaining questions are available in Appendix B.

Student Study Guide by Chad Burton, University of Missouri, Columbia The Student Study Guide promotes an active learning approach, with its chapter-by-chapter learning goals, chapter outlines, practice tests, and appreciative view exercises. Emphasizing successful results, the guide develops good study skills and emphasizes their importance in helping students to comprehend and retain the key information from the textbook. The guide coaches students in learning what needs to be included in a good chapter outline by demonstrating these essentials in the first few chapters and then gradually removing material as the chapters—and students' study skills—progress.

Student Online Learning Center by Nathan Smith, Texas Woman's University The Student Online Learning Center contains chapter-by-chapter quizzes, outlines, learning objectives, and key terms in English and Spanish. The Multiple Choice, Fill-in-the-Blank, and True/False quizzes ask questions that build on conscientious use of the Student Study Guide. To access the Online Learning Center, go to **www.mhhe. com/king1.**

PsychInteractive Online PsychInteractive Online (www.mhhe. com/psychinteractive) provides a wealth of interactive activities, self-assessments, and study aids that focus on students' mastery of core concepts in psychology. The lab activities cover over 45 key concepts in introductory psychology. And for courses taught wholly online and those supported by course Web sites, the content is fully integrated within course management cartridges. PsychInteractive Online may be used by students or by instructors. Additional instructional assets for teaching the course are also available for lecture and demonstration on PrepCenter. The newly developed activities cover research methods, shaping, memory, reinforcement, classical conditioning, infant vision, and observational learning.

ACKNOWLEDGMENTS

The quality of this book is a testament to the skills and abilities of so many people, and I am tremendously grateful to the following individuals whose insightful contributions during the book's development and production have improved it immeasurably.

Manuscript Reviewers

Debra Ahola, *Schenectady County Community College*
Julie Wargo Aikins, *University of Connecticut*
Jim Backlund, *Kirkland Community College*
Michelle Bannoura, *Hudson Valley Community College*
Joyce Bateman-Jones, *Central Texas College*
Craig Bowden, *University of Wisconsin, Green Bay*
Josh Burke, *College of William and Mary*
Cari Cannon, *Santiago Canyon College*
Chrisanne Christensen, *Southern Arkansas University*
Diana Ciesko, *Valencia Community College*
Jane Marie Cirillo, *Houston Community College, Central Campus*
Jennifer A. Clark, *University of Kentucky*
Patrick Courtney, *Central Ohio Tech College*
Don Daughtry, *Texas A & M*
Neil Carter Davis, *University of West Florida*
Neeru Deep, *Northwestern State University of Louisiana*
Lynne Dodson, *Seattle Community College*
Delores Doench, *Southwestern Community College*
Heather Dore, *Florida Community College at Jacksonville, South Campus*
Kimberley Duff, *Cerritos College*
Chris S. Dula, *East Tennessee State University*
Curt Dunkel, *Illinois Central College*
Robert Dunkle, *Ivy Tech Community College of Indiana*
Sheri Dunlavy, *Ivy Tech Community College of Indiana*
Tami J. Eggleston, *McKendree College*
Kenneth C. Elliott, *University of Maine, Augusta*
Scott Engel, *Sheridan College*
Tom Ersfeld, *Central Lakes College*
Dan Fawaz, *Georgia Perimeter College*
Gwen Fischer, *Hiram College*
William F. Ford, *Bucks County Community College*
Betty Jane Fratzke, *Indiana Wesleyan University*
Katrina Gantly, *Camosun College, Canada*
Barbara Gfellner, *Brandon University, Canada*
Jessica Gilbert, *Northern Virginia Community College*
Vicki S. Gier, *University of West Florida*
Peter Gram, *Pensacola Junior College*
Troianne Grayson, *Florida Community College, Jacksonville*
Jeffrey Green, *Virginia Commonwealth University*

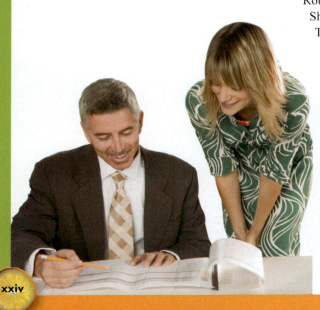

Janelle Grellner, *University of Central Oklahoma*
Laura Gruntmeir, *Redlands Community College*
Elizabeth Yost Hammer, *Loyola University*
Greg E. Harris, *Polk Community College*
Carmon W. Hicks, *Ivy Tech Community College of Indiana*
Cynthia M. Hoffman, *Indiana University*
Rachel Hull, *Texas A&M University*
Jean W. Hunt, *University of the Cumberlands*
Heather Jennings, *Mercer County Community College*
Brian Johnson, *University of Tennessee, Martin*
Arthur Kemp, *University of Central Missouri*
Sheryl Leytham, *Grand View College*
Angelina S. MacKewn, *University of Tennessee*
Nancy Mann, *Southern Wesleyan University*
Amy J. Marin, *Phoenix College*
Randy Martinez, *Cypress College*
Jane Martino, *Des Moines Area Community College*
Jason McCartney, *Salisbury University*
David McCone, *United States Air Force Academy*
Lisa McCone, *Pine Creek High School*
Will Mcintosh, *Georgia Southern University*
Ron Mulson, *Hudson Valley Community College*
Mar Navarro, *Valencia Community College*
Geoffrey O'Shea, *State University of New York, College at Oneonta*
Barbara Oswald, *Midlands Technical College*
Laura Gunter Overstreet, *Tarrant County College*
Shana Pack, *Western Kentucky University*
Jennifer P. Peluso, *Florida Atlantic University*
Stewart Perry, *American River College, Sacramento*
Deborah S. Podwika, *Kankakee Community College*
Charlotte Prokop, *Dutchess Community College*
Amanda Rabidue Bozack, *University of Arizona*
Betsye Robinette, *Indiana Wesleyan University*
Traci L. Sachteleben, *Southwestern Illinois College*
Sherry Schnake, *St. Mary of the Woods College*
John Schulte, *Cape Fear Community College*
Janis Wilson Seeley, *Luzerne County Community College*
David W. Shwalb, *Southeastern Louisiana University*
Carrie Veronica Smith, *University of Delaware*
Jason S. Spiegelman, *The Community College of Baltimore County–Catonsville*
Nelly Stadler, *University of Pittsburgh*
David Thompson, *Wake Technical Community College*
Martin van den Berg, *California State University, Chico*
Angela Vaughn, *Wesley College*
Shelly Warm, *Palm Beach Community College*
Mary E. Wells, *Sinclair Community College (Ohio)*
Molly A. Wernli, *College of Saint Mary*
Melissa B. Weston, *El Centro College*
Theodore W. Whitley, *East Carolina University*
Colin William, *Ivy Tech Community College of Indiana*

At last, someone has caught up with the 21st century and sees the importance of talking about how people develop healthy psyches!

—Debra Ahola, Schenectady County Community College

Introductory Psychology Symposia

Every year McGraw-Hill conducts several Introductory Psychology Symposia, which are attended by instructors from across the country. These events are an opportunity for editors from McGraw-Hill to gather information about the needs and challenges of instructors teaching the introductory psychology course. They also offer a forum for the attendees to exchange ideas and experiences with colleagues they might not have otherwise met. The feedback we have received has been invaluable and has contributed—directly or indirectly—to the development of *The Science of Psychology: An Appreciative View* and its supplements.

Mark Alicke, *Ohio University*
Cheryl Almeida, *Johnson and Wales University*
Dan Bellack, *Trident Technical College*
Jeffrey Blum, *Los Angeles City College*
Tamara Brown, *University of Kentucky*
Nicole Judith Campbell, *University of Oklahoma*
Alexis Collier, *Ohio State University*
Layton Curl, *Metropolitan State College, Denver*
Neeru Deep, *Northwestern State University of Louisiana*
Barb DeFilippo, *Lane Community College*
Suzanne Delaney, *University of Arizona, Tucson*
Tom DiLorenzo, *University of Delaware*
Peggy Dombrowski, *Harrisburg Area Community College–Lancaster Campus*
Carol Donnelly, *Purdue University*
Joan Doolittle, *Anne Arundel Community College*
Dale Doty, *Monroe Community College*
Joelle Elicker, *University of Akron*
Jay Brophy Ellison, *University of Central Florida*
Dan Fawaz, *Georgia Perimeter College*
Raymond Fleming, *University of Wisconsin–Milwaukee*
Don Forsyth, *Virginia Commonwealth University*
Eric Fox, *Western Michigan University*
Sara Grison, *University of Illinois–Champaign*
Regan Gurung, *University of Wisconsin–Green Bay*
Mike Hackett, *Westchester Community College*
Robin Hailstorks, *Prince George Community College*
Erin Hardin, *Texas Tech University*
Jeffrey B. Henriques, *University of Wisconsin, Madison*
Debra Hollister, *Valencia Community College*
Theresa Holt, *Middlesex City College*
Mark Hoyert, *Indiana University Northwest*
John Huber, *Texas State University–San Marcos*
Charlie Huffman, *James Madison University*
Natalie Kerr, *James Madison University*
Shirin Khosropour, *Austin Community College*
Mark Laumakis, *San Diego State University*
Philip K. Lehman, *Virginia Tech*
Veronica Evans Lewis, *University of Louisiana, Monroe*
Mark Licht, *Florida State University*
Clem Magner, *Milwaukee Area Technical College*

Randall Martinez, *Cypress College*

Charlene Melrose, *Orange Coast College*

Glen Musgrove, *Broward Community College*

Jeff Neubauer, *Pima Community College*

John Nezlek, *College of William and Mary*

Glenda Nichols, *Tarrant County College*

Randall Osborne, *Texas State University, San Marcos*

John Pellew, *Greenville Tech College*

Jennifer Peluso, *Florida Atlantic University*

Claire St. Peter Pipkin, *West Virginia University*

Deborah S. Podwika, *Kankakee Community College*

Susan Pollock, *Mesa Community College*

Bryan Porter, *Old Dominion University*

Alida Quick, *Wayne County Community College*

Christopher K. Randall, *Kennesaw State University*

Diane Reddy, *University of Wisconsin–Milwaukee*

Laura Reichel, *Front Range Community College*

Tanya Renner, *Kapi'olani Community College; University of Hawaii*

Tonja Ringgold, *Baltimore City Community College*

Edna Ross, *University of Louisville*

David A. Schroeder, *University of Arkansas*

Wayne Shebilske, *Wright State University*

Elisabeth Sherwin, *University of Arkansas at Little Rock*

Harvey Shulman, *Ohio State University*

Jennifer Siciliani, *University of Missouri, St. Louis*

Nancy Simpson, *Trident Tech College*

Jamie Smith, *Ohio State University*

Vivian Smith, *Lakeland Community College*

Genevieve Stevens, *Houston Community College–Central Campus*

Mark Stewart, *American River College*

Pam Stewart, *Northern Virginia Community College*

Nina Tarner, *Sacred Heart University*

Stephen Tracy, *Community College of Southern Nevada*

Lisa Valentino, *Seminole Community College*

Anre Venter, *University of Notre Dame*

Eduardo Vianna, *LaGuardia Community College*

Ruth Wallace, *Butler Community College*

Fred Whitford, *University of Montana*

Supplements Team

Chad Burton, *University of Missouri, Columbia*

Christopher K. Randall, *Kennesaw State University*

Edna Ross, *University of Louisville*

Nathan Smith, *Texas Women's University*

Nina Tarner, *Sacred Heart University*

MaryAnne Taylor, *Clemson University*

Biological Art Consultants

Nicole Judith Campbell, *University of Oklahoma*
Neeru Deep, *Northwestern State University of Louisiana*
Carlos Grijalva, *University of California, Los Angeles*
Erin Hardin, *Texas Tech University*
Jeffrey B. Henriques, *University of Wisconsin, Madison*
Debra Hollister, *Valencia Community College*
Philip K. Lehman, *Virginia Tech*
Christopher K. Randall, *Kennesaw State University*
Genevieve Stevens, *Houston Community College, Central Campus*
Ruth Wallace, *Butler Community College*

Design Consultants

Julie Wargo Aikens, *University of Connecticut*
Cheryl Almeida, *Johnson and Wales University*
Michelle Bannoura, *Hudson Valley Community College*
Joyce Bateman-Jones, *Central Texas College*
Craig Bowden, *University of Wisconsin–Green Bay*
Diana Ciesko, *Valencia Community College*
Jennifer Clarke, *University of Kentucky*
Patrick Courtney, *Central Ohio Tech College*
Neeru Deep, *Northwestern State University of Louisiana*
Delores Doench, *Southwestern Community College*
Joan Doolittle, *Anne Arundel Community College*
Sheri Dunlavy, *Ivy Tech Community College of Indiana*
Tami J. Eggleston, *McKendree College*
Kenneth Elliot, *University of Maine, Augusta*
Scott Engel, *Sheridan College*
Jeffrey Green, *Virginia Commonwealth University*
Laura Gruntmeir, *Redlands Community College*
Regan Gurung, *University of Wisconsin, Green Bay*
Jeffrey B. Henriques, *University of Wisconsin, Madison*
Carmon Hicks, *Ivy Tech Community College of Indiana*

Brian Johnson, *University of Tennessee, Martin*
Nicole T. Judice-Campbell, *University of Oklahoma*
Nancy Mann, *Southern Wesleyan University*
Amy J. Marin, *Phoenix College*
David McCone, *United States Air Force Academy*
Deborah S. Podwika, *Kankakee Community College*
Amanda Rabidue, *University of Arizona*
Betsye Robinette, *Indiana Wesleyan University*
Sherry Schnake, *St. Mary College of the Woods*
David A. Schroeder, *University of Arkansas*
John Schulte, *Cape Fear Community College*
Janis Wilson Seeley, *Luzerne County Community College*
Mary Anne Taylor, *Clemson University*
Donald Thompson, *Wake Technical Community College*
Eduardo Vianna, *LaGuardia Community College*
Shelley Warm, *Palm Beach Community College*
Molly Wernli, *College of St. Mary*
Melissa Weston, *El Centro College*

Expert Reviewers

Jamie Arndt, *University of Missouri, Columbia*
Bruce Bartholow, *University of Missouri, Columbia*
Scott Geller, *Virginia Tech*
Carlos Grijalva, *University of California, Los Angeles*
Christopher Robert, *University of Missouri, Columbia*
Amanda Rose, *University of Missouri, Columbia*
Timothy Trull, *University of Missouri, Columbia*
David Wolitzky, *New York University*

Study Edition Consultants

Diana Ciesko, *Valencia Community College*
Lloyd Pilkington, *Midlands Technical College*

Class Testers

Diane Roche Benson, *Miller-Motte Technical College*
Christina Brown, *Miami University (Oxford, OH)*
Emily Cheng, *California State University–Fullerton*
Wanda Clark, *South Plains College*
Diana Ciesko, *Valencia Community College*
Mark Cooksey, *Liberty University*
Patrick Courtney, *Central Ohio Tech College*
Mathew Diggs, *El Centro College*
Michael Earhart, *Metropolitan State University*
Tami J. Eggleston, *McKendree College*
Gladys Green, *Manatee Community College*
Gregory Harris, *Polk Community College*
Denise Jones, *University of Tennessee at Martin*
Richard Kandus, *Mt. San Jacinto College–Menifee Campus*
Barbara Keesling, *California State University–Fullerton*
Julie Kiotas, *Pasadena Community College*
Cheri Kittrell, *Manatee Community College*
Caroline Kozoje, *Jamestown College*
Thomas Kruggel, *Towson University*
Dana Kuehn, *Florida Community College–Jacksonville*
Sheryl Leytham, *Grand View College*

Maria Lopez-Moreno, *Mt. San Jacinto College–San Jacinto Campus*

Angie MacKewn, *University of Tennessee, Martin*

Dennis Macklin, *Century Community College*

Maryanne Michaloski, *Towson University*

Daniel Montoya, *Fayetteville State University*

Mar Navarro, *Valencia Community College*

Jane Noll, *University of South Florida*

Debra Parish, *Tomball College*

Elizabeth Pete, *Gibbs College of New Jersey*

Marianna Rader, *Florida Community College at Jacksonville, Downtown Campus*

Jonathan Reed, *East Carolina University*

Adya Riss, *Moorpark College*

Steven Samuels, *U.S. Air Force Academy*

Christine Selby, *University College of Bangor*

Scott Smith, *University of Louisiana at Lafayette*

Jason Spiegelman, *Villa Julie College*

William E. Thomas, *Louisiana Technical College, Sabine Valley Campus*

Jean Volckmann, *Pasadena Community College*

Roger A. Ward, *University of Cincinnati (Raymond Walters)*

Melissa Weston, *El Centro College*

Andrew Woster, *South Dakota State University*

Transparency Overlay Reviewers

Randolph C. Arnau, *University of Southern Mississippi*

Grace Austin, *Sierra College*

Glen Bradley, *Pensacola Junior College*

Jane Marie Cirillo, *Houston Community College, Southeast*

Lorry Cologny, *Owens Community College*

Robert Fisher, *Lee University*

Erin Hardin, *Texas Tech University*

Sherry Denise Jones, *University of Tennessee at Martin*

Dana L. Kuehn, *Florida Community College at Jacksonville, Deerwood Center*

Maria E. Lopez, *Mt. San Jacinto College*

Ronnie Rothschild, *Broward Community College*

Carol Shoptaugh, *Missouri State*

Martin van den Berg, *California State University, Chico*

Frederick (Charlie) Wiss, *The University of North Carolina–Chapel Hill*

PsychInteractive Advisory Board

The following advisory board members continually provide input that will undoubtedly improve all of the activities found on PsychInteractive Online. These board members have been working to help us create a series of new interactivities that will broaden the scope and effectiveness of our interactivity offerings.

Melissa Acevedo, *Westchester Community College*

Jennifer Brooks, *Collin County Community College*

Jeffrey Green, *Virginia Commonwealth University*

Julie Bauer Morrison, *Glendale Community College*

Phil Pegg, *Western Kentucky University*

Tanya Renner, *Kapi'olani Community College; University of Hawaii*

Carla Strassle, *York College of Pennsylvania*

Jim Stringham, *University of Georgia*

> *These are great! It is nice to connect information between chapters (and helps students elaborate on the information). This forces students to think deeply about the content from earlier chapters rather than "dump" information when they've finished chapters. The example on smell and memory is perfect, because it connects sensation & perception, memory, and emotions in a concrete way.*
>
> –Cari B. Cannon, Santiago Canyon College

Student Focus Groups

Joseph Aning, *City College of New York*

Melanie Bigenho, *San Francisco State University*

Allison Carroll, *San Francisco State University*

Diana Castro, *San Francisco State University*

Doris Corniell, *City University of New York, Brooklyn*

Tara Demoulin, *City College of San Francisco*

Jessica Frost, *San Francisco State University*

Marissa Holmes, *San Francisco State University*

Samula Jones, *City College of San Francisco*

Krupa Kothari, *San Francisco State University*

Ling Jung Li, *New York University*

Kyle Limin, *San Francisco State University*

Shi Yun Kristy Lin, *Cornell University*

Medeona Muca, *College of Staten Island*

Christina Ng, *State University of New York, Stony Brook*

Veronica Roman, *College of Staten Island*

Matt Russo, *State University of New York, Binghamton*

Brian Yu, *University of Michigan*

Student Reviewers

Melanie Bigenho, *San Francisco State University*

Andrea Brown, *State University of New York, New Paltz*

Allison Carroll, *San Francisco State University*

Xiao Xiao Chen, *Baruch College, City University of New York*

King Moon Chu, *Boston University*

Tara DeMoulin, *City College of San Francisco*

Stephanie Glass, *University of North Dakota*

Marissa Holmes, *San Francisco State University*

Samuel Jones, *City College of San Francisco*

Krupa Kothari, *San Francisco State University*

Kyle Limin, *San Francisco State University*

Patrick Reidy, *University of Northern Iowa*

David Zeng, *Baruch College, City University of New York*

Teleconference Attendees

Thomas Brandon, *University of South Florida, Tampa*
Julia Daniels, *West Chester Community College*
Don Daughtry, *South Texas College*
Robert Dunkle, *Ivy Tech Community College of Indiana*
Jamie Goldenberg, *University of South Florida, Tampa*
Natalie Kerr, *James Madison University*
Chris LeGrow, *Marshall University*
Randall Martinez, *Cypress College*
Patrick McCarthy, *Middle Tennessee State University*
Steve Mewaldt, *Marshall University*
Julie Penley, *El Paso Community College*
Roger Pfeifer, *Valdosta State University*
Sandra Prince-Madison, *Delgado Community College*
Traci Sachteleben, *Southwestern Illinois College*

King Regional Sales Champions

Jesse Cruz	Melissa Kumle
Jennifer Edwards	Steve Magdzinski
Rachel Egan	Tim Rutherford
Kristi Gordon	Denise Skaggs
Drew Holder	Nenden Stillman

Personal Acknowledgments

Instructors who teach introductory psychology have an amazing opportunity to present psychology to the uninitiated. This book reflects the efforts of a teacher and researcher. There is certainly no substitute for the vital human being standing before students (even on a TV screen or computer monitor) sharing his or her own enthusiastic and scholarly approach to the science of psychology. My hope is that in this book, I have provided a useful tool in this important endeavor, one that will supplement and bolster the efforts of instructors in providing students with a firm grounding in the science that fascinates us.

In the last year, many friends and colleagues have asked me to describe the experience of writing this book. The most exact and honest answer I have been able to give is, "It's just like Intro, only I miss the students." To me, teaching and writing about introductory psychology are about telling the story of psychology in an unforgettable, personal way that does justice to the passion of the individuals who have created the broad base of knowledge that is psychology. Indeed, I have approached every chapter in this book as if it is the first day of lecture for each topic and as if I am seeking to give students the essence of what they need to know about the topic, why it has been a source of fascination to psychologists, and how it can help individuals like themselves to live a good life.

I would like to thank the staff at McGraw-Hill for their confidence in my vision of introductory psychology, especially Mike Sugarman, whose support and encouragement throughout this process have been invaluable. This book would not exist were it not for Mike's own vision. I owe an enormous debt of gratitude to Sylvia Mallory, whose dedication to quality can be seen throughout this book. She wore many hats, including kindergarten teacher, coach, advocate, sounding board, comrade in arms, and (occasionally) task master. At every step, her commitment to making this book—every page, sentence, picture, citation, and feature—the very best it could be has paid off in ways that astonish me. Thanks also to Sheryl Adams, Dawn Groundwater, and Beth Mejia for amazing ideas and contributions along the way, as well as to James Headley and Sarah Martin for finding ways to "let me be me" in the service of the book. Thanks, too, to Meghan Campbell for her tireless work on the supplements, and to copyeditor Jennifer Gordon, production editor Catherine Morris, designer Kim Menning and art manager Robin Mouat. My appreciation also goes to the many sales representatives who have taken the time to get to know me and this book and whose enthusiasm has been inspiring.

I thank, in addition, all of my colleagues at Mizzou, who fielded innumerable random questions as I made my way through their specialties, especially Amanda Rose, Chris Robert, Jamie Arndt, Ken Sheldon, Kristin Hawley, Chuck Borduin, Tim Trull, Denis McCarthy, and Dennis Miller. And my gratitude goes as well to my graduate students—Chad Burton, Josh Hicks, and Aaron Geise—who kept my scholarship alive even as I was deep in the trenches of textbook writing. A special thanks to Carlos Grijalva of UCLA for his help and expertise in developing the biological transparency overlays. Carlos's dedication and keen eye for detail helped create an innovative way for students to learn and master key biological concepts. I extend my thanks too to John Santrock, who initially entrusted me as co-author and provided support and guidance throughout the writing process.

The mainstays of my survival during these last months of the publishing process have been caffeine, people, and music. As such, I never could have completed this book without the encouragement of my pals at Coffeezone in Columbia, whose regular greetings of "Hey Doc! How's that book coming?" kept me on task even during gossip breaks. Anyone who knows me knows I cannot think without music playing in the background. So I must also acknowledge the musicians, singers, and songwriters who kept me alive while writing, including Rufus Wainwright, Regina Spector, Tori Amos, Joni Mitchell, David Gray, Ella Fitzgerald, Billie Holiday, Chet Baker, and Connee Boswell.

In many ways this book is a tribute to the wonderful teachers I have had throughout my life. Robert Hare and Rich Jagunic fostered my loves of science and writing. My psychology professors at Kenyon College, especially Michael Levine and Jon Williams, though puzzled by the English major who kept taking their classes, allowed me to see that the science of human behavior was a lifelong passion. Thanks as well to Bill Klein, the English professor who once told me, "There is nothing you could write that would be so bad that I would tell you to stop writing!" Also, I owe deep gratitude to the late scholars, Gerrit Roelofs and Phil Church, English professors at Kenyon. They probably never knew I was a psychology major, but their profound impact on me is evident in my teaching and in this book. Finally, I must acknowledge my mentors (formal and informal) Bob Emmons, Jamie Pennebaker, and Ed Diener.

Thanks to my family for their constant support and faith in me, including Lisa Jensen, Becky Dills, Robert C. King, Robert W. King, and Shirley Jensen, and especially to Jim Jensen and Rob Dills, whose unwavering enthusiasm for this project, from beginning to end, inspired me deeply. I also owe so much to the many strong women in my life who have served as real-life examples of the amazing capacity of human beings to thrive: Shirley Jensen, Cyndi King, Teresa Williams, Judy Mantle, Dolores Hayes, Laura Renner, Joanne Manzella, Fatty Snyder, Mary Lee Maloney, and most especially my mother, Ida King, who would have been very proud of this book. When I was 7 years old, I told her I was going to be a psychologist to find out what was wrong with her. She took it with a big, warm smile, maybe knowing even then that that was not the kind of psychologist I was going to be after all.

L. A. K.

APA Learning Goals

BOOK FEATURES	Knowledge Base of Psychology	Research Methods in Psychology	Critical Thinking Skills in Psychology	Application of Psychology	Values in Psychology	Information and Technological Literacy	Communication Skills
Chapter Contents	●	●	●	●	●	●	●
Experiencing Psychology	●			●	●		
Preview	●						●
Review, Assess, and Sharpen Your Thinking	●		●	●			●
Intersections	●	●	●	●	●		●
Critical Controversy	●	●	●	●	●		●
Psychology and Life	●		●	●	●		●
Running glossary	●			●		●	●
Summary	●		●	●		●	●
Assess Your Knowledge	●		●	●			
Apply Your Knowledge	●		●	●	●		●
Touring the Brain & Nervous System; Touring the Senses	●	●	●			●	●
Practice Mid-term and Final Exams	●		●	●	●		

PSYCHOLOGY

THE SCIENCE OF

THE SCIENCE OF

AN APPRECIATIVE VIEW

STUDY EDITION

CHAPTER 1

WHAT IS PSYCHOLOGY?

Experiencing Psychology

THE MYSTERY THAT IS YOU

Do you have a hero? When you think about someone you truly admire, does a high-achieving celebrity or sports figure come to mind? If so, you are in good company, because individuals such as Tiger Woods, Oprah Winfrey, and Mother Teresa show up on many lists of most admired people. In a December 2006 Gallup poll, the most admired man was George W. Bush, followed by Bill Clinton, Jimmy Carter, Barack Obama, Colin Powell, and the Reverend Billy Graham (Jones, 2006). The most admired women were Hillary Clinton, Oprah Winfrey, Condoleezza Rice, Laura Bush, former British prime minister Margaret Thatcher, and Angelina Jolie. These are individuals who have made significant contributions in public life, many of them throughout long careers.

But at the right moment, an ordinary individual can become a hero. Jabbar Gibson was a teenager when Hurricane Katrina struck New Orleans, leaving him among the masses of people ravaged and stranded by the storm ("Editorial," 2005). After 2 days of wading alone in the filthy flood waters, he made a drastic move to save himself. He broke into a school, took the keys to a yellow school bus parked outside, and set off for Houston. Once on the way, Gibson's desperate act of self-preservation turned into something quite different: heroism. As he drove along Highway 10 (he never had driven a bus before), Gibson started picking up people stranded by the road. Soon his bus carried dozens of frightened but thankful individuals from all walks of life, including new babies with their mothers, as well as elderly people, all relying on young Gibson to get them to safety. The harrowing 8-hour, 300-mile journey included a stop for gas, paid for with spare change the passengers collected. When Gibson and his weary riders arrived in Houston, it occurred to him that he might be in trouble for taking the bus. But true to the spirit of the hero he had become, Gibson concluded, "I don't care if I get blamed for it so long as I saved my people" ("Editorial," 2005). In the aftermath of Katrina, Gibson was hardly the only hero to emerge; many doctors, nurses, and other citizens rode out the tempest and stayed to help others. Every catastrophe has its heroes.

Does it take a disaster to be a hero? The answer is no, because even in more ordinary daily circumstances, people make choices that might reasonably be called heroic. People are kind to individuals in need when they could be thoughtless or cruel. They are generous when they might be selfish. They work hard when they could slack off. When we think about the admirable people we encounter every day, we can see how ordinary human behavior can be extraordinary if viewed in the right light.

Similarly, many other aspects of human life take on extraordinary dimensions when looked at with a close lens. Scientists bring such powerful observations to their efforts. Consider astronomers, who wonder at the stars, and zoologists, who marvel at the varied creatures that populate the earth. As scientists, psychologists too are passionate about what they study, and what they study is you. Right now, as you are reading this book, thousands of dedicated scientists are studying things about you that you might have never considered, such as how your brain responds to a picture flashed on a screen or how your eyes adjust to a sunny day. It is hard to imagine a single thing about you that is not fascinating to some psychologist somewhere. As a human being you have been endowed with remarkable gifts—from the capacities to see, hear, smell, think, reason, and remember to the abilities to fall in love, strive for goals, and become someone's hero. As you interact with the world every day, you manifest these gifts in a variety of ways that psychologists find fascinating to study.

So, although psychology shares many similarities with other sciences, especially in how it studies the world, it is different from other sciences because of what it studies: the many facets of you. As you learn more about psychology, you will also be learning about more aspects of yourself than you ever imagined existed. Throughout this book and your introductory psychology class, you will join in the passionate scientific inquiry that seeks to unravel the mystery that is you. ■

PREVIEW

This chapter begins by defining psychology more formally, and then gives context to that definition by reviewing the history and the intellectual underpinnings of the field. We next examine a number of contemporary approaches to the subject, as well as areas of specialization and potential careers. Our introduction to this dynamic, practical field closes by looking into how psychology can play a key role in human health and wellness.

1 Defining Psychology

Explain what psychology is and describe the positive psychology movement.

What is psychology? When asked this question, if you are like most people, you think of therapy. You probably imagine a situation where a clinical psychologist, be it Sigmund Freud or Dr. Phil, sees clients and tries to help them deal with a variety of mental problems. Yet formally defined, **psychology** is the scientific study of behavior and mental processes. There are three key terms in this definition: *science, behavior,* and *mental processes.*

psychology The scientific study of behavior and mental processes.

Behavior includes the observable act of two people kissing; mental processes include their unobservable thoughts about kissing.

As a **science,** psychology uses the systematic methods of science to observe human behavior and draw conclusions. The goals of psychological science are to describe, predict, and explain behavior. Researchers might be interested in knowing whether individuals will help a stranger who has fallen down. The researchers could devise a study in which they observe people walking past a person who needs help. Through many observations, the researchers could come to describe helping behavior by counting how many times it occurs in particular circumstances. The researchers may also try to *predict* who will help, and when, by examining characteristics of the individuals studied. Are happy people more likely to help? Are women or men more likely to help? What circumstances promote helping? After psychologists have analyzed their data, they also will want to *explain* why helping behavior occurred when it did.

Behavior is everything we do that can be directly observed—two people kissing, a baby crying, a college student riding a motorcycle. **Mental processes** are the thoughts, feelings, and motives that each of us experiences privately but that cannot be observed directly. Although we cannot directly see thoughts and feelings, they are nonetheless real. They include *thinking* about kissing someone, a baby's *feelings* when its mother leaves the room, and a college student's *memory* of a motorcycle ride.

science In psychology, the use of systematic methods to observe, describe, predict, and explain behavior.

behavior Everything we do that can be directly observed.

mental processes The thoughts, feelings, and motives that each of us experiences privately but that cannot be observed directly.

Psychology Versus Common Sense: What Don't You Already Know About Psychology?

One of the challenges facing teachers and practitioners of the science of psychology is overcoming the sense that everybody "knows" everything there is to know about psychology because we are all people. Of course, we all have brains—but we do not necessarily know how they work! So, it is worthwhile to ask the question, How is psychology different from our common knowledge about ourselves and one another?

You may think that psychology is the same as simple common sense about people. But, in fact, researchers often turn up the unexpected in human behavior. For example, it may seem obvious that couples who live together (cohabit) before marriage have a better chance of making the marriage last. After all, practice makes perfect, doesn't it? However, researchers have found a higher rate of success for couples who marry before living together (Liefbroer & Dourleijn, 2006; Popenoe & Whitehead, 2005; Seltzer, 2004). It also might seem obvious that we would experience more stress and be less happy if we had to function in many different roles than if we functioned in only one role. Yet women who engage in multiple, such as wife, mother, and

career woman—report more satisfaction with their lives than women who perform a single role or fewer roles, such as wife or wife and mother (Barnett & Hyde, 2001; Bennett & McDaniel, 2006).

As you read this book, you will encounter some findings that fit well with what you already know about people, but other conclusions will seem counterintuitive. Keep in mind that "what everybody knows" is a category that is influenced by historical and cultural context. Although it is shocking and incredible from our present-day perspective, there was a time when "everybody knew" that African Americans were innately intellectually inferior to Whites and that women were morally inferior to men. As you will see, psychology does not accept assumptions at face value. Psychology is a rigorous discipline that tests assumptions, bringing scientific data to bear on the questions of central interest to human beings (McBurney & White, 2007; Stanovich, 2007).

Thinking Like a Psychologist Means Thinking Like a Scientist

Psychologists approach human behavior as scientists. As scientific thinkers, they examine the available evidence about some aspect of mind and behavior, evaluate how strongly the data (information) support their hunches, analyze disconfirming evidence, and carefully consider whether they have explored all of the possible factors and explanations (Sternberg, Roediger, & Halpern, 2007). It is important to underscore how critical it is that psychologists look for biases in the way people think and behave. Consider, for example, a person who expresses wild enthusiasm about the remarkable effects of exercise on health when responding to survey questions about health awareness. It would be crucial for a researcher to uncover the fact that this particular individual sells exercise videos on the side and thus perhaps is communicating a biased perspective.

Psychologists, like other scientists, rely on critical thinking. **Critical thinking** is the process of thinking reflectively and productively and evaluating the evidence. Thinking critically means asking ourselves how we know something. Too often we have a tendency to recite, define, describe, state, and list rather than to analyze, infer, connect, synthesize, criticize, create, evaluate, think, and rethink (Brooks & Brooks, 2001). Thinking critically is an important aspect of psychology, as it is in all disciplines (Sternberg, 2007; Sternberg, Roediger, & Halpern, 2007). The ability to evaluate information critically is also essential to all areas of daily life (Halpern, 2003, 2007). For example, if you are planning to buy a car, you might want to collect information about different makes and models and evaluate their features and costs before deciding which one(s) to test drive. This is an exercise in critical thinking.

Critical thinking is not a spectator sport. It means actively engaging with ideas and not settling for easy answers. Critical thinking means being open-minded, curious, and careful.

As you will see throughout this book, psychologists do not agree on everything. Instead, psychology, like any science, is filled with debate and controversy. How might psychology benefit from these controversies? Psychology has advanced as a field because it does not accept simple explanations and because psychologists do not always concur with one another about why mind and behavior work the way they do. Psychologists have reached a more accurate understanding of mind and behavior *because* psychology fosters controversies and *because* psychologists think deeply and reflectively and examine the evidence on all sides.

What are some of psychology's controversies? Here is a brief sample:

- Are memories of sexual abuse real or imagined?
- Can personality change?
- Is self-esteem always a good thing?
- Should the psychological disorders of children be treated with drugs?

Because it is important for you to think critically about controversies, each chapter of this book has a Critical Controversy feature that presents an issue of disagreement or

critical thinking The process of thinking reflectively and productively, as well as evaluating evidence.

debate in contemporary psychology. Psychology is a science that is alive and constantly changing. Reviewing these controversies gives you a chance to see how scientists grapple with the ever-changing questions presented by their continuously emerging knowledge about human behavior.

One controversy in psychology centers on the growing popularity of a new approach to the field. That new perspective is called positive psychology.

Positive Psychology

So, psychology is the science of human behavior. As you consider this general definition of psychology, you might be thinking, Okay, where's the couch? Where's the mental illness? The science of psychology certainly includes the study of therapy and psychological disorders, but by definition psychology is a much more general science (Ash & Sturm, 2007). This discrepancy between popular beliefs and the reality of psychology was one motivating factor behind the debate in the discipline that began at the beginning of the twenty-first century. A number of scholars noted that psychology had become far too negative, focusing on what can go wrong in people's lives rather than on what they can do competently and what can go right (Seligman & Csikszentmihalyi, 2000). Too often, they said, psychology has characterized people as passive and victimized. The desire to study the full range of human experience motivated the **positive psychology movement:** the push for a stronger emphasis on research involving the experiences that people value (such as hope, optimism, and happiness), the traits associated with optimal capacities for love and work, and positive group and civic values (such as responsibility, civility, and tolerance) (Csikszentmihalyi & Csikszentmihalyi, 2006; Diener, 2000; Emmons, 2007; Peterson, Park, & Seligman, 2006; Rathunde & Csikszentmihalyi, 2006; Snyder & Lopez, 2006).

To get a sense of why positive psychology is a valuable perspective, imagine that you have been asked to create a science of "watchology." You have two watches that have both had the unfortunate trauma of being left in the pocket of a pair of jeans as they churned and tumbled through the washer and dryer. One watch has suffered the worst possible fate—it no longer tells time. The other has emerged from the traumatic event still ticking. Which watch will you want to use in developing your theory of watchology? You quite reasonably conclude that the working watch will help you understand watches better than the broken one.

What does watchology have to do with psychology? When they think of psychology, many people think of Sigmund Freud. Certainly, Freud has had a lasting impact on the field and on the larger society. (As recently as March 2006, on the occasion of his 150th birthday, Freud was featured on the cover of *Newsweek*.) But it is important to keep in mind that Freud based his ideas about human nature on the patients that he saw in his clinical practice—individuals who were struggling with psychological problems. His experiences with these individuals colored his outlook on all of humanity. Freud (1918/1996) once wrote, "I have found little that is 'good' about human beings on the whole. In my experience most of them are trash."

This negative view of human nature has crept into general perceptions of what psychology is all about. Imagine, for example, that you are seated on a plane, having a pleasant conversation with the stranger sitting next to you. At some point you ask your seatmate what she does for a living, and she informs you she is a psychologist. You might think to yourself, "Uh-oh. What have I already told this person? What secrets does she know about me that I don't know about myself? Has she been analyzing me this whole time?" Would you be surprised to discover that this psychologist studies happiness? Or intelligence? Or the processes related to the experience of vision? The study of abnormal problems is a very important aspect of psychology, but to equate the science of psychology entirely with the study of abnormal problems is like equating biology with the field of medicine or a cellular biologist with a medical doctor (which, as any pre-med major will assure you, is a mistake). As you read further, you will discover that psychology is a diverse field and that psychologists have wide-ranging interests. Psychologists have made extraordinary advances in understanding psychological

positive psychology movement The push for a stronger emphasis on research involving the experiences that people value, the traits associated with optimal capacities for love and work, and positive group and civic values.

The murder in 2006 of five Amish schoolgirls evoked feelings in the community not of hatred and revenge but of forgiveness.

disorders and treatment, and these topics are essential to an understanding of the science of psychology. At the same time, the field of psychology is broader than these topics.

In this book, we consider the full range of human behavior, including strengths and capacities as well as disorders and dysfunction. Psychology is interested in understanding the rich truths of human life in all its dimensions, including people's best and worst experiences. Psychologists acknowledge that, as in the heroism of Jabbar Gibson, sometimes individuals' best moments emerge amid the most difficult circumstances.

Research on the human capacity for forgiveness demonstrates this point (Cohen & others, 2006; Legaree, Turner, & Lollis, 2007; McCullough, Bono, & Root, 2007; Ross, Hertenstein, & Wrobel, 2007). Forgiveness is the act of letting go of our anger and resentment toward someone who has done something harmful to us. With forgiveness we cease seeking revenge or avoiding the person who did us harm, and we might even wish that person well. Most world religions place value on the sometimes challenging act of forgiveness. In October 2006, after Charles Carl Roberts IV took 10 young Amish girls hostage in a one-room schoolhouse in Pennsylvania, eventually killing 5 of them and wounding 5 others before killing himself, the grief-stricken Amish community focused not on hatred and revenge but on forgiveness. As funds were being set up for the victims' families, the Amish insisted that one be established for the murderer's family. As they prepared simple funerals for the dead girls, the community invited the wife of the killer to attend.

The willingness of the Amish people to forgive this horrible crime is both remarkable and puzzling. Can we scientifically understand the human ability to forgive even what might seem to be unforgivable? A number of psychologists have taken up the topic of forgiveness in research and clinical practice (Bono & McCullough, 2006; Cohen & others, 2006). Michael McCullough and his colleagues (2007) have shown that the capacity to forgive is an unfolding process that often takes time. Furthermore, sometimes forgiveness is a dynamic process—we might forgive someone for an offense immediately but then later return to thoughts of revenge or punishment. For the Amish, their deep religious faith led them to embrace forgiveness, where many people might have been motivated to seek revenge and retribution. Researchers also have explored the relation between religious commitment and forgiveness (Cohen & others, 2006; McCullough, Bono, & Root, 2007; Tsang, McCullough, & Hoyt, 2005).

The positive psychology movement is certainly not without controversy and critics (Lazarus, 2003). As already noted, however, controversy is a part of any science. Healthy debate characterizes the field of psychology, and a new psychological perspective has sometimes arisen when one scientist questions the views of another. Such ongoing debate and controversy are signs of a vigorous, vital discipline. Indeed, the very birth of the field was itself marked with controversy and debate. As we will see, great minds do not always think alike, especially when they are thinking about psychology.

 ## REVIEW, ASSESS, AND SHARPEN YOUR THINKING

Review

1 Explain what psychology is and describe the positive psychology movement.
- Define psychology and discuss how psychology differs from our common knowledge about ourselves and others.
- Discuss the role of critical thinking in scientific thought.
- Outline the objectives of positive psychology and discuss why they are important.

Assess

1. How are psychology and common sense different in the study of people?

A. They are not different. Psychology is the study of what we know about ourselves and others.

B. Psychology uses the scientific method to answer questions about human behavior while common sense implies that everything is known, as through intuition.

C. Psychology focuses on behavior, while common sense focuses on thoughts.

D. Psychological findings are counterintuitive.

2. **Which of the following statements is correct?**
   A. Positive psychology focuses on human strengths and signs of resilience that often emerge out of a negative life experience, but does not examine negative aspects of life.
   B. Positive psychology has a long tradition in the field of psychology, dating back over 100 years.
   C. Positive psychology focuses only on persons in therapy.
   D. Positive psychology is based on Freud's ideas about human nature.

3. **On which of the following topics would a positive psychologist likely focus?**
   A. the relationship between combat and post-traumatic stress disorder
   B. the relationship between well-being and income
   C. the effectiveness of cognitive-behavioral therapy with persons with bipolar disorder
   D. the rates of neuronal death in brain injured individuals

4. **Which of the following is not a mental process?**
   A. Thoughts
   B. Behaviors
   C. Emotions
   D. Motives

5. **The goals of psychology include:**
   A. The study of human behavior
   B. The description, prediction, and explanation of behavior
   C. The confirmation of intuition
   D. The study of thinking

Sharpen Your Thinking

The human capacity for forgiveness is a topic that interests psychologists. What is an important strength of your own that you think should be included in psychology's research agenda? Why?

2 The Roots and Early Scientific Approaches of Psychology

Discuss the roots and early scientific foundations of psychology.

Psychology seeks to answer questions that people have been asking for thousands of years. For example:

- How do our senses perceive the world?
- How do we learn?
- What is memory?
- Why does one person grow and flourish, whereas another person struggles in life?
- Do dreams matter?
- Can people learn to be happier and more optimistic?

The notion that these questions might be answered by scientific inquiry is a relatively new idea. From the time human language included the word *why* and became rich enough to let people talk about the past, we have been creating myths to explain why things are the way they are. Ancient myths attributed most important events to the pleasure or displeasure of the gods: When a volcano erupted, the gods were angry; if two people fell in love, they had been struck by Cupid's arrows. Gradually, myths gave way to philosophy—the rational investigation of the underlying principles of being and knowledge. People attempted to explain events in terms of natural rather than supernatural causes (Viney & King, 2003).

Western philosophy came of age in ancient Greece in the fourth and fifth centuries B.C.E. Socrates, Plato, Aristotle, and others debated the nature of thought and behavior, including the possible link between the mind and the body. Later philosophers, especially René Descartes, argued that the mind and body were completely separate and focused their attention on the mind. Psychology grew out of this tradition of thinking about the mind and body. The influence of philosophy on contemporary psychology persists today,

Wilhelm Wundt (1832–1920)
Wundt founded the first psychology laboratory (with his co-workers) in 1879 at the University of Leipzig in Germany.

as researchers who study emotion still talk about Descartes, and scientists who study happiness refer back to Aristotle.

Philosophy was not the only discipline from which psychology emerged. Psychology also has roots in the natural sciences of biology and physiology (Johnson, 2008; Kalat, 2007). Indeed, it was Wilhelm Wundt (1832–1920), a German philosopher-physician, who put the pieces of the philosophy–natural science puzzle together to create the academic discipline of psychology.

Some historians like to say that modern psychology was born in December 1879 at the University of Leipzig, when Wundt and two young students performed an experiment to measure the time lag between the instant at which a person heard a sound and the instant at which that person actually pressed a telegraph key to signal that he had heard. The experiment was one of many attempts to measure human behavior through physiological measurement.

What was so special about this experiment? Wundt's experiment was about the workings of the brain: He was trying to measure the time it took the human brain and nervous system to translate information into action. At the heart of this experiment was the idea that mental processes could be studied quantitatively—that is, that they could be measured. This focus ushered in the new science of psychology.

Structuralism

The main research conducted by Wundt and his collaborators focused on trying to discover basic elements, or "structures," of mental processes. For example, they described three different dimensions of *feeling:* pleasure/displeasure, tension/relaxation, and excitement/depression. A student of Wundt's, E. B. Titchener (1867–1927), gave Wundt's approach the label of **structuralism** because of its focus on identifying the structures of the human mind.

The method used in the study of mental structures was *introspection* (literally, "looking inside"). For this type of experiment, a person was placed in a laboratory setting and was asked to think (introspect) about what was going on mentally as various events took place. For example, the individual might be subjected to a sharp, repetitive clicking sound and asked to report whatever conscious feelings the clicking produced. What made this method scientific was the systematic, detailed self-reports required of the person in the controlled laboratory setting.

These studies focused mainly on sensation and perception because they were the easiest processes to break down into component parts. For example, Titchener used the introspective method to study taste. He trained participants to identify and record their taste sensations. The outcome was the identification of four components of taste: bitter, sweet, salty, and sour. In the long run, though, conscious introspection was not a very productive method of exploring the basic elements of human behavior. You might be able to describe to someone how you solved a math problem using introspection, but could you explain the process by which you remember, say, your own phone number? It seems to pop into consciousness without your awareness of the operations that must be involved. Where did it come from? Where was it stored? How did you find it?

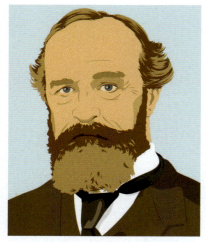

William James (1842–1910)
James's approach became known as functionalism.

Functionalism

Although Wundt is most often regarded as the founding father of modern psychology, it was William James (1842–1910), perhaps more than any other person, who gave the field an American stamp. James's approach to psychology developed out of his interest in the school of philosophy called *pragmatism,* which essentially holds that to find out the meaning of an idea, you must determine its consequences. So, an idea is evaluated based on how useful it is. From a pragmatic perspective, then, the question is not so much what the mind is (that is, its structures) as what it is for (its purpose or functions). This interest in the outcome of mental processes led James to emphasize cause and effect, prediction and control, and the important interaction of the environment and behavior. James's view was eventually named *functionalism.*

In contrast to structuralism, which emphasized the components of the mind, **functionalism** was concerned with the functions and purposes of the mind and behavior

structuralism An early school of psychology that attempted to identify the structures of the human mind.

functionalism An early school of psychology that was concerned with the functions and purposes of the mind and behavior in individuals' adaptation to the environment.

in individuals' adaptation to the environment. Structuralists were not interested in an individual's interaction with the environment, but this activity was a major functionalist theme. Whereas the structuralists were looking *inside* the mind, searching for its structures, the functionalists were focusing more on what was going on in human interactions with the *outside* world. If structuralism is about the "what" of the mind, functionalism is about the "why."

Central to functionalism is the question of why it is adaptive that people think the way they do. James and other functionalists did not believe in the existence of elementary, rigid structures of the mind. Instead, James saw the mind as flexible and fluid, characterized by constant change and adaptation in response to a continuous flow of information. James objected to the tendency of structuralists to break mental processes down into minute, separate components. Not surprisingly then, he called the natural flow of thought a *stream of consciousness.*

Functionalism meshed well with another important intellectual development at the time, the work of British naturalist Charles Darwin (1809–1882). In 1859, Darwin published his ideas in *On the Origin of Species.* He proposed the principle of **natural selection,** an evolutionary process that favors organisms' traits or characteristics that are best adapted to reproduce and survive. He believed that organisms reproduce at rates that would cause enormous increases in the population of most species, yet noted that populations remain nearly constant. Darwin reasoned that an intense, constant struggle for food, water, and resources must occur among the young born in each generation, because many of the young do not survive. Those that do survive to adulthood pass their genes on to the next generation. Darwin concluded that organisms with biological features that led to more successful reproduction were better represented in subsequent generations. Over many generations, organisms with these characteristics would constitute a larger percentage of the population. Eventually this process could modify a whole population. If environmental conditions changed, however, other characteristics might become favored by natural selection, moving the process in a different direction.

If you are unfamiliar with Darwin's theory of evolution, it might be useful to review these ideas through a simple example. Consider the question, Why do giraffes have long necks? An early explanation of this characteristic might be that giraffes live in places where the trees are very high, and so the giraffes must stretch their necks to get to their favorite food—leaves. Lots of stretching might lead to giraffes with longer necks. The problem with this explanation is that it does not tell us why giraffes are born with long necks. A characteristic cannot be passed from one generation to the next unless it is recorded in the genes. According to evolutionary theory, species change through random genetic mutation, so that presumably long, long ago, some giraffes were genetically predisposed to have longer necks, and some giraffes were genetically predisposed to have shorter necks. Only those with the long necks survived to reproduce, giving us the giraffes we see today. The survival of the giraffes with long necks is a product of natural selection. Natural selection favors organisms' traits or characteristics that are best adapted to survive in a particular environment. Evolutionary theory fits well with the functionalist perspective since it emphasizes the survival function of characteristics. Evolutionary theory implies that the way we are, at least partially, is the way that is best suited to surviving in our environment (Kardong, 2008). James was certainly influenced by Darwin's work (Myers, 1986). The influence of functionalism on psychology is apparent today in the application of the psychology to areas such as business and education (Kreitner & Kinicki, 2007; Santrock, 2008).

Wundt and James were each generally unimpressed with the other's perspective. Wundt famously compared James's masterwork *The Principles of Psychology* to literature: "It is beautiful but it is not psychology" (Fancher, 1996, p. 266). In turn, James wrote that Wundt's structuralist school of thought had "plenty of school, but no thought" (James, 1904, p.1). Nonetheless, although these two great minds did not agree, each had a profound influence on the science of psychology. Indeed, if you trace the intellectual history of any living psychologist, the academic family tree will end with one of these notable figures.

natural selection An evolutionary process that favors organisms' traits or characteristics that are best adapted to reproduce and survive.

The survival of giraffes with long necks (and not giraffes with short necks) vividly illustrates natural selection at work.

REVIEW, ASSESS, AND SHARPEN YOUR THINKING

Review

2 Discuss the roots and early scientific foundations of psychology.
- Summarize the roots of psychology and the view of psychology called structuralism.
- Define functionalism and explain the differing emphases of structuralists and functionalists.

Assess

1. Who is considered the founder of functionalism?
   A. Wilhelm Wundt
   B. Sigmund Freud
   C. William James
   D. Socrates

2. Which of the following statements is correct?
   A. Structuralism focuses on the purpose of the mind.
   B. Functionalism focuses on the structures of the brain.
   C. Functionalism led to the identification of the components of taste.
   D. Structuralism employs the method of introspection.

3. Who wrote *The Principles of Psychology?*
   A. William James
   B. Charles Darwin
   C. Wilhelm Wundt
   D. Rene Descartes

4. Wundt is considered the founder of modern psychology because he
   A. used animal research to understand the human mind.
   B. studied mental processes using quantitative experiments.
   C. used more philosophy than biology to understand the mind.
   D. tried to prove that the mind and body are completely separate.

5. Why is Charles Darwin's work relevant to psychology?
   A. Darwin's research demonstrated that there are few differences between humans and animals.
   B. Darwin's principle of natural selection suggests that human behavior is partially a result of efforts to survive.
   C. Darwin stated that humans descended from apes, which allows psychology to use animal research to understand human behavior.
   D. Darwin disproved functionalism.

Sharpen Your Thinking

List some questions about your mind and behavior that a deeper understanding of psychology might help you to answer.

3 Contemporary Approaches to Psychology

Summarize the main themes of seven approaches to psychology.

If structuralism won the battle to be the birthplace of psychology, it is safe to say that functionalism won the war. Today most psychologists talk about the adaptiveness of behavior and mental processes and rely on methods beyond introspection to understand the complex processes of the human mind (Strack & Schwarz, 2007). In the century since Wundt and James debated the best way to think about psychology, a number of broad approaches have emerged. In this section we briefly survey seven different approaches that represent the intellectual backdrop of psychological science: biological, behavioral, psychodynamic, humanistic, cognitive, evolutionary, and sociocultural.

The Biological Approach

Some psychologists examine behavior and mental processes through the **biological approach,** which is a focus on the body, especially the brain and nervous system. For example, researchers might investigate the way your heart races when you are afraid or how your hands sweat when you tell a lie. Although a number of physiological systems may be involved in thoughts and feelings, perhaps the largest contribution to physiological psychology has come through the emergence of neuroscience (Bosel, 2007; Hagner, 2007).

   Neuroscience is the scientific study of the structure, function, development, genetics, and biochemistry of the nervous system. Neuroscience emphasizes that the brain and nervous

biological approach A psychological perspective that examines behavior and mental processes through a focus on the body, especially the brain and nervous system.

neuroscience The scientific study of the structure, function, development, genetics, and biochemistry of the nervous system.

system are central to understanding behavior, thought, and emotion. Neuroscientists believe that thoughts and emotions have a physical basis in the brain. Electrical impulses zoom throughout the brain's cells, releasing chemical substances that enable us to think, feel, and behave. Our remarkable human capabilities would not be possible without the brain and nervous system, which constitute the most complex, intricate, and elegant system imaginable. Although biological approaches might sometimes seem to reduce complex human experience into simple physical structures, developments in neuroscience have allowed psychologists to understand the brain as an amazingly complex organ, perhaps just as complex as the psychological processes linked to its functioning.

The Behavioral Approach

The **behavioral approach** emphasizes the scientific study of observable behavioral responses and their environmental determinants. In other words, the behavioral approach focuses on interactions with the environment that can be seen and measured. The principles of the behavioral approach also have been widely applied to help people change their behavior for the better (Martin & Pear, 2007; Watson & Tharp, 2007). The psychologists who adopt this approach are called *behaviorists*. Under the intellectual leadership of John B. Watson (1878–1958) and B. F. Skinner (1904–1990), behaviorism dominated psychological research during the first half of the twentieth century.

B. F. Skinner was a tinkerer who liked to make new gadgets. The younger of his two daughters, Deborah, was raised in Skinner's enclosed Air-Crib. Some critics accused Skinner of monstrous experimentation with his children; however, the early controlled environment has not had any noticeable harmful effects. Deborah, shown here as a child with her parents, is today a successful artist whose work strongly reflects her unique early childhood experience.

Many studies with a behavioral approach take place in experimental laboratories under carefully controlled conditions. When behaviorism was in its infancy, virtually all behavioral studies were conducted in the laboratory, although today many take place outside the laboratory in natural settings such as schools and homes.

Skinner emphasized that what we *do* is the ultimate test of who we are. He believed that rewards and punishments determine our behavior. For example, a child might behave in a well-mannered fashion because her parents have rewarded this behavior. An adult might work hard at a job because of the money he gets for his effort. We do these things, say behaviorists, not because of an inborn motivation to be competent people but rather because of the environmental conditions we have experienced and continue to experience (Skinner, 1938).

Contemporary behaviorists still emphasize the importance of observing behavior to understand an individual, and they continue to use the rigorous sorts of experimental methods advocated by Watson and Skinner (Cooper, Heron, & Heward, 2007). They also continue to stress the importance of environmental determinants of behavior (DeSantis-Moniaci & Altshuler, 2007). However, not every behaviorist today accepts the earlier behaviorists' rejection of thought processes (often called *cognition*) (Kushner, 2007).

The Psychodynamic Approach

The **psychodynamic approach** emphasizes unconscious thought, the conflict between biological instincts and society's demands, and early family experiences. This approach argues that unlearned biological instincts, especially sexual and aggressive impulses, influence the way people think, feel, and behave. These instincts, buried deep within the unconscious mind, are often at odds with society's demands. Although Sigmund Freud (1856–1939), the founding father of the psychodynamic approach, saw much of psychological development as instinctual, he theorized that early relationships with parents are the chief forces that shape an

behavioral approach A psychological perspective emphasizing the scientific study of observable behavioral responses and their environmental determinants.

psychodynamic approach A psychological perspective emphasizing unconscious thought, the conflict between biological instincts and society's demands, and early family experiences.

Sigmund Freud (1856–1939)
Freud was the founding father of the psychodynamic approach.

humanistic approach A psychological perspective that emphasizes a person's positive qualities, capacity for positive growth, and the freedom to choose any destiny.

cognitive approach A psychological perspective that focuses on the mental processes involved in knowing: how we direct our attention, perceive, remember, think, and solve problems.

According to humanistic psychologists, warm, supportive behavior toward others helps us to realize our tremendous capacity for self-understanding.

individual's personality. Freud's (1917) theory was the basis for the therapeutic technique that he called *psychoanalysis.* His approach was controversial when he introduced it in Vienna at the beginning of the twentieth century. However, his ideas flourished, and many clinicians still find value in his insights into human behavior.

Unlike the behavioral approach, the psychodynamic approach focuses almost exclusively on clinical applications rather than on experimental research. For this reason, psychodynamic theories always have been controversial and difficult to validate. Nonetheless, they are an important part of psychology. Today's psychodynamic theories tend to place less emphasis on sexual instincts and more on cultural experiences as determinants of behavior.

The Humanistic Approach

The **humanistic approach** emphasizes a person's positive qualities, the capacity for positive growth, and the freedom to choose any destiny. Humanistic psychologists stress that people have the ability to control their lives and avoid being manipulated by the environment (Maslow, 1971; Rogers, 1961). They theorize that, rather than being driven by unconscious impulses (as the psychodynamic approach dictates) or by external rewards (as the behavioral approach emphasizes), people can choose to live by higher human values, such as altruism—unselfish concern for other people's well-being—and free will. Humanistic psychologists also think that people have a tremendous potential for self-understanding and that the way to help others achieve self-understanding is by being warm and supportive. Many aspects of this optimistic approach appear in research on motivation, emotion, and personality, and in many ways the humanistic perspective provides a foundation for positive psychology (Diaz-Laplante, 2007; Patterson & Joseph, 2007).

The Cognitive Approach

According to cognitive psychologists, your brain hosts or embodies a "mind" whose mental processes allow you to remember, make decisions, plan, set goals, and be creative (Gluck & others, 2007; Sternberg, 2008). The **cognitive approach,** then, emphasizes the mental processes involved in knowing: how we direct our attention, how we perceive, how we remember, and how we think and solve problems. For example, cognitive psychologists want to know how we solve algebraic equations, why we remember some things for only a short time but remember others for a lifetime, and how we can use imagery to plan for the future.

Cognitive psychologists view the mind as an active and aware problem-solving system (Plessner, Betsch, & Betsch, 2007). This positive view contrasts with the behavioral view, which portrays behavior as controlled by external environmental forces. The cognitive view also contrasts with pessimistic views (such as those of Freud) that see human behavior as being controlled by instincts or other unconscious forces. In the cognitive view, an individual's mental processes are in control of behavior through memories, perceptions, images, and thinking.

The Evolutionary Approach

Although arguably all of psychology emerges out of evolutionary theory, some psychologists emphasize an **evolutionary approach** that uses evolutionary ideas such as adaptation, reproduction, and "survival of the fittest" as the basis for explaining specific human behaviors. David Buss (1995, 2008) argues that just as evolution shapes our physical features, such as body shape, it also influences our decision making, level of aggressiveness, fears, and mating patterns. Thus, evolutionary psychologists argue, the way we adapt can be traced to problems animals and early humans faced in adapting to their environments (Dunbar & Barrett, 2007).

Evolutionary psychologists believe that their approach provides an umbrella that unifies the diverse fields of psychology (Bjorklund, 2007; Geary, 2006). Not all psychologists agree with this conclusion. For example, some critics stress that the evolutionary approach provides an inaccurate account of why men and women have different social roles and does not adequately account for cultural diversity and experiences (Wood & Eagly, 2007). But the evolutionary approach is young, and its future may be fruitful.

F-Minus: © United Feature Syndicate, Inc.

The Sociocultural Approach

The **sociocultural approach** examines the ways in which the social and cultural environments influence behavior. Socioculturalists argue that a full understanding of a person's behavior requires knowing about the cultural context in which the behavior occurs (Kagitcibasi, 2007; Shiraev & Levy, 2007). For example, in some cultures, including the United States, it may be entirely acceptable for a woman to be assertive, but in other cultures, such as in Iran, the same behavior may be considered inappropriate.

We find an example of the sociocultural approach in recent research examining motivation in Western versus Eastern cultures. Imagine that you are in a psychological study in which you are asked to solve a number of puzzles. Some of the puzzles are quite easy, and you complete them with no problem. The other puzzles are more difficult; try as you might, you cannot figure them out. After the study you are left alone with the puzzles, and the researcher informs you that if you like, you can keep playing with the puzzles while she prepares the rest of the study materials. Which puzzles would you be likely to work on?

If you are like most U.S. college students, you will gravitate toward the easy puzzles, choosing to work on what you know you are already good at. However, if you are like most Asian students, you will pick up the difficult puzzles and keep working on those that you have not yet solved (Heine, 2005; Norenzayan & Heine, 2005). These cultural differences are thought to emerge out of differing views of the self, goals, and learning. It has been suggested that Asian students show a particularly adaptive response to task difficulty and failure and that U.S. students might benefit from looking at failure as an opportunity to learn rather than as something to avoid.

The sociocultural approach focuses not only on comparisons of behavior across countries but also on the behavior of individuals from different ethnic and cultural groups within a country (Berry, 2007). Thus there is increasing interest in the behavior of African Americans, Latinos, and Asian Americans, especially in terms of the factors that have restricted or enhanced their ability to adapt and cope with living in a predominantly White society (Banks, 2008; Bennett, 2007).

These seven approaches to understanding psychology provide different and often complementary views of the same behavior. Think about a simple event you might experience—say, seeing a cute puppy. Seeing that puppy involves physical processes in the eyes, nervous system, and brain. But the moment you spot that puppy, you might smile without thinking. You might feel the cuteness of the puppy give your heart a little squeeze. Such an emotional reaction might be a response to your past learning experiences with animals, or to your unconscious memories of a childhood dog, or even to evolutionary processes that promoted cuteness as a way for helpless offspring to survive. You might find yourself tempted to pick up and cuddle the little guy. Sociocultural factors might play a role in your decision about whether to ask the owner if holding the puppy would be okay, whether to share those warm feelings about the puppy with others, and even whether (as in some cultures) to view that puppy as food.

The sociocultural approach especially contrasts with the evolutionary approach. To read about how these two approaches view altruism, see the Critical Controversy.

evolutionary approach A psychological perspective that uses evolutionary ideas such as adaptation, reproduction, and "survival of the fittest" as the basis for explaining specific human behaviors.

sociocultural approach A psychological perspective that examines the ways in which the social and cultural environments influence behavior.

Critical Controversy   Can Humans Really Be Altruistic?

If there was a silver lining in the dark cloud of September 11, 2001, it was that firefighters, police officers, emergency medical personnel, and many ordinary individuals altruistically risked their own lives to help people caught in the collapse of the twin towers of the World Trade Center in New York City. Other heroes of 9/11 included the passengers aboard United Flight 93 who selflessly forced the plane to crash in a field instead of allowing it to hit the intended target.

Altruistic behavior is often defined as voluntary behavior that is intended to benefit others and is not motivated by any expectation of personal gain. The most extreme form of altruism is giving one's life to save someone else, as did many responding to the attacks of September 11.

Altruism poses an important problem for the evolutionary approach to psychology (Van Lange & others, 2007). According to Darwin's theory of evolution, behaviors that favor an organism's reproductive success are likely to be passed on to future generations. In fact, altruistic behavior *reduces* a person's chances of reproductive success, to the extent that it means providing one's resources to another with no apparent gain. Therefore, altruists should be at a clear evolutionary disadvantage compared to those who act more selfishly and thereby ensure the propagation of their own genes. Over many generations, selfish behavior should be favored and altruistic behavior should die out, according to the evolutionary view.

Seen in this way through the Darwinian lens of the survival of the fittest, human altruism is hard to understand. The concept of *kin selection*, however, provides one way to reconcile altruism with evolutionary theory. According to this concept, our genes survive not just when we reproduce but also when our relatives reproduce. Kin selection includes the idea of *inclusive fitness*, which means that a gene may be considered successfully adaptive if it benefits not only the individual who possesses it but also anyone who is genetically related to that person (Caporael, 2007). Indeed, from an evolutionary perspective, the individuals who carry our genes—our children—have a special place in the domain of altruism. Natural selection favors parents who care for their children and improve their probability of surviving. Human parents who feed their young are performing a biologically altruistic act because feeding increases their offsprings' chances of survival. So is a mother bird that altruistically tries to drive predators away from the fledglings in her nest. She is willing to sacrifice herself so that three or four of her young offspring will have the chance to survive, thus preserving her genes.

The theory of kin selection can explain why some

Firefighters helping victims of the September 11, 2001, terrorist attack on the World Trade Center in New York City.

people forgo having their own children and choose instead to care for relatives and relatives' children. What this theory cannot explain is altruism directed toward people outside the family—and especially toward strangers. However, evolutionary psychologists believe that tremendous benefits can come to individuals who form cooperative, reciprocal relationships (Bernhard, Fischbacher, & Fehr, 2006; Wenseleers & Ratnieks, 2006). By being good to someone now, individuals increase the likelihood that they will receive a benefit from the other person in the future. Through this reciprocal process, both gain something beyond what they could have gained by acting alone.

In contrast to the evolutionary interpretation, the sociocultural approach attempts to explain altruistic behavior as being the result of social and cultural experiences. According to the sociocultural approach, each of us is a product of many culturally and socially derived relationships, which continually unfold over time (Newson, Richerson, & Boyd, 2007; Shiraev & Levy, 2007). Because our relationships within our culture are open-ended and adaptable rather than rigidly determined by our genes, genuine acts of altruism

(continued)

are possible. Simply put, if our culture teaches us to be kind without regard for our own gain, then we can become true altruists.

By providing a theory that emphasizes the importance of adaptation and natural selection in explaining all behavior, the evolutionary approach has much to recommend it (Fletcher & Zwick, 2006; Freeman & Herron, 2007). It forces us to look at our capacity for selfishness and to refine our notions of kindness and altruism. Yet the sociocultural approach also is attractive, because it stresses that people can be genuinely altruistic (Eisenberg, Fabes, & Spinrad, 2006). This possibility is what comes to mind when we think about the firefighters, police officers, and passengers who sacrificed their lives on September 11, 2001. In the end, this

contrast in views may well sharpen our understanding of what it is to be fully human.

What Do You Think?

- Are people ever truly altruistic? Or are they operating according to selfish motives?

- Have you ever acted in a genuinely altruistic fashion? If so, when and how? Could your behavior be explained instead by theories of kin selection?

- What kind of research might settle the question of whether humans are capable of genuine altruism?

 REVIEW, ASSESS, AND SHARPEN YOUR THINKING

Review

3 Summarize the main themes of seven approaches to psychology.
- Describe the biological approach.
- Discuss the behavioral approach.
- Summarize the psychodynamic approach.
- Explain the humanistic approach.
- Provide an overview of the cognitive approach.
- Review the evolutionary approach.
- Recap the sociocultural approach.

Assess

1. Which of the following areas of psychology is most interested in the impact of early family experiences?
   A. positive psychology   B. cognitive psychology
   C. psychodynamic psychology   D. behavioral psychology

2. Which of the following approaches would view learning as a combination of perceptual and memory processes?
   A. the positive psychology approach
   B. the behavioral approach
   C. the sociocultural approach
   D. the cognitive approach

3. A psychologist who examines the role of political messages in the well-being of lesbian, gay, and bisexual people would be most closely associated with which of the following approaches?
   A. the cognitive approach   B. the evolutionary approach
   C. the sociocultural approach   D. the psychodynamic approach

4. Which of the following approaches would focus on self-fulfillment, altruism, and personal growth?
   A. the cognitive approach
   B. the behavioral approach
   C. the psychodynamic approach
   D. the humanistic approach

5. A psychologist who conducts studies of identical twins to determine if having a twin with a psychological disorder increases the risk of the other twin developing the same disorder would be most closely associated with
   A. the evolutionary approach.
   B. the psychodynamic approach.
   C. the behavioral approach.
   D. the biological approach.

Sharpen Your Thinking

Suppose you could talk with a psychologist specializing in each of the seven approaches. Think about the members of your family and other people you know. Write down at least one question you might want to ask about the thoughts and behaviors of these people.

Richard J. Davidson of the University of Wisconsin, Madison, shown with the Dalai Lama, is a leading researcher in behavioral neuroscience.

4 Areas of Specialization and Careers in Psychology

Evaluate areas of specialization and careers in psychology.

If you were to go to graduate school to earn an advanced degree in psychology, you would be required to specialize in a particular area. Here we review the major areas of psychology that are the focus of this book. It is important to keep in mind that these specializations are not mutually exclusive. Indeed, the boundaries that separate these areas are quite fuzzy, and psychologists in one field may collaborate with researchers in another. Throughout this book, in a feature called Intersection (see page 21 of this chapter for the first example), we highlight areas where different fields of psychology come together to address important and often intriguing research questions.

Areas of Specialization

Psychology has many areas of specialization. In 2007, there were 56 divisions in the American Psychological Association, each focusing on a specific area of psychology. The most recent division to be added was trauma psychology. Here we describe some of the main specializations in the field of psychology.

Physiological Psychology and Behavioral Neuroscience Researchers who study physiological psychology are interested in the physical processes that underlie mental processes such as vision and memory. Physiological psychologists may use animal models (that is, they may use animals, such as rats, to study processes that are difficult or impossible to study in the same way in humans) to examine such topics as the development of the nervous system. The field of behavioral neuroscience also focuses on biological processes, especially the brain's role in behavior (Kolb & Whishaw, 2007). In Chapter 3 we examine the many ways that physiological processes relate to psychological experience.

Developmental Psychology *Developmental psychology* is concerned with how people become who they are, from conception to death. In particular, developmental psychologists concentrate on the biological and environmental factors that contribute to human development. For many years the major emphasis of developmentalists was child development. However, an increasing number of today's developmental psychologists show a strong interest in adult development and aging (Birren & Schaie, 2007; Schaie, 2007). Their inquiries range across the biological, cognitive, and social domains of life. Chapter 4 reviews the key findings in this fascinating area.

The research of Carol S. Dweck of Stanford University spans the fields of developmental and social psychology. Her influential work looks at how our ideas of self play a role in motivation, self-regulation, and achievement.

Sensation and Perception Researchers who study sensation and perception focus on the physical systems and psychological processes that allow us to experience the world—to smell the Thanksgiving turkey in the oven and to see the beauty of a sunset. These complex processes are the subject of Chapter 5.

Cognitive Psychology *Cognitive psychology* (addressed in Chapters 8 and 9) is the broad name given to the field of psychology that examines attention, consciousness, information processing, and memory. Cognitive psychologists are also interested in cognitive skills and abilities such as problem solving, decision making, expertise, and intelligence, topics covered in Chapter 9 (Gluck & others, 2007; Sternberg, 2006). Researchers in cognitive psychology and sensation perception are sometimes called experimental psychologists.

Learning *Learning* is the complex process by which behavior changes to adapt to changing circumstances. Learning has been addressed from the behavioral and cognitive perspectives, and this topic is covered in Chapter 7 (Bandura, 2007a, 2007b).

Motivation and Emotion   Researchers from a variety of specializations are interested in these two important aspects of experience. Research questions addressed by scientists who study motivation include how individuals persist to attain a difficult goal and how rewards affect the experience of motivation (Fishbach & Ferguson, 2007). Emotion researchers delve into such topics as the physiological and brain processes that underlie emotional experience, the role of emotional expression in health, and the possibility that emotions are universal (Barrett & others, 2007; Frijda, 2007). These fascinating questions are examined in Chapter 10.

Personality Psychology   *Personality psychology* focuses on the relatively enduring characteristics of individuals. Personality psychologists study such topics as traits, goals, motives, genetics, personality development, and well-being (Cloninger, 2008). Researchers in personality psychology are interested in those aspects of your psychological makeup that make you uniquely you. The field of personality is explored fully in Chapter 11.

"Well, you don't look like an experimental psychologist to me."

Social Psychology   *Social psychology* deals with people's social interactions, relationships, social perceptions, social cognition, and attitudes. Social psychologists are interested in the influence of groups on individuals' thinking and behavior and in the ways that the groups to which we belong influence our attitudes (Brewer, 2007). Some of the research questions that concern social psychologists include understanding and working to reduce racial prejudice, determining whether two heads really are better than one, and exploring how the presence of others influences performance (Mays, Cochran, & Barnes, 2007). Social psychologists believe that we can better understand mind and behavior if we know how people function in groups. Chapter 12 reviews the major research findings of social psychology.

Clinical and Counseling Psychology   *Clinical and counseling psychology* is the most widely practiced specialization in psychology. Clinical and counseling psychologists diagnose and treat people with psychological problems (Nolen-Hoeksema, 2007; Prochaska & Norcross, 2007). Counseling psychologists sometimes deal with people who have less serious problems (Santee, 2007). For example, counseling psychologists may work with students, advising them about personal problems and career planning.

   A clinical psychologist typically has a doctoral degree in psychology, which requires 3 to 4 years of graduate work and 1 year of internship in a mental health facility. Clinical psychologists are different from psychiatrists, who study *psychiatry,* which is a branch of medicine. Psychiatrists are physicians with a doctor of medicine (MD) degree who subsequently specialize in abnormal behavior and psychotherapy. Despite their different training, clinical psychologists and psychiatrists are alike in sharing a common interest in improving the lives of people with mental health problems. One important distinction is that psychiatrists can prescribe drugs, whereas clinical psychologists generally cannot. Chapters 14 and 15 address the intriguing world of psychological disorders and treatment.

Health Psychology   *Health psychology* is a multidimensional approach to health that emphasizes psychological factors, lifestyle, and the nature of the healthcare delivery system (Taylor, 2007). Many health psychologists study the roles of stress and coping in people's lives (Stanton, Revenson, & Tennen, 2007). Health psychologists may work in physical or mental health areas. Some are members of multidisciplinary teams that conduct research or provide clinical services. Health psychology is examined in Chapter 16.

James W. Pennebaker of the University of Texas, Austin, is a distinguished social psychologist. His research probes the connections among traumatic life experience, expressive writing, physical and mental health, and work performance.

Social psychologists explore the powerful influence of groups (such as, clockwise, Chinese Americans, members of motorcycle clubs, gay dads, military families, and inner-city youths) on individuals' attitudes, thinking, and behavior.

"I thought we'd look at reducing your medication and replacing it with eight hugs a day before and after meals."

© CartoonStock.com

The psychology specialties that we have discussed so far are the main areas of psychology that we cover in this book. However, they do not represent an exhaustive list of the interests of the field. Other specializations in psychology include the following.

Industrial and Organizational Psychology *Industrial and organizational psychology (I/O psychology)* centers on the workplace—both on the workers and on the organizations that employ them. I/O psychology is often divided into industrial psychology and organizational psychology. Among the main concerns of industrial psychology are personnel matters and human resource management (Fouad, 2007). Thus, industrial psychology is increasingly referred to as *personnel psychology*. Organizational psychology examines the social and group influences of the organization (McShane & von Glinow, 2007). I/O psychology is the focus of the online chapter.

Community Psychology *Community psychology* is concerned with providing accessible care for people with psychological problems. Community-based mental health centers are one means of delivering services such as outreach programs to people in need, especially those who traditionally have been underserved by mental health professionals (Dalton, Elias, & Wandersman, 2007). Community psychologists view human behavior in terms of adaptation to resources and the specific situation. They work to create communities that are more supportive of residents by pinpointing needs, providing needed services, and teaching people how to gain access to resources that are already available (Beeson & others, 2006). Community psychologists are also concerned with prevention. That is, they try to prevent mental health problems by identifying high-risk groups and then intervening with appropriate services and by stimulating new opportunities in the community.

School and Educational Psychology *School and educational psychology* centrally concerns children's learning and adjustment in school. School psychologists in elementary and secondary school systems test children, make recommendations about educational placement, and work on educational planning teams. Educational psychologists work at colleges and universities, teach classes, and do research on teaching and learning (Alexander & Winne, 2006).

Environmental Psychology *Environmental psychology* is the study of the interactions between people and the physical environment. Environmental psychologists explore the effects of physical settings in most major areas of psychology, including perception, cognition, learning, development, abnormal behavior, and social relations (Israel & others, 2006; Sallis & Glanz, 2006). Topics that an environmental psychologist might study range from how different building and room arrangements influence behavior to what strategies might be used to reduce human behavior that harms the environment.

Psychology of Women The *psychology of women* studies psychological, social, and cultural influences on women's development and behavior. This field stresses the importance of integrating information about women with current psychological knowledge and beliefs and applying the information to society and its institutions (Hyde, 2007; Smith, 2007).

Forensic Psychology *Forensic psychology* is the field of psychology that applies psychological concepts to the legal system (Fradella, 2006). Social and cognitive psychologists increasingly conduct research on topics related to psychology and law. Forensic psychologists are hired by legal teams to provide input about many aspects of a trial, such as jury selection. Forensic psychologists with clinical training may also provide expert testimony in trials, particularly to add their expertise to the question of whether a criminal is likely to be a danger to society.

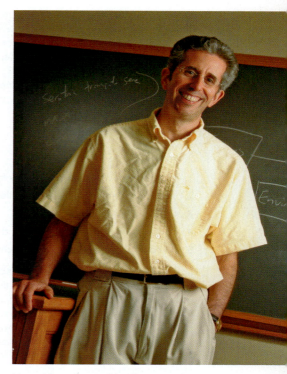

Howard Berenbaum of the University of Illinois, Urbana-Champaign, is a well-known clinical psychologist. His primary research delves into the roots of, and relationships among, various symptoms of mental disorders.

Sport Psychology *Sport psychology* applies psychology's principles to improving sport performance and enjoying sport participation (Cox, 2007; Williams, 2006). Sport psychology is a relatively new field, but it is rapidly gaining acceptance. It is now common to hear about elite athletes working with a sport psychologist to improve their games.

Cross-Cultural Psychology *Cross-cultural psychology* is the study of culture's role in understanding behavior, thought, and emotion (Kagitcibasi, 2007; Kitayama & Cohen, 2007). Cross-cultural psychologists compare the nature of psychological processes in different cultures with a special interest in whether psychological phenomena are universal or culture-specific. The International Association for Cross-Cultural Psychology promotes research on cross-cultural comparisons and awareness of culture's role in psychology. To read about some cross-cultural research on a topic of interest to almost everyone, see the Intersection on how culture influences happiness.

Careers

Psychologists do not pass all of their time in a laboratory, white-smocked with clipboard in hand, observing rats and crunching numbers. Some psychologists spend their days seeing individuals with problems; others teach at universities and conduct research. Still others work in business and industry, designing more efficient criteria for hiring. In short, psychology is a field with many areas of specialization.

Could you get passionate about psychology? Have you ever thought about majoring in psychology? Students who major in psychology often find the subject matter highly interesting (Kuther & Morgan, 2007; Landrum & Davis, 2007). In the remaining chapters of this book, you will encounter hundreds of truly fascinating inquiries in psychology.

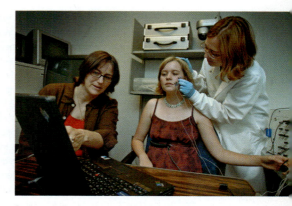

Barbara L. Frederickson (left) of the University of North Carolina, Chapel Hill, is a leading specialist in social psychology, the psychology of women, and positive psychology. Her research investigates topics such as positive emotions and human flourishing.

Cross-Cultural Psychology and Emotion: Are Some Cultures Happier Than Others?

When you think of all the things that might make a life good, you would probably include happiness. When asked to make three wishes for anything at all, many people wish for happiness (King & Broyles, 1997). And worldwide, people value being happy (Inglehart, 1990).

How do psychologists study happiness? Using the 1–7 scale, read the 5 statements below and indicate your agreement with each item.

7	6	5	4	3	2	1
Strongly Agree	Agree	Slightly Agree	Neither Agree Nor Disagree	Slightly Disagree	Disagree	Strongly Disagree

1. In most ways my life is close to my ideal.
2. The conditions of my life are excellent.
3. I am satisfied with my life.
4. So far I have gotten the important things I want in life.
5. If I could live my life over, I would change almost nothing.

You have just completed the Satisfaction with Life Scale (Diener & others, 1985), a commonly used questionnaire that measures how generally happy people are with their lives. To find out how happy you perceive yourself to be, add up your ratings and divide by 5. This average rating could be considered your level of general happiness. This scale and others like it have been used to measure happiness levels in a broad range of studies in many different countries.

Based on such research, Ed and Carol Diener (1996) have declared that "most people are pretty happy," scoring above the midpoint on the scale you just completed. These researchers concluded that being generally happy might be a characteristic of most people and that evolution may have endowed us with a propensity to be moderately happy most of the time. Still, research on happiness in various cultures has generally centered on relatively industrialized countries. What about truly nonindustrialized cultures?

When asked to make three wishes for anything at all, many people wish for happiness.

In a recent study, levels of happiness were examined in groups of people who have not generally been included in psychological studies (Biswas-Diener, Vitterso, & Diener, 2005). The research included three groups: the Inuits of Greenland, the Masai of southern Kenya, and American Old Order Amish. All three groups completed measures essentially the same as the one you just did. The Inuit tribe studied (the Inughuit) live at 79 degrees latitude (very far north!), in the harshest climate inhabited by a traditional human society. The landscape consists of rocks, glaciers, and the sea. Farming is impossible. The Inughuits do have some modern conveniences, such as electricity and running water, but they generally adhere to a traditional hunting culture. It is not uncommon to find an Inughuit hunter carving a seal or caribou on the kitchen floor while children in the next room watch TV. Most of us might feel a little blue in the winter months when gloomy weather seems to stretch on, day after day.

For the Inughuits, however, the sun never rises at all throughout the winter months, and in the summer, it never sets. How happy could an individual be in such a difficult setting? Pretty happy, it turns out, as the Inughuits averaged a 5.0 on the Satisfaction with Life Scale.

The Masai are an indigenous African nomadic group who live in villages of about 20 people, with little exposure to the West. The Masai are known to be fierce warriors, and their culture has many traditional ceremonies built around a boy's passage from childhood to manhood. Boys are circumcised between the ages of 15 and 22, and they are forbidden from moving or making a sound during the procedure. Girls also experience circumcision as they enter puberty, a controversial rite that involves the removal of the clitoris and that makes childbirth extremely difficult. The Masai practice child marriage and polygamy, and each tribe has a "medicine man." Women in Masai culture have very little power and are generally expected to do most of the work. How happy could an individual be in this context? Masai men and women who completed the measure orally in their native tongue, Maa, averaged a 5.4 on the life satisfaction scale (Biswas-Diener, Vitterso, & Diener, 2005).

Finally, the Old Order Amish belong to a strict religious sect that explicitly rejects modern aspects of life. The Amish separate themselves from mainstream society and can be seen on horse and buggy in various areas of the midwestern and northeastern United States. The women wear bonnets, and the men sport beards, dark clothes, and old-fashioned brimmed hats. Children are schooled only to the 8th grade. The people farm without modern machinery and dedicate their lives to simplicity—without radios, TVs, CDs, DVDs, iPods, cell phones, washing machines, and cars. But the Amish are still relatively happy, averaging 4.4 on the 7-point happiness scale (Biswas-Diener, Vitterso, & Diener, 2005).

These results converge with the findings of a host of other studies on happiness indicating that most individuals are indeed happy. But there is evidence for national differences in happiness. In one study, levels of happiness were examined in over 100,000 people from 55 nations (Diener, Diener, & Diener, 1995). The happiest countries were Iceland, Sweden, Australia,

(continued)

Denmark, Canada, Switzerland, and the United States. The least happy nations were the Dominican Republic, Cameroon, China, Russia, and South Korea. What might account for national differences in general happiness? Among the factors that were found to relate to increased national well-being were income, civil rights, and social equality (including the number of girls enrolled in secondary school).

Research on cultural factors in well-being suggests that even if most people are indeed reasonably happy, the factors that affect happiness may be culture-specific (Tov & Diener, 2007). Researchers have distinguished individualistic cultures from collectivistic cultures (Triandis, 2007). *Individualistic cultures* (such as the United States and western European nations) emphasize the uniqueness of each individual and his or her thoughts, feelings, and choices. Individualistic cultures view the person as having an independent sense of self, separate from his or her social group. In contrast, *collectivistic cultures* (such as those in East Asia) emphasize the social group and the roles the individual plays in that larger group. Collectivistic cultures view the person as embedded in the social network or having an interdependent sense of self. Researchers have found that the individualism is associated with higher levels of personal happiness (Diener, 2000; Diener, Diener, & Diener, 1995).

This difference between individualistic and collectivistic cultures is all the more interesting when we consider that although individualistic cultures report higher levels of personal happiness, they also have higher suicide rates. Similarly, individualistic cultures are characterized by higher levels of marital satisfaction but also higher divorce rates (Diener, 2000).

It may be that individuals in collectivistic cultures are more likely to sacrifice personal happiness for the sake of duty—for instance, staying in an unsatisfying marriage. Indeed, personal happiness is higher for individuals in collectivistic cultures when their personal goals and values fit societal dictates (Lu, 2006).

One factor that differs across cultures in relation to happiness is the individual's level of consistency across various situations. Are you essentially the same person at work, at school, and in your interactions with friends, family members, and romantic partners? In the West, being consistent across different situations is often considered an aspect of psychological health and of living in a way that is "true to yourself." In addition, in the West, when individuals perceive themselves to be consistent across different situations, they report higher levels of happiness. However, in other cultures, among them Korea (a collectivistic culture), consistency is unrelated to well-being (Suh, 2002). In more collectivistic cultures, tailoring one's behavior to social situations and roles is not experienced as being fake but rather as pursuing the goal of harmony with others.

This research shows how putting the central questions of psychology in a cross-cultural context can illuminate not only general human characteristics (such as happiness) but also differences in the culture-bound processes that lead to these characteristics (such as individualism versus collectivism). Further, cross-cultural research can help us to identify important characteristics within members of the same culture that influence the process by which individuals define and lead happy lives (Cross, Gore, & Morris, 2003; Kagitcibasi, 2007; Shiraev & Levy, 2007; Tov & Diener, 2007).

Not only do you gain considerable knowledge and understanding of the mind and behavior, but majoring in psychology equips you with a rich and diverse portfolio of skills that serve you well in many different types of work, both practical and professional (Morgan & Korschgen, 2006). A psychology major helps you improve your skills in research, measurement and computing, problem solving, critical thinking, and writing. Integrating these skills, which span the arts and sciences, provides you with unique qualifications. And even if you are not a psychology major and do not plan to major in psychology, this course and others in psychology can give you a richer, deeper understanding of many areas of life.

Business	Social/Human Services	Research
• personnel administrator	• case worker	• research assistant
• public relations	• youth counselor	• trainee for product research companies
• sales representative	• employment counselor	• marketing researcher
• admissions recruiter	• fund-raising specialist	• grant and report writer
• textbook representative	• alumni affairs coordinator	• information specialist/ researcher
• advertising	• mental health aide	• mental health aide
• insurance agent	• parent educator	• research analyst
• management trainee	• drug abuse counselor	• statistical assistant
• retail sales management		
• loan officer		

FIGURE 1.1

Some Job Possibilities for Students with an Undergraduate Degree in Psychology A psychology degree opens the door to many possible careers in the realms of business, social and human services, and research.

PSYCHOLOGY AND LIFE

Is Psychology in Your Future?

Instructions

Students who are successful as psychology majors have a profile that is related to the questions below. Answer true or false to each item.

		True	*False*
1.	I often think about what makes people do what they do.	_____	_____
2.	I like reading about new findings that scientists have discovered doing behavioral research.	_____	_____
3.	I am often skeptical when someone tries to persuade me about behavioral claims unless there is evidence to back up the claim.	_____	_____
4.	I like the prospect of measuring behavior and doing statistics to determine meaningful differences.	_____	_____
5.	I can usually come up with multiple explanations to account for behavior.	_____	_____
6.	I think I could come up with ideas to research to help explain behaviors I am curious about.	_____	_____
7.	I am often approached by others who want me to listen to their problems and share my ideas about what to do.	_____	_____
8.	I don't get especially frustrated if I can't get answers to my questions.	_____	_____
9.	I am usually careful with details.	_____	_____
10.	I enjoy writing and speaking about things I am learning.	_____	_____
11.	I like to solve puzzles.	_____	_____
12.	I feel comfortable that psychology can provide me with an education that will lead to a good job.	_____	_____

Scoring and Interpretation

If you answered true to a majority of the items, psychology is a major that likely matches up well with your interests. Although the items are not a perfect predictor of whether you will enjoy majoring in and pursuing a career in psychology, they can give you an indication of whether you might benefit from finding out more about what psychologists do and what is involved in becoming a psychologist. Your psychology professor or a career counselor at your college likely can inform you about the best way to pursue a career in psychology.

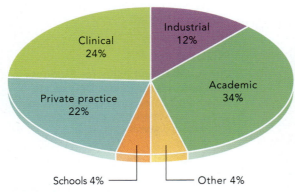

FIGURE 1.2

Settings in Which Psychologists Work More psychologists work in academic settings (34%), such as colleges and universities, than any other. However, clinical (24%) and private practice (22%) settings, both contexts in which many psychologists in the mental health professions work, together make up almost half of the total settings.

Psychology also pays reasonably well. Psychologists earn well above the median salary in the United States. It is unlikely that you would live in a palatial mansion because you majored in psychology, but it is also unlikely that you would go broke. A psychology major enables you to improve people's lives, to understand yourself and others, possibly to advance the state of knowledge in the field, and to have an enjoyable time while you are doing these things.

An undergraduate degree in psychology can give you access to a variety of jobs. For a list of some of the job possibilities in business, social and human services, and research that are open to students with such a degree, see Figure 1.1. If you choose a career in psychology, you can greatly expand your opportunities (and your income) by getting a graduate degree, either a master's or a doctorate.

Where do psychologists work? Slightly more than one-third are teachers, researchers, or counselors at colleges or universities. Most other psychologists work in clinical and private practice settings (Figure 1.2). To reflect on whether a career in psychology might be in your future, see the Psychology and Life box.

REVIEW, ASSESS, AND SHARPEN YOUR THINKING

Review

4 Evaluate areas of specialization and careers in psychology.

- Name and describe the various areas of specialization in psychology.
- Discuss career opportunities that are available to individuals who have an undergraduate degree in psychology.

Assess

1. Of the two types of psychologists listed in each option below, which would be most likely to spend the majority of their time doing research?
   A. social psychologists and personality psychologists
   B. counseling psychologists and clinical psychologists
   C. counseling psychologists and cognitive psychologists
   D. clinical psychologists and school psychologists

2. A researcher interested in the way in which our eyes are able to detect changes in the shape of an object would likely be associated with which of the following areas of specialization?
   A. motivation and learning
   B. developmental psychology
   C. industrial and organizational psychology
   D. sensation and perception

3. A psychologist who examines the role stress plays in triggering behaviors that are related to HIV transmission is most closely associated with which of the following specializations?
   A. health psychology
   C. community psychology
   B. social psychology
   D. physiological psychology

4. What is the difference between a psychologist and a psychiatrist?
   A. A psychiatrist has a doctoral degree, while a psychologist has a master's degree.
   B. A psychiatrist has a Ph.D. degree, while a psychologist has an M.D. degree.
   C. A psychiatrist cannot prescribe medication, while a psychologist can.
   D. A psychiatrist attends medical school, while a psychologist attends graduate school.

5. Which of the following specializations is most concerned with developing techniques to improve the hiring of employees for a company?
   A. Community psychology
   B. Industrial and organizational psychology
   C. Social psychology
   D. Personality psychology

Sharpen Your Thinking

Think of a career other than psychology that you might enter. In what ways might studying psychology be useful in that career?

5 Psychology and Health and Wellness

Describe the connections between the mind and the body.

One problem with the common tendency to equate the science of psychology with clinical psychology or with **psychopathology**—the study of mental illness—is that such a perspective limits the relevance of psychology to people with problems. This narrow way of viewing the field ignores the important question, What does psychology have to do with me and those around me? One of positive psychology's goals is to enhance general awareness of the role of psychological research in providing an understanding of "normal" people and their everyday lives. In this book, we seek to answer the question, What does psychology have to say about me? by tying research in psychology to your health and wellness. How better to show that psychology matters than to demonstrate how it matters to your ability to function as a healthy person every day?

psychopathology The study of mental illness.

How the Mind Impacts the Body

When you think of psychology, you might think first about the mind and its complex mental processes such as love, gratitude, hate, and anger. But psychology has come to recognize more and more that the mind we are studying is intricately connected to the body. As you will see when we examine neuroscience as an approach to psychology in Chapter 3, observations of the brain at work reveal that when mental processes change, so do physical processes (Hagner, 2007).

Health psychologists talk about "health behavior" as a subset of behaviors that are relevant to physical health. These behaviors might include eating well, exercising, not smoking, performing testicular and breast self-exams, brushing your teeth, and getting enough sleep. But think about your body for a moment. Are there really ever times when your behavior is not relevant to your body (and therefore your health)? Is there ever a time when you are doing anything—thinking, feeling, walking, running, singing—when your physical body is not present? As long as your body is there, with your heart, lungs, blood, and brain activated, your health is implicated. Everything we do, see, think, and feel is potentially important to our health and well-being.

It might be helpful to think about the ways the mind and body can relate to each other, even as they are united in the physical reality of a person. Let's say you experience a mental "event" such as seeing a "Buns of Steel" infomercial on TV. You decide to embark on a quest for these legendary buns of steel. Mental commitment, goal setting, and self-discipline will be the kinds of mental processes necessary to transform your body. The mind can work on the body, changing its shape and size.

How the Body Impacts the Mind

Similarly, the body can influence the mind in dramatic ways. Consider how fuzzy your thinking is after you stay out too late, and how much easier it is to solve life's problems when you have had a good night's sleep. Also consider your outlook on the first day of true recovery from a nagging cold: Everything just seems better. Your mood and your work improve. Clearly, physical states such as illness and health influence the way we think. So do physical conditions such as being hot or uncomfortable. Research has shown, for instance, that when people experience extreme heat, they can start to feel hostile and even act more aggressively than usual. A study by Doug Kenrick and Steve MacFarlane (1986) showed that during very hot weather, people without air conditioning in their cars were much more likely to honk their horns during a traffic jam.

The link between the mind and the body has fascinated philosophers for centuries. Psychology occupies the very spot where the mind and body meet. Throughout this book, we point out the ways that all of the various approaches to psychology matter to your well-being. Psychology is not only *about* you—it is *crucially about* you, essential to your understanding of your life, your goals, and the ways that you can use the insights of these thousands of scientists to make your life healthier and happier.

FRANK & ERNEST: © Thaves/Dist. by Newspaper Enterprise Association, Inc.

REVIEW, ASSESS, AND SHARPEN YOUR THINKING

Review

5 Describe the connections between the mind and the body.
- Summarize the ways that the mind can influence the body.
- Summarize the ways that the body can influence the mind.

Assess

1. Psychopathology is
   - A. another word for schizophrenia.
   - B. the study of healthy individuals.
   - C. the illness that affects all criminals.
   - D. a term that describes the study of mental illness.

2. Which of the following statements is most correct?
   - A. The mind has an impact on the body.
   - B. The body has an impact on the mind.
   - C. The link between the mind and body has not been established.
   - D. The mind and body impact each other.

3. Which of the following are health behaviors?
   - A. Smoking
   - B. Smiling
   - C. Eating
   - D. All of the above

4. Which of the following is an example of the mind impacting the body?
   - A. Exercise leading to elevated mood
   - B. Using alcohol to cope with a break-up
   - C. Setting a goal to run a marathon and starting training
   - D. Being in a hot room and feeling irritable

Sharpen Your Thinking

Consider your activities last night. What was your body doing, and what was your mind doing? Think of the various ways that these two aspects of yourself affected each other in one evening.

---

1 DEFINING PSYCHOLOGY

Explain what psychology is and describe the positive psychology movement.

Psychology Versus Common Sense: What Don't You Already Know About Psychology?

Psychology is the scientific study of behavior and mental processes. Science uses systematic methods to observe, describe, predict, and explain. Behavior includes everything organisms do that can be observed. Mental processes are thoughts, feelings, and motives. The science of psychology is different from common sense. Often, commonsense notions have been proven to be erroneous by sound scientific research.

Thinking Like a Psychologist Means Thinking Like a Scientist

Critical thinking involves thinking reflectively and productively and evaluating the evidence. It is important to maintain a healthy skepticism about anything that appears to be magical and wondrous. Psychology is full of controversies, and it is essential to think critically about these controversies. Most controversies are not completely resolved on one side or the other.

Positive Psychology

The positive psychology movement is a recent development, and the approach is not without controversy. Its proponents argue that

psychology has been too negative and needs to focus more on the positive aspects of people, such as their optimism, creativity, and civic values. Positive psychology draws attention to what works, as a basis for understanding what *does not* work.

2 THE ROOTS AND EARLY SCIENTIFIC APPROACHES OF PSYCHOLOGY

Discuss the roots and early scientific foundations of psychology.

Structuralism

Structuralism emphasized the study of the conscious mind and its structures. Wilhelm Wundt founded the first laboratory in psychology in 1879, dedicated to searching for the mind's elemental structures, and E. B. Titchener named the approach "structuralism."

Functionalism

Functionalism focused on the functions of the mind in adapting to the environment. William James was the leading functionalist theorist. The functionalist emphasis on the adaptive character of the mind fit well with the emerging understanding of Darwin's theory of evolution.

SUMMARY

3 CONTEMPORARY APPROACHES TO PSYCHOLOGY

Summarize the main themes of seven approaches to psychology.

The Biological Approach

The biological approach focuses on the body, especially the brain and nervous system. Technological advances in imaging the brain have allowed psychological researchers to examine the brain in all its complexity.

The Behavioral Approach

The behavioral approach emphasizes the scientific study of observable behavioral responses and their environmental determinants. John B. Watson and B. F. Skinner were important early behaviorists.

The Psychodynamic Approach

The psychodynamic approach emphasizes unconscious thought, the conflict between biological instincts and society's demands, and early family experiences. Sigmund Freud was the founding father of the psychodynamic approach.

The Humanistic Approach

The humanistic approach emphasizes a person's capacity for positive growth, freedom to choose a destiny, and positive qualities.

The Cognitive Approach

The cognitive approach emphasizes the mental processes involved in knowing. Cognitive psychologists study attention, thinking, problem solving, remembering, and learning.

The Evolutionary Approach

The evolutionary approach stresses the importance of adaptation, reproduction, and "survival of the fittest."

The Sociocultural Approach

The sociocultural approach focuses on the social and cultural determinants of behavior. This approach encourages us to attend to the ways that our behavior and mental processes are embedded in a social context.

4 AREAS OF SPECIALIZATION AND CAREERS IN PSYCHOLOGY

Evaluate areas of specialization and careers in psychology.

Areas of Specialization

Main areas of specialization in psychology include physiological psychology and behavioral neuroscience, developmental psychology, sensation and perception, cognitive psychology, learning, motivation and emotion, personality psychology, social psychology, industrial and organizational psychology, clinical and counseling psychology, and health psychology. Other specialties include community psychology, school and educational psychology, environmental psychology, the psychology of women, forensic psychology, sport psychology, and cross-cultural psychology.

Careers

Majoring in psychology can open up many career opportunities. Careers range from conducting therapy with people who have mental problems to teaching and conducting research at a university to working in advertising and public relations.

5 PSYCHOLOGY AND HEALTH AND WELLNESS

Describe the connections between the mind and the body.

How the Mind Impacts the Body

While philosophers have debated the relation between the mind and the body for centuries, psychologists have come to recognize that these two aspects of a human being are intricately related. The mind can influence the body. The way we think has implications for our nervous system and brain. Our motives and goals can influence our bodies as we strive to be physically fit and eat well.

How the Body Impacts the Mind

The body can have an influence over the mind. We think differently when our bodies are rested versus tired, healthy versus unhealthy, and hot versus comfortable.

Key Terms

psychology, p. 4
science, p. 5
behavior, p. 5
mental processes, p. 5
critical thinking, p. 6

positive psychology
    movement, p. 7
structuralism, p. 10
functionalism, p. 10
natural selection, p. 11

biological approach, p. 12
neuroscience, p. 12
behavioral approach, p. 13
psychodynamic approach, p. 13
humanistic approach, p. 14

cognitive approach, p. 14
evolutionary approach, p. 14
sociocultural approach, p. 15
psychopathology, p. 25

Assess Your Knowledge

1. A psychologist who focuses on how the brain processes information is most closely associated with
   A. the psychodynamic approach.
   B. the behavioral approach.
   C. the structural approach.
   D. the cognitive approach.

2. Which psychologist is able to diagnose a mental illness?
   A. a social psychologist
   B. a personality psychologist
   C. a counseling psychologist
   D. a physiological psychologist

3. Who is most closely associated with behaviorism?
   A. B. F. Skinner   B. Charles Darwin
   C. Wilhelm Wundt   D. David Buss

4. Which of the following areas of specialization would be most interested in the transitions that occur when someone retires?
   A. psychodynamic
   B. developmental
   C. cognitive
   D. health psychology

5. Which of the following is an example of a mental process?
   A. crying
   B. putting together the pieces of a jigsaw puzzle
   C. writing an outline for a paper
   D. feeling proud

6. What makes psychology a science?
   A. Psychologists have advanced degrees.
   B. Psychology proposes theories.
   C. Psychology uses systemic scientific methodology to observe behavior and to explain and predict behavior.
   D. Psychology is the same as the natural sciences.

7. Examining both why someone is depressed and why someone is hopeful is consistent with
   A. positive psychology.
   B. the behavioral approach.
   C. the scientific method.
   D. structuralism.

8. Structuralism focuses on _____ , while functionalism focuses on _____ .
   A. thoughts, behaviors
   B. the components of the mind, the purposes of the mind
   C. pragmatism, idealism
   D. natural selection, environment.

9. A psychologist who focuses on the impact of neural lesions on behavior uses which approach?
   A. behavioral
   B. cognitive
   C. health psychology
   D. biological

10. A researcher who examined the ways in which hot meal programs delivered at homeless shelters affected people's ability to obtain employment would likely be a(n)
    A. industrial/organizational psychologist.
    B. social psychologist.
    C. community psychologist.
    D. health psychologist.

11. Which of the following topics is most consistent with personality psychology?
    A. individual traits   B. groups
    C. stress   D. mental illness

12. _____ is associated with behaviorism; _____ is associated with the psychodynamic approach.
    A. B. F. Skinner, Freud
    B. Rene Descartes, Wilhelm Wundt
    C. William James, Wilhelm Wundt
    D. E. B. Titchener, William James

13. Which approach is concerned with people's capacity for growth and self-fulfillment?
    A. the humanistic approach
    B. the psychodynamic approach
    C. the evolutionary approach
    D. the sociocultural approach

14. Which of the following topics would be of most interest to a psychodynamic psychologist?
    A. altruism
    B. unconscious drives
    C. the adaptiveness of behaviors
    D. people's thought processes

15. What do clinical psychologists and psychiatrists have in common?
    A. their training
    B. their degree
    C. their focus on mental illness
    D. their ability to prescribe medications

Go to Appendix B for answers to these questions.

Apply Your Knowledge

1. Why are psychology and philosophy considered different disciplines? Research some of the questions addressed by both fields and the approaches each discipline uses to answer these questions.

2. Ask 10 friends and family members to tell you the first thing that comes to mind when they think of a psychologist. Do their responses reflect the need for positive psychology? Why or why not?

3. Visit the website of a major book retailer (like Amazon.com) and enter *psychology* as a search term. Examine descriptions of the five to seven most popular psychology books listed. How well do the themes covered represent your perceptions of what psychology is? How well do they represent the approaches to psychology discussed in the text? Are any perspectives over- or underrepresented? If so, why do you think that is?

4. In the faculty directory for your school (or for another institution), look up the psychology faculty. Select several faculty members and discover what the area of specialization is for each (be careful, it may not be the same as the classes they teach). How do you think their areas of academic training might affect the way they teach their classes?

5. Look at the health or science section of your local paper or favorite magazine. Evaluate the use of psychological research there. How are psychological studies presented in this publication?

CHAPTER 2

PSYCHOLOGY'S SCIENTIFIC METHOD

Experiencing Psychology

IN PURSUIT OF HAPPINESS

In 1981, Ed Diener, a professor of psychology at University of Illinois, Urbana-Champaign, was already an established researcher in the area of social influence. This subfield of psychology studies how the influence of others can make us engage in negative behavior that we otherwise would normally avoid—for example, participating in riots, mob behavior, and acts of aggression. Diener and his family were living in the Virgin Islands, where his wife, Carol (an accomplished clinical psychologist and attorney), was teaching. Perhaps inspired by the setting, Diener decided he would change his research focus to something more positive. Surveying the current psychological research, he noticed that the psychology of happiness was being all but ignored, and so he chose the experience of happiness, or what psychologists call "subjective well-being," as his new focus.

When he shared his plan with a former graduate school advisor, the response was less than enthusiastic: Who would be interested in knowing about such a thing? But, in fact, who (besides most psychologists prior to 1981) *wouldn't* be? Indeed, most of us are interested in what makes us happy and how we can be happier. In the 1980s alone, some 8,000 studies were published on the topic of happiness (a number of them by Diener himself). Diener's work provides one of the cornerstones of the exciting

new field known as positive psychology. Indeed, he is one of the creators of the Satisfaction with Life Scale you completed in Chapter 1 (his car license plate is SWLS).

Is there a danger in studying the sometimes mysterious experience of happiness? If we study it and try to put this complex emotion into words, will it lose its magic? A positive psychologist who was giving a talk on happiness was asked by a chemistry professor in the audience, "How can you study happiness? Isn't it ineffable?" By that the professor meant that he believed happiness cannot be put into words—that happiness goes beyond the reach of scientific inquiry. And if we cannot even describe it, how can we study it? In fact, now that so much research has focused on happiness, we have come to understand that happiness is quite effable. People know when they are happy and when they are unhappy, and we can use their expression of that knowledge to find out what causes enduring happiness and what the experience of happiness might lead to in people's lives. So, rather than spoiling the experience of happiness, a positive psychologist such as Diener would say that understanding this vital human experience provides a much better chance of increasing its occurrence in people's lives.

The striking popularity of self-help books—a half-trillion-dollar industry (Marketdata Enterprises, 2006)—attests to the fact that many people are struggling to experience happiness and other of life's elusive human rewards: enduring love, peace of mind, a sense of life's meaning, and more. Without psychologists' scientific research and the strong scientific evidence on which it rests, we would be left with only the shelves upon shelves of books in the self-help section of the bookstore, offering often contradictory suggestions. Should we follow the advice to "not sweat the small stuff" or "focus on the little things"? If Dr. Phil tells us something, is it so? The problem with relying on the authors of popular books, media figures, and even wise friends and family members to advise us on important questions about our psychological health and well-being is that we have no way of knowing whether what sounds like a good idea *really is* a good idea, one that will work reliably for us and for large numbers of people. The scientific method can lead us to the elusive answer. The scientific method allows researchers to test promising ideas not only about human happiness but also concerning many other questions, using objective methods to reach reliable findings. Accordingly, in recent years, the science of psychology has begun to examine the many aspects of the well-lived life, to enrich our understanding of life's sometimes mysterious pleasures without robbing them of their inherent value (Csikszentmihalyi & Csikszentmihalyi, 2006; Emmons, 2007; Tov & Diener, 2007).

PREVIEW

Being a psychologist means being a scientist who studies psychology. In this chapter, we review the scientific method. You will read about the ways that psychologists have applied this general method to a variety of important topics and about the steps that are involved in recognizing research questions, developing methods to test them, and using statistical techniques to understand the results. Later in the chapter we consider some of the ethical issues that are involved in scientific inquiry. Psychology shares a great deal with other sciences, but as you will see, topics that psychologists study sometimes require special methodological and ethical consideration.

1 Psychology's Scientific Method

Explain what makes psychology a science.

Science is not defined by *what* it investigates but by *how* it investigates. Whether you study photosynthesis, butterflies, Saturn's moons, or happiness, the *way* you study the question is what determines whether your approach is scientific. You can gain a clear understanding of science by knowing what it means to take a scientific approach, by realizing the importance of collaboration, and by learning about the scientific method.

A Scientific Approach

Central to the scientific approach are four attitudes: curiosity, skepticism, objectivity, and a willingness to think critically. A scientist is first and foremost *curious*. Why are some people happy and others not? What are the ingredients of a happy life? The scientist notices things in the world (a star in the sky, an insect, a happy person) and wants to know what it is and why it is that way. Science is about asking questions, even very big questions such as, Where did the earth come from? and How does love between two people endure for 50 years?

Scientists are also *skeptical*. Skeptical people question things that other people take for granted. They wonder whether a supposed fact is really true. There was a time when "everybody knew" that women were morally inferior to men, that race could influence a person's IQ, and that the earth was flat. A scientist looks at assumptions in a new and questioning way.

Science also means being *objective*. Scientists believe that one of the best ways to be objective is to conduct research studies (Martin, 2008; McBurney & White, 2007). Scientists use empirical methods to learn about the world. The empirical method means that for scientists knowledge comes from observation of events and logical reasoning. Being objective means trying to see things as they really are, not just as we would like them to be. It also means using methods of decision making that keep us in touch with the real world (Smith & Davis, 2007).

Last, science involves *thinking critically*. In Chapter 1, we saw that thinking critically consists of thinking reflectively, thinking productively, and evaluating the evidence. Critical thinkers question and test what some people say are facts. They examine research to see how sound its support of an idea really is (Stanovich, 2007).

These four attitudes are ideals. No scientist possesses them all at every moment. But the closer we embrace these attitudes, the better we are able to use the basic tools of scientific theory and objective observation. They reduce the likelihood that information will be based on unreliable personal beliefs, opinions, and emotions. As you go through this book, practice using these scientific attitudes. You also would do well to call on these attitudes whenever you hear people discussing "facts" and arguing about issues.

Collaboration

Science is a collaborative effort. Even when different groups of scientists seem to be competing to be the first to answer a particular question, they are part of a collective effort to increase an overall body of knowledge. More than that, no scientific finding has much impact until a community of scientists agrees, through the process of peer review, that the finding is true and important. Research psychologists share their work by publishing it in scientific and academic journals. In contrast to other types of periodicals, these journals publish mainly scholarly research and information—usually in a specific field such as the psychology of the workplace or human development. The peer review process means that nearly all scientific publications are reviewed by anonymous experts in the field who evaluate the methodological soundness, conceptual clarity, and importance of the work. Journals gather and preserve the core information of the discipline of psychology. Many journals are very selective about what they publish. The best journals maintain high standards, and some accept only 10 to 20 percent of the articles that are submitted to them. That is why evidence that appears in a

Science is defined not by what it studies but by how it investigates. Photosynthesis, butterflies, and relationships among people all can be studied in a scientific manner.

Research journals are the core of information in virtually every academic discipline. Those shown here represent some of the increasing number of research journals that publish information about psychology.

research journal is more likely to reflect valid processes than something that appears in a self-help book that is written, ultimately, to make a profit.

Within colleges and universities, psychologists share their findings with their colleagues and open their research to evaluation. Conferences conducted by national and international societies allow psychologists, and students of psychology as well, to share and discuss their findings.

One area in which the collaborative aspect of psychological research comes to the fore is in meta-analysis (Hyde, 2005, 2007). **Meta-analysis** is a method by which researchers can combine results across a variety of different studies to establish the strength of an effect. For instance, one meta-analysis of research revealed that frequently being in a positive mood often relates to success in life (Lyubomirsky, King, & Diener, 2005). The results of this analysis suggest that happiness not only comes from being successful in life but also predicts those successes. Examining hundreds of studies by a wide array of researchers, these researchers demonstrated that happy people may be more likely to get married, be promoted at work, and live long, healthy lives.

The Five Steps in the Scientific Method

One of the hallmarks of taking a scientific approach to psychology involves adopting the scientific method in studying topics in the field (Neuman, 2007). Indeed, most of the studies psychologists publish in research journals follow the scientific method, which is summarized in these five steps:

1. Observing some phenomenon.
2. Formulating hypotheses and predictions.
3. Testing through empirical research.
4. Drawing conclusions.
5. Evaluating conclusions.

The scientific method usually begins with one key idea: a theory. A **theory** is a broad idea or set of closely related ideas that attempts to explain certain observations. Theories try to explain why certain things have happened, and they can be used to make predictions about future observations.

In psychology, theories help to organize and connect observations and research. The overall meaning of the large numbers of research studies that are always being conducted in psychology would be difficult to grasp if theories did not provide a structure for summarizing and understanding them and putting them in a context with other research studies. In addition, good, testable theories generate interesting research questions and allow researchers to make observations that might answer those questions. Research may or may not support the theory in question, and theories may be revised in response to research findings. Scientists do not regard theories as being exactly, entirely, and permanently correct. A theory is judged by its ability to generate ideas about how the world works and to predict important events and behaviors. Depending on how well it predicts, a theory gains or loses support.

1. Observing Some Phenomenon The first step in conducting a scientific inquiry comes from observing some phenomenon in the world. The phenomena scientists study are called variables. A **variable** is anything that can change. The variable that interested Ed Diener was happiness. He noticed that some people seemed to be generally happier than others. What might account for these differences?

An important aspect of conceptualizing a research problem is coming up with a concrete way to measure the variables of interest. An **operational definition** is an objective description of how a research variable is going to be measured and observed. Operational definitions eliminate some of the fuzziness and loose ends that might creep into thinking about a problem.

meta-analysis A method that allows researchers to combine the results of several different studies on a similar topic in order to establish the strength of an effect.

theory A broad idea or set of closely related ideas that attempts to explain certain observations.

variable Anything that can change.

operational definition An objective description of how a research variable is going to be measured and observed.

To measure how happy a person is, Diener and his students (Diener & others, 1985) devised a self-report questionnaire that measures how satisfied a person is with his or her life. The scale includes items such as "The conditions of my life are excellent" and "On the whole I am satisfied with my life." Scores on the questionnaire are then used as measures of happiness.

Research using this scale and others like it has shown certain specific factors that are strongly related to being happy: marriage, religious faith, purpose in life, and good health (Diener, 1999). Interestingly, financial success is only weakly related to happiness. After a person has enough money to live comfortably, additional money does not seem to buy more happiness (Myers, 2000).

Importantly, there is not just one operational definition for something. For example, in a study that examined happiness as a *predictor* of important life outcomes, Lee Anne Harker and Dacher Keltner looked at the yearbook pictures of college women who had graduated 3 decades earlier. The researchers coded the pictures for the appearance of "Duchenne smiling." This type of smiling refers to genuine smiling—the kind that creates crow's feet, those little wrinkles around the outer corner of the eyes. Duchenne smiling has been shown to be a sign of genuine happiness. (If you want to see whether someone in a photograph is smiling genuinely, cover the bottom of the person's face. Can you still tell that he or she is smiling? A genuine smile can be seen in the eyes, not just the mouth.) So, while Diener and colleagues used the operationally defined (or "operationalized") happiness as a score on a questionnaire, Harker and Keltner operationalized happiness as Duchenne smiling. Harker and Keltner (2001) found that happiness, as displayed in these yearbook pictures, predicted positive life outcomes, such as successful marriages and satisfying lives, some 30 years later.

Researchers have identified Duchenne smiling (notice the wrinkles) as a sign of genuine happiness.

2. Formulating Hypotheses and Predictions

The second step in the scientific method is stating a hypothesis. A **hypothesis** is an idea that is arrived at logically from a theory. It is a prediction that can be tested. A hypothesis can be thought of as an educated guess, given existing theory and the application of logic.

For example, one theory of well-being is self-determination theory (Deci & Ryan, 2000). According to this theory, people are likely to feel fulfilled when their lives meet three important needs: relatedness (warm relations with others), autonomy (independence), and competence (mastering new skills). One hypothesis that follows logically from this theory is that people who value money, material possessions, prestige, and physical appearance (that is, *extrinsic rewards*) over the needs of relatedness, autonomy, and competence should be less fulfilled, less happy, and less well adjusted. In a series of studies entitled "The Dark Side of the American Dream," researchers Timothy Kasser and Richard Ryan have found that individuals who value materialistic rewards over more intrinsic rewards do indeed tend to suffer as predicted (Kasser & Ryan, 1993, 1996; Kasser & others, 2004).

The relationship between theories and hypotheses is not necessarily as straightforward as this simple example indicates. A theory can generate many hypotheses. If more and more hypotheses related to a theory turn out to be true, the theory gains in credibility. One reason that so many scientists hold the theory of evolution in high esteem is that it has been able to predict many observations.

3. Testing Through Empirical Research

The next step involved in the scientific method is the need to test the hypotheses by conducting empirical research, that is, collecting and analyzing data. Among the important decisions to be made about collecting data are whom to choose as the participants and which research methods to use. We will explore a number of research methods in some detail shortly; here, let's focus on the research participants.

Will the participants be people or animals? Will they be children, adults, or both? Will they be females, males, or both? Will they be of a single ethnicity, such as Anglo-American, or will they come from a diversity of ethnic groups?

When psychologists conduct a study, they usually want to be able to draw conclusions that will apply to a larger group of people (or animals) than the participants they actually study. Recall that research has shown that money does not buy happiness and in fact that

hypothesis An idea that is arrived at logically from a theory. It is a prediction that can be tested.

placing money above other values is quite bad for a person. A related question is, Do people think that money does buy happiness?

Christie Napa, an undergraduate researcher, was interested in finding out if people in general believe that it might be better to be rich and unhappy than poor and happy. With her advisor Laura King, she devised a research project in which undergraduate college students rated how good or desirable a life was when that life was described as happy or unhappy, meaningful or not meaningful, or wealthy or poor. Research on these undergraduates showed that the desirable life—the one that was rated as most like "the good life"—was the life that was happy and meaningful, with money having little impact on these desirability ratings (King & Napa, 1998).

The entire group about which the investigator wants to draw conclusions is the **population.** In this particular study of the good life, the population is all people in the United States. The subset of the population chosen by the investigator for study is a **sample.** In Napa's undergraduate thesis, the sample was a group of students. Now you might be thinking, "Some college students are naive—they don't realize how important money can be." With these concerns in mind, Napa collected more data, this time from adults who were waiting for jury duty. Even among these adults, similar results were found: the relative unimportance of money to the desirability of a life (King & Napa, 1998).

The target population to which the investigator wants to generalize varies with the study. The researcher might be interested only in a particular group, such as all children who are gifted and talented, all young women who embark on science and math careers, or all gay men. The key is that the sample studied must be representative of the population to which the investigator wants to generalize.

To mirror the population more closely, a researcher would use a **random sample,** a sample that gives every member of the population an equal chance of being selected. In the study of the good life, a representative sample would reflect the U.S. population's age, socioeconomic status, ethnic origins, marital status, geographic location, religion, and so forth. A random sample provides much better grounds for generalizing the results to a population than a nonrandom sample.

Investigators do not always use appropriate sampling methods (Jackson, 2008). Surveys by newspapers and magazines often ask people to mail or call in their opinions. However, the people who respond probably feel more strongly about the issue than do those who do not respond. In addition, the readers may feel differently about an issue than the population as a whole. Keep in mind that random sampling is important in some types of research but much less important in other kinds. If a researcher wants to know how often people donate money to charity in the United States, obtaining a random sample is important. However, in many research studies, psychologists are interested in studying specific aspects of behavior under specific conditions, in which case they deliberately do not obtain a random sample. In these studies, they might want people with certain characteristics to be well represented.

It is also noteworthy that, in many areas of psychology, generalization comes from similar findings across a number of studies rather than from random sampling within a single study. Imagine five or six studies conducted with varied samples and in different geographic locations, all examining views of the role of money judgments of the good life. Indeed, Christie Napa (who now goes by her married name, Scollon) eventually collected data on the topic of the good life from a variety of participants who were waiting for flights in airports all over the world (Scollon & King, 2004).

A key aspect of the process of testing hypotheses is data analysis. *Data* refers to all of the information researchers collect in a study. Data analysis involves the application of mathematical (or statistical) procedures to understand what the data mean (Aron, Aron, & Coops, 2008; Vogt, 2007). Later in this chapter, we examine two types of statistical procedures in some detail. Many students of psychology are surprised to hear that very much of the work that is done in psychological sciences relies heavily on sophisticated quantitative techniques.

4. Drawing Conclusions Based on the data analyses, scientists then draw conclusions from their research. It is important to keep in mind that a revision of theory usually occurs only after a number of studies produce similar results. Before we change a theory, we want

population The entire group about which the investigator wants to draw conclusions.

sample The subset of the population chosen by the investigator for study.

random sample A sample that gives every member of the population an equal chance of being selected.

to be sure that the research can be replicated. *Reliability* is the extent to which scientific research yields a consistent, reproducible result. If a research finding is shown again and again across different researchers and different specific methods, it is considered reliable.

5. Evaluating Conclusions   The final step in the scientific method is one that never really ends. Researchers submit their work for publication, and it undergoes rigorous review. Afterward, the published studies are there for all to see, read, and evaluate continuously. The research community maintains an active conversation about what we know, and conclusions are always questioned. A scholar may come up with a new idea based on published studies that will eventually change the way we think. Steps 3, 4, and 5 in the scientific method are understood as part of an iterative process. That is, researchers go back and do more research and continually revise theory, hone methods, and so on.

 REVIEW, ASSESS, AND SHARPEN YOUR THINKING

Review

1 Explain what makes psychology a science.
- Discuss the four attributes of a scientific attitude.
- Explain the need for collaboration in science.
- Name and describe the five steps in the scientific method.

Assess

1. Which of the following attitudes is not at the heart of the scientific approach?
   A. skepticism   B. critical thinking
   C. prejudging   D. curiosity

2. The statement "I predict this study will demonstrate that students who study in groups will get better grades than those who study alone" is an example of
   A. a theory.   B. an observation.
   C. a conclusion.   D. a hypothesis.

3. A group of 100 students is randomly chosen from Wilmington High School. Which of the following would be considered the population?
   A. the 100 students
   B. all the students at the Wilmington High School
   C. all high school students in America
   D. all high school students in the world

4. The ability of a study to yield a consistent result is referred to as
   A. validity.   B. reliability.
   C. prediction.   D. stability.

5. A(n) _____ is an objective description of how a variable will be measured.
   A. operational definition
   B. third variable
   C. prediction
   D. hypothesis

Sharpen Your Thinking

Create an operational definition of love. List several measurements that you might use to assess love.

2 Research Settings and Types of Research

Discuss common research settings and the three types of research that are used in psychology.

The collection of data is the fundamental means of testing hypotheses. In this section we investigate the major ways of gathering data about behavior and mental processes. We will find that three basic types of research are used in psychology: descriptive, correlational, and experimental.

Classrooms, playgrounds, sports arenas, shopping malls, and other places that people live in and frequent serve as ideal settings for naturalistic observations.

One concept that is central to all of these research approaches is that of a *variable,* a term referring to anything that varies. In a person, variables might include height, weight, IQ, religious faith, and the extent to which the individual feels happy or unhappy, for example. We can consider anything that differs among people or changes within a person to be a variable. In general, all forms of scientific inquiry in psychology are interested in how variables relate to one another. The type of methods researchers use is typically guided by their conceptual understanding of the variables of interest.

Another fundamental element of any research is the *setting* where such research may take place. We begin our look at common approaches to psychological research by considering the settings available to researchers.

Research Settings

All three types of research that we will discuss shortly—descriptive, correlational, and experimental—can be carried out in different settings. In other words, the setting of the research does not determine the type of research it is. Common settings include the research laboratory and natural settings.

Because psychological researchers often need to control certain factors that determine behavior but are not the focus of inquiry, much of their research is conducted in a *laboratory,* a controlled setting with many of the complex factors of the real world removed (Mitchell & Jolley, 2007).

Although laboratory research allows a great deal of control, doing research in the laboratory has some drawbacks. First, it is almost impossible to conduct research in the lab without the participants' knowing they are being studied. Second, the laboratory setting is unnatural and therefore can cause the participants to behave unnaturally. A third drawback of laboratory research is that people who are willing to go to a university laboratory may not fairly represent groups from diverse cultural backgrounds. Those who are unfamiliar with university settings and with the idea of "helping science" may be intimidated by the setting. Fourth, some aspects of the mind and behavior are difficult if not impossible to examine in the laboratory.

Laboratory studies of certain types of stress may even be unethical.

Research can also take place in a natural setting. Naturalistic observation provides insight that researchers sometimes cannot achieve in the laboratory (Bronfenbrenner & Morris, 2006). **Naturalistic observation** is observing behavior in real-world settings. Psychologists conduct naturalistic observations at sporting events, day-care centers, work settings, shopping malls, and other places that people frequent. Suppose that you wanted to study the level of civility on your campus. Most likely, you would include some naturalistic observation of how people treat one another in such gathering places as the cafeteria and the library reading room.

Naturalistic observation was used in one study that focused on conversations in a children's science museum (Crowley & others, 2001). The researchers' finding that parents were three times as likely to engage boys than girls in explanatory talk while visiting different exhibits suggests a

Jane Goodall was a young woman when she made her first trip to the Gombe Research Center in the African country of Tanzania. Fascinated by chimpanzees, she dreamed about a career that would allow her to explore her hunches about the nature of chimpanzees. A specialist in animal behavior, she embarked on a career in the bush that involved long and solitary hours of careful, patient observation. Her observations spanned 30 years, years that included her marriage, the birth of her son, untold hardship, and inestimable pleasure. Due to her efforts, our understanding of chimpanzees in natural settings dramatically improved.

gender bias that encourages boys more than girls in science (Figure 2.1). In another study, Mexican American parents who had completed high school used more explanations with their children when visiting a science museum than Mexican American parents who had not completed high school (Tenenbaum & others, 2002). Naturalistic observation allows the researcher access to a person's spontaneous behaviors; however, a key weakness of this method is the lack of control over the setting. For instance, imagine setting up one's research in a museum and having no one come by that day.

Descriptive Research

Some important psychological theories have grown out of descriptive research, which serves the purpose of observing and recording behavior. For example, a psychologist might observe the extent to which people are altruistic toward one another. By itself, descriptive research cannot prove what causes some phenomenon, but it can reveal important information about people's behaviors and attitudes. Descriptive research methods include observation, surveys and interviews, standardized tests, and case studies.

Observation   Imagine that you are interested in studying how children who are playing a game resolve conflicts that come up during the game. Thus, the data you are interested in concern conflict resolution. As a first step, you might go to a playground and simply observe what the children do—how often you see conflict resolution occur and how it unfolds. You would likely keep careful notes of what you observe.

This type of scientific observation requires an important set of skills. Unless we are trained observers and practice our skills regularly, we might not know what to look for, we might not remember what we saw, we might not realize that what we are looking for is changing from one moment to the next, and we might not communicate our observations effectively. Furthermore, it might be important to have more than one person do the observations as well, to develop a sense of how accurate your observations are. For observations to be effective, they must be systematic. We must have some idea of what we are looking for. We must know whom we are observing, when and where we will observe, and how we will make the observations. And we need to know in what form they will be recorded: in writing, by sound recording, or by video.

Surveys and Interviews   Sometimes the best and quickest way to get information about people is to ask them for it. One technique is to interview them directly. A related method that is especially useful when information from many people is needed is the survey, or questionnaire. A standard set of questions is used to obtain people's self-reported attitudes or beliefs about a particular topic. In a good survey, the questions are clear and unbiased, allowing respondents to answer unambiguously.

Surveys and interviews can probe into a wide range of topics, from religious beliefs to sexual habits to attitudes about gun control (Rosnow & Rosenthal, 2008). Surveys and interviews are conducted in person, by telephone, or (increasingly) over the Internet.

Some survey and interview questions are unstructured and open-ended, such as "Could you elaborate on your optimistic tendencies?" and "How fulfilling would you say your marriage is?" They allow for unique responses from each person surveyed. Other survey and interview questions are more structured and ask about quite specific things. For example, a structured survey or interview question might ask, "How many times have you talked with your partner about a personal problem in the past month: 0, 1–2, 3–5, 6–10, 11–30, every day?"

One problem with surveys and interviews is the tendency of participants to answer questions in a way that they think is socially acceptable or desirable rather than in a way that communicates what they truly think or feel (Nardi, 2006). For example, a person might exaggerate the amount of communication that goes on in a relationship in order to impress the interviewer.

One example of a survey conducted by the Gallup organization (1999) asked parents their beliefs about the most important problems facing schools. Forty-three percent cited drugs, 40 percent sex, 39 percent discipline in the classroom, 28 percent violence, and 25 percent social pressure among students to be popular. The survey was based on telephone interviews

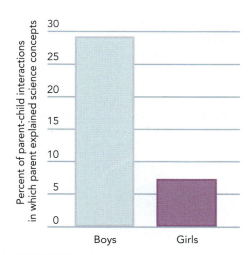

FIGURE 2.1

Parents' Explanations of Science to Sons and Daughters at a Science Museum In a naturalistic observation study at a children's science museum, parents were three times more likely to explain science to boys than to girls (Crowley & others, 2001). The gender difference occurred regardless of whether the father, the mother, or both parents were with the child, although the gender difference was greatest for fathers' science explanations to sons and daughters.

PSYCHOLOGY AND LIFE

Who Is the Healthiest Person You Know?

One way to study psychological variables is through case studies, or case histories. Researchers often use case studies to understand individuals who suffer from psychological disorders. But they might similarly use the case history approach to plumb the reasons why people are psychologically healthy.

Imagine that you have been asked to do a case study of psychological wellness. Think of the psychologically healthiest and happiest person you know. Consider the following questions about your hypothetical study:

- What makes this person a good example for a study of psychological health?
- How would you gather data for your case study?
- If you interviewed this person, what sorts of questions would you ask?
- What might we learn about psychological health, broadly speaking, from such a study?

with a randomly selected sample of 338 U.S. parents. Recall the discussion of random sampling earlier in the chapter. When surveys are conducted on a national basis, as Gallup polls are, random sampling is considered to be an important aspect of the survey process.

Standardized Tests A **standardized test** requires people to answer a series of written or oral questions or sometimes both (Gregory, 2007). A standardized test has two distinct features: An individual's answers are tallied to yield a single score, or set of scores, that reflects something about that individual; and the individual's score is compared with the scores of a large group of similar people to determine how the individual responded relative to others (Gronlund, 2006). One widely used standardized test in psychology is the Stanford-Binet intelligence test, which we consider in Chapter 9.

Scores on standardized tests are often stated in percentiles. Suppose you scored in the 92nd percentile on the Scholastic Assessment Test (SAT). This score would mean that 92 percent of a large group of individuals who previously took the test received scores lower than yours.

The main advantage of standardized tests is that they provide information about individual differences among people. But one problem with standardized tests is that they do not always predict behavior in nontest situations. Another problem is that standardized tests are based on the belief that a person's behavior is consistent and stable, yet personality and intelligence—two primary targets of standardized testing—can vary with the situation. For example, a woman may perform poorly on a standardized intelligence test in an office setting but score much higher at home, where she is less anxious. This criticism is especially relevant for members of minority groups, some of whom have been inaccurately classified as mentally retarded on the basis of their scores on intelligence tests (Hodapp & Dykens, 2006). In addition, cross-cultural psychologists caution that many psychological tests developed in Western cultures might not be appropriate in other cultures (Shiraev & Levy, 2007). People in other cultures may have had experiences that cause them to interpret and respond to questions much differently than the people on whom the test was standardized.

Case Studies A **case study**, or case history, is an in-depth look at a single individual. Case studies are performed mainly by clinical psychologists when, for either practical or ethical reasons, the unique aspects of an individual's life cannot be duplicated and tested in other individuals

standardized test A test that requires people to answer a series of written or oral questions or sometimes both.

case study An in-depth look at a single individual; also known as a case history.

Standardized tests require individuals to answer a series of written or oral questions. The individual on the left is taking a standardized test of intelligence.

(Dattilio, 2001). A case study provides information about one person's goals, hopes, fantasies, fears, traumatic experiences, family relationships, health, or anything else that helps the psychologist understand the person's mind and behavior. Sigmund Freud developed his theory of psychoanalysis based entirely on case studies of individuals suffering from psychological problems.

Another example of a case study is the analysis of India's spiritual leader Mahatma Gandhi by psychodynamic theorist Erik Erikson (1969). Erikson studied Gandhi's life in great depth to discover insights into how his positive spiritual identity developed, especially during his youth. In putting together the pieces of Gandhi's identity development, Erikson described the contributions of culture, history, family, and various other factors that might affect the way other people develop an identity.

Case histories provide dramatic, detailed portrayals of people's lives, but we must be cautious when generalizing from this information. The subject of a case study is unique, with a genetic makeup and personal history that no one else shares. In addition, case studies involve judgments of unknown reliability. However, case studies may be useful in generating ideas that could then be tested in empirical investigations using larger samples and correlational or experimental designs. To get a taste of how researchers approach a case study, see *Psychology and Life*.

Mahatma Gandhi was the spiritual leader of India in the middle of the twentieth century. Erik Erikson conducted an extensive case study of his life to determine what contributed to his identity development.

Correlational Research

Some psychological research relies on the systematic observation of variables within a sample of individuals. These studies are concerned with identifying the relationships between two or more variables in order to describe how these variables *change together*. This work is often called **correlational research** because of the statistical technique, referred to as correlation, that is typically used to analyze this type of data. The more strongly the two events are correlated (or related or associated), the more effectively we can predict one event from the other. The distinguishing feature of a correlational study is that the variables of interest are measured, not manipulated, by the researcher. That is, the researcher simply measures the variables of interest to see how they relate. No attempt is made to change the value of any of the variables.

The degree of relationship between two variables is expressed as a numerical value called a *correlational coefficient*. Let's assume that we have data on the relationship between how many hours individuals spend volunteering for a variety of charities (the *X* variable) as well as the level of life satisfaction these people experience (the *Y* variable). For the sake of this example, let's assume these data produce a correlation coefficient (represented by the letter *r*) of +.70. Remember this number, as we will soon use it to illustrate what a correlation coefficient tells you about the relationship between two events or characteristics.

For the moment, however, you need to know only that the number tells you the strength of the relationship between the two variables. The rule is simple: The closer the number is to 1.00, the stronger the correlation; conversely, the closer the number is to .00, the weaker the correlation. Figure 2.2 offers guidelines for interpreting correlational numbers. But perhaps you are wondering about the significance of the plus sign in the correlation coefficient of +.70 that we have calculated in our classroom study.

Positive and Negative Correlations The numerical value of a correlation coefficient always falls within the range from −1.00 to +1.00. The number of the correlation tells us about the strength of the relations, but the sign (+ or −) tells us about the direction of the relationship between the variables. So, negative numbers do not indicate a lower value than positive numbers. A correlation of −.65 is just as strong as a correlation of +.65. The plus or minus sign tells you nothing about the *strength* of the correlation. A correlation coefficient of −.87 is closer to −1.00 and thus indicates a stronger correlation than the coefficient of +.45 is to +1.00.

What the plus or minus sign does tell you is the direction of the relationship between the two variables. A *positive correlation* is a relationship in which the two factors vary in the same direction. Both factors tend to increase together, or both factors tend to decrease together. So, in the example above, the more time spent volunteering, the more satisfied

correlational research A research strategy that identifies the relationships between two or more variables in order to describe how these variables change together.

1.00	Perfect relationship; the two factors always occur together
.76–.99	Very strong relationship; the two factors occur together very often
.51–.75	Strong relationship; the two factors occur together frequently
.26–.50	Moderate relationship; the two factors occur together occasionally
.01–.25	Weak relationship; the two factors seldom occur together
.00	No relationship; the two factors never occur together

FIGURE 2.2

Guidelines for Interpreting Correlational Numbers The magnitude of a correlation tells us about the strength of the relationship between two variables.

people were with their lives. In addition, the positive correlation means that people who spent little time volunteering also showed lower life satisfaction. Either relationship represents a positive correlation. A *negative* correlation, in contrast, is a relationship in which increases in one variable are associated with decreases in the other. For instance, we might find that the number of hours spent watching TV is negatively correlated with life satisfaction. That means that the more TV a person watches, the lower his or her life satisfaction might be expected to be. Examples of scatter plots showing positive and negative correlations appear in Figure 2.3.

An example of a correlational research on happiness is a set of studies conducted by psychologists Sonja Lyubomirsky and Lee Ross. These researchers were interested in how happy and unhappy people feel about decisions they have made in their lives. Imagine, for example, that you are going to buy a new computer. You browse through plenty of stores, talk to friends, and read product reviews in *Consumer Reports* magazine. Finally, you make your choice. How are you likely to feel about it, and how will you feel about the computers you *almost* bought?

Lyubomirsky and Ross (1999) conducted a series of studies investigating the relationship between being happy and evaluations of one's choices as well one's feelings about what he or she did not get. In one study, Lyubomirsky and Ross studied high school students who were applying to colleges. These students completed a measure of how generally happy they were and provided information about the colleges to which they were applying. They also rated how positively they felt about each school. Three months later, after acceptance and rejection letters had been sent out (and students' decisions about which school to attend had been made), the students once again rated the schools to which they had applied. How did *knowing* that they were accepted, rejected, going to a particular school, or not going influence their feelings?

With regard to the college they had chosen to attend, happy students tended to be very excited about their chosen school—their assessment of the school had become even more

FIGURE 2.3

Scatter Plots Showing Positive and Negative Correlations A positive correlation is a relationship in which two factors vary in the same direction, as shown in the two scatter plots on the left. A negative correlation is a relationship in which two factors vary in opposite directions, as shown in the two scatter plots on the right.

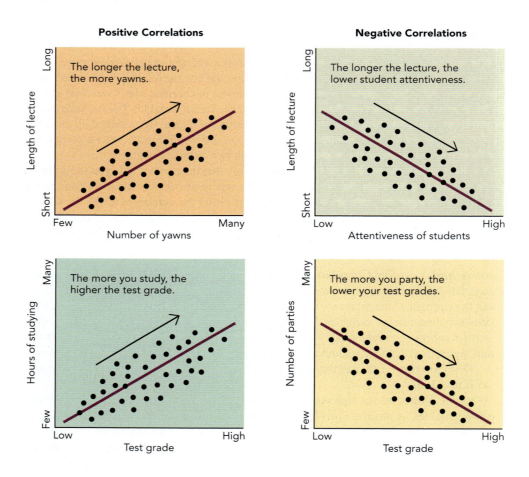

positive. In contrast, unhappy students did not show an increase in their feelings about the school they would be attending. Indeed, unhappy students tended to react somewhat negatively toward the school. With regard to schools that had accepted them but that they had declined to attend, happy students remained very positive about them. These schools, after all, had shown very good taste and judgment—the students' attendance there just was not meant to be.

In contrast, unhappy students tended to denigrate schools that had accepted them but that they had chosen not to attend. The comedian Groucho Marx once quipped that he would never want to join a club that would have him as a member, and the unhappy students tended to reflect this outlook: Any school that would take them could not be that great.

In a second study, conducted in the laboratory, happy and unhappy participants were presented with 10 fancy desserts to evaluate before and after they were told which one they would get to eat (Lyubomirsky & Ross, 1999). Participants were read descriptions of 10 different delicious desserts—cheesecake, lemon poppy seed cake, chocolate-on-chocolate cake, carrot cake, and so on. They were asked to rank the desserts in terms of how much they would want to try them. Participants were always told that they would be receiving their second choice. Before getting their dessert, however, participants were asked to rate the choices one more time—at this point they were presented with pictures of the desserts.

Once again, happy people showed a tendency to increase their liking of the dessert they were told they would be receiving, while unhappy people actually slightly decreased their liking for the dessert when they realized they would be getting it. In addition, when rating a dessert they would not be receiving, the unhappy people tended to derogate (that is, to belittle) the dessert; that slice of chocolate-on-chocolate cake suddenly looked much less appetizing when they knew it was not going to be theirs. These findings provide insight into the different thinking styles of happy and unhappy people. Compared to happy people, unhappy individuals appear to feel compelled to derogate alternatives they did not choose or could not have. Happy people, in contrast, appear to live in a world full of good things, and they tend to celebrate what they have received without feeling the need to boost its value by devaluing alternatives.

These studies are correlational in nature because in both studies happiness was measured, not manipulated—it was a variable that the participants brought with them into the studies. Lyubomirsky and Ross measured two variables: happiness (operationalized here by ratings on a happiness scale) and postdecisional judgments of alternatives that were either available or not (the ratings made of colleges and desserts before and after choices were made). They found that, compared to unhappy people, happy people were more likely to celebrate what they were getting (whether it was a college to attend or a dessert to eat). We might state this research result as, "Happiness was positively correlated with positivity about one's choices." As happiness increased, so did positive ratings of chosen schools and desserts. In addition, happiness was negatively correlated with derogating alternatives that were not chosen. As happiness increased, the tendency to view unchosen alternatives negatively decreased.

This example clarifies some key points about systematic observation. First, the setting of a study does not determine its methodology. Correlational studies can take place in a classroom, out in the world, or in a laboratory. Also, the methods for data analyses do not determine the design of a study. Lyubomirsky and Ross did not use correlation coefficients to analyze their data. Even though they are typically referred to as correlational studies, such investigations need not rely on correlation coefficients. Once again, the key defining feature of this type of research is that the variables are simply measured.

Correlation and Causation   In trying to make sense of the world, people often make a big mistake about correlation. Look at the terms in bold type in the following newspaper headlines:

Researchers **Link** Coffee Consumption to Cancer of Pancreas

Scientists Find **Connection** Between Ear Hair and Heart Attacks

Psychologists Discover **Relationship** Between Marital Status and Health

Reading these headlines, the general public would tend to jump to the conclusion that coffee causes cancer, ear hair causes heart attacks, and so on. But all of the words in bold type are synonymous only with correlation, not with causality. *Correlation does not equal causation.* Remember, correlation means only that two variables change together. Being able to predict one event based on the occurrence of another event does not necessarily tell us anything about the cause of either event (Howell, 2008). Sometimes an extraneous variable that has not been measured accounts for the relationship between two others. This circumstance is referred to as the **third variable problem.**

To understand the third variable problem, consider the following example. A researcher measures two variables: the number of ice cream cones sold in a town and the number of violent crimes that occur in that town throughout the year. She finds that ice cream cone sales and violent crimes are positively correlated, to the magnitude of +.50. This high positive correlation would indicate that as ice cream sales increase, so do violent crimes. Would it be reasonable for the local paper to run the headline "Ice Cream Consumption Leads to Violence"? Should protesters set themselves up outside the local *Frosty Freeze* to stop the madness? Probably not. Perhaps you have already thought of the third variable that might explain this correlation—heat. Indeed, when it is hot outside, people are more likely both to

purchase ice cream and to engage in aggressive acts (Anderson & Bushman, 2002). These "third variables" are also called *confounds.*

Given the potential problems with extraneous third variables, why do researchers conduct correlational studies? There are several very good reasons. One reason is that some important questions can be investigated only by using correlational designs. Such questions may involve variables that cannot be manipulated, such as biological sex, personality traits, genetic factors, and ethnic background. Another reason why researchers conduct correlational studies is that sometimes the variables of interest are real-world events that influence people's lives, such as the effects of the September 11 attack of the World Trade Center on New York City residents. Correlational research is also valuable in cases where it would not be ethical to carry out an experiment because of the dangers it poses, such as one in which expectant mothers are directed to smoke varying numbers of cigarettes so that the researcher can see how cigarette smoke affects birth weight and the fetal activity level.

Correlational studies are useful, too, when the issue under investigation is post hoc (after the fact) or historical, such as research into the childhood backgrounds of people who are particularly successful. And correlational research is used when researchers are interested in everyday experience, which is difficult to study by bringing people into the artificial setting of a laboratory. For example, correlational researchers have begun to use daily diary methodologies, known as the experience sampling method (ESM), to study people in their natural settings. These studies involve having people document their daily experiences in a diary a few times a day, or complete measures of their mood and behavior whenever they are beeped by an electronic organizer. One recent daily diary study examined the experience of the meaning in life on a daily basis. In this study, student volunteers rated their mood, activities, thoughts, and their sense of meaning in their life twice daily for a week. The data showed that the strongest predictor of a day being felt to be meaningful was the amount of positive mood the person experienced that day (King & others, 2006).

One way that correlational researchers can confront the problem of third variables is to include these variables in designs that adopt a *multivariate* approach—a method that involves more than just the two main variables of interest. If a variable is measured, it can be controlled for, if not experimentally then statistically. In this way, for example, we can show that the number of cigarettes a person smokes does predict the likelihood of developing lung cancer, controlling for such factors as alcohol consumption, diet, body weight, family background, exercise, and so on. Thus, although correlation cannot be assumed to imply a causal relationship, correlational studies can prove very useful in pinning down potentially causal relationships by employing multivariate approaches to problems that are difficult to study through experiments.

An interesting research question that has been addressed in this way is, Do happy people live longer? In one study, 2,000 older Mexican Americans were interviewed twice over the

third variable problem The situation where an extraneous variable that has not been measured accounts for the relationship between two others.

course of 2 years (Ostir & others, 2000). In the first assessment, participants completed measures of happiness but also reported about potential third variables such as diet, physical health, smoking, marital status, and distress. Two years later, the researchers contacted the participants again to see who was still alive. Results showed that, controlling for these many potential third variables, happiness predicted who was alive 2 years later.

Another way that correlational researchers can approach the issue of causation is to employ a special kind of systematic observation called a **longitudinal design.** Longitudinal research involves obtaining measures of the variables of interest in multiple waves over time. Longitudinal research can address the issue of causation because we can assume that if variable *X* causes changes in variable *Y, X* ought to, at least, precede *Y* over time.

One intriguing longitudinal study is the Nun Study, conducted by David Snowdon and his colleagues (Riley & others, 2005; Snowdon, 2003; Tyas & others, 2007). The study began in 1986 and has followed a sample of 678 School Sisters of Notre Dame ever since. The nuns ranged in age from 75 to 103 when the study began. These women complete a variety of psychological and physical measures annually. This sample is, of course, unique in many respects. However, some characteristics render the participants an excellent group for correlational research. For one thing, many potential extraneous third variables are relatively identical for all the women in the group. Their gender, living conditions, diet, activity levels, marital status, and religious participation are essentially held constant, providing little chance that differences in these variables can explain results. (If a variable does not change, it cannot *change with* or *correlate with* anything else.)

Researchers recently examined the question of the relation between happiness and longevity using this rich dataset. All of the nuns had been asked to write a spiritual autobiography when they entered the convent (for some, as many as 80 years before). Deborah Danner and her colleagues were given access to these documents and used them as indicators of happiness earlier in life, by counting the number of positive emotions expressed in the autobiographies (Danner, Snowdon, & Friesen, 2001). (Note that here we have yet another operational definition of happiness.) Higher levels of positive emotion expressed in autobiographies written at an average age of 22 were associated with a 2.5-fold difference in risk of mortality when the nuns were in their 80s and 90s. That is, women who included positive emotion in these autobiographies when they were in their early 20s were two-and-a-half times more likely to survive some 60 years later.

The use of multivariate approaches and longitudinal designs are ways that correlational researchers may attempt to indicate causal relations among variables. These are the kinds of studies that, along with experimental research using animal models, have allowed researchers to conclude that cigarette smoking *causes* cancer. Still, it is important to keep in mind that even the brightest scientist may not think of all of the potential third variables that might explain her results. Throughout this book you will read about numerous correlational research studies. Keep in mind how easy it is to assume causality when two events or characteristics are merely correlated. Think about those innocent ice cream cones, and critically evaluate conclusions that may be drawn from simple observation.

Experimental Research

If two variables are correlated, there might be a causal relationship between them; but if there is, we cannot be sure which way the causal arrow ought to point. Does *X* cause *Y,* or does *Y* cause *X*? Recent research on meaning in life provides a case in point.

Experiencing one's life as meaningful has long been assumed to be an important aspect of psychological well-being (Frankl, 1984; Steger & Frazier, 2005). Because measures of meaning in life and well-being have been shown to correlate positively (that is, the more meaning in life you have, the happier you are), the assumption has been that meaning in life caused the greater happiness. But because the studies involved in exploring this relationship have been correlational in nature, the causal pathway might well run in the other direction: Happiness might make people feel that their lives are more meaningful. A series of laboratory experiments has shown this very outcome. Laura King and colleagues (2006) have demonstrated that putting people in a good mood—by having them imagine themselves

longitudinal design A special kind of systematic observation that involves obtaining measures of the variables of interest in multiple waves over time.

being recognized as a hero for helping a lost child find his parents—caused them to rate their lives as more meaningful than individuals who were told to imagine a neutral experience.

To clarify the direction of causality, then, psychologists who are interested in determining the causal relationships that might exist between variables must turn to experimental methods (McBurney & White, 2007). An **experiment** is a carefully regulated procedure in which one or more variables believed to influence the behavior being studied are manipulated while all other variables are held constant.

If the behavior under study changes when a variable is manipulated, we say that the manipulated variable has caused the behavior to change. In other words, the experiment has demonstrated cause and effect. In the example above, positive mood was the cause, and meaning in life was the effect. This notion that experiments can demonstrate causation is based on the idea that if participants are randomly assigned to groups, the only systematic difference between them must be the manipulated variable. **Random assignment** means that researchers assign participants to groups by chance. This technique reduces the likelihood that the experiment's results will be due to any preexisting differences between groups (Martin, 2004). In the case of the study of meaning in life by King and others, because of random assignment we can assume that the groups (positive versus neutral mood) did not differ in meaning in life from the outset.

Independent and Dependent Variables   Experiments have two types of variables: independent and dependent. An **independent variable** is a manipulated experimental factor. It is a potential cause. The label "independent" is used because this variable can be manipulated independently of other factors to determine its effect. Researchers have a vast array of options open to them in selecting independent variables, and one experiment may include several independent variables. In the study of positive mood and meaning in life, the independent variable is mood (positive versus neutral).

A **dependent variable** is a factor that can change in an experiment in response to changes in the independent variable. As researchers manipulate the independent variable, they measure the dependent variable for any resulting effect. In the study of mood and meaning in life, meaning in life is the dependent variable.

Experimental and Control Groups   Experiments can involve one or more experimental groups and one or more control groups. An **experimental group** is a group whose experience is manipulated. A **control group** is as much like the experimental group as possible and is treated in every way like the experimental group except for the manipulated factor. The control group thus serves as a baseline against which the effects of the manipulated condition can be compared.

Some Cautions About Experimental Research   **Validity** refers to the soundness of the conclusions we draw from an experiment. Two types of validity matter to experimental designs. The first is **ecological validity,** which refers to the extent to which an experimental design is representative of the real-world issues it is supposed to address. That is, do the experimental methods and the results generalize to the real world?

Imagine that a researcher is interested in the influence of mood on creative problem solving. She randomly assigns individuals to listen to happy music (a positive mood induction) or sad music (a negative mood induction). She then gives all participants a chance to be creative by listing all of the uses they can think of for a cardboard box. Counting up the number of uses that people list, she finds that those in the happy-mood condition have generated more uses for the box. This finding might indicate that happiness is related to creativity. Considering the ecological validity of this study, we might ask the questions, How similar is the happy mood of participants in this study to the kinds of happy moods people experience in real life? and How much is listing the uses of a cardboard box really a sign of creativity? In other words, we ask, Do these methods do a good job of reflecting the real-world processes they are supposed to represent?

The second type of validity is **internal validity,** which refers to the extent to which changes in the dependent variable are due to the manipulation of the independent variable.

experiment A carefully regulated procedure in which one or more variables believed to influence the behavior being studied are manipulated while all other variables are held constant.

random assignment The assignment of participants to research groups by chance.

independent variable The manipulated experimental factor in an experiment.

dependent variable A factor that can change in an experiment in response to changes in the independent variable.

experimental group A group in the research study whose experience is manipulated.

control group A comparison group that is as much like the experimental group as possible and is treated in every way like the experimental group except for the manipulated factor.

validity The soundness of the conclusions we draw from an experiment.

ecological validity The extent to which an experimental design is representative of the real-world issues it is supposed to address.

internal validity The extent to which changes in the dependent variable are due to the manipulation of the independent variable.

In this case, we want to know if the experimental methods are free from biases and logical errors that may render the results suspect. Although experimental research is a powerful tool, it requires safeguards (Leary, 2008). Expectations and biases can, and sometimes do, tarnish results (Rosnow & Rosenthal, 2008).

Experimenter Bias   Experimenters may subtly (and often unknowingly) influence their research participants. **Experimenter bias** occurs when the experimenter's expectations influence the outcome of the research.

In a classic study, Robert Rosenthal (1966) turned college students into experimenters. He randomly assigned the participants rats from the same litter. However, half of the students were told that their rats were "maze bright," whereas the other half were told that their rats were "maze dull." The students then conducted experiments to test their rats' ability to navigate mazes. The results were stunning. The so-called maze-bright rats were more successful than the maze-dull rats at running the mazes. The only explanation for the results is that the college students' expectations affected the performance of the rats. In subsequent studies, researchers have demonstrated that experimenters' expectations influence not only rodent behavior but human behavior as well (Rosenthal, 1994).

Research Participant Bias and the Placebo Effect   Like the experimenters, research participants may have expectations about what they are supposed to do and how they should behave, and these expectations may affect the results of experiments (L. Christensen, 2007). **Research participant bias** occurs when the behavior of research participants during the experiment is influenced by how they think they are supposed to behave.

For example, in one study, the researchers first assessed participants' sensitivity to pain (Levine, Gordon, & Fields, 1979). Then they gave the participants an injection of a painkiller, or so the participants thought. Actually, they received a **placebo**—a harmless, inert substance that has no specific physiological effect. (A placebo can be given to participants instead of the presumed active agent, such as a drug, to determine if the placebo produces the effects thought to characterize the active agent.) Subsequently, when the experimenter administered painful stimuli, the participants perceived less pain than they had in the earlier assessment of their sensitivity to pain. This experiment demonstrated a **placebo effect,** which occurs when participants' expectations, rather than the experimental treatment, produce an experimental outcome.

U.S. television viewers are often exposed to advertisements for prescription drugs. These ads typically include a voice-over that describes the potential side effects. You may have heard the statement "Some individuals taking this drug complain of headaches or stomach discomfort, but these effects were no different from those experienced by people receiving the placebo or sugar pill." Experimenters use placebos to ensure that the effects of a medication are not simply due to expectations. Placebo effects can be surprisingly strong. Research has shown that a substantial part of the treatment effects for antidepressants, for example, may come out of the beliefs of the doctors and patients who use them (Kirsch & Sapirstein, 1999).

Another way to ensure that neither the experimenter's nor the participants' expectations affect the outcome is to design a **double-blind experiment.** In this design, neither the experimenter nor the participants are aware of which participants are in the experimental group and which are in the control group until the results are calculated.

experimenter bias The influence of the experimenter's own expectations on the outcome of the research.

research participant bias The influence of research participants' expectations on their behavior within an experiment.

placebo A harmless, inert substance that may be given to participants instead of a presumed active agent, such as a drug, and that has no specific physiological effect.

placebo effect The situation where participants' expectations, rather than the experimental treatment, produce an experimental outcome.

double-blind experiment An experiment that is conducted so that neither the experimenter nor the participants are aware of which participants are in the experimental group and which are in the control group until after the results are calculated.

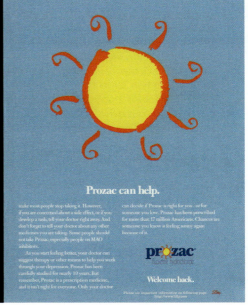

Advertisements for prescription drugs usually describe not only the side effects on people taking the actual drug but also the effects experienced by individuals receiving a placebo.

Anthropological Theory and Social Psychology: Can Reminders of Death Influence Political Allegiance?

At the beginning of this chapter, we considered a variety of life experiences that seem difficult to study through empirical research. We have found that even for something as potentially indescribable as happiness, psychologists can propose new theories, conduct studies, and describe results (with potential benefits to countless people) by employing the scientific method. Sometimes theories that are proposed to explain human behavior are quite abstract and even strange. Observing the world around them, scientists use their critical thinking and skepticism to devise explanations for a wide range of human behavior. These theories are sometimes counterintuitive, meaning that they run counter to common expectations or previously held notions. An example may help to illustrate how even abstract theory can be explored through empirical research.

In the 1970s anthropologist Ernest Becker (1972) drew together theory and research from a broad array of social sciences to devise a grand theory of human life and culture. According to Becker, an important human characteristic that has evolved over the centuries is our amazing intellectual capacity. One result of this capacity is that unlike other animals, we humans are aware of our own vulnerability, notably the reality of our own deaths. This awareness of our mortality creates the potential for overwhelming terror. Yet somehow we manage to go about our daily lives without being preoccupied by the terrifying reality of death. Why is this so?

According to Becker, as our intellectual capacity evolved, so did our capacity to create and invest in *culture*. Culture provides the customary beliefs, practices, religious rules, and social order for humans living together. People in the same culture often share attitudes, values, and goals. Our culture gives us the framework to understand what behavior is appropriate and what is not. Culture provides answers to questions such as, How many wives should a man have? and Should children work to support their family?

Becker asserted that being part of a larger culture shields us from the terror of our own mortality. He maintained that by investing in our cultural worldview (our beliefs, routine practices, and standards for conduct), we are able to enjoy real and symbolic immortality. Real immortality is provided by religious ideas about life after death. Symbolic immortality derives from our ability to contribute to a culture that will outlive us. As long as we feel that we are valued members of a culture, this status will buffer us against our fears of personal death. Becker's theory is known as terror management theory (TMT) (Solomon, Greenberg, & Pyszczynski, 1991).

TMT theory is abstract and not very intuitive. It might strike you as "out there." You might conclude that it is a theory that could not possibly be studied scientifically. How could one actually develop operational definitions for the variables in Becker's model? In fact, TMT has led to a number of provocative laboratory investigations that support Becker's views. Using the scientific method, social psychologists Jeff Greenberg, Sheldon Solomon, and Tom Pyszczynski (1997) derived some specific hypotheses from Becker's broad theory. One such hypothesis is that when people are reminded of their own death, we would expect them to show a tendency to champion their cultural worldview. That is, when our own death is made salient (real) to us, we should be more likely to defend ourselves against mortality by investing strongly in our cultural worldview. Thus, the awareness of death ought to lead to worldview defense.

Becker asserted that being part of a larger culture shields us from the terror of our own mortality.

How might we study this prediction empirically using an experimental design? First the variables must be operationalized. In this case, the independent variable (the cause) is death awareness. To make people more aware of their own deaths, these researchers asked participants to take a few minutes and to write a description of their own deaths—to describe what would happen to them physically and emotionally when they die (Arndt & others, 2005). This "mortality salience" condition is the experimental condition. The dependent variable in our prediction is the defense of one's worldview (the effect). How might this dependent variable be operationalized? One way that worldview defense might show itself is in attitudes about people who behave in ways that contradict the cultural worldview of what is appropriate—for example, criminals. In an early study, researchers asked a sample of 22 municipal court judges either to write about their own deaths or not to do this assignment, and then presented all of them with the same hypothetical case report of a woman arrested for prostitution (Rosenblatt & others, 1989). The judges were asked to set bail for the woman. Judges who had written about their own deaths gave the woman a much higher bond ($455 versus $50). In subsequent studies, these researchers and others have shown that reminding people of their own death tends to increase the tendency to judge harshly individuals who defy our cultural worldview and also to increase our own self-esteem.

Still, this research might seem artificial. How often do you sit down and write about your own death, and in this way get a reminder of your own mortality? Is this work ecologically valid—that is, does it represent how things work in the real world? Although you may not write such descriptions, reminders of death are in fact quite common: the violence we view on TV and in movies, news reports on war and acts of terrorism, the deaths of acquaintances, and even the cemetery or funeral home we drive by on our way home. These common experiences might serve as natural sources of mortality concern.

The terrorist attacks of September 11 might be thought of as a strong mortality salience manipulation. That is, thinking about 9/11 might cause individuals to feel a great deal of death anxiety. And from Becker's theory we would predict that thinking about 9/11 might require individuals to bolster their cultural worldview, just like the judges who were harsher toward a prostitute after thinking about their own deaths. Research has shown that reminders of September 11, such as the haunting images of the jet planes hitting the Trade Center towers, make death thoughts more accessible. For example, in one study, death accessibility (the dependent variable) was operationalized by having participants complete word fragments (Landau & others, 2004). After seeing reminders of 9/11, participants were more likely to complete the fragment COFF_ _ as *coffin* rather than *coffee*. Can such naturally occurring reminders of death influence our worldview in ways that matter?

A series of studies by Mark Landau and colleagues (2004) revealed how reminders of death can cause changes in political allegiances. This research was conducted prior to the November 2004 presidential election when the two main candidates for president were President George W. Bush and Senator John Kerry. In this research, students who were randomly assigned to complete the mortality salience condition (that is, write about their own deaths) or to write about the attacks of 9/11 were more likely than students who had written, for the same amount of time, about the experience of dental pain (a control condition meant to hold anxiety constant) to express increasing support for George W. Bush. That is, students who had written about their own deaths or the events of 9/11 expressed more favorable attitudes toward President Bush compared to those who wrote about dental pain.

In a final study, participants who wrote about their own mortality showed increases in their favorability ratings of George W. Bush and less favorable ratings of John Kerry, and they judged themselves as more likely to vote for Bush than Kerry (Landau & others, 2004). These provocative findings suggest that unconscious concerns about death heighten the appeal of a charismatic leader. It is interesting to note that on October 29, just prior to the 2004 presidential election, Osama bin Laden (certainly a powerful reminder of the events of 9/11) appeared in a video criticizing George W. Bush. Bush later noted that he felt bin Laden's speech only helped him win the election (Reuters, 2006). Indeed, he may have been correct if bin Laden's appearance heightened death concerns for U.S. viewers.

Terror management theory and research provide a powerful example of how broad theory can be translated into strong empirical research. This theory has also yielded surprising findings with regard to more positive human characteristics. Concerns about death can lead either to our becoming narrow and defensive or, conversely, to our becoming more creative and more concerned about leaving a good legacy for the future (Routledge, Arndt, & Sheldon, 2004). Relationships, religious faith, creativity, and sharing our values with others all have been shown to diminish the need to engage in worldview defense when individuals are reminded of their mortality (Jonas & Fischer, 2006; Mikulincer, Florian, & Hirschberger, 2004; Routledge, Arndt, & Sheldon, 2004). In this way, concern over mortality can be a strong motivator to contribute positively to the world.

A study of drug treatment for social phobia was conducted in a double-blind manner (Van Ameringen & others, 2001). Both the experimenter who administered the drug and the participants were kept in the dark about which individuals were receiving the drug and which were receiving a placebo that looked like the drug. This setup ensured that the experimenter could not, for example, make subtle gestures signaling who was receiving the drug and who was not. A double-blind study allows researchers to tease apart the actual effects of the independent variable from the possible effects of the experimenter's and the participants' expectations about it.

A final caution is worth noting in interpreting the results of an experiment. Even if the design was solid and free of obvious confounds or biases, some uncertainty may remain about precisely what aspect of the experimental manipulation caused the results in the dependent measure. An example is provided by the fascinating body of research on expressive writing begun by James Pennebaker. He and his colleagues (Pennebaker & Chung, 2007) conducted a number of studies that converge on the same conclusion: Writing about your deepest thoughts and feelings concerning your most traumatic life event leads to a number of health and well-being benefits.

In these studies, each participant is randomly assigned to write about one of two topics—either the individual's most traumatic life event or a relatively uninteresting topic (for example, his or her plans for the day). Assignment of the specific topic is meant to control for the act of writing itself (Pennebaker & Graybeal, 2001). The participants write about the same topic for 3 or 4 consecutive days for about 20 minutes each day. Weeks or months after writing, participants in the trauma writing group have better physical health than those in the control group. Since the first traumatic writing study, a host of researchers have replicated these effects, showing that writing about trauma is associated with superior immune function, better response to a vaccine, higher psychological well-being, better adjustment to coming to college, and more quickly finding employment after being laid off from work (Lepore & Smyth, 2002). Thus, we might conclude that documenting one's deepest thoughts and feelings about traumatic life events is necessary to attain what has been termed the "healing power" of writing.

Note, however, that the participants in the trauma group were not only writing about a trauma. They were also documenting an important personal experience. Is it necessary to focus on a trauma to benefit from writing? Might there not be other, less negative aspects of life that are equally meaningful and that might bring health benefits when they are the subject of personal writing? Indeed, researchers recently have begun to examine the impact of writing about a variety of topics for health and well-being. For example, research has shown that writing only about the benefits of a traumatic life event—how a person has grown or become a better person because of the event—also leads to health benefits (King & Miner, 2000; Low, Stanton, & Danoff-Burg, 2006).

In addition, writing about one's life dreams not only produced health benefits equal to writing about a traumatic life event but did so while also boosting positive mood (King, 2001). In one study, writing about one's most intensely positive experience also led to health benefits (Burton & King, 2004). These findings and others have prompted researchers to rethink what the mechanisms underlying writing benefits might be (King, 2002). It may be that writing about meaningful and important life experiences is what is needed to benefit from writing, regardless of whether these experiences are negative or positive. We will return to the power of writing for health and wellness in Chapter 12.

At this point, you have read about several different types of research in psychology. For another look at how these research methods differ, see Figure 2.4. And to read about how psychologists have used the experimental research method to translate a broad theory into testable findings about terrorism, death anxiety, and political allegiance, see the Intersection.

FIGURE 2.4

Psychology's Research Methods Applied to Dreaming Psychologists can apply very different methods to study the same phenomenon. Notice here how the object of study, dreams, can influence the usefulness of various methods.

Observation	Survey and Interview	Standardized Test	Case Study	Correlational Research	Experimental Research
Not an easy task, but researchers have observed that an individual's eyes move back and forth behind closed eyelids periodically during the night when dreams are occurring.	Individuals have been asked on surveys and in interviews to report what they dream about.	Psychologists have been ingenious at constructing psychological tests for many phenomena, but dreaming has not been one of them.	Analysis of all that was said by one individual during an hour in which a dream was related. Assessment might take place periodically during the individual's life.	There have been many correlational studies of dreams. For example, researchers have studied whether dreams are related to age, gender, and a person's cultural experiences.	Fewer experimental than correlational studies of dreaming have been conducted. However, in experimental research, individuals in drug-induced states often report a different profile of dreaming than those not under the influence of drugs.

REVIEW, ASSESS, AND SHARPEN YOUR THINKING

Review

2 Discuss common research settings and the three types of research that are used in psychology.

- Name and describe two common settings in which psychological research takes place.
- Name and describe four kinds of descriptive research and identify at least one advantage of each kind of study.
- State the goal of correlational research and explain the significance of the correlation coefficient.
- Discuss the experimental method, including its components. Include in your discussion the potential pitfalls of the experimental method and how to avoid them.

Assess

1. A correlation of −.67 indicates
   - A. a strong positive relationship.
   - B. a strong negative relationship.
   - C. a weak positive relationship.
   - D. a weak negative relationship.

2. A study on obesity had four groups: one group of participants was assigned to read a brochure about diet and nutrition; another group was assigned to a 30-minute counseling session with a nutritionist; a third group was assigned to read the newspaper; and a fourth group was assigned to watch a video about exercise and fitness. Which group is the control group?
   - A. the group that had a counseling session
   - B. the group that read the newspaper
   - C. the group that read the brochure
   - D. the group that watched the video

3. A researcher gives one group of participants an injection of epinephrine and another group an injection of a saline solution. The researcher then measures all participants' responses to completing a series of word puzzles. What is the dependent variable?
   - A. the epinephrine
   - B. the saline solution
   - C. the ages of the subjects
   - D. the word puzzles themselves

4. A study employed a double-blind methodology with random assignment to groups. All participants were first-year college students enrolled in an introductory psychology class. Which of the following could be a concern with this study?
   - A. experimenter bias
   - B. internal validity
   - C. research participant bias
   - D. ecological validity

5. Which of the following statements is correct?
   - A. Only correlational research allows researchers to determine causality.
   - B. Only experimental research allows researchers to determine causality.
   - C. Both correlational and experimental research allow researchers to determine causality.
   - D. Neither correlational nor experimental research allow researchers to determine causality.

Sharpen Your Thinking

Earlier, you were asked to give an operational definition for love. How would you use this definition to conduct research on the important construct of love? Would you use correlational or experimental methods? How would your study of this construct help us to better understand the experience of love?

3 Analyzing and Interpreting Data

Distinguish between descriptive statistics and inferential statistics.

As we have seen in the preceding discussion of the scientific method, after psychologists collect data, they analyze and interpret them. To do so, psychologists use *statistics,* which are mathematical methods for reporting data (Aron, Aron, & Coups, 2008). There are two basic categories of statistics: descriptive statistics, which are used to describe and summarize data, and inferential statistics, which are used to draw conclusions about those data.

Statistical analyses are vitally important to psychological research, and there is even a specific field of psychology, quantitative psychology, that is devoted to developing quantitative techniques to handle the most complex datasets (Jackson, 2006; Vogt, 2007). Psychology students are sometimes surprised to learn that a course in statistics is often a requirement for the major. In this section, as we look at how psychologists analyze and interpret research data, you will get a flavor of the ways in which math plays an important role in the science of psychology.

Descriptive Statistics

Most psychological studies generate considerable numerical data. Simply listing all of the scores generated by a study—for each individual in the study—is not very meaningful. **Descriptive statistics** are the mathematical procedures researchers have developed to describe and summarize sets of data in a meaningful way. Descriptive statistics show us the "big picture"—that is, the overall characteristics of the data and the significant variations among them (Neuman, 2007).

Measures of Central Tendency A *measure of central tendency* is a single number that tells you the overall characteristics of a set of data. The three measures of central tendency are the mean, the median, and the mode.

Most quantitative techniques in psychological science begin with the average, or the mean. The **mean** is what people often think of as the average. The mean is calculated by adding, for example, all the scores in a set of scores and then dividing by the number of scores. As a good indicator of the central tendency for a group of scores, the mean is the measure that is used most often. When your instructor provides students with their exam grades, he or she might mention the test mean, because this average gives the class a general idea of how the group performed.

The mean is not so helpful, however, when a group of scores contains a few extreme scores, especially if the number of such cases is small. Consider the annual earnings for the two groups of five people shown in the table below. Group 1 lists the earnings of five ordinary people. Group 2 is composed of the earnings of four ordinary people plus the approximate earnings of movie director Steven Spielberg. Now look at the means that have been calculated for the two groups. The vast difference between them is due to the one extreme score. In such a situation, one of the other two measures of central tendency, the median or the mode, would give a more accurate picture of the data overall.

The **median** is the score that falls exactly in the middle of the distribution of scores after they have been arranged (or ranked) from highest to lowest. When you have an odd number of scores (say, 5 or 7 scores), the median is the score with the same number of scores above it as below it. In the table below, each group has a median income of $23,000. Notice that, unlike the mean, the median is unaffected by extreme scores. The medians are the

descriptive statistics Mathematical procedures that are used to describe and summarize sets of data in a meaningful way.

mean A statistical measure of central tendency that is calculated by adding all the scores in a set and then dividing by the number of scores.

median A statistical measure of central tendency that falls exactly in the middle of a distribution of scores after they have been arranged (or ranked) from highest to lowest.

Group 1		Group 2	
	$19,000		$19,000
	19,000		19,000
	23,000		23,000
	24,000		24,000
	25,000		45,000,000
Mean	$22,000	Mean	$9,017,000
Median	$23,000	Median	$23,000
Mode	$19,000	Mode	$19,000

both groups ($23,000), but their means are extremely different ($22,000 versus $9,017,000). Of course, if there is an even number of scores, there is no "middle" score. This problem is dealt with by averaging the scores that share the middle location.

The **mode** is the score that occurs most often in a set of data. In our present example, the mode is $19,000, which occurs twice in each group. All of the other annual incomes occur only once. The mode is the least used measure of central tendency. But the mode can be particularly useful, for example, in cases in which information is desired about preference or popularity. Consider a teacher who wants to know the most popular or least popular child in her classroom. She might create a questionnaire and ask students which of their classmates they like the most or the least. The most frequently nominated child would be the mode in these instances.

Measures of Dispersion   In addition to revealing the central characteristics of a sample, descriptive statistics can also give us *measures of dispersion,* which describe how much the scores in a sample vary from one another. That is, these measures give us a sense of the *spread* of scores. Let's look at some common ways that researchers measure dispersion.

Imagine that four students rate their positive mood on a scale from 1 (not at all) to 7 (extremely much), as follows:

Positive mood

Sara	5
Sun Mee	4
Josh	1
Rodney	6

One common measure of dispersion is the **range,** which is the distance between the highest and the lowest scores. In the example above, the range in positive mood is 5 (6 – 1). Generally speaking, the range is a rather simplistic estimate of variability for a group of scores. More important, because the range takes into account only the lowest and highest scores, it can produce a misleading picture of the variability in a set of data. Note that for positive mood, most people in the example have fairly similar high scores, but using the range alone gives the impression that scores are very widely dispersed.

A more informative measure of dispersion, and the one most commonly used in psychological research, is the standard deviation. **Standard deviation** measures how much the scores vary, on the average, around the mean (which in our example of positive mood is 4) of the sample. There is a little hitch, however. One of the mathematical properties of the mean is that if you add up each person's difference from the mean, the sum will always be 0.

So, we cannot calculate the average deviation from the mean and get a meaningful answer. Instead, we calculate the average *squared* deviation from the mean and take the square root of that. The smaller the standard deviation, the less variability from the mean. To calculate the standard deviation in our positive mood example, we would do the following:

1. Subtract 4 (the mean) from all scores and in this way obtain a list of deviation scores: 1, 0, −3, and 2. (Notice that if you add these up, they equal 0.)

2. Square these deviation scores, thus getting 1, 0, 9, and 4.

3. Take the average of these scores by summing them (to get 14) and then dividing by 4 (to get 3.5).

4. Finally, take the square root of the average squared deviation from the mean (a mouthful, but essentially this is the definition of standard deviation) and get approximately 1.87. This is the standard deviation of our sample, which, compared to the range of 6, tells us that the group is actually fairly closely arranged around the mean.

Why do psychologists use the standard deviation so frequently? The reason is that the standard deviation tells them how far away a measured score is from the mean (Aron &

mode A statistical measure of central tendency; the score that occurs most often in a set of data.

range A statistical measure of variability that is the distance between the highest and lowest scores.

standard deviation A statistical measure of variability that involves how much the scores vary, on the average, around the mean of the sample.

"I think you're going to be very happy here."

Aron, 2003). The mean and standard deviation together yield a lot of information about a sample. Indeed, given the raw scores and the mean and standard deviations of two variables, we can calculate the correlation coefficient in no time.

Inferential Statistics

Imagine that you have conducted a study of the relation between expressions of positive emotion and interpersonal success. You have videotaped job candidates being interviewed, coded the tapes for Duchenne smiling by the candidates, and recorded who was called back for a second interview. Let's say you calculate that the mean number of smiles for candidates who were not called back was 3.5, and the mean number of smiles for candidates who were called back was 6.5. So, those who were called back generated, on average, 3 more smiles than those who were not called back. Does that difference matter? It seems pretty big, but is it big enough—should we believe that it represents a difference that is very unlikely to have happened by chance? Inferential statistics are the tools that can answer this question. More specifically, **inferential statistics** are the mathematical methods used to indicate whether data sufficiently support or confirm a research hypothesis (Sprinthall, 2007).

The logic behind inferential statistics is relatively simple. Inferential statistics yield a statement of probability about the differences observed between two or more groups; this probability statement gives the odds that the observed differences were due simply to chance.

If a probability statement tells you that the odds are 5 out of 100 (or .05) or less that the differences are due to chance, the results are considered statistically significant. In statistical language, this is referred to as the .05 *level of statistical significance,* or the .05 *confidence level.* Put another way, *statistical significance* means that the differences observed between two groups are so large that it is highly unlikely that those differences are merely due to chance.

The .05 level of statistical significance is considered the minimum level of probability that scientists will accept for concluding that the differences observed are real, thereby supporting a hypothesis. Some researchers prefer to use more rigorous levels of statistical significance, such as the .01 level of statistical significance (1 out of 100 odds or less that the differences are due to chance) or the .001 level of statistical significance (1 out of 1,000 odds or less). Note that the correlation coefficient that we have already discussed is an inferential statistic.

There are a few things to keep in mind with regard to interpreting statistical significance. First, significance tests are based in part on the number of cases in the sample. The higher the number of cases, the easier it is to get statistical significance. As a result, with a very large sample, even very small effects may be significant. Similarly, statistical significance is not the same thing as real-world significance. Even if a difference is found to be statistically significant, its "real-world value" remains to be evaluated by thinking scientists.

inferential statistics Mathematical methods that are used to indicate whether data sufficiently support or confirm a research hypothesis.

REVIEW, ASSESS, AND SHARPEN YOUR THINKING

Review

3 Distinguish between descriptive statistics and inferential statistics.
- Define descriptive statistics and identify three measures of central tendency and two measures of dispersion, stating the purpose of each.
- Define inferential statistics and discuss statistical significance and its importance in data interpretation.

Assess

1. Which of the following is not a measure of central tendency?
   A. standard deviation   B. mean
   C. median   D. mode

2. Which of the following statements is true?
   A. Inferential statistics describe a sample, while descriptive statistics describe a population.

B. Inferential statistics test hypotheses, while descriptive statistics summarize data.

C. Inferential statistics are based on measures of central tendency, while descriptive statistics are based on measures of dispersion.

D. Inferential statistics are based on a significance level of .01, while descriptive statistics are based on a significance level of .05.

3. You have obtained scores from five participants of 2, 2, 3, 3, and 10. What is the median?

   A. 2   B. 3

   C. 4   D. 10

4. There are 10 participants in a study. Nine of the participants scored between 1–5. The tenth participant has a score of 20.

What is the effect of this participant's score on the mean, median, and/or mode?

A. the mean will be most strongly affected

B. the median will be most strongly affected

C. the mode will be most strongly affected

D. the mean, median, and mode will all be affected equally

5. The standard deviation is

A. a measure of central tendency.

B. the same as the range.

C. the most commonly used measure of dispersion in psychological research.

D. the square root of the range.

Sharpen Your Thinking

Why is it important for you to develop a basic understanding of statistics?

4 The Challenges of Conducting and Evaluating Psychological Research

Discuss some research challenges that involve ethics, bias, and information.

The scientific and statistical foundation of psychological research helps to minimize the effect of individual researchers' biases and to maximize the objectivity of the results. Still, some subtle challenges remain to be fully resolved. One is to ensure that research is conducted in an ethical way; another is to recognize and try to overcome researchers' deeply buried personal biases. Researchers are not the only ones who face these challenges, however. So do you. Every time you encounter information about psychology, whether in the popular media or in academic journals, you face the challenge of evaluating the information objectively and making sure that you are not jumping to the wrong conclusions.

Conducting Ethical Research

Ethics is an important consideration for all science. This fact was brought to the fore in the aftermath of World War II, for example, when it became apparent that Nazi doctors had used concentration camp victims as guinea pigs in experiments. These atrocities spurred scientists to develop a code of appropriate behavior—a set of principles about the treatment that participants in research have a right to expect. In general, ethical principles of research focus on balancing the rights of the participants with the rights of the scientists to ask important research questions (Leary, 2008).

The issue of ethics in psychological research may affect you personally if at some point you serve as a participant in a study. In that event, you need to know your rights as a participant and the researchers' responsibilities in ensuring that these rights are safeguarded. Participants' experiences can have life-altering consequences if researchers fail to consider their well-being.

For example, one investigation of young dating couples asked them to complete a questionnaire that coincidentally stimulated some of the participants to think about potentially troublesome issues (Rubin & Mitchell, 1976). One year later, when the researchers followed up with the original sample, 9 of 10 participants said they had discussed their answers with their dating partners. In most instances, the discussions helped to strengthen the relationships. But in some cases, the participants used the questionnaire as a springboard to discuss problems or concerns previously hidden. One participant said, "The study definitely played a role in ending my relationship with Larry." In this case, the couple had different views about how long they expected to be together. She was thinking of a short-term dating relationship, whereas he was thinking in terms of a lifetime. Their answers to the questions brought the disparity in their views to the surface and led to the end of their relationship. Researchers have a responsibility to anticipate the personal problems their study might cause and, at least, to inform the participants of the possible fallout.

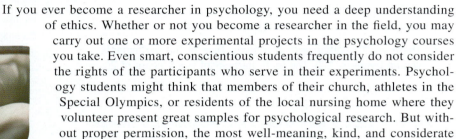

If you ever become a researcher in psychology, you need a deep understanding of ethics. Whether or not you become a researcher in the field, you may carry out one or more experimental projects in the psychology courses you take. Even smart, conscientious students frequently do not consider the rights of the participants who serve in their experiments. Psychology students might think that members of their church, athletes in the Special Olympics, or residents of the local nursing home where they volunteer present great samples for psychological research. But without proper permission, the most well-meaning, kind, and considerate studies still violate the rights of the participants.

Ethics Guidelines Safeguarding the rights of research participants is a challenge because the potential harm is not always obvious. At first glance, you might not imagine that a questionnaire on dating relationships among college students would have any substantial impact or that an experiment involving the treatment of memory loss would be anything but beneficial.

Today colleges and universities have a review board (typically called the institutional review board, or IRB) that evaluates the ethical nature of research conducted at their institutions. Proposed research plans must pass the scrutiny of a research ethics committee before the research can be initiated.

In addition, the American Psychological Association (APA) has developed ethics guidelines for its members. The code of ethics instructs psychologists to protect their participants from mental and physical harm. The participants' best interests need to be kept foremost in the researcher's mind (L. Christensen, 2007). APA's guidelines address four important issues:

- *Informed consent:* All participants must know what their participation will involve and what risks might develop. For example, participants in a study on dating should be told beforehand that a questionnaire might stimulate thoughts about issues in their relationships that they have not considered. Participants also should be informed that in some instances a discussion of the issues might improve their relationships but that in others it might worsen the relationships and even end them. Even after informed consent is given, participants must retain the right to withdraw from the study at any time and for any reason.

- *Confidentiality:* Researchers are responsible for keeping all of the data they gather on individuals completely confidential and, when possible, completely anonymous.

- *Debriefing:* After the study has been completed, participants should be informed of its purpose and the methods that were used. In most cases, the experimenter also can inform participants in a general manner beforehand about the purpose of the research without leading participants to behave in a way that they think that the experimenter is expecting. When preliminary information about the study is likely to affect the results, participants can at least be debriefed after the study has been completed.

- *Deception:* This is an ethical issue that psychologists debate extensively. In some circumstances, telling the participants beforehand what the research study is about substantially alters the participants' behavior and invalidates the researcher's data. For example, suppose a psychologist wants to know whether bystanders will report a theft. A mock theft is staged, and the psychologist observes which bystanders report it. Had the psychologist informed the participants beforehand that the study intended to discover the percentage of bystanders who will report a theft, the whole study would have been undermined. Thus, the researcher deceives participants about the purpose of the study, perhaps leading them to believe that it has some other purpose. In all cases of deception, however, the psychologist must ensure that the deception will not harm the participants and that the participants will be told the true nature of the study (will be debriefed) as soon as possible after the study is completed.

The federal government also takes a role in ensuring that research involving human participants is conducted ethically. The Federal Office for Protection from Research Risks is devoted to ensuring the well-being of participants in research studies. Over the years, the office has dealt with many challenging and controversial issues—among them, informed consent rules for research on mental disorders, regulations governing research on pregnant women and fetuses, and ethical issues regarding AIDS vaccine research.

Some people think of reality TV shows as natural social experiments. To read further about how psychologists view the ethical aspects of these shows, see the Critical Controversy.

The Ethics of Research with Animals   For generations psychologists have used animals in some research. Animal studies have provided a better understanding of and solutions for many human problems (Kalat, 2007; Wickens, 2005). Neal Miller, who has made important discoveries about the effects of biofeedback on health, listed the following areas in which animal research has benefited humans (Miller, 1985):

- Psychotherapy techniques and behavioral medicine
- Rehabilitation of neuromuscular disorders
- Alleviation of the effects of stress and pain
- Drugs to treat anxiety and severe mental illness
- Methods for avoiding drug addiction and relapse
- Treatments to help premature infants gain weight so they can leave the hospital sooner
- Methods used to alleviate memory deficits in old age

Only about 5 percent of APA members use animals in their research. Rats and mice account for 90 percent of all psychological research with animals. How widespread is abuse to animals in psychological research? Animal welfare and rights activists would have you believe that such abuse is extensive. It is true that researchers sometimes use procedures with animals that would be unethical with humans, but they are guided by a set of standards for housing, feeding, and maintaining the psychological and physical well-being of their animal subjects. Researchers are required to weigh potential benefits of the research against possible harm to the animal and to avoid inflicting unnecessary pain. Animal abuse simply is not as common as animal activist groups charge. Stringent ethical guidelines must be followed, whether animals or humans are the subjects in psychological research (Herzog, 1995).

Values   Questions are asked not only about the ethics of psychology but also about its values, its standards for judging what is worthwhile and desirable. Some psychologists argue that psychology should be value-free and morally neutral. From their perspective, the psychologist's role as a scientist is to present facts as objectively as possible.

Others believe that, because psychologists are human, they cannot possibly be value-free, even if they try. Indeed, some people even argue that psychologists *should* take stands on value-laden issues. For example, psychological research shows that children reared by gay and lesbian parents are no more likely to be gay than other

F-Minus © United Feature Syndicate, Inc.

Critical Controversy   Would Reality TV Pass the Institutional Review Board?

Survivor, Fear Factor, American Idol, The Bachelor, The Apprentice—these are just a few of the many extraordinarily popular reality shows that fill the U.S. television airwaves. The more pessimistic commentators view these shows as portents of the end of Western civilization; as a *Newsweek* article bemoaned, "Another Reality Show, Another IQ Point Disappears" (Peyser, 2001). More optimistically, some people see the programs as interesting social experiments. Indeed, reality TV watchers may think that they are learning a lot about human nature by tuning in to see who will get voted off, who will willingly eat ground-up rats, or who will be ridiculed by Simon Cowell.

For you as a student of psychology, an appropriate question might be, Would these reality TV shows ever gain the approval of the institutional review board (IRB) of an institution of higher learning? This issue was of interest to Barbara Spellman, a founding member of the American Psychological Society Committee on Human Subject Protection, who recently undertook a study of reality TV programming with an eye toward the ethical issues these shows present. If we were to consider reality TV from the perspective of the APA ethical guidelines we have considered in this chapter, at least five issues that Spellman identified would come to the fore.

First, how do reality shows achieve informed consent? The principle of informed consent means that all participants must know what their participation will involve and what risks might develop. Yet the very thing that makes reality shows exciting is the element of the unknown—the potential for surprise. Clearly the producers of *Fear Factor* are not going to inform contestants upfront that for their particular episode they will be asked to shave their heads, because the element of shock and the dramatic moment of the decision would diminish greatly if it occurred off camera while the person perused the consent form. On the other hand, we might note that it is highly unlikely that anyone who participates on such a show has not watched a few episodes, and therefore most participants will have a pretty good idea that they must expect the unexpected. On *American Idol,* as yet another contestant expresses dismay at the harsh treatment he or she has experienced courtesy of judge Simon Cowell, you may find yourself yelling at the TV, "What did you expect? Haven't you ever watched this show?"

A second, related problem with at least some reality shows is the use of deception. Fooling a group of women into believing that a semi-employed construction worker is actually a millionaire is probably not likely to satisfy APA ethical considerations.

A third issue that might arise is that of risk. As Spellman (2005) points out, many reality shows pose a great deal of psychological and/or physical risk. Some reality shows include children (for example, *Trading Spouses*), and it is very unlikely that an IRB would consider that posing any kind of risk to children could ever be justified. The most recent addition to reality TV, *Kid Nation,* would be particularly problematic, as it includes *only* children, with minimal

Reality TV shows such as American Idol *would face high hurdles in trying to win over members of the Institutional Review Board.*

adult supervision. The considerable physical risk common to reality TV, such as the extreme weight loss endured by *Survivor* contestants and the daunting physical challenges faced on *Fear Factor,* also would be likely to raise IRB eyebrows—and disapproval.

A fourth issue that Spellman identifies as a major stumbling block for reality TV is the potential for exorbitant award money. Participants in such "research" may feel persuaded to do things they would never "really" do because of the enormous financial incentives involved. Is it "really" lying if you are doing it in order to win a million dollars? If a person does something to "play the game" that he or she would never do outside of the game, haven't we shown that money has compelled the individual to act in ways he or she might later regret or be judged for? Indeed, Spellman suggests that one way to make the shows more likely to secure IRB approval would be to rework the payment structure so that financial gain is less likely to compel behavior.

Remember that ethical considerations involve balancing the rights of participants with the scientist's right to know. Thus, a fifth question pertinent to a study of reality TV is, What is the value of what we can learn from these "experiments"? This brings up the issue of how "natural" reality shows are. Are people truly themselves when the cameras are rolling? Can we learn much of value about human beings in these highly unusual circumstances?

Although we may not be able to discover much about the people who appear on the shows, perhaps we can learn something about the *viewers*. After all, the finale of *Survivor* attracted an audience of some 51 million. And even as the novelty of reality TV has worn off, the shows still remain unusually popular. Indeed, *American Idol* routinely trumped the Winter Olympics of 2006 in viewership. So, the question of why *do* people watch this stuff is one that researchers have begun to address. Steven Reiss and James Wiltz (2004) surveyed more than 10,000 individuals online and identified some of the motivations behind watching reality TV. Disturbingly, they found that what seemed to interest viewers was the enjoyment of watching other people being humiliated. Viewers tended to be high in motivations for status and vengeance (Reiss & Wiltz, 2004). Some psychologists are particularly concerned about the potential of reality shows to change our perceptions about what sort of behavior is appropriate or normal. As many of us complain about the loss of politeness and a growing crassness in human behavior, we might all need to be more mindful of how the things we watch on TV may influence our own behavior.

What Do You Think?

- Do reality TV shows represent natural human behavior? Explain.
- How could we possibly use reality TV in a way that might allow us to understand important psychological processes?
- Do you think that reality TV has affected the standards for behavior in your daily life? Why or why not?

children and tend to show levels of psychological functioning that are equal to or higher than those of children reared by heterosexual parents. To the extent that some have argued against the rights of gay individuals to adopt children or to retain custody of their biological children, psychologists may have a role to play in the debate about these issues. The underlying question is psychologists' scientific responsibilities versus their responsibilities to society as a whole.

Minimizing Bias

The debate over the place of values in psychology continues. But psychologists have generally come to agree that another type of personal objectivity is desirable when doing research. Specifically, psychological studies are most useful when they are conducted without bias or prejudice toward any particular group of people—especially biases based on sex or gender and on culture or ethnicity.

Gender Bias   For centuries, society has had a strong gender bias, a preconceived notion about varying abilities between women and men that prevented countless individuals from pursuing their own interests and achieving their potential. Many women have faced barriers in the academic world and in their careers. Within the field of psychology, gender bias also has had a less obvious effect (Hyde, 2007; Smith, 2007). Think about it: Psychology is the science of all human behavior. But historically, theory and research in psychology often started with just the male experience—not only because the researchers themselves were often male, but also because the research participants too were typically all men, since only men were available as participants when psychologists began to study undergraduates. Thus, too often psychological research has had a gender bias (Hyde, 2007; Kimmel & Crawford, 2002). For too long, the female experience has been subsumed under the male experience (Tetreault, 1997).

Florence Denmark and her colleagues (1988) argue as well that when gender differences are found, they are too often unduly magnified. For example, a researcher might report in a study that 74 percent of the men had high achievement expectations versus only 67 percent of the women, and might describe the difference in some detail. In reality, this might be a rather small difference. It also might disappear if the study were repeated or found to have methodological problems that do not allow such strong interpretations.

Researchers giving females equal rights in research have raised some new questions (Tetreault, 1997):

- How might gender bias influence the choice of hypotheses, participants, and research design? For example, the most widely known theory of moral development was proposed by a male (Lawrence Kohlberg) in a male-dominant society (the United States), and males were the main participants in research used to support the theory for many years.
- How might research on topics of primary interest to females—such as relationships, feelings, and empathy—challenge existing theory? For example, in the study of moral development, the highest level has often been portrayed as based on a principle of "justice for the individual" (Kohlberg, 1976). However, more recent theorizing notes that individuality and autonomy tend to be male concerns and suggests that a principle based on relationships and connections with others be added to our thinking about high-level moral development (Gilligan, 1982, 1996).
- How has research that has exaggerated gender differences between females and males influenced the way that people think about females? For example, some researchers believe that gender differences in mathematics have often been exaggerated and have been fueled by societal bias (Hyde, 2005, 2007). Such exaggeration of differences can lead to negative expectations for females' math performance.

Cultural and Ethnic Bias   The realization that psychological research needs to include more people from diverse ethnic groups has also been building (Berry & others, 2006; McLoyd, Aikens, & Burton, 2006). Historically, people from ethnic minority groups

Look at the two photographs, one of all White males, the other of a diverse group of females and males from different ethnic groups, including some White individuals. Consider a topic in psychology, such as parenting, love, or cultural values. If you were conducting two different research studies on this topic—one with the group on the left as participants, and the other with the group on the right—might the results be different? Why?

(African American, Latino, Asian American, and Native American) have been discounted from most research in the United States and simply thought of as variations from the norm, or average. Because their scores do not always fit neatly into measures of central tendency, minority individuals have been viewed as simply adding "noise" to the data. Consequently researchers have deliberately excluded them from the samples they have selected. Given the fact that individuals from diverse ethnic groups have been excluded from psychological research for so long, we might reasonably conclude that people's real lives are perhaps more varied than research data have indicated in the past.

Researchers also have tended to overgeneralize about ethnic groups (Banks, 2008). **Ethnic gloss** is using an ethnic label, such as "African American" or "Latino," in a superficial way that portrays an ethnic group as being more homogeneous than it really is. For example, a researcher might describe a research sample like this: "The participants were 20 Latinos and 20 Anglo-Americans." A more complete description of the Latino group might be something like this: "The 20 Latino participants were Mexican Americans from low-income neighborhoods in the southwestern area of Los Angeles. Twelve were from homes in which Spanish is the dominant language spoken, 8 from homes in which English is the main language spoken. Ten were born in the United States, 10 in Mexico. Ten described themselves as Mexican American, 5 as Mexican, 3 as American, 2 as Chicano, and 1 as Latino." Ethnic gloss can cause researchers to obtain samples of ethnic groups that are not representative of the group's diversity. Overgeneralization and stereotyping can result.

One psychologist interested in obtaining better research information about gender and ethnicity is Pam Reid (Reid, 2002; Reid & Zalk, 2001). Reid's research focuses on the ways in which gender, socioeconomic status, and ethnicity are involved in the development of social skills. Reid and her students study why middle school girls from various ethnic backgrounds stop taking classes in mathematics. Reid points out that many psychological findings have been based on research with middle socioeconomic status Euro-Americans. Taking into account the expectations, attitudes, and behaviors of diverse ethnic groups can only enrich psychological theory and practice.

ethnic gloss Using an ethnic label, such as "African American" or "Latino," in a superficial way that portrays the ethnic group as more homogeneous than it really is.

Being a Wise Consumer of Information About Psychology

Television, radio, newspapers, magazines, and the Internet all report on psychological research that is likely to be of interest to the general public. Much of the information has been published in professional journals or presented at national meetings, and most major colleges and universities have a media relations department that contacts the press about current research by their faculty.

You should be aware, however, that not all psychological information that is presented for public consumption comes from professionals with excellent credentials and reputations at colleges or universities or in applied mental health settings (Stanovich, 2007). Because journalists, television reporters, and other media personnel are not usually trained in psychological research, they often have trouble sorting through the widely varying material they find and making sound decisions about the best information to present to the public. In addition, the media often focus on sensationalistic and dramatic psychological findings to capture your attention. They tend to go beyond what actual research articles and clinical findings really say.

Even when the media present the results of excellent research, they have trouble adequately informing people about what has been found and the implications for people's lives. For example, this entire book is designed to carry out the task of carefully introducing, defining, and elaborating on key concepts and issues, research, and clinical findings. The media, however, do not have the luxury of so much time and space to detail and specify the limitations and qualifications of research. They often have only a few minutes or a few lines to summarize as best they can the complex findings of a study or a psychological concept.

In the end, you have to take responsibility for evaluating the reports on psychological research that you encounter in the media. To put it another way, you have to consume psychological information wisely. Five guidelines follow.

Distinguish Between Group Results and Individual Needs People who learn about psychological research through the media are likely to apply the results to their individual circumstances, yet most research focuses on groups, and individual variations in participants' responses are seldom emphasized. As a result, the ill-informed consumer of psychological research may get the wrong idea about the "normality" of his or her circumstances. For example, researchers interested in the effects of divorce on an adult's ability to cope with stress might conduct a study of 50 divorced women and 50 married women. They might conclude that the divorced women, as a group, cope more poorly with stress than the married women. In this particular study, however, some of the divorced women were likely to be coping better than some of the married women. Indeed, of the 100 women in the study, the 2 or 3 women who are best coping with stress may be the divorced women. It would be accurate to report the findings as showing that divorced women (as a group) coped less effectively with stress than married women (as a group) did. But it would not be sensible to conclude, after reading a summary of the results of the study, that your divorced sister may not be coping with stress as well as she thinks and to recommend that she see a therapist.

The failure of the media to distinguish adequately between research on groups and the individual needs of consumers is not entirely their fault. Researchers have not made the difference clear, either. They often fail to examine the overlap in the data on the groups they are comparing and focus only on the differences. And then, too often they highlight only these differences in their reports.

Remember, if you read a report in a research journal or the media that states that the divorced women coped more poorly with stress than the married women, you cannot conclude that all divorced women coped more poorly with stress. The only conclusion that you can reasonably draw is that more married women coped better than divorced women did.

Avoid Overgeneralizing from a Small Sample Media presentations of psychological information often do not have the space or time to go into details about the nature of the sample used in the study. Sometimes you will get basic information about the sample's size—whether it is based on 10 participants, 50 participants, or 200 participants. If you cannot learn anything else about the sample, at least pay attention to its number.

Small or very small samples require caution in generalizing to a larger population of individuals. For example, a sample of only 10 or 20 divorced women may have some unique characteristics that would make the study's finding inapplicable to many women. The women in the sample might all have high incomes, be White, be childless, live in a small southern town, and be undergoing psychotherapy. Divorced women who have moderate to low incomes, are from other ethnic backgrounds, have children, are living in different contexts, and are not undergoing psychotherapy might have given very different responses.

Look for Answers Beyond a Single Study   The media might identify an interesting piece of research or a clinical finding and claim that it is something phenomenal with far-reaching implications. Although such pivotal studies do occur, they are rare. It is safer to assume that no single study will provide conclusive answers to an important question, especially answers that apply to all people. In fact, in most psychological domains that prompt many investigations, conflicting results are common. Answers to questions in research usually emerge after many scientists have conducted similar investigations that yield similar conclusions.

If one study reports that a particular therapy conducted by a particular therapist has been especially effective with divorced adults, you should not conclude that the therapy will work as effectively with all divorced adults and with other therapists until more studies are conducted. Remember that you should not take a report of one research study as the absolute, final answer to a problem.

Avoid Attributing Causes Where None Have Been Found   Drawing causal conclusions from correlational studies is one of the most common mistakes made by the media. When a true experiment has not been conducted—that is, when participants have not been randomly assigned to treatments or experiences—two variables or factors might have only a noncausal relationship to each other (Leavitt, 2000). Remember from the discussion of correlation earlier in the chapter interpretations cannot be made when two or more factors are simply correlated. We cannot say that one *causes* the other.

In the case of divorce, imagine that you read this headline: "Low Income Causes Divorced Women to Have a High Degree of Stress." You should instantly be able to conclude that the story is about a correlational study, not an experimental study. The word *causes* is used in error. Why? For ethical and practical reasons, women participants cannot be randomly assigned to become divorced or stay married, and divorced women cannot be randomly assigned to be poor or rich. A more accurate heading might be "Low-Income Divorced Women Have a High Degree of Stress," meaning that the researchers found a correlation among being divorced, having a low income, and experiencing a lot of stress. Be skeptical of words indicating causation until you know more about the research they are describing.

Consider the Source of Psychological Information   Remember that studies conducted by psychologists are not automatically accepted by the rest of the research community. The researchers usually must submit their findings to a journal for review by their colleagues, who make a decision about whether to publish the paper, depending on the care taken in conducting the research. Although the quality of research and findings is not uniform among all psychology journals, in most cases journals submit the findings to far greater scrutiny than the popular media do (Stanovich, 2007).

Within the media, though, you can usually draw a distinction. The reports of psychological research in respected newspapers such as the *New York Times* and *Washington Post,* as well as in credible magazines such as *Time* and *Newsweek,* are far more trustworthy than reports in tabloids such as the *National Inquirer* and *Star.* But regardless of the source—serious publication, tabloid, or even academic journal—you are responsible for reading the details of the research behind the findings that are presented and analyzing the study's credibility.

In the next few days, look through several newspapers and magazines for reports about psychological research. Also notice what you see and hear on television about psychology. Try applying the guidelines for being a wise consumer of information about psychology to these media reports.

REVIEW, ASSESS, AND SHARPEN YOUR THINKING

Review

4 **Discuss some research challenges that involve ethics, bias, and information.**

- Describe researchers' ethical responsibilities to the humans and animals they study.
- Explain how gender, cultural, and ethnic bias can affect the outcome of a research study.
- List five key things to keep in mind when you come across information pertaining to psychological research.

Assess

1. Providing research participants with information about the purpose of a study at the study's conclusion is called
   - A. informed consent.
   - B. deception.
   - C. debriefing.
   - D. confidentiality.

2. Which organization provides ethical guidelines for psychologists?
   - A. The American Psychiatric Association
   - B. The Institutional Review Board
   - C. The American Medical Association
   - D. The American Psychological Association

3. Overgeneralizing about a racial or ethnic group is referred to as
   - A. gender bias.
   - B. ethnic bias.
   - C. ethnic gloss.
   - D. cultural bias.

4. What is the problem with small sample sizes?
   - A. Their results may be unrepresentative of the larger population.
   - B. They can only be studied with survey questions.
   - C. They are made up of unreliable sources.
   - D. They give only correlational information.

5. A study could possibly put participants at risk of harm but the participants are not told about the potential for harm. What ethical standard has been violated?
   - A. debriefing
   - B. informed consent
   - C. deception
   - D. confidentiality

Sharpen Your Thinking

What should society do with knowledge that is gained from research that is deemed unethical (for instance, research conducted on concentration camp victims)? Do you think the information should still be used to benefit society? Why or why not?

5 The Scientific Method and Health and Wellness

Discuss scientific studies on human happiness and the nature of their findings.

The Science of Increasing Happiness

The role of science in human health is obvious. Daily, we read or hear about important scientific discoveries that promise to help us prevent and cure disease. Research shows the benefits of exercising, eating right, and not smoking in enhancing our chances of living long, healthy lives. If science can be relied upon to help us be healthier, can scientific inquiry also help us to be happier?

The scientific study of happiness typically focuses on a variable called *subjective well-being*. Subjective well-being is an individual's personal assessment of how well things are going in his or her life: how much positive affect (that is, feeling) and negative affect the person experiences and how he or she feels about life in general. You can quickly assess your subjective well-being by answering the question, How satisfied are you with your life as a whole?

As we have considered throughout this chapter, happiness is best seen not only as an outcome of positive life events but also as a predictor of those events. Recall the description of the meta-analysis toward the beginning of the chapter that surveyed a broad array of studies in support of the notion that happiness is a correlate, predictor, and possible cause of life success (Lyubomirsky, King, & Diener, 2005). This meta-analysis presents compelling evidence from longitudinal research that demonstrates a link between positive affect and altruism, sociability, activity, self-esteem, other esteem, conflict resolution, physical health, and immune function. It seems likely that if we were to write a prescription for happiness, we might do well to include a good marriage, satisfying work, warm friendships, and a long, healthy life. Importantly, the results of the meta-analysis suggest not only that happiness is an outcome of these experiences but also that happiness may in fact foster them. Happiness is a precursor to a broad array of positive outcomes, including satisfying relationships (Lucas & others, 2003), career success (Staw, Sutton, & Pelled, 1994), superior coping (Aspinwall, 1998; Carver & others, 1993), physical health (Kubzansky & others, 2001), and even survival (Danner, Snowdon, & Friesen, 2001). Thus, happiness is a potential *cause* of life success.

In light of the significant benefits of happiness, what might we do to become happier? There are two important problems associated with attempts to enhance happiness: the so-called *hedonic treadmill* and the problem of pursuing happiness as a goal in and of itself.

The first key dilemma in increasing happiness is the hedonic (meaning "related to pleasure") treadmill (Brickman & Campbell, 1971; Fredrick & Loewenstein, 1999). The concept of the hedonic treadmill is that any aspect of life that enhances our positive feelings is likely to do so for only a short period of time. That is, we are likely to adapt quite rapidly to any change that might occur in our life that would presumably influence our happiness. So winning the lottery, moving to a dream home in California, or falling in love may lead to temporary gains in our experience of joy, but eventually we go back to our baseline (Schkade & Kahneman, 1998). Whether it is the switch from CDs to iTunes or from dial-up to wireless, what we first experience as a life-changing improvement eventually fades to a routine (but still necessary) aspect of life, all too soon to be taken for granted. So, how can we increase happiness if such happiness enhancers quickly lose their power?

A second challenge to the goal of enhancing happiness is that pursuing happiness for its own sake is rarely a good way to do it. When happiness is the goal, the pursuit is likely to backfire (Schooler, Ariely, & Loewenstein, 2003). Explicitly focusing on trying to be happier is not a good way to actually be happier. Indeed, those who explicitly link the pursuit of their everyday goals to happiness fare quite poorly (McIntosh, Harlow, & Martin, 1995).

How can the many among us who are interested in being happier navigate this difficult path? In other words, how can we enhance our happiness without having this new capacity for joy become ho-hum, and how might we pursue happiness without really pursuing it? One potentially useful approach is to commit ourselves to the pursuit of other personally meaningful goals.

Stop for a minute and write down the things you are typically trying to accomplish in your everyday behavior. You might identify a goal such as "to get better grades," "to be a good friend (or wife or mother)," or "to fight injustice when I see it happening." Such everyday goals and our pursuit of them have been shown to relate strongly to our subjective well-being (Brunstein, 1993; King, 2007; Sheldon, 2002). Research demonstrates that simply having important, valued goals is associated with subjective well-being, as is making progress on those goals. Personal goals have been shown to organize daily experience and influence the relationship between events and daily emotional life (Cantor & Sanderson, 1999; Diener & Fujita, 1995). Events matter to us to the extent that they affect our goals. Goal pursuit provides the glue that meaningfully relates a chain of life events, endowing life with beginnings, middles, and ends. To the extent that goals direct attention, draw our thoughts to them, and drive the extraction of meaning from life events, they are a kind of psychic hub in our mental lives (King, 2007).

Many people buy lottery tickets thinking that winning the jackpot will bring them greater happiness. Although lottery winners may experience some gains in joy, research shows that these are temporary and that people go back to their baseline level of happiness.

The considerable scholarly literature on goal investment offers a variety of ideas about the types of goals that are likely to enhance our subjective well-being. To optimize the happiness payoffs of goal processes, one ought to pursue goals that are important and personally valuable (Sheldon, 2002). These goals should be moderately challenging and should share an instrumental relationship with each other—so that the pursuit of one goal facilitates the accomplishment of another (Emmons & King, 1988). Having daily goals that serve the function of leading us to our broader life dreams is related to enhanced subjective well-being, and progress on those goals is particularly rewarding (King, Richards, & Stemmerich, 1998). Now pause and write down your daily goals and your life goals, and consider how these relate to each other. Are you pursuing the kinds of daily goals that will get you to the larger life dream you desire?

With regard to the hedonic treadmill, goal pursuit has a tremendous advantage over other ways of trying to enhance happiness. Goals change and are changed by life experience. As a result, goal pursuit may be less susceptible to adaptation over time. One reason why goals may allow us to maintain traction on the hedonic treadmill is that goals accentuate the positive but do not necessarily eliminate the negative. Goals may relate to either positive or negative emotional experiences, depending on how we are progressing in goal pursuit. Goals may increase not only subjective well-being, but also momentary unhappiness—the latter effect perhaps being a very good thing. Sometimes achieving a particular goal just does not work out, no matter how well we articulate it or how doggedly we pursue it. Indeed, setting a goal includes not only the promise of fulfillment but also the potential for failure, humiliation, and regret. Emotionally investing in one's daily life may mean experiencing worry over whether one will succeed (Pomerantz, Saxon, & Oishi, 2000) and experiencing disappointment when things do not go well (Kernis & others, 2000; Marsh, 1995).

So, overall, goal pursuit may lead to a happier life. But goals also keep life *affectively interesting*. By fostering a rich emotional life that is also coherent and comprehensible, goals keep the positive possible and interesting. The conclusion, for those who want to enhance happiness, is to strive mightily for the goals that you value. You may get lucky and fail now and then, but missing the mark will only make your successes all the sweeter. Another advantage of goals as an entryway to enhanced happiness is that goals allow you to enjoy happiness without necessarily pursuing it. Goals pave the way for you to pursue happiness while you are pursuing *other* things.

REVIEW, ASSESS, AND SHARPEN YOUR THINKING

Review

5 Discuss scientific studies on human happiness and the nature of their findings.

- Describe researchers' findings about how people can enhance their happiness, and discuss two challenges associated with attempts to become happier.

Assess

1. Which of the following is an example of the hedonic treadmill?

    A. a person continuing to seek out pleasure at the expense of his or her responsibilities

    B. a person feeling very happy when he or she buys a luxury car, but the feeling quickly fades

    C. a person pursuing a promotion in order to obtain more financial rewards

    D. a person working toward valued goals

2. Which of the following is least related to subjective well-being?

A. positive affect
B. negative affect
C. satisfaction with life
D. anxiety

3. To optimize your happiness, your goals should be

A. easy, attainable, and interesting.
B. moderately challenging, difficult to attain, and related to income.
C. easy, related to other goals, and personally meaningful.
D. moderately challenging, important, and personally valuable.

Sharpen Your Thinking

Do you think that increasing happiness is a worthwhile goal? Why or why not?

4. What is the relationship between positive life events and happiness?

A. Positive life events can predict happiness.
B. Happiness is a poor prediction of positive life events.
C. Happiness both predicts and is a positive outcome of positive life events.
D. There is very little relationship between positive life events and happiness.

1 PSYCHOLOGY'S SCIENTIFIC METHOD

Explain what makes psychology a science.

A Scientific Approach

A scientist's attitude is distinguished by four characteristics: being curious, being skeptical, being objective (by using empirical methods), and thinking critically.

Collaboration

Science takes place among a community of thinkers. Psychologists share their findings with others by making presentations at conferences and publishing their work in peer-reviewed journals. Through peer review, findings are evaluated critically by others, ensuring that the research published in academic journals represents the highest-quality knowledge.

The Five Steps in the Scientific Method

The scientific method involves five steps: (1) observing a phenomenon, (2) formulating hypotheses and predictions, (3) testing these hypotheses through empirical research, (4) drawing conclusions based on that research, and (5) evaluating conclusions.

2 RESEARCH SETTINGS AND TYPES OF RESEARCH

Discuss common research settings and the three types of research that are used in psychology.

Research Settings

Two common research settings are laboratories and natural settings. The research laboratory is a controlled setting where the complex factors of the real world can be closely controlled or eliminated. Natural settings are places in which behavior occurs naturally and without artificial control of outside factors.

Descriptive Research

Four types of descriptive research are observation, surveys and interviews, standardized tests, and case studies. Each type has certain strengths. Observation allows scientists to gain an understanding of behavior as it occurs naturally. Surveys and interviews allow researchers directly to ask people the questions they wish to know. Standardized tests provide a basis for comparing individuals. Case studies provide dramatic, in-depth portrayals of single individuals.

Correlational Research

The goal of correlational research is to determine whether two variables change together. The correlation coefficient is a statistic that conveys the direction of this covariation. In a positive correlation, the variables change in the same direction—if one increases, so does the other. In a negative correlation, as one variable increases, the other systematically decreases. Correlational studies are limited in that they cannot be used to determine causal relationships between variables.

Experimental Research

The experimental method involves a carefully regulated procedure that allows researchers to determine whether one variable causes changes in another. Experiments typically rely on random assignment to ensure that two groups do not differ systematically prior to the study. In an experiment, the independent variable is the one that is manipulated, allowing the researcher to examine its effects on the dependent variable. The independent variable is the "cause," and the dependent variable is the "effect." Generally, the experimental group is the group for whom the independent variable is manipulated. The control group is identical to the experimental group except for the manipulation of the independent variable.

Problems that can influence the validity of an experiment include experimenter bias, participant bias, and the placebo effect. Experimenter bias occurs when the experimenter's expectations influence the outcome of a study. Participant bias refers to the effects of a participant's expectations about a study. The placebo effect refers to the fact that sometimes a person's belief in a treatment can cause changes, even for individuals in the control condition. These biases can be avoided through the use of double-blind procedures, in which neither the experimenter nor the participant knows which treatment condition a person has been assigned to receive.

3 ANALYZING AND INTERPRETING DATA

Distinguish between descriptive statistics and inferential statistics.

Descriptive Statistics

Descriptive statistics are used to describe and summarize samples of data in a meaningful way. Two types of descriptive statistics are measures of central tendency and measures of variability. Measures of central tendency are the mean (or mathematical average), the median (the middle score), and the mode (the most common score). Measures of variability include the range (the difference between the highest and lowest scores) and the standard deviation (the square root of the average squared deviation from the mean).

Inferential Statistics

Inferential statistics are used to draw conclusions about data. Inferential statistics aim to uncover statistical significance, which means that the differences observed between groups (or the correlation between variables) are unlikely to be the result of chance.

4 THE CHALLENGES OF CONDUCTING AND EVALUATING PSYCHOLOGICAL RESEARCH

Discuss some research challenges that involve ethics, bias, and information.

Conducting Ethical Research

To conduct research ethically, the researcher's responsibilities include obtaining informed consent, ensuring confidentiality, debriefing participants about the purpose of the study and any consequences of participation, and avoiding the unnecessary use of deception. In animal research, ethical considerations include protecting animal subjects from unnecessary pain and discomfort, while weighing the potential benefits of research against the possible harm to animals.

Minimizing Bias

Psychologists must guard against gender, cultural, and ethnic biases in research. Research that relies on limited (for example, all male or all Euro-American) samples cannot be generalized to the entire population. Gender, cultural, and ethnic biases can lead to inaccurate conclusions in psychological research.

Being a Wise Consumer of Information About Psychology

When you read or hear about psychological research in the popular media, you should approach the information with a critical mind. This means distinguishing between group results and individual needs, not overgeneralizing based on a small sample or single study, and not drawing causal conclusions from correlational data. It is also important to evaluate the source of the information and its credibility.

5 THE SCIENTIFIC METHOD AND HEALTH AND WELLNESS

Discuss scientific studies on human happiness and the nature of their findings.

The Science of Increasing Happiness

The scientific study of happiness has shown that some strategies for enhancing happiness may work better than others. The hedonic tread-mill refers to the fact that many of the experiences that might temporarily enhance happiness eventually lose their novelty, causing levels of happiness to return to their previous levels. Goal pursuit is one way to enhance happiness without falling prey to the hedonic treadmill, because goals can enhance our happiness while also allowing us to lead emotionally rich lives.

Key Terms

meta-analysis, p. 34
theory, p. 34
variable, p. 34
operational definition, p. 34
hypothesis, p. 35
population, p. 36
sample, p. 36
random sample, p. 36
naturalistic observation, p. 39

standardized test, p. 40
case study, p. 40
correlational research, p. 41
third variable problem, p. 44
longitudinal design, p. 45
experiment, p. 46
random assignment, p. 46
independent variable, p. 46
dependent variable, p. 46

experimental group, p. 46
control group, p. 46
validity, p. 46
ecological validity, p. 46
internal validity, p. 46
experimenter bias, p. 47
research participant bias, p. 47
placebo, p. 47
placebo effect, p. 47

double-blind experiment, p. 47
descriptive statistics, p. 52
mean, p. 52
median, p. 52
mode, p. 53
range, p. 53
standard deviation, p. 53
inferential statistics, p. 54
ethnic gloss, p. 60

Assess Your Knowledge

1. Which of the following allows a researcher to test for causation?
   A. correlational design
   B. longitudinal design
   C. case study design
   D. experimental design

2. A researcher finds that as scores on optimism go up, scores on depression go down. Moreover, she finds that there is a strong relationship between optimism and depression. Which of the following correlation coefficients would be most consistent with her findings?
   A. .38
   B. .79
   C. −.11
   D. −.68

3. Examining 50 studies to determine the effects of parenting styles on children's well-being would be an example of
   A. developing a theory.
   B. testing a hypothesis.
   C. meta-analysis.
   D. an operational definition.

4. Which of the following is an example of a random sample?
   A. randomly choosing a group of 50 students from a roster of all students in a school
   B. randomly choosing a classroom from all classrooms in a school
   C. randomly choosing students who attended a soccer game
   D. choosing each 50th student who enters the building's front entrance

5. Michael scored in the 47th percentile on a standardized test. Which of the following statements is correct?
   A. Michael correctly answered 47% of the questions.
   B. Michael incorrectly answered 47% of the questions.
   C. Michael's score is worse than 47% of everyone who took the test.
   D. Michael's score is better than 47% of everyone who took the test.

6. What is the mode for the following set of numbers? 1, 1, 1, 3, 16, 23, 23, 45
   A. 1
   B. 9.5
   C. 14.125
   D. 45

7. To what does the .05 level of significance refer?
   A. There is a difference of 5 percentage points between groups.
   B. The research results are 95 percent reliable.
   C. There is a greater than 5 percent chance that the research results are due to chance.
   D. There is a 5 percent or less chance that the research results are due to chance.

8. _____ statistics are used to characterize a sample; _____ statistics are used to test a hypothesis.
   A. correlational, experimental
   B. experimental, correlational
   C. descriptive, inferential
   D. inferential, descriptive

9. An experimenter told a research participant that the purpose of the study was to examine people's reaction to media violence. In reality, the purpose of the study was to examine group dynamics. Which of the following would potentially be an ethical problem for this study?
   A. debriefing
   B. confidentiality
   C. informed consent
   D. deception

10. The statement "the study included 200 Asian participants" is problematic because of
    A. cultural bias.
    B. ethnic bias.
    C. ethnic gloss.
    D. ethnic misrepresentation.

11. Which of the following is not a measure of dispersion?
    A. standard deviation
    B. mean
    C. range
    D. spread

12. Alfonso is in a study testing the effectiveness of a new type of medication. He is given a pill that contains no actual medicine (a sugar pill). After taking the pill, he reports significantly fewer symptoms. Which of the following is at play?
    A. experimenter bias
    B. placebo effect
    C. ecological validity
    D. internal validity

13. Four groups of participants are enrolled in a study. One group is provided with a multiculturally-tailored therapy; the second is provided standard therapy; the third is provided group therapy; and the fourth receives no treatment. Which group is the control group?
    A. the multiculturally-tailored therapy group
    B. the standard therapy group
    C. the group therapy group
    D. the no-treatment group

14. A multivariate study is one that
    A. examines two or more variables of interest simultaneously.
    B. measures participant responses on more than one occasion.
    C. does not manipulate the independent variable.
    D. randomly assigns participants to groups.

15. A correlation of .78 probably means that
    A. there is a negative relationship between two variables.
    B. there is a weak relationship between two variables.
    C. there is no relationship between two variables.
    D. there is a very strong relationship between two variables.

16. Which of the following is not a part of the scientific method?
    A. Observation
    B. Formulation of hypotheses and predictions
    C. Making inferences
    D. Testing through empirical research

Go to Appendix B for answers to these questions.

Apply Your Knowledge

1. Astrology, ghostly hauntings, the power of crystals, UFOs, and extrasensory perception (ESP): Find a website dedicated to one of these phenomena. Using the four attributes of a scientific attitude, critically examine the claims made on the website. Describe the theory, the hypothesis, the data, and the analysis. Can you find all of this information on the website? If not, how would a scientist respond to the website?

2. Consider the following questions, which are the sort that might interest a psychologist. Describe a study you would use to address each of these questions, including what kind of research method you would employ, and evaluate the ethical considerations for your study.

   a. What percentage of people wash their hands after using the restroom?

   b. Does background music make people buy more at the supermarket?

   c. Is there a relationship between religious faith and helping others?

   d. Does drinking alcohol make people more creative?

3. Visit the library at your school and find an article in a psychology journal. Describe what kind of study was done—was it descriptive, correlational, or an experiment? If it was an experiment, what were the independent and dependent variables? What kind of statistics did the researchers use? Can you tell if the results are statistically significant?

4. Much of the experimental research in psychology has been conducted using undergraduate students. How might this choice influence the interpretation of the results to other groups, such as children or older adults? Describe some of the special ethical issues that might be involved in using children and older adults in psychological experiments.

CHAPTER 3

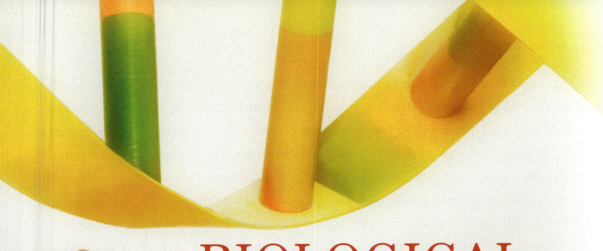

BIOLOGICAL FOUNDATIONS OF BEHAVIOR

Experiencing Psychology

TOMMY McHUGH: FROM VIOLENT HEROIN ADDICT TO ACCOMPLISHED ARTIST

Tommy McHugh had led a troubled life. He was a heroin addict who had spent time in jail. He was gruff and occasionally violent. Then, at the age of 51, he suffered a stroke. His doctors repaired two hemorrhages (or bleeds) in his brain (Lythgoe & others, 2005).

After the operations, Tommy began to recover. He was in a daze much of the time and could not remember much about his life prior to the stroke. During his recovery, he found himself talking in rhymes and then writing in rhymes. Those rhymes became poems. Soon he was writing poetry whenever he could. Then he started drawing and sculpting. This individual who had previously shown no interest in artistic expression was emerging as an accomplished and prolific artist. He described his creative process as "fairy liquid bubbles of intelligence . . . popping around me all the time" (reported in BBC News, 2004). Not only did Tommy become more artistically creative, but his personality changed in positive ways as well. After his stroke, he was happier and more contented. He declared the changes in his life to be "fantastic."

Tommy's experience is rare, but it does demonstrate some fascinating qualities of the human brain. First, the brain is a flexible organ, capable of adapting even to a major trauma such as a stroke. Second, hidden in the brain may be an untapped potential for creativity, positive functioning, and unknown abilities. Finally, the brain is the seat of our psychological characteristics. Changing the brain can change essential aspects of who we are, how we think, and what we do.

Our brain accounts for just 2 percent of our total body weight, yet this small organ is extraordinarily complex, containing about 100 billion nerve cells (Saladin, 2007). Learning about the brain can be, literally, mind blowing. Think about it. The very organ on which we are focusing in this chapter is the one that is doing the work of seeing, reading, understanding, and synthesizing the material. The brain is also the organ responsible for the research presented here. Thus, the brain is at once an object of study and *the studier*. You may view your "mind"—the kind of mind that is capable, for example, of doing such psychological research—as somehow separate from this peculiar-looking physical organ lodged within your skull. When you think about thinking, you likely see it as a mental process, not a physical one. Yet thinking *is* a physical event in the brain. Indeed, how we think has an impact on brain activity.

If a characteristic is shown to relate to some structure in the brain, we might think that brain structure must "cause" that characteristic. For instance, you might read a news article about brain differences between the sexes and think that these differences explain why men and women are different. However, and most significantly, the brain itself can be changed by experience. Although it took a stroke for Tommy McHugh to unlock his brain's capacities for creativity, the brain can be changed by far less invasive means—by simply altering our routine patterns of behavior and thought. For instance, research has demonstrated brain differences in London cab drivers who have developed a familiarity with the city. These individuals show increases in the size of the area of the brain thought to be responsible for reading maps (Maguire & others, 2000). Consider what this means: When you "change the way you think," you are *literally* changing physical structures and processes in the brain. When you learn a new skill or make a habit of thinking positively, you are actually paving new brain pathways.

We lose track of the real physical reality of the brain as we go about our lives. But imagine how we might feel about the brain if we could see it—if we had little windows in our foreheads so that we could observe people's brains and the remarkable activity that makes them work. And although we have no problem marveling at our eyes, ears, heart, or lungs, we underestimate the wonder of our brain. ▪

PREVIEW

In this chapter, we review what the brain has come to know about itself. We examine important biological foundations of human behavior. Our main focus is the nervous system and its command center—the brain. Tommy McHugh's experience is surely evidence of the great power, flexibility, and resilience of this internal command post. We also explore the genetic and evolutionary processes that have a significant influence on who we are as individuals and how we behave.

As we tour the physiological side of psychology, keep in mind that although all human brains are similar in some ways, in other ways each person's brain is unique. Hence, understanding the brain is not the same as understanding the heart or the stomach, which are essentially identical in healthy individuals. There is uniqueness from person to person in brain connections, in the use of particular structures for tasks, and in responses to brain injuries or insults. Thus, it is fitting that we close this chapter by considering how to unlock our brain's unique resources so that we may better handle life's challenges and maintain our health and well-being.

1 The Nervous System

Discuss the nature and basic functions of the nervous system.

The **nervous system** is the body's electrochemical communication circuitry. The field that studies the nervous system is called *neuroscience,* and the people who study it are *neuroscientists.*

The human nervous system is made up of billions of interconnected cells, and it is likely the most intricately organized aggregate of matter on the planet. A single cubic centimeter of the human brain consists of well over 50 million nerve cells, each of which communicates with many other nerve cells in information- processing networks that make the most elaborate computer seem primitive.

Characteristics

The brain and nervous system guide our interaction with the world around us, move the body through the world, and direct our adaptation to our environment. Several extraordinary characteristics allow the nervous system to direct our behavior: complexity, integration, adaptability, and electrochemical transmission.

Complexity   The brain and nervous system are enormously complex. The brain itself is composed of billions of nerve cells. The orchestration of all of these cells—to allow people to sing, dance, write, talk, and think—is an awe-inspiring task. As you are reading, your brain is carrying out a huge number of tasks—involved in breathing, seeing, thinking, moving—in which extensive assemblies of nerve cells are participating.

Integration   Neuroscientist Steven Hyman (2001) calls the brain the "great integrator." By this, he means that the brain does a wonderful job of pulling information together. Sounds, sights, touch, taste, smells, hearing, genes, environment—the brain integrates all of these as we function in our world.

The brain and the nervous system have different levels and many different parts. Brain activity is integrated across these levels through countless interconnections of brain cells and extensive pathways that link different parts of the brain. Each nerve cell communicates, on average, with 10,000 others, making up miles and miles of connections (Bloom, Nelson, & Lazerson, 2001). Consider what happens when a mosquito bites your arm. How does your brain know you were bitten and where? Bundles of interconnected nerve cells relay information about the bite from your arm through the nervous system in a very orderly fashion to the highest level of the brain.

Adaptability   The world around us is constantly changing. To survive, we must adapt to new conditions. Our brain and nervous system together serve as our agent in adapting to the world. Although nerve cells reside in certain brain regions, they are not fixed and immutable structures. They have a hereditary, biological foundation, but they are constantly adapting to changes in the body and the environment (Coch, Fischer, & Dawson, 2007).

The term **plasticity** denotes the brain's special capacity for modification and change. Tommy McHugh's amazing experience is an example of extreme plasticity. Less dramatic examples of plasticity occur in all of us. The experiences that we have contribute to the wiring or rewiring of the brain (Mills & Sheehan, 2007). For example, each time a baby tries to touch an object or gazes intently at a face, electrical impulses and chemical messengers shoot through the baby's brain, knitting brain cells together into pathways and networks.

Electrochemical Transmission   The brain and the nervous system function essentially as an information-processing system, powered by electrical impulses and chemical messengers (Chichilnisky, 2007). When people speak to each other, they use words. When neurons communicate with each other, they use chemicals.

The electrochemical communication system works effectively in most people to allow us to think and act. However, when the electrochemical system is short-circuited, as in the case

As we dance, write, play sports, talk, think, and connect with the world in countless other ways, the brain and the nervous system guide our every interaction, movement, and adaptation.

nervous system The body's electrochemical communication circuitry, made up of billions of interconnected cells.

plasticity The brain's special capacity for modification and change.

When we touch or gaze at an object, electrical charges and chemical messages pulse through our brain, knitting the cells together into pathways and networks for processing the information.

afferent nerves Sensory nerves that transport information to the brain.

efferent nerves Motor nerves that carry the brain's output.

neural networks Networks of nerve cells that integrate sensory input and motor output.

central nervous system (CNS) The brain and spinal cord.

of epilepsy, the flow of information is disrupted, the brain is unable to channel information accurately, and the person cannot effectively engage in mental processing and behavior. Epileptic seizures are the result of abnormal electrical discharges in the brain. Just as an electrical surge during a lightning storm can disrupt the circuits in a computer, the electrical surge that produces an epileptic seizure disrupts the brain's information-processing circuits. The brains of individuals with epilepsy work effectively to process information between seizures, unless the seizures occur with such regularity that they cause brain damage. In about 75 percent of epilepsy cases, seizures do not cause structural damage to the brain.

Pathways in the Nervous System

As we interact with and adapt to the world, the brain and the nervous system receive and transmit sensory input, integrate the information received from the environment, and direct the body's motor activities. Information flows into the brain through sensory input, becomes integrated within the brain, and then moves out of the brain to be connected with motor output (Fox, 2008).

The nervous system possesses specialized pathways that are adapted for different functions. These pathways are made up of afferent nerves, neural networks, and efferent nerves. **Afferent nerves,** or sensory nerves, carry information to the brain. The word *afferent* comes from the Latin word meaning "bring to." These sensory pathways communicate information about external and bodily environments from sensory receptors into and throughout the brain.

Efferent nerves, or motor nerves, carry the brain's output. The word *efferent* is derived from the Latin word meaning "bring forth." These motor pathways communicate information from the brain to the hands, feet, and other areas of the body that allow a person to engage in motor behavior.

Most information processing occurs when information moves through **neural networks.** These networks of nerve cells integrate sensory input and motor output. For example, as you read your class notes, the input from your eyes is transmitted to your brain and then passed through many neural networks, which translate your scratches into neural codes for letters, words, associations, and meaning. Some of the information is stored in the neural networks, and, if you read aloud, some is passed on as messages to your lips and tongue. Neural networks make up most of the brain.

Divisions of the Nervous System

When the nineteenth-century American poet and essayist Ralph Waldo Emerson said, "The world was built in order and the atoms march in tune," he must have had the human nervous system in mind. This truly elegant system is highly ordered and organized for effective function.

Figure 3.1 shows the two primary divisions of the human nervous system: the central nervous system and the peripheral nervous system. The **central nervous system (CNS)** is

FIGURE 3.1

Major Divisions of the Human Nervous System The nervous system is divided into two parts—the central nervous system (the brain and spinal cord) and the peripheral nervous system (the somatic and autonomic systems). These divisions work together to help us successfully navigate the world.

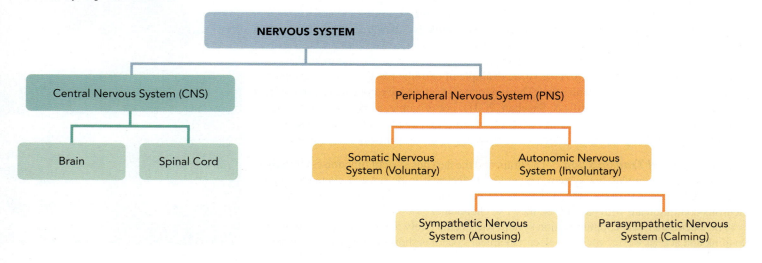

made up of the brain and spinal cord. More than 99 percent of all nerve cells in our body are located in the CNS. The **peripheral nervous system (PNS)** is the network of nerves that connects the brain and spinal cord to other parts of the body. The functions of the peripheral nervous system are to bring information to and from the brain and spinal cord and to carry out the commands of the CNS to execute various muscular and glandular activities.

The peripheral nervous system has two major divisions: the somatic nervous system and the autonomic nervous system. The **somatic nervous system** consists of sensory nerves, whose function is to convey information from the skin and muscles to the CNS about conditions such as pain and temperature, and motor nerves, whose function is to tell muscles what to do. The function of the **autonomic nervous system** is to take messages to and from the body's internal organs, monitoring such processes as breathing, heart rate, and digestion. The autonomic nervous system also is divided into two parts: the **sympathetic nervous system** arouses the body and the **parasympathetic nervous system** calms the body. You can remember that these very close words refer to different processes by keeping in mind that the sympathetic nervous system feels "sympathy" for you—when you are frightened or need to take action, the sympathetic nervous system kicks into action.

To better understand the various divisions of the nervous system, let's see what they do in a particular situation. Imagine that you are preparing to ask a judge to dismiss a parking ticket. As you are about to enter the courtroom, you scan a note card one last time to remember what you plan to say. Your *peripheral nervous system* carries the written marks from the note card to your central nervous system. Your *central nervous system* processes the marks, interpreting them as words, while you memorize key points and plan ways to keep the judge friendly. After studying the notes several minutes longer, you jot down an additional joke that you hope will amuse her. Again your *peripheral nervous system* is at work, conveying to the muscles in your arm and hand the information from your brain that enables you to make the marks on the paper. The information that is being transmitted from your eyes to your brain and to your hand is handled by the *somatic nervous system*. This is your first ticket hearing, so you are a little anxious. Your stomach feels queasy, and your heart begins to thump. This is the *sympathetic* division of the *autonomic nervous system* functioning as you become aroused. You regain your confidence after reminding yourself that you were parked in a legal spot. As you relax, the *parasympathetic* division of the *autonomic nervous system* is working.

peripheral nervous system (PNS) The network of nerves that connects the brain and spinal cord to other parts of the body. It is divided into the somatic nervous system and the autonomic nervous system.

somatic nervous system The division of the PNS consisting of sensory nerves, whose function is to convey information to the CNS, and motor nerves, whose function is to transmit information to the muscles.

autonomic nervous system The division of the PNS that communicates with the body's internal organs and monitors processes such as breathing, heart rate, and digestion. It consists of the sympathetic and parasympathetic nervous systems.

sympathetic nervous system The division of the autonomic nervous system that arouses the body.

parasympathetic nervous system The division of the autonomic nervous system that calms the body.

 REVIEW, ASSESS, AND SHARPEN YOUR THINKING

Review

 1 Discuss the nature and basic functions of the nervous system.

- Identify the fundamental characteristics of the brain and nervous system.
- Name and describe the pathways that allow the nervous system to carry out its three basic functions.
- Outline the divisions of the nervous system and explain their roles.

Assess

1. The _____ nervous system is to excitement as the _____ nervous system is to relaxation.
   - A. somatic, autonomic
   - B. autonomic, somatic
   - C. sympathetic, parasympathetic
   - D. parasympathetic, sympathetic

2. The peripheral nervous system is broken down into
   - A. the brain and the spinal cord.
   - B. the sympathetic nervous system and the parasympathetic nervous system.
   - C. the somatic nervous system and the autonomic nervous system.
   - D. the central nervous system and the somatic nervous system.

3. When you move your arm, your brain is sending information to your arm via
   - A. afferent nerves.
   - B. efferent nerves.
   - C. sensory neurons.
   - D. hippocampal neurons.

4. One nerve cell communicates with about _____ other nerve cells.
   A. 100
   B. 10,000
   C. 100,000
   D. 1,000,000

5. To what does the term *plasticity* refer?
   A. the ability of the brain to change
   B. the process of creating lesions in the brain
   C. the changing modes of communication between neurons
   D. the deactivation of the sympathetic nervous system

Sharpen Your Thinking

Try this exercise without looking at Figure 3.1. Suppose you (1) saw a person coming toward you, (2) realized it was someone famous, (3) got excited, (4) waved and shouted, (5) suddenly realized it was not a famous person, and (6) became suddenly calm again. Which part of your nervous system would have been heavily involved at each of these six points?

2 Neurons

Explain what neurons are and how they process information.

Within each division of the nervous system, much is happening at the cellular level. Nerve cells, chemicals, and electrical impulses work together to transmit information at speeds of up to 330 miles per hour. As a result, information can travel from your brain to your hands (or vice versa) in a matter of milliseconds (Shier, Butler, & Lewis, 2007).

There are two types of cells in the nervous system: neurons and glial cells. **Neurons** are the nerve cells that actually handle the information-processing function. The human brain contains about 100 billion neurons. The average neuron is as complex as a small computer and has as many as 10,000 physical connections with other cells. To have even the merest thought requires millions of neurons acting simultaneously.

Glial cells provide support and nutritional benefit functions in the nervous system (Bhat, 2007; Pav & others, 2007). Glial cells are not specialized to process information in the way that neurons are, although there are many more of them in the nervous system than there are neurons. In one study, neurons placed in a solution containing glial cells grew more rapidly and prolifically than neurons floating in the same solution without glial cells (Kennedy & Folk-Seang, 1986). This study indicates that glial cells function in a supportive or nutritive role for neurons.

Specialized Cell Structure

Not all neurons are alike. They are specialized to handle different information-processing functions. However, all neurons do have some common characteristics. Most neurons are created very early in life, but their shape, size, and connections can change throughout the life span. Thus the way neurons function reflects the major characteristic of the nervous system described at the beginning of the chapter: plasticity. They are not fixed and immutable but can change. Every neuron has a cell body, dendrites, and axon (Figure 3.2).

The **cell body** contains the nucleus, which directs the manufacture of substances that the neuron needs for growth and maintenance.

Dendrites receive and orient information toward the cell body. One of the most distinctive features of neurons is the treelike branching of their dendrites. Most nerve cells have

neurons Nerve cells that are specialized for processing information. Neurons are the basic units of the nervous system.

glial cells Cells that provide support and nutritional benefits in the nervous system.

cell body The part of the neuron that contains the nucleus, which directs the manufacture of substances that the neuron needs for growth and maintenance.

dendrites Branches of a neuron that receive and orient information toward the cell body; most neurons have numerous dendrites.

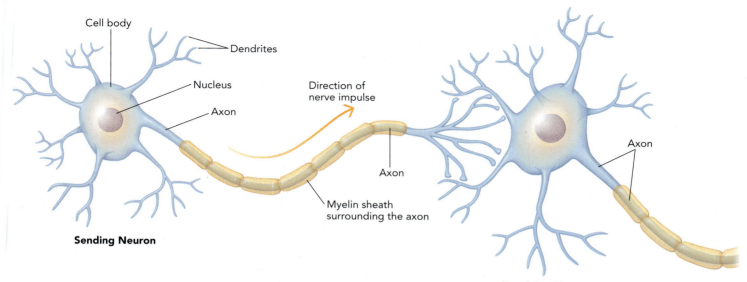

Cell body

Dendrites

Nucleus

Direction of
nerve impulse

Axon

Axon

Axon

Myelin sheath
surrounding the axon

Sending Neuron

Receiving Neuron

FIGURE 3.2

The Neuron The drawing shows the parts of a neuron and the connection between one neuron and another. Note the cell body, the branching of dendrites, and the axon with a myelin sheath.

numerous dendrites, which increase their surface area, allowing each neuron to receive input from many other neurons.

The **axon** is the part of the neuron that carries information away from the cell body toward other cells. Although very thin (1/10,000th of an inch), axons can be very long, with many branches. In fact, some extend more than 3 feet—all the way from the top of the brain to the base of the spinal cord.

Covering all surfaces of neurons, including the dendrites and axons, are very thin cellular membranes that are much like the surface of a bubble. The neuronal membranes are semipermeable, meaning that they contain tiny holes, or *channels,* that allow only certain substances to pass into and out of the neurons.

A **myelin sheath,** a layer of fat cells, encases and insulates most axons. By insulating axons, myelin sheaths speed up transmission of nerve impulses (Nave, 2007). Multiple sclerosis (MS), a degenerative disease of the nervous system in which a hardening of myelin tissue occurs, disrupts neuronal communication. *Sclerosis* means, literally, "scars," and indeed, in such disorders as MS, myelin is replaced by scar tissue. There are numerous disorders that involve problems in either the creation or maintenance of myelin. For instance, adrenoleukodystrophy (ALD) is a genetic disorder that generally affects boys. If you have seen the film *Lorenzo's Oil,* you are familiar with the story of Lorenzo Odone, a boy with ALD whose parents took it upon themselves to become experts on the biochemistry of myelinization so that they could search for a cure for their son. Although ALD remains an incurable disorder, some boys are spared its worst effects by the early introduction of Lorenzo's oil (actually, a mixture of oils) and an extremely low-fat diet that prevents the buildup of very long-chain fatty acids that results in demyelinization.

The myelin sheath developed as the brain evolved. As brain size increased, it became necessary for information to travel over longer distances in the nervous system. Axons without myelin sheaths are not very good conductors of electricity. With the insulation of myelin sheaths, axons transmit electrical impulses and convey information much more rapidly (Nave, 2007). We can compare the myelin sheath's development to the evolution of freeways as cities grew. A freeway is a shielded road. It keeps fast-moving, long-distance traffic from getting snarled by slow local traffic.

The Neural Impulse

To transmit information to other neurons, a neuron sends brief electrical impulses ("clicks") through its axon to the next neuron. As you reach to turn this page, hundreds of such

axon The part of the neuron that carries information away from the cell body to other cells.

myelin sheath The layer of fat cells that encases and insulates most axons. The myelin sheath speeds up the transmission of nerve impulses.

resting potential The stable, negative charge of an inactive neuron.

impulses will stream down the axons in your arm to tell your muscles just when to flex and how vigorously. By changing the rate and timing of the signals, or "clicks," the neuron can vary its message.

How does a neuron—a living cell—generate electrical impulses? To answer this question, we need to further examine the nature of a neuron and the fluids in which it floats. A neuron is like a balloon filled with one kind of fluid and surrounded by a slightly different kind of fluid. The axon is a piece of the "balloon" that has been stretched to form a long, hollow tube. The axon tube is so thin that a few dozen axons in a bundle would be about as thick as a human hair. Floating in the fluids inside and outside the tube are electrically charged particles called *ions*.

Some of these ions, notably sodium and potassium, carry positive charges. Negatively charged ions of chlorine and other elements also are present. The cell membrane prevents negative and positive ions from randomly flowing into or out of the cell. The neuron creates electrical signals by moving positive and negative ions back and forth through its outer membrane. How does the movement of ions across the membrane occur? It is fairly simple. Embedded in the membrane—the wall of our balloon—are hundreds of thousands of small gates, called *ion channels,* which open and close to let the ions pass into and out of the cell. Normally when the neuron is resting, not transmitting information, the ion channels are closed, and a slight negative charge is present along the inside of the cell membrane. On the outside of the cell membrane, the charge is positive. Because of the difference in charge, the membrane of the resting neuron is said to be *polarized,* like the ends of a flashlight battery, with all negatively charged ions on the inside of the cell and all positively charged ions on the outside. **Resting potential** is the stable, negative charge of an inactive neuron (Figure 3.3). That potential is between −60 and −75 millivolts, meaning it would take 75,000 of them to produce a single volt of electricity. In contrast, an electric eel's 8,400 neurons could generate 600 volts!

A neuron becomes activated when an incoming impulse—a reaction to, say, a pinprick or the sight of someone's face—raises the neuron's voltage, and the sodium gates at the base of the axon open briefly. This action allows positively charged sodium ions to flow into the neuron, creating a more positively charged neuron and *depolarizing* the membrane by decreasing the charge difference between the fluids inside and outside of the neuron. Then potassium channels open, and positively charged potassium ions move out through the neuron's semipermeable membrane. This outflow returns the neuron to a negative charge. Then the same process occurs as the next group of channels flips open briefly.

FIGURE 3.3

The Resting Potential An oscilloscope measures the difference in electrical potential between two electrodes. When one electrode is placed inside an axon at rest and one is placed outside, the electrical potential inside the cell is −70 millivolts (mV) relative to the outside. This potential difference is due to the separation of positive (+) and negative (−) charges along the membrane.

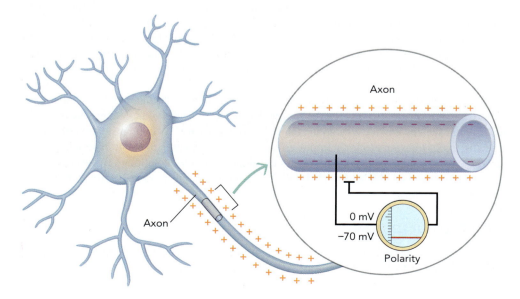

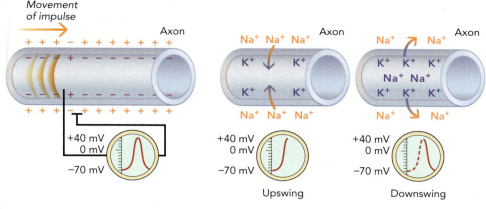

(a) Action potential generated by an impulse within a neuron

(b) Movement of sodium (NA⁺) and potassium (K⁺) ions responsible for the action potential

FIGURE 3.4

The Action Potential An action potential is a brief wave of positive electrical charge that sweeps down the axon as the sodium channels in the axon membrane open and close. (*a*) The action potential causes a change in electrical potential as it moves along the axon. (*b*) The movements of sodium ions (Na⁺) and potassium ions (K⁺) into and out of the axon cause the electrical changes.

And so it goes all the way down the axon, just like a long row of cabinet doors opening and closing in sequence.

The term **action potential** describes the brief wave of positive electrical charge that sweeps down the axon (Figure 3.4). An action potential lasts only about 1/1,000th of a second, because the sodium channels can stay open for only a very brief time. They quickly close again and become reset for the next action potential. When a neuron sends an action potential, it is commonly said to be "firing."

The action potential abides by the **all-or-none principle:** Once the electrical impulse reaches a certain level of intensity, called its *threshold,* it fires and moves all the way down the axon without losing any of its intensity. The impulse traveling down an axon can be compared to the burning fuse of a firecracker. Whether you use a match or blowtorch to light the fuse, once the fuse has been lit, the spark travels quickly and with the same intensity down the fuse.

Synapses and Neurotransmitters

What happens when a neural impulse reaches the end of the axon? Neurons do not touch each other directly, but they manage to communicate. The story of the connection between one neuron and another is one of the most intriguing and highly researched areas of contemporary neuroscience (McAllister, 2007). Figure 3.5 gives an overview of how this connection between neurons takes place.

Synaptic Transmission   **Synapses** are tiny junctions between neurons; the gap between neurons is referred to as a *synaptic gap.* Most synapses lie between the axon of one neuron and the dendrites or cell body of another neuron. Before an impulse can cross the synaptic gap, it must be converted into a chemical signal.

Each axon branches out into numerous fibers that end in structures called *terminal buttons.* Stored in minute synaptic vesicles (sacs) within the terminal buttons are chemical substances called **neurotransmitters.** As their name suggests, neurotransmitters transmit, or carry, information across the synaptic gap to the next neuron. When a nerve impulse reaches the terminal button, it triggers the release of neurotransmitter molecules from the synaptic vesicles (Brooks, 2006; Zhao & others, 2006). The neurotransmitter molecules flood the synaptic gap. Their movements are random, but some of them bump into receptor sites in the next neuron. If the shape of the receptor site corresponds to the shape of the neurotransmitter molecule, the neurotransmitter acts like a key to open the receptor site, so that the neuron can receive the signals coming from the previous neuron. After delivering its message, the neurotransmitter is reabsorbed by the axon that released it to await the next neural impulse.

action potential The brief wave of positive electrical charge that sweeps down the axon during the transmission of a nerve impulse.

all-or-none principle The idea that once an electrical impulse reaches a certain level of intensity, it fires and moves all the way down the axon without losing any of its intensity.

synapses Tiny junctions between two neurons, generally where the axon of one neuron meets the dendrites or cell body of another neuron.

neurotransmitters Chemicals substances that carry information across the synaptic gap from one neuron to the next.

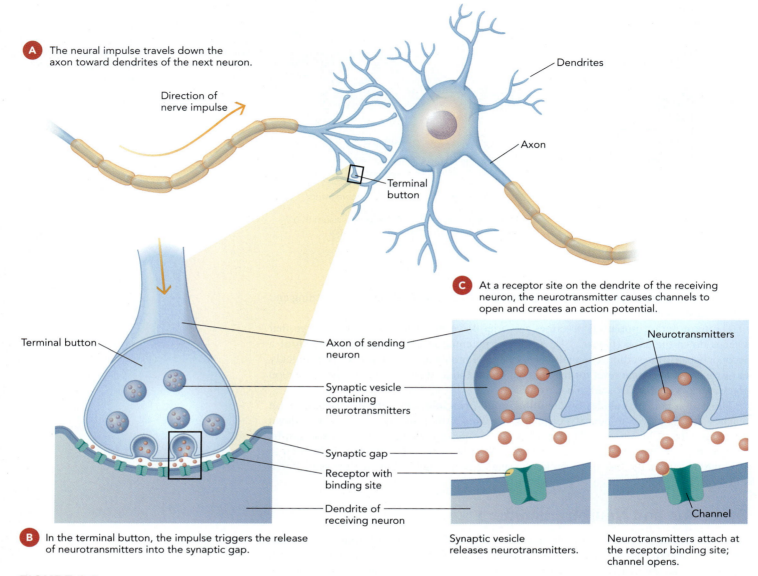

A The neural impulse travels down the axon toward dendrites of the next neuron.

Dendrites

Direction of nerve impulse

Axon

Terminal button

Terminal button

Axon of sending neuron

Synaptic vesicle containing neurotransmitters

Synaptic gap

Receptor with binding site

Dendrite of receiving neuron

B In the terminal button, the impulse triggers the release of neurotransmitters into the synaptic gap.

C At a receptor site on the dendrite of the receiving neuron, the neurotransmitter causes channels to open and creates an action potential.

Neurotransmitters

Channel

Synaptic vesicle releases neurotransmitters.

Neurotransmitters attach at the receptor binding site; channel opens.

FIGURE 3.5

How Synapses and Neurotransmitters Work (a) The axon of the *presynaptic* (sending) neuron meets dendrites of the *postsynaptic* (receiving) neuron. (b) This is an enlargement of one synapse, showing the synaptic gap between the two neurons, the terminal button, and the synaptic vesicles containing a neurotransmitter. (c) This is an enlargement of the receptor site. Note how the neurotransmitter opens the channel on the receptor site, triggering the neuron to fire.

Think of the synapse as a river that blocks a road. A grocery truck (the action potential) arrives at one bank of the river, crosses by ferry, and continues its journey to market. Similarly a message in the brain is "ferried" across the synapse by a neurotransmitter, which pours out of the terminal button just as the message approaches the synapse.

Neurochemical Messengers There are many different neurotransmitters. Each one plays a specific role and functions in a specific pathway. Whereas some neurotransmitters stimulate or excite neurons to fire, others can inhibit neurons from firing (von Bolhen und Halbach & Dermietzel, 2006). Some neurotransmitters are both excitatory and inhibitory. As the neurotransmitter moves across the synaptic gap to the receiving neuron, its molecules might spread out or be confined to a small space. The molecules might come in rapid sequence or be spaced out. The receiving neuron integrates this information before reacting to it.

Most neurons secrete only one type of neurotransmitter, but often many different neurons are simultaneously secreting different neurotransmitters into the synaptic gaps of a single neuron. At any given time, a neuron is receiving a mixture of messages from the neurotransmitters. At its receptor sites, the chemical molecules bind to the membrane and either excite the neuron, bringing it closer to the threshold at which it will fire, or inhibit the neuron from firing. Usually the binding of an excitatory neurotransmitter from one neuron will not be enough to trigger an action potential in the receiving neuron. Triggering an action potential often takes a number of neurons sending excitatory messages simultaneously or fewer neurons sending rapid-fire excitatory messages.

So far, researchers have identified more than 50 neurotransmitters, each with a unique chemical makeup. The rapidly growing list likely will grow to more than 100 (Johnson, 2003). In organisms ranging from snails to whales, neuroscientists have found the same neurotransmitter molecules that our own brains use. Many types of animal venom, such as that of the black widow spider, actually are neurotransmitter-like substances that do their harm by disturbing neurotransmission. To get a better sense of what neurotransmitters do, let's consider seven that have major effects on behavior.

The neurotransmitter-like venom of the black widow spider does its harm by disturbing neurotransmission.

Acetylcholine   *Acetylcholine (ACh)* usually stimulates the firing of neurons and is involved in the action of muscles, learning, and memory (Brooks, 2006). ACh is found throughout the central and peripheral nervous systems. The venom of the black widow spider causes ACh to gush out of the synapses between the spinal cord and skeletal muscles, producing violent spasms. The drug curare, which some South American native peoples apply to the tips of poison darts, blocks receptors for ACh, paralyzing muscles. In contrast, nicotine stimulates acetylcholine receptors. Individuals with Alzheimer disease, a degenerative brain disorder that involves a decline in memory, have an acetylcholine deficiency (Akaike, 2006; Born, Rasch, & Gais, 2006). Some of the drugs that alleviate the symptoms of Alzheimer disease do so by compensating for the loss of the brain's supply of acetylcholine.

GABA   *GABA (gamma aminobutyric acid)* is found throughout the central nervous system. It is believed to be the neurotransmitter in as many as one-third of the brain's synapses. GABA is important in the brain because it keeps many neurons from firing (Liu & Lachamp, 2006). In this way, it helps to control the precision of the signal being carried from one neuron to the next. Low levels of GABA are linked with anxiety. Valium and other antianxiety drugs increase the inhibiting effects of GABA.

Norepinephrine   *Norepinephrine* inhibits the firing of neurons in the central nervous system, but it excites the heart muscle, intestines, and urogenital tract. Stress stimulates the release of norepinephrine (Strawn & Geracioti, 2007). This neurotransmitter also helps to control alertness. Too little norepinephrine is associated with depression, and too much triggers agitated, manic states. For example, amphetamines and cocaine cause hyperactive, manic states of behavior by rapidly increasing brain levels of norepinephrine (Nelson & Gehlert, 2006).

Recall from the beginning of the chapter that one of the most important characteristics of the brain and nervous system is integration. In the case of neurotransmitters, they may work in teams of two or more. For example, norepinephrine works with acetylcholine to regulate states of sleep and wakefulness.

Dopamine   *Dopamine* helps to control voluntary movement and affects sleep, mood, attention, and learning (Monti & Monti, 2007). Stimulant drugs such as cocaine and amphetamines produce excitement, alertness, elevated mood, decreased fatigue, and sometimes increased motor activity mainly by activating dopamine receptors (Ikegami & others, 2007)

Low levels of dopamine are associated with Parkinson disease, in which physical movements deteriorate (Marvanova & Nichols, 2007). Although the actor Michael J. Fox contracted Parkinson disease in his late 20s, the disease is uncommon before the age of 30 and becomes more common as people age (Cantuti-Castelvetri, Shukitt-Hale, & Joseph, 2003). High levels of dopamine are associated with schizophrenia, a severe mental disorder that we will examine in Chapter 14.

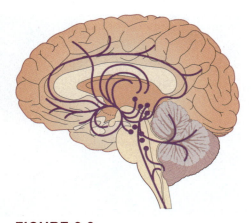

FIGURE 3.6

Serotonin Pathways Each of the neurotransmitters in the brain has specific pathways in which they function. Shown here are the pathways for serotonin.

agonist A drug that mimics or increases a neurotransmitter's effects.

antagonist A drug that blocks a neurotransmitter's effects.

Serotonin *Serotonin* is involved in the regulation of sleep, mood, attention, and learning. In regulating states of sleep and wakefulness, it teams with acetylcholine and norepinephrine (Miller & O'Callaghan, 2006). Lowered levels of serotonin are associated with depression (Leykin & others, 2007). The antidepressant drug Prozac works by increasing brain levels of serotonin (Little, Zhang, & Cook, 2006). Figure 3.6 shows the brain pathways for serotonin.

Endorphins *Endorphins* are natural opiates that mainly stimulate the firing of neurons. Endorphins shield the body from pain and elevate feelings of pleasure. A long-distance runner, a woman giving birth, and a person in shock after a car wreck all have elevated levels of endorphins (Armstrong & Hatfield, 2006).

As early as the fourth century B.C.E., the Greeks used wild poppies to induce euphoria. More than 2,000 years later, the magical formula behind opium's addictive action was finally discovered. In the early 1970s, scientists found that opium plugs into a sophisticated system of natural opiates that lie deep within the brain's pathways (Pert, 1999; Pert & Snyder, 1973). Morphine (the most important narcotic of opium) mimics the action of endorphins by stimulating receptors in the brain involved with pleasure and pain (Vetter & others, 2006).

Oxytocin *Oxytocin* is a hormone and neurotransmitter that plays an important role in the experience of love and human bonding. A powerful surge of oxytocin is released in mothers who have just given birth, and oxytocin is related to the onset of lactation and breast feeding. But oxytocin is not only involved in a mother's ability to provide nourishment for her baby (Carter & others, 2007). It is also a factor in the experience of parents who find themselves "in love at first sight" with their newborn (Febo, Numan, & Ferris, 2005; Numan, 2006). As well, oxytocin is released as part of the sexual orgasm and is thought to play a role in the human tendency to form emotional bonds with romantic partners (Neumann, 2007). Provocative research has related oxytocin to the way that women respond to stress. According to Shelley (2001, 2007), women under stress do not experience the classic "fight or flight" response—rather, the influx of oxytocin suggests that women may seek bonds with others when under stress. Taylor refers to this response as "tend and befriend."

Drugs and Neurotransmitters Most drugs that influence behavior do so mainly by interfering with the work of neurotransmitters (Fields, 2007). Drugs can mimic or increase the effects of a neurotransmitter, or they can block those effects. An **agonist** is a drug that mimics or increases a neurotransmitter's effects. For example, the drug morphine mimics the actions of endorphins by stimulating receptors in the brain and spinal cord associated with pleasure and pain. An **antagonist** is a drug that blocks a neurotransmitter's effects. For example, drugs used to treat schizophrenia interfere with the activity of dopamine.

Neural Networks

So far in the coverage of neurons, we have focused mainly on how a single neuron functions and on how a nerve impulse travels from one neuron to another. Now let's look at how large numbers of neurons work together to integrate incoming information and coordinate outgoing information.

At the beginning of the chapter, we imaged neural networks as clusters of neurons that are interconnected to process information. Figure 3.7 shows a simplified drawing of a neural network, or pathway. This diagram can give you an idea of how the activity of one neuron is linked with many others.

Some neurons have short axons and communicate with other, nearby neurons. Other neurons have long axons and

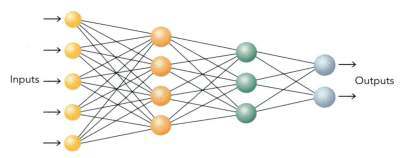

FIGURE 3.7

An Example of a Neural Network Inputs (information from the environment and sensory receptors, as when someone looks at a person's face) become embedded in extensive connections between neurons in the brain. This embedding process leads to outputs (such as remembering the person's face).

communicate with circuits of neurons some distance away. These neural networks are not static (Milton & others, 2007). They can be altered through changes in the strength of synaptic connections.

Any piece of information, such as a name, might be embedded in hundreds or even thousands of connections between neurons (Bota & Swanson, 2007). In this way, human activities such as being attentive, memorizing, and thinking are distributed over a wide range of connected neurons. The strength of these connected neurons determines how well you remember the information (Leibold & Kempter, 2006).

Let's see how the neural network concept might explain a typical memory, such as the name of a new acquaintance. Initially the processing of the person's face might activate a small number of weak neuronal connections that make you remember a general category ("interesting woman" or "attractive man"). However, repeated experience with that person will increase the strength and possibly the number of those connections, so you may remember the person's name as the neurons activated by the name become connected with the neurons that are activated by the face. Chapter 8 explores the nature of memory at greater length.

Our initial mental processing of a new acquaintance's face might activate just a small number of weak connections among neurons, leading us to remember only a general category (such as "interesting woman" or "attractive man"). As repeated experience with the person increases the strength (and possibly the number) of these connections, we remember the person's name and other details.

 REVIEW, ASSESS, AND SHARPEN YOUR THINKING

Review

2 **Explain what neurons are and how they process information.**
- Differentiate between neurons and glial cells, and describe the functions of the parts of a neuron.
- Explain what a neural impulse is and how it is generated.
- Discuss how a neural impulse is transmitted from one neuron to another.
- Describe the function of neural networks.

Assess

1. **In what part of the neuron is the nucleus contained?**
   A. the axon
   B. the dendrites
   C. the terminal buttons
   D. the cell body

2. **What is the direction of the neural impulse (from start to finish)?**
   A. dendrites, axon, cell body, and finally terminal buttons
   B. axon, cell body, terminal buttons, and finally dendrites
   C. dendrites, cell body, axon, and finally terminal buttons
   D. cell body, axon, dendrites, and finally terminal buttons

3. **During the depolarization of a neuron, which of the following occurs?**
   A. The inside of the cell becomes positively charged, increasing the charge difference across the membrane.
   B. The inside of the cell becomes positively charged, decreasing the charge difference across the membrane.

C. The inside of the cell becomes negatively charged, decreasing the charge difference across the membrane.
D. The inside of the cell becomes negatively charged, increasing the charge difference across the membrane.

4. **Cocaine acts as a(n) _____ on dopamine.**
   A. agonist
   B. antagonist
   C. neural depressant
   D. neural block

5. **Which of the following is implicated in love and bonding?**
   A. GABA
   B. Oxytocin
   C. Dopamine
   D. Norepinephrine

Sharpen Your Thinking

Why is it important to have so many connections and to have integration between neurons?

3 Structures of the Brain and Their Functions

Identify the brain's levels and structures, and summarize the functions of its structures.

The extensive and intricate networks of neurons that we have just studied are not visible to the naked eye. Fortunately technology is available to help neuroscientists form pictures of the structure and organization of neurons and the larger structures they make up without harming the organism being studied. This section explores some of the techniques that scientists use in brain research and discusses what they have shown us about the structures and functions of the brain. We pay special attention here to the cerebral cortex, the highest region of the brain.

How Researchers Study the Brain and Nervous System

Much of our early knowledge of the human brain came from clinical studies of individuals who suffered brain damage from injury or disease or who had brain surgery to relieve another condition (like Tommy McHugh, whose life-changing circumstances were described at the beginning of the chapter). Modern discoveries have relied largely on technology that enables researchers to "look inside" the brain while it is at work. Let's examine some of these innovative techniques.

Brain Lesioning *Brain lesioning* is an abnormal disruption in the tissue of the brain resulting from injury or disease. The study of naturally occurring brain lesions in humans has provided considerable information about how the brain functions.

Neuroscientists also produce lesions in laboratory animals to determine the effects on the animal's behavior (Deller & others, 2006). These lesions may be made by surgically removing brain tissue, destroying tissue with a laser, or eliminating tissue by injecting it with a drug (Martin & Clark, 2007). Sometimes transient lesions can be made by administering a drug that temporarily inactivates an area of the brain. The organism's behavior can be studied while the area is inactivated; after the effects of the drug have worn off, brain activity in the area returns to normal.

Staining A central interest in neuroscience is to identify the pathways of connectivity in the brain and nervous system that allow information to get from one place to another. This is not an easy task because of the complexity and extent of the interconnections. Much of the progress in charting these neural networks has come about through the use of stains, or dyes, that are selectively absorbed by neurons. A stain will coat only a small portion of neurons so that neuroscientists, using high-powered microscopes, can see which neurons absorb the stains and determine how they are connected (Buss, Sun, & Oppenheim, 2006; Zheng & others, 2007).

Electrical Recording Also widely used is the *electroencephalograph (EEG),* which records the electrical activity of the brain. Electrodes placed on the scalp detect brain-wave activity, which is recorded on a chart known as an electroencephalogram (Figure 3.8). This device can assess brain damage, epilepsy, and other problems (Salva & others, 2007). The electroencephalograph also has had extensive application in the study of the neuroscience of happiness, as we consider in the Intersection later in this chapter.

Not every recording of brain activity is made with surface electrodes. In *single-unit recording,* which provides information about a single neuron's electrical activity, a thin probe is inserted in or near an individual neuron (Cromwell, Klein, & Mears, 2007). The probe transmits the neuron's electrical activity to an amplifier so that researchers can "see" the activity (Zeitler, Fries, & Gielen, 2006).

Brain Imaging For years, X rays have been used to reveal damage inside or outside our bodies, both in the brain and in other locations. But a single X ray of the brain is hard to interpret because it shows a two-dimensional image of the three-dimensional interior of

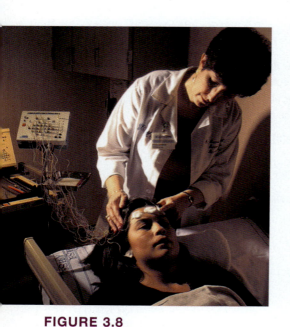

FIGURE 3.8

An EEG Recording The electroencephalograph (EEG) is widely used in sleep research. It has led to some major breakthroughs in understanding sleep by showing how the brain's electrical activity changes during sleep.

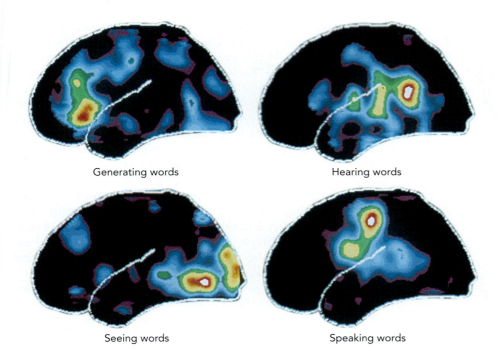

Generating words

Hearing words

Seeing words

Speaking words

FIGURE 3.9

PET Scan This PET scan of the left half of the brain contrasts the different areas used in aspects of language activity: generating words, hearing words, seeing words, and speaking words.

the brain. A newer technique called *computerized axial tomography (CAT scan* or *CT scan)* produces a three-dimensional image obtained from X rays of the head that are assembled into a composite image by a computer. The CT scan provides valuable information about the location and extent of damage involving stroke, language disorder, or loss of memory (Hankey, 2007).

Positron-emission tomography (PET scan) is based on metabolic changes in the brain related to activity. PET measures the amount of glucose in various areas of the brain and then sends this information to a computer for analysis. Because glucose levels vary with the levels of activity throughout the brain, tracing the amounts of glucose generates a picture of activity levels throughout the brain (Raichle & Mintun, 2006). Figure 3.9 shows PET scans of people's brain activity while they are hearing, seeing, speaking, and thinking.

An interesting application of the PET technique is the work of Stephen Kosslyn and his colleagues (1996) on mental imagery. Mental imagery is the brain's ability to create perceptual states in the absence of external stimuli. For instance, if you were to think of your favorite song right now, you could "hear" it in your mind's ear. Or you can think of your mother's face and "see" it in your mind's eye. Research using PET scans has shown that often the same area of the brain—a location called Area 17—is activated when we think of seeing something as when we are actually seeing it. However, Area 17 is not always activated for all of us when we imagine a visual image. Kosslyn and his colleagues asked their participants to visualize a letter in the alphabet and then asked those individuals to answer some "yes" or "no" questions about the letter. For instance, a person might be thinking of the letter "C" and have to answer the question "Does it have curvy lines?" The answer would be "yes." If the person was thinking of "F," the answer would be "no." The fascinating result of this work was that individuals who showed brain activation on the PET scan in Area 17 while engaged in the visualization task were faster to answer the questions than those who were not using Area 17. Again, not all brains are the same, and these differences might actually mean something with regard to task performance.

Another technique, *magnetic resonance imaging (MRI),* involves creating a magnetic field around a person's body and using radio waves to construct images of the person's tissues and biochemical activities (Raichle & Mintun, 2006). The magnetic field of the magnet used to create an MRI image is over 50,000 times more powerful

than the earth's magnetic field (Parry & Matthews, 2002). MRI takes advantage of the fact that our brains contain a great deal of water (like the rest of the body, the brain is 70 percent water). Within each water molecule there are hydrogen atoms (remember, water is H_2O). These hydrogen atoms can be thought of as tiny magnets. When these magnetlike hydrogen atoms encounter a very strong magnetic field, they align themselves with it. Neurons have more water in them than do other brain tissues, and that contrast is what provides the nuanced brain images that MRI is able to produce (Parry & Matthews, 2002).

MRI generates very clear pictures of the brain's interior, does not require injecting the brain with a substance, and (unlike X rays) does not pose a problem of radiation over-exposure (Nyberg, 2004). Getting an MRI scan involves lying completely still in a large metal barrellike tunnel. MRI scans provide an excellent picture of the structure of brain and allow us to see if and how experience affects brain structure. In one MRI study, Katrin Amunts and colleagues (1997) documented a link between the number of years a person has practiced musical skills (playing the piano or violin, for example) and the size of the brain region that is responsible for controlling hand movements. Clearly, our behavior can influence the very structure of our brains.

Although MRI scans can tell us a great deal about brain structure, they cannot provide information about the brain in action—the functioning of the brain. The newest method for studying brain function is *functional magnetic resonance imaging,* or *fMRI,* which allows us literally to see what is happening in the brain *while it is working.* Like the PET scan, fMRI is based on the idea that mental activity is associated with changes in the brain. While PET focuses on glucose levels reflecting metabolic work in the brain, fMRI exploits changes in blood oxygen that occur in association with metabolic changes. When part of the brain is working, oxygenated blood rushes into the area. This oxygen, however, is more than is actually needed. In a sense, fMRI is based on the fact that thinking is like running sprints—it is anaerobic exercise. When you run the 100-yard dash, blood rushes to the muscles in your legs, carrying oxygen. But right after you stop, you might feel a tightness in your leg, because the oxygen has not all been used in the exertion. Similarly, if an area of the brain is hard at work—for example, solving a math problem—there is an increase in metabolic activity that leads to a surplus of oxygenated blood. It turns out that for the magnetic signal used in the fMRI, oxygenated blood provides a stronger magnetic resonance than nonoxygenated blood. This is called the *blood oxygen level dependent contrast,* or BOLD (Hugdahl, 2001). When an area of the brain is hard at work, there is essentially a surplus of oxygenated blood. This "extra" oxygen allows the brain activity to be imaged. So the fMRI technology is based on the fact that the brain is a sprinter.

Getting an fMRI involves reclining in the same large metal barrel as does an MRI, but in the case of fMRI, the person is actively doing something during the procedure. For example, the individual may be listening to audio signals sent by the researcher through headphones. Or the person may be watching visual images that are presented on a screen mounted overhead (imagine a flat-screen TV on your bedroom ceiling). During these procedures, pictures of the brain are taken at different times: while the brain is at rest and while the brain is doing something, like listening to music. By subtracting the at-rest picture from the listening picture, fMRI gives an estimate of what specific brain activity is associated with the mental experience being studied.

FMRI is probably the most exciting methodological advance to hit psychology in a very long time. It has been used in just about every subfield of psychology, with each field studying the brain at work on whatever the topic of interest might be.

Levels of Organization in the Brain

As a human embryo develops inside its mother's womb, the nervous system begins forming as a long, hollow tube on the embryo's back. At 3 weeks or so after conception, cells making up the tube differentiate into a mass of neurons, most of which then develop into three major regions of the brain: the hindbrain, which is adjacent to the top part of the spinal cord; the

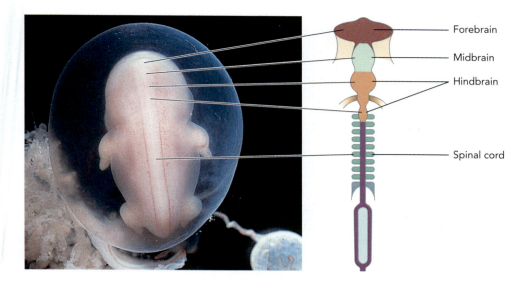

FIGURE 3.10

Embryological Development of the Nervous System The photograph shows the primitive, tubular appearance of the nervous system at 6 weeks in the human embryo. The drawing shows the major brain regions and spinal cord as they appear early in the development of a human embryo.

midbrain, which rises above the hindbrain; and the forebrain, which is the uppermost region of the brain (Figure 3.10).

Hindbrain   The **hindbrain,** located at the skull's rear, is the lowest portion of the brain. The three main parts of the hindbrain are the medulla, cerebellum, and pons. Figure 3.11 shows the location of these brain structures.

The *medulla* begins where the spinal cord enters the skull. It helps to control our breathing and regulates reflexes that allow us to maintain an upright posture.

The *cerebellum* extends from the rear of the hindbrain, just above the medulla. It consists of two rounded structures thought to play important roles in motor coordination (Fernandez Del Olmo & others, 2007). Leg and arm movements are coordinated by the cerebellum, for example. When we play golf, practice the piano, or learn a new dance, the cerebellum is hard at work. If a higher portion of the brain commands us to write the number *7,* it is the cerebellum that integrates the muscular activities required to do so. Damage to the cerebellum impairs the performance of coordinated movements. When this damage occurs, people's movements become uncoordinated and jerky. Extensive damage to the cerebellum even makes it impossible to stand up.

The *pons* is a bridge in the hindbrain. It contains several clusters of fibers involved in sleep and arousal (Stenberg, 2007).

Midbrain   The **midbrain,** located between the hindbrain and forebrain, is an area in which many nerve-fiber systems ascend and descend to connect the higher and lower portions of the brain (Prescott & Humphries, 2007). In particular, the midbrain relays information between the brain and the eyes and ears. The ability to attend to an object visually, for example, is linked to one bundle of neurons in the midbrain. Parkinson disease, a deterioration of movement that produces rigidity and tremors, damages a section near the bottom of the midbrain.

Two systems in the midbrain are of special interest. One is the **reticular formation** (see Figure 3.11), a diffuse collection of neurons involved in stereotyped patterns of behavior such as walking, sleeping, or turning to attend to a sudden noise (Alemdar, Kamaci, & Budak, 2006; McCarley, 2007). The other system consists of small groups of neurons that use the neurotransmitters serotonin, dopamine, and norepinephrine. Although these groups contain relatively few cells, they send their axons to a remarkable variety of brain regions, an operation that perhaps explains their involvement in high-level, integrative functions.

A region called the **brain stem** includes much of the hindbrain (it does not include the cerebellum) and midbrain and is so-called because it looks like a stem. Embedded deep within the brain, the brain stem connects with the spinal cord at its lower

hindbrain The lowest portion of the brain, consisting of the medulla, cerebellum, and pons.

midbrain Located between the hindbrain and forebrain, a region in which many nerve-fiber systems ascend and descend to connect the higher and lower portions of the brain.

reticular formation A midbrain system that consists of a diffuse collection of neurons involved in stereotypical behaviors, such as walking, sleeping, or turning to attend to a sudden noise.

brain stem The region of the brain that includes much of the hindbrain (excluding the cerebellum) and the midbrain.

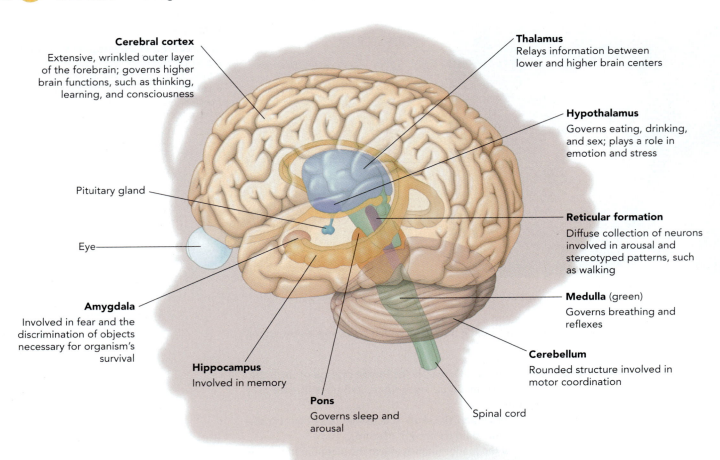

Cerebral cortex
Extensive, wrinkled outer layer of the forebrain; governs higher brain functions, such as thinking, learning, and consciousness

Pituitary gland

Eye

Amygdala
Involved in fear and the discrimination of objects necessary for organism's survival

Hippocampus
Involved in memory

Pons
Governs sleep and arousal

Thalamus
Relays information between lower and higher brain centers

Hypothalamus
Governs eating, drinking, and sex; plays a role in emotion and stress

Reticular formation
Diffuse collection of neurons involved in arousal and stereotyped patterns, such as walking

Medulla (green)
Governs breathing and reflexes

Cerebellum
Rounded structure involved in motor coordination

Spinal cord

FIGURE 3.11

Structure and Regions in the Human Brain To get a feel for where these structures are in your own brain, use the eye (pictured in the lower left of the figure) as a landmark. Note that structures such as the thalamus, hypothalamus, amygdala, pituitary gland, pons, and reticular formation reside deep within the brain.

forebrain The highest level of the brain. Key structures in the forebrain are the limbic system, thalamus, basal ganglia, hypothalamus, and cerebral cortex.

end and then extends upward to encase the reticular formation in the midbrain. The most ancient part of the brain, the brain stem evolved more than 500 million years ago (Carter, 1998). Clumps of cells in the brain stem determine alertness and regulate basic survival functions such as breathing, heartbeat, and blood pressure (Rollenhagen & Lubke, 2006).

Forebrain You try to understand what all of these terms and parts of the brain mean. You talk with friends and plan a party for this weekend. You remember that it has been 6 months since you went to the dentist. You are confident you will do well on the next exam in this course. All of these experiences and millions more would not be possible without the **forebrain,** the highest level of the human brain.

Before we explore the structures and function of the forebrain, though, let's stop for a moment and examine how the brain evolved. The brains of the earliest vertebrates were smaller and simpler than those of later animals. Genetic changes during the evolutionary process were responsible for the development of more complex brains with more parts and more interconnections (Johnson & Losos, 2008). Figure 3.12 compares the brains of a rat, cat, chimpanzee, and human. In both the chimpanzee's brain and (especially) the human's brain, the hindbrain and midbrain structures are covered by a forebrain structure called the cerebral cortex (Sun & others, 2006). The human hindbrain and midbrain are similar to those of other animals, so it is the forebrain structures that mainly differentiate the human brain from the brains of animals such as rats, cats, and chimps. The human forebrain's most important structures are the limbic system, thalamus, basal ganglia, hypothalamus, and cerebral cortex.

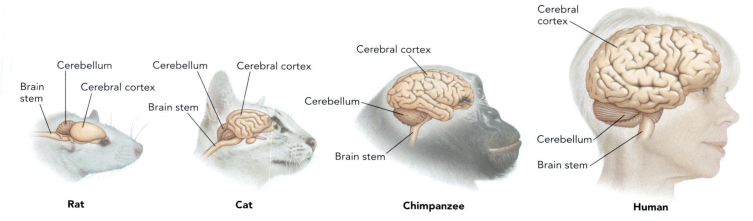

Rat Cat Chimpanzee Human

FIGURE 3.12
The Brain in Different Species
Note how much larger the cerebral cortex becomes as we go from the brain of a rat to the brain of a human.

Limbic System The **limbic system,** a loosely connected network of structures under the cerebral cortex, is important in both memory and emotion. Its two principal structures are the amygdala and hippocampus (see Figure 3.11).

The *amygdala* (from the Latin for "almond" shape) is located within the base of the temporal lobe. It is involved in the discrimination of objects that are necessary for the organism's survival, such as appropriate food, mates, and social rivals. Neurons in the amygdala often fire selectively at the sight of such stimuli, and lesions in the amygdala can cause animals to attempt to eat, fight, or mate with inappropriate objects such as chairs. The amygdala also is involved in emotional awareness and expression through its many connections with higher and lower regions of the brain (Sacchetti, Sacco, & Strata, 2007).

The *hippocampus* has a special role in the storage of memories (Cabeza & St. Jacques, 2007; Gold, Hopkins, & Squire, 2006). Individuals who suffer extensive hippocampal damage cannot retain any new conscious memories after the damage. It is fairly certain, though, that memories are not stored "in" the limbic system. Instead, the limbic system seems to determine what parts of the information passing through the cortex should be "printed" into durable, lasting neural traces in the cortex.

Thalamus The **thalamus** is a forebrain structure that sits at the top of the brain stem in the central core of the brain (see Figure 3.11). It serves as a very important relay station, functioning much like a server in a computer network. That is, an important function of the thalamus is to sort information and send it to the appropriate places in the forebrain for further integration and interpretation (Gheorghita & others, 2006). For example, one area of the thalamus receives information from the cerebellum and projects it to the motor area of the cerebral cortex. Indeed, most neural input to the cerebral cortex goes through the thalamus. Whereas one area of the thalamus works to orient information from the sense receptors (hearing, seeing, and so on), another region seems to be involved in sleep and wakefulness, having ties with the reticular formation.

Basal Ganglia Above the thalamus and under the cerebral cortex lie large clusters, or *ganglia,* of neurons called basal ganglia. The **basal ganglia** work with the cerebellum and the cerebral cortex to control and coordinate voluntary movements. Basal ganglia enable people to engage in habitual behaviors such as riding a bicycle. Individuals with damage to basal ganglia suffer from either unwanted movement, such as constant writhing or jerking of limbs, or too little movement, as in the slow and deliberate movements of people with Parkinson disease (Gale & others, 2007).

Hypothalamus The **hypothalamus,** a small forebrain structure just below the thalamus, monitors three pleasurable activities—eating, drinking, and sex—as well as emotion, stress, and reward (see Figure 3.11 for the location of the hypothalamus). As we will see later, the hypothalamus also helps direct the endocrine system. Perhaps the best way to describe the function of the hypothalamus is as a regulator of the body's internal state. It is sensitive

limbic system Loosely connected network of structures—including the amygdala and hippocampus—that play important roles in memory and emotion.

thalamus Forebrain structure that functions as a relay station to sort information and send it to appropriate areas in the forebrain for further integration and interpretation.

basal ganglia Large clusters of neurons, located above the thalamus and under the cerebral cortex, that work with the cerebellum and the cerebral cortex to control and coordinate voluntary movements.

hypothalamus Small forebrain structure involved in regulating eating, drinking, and sex; directing the endocrine system; and monitoring emotion, stress, and reward.

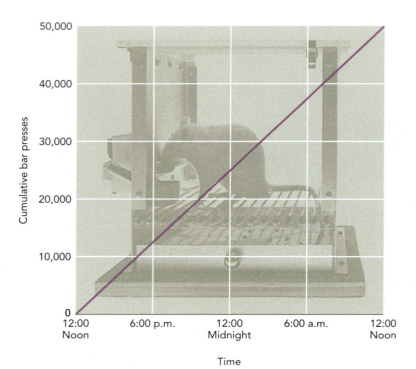

FIGURE 3.13

Results of the Experiment by Olds (1958) on the Role of the Hypothalamus in Pleasure The graphed results for one rat show that it pressed the bar more than 2,000 times an hour for a period of 24 hours to receive stimulation to its hypothalamus. One of the rats in Olds and Milner's experiments is shown pressing the bar.

cerebral cortex Highest level of the forebrain, where the highest mental functions, such as thinking and planning, take place.

occipital lobe The part of the cerebral cortex at the back of the head that is involved in vision.

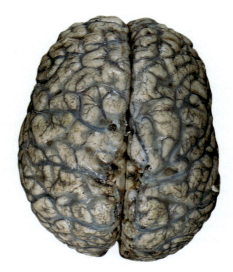

FIGURE 3.14

The Human Brain's Hemispheres

The two halves (hemispheres) of the human brain can be seen clearly in this photograph.

to changes in the blood and neural input, and it responds by influencing the secretion of hormones and neural outputs. For example, if the temperature of circulating blood near the hypothalamus is increased by just 1 or 2 degrees, certain cells in the hypothalamus start increasing their rate of firing. As a result, a chain of events is set in motion. Increased circulation through the skin and sweat glands occurs immediately to release this heat from the body. The cooled blood circulating to the hypothalamus slows down the activity of some of the neurons there, stopping the process when the temperature is just right—37.1 degrees Celsius. These temperature-sensitive neurons function like a finely tuned thermostat in maintaining the body in a balanced state.

The hypothalamus also is involved in emotional states and stress, playing an important role as an integrative location for handling stress. Much of this integration is accomplished through the hypothalamus's action on the pituitary gland, an important endocrine gland located just below it (Peters & others, 2007).

If certain areas of the hypothalamus are electrically stimulated, a feeling of pleasure results (Schultz, 2006). In a classic experiment, James Olds and Peter Milner (1954) implanted an electrode in the hypothalamus of a rat's brain. When the rat ran to a corner of an enclosed area, a mild electric current was delivered to its hypothalamus. The researchers thought the electric current would cause the rat to avoid the corner. Much to their surprise, the rat kept returning to the corner. Olds and Milner believed they had discovered a pleasure center in the hypothalamus. Olds (1958) conducted further experiments and found that rats would press bars until they dropped over from exhaustion just to continue to receive a mild electric shock to their hypothalamus. One rat pressed a bar more than 2,000 times an hour for a period of 24 hours to receive the stimulation to its hypothalamus (Figure 3.13). Today researchers agree that the hypothalamus is involved in pleasurable feelings but that other areas of the brain, such as the limbic system and a bundle of fibers in the forebrain, are also important in the link between the brain and pleasure.

The Olds studies have implications for drug addiction. In these studies, the rat pressed the bar mainly because it produced a positive, rewarding effect (pleasure), not because it wanted to avoid or escape a negative effect (pain). Cocaine users talk about the drug's ability to heighten pleasure in food, in sex, and in a variety of activities, highlighting the reward aspects of the drug (Hyman, Malenka, & Nestler, 2006; Kalivas, 2007).

The Cerebral Cortex

The **cerebral cortex** is the highest region of the forebrain and is the most recently developed part of the brain in the evolutionary scheme. It is in the cerebral cortex that the highest mental functions, such as thinking and planning, take place. The neural tissue that makes up the cerebral cortex covers the lower portions of the brain like a large cap. In humans the cerebral cortex is greatly convoluted with lots of grooves and bulges, and these considerably enlarge its surface area (compared with a brain with a smooth surface). The cerebral cortex is highly connected with other parts of the brain. Literally millions of axons connect the neurons of the cerebral cortex with those located elsewhere in the brain.

Lobes The wrinkled surface of the cerebral cortex is divided into two halves called *hemispheres* (Figure 3.14). Each hemisphere is subdivided into four regions—the frontal lobe, the parietal lobe, the temporal lobe, and the occipital lobe (Figure 3.15).

The **occipital lobe,** at the back of the head, responds to visual stimuli. Different areas of the occipital lobes are connected to process information about such aspects of visual stimuli as their color, shape, and motion. A stroke or wound in the occipital lobe can cause blindness or, at a minimum, wipe out a portion of the person's visual field.

The **temporal lobe,** the portion of the cerebral cortex just above the ears, is involved in hearing, language processing, and memory. The temporal lobes have a number of connections to the limbic system. For this reason, people with damage to the temporal lobes cannot file experiences into long-term memory. Some researchers argue that the temporal lobe is where humans' ability to process information about faces is localized. To read further about this topic, see the Critical Controversy.

So far, we have explored the occipital and temporal lobes of the frontal cortex. Another lobe, the **frontal lobe,** the portion of the cerebral cortex behind the forehead, is involved in the control of voluntary muscles, intelligence, and personality. One fascinating case study illustrates how damage to the frontal lobe can significantly alter personality. Phineas T. Gage, a 25-year-old foreman who worked for the Rutland and Burlington Railroad, met with an accident on September 13, 1848. Phineas and several co-workers were using blasting powder to construct a roadbed. The crew drilled holes in the rock and gravel, poured in the blasting powder, and then tamped down the powder with an iron rod. While Phineas was still tamping it down, the powder exploded, driving the iron rod up through the left side of his face and out through the top of his head. Although the wound in his skull healed in a matter of weeks, Phineas had become a different person. He had been a mild-mannered, hardworking, emotionally calm individual prior to the accident, well liked by all who knew him. Afterward he was obstinate, moody, irresponsible, selfish, and incapable of participating in any planned activities. Damage to the frontal lobe of his brain dramatically altered Phineas's personality.

Without intact frontal lobes, humans are emotionally shallow, distractible, listless, and so insensitive to social contexts that they may belch with abandon at dinner parties. Individuals with frontal lobe damage become so distracted by irrelevant stimuli that they often cannot carry out some basic directions. In one such case, an individual, when asked to light a candle, struck a match correctly but instead of lighting the candle he put the candle in his mouth and acted as if he were smoking it (Luria, 1973).

The frontal lobes of humans are especially large when compared with those of other animals. For example, the frontal cortex of rats barely exists; in cats, it occupies a paltry 3.5 percent of the cerebral cortex; in chimpanzees, 17 percent; and in humans, approximately 30 percent. Some neuroscientists maintain that the frontal cortex is a significant index of evolutionary advancement (Hooper & Teresi, 1993).

An important part of the frontal lobes is the *prefrontal cortex,* which is at the front of the motor cortex (see Figure 3.15). The prefrontal cortex is involved in higher cognitive functions such as planning, reasoning, and self-control (Yurgelun-Todd, 2007). Some neuroscientists refer to the prefrontal cortex as an executive control system because of its role in monitoring and organizing thinking (Kuhn & Franklin, 2006).

The **parietal lobe,** located at the top and toward the rear of the head, is involved in registering spatial location, attention, and motor control (Nachev & Husain, 2006). Thus the parietal lobes are at work when you are judging how far you have to throw a ball to get it to someone else, when you shift your attention from one activity to another (turn your attention away from the TV to a noise outside), and when you turn the pages of this book. The brilliant physicist Albert Einstein said that his reasoning often was best when he imagined

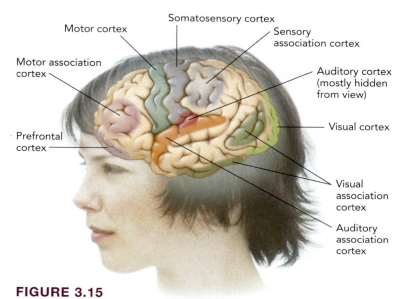

Lobes of the brain

Frontal lobe — Parietal lobe — Occipital lobe — Temporal lobe

Functional regions within the lobes

Motor cortex — Somatosensory cortex — Sensory association cortex — Motor association cortex — Auditory cortex (mostly hidden from view) — Prefrontal cortex — Visual cortex — Visual association cortex — Auditory association cortex

FIGURE 3.15

The Cerebral Cortex's Lobes and Association Areas The cerebral cortex (*top*) is roughly divided into four lobes: occipital, temporal, frontal, and parietal. The cerebral cortex (*bottom*) also consists of the motor cortex and somatosensory cortex. Further, the cerebral cortex includes association areas, such as the visual association cortex, auditory association cortex, and sensory association cortex.

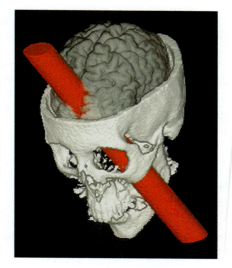

A computerized reconstruction of Phineas T. Gage's accident, based on measurements taken of his skull.

Critical Controversy   Are Human Brains Uniquely Wired to Recognize Faces?

One area of controversy in the study of neuroscience is the question of whether the human brain has a special place for processing information about faces. It seems hard to argue with the idea that faces have a unique importance to all of us. And faces have a special capacity to attract our attention. Even infants are drawn to human faces when given a choice of things to look at. Moreover, there is a specific disorder *(prosopagnosia)* that involves the inability to recognize faces but not other objects, and this condition would seem to suggest a specific region of brain damage. If faces are special in terms of perception and memory, it makes sense that there might be a special place in the brain for processing faces.

Research by Nancy Kanwisher and colleagues has provided evidence that there is indeed a specialized area in the brain for processing faces (Kanwisher, 2006; Kanwisher, Livingstone, & Tsao, 2007; Kanwisher, Stanley, & Harris, 1999). This area is located in the fusiform gyrus in the right temporal lobe and is therefore called the fusiform face area (FFA). The FFA is a small spot in the right temporal lobe, just behind your ear. Using fMRI, researchers have shown that the FFA is especially active when a person is viewing a face—a human face, a cat's face, or a cartoon face—but not cars, butterflies, or other objects (Tong & others, 2000). The theory that humans have a brain area specialized to process the most important visual information of life—other people's faces—makes sense. However, other researchers have challenged this idea along the following line of argument. As human beings, we are all experts in perceiving humans. We have been doing it since birth. So, what if the FFA is in fact more involved with processing expert knowledge generally rather than with processing faces per se?

To explore this alternative theory, Isabel Gauthier and her colleagues have conducted a number of studies (Bukach & others, 2006; Gauthier, Behrmann, & Tarr, 2004; Gauthier & Bukach, 2006; Gauthier & others, 2003). In one investigation, Gauthier and her colleagues (2000) examined individuals who were experts on cars or birds. The FFAs of these experts "lit up" when the individuals were presented with the objects about which they had expertise. In a provocative study, participants were trained to recognize imaginary, faceless creatures called *greebles*, small plantlike objects made of pink clay (Tarr & Gauthier, 2000) (Figure 3.16 shows some greebles used in this study). Participants quickly learned to classify the greebles according to sex and family. During fMRI, the FFA was active during these judgments, suggesting that the FFA is concerned with recognition more generally rather than just with recognition of faces. These results have been countered by studies showing that, at the very least, the FFA is far

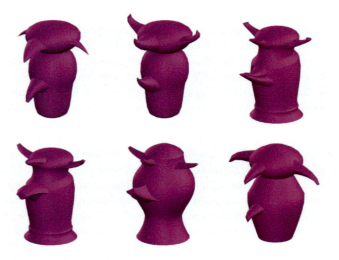

FIGURE 3.16

Some Greebles Used in Gauthier's Study The illustration shows sample greebles used in Gauthier's research. In individuals who had reached a level of expertise in recognizing these strange, faceless creatures, the fusiform face area became active during greeble identification.

more activated during facial recognition than during recognition of other objects (Tong & others, 2000).

The status of the FFA as a specific brain area for face recognition is at the center of a lively debate in neuroscience (Gauthier & Bukach, 2006; Kanwisher, 2006; McKone, Kanwisher, & Duchaine, 2007; McKone & Robbins, 2006). This area of research demonstrates the ways that, as scientists' experimental tools develop, so does their understanding of the brain. Moreover, the new questions they are asking and the way they are asking them can have a profound impact on the development of scientific knowledge.

What Do You Think?

- Why might it be that humans would evolve a brain area specialized just for recognizing faces?
- Are there other aspects of our social worlds that you might expect the brain to be especially designed to perceive? What might those be?
- How does the debate over the FFA illustrate the role of controversy in science more generally?

---

temporal lobe The portion of the cerebral cortex just above the ears that is involved in hearing, language processing, and memory.

frontal lobe The part of the cerebral cortex just behind the forehead that is involved in the control of voluntary muscles, intelligence, and personality.

parietal lobe Area of the cerebral cortex at the top of the head that is involved in registering spatial location, attention, and motor control.

objects in space. It turns out that his parietal lobes were 15 percent larger than average (Witelson, Kigar, & Harvey, 1999).

A word of caution is in order about going too far in localizing function within a particular lobe. Although this discussion has attributed specific functions to a particular lobe (such as vision in the occipital lobe), there are considerable integration and connection between any two or more lobes and between lobes and other parts of the brain.

Somatosensory Cortex and Motor Cortex   Two other important regions of the cerebral cortex are the somatosensory cortex and the motor cortex (see Figure 3.15). The

Touring the Nervous System and the Brain

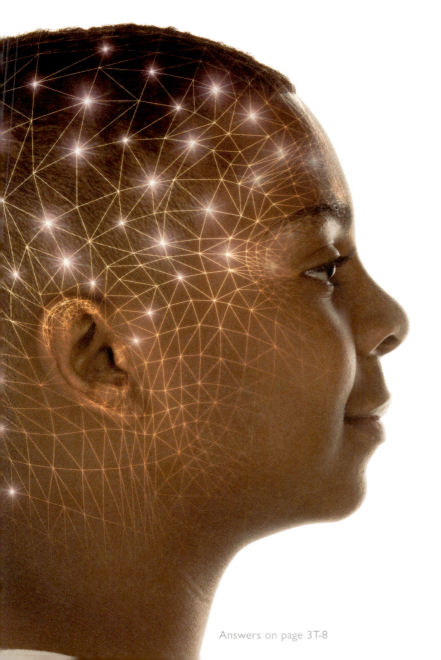

GOALS OF THE TOUR

1 **The Neuron and Synapse.** You will be able to identify parts of the neuron and synapse and describe how they communicate information.

2 **The Resting Potential and Action Potential.** You will be able to describe the ions used in maintaining the resting potential and in producing the action potential.

3 **Structures and Functions in the Human Brain.** You will be able to identify the brain's key structures and functions.

4 **Cerebral Cortex Lobes and Association Areas.** You will be able to identify the location and describe the function of the four cerebral lobes.

5 **Visual Information in the Split-Brain.** You will be able to describe hemispheric lateralization and communication in the brain.

6 **Central and Peripheral Nervous Systems.** You will be able to identify the parts of the central and peripheral nervous systems and describe the body functions they control.

The Neuron and the Synapse

1 Identify parts of the neuron and synapse and describe how they communicate information.

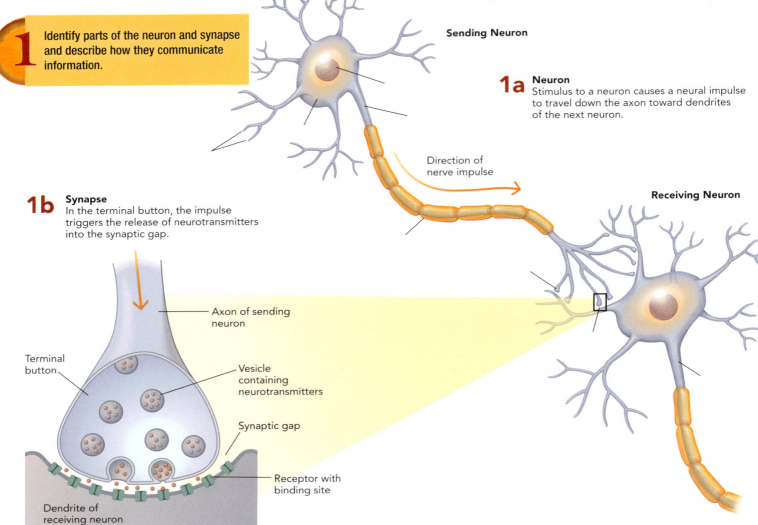

Sending Neuron

1a **Neuron**
Stimulus to a neuron causes a neural impulse to travel down the axon toward dendrites of the next neuron.

Direction of nerve impulse

Receiving Neuron

1b **Synapse**
In the terminal button, the impulse triggers the release of neurotransmitters into the synaptic gap.

Axon of sending neuron

Terminal button

Vesicle containing neurotransmitters

Synaptic gap

Receptor with binding site

Dendrite of receiving neuron

The Resting Potential and Action Potential

2a Resting Potential

The electrical potential across the membrane when the neuron is not stimulated. −70 mV inside relative to the outside of the membrane.

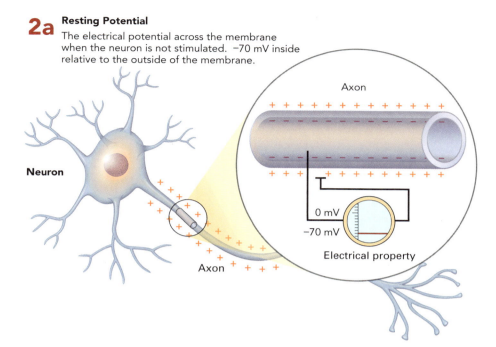

Neuron

Axon

Axon

0 mV

−70 mV

Electrical property

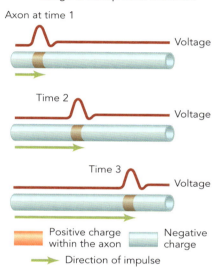

Describe the ions used in maintaining the resting potential and in producing the action potential.

2

2b Action Potential

The action potential is generated by an impulse within a neuron that causes a brief wave of positive electrical charge to sweep down the axon.

Axon at time 1

Voltage

Time 2

Voltage

Time 3

Voltage

Positive charge within the axon

Negative charge

Direction of impulse

Structures and Functions of the Human Brain

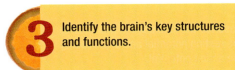

3 Identify the brain's key structures and functions.

3a Brain Stem Structures

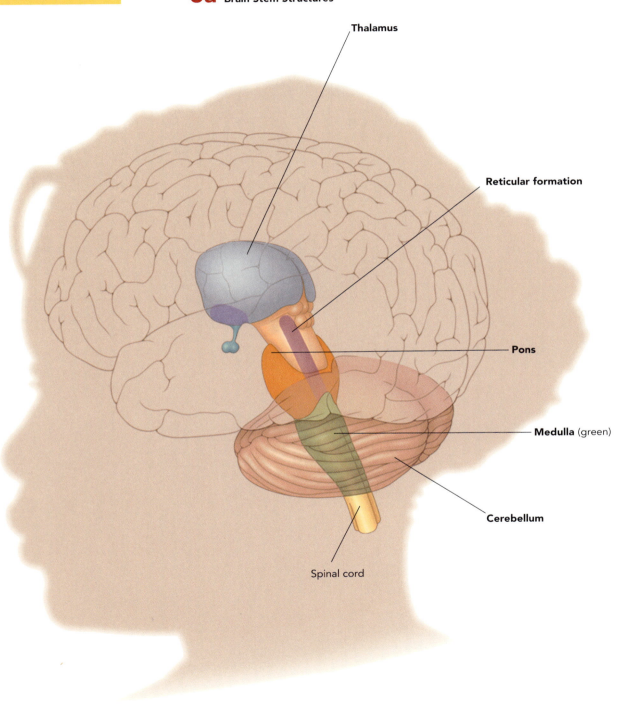

Thalamus

Reticular formation

Pons

Medulla (green)

Cerebellum

Spinal cord

Cerebral Cortex Lobes and Association Areas

Identify the location of the four cerebral cortex lobes and describe their primary functions.

4

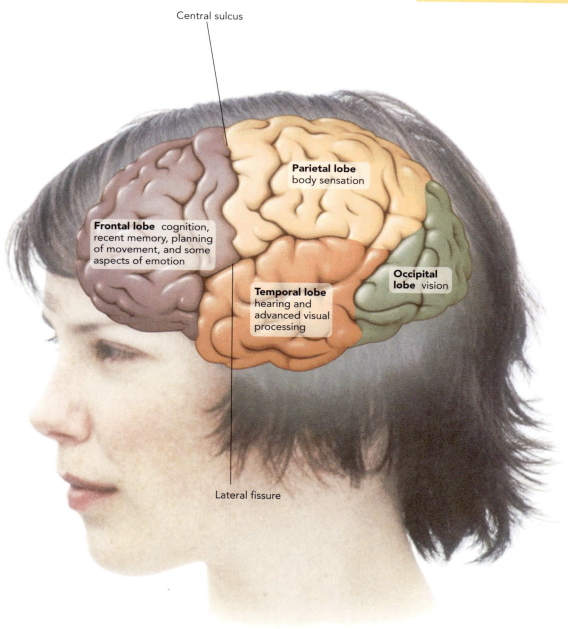

Central sulcus

Parietal lobe body sensation

Frontal lobe cognition, recent memory, planning of movement, and some aspects of emotion

Occipital lobe vision

Temporal lobe hearing and advanced visual processing

Lateral fissure

Visual Information in the Split Brain

5 Describe hemispheric lateralization and communication in the brain.

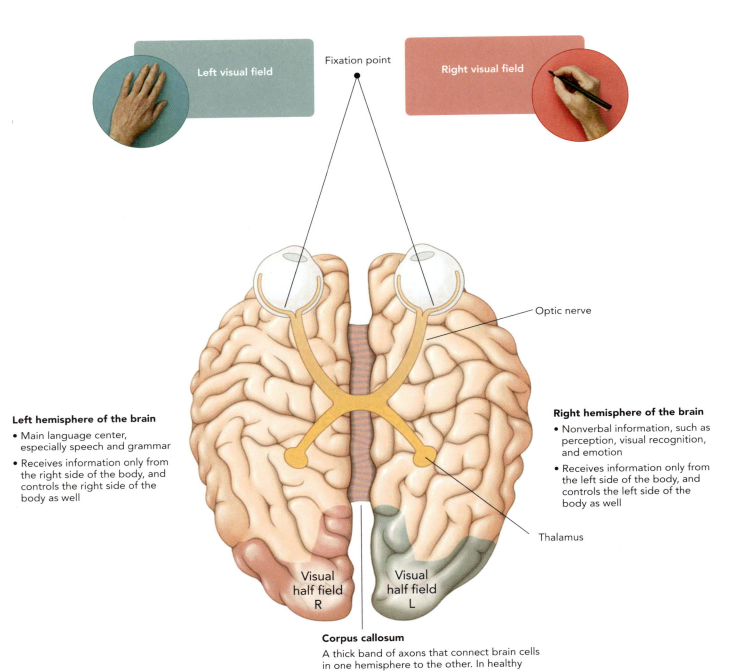

Left visual field

Fixation point

Right visual field

Optic nerve

Left hemisphere of the brain
- Main language center, especially speech and grammar
- Receives information only from the right side of the body, and controls the right side of the body as well

Right hemisphere of the brain
- Nonverbal information, such as perception, visual recognition, and emotion
- Receives information only from the left side of the body, and controls the left side of the body as well

Thalamus

Visual half field R

Visual half field L

Corpus callosum

A thick band of axons that connect brain cells in one hemisphere to the other. In healthy brains, the two sides engage in a continuous flow of information via this neural bridge and share information.

Central and Peripheral Nervous Systems

6a **The Central Nervous System**

● Central nervous system

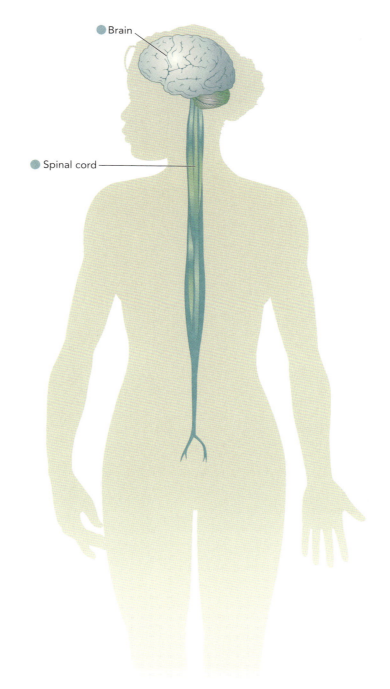

● Brain

● Spinal cord

Identify the parts of the central and peripheral nervous systems and describe the body functions they control.

6

ANSWERS

1. THE NEURON AND SYNAPSE

The *neuron* consists of a *cell body*, *dendrites*, and an *axon*. The cell body is the structure of the neuron that contains the nucleus, which consists of the genetic material including the chromosomes. The dendrites are branches of the neuron that receive information from other neurons. The axon sends information away from the cell body to other neurons or cells.

When a neuron fires, it sends an electrical impulse down the axon, known as the *action potential*. When the impulse arrives at the axon terminal buttons, it causes the release of *neurotransmitter* molecules into the *synapse*. The synapse is the gap junction between two neurons. Neurons communicate with one another by means of chemical signals provided by neurotransmitters that cross the synapse.

The neurotransmitter released by the sending neuron enters the synaptic gap and attaches to a *binding site* located on a *receptor* on the receiving neuron. The receptor contains a channel that is typically closed when the receiving neuron is in the resting state (*resting potential*). When the neurotransmitter binds to the receptor, it causes an opening of the receptor channel that then allows a particular *ion* to enter or leave the receiving neuron. If a neurotransmitter causes the opening of channels on the receiving neuron to a positively charged ion like sodium (Na^+), it will become less negative in charge. The entry of sodium will cause a change in the electrical charge (potential) of the receiving neuron that may make it more likely to generate its own action potential.

2. THE RESTING POTENTIAL AND ACTION POTENTIAL

The neuron maintains electrical properties called an *electrical gradient*, displaying a difference in the electrical charge inside and outside of the cell. The electrical gradient is created because the membrane of the neuron is *selectively permeable*. Some molecules can pass through it more freely than others. The membrane is not permeable to large negatively charged protein molecules that are trapped inside the neuron. Inside and outside of the neuron are various electrically charged particles called *ions* that vary in concentrations. The ions that play an important role in the function of the neuron are sodium (Na^+), potassium (K^+), and chloride (Cl^-). These ions enter or leave the neuron through special channels provided by protein molecules that line the neuron.

The *resting potential* is the electrical property of the neuron when it is not stimulated or not sending a nerve impulse. In a typical neuron this is seen as a -70 mV charge inside relative to the outside of the membrane. During the resting potential, the sodium channels are closed, leaving a higher concentration of sodium ions outside of the neuron membrane. The negative charge of a neuron during the resting state is largely maintained by the negatively charged protein molecules trapped inside the neuron and by the inability of positively charged sodium ions to cross the membrane into the neuron.

The *action potential* occurs when the neuron is stimulated to generate a nerve impulse down the axon. This is often referred to as the firing of the neuron. During the action potential, there is a rapid and slight reversal in the electrical charge from -70 mV to +40 mV. The action potential occurs as a brief wave of positive charge that sweeps down the axon.

3. STRUCTURES AND FUNCTIONS IN THE HUMAN BRAIN

The brain stem structures are embedded within the core of the brain and provide a number of vital functions for survival. These include the medulla, pons, cerebellum, reticular formation, and the thalamus.

The *medulla* is a brain structure just above the spinal cord. It controls a number of life-sustaining reflexes and functions including breathing, coughing, vomiting, and heart rate. The *pons* lies just above the medulla and is involved in functions including sleep and arousal. The *cerebellum* is a large structure at the base of the brain with many folds. It is traditionally known to be involved in motor coordination and balance but also plays a role in attention of visual and auditory stimuli and the timing of movements. The *reticular formation* is an elaborate diffuse network of neurons that runs through the core of the medulla and pons to the base of the thalamus. It plays a role in arousal, attention, sleep patterns, and stereotyped patterns such as posture and locomotion. The *thalamus* is a central structure in the brain that relays auditory, visual, and somatosensory (body senses) information to the cerebral cortex.

The limbic system comprises a number of brain structures involved in motivation, emotion, and memory. The *hypothalamus* is a small structure that is located just below the thalamus. It controls the autonomic nervous system as well as the release of hormones from the pituitary gland. It is involved in a number of functions including eating, drinking, and sexual behavior, and plays an important role in the expression of emotions and stress responses. The *hippocampus* is located in the temporal lobe and plays a role in learning and memory. Adjacent to the hippocampus is the amygdala, which is involved in fear and anxiety.

The *cerebral cortex* is the outer layer of the brain and is involved in higher-order functions such as thinking, learning, consciousness, and memory.

4. CEREBRAL CORTEX LOBES AND ASSOCIATION AREAS

The *cerebral cortex* is anatomically divided into four lobes: occipital lobe, parietal lobe, temporal lobe, and frontal lobe. The *occipital lobe* is located in the posterior end (back region) of the cortex and is involved in processing *visual information*. The *parietal lobe* lies between the occipital lobe and the *central sulcus*, which is one of the deepest grooves in the surface of the cortex. The parietal lobe is involved in *bodily senses*. The area just posterior to the central sulcus is called the primary somatosensory cortex because it is the primary target for the *touch senses* of the body and information for muscle-stretch receptors and joint receptors. The *temporal lobe* is the large portion of each hemisphere near the temples and lies behind the frontal lobe and below the *lateral fissure*. It is the primary region of the cortex that processes *auditory information*. The *frontal lobe* extends from the central sulcus to the anterior limit (forward region) of the brain. The region of the frontal lobe immediately adjacent to the central sulcus is called the *motor cortex* because it controls *fine movements*. The most anterior region is called the *prefrontal cortex;* it is involved in higher brain functions including *cognition* (thought processes), recent *memory*, the *planning of movement*, and some aspects of *emotion*.

Association areas are not primarily sensory or motor areas but, rather, associate sensory and motor inputs that give rise to higher mental functions such as perception, learning, remembering, thinking, and speaking.

5. VISUAL INFORMATION IN THE SPLIT-BRAIN

Lateralization refers to the division of labor between the two cerebral hemispheres of the brain. The *left hemisphere* receives sensory information from and controls the movements in the right side of the body. Likewise, images of objects in the right visual field are projected to the left half of the retina of each eye, which in turn sends the information to the visual cortex in the left hemisphere. The left hemisphere also contains the main language area involved in the comprehension and production of language.

The *right hemisphere* receives sensory information from and controls the movements in the left side of the body. Likewise, images of objects in the left visual field are projected to the right half of the retina of each eye, which in turn sends the information to the visual cortex in the right hemisphere. The right hemisphere processes nonverbal information, such as perception, visual recognition, and emotion.

In the healthy brain the two cerebral hemispheres share information with each other across the broad band of axons called the *corpus callosum*. In some instances the corpus callosum is surgically cut, a procedure called the *split-brain*. In the split-brain, information in one cerebral hemisphere is confined to that side of the brain.

6. CENTRAL AND PERIPHERAL NERVOUS SYSTEMS

The nervous system is made up of the *central nervous system* and the *peripheral nervous system*. The central nervous system is comprised of the brain and the spinal cord. The peripheral nervous system consists of all nerve fibers outside of the brain and spinal cord. The peripheral nervous system is made up of two major divisions: the *somatic division* and the *autonomic division*.

The *somatic division* consists of nerve fibers conveying information from the brain and spinal cord to skeletal muscles; this information controls movement and sends information back to the brain via the spinal cord from sensory receptors located in various parts of the body.

The *autonomic division* controls the glands and muscles of the internal organs such as the heart, digestive system, lungs, and salivary glands, and it consists of the sympathetic and the parasympathetic branches. The *sympathetic branch* arouses the body, mobilizes its energy during physical exercise and in stressful situations, and activates the adrenal gland to release epinephrine into the bloodstream. The *parasympathetic branch* calms the body and conserves and replenishes energy.

somatosensory cortex processes information about body sensations. It is located at the front of the parietal lobes. The **motor cortex,** just behind the frontal lobes, processes information about voluntary movement.

The map in Figure 3.17 shows which parts of the somatosensory and motor cortexes are associated with different parts of the body. It is based on research done by Wilder Penfield (1947), a neurosurgeon at the Montreal Neurological Institute. He worked with patients who had severe epilepsy and often performed surgery to remove portions of the epileptic patients' brains. However, he was concerned that removing a portion of the brain might impair some of the individuals' functions. Penfield's solution was to map the cortex during surgery by stimulating different cortical areas and observing the responses of the patients, who were given a local anesthetic so they would remain awake during the operation. He found that, when he stimulated certain somatosensory and motor areas of the brain, different parts of a patient's body moved. For both somatosensory and motor areas, there is a point-to-point relation between a part of the body and a location on the cerebral cortex. In Figure 3.17, the face and hands are given proportionately more space than other body parts because the face and hands are capable of finer perceptions and movements than are other body areas and therefore need more cerebral cortex representation.

somatosensory cortex Area of the cerebral cortex that processes information about body sensations.

motor cortex Area of the cerebral cortex that processes information about voluntary movement.

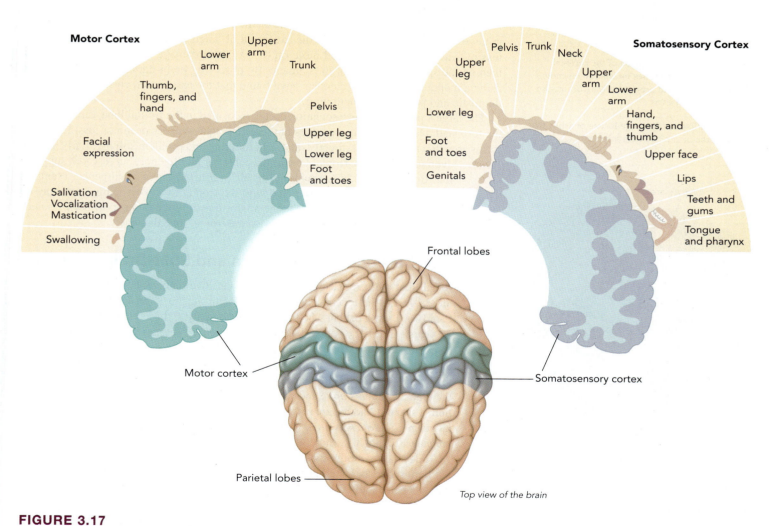

FIGURE 3.17

Disproportionate Representation of Body Parts in the Motor and Somatosensory Areas of the Cortex

The amount of cortex allotted to a body part is not proportionate to the body part's size. Instead, the brain has more space for body parts that require precision and control. Thus the thumb, fingers, and hand require more brain tissue than does the arm.

Neural pathways sometimes get connected the wrong way. A genetic defect in many Siamese cats causes the pathways from their eyes to connect to the wrong parts of the visual cortex during development. As a result, these cats end up looking at the world cross-eyed in an effort to "straighten out" the visual image of their visual cortex.

association cortex Region of the cerebral cortex in which the highest intellectual functions, including thinking and problem solving, occur; also called association areas.

corpus callosum The large bundle of axons that connects the brain's two hemispheres.

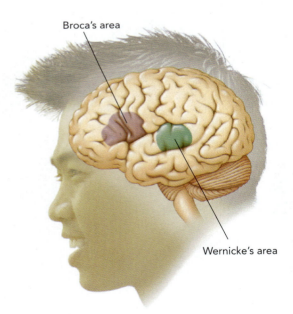

Broca's area

Wernicke's area

FIGURE 3.18

Broca's Area and Wernicke's Area Broca's area is located in the brain's left hemisphere, and it is involved in the control of speech. Individuals with damage to Broca's area have problems saying words correctly. Also shown is Wernicke's area, the portion of the left hemisphere that is involved in understanding language. Individuals with damage to this area cannot comprehend words; that is, they hear the words but do not know what they mean.

The point-to-point mapping of somatosensory fields onto the cortex's surface is the basis of our orderly and accurate perception of the world (Christensen & others, 2007; Zhu & others, 2007). When something touches your lip, for example, your brain knows what body part has been touched because the nerve pathways from your lip are the only pathways that project to the lip region of the somatosensory cortex.

Siamese cats provide an example of what happens when these neural pathways get connected the wrong way. Many Siamese have a genetic defect that causes the pathways from the eyes to connect to the wrong parts of the visual cortex during development. The result is that these cats spend their lives looking at things cross-eyed in an effort to "straighten out" the visual image of their visual cortex.

The Association Cortex Embedded in the brain's lobes, the association cortex makes up 75 percent of the cerebral cortex (see Figure 3.15). Processing information about sensory input and motor output is not all that is taking place in the cerebral cortex. The **association cortex** (sometimes called *association areas*) is the region of the cerebral cortex that integrates this information. The highest intellectual functions, such as thinking and problem solving, occur in the association cortex.

Interestingly, damage to a specific part of the association cortex often does not result in a specific loss of function. With the exception of language areas (which are localized), loss of function seems to depend more on the extent of damage to the association cortex than on the specific location of the damage. By observing brain-damaged individuals and using a mapping technique, scientists have found that the association cortex is involved in linguistic and perceptual functioning.

The largest portion of the association cortex is located in the frontal lobe, directly under the forehead. Damage to this area does not lead to somatosensory or motor loss. Indeed, it is this area that may be most directly related to thinking and problem solving. Early studies even referred to the frontal lobe as the center of intelligence, but research suggests that frontal lobe damage may not result in a lowering of intelligence. Planning and judgment are often associated with the frontal lobe. Personality also may be linked to the frontal lobe. Recall the misfortune of Phineas Gage, whose personality radically changed after he experienced frontal lobe damage.

The Cerebral Hemispheres and Split-Brain Research

Recall that the cerebral cortex is divided into two halves—left and right (see Figure 3.14). Do these hemispheres have different functions? In 1861, French surgeon Paul Broca saw a patient who had received an injury to the left side of his brain about 30 years earlier. The patient became known as Tan, because *Tan* was the only word he could speak. Tan suffered from *aphasia*, a language disorder associated with brain damage. Tan died several days after Broca evaluated him, and an autopsy revealed that the injury was to a precise area of the left hemisphere. Today we refer to this area of the brain as *Broca's area*, and we know that it plays an important role in the production of speech. Another area of the brain's left hemisphere that has an important role in language is *Wernicke's area*, which, if damaged, causes problems in comprehending language. Figure 3.18 shows the locations of Broca's area and Wernicke's area.

Today there continues to be considerable interest in the degree to which the brain's left hemisphere or right hemisphere is involved in various aspects of thinking, feeling, and behavior (Corballis, 2004; Corballis, Funnell, & Gazzaniga, 2002; Stephan & others, 2003). For many years, scientists speculated that the **corpus callosum,** the large bundle of axons that connects the brain's two hemispheres, has something to do with relaying information between the two sides (Figure 3.19). Roger Sperry (1974) confirmed this in an experiment in which he cut the corpus callosum in cats. He also severed certain nerves leading from the eyes to the brain. After the operation, Sperry trained the cats to solve a series of visual problems with one eye blindfolded.

After the cat learned the task—say, with only its left eye uncovered—its other eye was blindfolded and the animal was tested again. The "split-brain" cat behaved as if it had never learned the task. It seems that the memory was stored only in the left hemisphere, which could no longer directly communicate with the right hemisphere.

Further evidence of the corpus callosum's function has come from studies of patients with severe, even life-threatening, forms of epilepsy. Epilepsy is caused by electrical "brain-storms" that flash uncontrollably across the corpus callosum. In one famous case, neurosurgeons severed the corpus callosum of an epileptic patient now known as W. J. in a final attempt to reduce his unbearable seizures. Sperry (1968) examined W. J. and found that the corpus callosum functions the same in humans as in animals—cutting the corpus callosum seemed to leave the patient with "two separate minds" that learned and operated independently.

As it turns out, the right hemisphere receives information only from the left side of the body, and the left hemisphere receives information only from the right side of the body. When you hold an object in your left hand, for example, only the right hemisphere of your brain detects the object. When you hold an object in your right hand, only the left hemisphere of the brain detects the object (Figure 3.20). In a normally functioning corpus callosum, both hemispheres receive this information.

In people with intact brains, specialization of function occurs in some areas. Following are the main areas in which the brain tends to divide its functioning into one hemisphere or the other:

- *Verbal processing:* The most extensive research on the brain's two hemispheres has focused on language. Speech and grammar are localized to the left hemisphere (Bethmann & others, 2007; Powell & others, 2006). A common misconception, though, is that *all* language processing is carried out in the brain's left hemisphere. However, such aspects of language as appropriate use of language in different contexts, and much of our sense of humor reside in the right hemisphere (Coulson & Wu, 2005).

- *Nonverbal processing:* The right hemisphere is more dominant in processing nonverbal information such as spatial perception, visual recognition, and emotion (Bartolomeo, 2006). For example, as we saw earlier in the Critical Controversy feature, the right hemisphere is mainly at work when we are processing information about people's faces (Kanwisher, 2006). The right hemisphere also may be more involved in processing information about emotions, both when we express emotions ourselves and when we recognize others' emotions (Workman & others, 2006).

Because differences in the functioning of the brain's two hemispheres are known to exist, people commonly use the phrases *left-brained* and *right-brained* as a way of categorizing themselves and others. Such generalizations have little scientific basis. The most common myth about hemispheric specialization is that the left brain is logical and the right brain is creative. The left-brain, right-brain myth started with the publication of Roger Sperry's classic split-brain studies. As Sperry's findings made their way into the media, they became oversimplified, and people were labeled either right-brained (artistic) or left-brained (logical).

Sperry did discover that the *left* hemisphere is superior in the kind of logic used to prove geometric theorems. But in everyday life, our logic problems involve integrating information and drawing conclusions. In these instances, the *right* hemisphere is crucial. In most complex activities in which people engage, interplay occurs between the brain's two hemispheres (Salvador & others, 2005). For example, in reading, the left hemisphere comprehends syntax and grammar, which the right hemisphere does not. However, the right brain is better at understanding a story's intonation and emotion. A similar interplay is observed in music and art. Pop psychology assigns both music and art to the right brain. The right hemisphere is better at some musical skills, such as recognizing chords. But the left hemisphere is better at others, such as distinguishing which of two sounds occurs first.

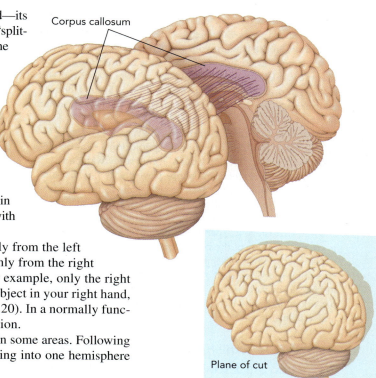

Corpus callosum

Plane of cut

FIGURE 3.19

The Corpus Callosum The corpus callosum is a thick band of about 80 million axons that connects the brain cells in one hemisphere to those in the other. In healthy brains, the two sides engage in a continuous flow of information via this neural bridge.

Emotion and Neuroscience: Is Your Brain Happy?

Are some brains happier than others? Put your hand over your forehead. The answer to the happy brain question is lying right there in the palm of your hand. Research using a variety of techniques to study the neuroscience of emotion suggests that there might be a pattern of brain activity associated with feeling good, and that this activity takes place in the front of your brain, in what are called the *prefrontal lobes* (van Reekum & others, 2007).

Paul Ekman, Richard Davidson, and Wallace Friesen (1990) measured EEG activity during emotional experiences provoked by film clips. Individuals in this study watched amusing film clips (such as a puppy playing with flowers and monkeys taking a bath) as well as clips likely to provoke fear or disgust (a leg amputation and a third-degree burn victim). How does the brain respond to such stimuli? This research showed that there is a particular type of asymmetry in the prefrontal regions of the brain associated with emotional experiences. While watching the amusing clips, people tended to exhibit more left than right prefrontal activity, as shown in EEGs. In contrast, when the participants viewed the fear-provoking films, the right prefrontal area was generally more active than the left.

> ### While watching the amusing clips, people show more left than right prefrontal brain activity.

Other research supports the idea that relatively more right than left prefrontal activation is associated with showing larger negative emotional responses to stimuli (Wheeler, Davidson, & Tomarken, 1993). These sorts of responses to stimuli represent what may be more general baseline differences between happy and unhappy people. Heather Urry and her colleagues (2004) found that individuals who have relatively more left than right prefrontal activity generally tend to rate themselves higher on a number of measures of well-being, including self-acceptance, positive relations with others, purpose in life, and life satisfaction. Happy and unhappy brains can even be identified in infants. In one study, 10-month-old infants who showed relatively greater right than left prefrontal activation at baseline were more likely to cry when separated from their mothers (Davidson & Fox, 1982).

Of course, by definition, research on the neural correlates of experience are *correlational* studies, and that means that it is not possible to establish causal conclusions from this work (as you might recall from Chapter 2). The fact that certain neurons are active during an activity does not prove that these brain processes cause the experience under study.

It might seem like a challenge to manipulate brain activity in the laboratory, but in a clever experiment, John Allen and his colleagues (Allen, Harmon-Jones, & Cavender, 2001) did just that. These researchers provide some experimental evidence

supporting the role of prefrontal asymmetry in emotional responses. They used biofeedback to train college women to increase right or left frontal activation. Specifically, these participants wore an electrode cap for EEG measurement and were hooked up to a computer that sounded a tone when they had effectively changed the symmetry of their brain activation in a particular direction. Half of the women were trained to increase activation of the left hemisphere, and half were trained to increase activation in the right hemisphere. Using this training, participants were generally able to accomplish the goal of changing their brain activation, without any mention of emotional processes at all. After the training, researchers found that women who were trained to activate the left more than the right side of the prefrontal brain area were less likely to frown while watching a negative clip, whereas those who were trained to activate the right side more than the left responded with less smiling to the happy clips. Among the women who were especially responsive to the biofeedback training, those who had been trained to activate the right side expressed less interest, amusement, and happiness than those who had been trained to activate the left side.

There may in fact be a causal link between prefrontal asymmetry and emotional experience. Indeed, Davidson and colleagues (2003) have shown that mindfulness meditation training can enhance left frontal activation and even promote immune system functioning. *Mindfulness meditation* (also called *awareness meditation*) involves maintaining a floating state of consciousness that encourages individuals to focus on whatever comes to mind—a sensation, a thought—at that particular moment (Bishop, 2002; Carlson & others, 2001). Remember that brain structure and function depend on experience. Maybe savoring every enjoyable moment of life—the flowers in your garden, a phone call from a friend, a sunny spring day—could be an opportunity to train your brain to be happy.

Although there is some specialization of function, in many complex tasks in which humans engage in their everyday lives, integration across the hemispheres is common. For example, enjoying or creating music requires the use of both hemispheres (Brown, Martinez, & Parsons, 2006). To read further about ways that the left and right hemispheres might be involved in your happiness, see the Intersection.

Integration of Function in the Brain

How do all of the regions of the brain cooperate to produce the wondrous complexity of thought and behavior that characterizes humans? Neuroscience still does not have answers to such questions as how the brain solves a murder mystery or writes a poem or an essay. But we can get a sense of integrative brain function by considering something like the act of escaping from a burning building.

Imagine you are sitting at your desk, writing letters, when fire breaks out behind you. The sound of crackling flames is relayed from your ear through the thalamus, to the auditory cortex, and on to the auditory association cortex. At each stage, the stimulus is processed to extract information, and at some stage, probably at the association cortex level, the sounds are finally matched with something like a neural memory representing sounds of fires you have heard previously. The association "fire" sets new machinery in motion. Your attention (guided in part by the reticular formation) shifts to the auditory signal being held in your association cortex and on to your auditory association cortex, and simultaneously (again guided by reticular systems) your head turns toward the noise. Now your visual association cortex reports in: "Objects matching flames are present." In other regions of the association cortex, the visual and auditory reports are synthesized ("We have things that look and sound like fire"), and neural associations representing potential actions ("flee") are activated. However, firing the neurons that code the plan to flee will not get you out of the chair. The basal ganglia must become engaged, and from there the commands will arise to set the brain stem, motor cortex, and cerebellum to the task of actually transporting you out of the room.

Which part of your brain did you use to escape? Virtually all systems had a role. By the way, you would probably remember this event because your limbic circuitry would likely have started memory formation when the association "fire" was triggered. The next time the sounds of crackling flames reach your auditory association cortex, the associations triggered would include this most recent escape. In sum, considerable integration of function takes place in the brain (Fusar-Poli & Broome, 2006; Mollet & Harrison, 2006).

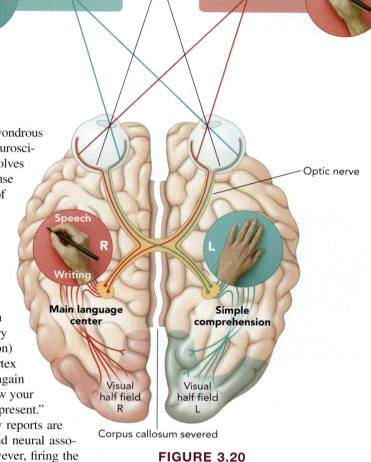

FIGURE 3.20

Visual Information in the Split Brain

In a split-brain patient, information from the visual field's left side projects only to the right hemisphere. Information from the visual field's right side projects only to the left hemisphere. Because of these projections, stimuli can be presented to only one of a split-brain patient's hemispheres.

 REVIEW, ASSESS, AND SHARPEN YOUR THINKING

Review

3 Identify the brain's levels and structures, and summarize the functions of its structures.

- Specify four techniques that are used to study the brain and the nervous system.
- Outline the levels of organization in the human brain.
- Discuss the areas of the cerebral cortex and their functions.
- Explain how split-brain research has increased our understanding of the way the cerebral hemispheres function.
- Describe the integration of function in the brain.

Assess

1. A person who experiences problems with visual stimuli may have damage to
   A. the occipital lobe.
   B. the temporal lobe.
   C. the parietal lobe.
   D. the frontal lobe.

2. Which of the following brain imaging techniques works by recording metabolic changes in the brain?
   A. positron-emission tomography
   B. magnetic resonance imaging
   C. functional magnetic resonance imaging
   D. blood oxygen level dependent contrast

3. Tamara is studying for an important test and is attempting to remember a number of concepts. If Tamara suffered extensive damage to the _____, she would not be able to remember any of the new concepts she is learning.
   A. amygdala
   B. basal ganglia

C. hypothalamus
D. hippocampus

4. Someone with damage to Wernicke's area would have problems
   A. understanding what others say.
   B. coordinating movements.
   C. producing speech.
   D. with sleep regulation.

5. In which part of the brain is the somatosensory cortex located?
   A. limbic system
   B. parietal lobe
   C. frontal lobe
   D. pons

Sharpen Your Thinking

In your experience, does human behavior differ in important ways from the behavior of other animals? What tasks are human brains able to accomplish that other animals may not be able to?

4 The Endocrine System

State what the endocrine system is and how it affects behavior.

Endocrine System Structures and Functions

The **endocrine system** is a set of glands that regulate the activities of certain organs by releasing their chemical products into the bloodstream. In the past, the endocrine system was considered separate from the nervous system. However, today neuroscientists know that these two systems are often interconnected.

Hormones are the chemical messengers that are manufactured by the endocrine glands. Hormones travel more slowly than nerve impulses. The bloodstream conveys hormones to all parts of the body, and the membrane of every cell has receptors for one or more hormones.

The endocrine glands consist of the pituitary gland, the thyroid and parathyroid glands, the adrenal glands, the pancreas, and the ovaries in women and the testes in men (Figure 3.21). In much the same way that the brain's control of muscular activity is constantly monitored and altered to suit the information received by the brain, the action of the endocrine glands is continuously monitored and changed by nervous, hormonal, and chemical signals (Johnson, 2008). Recall from earlier in the chapter that the autonomic nervous system regulates processes such as respiration, heart rate, and digestion. The autonomic nervous system acts on the endocrine glands to produce a number of important physiological reactions to strong emotions, such as rage and fear.

The **pituitary gland,** a pea-sized gland that sits at the base of the skull, controls growth and regulates other glands (Figure 3.22). The anterior (front) part of the pituitary is known as the

endocrine system A set of glands that regulate the activities of certain organs by releasing their chemical products (hormones) into the bloodstream.

hormones Chemical messengers manufactured by the endocrine glands.

pituitary gland An important endocrine gland at the base of the skull that controls growth and regulates other glands.

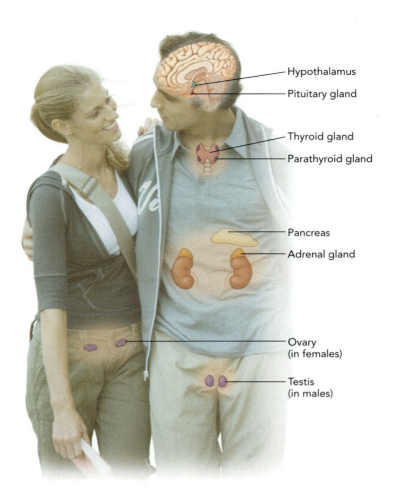

Hypothalamus

Pituitary gland

Thyroid gland

Parathyroid gland

Pancreas

Adrenal gland

Ovary
(in females)

Testis
(in males)

FIGURE 3.21

The Major Endocrine Glands The pituitary gland releases hormones that regulate the hormone secretions of the other glands. The pituitary gland is regulated by the hypothalamus.

master gland, because almost all of its hormones direct the activity of target glands elsewhere in the body. In turn, the anterior pituitary gland is controlled by the hypothalamus.

The **adrenal glands** are instrumental in regulating moods, energy level, and the ability to cope with stress (Ferreira & others, 2007). Each adrenal gland secretes epinephrine (also called adrenaline) and norepinephrine (also called noradrenaline). Unlike most hormones, epinephrine and norepinephrine act quickly. Epinephrine helps a person get ready for an emergency by acting on smooth muscles, the heart, stomach, intestines, and sweat glands. In addition, epinephrine stimulates the reticular formation, which in turn arouses the sympathetic nervous system, and this system subsequently excites the adrenal glands to produce more epinephrine. Norepinephrine also alerts the individual to emergency situations by interacting with the pituitary and the liver. You may remember that norepinephrine functions as a neurotransmitter when it is released by neurons. In the adrenal glands, norepinephrine is released as a hormone. In both instances, norepinephrine conveys information—in the first case, to neurons; in the second case, to glands (Mader, 2008).

adrenal glands Important endocrine glands that are instrumental in regulating moods, energy level, and the ability to cope with stress.

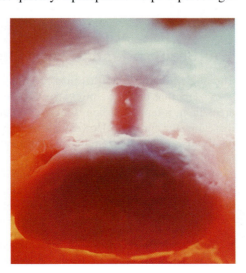

FIGURE 3.22

The Pituitary Gland The pituitary gland, which hangs by a short stalk from the hypothalamus, regulates the hormone production of many of the body's endocrine glands. Here it is enlarged 30 times.

REVIEW, ASSESS, AND SHARPEN YOUR THINKING

Review

4 State what the endocrine system is and explain how it affects behavior.
  • Describe the endocrine system, its glands, and their functions.

Assess

1. Which part of the endocrine system is known as the master gland?
   A. adrenal gland
   B. pituitary gland
   C. pancreas
   D. ovaries or testes

2. Which structure controls the pituitary gland?
   A. hypothalamus
   B. adrenal gland
   C. hormones
   D. basal ganglia

3. Which of the following statements is true?
   A. Hormones are created by neurons, whereas neurotransmitters are created by glands.
   B. Epinephrine is created by both neurons and glands.
   C. The endocrine system works chemically, whereas the nervous system works electrically.
   D. Dopamine is an example of a hormone.

Sharpen Your Thinking

Is the behavior of animals such as rats, rabbits, and bulls more likely to be strongly controlled by hormones than that of humans? In answering this question, think about the differences in the structures of the brains of humans and those animals that were described earlier in the chapter.

5 Brain Damage, Plasticity, and Repair

Describe the brain's capacity for recovery and repair.

Recall from the discussion of the brain's important characteristics earlier in the chapter that plasticity is an example of the brain's remarkable adaptability. Neuroscientists have studied plasticity especially following brain damage and have charted the brain's ability to repair itself (Greenberg & Jin, 2006; Sabatini, 2007). Brain damage can produce horrific effects, including paralysis, sensory loss, memory loss, and personality deterioration. When such damage occurs, can the brain recover some or all of its functions? Recovery from brain damage varies considerably, depending on the age of the individual and the extent of the damage (Kochanek, 2006; Nelson, Thomas, & de Haan, 2006).

The Brain's Plasticity and Capacity for Repair

The human brain shows the most plasticity in young children before the functions of the cortical regions become entirely fixed (Leblanc & others, 2006). For example, if the speech areas in an infant's left hemisphere are damaged, the right hemisphere assumes much of this language function. However, after age 5, damage to the left hemisphere can permanently disrupt language ability. We further examine the brain's plasticity in Chapter 4 on development throughout the life span.

A key factor in recovery is whether some or all of the neurons in an affected area are just damaged or are completely destroyed (Bahr & Lingor, 2006). If the neurons have not been destroyed, brain function often becomes restored over time.

There are three ways in which repair of the damaged brain might take place:

• *Collateral sprouting,* in which the axons of some healthy neurons adjacent to damaged cells grow new branches (Deller & others, 2006).

Actor Patricia Neal suffered a stroke when she was 39 years old. The stroke paralyzed one of her legs and left her unable to read, write, or speak. However, an intensive rehabilitation program and the human brain's plasticity allowed her to recover her functioning to the point that she resumed her career as an actor 4 years later.

- *Substitution of function,* in which the damaged region's function is taken over by another area or areas of the brain.
- *Neurogenesis,* the process by which new neurons are generated. Researchers have found that neurogenesis does occur in mammals such as mice (Gould & others, 1999). Also, exercise and a complex environment can generate new brain cells in mice. It is now accepted that neurogenesis can occur in humans, but to date the presence of new neurons has only been documented in the hippocampus, which is involved in memory, and the olfactory bulb, which is involved in the sense of smell (Elder, De Gasperi, & Gama Sosa, 2006). If researchers can discover how new neurons are generated, possibly the information can be used to fight degenerative diseases of the brain such as Alzheimer disease and Parkinson disease (Brinton & Wang, 2006).

Brain Tissue Implants

The brain naturally recovers some functions that are lost following damage, but not all. Recent research has generated considerable excitement about *brain grafts*—implants of healthy tissue into damaged brains (Farrington & others, 2006). The potential success of brain grafts is much better when brain tissue from the fetal stage (an early stage in prenatal development) is used (Dobkin, Curt, & Guest, 2006; Shanthly & others, 2006). The neurons of the fetus are still growing and have a much higher probability of making connections with other neurons than do the neurons of adults. In a number of studies, researchers have damaged part of an adult rat's (or some other animal's) brain, waited until the animal recovered as much as possible by itself, and assessed its behavioral deficits. Then they took the corresponding area of a fetal rat's brain and transplanted it into the damaged brain of the adult rat. In these studies, the rats that received the brain transplants demonstrated considerable behavioral recovery (Dunnett, 1989).

The late actor Christopher Reeve became paralyzed as the result of a horse riding accident during a competition. Reeve and his wife, Dana, with whom he is shown, worked tirelessly to promote stem cell research.

Might such brain grafts be successful with humans suffering from brain damage? Research suggests that they might, but finding donors is a problem (Ghen & others, 2006). Aborted fetuses are a possibility, but using them as a source of graft tissue raises ethical issues. Another type of treatment has been attempted with individuals who have Parkinson disease, a neurological disorder that affects about a million people in the United States (Clarke & Moore, 2007). Parkinson disease impairs coordinated movement to the point that just walking across a room can be a major ordeal. In one study, brain grafts of embryonic dopamine neurons from aborted fetuses into individuals with Parkinson disease resulted in a decrease of negative symptoms in individuals under 60 years of age but not in patients over 60 (Freed & others, 2001).

In another study, neuronal cells were transplanted into stroke victims (Kondziolka & others, 2000). The motor and cognitive skills of 12 patients who had experienced strokes improved markedly after the healthy neuron cells were implanted in the midbrain.

The potential for brain grafts also exists for individuals with Alzheimer disease, which is characterized by progressive decline in intellectual functioning resulting from the degeneration of neurons that function in memory (Eve & Sanberg, 2007). Such degenerative changes can be reversed in rats (Gage & Bjorklund, 1986). As yet, though, no successful brain grafts have been reported for Alzheimer patients.

Perhaps one of the most heated debates in recent years has concerned the use of human embryonic stem cells in research and treatment (Bianchi & Fisk, 2007; Holden, 2007). The human body contains more than 220 different types of cells, but stem cells are unique because they are primitive cells that have the capacity to develop into most types of human cells. Stem cells were first harvested from embryos by researchers at the University of Wisconsin, Madison, and Johns Hopkins University, in 1998. Because of their amazing plasticity, stem cells could potentially be used to replace a variety of damaged cells in the human body, including those involved in spinal cord injury, brain damage, and so on. Typically, researchers have harvested the stem cells from frozen embryos left over from in vitro fertilization procedures. In these procedures, a number of eggs, or ova, are collected from a woman's ovaries in order to be fertilized in a lab (rather than in the woman's body). In successful in vitro fertilization, the ova are brought together with sperm, producing human embryos. Because the procedure is difficult and delicate, doctors typically fertilize a large number of eggs with the hope that some will survive when implanted in the woman's uterus. In the typical procedure, there are leftover embryos. These embryos are in the *blastocyst* stage, which occurs 5 days after conception. At this stage the embryo has not yet attached to the uterus. The blastocyst has no brain, no central nervous system, and no mouth—it is an undifferentiated ball of cells.

Some supporters of stem cell technology (among them, the late actor Christopher Reeve, 2000) emphasize that we might relieve a great deal of human suffering by using these cells for research and treatment. Opponents of abortion disagree with the use of stem cells in research or treatment because the embryos die when the stem cells are removed. But in fact, leftover embryos are likely to be destroyed in any case. A compromise settled on by President George W. Bush was to permit research to continue only on existing cell lines but to allow no new lines to be harvested.

REVIEW, ASSESS, AND SHARPEN YOUR THINKING

Review

5 **Describe the brain's capacity for recovery and repair.**
- State the factors that favor recovery of function in damaged brains, and list three ways in which the brain may recover.
- Discuss the possibility of repairing damaged brains with tissue grafts and stem cells.

Assess

1. **Neurogenesis has been demonstrated in which of the following parts of the brain?**
   A. frontal lobe
   B. pons
   C. Broca's area
   D. hippocampus

2. **Which of the following statements is correct?**
   A. Brain grafts are easier to obtain than stem cells.
   B. Both brain grafts and stem cells are obtained from aborted fetuses.
   C. Both brain grafts and stem cells have been extensively used in humans.
   D. Stem cells can be obtained from embryos.

3. **Which of the following is true about stem cells?**
   A. Stem cells are undifferentiated and could be used to replace many different cells.

B. Stem cells have only been demonstrated to be effective at mimicking endocrine cells.
   C. Stem cells can be easily obtained from living adults.
   D. Currently, the United States government allows new embryos to be created for stem cell research.

4. **The creation of new neurons is known as**
   A. blasocystic regeneration
   B. neurogenesis
   C. plasticity
   D. collateral sprouting

5. **Which of the following statements is correct?**
   A. Neurogenesis refers to one area of the brain taking over the functions of another.
   B. Collateral sprouting refers to healthy neurons growing new branches when close to damaged neurons.
   C. Both neurogenesis and collateral sprouting must be present in order for brain repair to occur.
   D. Plasticity is most evident in middle age.

Sharpen Your Thinking

Suppose someone has suffered mild brain damage. What questions might you ask to determine whether the person's brain will likely be able either to compensate or to repair itself?

6 Genetics and Behavior

Explain how genetics increases our understanding of behavior.

In addition to the brain and nervous system, other aspects of our physiology also have consequences for psychological processes. Genes are one important contributor to these processes.

Chromosomes, Genes, and DNA

Within the human body are literally trillions of cells. The nucleus of each human cell contains 46 **chromosomes,** which are threadlike structures that come in 23 pairs, one member of each pair originating from each parent. Chromosomes contain the remarkable substance **deoxyribonucleic acid,** or **DNA,** a complex molecule that carries genetic information. **Genes,** the units of hereditary information, are short segments of chromosomes composed of DNA. Genes enable cells to reproduce and manufacture the proteins that are necessary for maintaining life. The relation among cells, chromosomes, genes, and DNA is illustrated in Figure 3.23.

The Human Genome Project recently documented that humans have exactly 21,774 genes (Ensembl Human, 2007). When these 21,000-plus genes from one parent combine at conception with the same amount of genes from the other parent, the number of possibilities are staggering. Although scientists are still a long way from unraveling all the mysteries about the way genes work, some aspects of this process are well understood, starting with the fact that multiple genes interact to give rise to observable characteristics (Lewis, 2007).

In some gene pairs, one gene is dominant over the other. If one gene of a pair is dominant and one is recessive, according to the **dominant-recessive genes principle,** the dominant gene overrides the recessive gene. A recessive gene exerts its influence only if both genes of a pair are recessive. If you inherit a recessive gene from only one parent, you may never know you carry the gene. In the world of dominant-recessive genes, brown eyes, farsightedness, and dimples rule over blue eyes, nearsightedness, and freckles. If you inherit a recessive gene for a trait from both of your parents, you will show the trait. That is why two brown-eyed parents can have a blue-eyed child: Each parent would have a dominant gene for brown eyes and a recessive gene for blue eyes. Because dominant genes override

chromosomes Threadlike structures that contain genes and DNA. Humans have 23 chromosome pairs in the nucleus of every cell. Each parent contributes one chromosome to each pair.

deoxyribonucleic acid (DNA) A complex molecule that contains genetic information; makes up chromosomes.

genes The units of hereditary information. They are short segments of chromosomes, composed of DNA.

dominant-recessive genes principle The principle that, if one gene of a pair governing a given characteristic (such as eye color) is dominant and one is recessive, the dominant gene overrides the recessive gene. A recessive gene exerts its influence only if both genes in a pair are recessive.

FIGURE 3.23

Cells, Chromosomes, Genes, and DNA

(*Left*) The body contains trillions of cells, which are the basic structural units of life. Each cell contains a central structure, the nucleus. (*Middle*) Chromosomes and genes are located in the nucleus of the cell. Chromosomes are made up of threadlike structures composed mainly of DNA molecules. (*Right*) A gene is a segment of DNA that contains the hereditary code. The structure of DNA resembles a spiral ladder.

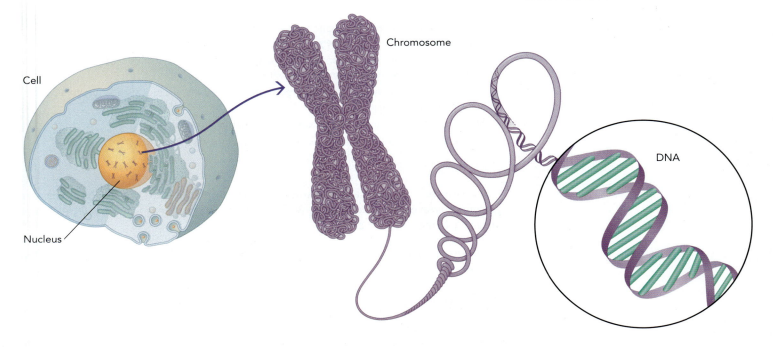

Cell

Nucleus

Chromosome

DNA

PSYCHOLOGY AND LIFE

The Human Genome Project and Your Genetic Future

The Human Genome Project, begun in the 1970s, has made stunning progress in mapping the human genome. The Human Genome Project has linked specific DNA variations with increased risk for a number of diseases and conditions, including Huntington disease (in which the central nervous system deteriorates), some forms of cancer, asthma, diabetes, hypertension, and Alzheimer disease (Reiman, 2007; Woodward, Lucci, & Cristofanilli, 2007). Other documented DNA variations affect the way people react to certain drugs.

A positive result from the Human Genome Project. Shortly after Andrew Gobea was born, his cells were genetically altered to prevent his immune system from failing.

Every individual carries a number of DNA variations that might predispose that person to a serious physical disease or mental disorder. Identifying these flaws could enable doctors to estimate an individual's disease risks, recommend healthy lifestyle regimens, and prescribe the safest and most effective drugs. A decade or two from now, parents of a newborn baby may be able to leave the hospital with a full genome analysis of their offspring that reveals various disease risks.

However, mining DNA variations to discover health risks might increasingly threaten an individual's ability to obtain and hold jobs, obtain insurance, and keep genetic profiles private. For example, should an airline pilot or a neurosurgeon, who one day may develop a disorder that makes the hands shake, be required to leave that job early?

Answering the following questions should encourage you to think further about issues involved in our genetic future (NOVA, 2001):

- Would you want yourself or a loved one to be tested for a gene that increases your risk for a disease but does not determine whether you will actually develop the disease?

- Would you want yourself and your mate tested before having offspring to determine your risk for having a child who is likely to contract various diseases?

- Should testing of fetuses be restricted to traits that are commonly considered to have negative outcomes, such as Huntington disease?

- Should altering a newly conceived embryo's genes to improve qualities such as intelligence, appearance, and strength be allowed?

- Should employers be permitted access to your genetic information?

- Should life insurance companies have access to your genetic information?

recessive genes, the parents have brown eyes. However, the child can inherit a recessive gene for blue eyes from each parent. With no dominant gene to override them, the recessive genes make the child's eyes blue.

Unlike eye color, complex human characteristics such as personality and intelligence are likely influenced by many different genes. The term *polygenic inheritance* is used to describe the influences of multiple genes on behavior.

The Study of Genetics

Historically speaking, genetics is a relatively young science. Its origins go back to the mid-nineteenth century, when an Austrian monk named Gregor Mendel studied heredity in generations of pea plants. By cross-breeding plants with different characteristics and noting the characteristics of the offspring, Mendel discovered predictable patterns of heredity and laid the foundation for modern genetics. Today researchers continue to apply Mendel's methods, as well as modern technology, in their quest to expand our knowledge of genetics. This section discusses three ways to study genetics: molecular genetics, selective breeding, and behavior genetics.

Molecular Genetics   The field of *molecular genetics* involves the actual manipulation of genes using technology to determine their effect on behavior. There is currently a great deal of enthusiasm about the use of molecular genetics to discover the specific locations on genes that determine an individual's susceptibility to many diseases and other aspects of health and well-being (Hartwell, 2008; Klug, Cummings, & Spencer, 2007).

The term *genome* refers to the complete set of instructions for making an organism. A genome contains the master blueprint for all cellular structures and activities for the life span of the organism. Read about the Human Genome Project and its possible applications in the Psychology and Life feature.

Selective Breeding   *Selective breeding* is a genetic method in which organisms are chosen for reproduction based on how much of a particular trait they display. Mendel developed this technique in his studies of pea plants. A more recent example involving behavior is the classic selective breeding study conducted by Robert Tryon (1940). He chose to study maze-running ability in rats. After he trained a large number of rats to run a complex maze, he then mated the rats that were the best at maze running ("maze bright") with each other and the ones that were the worst ("maze dull") with each other. He continued this process with 21 generations of rats. As Figure 3.24 shows, after several generations, the maze-bright rats significantly outperformed the maze-dull rats.

Selective breeding studies have demonstrated that genes are an important influence on behavior, but that does not mean that experience is unimportant (Bronikowski & others, 2006). For example, in another study, maze-bright and maze-dull rats were reared in one of two environments: (1) an impoverished environment that consisted of a barren wire-mesh group cage or (2) an enriched environment that contained tunnels, ramps, visual displays, and other stimulating objects (Cooper & Zubeck, 1958). When they reached maturity, only the maze-dull rats that had been reared in an impoverished environment made more maze-learning errors than the maze-bright rats.

An example of recent research using selective breeding involves drinking alcohol. The alcohol-preferring or "P" rat was developed by selective breeding to examine alcohol drinking (Bell & others, 2006). Genetically selected P rats show a predisposition for binge drinking.

Behavior Genetics   *Behavior genetics* is the study of the degree and nature of heredity's influence on behavior. Behavior genetics is less invasive than molecular genetics and selective breeding. Using methods such as the *twin study,* behavior geneticists examine the extent to which individuals are shaped by their heredity and their environmental experiences (Plomin, DeFries, & Fulker, 2007).

In the most common type of twin study, the behavioral similarity of identical twins is compared with the behavioral similarity of fraternal twins (Whitfield & others, 2007). *Identical twins* develop from a single fertilized egg that splits into two genetically identical embryos, each of which becomes a person. *Fraternal twins* develop from separate eggs and separate sperm, and so they are genetically no more similar than non-twin siblings. They may even be of different sexes.

By comparing groups of identical and fraternal twins, behavior geneticists capitalize on the fact that identical twins are more similar genetically than are fraternal twins. In one

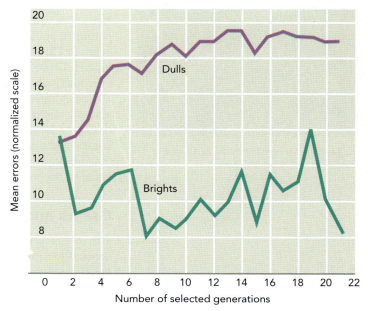

FIGURE 3.24

Results of Tryon's Selective Breeding Experiment with Maze-Bright and Maze-Dull Rats These results demonstrate genetic influences on behavior.

The twin-study method allows behavior geneticists to investigate the extent to which individuals are shaped respectively by their heredity and by their environment.

twin study, 7,000 pairs of Finnish identical and fraternal twins were compared on the personality traits of extraversion (being outgoing) and neuroticism (being psychologically unstable) (Rose & others, 1988). The identical twins were much more alike than the fraternal twins on both of these personality traits, suggesting that genes influence both traits.

One problem with twin studies is that adults might stress the similarities of identical twin children more than those of fraternal twins, and identical twins might perceive themselves as a "set" and play together more than fraternal twins do. If so, observed similarities in identical twins might be more strongly influenced by environmental factors than usually thought.

In another type of twin study, researchers evaluate identical twins who have been reared in separate environments. If their behavior is similar, the assumption is that heredity has played an important role in shaping their behavior. This strategy is the basis for the Minnesota Study of Twins Reared Apart, directed by Thomas Bouchard and his colleagues (1996). They bring identical twins who have been reared apart to Minneapolis from all over the world to study their behavior. They ask thousands of questions about their family, childhood, interests, and values. Detailed medical histories are obtained, including information about diet, smoking, and exercise habits.

One pair of twins in the Minnesota study, Jim Springer and Jim Lewis, were separated at 4 weeks of age and did not see each other again until they were 39 years old. They had an uncanny number of similarities, even though they had lived apart. For example, they both worked as part-time deputy sheriffs, had vacationed in Florida, had owned Chevrolets, had dogs named Toy, and had married and divorced women named Betty. Both liked math but not spelling. Both were good at mechanical drawing. Both put on 10 pounds at about the same time in their lives, and both started suffering headaches at 18 years of age. They did have a few differences. For example, one expressed himself better orally, and the other was more proficient at writing. One parted his hair over his forehead; the other wore his hair slicked back with sideburns.

Critics argue that some of the separated twins in the Minnesota study had been together several months prior to their adoption, that some had been reunited prior to testing (in certain cases, for a number of years), that adoption agencies often put identical twins in similar homes, and that even strangers are likely to have some coincidental similarities (Joseph, 2006). Still, it seems unlikely that all of the similarities in the identical twins reared apart could be due to experience alone.

The Jim twins: Springer (right) and Lewis were unaware of each other for 39 years.

Genes and the Environment

The role of genetics in some characteristics may seem pretty obvious. How tall you are depends to a large degree on how tall your parents are. But imagine a person growing up in a severely impoverished environment—with poor nutrition, inadequate shelter, little or no medical care, and a mother who had received no prenatal care. This person may have genes that call for the height of an NBA or WNBA center, but without environmental support for this genetic capacity, he or she may never reach that "genetically programmed" height. Thus, the relation between a person's genes and the actual person we see before us is not a perfect, isomorphic one. Even for a characteristic such as height, genes do not fully determine where a person will stand on this variable. We need to account for the role of environmental factors in the actual characteristics we see in the fully grown person.

If the environment matters for an apparently simple characteristic such as height, then imagine the role it might play in complex characteristics such as traits and intelligence. For these psychological characteristics, genes are, again, not directly reflected in the characteristics of the person. Rather, there is a probabilistic relationship between one's genetic heritage and the actual manifestations of this genetic information. To account for this gap between genes and actual observable characteristics, scientists make a distinction between a genotype and a phenotype. A **genotype** is a person's genetic heritage, his or her actual genetic material. A **phenotype** is the individual's observable characteristics. The phenotype is influenced by the genotype but also by environmental factors. *Phenotype* refers to both physical and psychological characteristics. Consider a trait such as extraversion, a person's tendency to be outgoing and sociable. Even if we knew the exact genetic recipe for extraversion, we still could not perfectly predict a person's level of (phenotypic) extraversion from his or her genes, because at least some of this trait comes from the person's experience.

One of the big surprises of the Human Genome Project was a report indicating that humans have only 21,000+ genes (Ensembl Human, 2007). Scientists had thought that humans had as many as 100,000 or more genes and that each gene programmed just one protein. In fact, humans have far more proteins than they have genes, so there cannot be a one-to-one correspondence between genes and proteins (Commoner, 2002; Moore, 2001). Each gene is not translated, in automatonlike fashion, into one and only one protein. A gene does not act independently, as emphasized by developmental psychologist David Moore in his book *The Dependent Gene* (2001).

Rather than being a group of independent genes, the human genome consists of many genes that collaborate both with each other and with nongenetic factors inside and outside the body. The collaboration operates at many points. For example, the cellular machinery mixes, matches, and links small pieces of DNA to reproduce the genes, and that machinery is influenced by what is going on around it.

Whether a gene is turned "on"—working to assemble proteins—is also a matter of collaboration. The activity of genes (*genetic expression*) is affected by their environment (Gottlieb, 2007). For example, hormones that circulate in the blood make their way into the cell where they can turn genes "on" and "off." And the flow of hormones can be affected by environmental conditions, such as light, day length, nutrition, and behavior. Numerous studies have shown that external events outside of the original cell and the person, as well as events inside the cell, can excite or inhibit gene expression (Gottlieb, 2007). For example, one recent study revealed that an increase in the concentration of stress hormones such as cortisol produced a 5-fold increase in DNA damage (Flint & others, 2007).

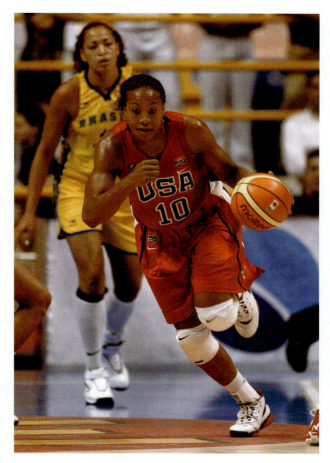

Our height depends significantly on the genes we inherit. But even if we have genes that call for the stature of a basketball center, we may not reach that "genetically programmed" height if we lack good nutrition, adequate shelter, and medical care.

genotype An individual's genetic heritage; his or her actual genetic material.

phenotype The expression of an individual's genotype in observable, measurable characteristics.

 REVIEW, ASSESS, AND SHARPEN YOUR THINKING

Review

6 Explain how genetics increases our understanding of behavior.

- Discuss the structures and functions of chromosomes, genes, and DNA.
- Describe three methods for studying genetics.
- Summarize the links between genes and the environment.

Assess

1. _____ refers to our genetic makeup, whereas _____ refers to the expression of that genetic makeup.
   - A. Genotype, phenotype
   - B. Phenotype, genotype
   - C. Dependent gene, independent gene
   - D. Independent gene, dependent gene

2. An experimental psychologist found that some cats are more apt to walk on a leash than others. She then separated the two groups of cats and allowed the cats to only reproduce with cats that had the same propensity to walk on a leash. She then examined the ability of the cats' offspring to walk on a leash. Her study is an example of
   - A. molecular genetics.
   - B. behavior genetics.
   - C. selective breeding.
   - D. the dominant-recessive genes principle.

3. According to the dominant-recessive genes principle, if brown hair is a dominant trait, then two brown-haired parents could have a blonde-haired child if
   - A. blonde hair is a selective trait.
   - B. neither parent had a gene for brown hair.
   - C. one parent had a gene for blonde hair but the other did not.
   - D. both parents had a recessive gene for blonde hair.

4. How many chromosomes do we have?
   - A. 16
   - B. 23
   - C. 46
   - D. 21,774

5. What is the relationship between chromosomes, genes, and DNA?
   - A. DNA is made up of chromosomes; there are two genes on each DNA.
   - B. Chromosomes are made up of DNA; genes are DNA segments.
   - C. Genes are made up of chromosomes; DNA allows the genes to combine together.
   - D. Chromosomes are made up of both genes and DNA.

Sharpen Your Thinking

What are some possible ethical issues regarding genetics and development that might arise in the future?

7 Psychology's Biological Foundations and Health and Wellness

Describe the role of the biological foundations of human psychology in the body's stress response.

Is stress a sign of our times? According to the American Academy of Family Physicians, two-thirds of office visits to family doctors these days are for stress-related symptoms. Stress is believed to be a major contributor to coronary heart disease, cancer, lung problems, accidental injuries, cirrhosis of the liver, and suicide—six of the leading causes of death in the United States. Antianxiety drugs and ulcer medications are among the best-selling prescription drugs in the United States. Further, people everywhere seem to be trying to reduce or counter the effects of excessive tension by jogging, going to health clubs, practicing various relaxation regimens, and following special diets. Even corporations have developed elaborate stress management programs. No one knows whether we truly experience more stress than our parents and grandparents did, but it *seems* as if we do. The nervous system that has been our focus in this chapter is central to the experience of stress—and also is itself affected by stress.

Stress and Stressors

Initially, the word *stress* was loosely borrowed from physics. Humans, it was thought, are in some ways similar to physical objects, such as metals, that resist moderate outside forces but lose their resiliency under greater pressure. But unlike metals, human beings can think and reason, and they experience a myriad of social and environmental circumstances that make defining stress far more complex in psychology than in physics (Hobfoll, 1989). Thus, in psychological terms, we can define **stress** as the response of individuals to **stressors,** which are the circumstances and events that threaten them and tax their coping abilities.

When we experience stress, our body readies itself to handle the assault of stress; a number of physiological changes take place. Those changes were the main interest of Hans Selye

stress The response of individuals to changes in circumstances and events that threaten their coping abilities.

stressors Circumstances and events that threaten individuals and tax their coping abilities.

(1974, 1983), the Austrian-born founder of stress research. Selye defined stress as the wear and tear on the body due to the demands placed on it. After observing patients with different problems—the death of someone close, loss of income, arrest for embezzlement—Selye concluded that any number of environmental events and stimuli will produce the same stress response. Regardless of which problem the patient had, similar symptoms appeared: loss of appetite, muscular weakness, and decreased interest in the world. You certainly know what stress feels like: Imagine, for example, that you show up for class one morning, and it looks as if everyone else knows that there is a test that day. You hear others talking about how much they studied and begin to get nervous: "Test? What test?!" You might start to sweat and your heart might be beating faster than usual. Sure enough, the professor shows up with a stack of exams; you are about to be tested on material you have not even thought about, much less studied.

That familiar feeling of anxiety can strike in response to many things—a near-miss car accident, a dental appointment, just having too much to do in too little time. The stress response begins with a "fight or flight" reaction. This reaction mobilizes the body's physiological resources quickly to prepare the organism to deal with threats to survival. Clearly, an unexpected exam is not literally a threat to your survival, but the human stress response is such that it can occur in response to any threat to personally important motives (Sapolsky, 2004).

The biological foundations of human psychology play a strong role throughout the stress response. When you feel your heart pounding and your hands sweating under stress, those experiences reveal the sympathetic nervous system in action. Recall that the sympathetic nervous system is the division of the autonomic nervous system that prepares you to take action when necessary. If you need to run away from a stressor, the sympathetic nervous system sends blood out to your extremities to get you ready to take off. When we undergo stress, we also experience the release of cortisol, a powerful hormone that we will examine later in this book. Cortisol in the brain allows us to focus our attention on what needs to be done *now*. For example, in an emergency, people sometimes report feeling strangely calm and just doing what has to be done, whether it is calling 911 or applying pressure to a cut. Such experiences show the good that cortisol can do for humans in times of extreme acute stress. Acute stress is the momentary stress that occurs in response to life experiences. When the scary situation ends, so does the acute stress.

However, most of the time when we experience stress, we are not in a live-or-die situation. Indeed, we can sometimes "stress ourselves out" just by thinking. *Chronic stress,* that is, stress that goes on continuously, may lead to persistent autonomic nervous system arousal and long-lasting high levels of testosterone in the brain. When the brain is bathed in testosterone for a long period of time, the testosterone that would be helpful in an acute stress reaction can become harmful. A chronically high level of cortisol in the brain actually *ages* the brain (Sapolsky, 2004). Chronic autonomic nervous system activity can be associated with the breakdown of the immune system as well. Recall that the parasympathetic nervous system is concerned with calming the body down and tending to systems in the body that require repair. If your body never stops reacting to stress, these maintenance functions are never taken care of. And the body breaks down.

Managing Stress Through Self-Talk

Clearly, chronic stress is best avoided. But this objective is easier said than done. Importantly, the brain, which is so deeply affected by chronic stress, is also the organ that can help us avoid chronic stress. When a challenging situation arises, is it inevitable that we see it as a threat? Perhaps we could use the brain's amazing abilities to interpret experience in a different way—one that is not so stressful. In the tragic play *Hamlet,* William Shakespeare noted that "there is nothing either good or bad, but thinking makes it so" (Act II, Scene 2). Might we use the brain's ability to reinterpret situations so they are not so likely to lead to stress? Many cognitive therapists believe that the process of *cognitive restructuring*—modifying the thoughts, ideas, and beliefs that sustain an individual's problems—can also be used to get people to think more positively and optimistically (Martin & Pear, 2007; Watson & Tharp, 2007). The process is often aided by changes in *self-talk* (also called *self-statements*), the soundless mental speech that we use when we think, plan, and

"I can't worry about that right now. I'm worrying about something else."

solve problems. Positive self-talk can foster the confidence that frees us to use our talents to the fullest. Because self-talk has a way of being self-fulfilling, unchallenged negative thinking can spell trouble. That is why it is so important to monitor your self-talk.

Several strategies can help you to monitor your self-talk. First, at random times during the day, ask yourself, "What am I saying to myself right now?" Then, if you can, write down your thoughts, along with a few notes about the situation you are in and how you are feeling. At the beginning, it is important to record your self-talk without any censorship. But your goal is to fine-tune your self-talk to make it as accurate and positive as possible.

Situations that you anticipate might be difficult for you also provide excellent opportunities to assess your self-talk. Write down a description of the coming event. Then ask yourself, "What am I saying to myself about this event?" If your thoughts are negative, think how you can use your strengths to turn these disruptive feelings into more positive ones and help turn a potentially difficult experience into a success. You can also use uncomfortable emotions or moods—such as stress, depression, and anxiety—as cues for listening to your self-talk. When such an emotion arises, identify the feeling as accurately as possible. Then ask yourself, "What was I saying to myself right before I started feeling this way?" or "What have I been saying to myself since I've been feeling this way?"

It may seem very difficult at first to change your thoughts about stressful life events. But keep in mind that when you change the way you think, you are literally forging new pathways in your brain. With practice, you can train your brain to recognize that the challenges that life presents are *just* challenges, not threats—that you can handle difficult circumstances. Your brain's remarkable ability to create a solution for dealing with life's problems might surprise you.

REVIEW, ASSESS, AND SHARPEN YOUR THINKING

Review

7 Describe the role of the biological foundations of human psychology in the body's stress response.
- Define stress and describe its physical symptoms and the body's stress response.
- Describe strategies for monitoring and adjusting your self-talk.

Assess

1. **Stress releases which hormone?**
   A. norepinephrine   B. epinephrine
   C. cortisol   D. progesterone

2. **Viewing an upcoming test as a challenge rather than something that will make you fail a course is an example of**
   A. negative self-talk.
   B. inevitable self-statements.
   C. cognitive restructuring.
   D. pessimistic realism.

3. **What is the difference between stress and a stressor?**
   A. Stress will cause stressors.
   B. A stressor is an event that taxes resources; stress is the reaction to the stressor.
   C. Stress is an event that taxes resources; a stressor is the reaction to the stressor.
   D. Stressors will cause stress.

4. **Why is chronic stress harmful?**
   A. Because it makes us feel badly about ourselves.
   B. Because it releases cortisol.
   C. Because it activates the sympathetic nervous system.
   D. Because it increases the body's maintenance functions.

Sharpen Your Thinking

Do you think life today, in the twenty-first century, might be more stressful than life 100 years ago? Why or why not?

1 THE NERVOUS SYSTEM

Discuss the nature and basic functions of the nervous system.

Characteristics

The nervous system is the body's electrochemical communication circuitry. Four important characteristics of the brain and nervous system are complexity, integration, adaptability, and electrochemical transmission. The brain's special ability to adapt and change is called plasticity.

Pathways in the Nervous System

Decision making in the nervous system occurs in specialized pathways of nerve cells. Three of these pathways involve sensory input, motor output, and neural networks.

Divisions of the Nervous System

The nervous system is divided into two main parts: central (CNS) and peripheral (PNS). The CNS consists of the brain and spinal cord. The PNS has two major divisions: somatic and autonomic. The autonomic nervous system consists of two main divisions: sympathetic and parasympathetic.

2 NEURONS

Explain what neurons are and how they process information.

Specialized Cell Structure

Neurons are cells that specialize in processing information. They make up the communication network of the nervous system. Glial cells perform supportive and nutritive functions for neurons. The three main parts of the neuron are the cell body, dendrite (receiving part), and axon (sending part). A myelin sheath encases and insulates most axons and speeds up transmission of neural impulses.

The Neural Impulse

A neuron sends information along its axon in the form of brief electric impulses or waves. Resting potential is the stable, slightly negative charge of an inactive neuron. When the electrical signals exceed a certain activation threshold, positively charged sodium ions rush into the neuron. The brief wave of electrical charge that sweeps down the axon is called the action potential. The neuron returns to a resting potential as positively charged potassium ions move out of it, returning the neuron to a negative charge. The action potential abides by the all-or-none principle: Its strength does not change during transmission.

Synapses and Neurotransmitters

To go from one neuron to another, information must be converted from an electrical impulse to a chemical messenger called a neurotransmitter. At the synapse where neurons meet, neurotransmitters are released into the narrow gap that separates them. There some neurotransmitter molecules attach to receptor sites on the receiving neuron, where they stimulate another electrical impulse. Neurotransmitters can be excitatory or inhibitory, depending on the nature of the neural impulse. Neurotransmitters include acetylcholine, GABA, norepinephrine, dopamine, serotonin, and endorphins. Most drugs that influence behavior do so mainly by mimicking neurotransmitters or interfering with their activity.

Neural Networks

Neural networks are clusters of neurons that are interconnected to process information.

3 STRUCTURES OF THE BRAIN AND THEIR FUNCTIONS

Identify the brain's levels and structures, and summarize the functions of its structures.

How Researchers Study the Brain and Nervous System

The main techniques used to study the brain are brain lesioning, staining, electrical recording, and brain imaging.

Levels of Organization in the Brain

The three major levels of the brain are the hindbrain, midbrain, and forebrain. The hindbrain is the lowest portion of the brain. The hindbrain's three main parts are the medulla (involved in controlling breathing and posture), cerebellum (involved in motor coordination), and pons (involved in sleep and arousal).

From the midbrain, many nerve-fiber systems ascend and descend to connect to higher and lower levels of the brain. The midbrain contains the reticular formation, which is involved in stereotypical patterns of behavior (such as walking and sleeping), and small groups of neurons that communicate with many areas in the brain. The brain stem consists of much of the hindbrain (excluding the cerebellum) and the midbrain.

The forebrain is the highest level of the brain. The key forebrain structures are the limbic system, thalamus, basal ganglia, hypothalamus, and cerebral cortex. The limbic system is involved in memory and emotion through its two structures, the amygdala (which plays roles in survival and emotion) and the hippocampus (which functions in the storage of memories). The thalamus is a forebrain structure that serves as an important relay station for processing information. The basal ganglia are forebrain structures that help to control and coordinate voluntary movements. The hypothalamus is a forebrain structure that monitors eating, drinking, and sex; directs the endocrine system through the pituitary gland; and is involved in emotion, stress, and reward.

The Cerebral Cortex

The cerebral cortex makes up most of the outer layer of the brain. Higher mental functions, such as thinking and planning, take place in the cerebral cortex. The wrinkled surface of the cerebral cortex is divided into hemispheres, each with four lobes: occipital, temporal, frontal, and parietal. There is considerable integration and connection between the brain's lobes. The somatosensory cortex processes information about body sensations. The motor cortex processes information about voluntary movement. Specific areas in the brain correspond to specific parts of the body and can be mapped on the cortex's surface. The association cortex, which makes up 75 percent of the cerebral cortex, is instrumental in integrating information, especially about the highest intellectual functions.

The Cerebral Hemispheres and Split-Brain Research

A controversial topic is the extent to which the brain's left and right hemispheres are involved in different functions. Two areas in the left hemisphere that involve specific language functions are Broca's area (speech) and Wernicke's area (comprehending language). The corpus callosum is a large bundle of fibers that connects the two hemispheres. Researchers have studied what happens when the corpus callosum has to be severed, as in some cases of severe epilepsy. Research suggests that the left brain is more dominant in processing verbal information (such as language) and the right brain in processing nonverbal information (such as spatial perception, visual recognition, and emotion). Nonetheless, in a normal individual whose corpus callosum is intact, both hemispheres of the cerebral cortex are involved in most complex human functioning.

Integration of Function in the Brain

Generally, brain function is integrated and involves connections between different parts of the brain. Pathways of neurons involved in a particular function, such as memory, are integrated across different parts and levels of the brain.

4 THE ENDOCRINE SYSTEM

State what the endocrine system is and explain how it affects behavior.

Endocrine System Structures and Functions

The endocrine glands release hormones directly into the bloodstream for distribution throughout the body. The pituitary gland is the master endocrine gland. The adrenal glands play important roles in moods, energy level, and ability to cope with stress.

5 BRAIN DAMAGE, PLASTICITY, AND REPAIR

Describe the brain's capacity for recovery and repair.

The Brain's Plasticity and Capacity for Repair

The human brain has considerable plasticity, although this plasticity is greater in young children than later in development. Three ways in which a damaged brain might repair itself are collateral sprouting, substitution of function, and neurogenesis.

Brain Tissue Implants

Brain grafts are implants of healthy tissue into damaged brains. Brain grafts are more successful when fetal tissue is used. Stem cell research is one controversial new area of science that may allow for new treatments of damage to the nervous system.

6 GENETICS AND BEHAVIOR

Explain how genetics increases our understanding of behavior.

Chromosomes, Genes, and DNA

Chromosomes are threadlike structures that occur in 23 pairs, one member of each pair coming from each parent. Chromosomes contain the genetic substance deoxyribonucleic acid (DNA). Genes, the units of hereditary information, are short segments of chromosomes composed of DNA. The dominant-recessive genes principle states that, if one gene of a pair is dominant and one is recessive, the dominant gene overrides the recessive gene.

The Study of Genetics

Two important concepts in the study of genetics are the genotype and phenotype. The genotype is an individual's actual genetic material. The phenotype refers to the observable characteristics of the person. Three methods of studying heredity's influence are molecular genetics, selective breeding, and behavior genetics. Two methods used by behavior geneticists are twin studies and adoption studies.

Genes and the Environment

Both genes and environment play a role in determining the phenotype of an individual. Even for characteristics in which genes play a large role (such as height and eye color), the environment plays a role.

7 PSYCHOLOGY'S BIOLOGICAL FOUNDATIONS AND HEALTH AND WELLNESS

Describe the role of the biological foundations of human psychology in the body's stress response.

Stress and Stressors

Stress is the body's response to changes in the environment. Stressors are those changes themselves. The body's stress response is largely a function of sympathetic nervous system activation that prepares us for action in the face of a threat. The stress response involves slowing down maintenance processes (such as our immune function and digestion) in favor of rapid action. Acute stress is an adaptive response, but chronic stress can have negative consequences for our health. Although stress may be inevitable, our reaction to a stressful event is largely a function of how we think about it.

Managing Stress Through Self-Talk

One way to manage stress is to change the way we think about important life changes. Construing an event as a challenge rather than a threat allows us to avoid the negative effects of stress. We can prevent and manage stress by modifying our thoughts, ideas, and beliefs about the meaning of life events. Self-talk refers to the soundless mental speech we use when we think, plan, and solve problems. Positive self-talk can foster the confidence that frees us to use our talents to the fullest.

Key Terms

nervous system, p. 73

plasticity, p. 73

afferent nerves, p. 74

efferent nerves, p. 74

neural networks, p. 74

central nervous system (CNS), p. 74

peripheral nervous system (PNS), p. 75

somatic nervous system, p. 75

autonomic nervous system, p. 75

sympathetic nervous system, p. 75

parasympathetic nervous system, p. 75

neurons, p. 76

glial cells, p. 76

cell body, p. 76

dendrites, p. 76

axon, p. 77

myelin sheath, p. 77

resting potential, p. 78

action potential, p. 79

all-or-none principle, p. 79

synapses, p. 79

neurotransmitters, p. 79

agonist, p. 82

antagonist, p. 82

hindbrain, p. 87

midbrain, p. 87

reticular formation, p. 87

brain stem, p. 87

forebrain, p. 88

limbic system, p. 89

thalamus, p. 89

basal ganglia, p. 89

hypothalamus, p. 89

cerebral cortex, p. 90

occipital lobe, p. 90

temporal lobe, p. 91

frontal lobe, p. 91

parietal lobe, p. 91

Assess Your Knowledge

1. The nervous system is divided into
   A. the brain and spinal cord.
   B. the somatic nervous system and the autonomic nervous system.
   C. the sympathetic nervous system and the parasympathetic nervous system.
   D. the central nervous system and the peripheral nervous system.

2. When you wake up in the middle of the night and stub your toe on the bed frame, which of the following informs your brain of what has happened?
   A. efferent nerves
   B. afferent nerves
   C. sympathetic nervous system
   D. parasympathetic nervous system

3. What is the resting potential of a neuron?
   A. 60 to 75 millivolts
   B. −60 to −75 millivolts
   C. 800 to 1000 millivolts
   D. −800 to −1000 millivolts

4. The _____ release neurotransmitters into the synaptic gap; the _____ receives neurotransmitters in the synaptic gap.
   A. Axon, cell body
   B. Cell body, axon
   C. Dendrite, terminal button
   D. Terminal button, dendrite

5. Which of the following is a natural opiate?
   A. serotonin
   B. oxytocin
   C. endorphins
   D. acetylcholine

6. Morphine is an agonist for which of the following?
   A. acetylcholine
   B. GABA
   C. serotonin
   D. endorphins

7. Which gland is most involved in preparing the body to respond to stress?
   A. pituitary gland
   B. thyroid gland
   C. parathyroid gland
   D. adrenal gland

8. Which structure is responsible for relaying information between the left and right hemispheres of the brain?
   A. association cortex
   B. corpus callosum
   C. Broca's area
   D. somatosensory cortex

9. The _____ lobe is involved in hearing.
   A. occipital
   B. parietal
   C. frontal
   D. temporal

10. Which method of brain imaging measures changes in glucose levels?
    A. MRI
    B. fMRI
    C. PET scan
    D. CT scan

11. A drug that blocks a neurotransmitter's effect is called a(n)
    A. synaptic gap.
    B. agonist.
    C. serotonin.
    D. antagonist.

12. The medulla is located in the
    A. hindbrain.
    B. midbrain.
    C. forebrain.
    D. cerebral cortex.

13. Which structure is responsible for regulating sleep?
    A. cerebellum
    B. hippocampus
    C. reticular formation
    D. thalamus

14. Phineas Gage sustained damage to the _____, which resulted in a change in his personality.
    A. occipital lobe
    B. parietal lobe
    C. frontal lobe
    D. temporal lobe

15. Aphasia refers to problems with
    A. visual processing.
    B. language processing.
    C. auditory processing.
    D. motor coordination.

Go to Appendix B for answers to these questions.

Apply Your Knowledge

1. Consider the four characteristics of the nervous system. Suppose you had to do without one of them. Which would you choose, and what would be the consequences of your decision for your behavior?

2. Do an Internet search for "nutrition" and "the brain." Examine the claims made by one or more of the websites. Based on what you learned in the chapter about the nervous system, how could nutrition affect brain function? Based on your scientific knowledge, how believable are the claims on the website?

3. Imagine that you could make one part of your brain twice as big as it is right now. Which part would it be, and how do you think your behavior would change as a result? What if you had to make another part of your brain half its current size? Which part would you choose to shrink, and what would the effects be?

4. Search the Web for information about a "happiness gene." How would you evaluate research on such a gene given what you have read in this book? What (if anything) would the existence of such a gene mean for your ability to find happiness in your life?

CHAPTER 4

HUMAN DEVELOPMENT

Experiencing Psychology

SHILOH NOUVEL JOLIE-PITT AND KYLIE JADE WALTON

On May 27, 2006, with a worldwide media frenzy as the backdrop, Shiloh Nouvel Jolie-Pitt was born to doting parents Angelina Jolie and Brad Pitt in the African country of Namibia. On that same day, about 383,999 other babies were born throughout the world, to much less fanfare and to far less famous parents. About 16,000 babies are born every hour; in fact, in the time it has taken you to read these few sentences, about 16 people have entered the world. Children are being born, literally, all the time, in homes and hospitals, at birthing centers, on highways, and even in parking lots—as was the case for Kylie Jade Walton, who was born in her parents' parked car outside a hospital in Vancouver, Washington, a couple of weeks before Shiloh Jolie-Pitt. Consider this: In that car, in that parking lot, there were two people, and then, miraculously, there were three.

Newborn babies are cute, fascinating and mysterious—a few pounds of complete enigma. Is it a boy or a girl? Whom does she look like? What will her personality and physical appearance be? What will she like?

Think about your own birthday—not the date or the gifts you want but the actual day you were born. You cannot remember it, but you know that you were much smaller, completely helpless, and full of possibilities. Those possibilities have been unfolding throughout your life, and here you are. How is it going so far? You are quite a bit taller and heavier, not to mention toilet trained. Some of these changes—physical growth, for instance—have "just happened." Some you have learned from instruction, and some have happened because you have wanted them to. Just as learning to walk was a developmental milestone, accomplishing the goals you set for yourself as a mature adult may also qualify as developmental changes. Consider what that word *mature* means to you. Who is the most mature person you know, and what characteristics make that individual mature? ▪

PREVIEW

This chapter explores the field of developmental psychology. Developmental psychologists are interested in tracking and understanding the changes that occur throughout a person's life—all the steps toward being the person you are now and the person you are becoming. We begin by examining the meaning of development and some key issues in the field. Then we review the processes of development throughout the life span: prenatally, during childhood, and in adolescence and adulthood. Finally we look at what developmental psychology has to say about health and wellness. Throughout, we consider how the active developer—whether he or she is an infant, a toddler, a teenager, or an adult—can influence the meaning of development itself.

1 Exploring Human Development

Explain how psychologists think about development.

Development refers to the pattern of continuity and change in human capabilities that occurs throughout the course of life. Most development involves growth, although it also consists of decline (for example, processing information becomes slower for older adults). Researchers who study development are intrigued by its universal characteristics and by its individual variations. The pattern of development is complex because it is the product of several processes:

- *Physical processes* involve changes in an individual's biological nature. Genes inherited from parents, the hormonal changes of puberty and menopause, and changes throughout life in the brain, height and weight, and motor skills all reflect the developmental role of biological processes. Psychologists refer to such biological growth processes as *maturation*.

- *Cognitive processes* involve changes in an individual's thought, intelligence, and language. Observing a colorful mobile as it swings above a crib, constructing a sentence about the future, imagining oneself as a movie star, memorizing a new telephone number—all these activities reflect the role of cognitive processes in development.

development The pattern of continuity and change in human capabilities that occurs throughout the course of life.

Human development is complex because it is the product of several processes. The hormonal changes of puberty, a baby's observation of a mobile, and an older couple's embrace reflect physical, cognitive, and socioemotional processes, respectively.

- *Socioemotional processes* involve changes in an individual's relationships with other people, changes in emotions, and changes in personality. An infant's smile in response to her mother's touch, a girl's development of assertiveness, an adolescent's joy at the senior prom, a young man's aggressiveness in sport, and an older couple's affection for each other all reflect the role of socioemotional processes.

Physical, cognitive, and socioemotional processes are intricately interwoven, as Figure 4.1 shows. For example, socioemotional processes shape cognitive processes, cognitive processes promote or restrict socioemotional processes, and physical processes influence cognitive processes. Although the three processes of development are discussed in separate sections of the chapter, keep in mind that you are studying the development of an integrated human being in whom body, mind, and emotion are interdependent.

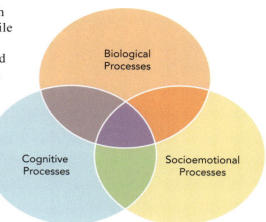

FIGURE 4.1

Developmental Changes Are the Result of Biological, Cognitive, and Socioemotional Processes
These processes are interwoven as individuals develop.

How Do Nature and Nurture Influence Development?

In Chapter 3 we examined the relation between genetics and behavior. We considered the concepts of *genotype* (the individual's genetic heritage—the actual genetic material) and *phenotype* (the person's observable characteristics). Although genes play an important role in human behavior, genes alone do not determine who we are. Genes exist within the context of a complex environment that is necessary for an organism to even exist. Environment includes all of the surrounding physical and social conditions and influences that affect the development of living things. Biologists who study even the simplest animals agree that separating the effects of the animals' genes from the effects of their environment is virtually impossible (Hartwell, 2008; Lewis, 2007).

Recall that the genotype may be expressed differently, depending on the environment. Thus, a person's observable and measurable characteristics (or phenotype) might not reflect his or her genetic heritage very precisely because of the particular experiences the person has had. For each genotype, a range of phenotypes can be expressed. An individual can inherit the genetic potential to grow very tall, but good nutrition will also be important in achieving that potential. In addition, while the environment may influence the expression of the genotype in the person, genotypic characteristics in turn may influence how the individual is treated in the environment. Thus, a child who is particularly physically attractive (a characteristic that is likely to be the result of genetics) may receive different treatment from the environment than one who is not. "The active genotype" means that genes, rather than passively waiting for the environment to "turn them on," may shape the treatment a person receives from the environment and in this way may exert a powerful force on the social world (Scarr, 1988, 1993).

Exploring Nature and Nurture   Related to the distinction between genotype and phenotype is a broader distinction between nature and nurture. The term **nature** refers to an organism's biological inheritance. The term **nurture** refers to an organism's environmental experiences. The interaction of nature and nurture, of genes and environment, influences every aspect of mind and behavior to a degree. Neither factor operates alone (Gottlieb, 2007; Mader, 2008; Rutter, 2007).

Psychologists are starting to agree that many complex behaviors have some genetic loading that makes people likely to develop in a particular way. But our actual development also depends on what we experience in our environment. And that environment is complex, as is the mixture of genes that we inherit. Environmental influences range from the things we lump together under "nurture" (such as parenting, family dynamics, peer relations, schooling, and neighborhood quality) to biological encounters (such as viruses, birth complications, and even cellular activities).

Development is not best understood as all nature or nurture. It is an *interaction* of the two. Heredity and environment operate together to produce temperament, height, weight,

nature An organism's biological inheritance.

nurture An organism's environmental experiences.

ability to pitch a baseball, reading ability, and so on (Gottlieb, Wahlsten, & Lickliter, 2006). According to William Greenough (2001), who studies heredity and environment issues, "The interaction of heredity and environment is so extensive that to ask which is more important, nature or nurture, is like asking which is more important to a rectangle, height or width?"

Optimal Experiences Although both nature and nurture are important in development, so is the actual developing human being. Developmental psychologists are increasingly acknowledging the active role of the person in his or her own development (Brandstadter, 2006). You might think of nature and nurture as the raw ingredients of yourself as a person; but you yourself take those ingredients and make them into the person you are. Indeed, some psychologists believe we can develop beyond what our genetic inheritance and our environment give us. They argue that a key aspect of development involves seeking optimal experiences in life (Massimini & Delle Fave, 2000). They cite examples of individuals who go beyond simple biological adaptation and actively choose from the environment the things that serve their purposes. These individuals build and construct their own lives, authoring a unique developmental path.

In our effort to experience our lives in optimal ways, we develop *life themes* that involve activities, social relationships, and life goals (Csikszentmihalyi & Rathunde, 1998; Nakamura & Csikszentmihalyi, 2002; Rathunde & Csikszentmihalyi, 2006). One example of an optimal life theme is to make the decision to go beyond selfish reproduction and competition in order to foster understanding, tolerance, and cooperation among all human beings.

Some individuals are more successful at constructing optimal life experiences than others. Among individuals who have succeeded are Franklin Roosevelt, Martin Luther King, Jr., Mother Teresa, Nelson Mandela, Bill and Melinda Gates, and Oprah Winfrey. These people looked for and found meaningful life themes as they developed. Their lives were not restricted to simple biological survival or passive acceptance of environmental dictates.

Do Early Experiences Rule Us for Life?

A key question in developmental psychology is the extent to which "the child is the father of the man"—that is, how much do childhood experiences determine aspects of later life? As psychologists study development, they debate whether early experiences or later experiences are more important (Baltes, Lindenberger, & Staudinger, 2006; Laible & Thompson, 2007). Some psychologists believe that, unless infants experience warm, nurturing caregiving in the first year or so of life, they will not develop to their full potential (Sroufe & others, 2005). This *early experience* doctrine suggests that, after a period of early development, we become relatively fixed and permanent in our makeup. It rests on the belief that each life is an unbroken trail on which a psychological quality can be traced back to its origin (Kagan, 1992, 2003).

In contrast, some psychologists emphasize the power of later experience and liken development in later years to the ebb and flow of a river. The *later experience* advocates argue that children are responsive to change and that sensitive caregiving is just as important later as it is earlier. A number of life-span developmentalists, who focus on both children and adults, stress that too little attention has been given to adult development (Baltes, Lindenberger, & Staudinger, 2006; Birren & Schaie, 2006; Schaie, 2007). They argue that, although early experiences are important contributors to development, they are not necessarily more important than later experiences.

Most developmentalists do not take extreme positions on the issue of early versus later experience (Tomasello, 2006). They believe that, although early experience can create a foundation for later experience, both make important contributions to development. Indeed, in talking about life-span development, we make the assumption that real developmental changes occur throughout life.

Microsoft founder Bill Gates and his wife, Melinda, along with TV talk show diva Oprah Winfrey, have quested after—and carved out—meaningful life experiences as they have progressed through their development.

REVIEW, ASSESS, AND SHARPEN YOUR THINKING

Review

1 Explain how psychologists think about development.

- Evaluate the influences of nature and nurture on human development.
- Discuss the influence of early and later experiences on human development.

Assess

1. Nature is to _____ as nurture is to _____.
   - A. genotype, phenotype
   - B. phenotype, genotype
   - C. development, maturation
   - D. maturation, development

2. Which of the following is not a developmental process?
   - A. physical processes
   - B. cognitive processes
   - C. genotype processes
   - D. socioemotional processes

3. The late Diana, Princess of Wales, devoted a considerable amount of her time on efforts to eradicate land mines. This endeavor is an example of
   - A. a life theme.
   - B. an early experience.
   - C. a socioemotional process.
   - D. a phenotype.

4. Which of the following is an example of an optimal experience?
   - A. Cooking food to eat
   - B. Having sex
   - C. Volunteering time teaching adults to read
   - D. Competing with others

Sharpen Your Thinking

Your development as a human being is determined by multiple factors. Think about what you are like as a person today and reflect on the processes in your development that made you who you are.

2 Child Development

Describe children's development from prenatal stages to adolescence.

How children develop has special importance because children are the future of any society. Our journey through childhood begins with conception and continues through the elementary school years. In this section we focus on the three fundamental developmental processes—physical, cognitive, and socioemotional. We revisit the nature and nurture theme along the journey, and also explore the importance of taking a positive view of childhood.

Prenatal Development

Many special things have taken place in your life since you were born. But imagine . . . at one time you were a microscopic organism floating in a sea of fluid in your mother's womb. As the nineteenth-century American poet-essayist Samuel Taylor remarked, "The history of man for nine months preceding his birth is probably far more interesting and contains more stunning events than all the years that follow."

The Course of Prenatal Development   *Conception* occurs when a single sperm cell from the male penetrates the female's ovum (egg). This process is also called *fertilization.* A *zygote* is a fertilized egg.

Prenatal development is divided into three periods:

- *Germinal period—weeks 1 and 2:* The germinal period begins with conception. The fertilized egg, a zygote, is a single cell with 23 chromosomes from the mother and 23 from the father. After 1 week and many cell divisions, the zygote is made up of 100 to 150 cells. By the end of 2 weeks, the mass of cells has attached to the uterine wall.

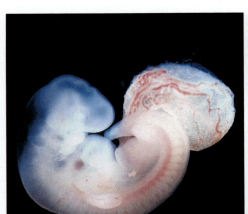

(a)

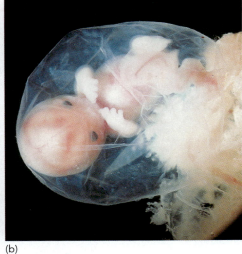

(b)

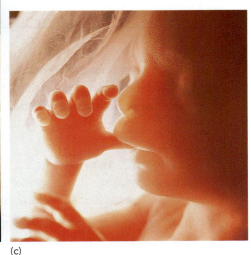

(c)

FIGURE 4.2

From Embryo to Fetus (*a*) At about 4 weeks, an embryo is about 0.2 inch (less than 1 centimeter) long. The head, eyes, and ears begin to show; the head and neck are half the length of the body; the shoulders will be located where the whitish arm buds are attached. (*b*) At 8 weeks, the developing individual is about 1.6 inches (4 centimeters) long and has reached the end of its embryonic phase. It has become a fetus. Everything that will be found in the fully developed human being has now begun to form. The fetal stage is a period of growth and perfection of detail. The heart has been beating for a month, and the muscles have just begun their first exercises. (*c*) At 4½ months, the fetus is just over 7 inches (about 18 centimeters) long. When the thumb comes close to the mouth, the head may turn, and lips and tongue begin their sucking motions—a reflex for survival.

- *Embryonic period—weeks 3 through 8:* Before most women even know they are pregnant, the rate of cell differentiation intensifies, support systems for the cells form, and the beginnings of organs appear. In the third week, the neural tube, which eventually becomes the spinal cord, starts to form. At about 21 days, eyes begin to appear, and by 24 days the cells of the heart have begun to differentiate. During the fourth week, arm and leg buds emerge (Figure 4.2a). At 5 to 8 weeks, the heart begins to beat, arms and legs become more differentiated, the face starts to form, and the intestinal tract appears (Figure 4.2b).

- *Fetal period—months 2 through 9:* Organs mature to the point at which life can be sustained outside the womb, and muscles begin their first exercises. The mother feels the fetus move for the first time. At 6 months after conception, the eyes and eyelids are completely formed, a fine layer of hair covers the fetus, the grasping reflex appears, and irregular breathing begins. At 7 to 9 months, the fetus is much longer and weighs considerably more. In addition, the functioning of various organs steps up.

In 9 short months, a single cell has developed the capacity to live and function as a human being, with the potential for further physical, cognitive, and socioemotional changes. Sometimes, however, normal development is disrupted.

Threats to the Fetus Old family pictures sometimes include images of pregnant relatives enjoying a cocktail or a cigarette at a family function. Until about 50 years ago, mothers and their doctors were unaware of the role that maternal diet and behavior might play for the developing fetus. Today some pregnant women avoid such potentially risky behaviors in the belief that everything they do has a direct effect on the unborn child. Others behave more casually, assuming their experiences have little effect. The truth lies somewhere between these extremes. Although it floats in a comfortable, well-protected environment, the fetus is not totally immune to the larger environment surrounding the mother (Derbyshire, 2007; Shankaran & others, 2007).

A *teratogen* (from the Greek word *tera,* meaning "monster") is any agent that causes a birth defect. Teratogens can be chemical substances ingested by the mother or an illness such as rubella (German measles). In 1960, the prescription drug thalidomide was given to pregnant women to treat nausea. The effects were often horrific. Children whose mothers took thalidomide were more likely to be born without ears or limbs. Heroin is another example of a teratogen. Babies born to heroin users are at risk for many problems, including premature birth, low birth weight, physical defects, breathing problems, and death.

Heavy drinking by pregnant women can also have devastating effects on their offspring (Spohr, Willms, & Steinhausen, 2007). *Fetal alcohol syndrome (FAS)* is a cluster of abnormalities that occurs in children born to mothers who are heavy drinkers. These abnormalities include a small head (microcephaly), facial characteristics such as wide-spaced eyes, a flattened nose, an underdeveloped upper lip, and defective limbs and heart defects (Abel, 2006). Most FAS children are also below average in intelligence. Concern has increased about the well-being of the fetus when pregnant women drink even small amounts of alcohol. Even moderate drinking can lead to serious problems (Pollard, 2007; Sayal & others, 2007). The best advice is that a woman who is pregnant or anticipates becoming pregnant should not drink any alcohol.

The effects of teratogens vary depending on a variety of factors. Timing of exposure is key because the body part or organ system that is developing when the fetus encounters the teratogen is most vulnerable. In addition, genetic characteristics may buffer or exacerbate the effects of a teratogen. Different teratogens can cause the same defect, and one teratogen can cause a host of defects. Perhaps most importantly, the postnatal environment can influence the ultimate effects of prenatal insults.

A variety of other problems may short-circuit prenatal development. Full-term infants, those who grew in the womb for 38 to 42 weeks between conception and delivery, have the best chances of normal development in childhood. A *preterm infant,* who is born prior to 38 weeks after conception, is at greater risk. Whether a preterm infant will have developmental problems is a complex issue, however. Very small preterm infants are more likely than their larger counterparts to have developmental problems (Mufti, Setna, & Nazir, 2006; Wocadlo & Rieger, 2006).

Also, preterm infants who grow up in poverty are more likely to have problems than are those who live in better socioeconomic conditions (Daniels, Noe, & Mayberry, 2006; Madan & others, 2006). Indeed, many larger preterm infants from middle- and high-income families do not have developmental problems. Nonetheless, more preterm infants than full-term infants have learning disorders (Litt & others, 2005).

As is the case with teratogen exposure, postnatal experience plays a crucial role in determining the ultimate effects of preterm birth. Tiffany Field's research has shown that massage might improve the developmental outcomes of premature infants (Field, 1998, 2001, 2003, 2007; Field, Diego, & Hernandez-Reif, 2007; Field & others, 2006). In one study, massaging infants for 15 minutes three times a day led to 47 percent more weight gain than standard medical treatment (Field & others, 1986) (Figure 4.3). Massaged infants also were more active and alert and performed better on developmental tests.

Prenatal and newborn development sets the stage for development in childhood. The changes in every realm of childhood—physical, cognitive, and socioemotional—establish the foundation for our development as adults.

Physical Development in Childhood

Human infants are among the most helpless newborns on earth. One reason for their helplessness is that they are born not quite finished. From an evolutionary perspective, what sets humans apart from other animals is our enormous brain. Getting that big brain out of the relatively small birth canal is a challenge, and nature has met that challenge by sending human babies out of the womb before they are fully "cooked." The first months and years of life allow the developing human to put the finishing touches on that important organ. Infancy (the developmental period from birth to about 18 to 24 months of age) is second only to prenatal development in terms of the extensive physical changes that take place. During infancy children change from virtually immobile beings to creatures who toddle as fast as their legs can carry them.

Reflexes   Newborns are not empty-headed. They come into the world equipped with several genetically wired reflexes that are crucial for survival. Babies are born "knowing" how to swallow. If they are dropped in water, they will naturally hold their breath and contract their throats to keep water out—and move their arms and legs to stay afloat at least briefly.

Some reflexes persist throughout life—coughing, blinking, and yawning, for example. Others, such as automatically grasping something that touches the fingers or sucking on anything put in the mouth, disappear in the months following birth as higher brain functions mature and infants develop voluntary control over many behaviors.

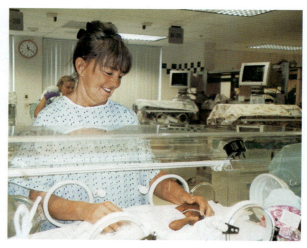

Tiffany Field massages a newborn infant. Her research has demonstrated the power of massage in improving the developmental outcome of at-risk infants. Under her direction, the Touch Research Institute in Miami, Florida, investigates the role of touch in a number of domains of health and well-being.

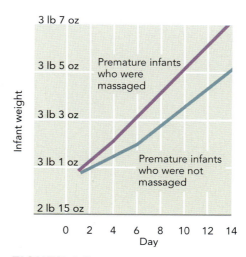

FIGURE 4.3

Weight Gain Comparison of Premature Infants Who Were Massaged or Not Massaged The graph shows that the mean daily gain of premature infants who were massaged was greater than that of premature infants who were not massaged.

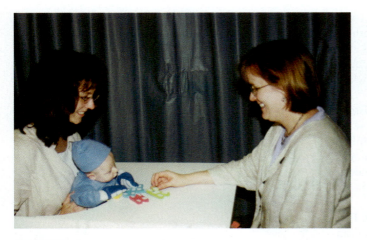

FIGURE 4.4

Infant's Use of "Sticky Mittens" to Explore Objects Amy Needham and her colleagues (2002) found that "sticky mittens" enhanced young infants' object exploration skills.

Motor and Perceptual Skills Relative to the rest of the body, a newborn's head is gigantic, and it flops around uncontrollably. Within 12 months, the infant becomes capable of sitting upright, standing, stooping, climbing, and often walking. During the second year, growth decelerates, but rapid gains occur in such activities as running and climbing.

The study of motor development has seen a renaissance in the past decade. Historically, researchers such as Arnold Gesell (1934) assumed that motor milestones unfolded as part of a genetic plan. However, psychologists now recognize that motor development is not the consequence of nature or nurture alone. The focus of research has shifted to discovering *how* motor skills develop and away from simply describing the age at which they develop (Adolph & Berger, 2006; Adolph & Joh, 2007).

In addition, when infants are motivated to do something, they may create a new motor behavior (Thelen & Smith, 2006). That new behavior is the result of many converging factors: the developing nervous system, the body's physical properties and its movement possibilities, the goal the infant is motivated to reach, and environmental support for the skill.

Environmental experiences play a role in reaching and grasping (Needham, 2008). In one study, 3-month-old infants participated in play sessions wearing "sticky mittens"—mittens with palms that stick to the edges of toys and allow the infants to pick up the toys (Needham, Barrett, & Peterman, 2002, p. 279) (Figure 4.4). Infants who participated in sessions with the mittens grasped and manipulated objects earlier in their development than a control group of infants who did not receive the "mitten" experience. The experienced infants looked at the objects longer, swatted at them more during visual contact, and were more likely to mouth the objects.

Psychologists also believe that motor skills and perceptual skills are coupled. Babies are continually coordinating their movements with information they perceive through their senses to learn how to maintain their balance, reach for objects in space, and move across various surfaces and terrains (Thelen & Smith, 2006). Consider what happens when a baby sees an attractive object across the room. She must perceive the current state of her body and learn how to use her limbs to get to the goal. Although infants' movements at first are awkward and uncoordinated, they soon learn to move in ways that are appropriate for reaching their goals.

Action also educates perception. For example, watching an object while holding and touching it helps infants to learn about its texture, size, and hardness. Moving from place to place in the environment teaches babies how objects and people look from different perspectives and whether surfaces will support their weight (Gibson, 2001).

Watching other people is also a way infants acquire knowledge about the world. Human infants differ from baby monkeys, for instance, in their strong reliance on imitation (MacLeod, 2006). Human infants are more likely than other primates to follow an example in a rote fashion. A baby monkey will figure out his own way to solve a problem, but a human infant will do what the model did, exactly. This reliance on imitation may be a way to solve the huge problem faced by the baby human: to learn the vast amount of cultural knowledge that is part of human life. Many of our behaviors are rather arbitrary. Why do we clap to show approval, for example, or wave "hello" or "bye-bye"? The human infant has a lot to learn and may be well served to follow the old adage, "When in Rome, do as the Romans do!" Imitation may be the quickest way to immerse oneself in the new world. It has been suggested that humans are particularly well adapted for imitation: We are one of the few animals with prominent whites in our eyes, which allow an observer to see what we are looking at.

Psychologists face a daunting challenge in studying infant perception. The word *infant* comes from the Latin *in fans,* which means "unable to speak." If the infant cannot talk, how can scientists learn whether or not she can see or hear certain things? Psychologists who study infants have no choice but to become extraordinarily clever methodologists. One way to study infant perception is to examine systematically what the baby looks at. The **preferential looking** technique involves giving the infant a choice of what object to look at. If an infant shows a reliable preference for one stimulus (for example, a picture of a face) over another (a scrambled picture of a face) when these are repeatedly presented in differing locations, we can infer that the infant can tell the two images apart.

preferential looking A test of perception that involves giving an infant a choice of what object to look at and that is used to determine whether infants can distinguish between objects.

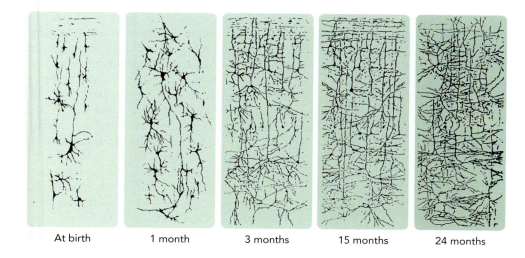

| At birth | 1 month | 3 months | 15 months | 24 months |

FIGURE 4.5

Dendritic Spreading Note the increase in connections among neurons over the course of the first 2 years of life. Reprinted by permission of the publisher from *The Postnatal Development of the Human Cerebral Cortex, Vols. I–VIII* by Jesse LeRoy Conel, Cambridge, Mass.: Harvard University Press, Copyright © 1939, 1975 by the President and Fellows of Harvard College.

Another way to examine infant perception is to habituate the infant on a particular stimulus. **Habituation** refers to decreased responsiveness to a stimulus after repeated presentations (Bendersky & Sullivan, 2007). For example, a square filled with vertical black and white stripes is presented to the infant multiple times until it is no longer interesting to the infant. Then a new stimulus (such as a square with slightly broader stripes) is presented. If the infant does not notice the change, we can infer that he or she does not perceive the new stimulus as different from the first.

Using these techniques, researchers have found that as early as 7 days old, infants are already engaged in organized perception of faces and are able to synchronize auditory and visual stimulation (Kellman & Arterberry, 2006). At 3 months, they prefer real faces to scrambled faces, and their mother's face to a stranger's (Slater, Field, & Reif-Hernandez, 2007). These techniques have provided a great deal of information about infants' remarkable abilities, but they are also limited. Indeed, research using brain imaging shows that infants may know more than even these clever strategies can tell us.

The Brain   As an infant walks, talks, runs, shakes a rattle, smiles, and frowns, his or her brain is changing dramatically. At birth and in early infancy, the brain's 100 billion neurons have only minimal connections. But as the infant ages from birth to 2 years, the dendrites of the neurons branch out, and the neurons become far more interconnected (Figure 4.5). The infant's brain literally is ready and waiting for the experiences that will create the connections (Nelson, 2007; Nelson, Thomas, & de Haan, 2006).

Recall from Chapter 3 that a *myelin sheath* encases most axons. The sheath insulates neurons and helps nerve impulses travel faster. Myelination, the process of encasing axons with fat cells, begins prenatally and continues after birth. Myelination for visual pathways occurs rapidly after birth and is completed in the first 6 months. Auditory myelination is not completed until 4 to 5 years of age. Some aspects of myelination continue into adolescence.

Another important aspect of the brain's development in childhood is the dramatic increase in *synaptic connections* (Webster & others, 2006). Recall from Chapter 3 that a *synapse* is a gap between neurons that is bridged by chemical neurotransmitters. Researchers have discovered that nearly twice as many synapses are available as will ever be used (Huttenlocher & Dabholkar, 1997). The connections that are made become stronger and will survive; the unused ones will be replaced by other neural pathways or disappear. In the language of neuroscience, these unused connections will be "pruned." Figure 4.6 vividly illustrates the dramatic growth and later pruning of synapses during infancy in specific areas of the brain.

Brain scanning techniques such as MRI and CT are improving the detection of developmental changes in the brain (Toga, Thompson, & Sowell, 2006). Using these tools, scientists have discovered that children's brains undergo dramatic anatomical changes between the ages of 3 and 15 (Thompson & others, 2000). By repeatedly obtaining brain scans of the same children for up to 4 years, they found that the amount of brain material in some areas

habituation Decreased responsiveness to a stimulus after repeated presentations. Habituation is used in infant research to examine if an infant can discriminate between an old stimulus and a new one.

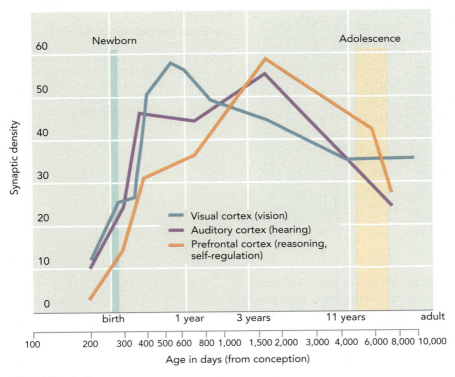

FIGURE 4.6

Synaptic Density in the Human Brain from Infancy to Adulthood The graph shows the dramatic increase and then pruning in synaptic density in three regions of the brain: visual cortex, auditory cortex, and prefrontal cortex. Synaptic density is believed to be an important indication of the extent of connectivity between neurons.

can nearly double within as little as a year, followed by a drastic loss of tissue as unneeded cells are purged and the brain continues to reorganize itself. The overall size of the brain does not show dramatic growth, but local patterns within the brain change dramatically. From 3 to 6 years of age, the most rapid growth takes place in the frontal lobe areas, which are involved in planning and organizing new actions and in maintaining attention to tasks (Thompson & others, 2000).

Of course, if the dendrites and synapses are not being stimulated by a wealth of new experiences, children's brains are less likely to develop normally (Nelson, Thomas, & de Haan, 2006). Thus, as in other areas of development, nature and nurture operate together.

Cognitive Development in Childhood

As amazing as physical development is in childhood, it is easily matched by cognitive development. *Cognitive development* refers to how thought, intelligence, and language processes change as people mature.

Until the mid-1900s, American psychologists had no useful theory for explaining how children's minds change as they age. Psychologists who were interested in the topic had to view it through the lens of behaviorism, which emphasizes that children merely receive information from the environment, or through the lens of the IQ testing approach, which emphasizes individual differences in children's intelligence. But then Jean Piaget (1896–1980), the famous Swiss developmental psychologist, changed the way we think about children's minds. When Piaget's ideas were introduced in the United States in the 1960s, American psychologists embraced his view that children *actively construct* their cognitive world as they go through a series of stages.

Piaget's Theory of Cognitive Development In Piaget's view, children actively construct their cognitive world, using schemas to make sense of what they experience. A **schema** is a concept or framework that already exists at a given moment in a person's mind and that organizes information and provides a structure for interpreting it. Schemas are expressed as various behaviors and skills that the child can exercise in relation to objects or situations. For example, sucking is an early, simple schema. Later, more complex schemas include licking, blowing, crawling, hiding, and so forth. Piaget's interest in schemas had to do with how they help in organizing and making sense out of current experience. In Chapter 8, you will see how schemas also help us to understand why people do not remember the past in an exact way but reconstruct it instead.

Piaget (1952) said that two processes are responsible for how people use and adapt their schemas:

- **Assimilation** occurs when individuals incorporate new information into existing knowledge. That is, people *assimilate* the environment into a schema. For example, a schema in the child's mind might provide the information that some objects can be picked up. The first time a child realizes that she might pick up a set of keys, she is assimilating the category "keys" into the schema of "picking up."

- **Accommodation** occurs when individuals adjust their schemas to new information. That is, people *accommodate* their schemas to the environment. For example, a child might

Jean Piaget (1896–1980) the famous Swiss developmental psychologist, changed the way we think about the development of children's minds.

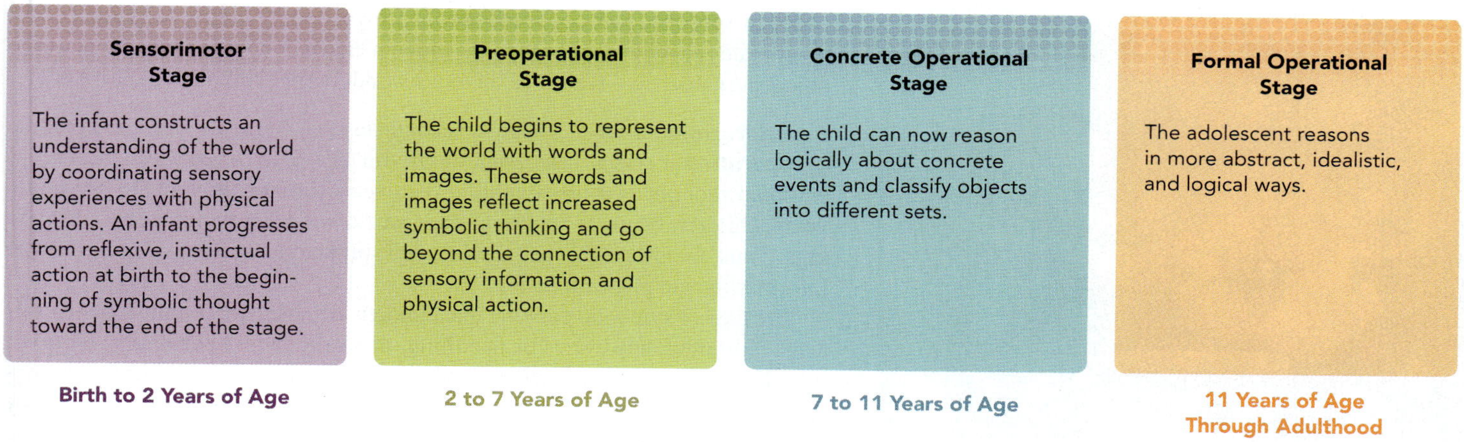

Sensorimotor Stage	Preoperational Stage	Concrete Operational Stage	Formal Operational Stage
The infant constructs an understanding of the world by coordinating sensory experiences with physical actions. An infant progresses from reflexive, instinctual action at birth to the beginning of symbolic thought toward the end of the stage.	The child begins to represent the world with words and images. These words and images reflect increased symbolic thinking and go beyond the connection of sensory information and physical action.	The child can now reason logically about concrete events and classify objects into different sets.	The adolescent reasons in more abstract, idealistic, and logical ways.
Birth to 2 Years of Age	**2 to 7 Years of Age**	**7 to 11 Years of Age**	**11 Years of Age Through Adulthood**

FIGURE 4.7

Piaget's Four Stages of Cognitive Development Jean Piaget described how human beings, through development, become ever more sophisticated thinkers about the world.

possess the schema of "picking up." With experience the child might learn that some things can be picked up easily between two fingers, that other things might require both hands and strong use of the arms, and that still other things cannot be picked up at all because they are too hot or too heavy. Thus, the schema "picking up" becomes modified into different schemas that *accommodate* the realities of different types of objects.

Assimilation and accommodation develop over time and through many repetitions of experience. Consider the schema of "sucking." Newborns reflexively suck everything that touches their lips. Their experience in sucking various objects allows them to assimilate those objects into other schemas of taste, texture, shape, and so on. After several months of experience, though, they accommodate the sucking schema by being more selective with it. For example, they discover that some objects, such as fingers and the mother's breasts, can be sucked, whereas others, such as fuzzy blankets, are better not.

Another important element of Piaget's theory is his observation that we go through four stages in understanding the world (Figure 4.7). Each of the stages is age-related and consists of distinct ways of thinking. In Piaget's view, it is not simply knowing more information that makes a child's thinking more advanced with each stage. Rather, it is the different way of understanding the world that makes one stage more advanced than another. The child's cognition is qualitatively different from one stage to the next.

Sensorimotor Stage The first stage identified by Piaget, the **sensorimotor stage,** lasts from birth to about 2 years of age. In this stage, infants construct an understanding of the world by coordinating sensory experiences (such as seeing and hearing) with motor (physical) actions—hence the term *sensorimotor*. As newborns they have little more than reflexive patterns with which to work. By the end of this stage, 2-year-olds show complex sensorimotor patterns and are beginning to use symbols in their thinking.

Imagine how you might experience the world if you were 5 months old. You are in a playpen filled with toys. One of the toys, a monkey, falls out of your grasp and rolls behind a larger toy, a hippopotamus. Would you know the monkey is behind the hippopotamus, or would you think it is completely gone? Piaget believed that "out of sight" literally was "out of mind" for young infants. At 5 months of age, you would not have reached for the monkey when it fell behind the hippopotamus. At 8 months of age, though, infants begin to understand that out of sight is not out of mind. At this point, you probably would have reached behind the hippopotamus to search for the monkey, coordinating your senses with your movements.

Object permanence is Piaget's term for this crucial accomplishment: understanding that objects and events continue to exist even when they cannot directly be seen, heard, or touched. The most common way to study object permanence is to show an infant an interesting toy and then cover the toy with a blanket. If infants understand that the toy still exists, they try to uncover it (Figure 4.8). Object permanence continues to develop throughout the sensorimotor period. For example, when infants initially understand that objects exist even when out of sight, they look only briefly for them. At the end of the sensorimotor stage, infants engage in a more prolonged and sophisticated search for an object.

schema A concept or framework that already exists at a given moment in a person's mind and that organizes information and provides a structure for interpreting it.

assimilation An individual's incorporation of new information into existing knowledge.

accommodation An individual's adjustment of a schema to new information.

sensorimotor stage The first Piagetian stage of cognitive development (birth to about 2 years of age), in which infants construct an understanding of the world by coordinating sensory experiences (such as seeing and hearing) with motor (physical) actions.

FIGURE 4.8

Object Permanence Piaget thought that object permanence was one of infancy's landmark cognitive accomplishments. For this 5-month-old boy, out of sight is literally out of mind. The infant looks at the toy dog (*top*), but when his view of the toy is blocked (*bottom*), he does not search for it. In a few more months, he will search for hidden toys, reflecting the presence of object permanence.

preoperational stage The second Piagetian stage of cognitive development (approximately 2 to 7 years of age), in which thought becomes more symbolic than in the sensorimotor stage but the child cannot yet perform operations.

concrete operational stage The third Piagetian stage of cognitive development (approximately 7 to 11 years of age), in which thought becomes operational and intuitive reasoning is replaced by logical reasoning in concrete situations.

From sensorimotor cognition—which involves the ability to organize and coordinate sensations with physical movements and includes the realization of object permanence—we move on to a second, more symbolic cognitive stage.

Preoperational Stage Piaget's second stage of cognitive development, the **preoperational stage,** lasts from approximately 2 to 7 years of age. Preoperational thought is more symbolic than sensorimotor thought. In preschool years, children begin to represent their world with words, images, and drawings. Thus, their thoughts begin to exceed simple connections of sensorimotor information and physical action.

The type of symbolic thinking that children are able to accomplish during this stage is limited, however. For one thing, they still cannot perform *operations,* by which Piaget meant mental representations that are "reversible." Preoperational children have difficulty understanding that reversing an action may restore the original conditions from which the action began. For example, the preoperational child may know that 4 plus 2 equals 6 but not understand that the reverse, 6 minus 2 equals 4, is also necessarily true according to the principle of reversibility. Or a preoperational child may walk a short distance to his friend's house each day but always gets a ride home. If you asked him to walk home one day, he would probably reply that he did not know the way because he had never walked home before.

A well-known test of whether a child can think "operationally" is to present a child with two identical beakers, A and B, filled with liquid to the same height (Figure 4.9). Next to them is a third beaker, C. Beaker C is tall and thin, whereas beakers A and B are short and wide. The liquid is poured from B into C, and the child is asked whether the amounts in A and C are the same. The 4-year-old child invariably says that the amount of liquid in the tall, thin beaker (C) is greater than that in the short, wide beaker (A). The 8-year-old child consistently says the amounts are the same. The 4-year-old child, a preoperational thinker, cannot mentally reverse the pouring action; that is, she cannot imagine the liquid going back from container C to container B. Piaget said that such a child has not grasped the concept of *conservation,* a belief in the permanence of certain attributes of objects or situations in spite of superficial changes.

The child's thought in the preoperational stage is also limited in that it is egocentric. By *egocentrism,* Piaget meant the inability to distinguish between one's own perspective and someone else's perspective. Piaget and Barbel Inhelder (1969) initially studied young children's egocentrism by devising the three-mountains task (Figure 4.10). The child walks around the model of the mountains and becomes familiar with what the mountains look like from different perspectives. The child can see that different objects are on the mountains as well. The child is then seated on one side of the table on which the mountains are placed. The experimenter takes a doll and moves it to different locations around the table, at each location asking the child to select one photo from a series of photos that most accurately reflects the view the doll is seeing. Children in the preoperational stage often pick the photo that shows the view they have, rather than the view the doll has.

Another limitation of preoperational thought is that it is *intuitive.* When Piaget asked children why they knew something, they often did not give logical answers but offered personal insights or guesses instead. Preoperational children do not seem to be bothered by the absence of logic in their thinking. As Piaget observed, they often seem very sure that they know something, even though they do not use logical reasoning to arrive at the answer.

Overall, then, preoperational thought is more symbolic than sensorimotor thought, but it is egocentric and intuitive rather than logical, and it does not include the ability to perform operations. But in reaching a basic level of operational understanding, the child progresses to the third of Piaget's cognitive stages.

Concrete Operational Stage Piaget's **concrete operational stage** occurs from approximately 7 to 11 years of age. Concrete operational thought involves using operations and replacing intuitive reasoning with logical reasoning in concrete situations. Classification skills are present, but abstract thinking is not yet developed.

Earlier you read about the beaker task, which preoperational children cannot do. Another well-known task for demonstrating operational thinking involves two identical balls of clay (Figure 4.11). As the child watches, the experimenter rolls one ball into a long, thin rod and leaves the other ball in its original spherical shape. Then the child is asked if more clay is in the ball or in the long, thin rod. By the time children reach 7 to 8 years of age, most answer that the amount of clay is the same. To solve this problem correctly, children have to recall that the ball was rolled into the shape of a rod and imagine the rod being returned to its original round shape—imagination that involves a reversible mental action. In this experiment and in the beaker experiment, the child who performs concrete operational thinking is able to mentally coordinate several characteristics or dimensions of an object rather than focusing on a single one. In the clay example, the preoperational child is likely to focus on either height or width. The child who has reached the stage of concrete operational thought coordinates information about both dimensions.

FIGURE 4.9

Piaget's Conservation Task The beaker test determines whether a child can think operationally—that is, can mentally reverse actions and understand conservation of the substance. (*a*) Two identical beakers are presented to the child, each containing the same amount of liquid. As the child watches, the experimenter pours the liquid from B into C, which is taller and thinner than A and B. (*b*) The experimenter then asks the child whether beakers A and C have the same amount of liquid. The preoperational child says no. When asked to point to the beaker that has more liquid, the child points to the tall, thin beaker.

Many of the concrete operations identified by Piaget are related to the properties of objects. One important skill at this stage of reasoning is the ability to classify or divide things into different sets or subsets and to consider their interrelations. Figure 4.12 shows an example of a classification task that concrete operational children can perform.

In sum, concrete operational thought involves operational thinking, classification skills, and logical reasoning in concrete, but not abstract, contexts. According to Piaget, reasoning in abstract contexts develops in the fourth, and final, cognitive stage.

Formal Operational Stage In Piaget's theory, individuals enter the **formal operational stage** of cognitive development at 11 to 15 years of age, and this stage continues through the adult years. Formal operational thought is more abstract, idealistic, and logical than concrete operational thought.

Unlike elementary school children, adolescents are no longer limited to actual concrete experience as the anchor of thought. They can conceive of hypothetical possibilities, which are purely abstract.

Thought also becomes more idealistic. Adolescents often compare themselves and others with ideal standards. And they think about what an ideal world would be like, wondering if they could carve out a better world than the one the adult generation has handed to them.

formal operational stage The fourth and final Piagetian stage of cognitive development (emerging from about 11 to 15 years of age), in which thinking becomes more abstract, idealistic, and logical.

FIGURE 4.10

The Three-Mountains Task The mountain model on the far left shows the child's perspective from view A, where he or she is sitting. The four squares represent photos showing the mountains from four different viewpoints of the model—A, B, C, and D. The experimenter asks the child to identify the photo in which the mountains look as they would from position B. To identify the photo correctly, the child has to take the perspective of a person sitting at spot B. Invariably, a child who thinks in a preoperational way cannot perform this task. When asked what a view of the mountains looks like from position B, the child selects Photo 1, taken from location A (the child's own view at the time) instead of Photo 2, the correct view.

Model of Mountains

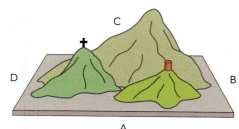

A
Child seated here

Photo 1
(View from A)

Photo 2
(View from B)

Photo 3
(View from C)

Photo 4
(View from D)

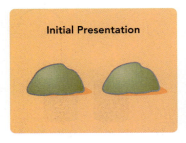

Initial Presentation

Two identical balls of clay are shown to the child. The child agrees that they are equal.

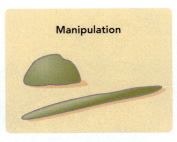

Manipulation

The experimenter changes the shape of one of the balls and asks the child whether they still contain equal amounts of clay.

Preoperational Child's Answer

No, the longer one has more.

Concrete Operational Child's Answer

Yes, they still have equal amounts.

FIGURE 4.11

Preoperational and Concrete Operational Children: The Clay Example Early on, relying on the shape—not the amount—of clay leads a preoperational child to make an error in judgment. By the concrete operational stage, the child is able to recognize that the piece of clay is the same amount, regardless of its shape.

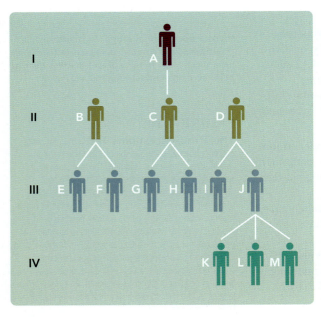

FIGURE 4.12

Classification Involving a Family Tree One way to determine if children possess classification skills is to see if they can understand a family tree of four generations (Furth & Wachs, 1975). This family tree suggests that the grandfather (A) has three sons (B, C, & D), each of whom has two sons (E through J), and that one of these sons (J) has three sons (K, L, & M). A child who comprehends this classification system can move up and down a level (vertically), across a level (horizontally), and up and down and across a level (obliquely) within the system. A child who thinks in a concrete operational way understands that person J can, at the same time, be father, brother, and grandson, for example. A preoperational child cannot perform this classification and says that a father cannot fulfill the other roles.

At the same time at which adolescents think more abstractly and idealistically, they also think more logically. Adolescents begin to think more in the way a scientist thinks, devising plans to solve problems and systematically testing solutions. Piaget gave this type of problem solving an imposing title: *hypothetical-deductive reasoning*. The phrase denotes adolescents' ability to develop hypotheses, or best hunches, about ways to solve problems, such as an algebraic equation. It also denotes their ability to systematically deduce, or conclude, the best path to follow to solve the problem. In contrast, before adolescence, children are likelier to solve problems by trial and error.

Thus, over the course of Piaget's four developmental stages, a person progresses from sensorimotor cognition to abstract, idealistic, and logical thought. Piaget based his stages on careful observation of children's behavior, but there is always room to evaluate theory and research. Let's consider the current thinking about Piaget's ideas about the development of cognition.

Evaluating Piaget Piaget opened up a new way of looking at how children's minds develop. We owe him for a long list of masterful concepts that have enduring power and fascination. These include the concepts of schemas, assimilation, accommodation, cognitive stages, object permanence, egocentrism, and conservation. We also owe Piaget for the currently accepted vision of children as active, constructive thinkers who manufacture (in part) their own development.

But just as other psychological theories have been criticized and amended, so have Piaget's. As methods improve for testing infants and children, researchers have found that certain cognitive abilities emerge earlier in some children than Piaget thought (Cohen & Cashon, 2006; Kellman & Arterberry, 2006). Renee Baillargeon (1997) has documented that infants as young as 4 months of age know that objects continue to exist even when hidden (an understanding Piaget did not think was possible until 8 months of age). In one study, 5-month-old infants showed an ability to attribute goals to people and objects (Luo & Baillargeon, 2005). By examining where the infants looked, these researchers were able to examine infants' expectations for the behavior of person or object. Also, memory and other forms of symbolic activity occur by at least the first half of the first year—much earlier than Piaget thought possible) (Bauer, 2006, 2007, 2008). Nor does formal operational thought emerge as consistently in early adolescence as Piaget envisioned (Kuhn & Franklin, 2006). Many adolescents and even adults do not reason as logically as Piaget proposed. Thus, infants are more cognitively competent than Piaget thought, and adolescents and adults are less competent.

Piaget has also been criticized on broader grounds. He was interested in examining the human species and general ways in which all people go through cognitive stages at particular ages. Not surprisingly, then, critics have faulted him for ignoring individual differences. In another broad criticism, psychologists who specialize in information processing argue that

Piaget's view places too much emphasis on grand stages and not enough on smaller, precise steps in solving problems. These psychologists believe that children's minds can be best understood by focusing more on their thinking strategies and their speed and efficiency in processing information (Munakata, 2006; Siegler, 2006).

The sociocultural perspective gives us yet another view of the shortcomings of Piaget's work. Piaget did not believe that culture and education play important roles in children's cognitive development. However, researchers have found that the age at which children acquire conservation skills is related to some extent to whether or not their culture provides relevant practice (Cole & Gajdamaschko, 2007). The Russian psychologist Lev Vygotsky (1962) recognized that cognitive development does not occur in a sociocultural vacuum. In Vygotsky's view, the goal of cognitive development is to learn the skills that will allow you to be competent in your culture. Thus, it is important to be guided and assisted by skilled members of the culture, much like being a cognitive apprentice (Bodrova & Leong, 2007; Hyson, Copple, & Jones, 2006). Vygotsky's view has become increasingly popular in educational psychology because of its emphasis on collaborative learning through interaction with skilled others.

Thus, today children's cognitive development is approached from several perspectives (Newman & Newman, 2007). However, Piaget still stands head and shoulders above all other developmental psychologists in creating a foundation for understanding how children's minds change in orderly, sequential ways.

Socioemotional Development in Childhood

As children grow and develop, they are socialized by and socialize others, such as parents, siblings, peers, and teachers. Their small world widens as they grow older. This section probes into several key topics related to children's socioemotional development: Erikson's theory of socioemotional development, attachment between infants and their caregivers, temperament, parenting, the wider social world, Kohlberg's theory of moral development, and gender development.

Erikson's Theory of Socioemotional Development   Erik Erikson (1902–1994) spent his early life in Europe. After working as a psychoanalyst under Sigmund Freud's direction, he came to the United States and taught at Harvard University. Although he accepted some of Freud's beliefs, he disagreed with others. For example, Freud stressed that personality is shaped mainly in the first 5 years of life. By contrast, Erikson emphasized lifelong development.

Erikson's theory of life-span development proposes eight psychosocial stages of development from infancy through old age. In Erikson's (1968) view, the first four stages take place in childhood; the last four, in adolescence and adulthood (Figure 4.13). Each stage represents a developmental task, or crisis, that a person must negotiate. The crises pit one outcome with another, such as trust versus mistrust. For Erikson, each stage is a turning point with two opposing possible outcomes: one, greater personal competence; and the other, greater weakness and vulnerability. The more successfully people resolve the issues at each stage, the more competent they are likely to become.

Erikson's Childhood Stages   We examine Erikson's adolescence and adult stages later in this chapter. His four childhood stages are as follows:

1. *Trust versus mistrust* occurs during approximately the first 1½ years of life. Trust is built when a baby's basic needs—such as comfort, food, and warmth—are met. If infants' needs are not met by responsive, sensitive caregivers, the result is mistrust. Trust in infancy sets the stage for a lifelong expectation that the world will be a good and pleasant place to live.

2. *Autonomy versus shame and doubt* occurs from about 1½ through 3 years of age. In this stage, children can develop either a positive sense of independence and autonomy or negative feelings of shame and doubt. In seeking autonomy, they are likely to develop a strong sense of independence.

3. *Initiative versus guilt* occurs from 3 to 5 years of age, the preschool years. During these years, children's social worlds are widening. When asked to assume more responsibility for themselves, children can develop initiative. When allowed to be irresponsible or made to

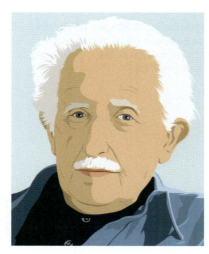

Erik Erikson (1902–1994) generated one of the most important developmental theories of the twentieth century.

Erikson's Stages	Developmental Period	Characteristics
Trust versus mistrust	Infancy (Birth to 1½ years)	A sense of trust requires a feeling of physical comfort and minimal amount of fear about the future. Infants' basic needs are met by responsive, sensitive caregivers.
Autonomy versus shame and doubt	Toddlerhood (1½ to 3 years)	After gaining trust in their caregivers, infants start to discover that they have a will of their own. They assert their sense of autonomy, or independence. They realize their will. If infants are restrained too much or punished too harshly, they are likely to develop a sense of shame and doubt.
Initiative versus guilt	Early childhood (preschool years, ages 3–5)	As preschool children encounter a widening social world, they are challenged more and need to develop more purposeful behavior to cope with these challenges. Children are now asked to assume more responsibility. Uncomfortable guilt feelings may arise, though, if the children are irresponsible and are made to feel too anxious.
Industry versus inferiority	Middle and late childhood (elementary school years, 6 years–puberty)	At no other time are children more enthusiastic than at the end of early childhood's period of expansive imagination. As children move into the elementary school years, they direct their energy toward mastering knowledge and intellectual skills. The danger at this stage involves feeling incompetent and unproductive.
Identity versus identity confusion	Adolescence (10–20 years)	Individuals are faced with finding out who they are, what they are all about, and where they are going in life. An important dimension is the exploration of alternative solutions to roles. Career exploration is important.
Intimacy versus isolation	Eary adulthood (20s, 30s)	Individuals face the developmental task of forming intimate relationships with others. Erikson described intimacy as finding oneself yet losing oneself in another person.
Generativity versus stagnation	Middle adulthood (40s, 50s)	A chief concern is to assist the younger generation in developing and leading useful lives.
Integrity versus despair	Late adulthood (60s–)	Individuals look back and evaluate what they have done with their lives. The retrospective glances can be either positive (integrity) or negative (despair).

FIGURE 4.13

Erikson's Eight Stages of Human Development Erikson changed the way psychologists think about development by tracing the process of growth over the entire life span.

feel anxious, they can develop too much guilt. Erikson argued that young children are resilient. He said that a sense of accomplishment quickly compensates for most guilt feelings.

4. *Industry versus inferiority* occurs from about the age of 6 until puberty. Children can achieve industry by mastering knowledge and intellectual skills. When they do not, they can feel inferior. At the end of early childhood, children are ready to turn their energy to learning academic skills. If they do not, they can develop a sense of being incompetent and unproductive.

Evaluating Erikson's Theory At a time when people believed that most development takes place in childhood, Erikson charted development as a lifelong challenge. His insights also helped to move psychology away from Freud's focus on sexuality and toward an understanding of the importance of successfully resolving various socioemotional tasks at different points in human life. Erikson's ideas changed conventional thinking about some periods of development. For example, Erikson encouraged looking at adolescents not just as sexual beings but as individuals seeking to find out who they are and searching to find their niche in the world.

But like Piaget's theory, Erikson's also has been criticized (Kroger, 2007). Erikson himself mainly practiced case study research. Critics argue that a firmer research base for

Erikson's entire theory has not been developed. However, research on specific stages of the theory reveals that there are important developmental tasks at certain points in our lives.

Critics also say that Erikson's attempt to capture each stage with a single concept sometimes leaves out other important developmental tasks. For example, Erikson said that the main task for young adults is to resolve the conflict between intimacy and isolation. However, another important developmental task in early adulthood involves careers and work.

Such criticisms do not tarnish Erikson's monumental contributions, however. He, like Piaget, is a giant in developmental psychology.

Attachment in Infancy The word *attachment* usually refers to a strong relationship between two people in which each person does a number of things to continue the relationship. Many types of people are attached: relatives, lovers, a teacher and a student. In the language of developmental psychology, however, **attachment** is the close emotional bond between an infant and its caregiver.

A number of developmental psychologists believe that attachment to the caregiver during the first year provides an important foundation for later development (Juffer, Bakermans-Kranenburg, & van Ijzendoorn, 2007; Sroufe & others, 2005; Thompson, 2006). British psychiatrist John Bowlby (1969, 1989) theorized that the infant and the mother instinctively form an attachment. He viewed the newborn as innately equipped to stimulate the caregiver to respond; it cries, clings, smiles, and coos. Later the infant crawls, walks, and follows the mother. The infant's goal is to keep the mother nearby. Research on attachment supports Bowlby's view that the infant's attachment to its caregiver intensifies at about 6 to 7 months (Thompson, 2006). Bowlby refined his theory of attachment until his death in 1990, and his work continues to have an impact on research in developmental and social psychology.

A classic study by Harry Harlow (1958) demonstrates the importance of warm contact to infant attachment. Harlow separated infant monkeys from their mothers at birth and placed them in cages in which they had access to two artificial "mothers." One of the mothers was a physically cold wire mother; the other was a warm, fuzzy cloth mother (the "contact comfort" mother). Each mother could be outfitted with a feeding mechanism. Half of the infant monkeys were fed by the wire mother, half by the cloth mother. The infant monkeys nestled close to the cloth mother and spent little time on the wire one, even if it was the wire mother that gave them milk (Figure 4.14). When afraid, the infant monkeys

attachment The close emotional bond between an infant and its caregiver.

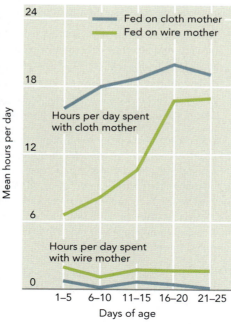

FIGURE 4.14

Contact Time with Wire and Cloth Surrogate Mothers Regardless of whether the infant monkeys were fed by a wire or a cloth mother, they overwhelmingly preferred to spend contact time with the cloth mother.

In the Hausa culture, siblings and grandmothers provide a significant amount of care for infants.

ran to the comfy mom. This study clearly demonstrates that what the researchers described as "contact comfort," not feeding, is the crucial element in the attachment process.

Mary Ainsworth devised a way to study differences in children's attachment. She called the procedure the *strange situation* (Ainsworth, 1979; Ainsworth & others, 1978). In this experiment, caregivers leave infants alone with a stranger and then return. Responses of children to this situation are used to classify their attachment style. Ainsworth devised the term **secure attachment** to describe how infants use the caregiver, usually the mother, as a secure base from which to explore the environment. In the strange situation, the secure infant is upset when the mother leaves but calms down and appears happy to see her when she returns. Infants who are securely attached are more likely to have mothers who are responsive and accepting and who express affection toward them than are infants who are insecurely attached (Sroufe & others, 2005). The securely attached infant moves freely away from the mother but also keeps tabs on her by periodically glancing at her. The securely attached infant responds positively to being picked up by others and, when put back down, happily moves away to play. An insecurely attached infant, in contrast, avoids the mother or is ambivalent toward her. In the strange situation, such an infant might not even notice the mother has gone or, conversely, might respond with intense distress, only to rage at the mother when she returns. The insecurely attached infant fears strangers and is upset by minor sensations.

One criticism of attachment theory is that it does not adequately account for cultural variations (Cole & Tan, 2007; Kagitcibasi, 2007). For example, in some cultures infants show strong attachments to many people, not just their primary caregiver. In the African Hausa culture, both grandmothers and siblings provide a significant amount of care to infants (Harkness & Super, 1995). Infants in agricultural societies tend to form attachments to older siblings who are assigned a major responsibility for younger siblings' care. The attachments formed by infants in group care in Israeli kibbutzim provide another variation.

Psychologists accept the importance of competent, nurturing caregivers in an infant's development (Powell, 2006; Ramey, Ramey, & Lanzi, 2006). Still at issue, though, is whether secure attachment, especially to a single caregiver, is necessary for healthy development and whether attachment, once established in childhood, changes throughout the course of life (Thompson, 2006).

Temperament   One factor that some psychologists believe is critical to understanding child development is **temperament,** an individual's behavioral style and characteristic way of responding. Psychiatrists Alexander Chess and Stella Thomas (1977) identify three basic types, or clusters, of temperament in children:

- *The easy child:* generally is in a positive mood, quickly establishes regular routines in infancy, and adapts easily to new experiences.
- *The difficult child:* tends to react negatively and cry frequently, engages in irregular daily routines, and is slow to accept new experiences.
- *The slow-to-warm-up child:* has a low activity level, is somewhat negative, shows low adaptability, and displays a low intensity of mood.

Other researchers propose different dimensions as the core of temperament, such as *effortful control* or *self-regulation* (controlling arousal and not being easily agitated), *inhibition* (being shy and showing distress in an unfamiliar situation), and *negative affectivity* (tending to be frustrated or sad) (Kagan & Fox, 2006; Rothbart & Bates, 2006). Thus, agreement about the basic core dimensions of temperament has not been reached (Bates & Pettit, 2007).

Many first-time parents do not recognize the importance of temperament. The picture changes for them, however, when they have their second child and find out that what worked with the first child does not work with the second (Putnam, Sanson, & Rothbart, 2002).

Parenting   Even though many American children spend a great deal of time in child care in their early years and nearly all children in the United States spend many hours in school as they grow older, parents are still the main caregivers for most children.

Parenting Styles   Ideas about the best way to rear children have gone through a lot of changes over the years and may vary across cultures. At one time, and in some cultures still, parents were advised to impose strict discipline along the lines of such adages as "Spare the rod and

secure attachment An important aspect of socioemotional development in which infants use the caregiver, usually the mother, as a secure base from which to explore the environment.

temperament An individual's behavioral style and characteristic way of responding.

Style	Parental Behavior	Common Outcome in Children
Authoritarian	Restrict and punish. Orders not to be questioned. Little verbal exchange.	Anxiety about social comparison, lack of initiative, poor communication skills.
Authoritative	Encourage independence within limits. Extensive verbal give-and-take. Warmth, nurturance.	Social competence, self-reliance, social responsibility.
Neglectful	Little involvement in the child's life. Unaware of what the child is doing.	Anxiety about social comparison, lack of initiative, poor communication skills.
Indulgent	Involved with the child but without placing demands. Highly permissive.	Anxiety about social comparison, lack of initiative, poor communication skills.

FIGURE 4.15

Parenting Styles and Child Outcomes
Research has demonstrated that parenting styles can be understood through four types that have important implications for children.

spoil the child" and "Children should be seen and not heard." But attitudes toward children—and how best to parent them—have changed to encompass more nurturing and caring.

Diana Baumrind (1991, 1993) believes that parents interact with their children in one of four basic ways:

- **Authoritarian parenting** is a restrictive, punitive style in which the parent exhorts the child to follow the parent's directions and to value hard work and effort. The authoritarian parent firmly limits and controls the child with little verbal exchange. In a difference of opinion about how to do something, for example, the authoritarian parent might say, "You do it my way or else. No backtalk." Authoritarian parenting is associated with children's social incompetence. Children of authoritarian parents often fail to initiate activity, have poor communication skills, and compare themselves with others.

- **Authoritative parenting** encourages children to be independent but still places limits and controls on their behavior. Extensive verbal give-and-take is allowed, and parents are warm and nurturing toward the child. An authoritative father might put his arm around the child in a comforting way and say, "You know you should not have done that; let's talk about how you can handle the situation better next time." Children whose parents are authoritative tend to be socially competent, self-reliant, and socially responsible.

- **Neglectful parenting** is a style in which parents are uninvolved in their child's life. Ask such parents, "It's 10 P.M. Do you know where your child is?" and they are likely to answer "No." Yet children have a strong need for their parents to care about them. Children whose parents are neglectful might develop a sense that other aspects of the parents' lives are more important than they are. Children whose parents are neglectful tend to be less competent socially, to handle independence poorly, and, especially, to show poor self-control.

- **Indulgent parenting** is a style in which parents are involved with their children but place few limits on them. Such parents let their children do what they want. Some parents deliberately rear their children in this way because they believe the combination of warm involvement with few restraints will produce a creative, confident child. But children whose parents are indulgent often rate poorly in social competence. They often fail to learn respect for others, expect to get their own way, and have difficulty controlling their behavior.

Figure 4.15 summarizes Baumrind's parenting styles and their child outcomes.

Although useful, Baumrind's findings leave many questions about parenting unanswered, and there is more to understanding parent–child relationships than parenting style (Grusec & Davidov, 2007). One key issue is whether parenting style is really a product of the parents alone. For many years, the socialization of children was viewed as a straightforward, one-way matter of repeated instruction—telling small children about using spoons and potties, saying "thank you," and not killing the baby brother. The basic philosophy was that children had to be trained to fit into the social world, so their behavior had to be shaped into that of

authoritarian parenting A restrictive, punitive parenting style in which the parent exhorts the child to follow the parent's directions and to value hard work and effort.

authoritative parenting A parenting style that encourages children's independence (but still places limits and controls on their behavior); it includes extensive verbal give-and-take, and warm and nurturing interactions with the child.

neglectful parenting A parenting style in which parents are uninvolved in their child's life.

indulgent parenting A parenting style in which parents are involved with their children but place few limits on them.

Critical Controversy   Parents Matter, Don't They?

The role of parents in the lives of the developing child would seem to be pretty obvious. But whether parenting matters has been an issue of some controversy. In the provocative book *The Nurture Assumption*, Judith Harris (1998) argues that what parents do does not make a difference in their children's behavior. Spank them. Hug them. Read to them. Ignore them. Harris says it will not influence how they turn out. She argues that children's genes and their peers are far more important than parents in children's development. In addition, Harris emphasizes that children learn from many sources and that their learning is specific to certain contexts. Although children imitate their parents to learn how to behave at home, they imitate other people to learn how to behave outside the home. Harris singles out children's peer relations as an especially important aspect of the nurture part of the nature/nurture equation. For Harris, children would develop into the same types of adults if we left them in their homes, schools, neighborhoods, peer groups, and culture but switched their parents around.

How far-fetched is Harris's view? Some psychologists believe that it is more plausible than it first appears. Sandra Scarr (1992, 2000) has said it all before. A retired professor and a well-known developmental researcher, Scarr suggests that "super parenting" is unnecessary. She asserts that while behaviorists believe that experience is crucial to behavior, the active genotype is so strong that it makes most environmental experiences unimportant. Scarr suggests that the only parenting that has a negative effect on a child is parenting that is far outside the normal range—for example, chronic physical abuse (Cicchetti & Toth, 2006; Pipes & others, 2007). Apart from such extreme cases, Scarr asserts, genes are the primary determinant of developmental outcomes. Thus, once parents have passed on their genes to their children, the most important work is done. Parenting that is "good enough" is all that is required for the development of healthy, well-adjusted children. Even behaviors that psychologists often see as negative (such as spanking) are not necessarily damaging, Scarr maintains.

But Scarr's claims encountered a firestorm of criticism. Diane Baumrind (1993) countered that "good enough" parenting *wasn't*

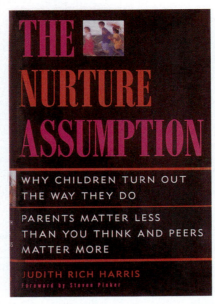

Harris's controversial book identifies children's relations with their peers as an especially important aspect of the nurture part of the nature/nurture equation.

good enough, and cited evidence that highly demanding and highly responsive parents are more likely to have high-achieving and socially well-adjusted children. A longitudinal study by W. Andrew Collins and his colleagues (2000) supported Baumrind's claims; it showed that even with genetic influences taken into account, parenting practices made a difference in children's lives. Baumrind also expressed concern that Scarr's opinion might lead parents to give up the important responsibility of child rearing or to conclude that their efforts on behalf of their children are not worthwhile. Others joined Baumrind in voicing worries that Scarr's views might lead public policymakers to reduce support for intervention programs that help children and parents (Jackson, 1993).

Indeed, studies of positive intervention especially have the ability to demonstrate whether parenting plays an important role in children's development (Bornstein, 2006; Clarke-Stewart, 2006; Collins & others, 2000; Dunifon, Duncan, & Brooks-Gunn, 2004; Juffer, Bakermans-Kranenburg, & van Ijzendoorn, 2007; Maccoby, 2007; Powell, 2006; Sroufe & others, 2005). In one study, training low-income mothers to respond sensitively to their infants both changed the negative responses of mothers when their infants became irritable and reduced the likelihood that distressed infants would avoid their mothers (Van den Boom, 1994). In another study, parents' participation in 16-week discussion groups on effective parenting just prior to their children's entry into kindergarten resulted in better school adjustment and higher academic achievement for their children than for children whose parents attended discussion groups without the effective parenting emphasis (Cowan & Cowan, 2001).

What Do You Think?

- Do you think that your personality was formed more by nature or nurture? In other words, was your personality shaped more by your genes or by your life experiences?

- If you have children or decide to have them in the future, how do you think this information might affect your approach to parenting?

a mature adult. However, as research on temperament suggests, the young child is not like the blob of clay from which a sculptor builds a statue. Through the process of *reciprocal socialization,* children socialize their parents just as parents socialize their children. For example, children's smiles usually elicit positive overtures by parents. However, when children are difficult and aggressive, their parents are more likely to punish them. Or consider adolescents: They promote guilt feelings in parents, just as parents promote guilt feelings in them. In other words, parenting styles may be influenced by children's behavior.

A recent debate about parenting focuses on the nature versus nurture issue. To examine this issue, see the Critical Controversy.

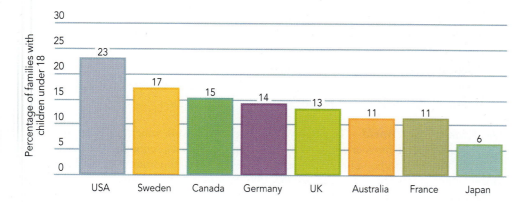

FIGURE 4.16
Single-Parent Families in Different
Countries The percentage of families with children
that are headed by a single adult differs across countries.
What do you think might explain these differences?

Divorce Although the U.S. divorce rate has been declining in the last two decades, the rate is still very high (Amato, 2006). As a result, as shown in Figure 4.16, the United States has the highest percentage of children growing up in single-parent families (many of which are the result of divorce) of all industrialized countries.

Many children are highly vulnerable to stress during the experience of divorce (Clarke-Stewart & Brentano, 2006; Fine & Harvey, 2006). Research shows that children from divorced families are more poorly adjusted and more likely to have psychological problems, such as being overly aggressive or depressed, than children from non-divorced families (Hetherington, 2006). Those who have experienced multiple divorces are at an even greater risk. What percentage of children from divorced families has adjustment problems? According to leading researcher E. Mavis Hetherington (2006; Hetherington & Stanley-Hagen, 2002), adjustment difficulties characterize approximately 25 percent of children and adolescents in divorced families, compared with only 10 percent of children and adolescents in non-divorced families. This finding means, however, that approximately 75 percent of children in divorced families do *not* have adjustment problems—a statistic that runs counter to stereotypical beliefs about children of divorce. Among the factors that predict better adjustment for children in divorced families are harmony between the divorced parents, authoritative parenting, good schools, and the child's possession of an easy rather than a difficult temperament (Amato, 2006; Fine & Harvey, 2006; Hetherington, 2006).

Positive Parenting We already have examined some important aspects of positive parenting, especially an authoritative parenting style. Another aspect is recognizing that parenting takes time and effort. Suggestions that parenting can be done quickly and with little or no inconvenience are quite common today (Sroufe, 2000). However, researchers have found that competent parenting takes time and effort (Bornstein, 2006; Parke & Buriel, 2006; Powell, 2006).

Another aspect of positive parenting is coaching children about how to control their emotions (Katz, 1999). "Emotion-coaching parents" monitor their children's emotions, view their children's negative emotions as opportunities for teaching about emotion, and provide guidance in effectively dealing with emotions. In research, emotion-coaching parents have been observed to reject their children less, praise them more, and be more nurturing toward them than "emotion-dismissing parents" (Gottman, Katz, & Hooven, 1997). The children of the emotion-coaching parents in this research were better at toning down the intensity of their negative emotions and at focusing their attention and had fewer behavior problems than the children of emotion-dismissing parents.

Still another dimension of positive parenting is using strategies for raising a moral child. The goal is to raise a child who is considerate of others, understands the difference between right and wrong, and is less likely to lie, cheat, or steal. The following positive parenting strategies have most often been found to be helpful in raising a moral child (Eisenberg, Fabes, & Spinrad, 2006; Eisenberg & Murphy, 1995; Eisenberg & Valiente, 2002):

• Being warm and supportive rather than punitive
• When disciplining, using reasoning the child can understand

- Providing opportunities for the child to learn about others' perspectives and feelings
- Involving children in family decision making and in thinking about moral decisions
- Modeling moral behaviors and thinking, and providing children with opportunities to engage in such behaviors and thought
- Providing information to children about what behaviors are expected and why
- Fostering an internal rather than an external moral orientation

The Wider Social World   The family is one social context in which children's development occurs. But the broader culture—the child's peer relations, school influences, and the quality of the neighborhood in which the child lives—also is important (Bronfenbrenner & Morris, 2006; Rubin, Bukowski, & Parker, 2006; Wigfield & others, 2006).

Today psychologists are especially interested in improving the lives of children who live in impoverished neighborhoods and attend ineffective schools (Fuligni & Fuligni, 2007; Huston & Ripke, 2006). They also are increasingly interested in studying children from ethnic minority groups. Although many ethnic minority families are not poor, poverty can contribute to the stressful life experiences of minority children, creating a double disadvantage for them (McLoyd, Aikens, & Burton, 2006): prejudice, discrimination, and bias because of their ethnic minority background and the stressful effects of poverty.

Developmental psychologists also are intrigued by cultural comparisons of children in the United States and other countries. For example, parents in the United States tend to rear their children to be more independent than do their counterparts in Japan and other Asian countries (Greenfield, Suzuki, & Rothstein-Fisch, 2006; Rothbaum & Trommsdorff, 2007). Such cross-cultural variations reflect the nurture part of the nature versus nurture issue.

Moral Development   Moral development involves changes with age in thoughts, feelings, and behaviors regarding the principles and values that guide what people should do. Moral development has both an intrapersonal dimension (a person's basic values and sense of self) and an interpersonal dimension (what people should do in their interactions with other people) (Lapsley & Narvaez, 2006; Turiel, 2006).

Psychologists have studied how people reason and think about moral matters, how they feel about them, and how they actually behave. Research on moral reasoning and thinking has revolved around Lawrence Kohlberg's theory of moral development and reactions to it.

Kohlberg's Theory   Kohlberg (1958) began his study of moral thinking by creating 11 stories and asking children, adolescents, and adults questions about the stories. One of the stories (set in Europe) goes like this:

> A woman was near death from a special kind of cancer. There was one drug that the doctors thought might save her. It was a form of radium that a druggist in the same town had recently discovered. The drug was expensive to make, but the druggist was charging ten times what the drug cost him to make. He paid $200 for the radium and charged $2,000 for a small dose of the drug. The sick woman's husband, Heinz, went to everyone he knew to borrow the money, but he could get together only $1,000. He told the druggist that his wife was dying and asked him to sell it cheaper or let him pay later. But the druggist said, "No. I discovered the drug, and I am going to make money from it." Desperate, Heinz broke into the man's store to steal the drug for his wife. (Kohlberg, 1969)

After reading the story, the interviewee was asked a series of questions about the moral dilemma. Should Heinz have stolen the drug? Was stealing it right or wrong? Why? Is it a husband's duty to steal a lifesaving drug for his wife if he can get it in no other way? Would a good husband do it? Did the druggist have the right to charge so much in the absence of a law setting a limit on the price? Why or why not? Based on the answers that people gave to the questions about this story and other moral dilemmas, Kohlberg constructed a theory.

Kohlberg (1986) proposed that moral development consists of three levels, with two stages at each level (Figure 4.17):

1. The *preconventional level* is based primarily on punishments (stage 1) or rewards (stage 2) that come from the external world. In regard to the Heinz story, at stage 1 an individual might say that Heinz should not steal the drug because he might get caught

Lawrence Kohlberg (1927–1987) created a provocative theory of moral development. In his view, "Moral development consists of a sequence of qualitative changes in the way an individual thinks."

LEVEL 1 **Preconventional Level** **No Internalization**	**LEVEL 2** **Conventional Level** **Intermediate Internalization**	**LEVEL 3** **Postconventional Level** **Full Internalization**
Stage 1 Heteronomous Morality *Individuals pursue their own interests but let others do the same. What is right involves equal exchange.*	**Stage 3** Mutual Interpersonal Expectations, Relationships, and Interpersonal Conformity *Individuals value trust, caring, and loyalty to others as a basis for moral judgments.*	**Stage 5** Social Contract or Utility and Individual Rights *Individuals reason that values, rights, and principles undergird or transcend the law.*
Stage 2 Individualism, Purpose, and Exchange *Children obey because adults tell them to obey. People base their moral decisions on fear of punishment.*	**Stage 4** Social System Morality *Moral judgments are based on understanding and the social order, law, justice, and duty.*	**Stage 6** Universal Ethical Principles *The person has developed moral judgments that are based on universal human rights. When faced with a dilemma between law and conscience, a personal, individualized conscience is followed.*

FIGURE 4.17

Kohlberg's Three Levels and Six Stages of Moral Development Kohlberg proposed that human moral development could be characterized by a sequence of age-related changes.

and sent to jail. At stage 2, the person might say he should not steal the drug because the druggist needs to make a profit on the drug.

2. At the *conventional level,* the individual abides by standards such as those learned from parents (stage 3) or society's laws (stage 4). At stage 3, an individual might say that Heinz should steal the drug for his wife because that is what people expect a good husband to do. At stage 4, the person might say that it is natural for Heinz to want to save his wife but that the law says it still is always wrong to steal.

3. At the *postconventional level,* the individual recognizes alternative moral courses, explores the options, and then develops a personal moral code. The code reflects the principles generally accepted by the community (stage 5) or it reflects more abstract principles for all of humanity (stage 6). At stage 5, a person might say that the law was not set up for these circumstances, so Heinz can steal the drug. It is not really right, but he is justified in doing it. At stage 6, the individual evaluates alternatives but recognizes that Heinz's wife's life is more important than a law.

Kohlberg believed that these levels and stages develop in a sequence and are age-related. Some evidence for the sequence of Kohlberg's stages has been found, although few people reach stage 6 (Colby & others, 1983). Children are often in stages 1 and 2, although in the later elementary school years they may be in stage 3. Most adolescents are at stage 3 or 4.

Kohlberg also thought that advances in moral development take place because of the maturation of thought, opportunities for role taking, and opportunities to discuss moral issues with a person who reasons at a stage just above one's own. In Kohlberg's view, parents contribute little to children's moral thinking because parent–child relationships are often too power-oriented.

Evaluating Kohlberg's Theory   Kohlberg's ideas have stimulated considerable research about how people think about moral issues (Lapsley, 2006; Killen & Smetana, 2006). At the same time, his theory has numerous critics. One criticism is that moral *reasoning* does not necessarily mean moral *behavior.* When people are asked about their moral reasoning, what they say might fit into Kohlberg's advanced stages, but their actual behavior might involve cheating, lying, and stealing. The cheaters, liars, and thieves might know what is right and what is wrong but still do what is wrong.

Another criticism is that Kohlberg's view does not adequately reflect interpersonal relationships and concerns for others—that it focuses too much on the intrapersonal dimension of moral development (Carlo, 2006). Kohlberg's theory is thus a *justice perspective* concerned with the rights of "the individual," who stands alone and independently makes moral decisions. In contrast, the *care perspective,* which lies at the heart of Carol Gilligan's

Carol Gilligan (1936–) argues that Kohlberg's view does not give adequate attention to relationships. In Gilligan's view, "Many girls seem to fear, most of all, being alone— without friends, family, and relationships."

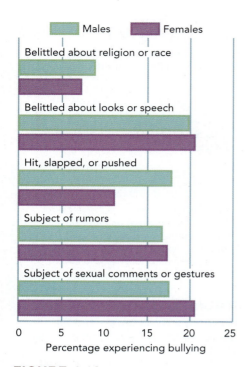

FIGURE 4.18

Bullying Behaviors Among U.S. Youth

This graph shows the type of bullying most often experienced by U.S. youth. The percentages reflect the extent to which bullied students said that they had experienced a particular type of bullying. In terms of gender, note that when they were bullied, boys were more likely to be hit, slapped, or pushed than girls were.

prosocial behavior Behavior that is intended to benefit other people.

(1982) approach to moral development, views people in terms of their connectedness with others and focuses on interpersonal communication, relationships, and concern for others. From Gilligan's perspective this weakness in Kohlberg's approach explains why, using his measures, women generally score lower than men on moral development. From Gilligan's view, at the highest level of moral development, the individual and relationship aspects of moral reasoning are likely to be integrated.

Recent Studies of Moral Development You have just read criticisms of Kohlberg's theory that indicate his theory does not give adequate attention to moral behavior—that is, what people morally do, and that it does not adequately focus on caring for others. In recent years, researchers have increasingly studied **prosocial behavior,** behavior that is intended to benefit other people (Eisenberg, Fabes, & Spinrad, 2006; Eisenberg, Spinrad, & Sadovsky, 2006). For example, researchers are probing how, when, and why children engage in everyday acts of kindness toward others (Carlo, 2006; Killen & Smetana, 2006). Also, researchers are finding that supportive parenting and parental monitoring relate to less aggression in their children and increased helping and comforting of others (Dodge, Coie, & Lynam, 2006; Eisenberg, Fabes, & Spinrad, 2006).

Other recent work focuses on when a child first shows signs of possessing a conscience (Saarni & others, 2006; Thompson, 2006). Having a conscience means hearing that voice in our head that tells us that something is morally good or bad. Deborah Laible and Ross Thompson (2000, 2002) have examined the conversations between mothers and toddlers at times when the child did something well or got into trouble. They have found that by 3 years of age, children begin to show signs of early conscience development. This development is fostered by parent–child interactions that are clear, elaborate, and rich with emotional content and that include shared positive emotion. Researchers also have revealed that kind, moral children are more likely to be kind moral adults (Eisenberg, Fabes, & Spinrad, 2006).

Another form of behavior in childhood that is relevant to morality and empathy is bullying—physically or verbally coercing someone of lesser power to do something (Hyman & others, 2006). Bullying, which includes aggression and implied aggression (as when someone is threatened), involves a desire to hurt the other person. Bullying has recently been recognized as a serious problem in children's lives, with many children reporting that they have been taunted, belittled, or otherwise victimized repeatedly by bullies at school. One survey revealed that as many as 25 percent of children are regularly bullied (Nansel & others, 2001) (Figure 4.18). Bullying can have severe negative effects on the victim, including low self-esteem, depression, low interest in school, and high stress (Dao & others, 2006; Gladstone, Parker, & Malhi, 2006). Moreover, bullies themselves are also likely to show negative consequences (Nansel & others, 2001). In one study, 60 percent of boys who were bullies in middle school had at least one criminal conviction by the age of 24 (Olweus, 1993). As parents and educators have become more aware of the profound effects of bullying, more programs are being developed to combat this problem (Fekkes, Pijpers, & Verlove-Vanhorick, 2006; Weinstein, 2007).

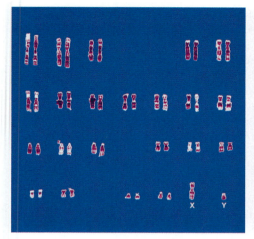 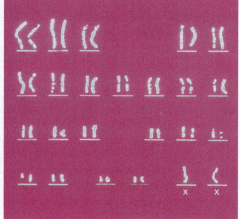

FIGURE 4.19

The Genetic Difference Between Males and Females The chromosome structures of a male (*left*) and female (*right*). The 23rd pair is shown at bottom right. Notice that the male's Y chromosome is smaller than his X chromosome. To obtain pictures of chromosomes, a cell is removed from a person's body, usually from inside the mouth, and the chromosomes are photographed under magnification.

Gender Development Following prenatal tests, or when a baby is born, the first question often is "Is it a boy or a girl?" *Gender* refers to the social and psychological aspects of being female and male. Gender includes not only biological sex but also one's understanding of the meaning of gender in one's life. Although checking off "male" or "female" on a questionnaire may seem like a pretty simple decision, gender is a complex variable influenced by both nature (biological factors) and nurture (social and environmental factors).

Biology and Gender Development In the 1920s researchers confirmed the existence of human sex chromosomes, the genetic material that determines our sex. Anatomical differences were obvious, of course, but not the underlying biological elements that differentiate the sexes. Humans normally have 46 chromosomes arranged in pairs. The 23rd pair may have two X-shaped chromosomes, which produces a female, or it may have both an X-shaped and a Y-shaped chromosome, which produces a male (Figure 4.19).

In the first few weeks after conception, male and female embryos look alike. When the Y chromosome in the male embryo triggers the secretion of **androgens,** the main class of male sex hormones, male sex organs start to differentiate from female sex organs. (Recall from Chapter 3 that hormones are powerful chemical substances secreted by the endocrine glands and carried by the blood throughout the body.) Low levels of androgen in a female embryo allow the normal development of female sex organs—essentially the female genitals are the default. Not until about the seventh week after conception can the developing genitals be observed externally. Long after conception, hormones still play a powerful role in shaping sex characteristics and possibly in influencing gender-related behaviors (Lippa, 2005; Ruble, Martin, & Berenbaum, 2006). You will soon read about the hormonal changes that take place in androgens and **estrogens,** the main class of female sex hormones, during puberty and adulthood.

As in other aspects of human development, in gender behavior, both biology and experience are likely at work. Evolutionary psychologists, however, emphasize the importance of biological processes in behavior (as you may recall from Chapter 1). In evolutionary psychology, differences in gender behavior are the product of gradual genetic adaptations (Buss, 2004; Freeman & Herron, 2007). Evolutionary psychologists argue that women and men have faced different pressures throughout human evolution (Geary, 2006). They stress that the sexes' different status in reproduction is the key to understanding how this evolution took place (Buss, 2004).

In this view, male competition led to a reproductive advantage for dominant males. Men adopted short-term mating practices because these allowed them to increase their reproductive advantage by fathering more children. In contrast, women devoted more effort to parenting and chose mates who could provide their offspring with resources for protection.

androgens The main class of male sex hormones.

estrogens The main class of female sex hormones.

gender roles Expectations for how females and males should think, act, and feel.

Because men competed with other men for access to women, men have evolved dispositions that favor violence and risk taking. Women have developed a preference for long-term mates who can support a family. Men strive to acquire more resources than other men in order to attract more women, and women seek to attract successful, ambitious men who can provide these resources.

Critics of evolutionary psychology theory argue that humans have the decision-making ability to change their gender behavior and thus are not locked into their evolutionary past. They cite extensive cross-cultural variation in gender behavior and mate preference as proof that social experience affects gender behavior (Matlin, 2008; Smith, 2007). For instance, the *social role* view of gender asserts that social experiences have caused differences in gender behavior (Eagly & Koenig, 2006; Wood & Eagly, 2007). The social role approach acknowledges the biological differences between men and women but stresses the ways these differences are played out in differing cultures and societal contexts. Social role theory asserts that, as women were forced to adapt to roles with less power and less status in society, they showed more cooperative and less dominant profiles than men. Indeed, in cultures that view the sexes more equally, women appear to be less likely to show the mate preferences thought to be dictated by evolution (Kasser & Sharma, 1999).

Social Experience and Gender Development How might children's social experiences influence their gender behavior? As children grow up, they adopt **gender roles,** which involve expectations for how females and males should think, act, and feel (Ruble, Martin, & Berenbaum, 2006).

How do children learn what girls and boys are supposed to be like? Recall from our earlier discussion of Piaget's theory that a schema is a mental framework that organizes and guides an individual's thoughts. A recent theory proposes that children develop a gender schema based on what is considered appropriate behavior for females and males in their culture (Martin & Dinella, 2001; Ruble, Martin, & Berenbaum, 2006). Their gender schema then serves as a cognitive framework for interpreting further experiences related to gender. As their gender schema develops, children knit together all sorts of ideas in the context of gender, such as "Girls are expected to be nurturing" and "Boys are expected to be independent." Very young children may not understand gender as a constant and may believe that a person's sex can change depending on very superficial features. They may reason, for instance, that girls have long hair and so if that hair is cut short, a girl becomes a boy.

Some cultures emphasize that children should be reared to adopt traditional gender roles (Shiraev & Levy, 2007). Boys are reared to be "masculine" (powerful, aggressive, and independent, for example) and girls brought up to be "feminine" (sensitive to others, good at relationships, and less assertive, for example). Other cultures, especially in recent times, have placed more emphasis on rearing boys and girls to be more similar—girls being raised to be just as assertive as boys, and boys being raised to be just as caring toward others as girls, for example. Egypt and China are two countries in which traditional gender roles continue to dominate, but the United States has moved toward more diversity in gender roles.

Still, much socialization in U.S. culture is gender based (Bornstein, 2006). Parents often apply the "pink" and "blue" treatment to infants, with boys dressed in blue and girls in pink. Boys receive trucks to play with; girls receive dolls. Parents let boys be more aggressive and require girls to be more reserved.

Peers also play an important role in gender development. Beginning in middle and late childhood (6 to 10 or 11 years of age or until puberty begins) especially, peer groups are often segregated into boy groups and girl groups (Maccoby, 1998, 2002) (Figure 4.20). Peers are stricter than most parents in rewarding gender-appropriate behavior in the culture and punishing gender-inappropriate behavior.

Psychologists have increasingly viewed gender, like many other aspects of human life, as a complex product of nature and nurture (Hyde, 2007; Lippa, 2005; Ruble, Martin, & Berenbaum, 2006). John Money, a well-known sex researcher who coined the term *gender*

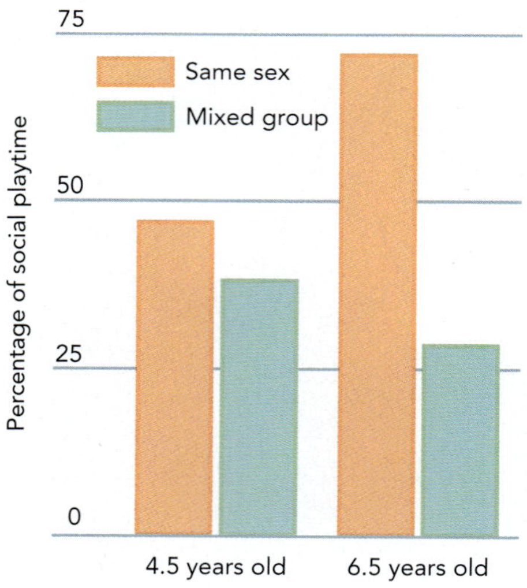

FIGURE 4.20

Developmental Changes in Percentage of Time Spent in Same-Sex and Mixed-Group Settings Observations of children show that they are more likely to play in same-sex than mixed-sex groups. This tendency increases between 4 and 6 years of age.

role, believed strongly that nurture was the most important determinant of gender behavior. In the late 1960s a case presented itself that gave Money the opportunity to test this theory. In 1965 twin boys were born, and a few months after birth, one twin's penis was mutilated during circumcision. The boy's penis was destroyed. Money persuaded the boy's parents to allow him to perform sex-reassignment surgery, that is, to surgically transform the injured male genitals into female genitals and to agree to raise the child as a girl. The "John/Joan" case became famous—the former boy was reared as a girl, dressed like a girl, and treated like a girl in every way possible (Money & Tucker, 1975).

For many years, this case was used as evidence for the amazing flexibility of gender. In fact, until recently, many psychology textbooks still described the case of "John/Joan" as a story of the success of nurture over nature. However, Milton Diamond, a biologist and strong critic of Money's theory, decided to follow up on Money's most famous case study (Diamond & Sigmundson, 1997). Diamond found that over time, "Joan" became less and less interested in being a girl and eventually refused to continue the process of feminization that Money had devised. Indeed, we now know that "Joan" was really David, whose biography, *As Nature Made Him,* written by John Colapinto (2000), revealed the difficulties of his life as a boy, then girl, then boy, and finally man. David struggled with traumatic gender-related life experiences and also depression, eventually committing suicide in 2004. Although this case seems to indicate that nature is quite powerful, similar cases have been studied that have more positive outcomes in favor of nurture (Bradley & others, 1998; Lippa, 2005).

Earlier in our discussion of socioemotional development in childhood, we indicated that experiences outside the home, such as peer relations, are important influences on children's development. And we just described the importance of peer relations in children's gender development. As we see in the Intersection, an aspect of peer relations—friendship—plays a key role in children's development.

Extrafamilial factors such as contact with supportive, competent adults outside the home can contribute powerfully to childhood resiliency.

Positive Psychology and Children's Development: Resilient Children

We cannot fully understand children's development without examining their competence and adaptive capabilities. The concept of resilience highlights this competence and adaptability. **Resilience** refers to a person's ability to recover from or adapt to difficult times. Resilience is a key aspect of thriving—making the most out of life.

Despite hardship, time and time again, resilient children grow up to be capable adults. But why does one person who is subjected to violence, poverty, racism, or the divorce of parents remain mired in lifelong misfortune, whereas another rises above those obstacles to succeed in business, the community, or family life?

Researchers have found that resilient children have one or more advantages that help them to overcome their disadvantages (Masten, 2001; Masten & Coatsworth, 1998; Masten, Obradovic, & Burt, 2006; Masten & Shaffer, 2006). These advantages include individual factors (such as good intellectual functioning), family factors (such as a close, caring relationship with at least one parent), and extrafamilial factors (such as bonds to supportive, competent adults outside the family) (Figure 4.21). Not all of them need to be present to help a child develop successfully. If a child does not have responsible, caring parents, then high self-esteem and a bond to a caring adult outside the home could make the child resilient enough to overcome negative family factors.

The study of resilient children raises questions about what optimal functioning in children is like and which factors contribute to positive development (Leckman & Mayes, 2007). The same characteristics that show up in resilient children are those that appear in competent children who do not face adverse circumstances.

resilience A person's ability to recover from or adapt to difficult times.

Source	Characteristic
Individual	Good intellectual functioning Appealing, sociable, easygoing disposition Self-confidence, high self-esteem Talents Faith
Family	Close relationship to caring parent figure Authoritative parenting: warmth, structure, high expectations Socioeconomic advantages Connections to extended supportive family networks
Extrafamilial Context	Bonds to caring adults outside the family Connections to positive organizations Attending effective schools

FIGURE 4.21

Characteristics of Resilient Children and Their Contexts Resilient children thrive even in the face of hardship. The characteristics in one source can help to compensate for deficiencies in another source.

Developmental Psychology and Social Psychology: What Are Friends For?

Someone once quipped that "friends are God's way of apologizing to us for our families." And it is an interesting attribute of friends that they are not (necessarily) family. Friendships are relationships that are constructed by human beings, not nature. Social relationships such as friendships are crucial to health and well-being throughout our lives (Carstensen, 2006; Giles & others, 2005; Rubin, Bukowski, & Parker, 2006). Researchers have found that "discretionary" social relationships (that is, friendships)—relationships we engage in because we want to, not because we have to—are especially important to well-being (Sherman, Lansford, & Volling, 2006).

Friends are a vital part of life because friends are "there for us," providing us with a sounding board, a shoulder to cry on, and occasionally a much needed reality check. We can count on friends in good times and bad. They celebrate our triumphs and see us through our defeats. A friend is the first person we think to call when we find out we got that important job (or not). We can phone a friend at 7 A.M. when we discover our car battery is dead or at midnight to come get us when that date didn't work out. As American poet Emily Dickinson famously declared, "My friends are my estate."

We can count on friends in good times and bad.

Making friends, keeping friends, and being a friend are all tasks that face the developing human being. Friends are important to children's self-esteem, well-being, and school adjustment (Rubin, Bukowski, & Parker, 2006). Friends (and especially having a best friend) can also be a buffer against the effects of victimization by bullies (Fox & Boulton, 2006). Understanding the processes that contribute to children's ability to make and keep friends is important to our understanding of socioemotional development more broadly.

One important aspect of being a friend is helping. Friendship implies a willingness to help and be helped. An interesting developmental question is whether children understand the central role of helping in friendships. Amanda Rose and Steve Asher (2004) asked 511 fifth-graders to tell them about how they would respond to a friend in need and how they would turn to a friend for help. For example, they asked the children to imagine that their best friend had done poorly on an oral report in class—what would they do for their friend during recess? They also asked the children to imagine themselves in a stressful situation such as being teased in a mean way by peers—how might they approach their best friend for help? The researchers further asked these 10- and 11-year-olds to circle the names of their three best friends on a class roster. In this way the researchers could discover whether the friendships were reciprocated, meaning that if Jeremy circled Jose's name, Jose also circled Jeremy's name.

Rose and Asher were interested in knowing how the children's responses to requests of help related to the number of friends the kids had. They found that children who said that they would "help" a friend in need by pointing out his or her own responsibility or blame for the situation were likely to have fewer friends. Those who said they would try to avoid a friend who had just had a bad experience also had fewer friends. With regard to seeking help from others, those who said they would try not to look dumb or who were concerned about not letting the friend know they had a problem were also likely to have fewer friends. Essentially, children who were uncomfortable giving or receiving help tended to have fewer friends.

Friendships are such a central aspect of our lives that it may be difficult to realize that learning to be a friend is not an innate developmental skill: We are not born with it. We *learn* to let people into our lives—to help others and to ask for help. Perhaps maturity means coming to an understanding that one of the reasons we need friends is to be needed.

REVIEW, ASSESS, AND SHARPEN YOUR THINKING

Review

2 Describe children's development from prenatal stages to adolescence.

- Identify the stages of prenatal development and describe the risks associated with this period.
- Summarize the physical changes after birth that make possible rapid cognitive and socioemotional growth in childhood.
- Explain Piaget's theory of cognitive development and the key criticisms of it.
- Discuss Erikson's theory of psychosocial development and other key research on specific factors believed to have an influence on children's socioemotional development.
- Describe the various advantages of resilient children that help them to overcome their disadvantages.

Assess

1. A parent who allows his children to make choices about their behavior but who still places limitations on what they can do is engaging in
   - A. neglectful parenting.
   - B. authoritarian parenting.
   - C. indulgent parenting.
   - D. authoritative parenting.

2. Which of Erickson's stages of socioemotional development happens during late adulthood?
   - A. intimacy versus isolation
   - B. integrity versus despair
   - C. generativity versus stagnation
   - D. industry versus inferiority

3. Object permanence occurs in which of Piaget's stages of cognitive development?
   - A. concrete operational stage
   - B. formal operational stage
   - C. preoperational stage
   - D. sensorimotor stage

4. The first two weeks after conception are referred to as the
   - A. fetal period.
   - B. germinal period.
   - C. embryonic period.
   - D. zygotic period.

5. What is the name of the technique used to determine if infants can differentiate between objects?
   - A. sticky mittens
   - B. habituation
   - C. preferential looking
   - D. reflexes

Sharpen Your Thinking

Is there a best way to parent? Explain.

---

3 Adolescence

Identify the most important changes that occur in adolescence.

Adolescence is the developmental period of transition from childhood to adulthood. It begins around 10 to 12 years of age and ends at 18 to 21 years of age. In exploring adolescence, we must keep in mind that adolescents are not all the same (Dryfoos & Barkin, 2006). Ethnic, cultural, historical, gender, socioeconomic, and lifestyle variations characterize their life trajectories (Benson & others, 2006; Eccles, 2007). Our image of adolescents should take into account the particular adolescent or group of adolescents we are considering.

Physical Development in Adolescence

Dramatic physical changes characterize adolescence, especially early adolescence. Among the major physical changes of adolescence are those involving puberty and the brain.

Pubertal Change   The signature physical change in adolescence is **puberty,** a period of rapid skeletal and sexual maturation that occurs mainly in early adolescence. In general, we

puberty A period of rapid skeletal and sexual maturation that occurs mainly in early adolescence.

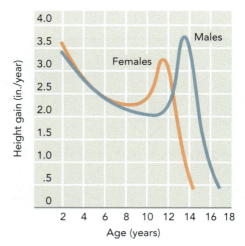

FIGURE 4.22

Pubertal Growth Spurt On average, the pubertal growth spurt begins and peaks about 2 years earlier for girls (starts at 9, peaks at 11½) than for boys (starts at 11½, peaks at 13½). From J. M. Tanner et al., in *Archives of Diseases in Childhood* 41, 1966. Reproduced with permission from the BMJ Publishing Group.

know when an individual is going through puberty, but we have a hard time pinpointing its beginning and its end. Except for menarche (girls' first menstrual cycle), no single marker defines it. For boys the first whisker or first wet dream could mark its appearance, but both may go unnoticed.

The spurt in height and weight that characterizes pubertal change occurs about 2 years earlier for girls than for boys (Figure 4.22). In the United States today, the mean beginning of the spurt is 9 years of age for girls and 11 years for boys. The peak of pubertal change occurs at an average age of 11½ for girls and 13½ for boys.

Hormonal changes lie at the core of pubertal development. The concentrations of certain hormones increase dramatically during puberty (Dorn & others, 2006). *Testosterone,* an androgen, is associated in boys with the development of genitals, an increase in height, and voice change. *Estradiol,* an estrogen, is associated in girls with breast, uterine, and skeletal development. In one study, testosterone levels doubled in girls but increased 18-fold in boys during puberty; similarly, estradiol doubled in boys but increased 8-fold in girls (Nottelmann & others, 1987).

Are concentrations of hormones and adolescents' behavior linked? Developmental psychologists believe that hormonal changes account for at least some of the emotional ups and downs of adolescence (Archibald, Graber, & Brooks-Gunn, 2003; Graber, Brooks-Gunn, & Warren, 2006). But hormones alone are not responsible for adolescent behavior (DeRose, Wright, & Brooks-Gunn, 2006). For example, in one study, social factors (such as stress, bad grades, and relationship problems) explained differences in young girls' depression and anger much more powerfully than did hormonal factors (Brooks-Gunn & Warren, 1989). Moreover, stress, eating patterns, sexual activity, and depression can either activate or suppress hormones (Alan Guttmacher Institute, 2000).

Earlier we considered that physical and socioemotional development are intertwined. Nowhere is this link more apparent than in the timing of puberty. Boys who mature earlier than their peers tend to show more positive socioemotional outcomes, such as being popular with their peers and having higher self-esteem (Graber, Brooks-Gunn, & Warren, 2006). In one recent study, boys who matured early in adolescence were more successful and less likely to drink alcohol or smoke cigarettes than late maturing boys 39 years later in middle adulthood (Taga, Markey, & Friedman, 2006). In contrast, girls who are "early bloomers" tend to be less outgoing and less popular, and they are more likely to smoke, use drugs, become sexually active, and engage less in academic pursuits (Graber, Brooks-Gunn, & Warren, 2006).

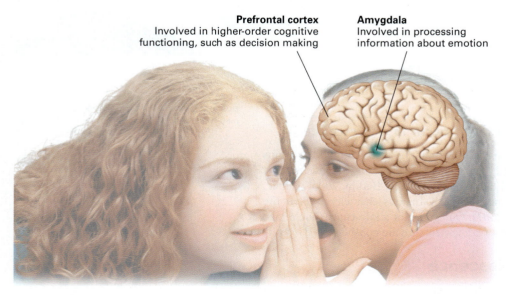

Prefrontal cortex
Involved in higher-order cognitive functioning, such as decision making

Amygdala
Involved in processing information about emotion

FIGURE 4.23

Development Changes in the Adolescent's Brain The amygdala, which is responsible for processing information about emotion, matures earlier than the prefrontal cortex, which is responsible for making decisions and other higher-order cognitive functions.

The Brain The advances in imaging of the human brain have allowed researchers to discover some important changes in the brain during adolescence (Giedd & others, 2006; Nelson, Thomas, & de Haan, 2006; Whitford & others, 2006). These changes focus on the earlier development of the amygdala, which involves emotion, and the later development of the prefrontal cortex, the highest level of the brain that involves reasoning and decision-making (Figure 4.23). Neuroscientists and developmental psychologists who study adolescents are concluding that these changes in the brain may help to explain why adolescents often display very strong emotions but cannot yet control these passions. It is as if their brain does not have the brakes to slow down their emotions. Because of the relatively slow development of the prefrontal cortex, which continues to mature into early adulthood, adolescents may lack the cognitive skills to control their pleasure seeking effectively. This developmental disjunction may account for increased risk taking and other problems in adolescence (Steinberg, 2005, 2006, 2007).

Does what we now know about the adolescent's still developing brain have implications for the legal system? For example, can the recent brain research just discussed be used to argue that because the adolescent's brain, especially the higher-level prefrontal cortex, is still developing, adolescents should not be subject to the death penalty? Some scientists argue that although criminal behavior in adolescence should not be excused, adolescents should not be given the death penalty (Fassler, 2004). Other scientists, such as Jerome Kagan (2004), stress that whether adolescents should be given the death penalty is an ethical issue and that the brain research does not show that adolescents have a reduced blame for committing crimes. Some of the leading neuroscientists studying brain development in adolescence take a similar stance. Elizabeth Sowell (2004) says, "We couldn't just do a scan on a kid and decide if he should be tried as an adult" (p. 599). In 2005, the Supreme Court prohibited the death penalty for adolescents (under the age of 18), but the issue continues to be debated (Ash, 2006).

Cognitive Development in Adolescence

Adolescents undergo significant cognitive changes (Keating, 2004; Kuhn & Franklin, 2006). One is the advance to Piaget's stage of formal operational thinking, which we examined earlier. Another change has to do with adolescent egocentrism.

Piaget's Formal Operational Stage   Piaget said that adolescents enter a fourth, most advanced stage of cognitive development, which he called the formal operational stage, at about 11 to 15 years of age. It is characterized by thought that is abstract, idealistic, and logical.

The abstract quality of thought at the formal operational level is evident in the adolescent's new verbal problem-solving ability. The concrete operational thinker would need to see the concrete elements A, B, and C to be able to make the logical inference that, if A = B = C, then A = C. But the formal operational thinker can solve this problem merely through verbal presentation.

Another indication of the abstract quality of adolescents' thought is their increased tendency to think about thought itself. One adolescent commented, "I began thinking about why I was thinking what I was. Then I began thinking about why I was thinking about why I was thinking about what I was." If these statements sound abstract, they are.

Formal operational thought is also full of idealism and possibilities. Children often think in concrete ways or in terms of what is real and limited. Adolescents begin to engage in extended speculation about the qualities they desire in themselves and in others. In search of the ideal, adolescents' thoughts may take fantasy flights into future possibilities. It is not unusual for adolescents to become impatient with these newfound ideals, however, and to be perplexed over which of many ideal standards to adopt.

At the same time at which adolescents start to think more abstractly and idealistically, they begin to think more logically about problems and possible solutions. This hypothetical-deductive reasoning, as Piaget called it, refers to the ability to develop hypotheses, or best hunches, about ways to solve problems and then to deduce or conclude the best way to solve the problem.

Not all adolescents engage in formal operational thought, especially in hypothetical-deductive reasoning (Kuhn & Franklin, 2006; Wigfield, Byrnes, & Eccles, 2006). Some adolescents and adults remain at Piaget's concrete operational stage.

Adolescent Egocentrism   Especially in early adolescence, adolescent thought is egocentric. *Adolescent egocentrism* involves the beliefs that others are as preoccupied with the adolescent as he or she is, that one is unique, and that one is invincible (Elkind, 1978). Adolescent egocentrism means that adolescents perceive others to be noticing and watching them more than actually is the case. Think of the eighth-grade boy who senses that everyone else has noticed the small pimple on his face or the teenage girl who says, "My mother has no idea about how much pain I'm going through. She has never been hurt like I have. Why did he break up with me?"

The aspect of adolescent egocentrism that can produce the most harm is a sense of invincibility. This belief may lead to behaviors such as drag racing, drug use, suicide attempts, or unsafe sex leading to sexually transmitted diseases or adolescent pregnancy. Imagine the adolescent girl who hears that a friend has become pregnant. She may say, "I won't ever let that happen to me"—and then have unprotected sex the next week. Her sense of invincibility causes her to behave in a high-risk manner.

A recent study of sixth- through twelfth-graders revealed that a sense of invincibility was linked to engaging in risky behaviors such as smoking cigarettes, drinking alcohol, and delinquency (Aalsma, Lapsley, & Flannery, 2006). On a positive note, the adolescent's sense of invincibility may also lead to courageous efforts to save people's lives in hazardous circumstances, as when Jabbar Gibson commandeered a school bus to rescue people from New Orleans after Hurricane Katrina.

Socioemotional Development in Adolescence

The increase in abstract and idealistic thought during adolescence serves as a foundation for exploring one's identity. Many aspects of socioemotional development—such as relationships with parents, peer interaction and friendships, and cultural and ethnic values—contribute to an adolescent's identity development. Erikson's theory addresses the manner in which adolescents seek their identities.

Erikson's Theory and Identity Development   As we saw in the section on children's socioemotional development, Erik Erikson's life-span theory states that people go through eight psychosocial stages of development. Within the eight stages that Erikson (1968) proposed, his ideas about the formation of identity during adolescence are among his most important contributions to psychology. They changed the way we think about adolescence (Kroger, 2007). For example, Erikson encouraged us to look at adolescents not just as hormone-driven beings but also as individuals finding out who they are and searching for their niche in the world.

Erikson's theory characterizes the main concern of the fifth stage of socioemotional development as **identity versus identity confusion.** In seeking an *identity,* adolescents face the challenges of finding out who they are, what they are all about, and where they are going in life. Adolescents are confronted with many new roles and adult statuses—from the vocational to the romantic. If they do not adequately explore their identities during this stage, they emerge confused about who they are. Therefore, Erikson argues, parents should allow adolescents to explore many different roles and many paths within a particular role and not push an identity on them.

Erikson described adolescence as a moratorium, by which he meant a gap in time and in the developing mind between the security of childhood and the autonomy of adulthood. Adolescents who use the moratorium to explore alternatives can reach some resolution of the identity crisis and emerge with a new sense of self that is both refreshing and acceptable. Those who do not successfully resolve the crisis become confused, suffering what Erikson calls *identity confusion.* This confusion is expressed in one of two ways: Either individuals withdraw, isolating themselves from peers and family, or they lose themselves in the crowd.

Erikson noted that in U.S. culture, adolescents want to decide for themselves such matters as what careers they will pursue, whether they will go to college, and whether they will marry. They want to free themselves from the control of their parents and other adults and make their own choices. At the same time, many deeply fear making the wrong decisions—and failing. In some cases, the problem may be simply that adolescents have not yet realized their own growing cognitive abilities. One strength that equips them to pursue their identities effectively is the growing abstractness and logic of their thought, by which they can reason with increasing sophistication.

Identity Status   Building on Erikson's ideas, James Marcia (1980, 2002) proposed the concept of *identity status* to describe a person's position in the development of an identity. In his view, two dimensions of identity are important. *Exploration* refers to a person's exploring various options for a career and for personal values. *Commitment* involves making a decision about which identity path to follow and making a personal investment in attaining that identity.

identity versus identity confusion Erikson's fifth psychological stage in which adolescents face the challenge of finding out who they are, what they are all about, and where they are going in life.

Various combinations of exploration and commitment give rise to one of four identity statuses (Figure 4.24):

- *Identity diffusion:* A person has not yet explored meaningful alternatives and has not made a commitment. Many young adolescents have a diffuse (unclear) identity status. They have not yet begun to explore different career options and personal values.

- *Identity foreclosure:* A person makes a commitment to an identity before adequately exploring various options. For example, an adolescent might say that she wants to be a doctor because that is what her parents want her to be, rather than exploring career options and then deciding on her own to be a doctor.

- *Identity moratorium:* A person is exploring alternative paths but has not yet made a commitment. Many college students are in a moratorium status with regard to a major field of study or a career.

- *Identity achievement:* A person has explored alternative paths and made a commitment. For example, an individual might have examined a number of careers over an extended period of time and decided to pursue one wholeheartedly.

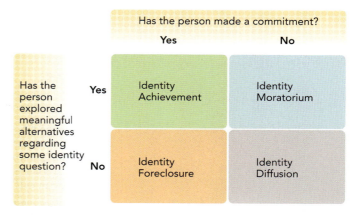

FIGURE 4.24

Marcia's Four Statuses of Identity Who are you? When you think of how you have come to identify yourself, which of these four statuses does your answer best represent?

Ethnic Identity   Developing an identity in adolescence can be especially challenging for individuals from ethnic minority groups (Phinney, 2003, 2006; Spencer, 2006). As they mature cognitively, many adolescents become acutely aware of the evaluation of their ethnic group by the majority culture. In addition, an increasing number of minority adolescents face the challenge of biculturalism—identifying in some ways with their ethnic minority group and in other ways with the majority culture (Phinney & others, 2006).

In one study, a researcher examined the development of ethnic identity in Asian American, African American, Latino, and White tenth-grade students in Los Angeles (Phinney, 1989). Adolescents from each of the three ethnic minority groups faced a similar need to deal with their ethnic-group identity in a predominately White, Euro-American culture. But the three groups faced different challenges. For Asian American adolescents, the pressure to achieve academically was an important identity concern. Female African American adolescents were concerned that White standards of beauty (especially hair and skin color) did not apply to them. Male African American adolescents were concerned with possible job discrimination and the need to distinguish themselves from a negative societal image. For Latino adolescents, prejudice was a recurrent theme, as was the conflict in values between their cultural heritage and the majority culture. Although it might seem that being a member of an ethnic minority would make life more stressful, research has shown that having a strong ethnic identity can be a resource that buffers adolescents from the effects of discrimination (Sellers & Shelton, 2003; Sellers & others, 2006).

For both minority and majority adolescents, however, developing a positive identity is an important life theme (Kroger, 2007; Phinney, 2006). Read more about how to develop a positive identity in the Psychology and Life feature.

Parents and Peers   Parents and peers are both powerful influences on adolescents' development (Bukowski, Brendgen, & Vitaro, 2007; Grusec & Davidov, 2007). An important developmental task in adolescence is to acquire the ability to make competent decisions in an increasingly independent manner (Collins & Steinberg, 2006). To help adolescents reach their full potential, an important parental role is to be an effective manager—one who locates information, makes contacts, helps to structure their offspring's choices, and provides guidance. By assuming this managerial role, parents help adolescents to avoid pitfalls and to work their way through the myriad of choices and decisions they face (Parke & Buriel, 2006).

A key aspect of the managerial role of parenting is effective monitoring of the adolescent (Collins & Steinberg, 2006; Dodge, Coie, & Lynam, 2006). Monitoring includes supervising the adolescent's choice of social settings, activities, and friends, as well as academic efforts. A recent research review concluded that when African American parents

Michelle Chin, age 16, reflecting on her identity, commented, "Parents do not understand that teenagers need to find out who they are, which means a lot of experimenting, a lot of mood swings, a lot of emotions and awkwardness. Like any teenager, I am facing an identity crisis. I am still trying to figure out whether I am a Chinese American or an American with Asian eyes."

PSYCHOLOGY AND LIFE

Developing a Positive Identity

Following are some helpful attitudes for developing a positive identity:

- *Be aware that your identity is complex and takes a long time to develop.* Your identity has many components. One of your main identity tasks is to integrate all of these parts into a meaningful whole. Your identity does not arise in a sudden burst of insight. It is achieved in bits and pieces over your lifetime. What are some of the bits and pieces of your identity development?

- *Make the most of your college years.* For many individuals, the college years are an important time for identity development. College by its very nature encourages exploration and exposure to a wide variety of ideas and values. Your views likely will be challenged by instructors and classmates, and these challenges may motivate you to change some aspects of your identity.

- *Examine whether your identity is your own or your parents'.* Some college students have foreclosed on an identity without adequately considering alternatives. Identity foreclosure occurs especially when individuals accept their parents' views without deeply questioning whether they want to be just like them. Individuals might come to an identity similar to that of their parents; but while evaluating different paths, they may discover a more suitable identity. Have you genuinely developed an identity that is your own?

monitored their son's academic achievement—by ensuring that he completed homework and restricted the time spent on nonproductive distractions (such as video games and TV) and by participating in a consistent, positive dialogue with teachers and school officials—their son's academic achievement benefited (Mandara, 2006).

During adolescence, individuals spend more time with peers than they did in childhood. These peer influences can be positive or negative (Rubin, Bukowski, & Parker, 2006). As we saw earlier in the chapter, a key aspect of positive peer relations is having one or more close friends. Adolescents can learn to be skilled and sensitive partners in intimate relationships by forging close friendships with selected peers.

Of course, some peers and friends can have a negative influence on adolescents' development. Consider the findings of three recent studies: Hanging out with antisocial peers in adolescence was a stronger predictor of substance abuse than relationships with parents (Nation & Heflinger, 2006); higher levels of antisocial peer involvement in early adolescence (13–16 years of age) were linked with higher rates of delinquent behavior in late adolescence (17–18 years of age) (Laird & others, 2005); and deviant peer affiliation was related to adolescents' depressive symptoms (Connell & Dishion, 2006).

Positive Psychology and Adolescence

Too often adolescents have been stereotyped as abnormal and deviant. Young people of every generation have seemed radical, unnerving, and different to adults—different in how they look and behave and even different in the music they enjoy. But adolescence is more accurately viewed as a time of evaluation, a time of decision making, and a time of commitment as young people carve out their place in the world (Hunter & Csikszentmihalyi, 2003; Kroger, 2007). It is an enormous error to confuse the adolescent's enthusiasm for trying on new identities

The managerial role of parenting is effective monitoring of the adolescent's friends, social activities, and efforts in school.

and enjoying moderate amounts of outrageous behavior with hostility toward parents and society. Searching for an identity is a time-honored way in which adolescents move toward accepting, rather than rejecting, parental and societal values.

How competent adolescents will eventually become often depends on their access to legitimate opportunities for growth such as a quality education, community and societal support for achievement and involvement, and access to good jobs. Especially important in adolescents' development is long-term support from adults who deeply care about them (Benson, 2007; Silbereisen & Lerner, 2007).

As evidence that the majority of adolescents develop more positively than is commonly believed, consider a research study conducted by Daniel Offer and his colleagues (1988) that sampled the self-images of adolescents around the world— in the United States, Australia, Bangladesh, Hungary, Israel, Italy, Japan, Taiwan, Turkey, and West Germany. About three of every four of these adolescents had healthy self-images. Most were happy, enjoyed life, and believed they had the ability to cope effectively with stress. They valued school and work.

But what about the one in four adolescents who did not have positive self-images? What might be done to help them negotiate adolescence? Reed Larson (2000, 2007) argues that adolescents need more opportunities to develop the capacity for initiative, which he defines as becoming self-motivated and expending effort to reach challenging goals. Too often adolescents find themselves bored with life. To counter this boredom and help adolescents develop more initiative, Larson recommends structured voluntary activities such as sports, the arts, and participation in organizations.

 REVIEW, ASSESS, AND SHARPEN YOUR THINKING

Review

3 Identify the most important changes that occur in adolescence.

- Discuss the nature of puberty.
- Describe the key aspects of cognitive development during adolescence.
- Explain identity development in adolescence and describe the importance of parents and peers in adolescent development.
- Explore the contribution of positive psychology to our thinking about adolescent development.

Assess

1. Jocelyn is a 19 year old college student and has taken classes in a variety of disciplines. After sampling from many different majors, she decides to be a biology major. In what stage of identity status is Jocelyn?

   A. identity diffusion

   B. identity moratorium

   C. identity achievement

   D. identity foreclosure

2. Risk-taking behaviors in adolescents may be a result of

   A. identity foreclosure.

   B. identity confusion.

   C. the industry versus guilt stage.

   D. adolescent egocentrism.

3. Levels of which hormone increase drastically in girls during puberty?

   A. testosterone

   B. estradiol

   C. androgen

   D. norepinephrine

4. It is thought that the increase in emotionality that happen during puberty are a result of early development of the _____ but later development of the _____.

   A. amygdala, prefrontal cortex

   B. prefrontal cortex, amygdala

   C. hippocampus, thalamus

   D. thalamus, hippocampus

5. What does the psychological research tell us about ethnic identity?

A. Adolescents who downplay the importance of their ethnic identity fare better in school.

B. Adolescents use their ethnic identity to avoid other developmental tasks.

C. Adolescents who have a strong ethnic identity are better able to cope with the effects of discrimination.

D. Adolescents from different racial groups have the same challenges to their ethnic identity.

Sharpen Your Thinking

Are Marcia's identity statuses useful to you in thinking about your own identity development? To explore this question, evaluate your levels of exploration and commitment in regard to career and personal values. Into which identity status would you place yourself?

4 Adult Development and Aging

Discuss adult development and the positive dimensions of aging.

Development continues throughout the roughly 60 (and often more) years of adulthood. Developmental psychologists identify three approximate periods in adult development: early adulthood (20s and 30s), middle adulthood (40s and 50s), and late adulthood (60s until death). Each phase features some distinctive physical, cognitive, and socioemotional changes. However, before we examine these three main age periods, we will survey the transition from adolescence to adulthood and the period called *emerging adulthood*. If you are a traditional-aged college student, this is the time frame in the life span in which you are now living.

Emerging Adulthood

The transition from adolescence to adulthood is now referred to as **emerging adulthood** (Arnett, 2004, 2006, 2007). Like youth, the age range for emerging adulthood is approximately 18 to 25 years of age. Experimentation and exploration characterize the emerging adult. At this point in their development, many individuals are still exploring which career path they want to follow, what they want their identity to be, and which lifestyle they want to adopt (for example, single, cohabiting, or married).

Jeffrey Arnett (2006) recently concluded that five key features characterize emerging adulthood:

- *Identity exploration, especially in love and work:* Emerging adulthood is the time during which key changes in identity take place for many individuals.
- *Instability:* Residential changes peak during early adulthood, a time during which there also is often instability in love, work, and education.
- *Self-focused:* According to Arnett, emerging adults "are self-focused in the sense that they have little in the way of social obligations, little in the way of duties and commitments to others, which leaves them with a great deal of autonomy in running their own lives" (2006, p. 10).
- *Feeling "in between":* Many emerging adults do not consider themselves adolescents or full-fledged adults.
- *The age of possibilities, a time when individuals have an opportunity to transform their lives:* Arnett (2006) describes two ways in which emerging adulthood is the age of possibilities: (1) Many emerging adults are optimistic about their future, and (2) for emerging adults who have experienced difficult times while growing up, emerging adulthood presents an opportunity to direct their lives in a more positive direction (Masten, Obradovic, & Burt, 2006; Schulenberg & Zarrett, 2006).

emerging adulthood The transition from adolescence to adulthood.

Does life get better for individuals when they become emerging adults? John Schulenberg and Nicole Zarrett (2006) have examined this question. For the most part, life does get better for most emerging adults. For example, Figure 4.25 shows a steady increase in self-reported well-being from 18 years of age through 26 years of age. Figure 4.26 indicates that risk taking decreases during the same time frame.

Why do the health and well-being of emerging adults improve over their adolescent levels? One possibility is that individuals have increasing choices in their daily living and life decisions during emerging adulthood. This increase can lead to more opportunities for individuals to exercise self-control in their lives. Also, emerging adulthood provides an opportunity for individuals who engaged in problem behavior during adolescence to get their lives together. However, the lack of structure and support that often characterizes emerging adulthood can produce a downturn in health and well-being for some individuals (Schulenberg & Zarrett, 2006).

One individual who got his life together in emerging adulthood is Michael Maddaus (Broderick, 2003; Masten, Obradovic, & Burt, 2006). During Michael's childhood and adolescence in Minneapolis, his mother drank heavily and his stepfather abused him. Michael coped by spending increasing time on the streets. Arrested more than 20 times for his delinquency, and frequently placed in detention centers, he rarely went to school. At 17, he joined the navy, and the experience helped him to gain self-discipline and hope. After his brief stint in the navy, he completed a GED and began taking community college classes. However, he continued to have some setbacks with drugs and alcohol. A defining moment as an emerging adult came when he delivered furniture to a surgeon's home. The surgeon became interested in helping Michael, and his mentorship led to Michael's volunteering at a rehabilitation center and then to a job with a neurosurgeon. Eventually, Michael obtained his undergraduate degree, went to medical school, got married, and started a family. Today, Michael Maddaus is a successful surgeon whose activities include telling his story to troubled youth. Maddaus is an excellent exemplar of the concept of resilience that we discussed earlier in the chapter.

Physical Development in Adulthood

Singer-actress Bette Midler once remarked that after age 30 a body has a mind of its own. How do we age physically as we go through the adult years?

Physical Changes in Early Adulthood   Most adults reach their peak physical development during their 20s and are the healthiest then. For athletes—not only at the Olympic level but also the average athlete—performance peaks in the 20s, especially for strength and speed events such as weight lifting and the 100-meter dash (Schultz & Curnow, 1988). The main exceptions are female gymnasts and swimmers, who often peak in adolescence, and marathon runners, who tend to peak in their late 30s.

Unfortunately, early adulthood also is the time when many physical skills begin to decline. The decline in strength and speed often is noticeable in the 30s.

Perhaps because of their robust physical skills and overall health, young adults rarely recognize that bad eating habits, heavy drinking, and smoking in early adulthood can impair their health as they age. Despite warnings on packages and in advertisements that cigarettes are hazardous to health, individuals increase their use of cigarettes as they enter early adulthood (Johnston, Bachman, & O'Malley, 1989). They also increase their use of alcohol, marijuana, amphetamines, barbiturates, and hallucinogens.

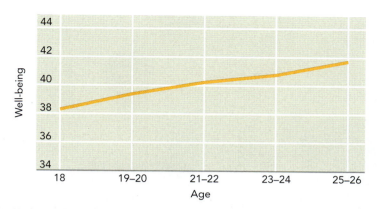

FIGURE 4.25

Well-Being Through Emerging Adulthood Well-being (measured here by a composite that includes self-esteem, self-efficacy, and social support) shows a steady increase over emerging adulthood. The highest possible score was 95.

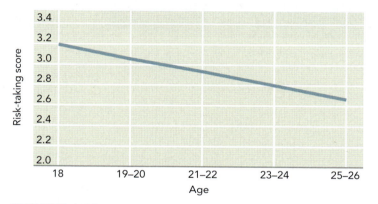

FIGURE 4.26

Risk Taking Through Emerging Adulthood Risk taking (measured here with two items asking young adults if they "got a kick out of doing things that are a little dangerous" and "enjoyed doing something a little risky") shows a steady decrease over emerging adulthood. The highest possible score was 5.

We go through many observable and unobservable changes as we age.

A special concern is heavy drinking by college students (Johnston & others, 2006; Karam, Kypri, & Salamoun, 2007). In a study of 14,000 college students, approximately 40 percent said they had engaged in binge drinking (drinking five or more drinks in a row for men and four or more in a row for women) at least once a week in the 2 weeks before they were surveyed (Wechsler & others, 2000). Heavy drinking can take a toll on college students and threaten their future. In one study at 140 colleges, binge drinking was associated with class absences, physical injuries, troubles with police, and unprotected sex (Wechsler & others, 1994).

Fortunately, by the time individuals reach their mid-20s, many have reduced their use of alcohol and other drugs. Wendy Slutske (2005) reported the results of a recent national survey of 6,352 young adults showing that college-attending young adults were no more likely than adults who did not attend college to receive a diagnosis of alcohol dependency. Slutske found that college students are more likely to abuse alcohol but are no more likely to become alcoholics.

Physical Changes in Middle Adulthood   One of the most visible physical changes in middle adulthood is appearance. By the 40s or 50s, the skin has begun to wrinkle and sag because of a loss of fat and collagen in underlying tissues. Small, localized areas of pigmentation in the skin produce age spots, especially in areas exposed to sunlight such as the hands and face (McCullough & Kelly, 2006). Hair becomes thinner and grayer due to a lower replacement rate and a decline in melanin production.

Individuals lose height in middle age, and many gain weight (McDermott & others, 2006). On average, from 30 to 50 years of age, men lose about ½ inch in height, and then might lose another ¾ inch from 50 to 70 years of age (Hoyer & Roodin, 2003). The height loss for women can be as much as 2 inches from 25 to 75 years of age. Note that there are large variations in the extent to which individuals become shorter with aging. The decrease in height is due to bone loss in the vertebrae. On average, body fat accounts for about 10 percent of body weight in adolescence; it makes up 20 percent or more in middle age.

Perhaps because the signs of aging are all too visible to us, we become more acutely concerned about our health in our 40s. In fact, most individuals do experience a general decline in physical fitness in middle adulthood and some deterioration in health. The three greatest health concerns at this age are heart disease, cancer, and weight. Cancer related to smoking often surfaces in middle adulthood.

Because U.S. culture values a youthful appearance, the physical deterioration that takes place in middle adulthood—graying hair, wrinkling skin, and a sagging body—can be difficult for the individual to handle. Many middle-aged adults dye their hair and join weight reduction programs; some undergo cosmetic treatments and even surgery to look young.

For women, entering middle age also means that menopause will soon occur. Usually in the late 40s or early 50s, a woman's menstrual periods cease completely. The average age at which women have their last period is 52, but 10 percent of women undergo menopause before age 40.

With menopause comes a dramatic decline in the ovaries' production of estrogen. Estrogen decline produces uncomfortable symptoms in some menopausal women, such as hot flashes (sudden, brief flushing of the skin and a feeling of elevated body temperature), nausea, fatigue, and rapid heartbeat. Some menopausal women report depression and irritability (Matthews & others, 2007), but in some instances these feelings are related to other circumstances in the women's lives, such as becoming divorced, losing a job, or caring for a sick parent (Schmidt & others, 2004). Research reveals that menopause does not produce psychological or physical problems for most women (Wise, 2006).

Although menopause is not the negative experience for most women that it was once thought to be, the loss of fertility is an important marker for women: Its approach means that they have to make final decisions about having children. Women in their 30s who have never had children sometimes speak about being "up against the biological clock" because they cannot postpone the decision much longer.

Physical Changes in Late Adulthood   The concept of a period called "late adulthood" is a recent one: Until the twentieth century, most individuals died before they were 65. Many societies around the world have become less youthful, however, and so we need to develop a better understanding of the later years of life (Birren & Schaie, 2006; Markides, 2007; Schaie, 2007).

Developmentalists distinguish between life span and life expectancy. The term *life span* is used to describe the upper boundary of a species' life, the maximum number of years an individual can expect to live. The maximum number of years human beings can live is about 120. As can be seen in Figure 4.27, *Homo sapiens* is believed to have one of the longest life spans, if not the longest.

The term *life expectancy* describes the number of years that will probably be lived by the average person born in a particular year. Improvements in medicine, nutrition, exercise, and lifestyle have increased our life expectancy an average of 31 additional years since 1900 (Figure 4.28). According to the National Center for Health Statistics (Miniño, Heron, & Smith, 2004), the life expectancy of individuals born today in the United States is 77.9 years (80.4 for women, 75.2 for men). One in three women born today is expected to live to be 100 or more. According to the United Nations (2002), the world's population of individuals 65 years and older tripled from 1950 to 2000, and the fastest-growing segment of the population is 85 years and older. Individuals over the age of 80 currently make up 11 percent of the over-60 age group and will grow to 19 percent by 2050. By 2050, the number of older adults will exceed the number of younger adults for the first time in history.

Although life expectancy has risen dramatically, life span does not seem to have increased since the beginning of recorded history. Even if we are remarkably healthy through our adult lives, we begin to age at some point.

Biological Theories of Aging   Of the many proposed biological theories of aging, two especially merit attention: the cellular-clock theory and the free-radical theory. Both of these theories look within the body's cells for causes of aging. The *cellular-clock theory* is Leonard Hayflick's (1977) view that cells can divide a maximum of about 100 times and that, as we age, our cells become less capable of dividing. Hayflick found that cells extracted from adults in their 50s to 70s had divided fewer than 100 times. The total number of cell divisions was roughly related to the age of the individual. Based on the way cells divide, Hayflick places the upper limit of the human life span at about 120 years.

In the past decade, scientists have tried to explain why cells lose their ability to divide (Chai & others, 2006). The answer may lie at the tips of chromosomes. Each time a cell divides, the *telomeres* that protect the ends of chromosomes become shorter and shorter (Figure 4.29). After about 100 replications, the telomeres are dramatically reduced, and the cell no longer can reproduce (Shay & Wright, 2005, 2006, 2007). In one study, age-related telomere erosion was linked with an inability to recover from stress and an increase in cancer (Rudolf & others, 1999).

Another biological theory of aging is *free-radical theory*, which states that people age because inside their cells unstable oxygen molecules known as free radicals are produced. These molecules ricochet around in the cells, damaging DNA and other cellular structures (Chandel & Budinger, 2007; Liu & others, 2007). The damage done by free radicals may lead to a range of disorders, including cancer and arthritis.

The Brain and Alzheimer Disease   Just as the aging body has been found to have a greater capacity for renewal than previously thought, so has the aging brain (Dempsey &

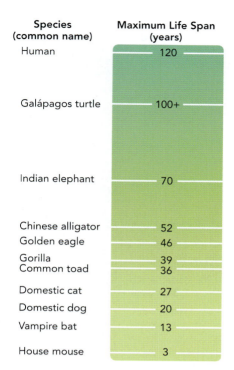

Species (common name)	Maximum Life Span (years)
Human	120
Galápagos turtle	100+
Indian elephant	70
Chinese alligator	52
Golden eagle	46
Gorilla	39
Common toad	36
Domestic cat	27
Domestic dog	20
Vampire bat	13
House mouse	3

FIGURE 4.27

Maximum Recorded Life Spans of Various Species Although the sight of a mouse scurrying around your kitchen can be quite terrifying, you can take comfort in the fact that he has only a couple of years to live, unless you catch him first.

Frenchwoman Jeanne Louise Calment pushed the upper boundary of the human life span, dying in 1997 at the age of 122. Asked on her 120th birthday about the kind of future she expected, Calment replied, "A very short one." Greater ages have been claimed, but scientists say that the human life span is approximately 120 years. However, as genetic engineering continues to make progress, the possibility of altering cellular functioning to increase the human life span is raised. Some biologists even have brought up the possibility that in the future humans might live 400 years!

Time Period	Average Life Expectancy (in years)
2004, USA	78
1954, USA	70
1915, USA	54
1900, USA	47
19th century, England	41
1620, Massachusetts Bay Colony	35
Middle Ages, England	33
Ancient Greece	20
Prehistoric times	18

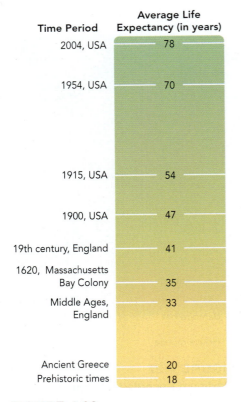

FIGURE 4.28

Human Life Expectancy at Birth from Prehistoric to Contemporary Times
Advances in nutrition and medicine have led to a dramatic increase in human life expectancy. Longer lives mean new research questions for psychologists interested in coping with the effects of aging.

Kalluri, 2007; Kramer, Fabiani, & Colcombe, 2006). For decades, scientists believed that no new brain cells are generated past early childhood. However, as mentioned in Chapter 3, researchers recently discovered that adults can grow new brain cells throughout their lives (Briones, 2006; Chopp, Zhang, & Jiang, 2007; Gould & others, 1999). In one study, the growth of dendrites (the receiving, branching part of the neuron, or nerve cell) continued through the 70s, although no new dendritic growth was discovered in people in their 90s (Coleman, 1986).

Even in late adulthood, the brain has remarkable repair capability. Stanley Rapaport (1994) compared the brains of younger and older adults when they were engaged in the same tasks. The older adults' brains literally rewired themselves to compensate for losses. If one neuron was not up to the job, neighboring neurons helped to pick up the slack. Rapaport concluded that, as brains age, they can shift responsibilities for a given task from one region to another.

Changes in lateralization may provide one type of adaptation in aging adults (Kramer, Fabiani, & Colcombe, 2006). Lateralization is the specialization of function in one hemisphere of the brain or the other. Using neuroimaging techniques, researchers recently found that brain activity in the prefrontal cortex is lateralized less in older adults than in younger adults when they are engaging in cognitive tasks (Cabeza, 2002; Cabeza, Nyberg, & Park, 2005; Rossi & others, 2005). For example, Figure 4.30 shows that when younger adults are given the task of recognizing words they have previously seen, they process the information primarily in the right hemisphere; older adults are more likely to use both hemispheres (Madden & others, 1999). The decrease in lateralization in older adults might play a compensatory role in the aging brain. That is, using both hemispheres may improve the cognitive functioning of older adults.

Alzheimer disease—a progressive, irreversible brain disorder that is characterized by gradual deterioration of memory, reasoning, language, and eventually physical functioning—does not present such encouraging prospects (Thompson & others, 2007). Approximately 2.5 million people over the age of 65 in the United States have Alzheimer disease; the percentage of people who have it doubles for every 5 years beyond age 65. As Alzheimer disease progresses, the brain deteriorates and shrinks (Harman, 2006).

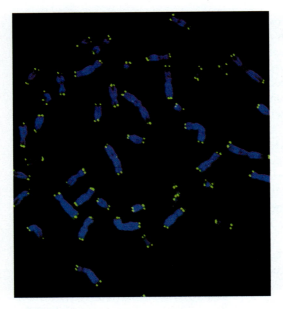

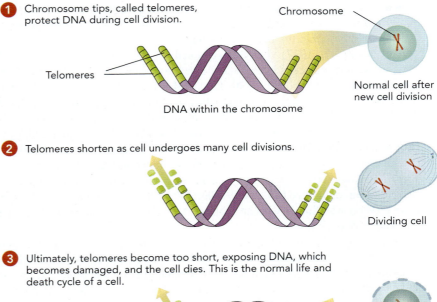

1. Chromosome tips, called telomeres, protect DNA during cell division.

Chromosome

Telomeres

DNA within the chromosome

Normal cell after new cell division

2. Telomeres shorten as cell undergoes many cell divisions.

Dividing cell

3. Ultimately, telomeres become too short, exposing DNA, which becomes damaged, and the cell dies. This is the normal life and death cycle of a cell.

Cell death

FIGURE 4.29

Telomeres and Aging The photograph shows telomeres lighting up the tips of chromosomes. The figure illustrates how the telomeres shorten every time a cell divides. Eventually, after about 100 divisions, the telomeres are greatly reduced in length. As a result, the cell can no longer reproduce, and it dies.

Figure 4.31 strikingly contrasts the brain of a normal aging individual with the brain of an individual who has Alzheimer disease. Among the main characteristics of Alzheimer disease are the increasing number of tangles (tied bundles of proteins that impair the function of neurons) and plaques (deposits that accumulate in the brain's blood vessels). The formation of tangles and plaques is a normal part of aging, but it is far more pronounced in Alzheimer disease.

Alzheimer disease also involves a deficiency in acetylcholine, which you read about in Chapter 3 (Holzgrabe & others, 2007). This neurotransmitter plays an important role in memory. The main drug currently used to treat Alzheimer disease is Aricept, which blocks chemicals that cut acetylcholine apart (Birks, 2006). However, such drugs do not prevent the brain from continuing to deteriorate in Alzheimer patients.

Research on the aging brain does give cause for hope. One ongoing study, the Nun Study described in Chapter 2, involves nearly 700 nuns in a convent in Mankato, Minnesota (Snowdon, 1995, 1997, 2001, 2003, 2007) (Figure 4.32). Although in Chapter 2 we examined the aspects of the study related to happiness, this research has also examined brain functioning and Alzheimer disease. By examining the nuns' donated brains as well as others, neuroscientists have documented the remarkable ability of the aging brain to grow and change. Even the oldest Mankato nuns lead intellectually challenging lives, and neuroscientists believe that stimulating mental activities increase dendritic branching. The researchers are also intrigued to find that the nuns are showing almost no signs of Alzheimer disease. Indeed, researchers have consistently found support for the "use it or lose it" concept: The cognitive skills of older adults benefit considerably when they engage in challenging intellectual activities (Baltes, Lindenberger, & Staudinger, 2006; Willis & Schaie, 2005).

Cognitive Development in Adulthood

Earlier in the chapter, you learned that considerable changes take place in children's and adolescents' cognitive development. What kind of cognitive changes occur in adults?

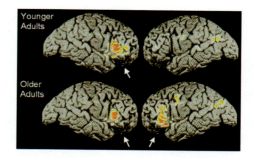

FIGURE 4.30

The Decrease in Brain Lateralization in Older Adults Younger adults primarily used the right prefrontal region of the brain (*top left photo*) during a recall memory task, while older adults used both the left and right prefrontal regions (*bottom two photos*).

crystallized intelligence An individual's accumulated information and verbal skills.

fluid intelligence An individual's ability to reason abstractly.

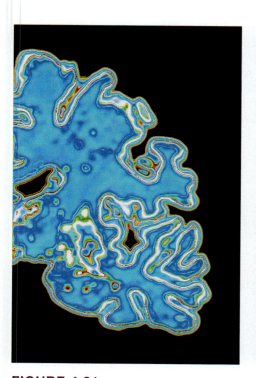
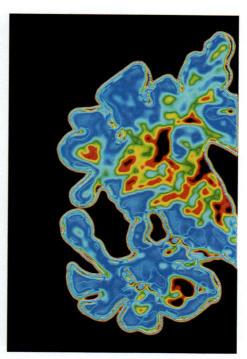

FIGURE 4.31

Two Brains: Normal Aging and Alzheimer Disease (*Left*) A slice of a normally aging brain. (*Right*) A slice of a brain ravaged by Alzheimer disease. Notice the deterioration and shrinking in the Alzheimer-diseased brain.

FIGURE 4.32

The Brains of the Mankato Nuns

At 90 years old, Nun Study participant Sister Rosella Kreuzer, SSND, remains an active, contributing member of her community of sisters. Sister Rosella designed the Nun Study logo, *That You May Have Life to the Full.* (*Inset*) A neuroscientist holds a brain donated by one of the Mankato Nun Study participants.

FIGURE 4.33

Fluid and Crystallized Intellectual Development Across the Life Span

According to Horn, crystallized intelligence (based on cumulative learning experiences) increases throughout the life span, but fluid intelligence (the ability to perceive and manipulate information) steadily declines from middle adulthood.

Cognition in Early Adulthood Piaget theorized that formal operational thought is the highest level of thinking, and he argued that no new qualitative changes in cognition take place in adulthood. He did not believe that a person with a PhD in physics thinks any differently than a young adolescent who has reached the stage of formal operational thought. The only difference is that the physicist has more knowledge in a specific scientific domain. The physicist and the young adolescent both use logical thought to develop alternatives for solving a problem and to deduce a solution from the options.

Piaget was right about some adolescents and some adults—but not about all of them. As you learned earlier, some adolescents are not formal operational thinkers; as well, many adults never reach that stage.

Yet some experts on cognitive development argue that the typical idealism of Piaget's formal operational stage is replaced in young adulthood by more realistic, pragmatic thinking (Labouvie-Vief, 1986). Also, adolescents tend to think in absolute terms—things are either all this way or that way. As they go through the college years, individuals often begin to think in more relative and reflective ways (Kitchener & King, 1981). Gisela Labouvie-Vief (2006) recently proposed that the increasing complexity of cultures in the past century has generated a greater need for reflective, more complex thinking that takes into account the changing nature of knowledge and challenges. She also emphasizes that key aspects of cognitive development for young adults include deciding on a particular worldview, recognizing that the worldview is subjective, and understanding that diverse worldviews should be acknowledged. In her perspective, considerable individual variation characterizes the thinking of emerging adults, with the highest level of thinking attained only by some. She argues that the level of education individuals achieve influences how likely they will maximize their thinking potential.

In sum, for the most part, intellectual skills are strong in early adulthood (Kitchener, King, & DeLuca, 2006). Do they begin to decline in middle age?

Cognition in Middle Adulthood John Horn's view is that some intellectual abilities begin to decline in middle age, whereas others increase (Horn & Donaldson, 1980). He believes that **crystallized intelligence,** an individual's accumulated information and verbal skills, increases in middle adulthood. By contrast, **fluid intelligence,** one's ability to reason abstractly, begins to decline in middle adulthood (Figure 4.33).

Horn's view is based on data he collected in a *cross-sectional study,* which assesses a number of people all at one point in time. A cross-sectional study, for example, might assess the intelligence of six hundred 40-, 50-, and 60-year-olds in a single evaluation in January 2007. In a cross-sectional study, differences on intelligence tests might be due to *cohort effects,* the effects of living through a certain historical time in a certain culture, rather than to age. The 40-year-olds and the 60-year-olds were born in different eras that offered different economic, educational, and health opportunities. For example, as the 60-year-olds grew up, they likely had fewer educational opportunities than the 40-year-olds had, and this difference may influence their performance on intelligence tests.

In contrast, a *longitudinal study* assesses the same participants over a lengthy period. A longitudinal study of intelligence in middle adulthood might consist of giving the

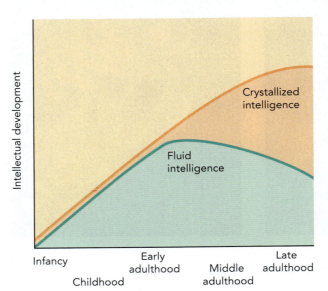

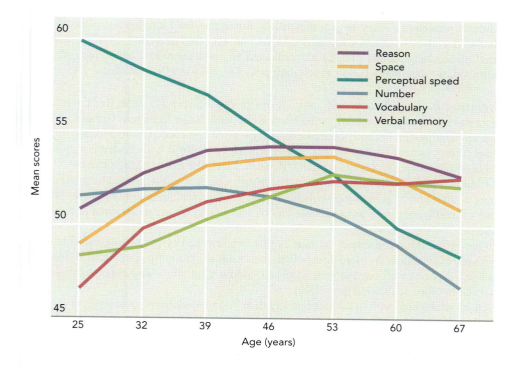

same intelligence test to the same individuals over a 20-year time span, when they are 40, 50, and 60 years of age. As we consider next, whether data on intelligence are collected cross-sectionally or longitudinally can make a difference in the results.

K. Warner Schaie is conducting an extensive longitudinal study of intellectual abilities in adulthood. Five hundred individuals initially were tested in 1956 (Schaie, 1994, 2006, 2007; Schaie & Zanjani, 2006; Willis & Schaie, 2005). New waves of participants are added periodically. The main abilities tested by Schaie are:

- *Vocabulary:* ability to encode and understand ideas expressed in words
- *Verbal memory:* ability to encode and recall meaningful language units, such as a list of words
- *Number:* ability to perform simple mathematical computations, such as addition, subtraction, and multiplication
- *Spatial orientation:* ability to visualize and mentally rotate stimuli in two- and three-dimensional space
- *Inductive reasoning:* ability to recognize and understand patterns and relationships in a problem and use this understanding to solve other instances of the problem
- *Perceptual speed:* ability to quickly and accurately make simple discriminations in visual stimuli

As shown in Figure 4.34, the highest level of functioning for four of the six intellectual abilities—vocabulary, verbal memory, inductive reasoning, and spatial orientation—occurred in middle adulthood (Schaie, 2006; Willis & Schaie, 2005). Only two of the six abilities—numerical ability and perceptual speed—declined in middle age. Perceptual speed showed the earliest decline, beginning in early adulthood.

These are encouraging results, but should we accept them uncritically? When Schaie (1994) assessed intellectual skills both cross-sectionally and longitudinally, he found more decline in middle age in the cross-sectional assessment. For example, as shown in Figure 4.35, when he assessed inductive reasoning longitudinally, it increased until the end of middle adulthood, at which point it began a slight decline. By contrast, when he assessed it cross-sectionally, inductive reasoning already was declining at the beginning of middle adulthood.

Schaie found middle adulthood to be a time of peak performance for some aspects of both crystallized intelligence (vocabulary) and fluid intelligence (spatial orientation and

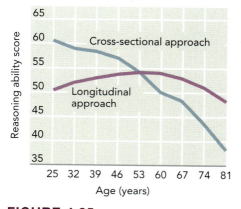

FIGURE 4.35

Cross-Sectional and Longitudinal Comparisons of Reasoning Ability Across the Adulthood Years In Schaie's research (1994), the cross-sectional approach revealed declining scores with age; the longitudinal approach showed a slight rise of scores in middle adulthood and only a slight decline beginning in the early part of late adulthood.

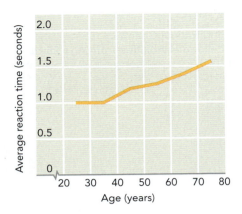

FIGURE 4.36

The Relation of Age to Reaction Time
In one study, the average reaction time began to slow in the 40s, and this decline accelerated in the 60s and 70s (Salthouse, 1994). The task used to assess reaction time required individuals to match numbers with symbols on a computer screen.

inductive reasoning). Horn, as you may recall, found that fluid intelligence peaks in early adulthood and crystallized intelligence in middle age. Schaie (2006, 2007) concluded, based on the longitudinal data he has collected so far, that middle adulthood, not early adulthood, is when many people reach their peak for many intellectual skills.

Cognition in Late Adulthood At age 70, medical researcher John Rock introduced the birth control pill. At age 76, Anna Mary Robertson, better known as Grandma Moses, took up painting and became internationally famous. When Pablo Casals reached 95 years of age, a reporter called him the greatest cellist who ever lived but wondered why he still practiced 6 hours a day. Casals replied, "Because I feel like I am making progress."

Claims about intellectual functioning through the late adult years are provocative. Many contemporary psychologists believe that, as with middle adulthood, some dimensions of intelligence decline in late adulthood, whereas others are maintained or may even increase.

One of the most consistent findings is that, when speed of processing information is involved, older adults do more poorly than their younger counterparts (Figure 4.36). This decline in speed of processing is apparent in middle-aged adults and becomes more pronounced in older adults (Hartley, 2006).

Older adults also tend to do more poorly than younger adults in most areas of memory (Craik & Bialystok, 2006; Hoyer & Verhaeghen, 2006). Older adults do not remember the "where" and "when" of life's happenings as well as younger adults (Tulving, 2000). For example, older adults do not remember their high school classmates or the names of their teachers as well as younger adults do. In the area of memory involving knowledge of the world (for instance, the capital of Peru or the chemical formula for water), older adults usually take longer than younger adults to retrieve the information, but they often are able to retrieve it. And in the important area of memory in which individuals manipulate and assemble information to solve problems and make decisions, decline occurs in older adults (Marsiske & Margrett, 2006).

However, some aspects of cognition might improve with age. One candidate is **wisdom,** expert knowledge about the practical aspects of life. Wisdom may increase with age because of the buildup of life experiences. However, not every older person has wisdom (Brugman, 2006; Baltes, Lindenberger, & Staudinger, 2006). Individual variations characterize all aspects of our cognitive lives.

Do we all face the prospect, then, of gradually becoming less competent intellectually? Not necessarily, as the study of the Mankato nuns suggests. Even for those aspects of cognitive aging that decline, training older adults can improve their cognitive skills (Schaie, 2006; Willis & Schaie, 2005). Researchers have demonstrated that training older adults to use certain strategies can even improve their memories (Willis & Schaie, 2005). However, many experts believe that older adults are less able to adapt than younger adults and thus are limited in how much they can improve their cognitive skills (Baltes, Lindenberger, & Staudinger, 2006).

Socioemotional Development in Adulthood

Infancy, childhood, and adolescence all have demarcated time periods—they begin and end and lead to another period of development. We know what the milestones are for an infant. Adulthood, in contrast, may be more ambiguous. Our adult life is driven less by physical change and more by what we are interested in doing, pursuing those life goals that promise fulfillment. In order to examine what psychologists have learned about socioemotional development in adulthood, let's return to Erikson's stage theory of life-span development.

Erikson's Adult Stages Recall that Erikson's eight stages of the human life span include one stage for early adulthood, one for middle adulthood, and one for late adulthood. Erikson (1968) said that individuals enter the sixth stage of *intimacy versus isolation* during early adulthood. At this time, people face the developmental task of

wisdom Expert knowledge about the practical aspects of life.

either forming intimate relationships with others or becoming socially isolated. Erikson describes intimacy as both finding oneself and losing oneself in another. If the young adult develops healthy friendships and an intimate relationship with a partner, intimacy will likely be achieved.

Generativity versus stagnation, Erikson's seventh stage, occurs in middle adulthood. A main concern in middle adulthood is to help the younger generation in developing useful lives—this is what Erikson means by *generativity.* The feeling of having done nothing to help the next generation is *stagnation.*

Integrity versus despair, Erikson's eighth stage, occurs in late adulthood. In the later years of life, we look back and evaluate what we have done with our lives. If the older adult has resolved many of the earlier stages negatively, looking back likely will produce doubt or gloom—the *despair* Erikson speaks of. But if the older adult has successfully negotiated most or all of the previous stages of development, the looking back will reveal a picture of a life well spent, and the person will feel a sense of satisfaction—*integrity* will be attained.

Marriage, Parenting, and Adulthood   Until about 1930, a stable marriage was accepted as a legitimate end point of adult development. In the past 70 years, however, the desire for personal fulfillment—both inside and outside a marriage—has become an equally legitimate goal. The decline of marriage is regularly heralded in the media. On January 2, 2005, a *Cleveland Plain Dealer* article was headlined, "Culture of Marriage Disappearing." Yet the truth behind the uproar is somewhat less shocking. Most people will eventually marry. And even among those who have divorced, remarriage is the norm (Popenoe & Whitehead, 2006).

In the last two decades or so, it is clear that men and women are waiting longer to marry. In the 1970s, for example, the median age for first marriages was 20.8 for women and 23.2 for men, compared with 25 for women and 26.8 for men in 2000 (Stevenson & Wolfers, 2007). People sometimes compare these figures to data from the 1950s and suggest that something has gone wrong. However, it is important to note the 1950s were a "marrying" time and that recent statistics are more similar to trends from 1890 to 1940.

The rising age of individuals at first marriage may be good news. The age of a woman at her first marriage is related to the ultimate survival of the marriage. As many as 59 percent of marriages in which the wife is less than 18 years old end in divorce within 15 years, compared to just 36 percent of marriages in which the woman is age 20 or older (Center for Family and Demographic Research, 2002). The U.S. divorce rate, although it has slowed down in recent years, increased astronomically in the 1970s and remains high—the highest rate of any industrialized society. The average duration of a marriage in the United States currently is just over 9 years.

What makes a marriage work? Research shows that whether wives or husbands feel satisfied with the sex, romance, and passion in their marriage depends on the extent to which the couples are good friends (Gottman & Silver, 1999). John Gottman has been studying married couples' lives since the early 1970s (Gottman, 1994, 2006; Gottman, Gottman, & Declaire, 2006; Gottman & Silver, 1999; Gottman & others, 1998, 2002). He interviews couples about the history of their marriage, their philosophy about marriage, and their views of their parents' marriages. He videotapes them talking with each other about how their day went and evaluates what they say about the good and bad times of their marriage. He uses physiological measures to assess their heart rate, blood flow, blood pressure, and immune functioning moment by moment while they discuss these topics. He also checks back with the couples every year to see how their marriages are faring. He and his colleagues continue to follow married couples, as well as same-sex partners, to try to understand what makes relationships work. One of the key issues, according to Gottman, is getting past the notion that love is a magical thing. Gottman (2006) stresses that love is a decision and a responsibility and that we have control over extramarital temptations (Gottman, Gottman, & Declaire, 2006).

In his exceptionally thorough research, Gottman (2006) has found these four principles at work in successful marriages:

- *Nurturing fondness and admiration:* In successful marriages, partners sing each other's praises. When couples put a positive spin on their talk with and about each other, the marriage tends to work.

- *Turning toward each other as friends:* In good marriages, partners see each other as friends and turn toward each other for support in times of stress and difficulty.
- *Giving up some power:* Bad marriages often involve one partner who is a power monger. This is more common in husbands, but some wives have the problem as well.
- *Solving conflicts together:* In successful marriages, couples work to solve problems, regulate their emotion during times of conflict, and compromise to accommodate each other.

Parenting is a key way by which individuals meet Erikson's challenge of generativity. By procreating, they contribute to the next generation. As we have previously considered, parenting can be hard work. However, research shows that engaged parenting may have benefits not only for children but for parents as well. John Snarey (1993) followed fathers and their children for 4 decades. He found that children, especially girls, were better off if their fathers were actively engaged in their lives—especially with regard to athletic pursuits. In addition, and perhaps more importantly for fathers, those who were constructively engaged in child rearing were themselves better off in terms of marital satisfaction, life satisfaction, and even career mobility and enhanced career success.

Midlife Crises If a man turns 50 and suddenly buys a hot new red Bentley Continental GT or a bright yellow Hummer, family and friends might roll their eyes and conclude, "Midlife crisis strikes!" The notion of midlife crisis was introduced by Daniel Levinson (1978) in his book, *The Seasons of a Man's Life*. But research on middle-aged adults reveals that few experience what people think of as a midlife crisis (Kirasic, 2004; Lachman, 2004). Individuals vary extensively in how they cope with and perceive midlife (Vaillant, 1977). In a large-scale study of 3,032 U.S. adults 25 to 74 years of age, the portrait of midlife was mainly positive (Brim, 1999). Only about 10 percent of individuals described themselves as experiencing a midlife crisis. In fact, middle-aged individuals (40–65 years old) had lower anxiety levels and worried less than people under 40. The middle-aged individuals did report more negative life events than people under 40, but they showed considerable resilience and good coping skills in facing these stresses. The midlife individuals generally had few illnesses but poor physical fitness.

More accurate than the phrase "midlife crisis" might be the phrase "midlife consciousness" (Santrock, 2007). That is, during middle age, people do become aware of the gap between being young and being old and the shrinking time left in their lives. They do think about their role in contributing to the next generation. They do contemplate the meaning of life. But for most people, midlife consciousness does not become tumultuous and take on crisis proportions.

Socioemotional Aspects of Aging Although we are in the evening of our lives in late adulthood, we need not live out our remaining years lonely and unhappy. The more active and involved older people are, the more satisfied they are and the more likely they are to stay healthy (Hendricks & Hatch, 2006). Researchers have found that older people who go to church, attend meetings, take trips, and exercise are happier than those who simply sit at home (George, 2006).

However, older adults may become more selective about their social networks, according to one theory (Carstensen, 1995, 1998, 2006; Carstensen, Mikels, & Mather, 2006; Carstensen & others, 2003). Because they place a high value on emotional satisfaction, older adults often are motivated to spend more time with familiar individuals—close friends and family members—with whom they have had rewarding relationships. They may deliberately withdraw from social contact with individuals on the fringes of their lives. This narrowing of social interaction maximizes positive emotional experiences and minimizes emotional risks as individuals become older. Researchers have found support for this theory (Carstensen, Mikels, & Mather, 2006; Charles & Carstensen, 2004).

Studies also have found that across diverse samples—Norwegians, Catholic nuns, African Americans, Chinese Americans, and Euro-Americans—older adults report better control of their emotions than

"Goodbye, Alice, I've got to get this California thing out of my system."

Research shows that the more active and involved older people are, the more life satisfaction they feel, and the more likely they are to remain healthy.

younger adults (Carstensen & Charles, 2003; Carstensen, Gottman, & Levensen, 1995). Stereotypes would lead us to expect that most older adults live sad, lonely lives. However, research has revealed a different picture. For example, one study of a very large U.S. sample examined emotions at different ages (Mroczek & Kolarz, 1998). Older adults reported experiencing more positive emotion and less negative emotion than younger adults, and positive emotion increased with age in adults at an accelerating rate (Figure 4.37).

Positive Psychology and Aging

Until fairly recently, middle-aged and older adults were perceived as enduring a long decline in physical, cognitive, and socioemotional functioning, and the positive dimensions of aging were ignored (Rowe & Kahn, 1997). Throughout this section, however, we have seen examples and evidence of successful aging. The earlier stereotypes of aging are being overturned as researchers discover that being a middle-aged or an older adult has many positive aspects (Aldwin, Spiro, & Park, 2006).

Once developmental psychologists began focusing on the positive aspects of aging, they discovered that far more robust, healthy middle-aged and older adults are among us than they previously envisioned. A longitudinal study of aging documented some of the ways that positive aging can be attained (Vaillant, 2002). Individuals were assessed at age 50 and then again at 75 to 80 years of age. As shown in Figure 4.38, when individuals at 50 years of age were not heavy smokers, did not abuse alcohol, had a stable marriage, exercised, maintained a normal weight, and had good coping skills, they were more likely to be alive and happy at 75 to 80 years of age.

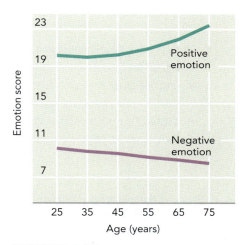

FIGURE 4.37

Changes in Positive and Negative Emotion Across the Adult Years Positive and negative scores had a possible range of 6 to 30, with higher scores reflecting positive emotion and lower scores negative emotion. Positive emotion increased in the middle adulthood and late adulthood years while negative emotion declined.

FIGURE 4.38

Linkage Between Characteristics at Age 50 and Health and Happiness at Age 75 to 80 In a longitudinal study, the characteristics shown at age 50 were related to whether individuals were happy-well, sad-sick, or dead at age 75 to 80 (Vaillant, 2002).

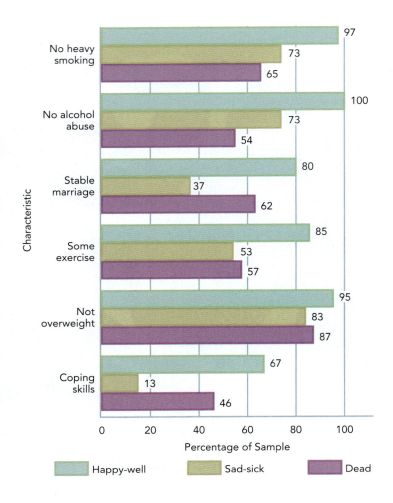

REVIEW, ASSESS, AND SHARPEN YOUR THINKING

Review

4 Discuss adult development and the positive dimensions of aging.

- Explain the concept of emerging adulthood and identify its five key features.
- Describe physical development throughout adulthood.
- Identify major changes in cognitive development in adulthood.
- Discuss the main aspects of socioemotional development in adulthood.
- Summarize the positive view of aging that now exists.

Assess

1. Which of the following statements about cognitive development in adulthood is most accurate?

   A. Crystallized and fluid intelligence both peak in late adulthood.

   B. Fluid intelligence is more important to overall IQ than crystallized intelligence.

   C. Fluid intelligence tends to peak long after crystallized intelligence.

   D. Fluid intelligence deals with abstract reasoning and crystallized intelligence deals with information and verbal skills.

2. What age range is considered emerging adulthood?

   A. 16–18

   B. 16–21

   C. 18–25

   D. 21–27

3. _____ is the cessation of a woman's menstrual cycle.
   A. Menarche
   B. Maturation
   C. Uterine shedding
   D. Menopause

4. The life expectancy of humans born in the United States is currently
   A. approximately 50 years.
   B. approximately 65 years.

C. approximately 80 years.
D. approximately 95 years.

5. The theory of aging that states that aging is caused by damage to DNA is
   A. the cellular-clock theory.
   B. the life-expectancy theory.
   C. the genetic-deficiency theory.
   D. the free-radical theory.

Sharpen Your Thinking

Suppose that you wanted to construct a test for wisdom that would be fair to adults of all ages. Write down two or three questions or items that you would want to include in your test.

5 Developmental Psychology and Health and Wellness

Discuss important factors in successful adult psychological development.

When you think about developmental psychology, child development may still be the first thing to pop into your mind. And for good reason: In childhood, the physical and psychological changes that occur are truly awe inspiring. In adulthood, however, we typically do not see this dual physical and psychological development. In fact, physical and psychological decline may be part of the developmental process in adulthood.

You might ask, Graying hair? Loss of mobility? Cognitive decline? How can all that be considered development? In fact, it may be that adult development is particularly important *because* it occurs in the context of some declines. Unlike childhood growth, adult growth is more likely to be a conscious process and therefore a truer marker of an individual's accomplishment (Levenson & Crumpler, 1996).

Coping and Development

How do adults "grow themselves"? One way that adults develop is through coping with life's difficulties. Psychologist Carolyn Aldwin and her colleagues have suggested that stress and coping should be understood as having developmental implications (Aldwin, 2007; Aldwin, Spiro, & Park, 2006; Aldwin, Yancura, & Boeninger, 2007; Levenson & Aldwin, 2006). When we encounter a negative life circumstance such as an illness or a loss, we have the opportunity to develop and to mature (Davis & others, 2007). Recall Piaget's ideas of assimilation and accommodation in cognitive development. These processes can be applied to adult development as well (Block, 1982). In assimilation, existing cognitive structures are used to make sense out of the current environment. Assimilation allows the person to enjoy a feeling of meaning because experiences fit into his or her preexisting meaning structures. But life does not always conform to our expectations. When our experience conflicts with our existing cognitive structures, it is necessary to modify current ways of thinking. Accommodation is this process, whereby existing cognitive structures are modified or new structures are developed. Accommodation helps us to change so that we can make sense of life's previously incomprehensible events. Indeed, research suggests that individuals who are faced with difficulties in life are more likely to come to a rich, complex view of themselves and the world (Helson, 1992; Helson & Roberts, 1994).

Life Themes and Life-Span Development

One of the negative events that people begin to experience in middle adulthood is death, especially the death of parents and older relatives. Also faced with less time in their own lives, many individuals think more deeply than before about what life is all about and what they want the rest of their lives to be like.

Austrian psychiatrist Victor Frankl confronted this issue personally and then shared his insights with the world. His mother, father, brother, and wife died in the concentration camps and gas chambers in Auschwitz, Germany. Frankl survived the camps and went on to write *Man's Search for Meaning* (1984), in which he emphasized each person's uniqueness and the finiteness of life. If life were not finite, said Frankl, we could spend our lives doing just about anything we please because time would go on forever. Frankl proposed that people need to ask themselves such questions as why they exist, what they want from life, and what their lives really mean.

Frankl's ideas fit with the concept of *life themes* introduced earlier in this chapter. Recall that life themes involve people's efforts to cultivate meaningful optimal experiences (Csikszentmihalyi & Rathunde, 1998; Massimini & Delle Fave, 2000; Rathunde & Csikszentmihalyi, 2006). Thus, some people who have spent much of their adult lives pursuing wealth and career success turn in middle age to more selfless pursuits. To contribute to the well-being of the next generation, they devote more energy and resources to helping others—for example, by volunteering or working with young people. This reorientation can ease individuals into a positive and meaningful old age. Remaining actively engaged in life is an essential part of successful adulthood (Kramer, Fabiani, & Colcombe, 2006; Sumic & others, 2007).

These motivations are demonstrated dramatically by numerous individuals who have chosen to use their successes for the betterment of the world. Consider, for example, businessman and philanthropist Warren Buffett, the man whom *Forbes* magazine ranks as the world's second-wealthiest person (behind Microsoft founder Bill Gates). Worth an estimated $42 billion, Buffett has always been known for his down-to-earth, frugal lifestyle. He still lives in the house he bought in Omaha, Nebraska, in 1958 (for less than $32,000), although he now owns other homes. In June 2006, Buffett committed approximately 85 percent of his wealth to charity, the largest charitable donation in history, most of it going to the Bill and Melinda Gates Foundation.

Or consider Bono, the lead singer of the rock group U2. Enriched by tremendous music sales and concert proceeds, the Grammy Award winner has turned his energies to addressing some of the world's most urgent problems, including poverty and AIDS. He has spent the last few years lobbying political leaders on behalf of African nations beset with debt. In 2005, he and others launched the socially conscious fashion line EDUN that uses factories in Africa, turning the focus on developing countries from aid to trade.

Similarly, former U.S. president Jimmy Carter has used his status as an elder statesman to mediate for peace and to press for human rights around the world. He and his wife Rosalynn have worked tirelessly for the organization Habitat for Humanity. In addition, Carter has become an accomplished author and poet.

Earlier in this chapter, you were asked about the meaning of the word *maturity*. You might have thought of happiness, kindness, or wisdom. George Vaillant and Kenneth Mukamal (2001) reviewed the qualities that we associate with successful aging and concluded that many of them are within the individual's control. Indeed, perhaps the strongest predictor of successful aging is remaining physically active.

If all of this sounds like a lot of hard work, there is some good news: Successful aging implies happy aging, and research has shown that happiness may well increase with age (Mroczek & Spiro, 2005; Mroczek, Spiro, & Griffin, 2006; Sheldon & Kasser, 2001; Vaillant & Mukamal, 2001).

Bono has turned his energies and celebrity to addressing urgent global problems such as poverty and AIDS.

As children, our psychological development occurs in tandem with physical development. As we become strong and skilled enough to walk, the horizons of our world open up to new discoveries. In adulthood, we receive our developmental cues from ourselves—where do we go, once we have managed the many tasks that human beings face in childhood and adolescence? This chapter began by reminding you of the day of your birth, a day when you were the center of attention and a mystery waiting to unfold. From a developmental psychology perspective, today could be as important a day as that one. On the day you were born, you were full of possibilities. And you still are.

 REVIEW, ASSESS, AND SHARPEN YOUR THINKING

Review

5 Discuss important factors in successful adult psychological development.

- Explain the role of coping in adult development, including the application of Piaget's ideas of assimilation and accommodation to adult development.
- Describe the idea of life themes and discuss how they might change over the life span.

Assess

1. Which of the following statements is true?
   A. Avoiding stressors helps people to mature.
   B. Stressors prevent people from maturing.
   C. Stressors are unrelated to maturation.
   D. Stressors encourage people to mature.

2. What is the relationship between life themes and aging?
   A. People are more likely to develop life themes early in life.
   B. The development of life themes can facilitate integrity in later life.

   C. Only older individuals have the ability to develop life themes.
   D. Life themes and maturation are unrelated.

3. Who wrote *Man's Search for Meaning*?
   A. Victor Frankl
   B. Erik Erikson
   C. Jean Piaget
   D. Carol Gilligan

Sharpen Your Thinking

How would you describe your top three life pursuits at present? How do you think these might change 25 years from now? Why?

1 EXPLORING HUMAN DEVELOPMENT

Explain how psychologists think about development.

How Do Nature and Nurture Influence Development?

Development refers to the pattern of change in human capabilities that begins at conception and continues throughout the life span. Both nature (biological inheritance) and nurture (environmental experience) influence development extensively. However, people are at the mercy of neither their genes nor their environment when they actively construct optimal experiences. History is filled with examples of individuals who have contributed greatly to society despite early difficulties.

Do Early Experiences Rule Us for Life?

Developmental psychologists debate the extent to which early experience (as in infancy or early childhood) is more important than later experience in development. Most agree that both early and later experiences influence development.

2 CHILD DEVELOPMENT

Describe children's development from prenatal stages to adolescence.

Prenatal Development

Prenatal development progresses through the germinal, embryonic, and fetal periods. Certain drugs, such as alcohol, can have an adverse effect on the fetus. Preterm birth is another potential problem, especially if the infant is very small or grows up in an adverse environment.

Physical Development in Childhood

The newborn comes into the world with several genetically wired reflexes, including grasping and sucking. The infant's physical development is dramatic in the first year, and a number of motor milestones are reached in infancy. Motor behaviors are assembled for perceiving and acting, drawing on the infant's physical abilities, perceptual skills, and factors in the environment. Extensive changes in the brain,

including denser connections between synapses, take place in infancy and childhood.

Cognitive Development in Childhood

In Piaget's view, children use schemas to actively construct their world, either assimilating new information into existing schemas or adjusting schemas to accommodate it. Piaget also said that people go through four stages of cognitive development: (1) the sensorimotor stage (birth to 2 years of age); (2) the preoperational stage (2 to 7 years of age); (3) the concrete operational stage (7 to 11 years of age); and (4) the formal operational stage (11 to 15 years of age through adulthood). Piaget opened up new ways of looking at how children's minds develop, and he gave us the model of a child as an active, constructivist thinker. However, critics believe that Piaget's stages are too rigid and do not adequately take into account the influence of culture and education on cognitive development.

Socioemotional Development in Childhood

Erikson presented a major, eight-stage psychosocial view of life-span development; its first four stages occur in childhood. In each stage, the individual seeks to resolve a particular socioemotional conflict. Other researchers have focused on specific aspects of socioemotional development in childhood. For instance, Bowlby and Ainsworth theorized that the first year of life is crucial for the formation of a secure attachment between infant and caregiver. Development also depends on temperament, an individual's behavioral style or characteristic way of responding, as well as on parenting. Among the important aspects of parenting are parenting style, divorce, and positive parenting. The family is an important context for children's development, but other social contexts—such as peers, schools, neighborhood quality, and culture—are also important. Kohlberg proposed a major cognitive-developmental theory of moral development with three levels (preconventional, conventional, and postconventional) and two stages at each level. Gilligan presented an alternative view of moral development that emphasizes interpersonal relationships more heavily than does Kohlberg's theory. Finally, gender development includes biology, social experience, and cognitive factors.

Positive Psychology and Children's Development: Resilient Children

Positive psychology emphasizes children's resiliency and focuses on improving children's lives.

3 ADOLESCENCE

Identify the most important changes that occur in adolescence.

Physical Development in Adolescence

Puberty is a period of rapid skeletal and sexual maturation that occurs mainly in early adolescence. It occurs about 2 years earlier in girls than in boys. Hormonal changes lie at the core of pubertal development.

Cognitive Development in Adolescence

According to Piaget, cognitive development in adolescence is characterized by the appearance of formal operational thought, the final stage in his theory. He believed that children enter this stage between 11 and 15 years of age. This stage involves abstract, idealistic, and logical thought. *Hypothetical-deductive reasoning* is Piaget's term for adolescents' logical thought. Another key feature of cognitive development, especially in early adolescence, is egocentric thought.

Socioemotional Development in Adolescence

One of the most important aspects of socioemotional development in adolescence is identity. Erikson's fifth stage of psychosocial development is identity versus identity confusion. Marcia proposed four statuses of identity based on crisis and commitment. A special concern is the development of ethnic identity. Successful programs for intervening in adolescent problems involve individual attention and communitywide interventions.

Positive Psychology and Adolescence

Positive psychology views adolescence as a time of evaluation, decision making, and commitment. Adolescents are not all alike, but the majority of them develop competently.

4 ADULT DEVELOPMENT AND AGING

Discuss adult development and the positive dimensions of aging.

Emerging Adulthood

Psychologists refer to the period between adolescence and adulthood as emerging adulthood. This period (typically between 18 and 25 years of age) is characterized by the exploration of identity through work and relationships, instability, and self-focus. Emerging adults may feel "in between"—not quite adults but certainly no longer adolescents. Emerging adulthood is experienced as a time of enormous possibility and a chance for life transformation.

Physical Development in Adulthood

Most adults reach their peak physical performance during their 20s and are healthiest then. However, physical skills begin to decline during the 30s. Changes in physical appearance are among the most visible signs of aging in middle adulthood. Menopause, which also takes place during middle adulthood, has been stereotyped as more negative than it actually is. The cellular-clock and free-radical theories are two important biological theories of aging. Alzheimer disease is a special concern. Even in late adulthood, the brain has remarkable repair capacity and plasticity.

Cognitive Development in Adulthood

Piaget argued that no new cognitive changes occur in adulthood. However, some psychologists have proposed that the idealistic thinking of adolescents is replaced by the more realistic, pragmatic thinking of young adults. Horn argued that crystallized intelligence increases in middle age, whereas fluid intelligence declines. Schaie conducted a longitudinal study of intelligence and found that many cognitive skills peak in middle age. Overall, older adults do not do as well on memory and other cognitive tasks and are slower to process information than younger adults. But older adults may have greater wisdom than younger adults.

Socioemotional Development in Adulthood

Erikson's three stages of socioemotional development in adulthood are intimacy versus isolation (early adulthood), generativity versus stagnation (middle adulthood), and integrity versus despair (late adulthood). Career and work become central themes in the lives of young adults. Lifestyles, marriage, and commitment also become important aspects of adult life for most people. In middle adulthood, people begin to realize the limits of their ideals and dreams. Levinson proposed that a majority of people experience midlife crises as a result, but researchers have found that only a small percentage of middle-aged adults undergo such a crisis. Nevertheless, a special concern, beginning in the 50s, is understanding the meaning of life. Researchers have found that remaining active increases the likelihood that older adults will be happier and healthier. They also have found that older adults often reduce their general social affiliations. Instead, they are motivated to spend more time with close friends and family members.

Positive Psychology and Aging

The positive dimensions of aging were largely ignored until recently. Developmentalists now recognize that many adults can sustain or even improve their functioning as they age.

5 DEVELOPMENTAL PSYCHOLOGY AND HEALTH AND WELLNESS

Discuss important factors in successful adult psychological development.

Coping and Development

Though often associated with childhood, psychological development can continue throughout life. Psychologists have suggested that coping with life's difficulties is one way in which adults may develop. For adults, taking an active approach to developing oneself may be a key motivator in development. Piaget's concepts of assimilation and accommodation have been applied to the process of developing through difficult times. An individual may experience meaning in life experience by applying his or her current understanding of the world (assimilation). In contrast, the individual may find that some experiences require a revision of that understanding (accommodation).

Life Themes and Life-Span Development

In adulthood, we have the opportunity to pursue new goals that represent important life themes, such as leaving a legacy for the future. Development in adulthood can be viewed as a self-motivated process whose limits are set by the individual's capacity to imagine.

Key Terms

development, p. 116
nature, p. 119
nurture, p. 119
preferential looking, p. 122
habituation, p. 123
schema, p. 124
assimilation, p. 124
accommodation, p. 124

sensorimotor stage, p. 125
preoperational stage, p. 126
concrete operational stage, p. 126
formal operational stage, p. 127
attachment, p. 131
secure attachment, p. 132
temperament, p. 132
authoritarian parenting, p. 133

authoritative parenting, p. 133
neglectful parenting, p. 133
indulgent parenting, p. 133
prosocial behavior, p. 138
androgens, p. 139
estrogens, p. 139
gender roles, p. 140
resilience, p. 141

puberty, p. 143
identity versus identity confusion, p. 146
emerging adulthood, p. 150
crystallized intelligence, p. 156
fluid intelligence, p. 156
wisdom, p. 158

Assess Your Knowledge

1. The phrase "out of sight, out of mind" is true of children's cognitive processing in which stage of development?
   A. sensorimotor stage
   B. preoperational stage
   C. concrete operational stage
   D. formal operational stage

2. Which period of prenatal development occurs just before birth?
   A. embryonic period   B. zygotic period
   C. fetal period   D. germinal period

3. Which of the following activities would be consistent with the concept of a life theme?
   A. competing against others
   B. making a great deal of money
   C. procreating
   D. being altruistic

4. A baby that is shown an image of a lion and an image of a tractor gazes at the tractor more. This finding is an example of
   A. preferential looking.   B. visual development.
   C. habituation.   D. object permanence.

5. A child who during play asks a parent to ignore the cries of a younger sibling until their game is finished is in which stage of cognitive development?
   A. operational
   B. preoperational
   C. sensorimotor
   D. concrete operational

6. When something is put close to an infant's mouth, the infant will suck at the object. The sucking is an example of
   A. a motor skill.   B. a reflex.
   C. voluntary habituated response.   D. the preoperational stage.

7. Which of the following stages occurs during the preschool years?
   A. identity versus identity confusion
   B. trust versus mistrust
   C. intimacy versus isolation
   D. initiative versus guilt

8. Of the following, who is known for a theory of moral development?
   A. Erik Erikson   B. Jean Piaget
   C. James Marcia   D. Lawrence Kohlberg

9. Which of the following statements is correct?
   A. Ethnic identity is consistent across different ethnic and racial groups.
   B. Ethnic identity is unrelated to well-being.
   C. Ethnic identity does not exist for White individuals.
   D. A strong ethnic identity can buffer the effects of discrimination.

10. The _____ theory of aging focuses on the limited number of times a cell can divide.
    A. telomeres
    B. life-expectancy
    C. cellular-clock
    D. free-radical

11. The ability to think abstractly is known as
    A. fluid intelligence.
    B. cohort effects.
    C. crystallized intelligence.
    D. accommodation.

12. Which parenting style is characterized by high parental control and little verbal exchange?
    A. authoritarian
    B. authoritative
    C. neglectful
    D. indulgent

13. A person who does not do something because he or she is fearful of getting in trouble is at which level of moral reasoning?
    A. preconventional
    B. conventional
    C. postconventional
    D. formal operational

14. Who is associated with the theory that moral development relies on an individual's connectedness and relationships with other people?
    A. Lawrence Kohlberg
    B. Erik Erikson
    C. Carol Gilligan
    D. James Marcia

15. Which of the following is involved in successfully overcoming a trauma?
    A. assimilation
    B. accommodation
    C. generativity
    D. a midlife crisis

Go to Appendix B for answers to these questions.

Apply Your Knowledge

1. The possibility of human cloning has received extensive media coverage. If you could clone yourself, your clone would have the same genetic makeup as you have. Take a quick survey of some friends to ask whether they would clone themselves if they were given the opportunity. Ask them to explain their answers and critically examine their reasons, keeping in mind the lessons on nature and nurture in the text. Do you think the phenotype of your clone would most resemble you physically, cognitively, or socioemotionally? Why?

2. Find a copy of a popular child-rearing book. Read a few pages and comment on how the perspective on children's development in the popular book relates to the scientific perspectives on children's development in the text. Are all perspectives represented, or does one view dominate?

3. "Emerging adulthood" is a relatively new designation for the period of time between the ages of 18 and 25. It has been suggested that Americans tend to put off becoming full-fledged adults. What are your views of this new stage? What factors may contribute to postponing being an adult?

4. Visit the website of the National Center for Health Statistics maintained by the Centers for Disease Control and Prevention **http://www.cdc.gov/nchs/about/otheract/aging/trendsoverview.htm** and examine one or more of the aging trends described. How well do these trends correspond to your perception of what happens as we age?

5. Consider the definition of wisdom given in this chapter and make arrangements to interview the wisest person you know. Ask the person about important life themes—experiences that have had an impact on his or her life. Examine the person's responses for indications of resilience, assimilation, and accommodation.

CHAPTER 5

SENSATION AND PERCEPTION

Experiencing Psychology

ELEVEN-YEAR-OLD DESTINY DIAZ, SEEING THE WORLD FOR THE FIRST TIME

"I can see Mariah Carey. She's American and she has the same skin as me. Her pants are red." Thus exclaimed Destiny Diaz, an 11-year-old who had been legally blind since birth, after she received an artificial cornea in the fall of 2005. Just 24 hours after her transplant—an artificial cornea was used because her immune system had rejected human transplants—Destiny's doctor held up his fingers and asked her to tell him how many there were. Then he asked her to touch his nose. And as she reached out and touched it, her aunts, watching in a corner of the room, wept with joy. This formerly blind little girl could see.

The first organ transplant in history was a double cornea transplant, performed about a century ago by a Czech doctor named Eduard Zirm on a 43-year-old man named Alois Gloger. The corneas came from an 11-year-old boy whose eyes (but not corneas) had been damaged in an accident. After the surgery, Gloger had to endure having his eyes sewn shut for 10 days, but ultimately he was able to see. Today, 40,000 cornea transplants are performed each year. The transplants generally depend on eye banks, to which individuals can promise to donate their precious organs at their death. The operation is now done on an outpatient basis; it is complex but not nearly as difficult as that first one. For adults, the odds of rejection are quite low because the cornea has a very low blood supply. (Children, however, like Destiny, have a higher rate of rejection.) Imagine 40,000 people a year undergoing this procedure—in some cases seeing for the first time. Sight is truly a gift for these previously non-seeing people, bestowed not by nature but by science, technology, and the generosity of others.

Seeing is a vital way that we experience life. Our senses, collectively speaking, connect us to the world. We see a beloved friend's face, feel a comforting hand on our shoulder, or hear our name called from across a room. Our ability to perceive the world is what allows us to reach out into that world in the many ways we do every day.

Sensation and perception are processes at the core of our most wonderful experiences. Visiting the Grand Canyon, for example, is often described as awe-inspiring and beyond words. Experiencing the depth, vastness, wild beauty, and haunting sounds of this giant hole in the earth is a moment that few ever forget. Yet, without our senses, the occasion would be lost on us. ▪

PREVIEW

Psychology is keenly interested in the ways we sense the world. Sensation and perception researchers represent a broad range of specialties, including *ophthalmology,* the study of the eye's structure, function, and diseases; *audiology,* the science concerned with hearing; *neurology,* the scientific study of the nervous system; and many others. Understanding sensation and perception requires comprehending the physical properties of the objects of our perception—light, sound, texture, and so on. The psychological approach to these processes involves understanding the physical structures and functions of the sense organs, as well as the brain's conversion of the information from these organs into experience.

As we begin to explore what psychologists know about sensation and perception, you might wonder what the mechanics of vision, hearing, taste, smell, and touch have to do with psychology. Do students of astronomy have to know how telescopes are made? Do biology students study the components and workings of microscopes? Importantly, human sensory organs and our perceptual abilities are not analogous to telescopes and microscopes and how they work. Telescopes give astronomers an objective portrait of the night sky. Microscopes give biologists an objective picture of cells and other minute objects. But it is the eyes and brains of astronomers and biologists that play an active role in what these scientists "see." Perception is not a direct reflection of the real world but rather a computed interpretation, a constructive and integrative process. We will see startling proof of the creativity with which our brain approaches reality through the "blind spot" demonstration later in this chapter.

As we plumb the complexities of sensation and perception, you will come to appreciate such remarkable abilities as how our brain creatively interprets visual input and how smells lead to "chemistry" between people. We first explore the processes of sensation and perception. After reviewing these general concepts, we examine vision, the sense about which scientists know the most. We next probe the nature of hearing, the skin senses, taste, smell, and the kinesthetic and vestibular senses. We conclude by considering the place of sensation and perception in health and wellness.

1 How We Sense and Perceive the World

Discuss basic principles of sensation and perception.

When blind musician Stevie Wonder's hands touch the keys of a piano, his brain recognizes the sensation and directs his fingers to press one or more of the keys. He begins to play. His brain automatically interprets the information it receives from the fingers as they feel the keys and responds to its sensation. The seemingly simple act of playing one note on the piano is, in fact, the outcome of two complex and virtually inseparable processes: sensation and perception.

Detecting, Processing, and Interpreting Experiences

Sensation is the process of receiving stimulus energies from the external environment. Stimuli consist of physical energy—light, sound, and heat, for example. A stimulus is detected by specialized receptor cells in the sense organs—eyes, ears, skin, nose, and tongue. When the receptor cells have registered a stimulus, the energy is converted to an electrochemical impulse. The process of transforming physical energy into electrochemical energy is called **transduction.** Transduction produces an action potential that relays information about the stimulus through the nervous system to the brain (Jia, Dallos, & He, 2007; Lumpkin & Caterina, 2007). When it reaches the brain, the information travels to the appropriate area of the cerebral cortex (Pasupathy, 2006).

The brain gives meaning to sensation through perception. **Perception** is the process of organizing and interpreting sensory information to give it meaning. Receptor cells in our eyes record a silver object in the sky, but they do not "see" a jet plane; receptor cells in the ear vibrate in a particular way, but they do not "hear" a symphony. Finding meaningful patterns in sensory information is perception. Sensing and perceiving give us three-dimensional views of the setting sun, the sounds of a rock concert, the touch of soft caresses, the taste of sweets, and the fragrances of flowers and peppermint.

Bottom-Up and Top-Down Processing   Psychologists distinguish between bottom-up and top-down processing in sensation and perception. In **bottom-up processing,** sensory receptors register information about the external environment and send it up to the brain for analysis and interpretation. Bottom-up processing is initiated by stimulus input (Prouix, 2007; Wei & Zhou, 2006). It means taking in information from the environment and trying to make sense of it. An example of bottom-up processing might be the way you experienced your favorite song the first time you heard it: You had to listen carefully to get a "feel" for it. In contrast, **top-down processing** starts out with cognitive processing at the higher levels of the brain (Schlack & Albright, 2007; Zhaoping & Guyader, 2007). Top-down processing means we start with some sense of what is happening and apply that framework to information from the world. These cognitive processes include knowledge, beliefs, and expectations. Thus, top-down processing does not start with the detection of a stimulus, as bottom-up processing does. You can experience top-down processing by "listening" to your favorite song in your head right now. As you "hear" the song in your mind's ear, you are engaged in perceptual experience.

Clearly both bottom-up and top-down processing take place in sensing and perceiving the world (Schill, Zetzsche, & Wolter, 2006). By themselves our ears provide only incoming information about sound in the environment. Only when we consider both what the ears hear (bottom-up processing) and what the brain interprets (top-down processing) can we fully understand how we perceive sounds in our world.

Doing a jigsaw puzzle is another activity in which bottom-up and top-down processing might be involved (Friedrich, 2001). If you have ever tried to put together a jigsaw puzzle without the puzzle's original box, you understand how difficult it is to assemble the pieces without knowing what the finished picture looks like. You have to proceed on the basis of the shapes and colors of the pieces to determine how they fit together. That is essentially bottom-up processing. However, if you have a picture of the finished product, you can select a particular area to work on. If you know that there will be a castle on the right side of the puzzle, you can go through the pieces and pick out in advance those that look like they are part of a castle. That makes your task of fitting the pieces together much easier—you have fewer to work with and have a general idea of how they should look once they are put together. Your selection process based on prior knowledge is an example of top-down processing.

In everyday life, the two processes of sensation and perception are essentially inseparable. The brain automatically perceives the information it receives from the sense organs.

Through sensation we take in information from the world; through perception we identify meaningful patterns in that information. Thus sensation and perception work hand in hand when we enjoy a hug and the sweet fragrance of a flower.

sensation The process of receiving stimulus energies from the environment.

transduction The process of transforming physical energy into electrochemical energy.

perception The brain's process of organizing and interpreting sensory information to give it meaning.

bottom-up processing Processing that begins with sensory receptors registering environmental information and sending it to the brain for analysis and interpretation.

top-down processing Processing of perceptual information that starts out with cognitive processing at the higher levels of the brain.

Most predatory animals have eyes at the front of their faces; most animals that are prey have eyes on the side of their heads. Through these adaptations, predators perceive their prey accurately, and preys gain a measure of safety from their panoramic view of their environment.

sensory receptors Specialized cells that detect stimulus information and transmit it to sensory (afferent) nerves and the brain.

Anableps microlepis, a fish with four eyes. Two eyes allow it to observe the world above water, two the world below water, as it swims just at the surface.

For this reason, most psychologists refer to sensation and perception as a unified information-processing system (Goldstein, 2007).

The Purpose of Perception We can gain important insights into perception by asking the simple question "What is its purpose?" According to a leading expert in this field, David Marr (1982), the purpose of perception is to represent information from the outside world internally. For example, the purpose of vision is to create a three-dimensional representation, or map, of the world in the brain.

From an evolutionary perspective, the purpose of sensation and perception is adaptation that improves a species' chances for survival (Freeman & Herron, 2007; Kardong, 2008). An organism must be able to sense and respond quickly and accurately to events in the immediate environment, such as the approach of a predator, the presence of prey, or the appearance of a potential mate. Thus, it is not surprising that most animals—from goldfish to elephants to humans—have eyes and ears, as well as sensitivities to touch and chemicals (smell and taste). However, a close comparison of sensory systems in animals reveals that each species is exquisitely adapted to the habitat in which it evolved (Park, 2008). Animals that are primarily predators generally have their eyes at the front of their faces so that they can perceive their prey accurately. In contrast, animals that are more likely to be someone else's lunch have their eyes on either side of their heads. This adaptation gives them a wide view of their surroundings at all times.

A marvelous example of evolutionary accomplishment appears in a fish called *Anableps microlepis,* which has four eyes! To survive, *Anableps microlepis* swims just at the surface of the water, with two aerial eyes monitoring the visual field above the water and two aquatic eyes monitoring the visual field underwater. This remarkable adaptation enables *Anableps microlepis* to search for food while watching for predators.

Sensory Receptors and the Brain

All sensation begins with sensory receptors. **Sensory receptors** are specialized cells that detect stimulus information and transmit it to sensory (afferent) nerves and the brain (Lewis & others, 2007). Sensory receptors are the openings through which the brain and nervous system experience the world. Figure 5.1 shows the types of sensory receptors for each of the five senses in humans.

The sensory receptors of every animal species have evolved to fit their environments. For example, the sensory receptors that a bat uses to find food are very different from but no more specialized than those that an eagle uses. Bats use sound to locate prey at night, whereas eagles hunt with their eyes from great heights to avoid detection from potential prey.

Figure 5.2 depicts the general flow of information from the environment to the brain. Sensory receptors take in information from the environment, creating local electrical currents. These currents are *graded;* that means they are sensitive to the intensity of stimulation, such as the difference between a dim and bright light. These receptors trigger action potentials in sensory neurons, which carry that information to the central nervous system. Recall from Chapter 3 that an action potential is the brief wave of electrical charge that sweeps down the axon of a neuron for possible transmission to another neuron. Because sensory neurons follow the all-or-none principle, the intensity of the stimulus cannot be communicated to the brain by changing the strength of the action potential. Instead, the receptor varies the *frequency* of action potentials sent to the brain. So, if a stimulus is very intense, like the bright sun on a hot day, the neuron will fire more frequently (but with the same strength), to let the brain know the light is, indeed, very very bright.

Other than frequency, the action potentials of all sensory nerves are alike. This sameness raises an intriguing question: How can an animal distinguish among sight, sound, odor, taste, and touch? The answer is that sensory receptors are selective and have different neural pathways. They are specialized to absorb a particular type of energy—light energy, mechanical energy (such as sound vibrations), or chemical energy, for example—and transduce (convert) it into the electrochemical energy of an action potential. But there are rare cases in which the senses can become confused. The term *synaesthesia* describes an experience in which one sense (say, sight) induces an experience in another sense (say, hearing). Some individuals "see" music or "taste" a color, for example. One woman was able to taste sounds (Beeli, Esslen, & Jancke, 2005). The most common form of synaesthesia is called lexical or grapheme synaesthesia, in which letters and numbers each have shades or tints of individual colors (Jansari, Spiller, & Redfern, 2006; Pearce, 2007). Thus, an individual might experience the letter "A" as having a yellow sunflower tint and the number 2 as the color of wet gray cement. Scientists are exploring the neuroscience connections of synaesthesia, especially in the various sensory regions of the cerebral cortex (Cohen & Henik, 2007). One proposal is that the posterior parietal cortex, which is linked to normal sensory integration, is a key brain region involved in synaesthesia (Muggleton & others 2007; Mulvenna & Walsh, 2006). Senses can be confused, even in people without synaesthesia. For instance, in a series of studies in which participants' actual hands were hidden from view, 66 percent reported "feeling" the touch of a laser beam on a rubber hand that was placed in the same position as their actual hands (Durgin & others, 2007). This rubber hand illusion demonstrates the way that our senses (in this case, vision and sense of touch) work together in an integrative fashion to produce experience.

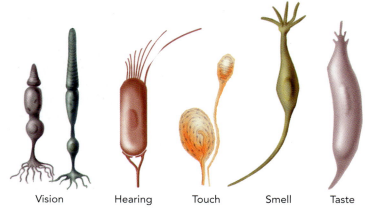

FIGURE 5.1
Sensory Receptor Cells These cells are specialized to detect particular stimuli.

FIGURE 5.2
Information Flow in Senses The diagram shows a general flow of sensory information from energy stimulus to sensory receptor cell to sensory neuron to sensation and perception.

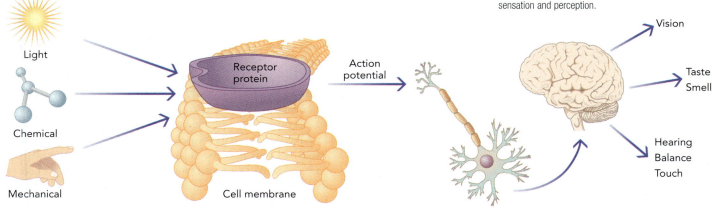

Energy Stimulus   **Sensory Receptor Cell**   **Sensory Neuron**   **Sensation and Perception**

Humans have multiple receptors that provide a rich tapestry of sensations (Lewis & others, 2007). Your skin, for example, contains 4 million pain receptors, 500,000 pressure receptors, 150,000 receptors for cold, and 16,000 receptors for heat. Specialized receptors in the joints, ligaments, and muscles produce information that is combined with information from other receptors, such as those in the eyes and ears, to give us a sense of where certain body parts are in relation to other body parts. Vision, hearing, touch, taste, and smell are only the best known of a wide spectrum of sensations.

The sense organs and sensory receptors fall into several main classes based on the type of energy that is transmitted. These include:

- *Photoreception:* detection of light, perceived as sight
- *Mechanoreception:* detection of pressure, vibration, and movement, perceived as touch, hearing, and equilibrium
- *Chemoreception:* detection of chemical stimuli, perceived as smell and taste

In the brain, nearly all sensory signals go through the thalamus. Recall from Chapter 3 that the thalamus is the brain's great relay station. From the thalamus, the signals go to the sensory areas of the cerebral cortex, where they are modified and distributed throughout a vast network of neurons.

Also recall from Chapter 3 that certain areas of the cerebral cortex are specialized to handle different sensory functions. Visual information is processed mainly in the occipital lobes; hearing in the temporal lobes; and pain, touch, and temperature in the parietal lobes. Keep in mind, however, that the interactions and pathways of sensory information are complex, and the brain often must coordinate extensive information and interpret it (Horowitz, Tanyu, & Simmons, 2007). Vision and the other senses evolved to help animals solve important problems, such as knowing when to flee and understanding how to build a shelter. Large numbers of sensory neurons make this behavior possible. As they do so, they allow us to perceive the world in a unified way.

An important part of perception is figuring out what the sensory messages mean (Blake & Sekuler, 2006). Many top-down factors determine this meaning, including signals from different parts of the brain, prior learning, the person's goals, and his or her degree of arousal (Ciaramelli & others, 2007). Moving in the opposite direction, bottom-up signals from a sensory area may help other parts of the brain maintain arousal, form an image of where the body is in space, or regulate movement (Stuss, 2006).

Thresholds

How close does an approaching bumblebee have to be for you to hear its buzzing? How far away from a brewing coffeemaker can you be and still detect the smell of coffee? How different does the percentage of fat in the low-fat and regular versions of your favorite ice cream have to be for you to taste a difference? Such questions are answered by **psychophysics,** the field that studies links between the physical properties of stimuli and a person's experience of them (Meddis, 2006; Meese & others, 2007). For example, an experiment in psychophysics might examine the relation between the rate at which a light flashes and a participant's ability to see individual flashes.

Absolute Threshold Any sensory system must be able to detect varying degrees of energy. This energy can take the form of light, sound, chemical, or mechanical stimulation. How much of a stimulus is necessary for you to see, hear, taste, smell, or feel something? One way to address this question is to assume that there is an **absolute threshold,** or minimum amount of stimulus energy that a person can detect. When the energy of a stimulus falls below this absolute threshold, we cannot detect its presence; when the energy of the stimulus rises above the absolute threshold, we can detect the stimulus (Glasberg & Moore, 2006). As an example, find a clock that ticks; put it on a table and walk far enough away that you no longer hear it. Then gradually move toward the clock. At some point, you will begin to hear it ticking. Hold your position and notice that occasionally the ticking fades, and you may have to move forward to reach the threshold; at other times, it may become loud, and you can move backward.

psychophysics The field that studies links between the physical properties of stimuli and a person's experience of them.

absolute threshold The minimum amount of stimulus energy that a person can detect.

In this experiment, if you measure your absolute threshold several times, you likely will record several different distances for detecting the stimulus. For example, the first time you try it, you might hear the ticking at 25 feet from the clock. But you probably will not hear it every time at 25 feet. Maybe you hear it only 38 percent of the time at this distance, but you hear it 50 percent of the time at 20 feet away and 65 percent of the time at 15 feet. Also, people have different thresholds because some have better hearing than others, and some have better vision than others. Figure 5.3 shows one person's measured absolute threshold for detecting a clock's ticking sound. Psychologists have arbitrarily decided that absolute threshold is the point at which the individual detects the stimulus 50 percent of the time—in this case, 20 feet away. Using the same clock, another person might have a measured absolute threshold of 26 feet, and yet another, 18 feet. Figure 5.4 lists the approximate absolute thresholds of five senses.

Under ideal circumstances, our senses have very low absolute thresholds, so we can be remarkably good at detecting small amounts of stimulus energy. You can demonstrate this to yourself by using a sharp pencil point to carefully lift a single hair on your forearm. Most people can easily detect this tiny bit of pressure on the skin. You might be surprised to learn that the human eye can see a candle flame at 30 miles on a dark, clear night.

But our environment seldom gives us ideal conditions with which to detect stimuli. If the night were cloudy or the air were polluted, for example, you would have to be much closer to see the candle flame. And other lights on the horizon—car or house lights—would hinder your ability to detect the candle's flicker. **Noise** is the term given to irrelevant and competing stimuli. For example, suppose someone speaks to you from the doorway of the room in which you are sitting. You might fail to respond because your roommate is talking on the phone, and a CD player is blaring out your favorite song. We usually think of noise as being auditory, but the psychological meaning of *noise* also involves other senses (Lindgren, Andersson, & Norback, 2006; Schwela, Kephalopoulous, & Prasher, 2005). Air pollution, cloudiness, car lights, and house lights are forms of visual noise that hamper your ability to see a candle flame from a great distance.

Subliminal Perception   Is it possible for us to be affected by sensations at levels below our absolute threshold without being aware of them? **Subliminal perception**—the detection of information below the level of conscious awareness—was once a subject of controversy. Research has shown that we *can* be influenced by information that is presented below the conscious threshold. In a recent study, participants were exposed to subliminal words such as *happy, joyful,* and *proud.* The words were shown too quickly (mere milliseconds) to be consciously "seen." But after viewing these words, college students rated their lives as more meaningful than students who had been exposed to the words *violin, hubcap,* and *puddle* for the same brief time (King & others, 2006). Research has verified that people's performance is affected by stimuli that are too faint to be recognized at a conscious level (Cleeremans & Sarrazin, 2007; Wiens, 2006; Wolbers & others, 2006). We examine these kinds of effects further in Chapter 8's discussion of priming.

Difference Threshold   In addition to studying how much energy is required for a stimulus to be detected, psychologists investigate the degree of *difference* that must exist between two stimuli before the difference is detected. This is the **difference threshold,** or

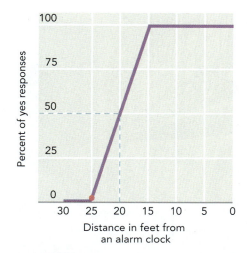

FIGURE 5.3

Measuring Absolute Threshold Absolute threshold is the minimum amount of energy we can detect. To measure absolute threshold, psychologists have arbitrarily decided to use the criterion of detecting the stimulus 50 percent of the time. In this graph, the person's absolute threshold for detecting the ticking clock is at a distance of 20 feet.

noise Irrelevant and competing stimuli.

subliminal perception The detection of information below the level of conscious awareness.

difference threshold The smallest difference in stimulation required to discriminate one stimulus from another 50 percent of the time; also called *just noticeable difference.*

FIGURE 5.4

Approximate Absolute Thresholds for Five Senses These thresholds show the amazing power of our senses to detect even very slight variations in the environment.

Vision   A candle flame at 30 miles on a dark, clear night
Hearing   A ticking watch at 20 feet under quiet conditions
Smell   One drop of perfume diffused throughout three rooms
Taste   A teaspoon of sugar in 2 gallons of water
Touch   The wing of a fly falling on your neck from a distance of 1 centimeter

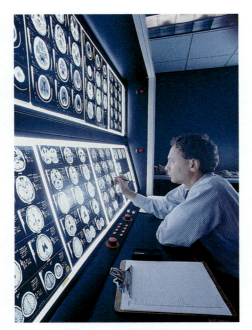

Signal detection theory has important applications in many areas, including medicine.

just noticeable difference. An artist might detect the difference between two similar shades of color. A tailor might determine a difference in the texture of two fabrics. How different must the colors and textures be to determine the difference? Just as the absolute threshold is determined by a 50 percent detection rate, the difference threshold is the smallest difference in stimulation required to discriminate one stimulus from another 50 percent of the time.

An important aspect of difference thresholds is that the threshold increases with the magnitude of the stimulus. When music is playing softly, you may notice when your roommate increases the volume by even a small amount. But if he or she turns the volume up an equal amount when the music is playing very loudly, you may not notice. More than 150 years ago, E. H. Weber, a German physiologist, noticed that, regardless of their magnitude, two stimuli must differ by a constant proportion to be detected. **Weber's law** is the principle that two stimuli must differ by a constant minimum percentage (rather than a constant amount) to be perceived as different. Weber's law generally holds true (Deco & Rolls, 2006; van Marie & Wynn, 2006). For example, we add 1 candle to 60 candles and notice a difference in the brightness of the candles; we add 1 candle to 120 candles and do not notice a difference. We discover, though, that adding 2 candles to 120 candles does produce a difference in brightness. Adding 2 candles to 120 candles is the same proportionately as adding 1 candle to 60 candles. The exact proportion varies with the stimulus involved. For example, a change of 3 percent in a tone's pitch can be detected, but a 20 percent change is required for a person to detect a difference in taste, and a 25 percent change in smell is required.

Signal Detection Theory

Nearly all reasoning and decision making takes place with some degree of uncertainty. One theory about perception—**signal detection theory**—focuses on decision making about stimuli in the presence of uncertainty. In signal detection theory, detection of sensory stimuli depends on a variety of factors besides the physical intensity of the stimulus and the sensory abilities of the observer. These factors include individual and contextual variations, such as fatigue, expectancy, and the urgency of the moment (Demeyer, Zaenen, & Wagemans, 2007; Kornbrot, 2006; Lu & Eskew, 2007).

Consider the case of two air traffic controllers with exactly the same sensory ability to detect blips on a radar screen. One is monitoring the radar screen while working overtime late into the night and feeling fatigued. The other is watching the screen in the morning after having had a good night's sleep. The fatigued radar operator fails to see a blip indicating that a small private plane is flying too close to a large passenger jet, and the two collide. However, in a similar situation, the well-rested controller detects a private plane intruding in the air space of a large passenger jet and contacts the small private plane's pilot, who then changes course. Consider also two people at a dentist's office. One "feels" pain the instant the drill touches the tooth's surface; the other does not "feel" pain until the dentist drills deeply into a cavity.

Signal detection theory provides a precise language and graphic representation for analyzing decision making in the presence of uncertainty. To see how signal detection theory works, consider the following medical context (Heeger, 1997). A radiologist is scanning an image of the brain created by magnetic resonance imaging (MRI) to determine if a tumor is present. Either there is a tumor (signal present) or there is not (signal absent). Either the radiologist sees the tumor (responding "yes") or does not (responding "no"). This leads to four possible outcomes: (1) hit (tumor present and doctor says, "Yes, I see it"); (2) miss (tumor present and doctor says, "No, I don't see it"); (3) false alarm (tumor absent and doctor says, "Yes, I see it"); and (4) correct rejection (tumor absent and doctor says, "No, I don't see it") (Figure 5.5).

Decision making in signal detection theory has two main components: information acquisition and criterion. In terms of *information acquisition,* the question is "What information is in the image produced by the brain scan?" For example, a healthy brain has a characteristic shape; a tumor might distort that shape. Tumors might have different image characteristics, such as brightness or darkness.

The *criterion* component of signal detection theory is the basis for making a judgment about the available information. That is,

Weber's law The principle that two stimuli must differ by a constant minimum percentage (rather than a constant amount) to be perceived as different.

signal detection theory The theory about perception that focuses on decision making about stimuli in the presence of uncertainty; detection depends on a variety of factors besides the physical intensity of the stimulus and the sensory abilities of the observer.

FIGURE 5.5

Four Outcomes in Signal Detection
Signal detection research helps to explain when and how responses are correct or mistaken.

	Observer's Response	
	"Yes, I see it"	*"No, I don't see it"*
Signal Present	Hit (correct)	Miss (mistake)
Signal Absent	False alarm (mistake)	Correct rejection (correct)

responses depend on the criterion that decision makers set for determining whether a stimulus is present or not. The criterion depends on more than the information provided by the environmental stimuli. For example, in addition to relying on technology or testing to provide information, doctors also make judgments about the information. They may feel that different types of errors are not equal. For example, a doctor may believe that missing an opportunity for early diagnosis may mean the difference between life and death, whereas a false alarm may simply result in a routine biopsy operation. This type of doctor may err on the side of "yes" (tumor present) decisions. However, another doctor may believe that unnecessary surgeries, even routine biopsies, should not be done because of the expense and the patient stress. Such a doctor may tend to be conservative and say "no" (tumor absent) more often. This doctor may miss more tumors but will reduce unnecessary surgeries. The conservative doctor also may believe that, if a tumor is present, it will be detected in time on the next checkup.

Perceiving Sensory Stimuli

As we just saw, the perception of stimuli is influenced by more than the characteristics of the environmental stimuli themselves. Two important factors in perceiving sensory stimuli are attention and perceptual set.

Attention   The world holds a lot of information to perceive. At this moment you are perceiving the letters and words that make up this sentence. Now gaze around you and pick out something other than this book to look at. Afterward, curl up the toes on your right foot. In each of these circumstances, you engaged in **selective attention,** which involves focusing on a specific aspect of experience while ignoring others (Melcher & Gruber, 2006; Richards & others, 2007). A familiar example of selective attention is the ability to focus on one voice among many in a crowded room or a noisy restaurant. Psychologists call this common occurrence the "cocktail party effect."

Not only is attention selective, but it also is *shiftable*. For example, if someone calls your name in a crowded room, you can shift your attention to that person. Or if you go to an art museum, you look at one painting, then another, then others, moving your attention from one painting to the next. And as you look at each painting, you shift your vision from one part of the painting to another, seeking to understand it better. The fact that we can attend selectively to one thing and shift it readily to something else indicates that we must be monitoring many things at once.

Certain features of stimuli cause people to attend to them. Novel stimuli (those that are new, different, or unusual) often attract our attention. If a Ferrari convertible whizzes by, you are more likely to notice it than you would a Ford. Size, color, and movement also influence our attention. Objects that are large, vividly colored, or moving are more likely to grab our attention than objects that are small, dull-colored, or stationary.

Highly practiced and familiar stimuli, such as your own name or hometown, often are perceived so automatically that it is almost impossible to ignore them. The *Stroop effect* is an example of an automatic perception whereby it is difficult to name the colors in which words are printed when the words name different colors (Cho, Lien, & Proctor, 2006; Goldfarb & Tzelgov, 2007). To experience the Stroop effect, see Figure 5.6. Most of the time, the highly practiced and almost automatic perception of word meaning makes reading easier. However, this automaticity makes it hard to ignore the meaning of the words for colors (such as *blue*) when they are printed in a different color (such as orange). Thus, the Stroop effect represents a failure of selective attention.

Psychologists also are interested in the top-down and bottom-up processing aspects of attention (Moradi, Hipp, & Koch, 2007). For example, the Stroop effect is an example of *bottom-up processing,* in which attention is stimulus-driven (Banaschewski & others, 2006). However, attention also involves *top-down processing,* in which attention is due to decisions to initiate attention (Womelsdorf & others, 2006). Thus, you can decide to look at your watch to see how much more time you have to study this book today.

selective attention Focusing on a specific aspect of experience while ignoring others.

As fast as you can, name each color of ink used to print each of the rectangles below.

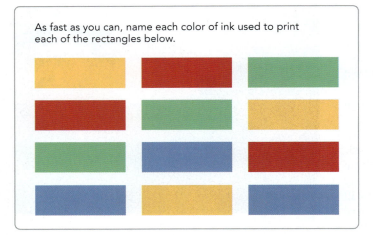

Now, as fast as you can, name the color of ink used to print each word shown below, ignoring what each word says.

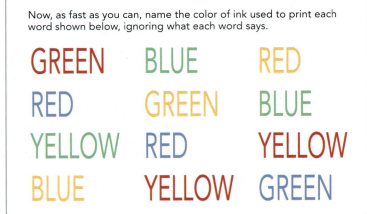

GREEN BLUE RED
RED GREEN BLUE
YELLOW RED YELLOW
BLUE YELLOW GREEN

FIGURE 5.6

The Stroop Effect Before reading further, read the instructions above and complete the tasks. You probably had little or no difficulty naming the colors of the rectangles in the set on the left. However, you likely stumbled more when you were asked to name the color of ink used to print each word in the set on the right. This automaticity in perception is the Stroop effect.

Perceptual Set   Place your hand over the playing cards on the right in the illustration and look at the playing cards on the left. As quickly as you can, count how many aces of spades you see. Then place your hand over the cards on the left and count the number of aces of spades among the cards on the right.

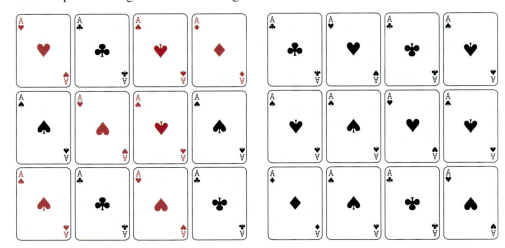

Most people report that they see two or three aces of spades in the set of 12 cards on the left. However, if you look closely, you will see that there are five. Two of the aces of spades are black and three are red. When people look at the set of 12 cards on the right, they are more likely to count five aces of spades. Why do we perceive the two sets of cards differently? We expect the ace of spades to be black because it is always black in a regular deck of cards. We do not expect it to be red, so we skip right over the red ones. Our expectations influence our perceptions.

Psychologists refer to a predisposition, or readiness, to perceive something in a particular way as a **perceptual set**. Perceptual sets act as "psychological" filters in processing information about the environment (Fei-Fei & others, 2007). Interpretation is another consequence of a perceptual set. Interpretation can occur even before a stimulus or signal appears, as in the case of a runner waiting for a starting signal.

Interestingly, young children are more accurate at the task involving the ace of spades than adults are. Why? Because they have not built up the perceptual set that the ace of spades is black. The underestimation of aces of spades in the left set of 12 cards reflects the concept of top-down processing. To read further about how perceptual sets can influence perceptions and subsequent actions, see the Intersection.

Sensory Adaptation

perceptual set A predisposition, or readiness, to perceive something in a particular way.

Turning out the lights in your bedroom at night, you stumble across the room to your bed, completely blind to the objects around you. Gradually the objects reappear and become

Perception and Social Psychology: Was That a Gun or a Cell Phone?

It was midnight on a cold February night in 1999. Amadou Diallo, a 22-year-old Black man from West Africa who had come to New York City to pursue his interest in computer science, was returning home from a late meal. Outside his apartment building, he was approached by four White plainclothes police officers, who told him to stop. As Diallo reached into his pocket, one of the officers shouted "Gun!" setting off a flurry of 41 gunshots. Nineteen bullets hit Diallo, killing him. The object in his hand was, in fact, not a gun but his wallet. Two years earlier, on Christmas day, William J. Whitfield, an unarmed African American in a New York supermarket, was shot dead by police who mistook the keys he was carrying for a gun. And in Shreveport, Louisiana, Marquise Hudspeth, a 25-year-old African American, was shot and killed by three White police officers who mistook his cell phone for a gun.

> ### Three White police officers . . . mistook his cell phone for a gun.

In all of these cases, the police officers were acquitted of any wrongdoing in their trials. Juries and judges concluded that they had made terrible but honest mistakes. These and similar cases incited critical public and media interest. Could it be a coincidence that the unarmed dead men were all African Americans? What role did ethnicity play in these "honest" perceptual mistakes?

Inspired by such cases, social psychologist Keith Payne (2001) examined how ethnicity might influence the tendency to misperceive harmless objects such as wallets, car keys, and cell phones as handguns. Participants in the study were told that they would see two pictures on a computer screen. Their job was to decide, as quickly and accurately as possible, if the second picture was a gun or a tool. The first picture—always a picture of an African American man or a White man—was

a cue for the participants that the real judgment was coming. Payne found that after seeing an African American man's face, participants were quicker to recognize guns accurately in the second picture. Then, in a second study using the same sequence of images, participants were required to respond very quickly. Like the police officers in the real-life examples, participants were more likely to misperceive tools as guns when the tools were shown after a picture of an African American man.

Subsequent research has extended Payne's findings by employing video games in which participants must decide whether to shoot or not shoot a potential suspect who is holding either a gun or some harmless object. In these studies, both African American and White participants have been found to shoot more quickly at an armed African American man and to decide more quickly not to shoot at an unarmed White man (Correll & others, 2002). Because African Americans and Whites were equally disposed to react in these ways, the researchers concluded that personal prejudice did not predict the tendency to let ethnicity guide the decision to shoot or not shoot a suspect. Instead, knowledge of the cultural stereotypes—or generalizations—about different ethnicities did.

In a more recent study, 48 police officers, Whites and African Americans, played a video game in which they had to decide whether to shoot or not shoot the suspects in the game (Plant & Peruche, 2005). The suspects were African American or White and were holding guns or other objects. The researchers were interested in whether practice with the game—in which African American and White suspects were randomly determined to be holding a gun or another object—would help the officers become less ethnically biased in their perceptions. Would experience with the fact that there was no systematic relation between ethnicity and whether a person was likely to be armed and dangerous reduce the tendency to perceive harmless objects as guns? In the early trials the police officers were more likely to mistakenly shoot an unarmed suspect when he was African American. But by the experiment's end, this tendency had faded, and the officers treated African American and White suspects with equal levels of restraint.

Let's return to the case of Amadou Diallo. A deeply religious young man who worked 12 hours a day, 6 days a week, Diallo loved reading, music, and sports, especially basketball. He had dreamed of going to school in the United States. But his life was cut tragically short because someone "saw" a gun where there was only a wallet. His death has become a touchstone for those who are concerned about civil rights, police brutality, and the role of ethnicity in American life. Hip hop artists such as Wyclef Jean and Mos Def, rock singer Bruce Springsteen, and alternative songwriter and lead singer Zack de la Rocha, formerly of Rage Against the Machine, have all written songs or spoken publicly about the Diallo case.

Although the mistake police made on that February night may have been an honest one, it was not inevitable. Cases such as Diallo's highlight the crucial role of cultural beliefs and the social world in the basic process of perception. In a society in which ethnic minority individuals are not viewed as dangerous, aggressive, or likely to be criminals, wallets, car keys, and cell phones might no longer be misperceived as weapons, and such tragedies might be avoided.

clearer. The ability of the visual system to adjust to a darkened room is an example of **sensory adaptation**—a change in the responsiveness of the sensory system based on the average level of surrounding stimulation (Jiang, Blanz, & O'Toole, 2006; Parra & Pearlmutter, 2007). You have experienced sensory adaptation countless times in your life—adapting to the temperature of a shower, to the water in an initially "freezing" swimming pool, and to the smell of the Thanksgiving dinner that is wonderful to you as an arriving guest but almost undetectable to the cook who spent all day laboring over it. When you first enter a room, you might be bothered by the hum of the air conditioner or the buzz of the fluorescent lights, but after a while you get used to these mild irritations. You have experienced adaptation.

In the example of adapting to the dark, when you turn out the lights, everything is black. Conversely, when you step out into the bright sunshine after spending time in a dark basement, your eyes are flooded with light and everything appears light. An important function of the eye is to get a good picture of the world. Good pictures have sharp contrasts between dark and light parts. The pupil of the eye adjusts the amount of light that gets into the eye and therefore helps to preserve the contrast between dark and light areas in our picture. Additional structures throughout the visual system adapt. You may have noticed that the change in the size of the pupil as you dim or brighten the lights happens very quickly. You also may have noticed that, when you turn out the lights in your bedroom, the contrast between dark and light continues to improve for nearly 45 minutes. The reason is that the sensory receptors in your visual system adjust their response rates on the basis of the average light level of the surrounding room. This adaptation takes longer than it does for the pupil to adjust.

All of these mechanisms allow the visual system to preserve contrast over an extremely large range of background illumination conditions. The price we pay for our ability to adapt to the mean light level is *time*. Driving out of a dark tunnel under a mountain into the glistening and blinding reflection of the sun off the snow reminds us of this trade-off.

sensory adaptation A change in the responsiveness of the sensory system based on the average level of surrounding stimulation.

REVIEW, ASSESS, AND SHARPEN YOUR THINKING

Review

1 Discuss basic principles of sensation and perception.
- Explain what *sensation* and *perception* mean.
- Outline the sensory reception process, and define three types of sensory reception.
- Distinguish between absolute threshold and difference threshold, and evaluate subliminal perception.
- Explain how signal detection theory accounts for the effect of uncertainty on perception.
- Discuss these aspects of perception: attention and perceptual set.
- Describe sensory adaptation.

Assess

1. An example of _____ is hearing the sounds that come out of a stereo; an example of _____ is recognizing the sound to be your favorite singer.
   A. transduction, perception
   B. perception, transduction
   C. sensation, perception
   D. perception, sensation

2. Which form of processing proceeds from the detection of a stimulus to its implantation?
   A. top-down processing
   B. bottom-up processing
   C. transduction processing
   D. perception processing

3. Being in a movie theater and having the ability to focus on the movie despite someone near you talking is an example of
   A. signal detection theory.
   B. selective attention.
   C. sensory adaptation.
   D. a perceptual set.

4. A video that helps children learn math skills has brief clips of encouraging words, such as "smart," "success," and "competent." These words are not shown long enough to consciously register and can only be seen when the video is slowed down. Which of the following is being used?
   A. the difference threshold
   B. the absolute threshold
   C. subliminal perception
   D. sensory adaptation

5. Shelley has been studying late into the night and does not feel pain when an insect stings her. According to signal detection theory, which of the following outcomes best describes Shelley's response?

A. hit
B. miss
C. false alarm
D. correct rejection

Sharpen Your Thinking

Try the absolute threshold experiment described on page 176–177. Discuss your results with others in your class who tried the experiment.

2 The Visual System

Explain how the visual system enables us to see and, by communicating with the brain, to perceive the world.

Michael May, from Davis, California, was blinded at the age of 3 when an accident left him with only the ability to perceive the difference between night and day. He lived a rich, full life, marrying and having children, founding a successful company, and becoming an expert skier. After 25 years of blindness, a new procedure, in which stem cells were transplanted into his right eye, gave him partial sight (Kurson, 2007). May can now see; his right eye is functional and allows him to detect color and negotiate the world without the use of a cane or reliance on his seeing-eye dog. But his visual experience remains unusual: He sees the world as if it were an abstract painting. He can catch a ball thrown to him by his sons, but he cannot recognize his wife's face. His brain has to work at interpreting the new information that his right eye is providing.

May's experience highlights the intimate connection between the brain and the sense organs in producing perception. Vision is a remarkable process that involves the brain's interpretation of what the eyes see. We now explore the physical foundations of the visual system.

The Visual Stimulus and the Eye

Our ability to detect visual stimuli depends on the sensitivity of our eyes to differences in light. This section covers some basic facts about light energy and the complex structure of the eye.

Light   *Light* is a form of electromagnetic energy that can be described in terms of wavelengths. Like ocean waves moving toward the beach, light travels through space in waves. The *wavelength* of light is the distance from the peak of one wave to the peak of the next. Wavelengths of visible light range from about 400 to 700 nanometers (a nanometer is 1-billionth of a meter and is abbreviated nm).

Outside the range of visible light are longer radio and infrared radiation waves and shorter ultraviolet and X rays (Figure 5.7). These other forms of electromagnetic energy continually bombard us, but we do not see them. Why do we see only the narrow band of electromagnetic energy with wavelengths between 400 and 700 nanometers? The most likely answer is that our visual system evolved in the sun's light. Thus, our visual system is able to perceive the range of energy emitted by the sun. By the time sunlight reaches the earth's surface, it is strongest in the 400 to 700 nanometer range. The wavelength of light that is reflected by a visual stimulus determines its *hue,* or color.

Two other characteristics of light waves are amplitude and purity. *Amplitude* refers to the height of a wave, and it is linked with the brightness of a visual stimulus (Figure 5.8). *Purity,* the mixture of wavelengths in light, is related to the perceived saturation, or richness, of a visual stimulus. The color tree shown in Figure 5.9 can help you to understand

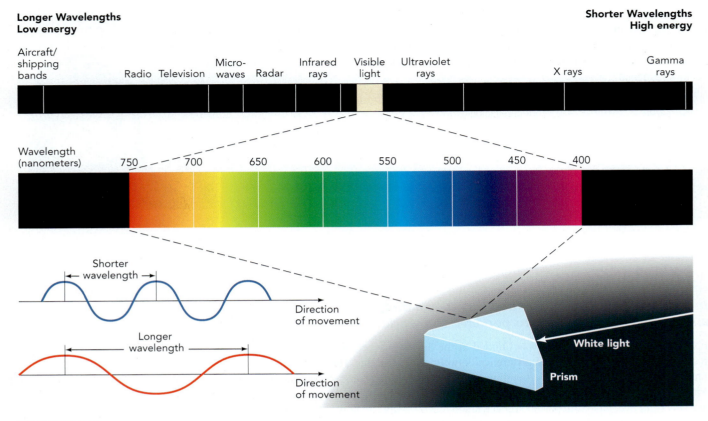

FIGURE 5.7

The Electromagnetic Spectrum and Visible Light (*Top*) Visible light is only a narrow band in the electromagnetic spectrum. Visible light wavelengths range from about 400 to 700 nm. X rays are much shorter, radio waves much longer. (*Bottom*) The two graphs show how waves vary in length between successive peaks. Shorter wavelengths are higher in frequency, as reflected in blue colors; longer wavelengths are lower in frequency, as reflected in red colors.

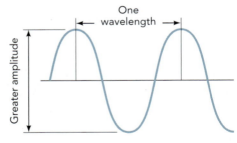

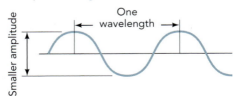

FIGURE 5.8

Light Waves of Varying Amplitude The top graph might suggest a spotlight on a concert stage, while the bottom figure might represent a romantic candlelight dinner.

saturation. Colors that are very pure have no white light in them. They are located on the outside of the color tree. Notice how the saturation of a color changes toward the interior of the color tree. The closer we get to the center, the more white light has been added to the single wavelength of a particular color. In other words, the deep colors at the edge fade into pastel colors toward the center.

The Structure of the Eye   The eye, like a camera, is constructed to get the best possible picture of the world. Let's see how the eye performs this task.

Getting the Best Picture of the World   A good picture is in focus, is not too dark or too light, and has good contrast between the dark and light parts. Each of several structures in the eye plays an important role in this process. If you look closely at your eyes in the mirror, you will notice three parts—the sclera, iris, and pupil (Figure 5.10). The *sclera* is the white, outer part of the eye that helps to maintain the shape of the eye and to protect it from injury. The *iris* is the colored part of the eye, which might be light blue in one individual and dark brown in another. The *pupil,* which appears black, is the opening in the center of the iris. The iris contains muscles that control the size of the pupil and, hence, the amount of light that gets into the eye. This allows the eye to function optimally under different conditions of illumination, which can range in the course of a normal day from the darkest moonless night to the brightest summer sunshine. To get a good picture of the world, the eye needs to be able to adjust the amount of light that enters. In this sense, the pupil acts like the aperture of a camera, opening to let in more light when it is needed and closing to let in less light when there is too much.

You can demonstrate changes in the size of the pupil by looking at your eyes in the mirror and turning the room lights up and down. (You need to try this experiment in a room with sufficient light to be able to see your eyes even when the lights are turned all the way down.) As you dim the light, your pupils will begin to enlarge to let in more light; as you turn the room lights back up, the pupil opening will shrink to let in less light.

If the eye acts like a camera, then, in addition to having the right amount of light, the image has to be in focus at the back of the eye. Two structures serve this purpose: the *cornea,* which is a clear membrane just in front of the eye, and the *lens* of the eye, which is a transparent and somewhat flexible, disklike entity filled with a gelatinous material. The function of both of these structures is to bend the light falling on the surface of the eye just enough to focus it at the back of the eye. The curved surface of the cornea does most of this bending, while the lens fine-tunes the focus. When you are looking at faraway objects, the lens has a relatively flat shape, because the light reaching the eye from faraway objects is parallel and the bending power of the cornea is sufficient to keep things in focus. However, the light reaching the eye from objects that are close is more scattered, so more bending of the light is required to achieve focus.

Without this ability of the lens to change its curvature, the eye would have a tough time focusing on objects that are close to us, such as needlework or reading. As we get older, the lens of our eye begins to lose its flexibility and, hence, its ability to change from its normal flattened shape to the rounder shape needed to bring close objects into focus. This is the reason that many people whose vision is normal throughout their young adult lives will require reading glasses when they get older.

Recording Images on the Retina   The parts of the eye we have considered so far work together to get the best possible picture of the world. This effort, however, would be useless without a method for keeping, or recording, the images we take of the world. In a camera, film serves just such a purpose. Film is made of a material that responds to light. At the back of the eye, the multilayered **retina** is the light-sensitive surface that records what we see and converts it to neural impulses for processing in the brain.

But making a comparison between the film in a camera and the retina vastly underestimates the complexity and elegance of the retina's design. The retina is, in fact, the primary mechanism of sight, but even after decades of intense study, the full marvel of this structure is far from understood (Field & Chichilnisky, 2007; van Hateren, 2007).

The human retina has approximately 126 million receptor cells. They turn the electromagnetic energy of light into a form of energy that the nervous system can process. There are two kinds of visual receptor cells: rods and cones. Rods and cones differ both in how they respond to light and in their patterns of distribution on the surface of the retina (Foster, Hankins, & Peirson, 2007; Pan & Massey, 2007). **Rods** are the receptors in the retina that are sensitive to light, but they are not very useful for color vision. Thus, they function

FIGURE 5.9

A Color Tree Showing Color's Three Dimensions: Hue, Saturation, and Brightness Hue is represented around the color tree, saturation horizontally, and brightness vertically.

retina The light-sensitive surface in the back of the eye that records what we see and converts it to neural impulses for processing in the brain.

rods The receptors in the retina that are sensitive to light but are not very useful for color vision.

FIGURE 5.10

Parts of the Eye Note that the image of the butterfly on the retina is upside down. The brain allows us to see the image right side up.

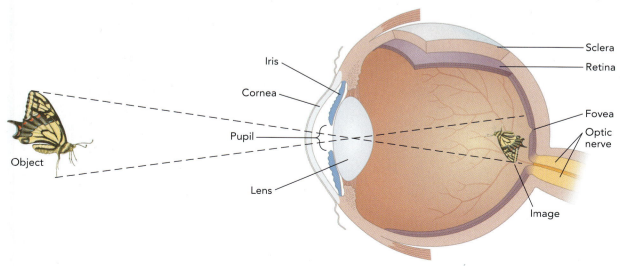

FIGURE 5.11

Rods and Cones In real life, rods and cones look somewhat like stumps and corncobs.

cones The receptors in the retina that process information about color.

well under low illumination; as you might expect, they are hard at work at night. Humans have about 120 million rods. **Cones** are the receptors that we use for color perception. Like the rods, cones are light-sensitive. However, they require a larger amount of light than the rods do to respond, so they operate best in daylight or under high illumination. There are about 6 million cone cells in human eyes. Figure 5.11 shows what rods and cones look like.

The most important part of the retina is the *fovea,* a minute area in the center of the retina at which vision is at its best (see Figure 5.10). The fovea contains only cones and is vital to many visual tasks (try reading out of the corner of your eye!). Rods are found almost everywhere on the retina except in the fovea. Because rods require little light, they work best under conditions of low illumination. This light sensitivity and the rods' location on the retina give us the ability to detect fainter spots of light on the peripheral retina than at the fovea. Thus, if you want to see a very faint star, you should gaze slightly away from it.

Figure 5.12 shows how the rods and cones at the back of the retina transduce light into electrochemical impulses. The signal is transmitted to the *bipolar cells* and then moves on to another layer of specialized cells called *ganglion cells* (tom Dieck & Brandstatter, 2006). The axons of the ganglion cells make up the optic nerve, which carries the visual information to the brain for further processing.

There is one place on the retina that contains neither rods nor cones. Not surprisingly, this area is called the *blind spot;* it is the place on the retina where the optic nerve leaves the eye on its way to the brain (see Figure 5.12). We cannot see anything that reaches only this part of the retina. To prove to yourself that you have a blind spot, take a look at Figure 5.13. Once you have seen the yellow pepper disappear, you have probably noticed it took a while to succeed at this task. Now shut one eye and look around. You see a perfectly continuous picture of the world around you; there is no blind spot. This is a great example of top-down processing and a demonstration of the constructive aspect of perception. Your brain fills in the gap for you (the one that ought to be left by your blind spot) with some pretty good guesses about what must be in that spot. Your brain is a creative artist, painting in the blind spot.

A summary of the characteristics of rods and cones is presented in Figure 5.14.

FIGURE 5.12

Direction of Light in the Retina After light passes through the cornea, pupil, and lens, it falls on the retina. Three layers of specialized cells in the retina convert the image into a neural signal that can be transmitted to the brain. First, light triggers a reaction in the rods and cones at the back of the retina, transducing light energy into electrochemical neural impulses. The neural impulses activate the bipolar cells, which in turn activate the ganglion cells. Then light information is transmitted to the optic nerve, which conveys it to the brain. The arrows indicate the sequence in which light information moves in the retina.

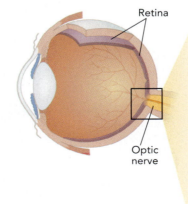

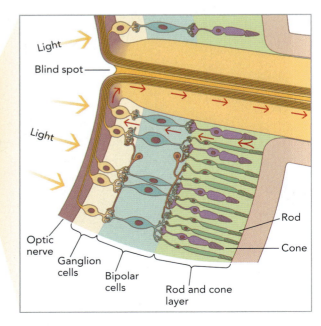

Visual Processing in the Brain

The eyes are just the beginning of visual perception. The next step occurs when neural impulses generated in the retina are dispatched to the brain for analysis and integration.

The optic nerve leaves the eye, carrying information about light toward the brain. Light travels in a straight line; therefore, stimuli in the left visual field are registered in the right half of the retina in both eyes, and stimuli in the right visual field are registered in the left half of the retina in both eyes (Figure 5.15). In the brain, at a point called the *optic chiasm,* the optic nerve fibers divide, and approximately half of the nerve fibers cross over the midline of the brain. As a result, the visual information originating in the right halves of the two retinas is transmitted to the left side of the occipital lobe in the cerebral cortex, and the visual information coming from the left halves of the retinas is transmitted to the right side of the occipital lobe. These crossings mean that what we see in the left side of our visual field is registered in the right side of the brain, and what we see in the right visual field is registered in the left side of the brain (see Figure 5.15). Then this information is processed and combined into a recognizable object or scene in the visual cortex.

FIGURE 5.13

The Eye's Blind Spot There is a normal blind spot in your eye, a small area where the optic nerve leads to the brain. To find your blind spot, hold this book at arm's length, cover your left eye, and stare at the red pepper on the left with your right eye. Move the book slowly toward you until the yellow pepper disappears. To find the blind spot in your left eye, cover your right eye, stare at the yellow pepper, and adjust the book until the red pepper disappears.

The Visual Cortex   The *visual cortex,* located in the occipital lobe of the brain, is the part of the cerebral cortex that functions in vision. Most visual information travels to the primary visual cortex, where it is processed, before moving to other visual areas for further analysis (Shevelev & Lazareva, 2007).

An important aspect of visual information processing is the specialization of neurons. Like the cells in the retina, many cells in the primary visual cortex are highly specialized (Horridge, 2006). **Feature detectors** are neurons in the brain's visual system that respond to particular features of a stimulus. David Hubel and Torsten Wiesel (1965) won a Nobel Prize for their research on feature detectors. By recording the activity of a *single* neuron in a cat while it looked at patterns that varied in size, shape, color, and movement, the researchers found that the visual cortex has neurons that are individually sensitive to different types of lines and angles. One neuron might show a sudden burst of activity when stimulated by lines of a particular angle; another neuron might fire only when moving stimuli appear; yet another neuron might be stimulated when the object in the visual field has a combination of certain angles, sizes, and shapes.

Hubel and Wiesel also noted that when deprived of certain types of visual stimulation early on, kittens lost the ability to perceive these patterns. This finding suggested that there might be a critical period in visual development and that the brain requires stimulation in its efforts to delegate its resources to different perceptual tasks. The brain's "learning" to perceive through experience is a crucial aspect of sensation and perception. It is the reason for Michael May's unusual experience that was described at the beginning of our coverage of the visual system. Once deprived of stimulation, the brain will redistribute its resources to other tasks.

Parallel Processing   "What?" and "Where?" are two basic questions that need to be answered in visual perception. Not only must people realize what they are looking at, but they also need to know where it is in order to respond appropriately. The elegantly organized brain has two pathways—dubbed "what" and "where"—to handle these important vision tasks (Figure 5.16) (Ungerleider & Mishkin, 1982).

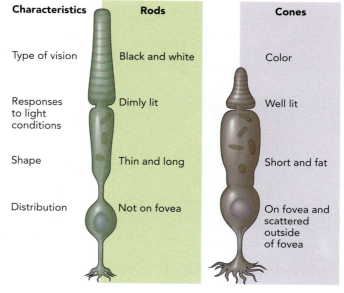

Characteristics	Rods	Cones
Type of vision	Black and white	Color
Responses to light conditions	Dimly lit	Well lit
Shape	Thin and long	Short and fat
Distribution	Not on fovea	On fovea and scattered outside of fovea

FIGURE 5.14

Characteristics of Rods and Cones Rods and cones differ in shape, location, and function.

feature detectors Neurons in the brain's visual system that respond to particular features of a stimulus.

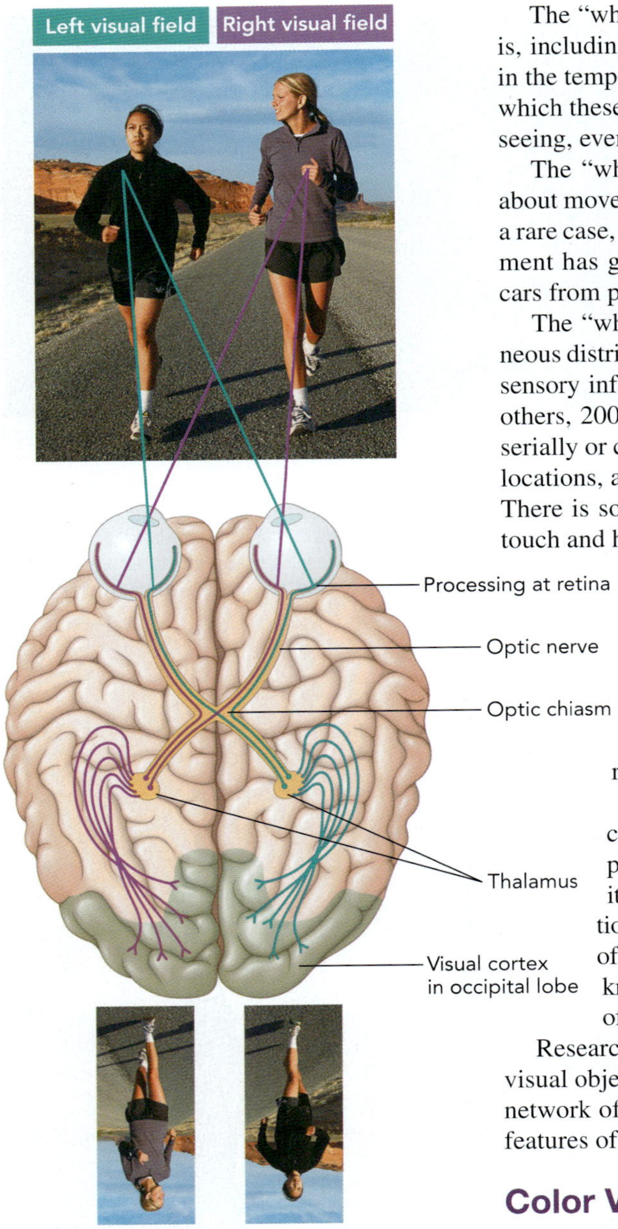

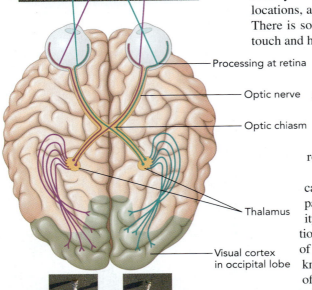

FIGURE 5.15

Visual Pathways to and Through the Brain Light from each side of the visual field falls on the opposite side of each eye's retina. Visual information then travels along the optic nerve to the optic chiasm, where most of the visual information crosses over to the other side of the brain. From there visual information goes to the occipital lobe at the rear of the brain. All these crossings mean that what we see in the left side of our visual field (here, the shorter, dark-haired woman) is registered in the right side of our brain, and what we see in the right visual field (the taller, blond woman) is registered in the left side of our brain.

Labels on figure:
- Left visual field
- Right visual field
- Processing at retina
- Optic nerve
- Optic chiasm
- Thalamus
- Visual cortex in occipital lobe

parallel processing The simultaneous distribution of information across different neural pathways.

binding The bringing together and integration of what is processed through different pathways or cells.

The "what" pathway in the temporal lobe processes information about what the object is, including its color, form, and texture. For instance, an area along the "what" pathway in the temporal lobe is activated when we try to recognize someone's face. In rare cases in which these areas are damaged, individuals have difficulty recognizing the person they are seeing, even though they know they are seeing a face.

The "where" pathway processes information on an object's location, including input about movement and the depth of the object. This pathway is located in the parietal lobe. In a rare case, a woman with damage in an area of the parietal lobe that is activated by movement has great difficulty crossing the street because she cannot distinguish approaching cars from parked cars (Zeki, 1991).

The "what" and "where" pathways are examples of **parallel processing,** the simultaneous distribution of information across different neural pathways. Parallel processing helps sensory information travel rapidly through the brain (Altmann & others, 2007; Sestieri & others, 2006). A sensory system designed to process information about sensory qualities serially or consecutively (such as the shapes of images, their colors, their movements, their locations, and so on) would be too slow to keep us current with a rapidly changing world. There is some evidence suggesting that parallel processing also occurs for sensations of touch and hearing (Ahveninen & others, 2006).

Binding Although the "what" and "where" pathways work in parallel, connections between them unify sensory information into a complete picture of all we see. For instance, if you look at a parrot, visual information about the parrot enters the visual system through your eyes as a complete object. However, as we have seen, the sensory system breaks down this visual information and transmits it in distributed pathways to specific neurons. Seeing the whole parrot requires reassembling the information.

One of the most exciting topics in visual perception today is what neuroscientists call **binding,** the bringing together and integration of what is processed by different pathways or cells (Olson & others, 2006). Binding involves the coupling of the activity of various cells and pathways. Thus, through binding, you can integrate information about the parrot's shape, size, location, color, and motion into a complete image of the parrot in the cerebral cortex. Exactly how binding occurs is not completely known at this time, but the process is a major focus of research in the neuroscience of visual perception today (Giersch & others, 2006; Taylor & others, 2006).

Researchers have found that all the neurons throughout pathways that are activated by a visual object pulse together at the same frequency (Engel & Singer, 2001). Within the vast network of cells in the cerebral cortex, this set of neurons appears to *bind* together all the features of the objects into a unified perception.

Color Vision

Imagine how dull a world without color would be. Art museums are filled with paintings that are remarkable for their use of color, and flowers would lose much of their beauty if we could not see their rich colors. The ability to see color evolved because it provides many advantages to animals, including the ability to detect and discriminate among various objects (Blake & Sekuler, 2006). For example, the edibility of foods depends on ripeness, which is reflected in color.

Color is a pattern of neural responses, not the wavelengths of light themselves, that generate color vision (Solomon & Lennie, 2007; Vanni & others, 2006). The study of human color vision using psychological methods has a long and distinguished history. A full century before the methods existed to study the anatomical and neurophysiological bases of color perception, psychological studies had discovered many of the basic principles of our color vision system. These studies produced two main theories: trichromatic theory and opponent-process theory. Both turned out to be correct.

The **trichromatic theory** states that color perception is produced by three types of receptors (cone cells in the retina) that are particularly sensitive to different, but overlapping, ranges of wavelengths. The trichromatic theory of color vision was proposed by Thomas Young in 1802 and extended by Hermann von Helmholtz in 1852. The theory is

Touring the Senses

GOALS OF THE TOUR

1 **Parts of the Eye.** You will be able to identify the structures of the human eye and describe their functions.

2 **Visual Pathways.** You will be able to identify the pathways for visual stimulation and describe the brain's role in visual information processing.

3 **Parts of the Ear.** You will be able to identify the three areas of the ear and describe the key structures of the inner ear.

4 **The Olfactory Sense.** You will be able to describe how the olfactory sense processes a smell or odor.

Parts of the Eye and Visual Pathways

Object

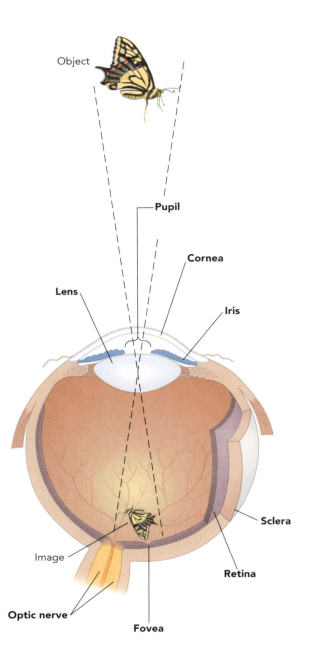

Lens

Pupil

Cornea

Iris

Sclera

Image

Retina

Optic nerve

Fovea

 2 Identify the pathways for visual stimulation and describe the brain's role in visual information processing.

Left visual field   Right visual field

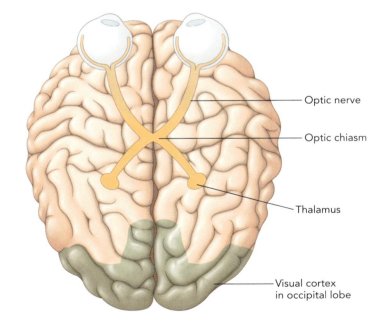

Optic nerve

Optic chiasm

Thalamus

Visual cortex in occipital lobe

Parts of the Ear and the Olfactory Sense

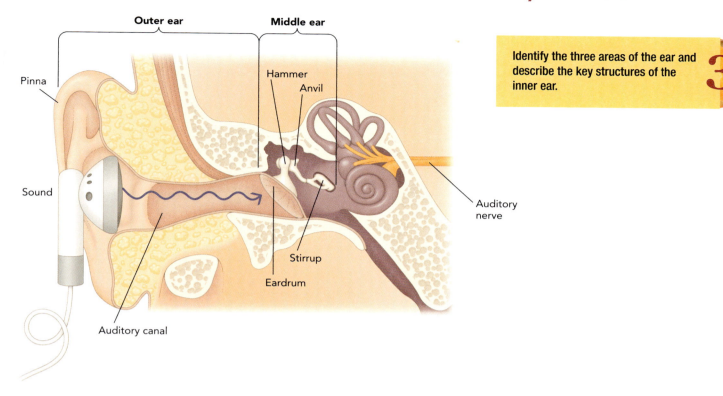

Outer ear

Middle ear

Pinna

Sound

Auditory canal

Hammer

Anvil

Stirrup

Eardrum

Auditory nerve

3 Identify the three areas of the ear and describe the key structures of the inner ear.

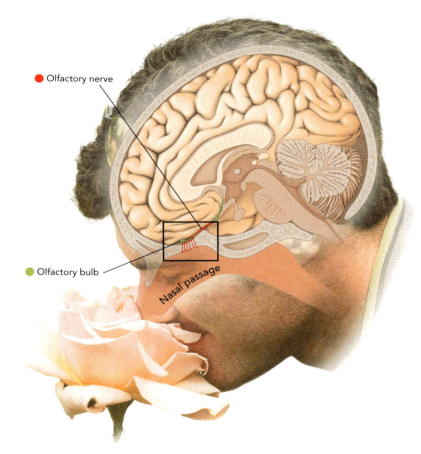

● Olfactory nerve

● Olfactory bulb

Nasal passage

4 Describe how the olfactory sense processes a smell or odor.

ANSWERS

1. PARTS OF THE EYE

The *sclera* is the outer membrane of the eyeball that makes up the white of the eye.

The *retina* is made up of a layer of cells in the interior of the eye that contain the *photoreceptors*, the rods and the cones.

The *cornea* is the transparent membrane in the front of the eye that protects the eye and bends light to provide focus.

The *pupil* is the opening that allows light to enter the eye.

The *iris* is the colored muscle that surrounds the pupil and adjusts the amount of light entering into the eye through the pupil. It dilates (opens) or constricts (closes) in response to the intensity (brightness) of the light. It also dilates in response to certain emotions.

The *lens* focuses the image onto the retinal layer on the back surface of the eye. As in a camera, the image projected by the lens onto the retina is reversed.

The *fovea* is the region of the retina that is directly in line with the pupil and contains mostly cones, which are involved in color perception and visual acuity (sharpness).

The *optic nerve* receives inputs from the photoreceptors and sends information to the brain.

2. VISUAL PATHWAYS

Images of objects in the right visual field are projected to the left half of the retina of each eye, which in turn sends the information first to the thalamus for initial processing and then to the visual cortex in the left hemisphere where perception takes place. Likewise, images of objects in the left visual field are projected to the right half of the retina of each eye, which in turn sends the information to the thalamus and then to the visual cortex in the right hemisphere.

3. PARTS OF THE EAR

The *outer ear* is the visible portion of the ear and the auditory canal (ear canal) that funnels sound waves to the eardrum.

The *middle ear* includes the eardrum and three tiny bones (hammer, anvil, and stirrup) that transmit the eardrum's vibrations to a membrane on the cochlea called the oval window.

The *inner ear* includes the snail-shaped tube called the *cochlea*, which translates sound waves into fluid waves, and the semicircular canals, which sense equilibrium.

4. THE OLFACTORY SENSE

Airborne molecules (olfactory chemicals) enter the nasal passage and reach receptor cells located in the olfactory epithelium of the upper nasal passage. The receptors send messages to the brain's olfactory bulb and then onward to the primary smell cortex located in the temporal lobes.

based on the results of experiments on human color-matching abilities, which show that a person with normal vision can match any color in the spectrum by combining three other wavelengths. In this type of experiment, individuals are given a light of a single wavelength and are asked to combine three other single-wavelength lights to match the first light. They can do this by changing the relative intensities of the three lights until the color of the combination light is indistinguishable from the color of the first light. Young and Helmholtz reasoned that, if the combination of any three wavelengths of different intensities is indistinguishable from any single pure wavelength, the visual system must base its perception of color on the relative responses of three receptor systems.

The study of defective color vision, commonly referred to as color blindness (Figure 5.17), provides further support for the trichromatic theory. The term *color blind* is misleading because it suggests that a color-blind person cannot see color at all. Complete color blindness is rare; most people who are color blind, the vast majority of whom are men, can see some colors but not others. The nature of color blindness depends on which of the three kinds of cones is inoperative (Deeb, 2006). The three cone systems are green, red, and blue. In the most common form of color blindness, the green cone system malfunctions in some way, rendering green indistinguishable from certain combinations of blue and red. Color-matching experiments performed by people with this form of color blindness show that they need only two other colors to match a pure color and, hence, have dichromatic color perception. *Dichromats* are people with only two kinds of cones. *Trichromats* have three kinds of cone receptors and normal color vision.

In 1878, the German physiologist Ewald Hering observed that some colors cannot exist together, whereas others can. For example, it is easy to imagine a greenish blue or a reddish yellow but nearly impossible to imagine a reddish green or a bluish yellow. Hering also noticed that trichromatic theory could not adequately explain *afterimages,* sensations that remain after a stimulus is removed (see Figure 5.18 to experience an afterimage). Color afterimages are common and involve complementary colors. One example of afterimages occurs after prolonged exposure to a computer terminal screen with green lettering, such as those used in many businesses. Working all day with such a computer can cause white

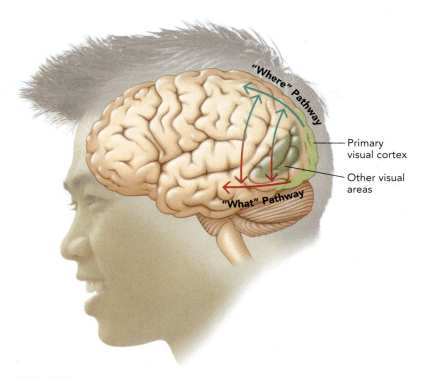

FIGURE 5.16

The What and Where Pathways for Visual Information These parallel neural pathways process information about an object's characteristics ("what") and location ("where"). Note the interconnecting arrows between the pathways. As the "what" and "where" pathways carry information to other areas of the cerebral cortex, they are not completely isolated: Connections between them contribute to the integration of "what" and "where" information.

trichromatic theory Theory stating that color perception is produced by three types of receptors (cone cells in the retina) that are particularly sensitive to different, but overlapping, ranges of wavelengths.

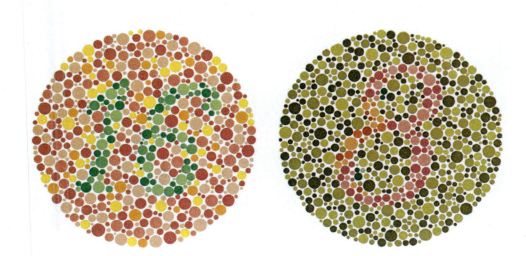

FIGURE 5.17

Examples of Stimuli Used to Test for Color Blindness People with normal vision see the number 16 in the left circle and the number 8 in the right circle. People with red-green color blindness may see just the 16, just the 8, or neither. A complete color blindness assessment involves the use of 15 stimuli.

FIGURE 5.18

Negative Afterimage—Complementary Colors If you gaze steadily at the dot in the colored panel on the left for a few moments, then shift your gaze to the gray box on the right, you will see the original hues' complementary colors. The blue appears as yellow, the red as green, the green as red, and the yellow as blue. This pairing of colors has to do with the fact that color receptors in the eye are apparently sensitive as pairs: When one color is turned off (when you stop staring at the panel), the other color in the receptor is briefly turned on. The afterimage effect is especially noticeable with bright colors.

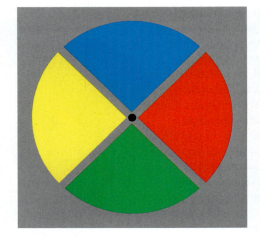

opponent-process theory Theory stating that cells in the visual system respond to red-green and blue-yellow colors; a given cell might be excited by red and inhibited by green, whereas another might be excited by yellow and inhibited by blue.

objects and walls to appear reddish. Conversely, if you look at red long enough, eventually a green afterimage will appear. And if you look at yellow long enough, eventually a blue afterimage will appear. Such afterimages are examples of bottom-up processing.

Hering's observations led him to propose that the visual system treats colors as complementary pairs: red-green and blue-yellow. Hering's view is called **opponent-process theory,** which states that cells in the visual system respond to red-green and blue-yellow colors; a given cell might be excited by red and inhibited by green, whereas another cell might be excited by yellow and inhibited by blue. Researchers have found that opponent-process theory does, indeed, explain afterimages (Hurvich & Jameson, 1969; Jameson & Hurvich, 1989). If you stare at red, for instance, your red-green system seems to "tire," and when you look away, it rebounds and gives you a green afterimage. Also, if you mix equal amounts of opponent colors, such as blue and yellow, you see gray; Figure 5.19 illustrates this principle.

If the trichromatic theory of color perception is correct and we do, in fact, have three kinds of cone receptors like those predicted by Young and Helmholtz, then how can the

FIGURE 5.19

Color Wheel Colors opposite each other produce the neutral gray in the center when they are mixed.

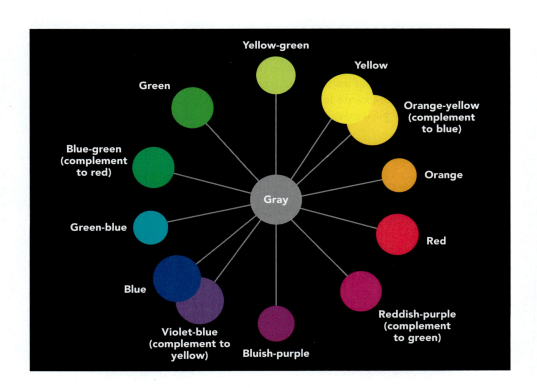

opponent-process theory also be correct? The answer is that the red, blue, and green cones in the retina are connected to retinal ganglion cells in such a way that the three-color code is immediately translated into the opponent-process code (Figure 5.20). For example, a green cone might inhibit and a red cone might excite a particular ganglion cell. Thus, *both* the trichromatic and opponent-process theories are correct—the eye and the brain use both methods to code colors.

This discussion of theories of color vision illustrates an important feature of psychology: Science often progresses when conflicting ideas are posed and investigated. In many instances, as with color vision, seemingly conflicting ideas or systems may actually work, and even work best, together.

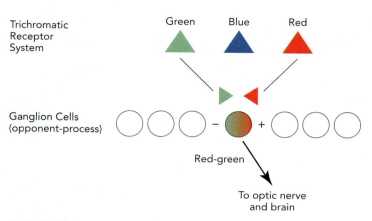

FIGURE 5.20

Trichromatic and Opponent-Process Theories: Transmission of Color Information in the Retina Cones responsive to green, blue, or red light form a trichromatic receptor system in the retina. As information is transmitted to the retina's ganglion cells, opponent-process cells are activated. As shown here, a retinal ganglion cell is inhibited by a green cone (–) and excited by a red cone (+), producing red-green color information.

Perceiving Shape, Depth, Motion, and Constancy

Perceiving visual stimuli means organizing and interpreting the fragments of information that the eye sends to the visual cortex. Information about the dimensions of what we are seeing is critical to this process. Among these dimensions are shape, depth, motion, and constancy.

Think about the visible world and its shapes—buildings against the sky, boats on the horizon, letters on this page. We see these shapes because they are marked off from the rest of what we see by *contour,* a location at which a sudden change of brightness occurs (Breitmeyer & others, 2006; Van Es, Vladusich, & Cornelissen, 2007). Now think about the letters on this page. As you look at the page, you see letters, which are shapes, in a field or background—the white page. The **figure-ground relationship** is the principle by which we organize the perceptual field into stimuli that stand out (*figure*) and those that are left over (*background,* or *ground*). Generally this principle works well for us, but some figure-ground relationships are highly ambiguous, and it may be difficult to tell what is figure and what is ground. A well-known ambiguous figure-ground relationship is shown in Figure 5.21. As you look at the figure, your perception is likely to shift from seeing two faces to seeing a single goblet. The work of artist M. C. Escher, which does not provide spatial location and depth cues, also illustrates figure-ground ambiguity (Figure 5.22).

One school of psychology has been especially intrigued by how we perceive shapes. According to **gestalt psychology,** people naturally organize their perceptions according to certain patterns (*gestalt* is German for "configuration" or "form"). One of gestalt psychology's main principles is that the whole is different from the sum of its parts. For example, when you watch a movie, the "motion" you see in the film cannot be found in the film itself; if you examine the film, you see only separate frames. When you watch the film, the frames move past a light source at a rate of many per second, and you perceive a whole that is very different from the separate frames that are the film's parts. Thus, also, thousands of tiny dots (parts) make up an image (whole) in a newspaper or on a computer screen.

The figure-ground relationship is also a gestalt principle. Three other gestalt principles are closure, proximity, and similarity. The principle of *closure* states that when individuals see a disconnected or incomplete figure, they fill in the spaces and see it as a complete figure (Figure 5.23a). The principle of *proximity* states that when individuals see objects close to each other, they tend to group them together (Figure 5.23b). The principle of *similarity* states that when objects are similar, individuals tend to group them together (Figure 5.23c).

Depth Perception Images appear on our retinas in two-dimensional form, yet remarkably we see a three-dimensional world. **Depth perception** is the ability to perceive objects three-dimensionally. Look around you. You do not see your surroundings as flat. You see some objects farther away, some closer. Some objects overlap each other. The scene and objects that you are looking at have depth. How do you see depth? To see a world of depth, we use two kinds of information, or cues—binocular and monocular.

FIGURE 5.21

Reversible Figure-Ground Pattern Do you see the silhouette of a goblet or a pair of faces in profile?

figure-ground relationship Principle by which individuals organize the perceptual field into stimuli that stand out (*figure*) and those that are left over (*background,* or *ground*).

gestalt psychology School of psychology emphasizing that people naturally organize their perceptions according to certain patterns.

depth perception The ability to perceive objects three-dimensionally.

FIGURE 5.22

Sophisticated Use of the Figure-Ground Relationship in Escher's Woodcut *Relativity* **(1938)** If you are new to your campus, you might think that you are looking at a map of the student union. Note, however, that as your eye follows a specific staircase, your brain tries to make sense of this chaotic image.

Because we have two eyes, we get two views of the world, one from each eye. **Binocular cues** are depth cues that depend on the combination of the images in the left and right eyes and on the way the two eyes work together. The pictures are slightly different because the eyes are in slightly different positions. Try holding your hand about 10 inches from your face. Alternately close and open your left and right eyes, so that only one eye is open at a time. The image of your hand will appear to jump back and forth because the image of your hand is in a slightly different place on the left and right retinas. The *disparity,* or difference, between the images in the two eyes is the binocular cue the brain uses to determine the depth, or distance, of an object. The combination of the two images in the brain, and the disparity between them in the eyes, give us information about the three-dimensionality of the world (Ding & Sperling, 2006).

The perception of depth from disparity can be demonstrated with Figure 5.24, based on a principle for presenting stereoscopic information from a single two-dimensional image

binocular cues Depth cues that are based on the combination of the images on the left and right eyes and on the way the two eyes work together.

(a)

(b)

(c)

FIGURE 5.23

Gestalt Principles of Closure, Proximity, and Similarity (a) *Closure:* When we see disconnected or incomplete figures, we fill in the spaces and see them as complete figures. (b) *Proximity:* When we see objects that are near each other, they tend to be seen as a unit. You are likely to perceive the grouping as 4 columns of 4 squares, not 1 set of 16 squares. (c) *Similarity:* When we see objects that are similar to each other, they tend to be seen as a unit. Here, you are likely to see vertical columns of circles and squares in the left box but horizontal rows of circles and squares in the right box.

FIGURE 5.24

A Stereogram Seen in the right way, this figure contains 3 three-dimensional objects:

- a sphere in the top left
- a pyramid in the top right
- a curved, pointed conical figure in the center at the bottom

There are two ways to see these three-dimensional objects:

- *Technique 1:* Cross your eyes by holding your finger up between your face and the figure. Look at your fingertip and then slowly move your finger back and forth, toward and away from the figure, being careful to keep your focus on your finger. When you reach the correct distance, the three-dimensional objects will pop out at you.
- *Technique 2:* Put your face very close to the figure so that it is difficult to focus or converge your eyes. Wait a moment, and begin to pull your face very slowly back from the figure. The picture should appear blurred for a bit, but when you reach the right distance, it should snap into three-dimensionality.

You may need to try one or both of these techniques a few times. The difficulty is that your eyes will try to converge at the distance of the page, so you must trick them into converging elsewhere, such as in front of the page, as in technique 1, or into staying perfectly parallel and unconverged, as in technique 2.

Some people will be unable to see the three-dimensionality in these figures, for one of these reasons:

- Some individuals' eyes are so well adapted to the real world that they cannot converge in the "wrong place" given the image data appearing on the retinas.
- Certain very common visual deficits that can yield appreciable differences between the quality of the image on the left and right retinas can affect the development of normal binocular vision. The brain requires comparable image quality from the two eyes in the first few years of life in order to develop a high degree of stereoacuity. When this fails to happen, the development of binocular neural mechanisms, which need to compare information in the two eyes, can be affected and can pose problems in processing *pure* stereoscopic information as in this figure. The information here is purely stereoscopic because other, monocular kinds of cues to depth, such as shading and perspective, are not available.

FIGURE 5.25

An Artist's Use of the Monocular Cue of Linear Perspective Famous landscape artist J. M. W. Turner used linear perspective to give the perception of depth in *Rain, Steam, and Speed.*

monocular cues Depth cues that are available from the image in either eye.

(Farell, 2006; Grove & others, 2006). These kinds of displays have become extremely popular and can be found in art books, on greeting cards, and on posters in specialty shops. In the late nineteenth century, stereograms were similarly popular when stereoviewers became easily available.

In addition to using binocular cues to get an idea of the depth of objects, we use a number of **monocular cues,** or depth cues, available from the image in one eye, either right or left. These are powerful cues and under normal circumstances can provide a very compelling impression of depth. Try closing one eye—your perception of the world still retains many of its three-dimensional qualities. Some examples of monocular cues are as follows:

1. *Familiar size:* This cue to the depth and distance of objects is based on what we have learned from experience about the standard sizes of objects. We know how large oranges tend to be, so we can tell something about how far away an orange is likely to be by the size of its image on the retina.

2. *Height in the field of view:* All other things being equal, objects positioned higher in a picture are seen as farther away.

3. *Linear perspective:* Objects that are farther away take up less space on the retina. As an object recedes into the distance, parallel lines in the scene appear to converge (Figure 5.25).

4. *Overlap:* An object that partially conceals or overlaps another object is perceived as closer.

5. *Shading:* This cue involves changes in perception due to the position of the light and the position of the viewer. Consider an egg under a desk lamp. If you walk around the desk, you will see different shading patterns on the egg.

6. *Texture gradient:* Texture becomes denser and finer the farther away it is from the viewer (Figure 5.26).

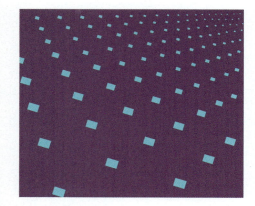

FIGURE 5.26

Texture Gradient The gradients of texture create an impression of depth on a flat surface.

Depth perception is especially intriguing to artists who seek to paint a three-dimensional world on a two-dimensional canvas. Artists often use monocular cues to give the feeling of

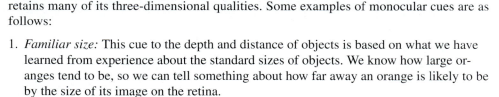

depth to their paintings. Indeed, monocular cues have become so widely used by artists that they also are called *pictorial cues.*

Depth perception is a remarkably complex adaptation. Individuals with only one functioning eye cannot see depth in the way that those with two eyes can. Other disorders of the eye can also lead to a lack of depth perception. Oliver Sacks (2006) described the case of Susan Barry, a woman who had been born with crossed eyes. The operation to correct her eyes left her cosmetically normal, but she was unable to perceive depth throughout her life. As an adult, she became determined to see depth. With the aid of a doctor, she found special glasses and undertook a process of eye muscle exercises to improve her chances of perceiving in three dimensions. It was a difficult and long process, but one day she noticed things starting to "stick out" at her—as you might when watching a film in "3-D." Although Barry had successfully adapted to life in a "flat" visual world, she came to realize that relying on monocular cues was not the same as experiencing the rich visual world of binocular vision. She described flowers as suddenly appearing "inflated." She noted how "ordinary things looked extraordinary" as she saw the leaves of a tree, an empty chair, and her office door projecting out from the background. For the first time, she had a sense of being inside the world she was viewing.

Motion Perception Motion perception plays an important role in the lives of many species (Murakami, 2006; Webb, 2007). Indeed, for some animals, motion perception is critical for survival. Both predators and their prey depend on being able to detect motion quickly. Frogs and some other simple vertebrates may not even see an object unless it is moving. For example, if a dead fly is dangled motionlessly in front of a frog, the frog cannot sense its winged meal. The bug-detecting cells in the frog's retinas are wired only to sense movement.

Whereas the retinas of frogs can detect movement, the retinas of humans and other primates cannot. According to one neuroscientist, "The dumber the animal, the 'smarter' the retina" (Baylor, 2001). In humans the brain takes over the job of analyzing motion through highly specialized pathways (Kamitani & Tong, 2006). Recall from our discussion of the brain pathways in vision that the "where" pathway is involved in motion detection.

How do humans perceive motion? First, we have neurons that are specialized to detect motion. Second, feedback from our body tells us whether we are moving or whether someone or some object is moving. For example, you move your eye muscles as you watch a ball coming toward you. Third, the environment we see is rich in cues that give us information about movement (Badler & Heinen, 2006; Engel, Remus, & Sainath, 2006). For example, when we run, our surroundings appear to be moving.

Psychologists are interested in both real movement and **apparent movement,** which occurs when an object is stationary, but we perceive it as moving. Apparent movement can be experienced at IMAX movie theaters. In watching a film of a climb of Mount Everest, you may find yourself feeling breathless as your visual field is filled with startling images. In theaters without seats, viewers of these films are often warned to hold the handrail because perceived movement is so realistic that they might fall. In theaters with seats, the screens are designed to match the curve of peripheral vision (both vertically and horizontally), and the seats are placed at a steep incline to provide a sense of being truly engulfed in the experience.

Two forms of apparent motion are stroboscopic motion and movement aftereffects. *Stroboscopic motion* is the illusion of movement created when a rapid stimulation of different parts of the retina occurs (Sokolov & Pavlova, 2006). Motion pictures are a form of stroboscopic motion. *Movement aftereffects* happen when we watch continuous movement and then look at another surface, which then appears to move in the opposite direction (Bulakowski, Koldewyn, & Whitney, 2007; Shim & Cavanaugh, 2006). Figure 5.27 provides an opportunity to experience movement aftereffects.

Perceptual Constancy Retinal images are constantly changing. Yet even though the stimuli that fall on our retinas change as we move closer to or farther away from objects or as we look at objects from different orientations and in light or dark settings, our perception of them remains stable. **Perceptual constancy** is the recognition that objects are constant and unchanging even though sensory input about them is changing.

apparent movement The perception that a stationary object is moving.

perceptual constancy Recognition that objects are constant and unchanging even though sensory input about them is changing.

FIGURE 5.27

Movement Aftereffects This is an example of a geometric pattern that produces afterimages in which motion can be perceived. Stare at the center of the pattern for about 10 seconds; then look at a white sheet of paper. You should perceive rotary motion on the paper.

FIGURE 5.28

Size Constancy Even though our retinal images of the hot air balloons vary, we still realize the balloons are approximately the same size. This illustrates the principle of size constancy.

© ScienceCartoonsPlus.com

We experience three types of perceptual constancy: size constancy, shape constancy, and brightness constancy. *Size constancy* is the recognition that an object remains the same size even though the retinal image of the object changes (Figure 5.28). *Shape constancy* is the recognition that an object retains the same shape even though its orientation to us changes. Look around. You probably see objects of various shapes—chairs and tables, for example. If you walk around the room, you will see these objects from different sides and angles. Even though the retinal image of the object changes as you walk, you still perceive the objects as having the same shape (Figure 5.29). *Brightness constancy* is the recognition that an object retains the same degree of brightness even though different amounts of light fall on it. For example, regardless of whether you are reading this book indoors or outdoors, the white pages and the black print do not look any different to you in terms of their whiteness or blackness.

How are we able to resolve the discrepancy between a retinal image of an object and its actual size, shape, and brightness? Experience is important. For example, no matter how far away you are from your car, you know how large it is. Binocular and monocular distance cues also provide information about an object's size. Many visual illusions are influenced by our perception of size constancy.

Illusions

Our perceptual interpretations are usually correct. For example, on the basis of differences in color or texture, we can conclude that a dog is on the rug. On the basis of a continuous increase in size, we conclude that a train is coming toward us. Sometimes, though, the interpretations or inferences are wrong, with the results being an illusion. A **visual illusion** occurs when there is a discrepancy between reality and the perceptual representation of it. Illusions are incorrect, but they are not abnormal. They can provide insight into how our perceptual processes work (Eagleman & Sejnowski, 2007; Jazayeri & Movshon, 2007). More than 200 types of illusions have been discovered. Following are six of them.

One of the most famous visual illusions is the Müller-Lyer illusion, illustrated in Figure 5.30. The two horizontal lines are exactly the same length, although (b) looks longer than (a). Another illusion is the horizontal-vertical illusion, in which a vertical line looks longer than a horizontal line even though the two are equal (Figure 5.31). In the Ponzo illusion, the top line looks much longer than the bottom line (Figure 5.32).

Why do these illusions trick us? One reason is that we mistakenly use certain cues for maintaining size constancy. For example, in the Ponzo illusion we see the upper line as being farther away (remember that objects higher in a picture are perceived as being farther away). The Müller-Lyer illusion, though, is not so easily explained. We might make judgments about the lines by comparing incorrect parts of the figures. For example, when the wings are a different color than the horizontal lines in the Müller-Lyer illusion, the illusion is less pronounced (Coren & Girus, 1972).

FIGURE 5.29

Shape Constancy The various projected images from an opening door are quite different, yet you perceive a rectangular door.

visual illusion A discrepancy between reality and the perceptual representation of it.

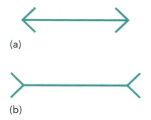

(a)

(b)

FIGURE 5.30

Müller-Lyer Illusion The two lines are exactly the same length, although (*b*) looks longer than (*a*). This illusion was created by Franz Müller-Lyer in the late nineteenth century.

FIGURE 5.31

Horizontal-Vertical Illusion The vertical line looks longer than the horizontal line, but they are the same length.

FIGURE 5.32

Ponzo Illusion The top line looks much longer than the bottom line, but they are the same length.

Another well-known illusion is the moon illusion (Figure 5.33). The moon is 2,000 miles in diameter and 289,000 miles away. Because both the moon's size and its distance from us are beyond our own experience, we have difficulty judging just how far away it really is. When the moon is high in the sky, directly above us, little information is present to help us judge its distance—no texture gradients or stereoscopic cues exist, for example. But when the moon is on the horizon, we can judge its distance in relation to familiar objects—trees and buildings, for example—which make it appear farther away. The result is that we estimate the size of the moon as much larger when it is on the horizon than when it is overhead (Kaufman & others, 2007).

The devil's tuning fork is another fascinating illusion. Look at Figure 5.34 for about 30 seconds; then close the book. Now try to draw the tuning fork. You undoubtedly found this a difficult, if not impossible, task. Why? Look carefully at the figure again. You will see that the figure's depth cues are ambiguous.

In our final example of an illusion, a "doctored" face seen upside down goes unnoticed. Look at Figure 5.35—you probably recognize this famous face as President George W. Bush. In what seems to be an ordinary portrait, however, the mouth and eyes have been cut

FIGURE 5.33

Moon Illusion When the moon is on the horizon, it looks much larger than when it is high in the sky, directly above us.

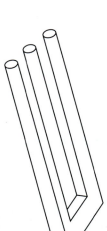

FIGURE 5.34

Devil's Tuning Fork An example of a two-dimensional representation of an impossible three-dimensional figure.

FIGURE 5.35

Why Does This Famous Face Look So Different When You Turn the Book Upside Down?

out from the original and pasted back on upside down. If you turn this book upside down, the horrific look is easily seen. The "Bush" illusion may take place because the mouth is so far out of alignment that we simply cannot respond to its expression; it is still a fearsome face, but we do not see that, and we may have a difficult time telling what really is the top of the mouth in the picture.

REVIEW, ASSESS, AND SHARPEN YOUR THINKING

Review

2 **Explain how the visual system enables us to see and, by communicating with the brain, to perceive the world.**
- Explain the nature of light and how it is detected and transduced into neural impulses in the human eye.
- Describe how neural impulses are processed in the brain and reassembled into a single image.
- Discuss the trichromatic and opponent-process theories of color vision.
- State how shape, depth, motion, and perceptual constancy enable us to transform flat images into three-dimensional objects and scenes.
- Give an explanation for visual illusions and cite examples.

Assess

1. A very bright light has a
   A. high wavelength.
   B. low wavelength.
   C. high amplitude.
   D. low amplitude.

2. _____ are used to detect stimuli in low light; _____ are used for color vision.
   A. Retinas, optic nerves
   B. Optic nerves, retinas
   C. Cones, rods.
   D. Rods, cones.

3. Which structure of the eye causes the pupil to change its size?
   A. sclera   B. iris
   C. cornea   D. lens

4. When you close one eye, you can still detect depth because of
   A. binocular cues.
   B. closure.
   C. monocular cues.
   D. proximity.

5. After staring at something that is red, when you look away you see an afterimage of green. Which theory accounts for this phenomenon?

   A. opponent-process theory

   B. trichromatic theory

   C. Gestalt theory

   D. dichromatic theory

Sharpen Your Thinking

Try to think of at least one perceptual illusion involving a sense other than vision.

3 The Auditory System

Understand how the auditory system registers sound and how it connects with the brain to perceive it.

In 1997, *The Washington Post* carried the story of Louis Weiss, then a 17-year-old senior honors student in high school. Weiss spoke English, French, and Spanish; scored 700 on the math SAT; and wanted to be an aeronautical engineer (Arana-Ward, 1997). But back when Louis was 10 months old, he had contracted meningitis, which left him profoundly deaf. When he was 3, Louis had undergone an operation to insert a cochlear implant in his ear. After the procedure, Louis experienced a sensory rush of noise, but over time he was able to sort through that rush and understand it as the sounds of cars, music, nature, and people.

Louis's success story following the implant highlights the importance of hearing in our world. His parents had dedicated themselves to their son's learning to speak and fully function in the hearing world. However, this case also sparked controversy, as we will review later.

Just as light provides us with information about the environment, so does sound. What would Louis Weiss's life be like without music, the crashing sound of ocean waves, or the voices of his parents and friends? Sounds tell us about the presence of a person behind us, the approach of an oncoming car, the force of the wind outside, or the mischief of a 2-year-old. Perhaps most important, sounds allow us to communicate through language and song.

The Nature of Sound and How We Experience It

At a fireworks display, you may feel the loud "boom" of the explosion in your chest. At a concert, you might have sensed that the air around you was vibrating. Bass instruments are especially effective at creating mechanical pulsations, even causing the floor to vibrate. When the bass is played loudly, we can sense air molecules being pushed forward in waves from the speaker. How does sound generate these sensations?

Sounds, or sound waves, are vibrations in the air that are processed by the auditory (or hearing) system. Remember that light waves are much like the waves in the ocean moving toward the beach. Sound waves are similar. Sound waves also vary in wavelength. Wavelength determines the *frequency* of the sound wave, or the number of cycles (full wavelengths) that pass through a point in a given time. *Pitch* is the perceptual interpretation of the frequency of a sound. High-frequency sounds are perceived as having a high pitch; low-frequency sounds, as having a low pitch. A soprano voice sounds high-pitched.

FIGURE 5.36

Physical Differences in Sound Waves and the Qualities of Sound They Produce Here we can see how the input of sound stimuli requires our ears and brain to attend to varying characteristics of the rich sensory information that is sound.

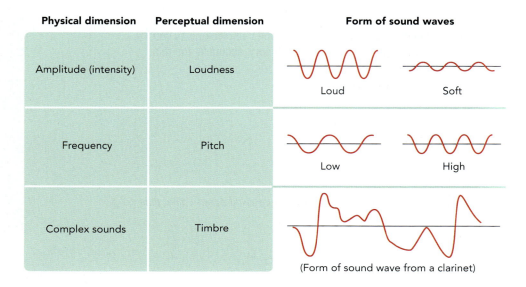

Physical dimension	Perceptual dimension	Form of sound waves
Amplitude (intensity)	Loudness	Loud Soft
Frequency	Pitch	Low High
Complex sounds	Timbre	(Form of sound wave from a clarinet)

A bass voice has a low pitch. As with the wavelengths of light, human sensitivity is limited to a range of sound frequencies. It is common knowledge that dogs, for example, can hear higher frequencies than can humans. Sound waves vary not only in frequency but also, like light waves, in amplitude (see Figure 5.8). *Amplitude* of a sound wave, measured in decibels (dB), is the amount of pressure produced by a sound wave relative to a standard. The typical standard—0 decibels—is the weakest sound the human ear can detect. *Loudness* is the perception of the sound wave's amplitude. In general, the higher the amplitude of the sound wave, or the higher the decibel level, the louder the sound is perceived to be. In the world of amplitude, this means that the air is pressing more forcibly against you and your ears during loud sounds and more gently during quiet sounds.

So far we have been describing a single sound wave with just one frequency. A single sound wave is similar to the single wavelength of pure colored light, discussed in the context of color matching. Most sounds, including those of speech and music, are *complex sounds,* those in which numerous frequencies of sound blend together. *Timbre* is the tone saturation, or the perceptual quality, of a sound. Timbre is responsible for the perceptual difference between a trumpet and a trombone playing the same note and for the quality differences we hear in human voices. Figure 5.36 illustrates the physical differences in sound waves that produce the different qualities of sounds.

Structures and Functions of the Ear

What happens to sound waves once they reach your ear? How do various structures of the ear transform sound waves into signals that the brain will recognize as sound? Functionally the ear is analogous to the eye. The ear serves the purpose of transmitting a high-fidelity version of sounds in the world to the brain for analysis and interpretation. Just as an image needs to be in focus and sufficiently bright for the brain to interpret it, a sound needs to be transmitted in a way that preserves information about its location, its frequency (which helps us distinguish the voice of a child from that of an adult), and its timbre (which allows us to identify the voice of a friend on the telephone).

The ear is divided into three parts: *outer ear, middle ear,* and *inner ear* (Figure 5.37).

Outer Ear The **outer ear** consists of the pinna and the external auditory canal. The funnel-shaped *pinna* (plural, *pinnae*) is the outer, visible part of the ear. (Elephants have very large pinnae.) The pinna collects sounds and channels them into the interior of the ear. The pinnae of many animals, such as cats, are movable and serve a more important role in sound localization than do the pinnae of humans. Cats turn their ears in the direction of a faint and interesting sound.

outer ear Consists of pinna and external auditory canal.

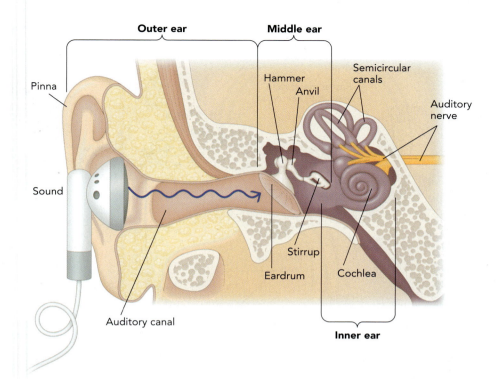

FIGURE 5.37
The Outer, Middle, and Inner Ear On entering the outer ear, sound waves travel through the auditory canal, where they generate vibrations in the eardrum. These vibrations are transferred via the hammer, anvil, and stirrup to the fluid-filled cochlea in the inner ear. There the mechanical vibrations are converted to an electrochemical signal that the brain will recognize as sound.

Middle Ear After passing the pinna, sound waves move through the auditory canal to the middle ear. The **middle ear** channels the sound through the eardrum, hammer, anvil, and stirrup to the inner ear. The *eardrum* is a membrane that vibrates in response to sound. It is the first structure that sound touches in the middle ear. The *hammer, anvil,* and *stirrup* are a connected chain of the three smallest bones in the human body. When they vibrate, they transmit sound waves to the fluid-filled inner ear (Stenfelt, 2006).

If you are a swimmer, you know that sound travels far more easily in air than in water. Sound waves entering the ear travel in air until they reach the inner ear. At this border between air and fluid, sound meets the same kind of resistance encountered by shouts directed at an underwater swimmer when they hit the surface of the water. To compensate, the hammer, anvil, and stirrup also amplify the sound waves.

Inner Ear The function of the **inner ear,** which includes the oval window, cochlea, and basilar membrane, is to transduce sound waves into neural impulses and send them on to the brain (Zou & others, 2006). The stirrup is connected to the membranous *oval window,* which transmits sound waves to the cochlea. The *cochlea* is a tubular, fluid-filled structure that is coiled up like a snail (Figure 5.38). The *basilar membrane* lines the inner wall of the cochlea and runs its entire length. It is narrow and rigid at the base of the cochlea but widens and becomes more flexible at the top. The variation in width and flexibility allows different areas of the basilar membrane to vibrate more intensely when exposed to different sound frequencies (Dubno, Horwitz, & Ahlstrom, 2007). For example, the high-pitched tinkle of a bell stimulates the narrow region of the basilar membrane at the base of the cochlea, whereas the low-pitched tones of a tugboat whistle stimulate the wide end.

In humans and other mammals, hair cells line the basilar membrane (see Figure 5.38). These *hair cells* are the sensory receptors of the ear (Vollrath, Kwan, & Corey, 2007). They are called hair cells because of the tufts of fine bristles, or cilia, that sprout from the top of them. The movement of the hair cells against the *tectorial membrane,* a jellylike flap above them, generates resulting impulses that are interpreted as sound by the brain (Gueta & others, 2006). Hair cells are delicate and can be destroyed by exposure to loud noise. Autopsies of factory workers who have worked around loud machinery have shown that

middle ear Consists of the eardrum, hammer, anvil, and stirrup.

inner ear Consists of the oval window, cochlea, and basilar membrane.

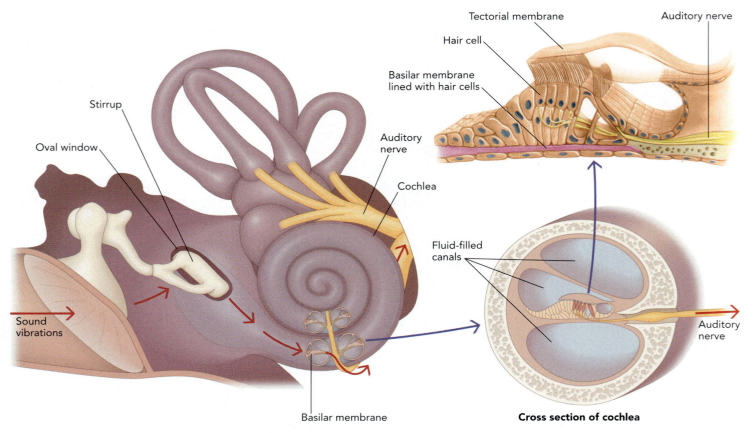

FIGURE 5.38

The Cochlea The cochlea is a spiral structure consisting of fluid-filled canals. When the stirrup vibrates against the oval window, the fluid in the canals vibrates. Vibrations along portions of the basilar membrane correspond to different sound frequencies. The vibrations exert pressure on the hair cells (between the basilar and tectorial membranes); the hair cells in turn push against the tectorial membrane, and this pressure bends the hairs. This triggers an action potential in the auditory nerve.

they all have the same area of hair cells missing. Another result of damage to hair cells is *tinnitus*. Tinnitus is ringing in the ears that occurs even though no sound is present. Tinnitus sufferers may also "hear" rushing or roaring. Some individuals who have tinnitus are not bothered by it, but others find it quite problematic.

Theories of Hearing

One of the auditory system's mysteries is how the inner ear registers the frequency of sound. Two theories have been proposed to explain this mystery: place theory and frequency theory.

Place theory states that each frequency produces vibrations at a particular spot on the basilar membrane. Georg von Békésy (1960) studied the effects of vibration applied at the oval window on the basilar membrane of human cadavers. Through a microscope, he saw that this stimulation produced a traveling wave on the basilar membrane. A traveling wave is like the ripples that appear in a pond when you throw in a stone. However, because the cochlea is a long tube, the ripples can travel in only one direction, from the oval window at one end of the cochlea to the far tip of the cochlea. High-frequency vibrations create traveling waves that maximally displace, or move, the area of the basilar membrane next to the oval window; low-frequency vibrations maximally displace areas of the membrane closer to the tip of the cochlea. Békésy won a Nobel Prize in 1961 for his research on the basilar membrane.

place theory The theory of hearing that states that each frequency produces vibrations at a particular spot on the basilar membrane.

PSYCHOLOGY AND LIFE

Is Your iPod Hurting Your Hearing?

Many of us enjoy listening to our favorite tunes on a portable media player, whether it is an iPod or another model (say, the Meizu miniPlayer or the iRiver T10). As these devices have become smaller and smaller, they have grown increasingly popular—we use them whenever we desire and wherever we are. These players differ from the Walkman of the 1980s in that they use earbuds that transmit sound directly into the ear canal, rather than the headphones that were common previously. What are the implications of this change in the technology for our hearing?

A recent study examined the safety of iPods for the hearing of listeners. Cory Portnuff and Brian Fligor (2006) found that a typical person could safely listen to an iPod for nearly 5 hours at 70 percent volume. The researchers concluded that those who like their tunes louder should not listen as long; if you listen at 90 percent volume, for example, keep yourself plugged in for no more than 90 minutes. One important issue is the environment in which the person is listening. Participants in the study were more likely to pump up the volume if they were listening to their iPods in environments that were already noisy. This new research also found that earbuds were no more dangerous to hearing than headphones (Portnuff & Fligor, 2006). Interestingly, effects on hearing did not depend on the participants' choice of music. So, whether it is the Black Eyed Peas, Barry Manilow, or Mozart, sensible listening is wise.

Place theory adequately explains high-frequency sounds but not low-frequency sounds. A high-frequency sound stimulates a very precise area on the basilar membrane. By contrast, a low-frequency sound causes such a large part of the basilar membrane to be displaced that it is hard to localize the maximal displacement. Because humans can hear low-frequency sounds better than can be predicted by looking at the basilar membrane's response to these sounds, some other factors must be involved. **Frequency theory** addresses this problem by stating that the perception of a sound's frequency depends on how often the auditory nerve fires. Higher-frequency sounds cause the auditory nerve to fire more often than do lower-frequency sounds. One limitation of frequency theory is that a single neuron has a maximum firing rate of about 1,000 times per second. Therefore, frequency theory cannot be applied to tones with frequencies that would require a neuron to fire more rapidly.

To deal with this limitation, a modification of frequency theory called the **volley principle** states that a cluster of nerve cells can fire neural impulses in rapid succession, producing a volley of impulses. Individual neurons cannot fire faster than 1,000 times per second. But if the neurons team up and alternate their neural firing, they can attain a combined frequency above that rate. Thus, frequency theory better explains the perception of sounds below 1,000 times per second, whereas a combination of frequency and place theory is needed for those above 1,000 times per second. The Psychology and Life feature explores possible ways that we are harming our hearing through our toys.

Auditory Processing in the Brain

As you saw in the discussion of the visual system, once energy from the environment is picked up by our receptors, it must be transmitted to the brain for processing and interpretation. An image on the retina does not a Picasso make—likewise, a pattern of receptor responses in the cochlea does not a symphony make. We saw that, in the retina, the responses of the rod and cone receptors feed into ganglion cells in the retina and leave the eye via the optic nerve. In the auditory system, information about sound moves from

frequency theory Theory stating that perception of a sound's frequency depends on how often the auditory nerve fires.

volley principle Modification of frequency theory stating that a cluster of nerve cells can fire neural impulses in rapid succession, producing a volley of impulses.

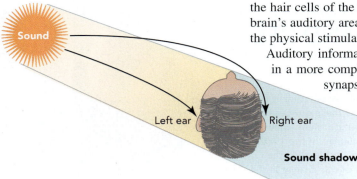

FIGURE 5.39

The Sound Shadow The sound shadow is caused by the listener's head, which forms a barrier that reduces the sound's intensity. Here the sound is to the person's left, so the sound shadow will reduce the intensity of the sound that reaches the right ear.

auditory nerve Nerve that carries neural impulses to the brain's auditory areas.

The amazing echolocation ability of bats allows them to navigate through their environment with speed and precision and makes them very successful hunters.

the hair cells of the inner ear to the **auditory nerve,** which carries neural impulses to the brain's auditory areas. Remember that it is the movement of the hair cells that transforms the physical stimulation of sound waves into the action potential of neural impulses.

Auditory information moves up the auditory pathway via electrochemical transmission in a more complex manner than does visual information in the visual pathway. Many synapses occur in the ascending auditory pathway, with most fibers crossing over the midline between the hemispheres of the cerebral cortex, although some proceed directly to the hemisphere on the same side as the ear of reception (Fuchs, 2006; Moser, Brandt, & Lysakowski, 2006). This means that most of the auditory information from the left ear goes to the right side of the brain, but some also goes to the left side of the brain. The auditory nerve extends from the cochlea to the brain stem, with some fibers crossing over the midline. The cortical destination of most of these fibers is the temporal lobes of the brain (beneath the temples of the head). As in the case of visual information, researchers have found that features are extracted from auditory information and transmitted along parallel "what" and "where" pathways in the brain (Ahveninen & others, 2006; Recanzone & Sutter, 2008).

Localizing Sound

When we hear the siren of a fire engine or the bark of a dog, how do we know where the sound is coming from? The basilar membrane gives us information about the frequency, pitch, and complexity of a sound, but it does not tell us where a sound is located.

Earlier in the chapter we saw that because our two eyes see slightly different images, we can determine how near or far away an object is. Similarly, having two ears helps us to localize a sound because each receives somewhat different stimuli from the sound source. A sound coming from the left has to travel different distances to the two ears, so if a barking dog is to your left, your left ear receives the sound sooner than your right ear. Also, your left ear will receive a slightly more intense sound than your right ear in this case. The sound reaching one ear is more intense than the sound reaching the other ear for two reasons: (1) It has traveled less distance and (2) the other ear is in what is called the *sound shadow* of the listener's head, which provides a barrier that reduces the sound's intensity (Figure 5.39). The sound shadow is one means that blind individuals use for orientation.

Thus, differences in both the *timing* of the sound and the *intensity* of the sound help us to localize a sound (Wright & Zhang, 2006). Humans often have difficulty localizing a sound that is coming from a source that is directly in front of them because it reaches both ears simultaneously. The same is true for sounds directly above your head or directly behind you.

Compared with some animals, humans are not very accurate at locating sounds (Houser & Finneran, 2006; Lomber, Malhotra, & Hall, 2007). For example, bats are able to hunt insects at night because of their exquisitely developed sensitivity to their own echoes. They emit sounds and then listen to the echoes coming back. Using this system—called *echolocation*—bats can fly through their environment at high speeds, avoid predators, and find prey (Russo, Jones, & Arlettaz, 2007). Why has evolution provided bats with such superb hearing? The answer is simple. Vision requires light, and bats are nocturnal animals. Any method of building internal representations of the environment that requires light would not be an effective perceptual system for the bat. Humans do not need the bat's echolocation ability because we do not hunt bugs at night. Rather, we use our eyes to pursue food by day. Nonetheless, humans are fairly accurate at localizing sounds.

Our study of the auditory system began with the story of Louis Weiss, who received a cochlear implant when he was 3 years old, allowing him to hear. We conclude our discussion of the sense of hearing in the Critical Controversy, which explores the debate over cochlear implants.

Critical Controversy   Are Cochlear Implants a "Cure" for Deafness?

Hearing, like seeing, is a fantastic gift that many of us take for granted. Listen for a moment to the sounds around you in the place where you are reading this book. Perhaps you hear music playing, the hum of a ventilation system, the songs of birds, or rain tapping against the window. If the phone rings, you pick it up and hear the voice of a friend. For those of us who can hear, the thought of losing the experience of hearing is a terrible one.

Cochlear implants—small electronic devices that are surgically implanted into a person's ear and head—allow deaf or profoundly hard-of-hearing individuals to detect sound. Unlike a hearing aid, an implant does not amplify sound. Instead, it works by directly stimulating whatever working auditory nerves the recipient has in his or her cochlea with electronic impulses. A cochlear implant involves a receiver and stimulator, which are internally secured to the bone behind the ear, as well as a microphone, speech processor, and transmitter, which are worn on the outside of the person's ear. The speech processor filters out background noise and is tuned to prioritize spoken language.

The U.S. Food and Drug Administration (FDA) approved the use of cochlear implants for adults in 1985 and for children in 1990. In the United States, 22,000 adults and nearly 15,000 children have had cochlear implants (FDA, 2005). Roughly 100,000 individuals—about half of them children—have received such implants worldwide (University of Michigan, 2006).

Cochlear implants have been a focus of particular concern for two groups—adults who have experienced hearing loss and parents of children who are born deaf or who have gone deaf in childhood (Gordon, Valero, & Papsin, 2007; Hyde & Power, 2006). For deaf adults who previously were able to hear and speak, implants work best if they are inserted shortly after the hearing loss. The reason? The brain, as we have seen, is a remarkably flexible organ. If a person is deaf for a long time, the brain adapts to this change and uses the auditory cortex for other tasks. Indeed, for older adults who receive a cochlear implant, the length of time spent profoundly deaf and the percentage of one's life lived as deaf are much stronger predictors of hearing success than age at implantation (Leung & others, 2005). Conservative radio personality Rush Limbaugh received a cochlear implant in late 2001 after experiencing sudden deafness. He has said that his hearing is close to normal, although he cannot pick out the melody of songs he had not heard before going deaf.

For the parents of a child with a hearing impairment, cochlear implants may be a way of improving the chances that the child will develop speech and communication skills. Anna Geers (2002) reported normal speech and language abilities in 80 percent of children who were deafened after birth (not born deaf) and received the implant within a year of deafening. The success of the implant is time sensitive. There are appreciable differences between the abilities of children implanted at the age of 2 versus those who wait until the age of 4 (Niparko, 2004). Although it might be preferable to ask the child for his or her opinion, many parents are motivated to have their child receive the implant as early as possible. And this is where the controversy comes in. The brain is quite sensitive and responsive to sensory processes, and in a manner of speaking, a young child's brain remains somewhat "up for grabs." It can be used to process sound or other stimuli, but once it dedicates itself, change is difficult.

Some critics say that parents who opt for a cochlear implant for their deaf daughter or son deprive the child of participation in the unique language and culture that is the child's right.

The deaf community was initially skeptical of the prospect of implants, especially for children. Throughout the 1990s a debate raged over the pros, cons, and ethics of implants. On one side stood parents of deaf children, late-deafened adults, and medical professionals. On the other side were members of the deaf community. This debate reinvigorated a decades-old disagreement over how deaf children should be trained to communicate and how they should be viewed in the world. Should they use sign language or speech? Should society see them as a part of the deaf world or the hearing world? The debate over cochlear implants seemed to cast the divide between these two worlds in very rigid terms, perhaps ignoring the larger truth that these worlds overlap to a great degree.

Your first reaction might be, "What parent wouldn't want a deaf son or daughter to be able to hear?" In response, a deaf adult might point out that life as a deaf person can be rich, rewarding, and successful. Deaf culture has its own language, opportunities, and unique and valuable perspectives. Perhaps, the deaf adult might argue, hearing parents simply do not want to take on the daunting tasks of learning a new language and navigating this new world. Moreover, the use of cochlear implants in children implies that deafness is somehow a problem that must be fixed, and in this way the procedure further undermines the many positive aspects of deaf culture.

In all cases, we must take care not to equate the abilities to speak and to hear with intelligence or with a person's capacity for well-being or success. The Academy Award–nominated documentary *Sound and Fury,* directed by Josh Aronson, depicts the struggle of a family (with some deaf and some hearing members) dealing with the array of issues surrounding this complex dilemma. These include questions such as, Does the use of a cochlear implant deny a child an identity as a deaf person? Does rejecting such an implant deny the child the benefit of hearing? A deaf mother in the film explains that being deaf is more than not being able to hear; it means "membership in a close-knit supportive community based on a rich history and beautiful language" (quoted from pbs.org, 2007).

Some in the deaf community share this perspective and argue that parents who opt for cochlear implants for their children

(continued)

(and who strive mightily to ensure that the children communicate through speech rather than sign language) are depriving their children of the unique language and culture that are their right as deaf people. Psychologist David Myers (2000), who has chronicled his own hearing loss in his book *A Quiet World,* has noted the uniqueness of hearing impairment. Myers suggests that there is little doubt that a blind person would opt to see, if sight were possible; but among the deaf, there is a stronger sense that if deafness were "cured," a valuable part of their world would be lost.

In 2001 the National Association of the Deaf (or NAD, an education and advocacy group for the civil rights of deaf and hard-of-hearing people in the United States) issued a statement on cochlear implants that somewhat quieted the debate. The group emphasized that whether or not a child receives an implant, he or she will always live, simultaneously, in two worlds—the deaf world and the hearing world. The NAD also stressed the importance of parents' and professionals' having a realistic view of the promises and limitations of cochlear implants.

A cochlear implant does not provide "normal" hearing. We have seen that the human ear is a complex apparatus. The cochlear implant substitutes just 22 electrodes wound around the cochlea for the 16,000 delicate hairs that exist in the intact cochlea. Hence the auditory experience of a person who has a cochlear implant is limited compared with that of a hearing individual. But cochlear implants can allow a person to comprehend spoken language, to communicate on the phone, and to hear his or her own voice—in this way facilitating speech and conversation. A cochlear implant does not "cure" deafness. When the external apparatus is removed, the person can no longer detect sound.

The reality of cochlear implants is not like what might be depicted in a Hollywood movie. The recipient does not wake up from the operation and announce "I can hear!" Rather, after a healing process of about a month, the hard work begins. Because hearing is as much

about the brain as it is about the ear, the recipient's brain must begin to process a new type of information and make it sensible. For deaf children, cochlear implantation is thus the beginning of a long process of speech therapy and lip reading (Connor & Zwolan, 2004). Further, all children require a rich social environment in which to master the art of communication (as we will see in Chapter 9), and deaf children are no exception. Visual stimulation may always be especially important to these children.

Conflict is likely to continue over cochlear implants and the appropriate communication training for deaf children. Although sign language is a vital part of deaf culture, reliance on visual language might interfere with speech training. Parents of children who receive cochlear implants may be encouraged to rely on speech (not signing) as a primary form of communication. Yet speech training is a difficult and laborious process that might ultimately detract from the child's capacity to more rapidly and easily communicate using signing. Importantly, the NAD has recognized that the deaf community itself is diverse—and emphasizes that all individuals are unique. There is no one right answer to these dilemmas. As the motto of Hands and Voices, another deaf and hard-of-hearing advocacy group, stresses, "What works for your child is what makes the choice right."

What Do You Think?

- Does the use of cochlear implants imply that deaf people are "broken"?
- What values of deaf culture might be lost if deafness were "cured"?
- Why might Rush Limbaugh have trouble picking out a new song? What is the role of top-down and bottom-up processing in the hearing of someone like Limbaugh, who received an implant shortly after experiencing deafness?

REVIEW, ASSESS, AND SHARPEN YOUR THINKING

Review

③ Understand how the auditory system registers sound and how it connects with the brain to perceive it.
- Describe the nature of sound and how it is experienced.
- Identify the structures of the ear and their functions.
- Discuss three theories of hearing.
- Explain how auditory signals are transmitted to the brain for processing.
- Describe sound localization.

Assess

1. Which of the following is found in the middle ear?
   A. hammer   B. cochlea
   C. pinna   D. basilar membrane

2. The pitches played by a bass guitar have a
   A. high amplitude.   B. low amplitude.
   C. high frequency.   D. low frequency.

3. What is the first structure with which a sound comes into contact?
   A. eardrum
   B. pinna
   C. tectorial membrane
   D. hammer

4. Which theory of hearing focuses on the number of times an auditory nerve fires?
   A. place theory
   B. volley principle theory
   C. intensity theory
   D. frequency theory

5. What is a sound shadow?
   A. an echo that happens after a sound has been emitted
   B. a sound that is at the threshold of perception
   C. an area where the sound is less intense because of the barrier created by the head
   D. the timing of a sound

Sharpen Your Thinking

Suppose you were in an accident and, in order to survive, had to sacrifice either your vision or your hearing. Which sense would you preserve? Why?

4 Other Senses

Explain how the skin, chemical, kinesthetic, and vestibular senses work.

Having studied the visual and auditory systems, we turn now to our other sensory systems. You are familiar with the skin senses and the chemical senses (smell and taste). The lesser-known kinesthetic and vestibular senses enable us to stay upright and to coordinate our movements. Some individuals also claim to have another sense that enables them to read other people's minds, for example, or foresee the future. Such claims have not held up under scientific scrutiny.

The Skin Senses

You know when a friend has a fever by putting your hand to her head; you know how to find your way to the light switch in a darkened room by groping along the wall; and you know whether or not a pair of shoes is too tight by the way the shoes touch different parts of your feet when you walk. Many of us think of our skin as a canvas rather than a sense. We color it with cosmetics, dyes, and tattoos. But the skin is our largest sensory system, draped over the body with receptors for touch, temperature, and pain. These three kinds of receptors form the *cutaneous senses*. Standing in front of a vending machine, you reach into your pocket. You need a nickel. Without looking, you are somehow able to pull out the right piece of change to get your snack. That might seem like a small accomplishment, but it is something you can do that no robot can. Engineers who design robots to be used, for instance, in surgical procedures have been unable to match the amazing sensitivity of the human hand.

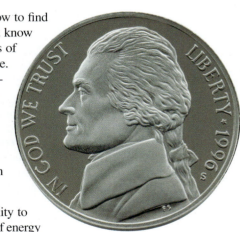

Touch   Touch is one of the senses that we most often take for granted, yet our ability to respond to touch is astounding. What do we detect when we feel "touch"? What kind of energy does our sense of touch pick up from our external environment?

Processing Information About Touch   In vision we detect light energy. In hearing we detect the vibrations of air or sound waves pressing against our eardrums. In touch we detect mechanical energy, or pressure against the skin. The lifting of a single hair causes pressure on the skin around the shaft of hair. This tiny bit of mechanical pressure at the base of the hair is sufficient for us to detect the touch of a pencil point. More commonly we detect the mechanical energy of the pressure of a car seat against our buttocks or the pressure of a pencil in our hands. Is this kind of energy so different from the kind of energy we detect in vision or hearing? Sometimes the only difference is one of intensity—the sound of a rock band playing softly is an auditory stimulus, but at the high volumes that make a concert hall reverberate, this auditory stimulus is also *felt* as mechanical energy pressing against our skin.

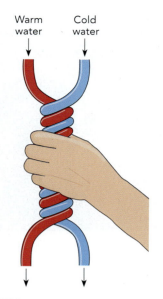

Warm water   Cold water

FIGURE 5.40

A "Hot" Experience When two pipes, one containing cold water and the other warm water, are braided together, a person touching the pipes feels a sensation of "hot." The perceived heat coming from the pipes is so intense that a person cannot touch them for longer than a couple of seconds.

How does information about touch travel from the skin through the nervous system? Sensory fibers arising from receptors in the skin enter the spinal cord. From there the information travels to the brain stem, at which point most fibers from each side of the body cross over to the opposite side of the brain. Then the information about touch moves on to the thalamus, which serves as a relay station. The thalamus then projects the map of the body's surface onto the somatosensory areas of the parietal lobes in the cerebral cortex (Hlushchuk & Hari, 2006).

As in the visual and auditory systems, both feature detection and parallel processing occur when information about touch is processed. Some cells in the somatosensory cortex respond to specific aspects of touch, such as movement across the skin. Also, features of tactile sensation, such as pressure, temperature, and movement, may be reassembled in the somatosensory cortex in the same way as in vision (Bloom, Nelson, & Lazerson, 2001).

Just as the visual system is more sensitive to images on the fovea than to images in the peripheral retina, our sensitivity to touch is not equally good across all areas of the skin. As you might expect, human toolmakers need to have excellent touch discrimination in their hands, but they require much less touch discrimination in other parts of the body, such as the torso or legs. Because of this, the brain devotes more space to analyzing touch signals coming from the hands than from the legs.

Exploring Touch in Life Psychologists Susan Lederman and Roberta Klatsky are working with engineers to determine whether touch input is important for such jobs as operating robots from afar and performing microsurgery (Klatsky & Lederman, 2003, 2006; Lederman & Klatsky, 1998). This research focuses mainly on the hands because the fingertips contain the highest densities of tactile receptors. In one study, the researchers tested individuals' ability to perform several tasks with and without feedback to their index fingers (Lederman & Klatsky, 1998). They measured people's ability to feel vibrations, to sense whether they could feel two distinct objects or just one, and to detect the presence of a thin nylon hair. They also tested perceptual abilities, such as the ability to judge how rough a surface was and to compare the roughness of the two surfaces. To simulate a no-feedback situation, they covered participants' fingertips with a fiberglass sheath. The sheath had a dramatic impact on the participants' perceptual judgments. For example, their ability to sense the thin hair declined 73 percent, and their skill in detecting two objects as opposed to one dropped 32 percent.

Newborns can feel touch better than they can see, hear, or even taste (Eliot, 2001). Newborn girls are more sensitive to touch than their male counterparts, and this gender difference remains throughout life. The sense of touch is crucial to infants, as it helps them detect and explore the physical world and is important for health and emotional well-being. As we saw in Chapter 4, touch is a key aspect of attachment, and massage therapy can help preterm infants become healthier.

Temperature Even in the absence of direct contact with the skin, we need to detect temperature. **Thermoreceptors,** which are located under the skin, respond to changes in temperature at or near the skin and provide input to keep the body's temperature at 98.6 degrees Fahrenheit. There are two types of thermoreceptors: warm and cold. Warm thermoreceptors respond to the warming of the skin, and cold thermoreceptors respond to the cooling of the skin. Somewhat surprisingly, when warm and cold receptors that are close to each other in the skin are stimulated simultaneously, we experience the sensation of hotness. Figure 5.40 illustrates this "hot" experience.

Pain When contact with the skin takes the form of a sharp pinch, our sensation of mechanical pressure changes from touch to pain. When a pot handle is so hot that it burns your hand, your sensation of temperature becomes one of pain. Many kinds of stimuli can cause pain. Intense stimulation of any one of the senses can produce pain—too much light, very loud sounds, or very spicy food, for example. Our ability to sense pain is vital for our survival as a species. **Pain** is the sensation that warns us of damage to our bodies. It functions as a quick-acting system that tells the motor systems of the brain that they must act to minimize or eliminate this damage. A hand touching a hot stove must be pulled away; ears should be covered up when one walks by a loud pavement drill; fiery-hot chili should be buffered with some crackers.

thermoreceptors Sensory receptors, located under the skin, that respond to changes in temperature at or near the skin and provide input to keep the body's temperature at 98.6 degrees Fahrenheit.

pain The sensation that warns us that damage to our bodies is occurring.

Pathways of Pain   Pain receptors are dispersed widely throughout the body—in the skin, in the sheath tissue surrounding muscles, in internal organs, and in the membranes around bone. Although all pain receptors are anatomically similar, they differ in the type of physical stimuli to which they most readily respond. Mechanical pain receptors respond mainly to pressure, such as when a sharp object is encountered. Heat pain receptors respond primarily to strong heat that is capable of burning the tissue in which the receptors are embedded. Other pain receptors have a mixed function, responding to both types of painful stimuli. Many pain receptors are chemically sensitive and respond to a range of pain-producing substances.

Pain receptors have a much higher threshold for firing than receptors for temperature and touch (Bloom, Nelson, & Lazerson, 2001). Pain receptors react mainly to physical stimuli that distort them or to chemical stimuli that "irritate" them into action. Inflamed joints or sore, torn muscles produce *prostaglandins,* which stimulate the receptors and cause the experience of pain. Drugs such as aspirin likely reduce the feeling of pain by reducing the body's production of prostaglandins.

Two different neural pathways transmit pain messages to the brain: a fast pathway and a slow pathway (Bloom, Nelson, & Lazerson, 2001). In the *fast pathway,* fibers connect directly with the thalamus, then to the motor and sensory areas of the cerebral cortex. This pathway transmits information about sharp, localized pain, as when you cut your skin. The fast pathway may serve as a warning system, providing immediate information about an injury—it takes less than a second for the information in this pathway to reach the cerebral cortex. In the *slow pathway,* pain information travels through the limbic system, a detour that delays the arrival of information at the cerebral cortex by seconds. The unpleasant, nagging pain that characterizes the slow pathway may function to remind the brain that an injury has occurred, that normal activity needs to be restricted, and that the pain needs to be monitored.

In the 1960s, Ronald Melzack and Patricia Wall (1965) proposed the **gate-control theory of pain,** which states that the spinal column contains a neural gate that can be opened (allowing the perception of pain) or closed (blocking the perception of pain). The brain can send signals downward to the spinal cord to close the gate and thus suppress the sensation of pain. The gate-control theory was proposed as an explanation for the effects of *acupuncture,* a technique in which thin needles are inserted at specific points in the body to produce various effects, such as local anesthesia (Figure 5.41). The gate-control theory assumes that the presence of acupuncture needles somehow manages to shut the pain gate, inhibiting the experience of pain. The gate-control theory has been revised in response to new findings about the complexity of pain neurophysiology (Melzack & Katz, 2006; Wall & Melzack, 1999). Although some pain originates in signals coming through the spinal cord gate, it is now clear that ultimately the brain generates the experience of pain.

Although the original conception of gate-control theory has been abandoned, there is evidence that turning pain signals on and off is a chemical process that probably involves *endorphins.* Recall from Chapter 3 that endorphins are neurotransmitters that function as natural opiates in producing pleasure and pain (Vetter & others, 2006). Endorphins are believed to be released mainly in the synapses of the slow pathway.

Perception of pain is complex and often varies from one person to the next (Lund & Lundeberg, 2006; Oshiro & others, 2007). Some people rarely feel pain; others seem to be in great pain if they experience a minor bump or bruise. To some degree, these individual variations may be physiological. A person who experiences considerable pain even with a minor injury may have a neurotransmitter system that is deficient in endorphin production.

However, perception of pain goes beyond physiology. Although it is true that all sensations are affected by factors such as motivation, expectation, and other related decision factors, the perception of pain is especially susceptible to these factors (Watson & others, 2006). Cultural and ethnic contexts also can greatly determine the degree to which an individual experiences pain (Hernandez & Sachs-Ericsson, 2006). For example, one pain researcher described a ritual performed in India in which a chosen person travels from town to town delivering blessings to the children and the crops while suspended from metal hooks embedded in his back (Melzak, 1973). The individual apparently reports no sensation of pain and appears to be in ecstasy (Figure 5.42).

gate-control theory of pain Theory stating that the spinal column contains a neural gate that can be opened (allowing the perception of pain) or closed (blocking the perception of pain).

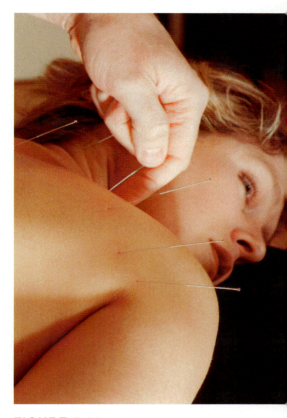

FIGURE 5.41
Acupuncture This woman is being treated for pain by an acupuncturist.

FIGURE 5.42
Indian Hook-Swinging Ritual In this traditional ceremony, steel hooks are inserted in the backs of participants, who then are conveyed through the villages to give their blessings to children and crops as they swing freely, suspended by the hooks.

Nowhere is cultural variation more pronounced than in the perception of pain in childbirth. In some cultures, women do not expect childbirth to be painful. They may have their babies and in a matter of hours go back to their normal activities. However, in the United States and most other Western cultures, women expect childbirth to involve considerable pain. The Lamaze method of childbirth (natural childbirth) seeks to reduce this fear of pain by training women's muscle tone and breathing patterns. Women who use the Lamaze method experience reduced perception of pain in childbirth.

Pain Control and Treatment Most acute pain decreases over time with avoidance of activity or with pain-reducing medication. Treatment of chronic pain is often more complex. Often the most successful treatment of pain involves a combination of physical and psychological techniques (Watkins & Maier, 2000). A pain clinic may select one or more of the following techniques to treat an individual's pain: surgery, drugs, acupuncture, electrical stimulation, massage, exercise, hypnosis, relaxation, and thought distraction (Hahn, Payne, & Lucas, 2007; Insel & Roth, 2008). We discuss hypnosis further in Chapter 6.

Other strategies for reducing acute pain include:

- *Distraction:* When you are about to get an injection, do you focus on the needle as it is about to plunge into your flesh, or do you turn your gaze and concentrate on something else? Distraction is usually the best way to reduce pain, because attention to the sensation can magnify it. You might focus instead on your plans for the coming weekend, for example.
- *Focused breathing:* The next time you stub your toe, try panting—using short, fast breaths (similar to the breathing practiced in Lamaze childbirth). Focused breathing may diminish your agony.
- *Counterstimulation:* If you pinch your cheek in the aftermath of a bad cut, it likely will mute your pain. Applying ice to a sprained or swollen area not only reduces the pain but also can keep the swelling down.

The Chemical Senses

The information processed through our senses comes in many diverse forms: electromagnetic energy in vision, sound waves in hearing, and mechanical pressure and temperature in the skin senses. The two senses discussed below, smell and taste, are responsible for processing chemicals in our environment. With the sense of smell, we detect airborne chemicals, and with taste we detect chemicals that have been dissolved in saliva. Smell and taste are frequently stimulated simultaneously. We sometimes realize the strong links between the two senses only when a nasty cold and nasal congestion seem to take the pleasure out of eating. Our favorite foods become "tasteless" without the smells that characterize them. Despite this link, taste and smell are indeed two distinct systems.

Taste What is your favorite food? Why do you like it? Imagine that food without its flavor. The thought of giving up a favorite taste, such as chocolate or butter, can be depressing. We use our sense of taste to select food and to regulate food intake. Although it is not so easy to see or smell mold on a blueberry, a small taste is enough to prompt you to sense that the fruit is no longer fit for consumption. Beyond that, the pleasure associated with the taste of food depends on many aspects of our body's need for a particular food (Bartoshuk & Beauchamp, 1994). The taste of devil's food cake can be very pleasurable when we are hungry but downright revolting after we eat a banana split.

It is not the prettiest sight you have ever seen, but try this anyway. Take a drink of milk and allow it to coat your tongue. Then go to a mirror, stick out your tongue, and look carefully at its surface. You should be able to see rounded bumps above the surface of your tongue. Those bumps, called **papillae,** contain taste buds, which are the receptors for taste. Your tongue houses about 10,000 taste buds. As with all of the other sensory systems we have considered, the information picked up by these receptors is transmitted to the brain for analysis and, when necessary, for a response (spitting something out, for example).

papillae Bumps on the tongue that contain taste buds, the receptors for taste.

The taste qualities we respond to can be categorized as sweet, sour, bitter, and salty (Scott, 2000). Though all areas of the tongue can detect each of the four tastes, different regions of the tongue are more sensitive to some tastes than others. The tip of the tongue is the most sensitive to sweet and salty substances, the sides to sour, and the rear to bitter (Figure 5.43) (Bloom, Nelson, & Lazerson, 2001).

Today, many neuroscientists believe that the breakdown of taste into four independent, elementary categories is overdrawn (Cauller, 2001). The taste fibers leading from a taste bud to the brain often respond strongly to a range of chemicals spanning multiple taste elements, such as salty and sour (Smith & Margolskee, 2001). The brain processes these somewhat ambiguous incoming signals and integrates them into a perception of taste (Bartoshuk, 2008; Verhagen & Engelen, 2006).

People still often categorize taste sensations along the four dimensions of sweet, bitter, salty, and sour. Our tasting ability, however, goes far beyond these. Think of the remarkable range of tastes you have experienced that are generated by variations and combinations of sweet, sour, bitter, and salty.

Taste is certainly influenced by culture. Any American who has watched the Japanese version of the TV series *Iron Chef* quickly notes that some people enjoy the flavor of sea urchin, while others just do not get the appeal. In some cultures, food that is so spicy as to be practically inedible for the outsider may be viewed as quite delicious.

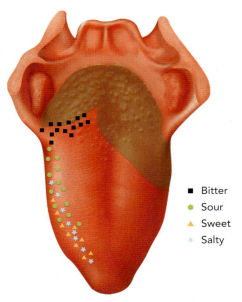

FIGURE 5.43

Location on the Tongue of Sensitivity to Sweet, Salty, Sour, and Bitter Substances Note how different areas of the tongue are sensitive to the differing tastes of bitter, sour, sweet, and salty.

Smell A good way to begin the discussion of smell is to consider the many functions it serves. It is often easier to understand the importance of smell when we think about animals with more sophisticated senses of smell than our own. A dog, for example, can use its sense of smell to find its way back from a long stroll, to distinguish friend from foe, or even (with practice) to detect illegal drugs concealed in a suitcase. In fact, dogs can detect odors in concentrations 100 times lower than those detectable by humans. Given the nasal feats of the average dog, we might be tempted to believe that the sense of smell has outlived its usefulness in humans.

What do we use smell for? For one thing, humans need the sense of smell to decide what to eat. We can distinguish rotten food from fresh food and remember (all too well) which foods have made us ill in the past. The smell of a food that has previously made us sick is often, by itself, enough to make us feel nauseated. Second, although tracking is a function of smell that we often associate only with animals, humans are competent odor trackers. We can follow the odor of gas to a leak, the smell of smoke to a fire, and the aroma of a hot apple pie to a windowsill.

olfactory epithelium A sheet of receptor cells for smell that lines the roof of the nasal cavity.

What physical equipment do we use to process odor information? Just as the eyes scan the visual field for objects of interest and the pinnae prick up to direct attention to sounds of interest, the nose is an active instrument. We actively sniff when we are trying to track down the source of a fire or of an unfamiliar chemical odor. The **olfactory epithelium,** lining the roof of the nasal cavity, contains a sheet of receptor cells for smell (Figure 5.44), so sniffing maximizes the chances of detecting an odor. The receptor cells are covered with millions of minute, hairlike antennae that project through the mucus in the top of the nasal cavity and make contact with air on its way to the throat and lungs (Bartoshuk, 2008; Rawson & Yee, 2006). Interestingly, unlike the neurons of most sensory systems, the neurons in the olfactory epithelium tend to replace themselves after injury (Doty, 2001).

What is the neural pathway for information about smell? Although all other sensory

Many animals have a stronger sense of smell than humans do. Dogs especially have a powerful olfactory sense. Watson, a Labrador retriever, reliably paws his owner 45 minutes before her epileptic seizures begin, giving her time to move to a safe place. How does Watson do this? The best hypothesis is that the dog smells the chemical changes known to precede epileptic seizures.

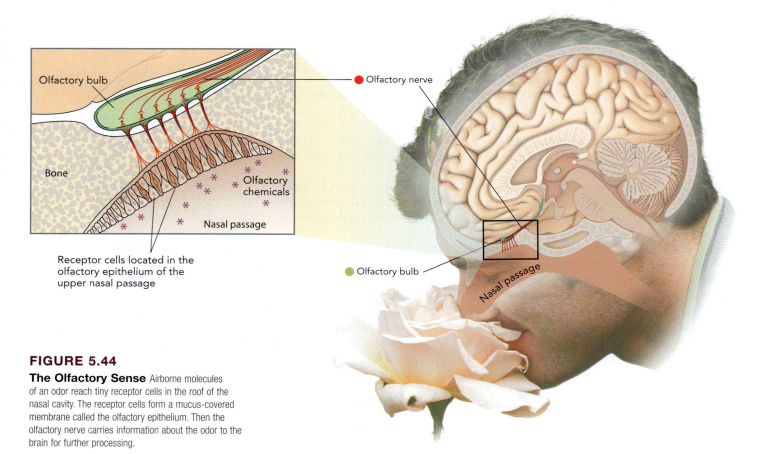

Olfactory bulb

Bone

Olfactory chemicals

Nasal passage

Receptor cells located in the olfactory epithelium of the upper nasal passage

● Olfactory nerve

● Olfactory bulb

Nasal passage

FIGURE 5.44

The Olfactory Sense Airborne molecules of an odor reach tiny receptor cells in the roof of the nasal cavity. The receptor cells form a mucus-covered membrane called the olfactory epithelium. Then the olfactory nerve carries information about the odor to the brain for further processing.

pathways pass through the thalamus, the pathway for smell does not. In smell the neural pathway first goes to the olfactory areas in the temporal lobes and then projects to various brain regions, especially the limbic system, which is involved in emotion and memory (Breer, Fleischer, & Strotmann, 2006). For many people, smells have a way of generating memories—often emotion-laden ones—undoubtedly because of the neural pathways that smell takes through the limbic system (Bloom, Nelson, & Lazerson, 2001).

We have called the sense of smell a chemical sense, and smell might have a role to play in another kind of chemistry—interpersonal attraction. From an evolutionary perspective, the goal of human mating is to find someone with whom to produce the healthiest offspring. Mates with differing sets of genes (known as the major histocompatibility complex, or MHC) produce healthier offspring with the broadest immune systems. How do we find these people, short of taking a blood test? Martie Haselton (2006) has conducted a number of studies on interpersonal attraction using the "smelly T-shirt" paradigm. In this research, men are asked to wear a T-shirt to bed every day for a week without washing it. After they have been thoroughly imbued with a male's personal scent, the T-shirts are presented to women to smell and rate for attractiveness. Women reliably rate men whose MHCs are different from their own as more attractive, on the basis of the aroma of the T-shirts. Thus, although the eyes may be the window to the soul, the nose might be the gateway to love. There is an interesting exception, however: These effects have not been found for women who are taking contraceptives that alter their hormonal cycles.

The Kinesthetic and Vestibular Senses

You know the difference between walking and running and between lying down and sitting up. To perform even the simplest act of motor coordination, such as reaching out to take a book off a shelf or getting up out of a chair, the brain must constantly receive and coordinate information from every part of the body. Your body has two kinds of senses that give you information about your movement and orientation in space, as well as help you to maintain balance. The **kinesthetic senses** provide information about movement, posture, and orientation. The **vestibular sense** provides information about balance and movement.

No specific organ contains the kinesthetic senses. Instead, they are embedded in muscle fibers and joints. As we stretch and move, these receptors signal the state of the muscle. Kinesthesia is a sense that you often do not even notice until it is gone. Try walking when your leg is "asleep" or smiling (never mind talking) when you have just come from a dentist's office and are still under the effects of novocaine.

Perhaps the sophistication of kinesthesis can be best appreciated when we think in terms of memory. Even a mediocre typist can bang out 20 words per minute—but how many of us could write down the order of the letters on a keyboard without looking? Typing is a skill that relies on very coordinated sensitivity to the orientation, position, and movements of our fingers. We say that our fingers remember the positions of the keys. Likewise, the complicated movements a pitcher uses to throw a baseball cannot be written down or communicated easily using language. They involve nearly every muscle and joint in the body. Most information about the kinesthetic senses is transmitted from the joints and muscles along the same pathways to the brain as information about touch.

The vestibular sense tells us whether our head (and hence usually our body) is tilted, moving, slowing down, or speeding up. It works in concert with the kinesthetic senses to coordinate our *proprioceptive feedback,* which is information about the position of our limbs and body parts in relation to other body parts. Consider the combination of sensory abilities involved in the motion of an ice hockey player skating down the ice, cradling the puck, and pushing it forward with the hockey stick. The hockey player is responding simultaneously to a multitude of sensations, including those produced by the slickness of the ice, the position of the puck, the speed and momentum of the forward progression, and the requirements of the play to turn and to track the other players on the ice.

The **semicircular canals,** located in the inner ear, contain the sensory receptors that detect head motion caused when we tilt or move our heads and/or bodies (Figure 5.45). These canals consist of three fluid-filled, circular tubes that lie in the three planes of the body—right-left, front-back, and up-down. We can picture these as three intersecting hula hoops. As you move your head, the fluid of the semicircular canals flows in different directions and at different speeds (depending on the force of the head movement). Our perception of head movement and position is determined by the movements of these receptor cells (Tribukait, 2006). This ingenious system of using the motion of fluid in tubes to sense head position is not unlike the auditory system found in the inner ear. However, the fluid movement in the cochlea is caused by the pressure sound exerts on the oval window, whereas the movements in the semicircular canals reflect physical movements of the head and body. Vestibular sacs in the semicircular canals contain hair cells embedded in a gelatin-like mass. Just as the hair cells in the cochlea trigger hearing impulses in the brain, the hair cells in the semicircular canals transmit information about balance and movement.

The brain pathways for the vestibular sense begin in the auditory nerve, which contains both the cochlear nerve (with information about sound) and the vestibular nerve (which has information about balance and movement). Most of the axons of the vestibular nerve connect with the medulla, although some go directly to the cerebellum. There also appear to be vestibular projections to the temporal cortex, although their specific pathways have not been fully charted. Most neuroscientists believe that the projections to the cerebral cortex are responsible for dizziness, whereas the connections to the lower brain stem produce the nausea and vomiting that accompany motion sickness (Carlson, 2001).

The combination of kinesthetic and vestibular senses is supplemented by information from vision. This simple principle has made IMAX theaters profitable. When films are shown on screens that are large enough to fill our visual field, such as those found in many theme parks, the motion you perceive on the screen can make you feel as if you are moving. This is the same principle that causes a motorist to slam on the brakes in his tiny sports car when the big truck next to him starts to move forward. When everything in our visual field appears to be moving, it is generally because we are moving. Motion sickness is particularly problematic when people are receiving conflicting messages from their senses. If you are feeling motion sickness during a car ride, whatever you do, do not lie down. Let your eyes help convey as much consistent information as possible to your brain.

kinesthetic senses Senses that provide information about movement, posture, and orientation.

vestibular sense Senses that provide information about balance and movement.

semicircular canals Structure in the inner ear containing the sensory receptors that detect head motion.

FIGURE 5.45

The Semicircular Canals and Vestibular Sense The semicircular canals provide feedback to the gymnast's brain as her head and body tilt in different directions. Any angle of head rotation is registered by hair cells in one or more semicircular canals in both ears. (*Inset*) The semicircular canals.

REVIEW, ASSESS, AND SHARPEN YOUR THINKING

Review

4 **Explain how the skin, chemical, kinesthetic, and vestibular senses work.**

- Relate how the skin monitors touch, temperature, and pain.
- Discuss the chemical senses of taste and smell.
- Describe how the kinesthetic and vestibular senses function.

Assess

1. How many types of sensory receptors are in our skin?

A. one   B. two

C. three   D. four

2. How do the fast and slow neural pathways for pain differ?

A. The slow pathway serves as an early warning system.

B. The fast pathway travels directly to the thalamus.

C. The slow pathway is used for localized pain.

D. The fast pathway includes the limbic system.

3. The rear of the tongue is most sensitive to substances that are

A. sweet.

B. bitter.

C. salty.

D. sour.

4. Which pathway for smell accounts for the fact that certain smells trigger vivid memories?

A. The neural pathway for smell that passes through the thalamus.

B. The neural pathway for smell that passes through the temporal lobes.

C. The neural pathway for smell that passes through the limbic system.

D. The neural pathway for smell that passes through the olfactory epithelium.

5. Which structure is responsible for detecting the position of the head?

A. semicircular canals

B. cochlea

C. cochlear nerve

D. vestibular nerve

Sharpen Your Thinking

Why can some individuals stand more pain than others?

5 Sensation, Perception, and Health and Wellness

Discuss the everyday practices associated with protecting vision and hearing.

Taking Care of Our Senses—and Enjoying the Rewards

Our senses are a vital connection to the world and to our experience, and we should not take them for granted. Ensuring the health of our senses means caring for our precious sensory organs—for example, by getting vision and hearing screenings and noting changes that might occur in our sensory experiences (Insel & Roth, 2008).

Taking care of your eyes means avoiding high-fat food, not smoking, and eating a diet rich in vitamins A, E, and C, zinc, and beta carotene. This means consuming a wide variety of fruits and vegetables (including your spinach). It also means reading with appropriate lighting (three times brighter than the rest of the room light) and with your work at eye level—about 16 inches away—and wearing sunglasses that protect your eyes from UVA and UVB, the sun's damaging rays. Some of the common causes of blindness are preventable but also undetectable. A glaucoma test is especially important after the age of 60. Staying active and eating healthy are important for avoiding another cause of blindness: diabetic retinopathy.

With respect to our hearing, perhaps the most dangerous threat comes from loud noise. HEAR (Hearing Education and Awareness for Rockers) was founded by rock musicians whose hearing had been damaged by their exposure to high volumes of rock music. Hearing loss, which is common among rock musicians, limits what they are able to do later in their lives. Other noisy environments, such as production factories and airports, may pose threats to your hearing.

To determine how well you protect your hearing, answer these questions:

- Do you work in a noisy environment? If so, ask your employer to inform you about the level of noise and company policy on protecting your hearing.
- If you use power equipment, are you using earplugs or other ear protectors?
- Do you go to rock concerts? According to HEAR, the sound level at a rock concert can be as high as 140 dB in front of the speakers, which can damage hearing, and above 100 dB behind the speakers, still very loud and potentially dangerous. Lars Ulrich of Metallica says, "Three of the four members of Metallica wear earplugs. Some people think earplugs are for wimps. But if you don't want to hear records in 5 or 10 years, that's your decision."

Through our senses we experience the world in all its richness. When his sight was restored after 25 years of blindness, Michael May could not believe that the thousands of twinkling stars in the night sky were real.

Throughout this chapter we have viewed sensation and perception as our connections to the world. How about treating your senses by taking them outside? Research has shown that exposure to nature can be a vital refresher for our senses, broadening our attention and improving our well-being. For instance, researchers have found that children who are exposed to nature are better able to manage stress (Wells & Evans, 2003). Few things engage all of our senses like being outside in a natural environment. And experiences with the natural world have been shown to improve overall physical and psychological well-being (Devlin & Arneill, 2003; Gulwadi, 2006; Ulrich, 1991). Hospital patients recover more quickly if they have a window that looks out onto trees, sky, and plants (Ulrich, 1991). Taking a walk outside is an excellent way to get exercise as well as to open up your senses to the world around you. And while you are walking, do not forget to stop and smell the flowers—literally. Flowers are visually pleasant and they smell good, so they are a natural mood booster for both men and women (Haviland-Jones & others, 2005). They appear to be designed by nature to make people happy (Haviland-Jones & others, 2005).

Our senses allow us to experience the world in all its vibrancy. Sue Berry, who achieved the ability to perceive depth only after a long, arduous effort, described her encounter with nature on a snowy day. "I felt myself within the snow fall, among the snowflakes. . . . I was overcome with a sense of joy. A snow fall can be quite beautiful—especially when you see it for the first time" (quoted in Sacks, 2006, p. 73). Recall the example of Michael May who was able to see after 25 years of blindness. One night, with his seeing-eye dog Josh at his side, he decided to go look at the sky. Lying on the grass in a field, he opened his eyes. He thought he was "seeing stars"—in the metaphorical sense. He thought that the thousands of white lights in the sky could not really be real, but they were. As he remarked in his "vision diary": "How sweet it is" (May, 2003; Stein, 2003).

 REVIEW, ASSESS, AND SHARPEN YOUR THINKING

Review

5 Discuss the everyday practices associated with protecting vision and hearing.

- Identify actions you should take and those you should avoid to protect your vision and hearing.
- Describe research findings about how exposure to nature benefits the senses and promotes well-being.

SUMMARY

1 HOW WE SENSE AND PERCEIVE THE WORLD

Discuss basic principles of sensation and perception.

Detecting, Processing, and Interpreting Experiences

Sensation is the process of receiving stimulus energies from the environment. Perception is the process of organizing and interpreting sensory information to give it meaning. Sensation and perception are integrated. Perceiving the world involves both bottom-up and top-down processing.

Sensory Receptors and the Brain

All sensation begins with sensory receptors, specialized cells that detect and transmit information about a stimulus to sensory neurons and the brain. Sensory receptors are selective and have different neural pathways. The three main classes of sense organs and receptors are photoreception, mechanoreception, and chemoreception.

Thresholds

Psychophysics—the field that studies links between the physical properties of stimuli and a person's experience of them—defines absolute threshold as the minimum amount of energy that people can detect. There is no evidence that subliminal perception—the ability to detect information below the level of conscious awareness—has any substantial influence on our thoughts and behavior. The difference threshold, or just noticeable difference, is the smallest difference in stimulation required to discriminate one stimulus from another 50 percent of the time. Weber's law holds that two stimuli must differ by a constant minimum percentage to be perceived as different.

Signal Detection Theory

Signal detection theory focuses on decision making about stimuli in the presence of uncertainty. In this theory, detection of sensory stimuli depends on many factors other than the physical properties of the stimuli, and differences in these other factors may lead different people to make different decisions about identical stimuli.

Perceiving Sensory Stimuli

What we perceive depends in part on which stimuli engage our attention and on a tendency to perceive things according to our beliefs and expectations. Selective attention involves focusing on a specific aspect of experience while ignoring others. Attention may involve bottom-up or top-down processing. A perceptual set is a collection of experiences and expectations that influence perception.

Sensory Adaptation

Sensory adaptation is a change in the responsiveness of the sensory system based on the average level of surrounding stimulation.

2 THE VISUAL SYSTEM

Explain how the visual system enables us to see and, by communicating with the brain, to perceive the world.

The Visual Stimulus and the Eye

Light is a form of electromagnetic energy that can be described in terms of wavelengths. Three characteristics of light are hue, amplitude, and purity. The eye responds to light within a narrow range of wavelengths (400–700 nm). Light passes through the cornea and lens to the retina, the light-sensitive surface in the back of the eye that houses light receptors called rods (which function in low illumination) and cones (which react to color). The fovea of the retina contains only cones and sharpens detail in an image. Ganglion cells interpret incoming visual information and send it to the brain.

Visual Processing in the Brain

The optic nerve transmits neural impulses to the brain. There it diverges at the optic chiasm, so that what we see in the left visual field is registered in the right side of the brain and vice versa. In the occipital lobes of the cerebral cortex, the information is integrated. Visual information processing involves feature detection, parallel processing, and binding.

Color Vision

The trichromatic theory of color perception stipulates that three types of color receptors in the retina allow us to perceive three colors (green, red, and blue). The opponent-process theory states that cells in the visual system respond to red-green and blue-yellow colors. Both theories are probably correct—the eye and the brain use both methods to code colors.

Perceiving Shape, Depth, Motion, and Constancy

Shape perception is the ability to distinguish objects from their background. This figure-ground relationship is a principle of gestalt psychology, which emphasizes that people naturally organize their perceptions according to patterns. Depth perception is the ability to perceive objects three-dimensionally. Depth perception depends on binocular cues and monocular cues. Motion perception by humans depends on specialized neurons, feedback from the body, and environmental cues. Psychologists are interested in both real and apparent movement. Perceptual constancy is the recognition that objects are stable despite changes in the way we see them. Three types of perceptual constancy are size constancy, shape constancy, and brightness constancy.

Illusions

A visual illusion is the result of a discrepancy between reality and the perceptual representation of it. Examples are the Müller-Lyer illusion, the moon illusion, the horizontal-vertical illusion, the Ponzo illusion, and the devil's tuning fork.

3 THE AUDITORY SYSTEM

Understand how the auditory system registers sound and how it connects with the brain to perceive it.

The Nature of Sound and How We Experience It

Sounds, or sound waves, are vibrations in the air that are processed by the auditory system. Sound waves vary in wavelength. Wavelength determines frequency. Pitch is the perceptual interpretation of frequency. Amplitude, measured in decibels, is perceived as loudness. Complex sounds involve a blending of frequencies. Timbre is the tone saturation, or perceptual quality, of a sound.

Structures and Functions of the Ear

The outer ear consists of the pinna and external auditory canal and acts to funnel sound to the middle ear. In the middle ear, the eardrum, hammer, anvil, and stirrup vibrate in response to sound and transfer the vibrations to the inner ear. Important parts of the fluid-filled inner ear are the oval window, cochlea, and basilar membrane. The movement of hair cells between the basilar membrane and the tectorial membrane generates nerve impulses.

Theories of Hearing

Place theory states that each frequency produces vibrations at a particular spot on the basilar membrane. Place theory adequately explains high-frequency sounds but not low-frequency sounds. Frequency theory states that the perception of a sound's frequency depends on how often the auditory nerve fires. A modification of frequency theory, the volley principle, states that a cluster of neurons can fire impulses in rapid succession, producing a volley of impulses.

Auditory Processing in the Brain

Information about sound moves from the hair cells to the auditory nerve, which carries information to the brain's auditory areas. The cortical destination of most fibers is the temporal lobes of the cerebral cortex.

Localizing Sound

Localizing sound involves both the timing of the sound and the intensity of the sound arriving at each ear.

4 OTHER SENSES

Explain how the skin, chemical, kinesthetic, and vestibular senses work.

The Skin Senses

Touch is the detection of mechanical energy, or pressure, against the skin. Touch information travels through the spinal cord, brain stem, and thalamus and on to the somatosensory areas of the parietal lobes. Psychologists are studying the role of touch in various jobs and in infant development. Thermoreceptors under the skin respond to increases and decreases in temperature. Pain is the sensation that warns us about damage to our bodies. Two different neural pathways—one fast and the other slow—transmit information about pain. One theory of pain is gate-control theory. Many physical and psychological techniques are used to control pain.

The Chemical Senses

Taste and smell enable us to detect and process chemicals in the environment. Papillae are bumps on the tongue that contain taste buds, the receptors for taste. The taste qualities we respond to are categorized as sweet, sour, bitter, and salty, although our tasting ability goes beyond these four qualities. The olfactory epithelium contains a sheet of receptor cells for smell in the roof of the nose.

The Kinesthetic and Vestibular Senses

The kinesthetic senses provide information about movement, posture, and orientation. The vestibular sense provides information about balance and movement. Receptors for the kinesthetic senses are embedded in muscle fibers and joints. The semicircular canals in the inner ear contain the sensory receptors that detect head motion.

5 SENSATION, PERCEPTION, AND HEALTH AND WELLNESS

Discuss the everyday practices associated with protecting vision and hearing.

Taking Care of Our Senses—and Enjoying the Rewards

Our senses connect us to the world. Taking care of these precious organs means adopting healthy practices such as eating a low-fat diet rich in vitamins and beta carotene. Caring for your eyes means wearing protective lenses when you are in the bright sun. Protecting your hearing requires avoiding dangerously loud noises. Noise at 80 decibels or higher, if heard for prolonged periods of time, can damage hearing. Experiences in nature have been shown to reduce stress and enhance well-being.

Key Terms

Assess Your Knowledge

1. Weber's law explains which of the following?
   A. our tendency to group different objects into a set
   B. feeling hotness when we simultaneously touch something warm and something cold
   C. why certain colors can be seen better in the dark
   D. noticing a 1 dB change in volume at low levels rather than at high levels

2. Someone being able to smell color is an example of
   A. the absolute threshold.
   B. synaesthesia.
   C. subliminal perception.
   D. olfactory compensation.

3. To determine a person's absolute threshold, you need to know how much of a stimulus is needed to be detected ___ percent of the time.
   A. 25   B. 50
   C. 75   D. 100

4. Martin sees a deep red pillow in the store and is attracted to the richness of the color. He is focusing on the
   A. purity.   B. amplitude.
   C. wavelength.   D. hue.

5. Images are first projected onto what structure of the eye?
   A. sclera   B. retina
   C. iris   D. visual cortex

6. One neuron in the visual system is sensitive to motion while another is sensitive to specific shapes. These neurons are known as
   A. rods.   B. cones.
   C. binding neurons.   D. feature detectors.

7. Which theory accounts for color blindness?
   A. bottom-up processing theory
   B. top-down processing theory
   C. trichromatic theory
   D. opponent-process theory

8. Which of the following does not belong with the others?
   A. stirrup   B. pinna
   C. hammer   D. anvil

9. Which structure of the ear responds to the movement of hair cells?
   A. basilar membrane
   B. eardrum
   C. oval window
   D. tectorial membrane

10. The side of the tongue is most sensitive to tastes that are
    A. bitter.   B. sweet.
    C. salty.   D. sour.

11. To what does the term *propioceptive feedback* refer?
    A. the integration of olfactory senses
    B. information about the position of our body parts
    C. the use of monocular cues in vision
    D. information about the location of stimuli on the tongue.

12. Which structure contains the taste buds?
    A. papillae
    B. semicircular canals
    C. olfactory bulb
    D. basilar membrane

13. Which part of the body's nervous system is thought to contain the neural gates proposed in to the gate-control theory of pain?
    A. spinal column   B. thermoreceptors
    C. cerebral cortex   D. thalamus

14. Which of the following is the origin of brain pathways for the vestibular senses?
    A. olfactory nerve
    B. visual nerve
    C. auditory nerve
    D. taste nerve

15. Which theory focuses on the location of vibration of the basilar membrane?
    A. frequency theory
    B. gate-control theory
    C. place theory
    D. trichromatic theory

Go to Appendix B for answers to these questions.

Apply Your Knowledge

1. Find a partner and test your absolute threshold for sugar. Have your partner set up the following sugar-and-water mixtures. Mix 2 teaspoons of sugar in 4 cups of water. Label this solution ("solution X," for example). Take 2 cups of solution X, add 2 cups of water, and give this solution a second label ("solution D," for example). Then take 2 cups of solution D, add 2 cups of water, and give this a third label ("solution Q"). Continue taking 2 cups from each successive solution until you have a total of eight solutions, making sure to keep track of which solution is which. When you are done, the concentration of the solutions should be equivalent to 1 teaspoon in each of the following amounts of water: 1 pint (2 cups), 1 quart, 1 half-gallon, 1 gallon, 2 gallons, 4 gallons, and 8 gallons. Your partner should place a sample of one of the solutions in a cup and a sample of plain water in another, identical cup. You should taste the solution in each cup and decide which one is the sugar solution. Do this with all of the solutions until you can decide what your absolute threshold is according to the definition in the text. Do you think your absolute threshold would vary depending on what you had recently eaten? Why or why not?

2. Imagine that you have two sets of dominoes. Each set contains 100 dominoes. With the first set, you make a straight line of 100. With the second set, you make an arrangement in which tipping a single domino causes five separate lines of dominoes to fall down simultaneously. Which set of dominoes will fall the fastest? How is this set of dominoes similar to the way we process visual information?

3. Compare and contrast the consequences of losing vision in one eye versus losing hearing in one ear.

4. It has been said that we taste with our eyes first. Professional chefs give great thought to the presentation of foods. Think about your favorite food and focus not on how it tastes but on how it looks. Now think about how it smells. How do vision, smell, and taste work together to produce the experience of your favorite dish? Would your favorite beef stew be just as appetizing if it were served in a dog food dish?

5. Jot down all the foods you have eaten today. Search the web for the nutritional information on these—and evaluate how good you have been to your eyes today.

CHAPTER 6

STATES OF CONSCIOUSNESS

Experiencing Psychology

TERRY WALLIS—AWAKENED AFTER ALMOST 20 YEARS

Imagine falling asleep at the age of 19 and waking up nearly 20 years later. With no memories of the last 2 decades, you open your eyes to a world that has changed drastically. You see that the people you love have aged, seemingly quite suddenly. Meanwhile, you are oblivious to the fact that they have held a worried vigil at your bedside for weeks and months that turned into years and years.

This story is Terry Wallis's story. He was 19 years old in 1984 when the pickup truck he was driving went through a guardrail and dove off a 25-foot bluff. Terry was found paralyzed and in a coma, unable to communicate. For the next 19 years, he persisted in a state of minimal consciousness, occasionally grunting or nodding, seemingly awake but not communicative. His parents took him home every other week and continued to talk to him, but they never knew if he had any awareness of what was going on. Then, one day in 2003, Terry shocked everyone by answering "Mom" when one of his nursing home caretakers asked him who his visitor was that day.

The last 3 years have seen improvements in Terry's functioning. He is now able to count to 25. But more important, to his family he has become "himself" again, making jokes and expressing joy at being alive. A real-life Rip Van Winkle, Terry Wallis has taken a while to accommodate to his new world. He still believes that Ronald Reagan is president, and until recently he could not imagine that he was 42 years old, not a young adult of 20.

Recoveries such as Terry's are extremely rare. And now, for the first time, scientists have evidence of how he recovered. In the summer of 2006, neuroscientists Henning Voss and his colleagues (2006) published the first proof that Terry's brain had actually *rewired* itself, allowing him to regain consciousness. Using the new technology of diffusion tensor imaging, or DTI, the researchers showed that nerve cells in Terry's brain (cells that were damaged but not destroyed by his accident) had made new connections, over time restoring him to consciousness. During what seemed like a long wait to everyone who loved him, Terry's brain was engaged in a complex process of healing, with his brain cells slowly forming new connections and finally making enough to form a network. Terry's return to conscious life and his sense that he is himself again are based on the recovery of conscious awareness. ▪

PREVIEW

Such is the enormous importance of consciousness in human life, the focus of this chapter. We first review the meaning of various states of consciousness. We next explore the intriguing world of sleep and dreams, states in which most of us spend a great deal of time. Then we turn to the topic of hypnosis—a technique that may provide ways to harness altered consciousness—before exploring various altered states of consciousness produced by psychoactive drugs. The chapter closes with a look at the important role of consciousness in health and wellness.

1 The Nature of Consciousness

Discuss the nature of consciousness.

In his entry for *consciousness* in the 1989 *Dictionary of Psychology,* British psychologist Stuart Sutherland gave the following pessimistic assessment: "Consciousness is a fascinating but elusive phenomenon; it is impossible to specify what it is, what it does, or why it evolved. Nothing worth reading has ever been written about it." Although Sutherland dismissed the potential for scientific research on consciousness, this "fascinating but elusive" aspect of life has interested psychologists for centuries, down to the present day, and for good reason: Consciousness is a crucial part of many human experiences (Owen & others, 2006; Pinker, 2007).

On an autumn afternoon, when you see a beautiful tree, vibrant with color, you are not simply perceiving the colors; you are aware as well that you are seeing them. Many emotional experiences also rely on consciousness. You would never feel embarrassment, for example, except that you have conscious awareness of yourself as a social object. *Metacognition* refers to thinking about thinking (Pressley & Harris, 2006). When you think about your thoughts—for example, when you reflect on why you are so nervous before an exam—you are using your conscious awareness to examine your own thought processes. This awareness might even have significance for survival. Recently it has been argued that consciousness is adaptive, because it gives us a feeling that we are truly special, heightening our motivation to survive (Humphrey, 2006).

In the late nineteenth and early twentieth centuries, psychology pioneers such as Sigmund Freud and William James took great interest in the study of the conscious and unconscious mind. However, for much of the twentieth century, psychologists shifted instead to a focus on behaviors and on the rewards and punishments that determined those behaviors (Skinner, 1938; Watson, 1913). In the past decade, though, the study of consciousness has gained widespread respectability in psychology (Mashour, 2006). For the first time in many decades, psychologists from many different fields are interested in consciousness, including its relation to subconsciousness (Hebb, 2002; Lamme, 2006; Wiens, 2006).

Although there is disagreement about a proper definition, we can define consciousness in terms of its two parts: awareness and arousal. **Consciousness** refers to *awareness* of external events and internal sensations, including awareness of the self and thoughts about one's experiences; this awareness occurs under a condition of *arousal,* the physiological state of being engaged with the environment. Thus, a sleeping person is not conscious in the same way as he or she would be while awake.

The contents of our awareness change from moment to moment. Information moves rapidly in and out of consciousness. William James (1890/1950) described the mind as a **stream of consciousness**—a continuous flow of changing sensations, images, thoughts, and feelings. Our minds can race from one topic to the next: from thinking about the person approaching us to our physical state today to our strategy for the test tomorrow to the café where we are going to have lunch.

consciousness Awareness of external events and internal sensations, including awareness of the self and thoughts about one's experiences; this awareness occurs under a condition of arousal.

stream of consciousness James's concept that the mind is a continuous flow of changing sensations, images, thoughts, and feelings.

Consciousness and the Brain

One of the great unanswered questions about consciousness involves its location. Does consciousness stand alone (located in what might be called the *mind*), separate in some way from the brain (Livaditis & Tsatalmpasidou, 2007)? Or is it an intrinsic aspect of the brain's functioning? If consciousness is in the brain, is there a particular location that is the seat of consciousness, or is consciousness distributed across different areas (Arshavsky, 2006)?

Most neuroscientists do not believe that a specific location in the brain takes incoming information from one's body and the world and converts it into the conscious world we are aware of and can report on. Rather, it is likely that separate distributed processing systems connect to produce consciousness. Depending on what a person is aware of at a particular point in time, different areas of the brain "light up," or are activated (Nunez & Srinivasan, 2006; Seth & others, 2006).

The two aspects of consciousness, awareness and arousal, are associated with different parts of the brain. Awareness, the subjective state of being conscious of what is going on, typically involves the cerebral cortex, especially its association areas and frontal lobes (Macknik, 2006; Rees, 2007). It may be that the integration of input from the senses, along with information about emotions and memories in the association areas, creates consciousness (Bloom, Nelson, & Lazerson, 2001). Arousal is a physiological state determined by the reticular activating system, a network of structures including the brain stem, medulla, and thalamus. Damage to either of the two areas related to consciousness may cause a coma.

Levels of Awareness

The flow of sensations, images, thoughts, and feelings that William James spoke of can occur at different levels of awareness. Although we might think of consciousness as either present or not, there are in fact shades of awareness, observed in coma patients as well as in everyday life. Here we consider five levels of awareness: higher-level consciousness, lower-level consciousness, altered states of consciousness, subconscious awareness, and no awareness (Figure 6.1).

Level of Awareness	Description	Examples
Higher-Level Consciousness	Involves controlled processing, in which individuals actively focus their efforts on attaining a goal; the most alert state of consciousness.	Doing a math or science problem; preparing for a debate; taking an at-bat in a baseball game.
Lower-Level Consciousness	Includes automatic processing that requires little attention, as well as daydreaming.	Punching in a number on a cell phone; typing on a keyboard when one is an expert; gazing at a sunset.
Altered States of Consciousness	Can be produced by drugs, trauma, fatigue, possibly hypnosis, and sensory deprivation.	Feeling the effects of having taken alcohol or psychedelic drugs; undergoing hypnosis to quit smoking or lose weight.
Subconscious Awareness	Can occur when people are awake, as well as when they are sleeping and dreaming.	Sleeping and dreaming.
No Awareness	Freud's belief that some unconscious thoughts are too laden with anxiety and other negative emotions for consciousness to admit them.	Having unconscious thoughts; being knocked out by a blow or anesthetized.

FIGURE 6.1

Levels of Awareness Each level of awareness has its time and place in human life.

"If you ask me, all three of us are in different states of awareness."
© The New Yorker Collection 1983 Edward Frascino from cartoonbank.com.
All Rights Reserved.

Higher-Level Consciousness **Controlled processes** represent the most alert states of human consciousness, in which individuals actively focus their efforts toward a goal (Tanida & Poppel, 2006). Watch Maria as she struggles to master the unfamiliar buttons on her new 10-function cell phone. She does not hear you humming to yourself or notice the intriguing shadow on the wall. Her state of focused awareness is what is meant by controlled processes.

Chapter 5 described the role of attention in perception. Controlled processes require selective attention, the ability to focus on a specific aspect of experience while ignoring others (Gunstad & others, 2006).

Lower-Level Awareness Beneath the level of controlled processes are other levels of conscious awareness. Lower levels of awareness include automatic processes and the familiar state of daydreaming.

Automatic Processes A few weeks after acquiring her cell phone, Maria flips it open and sends a text message in the middle of a conversation with you. Her fingers fly almost automatically across the buttons. She does not have to concentrate on the keys now and hardly seems aware of the gadget in her hand as she continues to talk to you while finishing her lunch. For her, using her cell phone has reached the point of automatic processing. **Automatic processes** are states of consciousness that require little attention and do not interfere with other ongoing activities. Automatic processes require less conscious effort than controlled processes (Aarts, Custers, & Holland, 2007; Lieberman, 2007; Moors & De Houwer, 2006). When we are awake, our automatic behaviors occur at a lower level of awareness than controlled processes, but they are still conscious behaviors. Maria pushed the right buttons, so at some level she apparently was aware of what she was doing.

Daydreaming Another state of consciousness that involves a low level of conscious effort, *daydreaming* lies somewhere between active consciousness and dreaming while we are asleep. It is a little like dreaming while we are awake. Daydreams usually begin spontaneously when we are doing something that requires less than our full attention.

Mind wandering is probably the most obvious type of daydreaming. We regularly take brief side trips into our own private kingdoms of imagery and memory while reading, listening, or working. When we daydream, we drift into a world of fantasy. We imagine ourselves on dates, at parties, on television, in faraway places, at another time in our lives, and so on. Sometimes our daydreams are about everyday events such as paying the rent, going to the dentist, and meeting with somebody at school or work.

The semiautomatic flow of daydreaming can be useful. As you daydream while you shave, iron a pair of pants, or walk to the store, you may make plans, solve a problem, or come up with a creative idea. Daydreams can remind us of important things ahead. Daydreaming keeps our minds active while helping us to cope, create, and fantasize (Klinger, 2000).

Altered States of Consciousness *Altered states of consciousness or awareness* are mental states that are noticeably different from normal awareness. They can be produced by drugs, trauma, fatigue, possibly hypnosis, and sensory deprivation (Avner, 2006). In some cases, drug use may create a higher level of awareness (Fields, 2007). The popularity of coffee and other beverages that contain caffeine, a stimulant drug, provides evidence of the widespread belief that caffeine increases alertness. Awareness also may be altered to a lower level. Alcohol has this effect.

Subconscious Awareness In Chapter 5, we saw that a great deal of brain activity is going on beneath the level of conscious awareness. Psychologists are increasingly interested in subconscious processing of information, which can take place while we are awake or asleep (Gaillard & others, 2006).

Waking Subconscious Awareness When we are awake, processes are going on just below the surface of awareness. For example, while you are grappling with a problem,

controlled processes The most alert states of consciousness, in which individuals actively focus their efforts toward a goal.

automatic processes States of consciousness that require little attention and do not interfere with other ongoing activities.

the solution may just "pop" into your head. Such insights can occur when a subconscious connection between ideas is so strong that it rises into awareness, somewhat the way a cork held underwater bobs to the surface as soon as it is released (Csikszentmihalyi, 1995).

Evidence that we are not always aware of the processing of information in our brains comes from studies of individuals with certain neurological disorders. In one case, a woman who suffered neurological damage was unable to describe or report the shape or size of objects in her visual field, although she was capable of describing other physical perceptions that she had (Milner & Goodale, 1995). Yet when she reached for an object, she could accurately adjust the size of her grip to allow her to grasp the object. Thus, she did possess some subconscious knowledge of the size and shape of objects, even though she had no awareness of this knowledge.

Subconscious information processing can occur simultaneously in a distributed manner along many parallel tracks. (Recall the discussion of parallel processing of visual information in Chapter 5.) For example, when you look at a dog running down the street, you are consciously aware of the event but not of the subconscious processing of the object's identity (a dog), its color (black), and its movement (fast). In contrast, conscious processing is *serial*. That is, it occurs in sequence and is slower than much subconscious processing.

Sleep and Dreams   When we sleep and dream, our level of awareness is lower than when we daydream, but sleep and dreams are not best regarded as the absence of consciousness (Zeman, 2006). Rather, they are low levels of consciousness.

Consider the German chemist August Kekulé, who in 1865 developed the insight that the benzene molecule might be shaped like a ring. This idea occurred to him after he fell asleep while watching sparks in the fireplace make circles in the air. If he had remained awake, Kekulé would likely have rejected as ridiculous the notion of a link between the sparks and the shape of the benzene molecule. However, in his subconscious mind rational thought could not censor the connection, so when Kekulé woke up he could not ignore its possibility. It may be that irrelevant connections fade away and disappear but those that are robust survive long enough to emerge eventually into consciousness (Csikszentmihalyi, 1995).

Researchers have found that when people are asleep, they remain aware of external stimuli to some degree. For example, in sleep laboratories, when people are clearly asleep (as determined by physiological monitoring devices), they are able to respond to faint tones by pressing a handheld button (Ogilvie & Wilkinson, 1988). In one study, the presentation of pure auditory tones to sleeping individuals activated auditory processing regions of the brain, whereas participants' names activated language areas, the amygdala, and the prefrontal cortex (Stickgold, 2001). We return to the topics of sleep and dreams in the next section.

No Awareness   The term *unconscious* generally applies to someone who has been knocked out by a blow or anesthetized, or who has fallen into a deep, prolonged unconscious state (Harden, Dey, & Gawne-Cain, 2007; Valentine & Curl, 2006). However, Sigmund Freud (1917) used the term *unconscious* in a very different way. At about the same time that William James was charting the shifting nature of our stream of consciousness, Freud concluded that most of our thoughts are unconscious. **Unconscious thought,** said Freud, is a reservoir of unacceptable wishes, feelings, and thoughts that are beyond conscious awareness.

Freud's interpretation viewed the unconscious as a storehouse for vile thoughts. Freud believed that some aspects of our experience remain unconscious for good reason, as if we are better off not knowing about them. Although Freud's ideas remain controversial, psychologists now widely accept the notion that unconscious processes do exist (Cramer, 2000). Recently, researchers have found that many mental processes (thoughts, emotions, and perceptions) can occur outside of awareness. Some psychologists term these processes *nonconscious* rather than *unconscious,* to avoid the Freudian connotation (Bargh, 2006).

For further insights on consciousness, see the Intersection, which explores children's beliefs and understanding of how the mind works and the implications of these beliefs and understanding for their social functioning.

Among those who practice altered states of consciousness are Zen monks who explore the Buddha-nature at the center of their beings.

unconscious thought Freud's concept of a reservoir of unacceptable wishes, feelings, and thoughts that are beyond conscious awareness.

Consciousness and Developmental Psychology: How Do We Develop a Sense for the Minds of Others?

Imagine yourself in a conversation with a friend, describing a complex issue you have been thinking about. While talking, you search your friend's face for signs of understanding. Does she nod? Does her brow furrow? As you talk, you watch her face and body for signs of what you think is going on in her head. In a sense, although you may have never thought of it this way, these observations reveal your belief in your friend's consciousness. You pause and ask, "Do you see what I mean?" When you do, you are checking in on your conversation partner's mind.

> **There is perhaps no greater mystery than what is going on behind another person's eyes.**

The way human beings interact in a situation such as this gives us clues about how we think others think. It might seem obvious that other people have "minds of their own," but the human ability to recognize the subjective experience of another is a true developmental accomplishment. Developmental psychologists who study children's ideas about mental states use the phrase *theory of mind* to refer to individuals' understanding that they and others think, feel, perceive, and have private experiences (Pressley & Hilden, 2006).

In subtle ways, children reveal very early in life their sense that other people think. For example, if a 6-month-old sees a person talking to someone who is hidden behind a curtain, the child will be surprised if the curtain is

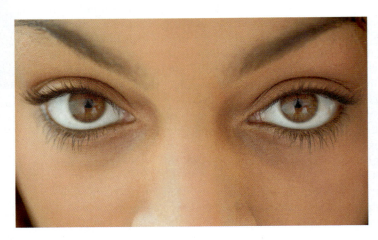

opened to reveal an object rather than another person. This outcome suggests that even an infant "knows" that people talk to people (Legerstee, Barna, & DiAdamo, 2000). When a 9-month-old points to something he or she wants, these actions imply that the infant recognizes that the other person can understand that he or she wants something (Tomasello, 2006). If a toddler sees someone express disgust for a particular food, such as a cookie, she will know that the person would prefer some other food over the cookie that she herself prefers (Repacholi & Gopnik, 1997). At around ages 2 and 3, children can talk about mental states—indicating, for example, that they know that someone might feel sad if he or she does not get a hoped-for present (Wellman, Philips, & Rodriguez, 2000). Around that same time, children understand that they can know something someone else does not know, and they start telling fibs (Harris, 2006).

Developmental psychologists have used a clever procedure called the false belief task to examine children's theory of mind (Sabbagh, Moses, & Shiverick, 2006). In one version of the false belief task, the child is asked to consider the

following situation (Wellman & Woolley, 1990). Anna is a little girl who has some chocolate that she decides to save for later. She puts it in a blue cupboard and goes outside to play. While Anna is gone, her mother moves the chocolate to the red cupboard. When Anna comes back in, where will she look for her chocolate? Three-year-olds give the wrong answer—they assume that Anna will look in the red cupboard because they know (even though Anna does not) that Anna's mom moved the chocolate to the red one. But 4-year-olds answer correctly—they recognize that Anna does not know everything they do and that she will believe the chocolate is where she left it (Wellman & Woolley, 1990). Success at the false belief task is associated with social competence, and children who perform well at it are better liked by their peers (Cassidy & others, 2003; Leslie, German, & Polizzi, 2005).

Theory of mind is essential to many valuable social capacities, such as empathy and sympathy (Lockl & Schneider, 2007; Volim & others, 2006). We know we have found a true kindred spirit when someone really "gets" us—when a friend can say, "I know exactly what you mean." When we have a problem, we might look to someone we trust to get his or her point of view. Theory of mind means that we know that others *have* a point of view. Our desire that others should know all of what is going on in our head is demonstrated by the use of emoticons in e-mails and instant messages. Why is it important to include a :) or a ;) ? These icons fill in the missing pieces of our full intentions for our electronic correspondent.

Simon Baron-Cohen (1995, 2006) is an expert on autism, a disorder that affects communication and social interaction. He has proposed that the emergence of theory of mind is so central to human functioning that evolution would not leave it up to chance. Indeed, Baron-Cohen suggests that we are born with a brain mechanism that is ready to develop a theory of mind. This theory of mind mechanism (or TOMM) accounts for the fact that nearly all children over the age of 4 pass the false belief task, even children with the genetic disorder Down syndrome. Baron-Cohen has proposed that autistic individuals lack the TOMM, a condition that would explain their unique social deficits. Indeed, he has referred to autism as "mind blindness."

Fascinating research has revealed the very social nature of theory of mind. Using a procedure similar to the false belief test, researchers direct children to watch as a photograph is taken of Big Bird sitting on a bed. Before the photograph is developed, the kids observe Big Bird moving to the bathtub. The question for the child is, Where will Big Bird be in the photograph, once it is developed? In this situation, 3-year-olds perform quite poorly, thinking that Big Bird will be in the bathtub. But autistic children of a variety of ages get the answer right (Leslie & Thais, 1992; Zaitchik, 1990). In this situation, success at the task does not require a mental representation of another's mind.

We often use our own internal states as a "default" for judging how another person is feeling or thinking (Royzman, Cassidy, & Baron, 2003), but the autistic individual has no such luxury. Indeed, research has shown that the autistic amygdala has fewer neurons devoted to processing emotion than the non-autistic amygdala (Schumann & Amaral, 2006). Temple Grandin (2006), an accomplished scientist who is autistic, has described in her memoir *Thinking in Pictures* how she has had to memorize and practice the kinds of things that go on effortlessly in other people's heads. For example, she must commit to memory the fact that non-autistic people think in words, not images, and that their facial expressions reveal important information about their feelings. To support individuals who are coping with such challenges, researchers have designed special training programs for people who have Asperger syndrome (a type of autism typically associated with normal levels of IQ) and

high-functioning autism (a kind of autism in which individuals are able to function close to or above normal levels in society). The programs aim to help these individuals decode the complex emotional messages conveyed by facial expressions and tone of voice (Golan & Baron-Cohen, 2006). Researchers have found that such training increases activation of the fusiform face area in the brain, which, as discussed in Chapter 3, is vital in human face recognition (Bolte & others, 2006).

But even with our remarkable TOMM in full working order, our intuitions about others are sometimes inaccurate. We might love someone who does not return our feelings. Or we might trust a person who does not have our best interest at heart. There is perhaps no greater mystery than what is going on behind another person's eyes. What another person knows, thinks, believes, and wants—these are questions that have fascinated human beings since the beginning of our species.

 ## REVIEW, ASSESS, AND SHARPEN YOUR THINKING

Review

1 Discuss the nature of consciousness.
- Explain the brain's role in consciousness.
- Define consciousness and describe five levels of awareness.

Assess

1. The term *metacognition* refers to
   A. the study of cognitive research.
   B. thinking about thought processes.
   C. cognition that is subliminal.
   D. stream of consciousness thinking.

2. Which of the following is not an automatic process?
   A. a student solving a complex math problem
   B. an athlete jogging
   C. a person talking to a friend
   D. a student composing a research paper

3. Rank the following states of consciousness in order from least awareness to most.
   A. altered states of consciousness, subconscious awareness, lower-level consciousness
   B. altered states of consciousness, lower-level consciousness, subconscious awareness

   C. lower level consciousness, subconscious awareness, altered states of consciousness
   D. subconscious awareness, altered states of consciousness, lower-level consciousness

4. According to Freud, unconscious thought
   A. happens when someone is asleep or anesthetized.
   B. does not exist.
   C. consists of desires, feelings, and thoughts we cannot accept.
   D. is the stream of consciousness.

5. Processing of subconscious information is _____, whereas processing of conscious information is _____.
   A. parallel, serial
   B. serial, parallel
   C. instantaneous, distributed
   D. distributed, instantaneous

Sharpen Your Thinking

How many different states of awareness have you experienced? In one or two sentences each, describe the nature of your experience in each state.

2 Sleep and Dreams

Explain the nature of sleep and dreams.

Sleep claims about one-third of the time in our lives, more than any other pursuit. What is sleep, and why is it so important? This section explores the answers to these questions, as well as the fascinating world of dreams. First, let's see how sleep is linked to our internal biological rhythms.

Biological Rhythms and Sleep

Biological rhythms are periodic physiological fluctuations in the body. We are unaware of most biological rhythms, such as the rise and fall of hormones and accelerated and decelerated cycles of brain activity, but they can influence our behavior. These rhythms are controlled by biological clocks, which include

- *Annual or seasonal cycles,* such as the migration of birds, the hibernation of bears, and the seasonal fluctuations of humans' eating habits
- *Twenty-eight-day cycles,* such as the female menstrual cycle, which averages 28 days
- *Twenty-four-hour cycles,* such as the sleep/wake cycle and temperature changes in the body

Let's further explore the 24-hour cycles.

Circadian Rhythms A **circadian rhythm** is a daily behavioral or physiological cycle. Daily circadian rhythms involve the sleep/wake cycle, body temperature, blood pressure, and blood sugar level (Skene & Arendt, 2006). The term *circadian* comes from the Latin words *circa,* meaning "about," and *dies,* meaning "day." For example, body temperature fluctuates about 3 degrees Fahrenheit in a 24-hour day, peaking in the afternoon and reaching its lowest point between 2 A.M. and 5 A.M.

Researchers have discovered that the change from day to night is monitored by the **suprachiasmatic nucleus (SCN),** a small structure in the brain that synchronizes its own rhythm with the daily cycle of light and dark based on input from the retina (Michel & others, 2006). Output from the SCN allows the hypothalamus to regulate daily rhythms such as temperature and hunger and the reticular formation to regulate daily rhythms of sleep and wakefulness (Figure 6.2). Although a number of biological clocks or pacemakers seem to be involved in regulating circadian rhythms, researchers have found that the SCN is the most important one (Buijs & others, 2006).

Many individuals who are totally blind experience lifelong sleeping problems because their retinas are unable to detect light. These people have a kind of permanent jet lag and periodic insomnia because their circadian rhythms often do not follow a 24-hour cycle (National Institute of Neurological Disorders and Stroke, 2001).

Desynchronizing the Biological Clock Biological clocks can become desynchronized, or thrown off their regular schedules. Among the circumstances of modern life that can introduce irregularities into our sleep are jet travel, changing work shifts, and insomnia. What effects might such irregularities have on circadian rhythms?

If you fly from Los Angeles to New York and then go to bed at 11 P.M. eastern time, you may have trouble

biological rhythms Periodic physiological fluctuations in the body.

circadian rhythm A daily behavioral or physiological cycle, such as the sleep/wake cycle.

suprachiasmatic nucleus (SCN) A small structure in the brain that synchronizes its own rhythm with the daily cycle of light and dark based on input from the retina.

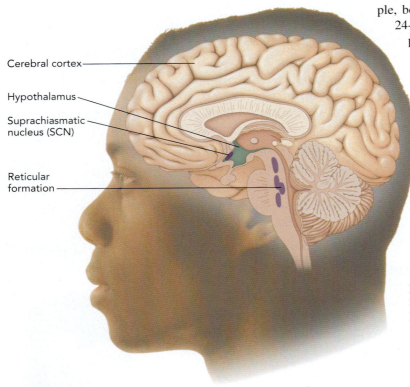

Cerebral cortex

Hypothalamus

Suprachiasmatic nucleus (SCN)

Reticular formation

FIGURE 6.2

Suprachiasmatic Nucleus The suprachiasmatic nucleus (SCN) plays an important role in keeping our biological clock running on time. The SCN is located in the hypothalamus. It receives information from the retina about light, which is the external stimulus that synchronizes the SCN. Output from the SCN is distributed to the rest of the hypothalamus and to the reticular formation.

Traveling by jet across a number of time zones and changing to a night-shift job can desynchronize our biological clocks and can affect our circadian rhythms and performance. Sleep deprivation has negative implications for academic performance.

falling asleep because your body is still on west coast time. Even if you sleep for 8 hours that night, you may have a hard time waking up at 7 A.M. eastern time, because your body thinks it is 4 A.M. If you stay in New York for several days, your body will adjust to this new schedule.

The jet lag you experience when you fly from Los Angeles to New York occurs because your body time is out of phase, or synchronization, with clock time (Lack & Wright, 2007). Jet lag is the result of two or more body rhythms being out of sync. You usually go to bed when your body temperature begins to drop, but in your new location, you might be trying to go to sleep when it is rising. In the morning, your adrenal glands release large doses of the hormone *cortisol* to help you wake up. In your new geographic time zone, the glands may be releasing this chemical just as you are getting ready for bed at night.

Circadian rhythms may also become desynchronized when shift workers change their work hours (Lee, Smith, & Eastman, 2006). A number of near accidents in air travel have been associated with pilots who have not yet become synchronized to their new shifts and are not working as efficiently as usual (Kim & Lee, 2007).

Shift-work problems most often affect night-shift workers who never fully adjust to sleeping in the daytime after their work shifts. Such workers may fall asleep at work and are at increased risk for heart disease and gastrointestinal disorders (Fujino & others, 2006). But not all shift workers are affected equally (Monk, 1993). Individuals older than 50, those who require more than 9 hours of sleep a night, and those with a tendency to be "morning types" (get up early, go to bed early) are the most adversely affected by shift work.

Resetting the Biological Clock   If your biological clock for sleeping and waking becomes desynchronized, how can you reset it? With regard to jet lag, if you take a transoceanic flight and arrive at your destination during the day, it is a good idea to spend as much time outside in the daylight as possible. Bright light during the day, especially in the morning, increases wakefulness, whereas bright light at night delays sleep (Oren & Terman, 1998).

Melatonin, a hormone that increases at night in humans, also is being studied for its possible effects in reducing jet lag (Pandi-Perumal & others, 2007). Recent studies have shown that a small dosage of melatonin can reduce jet lag by advancing the circadian clock, which makes it useful for eastward jet lag but not westward jet lag (Waterhouse & others, 2007).

Why Do We Need Sleep?

Everyone sleeps, and when we do not get enough sleep, we often do not function well, physically and mentally. The important benefits of sleep include restoration, adaptation, growth, and memory.

Because all animals require sleep, it seems that sleep is a fundamental mechanism for survival. Examining the evolutionary basis for sleep, scientists have proposed that sleep restores, replenishes, and rebuilds our brains and bodies, which can become worn out or used up by the day's waking activities. This idea fits with the feeling of being worn out or tired before we go to sleep and restored when we wake up.

In support of the restorative function of sleep, many of the body's cells show increased production and reduced breakdown of proteins during deep sleep (National Institute of Neurological Disorders and Stroke, 2001). Protein molecules are the building blocks needed for cell growth and for repair of damages from factors such as stress. Also, some neuroscientists believe that sleep gives neurons that are used while we are awake a chance to shut down and repair themselves (National Institute of Neurological Disorders and Stroke, 2001). Without sleep, neurons might become so depleted in energy or so polluted by the by-products of cellular activity that they begin to malfunction.

In addition to having a restorative function, sleep has had an adaptive evolutionary function. Sleep may have developed because animals needed to protect themselves. For example, for some animals the search for food and water is easier and safer when the sun is up. When it is dark, it is adaptive for these animals to save energy, prevent getting eaten, and avoid falling off a cliff that they cannot see. In general, animals that serve as food for other animals sleep the least. Figure 6.3 portrays the average amount of sleep per day of various animals.

Sleep also may be beneficial to physical growth and increased brain development in infants and children. For example, deep sleep coincides with the release of growth hormone in children (National Institute of Neurological Disorders and Stroke, 2001). The lack of sleep is stressful, and stress hormones may interfere with the creation of neurons in the hippocampus: the part of the brain most associated with memory (Mirescu & others, 2006).

In fact, the important role of sleep in the consolidation, storage, and maintenance of long-term memory is now recognized (Born, Rasch, & Gais, 2006; Walker & Stickgold, 2006). One possible explanation is that during sleep the cerebral cortex is not busy with the processing of sensory input, active awareness, and motor functions. Therefore, it is free to conduct activities that strengthen memory associations, so that memories formed during recent waking hours can be integrated into long-term memory storage.

Are you thinking about studying all night for the next test in one of your classes? You might want to think again. In one study, a good night's sleep helped the brain to store the memory of what had been learned during the day (Stickgold & Hobson, 2000). In the study, the memory of individuals who stayed up all night for one of the nights during the study was inferior to the memory of individuals who got a good night's sleep every night during the study. Lost sleep often results in lost memories (Kalia, 2006).

The Effects of Chronic Sleep Deprivation Testing the limits of his capacity to function without sleep, one 17-year-old high school student, Randy Gardner, went without sleep for 264 hours (about 11 days), the longest observed period of total sleep deprivation. He did it as part of a science fair project (Dement, 1978). Randy, who was carefully monitored by sleep researchers, did suffer some hallucinations, as well as speech and movement problems. However, on the last night, Randy played arcade games with sleep researcher William Dement and consistently beat him. Randy recovered fully, as well as could be detected, after a 14-hour, 40-minute restorative sleep. Randy's story is exceptional in that he was able to maintain a high level of physical activity and in that he received national TV coverage, which helped him to stay awake. Even so, he almost fell asleep several times, but his observers

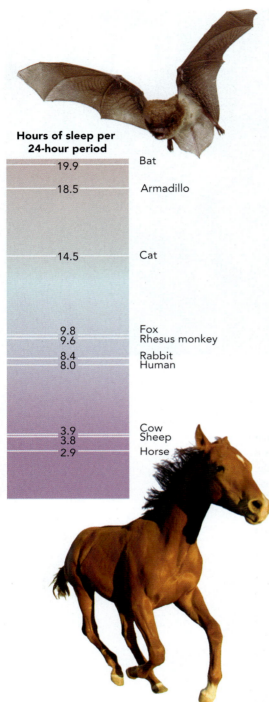

Hours of sleep per 24-hour period

19.9	Bat
18.5	Armadillo
14.5	Cat
9.8	Fox
9.6	Rhesus monkey
8.4	Rabbit
8.0	Human
3.9	Cow
3.8	Sheep
2.9	Horse

FIGURE 6.3

From Bats to Horses: The Wide Range of Sleep in Animals We might feel envious of bats, which sleep nearly 20 hours a day, and more than a little in awe of horses, still running on just under 3 hours of rest.

would not let him close his eyes. Under more normal circumstances, individuals have far more difficulty staying awake all night, especially between 3 A.M. and 6 A.M.

Although Randy Gardner went about 11 days without sleep, the following discussion should convince you that even getting 60 to 90 minutes less sleep than you need at night can harm your ability to perform optimally the next day. Optimal performance is enhanced by sleeping more than 8 hours a night and reduced by sleeping less (Habeck & others, 2004). Lack of sleep is stressful and has impact on our bodies (Goh & others, 2001) and, of course, our brains. For example, in one study, brain scans showed that sleep deprivation decreased brain activity in the thalamus and the prefrontal cortex (Thomas & others, 2001). Alertness and cognitive performance declined, along with brain activity. In another study, sleep deprivation was linked with an inability to sustain attention (Doran, Van Dongen, & Dinges, 2001). Research using EEGs of individuals deprived of sleep for 24 hours revealed a decline in the complexity of brain activity (Jeong & others, 2001). Research using fMRI has shown that when deprived of sleep, the brain must compensate by using other pathways for cognitive work (Drummond & others, 2005) and that interactions among areas of the brain differ during problem solving 0 (Stricker & others, 2006).

Sleep deprivation also can affect decision making, especially dealing with the unexpected, innovation, revising plans, and effective communication (Harrison & Horne, 2000). Sleep can also influence moral judgment. A recent study demonstrated that following 53 hours of wakefulness, participants had more difficulty making moral decisions and were more likely to agree with decisions that violated their personal standards (Killgore & others, 2007).

Sleep, then, is key to optimal performance, both physically and mentally. Yet, many of us do not get sufficient sleep. In a national survey of more than 1,000 American adults conducted by the National Sleep Foundation (2001), 63 percent said that they get less than 8 hours of sleep a night, and 31 percent said that they get less than 7 hours of sleep a night. Many said they try to catch up on their sleep on the weekend, but they still reported getting less than 8 hours on weekend nights. Forty percent of those surveyed said that they become so sleepy during the day that their work suffers at least a few days per month, and 22 percent said their work suffers a few days each week. Seven percent said sleepiness on the job is a daily problem for them. It is estimated that 50 to 70 million Americans chronically suffer from lack of sleep or a sleep disorder (Institute of Medicine, 2006). The Institute of Medicine declared that sleep deprivation is an unmet health problem in the United States (2006).

Why are Americans getting too little sleep? Work pressures, school pressures, family obligations, and social obligations often lead to long hours of wakefulness and irregular sleep/wake schedules (Kiernan & others, 2006). Not having enough hours to do all we want to do in a day, we cheat on our sleep. Most people need to get 60 to 90 minutes more sleep each night than they presently get.

Sleep Deprivation in Adolescents and Older Adults

Might changing sleep patterns in adolescence contribute to adolescents' health-compromising behaviors? Recently there has been a surge of interest in adolescent sleep patterns (Carskadon, 2005, 2006; Carskadon, Mindell, & Drake, 2006; Crowley, Acebo, & Carskadon, 2007; Dahl, 2006).

The National Sleep Foundation (2006) conducted a U.S. survey of 1,602 caregivers and their 11- to 17-year-olds. Forty-five percent of the adolescents got inadequate sleep on school nights (less than 8 hours). Older adolescents (ninth- to twelfth-graders) got markedly less sleep on school nights than younger adolescents (sixth- to eighth-graders)—specifically, 62 percent of the older adolescents got inadequate sleep compared to 21 percent of the younger adolescents. Adolescents who got inadequate sleep (8 hours or less) on school nights were more likely to feel more tired or sleepy, and more cranky and irritable; to fall asleep in school; to be in a depressed mood; and to drink caffeinated beverages than their counterparts who got optimal sleep (9 or more hours).

Many adolescents stay up later at night and sleep longer in the morning than they did when they were children, and this changing timetable has physiological underpinnings.

Sleep researchers record Randy Gardner's (he's the person doing push-ups) behavior during his 264-hour period of sleep deprivation. Most people who try to stay up even one night have difficulty remaining awake from 3 A.M. to 6 A.M.

Isabella Bannerman. King Features Syndicate.

Developmental changes in sleep patterns during adolescence can influence alertness at school.

These findings have implications for the hours during which adolescents learn most effectively in school (Carskadon, Mindell, & Drake, 2006; Hansen & others, 2005).

Mary Carskadon and her colleagues have conducted a number of research studies on adolescent sleep patterns (Carskadon, 2005, 2006; Carskadon, Acebo, & Jenni, 2004; Carskadon, Mindell, & Drake, 2006). They found that when given the opportunity, adolescents will sleep an average of 9 hours and 25 minutes a night. Most get considerably less than 9 hours of sleep, especially during the week. This shortfall creates a sleep deficit, which adolescents often attempt to make up on the weekend. The researchers also found that older adolescents tend to be sleepier during the day than younger adolescents. They theorized that this sleepiness was not due to academic work or social pressures. Rather, their research suggests that adolescents' biological clocks undergo a shift as they get older, delaying their period of wakefulness by about 1 hour. A delay in the nightly release of the sleep-inducing hormone melatonin, produced in the brain's pineal gland, seems to underlie this shift. Melatonin is secreted at about 9:30 P.M. in younger adolescents and approximately an hour later in older adolescents.

Carskadon has suggested that early school starting times may cause grogginess, inattention in class, and poor performance on tests. Based on her research, school officials in Edina, Minnesota, decided to start classes at 8:30 A.M. rather than the usual 7:25 A.M. Since then there have been fewer referrals for discipline problems, and the number of students who report being ill or depressed has decreased. The school system reports that test scores have improved for high school students, but not for middle school students. This finding supports Carskadon's suspicion that early start times are likely to be more stressful for older than for younger adolescents.

Sleep patterns also change as people age through the middle-adult (40s and 50s) and late-adult (60s and older) years (Ancoli-Israel, 2006; Dijk, 2006). Many adults go to bed earlier at night and wake up earlier in the morning. Thus, a clear reversal occurs in the time at which individuals go to bed—later to bed as adolescents, earlier to bed in middle age. Beginning in the 40s, individuals report that they are less likely to sleep through the entire night than when they were younger. Middle-aged adults also spend less time in the deepest sleep stage than when they were younger. More than 50 percent of individuals in late adulthood report that they experience some degree of insomnia (Kamel & Gammack, 2006; Wolkove & others, 2007).

Think about your own sleep patterns. Are you getting enough sleep? See the Psychology and Life box.

Sleep Stages

Have you ever been awakened from your sleep and been totally disoriented? Have you ever awakened in the middle of a dream and gone right back into the dream as if it were a movie running just under the surface of your consciousness? These two circumstances reflect two distinct stages in the sleep cycle.

Stages of sleep correspond to massive electrophysiological changes that occur throughout the brain as the fast, irregular, and low-amplitude electrical activity of wakefulness is replaced by the slow, regular, high-amplitude waves of deep sleep. Using the electroencephalograph (EEG) to monitor the brain's electrical activity, scientists have discovered five distinct stages of sleep and two stages of wakefulness.

When people are awake, their EEG patterns exhibit two types of waves: beta and alpha. *Beta waves* reflect wakefulness. These waves are the highest in frequency and lowest in amplitude. They also are more *desynchronous* than other waves. Desynchronous waves do not form a very consistent pattern. Inconsistent patterning makes sense, given the

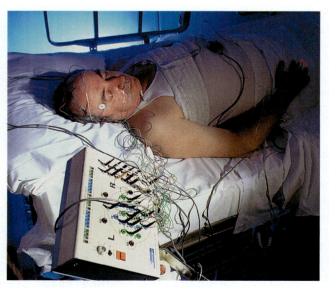

An individual being monitored by an EEG in a sleep experiment.

PSYCHOLOGY AND LIFE

Do You Get Enough Sleep?

Some people seem to take a "do it all" approach to life, pushing and pushing themselves without listening to what their body is telling them about its level of exhaustion (Aziz & Zickar, 2006). In fact, no amount of motivation is going to overcome the physical limits of our bodies. Sleep is an essential restorative element in a healthy life (Zheng & others, 2006).

Imagine how differently such people might view their lifestyle if insufficient sleep had consequences for their interactions with others. Think about it in personal terms: You would not stop brushing your teeth, because you would not want to have bad breath. You would not avoid showering for days on end, because your physical state would be socially unacceptable. What if tired people started to have bad breath or smell funky? Consider how much more support the world might provide for the occasional nap! Even though people generally do not smell bad when they are tired, they owe it to themselves to sleep when sleep is needed. The brain is a remarkable organ, capable of doing an awful lot for us, but it cannot work its best magic without reasonable time for refueling.

Many college students do not get enough sleep (Brown, Buboltz, & Soper, 2006). To evaluate whether you are sleep-deprived, place a check mark next to the following items.

Yes	No	
____	____	I need an alarm clock to wake up at the appropriate time.
____	____	It is a struggle for me to get out of bed in the morning.
____	____	I feel tired, irritable, and stressed out during the week.
____	____	I have trouble concentrating.
____	____	I have trouble remembering.
____	____	I feel slow with critical thinking, problem solving, and being creative.
____	____	I often fall asleep watching TV.
____	____	I often fall asleep in boring meetings or lectures in warm rooms.
____	____	I often fall asleep after heavy meals or after low doses of alcohol.
____	____	I often fall asleep within 5 minutes of getting into bed.
____	____	I often feel drowsy while driving.
____	____	I often sleep extra hours on weekend mornings.
____	____	I often need a nap to get through the day.
____	____	I have dark circles around my eyes.

According to sleep expert James Maas (1998), who developed this quiz, if you responded "yes" to three or more of these items, you probably are not getting enough sleep.

If you are not getting enough sleep, the following behavioral strategies for what sleep experts call "good sleep hygiene" might help you:

1. Reduce stress as much as possible.
2. Exercise regularly, but not just before you go to bed.
3. Keep mentally stimulated during the day.
4. Become a good time manager.
5. Eat a proper diet.
6. Stop smoking.
7. Reduce caffeine intake, especially in the afternoon.
8. Avoid alcohol, especially near bedtime.
9. Take a warm bath before bed.

(continued)

10. Maintain a relaxing atmosphere in the bedroom and keep the temperature cool.

11. Clear your mind at bedtime.

12. Before going to bed, use a relaxation technique, such as listening to a CD designed for relaxation.

13. Learn to value sleep.

14. Go to bed and wake up at the same time every day, even on weekends.

15. If necessary, contact the health service at your college or university for advice about your sleeping problem.

extensive variation in sensory input and activities we experience when we are awake. When we are relaxed but still awake, our brain waves slow down, increase in amplitude, and become more *synchronous,* or regular. These waves are called *alpha waves.* The five stages of sleep are differentiated by the types of wave patterns detected with an EEG, and the depth of sleep varies from one stage to another.

Stages 1–4 *Stage 1 sleep* is characterized by *theta waves,* which are even slower in frequency and greater in amplitude than alpha waves. The difference between just being relaxed and stage 1 sleep is gradual. Figure 6.4 shows the EEG pattern of stage 1 sleep, along with the EEG patterns for the other four sleep stages and beta and alpha waves.

In *stage 2 sleep,* theta waves continue but are interspersed with a defining characteristic of stage 2 sleep: *sleep spindles.* These involve a sudden increase in wave frequency (Fogel & Smith, 2006). Stages 1 and 2 are both relatively light stages of sleep, and if people awaken during one of these stages, they often report not having been asleep at all.

Stage 3 and *stage 4 sleep* are characterized by *delta waves,* the slowest and highest-amplitude brain waves during sleep. These two stages are often referred to as *delta sleep.* Distinguishing between stage 3 and stage 4 is difficult, although typically stage 3 is characterized by delta waves occurring less than 50 percent of the time and stage 4 by delta waves occurring more than 50 percent of the time. Delta sleep is our deepest sleep, the time when our brain waves are least like waking brain waves. It is during delta sleep that it is the most difficult to wake sleepers. When they are awakened during this stage, they usually are confused and disoriented.

REM sleep Rapid eye movement sleep; stage 5 of sleep, in which dreaming occurs.

REM Sleep After going through stages 1–4, sleepers drift up through the sleep stages toward wakefulness. But instead of reentering stage 1, they enter *stage 5,* a different form of sleep called *REM (rapid eye movement) sleep* (Dan & Boyd, 2006). **REM sleep** is an active stage of sleep during which dreaming occurs. During REM sleep, the EEG pattern shows fast waves similar to those of relaxed wakefulness, and the sleeper's eyeballs move up and down and from left to right (Figure 6.5).

Stages 1–4 are referred to as *non-REM sleep.* Non-REM sleep is characterized by a lack of rapid eye movement and little dreaming. A person who is awakened during REM sleep is more likely to report having dreamed than when awakened at any other stage (Ogawa, Nittono, & Hori, 2005). Even people who claim they rarely dream frequently report dreaming when they are awakened during REM sleep. The longer the period of REM sleep, the more likely it is that the person will report dreaming. Dreams also occur during slow-wave or non-REM sleep, but the frequency of dreams in these stages is relatively low (Takeuchi & others, 2001). Reports of dreaming by individuals awakened from REM sleep are typically longer, more vivid, more motorically animated, more emotionally charged, and less related to waking life than reports by those awakened from non-REM sleep (Hobson, 2004).

FIGURE 6.4

Characteristics and Formats of EEG Recordings During Stages of Sleep Even while we are sleeping, our brains are busy. No wonder we sometimes wake up feeling tired.

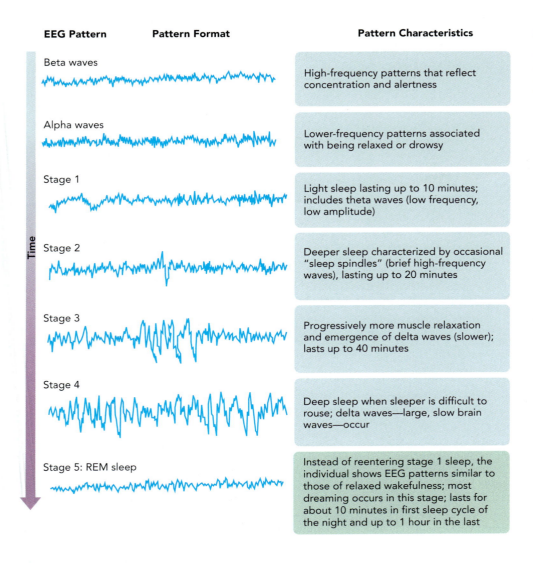

EEG Pattern	Pattern Format	Pattern Characteristics
Beta waves		High-frequency patterns that reflect concentration and alertness
Alpha waves		Lower-frequency patterns associated with being relaxed or drowsy
Stage 1		Light sleep lasting up to 10 minutes; includes theta waves (low frequency, low amplitude)
Stage 2		Deeper sleep characterized by occasional "sleep spindles" (brief high-frequency waves), lasting up to 20 minutes
Stage 3		Progressively more muscle relaxation and emergence of delta waves (slower); lasts up to 40 minutes
Stage 4		Deep sleep when sleeper is difficult to rouse; delta waves—large, slow brain waves—occur
Stage 5: REM sleep		Instead of reentering stage 1 sleep, the individual shows EEG patterns similar to those of relaxed wakefulness; most dreaming occurs in this stage; lasts for about 10 minutes in first sleep cycle of the night and up to 1 hour in the last

The amount of time we spend in REM sleep changes over the life span. As shown in Figure 6.6, the percentage of total sleep during a 24-hour period that consists of REM sleep is especially large during early infancy (almost 8 hours). Older adults experience less than 1 hour of REM sleep per 24-hour period. Figure 6.6 also reveals how the total amount of sleep changes from approximately 16 hours per 24-hour period for young infants to less than 6 hours for older adults.

These dramatic changes in sleep, especially REM sleep, raise questions about the function of sleep. For young infants, REM sleep may be nature's way of stimulating the brain and contributing to its growth.

REM sleep also likely plays a role in memory (Cipolli & others, 2006). Researchers have presented individuals with unique phrases before they go to bed. When they are awakened just before they begin REM sleep, they remember less the next morning than when they are awakened during the other sleep stages (Stickgold & Walker, 2005).

Sleep Cycling Through the Night   The five stages of sleep described here make up a normal cycle of sleep. As shown in Figure 6.7, one of these cycles lasts about 90 to 100 minutes and recurs several times during the night. The amount of deep sleep (stages 3 and 4) is much greater in the first half of a night's sleep than in the second half. Most REM sleep takes place toward the end of a night's sleep, when the REM stage becomes progressively longer. The night's first REM stage might last for only 10 minutes, and the final REM stage might continue for as long as an hour. During a normal night of sleep, individuals will

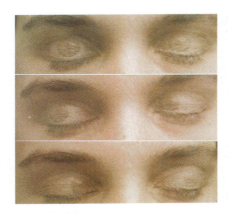

FIGURE 6.5

REM Sleep During REM sleep, your eyes move rapidly, as if following the images moving in your dreams.

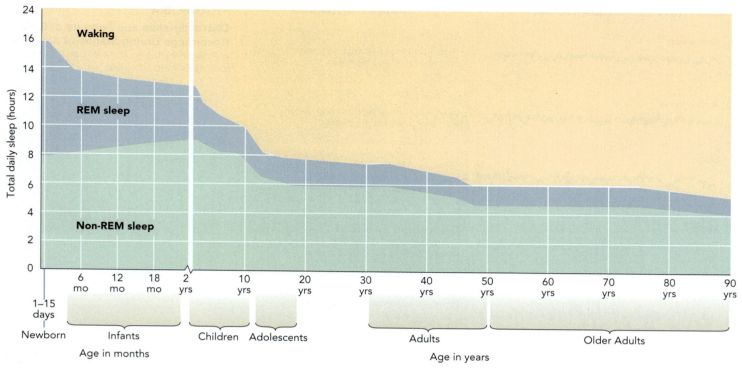

FIGURE 6.6

Sleep Across the Human Life Span With age, human beings require less sleep.

spend about 60 percent of sleep in light sleep (stages 1 and 2), 20 percent in delta or deep sleep, and 20 percent in REM sleep (Webb, 2000).

Sleep and the Brain The five sleep stages are associated with distinct patterns of neurotransmitter activity initiated in the reticular formation, the core of the brain stem. In all vertebrates, the reticular formation plays a crucial role in sleep and arousal (see Figure 6.2). As previously noted, damage to the reticular formation can result in coma and death.

Three important neurotransmitters involved in sleep are serotonin, epinephrine, and acetylcholine (Kalia, 2006). As sleep begins, the levels of neurotransmitters sent to the forebrain from the reticular formation start dropping, and they continue to fall until they reach their lowest levels during the deepest sleep stage—stage 4. REM sleep (stage 5) is initiated by a rise in acetylcholine, which activates the cerebral cortex while the rest of the brain remains relatively inactive. REM sleep is terminated by a rise in serotonin and norepinephrine, which increase the level of forebrain activity nearly to the awakened state (Miller & O'Callaghan, 2006). You are most likely to wake up just after a REM period. If you do not wake up then, the level of the neurotransmitters begins to fall again, and you enter another sleep cycle.

Another neurotransmitter associated with sleep is adenosine (Landolt & others, 2004). Adenosine builds up during our waking hours. At night, adenosine deaminase (or ADA) breaks down the adenosine, during slow-wave sleep. Caffeine stops adenosine from binding with receptors—and if the adenosine does not bind, you cannot fall asleep (Salin-Pascual & others, 2006).

FIGURE 6.7

Cycling Through a Night's Sleep During a night's sleep, we go through several cycles. Depth of sleep decreases and REM sleep (shown in light blue) increases as the night progresses. In this graph, the person is depicted as awakening at about 5 A.M. and then going back to sleep for another hour.

Sleep and Disease

Sleep plays a role in a large number of diseases and disorders (Costa & Silva, 2006). For example, stroke and asthma attacks are more common during the night and in the early morning, probably because of changes in hormones, heart rate, and other characteristics associated with sleep (Teodorescu & others, 2006). Sleeplessness is also associated with obesity and heart disease (Plante, 2006).

Neurons that control sleep interact closely with the immune system (Lange & others, 2006). As anyone who has had the flu knows, infectious diseases make us sleepy. The probable reason is that chemicals called *cytokines,* produced by the body's cells while we are fighting an infection, are powerful sleep-inducing chemicals (Opp, 2006). Sleep may help the body conserve energy and other resources that the body needs to overcome infection (Irwin & others, 2006).

Sleep problems afflict most people who have mental disorders, including those with depression (Agargun & others, 2006). Individuals with depression often awaken in the early hours of the morning and cannot get back to sleep, and they often spend less time in delta wave or deep sleep than do non-depressed individuals.

Sleep problems are common in many other disorders as well, including Alzheimer disease, stroke, and cancer (McEwen, 2006; Wu & Swaab, 2007). In some cases, however, these problems may be due not to the disease itself but to the drugs used to treat the disease.

Sleep Disorders

Many individuals suffer from undiagnosed and untreated sleep disorders that leave them struggling through the day, feeling unmotivated and exhausted (Culpepper, 2005; Ekstedt & others, 2006). Some of the major sleep problems are insomnia, sleepwalking and sleep talking, nightmares and night terrors, narcolepsy, and sleep apnea.

Insomnia   A common sleep problem is *insomnia,* the inability to sleep. Insomnia can involve a problem in falling asleep, waking up during the night, or waking up too early. In the United States, as many as one in five adults have insomnia (Pearson, Johnson, & Nahin, 2006). It is more common among women and older adults, as well as individuals who are thin, stressed, or depressed (Johnson, Roth, & Breslau, 2006). Women are more likely to suffer from insomnia than men, for a variety of factors, including iron deficiencies and hormonal changes (Kotani & others, 2007; Lee, 2006; Sanford & others, 2006). The National Sleep Foundation found that over 70 percent of women from all walks of life (stay-at-home moms, single mothers, working mothers, and so on) reported experiencing sleep problems (2007).

For short-term insomnia, most physicians prescribe sleeping pills (Becker, 2005). However, most sleeping pills stop working after several weeks of nightly use, and their long-term use can interfere with good sleep. Mild insomnia often can be reduced by simply practicing good sleep habits. In more serious cases, researchers are experimenting with light therapy, melatonin supplements, and other ways to alter circadian cycles (Cohen, 2002; Revell & Eastman, 2005). Also, in one study, behavioral changes helped insomniacs to increase their sleep time and to awaken less frequently in the night (Edinger & others, 2001). In this study, insomniacs were restricted from taking a nap during the day, and they were required to set an alarm and to force themselves to get out of bed in the morning. Thus, the longer they stayed awake during the day, the better they were able to sleep at night.

Sleepwalking and Sleep Talking   *Somnambulism* is the formal term for sleepwalking, which occurs during the deepest stages of sleep (Guilleminault & others, 2006). For many years, experts believed that somnambulists were just acting out their dreams. But somnambulism occurs during stages 3 and 4, usually early in the night, when a person is unlikely to be dreaming. There is nothing really abnormal about sleepwalking. Despite superstition, it is safe to awaken sleepwalkers; in fact, they probably should be awakened, as they may harm themselves wandering around in the dark (Swanson, 1999).

Another quirky night behavior is sleep talking (Hublin & others, 2001). If you interrogate sleep talkers, can you find out what they did, for instance, last Thursday night? Probably not. Although sleep talkers will converse with you and make fairly coherent statements, they are soundly asleep. Thus, even if a sleep talker mumbles a response to your question, do not count on its accuracy.

"I probably shouldn't wake him. He needs the exercise."

Recently, a few cases of an even rarer sleep behavior have come to light—sleep eating. Ambien is a widely prescribed sleep medication for insomnia. Some Ambien users began to notice odd things upon waking up from a much-needed good night's sleep: candy wrappers strewn around the room, crumbs in the bed, and food missing from the refrigerator. One woman gained 100 pounds without changing her waking, eating, or exercise habits. How could this be? Dr. Mark Mahowald, the medical director of the Minnesota Regional Sleep Disorders Center in Minneapolis, has confirmed that sleep eating may be a side effect of using Ambien (CBS News, 2006). The phenomenon of sleep eating highlights the fact that even when we feel fast asleep, we may be "half awake"—and capable of putting together some unusual late-night snacks, including buttered cigarettes, salt sandwiches, and raw bacon! The maker of Ambien has noted this unusual side effect on the label of the drug. Even more alarming than sleep eating may be recent reports of sleep driving under the influence of Ambien (Saul, 2006). Sleep experts agree that reports of sleep driving while taking Ambien are rare and extreme but are plausible, nonetheless.

Of course, no one should abruptly stop taking any medication without talking to his or her doctor. For individuals who are battling persistent insomnia, a drug that permits them to have a good night's rest may be worth the risk of these unusual side effects.

Nightmares and Night Terrors A *nightmare* is a frightening dream that awakens a dreamer from REM sleep (Zadra, Pilon, & Donderi, 2006). The nightmare's content invariably involves danger—the dreamer is chased, robbed, raped, murdered, or thrown off a cliff. Nightmares are common. Most of us have had them, especially as young children. Nightmares peak at 3 to 6 years of age and then decline, although the average college student experiences four to eight nightmares a year (Hartmann, 1993). Reported increases in nightmares or worsening nightmares are often associated with an increase in life stressors such as the loss of a relative or a job, conflicts, and other negative events.

A *night terror* is characterized by sudden arousal from sleep and intense fear. Night terrors are accompanied by a number of physiological reactions, such as rapid heart rate and breathing, loud screams, heavy perspiration, and movement (Mason & Pack, 2005). Night terrors are less common than nightmares. Unlike nightmares, night terrors occur during slow-wave, non-REM sleep. Night terrors peak at 5 to 7 years of age and decline thereafter.

Narcolepsy The overpowering urge to sleep is called *narcolepsy*. The urge is so strong that the person may fall asleep while talking or standing up. Narcoleptics immediately enter REM sleep rather than progressing through the first four sleep stages (Stores, Montgomery, & Wiggs, 2006). Researchers suspect that narcolepsy is inherited. Treatment usually involves counseling to discover potential causes of the excessive sleepiness (Morrish & others, 2004).

Sleep Apnea *Sleep apnea* is a sleep disorder in which individuals stop breathing because the windpipe fails to open or because brain processes involved in respiration fail to work properly. People with sleep apnea experience numerous brief awakenings during the night so that they can breathe better, although they usually are not aware of their awakened state. During the day, these people may feel sleepy because they were deprived of sleep at night. A common sign of sleep apnea is loud snoring, punctuated by silence (the apnea).

According to the American Sleep Apnea Association (ASAA), sleep apnea affects approximately 12 million Americans (ASAA, 2006). Sleep apnea is most common among infants and adults over the age of 65. Sleep apnea also occurs more frequently among obese individuals, men, and individuals with large necks and recessed chins (ASAA, 2006; Scott & others, 2006). Untreated sleep apnea can cause high blood pressure, stroke, and impotence. In addition, the daytime sleepiness it causes can result in accidents, lost productivity, and relationship problems (Hartenbaum & others, 2006).

Dreams

Have you ever had a dream in which you had a fight with someone, and then woken up still angry at the person? Have you had a dream in which you left your long-term romantic

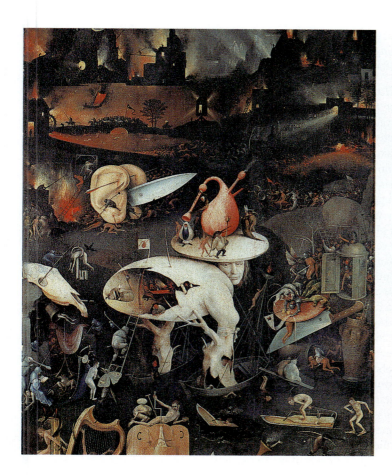 

FIGURE 6.8

Artists' Portrayals of Dreams Through the centuries, artists have been adept at capturing the enchanting or nightmarish characteristics of our dreams. (*Left*) Dutch painter Hieronymus Bosch (1450–1516) captured both the enchanting and the frightening world of dreams in *Garden of Earthly Delights*. (*Right*) Marc Chagall painted a world of dreams in *I and the Village*.

partner for a former flame? Would you tell your partner about that dream? Probably not. But you would likely wonder about the dream's meaning. The idea that dreams "mean" something has been with us for a very long time.

Ever since the dawn of language, human beings have imbued dreams with historical, personal, and religious significance. As early as 5000 B.C.E., Babylonians recorded and interpreted their dreams on clay tablets. Egyptians built temples in honor of Serapis, the god of dreams. Dreams are described at length in more than 70 passages in the Bible. Sigmund Freud put great stock in dreams as a key to our unconscious minds. He believed that dreams symbolize unconscious wishes, and that by analyzing dream symbols we could discover our hidden desires. Artists have sometimes incorporated the symbolic world of dreaming in their work (Figure 6.8). Because dreams are written in the mind with little or no conscious participation, it is difficult to unravel their mysteries. The most prominent theories that attempt to explain dreams are cognitive theory and activation-synthesis theory.

Subconscious Cognitive Processing

The **cognitive theory of dreaming** proposes that dreaming can be understood by applying the same cognitive concepts that are used in studying the waking mind. That is, dreaming involves information processing, memory, and problem solving. In the cognitive theory of dreaming, there is little or no search for the hidden, symbolic content of dreams that Freud sought (Foulkes, 1993, 1999).

From this perspective, dreams might be a mental realm in which we can solve problems and think creatively. For example, the Scottish author Robert Louis Stevenson (1850–1894) claimed that he got the idea for his story about Dr. Jekyll and Mr. Hyde in a dream. Elias Howe, attempting to invent a machine that sewed, reportedly dreamed that he was captured by savages carrying spears with holes in their tips. On waking, he realized that he should place the hole for the thread at the end of the needle, not in the middle. Dreams may spark such gifts of inspiration because, in unique and creative ways, they weave together current experiences with the past.

cognitive theory of dreaming Theory proposing that dreaming can be understood by applying the same cognitive concepts that are used in studying the waking mind.

activation-synthesis theory Theory stating that dreaming occurs when the cerebral cortex synthesizes neural signals generated from activity in the lower part of the brain.

Criticisms of the cognitive theory of dreaming focus on skepticism about the ability to resolve problems during sleep and the lack of attention to the roles of brain structures and activity in dreaming, the main emphasis of the activation-synthesis theory of dreams.

Finding Logic in Random Brain Activity **Activation-synthesis theory** states that dreaming occurs when the cerebral cortex synthesizes neural signals generated from activity in the lower part of the brain. In this view, dreams reflect the brain's efforts to make sense out of neural activity that takes place during sleep (Hobson, 1999).

When we are awake and alert, the contents of our conscious experience tend to be driven by external stimuli that result in specific motor behavior. During sleep, according to activation-synthesis theory, conscious experience is driven by internally generated stimuli that have no apparent behavioral consequence. You may have noticed how internal states influence your dreams if you have ever been very thirsty while sleeping and dream that you get a glass of water. A key source of internal stimulation is spontaneous neural activity in the reticular formation of the limbic system (Hobson, 2000).

Proponents of activation-synthesis theory have suggested that neural networks in other areas of the forebrain play a key role in dreaming (Hobson, Pace-Schott, & Stickgold, 2000). Specifically, they believe that the same regions of the forebrain that are involved in certain waking behaviors also function in particular aspects of dreaming (Lu & others, 2006). Thus, the primary motor and sensory areas of the forebrain would be activated in the sensorimotor aspects of the dream; the parietal lobe would be activated in the spatial organization of the dream; the visual aspects of the dream in the visual association cortex; the amygdala, hippocampus, and frontal lobe would be activated in the emotional aspects of a dream; and so on.

The sudden, uncoordinated eye movements of REM sleep make the dream world move in odd ways. For instance, a dream might include magic carpets flying over an undulating landscape. Dreams tend to truncate, dissolve, or shift suddenly in midstream. Freud explained this phenomenon as the dreamer's attempt to elude the unpleasant and the taboo. Activation-synthesis theorists say that this shifting is due to normal cycles of neural activation (Hobson, 2000, 2004). As levels of neurotransmitters rise and fall during the stages of sleep, some neural networks are activated, and others shut down. As a new cycle is activated, a new dream landscape emerges. In sum, in the activation-synthesis view, dreams are merely a glitzy sideshow, not the main event (Hooper & Teresi, 1993).

Like all dream theories, activation-synthesis theory has its critics. Among their criticisms are the beliefs that the brain stem is not the only starting point for neural activity in dreaming and that life experiences stimulate and shape dreaming more than activation-synthesis theory acknowledges (Domhoff, 2001).

REVIEW, ASSESS, AND SHARPEN YOUR THINKING

Review

2 Explain the nature of sleep and dreams.
- Describe the relationship between biological rhythms and sleep.
- Summarize the benefits of sleep and the effects of sleep deprivation.
- Describe the five stages of sleep and changes in the level of activity in the brain during sleep.
- Explain the links between sleep and disease.
- Name and describe five types of sleep disorders.
- Understand the nature of dreams, including theories of why people dream.

Assess

1. Which brain structure is most responsible for regulating circadian rhythms?
   A. cerebral cortex
   B. hypothalamus
   C. reticular formation
   D. suprachiasmatic nucleus

2. The release of a large amount of which hormone is implicated in waking up from sleep?
   A. epinephrine
   B. norepinephrine
   C. androgen
   D. cortisol

3. **Which of the following is characterized by individuals immediately entering REM sleep?**

   A. sleep apnea   B. narcolepsy

   C. night terrors   D. somnambulism

4. **Which brain waves are active when we are awake and focused?**

   A. alpha   B. beta

   C. delta   D. theta

5. **During which stage of sleep do sleep spindles occur?**

   A. stage 1

   B. stage 2

   C. stage 3

   D. stage 4

Sharpen Your Thinking

Do you know someone who might have a diagnosed or an undiagnosed sleep disorder? What might he or she be able to do about it?

3 Hypnosis

Describe hypnosis.

Fifty-three-year-old Shelley Thomas entered a London Hospital for a 30-minute pelvic surgery. Before the operation, with her hypnotherapist guiding her, Shelley counted backward from 100 and entered a hypnotic trance. Her surgery was performed with no anesthesia (Song, 2006); rather, Shelley relied on hypnosis to harness her mind's powers to overcome pain.

You may have seen a hypnotist on TV or in a nightclub, putting people into a trance and then making them act like chickens or pretend to be contestants on *American Idol.* When we see someone in such a trance, we might be convinced that hypnosis involves a powerful manipulation of another person's consciousness. But, what is hypnosis? The answer to this question, is, itself, the source of some debate. Some think of hypnosis as an altered state of consciousness, while others believe that hypnosis is simply a product of more mundane processes such as focused attention and expectation (Lynn, 2007; Raz, 2007). **Hypnosis** may be defined as an altered state of consciousness or simply a psychological state of altered attention and expectation, in which the individual is unusually receptive to suggestions. Basic hypnotic techniques have been used since the beginning of recorded history in association with religious ceremonies, magic, the supernatural, and many erroneous theories.

In the late nineteenth century, the Austrian physician Friedrich Anton Mesmer cured patients of various problems by passing magnets over their bodies. Mesmer credited his success to "animal magnetism," an intangible force that passes from therapist to patient. In reality, the cures were due to hypnotic suggestion. A committee was appointed by the French Academy of Science to investigate Mesmer's claims. The committee agreed that his treatment was effective. However, they disputed his theory about animal magnetism and prohibited him from practicing in Paris. Mesmer's theory was called "mesmerism," and even today we use the term *mesmerized* to mean hypnotized or enthralled.

Today, hypnosis is recognized as a legitimate process in psychology and medicine, although there is still much to learn about how it works. In addition, there is continuing debate about whether hypnosis truly is an altered state of consciousness (Chaves, 2000; Raz, 2007).

The Nature of Hypnosis

A common misconception is that the hypnotic state is much like a sleep state. However, unlike sleepers, hypnotized individuals are aware of what is happening and remember the experience later unless they are instructed to forget it. Evidence from studies involving EEGs documents that individuals show different patterns of brain

hypnosis An altered state of consciousness or simply a psychological state of altered attention and expectation, in which the individual is unusually receptive to suggestions.

The brain activity of a hypnotized individual is being monitored.

activity during hypnosis than they do when they are not under hypnosis (Gemignani & others, 2006). Individuals in a hypnotic state display a predominance of alpha and beta waves, characteristic of persons in a waking state, when monitored by an EEG (Williams & Gruzelier, 2001). In one study, hypnotized individuals' EEGs resembled those of a person in a relaxed waking state (Graffin, Ray, & Lundy, 1995). Also, in a recent brain-imaging study, widespread areas of the cerebral cortex—including the occipital lobes, parietal lobes, sensorimotor cortex, and prefrontal cortex—were activated when individuals were in a hypnotic state (Faymonville, Boly, & Laureys, 2006). A similar activation pattern is found in individuals in a nonhypnotic waking state who are engaging in mental imagery.

The Four Steps in Hypnosis Successful hypnosis involves four steps:

1. Distractions are minimized; the person to be hypnotized is made comfortable.
2. The hypnotist tells the person to concentrate on something specific, such as an imagined scene or the ticking of a watch.
3. The hypnotist tells the person what to expect in the hypnotic state, such as relaxation or a pleasant floating sensation.
4. The hypnotist suggests certain events or feelings he or she knows will occur or observes occurring, such as "Your eyes are getting tired." When the suggested effects occur, the person interprets them as being caused by the hypnotist's suggestions and accepts them as an indication that something is happening. This increase in the person's expectations that the hypnotist will make things happen in the future makes the person even more suggestible.

Individual Variations in Hypnosis Do you think you could be hypnotized? For as long as hypnosis has been studied (about 200 years), some people have been found to be more easily hypnotized than others. About 65 percent of individuals are moderately hypnotizable, with an additional 15 percent being highly susceptible to hypnosis (Song, 2006). Ten percent or fewer cannot be hypnotized at all, and the remainder fall somewhere in between (Hilgard, 1965).

There is no simple way to tell beforehand who can be hypnotized. But if you have the capacity to immerse yourself in imaginative activities—listening to a favorite piece of music or reading a novel, for example—you are a likely candidate. People susceptible to hypnosis become completely absorbed in what they are doing, removing the boundaries between themselves and what they are experiencing in their environment. Nonetheless, such absorption is best described as a weak rather than a strong predictor of a person's likelihood of being hypnotized (Nash, 2001).

Hypnosis and Will If you are in a hypnotic state, can the hypnotist make you do something against your will? Individuals being hypnotized surrender their responsibility to the hypnotist and follow the hypnotist's suggestions. However, when in a hypnotic state, they are unlikely to do anything that violates their morals or that is dangerous.

Explaining Hypnosis

Ever since Anton Mesmer proposed his theory of animal magnetism, psychologists have been trying to figure out why hypnosis works. Contemporary theorists are divided on their answers to the question, Is hypnosis a divided state of consciousness, or is it simply a form of learned social behavior?

A Divided State of Consciousness Ernest Hilgard (1977, 1992) proposed that hypnosis involves a special divided state of consciousness, a sort of splitting of consciousness into separate components. One component follows the hypnotist's commands, while another component acts as a "hidden observer."

In one situation, Hilgard placed one arm of hypnotized individuals in a bucket of ice-cold water and told them that they would not feel any pain but that another part of their minds—the hidden part that is aware of what is going on—could signal any true pain by pressing a key with the hand that was not submerged (Figure 6.9). The individuals

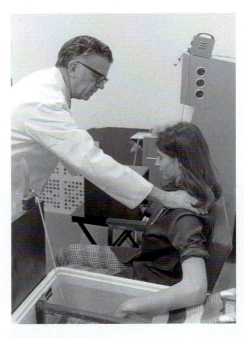

FIGURE 6.9

Divided Consciousness Ernest Hilgard tests a participant in the study in which he had individuals place one arm in ice-cold water.

under hypnosis reported afterward that they did not experience any pain, but while their arms were submerged in the ice-cold water, they had indeed pressed the key with their non-submerged hands, and they pressed it more frequently the longer their arms were in the cold water. Thus, in Hilgard's view, in hypnosis, consciousness has a hidden part that stays in contact with reality and feels pain while another part of consciousness feels no pain.

Social Cognitive Behavior Some experts are skeptical that hypnosis is truly an altered state of consciousness (Chaves, 2000; Lynn & others, 2006). In the **social cognitive behavior view of hypnosis,** hypnosis is a normal state in which the hypnotized person behaves the way he or she believes that a hypnotized person should behave. The social cognitive perspective frames the important questions about hypnosis around cognitive factors—the attitudes, expectations, and beliefs of good hypnotic participants—and around the social context in which hypnosis occurs (Lynn, 2007; Spanos & Chaves, 1989).

Applications of Hypnosis

In the United States, where it was first approved for medical use in 1958, hypnosis is used for a wide array of purposes. These include the treatment of alcoholism, somnambulism, suicidal tendencies, post-traumatic stress disorder, migraines, overeating, and smoking (Hammond, 2007; Holt & others, 2006; Lynn & Cardena, 2007; Sandor & Afra, 2005). Among the least effective, but most common, applications of hypnosis are those intended to help people stop overeating or quit smoking. Hypnotists direct individuals to cease these behaviors, but dramatic results rarely are achieved unless the individuals are already motivated to change. Hypnosis is most effective when combined with psychotherapy (Borckardt, 2002).

A long history of research and practice clearly has demonstrated that hypnosis can reduce the experience of pain (Jensen & Patterson, 2006). A fascinating study examined the pain perceptions of individuals who were hypnotized with the goal of changing their pain threshold. In that study, participants' brains were monitored while they received painful electrical shocks (rated 8 or higher on a 1 to 10 pain scale) (Schulz-Stubner & others, 2004). Those who were hypnotized to find the shocks less painful did indeed rate them as lower in pain (giving them a 3 or less). The brain-scanning results were most interesting: The subcortical brain areas (the brain stem and midbrain) of the hypnotized patients responded the same as those of the patients who were not hypnotized, suggesting that these lower brain structures recognized the painful stimulation. However, the sensory cortex was not activated in the hypnotized patients, suggesting that although they sensed pain on some level, they were never conscious of it. In essence, the "ouch" signal never made it to awareness.

Hypnosis is used more widely in Europe than in the United States as a pain-control technique during surgery—specifically, as a replacement for or complement to typical sedation and anesthesia. Hypnosedation involves the combination of hypnosis and administration of a local anesthetic (Pyati & Gan, 2007; Wobst, 2007). In hypnosedation, patients receive less than 1 percent of the typical amount of medication as in traditional surgery and report fewer side effects (Song, 2006). In one study comparing hypnosedation and typical anesthesia for thyroid surgery, individuals in the hypnosedation group returned to work 2 weeks earlier than patients who received standard procedures (Faymonville, Meurisse, & Fissette, 1999).

social cognitive behavior view of hypnosis
Perspective that views hypnosis as a normal state in which the hypnotized person behaves the way he or she believes a hypnotized person should behave.

Etzel Cardena is a hypnotherapist and a professor of psychology at the University of Texas at Pan American, and he has been president of Division 30 (Hypnosis) of the American Psychological Association. He is shown here hypnotizing a student. Cardena's first experiences with hypnosis were at his father's hypnosis workshops in Mexico. He moved to the United States to pursue a doctoral degree in psychology with an emphasis on altered states of consciousness. Cardena is especially interested in hypnosis as a dissociated state of consciousness and its use in helping people who have experienced trauma and various psychological disorders.

REVIEW, ASSESS, AND SHARPEN YOUR THINKING

Review

3 **Describe hypnosis.**
- Explain what hypnosis is.
- Discuss two theoretical explanations of hypnosis.
- Identify some applications of hypnosis.

Assess

1. What type of brain waves are displayed by persons who are hypnotized?
   A. alpha and beta   B. delta
   C. gamma   D. theta

2. What percentage of people cannot be hypnotized?
   A. 5%
   B. 10%
   C. 20%
   D. 50%

3. Which view of hypnosis states that persons under hypnosis behave in ways consistent with their expectations of how a hypnotized person should behave?
   A. divided-consciousness view
   B. free-will view
   C. social-cognitive behavior view
   D. suggestibility view

4. Which of the following does the research suggest hypnosis most effective at treating?
   A. overeating   B. smoking
   C. laziness   D. pain

Sharpen Your Thinking

Do you think you are a good candidate for hypnosis? Why or why not?

4 Psychoactive Drugs

Evaluate the uses and types of psychoactive drugs.

Illicit drug use is a global problem. More than 200 million people worldwide use drugs each year (UNDCP, 2007). Among those, 25 million individuals (or 2.7 percent of the world population) are characterized as problem drug users (UNDCP, 2007). Media images of drug abusers span all segments of society: the urban professional snorting cocaine in a downtown nightclub, the farmer addicted to the opium poppy he grows, the teenage Ecstasy user in a comfortable suburban home.

Drug use among youth is a special concern because of its relation to a variety of other problems, including unsafe sexual practices, sexually transmitted infections, unplanned pregnancy, depression, and school-related difficulties (Eaton & others, 2006; UNDCP, 2007).

What are some trends in drug use by U.S. adolescents? The use of drugs among U.S. secondary school students declined in the 1980s but began to increase in the early 1990s (Johnston & others, 2006). In the late 1990s and early part of the twenty-first century, the proportion of secondary school students reporting the use of any illicit drug has declined (Johnston & others, 2006). The overall decline in the use of illicit drugs by adolescents during this time frame is approximately one-third for eighth-graders, one-fourth for tenth-graders, and one-tenth for twelfth-graders. Figure 6.10 shows the overall trends in drug use by U.S. high school seniors since 1975 and by U.S. eighth- and tenth-graders since 1991. The most notable declines in drug use by U.S. adolescents in the twenty-first century have occurred for marijuana, LSD, Ecstasy, steroids, and cigarettes. Yet the United States still

FIGURE 6.10

Trends in Drug Use by U.S. High School Seniors This graph shows the percentage of high school seniors who say they have taken an illicit drug in the previous 30 days. Notice the increased use in the latter half of the 1970s, the decrease in the 1980s, the increase in the 1990s, and the recent leveling off.

has the highest rate of adolescent drug use of any industrialized nation (Johnston & others, 2006).

Although drug use is high among U.S. adolescents, it increases further in emerging adulthood. In one national survey, approximately 20 percent of 18- to 25-year-old Americans reported recent illicit drug use compared with 11 percent of adolescents (Substance Abuse and Mental Health Services Administration, 2006).

Uses of Psychoactive Drugs

Psychoactive drugs are substances that act on the nervous system to alter consciousness, modify perceptions, and change moods. People are attracted to psychoactive substances because they help them adapt to an ever-changing environment. Drinking, smoking, and taking drugs reduce tension, relieve boredom and fatigue, and in some cases help people to escape from the harsh realities of the world. Some people use drugs because they are curious about their effects. Others may take drugs for social reasons—for example, to feel more at ease and happier in interactions with others.

The use of psychoactive drugs for personal gratification and temporary adaptation can carry a high price tag: drug dependence, personal disarray, and a predisposition to serious, sometimes fatal diseases (Fields, 2007; McKim, 2007). What was initially intended to provide pleasure and adaptation can lead to enormous grief. For example, drinking alcohol may initially help people relax and forget about their worries. But if they turn more and more to alcohol to escape reality, they may develop a dependence that can destroy relationships, careers, and their bodies.

Continued use of psychoactive drugs leads to **tolerance,** which is the need to take increasing amounts of a drug to get the same effect (Holland, 2007; Ksir, Hart, & Ray, 2008). For example, the first time someone takes 5 milligrams of the tranquilizer Valium, the person feels very relaxed. However, after taking the pill every day for 6 months, the individual may need to consume 10 milligrams to achieve the same calming effect.

Continuing drug use can also result in **physical dependence,** the physiological need for a drug that causes unpleasant *withdrawal* symptoms, such as physical pain and a craving for the drug, when it is discontinued. **Psychological dependence** is the strong desire to repeat the use of a drug for emotional reasons, such as a feeling of well-being and reduction of stress. Experts on drug abuse use the term **addiction** to describe either a physical or psychological dependence, or both, on the drug (Hales, 2007). Physical and psychological dependence mean that the psychoactive drug is exerting a powerful influence over the person's behavior.

Can the brain become addicted? Psychoactive drugs increase dopamine levels in the brain's reward pathways (Schultz, 2006; Zhou & others, 2007). This reward pathway is located in the *ventral tegmental area (VTA)* and *nucleus accumbens* (Figure 6.11).

psychoactive drugs Substances that act on the nervous system to alter consciousness, modify perceptions, and change moods.

tolerance The need to take increasing amounts of a drug to produce the same effect.

physical dependence The physiological need for a drug, accompanied by unpleasant withdrawal symptoms, such as pain and craving, when the drug is discontinued.

psychological dependence The strong desire to repeat the use of a drug for emotional reasons, such as a feeling of well-being and stress reduction.

addiction Either a physical or a psychological dependence, or both, on a drug.

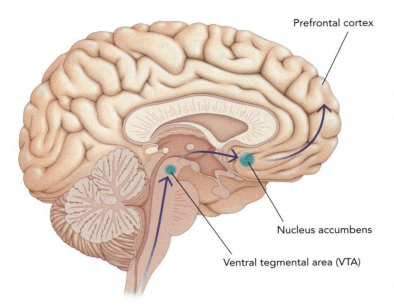

Prefrontal cortex

Nucleus accumbens

Ventral tegmental area (VTA)

FIGURE 6.11

The Brain's Reward Pathway for Psychoactive Drugs The ventral tegmental area (VTA) and nucleus accumbens are important locations in the reward pathway for psychoactive drugs. Information travels from the VTA to the nucleus accumbens and then up to the prefrontal cortex. The VTA is located in the midbrain just above the pons, and the nucleus accumbens is located in the forebrain, just beneath the prefrontal cortex.

Respond yes or no to the following items:

Yes	No	
☐	☐	I have gotten into problems because of using drugs.
☐	☐	Using alcohol or other drugs has made my college life unhappy at times.
☐	☐	Drinking alcohol or taking other drugs has been a factor in my losing a job.
☐	☐	Drinking alcohol or taking other drugs has interfered with my studying for exams.
☐	☐	Drinking alcohol or taking drugs has jeopardized my academic performance.
☐	☐	My ambition is not as strong since I've been drinking a lot or taking drugs.
☐	☐	Drinking or taking drugs has caused me to have difficulty sleeping.
☐	☐	I have felt remorse after drinking or taking drugs.
☐	☐	I crave a drink or other drugs at a definite time of the day.
☐	☐	I want a drink or other drug in the morning.
☐	☐	I have had a complete or partial loss of memory as a result of drinking or using other drugs.
☐	☐	Drinking or using other drugs is affecting my reputation.
☐	☐	I have been in the hospital or another institution because of my drinking or taking drugs.

College students who responded yes to items similar to these on the Rutgers Collegiate Abuse Screening Test were more likely to be substance abusers than those who answered no. If you responded yes to just 1 of the 13 items on this screening test, consider going to your college health or counseling center for further screening.

FIGURE 6.12

Do You Abuse Drugs? Take this short quiz to see if your use of drugs and alcohol might be a cause for concern.

Only the limbic and prefrontal areas of the brain are directly activated by dopamine, which comes from the VTA (Koob, 2006). Although different drugs have different mechanisms of action, each drug increases the activity of the reward pathway by increasing dopamine transmission. Recall from Chapter 3 that when a drug mimics a particular neurotransmitter or blocks its reuptake, it is referred to as an *agonist*. Thus, drugs that increase dopamine levels in the brain are agonists. In contrast, when a drug blocks a neurotransmitter or diminishes its release, it is called an *antagonist*.

Types of Psychoactive Drugs

Three main categories of psychoactive drugs are depressants, stimulants, and hallucinogens. All of them have the potential to cause health or behavior problems or both. To evaluate whether you abuse drugs, see Figure 6.12.

Depressants **Depressants** are psychoactive drugs that slow down mental and physical activity. Among the most widely used depressants are alcohol, barbiturates, tranquilizers, and opiates.

Alcohol Alcohol is a powerful drug. It acts on the body primarily as a depressant and slows down the brain's activities. This effect might seem surprising, as people who tend to be inhibited may begin to talk, dance, and socialize after a few drinks. However, people "loosen up" after a few drinks because the areas of the brain involved in inhibition and judgment slow down. As people drink more, their inhibitions decrease even further, and their judgment becomes increasingly impaired. Activities that require intellectual functioning and motor skills, such as driving, become harder to perform. Eventually the drinker falls asleep. With extreme intoxication, the person may lapse into a coma and die. Each of these effects varies with the way the individual's body metabolizes alcohol, body weight, the amount consumed, and whether previous drinking has led to tolerance (Fields, 2007).

How does alcohol affect the brain? Like other psychoactive drugs, alcohol goes to the ventral tegmental area (VTA) and the nucleus accumbens (NIDA, 2001). Alcohol also increases the concentration of the neurotransmitter gamma aminobutyric acid (GABA), which is widely distributed in many areas of the brain, including the cerebral cortex, cerebellum, hippocampus, amygdala, and nucleus accumbens (Krystal & others, 2006; Zhou & others, 2007). Researchers believe that the frontal cortex holds a memory of the pleasure involved in prior alcohol use and contributes to continued drinking. Alcohol consumption also may affect the areas of the frontal cortex involved in judgment and impulse control (Mantere & others, 2002). It is further believed that the basal ganglia, which are involved in compulsive behaviors, may lead to a greater demand for alcohol, regardless of reason and consequences (Brink, 2001).

After caffeine, alcohol is the most widely used drug in the United States. As many as two-thirds of U.S. adults drink beer, wine, or liquor at least occasionally, and in one recent survey approximately 30 percent reported drinking more than five drinks at one sitting at least once in the last year (National Center for Health Statistics, 2005).

Approximately 14 million people in the United States are alcoholics (Brink, 2001). Alcoholism is the third leading killer in the United States. Approximately 20,000 people are killed and 1.5 million injured by drunk drivers each year. Approximately 34 percent of all fatal crashes and 50 percent of those during holidays involve alcohol (U.S. Department of Transportation, 2005). It may be surprising that the vast majority of offenses for drinking under the influence are committed not by alcoholics but by social drinkers (Caetano & McGrath, 2005). An estimated 3 in 10 Americans will be involved in an alcohol-related crash (National Highway Traffic Safety Administration, 2001). Alcohol is also related to violence and aggression (Dawson & others, 2007). More than 60 percent of homicides involve alcohol use by either the offender or the victim, and 65 percent of aggressive sexual acts against women involve alcohol consumption by the offender.

A special concern is the high rate of alcohol use by U.S. secondary school and college students (Shillington & Clapp, 2006). In a recent national survey of more than 17,000 high school seniors in the United States, 75 percent had tried alcohol, and 41 percent had done so by the eighth grade (Johnston & others, 2007). In this survey, 57 percent of the twelfth-graders and 19 percent of the eighth-graders reported having been drunk at least once in their life. Thirty percent of the high school seniors had engaged in binge drinking (having five or more drinks in a row at least once in the previous 2 weeks) at least once during the previous month.

Two recent longitudinal studies have linked early onset of drinking to later alcohol problems. In one study, individuals who began drinking alcohol before 14 years of age were more likely to become alcohol dependent than their counterparts who began drinking alcohol at 21 years of age or older (Hingson, Heeren, & Winter, 2006). In a second study, individuals were assessed from the time they were 8 years old to 42 years old (Pitkanen, Lyyra, & Pulkkinen, 2005). Early onset of drinking was linked to an elevated risk of heavy drinking in middle age.

Heavy binge drinking often increases during the first 2 years of college, and it can take its toll on students (Park, 2004). Chronic binge drinking is more common among male college students than among females and among students living away from home, especially males residing in fraternity houses (Schulenberg & Zarrett, 2006). In a national survey of drinking patterns on college campuses, almost half of the binge drinkers reported problems that included missed classes, injuries, trouble with police, and unprotected sex (Wechsler & others, 2000; 2002) (Figure 6.13). Binge-drinking college students were 11 times more likely to fall behind in school, 10 times more likely to drive after drinking, and twice as likely to have unprotected sex as college students who did not binge drink. Many emerging

depressants Psychoactive drugs that slow down mental and physical activity.

The Troubles Frequent Binge Drinkers Create for . . .

Themselves[1]		and Others[2]	
(% of those surveyed who admitted having had the problem)		(% of those surveyed who had been affected)	
Missed class	61	Had study or sleep interrupted	68
Forgot where they were or what they did	54	Had to care for drunken student	54
Engaged in unplanned sex	41	Were insulted or humiliated	34
Got hurt	23	Experienced unwanted sexual advances	26
Had unprotected sex	22	Had serious argument	20
Damaged property	22	Had property damaged	15
Got into trouble with campus or local police	11	Were pushed or assaulted	13
Had five or more alcohol-related problems in school year	47	Had at least one of the above problems	87

[1] Frequent binge drinkers were defined as those who had at least four or five drinks at one time on at least three occasions in the previous two weeks.
[2] These figures are from colleges where at least 50 percent of students are binge drinkers.

FIGURE 6.13

Consequences of Binge Drinking Binge drinking has wide-ranging negative consequences.

adults decrease their use of alcohol as they move into adult roles such as a permanent job, marriage or cohabitation, and parenthood (Slutske, 2005).

Alcoholism is a disorder that involves long-term, repeated, uncontrolled, compulsive, and excessive use of alcoholic beverages and that impairs the drinker's health and social relationships. One in nine individuals who drink continues the path to alcoholism. Those who do are disproportionately related to alcoholics. Family studies consistently find a high frequency of alcoholism in the first-degree relatives of alcoholics (Edenberg & Foroud, 2006). Indeed, researchers have determined that heredity likely plays a role in alcoholism, with the gene associated with GABA being most likely implicated (Soyka & others, 2007). An estimated 50 to 60 percent of those who become alcoholics are believed to have a genetic predisposition for it (Quickfall & el-Guebaly, 2006).

One possible explanation is that the brains of people genetically predisposed to alcoholism may be unable to produce adequate dopamine, a neurotransmitter that can make us feel pleasure (Dick & Bierut, 2006). For these individuals, alcohol may increase dopamine concentration and resulting pleasure to the point at which it leads to addiction.

Although studies reveal a genetic influence on alcoholism, they also show that environmental factors play a role (Fromme, 2006). For example, family studies indicate that many alcoholics do not have close relatives who are alcoholics (Duncan & others, 2006).

What does it take to stop alcoholism? About one-third of alcoholics recover, whether they are in a treatment program or not. This finding came from a long-term study of 700 individuals over 50 years (Vaillant, 1983, 1992) and has consistently been confirmed by other researchers. George Vaillant formulated the one-third rule for alcoholism: By age 65, one-third are dead or in terrible shape; one-third are still trying to beat their addiction; and one-third are abstinent or drinking only socially. In his extensive research, Vaillant found that recovery from alcoholism was predicted by (1) having a strong negative experience with drinking, such as a serious medical emergency; (2) finding a substitute dependency, such as meditation, exercise, or overeating (which has its own adverse health effects); (3) developing new, positive relationships (such as with a concerned employer or a new spouse); and (4) joining a support group such as Alcoholics Anonymous or Rational Recovery.

Barbiturates **Barbiturates,** such as Nembutal and Seconal, are depressant drugs that decrease central nervous system activity. They were once widely prescribed as sleep aids. In heavy dosages, they can lead to impaired memory and decision making. When combined with alcohol (for example, sleeping pills taken after a night of binge drinking), barbiturates can be lethal. Heavy doses of barbiturates by themselves can cause death. For this reason, barbiturates are the drug most often used in suicide attempts. Abrupt withdrawal can produce seizures. Because of the addictive potential and relative ease of toxic overdose, barbiturates have been largely replaced by tranquilizers in the treatment of insomnia.

Tranquilizers **Tranquilizers,** such as Valium and Xanax, are depressant drugs that reduce anxiety and induce relaxation. Unlike barbiturates, which often are given to induce sleep, tranquilizers are usually prescribed to calm an anxious, nervous individual. Widely prescribed in the United States, tranquilizers can produce withdrawal symptoms when use is stopped (Voshaar & others, 2006).

Opiates Narcotics, or **opiates,** consist of opium and its derivatives and depress the central nervous system's activity. The most common opiate drugs—morphine and heroin—affect synapses in the brain that use endorphins as their neurotransmitter. When these drugs leave the brain, the affected synapses become understimulated. For several hours after taking an opiate, the person feels euphoric and pain-free and has an increased appetite for food and sex. Opiates are highly addictive drugs, leading to craving and painful withdrawal when the drug becomes unavailable.

Another hazardous consequence of opiate addiction is the risk of exposure to HIV, the virus that causes AIDS. Most heroin addicts inject the drug intravenously. When they share needles without sterilizing them, one infected addict can transmit the virus to others.

---

alcoholism A disorder that involves long-term, repeated, uncontrolled, compulsive, and excessive use of alcoholic beverages and that impairs the drinker's health and social relationships.

barbiturates Depressant drugs that decrease the activity of the central nervous system.

tranquilizers Depressant drugs that reduce anxiety and induce relaxation.

opiates Opium and its derivatives; they depress the central nervous system's activity.

Stimulants   **Stimulants** are psychoactive drugs that increase the central nervous system's activity. The most widely used stimulants are caffeine, nicotine, amphetamines, and cocaine.

Caffeine   Often overlooked as a drug, caffeine is the world's most widely used psychoactive drug. Caffeine is a stimulant and a natural component of the plants that are the sources of coffee, tea, and cola drinks. Caffeine also is present in chocolate and in many nonprescription medications. People often perceive the stimulating effects of caffeine as beneficial for boosting energy and alertness, but some experience unpleasant side effects.

Caffeinism refers to an overindulgence in caffeine. It is characterized by mood changes, anxiety, and sleep disruption. Caffeinism often develops in people who drink five or more cups of coffee (at least 500 milligrams) each day. Common symptoms are insomnia, irritability, headaches, ringing ears, dry mouth, increased blood pressure, and digestive problems (Hogan, Hornick, & Bouchoux, 2002).

Caffeine affects the brain's pleasure centers, so it is not surprising that it is difficult to kick the caffeine habit. When individuals who regularly consume caffeinated beverages remove caffeine from their diet, they typically experience headaches, lethargy, apathy, and concentration difficulties. These symptoms of withdrawal are usually mild and subside after several days.

Nicotine   Nicotine is the main psychoactive ingredient in all forms of smoking and smoke-less tobacco. Even with all the publicity given to the enormous health risks posed by tobacco, we sometimes overlook the highly addictive nature of nicotine. Nicotine stimulates the brain's reward centers by raising dopamine levels. Behavioral effects of nicotine include improved attention and alertness, reduced anger and anxiety, and pain relief (Knott & others, 2006).

Tolerance develops for nicotine both in the long run and on a daily basis, so that cigarettes smoked later in the day have less effect than those smoked earlier. Withdrawal from nicotine often quickly produces strong, unpleasant symptoms such as irritability, craving, inability to focus, sleep disturbance, and increased appetite. Withdrawal symptoms can persist for months or longer.

Despite the positive short-term effects of nicotine (such as increased energy and alertness), most smokers recognize the serious health risks of smoking and wish they could quit. Chapter 16 further explores the difficulty of giving up smoking and strategies for quitting.

Tobacco poses a much larger threat to public health than illegal drugs. A full 28 percent of the world's population between the ages of 15 and 64 smokes (UNDCP, 2007). Today there are approximately 1 billion smokers globally, and estimates are that by 2030, another 1 billion youth will have started to smoke (UN World Youth Report, 2005). In 2005, about 21 percent of U.S. adults smoked—a decline from 1996, when nearly a quarter of surveyed Americans smoked (Centers for Disease Control and Prevention, 2006).

Fortunately, cigarette smoking is decreasing among both adolescents and college students. In a national survey by the Institute of Social Research, the percentage of U.S. adolescents who are current cigarette smokers continued to decline in 2005 (Johnston & others, 2007). Cigarette smoking peaked in 1996 and 1997 and then declined 11 to 15 percent, depending on grade level, from 1998 to 2005 (Figure 6.14). The drop in cigarette use by U.S. youth may have several sources, including higher cigarette prices, less tobacco advertising reaching adolescents, more antismoking advertisements, and more negative publicity about the tobacco industry than before. Since the mid-1990s, a rising percentage of adolescents has reported perceiving cigarette smoking as dangerous, disapproving of it, becoming less accepting of being around smokers, and preferring to date nonsmokers (Johnston & others, 2007).

The devastating effects of early smoking were brought home in a research study that found that smoking in the adolescent years causes permanent genetic changes in the lungs and forever increases the risk of lung cancer, even if the smoker quits (Weineke & others, 1999). The damage was much less likely among smokers in the study who started in their 20s. One of the remarkable findings in the study was that the early age of onset of smoking was more important in predicting genetic damage than was how heavily the individuals smoked.

stimulants Psychoactive drugs that increase the central nervous system's activity.

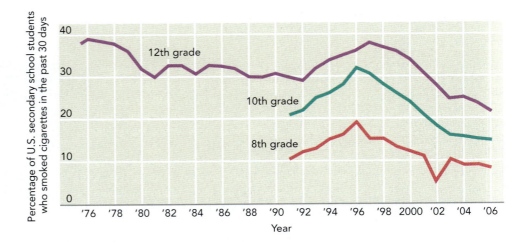

Although cigarette smoking by U.S. adolescents and adults in general has declined considerably in recent years, cigarette smoking by college students has shown a smaller decline, and little change has been revealed in young adults (Johnston & others, 2007). Among college students, the peak rate of smoking occurred in 1999 when 31 percent said they had smoked a cigarette in the past 30 days; this figure declined to 24 percent in 2005. Young adults 19 to 28 years of age showed little change in their smoking habits between 1996 and 2005, with approximately 30 percent reporting they had smoked a cigarette in the past 30 days.

Amphetamines Amphetamines, commonly called "pep pills" or "uppers," are stimulant drugs that people use to boost energy, stay awake, or lose weight. Amphetamines often are prescribed in the form of diet pills. These drugs increase the release of dopamine, which enhances the user's activity level and pleasurable feelings.

Perhaps the most insidious illicit drug for contemporary society is crystal methamphetamine, or crystal meth. Crystal meth (or "tina") is a synthetic stimulant that causes a very strong feeling of euphoria, particularly the first time it is ingested (it can be smoked, injected, or swallowed). Meth is made using household products such as battery acid, cold medicine, drain cleaner, and kitty litter, and its effects have been devastating, particularly in rural areas.

Crystal meth is highly addictive. The drug's extreme high drains the body of endorphins, causing a severe "come down" experience that is associated with strong cravings. The Drug Enforcement Agency (DEA) has committed some $145 million per year to combat methamphetamine (U.S. Department of Justice, 2006). Because the person's very first experience with crystal meth can lead to devastating consequences, the DEA has also started a website, designed by and targeted at teenagers, **http://www.justthinktwice.com,** to share the hard facts of the horrific effects of this and other illicit substances.

Cocaine Cocaine is an illegal drug that comes from the coca plant, native to Bolivia and Peru. For centuries, Bolivians and Peruvians have chewed the leaves of the plant to increase their stamina. Generally, however, cocaine is either snorted or injected in the form of crystals or powder. Used this way, cocaine can trigger a heart attack, stroke, or brain seizure.

When animals and humans chew coca leaves, small amounts of cocaine gradually enter the bloodstream, without any apparent adverse effects. However, when extracted cocaine is sniffed or injected, it enters the bloodstream very rapidly, producing a rush of euphoric feelings that lasts for about 15 to 30 minutes. Because the rush depletes the supply of the neurotransmitters dopamine, serotonin, and norepinephrine in the brain, an agitated, depressed mood usually follows as the drug's effects decline. Figure 6.15 shows how cocaine affects dopamine levels in the brain.

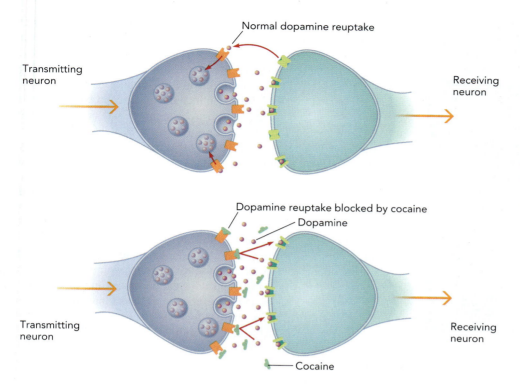

Normal dopamine reuptake

Transmitting neuron

Receiving neuron

Dopamine reuptake blocked by cocaine

Dopamine

Transmitting neuron

Receiving neuron

Cocaine

FIGURE 6.15

Cocaine and Neurotransmitters Cocaine concentrates in areas of the brain that are rich in dopamine synapses, such as the VTA and the nucleus accumbens. (*Top*) What happens in normal reuptake. The transmitting neuron releases dopamine, which stimulates the receiving neuron by binding to its receptor sites. After binding occurs, dopamine is carried back into the transmitting neuron for later release. (*Bottom*) What happens when cocaine is present in the synapse. Cocaine binds to the uptake pumps and prevents them from removing dopamine from the synapse. This results in more dopamine in the synapse, and more dopamine receptors are activated.

Crack is a potent form of cocaine, consisting of chips of pure cocaine that are usually smoked. Crack is believed to be one of the most addictive substances known, even more addictive than heroin, barbiturates, and alcohol.

Treatment of cocaine addiction has not been very successful (Hser & others, 2006). Cocaine's addictive properties are so strong that, 6 months after treatment, more than 50 percent of cocaine abusers return to the drug. Experts on drug abuse argue that prevention is the best approach to reducing cocaine use.

Inhalants   Although the consumption of illicit drugs generally appears to be declining, inhalant use has increased alarmingly. Inhalants are volatile substances that are intentionally breathed in to produce psychoactive effects. "Huffing" involves inhaling common household chemicals such as gasoline and paint thinner; aerosol sprays such as hairspray and deodorant; medical anesthetics such as ether; or nitrates (also called "poppers"). According to a 2004 survey, nearly 10 percent of the population over age 12 reported using inhalants (SAMHSA, 2005). Indeed, the National Institute on Drug Abuse (NIDA) found that over 17 percent of eighth-graders reported using inhalants, and 3 percent of children have tried inhalants before they reach the fourth grade (NIDA, 2005).

Most inhalants produce a rapid high and have an effect similar to anesthesia. Because the effects are quite short-lived, users may seek to prolong the experience by inhaling more, sometimes bringing on a loss of consciousness. Even a single use of inhalants can result in death by disrupting the person's heart rhythms (NIDA, 2005). These drugs often deprive the brain of oxygen and can produce lingering effects, including headache, lack of motor coordination, difficulty concentrating, memory loss, irritability, and depression (NIDA, 2005).

Hallucinogens   **Hallucinogens** are psychoactive drugs that modify a person's perceptual experiences and produce visual images that are not real. Hallucinogens are also called psychedelic (from the Greek meaning "mind-revealing") drugs. Marijuana has a mild hallucinogenic effect; LSD, a stronger one (Figure 6.16).

Marijuana   Marijuana is the dried leaves and flowers of the hemp plant *Cannabis sativa,* which originated in central Asia but is now grown in most parts of the world.

hallucinogens Psychoactive drugs that modify a person's perceptual experiences and produce visual images that are not real.

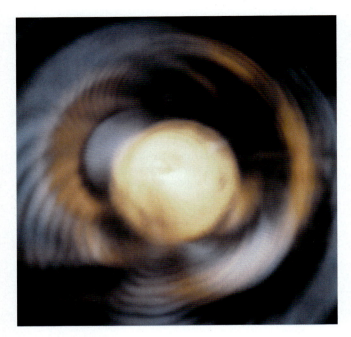

FIGURE 6.16

LSD-Induced Hallucination Under the influence of hallucinogenic drugs, such as LSD, several users have reported seeing tunnellike images.

The plant's dried resin is known as hashish. The active ingredient in marijuana is THC (delta-9-tetrahydrocannabinol). Unlike other psychoactive drugs, THC does not affect a specific neurotransmitter. Rather, marijuana disrupts the membranes of neurons and affects the functioning of a variety of neurotransmitters and hormones.

The physical effects of marijuana include increases in pulse rate and blood pressure, reddening of the eyes, coughing, and dryness of the mouth. Psychological effects include a mixture of excitatory, depressive, and mildly hallucinatory characteristics that make it difficult to classify the drug. Marijuana can trigger spontaneous unrelated ideas; distorted perceptions of time and place; increased sensitivity to sounds, tastes, smells, and colors; and erratic verbal behavior. Marijuana can also impair attention and memory. When used daily in large amounts, marijuana also can alter sperm count and change hormonal cycles (Close, Roberts, & Berger, 1990). It may be involved in some birth defects and less effective information processing in children. For example, a recent review of research concluded that marijuana use by pregnant women is related to negative outcomes in memory and information processing in their offspring (Kalant, 2004). On a positive note, researchers have found some medical uses for marijuana, such as treating glaucoma, chemotherapy-caused vomiting, and AIDS-related weight loss.

Marijuana is the illegal drug most widely used by high school students. As many as 32 percent of high school seniors in the United States say that they have used marijuana in the past year (Bureau of Justice Statistics, 2006).

MDMA (Ecstasy) MDMA is an illegal synthetic drug with both stimulant and hallucinogenic properties. Street names for MDMA include Ecstasy, X, XTC, hug, beans, and love drug. Ecstasy has been referred to as an "empathogen" because under its influence, users tend to feel warm bonds with others.

MDMA has adverse effects on memory and cognitive processing. Individuals who have been heavy users of Ecstasy, for example, show cognitive deficits (Dafters, 2006) that persist even *two years* after they begin to abstain (Ward, Hall, & Haslam, 2006). MDMA kills serotonergic axons, suggesting that repeated use might lead to susceptibility to depression (Guillot & Greenway, 2006).

LSD LSD (lysergic acid diethylamide) is a hallucinogen that even in low doses produces striking perceptual changes. Objects change their shapes and glow. Colors become kaleidoscopic, and fabulous images unfold. Designs swirl, colors shimmer, and bizarre scenes appear. LSD-induced images are sometimes pleasurable and sometimes grotesque. Figure 6.16 shows one kind of perceptual experience that a number of LSD users have reported. LSD can also influence a user's sense of time. Time seems to slow down dramatically, so that brief glances at objects are experienced as deep, penetrating, and lengthy examinations, and minutes seem to be hours or even days. A bad LSD trip can trigger extreme anxiety, paranoia, and suicidal or homicidal impulses.

LSD's effects on the body can include dizziness, nausea, and tremors. LSD acts primarily on the neurotransmitter serotonin in the brain, though it also can affect dopamine (Nichols & Sanders-Bush, 2002). Emotional and cognitive effects may include rapid mood swings and impaired attention and memory. LSD is one psychoactive drug that has no beneficial effects. Its effects are summarized in Figure 6.17, along with the characteristics of the other types of drugs that have been discussed.

The use of LSD peaked in the 1960s and 1970s. Its popularity declined after its unpredictable effects became publicized. However, in the 1990s, the use of LSD by high school students increased, although not to the level in the 1960s and 1970s, and its use has been decreasing in the twenty-first century (Johnston & others, 2007).

A current controversy involves the extent hallucinogenic drugs, such as LSD and marijuana, should be used for medical purposes. To read about this issue, see the Critical Controversy.

Drug Classification	Medical Uses	Short-Term Effects	Overdose Effects	Health Risks	Risk of Physical/ Psychological Dependence
Depressants					
Alcohol	Pain relief	Relaxation, depressed brain activity, slowed behavior, reduced inhibitions	Disorientation, loss of consciousness, even death at high blood-alcohol levels	Accidents, brain damage, liver disease, heart disease, ulcers, birth defects	Physical: moderate Psychological: moderate
Barbiturates	Sleeping pill	Relaxation, sleep	Breathing difficulty, coma, possible death	Accidents, coma, possible death	Physical and psychological: moderate to high
Tranquilizers	Anxiety reduction	Relaxation, slowed behavior	Breathing difficulty, coma, possible death	Accidents, coma, possible death	Physical: low to moderate Psychological: moderate to high
Opiates (narcotics)	Pain relief	Euphoric feelings, drowsiness, nausea	Convulsions, coma, possible death	Accidents, infectious diseases such as AIDS	Physical: high Psychological: moderate to high
Stimulants					
Amphetamines	Weight control	Increased alertness, excitability; decreased fatigue, irritability	Extreme irritability, feelings of persecution, convulsions	Insomnia, hypertension, malnutrition, possible death	Physical: possible Psychological: moderate to high
Cocaine	Local anesthetic	Increased alertness, excitability, euphoric feelings; decreased fatigue, irritability	Extreme irritability, feelings of persecution, convulsions, cardiac arrest, possible death	Insomnia, hypertension, malnutrition, possible death	Physical: possible Psychological: moderate (oral) to very high (injected or smoked)
MDMA (Ecstasy)	None	Mild amphetamine and hallucinogenic effects; high body temperature and dehydration; sense of well-being and social connectedness	Brain damage, especially memory and thinking	Cardiovascular problems; death	Physical: possible Psychological: moderate
Caffeine	None	Alertness and sense of well-being followed by fatigue	Nervousness, anxiety, disturbed sleep	Possible cardiovascular problems	Physical: moderate Psychological: moderate
Nicotine	None	Stimulation, stress reduction, followed by fatigue, anger	Nervousness, disturbed sleep	Cancer and cardio-vascular disease	Physical: high Psychological: high
Hallucinogens					
LSD	None	Strong hallucinations, distorted time perception	Severe mental disturbance, loss of contact with reality	Accidents	Physical: none Psychological: low
Marijuana	Treatment of the eye disorder glaucoma	Euphoric feelings, relaxation, mild hallucinations, time distortion, attention and memory impairment	Fatigue, disoriented behavior	Accidents, respiratory disease	Physical: very low Psychological: moderate

FIGURE 6.17

Categories of Psychoactive Drugs: Depressants, Stimulants, and Hallucinogens

Note that these various drugs have different effects and negative consequences.

Critical Controversy — Should Psychedelic Drugs Be Legalized for Medical Uses?

During one phase of his career, Sigmund Freud personally experimented with therapeutic uses of cocaine. He was searching for possible medical applications such as the drug's potential use as a painkiller during eye surgery.

He found that the drug induced feelings of ecstasy. Writing to his fiancée, he told her how just a small dose produced wonderful, lofty sensations. But as he heard stories about others who had become addicted and suffered overdoses, Freud quit using the drug.

The notion of exploring the use of mind-altering drugs for legitimate purposes is not exclusive to Freud. Psychedelic drugs such as LSD (acid), MDMA (Ecstasy), psilocybin (magic mushrooms), mescaline (peyote buttons), and cannabis (marijuana, or pot) all have mind-altering effects. Users sometimes talk about the amazing insights they have experienced under the influence of these substances, and some cultures and religions incorporate the use of hallucinogens in rituals. Could these effects be harnessed to promote healthier functioning in the mentally ill? Could they be used to promote well-being more generally? John Halpern, an associate director of addiction research at Harvard University's McLean Hospital, and his colleagues think so (Halpern, 2003; Halpern & Sewell, 2005; Halpern & others, 2005; Sewell, Halpern, & Pope, 2006).

They have been leading advocates for research using psychedelic drugs to treat addiction, anxiety, and other disorders.

Of course, these drugs are illegal today, but they were not always. The effects of LSD were discovered by a Swiss chemist who accidentally ingested LSD while working in a pharmaceutical lab. He described his "trip" as both terrifying and thrilling, and his experience led others to consider whether LSD might have a use in psychological treatment. During the 1960s, more than 100 peer-reviewed articles examining the effects and potential benefits of psychedelic drugs were published in scientific journals. During that time, more than 40,000 patients were given LSD for a variety of problems, including schizophrenia, alcoholism, and depression.

The benefits of LSD were championed especially passionately by the late Timothy Leary. In the 1960s, Leary, a Harvard psychologist, embarked on a research program dedicated to unlocking the secrets of consciousness through the use of LSD. Leary believed that LSD could be beneficial in freeing people from addiction, changing the behavior of criminals, and providing entry into mystical experience. Perhaps less interested in science than celebrity, however, Leary ultimately fell out of favor and lost his job over his and his research associates' tendencies to sample the

(continued)

The Supreme Court recently upheld the federal government's right to enforce drug laws strictly, regardless of state regulations such as those permitting medical usage of marijuana. Congress, as recently as June 2006, voted down a proposal that would have blocked drug enforcers' raids on patients using medical marijuana. Here protesters show their displeasure with these decisions.

research stimuli, sacrificing scientific rigor in favor of simply promoting the use of LSD (Greenfield, 2006). Certainly, Leary's controversial persona and behavior had a chilling effect on research into the potential applications of psychedelic drugs (Horgan, 2005; Sessa, 2007). By the late 1960s, LSD and other psychedelic drugs were outlawed in the United States, Canada, and Europe. In 1971, the *Journal of the American Medical Association* printed an editorial decrying the negative effects of LSD and warning that among those who had used the drug more than 50 times, only a lucky few escaped without severe "personality deterioration."

Slowly, however, researchers again have begun to consider the potential benefits of these now illegal substances. On the basis of a review of previous studies, Halpern (1996) concluded that LSD may help addicts avoid cravings. During the months following an acid trip, for example, addicts experience an "afterglow" in which they no longer have cravings for heroin or alcohol. Although government restrictions make the research difficult, a variety of scholars are examining the legitimate uses of psychedelic drugs for a broad range of problems. For example, psilocybin is being studied as a treatment for obsessive-compulsive disorder; MDMA, for anxiety and migraine headaches; and ketamin ("vitamin K," a veterinary tranquilizer), for alcoholism (Horgan, 2005). Promising initial results are leading some to consider whether these drugs should be legalized for medical use.

The controversy over medical marijuana illustrates the conflicts that can erupt over the possibility of an illicit drug's legalization. In the late 1970s, it became apparent that marijuana could be used as treatment for glaucoma (American Academy of Ophthalmology, 2003). More recently, marijuana has been recognized as a potential treatment for individuals who suffer from diseases such as AIDS and cancer (as well as the unpleasant side effects of treatments for these illnesses). For such individuals, "medical marijuana" may be a means to promote appetite, to calm anxiety, and to stimulate well-being (Joy, Watson, & Benson, 1999). If marijuana were legalized for medical purposes, would drug use rise more generally, as many believe (Schwartz & others, 2003)?

In 1996, California provided a natural experiment that addressed this very question when voters passed Proposition 215, legalizing the noncommercial possession, cultivation, and distribution of marijuana for medical purposes. Researchers looked at data from a survey of a broad sample of 16- to 25-year-old Californians that was begun before the passage of Proposition 215. The survey, which measured attitudes toward pot and self-reported usage, allowed researchers to gauge the effects of Proposition 215. They concluded that while attitudes about marijuana were more lenient in 1999 than in the years prior to the passage of the proposition, usage did not change (Khatapoush & Hallfors, 2004).

More recently, the U.S. Supreme Court upheld the right of the federal government strictly to enforce drug laws, regardless of state regulations (or lack thereof). The justices ruled that "medical necessity" is not a viable legal defense (Aggarwal, Carter, & Steinborn, 2005). As recently as June 2006, the U.S. Congress voted down a proposal that would have prevented drug enforcement officials from conducting raids on patients using medical marijuana in the 11 states in which such use is not illegal (Alaska, California, Colorado, Hawaii, Maine, Montana, Nevada, Oregon, Rhode Island, Vermont, and Washington). Legislators defeated this proposal despite support from both Democrats and Republicans.

Naturally, there are reasons why these drugs have been outlawed, including matters of safety. One issue is the occurrence of *flashbacks,* the experience in which a user is transported back into the hallucinogenic state even without the use of the drug. Another concern centers on the levels at which these drugs can be safely taken. Yet some advocates point out that the safety risks associated with some of the hallucinogenic substances are not different from those posed by alcohol and tobacco (Grinspoon, 2000).

The scientific study of the uses of these drugs is hampered not only by the legal issues involved but also by specific issues of research design. Indeed, drug research has faced a variety of challenges. First, in general, participants in studies of the effects of illegal drugs are by definition participating in illegal behavior, and this fact may make them less representative of the population as a whole. Second, older studies failed to measure preexisting psychiatric conditions, thus leaving the negative effects of drugs potentially attributable to these preexisting factors. In addition, many drug users ingest multiple drugs at the same time—for example, taking LSD or Ecstasy while drinking and smoking—so that teasing apart the specific causes of reactions is difficult. To avoid these pitfalls, some studies have focused on individuals who use psychedelic drugs only in religious contexts; this way, the researchers can examine the effects of specific drugs in the absence of any other substance use and without concern for legal issues (Doering-Silveira & others, 2005).

Another controversial question is whether such drugs ought to be legalized not just for medical purposes but for the enhancement of everyday life. Some people even argue that psychedelic drugs should be legalized because they are an avenue for gaining creative insight. "The illegality of cannabis is outrageous, an impediment to full utilization of a drug which helps produce serenity, insight, sensitivity and fellowship so desperately needed in this increasingly mad and dangerous world." This quote is from the late scientist and author Carl Sagan, writing as "Mr. X" in Lester Grinspoon's *Marihuana Reconsidered* (1994).

Whether hallucinogenic drugs provide us with insight into the great mysteries of life is certainly debatable. One of Timothy Leary's early participants noted that he had solved all the world's problems during an acid trip, yet the next day he could not remember how (Greenfield, 2006). The use of these drugs to help individuals struggling with serious life difficulties is certain to remain a subject of debate for years to come.

What Do You Think?

- Would the legalization of psychedelic drugs for medical purposes "send the wrong message" about drug use? Why or why not?
- Compare the legalization of illicit drugs for medical use versus for the enhancement of daily life. What are the different implications of each of these notions?
- How might the particular characteristics of an individual influence the person's experiences with hallucinogenic drugs? How might these experiences compare with those of others using the drugs?
- Would you support the legalization of drugs for medical purposes? Why or why not?

 **REVIEW, ASSESS, AND SHARPEN YOUR THINKING**

Review

4 Evaluate the uses and types of psychoactive drugs.

- Describe the effects of psychoactive drugs.
- Know the characteristics of the three main types of psychoactive drugs: depressants, stimulants, and hallucinogens.

Assess

1. Which type of drug is used most often for suicide attempts?
   A. opiates
   B. tranquilizers
   C. barbiturates
   D. alcohol

2. How does cocaine affect dopamine transmission?
   A. Cocaine causes the presynaptic neuron to release more dopamine.
   B. Cocaine causes the postsynaptic neuron to release more dopamine.
   C. Cocaine blocks the reuptake of dopamine by the presynaptic neuron.
   D. Cocaine blocks the reuptake of dopamine by the postsynaptic neuron.

3. Heroin is an example of
   A. a barbiturate.
   B. a hallucinogen.
   C. an amphetamine.
   D. an opiate.

4. Roger used to feel the effect of one or two alcoholic drinks; he now needs four or five to feel the same effect. Roger is experiencing
   A. physical dependence.
   B. psychological dependence.
   C. withdrawal symptoms.
   D. tolerance.

5. Which of the following is not a depressant?
   A. nicotine
   B. alcohol
   C. barbiturates
   D. opiates

Sharpen Your Thinking

Do you know someone who has a drug problem? If so, describe the nature of the problem. Is he or she willing to admit to having a problem?

5 Consciousness and Health and Wellness

Discuss the role of the conscious mind in constructing a happy and healthy life.

Positive and Negative Aspects of Our Thoughts

Consciousness is perhaps the central feature of the human mind—our internal running awareness of life's events and our thoughts and feelings. Being alone with our thoughts can be stressful, as when we are thinking about all the things we have to accomplish, the bills we neglected to pay, and the phone calls we forgot to return. But our inner life can also be a powerful tool for constructing a healthy life, as the experience of Melissa Munroe illustrates.

Munroe, a Canadian woman diagnosed with Hodgkin's lymphoma, found herself tormented by excruciating pain. Seeking ways to cope with the agony, Munroe enrolled in a meditation program. She was skeptical at first. "What I didn't realize," she said, "is that if people have ever found themselves taking a walk in the countryside or in the forest or on a nice pleasant autumn day . . . and find themselves in a contemplative state, that's a form of meditation." Monroe worked hard to use meditation to control her pain. Interestingly, the way she harnessed the power of her mind to overcome pain was by concentrating her thoughts on the pain—not trying to avoid it.

Using *mindfulness meditation,* a technique practiced by yoga enthusiasts and Buddhist monks, Monroe focused on her pain. By doing so, she was able to isolate the pain from her emotional response to it and to her cancer diagnosis. She grew to see her physical discomfort as something she could tolerate. Monroe's success shows that, contrary to what a non-meditator might think, meditation is not about avoiding one's thoughts. Indeed, the effort involved in avoiding steers the person away from the contemplative state. Munroe described her thoughts as like people striding by her on the street, walking in the other direction; she explained, "They come closer and closer, then they pass you by."

Jon Kabat-Zinn (2006) has pioneered the use of meditation techniques in medical settings. Research by Kabat-Zinn and colleagues has demonstrated the beneficial effects of mindfulness meditation for a variety of conditions, including depression, panic attacks, and anxiety (Miller, Fletcher, & Kabat-Zinn, 1995), chronic pain (Kabat-Zinn, Lipworth, & Burney, 1985), and stress and the skin condition psoriasis (Kabat-Zinn & others, 1998). Many of these effects have also been shown to be long-lasting.

As noted in Chapter 3, Richard Davidson and colleagues (including Jon Kabat-Zinn) studied the brain and immune system changes that might underlie the health and wellness effects of meditation (Davidson & others, 2003). They performed MRIs on the brains of individuals who were in a standard 8-week meditation training program. After the training program and as compared to a control group, those in the meditation program reported reduced anxiety and fewer negative emotions. Furthermore, brain scans revealed that these individuals showed increased activation in the left hemisphere—the "happy brain" described in Chapter 3. In addition, the meditators showed a better immune system response to a flu vaccine (Davidson & others, 2003). These results suggest that our conscious minds may have a role to play in enhancing our psychological and physical health (Arias & others, 2006; Ekman & others, 2005).

The Meditative State of Mind

What actually is the meditative state of mind? As a physiological state, meditation shows qualities of sleep *and* wakefulness, yet it is distinct from both. You may have experienced a state researchers call *hypnogogic reverie*—an overwhelming feeling of wellness right before you fall asleep, the sense that everything is going to work out. Meditation has been compared to this relaxed sense that all is well (Friedman, Myers, & Benson, 1998). In a study of Zen meditators, researchers were interested in examining what happens when people switch from their normal waking state to a meditative state (Ritskes & others, 2003). Using fMRI (described in Chapter 3), the researchers got images of the brain before and after the participants entered the meditative state. They found that the switch to meditation involved initial increases in activation in the basal ganglia and prefrontal cortex (the now familiar area that is often activated during consciousness). However, and interestingly, they also found that these initial activations led to decreases in the anterior cingulate, a brain area that is thought to be associated with acts of will. These results provide a picture of the physical events of the brain that are connected with the somewhat paradoxical state of meditation—controlling one's thoughts in order to let go of the need to control.

Would you like to experience what a state of meditation is like? If so, you can probably reach that state by following some simple instructions. First, you need a quiet place and a comfortable chair. Sit upright in the chair, rest your chin comfortably on your chest, and place your arms in your lap. Close your eyes. Now focus on your breathing. Every time you inhale and every time you exhale, pay attention to the sensations of air flowing through your body, the feeling of your lungs filling and emptying. After you have focused on several breaths, begin to repeat silently to yourself a single word every time you breathe out. The word you choose does not have to mean anything: You can make a word up, you can use the word *one,* or you can try a word associated with the emotion you want to produce, such as *trust, love, patience,* or *happy.* Experiment with several different words to see which one works for you. At first, you will find that thoughts are intruding and that you are no longer attending to your breathing. Just return to your breathing and say the word each time you exhale.

After you have practiced this exercise for 10 to 15 minutes, twice a day, every day for 2 weeks, you will be ready for a shortened version. If you notice that you are experiencing stressful thoughts or circumstances, simply meditate, on the spot, for several minutes. If

Regular meditation can help you to clarify your goals and purpose in life, strengthen your values, and improve your outlook.

Being alone with our thoughts can be a source of great stress or one of strength.

you are in public, you do not have to close your eyes; just fix your gaze on a nearby object, attend to your breathing, and say your word silently every time you exhale.

Meditation is an age-old practice. Without explicitly mentioning meditation, some religions advocate related practices such as daily prayer and peaceful introspection. Whether the practice involves praying over rosary beads, chanting before a Buddhist shrine, or simply taking a moment to commune with nature, a contemplative state clearly has broad appeal and conveys many benefits (Kabat-Zinn, 2006). Current research on the contemplative state suggests that there are good reasons why human beings have been harnessing its beneficial powers for centuries.

Being alone with your thoughts can be challenging. But with practice, meditation can help you to develop a clearer picture of your life, a stronger sense of your values, and ultimately a healthier and more positive perspective.

REVIEW, ASSESS, AND SHARPEN YOUR THINKING

Review

5 Discuss the role of the conscious mind in constructing a happy and healthy life.

- Give some positive and negative aspects of "being alone with one's thoughts."
- Describe the meditative state of mind and findings about the benefits of meditation to health and wellness.

Assess

1. A state of calmness and wellness characterized by optimism is called
   A. yoga.
   B. hypnogogic reverie.
   C. meditation.
   D. mindfulness.

2. Which of the following is true about mindfulness meditation?
   A. It involves clearing the mind of all thoughts.
   B. It has not been demonstrated to be effective in pain management.
   C. It increases activation of the right hemisphere of the brain.
   D. It increases awareness of thoughts, feelings, and specific bodily sensations.

3. Which part of the brain shows an increase in activation during mediation?

A. thalamus

B. reticular formation

C. prefrontal cortex

D. hippocampus

Sharpen Your Thinking

Try meditating for just 15 minutes when you finish reading this chapter. What was the experience like? How would you describe the quality of your thoughts? Were you able to "let go"? Why or why not? Is the skill of meditation something you would like to pursue?

1 THE NATURE OF CONSCIOUSNESS

Discuss the nature of consciousness.

Consciousness and the Brain

Consciousness is the awareness of external events and internal sensations, including awareness of the self and thoughts about experiences. Unanswered questions about consciousness concern its location—in the mind, in the brain?—and, if in the brain, whether there is a seat of consciousness or rather a distribution across different areas. Most experts agree that consciousness is likely distributed across the brain, although the association areas and prefrontal lobes are believed to play important roles in consciousness.

Levels of Awareness

William James described the mind as a stream of consciousness. Consciousness occurs at different levels of awareness that include higher-level awareness (controlled processes and selective attention), lower-level awareness (automatic processes and daydreaming), altered states of consciousness (produced by drugs, trauma, fatigue, and other factors), subconscious awareness (waking subconscious awareness, sleep, and dreams), and no awareness (unconscious thought).

2 SLEEP AND DREAMS

Explain the nature of sleep and dreams.

Biological Rhythms and Sleep

Biological rhythms are periodic physiological fluctuations. The biological rhythm that regulates the daily sleep/wake cycle is the circadian rhythm. The part of the brain that keeps our biological clocks synchronized is the suprachiasmatic nucleus, a small structure in the hypothalamus that registers light. Biological clocks can become desynchronized by such things as jet travel and work shifts. Some strategies are available for resetting the biological clock.

Why Do We Need Sleep?

We need sleep for physical restoration, adaptation, growth, and memory. Research studies increasingly reveal that people do not function optimally when they are sleep-deprived. In general, Americans—and adolescents and aging adults in particular—do not get enough sleep.

Sleep Stages

Stages of sleep correspond to massive electrophysiological changes that occur in the brain and that can be assessed by an EEG. Humans go through four stages of non-REM sleep and one stage of REM sleep, or rapid eye movement sleep. Most dreaming occurs during REM sleep. The amount of REM sleep changes over the life span. A sleep cycle of five stages lasts about 90 to 100 minutes and recurs several times during the night. The REM stage lasts longer toward the end of a night's sleep. The sleep stages are associated with distinct patterns of neurotransmitter activity. Levels of the neurotransmitters serotonin, norepinephrine, and acetylcholine decrease as the sleep cycle progresses from stage 1 through stage 4. Stage 5, REM sleep, begins when the reticular formation raises the level of acetylcholine.

Sleep and Disease

Sleep plays a role in a large number of diseases and disorders. Neurons that control sleep interact closely with the immune system, and when our bodies are fighting infection our cells produce a substance that makes us sleepy. Individuals with depression often have sleep problems.

Sleep Disorders

Many Americans suffer from chronic, long-term sleep disorders that can impair normal daily functioning. These include insomnia, sleepwalking and sleep talking, nightmares and night terrors, narcolepsy, and sleep apnea.

Dreams

There are cultural and gender variations in dreaming. People in primitive cultures more often tie dreaming to reality or to the spiritual than do people in modern cultures. In Freud's view, dreams represented symbols of unconscious wishes. The cognitive theory of dreaming attempts to explain dreaming in terms of the same cognitive concepts that are used in studying the waking mind. In this view, dreams might be an arena for solving problems and thinking creatively. According to activation-synthesis theory, dreaming occurs when the cerebral cortex synthesizes neural signals emanating from activity in the lower part of the brain. In this view, the rising level of acetylcholine during REM sleep plays a role in neural activity in the reticular formation of the limbic system that the cerebral cortex tries to make sense of.

3 HYPNOSIS

Describe hypnosis.

The Nature of Hypnosis

Hypnosis is a psychological state or possibly altered attention and awareness in which the individual is unusually receptive to suggestions. The hypnotic state is different from a sleep state, as confirmed

by EEG recordings. Inducing hypnosis involves four basic steps, beginning with minimizing distractions and making the person feel comfortable and ending with the hypnotist's suggesting certain events or feelings that he or she knows will occur or observes occurring. There are substantial individual variations in people's susceptibility to hypnosis. People in a hypnotic state are unlikely to do anything that violates their morals or that involves a real danger.

Explaining Hypnosis

Two theories have been proposed to explain hypnosis. In Hilgard's divided consciousness view, hypnosis involves a divided state of consciousness, a splitting of consciousness into separate components. One component follows the hypnotist's commands; the other acts as a "hidden observer." In the social cognitive behavior view, hypnotized individuals behave the way they believe hypnotized individuals are expected to behave.

Applications of Hypnosis

Hypnosis is widely used in psychotherapy and medicine and has become more popular in Europe as a complement to more standard anesthesia.

4 PSYCHOACTIVE DRUGS

Evaluate the uses and types of psychoactive drugs.

Uses of Psychoactive Drugs

Psychoactive drugs act on the nervous system to alter states of consciousness, modify perceptions, and change moods. Humans are attracted to these types of drugs because they help people adapt to change. Addictive drugs activate the brain's reward system by increasing dopamine concentration. The reward pathway involves the ventral tegmental area (VTA) and nucleus accumbens. The abuse of psychoactive drugs can lead to tolerance, psychological and physical dependence, and addiction—a pattern of behavior characterized by a preoccupation with using a drug and securing its supply.

Types of Psychoactive Drugs

Depressants slow down mental and physical activity. Among the most widely used depressants are alcohol, barbiturates, tranquilizers, and opiates. After caffeine, alcohol is the most widely used drug in America. The high rate of alcohol abuse by high school and college students is especially alarming. Alcoholism is a disorder that involves long-term, repeated, uncontrolled, compulsive, and excessive use of alcoholic beverages that impairs the drinker's health and work and social relationships. Stimulants increase the central nervous system's activity and include caffeine, nicotine, amphetamines, cocaine, and MDMA (Ecstasy). Hallucinogens modify a person's perceptual experiences and produce visual images that are not real. Marijuana has a mild hallucinogenic effect. LSD has a strong one.

5 CONSCIOUSNESS AND HEALTH AND WELLNESS

Discuss the role of the conscious mind in constructing a happy and healthy life.

Positive and Negative Aspects of Our Thoughts

How we think about our lives and experiences plays a role in determining whether we feel stressed and worried or challenged and excited about life. Seeking times of quiet contemplation can have a positive impact on our abilities to cope with life's ups and downs.

The Meditative State of Mind

One powerful tool for managing life's problems is mindfulness meditation. Meditation refers to a state of quiet reflection. Meditation has benefits for a wide range of psychological and physical illnesses. Meditation can also benefit the body's immune system. Research using fMRI suggests that meditation allows an individual to control his or her thoughts in order to "let go" of the need to control.

Key Terms

Assess Your Knowledge

1. Withdrawal symptoms including physical pain and craving are a sign of
   A. psychological dependence.
   B. tolerance.
   C. damage to the nucleus accumbens.
   D. physical dependence.

2. Which drug is used most by Americans?
   A. marijuana   B. alcohol
   C. nicotine   D. caffeine

3. Marijuana is classified as a
   A. stimulant.   B. hallucinogen.
   C. depressant.   D. legal drug.

4. How are amphetamines and cocaine different?
   A. Amphetamines are hallucinogens, whereas cocaine is a stimulant.
   B. Amphetamines are addictive, whereas cocaine is not.

C. Amphetamines are made from chemical products, whereas cocaine is made from plants.

D. Amphetamines are a more concentrated form of cocaine.

5. Joseph just realized that he was daydreaming. He began to think about the way that his mind wandered from what he was focusing on to what he was daydreaming. Joseph is now engaging in

A. daydreaming.   B. stream of consciousness.
C. metacognition.   D. subconscious awareness.

6. For an experienced driver, driving down her own street to get home is

A. a controlled process.
B. an example of subconscious awareness.
C. an altered state of consciousness.
D. an automatic process.

7. Our bodies know that it is day or night based on input from the retina that goes to the

A. occipital lobe.   B. suprachiasmatic nucleus.
C. limbic system.   D. thalamus.

8. During which stage of sleep are brain waves largest in amplitude for the longest period of time?

A. stage 2   B. stage 3
C. stage 4   D. stage 5

9. When someone is in the lightest state of sleep, which type of brain waves predominate?

A. alpha   B. beta
C. delta   D. theta

10. Problems with breathing during sleeping are referred to as

A. somnambulism.   B. sleep apnea.
C. narcolepsy.   D. night terrors.

11. Someone who has been hypnotized reports that she did not perceive pain when poked with a sharp object. However, she experienced physiological changes when poked. The _____ view of hypnosis would say that one part of her experienced the pain while another part of her did not.

A. unconscious
B. divided state of consciousness
C. hypnosedation
D. social cognitive behavior

12. What is the main way in which alcohol affects the brain?

A. It serves as an agonist for GABA.
B. It serves as an antagonist for GABA.
C. It serves as an agonist for acetylcholine.
D. It serves as an antagonist for acetylcholine.

13. Mindfulness meditation involves all of the following except:

A. clearing the mind of all thoughts.
B. increased immune functioning.
C. activation of the left hemisphere of the brain.
D. characteristics of both sleeping and waking.

14. Arousal is most associated with the

A. reticular formation.
B. cerebral cortex.
C. hippocampus.
D. suprachiasmatic nucleus.

15. Which theory states that dreams are triggered by internal stimuli, such as being hot or thirsty when sleeping?

A. social cognitive behavior
B. activation-synthesis
C. biological-clock
D. stream-of consciousness

Go to Appendix B for answers to these questions.

Apply Your Knowledge

1. We process information at many levels of consciousness. As an experiment, try to bring as much sensory information into the controlled process level of consciousness as you can. Pay attention to every sensation available to you. (Are your socks touching your ankles? How many sounds can you hear? What is available to your visual system? Is your stomach growling?) How long can you keep track of all of this sensory information, and what would happen if something important abruptly required your full attention? What does this exercise tell you about which levels of consciousness normally process all this information?

2. Keep a sleep journal for several nights. Compare your sleep patterns with those described in the text. Do you have a sleep debt? If so, which stages of sleep are you likely missing most? Does a good night's sleep affect your behavior? Keep a record of your mood and energy levels after a short night's sleep and then after you have had at least 8 hours sleep in one night. What changes do you notice, and how do they compare with the changes predicted by research on sleep deprivation described in the chapter?

3. You may recall the widely publicized controversy over Terri Schiavo, a woman who fell into a coma at the age of 26, never to recover. Eventually Schiavo was diagnosed as being in a "persistent vegetative state"—a state of wakefulness without awareness. Whether Schiavo had any consciousness at all was a key question in the debate that surrounded whether her feeding tube should be removed. After her death, an autopsy revealed that her cerebrum was severely damaged, supporting the notion that she had indeed been in a persistent vegetative state, with no conscious awareness. Search the web for information about the Schiavo case. Look for indicators of the crucial place that consciousness and theory of mind played in responses to the case.

4. The website of the National Institute on Drug Abuse maintains a series of reports on current scientific knowledge about many commonly abused drugs. Visit the site at **http://www.nida.nih.gov/ ResearchReports/ResearchIndex.html** and pick one of the listed reports. Using the report's information, compare the psychological effects and the risks associated with use of this drug with the psychological effects and risks of one of the psychoactive compounds described in the chapter.

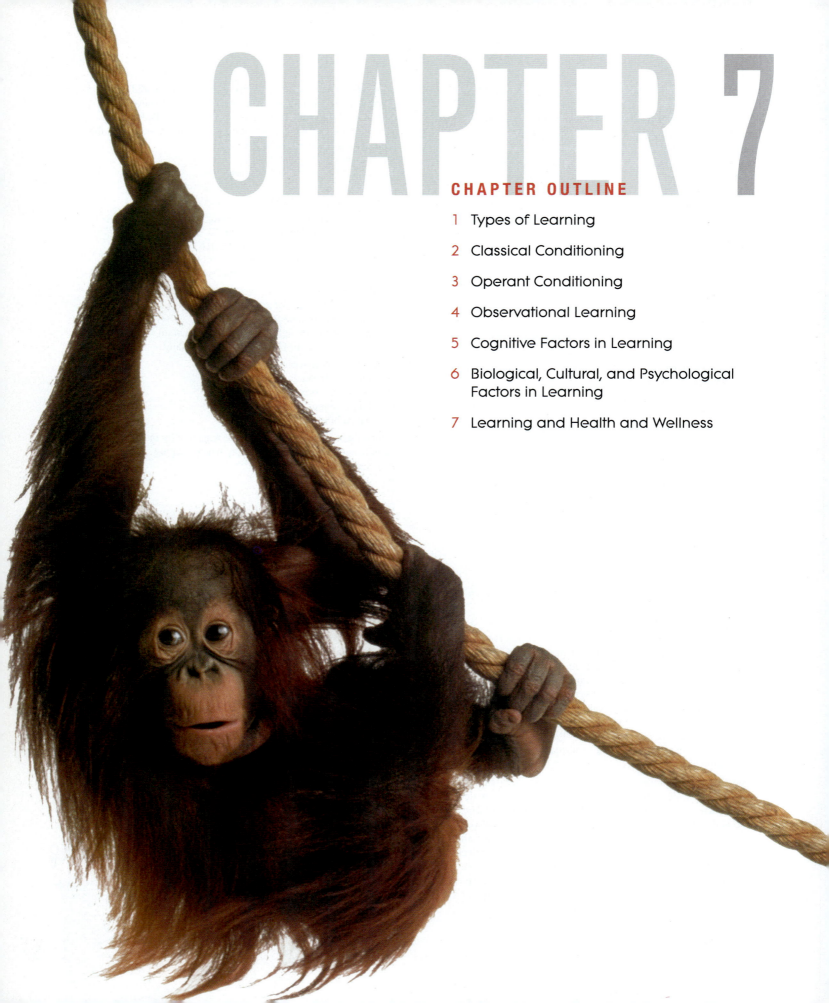

CHAPTER 7

LEARNING

Experiencing Psychology

A BOY AND HIS DOG

On December 27, 2003, the *San Diego Tribune* carried a story about a 6-year-old boy, Xavier Ivy-Parris. Like many other children, Xavier had received a puppy for Christmas. What made this particular gift noteworthy was that Xavier had suffered a traumatic brain injury that left him prone to blackouts and made concentrating difficult. As a result, he could not walk to school like his first-grade classmates. Xavier's puppy changed that and many other aspects of his life as well. His new puppy was not only a beloved pet but a service dog, trained to help him walk to school and to alert others if Xavier blacked out.

We have all seen such service dogs—on a city street, on a bus, or in a store—faithfully walking next to their human partners. The idea of guide dogs began in 1929, when Dorothy Eustis observed that the German military was using German shepherds as guides for war-blinded veterans of World War I. Although the first service dogs were seeing-eye dogs for the blind, today service dogs are trained to provide services to people with spinal cord and head injury, muscular dystrophy, visual and hearing loss, arthritis, and a long list of other disabilities.

According to the University of Arizona's Partners for Life program, there are approximately 15,000 service dogs in the United States (Partners for Life, 2007). The range of assistance these dogs provide is breathtaking. They lead, provide sound discrimination for the hearing impaired, assist with mobility, retrieve items, and locate people, bathrooms, elevators, and even lost cell phones. They open and close doors, help people dress and undress, carry items in a backpack, flush toilets, and even put clothes in a washer and dryer. Service dogs have become a common sight in the United States since 1990, when the Americans with Disabilities Act was passed. A portion of this act requires the admission of service dogs to the public places where their human partners wish to go.

In many ways, service dogs are highly skilled professionals. Anyone who has a lazy mutt at home might wonder how it is possible for dogs to acquire these skills. Service dogs have been trained to perform these complex acts using the principles that psychologists have uncovered in studying the processes that underlie *learning*. When you think about learning, your thoughts may turn to the teachers you have had and classes you have taken. Indeed, even though it has been a long time since you were Xavier's age, you probably remember the name of your first-grade teacher to this day—evidence of the importance of learning in your life. ■

PREVIEW

Although human learning may seem a far cry from even the most sophisticated dog training, many of the basic principles of learning apply to humans as well as to other animals. In this chapter, we first focus on two types of associative learning: classical conditioning and operant conditioning. These forms of conditioning help to illuminate the seemingly fantastic abilities of service dogs. Next, we survey observational learning, a form of learning that may be more common in humans. We then probe into the role of cognitive processes in learning and consider the biological, cultural, and psychological constraints on learning. Finally, we explore the implications of the basic learning principles for individuals' physical health and well-being. Throughout the chapter, you might ask yourself about your own beliefs about learning: What can be learned and what cannot? If a dog can learn to do the laundry, surely the human potential for learning has barely been tapped.

1 Types of Learning

Explain learning.

Learning anything new involves change. Once you learned the alphabet, it did not leave you. Once you learn how to drive a car, you do not have to go through the process again at a later time. If you ever decide to try out for the X-Games, you may break a few bones along the way, but at some point you probably will learn a trick or two, changing from a novice to an enthusiast who can at least stay on top of a skateboard. Learning involves a relatively permanent influence on behavior. You learned the alphabet through experience with the letters. Through experience, you also may have learned that you have to study to do well on a test, that there usually is an opening act at a rock concert, and that a field goal in U.S. football adds 3 points to the score. Putting these pieces together, we arrive at a definition of **learning:** a relatively permanent change in behavior that occurs through experience.

What psychologists have learned about learning comes from a perspective that started with rats, cats, pigeons, and even raccoons, not with a student like yourself who, in the course of reading this book and taking a class, is learning. So much research on learning has been done with lower animals largely because of the extensive control that researchers can exercise in studies on lower animals. A century of research on learning in lower animals and in humans suggests that many of the principles generated initially in research on lower animals also apply to humans (Domjan, 2006).

If someone were to ask you what you learned in class today, you might talk about new ideas you heard about, lists you memorized, or concepts you mastered. But how would you define your learning if you could not refer to the mind or to unobservable mental processes? You might follow the lead of behavioral psychologists.

Behaviorism is a theory of learning that focuses solely on observable behaviors, discounting the importance of such mental activity as thinking, wishing, and hoping. Psychologists who approach learning from a behavioral perspective define learning as relatively stable, observable changes in behavior.

The behavioral approach has emphasized general laws that guide behavior change and make sense of some of the puzzling aspects of human life. What does positive psychology have to say about the behavioral approach to human learning? As we will see, behaviorism is the area in which one of the founders of the positive psychology movement first had an impact on the field of psychology.

In this chapter we look at two types of learning, *associative learning* and *observational learning*. **Associative learning** occurs when a connection, or an association, is made between two events. *Conditioning* is the process of learning associations (Chance, 2006). There are two types of conditioning: classical and operant.

In *classical conditioning,* organisms learn the association between two stimuli. As a result of this association, organisms learn to anticipate events. For example, lightning is associated with thunder and regularly precedes it. Thus, when we see lightning, we anticipate that we will hear thunder soon afterward. Fans of horror films know the power of

learning A relatively permanent change in behavior that occurs through experience.

behaviorism A theory of learning that focuses solely on observable behaviors, discounting the importance of such mental activity as thinking, wishing, and hoping.

associative learning Learning in which a connection, or an association, is made between two events.

Classical Conditioning

Stimulus 1
Doctor's office

Stimulus 2
Shot

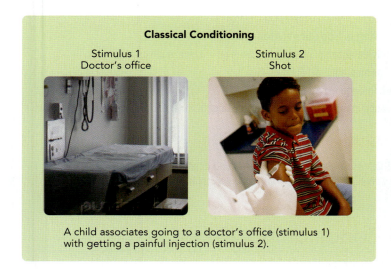

A child associates going to a doctor's office (stimulus 1) with getting a painful injection (stimulus 2).

Operant Conditioning

Behavior

Consequences

Performing well in a swimming competition (behavior) becomes associated with getting awards (consequences).

FIGURE 7.1

Associative Learning: Comparing Classical and Operant Conditioning
(*Left*) In this example of classical conditioning, a child associates a doctor's office (stimulus 1) with getting a painful injection (stimulus 2). (*Right*) In this example of operant conditioning, performing well in a swimming competition (behavior) becomes associated with getting awards (consequences).

classical conditioning. Watching one of the *Friday the 13th* movies, we find the tension building whenever we hear that familiar "Ch-ch-ch—ch-ha-ha-ha-ha" that signals Jason's arrival. During *Jaws,* we hear the telltale "Bah-bump bah-bump bah-bump," and we brace ourselves for the shark attack.

In *operant conditioning,* organisms learn the association between a behavior and a consequence. As a result of this association, organisms learn to increase behaviors that are followed by rewards and to decrease behaviors that are followed by punishment. For example, children are likely to repeat their good manners if their parents reward them with candy after they have shown good manners. Also, if children's bad manners are followed by scolding words and harsh glances by parents, the children are less likely to repeat the bad manners. Figure 7.1 compares classical and operant conditioning.

Much of what we learn, however, is not a matter of direct reinforcement but rather comes from our exposure to models performing a behavior or skill. For instance, watching someone shoot baskets, you might get a sense of how it is done. This process of learning that takes place when a person observes and imitates another's behavior is called **observational learning.** Observational learning is a common way that people learn in educational and other settings.

Learning applies to many areas of acquiring new behaviors, skills, and knowledge. Our focus in this chapter is on the two types of associative learning—classical conditioning and operant conditioning—and on observational learning.

observational learning Learning that occurs when a person observes and imitates another's behavior; also called imitation or modeling.

 REVIEW, ASSESS, AND SHARPEN YOUR THINKING

Review

1 Explain learning.
   - Define learning and distinguish between observational and associative learning.

Assess

1. A cat who associates the sound of a can opener with being fed has learned via what mechanism?

   A. behaviorism
   B. operant conditioning
   C. classical conditioning
   D. observational learning

2. A parent who gives a child ice cream when she gets good grades in school is using what type of learning technique?

   A. behaviorism
   B. operant conditioning
   C. classical conditioning
   D. observational learning

3. **Which of the following is true about learning?**

    A. Learning can only be accomplished by higher-level species, such as mammals.

    B. Learning is not permanent.

    C. Learning occurs through experience.

    D. Learning processes in humans is completely distinct from learning processes in animals.

Sharpen Your Thinking

How do you learn? Think of a behavior you engage in and describe how you learned it. Give an example of associative learning and operant conditioning from your own life.

2 Classical Conditioning

Describe classical conditioning.

It is a nice spring day. A father takes his baby out for a walk. The baby reaches over to touch a pink flower and is stung by the bumblebee sitting on the petals. The next day, the baby's mother brings home some pink flowers. She removes a flower from the arrangement and takes it over for her baby to smell. The baby cries loudly as soon as she sees the pink flower. The baby's panic at the sight of the pink flower illustrates the learning process of **classical conditioning,** in which a neutral stimulus (the flower) becomes associated with a meaningful stimulus (the pain of a bee sting) and acquires the capacity to elicit a similar response (fear).

Pavlov's Studies

In the early 1900s, the Russian physiologist Ivan Pavlov was interested in the way the body digests food. In his experiments, he routinely placed meat powder in a dog's mouth, causing the dog to salivate. Quite by accident, Pavlov noticed that the meat powder was not the only stimulus that caused the dog to salivate. The dog salivated in response to a number of stimuli associated with the food, such as the sight of the food dish, the sight of the individual who brought the food into the room, and the sound of the door closing when the food arrived. Pavlov recognized that the dog's association of these sights and sounds with the food was an important type of learning, which came to be called *classical conditioning.*

classical conditioning Learning by which a neutral stimulus becomes associated with a meaningful stimulus and acquires the capacity to elicit a similar response.

Pavlov (the white-bearded gentleman in the center) is shown demonstrating the nature of classical conditioning to students at the Military Medical Academy in Russia.

Before Conditioning

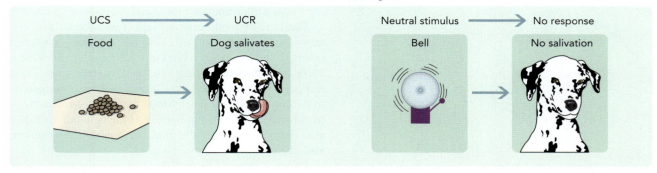

Conditioning

After Conditioning

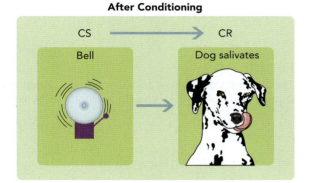

Pavlov wanted to know *why* the dog salivated in reaction to various sights and sounds before eating the meat powder. He observed that the dog's behavior included both learned and unlearned components. The unlearned part of classical conditioning is based on the fact that some stimuli automatically produce certain responses apart from any prior learning; in other words, they are inborn, or innate. *Reflexes* are such automatic stimulus–response connections. They include salivation in response to food, nausea in response to spoiled food, shivering in response to low temperature, coughing in response to throat congestion, pupil constriction in response to light, and withdrawal in response to blows or burns. An **unconditioned stimulus (UCS)** is a stimulus that produces a response without prior learning; food was the UCS in Pavlov's experiments. An **unconditioned response (UCR)** is an unlearned response that is automatically elicited by the UCS. In Pavlov's experiment, the saliva that flowed from the dog's mouth in response to food was the UCR.

In the case of the baby and the flower, the baby's learning and experience did not cause her to cry when the bee stung her. Her crying was unlearned and occurred automatically. The bee's sting was the UCS, and the crying was the UCR.

In classical conditioning, the **conditioned stimulus (CS)** is a previously neutral stimulus that eventually elicits the conditioned response after being associated with the unconditioned stimulus. The **conditioned response (CR)** is the learned response to the conditioned stimulus that occurs after CS–UCS pairing (Pavlov, 1927). In studying a dog's response to various stimuli associated with meat powder, Pavlov rang a bell before giving meat powder to the dog. Until then, ringing the bell did not have a particular effect on the dog, except perhaps to wake the dog from a nap. The bell was a neutral stimulus. But the dog began to associate the sound of the bell with the food and salivated when it heard the bell. The bell had become a conditioned (learned) stimulus (CS) and salivation was now a conditioned response (CR). For the unhappy baby, the flower was the "bell," or CS, and crying was the CR after the sting (UCS) and the flower (CS) were paired. A summary of how classical conditioning works is shown in Figure 7.2.

Acquisition   **Acquisition** in classical conditioning is the initial learning of the stimulus–response link. This involves a neutral stimulus being associated with the UCS and becoming

FIGURE 7.2

Pavlov's Classical Conditioning In one experiment, Pavlov presented a neutral stimulus (bell) just before an unconditioned stimulus (food). The neutral stimulus became a conditioned stimulus by being paired with the unconditioned stimulus. Subsequently, the conditioned stimulus (bell) by itself was able to elicit the dog's salivation.

unconditioned stimulus (UCS) A stimulus that produces a response without prior learning.

unconditioned response (UCR) An unlearned response that is automatically elicited by an unconditioned stimulus.

conditioned stimulus (CS) A previously neutral stimulus that eventually elicits the conditioned response after being associated with the unconditioned stimulus.

conditioned response (CR) The learned response to the conditioned stimulus that occurs after the pairing of a conditioned stimulus and an unconditioned stimulus.

acquisition (classical conditioning) The initial learning of the stimulus–response link, which involves a neutral stimulus being associated with an unconditioned stimulus and becoming the conditioned stimulus that elicits the conditioned response.

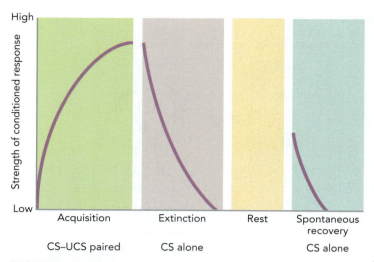

FIGURE 7.3

The Strength of a Classically Conditioned Response During Acquisition, Extinction, and Spontaneous Recovery During acquisition, the conditioned stimulus and unconditioned stimulus are associated. As seen in the graph, when this occurs, the strength of the conditioned response increases. During extinction, the conditioned stimulus is presented alone, and, as can be seen, this results in a decrease of the conditioned response. After a rest period, spontaneous recovery appears, although the strength of the conditioned response is not nearly as great at this point as it was after a number of CS–UCS pairings. When the CS is presented alone again, after spontaneous recovery, the response is extinguished rapidly.

generalization (classical conditioning) The tendency of a new stimulus that is similar to the original conditioned stimulus to elicit a response that is similar to the conditioned response.

discrimination (classical conditioning) The process of learning to respond to certain stimuli and not to others.

extinction (classical conditioning) The weakening of the conditioned response in the absence of the unconditioned stimulus.

spontaneous recovery The process in classical conditioning by which a conditioned response can recur after a time delay without further conditioning.

the conditioned stimulus (CS) that elicits the CR. Two important aspects of acquisition are timing and contingency/predictability.

The time interval between the CS and the UCS is one of the most important aspects of classical conditioning (Bangasser & others, 2006; McNally & Westbrook, 2006). It defines the *contiguity,* or connectedness in time and space, of the stimuli. Conditioned responses develop when the CS and UCS are contiguous, occurring close together. Often, optimal spacing is a fraction of a second (Kimble, 1961). In Pavlov's work, if the bell had rung 20 minutes after the presentation of the food, the dog probably would not have associated the bell with the food.

Robert Rescorla (1966, 1988) believes that for classical conditioning to take place, it is important to have not only a brief time interval in the CS–UCS connection but also contingency. *Contingency* in classical conditioning means the predictability of the occurrence of one stimulus from the presence of another. For example, as we considered earlier, a flash of lightning usually is followed by the sound of thunder. Thus, if you see lightning, you might put your hands over your ears or lean away in anticipation of the thunder.

Generalization and Discrimination Pavlov found that the dog salivated in response not only to the tone of the bell but also to other sounds, such as a whistle. Pavlov did not pair these sounds with the unconditioned stimulus of the food. He discovered that, the more similar the noise was to the original sound of the bell, the stronger was the dog's salivary flow. **Generalization** in classical conditioning is the tendency of a new stimulus that is similar to the original conditioned stimulus to elicit a response that is similar to the conditioned response (Rescorla, 2006a; Shaban & others, 2006). Generalization has value in preventing learning from being tied to specific stimuli. For example, we do not have to learn to drive all over again when we change cars or drive down a different road.

Stimulus generalization is not always beneficial. For example, the cat that generalizes from a harmless minnow to a dangerous piranha has a major problem; therefore, it is important to also discriminate between stimuli. **Discrimination** in classical conditioning is the process of learning to respond to certain stimuli and not to others (J. Harris, 2006; Murphy, Baker, & Fouquet, 2001). To produce discrimination, Pavlov gave food to the dog only after ringing the bell and not after any other sounds. In this way, the dog learned to distinguish between the bell and other sounds.

Extinction and Spontaneous Recovery After conditioning the dog to salivate at the sound of a bell, Pavlov rang the bell repeatedly in a single session and did not give the dog any food. Eventually the dog stopped salivating. This result is **extinction,** which in classical conditioning is the weakening of the conditioned response in the absence of the unconditioned stimulus (Barad, Gean, & Lutz, 2006; Joscelyne & Kehoe, 2007). Without continued association with the unconditioned stimulus (UCS), the conditioned stimulus (CS) loses its power to elicit the conditioned response (CR).

Extinction is not always the end of a conditioned response (Moody, Sunsay, & Bouton, 2006). The day after Pavlov extinguished the conditioned salivation to the sound of a bell, he took the dog to the laboratory and rang the bell, still not giving the dog any meat powder. The dog salivated, indicating that an extinguished response can spontaneously recur. **Spontaneous recovery** is the process in classical conditioning by which a conditioned response can recur after a time delay without further conditioning (Rescorla, 2005). Consider an example of spontaneous recovery you may have experienced: You thought that you had totally forgotten about (extinguished) an old lover you once had, but then, all of a sudden, you are in a particular context and you get a mental image of the person, accompanied by an emotional reaction to him or her from the past (spontaneous recovery).

Figure 7.3 shows the sequence of acquisition, extinction, and spontaneous recovery. Spontaneous recovery can occur several times, but as long as the conditioned stimulus is presented alone, spontaneous recovery becomes weaker and eventually ceases to occur.

To strengthen your grasp of acquisition, generalization, discrimination, and extinction in classical conditioning, consider how these concepts might reflect a young child's experience in going to see a dentist:

- *Acquisition:* The child learns to fear (CR) going to the dentist's office by associating the visit with the unlearned emotional response (UCR) to the pain of having a tooth cavity filled (UCS).
- *Generalization:* The child fears all dentists' offices and similar places, including doctors' offices and adults in them who wear white medical clothing, as well as the smells and sounds there.
- *Discrimination:* The child goes with his or her mother to the mother's doctor's office and learns that it is not associated with the pain of the UCS.
- *Extinction:* The child subsequently goes to the dentist on a number of occasions and does not have a painful experience, so the child's fear of dentists' offices goes away, at least for a while, until the child has another painful experience with a cavity being filled.

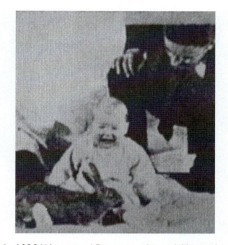

In 1920, Watson and Rayner conditioned 11-month-old Albert to fear a white rat by pairing the rat with a loud noise. When little Albert was subsequently presented with other stimuli similar to the white rat, such as the rabbit shown here with little Albert, he was afraid of them, too. This illustrates the principle of stimulus generalization in classical conditioning.

Researchers have found that the majority of dental fears originate in childhood, likely through classical conditioning, and that these fears can keep individuals from obtaining dental treatment as adults (Ost, 1991).

Interestingly, there are cultural variations in children's dental fear. Children in the United States have the most fear (20 percent have a high level of fear), and children in Norway and Sweden have the least fear (only 3 to 4 percent have a high level of fear) (Milgram, Vigehesa, & Weinstein, 1992; Neverlien & Johnsen, 1991). This cultural difference likely stems from the fact that dental care is part of a free, universal health care system in Norway and Sweden. Consequently, children there go to the dentist on a regular basis, regardless of whether they have a dental problem. By contrast, the United States does not have a universal health care system, and children often go to the dentist only when they have a problem. Thus, American children experience dental treatment as painful and something to be avoided. Possibly, then, differences in cultural experience influence the occurrence of conditioned emotional responses.

Classical Conditioning in Humans

Since Pavlov conducted his experiments, individuals have been conditioned to respond to the sound of a buzzer, a glimpse of light, a puff of air, or the touch of a hand (J. Harris, 2006). Classical conditioning has a great deal of survival value for the individual (McNally & Westbrook, 2006). Because of classical conditioning, we jerk our hands away before they are burned by fire. Classical conditioning also is at work when a novelist's description of a tranquil scene such as an empty beach with waves lapping the sand causes a harried executive to relax as if she were actually lying on that beach.

Explaining and Eliminating Fears   A *phobia* is an irrational fear. Classical conditioning provides an explanation of phobias and other fears (Hermans & others, 2006; Wood & others, 2007). John B. Watson (who coined the term *behaviorism*) and Rosalie Rayner (1920) demonstrated classical conditioning's role in phobias with an infant named Albert. They showed Albert a white laboratory rat to see if he was afraid of it. He was not. As Albert played with the rat, a loud noise was sounded behind his head. As you might imagine, the noise caused little Albert to cry. After only seven pairings of the loud noise with the white rat, Albert began to fear the rat even when the noise was not sounded. Albert's fear was generalized to a rabbit, a dog, and a sealskin coat.

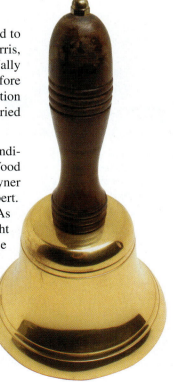

Today, Watson and Rayner's (1920) study would violate the ethical guidelines of the American Psychological Association. Especially noteworthy is the fact that they did not reverse Albert's fear of furry objects, so presumably this phobia remained with him after the experiment. In the early part of the twentieth century, when the experiment with little Albert was conducted, there was less concern about the ethical aspects of research. As we saw in Chapter 2, today, research psychologists must adhere to strict ethical guidelines.

A breathtaking rainbow or some other beautiful natural event that you observed can serve as a conditioned stimulus. So can a restaurant where you enjoyed a positive romantic experience.

Watson correctly concluded that we learn many of our fears through classical conditioning. We might develop a fear of the dentist because of a painful experience, fear of driving after having been in an automobile accident, and fear of dogs after having been bitten by one.

If we can produce fears through classical conditioning, then we should be able to eliminate them using conditioning procedures. **Counterconditioning** is a classical conditioning procedure for weakening a CR by associating the fear-provoking stimulus with a new response that is incompatible with the fear. Although Watson did not eliminate little Albert's fear of white rats, an associate of Watson's, Mary Cover Jones (1924), did eliminate the fears of a 3-year-old boy named Peter. Peter had many of the same fears as Albert; however, Peter's fears were not produced by Jones. Among Peter's fears were white rats, fur coats, frogs, fish, and mechanical toys. To eliminate these fears, Jones brought a rabbit into Peter's view but kept it far enough away that it would not upset him. At the same time that the rabbit was brought into view, Peter was fed crackers and milk. On each successive day, the rabbit was moved closer to Peter as he ate crackers and milk. Eventually Peter reached the point at which he would eat the food with one hand and pet the rabbit with the other. The feeling of pleasure produced by the crackers and milk was incompatible with the fear produced by the rabbit, and Peter's fear was extinguished through counterconditioning.

Explaining Pleasant Emotions Classical conditioning is not restricted to unpleasant emotions such as fear. Among the things in our lives that produce pleasure because they have become conditioned might be a rainbow, a sunny day, and a favorite song. If you have a positive romantic experience, the location in which that experience took place can become a conditioned stimulus. This is the result of the pairing of a place (CS) with the event (UCS). Stimuli that are often associated with sex, such as mood music, seductive clothing, and a romantic restaurant, likely become conditioned stimuli that produce sexual arousal.

Sometimes, though, classical conditioning involves an experience that is both pleasant and deviant from the norm. Consider the fetishist who becomes sexually aroused by the sight and touch of certain clothing, such as undergarments or shoes. The fetish may have developed when the fetish object (undergarment, shoe) was associated with sexual arousal, especially when the individual was young. The fetish object becomes a conditioned stimulus that can produce sexual arousal by itself (Chance, 2006).

Classical Conditioning and Advertising When John Watson left the field of psychology he went on, perhaps not surprisingly, to advertising. Many contemporary advertisers use classical conditioning in some way (Perner, 2001). Consider this sequence:

- Beautiful woman (UCS) → emotional arousal (UCR) in males
- Beautiful woman (UCS) paired with an automobile (not yet a CS) many times
- Automobile (CS) → emotional arousal (CR)

Recent research has shown that, if the conditioned stimulus is encountered outside of ads, it does not predict the UCS (Bettman, 2001). Thus, classical conditioning may work best for infrequently encountered products and cases in which the UCS is associated with only one brand. Also, classical conditioning usually works best when the CS precedes the UCS in ads.

counterconditioning A classical conditioning procedure for weakening a conditioned response by associating the fear-provoking stimulus with a new response that is incompatible with the fear.

Classical Conditioning and Drug Habituation   Classical conditioning also can be involved in certain aspects of drug use. Pavlov realized that conditioned reflexes are important in digestion. He said that the digestive process begins as soon as food is seen or smelled—in other words, the body starts the digestive process before the food arrives. This reaction is similar to the response that occurs in the body before a drug arrives. When drugs are administered in particular circumstances—at a particular time of day, in a particular location, or in a particular ritual—the body reacts in anticipation of receiving the drug.

This aspect of drug use, which involves classical conditioning, can play a role in deaths caused by drug overdoses. How might this process work? A user typically takes a drug in a particular setting, such as a bathroom, and acquires a conditioned response to this location (Siegel, 1988). Because of classical conditioning, as soon as the drug user walks into the bathroom, his or her body begins to prepare for and anticipate the drug dose in order to lessen the effect of the insult of the drug. However, if the user takes a drug in a location other than the usual one, such as at a rock concert, the effect of the drug is greater because no conditioned responses have built up in the new setting, and therefore the body is not prepared for the drug. In cases in which heroin causes death, researchers often have found that the individuals took the drug under unusual circumstances, at a different time, or in different place relative to the context in which they usually took the drug (Marlow, 1999).

 REVIEW, ASSESS, AND SHARPEN YOUR THINKING

Review

2 **Describe classical conditioning.**

- Summarize the classical conditioning process. Include the following terms in your description: *unconditioned stimulus (UCS)*, *conditioned stimulus (CS)*, *unconditioned response (UCR)*, and *conditioned response (CR)*, as well as *acquisition*, *generalization*, *discrimination*, and *extinction/spontaneous recovery*.
- Discuss the role of classical conditioning in human phobias and specify other types of behavior that involve classical conditioning.

Assess

1. A child went to the zoo for the first time with his father and sister. While looking at one of the bird displays, his sister sneaked up and startled him. He became very frightened at the zoo and now when he sees birds outside or on the television, he cries. What is the unconditioned response?

   A. fear from being startled   B. birds

   C. being startled by his sister   D. fear from seeing birds

2. Brandon's girlfriend Molly took him out for a romantic evening. Molly was wearing a new perfume that night. Now when Brandon smells that perfume, he feels aroused. What is the conditioned stimulus?

   A. the romantic evening   B. arousal

   C. perfume   D. Molly

3. A dog has learned to associate a small blue light coming on with being fed. However, when a small light of any color comes on, the dog salivates. What has happened?

   A. extinction   B. discrimination

   C. counterconditioning   D. generalization

4. In classical conditioning, to what does the term *contingency* refer?

   A. the ability of the UCS to predict the number of times a conditioned stimulus is paired with an unconditioned stimulus

   B. how much time lapses between the conditioned stimulus and the unconditioned stimulus

   C. a conditioned response weakening when the unconditioned stimulus is absent

   D. the conditioned response being activated by stimuli that are similar to the conditioned stimulus

5. Which of the following is an example of a reflex?

   A. feeling happy after seeing a rainbow

   B. feeling nauseated after eating spoiled food

   C. feeling fear after seeing a large dog

   D. feeling excited after hearing a song

Sharpen Your Thinking

Think about an attachment that you or someone you know has for a certain object or environment. Explain how classical conditioning might account for the pleasant association.

3 Operant Conditioning

Discuss operant conditioning.

Although classical conditioning helps us to explain a great deal of learning, it is far from a complete account of all the ways we learn. Classical conditioning describes an organism's *response* to the environment, a view that fails to capture the active nature of the organism and its influence on the environment. Another major form of learning—operant conditioning—places more emphasis on the organism's *activity* in the environment (Hergenhahn & Olson, 2001).

Defining Operant Conditioning

Recall from the beginning of the chapter that classical conditioning and operant conditioning are forms of associative learning, which involves learning that two events are connected. In classical conditioning, organisms learn the association between two stimuli (UCS and CS). Classical conditioning is a form of *respondent behavior,* behavior that occurs in automatic response to a stimulus such as a nausea-producing drug, and later to a conditioned stimulus such as sweet water that was paired with the drug. Classical conditioning excels at explaining how neutral stimuli become associated with unlearned, *involuntary responses,* but it is not as effective in explaining *voluntary behaviors* such as a student's studying hard for a test, a gambler's playing slot machines in Las Vegas, or a dog's finding his owner's lost cell phone. Operant conditioning is usually much better at explaining such voluntary behaviors.

The American psychologist B. F. Skinner (1938) developed the concept of operant conditioning. **Operant conditioning** (or instrumental conditioning) is a form of associative learning in which the consequences of a behavior change the probability of the behavior's occurrence. Skinner chose the term *operant* to describe the behavior of the organism—the behavior operates on the environment, and the environment in turn operates on the behavior. As an example, in operant conditioning, performing a great skating routine in competition (behavior) is likely to result in a high score from the judges (consequences), which in turn encourages the skater to continue training and competing. Thus, whereas classical conditioning involves respondent behavior, operant conditioning consists of *operant behavior,* voluntary behavior that acts, or operates, on the environment and produces rewarding or punishing stimuli.

Recall that earlier we saw how *contingency* is an important aspect of classical conditioning in which the occurrence of one stimulus can be predicted from the presence of another one. Contingency is also important in operant conditioning. For example, when a rat pushes a lever (behavior) that delivers food, the delivery of food (consequence) is *contingent* on that behavior. Note that this principle of contingency helps explain why passersby should never praise, pet, or feed a service dog while he is working (at least without asking first). Providing rewards during such times might interfere with the dog's training.

operant conditioning Also called instrumental conditioning; a form of associative learning in which the consequences of a behavior change the probability of the behavior's occurrence.

Operant conditioning explains voluntary behaviors such as studying hard for a test and playing a fierce game of Frisbee much better than does classical conditioning.

Thorndike's Law of Effect

Although Skinner emerged as the primary figure in operant conditioning, the experiments of E. L. Thorndike (1898) established the power of consequences in determining voluntary behavior. At about the same time that Pavlov was conducting classical conditioning experiments with salivating dogs, Thorndike, an American psychologist, was studying cats in puzzle boxes. Thorndike put a hungry cat inside a box and placed a piece of fish outside. To escape from the box and obtain the food, the cat had to learn to open the latch inside the box. At first the cat made a number of ineffective responses. It clawed or bit at the bars and thrust its paw through the openings. Eventually the cat accidentally stepped on the treadle that released the door bolt. When the cat returned to the box, it went through the same random activity until it stepped on the treadle once more. On subsequent trials, the cat made fewer and fewer random movements, until finally it immediately stepped on the treadle to open the door (Figure 7.4). The **law of effect,** developed by Thorndike, states that behaviors followed by positive outcomes are strengthened, whereas behaviors followed by negative outcomes are weakened.

The key question for Thorndike was how the correct stimulus–response bond strengthens and eventually dominates incorrect stimulus–response bonds. According to Thorndike, the correct stimulus–response (S–R) association strengthens and the incorrect association weakens because of the *consequences* of the organism's actions. Thorndike's view is called *S–R theory* because the organism's behavior is due to a connection between a stimulus and a response. As the next section explains, Skinner's operant conditioning approach expanded Thorndike's basic ideas.

Skinner's Approach to Operant Conditioning

Skinner strongly believed that the mechanisms of learning are the same for all species. This conviction led him to study animals in the hope that he could discover the basic mechanisms of learning with organisms simpler than humans. During World War II, Skinner

law of effect Thorndike's principle that behaviors followed by positive outcomes are strengthened, whereas behaviors followed by negative outcomes are weakened.

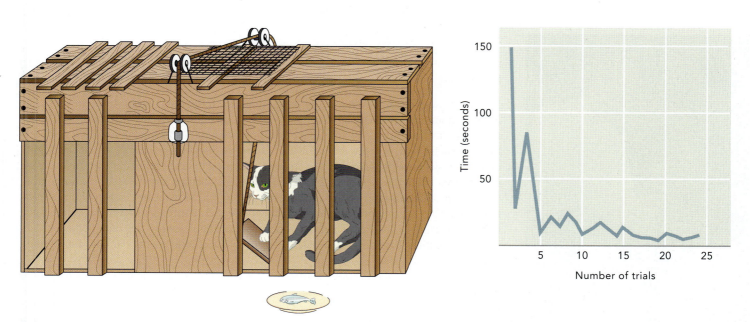

FIGURE 7.4

Thorndike's Puzzle Box and the Law of Effect (*Left*) A box typical of the puzzle boxes Thorndike used in his experiments with cats to study the law of effect. Stepping on the treadle released the door bolt; a weight attached to the door then pulled the door open and allowed the cat to escape. After accidentally pressing the treadle as it tried to get to the food, the cat learned to press the treadle when it wanted to escape the box. (*Right*) One cat's learning curve over 24 separate trials. Notice that the cat escaped much more quickly after about 5 trials. It had learned the consequences of its behavior.

FIGURE 7.5

Skinner's Pigeon-Guided Missile Skinner wanted to help the military during World War II by using pigeons' tracking behavior. A gold electrode covered the tip of the pigeons' beaks. Contact with the screen on which the image of the target was projected sent a signal informing the missile's control mechanism of the target's location. A few grains of food occasionally given to the pigeons maintained their tracking behavior.

shaping Rewarding approximations of a desired behavior.

FIGURE 7.6

The Skinner Box B. F. Skinner conducting an operant conditioning study in his behavioral laboratory. The rat being studied is in a Skinner box.

carried out an unusual study that involved a pigeon-guided missile. A pigeon in the warhead of the missile operated the flaps on the missile and guided it home by pecking at an image of a target. How could this possibly work? When the missile was in flight, the pigeon pecked the moving image on a screen, receiving a reward of food to keep the designated target in the center of the screen. This reward produced corrective signals to keep the missile on course. The pigeons did their job well in trial runs, but top navy officials just could not accept pigeons piloting their missiles in a war. Skinner, however, congratulated himself on the degree of control he was able to exercise over the pigeons (Figure 7.5).

Following the pigeon experiment, Skinner (1948) wrote *Walden Two,* a novel in which he presented his ideas about building a scientifically managed society. Skinner envisioned a utopian (perfect) society that could be engineered through operant conditioning. Skinner viewed existing societies as poorly managed because people believe in the myth of free will. He pointed out that humans are no freer than pigeons are; denying that our behavior is controlled by environmental forces is to ignore science and reality, he argued. Skinner believed that in the long run we would be much happier when we recognized such truths, especially his concept that operant conditioning would provide us with prosperous lives.

Skinner and other behaviorists made every effort to study organisms under precisely controlled conditions so that they could examine the connection between the operant and the specific consequences in minute detail (Lieberman, 2004). One of Skinner's creations in the 1930s to control experimental conditions was the Skinner box (Figure 7.6). A device in the box delivered food pellets into a tray at random. After a rat became accustomed to the box, Skinner installed a lever and observed the rat's behavior. As the hungry rat explored the box, it occasionally pressed the lever, and a food pellet was dispensed. Soon the rat learned that the consequences of pressing the lever were positive: It would be fed. Skinner achieved further control by soundproofing the box to ensure that the experimenter was the only influence on the organism. In many of the experiments, the responses were mechanically recorded, and the food (the stimulus) was dispensed automatically. Such precautions were designed to avoid human error.

Shaping

Imagine trying to teach even a really bright dog how to do the laundry. It might seem like an insurmountable challenge, particularly because it is quite unlikely that a dog will spontaneously start putting the clothes in the washing machine. A person could wait a very long time for such a feat! It is possible, however, to train a dog, or any animal, to perform highly complex tasks through the process of shaping. **Shaping** refers to rewarding approximations of a desired behavior (Peterson, 2004). For example, shaping can be used to train a rat to press a bar to obtain food. When a rat is first placed in a Skinner box, it rarely presses the bar. Thus, the experimenter may start off by giving the rat a food pellet if it is in the same half of the cage as the bar. Then the experimenter might reward the rat's behavior only when it is within 2 inches of the bar, then only when it touches the bar, and finally only when it presses the bar.

Returning to our service dog example, rather than waiting for the dog spontaneously to put the clothes in the washing machine, we might reward the dog for carrying the clothes to the laundry room and for bringing them closer and closer to the washing machine. Finally, we might reward the dog only when he gets the clothes inside the washer (desirably, sorted by color!). Indeed, shaping is extensively used in training animals to perform tricks. A dolphin that jumps through a hoop held high above the water has been trained to perform this behavior through shaping.

Shaping can be used effectively in educational classrooms (Alberto & Trautman, 2006). Suppose a teacher has a student who has never completed more than 50 percent of her math

Through operant conditioning, animal trainers can coax some amazing behaviors from their star performers.

assignments. The teacher sets the target behavior at 100 percent but rewards her for successive approximations to the target. The teacher initially might provide a reward (some type of privilege, for example) when the student completes 70 percent, then 80 percent, then 90 percent, and finally 100 percent. Shaping can be especially helpful for learning tasks that require time and persistence to complete. To experience these shaping principles at work, try the activities in the Psychology and Life box.

Principles of Reinforcement

Reinforcement is the process by which a stimulus or an event strengthens or increases the probability of a behavior or an event that it follows. Behavioral psychologists have developed a number of principles of reinforcement, including a distinction between positive and negative reinforcement.

Positive and Negative Reinforcement   In **positive reinforcement,** the frequency of a behavior increases because it is followed by a rewarding stimulus. For example, if someone you meet smiles at you after you say, "Hello, how are you?" and you keep talking, the smile has reinforced your talking. The same principle of positive reinforcement is at work when you teach a dog to "shake hands" by giving it a piece of food when it lifts its paw.

Conversely, in **negative reinforcement,** the frequency of a behavior increases because it is followed by the removal of an aversive (unpleasant) stimulus. For example, if your father nagged you to clean out the garage and kept nagging until you cleaned out the garage, your response (cleaning out the garage) removed the unpleasant stimulus (nagging). Taking an aspirin when you have a headache works the same way. A reduction of pain reinforces the act of taking an aspirin.

To understand the distinction between positive and negative reinforcement, remember that "positive" and "negative" do not have anything to do with "good" and "bad." Just keep in mind that they are processes in which something is given (positive reinforcement) or something is removed (negative reinforcement). Figure 7.7 provides further examples to help you understand the distinction between positive and negative reinforcement.

reinforcement The process by which a stimulus or an event strengthens or increases the probability of a behavior or an event that it follows.

positive reinforcement Following a behavior with a rewarding stimulus to increase the frequency of the behavior.

negative reinforcement Following a behavior with the removal of an aversive (unpleasant) stimulus to increase the frequency of the behavior.

"Once it became clear to me that, by responding correctly to certain stimuli, I could get all the bananas I wanted, getting this job was a pushover."

PSYCHOLOGY AND LIFE

Mind Games

Here are two mind games using the principles of operant conditioning for you to try out.

1. Enlist some of your classmates to play this mind game on your professor. Every time your instructor moves to the right side of the room during lecture, be more attentive, smile, and nod. Start out by shaping—every time he or she moves even a little to the right, give a smile or nod. Through this simple positive reinforcement, see how far you can get the professor to go toward the right corner of the room.

2. When you have a gathering of a few friends, play the party game known as the "dream game." In this game, one person (who is the victim) steps out of the room. The purpose of the game (or so the victim thinks) is to figure out the content of a dream that someone in the room had the night before. The victim will try to guess by asking "yes" or "no" questions about what was in the dream. After he or she has left the room, everyone in the room decides the actual rules, or reinforcement schedule, of the game. For instance, if the person guesses something that starts with the letters A through M, the answer will always be "yes" (the reward). If the person guesses something that starts with the letters L through Z, the answer will always be "no." When the victim returns, he or she begins asking "yes" or "no" questions about what was in the dream.

   You will notice two things. First, the "rules" or reinforcement schedule is very difficult for the victim to recognize. And second, the person will be astounded at the outlandish dream—which might perhaps include a cat, a dog, and Jessica Simpson but not SpongeBob SquarePants, a pizza, the sun, a taxi, or a yak. Making sense out of a "learning experience" can be a challenge for the human rat.

Operant conditioning can be more fun than you might have thought!

Primary and Secondary Reinforcement Positive reinforcement can be classified as primary reinforcement or secondary reinforcement, based on whether the behavior is inborn and unlearned or is learned. **Primary reinforcement** involves the use of reinforcers that are innately satisfying; that is, they do not take any learning on the organism's part to make them pleasurable. Food, water, and sexual satisfaction are primary reinforcers.

Secondary reinforcement acquires its positive value through experience; secondary reinforcers are learned or conditioned reinforcers. We encounter hundreds of secondary reinforcers in our lives, such as getting a pat on the back, praise, and eye contact.

The following example helps to illustrate the importance of secondary reinforcement in our everyday lives. When a student is given $25 for an *A* on her report card, the $25 is a secondary reinforcer. It is not innate, and it increases the likelihood that the student will work to get another *A* in the future. When an object can be exchanged for some other reinforcer, the object may have reinforcing value itself, so it is called a *token reinforcer.* Money, gift certificates, and poker chips are often referred to as token reinforcers.

Schedules of Reinforcement Most of the examples of reinforcement we have discussed so far have involved *continuous reinforcement,* in which a behavior is reinforced every time it occurs. When continuous reinforcement occurs, organisms learn rapidly. However, when reinforcement stops, extinction also takes place quickly. If a pay telephone we often use starts "eating" our coins and not giving us a dial tone, we quickly stop putting in more coins. However, several weeks later, we might try to use the phone again, hoping it now works properly (this behavior illustrates spontaneous recovery).

Partial reinforcement follows a behavior only a portion of the time (Shull & Grimes, 2006). Most of life's experiences involve partial reinforcement. A golfer does not win every tournament she enters; a chess whiz does not win every match he plays; a student is not patted on the back each time she solves a problem. **Schedules of reinforcement** are timetables that determine when a behavior will be reinforced (Lejeune, Richelle, &

primary reinforcement The use of reinforcers that are innately satisfying.

secondary reinforcement The use of reinforcers that are learned or conditioned.

schedules of reinforcement Timetables that determine when a behavior will be reinforced.

Positive Reinforcement

Behavior	Rewarding Stimulus Provided	Future Behavior
You turn in homework on time.	Teacher praises your performance.	You increasingly turn in homework on time.
You wax your skis.	The skis go faster.	You wax your skis the next time you go skiing.
You randomly press a button on the dashboard of a friend's car.	Great music begins to play.	You deliberately press the button again the next time you get into the car.

Negative Reinforcement

Behavior	Unpleasant Stimulus Removed	Future Behavior
You turn in homework on time.	Teacher stops criticizing late homework.	You increasingly turn in homework on time.
You wax your skis.	People stop zooming by you on the slope.	You wax your skis the next time you go skiing.
You randomly press a button on the dashboard of a friend's car.	An annoying song shuts off.	You deliberately press the button again the next time the annoying song is on.

FIGURE 7.7

Positive and Negative Reinforcement
Negative reinforcers involve taking something aversive away. Positive reinforcers mean adding something pleasant.

Slot machines are on a variable-ratio schedule of reinforcement.

Wearden, 2006; Roll & Shoptaw, 2006). The four main schedules of reinforcement are fixed-ratio, variable-ratio, fixed-interval, and variable-interval.

A *fixed-ratio schedule* reinforces a behavior after a set number of behaviors. For example, if you are playing the slot machines in Atlantic City and if the machines are on a fixed-ratio schedule, you might get $5 back every 20th time you put money in the machine. It would not take long to figure out that, if you watched someone else play the machine 18 or 19 times, not get any money back, and then walk away, you should step up, insert your coin, and get back $5. Fixed-ratio schedules often are used in business to increase production. For example, a factory might require a line worker to produce a certain number of items to get paid a particular amount. One characteristic of fixed-ratio schedules is that performance often drops off just after reinforcement.

Consequently, slot machines are on a *variable-ratio schedule,* a timetable in which behaviors are rewarded an average number of times but on an unpredictable basis. For example, a slot machine might pay off at an average of every 20th time, but the gambler does not know when this payoff will be. The slot machine might pay off twice in a row and then not again until after 58 coins have been inserted. This averages out to a reward for every 20 behavioral acts, but when the reward will be given is unpredictable. Variable-ratio schedules produce high, steady rates of behavior that are more resistant to extinction than the other three schedules.

The interval reinforcement schedules are determined by *time elapsed* since the last behavior was rewarded. A *fixed-interval schedule* reinforces the first appropriate behavior after a fixed amount of time has elapsed. For example, you might get a reward the first time you put money in a slot machine after every 10-minute period has elapsed. The behavior of politicians campaigning for reelection often reflects a fixed-interval schedule of reinforcement. After they have been elected, they reduce their campaigning and then do not pick it up again heavily until just before the next election (which can be 2 to 4 years later). On a fixed-interval schedule, few behaviors are enacted until the time approaches when the behavior likely will be reinforced (such as through getting reelected), and at that time the rate of behavior picks up rapidly.

A *variable-interval schedule* is a timetable in which a behavior is reinforced after a variable amount of time has elapsed (Staddon, Chelaru, & Higa, 2002). On this schedule, the

How might the campaigning behavior of a political officeholder reflect a fixed-interval schedule of reinforcement?

generalization (operant conditioning) The tendency to give the same response to similar stimuli.

discrimination (operant conditioning) The tendency to respond to stimuli that signal that a behavior will or will not be reinforced.

slot machines might reward you after 10 minutes, then after 2 minutes, then after 18 minutes, and so on. Pop quizzes occur on a variable-interval schedule. So does fishing—you do not know if the fish will bite in the next minute, in a half hour, in an hour, or at all. Because it is difficult to predict when a reward will come, behavior is slow and consistent on a variable-interval schedule (Staddon, Chelaru, & Higa, 2002).

Figure 7.8 shows how the different schedules of reinforcement result in different rates of responding.

Generalization, Discrimination, and Extinction   Remember that generalization, discrimination, and extinction are important classical conditioning principles. They also are important principles in operant conditioning, but they are defined somewhat differently.

Generalization   In operant conditioning, **generalization** means giving the same response to similar stimuli. For example, in one study pigeons were reinforced for pecking at a disk of a particular color (Guttman & Kalish, 1956). To assess stimulus generalization, researchers presented the pigeons with disks of varying colors. As Figure 7.9 shows, the pigeons were most likely to peck at disks closest in color to the original. An everyday example is a student who has great success in dating people who dress neatly but not such good results with people who dress sloppily. The student subsequently seeks dates with people who dress neatly (the more neatly, the better) and avoids dating sloppy dressers, especially the sloppiest.

Discrimination   In operant conditioning, **discrimination** means responding to stimuli that signal that a behavior will or will not be reinforced (Alsop & Porritt, 2006; de Wit & others, 2007). For example, you might go to a restaurant that has a "University Student Discount" sign in the front window. That sign tells you that pulling out your student ID is likely to get you a reward. On the other hand, without the sign, showing your ID might just get you a puzzled look, not cheap food. The principle of discrimination helps to explain how a service dog "knows" when he is working. Typically, these animals wear training harnesses while on duty but not at other times. Thus, when the dog is wearing its harness, it is quite important that he is treated like the professional that he is.

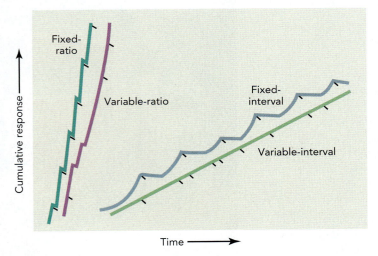

FIGURE 7.8

Schedules of Reinforcement and Different Patterns of Responding In this figure, each hash mark indicates the delivery of reinforcement. Notice on the fixed-ratio schedule the dropoff in responding after each response; on the variable-ratio schedule the high, steady rate of responding; on the fixed-interval schedule the immediate dropoff in responding after reinforcement and the increase in responding just before reinforcement (resulting in a scalloped curve); and on the variable-interval schedule the slow, steady rate of responding.

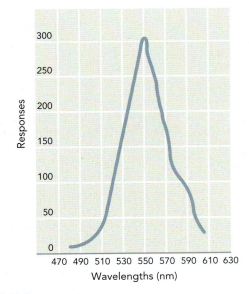

FIGURE 7.9

Stimulus Generalization In the experiment by Guttman and Kalish (1956), pigeons initially pecked a disk of a particular color (in this graph, a color with a wavelength of 550 nm) after they had been reinforced for this wavelength. Subsequently, when the pigeons were presented disks of colors with varying wavelengths, they were likelier to peck disks that were similar to the original disk.

Extinction   In operant conditioning, **extinction** occurs when a previously reinforced behavior is no longer reinforced, and there is a decreased tendency to perform the behavior (Leslie & others, 2006). For example, a factory worker gets a monthly bonus for producing more than her quota. Then, as a part of economic tightening, the company decides that it can no longer afford the bonuses. When the firm gave out the bonuses, the worker's productivity was above quota every month; once the bonuses ended, the woman's performance declined. Spontaneous recovery also characterizes the operant form of extinction.

Punishment   From the discussion of positive and negative reinforcement, you learned that both types of reinforcement strengthen behavior. In contrast, the effect of punishment is usually to weaken or extinguish a behavior. Let's explore the concept of punishment in the operant conditioning context and learn why psychologists generally disapprove of punishment.

What Is Punishment?   **Punishment** is a consequence that decreases the likelihood that a behavior will occur. For example, a child plays with an attractive matchbox and gets burned when one of the matches is lit. In the future, the child is less likely to play with matches. Or if a student interrupts the teacher and the teacher verbally reprimands the student, the student stops interrupting the teacher.

Punishment differs from reinforcement in that, in punishment, a behavior is weakened; in reinforcement, a behavior is strengthened. Thus, punishment is not the same as negative reinforcement. Also, in punishment, a response decreases because of its consequences; in negative reinforcement, a response increases because of its consequences. Figure 7.10 provides additional examples of the distinction between negative reinforcement and punishment.

Here is another example to help you distinguish between negative reinforcement and punishment. When an alcoholic consumes liquor to relieve uncomfortable withdrawal symptoms, the probability that the person will use alcohol in the future increases. The reduction of the withdrawal symptoms was a negative reinforcer for drinking. But if a drunken alcoholic is seriously injured in a car wreck and subsequently drinks less, the incident served as punishment because a behavior (drinking) was subsequently decreased.

The positive–negative distinction also can be applied to punishment, although it is not used as widely as in reinforcement. In **positive punishment,** a behavior decreases when it is followed by an unpleasant stimulus. In **negative punishment,** a behavior decreases when a positive stimulus is removed from it.

extinction (operant conditioning) The situation where, because a previously reinforced behavior is no longer reinforced, there is a decreased tendency to perform the behavior.

punishment A consequence that decreases the likelihood a behavior will occur.

positive punishment A behavior decreases when it is followed by an unpleasant stimulus.

negative punishment A behavior decreases when a positive stimulus is removed from it.

FIGURE 7.10

Punishment Versus Negative Reinforcement It is easy to confuse punishment and negative reinforcement. Just remember that punishment means adding something that is unpleasant in response to a behavior, while negative reinforcement means taking away something that is unpleasant.

Punishment

Behavior	Aversive Stimulus Presented	Future Behavior
You take medication to cure a headache.	You have a bad allergic reaction.	You avoid that medication in the future.
You show off to a friend by speeding past a police car.	You get a $200 ticket.	You stop speeding.

Negative Reinforcement

Behavior	Aversive Stimulus Removed	Future Behavior
You take medication to cure a headache.	The headache goes away.	You take more medication in the future.
You show off to a friend by speeding past a police car.	The officer pays no attention to you although officers have ticketed you in the past.	You continue to show off by speeding past police cars.

This second-grade student has been placed in time-out for misbehaving.

Time-out is a form of negative punishment in which a child is removed from a positive reinforcement. It generally is recommended over presenting an aversive stimulus (positive reinforcement), as typically is done when punishment is administered. If a child is behaving in disruptive ways in the classroom, the teacher might put the child in a chair in the corner of the room facing away from the class or take the child to a time-out room. Figure 7.11 compares positive reinforcement, negative reinforcement, positive punishment, and negative punishment.

Evaluating the Use of Punishment with Children   Many people associate punishment with yelling at children or spanking them. All too often, though, aversive stimuli do not do what they are intended to do—namely, decrease an unwanted behavior. Some people turn too quickly to aversive stimuli when trying to change a child's behavior (Alberto & Trautman, 2006; Cooper, Heron, & Heward, 2007). They might do so for several reasons: because they were harshly disciplined when they were growing up, and they are just repeating how their parents dealt with them; because they have developed a style of handling stress by yelling or screaming; because they feel they can effectively exercise power over their smaller charges; or because they are unaware of how positive reinforcement or other techniques, such as a time-out, can be used to improve children's behavior.

For more insight about whether punishing children is an effective strategy, see the Critical Controversy.

Timing, Reinforcement, and Punishment   How does the timing of reinforcement and punishment influence behavior? And does it matter whether the reinforcement is small or large?

Immediate Reinforcement and Delayed Reinforcement   As is the case in classical conditioning, in operant conditioning learning is more efficient when the interval between a behavior and its reinforcement is a few seconds rather than minutes or hours, especially in lower animals (Church & Kirkpatrick, 2001). If a food reward is delayed for more than 30 seconds after a rat presses a bar, it is virtually ineffective as reinforcement. Humans, however, have the ability to respond to delayed reinforcers (Holland, 1996).

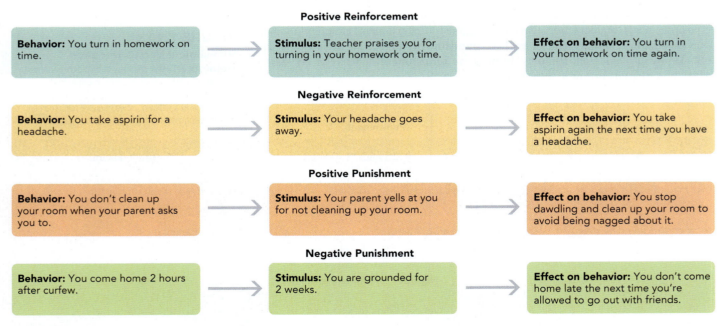

Positive Reinforcement

| **Behavior:** You turn in homework on time. | → | **Stimulus:** Teacher praises you for turning in your homework on time. | → | **Effect on behavior:** You turn in your homework on time again. |

Negative Reinforcement

| **Behavior:** You take aspirin for a headache. | → | **Stimulus:** Your headache goes away. | → | **Effect on behavior:** You take aspirin again the next time you have a headache. |

Positive Punishment

| **Behavior:** You don't clean up your room when your parent asks you to. | → | **Stimulus:** Your parent yells at you for not cleaning up your room. | → | **Effect on behavior:** You stop dawdling and clean up your room to avoid being nagged about it. |

Negative Punishment

| **Behavior:** You come home 2 hours after curfew. | → | **Stimulus:** You are grounded for 2 weeks. | → | **Effect on behavior:** You don't come home late the next time you're allowed to go out with friends. |

FIGURE 7.11

Positive Reinforcement, Negative Reinforcement, Positive Punishment, and Negative Punishment The fine distinctions here can sometimes confound students. Note that positive reinforcement means rewarding good behaviors. Negative reinforcement means taking away something aversive. The words *positive* and *negative* for punishment refer to whether the response to behavior is adding something aversive (positive punishment such as scolding) or taking away something pleasant (negative punishment such as a time-out).

Critical Controversy   Will Sparing the Rod Spoil the Child?

For centuries, corporal (physical) punishment such as spanking has been considered a necessary and even desirable method of disciplining children. The use of corporal punishment is legal in every U.S. state, and an estimated 70 to 90 percent of American parents have spanked their children (Straus, 1991). A cross-cultural comparison found that individuals in the United States and Canada were among the most favorable toward corporal punishment and remembered their parents' using it (Curran & others, 2001) (Figure 7.12).

Despite the widespread use of corporal punishment, there have been surprisingly few research studies on physical punishment, and those that have been conducted are correlational (Kazdin & Benjet, 2003). Clearly, it would be highly unethical to assign parents randomly to either spank or not spank their children in an experimental study. Recall that cause and effect cannot be determined in a correlational study. In one correlational study, spanking by parents was linked with children's antisocial behavior, including cheating, telling lies, being mean to others, bullying, getting into fights, and being disobedient (Strauss, Sugarman, & Giles-Sims, 1997).

In a longitudinal study of White, African American, and Latino families, spanking by parents predicted an increase in children's problems over time in all three groups (McLoyd & Smith, 2002). However, when parents showed strong emotional support of the child, the link between spanking and child problems was reduced. Another longitudinal study linked spanking before 2 years of age to behavioral problems in the elementary school years (Slade & Wissow, 2004).

A research review concluded that corporal punishment by parents is associated with children's higher levels of immediate compliance, aggression among children, and lower levels of moral internalization and mental health (Gershoff, 2002). High and harsh levels of corporal punishment have been shown to be particularly detrimental to children's well-being (Aucoin, Frick, & Bodin, 2006) and may affect them in adolescence as well (Bender & others, 2007). Some critics, though, argue that the research evidence is not yet sound enough to warrant making corporal punishment illegal, especially mild corporal punishment (Baumrind, Larzelere, & Cowan, 2002; Kauffman, 2005; Landrum & Kauffman, 2006). And animal studies reveal that punishment is often effective in reducing undesired behaviors (Domjan, 2006).

What are some reasons for avoiding spanking or similar punishments?

- When adults yell, scream, or spank, they are presenting children with out-of-control models for handling stressful situations (Sim & Ong, 2005). Children may imitate this aggressive, out-of-control behavior.
- Punishment can instill fear, rage, or avoidance. For example, spanking the child may cause the child to avoid being around the parent and to fear the parent.
- Punishment tells children what not to do rather than what to do. Instead, children should be given feedback such as "Why don't you try this?"
- Punishment can be abusive. When parents discipline their children, they might not intend to be abusive but might become so aroused during the act of punishing that they become abusive.

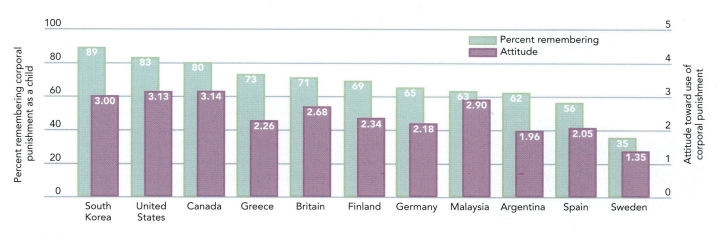

FIGURE 7.12

Corporal Punishment in Various Countries A 5-point scale was used to assess attitudes toward corporal punishment, with scores closer to 1 indicating an attitude against its use and scores closer to 5 suggesting an attitude for its use.

(continued)

For reasons such as these, Sweden passed a law in 1979 forbidding parents to punish (spank or slap, for example) children physically. Since the law was enacted, youth rates of delinquency, alcohol abuse, rape, and suicide have dropped in Sweden (Durrant, 2000). These improvements may have occurred for other reasons, such as changing attitudes and broadened opportunities for youth. Nonetheless, the Swedish experience suggests that the physical punishment of children may be unnecessary. Other countries that have passed antispanking laws include Finland, Denmark, Norway, Austria, Cyprus, Croatia, Latvia, Germany, and Israel.

When asked why they use corporal punishment, parents often respond that their children need strong discipline to learn how to behave. Parents also sometimes say that they were spanked by their own parents and they turned out okay, so there is nothing wrong with corporal punishment.

What Do You Think?

- Should the United States outlaw the physical punishment of children?
- Did your parents spank you when you were a child? If so, what effect do you think physical punishment had on your behavior?
- Might negative punishment, such as time-outs, be more effective than positive punishment, such as spanking? Explain.

Sometimes important life decisions involve whether to obtain a small, immediate reinforcer or to wait for a delayed but more highly valued reinforcer (Martin & Pear, 2007). For example, you can spend your money now on clothes, the latest iPod release, concert tickets, and so on, or you can save your money and buy a house and car later. You might play around and enjoy yourself now in return for immediate small reinforcers, or you can study hard over the long haul for delayed stronger reinforcers such as good grades, a scholarship to graduate school, and a better job.

Immediate Punishment and Delayed Punishment As with reinforcement, in most instances of research with lower animals, immediate punishment is more effective than delayed punishment in decreasing the occurrence of a behavior. However, also as with reinforcement, delayed punishment can have an effect on human behavior.

Why do so many of us postpone such activities as going to the dentist, scheduling minor surgery, and paying campus parking fines (Martin & Pear, 2007)? If we act immediately, we experience a weak punisher—it hurts to have our teeth drilled, it is painful to have minor surgery, and it is not pleasurable to pay a campus parking fine. However, the delayed consequences can be more punishing—our teeth might fall out, we may need major surgery, and our car might be towed or we might face even larger fines if we delay paying a campus parking fine.

Immediate and Delayed Reinforcement and Punishment How does receiving immediate small reinforcement versus delayed strong punishment affect human behavior (Martin & Pear, 2007)? One reason that obesity is such a major health problem is that eating is a behavior with immediate positive consequences—food tastes great and quickly provides a pleasurable, satisfied feeling. Although the potential delayed consequences of overeating are negative (obesity and other possible health risks), the immediate consequences are difficult to override. When the delayed consequences of behavior are punishing and the immediate consequences are reinforcing, the immediate consequences usually win, even when the immediate consequences are minor reinforcers, and the delayed consequences are major punishers.

Smoking and drinking follow a similar pattern. The immediate consequences of smoking are reinforcing for most smokers—the powerful combination of positive reinforcement (tension relief, energy boost) and negative reinforcement (removal of craving). The primarily long-term effects of smoking are punishing, such as shortness of breath, a chronic sore throat and/or coughing, emphysema, heart disease, and cancer. Likewise, the immediate pleasurable consequences of drinking override the delayed consequences of a hangover or even alcoholism and liver disease.

Now think about the following situations. Why are some of us so reluctant to take up a new sport, try a new dance step, go to a social gathering, or do almost anything different? One reason is that learning new skills often involves minor punishing consequences, such as initially looking and feeling stupid, not knowing what to do, and having to put up with sarcastic comments from onlookers. In these circumstances, reinforcing consequences are

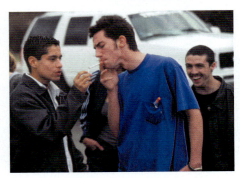

How might timing, reinforcement, and punishment be involved in overeating, drinking excessively, and smoking?

Behaviorism and Neuroscience: If It Feels Good, Is It Reinforcing?

When behaviorists talk about behaviors, they rarely talk about what is going on inside the head of the organism being studied. Yet with remarkable innovations in the technology of brain imaging, researchers—even those interested in associative learning—can now examine the neural underpinnings of the relationships that underlie behavior (Koob, 2006). In effect, researchers can now look inside the "black box" of the human brain and observe how learning takes place.

> **Researchers can now look inside the "black box" of the human brain and observe how learning takes place.**

A central idea behind operant conditioning is that behavior that is followed by reward is likely to be repeated. But what is rewarding about a reward? Food is one obvious reinforcement. Hungry rats will work hard for food. Neuroscientists (as described in Chapter 3) have identified a part of the midbrain called the nucleus accumbens (or NAc), an extension of the amygdala that plays a vital role in our learning to repeat a rewarded behavior (Schultz, 2006). In essence, a special input into the NAc tells the organism to "do it again." We can think of this reinforcement as literally reinforcing the synapses in the brain that connect the stimulus and response.

Researchers have found that dopamine plays a crucial role in the reinforcement of behaviors (Ahn & Phillips, 2006). An electrode that records dopamine cells in the brain of a monkey, for example, shows that dopamine is released not only when the monkey tastes food, but also

when it sees signals in the environment suggesting that food is available (Schultz, Dayan, & Montague, 1997). By comparison, imagine that you are walking through the mall. You see a "50 percent off" sign outside the shoe store. This sign might just start a dopamine explosion in your brain! The role of dopamine in the activation of reinforcement is also demonstrated in animals that lack dopamine. Animals that have been given a drug that blocks dopamine find rewards less rewarding. They treat sugar as less sweet and fail to react to reinforcers in the environment (Smith, 1995).

As researchers bring questions of basic learning principles into the neuroscience laboratory, they get ever-closer to understanding what "rewarding" really means.

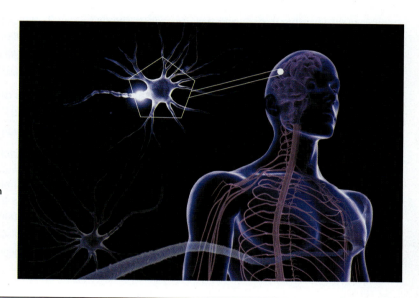

often delayed. For example, it may take a long time to become a good enough golfer or a good enough dancer to enjoy these activities.

Choosing Effective Reinforcers for Children In the case of children, not all reinforcers are the same for every child. Teachers can explore which reinforcers work best with which children—that is, they can individualize the use of particular reinforcers. For one child the most effective reinforcer might be praise, for another it might be getting to be hall monitor for a week, and for another it might be permission to surf the Internet. Natural reinforcers such as praise and privileges are generally recommended over material reinforcers such as stars and candy.

Activities are some of the most common reinforcers that teachers use. Named after psychologist David Premack, the *Premack principle* states that a high-probability activity can be used to reinforce a low-probability activity. The term *probability* here means likelihood of occurrence. For many children, playing a game on a computer has a higher likelihood of occurrence than doing a writing assignment. Thus, a teacher might tell a child, "When you complete your writing assignment, you can play a computer game." The Premack principle also can be used with an entire classroom of children. For example, a teacher might say, "If all of the class gets their homework done by Friday, we will take a field trip next week."

Recent research reveals considerable interest in discovering the links between brain activity and operant conditioning (Chester & others, 2006; Mitchell & others, 2006). To explore this topic, see the Intersection.

REVIEW, ASSESS, AND SHARPEN YOUR THINKING

Review

3 Discuss operant conditioning.

- Define operant conditioning and distinguish it from classical conditioning.
- Describe Thorndike's law of effect.
- Understand Skinner's operant conditioning.
- Discuss shaping.
- Identify the principles of reinforcement and explain how they affect behavior.

Assess

1. Matthew went to a theme park and was amazed at the live-action animal show he saw there. In the show, cats ran through a series of cones, dogs played basketball, and ducks flew under a horse. What type of technique was probably used to teach these animals to do these complex behaviors?

   A. negative reinforcement   B. the Premack principle

   C. extinction   D. shaping

2. A mother takes away her son's favorite toy when he misbehaves. Her action is an example of

   A. positive reinforcement.

   B. negative reinforcement.

   C. positive punishment.

   D. negative punishment.

3. Which schedule of reinforcement results in the greatest increase in desired behavior and is the most resistant to extinction?

   A. fixed ratio   B. variable ratio

   C. fixed interval   D. variable interval

4. Who developed the law of effect?

   A. B. F. Skinner   B. E. L. Thorndike

   C. Ivan Pavlov   D. Albert Bandura

5. A teacher gives his students a piece of candy when they get an A on a paper. He finds that more students are getting As on their papers. However, when he stops giving the candy, he finds that fewer students receive As on their papers. What has happened?

   A. discrimination   B. punishment

   C. generalization   D. extinction

Sharpen Your Thinking

Think of two behaviors, one that you really enjoy and one you do because you feel you have to. Try to use the Premack principle to use the first activity as a reward for the second. Do you think it will work? Why or why not?

4 Observational Learning

Understand observational learning.

Would it make sense to teach a 15-year-old boy how to drive by either classical conditioning or operant conditioning procedures? Driving a car is a voluntary behavior, so classical conditioning does not apply. In terms of operant conditioning, we could ask him to drive down the road and then reward his positive behaviors. Not many of us would want to be on the road, though, when he makes mistakes. Albert Bandura (2005, 2006, 2007b) believes that, if we learned only in such a trial-and-error fashion, learning would be exceedingly tedious and at times hazardous. Instead, he says, many complex behaviors are the result of exposure to competent models. By observing other people, we can acquire knowledge, skills, rules, strategies, beliefs, and attitudes (Schunk, 2008).

Bandura's Model of Observational Learning

In Chapter 1, we examined Bandura's social cognitive theory. This section discusses his view of observational learning further. *Observational learning,* also called *imitation* or *modeling,* is learning that occurs when a person observes and imitates behavior. The capacity to learn by observation eliminates trial-and-error learning. Often observational learning takes less time than operant conditioning.

Bandura (1986) described four main processes that are involved in observational learning: attention, retention, motor reproduction, and reinforcement. For observational learning to take place, the first process that must occur is *attention* (which we initially considered in Chapter 5 due to its important role in perception). In order to reproduce a model's actions, you must attend to what the model is saying or doing. You might not hear what a friend says if the stereo is blaring, and you might miss your professor's analysis of a problem if you are admiring someone sitting in the next row. Or imagine that you decide to take a class to improve your drawing skills. You need to attend to the instructor's words and hand movements. Attention to the model is influenced by a host of characteristics. For example, warm, powerful, atypical people command more attention than do cold, weak, typical people.

Retention is the second process required for observational learning to occur. To reproduce a model's actions, you must code the information and keep it in memory so that you can retrieve it. A simple verbal description, or a vivid image of what the model did, assists retention. (Memory is such an important cognitive process that Chapter 8 is devoted exclusively to it.) In the example of taking a class to sharpen your drawing skills, you will need to remember what the instructor said and did in modeling good drawing skills.

Motor reproduction is the process of imitating the model's actions. People might pay attention to a model and code in memory what they have seen, but limitations in motor development might make it difficult for them to reproduce the model's action. Thirteen-year-olds might see a professional basketball player do a reverse two-handed dunk, but might be unable to reproduce the pro's actions. Similarly, in a drawing class, you will need good motor reproduction skills to follow the instructor's example.

Reinforcement, or incentive conditions, is the final component of observational learning. On many occasions, we may attend to what a model says or does, retain the information in memory, and possess the motor capabilities to perform the action, but we might fail to repeat the behavior because of inadequate reinforcement. The importance of this step was demonstrated in one of Bandura's (1965) early studies, in which children who had seen a model punished for aggression reproduced the model's aggression only when they were offered an incentive to do so. In your art class, if the instructor chooses one of your drawings for display, the reinforcement encourages you to keep drawing and to take another art skills class.

Figure 7.13 summarizes Bandura's model of observational learning.

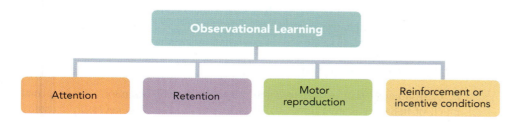

FIGURE 7.13

Bandura's Model of Observational Learning In terms of Bandura's model, if you are learning to ski, you need to attend to the instructor's words and demonstrations. You need to remember what the instructor did and his or her tips for avoiding disasters. You also need the motor abilities to reproduce what the instructor has shown you. And praise from the instructor after you have completed a few moves on the slopes should improve your motivation to continue skiing.

REVIEW, ASSESS, AND SHARPEN YOUR THINKING

Review

4 Understand observational learning.

- Define observational learning and outline the four steps in Bandura's model.

Assess

1. According to Bandura, which occurs first in observational learning?

   A. motor reproduction   B. retention

   C. attention   D. reinforcement

2. A friend shows you how to do a card trick. However, you forget the second step in the trick and are unable to replicate the card trick. There has been a failure in which of the following?

   A. motor reproduction

   B. retention

   C. attention

   D. reinforcement

3. Cindy often helps her father complete repairs to her car. She finds that she is very successful at repairing cars. However, Cindy does not enjoy working on cars and therefore tends to avoid this task. Which of the following is responsible for Cindy's avoidance working on cars?

   A. lack of reinforcement

   B. lack of attention

   C. lack of motor reproduction

   D. lack of retention

Sharpen Your Thinking

Who have been the most important models in your life? What have you learned from them?

5 Cognitive Factors in Learning

Discuss the role of cognition in learning.

In learning about learning, we have looked at cognitive processes only as they apply in observational learning. Skinner's operant conditioning approach and Pavlov's classical conditioning approach both ignore the possibility that cognitive factors such as memory, thinking, planning, and expectations might be important in learning. Skinnerian behaviorists point out that they do not deny the existence of thinking processes, but because such processes cannot be observed, they may interfere with the discovery of important environmental conditions that govern behavior.

But even within the behavior of animals, sometimes it seems that we must incorporate a consideration of cognitive factors to provide a complete picture of what is going on. As one example, an important aspect of the training of service dogs is the need for selective disobedience. Selective disobedience means that in addition to obeying commands from their human partners, these dogs must at times override such commands if their own assessment of the environment indicates there is reason to do so. So, if a guide dog is standing at the corner with his visually impaired human, and the human commands him to move forward, he might refuse, if he sees an oncoming car.

As we next consider, many contemporary psychologists, including behavioral revisionists who recognize the importance of cognition, believe that learning involves more than environment–behavior connections (Bandura, 2005, 2006, 2007a, 2007b; Zimmerman & Schunk, 2001). A good starting place is E. C. Tolman's contributions to the role of cognition in learning.

Purposive Behavior

E. C. Tolman (1932) emphasized the *purposiveness* of behavior—the idea that much of behavior is goal-directed. Tolman believed that it is necessary to study entire behavioral sequences in order to understand why people engage in particular actions. For example, high school students whose goal is to attend a leading college or university study hard in their classes. If we focused only on their studying, we would miss the purpose of their behavior. The students do not always study hard because they have been reinforced for studying in the past. Rather, studying is a means to intermediate goals (learning, high grades) that in turn improve their likelihood of getting into the college or university of their choice (Schunk, 2004).

We can see Tolman's legacy today in the extensive interest in the role of goal setting in human behavior (Gollwitzer & Oettingen, 2007; Zimmerman & Schunk, 2003). Researchers are especially curious about how people self-regulate and self-monitor their behavior to reach a goal (Boekaerts, 2006; Wigfield & others, 2006).

Expectancy Learning and Information   In studying the purposiveness of behavior, Tolman went beyond the stimuli and responses of Pavlov and Skinner to focus on cognitive mechanisms. Tolman said that, when classical and operant conditioning occur, the organism acquires certain expectations. In classical conditioning, the young boy fears the rabbit because he expects it will hurt him. In operant conditioning, a woman works hard all week because she expects to be paid on Friday. Expectancies are acquired from people's experiences with their environment.

Tolman (1932) emphasized that the information value of the CS is important as a signal or an expectation that a UCS will follow. Anticipating contemporary thinking, Tolman believed that the information that the CS provides is the key to understanding classical conditioning.

One contemporary view of classical conditioning describes an organism as an information seeker, using logical and perceptual relations among events, along with preconceptions, to form a representation of the world (Rescorla, 2003, 2004, 2005, 2006a, 2006b). A classic experiment conducted by Leon Kamin (1968) illustrates the importance of an organism's history and the information provided by a conditioned stimulus in classical conditioning. A rat was conditioned by repeatedly pairing a tone (CS) and a shock (UCS), until the tone alone produced fear (CR). Then the tone continued to be paired with the shock, but a light (a second CS) was turned on each time the tone was sounded. Even though the light (CS) and the shock (UCS) were repeatedly paired, the rat showed no conditioning to the light (the light by itself produced no CR). Conditioning to the light was blocked, almost as if the rat had not paid attention. The rat apparently used the tone as a signal to predict that a shock would be forthcoming; information about the light's pairing with the shock was redundant with the information already learned about the tone's pairing with the shock. In this experiment, conditioning was governed not by the contiguity of the CS and UCS but rather by the rat's history and the information it received. Contemporary classical conditioning researchers are further exploring the role of information in an organism's learning (Beckers & others, 2006; Mitchell & others, 2006).

One type of expectancy involves cognitive maps. Tolman (1948) believed that organisms form cognitive maps that are made up of expectancies about which actions are needed to attain a goal. A *cognitive map* is an organism's mental representation of the structure of physical space. His experiments with rats in a maze led Tolman to conclude that rats developed mental awareness of physical space and the elements in it. They used these cognitive maps to find the food at the end of the maze—their goal.

Tolman's idea of cognitive maps is alive and well today. As we move around in our environment, we develop a cognitive map of where things are located, on both small and large scales (Daniel & others, 2006; McNaughton & others, 2006). We have a cognitive map of the locations of rooms in our houses or apartments, and we have a cognitive map of our location in the United States, for example. A popular exercise is to draw a cognitive map reflecting our perception of the city or state in which we live, relative to the rest of the United States. Texans, for example, usually make the state of Texas about three-fourths the size of the entire United States. People living in New York City often draw it to be about nine-tenths the size of the United States. Of course, such cognitive maps deliberately distort the physical world, reflecting the perceivers' egocentric interest in their city or state.

latent learning (implicit learning)
Unreinforced learning that is not immediately reflected in behavior.

Latent Learning Experiments on latent learning provide other evidence to support the role of cognitive maps in learning. **Latent learning,** or **implicit learning,** is unreinforced learning that is not immediately reflected in behavior. In one study, researchers put two groups of hungry rats in a maze and required them to find their way from a starting point to an end point (Tolman & Honzik, 1930). The first group found food (a reinforcer) at the end point; the second group found nothing there. In the operant conditioning view, the first group should learn the maze better than the second group, which is exactly what happened. However, when Tolman subsequently took some of the rats from the non-reinforced group and gave them food at the end point of the maze, they began to run the maze as effectively as the reinforced group. The non-reinforced rats apparently had learned a great deal about the maze as they roamed around and explored it. However, their learning was *latent,* stored cognitively in their memories but not yet expressed behaviorally. When these rats were given a good reason (reinforcement with food) to run the maze speedily, they called on their latent learning to help them reach the end of the maze more quickly.

Outside of a laboratory, latent learning is evident in an animal's exploration of its surroundings. Learning the layout of its environment may bring the animal no immediate benefits, but it can prove critical in the future when the creature is fleeing a predator or searching for food.

Insight Learning

Tolman was not the only psychologist in the first half of the twentieth century who believed that cognitive factors play an important role in learning. So did the German gestalt psychologist Wolfgang Köhler. Köhler spent 4 months in the Canary Islands during World War I observing the behavior of apes. There he conducted two fascinating experiments. One is called the "stick problem"; the other, the "box problem." Although these two experiments are basically the same, the solutions to the problems are different. In both situations, the ape discovers that it cannot reach an alluring piece of fruit, either because the fruit is too high or because it is outside of the ape's cage and beyond reach. To solve the stick problem, the ape has to insert a small stick inside a larger stick to reach the fruit. To master the box problem, the ape must stack several boxes to reach the fruit (Figure 7.14).

According to Köhler (1925), solving these problems does not involve trial and error or simple connections between stimuli and responses. Rather, when the ape realizes that

FIGURE 7.14

Insight Learning Sultan, one of Köhler's brightest chimps, is faced with the problem of reaching a cluster of bananas overhead. He solves the problem by stacking boxes on top of one another to reach the bananas. Köhler called this type of problem solving insight learning.

its customary actions are not going to help it get the fruit, it often sits for a period of time and appears to ponder how to solve the problem. Then it quickly gets up, as if it has had a sudden flash of insight, piles the boxes on top of one another, and gets the fruit. Although Köhler's conclusions are not without their detractors (Windholz & Lamal, 2002), **insight learning** is a form of problem solving in which the organism develops a sudden insight into or understanding of a problem's solution.

REVIEW, ASSESS, AND SHARPEN YOUR THINKING

Review

5 Discuss the role of cognition in learning.

- Discuss the role of expectations, latent learning, and cognitive maps in learning.
- Explain insight learning.

Assess

1. **You are able to move around your home in the dark without bumping into too many things. However, if you were to walk around in the dark in an unfamiliar setting, you would likely bump into several things. Why?**

   A. You have developed a cognitive map of your house.

   B. Latent learning allows you to know where things are in your house.

   C. Walking around in your own home is purposive, but walking around in an unfamiliar setting is not.

   D. Insight learning allows you to know where things are in your house.

2. **When the answer to a problem just "pops" into your head, you have experienced**

   A. latent learning.   B. insight learning.

   C. implicit learning.   D. expectancy learning.

3. **Learning that has occurred but is not immediately demonstrated in behavior is called**

   A. problem solving.   B. insight learning.

   C. a cognitive map.   D. latent learning.

4. **_____ learning is a form of problem solving in which the learner develops an "aha" moment or understanding of the solution to the problem.**

   A. Insight learning

   B. Latent learning

   C. Expectancy learning

   D. Implicit learning

Sharpen Your Thinking

What are your career expectations? How might these expectations influence your behavior this term?

6 Biological, Cultural, and Psychological Factors in Learning

Identify biological, cultural, and psychological factors in learning.

Albert Einstein had many special talents. He combined enormous creativity with great analytic ability to develop some of the twentieth century's most important insights into the nature of matter and the universe. Genes obviously endowed Einstein with extraordinary intellectual skills that enabled him to think and reason on a very high plane, but cultural factors also contributed to Einstein's genius. Einstein received an excellent, rigorous European education, and later in the United States he experienced the freedom and support believed to be important in creative exploration. Would Einstein have been able fully to develop his intellectual skills and to make such brilliant insights if he had grown up in a developing country? It is unlikely. Clearly, both biological *and* cultural factors contribute to learning.

insight learning A form of problem solving in which the organism develops a sudden insight into or understanding of the problem's solution.

FIGURE 7.15

Instinctive Drift This raccoon's skill in using its hands made it an excellent basketball player, but because of instinctive drift, the raccoon had a much more difficult time dropping coins in a tray.

instinctive drift The tendency of animals to revert to instinctive behavior that interferes with learning.

preparedness The species-specific biological predisposition to learn in certain ways but not others.

Biological Constraints

We cannot breathe under water, fish cannot play table tennis, and cows cannot solve math problems. The structure of an organism's body permits certain kinds of learning and inhibits others (Chance, 2006). For example, chimpanzees cannot learn to speak English, because they lack the necessary vocal equipment. Service dogs also provide an illustration of the limits of learning principles. One type of service dog, the seizure-alert dog, warns individuals with epilepsy of an oncoming attack, minutes or hours before the seizure takes place. These dogs may whine, bark, or paw their owners prior to a seizure. No one knows how these dogs sense an oncoming seizure. Certainly, learning principles of reward are applied to seizure-alert dogs. Dogs that show sensitivity to seizures are rewarded with treats when they are successful. Seizure-alert dogs are also trained via rewards to stay with the person after a seizure and to press a button to call 911. But, as one trainer noted, "I can train a dog to sit, lay down, and fetch, but I can't teach a dog to alert" (Mott, 2004).

Instinctive Drift An example of biological influences on learning is **instinctive drift,** the tendency of animals to revert to instinctive behavior that interferes with learning. Consider the situation of Keller and Marion Breland (1961), students of B. F. Skinner, who used operant conditioning to train animals to perform at fairs, at conventions, and in television advertisements. They used Skinner's techniques to teach pigs to cart large wooden nickels to a piggy bank and deposit them. They also trained raccoons to pick up a coin and place it in a metal tray. Although the pigs and raccoons, as well as chickens and other animals, performed well at most of the tasks (raccoons became adept basketball players, for example—see Figure 7.15), some of the animals began acting strangely. Instead of picking up the large wooden nickels and carrying them to the piggy bank, the pigs dropped the nickels on the ground, shoved them with their snouts, tossed them in the air, and then repeated these actions. The raccoons began to hold on to their coins rather than dropping them into the metal tray. When two coins were introduced, the raccoons rubbed them together in a miserly fashion. Somehow these behaviors overwhelmed the strength of the reinforcement. Why were the pigs and the raccoons misbehaving? The pigs were rooting, an instinct that is used to uncover edible roots. The raccoons were engaging in an instinctive food-washing response. Their instinctive drift interfered with learning.

Preparedness and Taste Aversion Some animals learn readily in one situation but have difficulty learning in slightly different circumstances. The difficulty might result not from some aspect of the learning situation but from the organism's biological predisposition (Seligman, 1970). **Preparedness** is the species-specific biological predisposition to learn in certain ways but not others.

Much of the evidence for preparedness comes from research on taste aversion (Garcia, 1989). Consider this situation: A psychologist went to dinner with his wife and ordered filet mignon with béarnaise sauce, his favorite dish. Afterward they attended the opera. Several hours later, he became very ill with stomach pains and nausea. Several weeks later, he tried to eat béarnaise sauce but could not stand it. But importantly, the psychologist did not experience an aversion to opera, even though he had also attended the opera before getting sick. The psychologist's experience involved *taste aversion,* another biological constraint on learning (Ferreira & others, 2006; Masaki & Nakajima, 2006).

If an organism ingests a substance that poisons but does not kill it, the organism often develops considerable distaste for that substance—even with only a single conditioning trial. Rats that experience low levels of radiation after eating show a strong aversion to the food they were eating when the radiation made them ill. This aversion has been shown to last for as long as 32 days. Such long-term effects cannot be accounted for by classical conditioning, which would argue that a single pairing of the conditioned and unconditioned stimuli would not last that long (Garcia, Ervin, & Koelling, 1966). Note that it is highly adaptive to learn taste aversion in only one trial. An animal that required multiple pairings of taste with poison would likely not survive the acquisition phase! Radiation and chemical treatment of cancer often produce nausea in patients, and the resulting pattern of aversions often resembles the patterns shown by laboratory animals.

Knowledge about taste aversion has been used to discourage animals from preying on certain species. For example, wolves and coyotes may threaten the livestock of ranchers. Instead of killing these predators, the ranchers feed them the poisoned meat of their prey (cattle and sheep). The wolves and coyotes, poisoned but not killed, develop a taste aversion for cattle or sheep and hence become less of a threat to the ranchers and their livestock. In this way, ranchers, cattle, sheep, wolves, and coyotes can live in a semblance of ecological balance. Aversion learning is related to how species select their food. Thus, like other mammals that select food based on taste, human beings show taste aversion. In contrast, species (such as birds) that select food based on sight may show aversion learning to sickening colors rather than to tastes.

Cultural Constraints

Traditionally, researchers have given little attention to the influence of culture on learning. The behavioral orientation that dominated studies in psychology in the United States for much of the twentieth century does focus on the cultural contexts of learning, but the organisms in those contexts have typically been animals. There has been limited interest in the cultural context of human learning.

So, how does culture influence human learning? Most psychologists agree that the principles of classical conditioning, operant conditioning, and observational learning are universal and are powerful learning processes in every culture. However, culture can influence the *degree* to which these learning processes are used (Cole, 2006). For example, Mexican American students may learn more through observational learning, while Euro-American students may be more accustomed to learn through direct instruction (Mejia-Arauz, Rogoff, & Paradise, 2005). In addition, culture can also determine the *content* of learning. For example, punishment is a universal learning process, but its use and type show considerable sociocultural variation.

When behaviorism began its influential reign in the United States between 1910 and 1930, child-rearing experts regarded the infant as capable of being shaped into almost any type of child. Desirable social behavior could be achieved if the child's antisocial behaviors were always punished and never indulged and if positive behaviors were carefully conditioned and rewarded in a highly controlled and structured child-rearing regimen. John Watson (1928) authored a publication, *Psychological Care of the Infant and Child,* that became the official government guidebook for parents. This booklet advocated never letting children suck their thumbs and, if necessary, restraining the children by tying their hands to the crib at night and painting their fingers with foul-tasting liquids. Parents were advised to let infants "cry themselves out" rather than to reinforce this unacceptable behavior by picking them up to rock and soothe them.

From the 1930s to the 1960s, a more permissive attitude prevailed, and parents were advised to be concerned with the feelings and capacities of the child. Since the 1960s, there has been a continued emphasis on the role of parental love in children's socialization, but experts now advise parents to play a less permissive and more active role in shaping children's behavior. Experts stress that parents should set limits and make authoritative decisions in areas in which the child is not capable of reasonable judgment. However, they should listen and adapt to the child's point of view, should explain their restrictions and discipline, and should not discipline the child in a hostile, punitive manner.

Culture also influences the content of learning (Cole, 2006; Shiraev & Levy, 2007). We cannot learn about something we do not experience. The 4-year-old who grows up among the Bushmen of the Kalahari Desert is unlikely to learn about taking baths and pouring water from one glass into another. Similarly, a child growing up in Chicago is unlikely to be skilled at tracking animals and finding water-bearing roots in the desert. Learning often requires

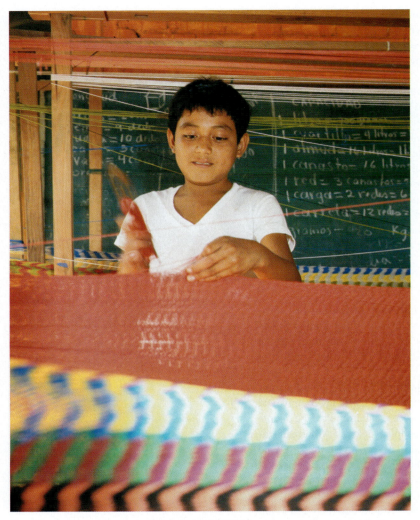

Our culture strongly influences what we learn. A child living in a rural village famed for its woven goods is more likely to become an expert weaver by working at the loom day after day than is a youth growing up in a village known exclusively for its clay pots.

practice, and certain behaviors are practiced more often in some cultures than in others. In Bali, many children are skilled dancers by the age of 6, whereas Norwegian children are much likelier to be good skiers and skaters by that age. Children growing up in a Mexican village famous for its pottery may work with clay day after day, whereas children in a nearby village renowned for woven rugs and sweaters rarely become experts at making clay pots.

Psychological Constraints

Are there psychological constraints on learning? For animals, the answer is probably no. For humans, the answer very well may be yes. This section opened with the claim that fish cannot play table tennis. The truth of this statement is clear. Biological circumstances render it simply impossible. If we put biological considerations aside, we might ask ourselves about times in our lives when we feel like a fish trying to play table tennis—when we feel that we just do not have what it takes to learn a skill or to master a task.

Carol Dweck (2006) recently used the term *mindset* to describe the way our beliefs about ability dictate what goals we set for ourselves, what we think we *can* learn, and ultimately what we *do* learn. Dweck and her colleagues have conducted a number of studies illustrating how our mindset is a powerful influence on whether we reach our potential (Dweck, 2002a, 2002b, 2006; Dweck & Leggett, 2000).

One aspect of their research focuses on how individuals define intellectual ability. Dweck and her colleagues found that some children defined intelligence as fixed (Dweck & Leggett, 2000). These children believed that when it comes to academic ability, either you have it or you do not. For these kids, having to work hard to achieve academic goals is a sign that you are just not gifted. Dweck calls such a belief about intelligence an *entity theory.* In contrast, other children defined intelligence as something that a person could increase and improve upon. For these kids, effort was just a sign of learning what you need to know. Dweck refers to this type of belief as an *incremental theory,* which emphasizes that we can become more intelligent by gaining skills and mastering difficult tasks.

These two definitions of ability have implications for the meaning of failure. From the perspective of entity theory, failure means lack of ability. But from the vantage point of incremental theory, failure tells the person what he or she still needs to learn. When faced with a challenging academic task (math problems that were beyond their age level), the children in Dweck's studies responded quite differently. Children whose views reflected an entity theory were threatened by the difficult task, withdrew from it, and were more likely to criticize the task and put themselves down. Indeed, Dweck described these children as showing **learned helplessness,** which is the phenomenon of learning through experience that outcomes are not controllable. In Dweck's studies, the children had come to believe that outcomes in their lives were simply not in their control. We will return to this topic later in this chapter.

In contrast, the children who revealed incremental views of intelligence seemed to be energized by the challenging tasks. They remained focused and persisted in trying to solve the "impossible" problems. Amazingly, some of them actually did—they achieved the impossible. Dweck has referred to entity beliefs of ability as "beliefs that make smart people dumb" (Dweck, 2002a).

learned helplessness The phenomenon of learning through experience that outcomes are not controllable.

Dweck's (2006) work challenges us to consider the limits we place on our own learning. Our beliefs about ability profoundly impact what we try to learn. When we think of the relative absence of women and minorities in math and science professions, we might consider the messages these groups have received about whether they have what it takes to succeed in these domains. When we see Tiger Woods playing golf or Maria Sharapova excelling on the tennis court, we often marvel at their natural ability. Importantly, we ought also to consider what we have not seen—the years of grueling practice and the monumental efforts that have contributed to their performances.

Dweck (2002b) and her colleagues have also examined how parents and teachers influence the development of ability beliefs in children. A child comes home with an *A* on a class project. What should parents do? Dweck has found that praising children for being smart after an achievement is actually associated with the development of entity beliefs. Parents, teachers, and children might be better served by praise directed at the hard work that led to that *A*.

 REVIEW, ASSESS, AND SHARPEN YOUR THINKING

Review

6 Identify biological, cultural, and psychological factors in learning.

- Discuss these biological constraints on learning: instinctive drift, preparedness, and taste aversion.
- Explain how culture can influence learning.
- Describe psychological constraints on learning.

Assess

1. A pig's rooting behavior interfering with learning is an example of
   - A. preparedness.
   - B. learned helplessness.
   - C. a taste aversion.
   - D. instinctive drift.

2. The view that intelligence can be increased is consistent with which theory?
   - A. learned helplessness theory
   - B. entity theory
   - C. preparedness theory
   - D. incremental theory

3. Believing that you have no control over the things that happen to you is known as
   - A. psychological constraints.
   - B. instinctive drift.
   - C. learned helplessness.
   - D. preparedness.

4. When humans become sick after eating a specific food, they attribute the sickness to the food rather than other stimuli that were present at the time. This tendency is because of
   - A. cultural constraints.
   - B. preparedness.
   - C. instinctive drift.
   - D. learned helplessness.

5. Believing that studying hard will result in a good grade in a course is an example of
   - A. a mindset.
   - B. entity theory.
   - C. preparedness.
   - D. incremental theory.

Sharpen Your Thinking

Do think that you have an entity or incremental theory of your ability to master the topics in psychology? How might this theory influence your performance in class and your decision whether to pursue a psychology major?

7 Learning and Health and Wellness

Describe how principles of learning apply to health and wellness.

So far in this chapter, we have examined the main psychological approaches to learning. These basic learning principles have implications for health and wellness. Here we consider how classical conditioning and operant conditioning relate to physical health, the experience of stress, and the modification of unhealthy behavior patterns.

Classical Conditioning: From Pavlov to You

In Chapter 1, we argued that experience is always relevant to our physical health. Nowhere is this point clearer than in the realm of classical conditioning. Because the unconditioned response is an automatic reflex, it is something that our body does without our control or conscious effort. In any given situation, our body can be learning associations through classical conditioning. Research on the immune system and drug habituation highlights the provocative possibility that our body is learning things even when we do not know it.

A fascinating finding from research using rats to examine classically conditioned illness is that the immune system can be conditioned to respond to a conditioned stimulus. Our immune system is the body's natural defense against disease. Robert Ader and Nicholas Cohen have conducted a number of studies that reveal that classical conditioning can produce *immunosuppression*, a decrease in the production of antibodies (Ader, 2000; Ader & Cohen, 1975, 2000). The initial discovery of this link between classical conditioning and immunosuppression came as a surprise. In the course of studying classical conditioning, Ader (1974) was examining how long a conditioned response would last in some laboratory rats. A conditioned stimulus (saccharin solution) was paired with an unconditioned stimulus, a drug called Cytoxan, which induces nausea. Afterward, while giving the rats saccharin-laced water without the accompanying Cytoxan, Ader watched to see how long it would take the rats to forget the association between the two.

Unexpectedly, in the second month of the study, the rats developed a disease and began to die off. In analyzing this unforeseen result, Ader looked into the properties of the nausea-inducing drug he had used. He discovered that one of its side effects was immunosuppression. It turned out that the rats had been classically conditioned to associate sweet water not only with nausea but also with the shutdown of the immune system. The sweet water apparently had become a conditioned stimulus for immunosuppression. Researchers have found that conditioned immune responses also may occur in humans (Ader, 2000; Voudouris, Peck, & Coleman, 1985).

Operant Conditioning: What a Rat Can Tell Us About Stress

A great deal of research in learning has relied primarily on animal models, such as rats, to understand the principles that underlie human learning. It may be surprising that this work has important implications for humans' health and well-being. Indeed, research on the stress response in rats provides interesting insights about how we humans can deal with stress.

Predictability One very powerful aspect of potentially stressful experiences is their predictability. For a rat, this might mean getting a warning buzzer before receiving a shock. Although the rat still experiences the shock, the buzzer causes less stress than a shock that is received with no warning (Abbott, Schoen, & Badia, 1984). Even getting positive things on a predictable schedule is less stressful than having good things happen at random times. For example, a rat might do very well receiving its daily chow at specific times during the day. But if the timing is instead random, the rat will experience stress. Similarly, when you receive a gift for your birthday or a holiday, it feels very good. But if someone surprises you with a gift out of the blue, you might experience some stress in wondering, "What is this person up to?" Classic research by Judith Rodin and colleagues demonstrated that nursing home residents showed better adjustment if they experienced a given number of visits at predictable times rather than the same number of visits at random times (Langer & Rodin, 1976).

Control Sometimes having control over situations can feel pretty stressful, but it turns out that control may be a key to avoiding feelings

"I feel better today too, but around here I've learned not to be too optimistic."

of stress over difficulties. Specifically, once you have experienced control over negative events, you may be "protected" from stress, even during difficult times.

Returning to our animal model, imagine, for example, a rat that has been trained to avoid a shock by pressing a lever. Later, even if the lever is no longer related to the shock, the rat will press it during the shock and experience less stress. We might imagine the rat thinking, "Gee, it could be really bad if I weren't pressing this lever!" Researchers have also found these links between having control and experiencing stress in humans—for example, nursing home residents are more likely to thrive if they receive visits at times they personally choose. In addition, simply having a plant to take care of was associated with living longer for nursing home residents (Langer & Rodin, 1976).

A lack of control over aversive stimuli can be particularly stressful. For example, individuals exposed to uncontrollable loud blasts of noise showed lowered immune system function (Sieber & others, 1992). One result of exposure to uncontrollable negative events is *learned helplessness,* which we discussed earlier in this chapter. Through experience, one has learned that outcomes are not controllable. A result of learned helplessness is that the organism stops trying to exert control at all.

Martin Seligman, a former president of the American Psychological Association and a founder of the positive psychology movement, began his career in the field of animal learning. He introduced the concept of learned helplessness to explain a pattern of behavior in dogs that were being trained in avoidance learning (Seligman, 1975). Avoidance occurs when an organism learns that it can completely avoid any aversive stimuli if it escapes from the aversive context. For instance, dogs that were trained to jump over a small barrier in their cages could avoid an electrical shock. However, dogs that had been previously exposed to an inescapable shock eventually failed even to try to escape. Using this animal research, Seligman developed an approach to human depression, suggesting that depressed individuals had learned to be helpless.

Improvement   Imagine that you have two mice, both of which are receiving mild electrical shocks. One of them, Gerry, receives 50 shocks every hour, and the other, Chuck-E, receives 10 shocks every hour. The next day both rats are switched to 25 shocks every hour. Which one is more stressed out at the end of the second day? The answer is that, even though Gerry has experienced more shocks in general, Chuck-E is more likely to show the wear and tear of stress. In Gerry's world, even with 25 shocks an hour, *things are getting better*. The perception of improvement, even in a situation that is objectively worse than another, is related to lowered stress (Sapolsky, 2004).

Outlets for Frustration   When things are not going well for us, it often feels good to seek out an outlet such as going for a jog or, perhaps even better, attending a kickboxing class. Likewise, for a rat, having an outlet for life's frustrations is related to lowered stress symptoms. Rats that have a wooden post to gnaw on or even a furry little friend to complain to are less stressed out in response to negative circumstances.

Behavior Modification

Although behaviorist approaches to psychology are often criticized for ignoring mental processes and focusing only on observable behavior, these approaches do provide an optimistic perspective for individuals interested in changing their behaviors. That is, rather than concentrating on factors such as the type of person you are, behavioral approaches imply that you can modify even longstanding habits by changing the reward contingencies that maintain those habits (Miller, 2006).

One way that operant conditioning principles have been used to promote better functioning is through behavior modification programs. **Applied behavior analysis (behavior modification)** is the application of operant conditioning principles to change human behavior. Consequences for behavior are established to ensure that more adaptive actions

applied behavior analysis (behavior modification) The application of operant conditioning principles to change human behavior.

1. Define the problem.

2. Commit to change.

3. Collect data about yourself.

4. Design a self-control program.

5. Make the program last—maintenance.

FIGURE 7.16

Five Steps in Developing a Self-Control Program These actions can help you combat harmful habits in your own life, one step at a time.

are reinforced and less adaptive ones are not (Martin & Pear, 2007; Umbreit & others, 2007). Advocates of behavior modification believe that many emotional and behavior problems stem from inadequate or inappropriate response consequences (Alberto & Trautman, 2006). The child who throws down his glasses and breaks them may be receiving too much attention from his teachers and peers for his behavior; they unwittingly may be reinforcing an unacceptable behavior. In this instance, the child's parents and teachers would be instructed to divert attention from the destructive behavior and transfer it to a more constructive behavior, such as working quietly or playing cooperatively with peers (Harris, Wolf, & Baer, 1964).

Behavior modification can help people improve their self-control in many aspects of mental and physical health (Watson & Tharp, 2007). Garry Martin and Joseph Pear (2007) created five steps to help individuals make gains in their self-control (Figure 7.16):

- *Step 1: Define the behavior to be changed in specific, concrete terms.* For Al, defining the behavior is easy—he is overweight and wants to lose 30 pounds. Stated even more precisely, he wants to consume about 1,000 fewer calories per day to achieve a weight loss of about 2 pounds per week. But some problems are more difficult to specify, such as "wasting time," "having a bad attitude toward school," "having a poor relationship with ——," and "being too nervous and worrying a lot." These types of problems have been called "fuzzies" because of their abstract nature (Mager, 1972). As a key step in behavior modification, it is important to make abstract problems specific and concrete. Problems can be made precise by writing out a goal and listing the things that would give clear evidence of having reached the goal.

- *Step 2: Make a commitment to change.* Researchers have shown that both a commitment to change and a knowledge of change techniques help college students become more effective self-managers of their smoking, eating, studying, and relationship problems (Alterman, Gariti, & Mulvaney, 2001; Perkins & others, 2001). Building a commitment to change requires doing things that increase the likelihood that you will stick to your project. First, tell others about your commitment to change—they will remind you to stick to your program. Second, rearrange your environment to provide frequent reminders of your goal, making sure the reminders are associated with the positive benefits of reaching your goal. Third, put substantial time and energy into planning your project. Make a list of statements about your project, such as "I've put a lot of time into this project; I am certainly not going to waste all of this effort now." Fourth, because you will invariably face temptations to backslide or quit your project, plan ahead for ways that you can deal with temptation, tailoring these plans to your problem.

- *Step 3: Collect data about your behavior.* Collecting data is especially important in decreasing excessive behaviors such as overeating and frequent smoking. One reason for tracking your behavior is that it provides a reference point for evaluating your progress. When recording the frequency of a behavior during initial observations, you should examine the immediate circumstances that could be maintaining the problem (Martin & Pear, 2007).

- *Step 4: Design a self-control program.* Many good self-control programs involve setting long-term and short-term goals and developing a plan for reaching the goals. Good self-control programs also usually include some type of self-talk, self-instruction, or self-reinforcement. For example, a person whose goal is to jog 30 minutes a day 5 days a week might say, "I'll never make it. It just won't work." This person can benefit by saying something like "I know it's going to be tough, but I can make it." Also, individuals can engage in self-reinforcing statements or treat themselves. This might involve saying something like "Way to go. You're up to 30 minutes three times a week. You're on your way." Or they might treat themselves to a reward such as a movie, a new piece of clothing, or a new CD.

- *Step 5: Make the program last—maintenance.* One strategy is to establish specific dates for postchecks and to plan a course of action if your postchecks are not favorable. For example, if your self-control program involves weight reduction, you might want to weigh yourself once a week. If your weight increases to a certain level, then you immediately go back on your self-control program. Another strategy is to establish a buddy system by finding a friend or someone with a similar problem. The two of you set mutual maintenance goals. Once a month, get together and check each other's behavior. If your goals have been maintained, celebrate together in an agreed-on way.

For other ideas on how to establish an effective self-control program tailored to your needs, you might contact the counseling center at your college or university. You also might consider consulting a good book on behavior modification or self-control, such as *Behavior Modification: What It Is and How to Do It* (Martin & Pear, 2007).

 REVIEW, ASSESS, AND SHARPEN YOUR THINKING

Review

7 **Describe how principles of learning apply to health and wellness.**
- Describe the relationships between classical conditioning and immune system functioning.
- Describe four conclusions from research using rats that help us understand stress.
- Describe the principles behind behavior modification.

Assess

1. **What is immunosuppression?**
   A. difficulty with acquisition of learning
   B. an interruption of the conditioned stimulus–unconditioned stimulus pairing
   C. a decrease in antibody production
   D. the desired outcome of behavior modification

2. **How would the theory of learned helplessness explain depression?**
   A. Depressed people stay depressed because they are rewarded by others for being depressed.
   B. Depressed people relate everyday events to negative outcomes.
   C. Depressed people stop trying because they have not been able to control things in their lives.
   D. Depressed people are waiting for things to change.

3. **Humberto has set a goal of becoming more assertive. According to principles of behavior modification, what would be the first step Humberto should take?**

   A. observe himself to see if he is being assertive or not
   B. set short-term and long-term goals
   C. concretely define what he means by being assertive
   D. reward himself for being assertive

4. **Which of the following would be consistent with the behavior modification stage of making a commitment to change?**
   A. putting reminders of the goal around your room
   B. operationally defining the behavior you want to change
   C. observing yourself to see if you are making progress
   D. rewarding yourself for making changes

Sharpen Your Thinking

What is a personal habit you would like to change? How would you use behavior modification to make the required change?

SUMMARY

1 TYPES OF LEARNING

Explain learning.

Learning is a relatively permanent change in behavior that occurs through experience. Observational learning is learning by watching what other people do. In associative learning, a connection is made between two events. Conditioning is the process by which associative learning occurs. In classical conditioning, organisms learn the association between two stimuli, and in operant conditioning, they learn the association between behavior and a consequence.

2 CLASSICAL CONDITIONING

Describe classical conditioning.

Pavlov's Studies

Classical conditioning occurs when a neutral stimulus becomes associated with a meaningful stimulus and comes to elicit a similar response. Pavlov discovered that an organism learns the association between an unconditioned stimulus (UCS) and a conditioned stimulus (CS). The UCS automatically produces the unconditioned response (UCR). After conditioning (CS–UCS pairing), the CS elicits the conditioned response (CR) by itself. Acquisition in classical conditioning is the initial linking of stimuli and responses, which involves a neutral stimulus being associated with the UCS so that the CS comes to elicit the CR.

Two important aspects of acquisition are contiguity and contingency/predictability. Generalization in classical conditioning is the tendency of a new stimulus that is similar to the original conditioned stimulus to elicit a response that is similar to the conditioned response. Discrimination in classical conditioning is the process of learning to respond to certain stimuli and not to others. Extinction in classical conditioning is the weakening of the CR in the absence of the UCS. Spontaneous recovery is the recurrence of a CR after a time delay without further conditioning.

Classical Conditioning in Humans

In humans, classical conditioning has been applied to explaining and eliminating fears. Counterconditioning, a classical conditioning procedure for weakening the CR by associating the fear-provoking stimulus with a new response that is incompatible with the fear, has been successful in eliminating fears. Classical conditioning can explain pleasant emotions, too. Classical conditioning also has been applied to consumer behavior and is an underlying principle in advertising. Some behaviors we associate with physical and mental disorders, including certain aspects of drug use, can involve classical conditioning.

3 OPERANT CONDITIONING

Discuss operant conditioning.

Defining Operant Conditioning

Operant conditioning is a form of learning in which the consequences of behavior produce changes in the probability of the behavior's occurrence. Skinner described the behavior of the organism as operant: The behavior operates on the environment, and the environment in turn operates on the organism. Whereas classical conditioning involves respondent behavior, operant conditioning involves operant behavior. In most instances, operant conditioning is better at explaining voluntary behavior than classical conditioning is.

Thorndike's Law of Effect

Thorndike's law of effect states that behaviors followed by positive outcomes are strengthened, whereas behaviors followed by negative outcomes are weakened. Thorndike's view that the organism's behavior is due to a connection between a stimulus and a response is called S–R theory.

Skinner's Approach to Operant Conditioning

Skinner believed that the mechanisms of learning are the same for all species. This conclusion led him to study lower animals extensively in the hope that the basic mechanisms of learning could be more easily understood in organisms simpler than humans. Like Skinner, contemporary behaviorists study organisms under precisely controlled conditions so that the connection between the operant behavior and the specific consequences can be examined in minute detail.

Shaping

Shaping is the process of rewarding approximations of desired behavior in order to shorten the learning process.

Principles of Reinforcement

Principles of reinforcement include the distinction between positive reinforcement (the frequency of a behavior increases because it is followed by a rewarding stimulus) and negative reinforcement (the frequency of behavior increases because it is followed by the removal of an aversive, or unpleasant, stimulus). Positive reinforcement can be classified as primary reinforcement (using reinforcers that are innately satisfying) and secondary reinforcement (using reinforcers that acquire positive value through experience). Reinforcement can also be continuous (a behavior is reinforced every time) or partial (a behavior is reinforced only a portion of the time). Schedules of reinforcement—fixed-ratio, variable-ratio, fixed-interval, and variable-interval—are timetables that determine when a behavior will be reinforced.

Operant conditioning involves generalization (giving the same response to similar stimuli), discrimination (responding to stimuli that signal that a behavior will or will not be reinforced), and extinction (a decreasing tendency to perform a previously reinforced behavior when reinforcement is stopped). Punishment is a consequence that decreases the likelihood a behavior will occur. Punishment, through which a behavior is weakened, is different from negative reinforcement, through which a behavior is strengthened. In positive punishment, a behavior decreases when it is followed by an unpleasant stimulus. In negative punishment, a behavior decreases when a positive stimulus is removed from it.

Time-out is a form of negative punishment. Most psychologists recommend that positive punishment not be used with children. Operant conditioning is more efficient, especially in lower animals, when the interval between behavior and its reinforcement or punishment is very brief. However, in humans, delayed reinforcement and punishment can have significant effects on behavior. Connections between the timing of reinforcement and punishment have implications for understanding health problems such as obesity and substance abuse.

4 OBSERVATIONAL LEARNING

Understand observational learning.

Bandura's Model of Observational Learning

Observational learning occurs when a person observes and imitates someone's behavior. Bandura identified four main processes in observational learning: attention, retention, motor reproduction, and reinforcement.

5 COGNITIVE FACTORS IN LEARNING

Discuss the role of cognition in learning.

Purposive Behavior

Tolman emphasized the purposiveness of behavior. *Purposiveness* refers to Tolman's belief that much of behavior is goal-directed. There is considerable interest in goal-directed behavior today. In studying purposiveness, Tolman went beyond stimuli and responses to discuss cognitive mechanisms. Tolman believed that expectancies, acquired through experiences with the environment, are an important cognitive mechanism in learning. Cognitive maps, an organism's mental representations of physical space, involve expectancies about which actions are needed to reach a goal.

Insight Learning

Köhler developed the concept of insight learning, a form of problem solving in which the organism develops a sudden insight into or understanding of a problem's solution.

6 BIOLOGICAL, CULTURAL, AND PSYCHOLOGICAL FACTORS IN LEARNING

Identify biological, cultural, and psychological factors in learning.

Biological Constraints

Biological constraints restrict what an organism can learn from experience. These constraints include instinctive drift (the tendency of animals to revert to instinctive behavior that interferes with learned behavior), preparedness (the species-specific biological predisposition to learn in certain ways but not in others), and taste aversion (the biological predisposition to avoid foods that have caused sickness in the past).

Cultural Constraints

Although most psychologists agree that the principles of classical conditioning, operant conditioning, and observational learning are universal, cultural customs can influence the degree to which these learning processes are used, and culture also often determines the content of learning.

Psychological Constraints

What we learn is determined in part by what we believe we can learn. According to Dweck, our implicit theories of ability play a large role in the goals we set for learning. An entity theory holds that ability is fixed and unchanging. An incremental theory holds that ability can change through learning. Those who adopt incremental theories of ability are more likely to persevere at a challenging task and to interpret failure not as indicative of low ability but as an opportunity to learn new skills.

7 LEARNING AND HEALTH AND WELLNESS

Describe how principles of learning apply to health and wellness.

Classical Conditioning: From Pavlov to You

Research has shown that the immune system is susceptible to the effects of classical conditioning.

Operant Conditioning: What a Rat Can Tell Us About Stress

Research using rats has demonstrated four important variables involved in the stress response: predictability, perceived control, perceptions of improvement, and outlets for frustration.

Behavior Modification

Behavior modification is the application of operant conditioning principles to change human behavior. It involves establishing consequences for behavior to reinforce more adaptive actions. Operant conditioning has been applied to mental and physical health, as well as to education.

Key Terms

learning, p. 264
behaviorism, p. 264
associative learning, p. 264
observational learning, p. 265
classical conditioning, p. 266
unconditioned stimulus (UCS), p. 267
unconditioned response (UCR), p. 267
conditioned stimulus (CS), p. 267
conditioned response (CR), p. 267

acquisition (classical conditioning), p. 267
generalization (classical conditioning), p. 268
discrimination (classical conditioning), p. 268
extinction (classical conditioning), p. 268
spontaneous recovery, p. 268
counterconditioning, p. 270
operant conditioning, p. 272
law of effect, p. 273

shaping, p. 274
reinforcement, p. 275
positive reinforcement, p. 275
negative reinforcement, p. 275
primary reinforcement, p. 276
secondary reinforcement, p. 276
schedules of reinforcement, p. 276
generalization (operant conditioning), p. 278
discrimination (operant conditioning), p. 278

extinction (operant conditioning), p. 279
punishment, p. 279
positive punishment, p. 279
negative punishment, p. 279
latent learning (implicit learning), p. 288
insight learning, p. 289
instinctive drift, p. 290
preparedness, p. 290
learned helplessness, p. 292
applied behavior analysis (behavior modification), p. 295

Assess Your Knowledge

1. Researchers found that raccoons who were trained to deposit coins in a tray began to rub the coins together instead of dropping them in the tray. Why?
   A. because of extinction
   B. because of spontaneous recovery
   C. because of instinctive drift
   D. because of counterconditioning

2. When a child hears a loud noise, he cries. The loud noise is
   A. the unconditioned stimulus.
   B. the conditioned stimulus.
   C. the unconditioned response.
   D. the conditioned response.

3. The first time Nikki goes to the dentist, she feels pain from the dentist's drill. The next time Nikki goes to the dentist, she hears the sound of the drill from the waiting room. Nikki begins to feel her heart beat faster and her palms sweat. What is the conditioned response?
   A. the drill
   B. pain from the drill
   C. sweating and heart racing from the sound
   D. the sound of the drill

4. Which of the following is consistent with the law of effect?
   A. A child who is rewarded for getting good grades begins to do poorly in school.
   B. A dog who is punished for barking barks more.
   C. A cat who is yelled at when she scratches the sofa stops scratching the sofa.
   D. An adult who is fired from his job for being late is late at his next job.

5. Meghan is scared of flying. When she goes on vacation with her husband, he helps her to relax by holding her hand, having her breathe deeply, and imagining herself on a sandy beach. After several flights with her husband, Meghan finds that she is no longer afraid of flying. Which of the following processes occurred?
   A. counterconditioning
   B. positive punishment
   C. discrimination
   D. spontaneous recovery

6. Kim has taught her dog to pick up a sponge, walk it to the sink on two legs, and drop it on the dishes. Kim has taught her dog to "wash the dishes" using which of the following techniques?
   A. classical conditioning
   B. instinctive drift
   C. generalization
   D. shaping

7. Every sixth time Miguel cleans his room, his mother takes him to dinner as a reward. On what type of reinforcement schedule is Miguel?
   A. variable-ratio schedule
   B. variable-interval schedule
   C. fixed-ratio schedule
   D. fixed-interval schedule

8. Which schedule of reinforcement is most resistant to extinction?
   A. variable-ratio schedule
   B. variable-interval schedule
   C. fixed-ratio schedule
   D. fixed-interval schedule

9. Kurt's older brother Rob repeatedly punches Kurt on the arm until Kurt takes out the trash. Rob punching Kurt is an example of a
   A. negative reinforcer.
   B. negative punisher.
   C. positive reinforcer.
   D. positive punisher.

10. Putting a child who misbehaves in time out is an example of a
    A. negative reinforcer.
    B. negative punishment.
    C. positive reinforcer.
    D. positive punishment.

11. Sally witnesses her friend get arrested for drug possession. As a result, Sally avoids drugs. Sally has experienced what type of learning?
    A. negative reinforcement
    B. classical conditioning
    C. operant learning
    D. observational learning

12. People who agree with the _____ approach are more likely to be energized by challenging tasks.
    A. entity theory
    B. learned helplessness
    C. incremental theory
    D. applied behavior analysis

13. _____ accounts for the finding that taste aversions develop more quickly than other types of learning.
    A. Instinctive drift
    B. Preparedness
    C. Insight learning
    D. Contingency

14. A stressor will be more easily managed when it
    A. is predictable and not controllable.
    B. is not predictable but is controllable.
    C. is neither predictable nor controllable.
    D. is predictable and controllable.

15. Each time a green light is shown to an animal, it receives a shock 1 minute later. The pairing of the conditioned stimulus with the unconditioned stimulus is characterized by which of the following?
    A. high contingency and low contiguity
    B. low contingency and high contiguity
    C. high contingency and high contiguity
    D. low contingency and low contiguity

Go to Appendix B for answers to these questions.

Apply Your Knowledge

1. One common association that people have is called a *conditioned taste aversion,* which occurs when you eat or drink something and then get sick. A conditioned taste aversion is most likely to occur when the food or drink is relatively unfamiliar. Suppose you have acquired a conditioned taste aversion to tequila. Identify the unconditioned stimulus, unconditioned response, conditioned stimulus, and conditioned response in this example.

2. Positive and negative reinforcement are often difficult concepts to understand. On the following website, examples and a practice exercise may help you figure out the distinction more easily: **http://psych.athabascau.ca/html/prtut/reinpair.htm**

3. Think of everything you have learned in the past several days. Write down an example involving each of the following types of learning: classical conditioning, operant conditioning, observational learning, latent learning, and insight learning. Which kind of learning do you use most frequently? Which is the least common for you? Are there types of learning you have done that do not seem to fit any category? If so, what aspects of those types exclude them from these categories?

4. Check out your local sports page for a report of a recent win or loss by your favorite team. Look for evidence of entity versus incremental theories of ability. To what extent is hard work versus natural ability mentioned?

CHAPTER 8

MEMORY

Experiencing Psychology

AKIRA HARAGUCHI AND HIS REMARKABLE MEMORY

On July 2, 2005, the British Broadcasting Company (BBC) reported that a Japanese mental health counselor, Akira Haraguchi, age 59, recited the digits of pi to the number's first 83,431 decimal places from memory, shattering the previous world record (BBC News, 2005). The recitation took several hours; Haraguchi had to start over after the first 3 hours because he lost his place. Imagine memorizing such a list, over 80,000 numbers long, with no apparent pattern or meaning. Surely Haraguchi's feat earns a place in a book of amazing acts of memory. Mnemonists are people who have astonishing memory abilities such as Haraguchi's, and as we will see, psychologists (including positive psychologists) have learned a good deal about memory from such individuals (Takahashi & others, 2006). Consider that the field of positive psychology stresses not only the very best of human capacities but also the *extraordinary* aspects of human ability in everyday experience. And daily life presents countless examples that demonstrate the amazing capacity of human memory.

Imagine for example that you are at an upscale restaurant with six friends. The server takes your order. After reciting your rather complicated dinner preferences, you note that he is not writing anything down. Now you wait patiently through your friends' orders and cannot help but wonder, "How can he possibly remember all this?" Surely, you will get blue cheese instead of ranch salad dressing, or a side of carrots instead of green beans, or your pasta will be covered with cheese when you specifically requested no cheese. But when the meal arrives, everything is exactly right. Waiters seem to commit amazing acts of memory routinely. How do they do it? Asked to share their secrets, a few college students who moonlight in food service explained their methods: "I always try to remember the person's face, and imagine him eating the food he's ordered"; "The more complicated the order is, the easier it is to remember"; "If it's something really off the wall, you'll never forget it"; "Repetition is the key!" As we will see, research studies on memory support these techniques surprisingly well.

Memories matter to us in a larger way as well. Recent controversies over the accuracy of memoirs demonstrate that memories have a special place, beyond that of fiction. Memories are a piece of "what really happened," and as such they have an unusual value to us. Even Oprah Winfrey was moved to apologize to her viewers for recommending James Frey's "nonfiction" book *A Million Little Pieces* when it was revealed that many of the experiences described were not, in fact, facts.

PREVIEW

Through our memory, we weave the past into the present. Memory can quietly stir, or spin off, with each thought we think and each word we utter. As twentieth-century American playwright Tennessee Williams once remarked, "Life is all memory except for the one present moment that goes by so quick you can hardly catch it going." In this chapter, we explore three key aspects of memory: how information gets into our memory, how we store the information, and how we retrieve it. We also examine fascinating aspects of why we sometimes forget, what the science of memory can tell us about improving our study habits, and how memory might even be involved in our health and wellness.

1 The Nature of Memory

Identify the three fundamental processes of memory.

The stars are shining, and the moon is full. A beautiful evening is coming to a close. You look at your significant other and think, "I'll never forget this night." How is it possible that, in fact, you never will forget it? Years from now, you might even tell your children about that one special night so many years ago, even if you had not thought about it in the years since. How does one perfect night become a part of our enduring life memories?

Psychologists define **memory** as the retention of information or experience over time. Memory occurs through three important processes: encoding, storage, and retrieval. For memory to work, we have to take in information (encode the sights and sounds of that night), store it or represent it in some manner (retain it in some mental storehouse), and then retrieve it for a later purpose (recall it when someone asks, "So how did you two end up together?"). The first three sections of the chapter focus on these phases of memory: encoding, storage, and retrieval (Figure 8.1).

Except for the annoying moments when our memory fails, or the situation where someone we know experiences memory loss, we do not think about how much everything we do or say depends on the smooth operation of our memory systems (Schacter, 1996, 2001, 2007; Schacter & Addis, 2007). Let's return to our server in the restaurant. He has to attend to the orders he receives—who is asking for what and how they would like it prepared. To do so, he must encode the information about each customer and each order. He might look at each customer and associate his or her face with the menu items requested. Without writing anything down, he must retain the information, at least until he gets the orders to the kitchen or onto the computer. He might rehearse the order over in his mind as he walks to the back of the restaurant. When delivering the food to the table, he must accurately retrieve the information about who ordered what. Human memory systems truly are remarkable when you think of how much information we put into our memories and how much we must retrieve to perform all of life's activities (Kellogg, 2007).

memory The retention of information over time through the processes of encoding, storage, and retrieval.

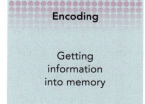

Encoding	Storage	Retrieval
Getting information into memory	Retaining information over time	Taking information out of storage

FIGURE 8.1

Processing Information in Memory As you read about the many aspects of memory in this chapter, think about the organization of memory in terms of these three main activities.

Review

1 Identify the three fundamental processes of memory.

- Define memory and briefly profile the three fundamental processes of memory.

Assess

1. You are trying to think of the name of the actor in the movie you saw last week, but you can't remember her name. You are having a problem with

   A. encoding.   B. retrieval.

   C. rehearsal.   D. storage.

2. Which of the following happens first?

   A. encoding   B. retrieval

   C. storage   D. forgetting

3. Which stage of the memory process is associated with information being retained?

   A. retrieval

   B. encoding

   C. storage

   D. elaborating

Sharpen Your Thinking

Imagine what life would be like without memory. Reflect on the activities you have engaged in today. When and how did memory influence your daily life? Think about what memory means with respect to social relationships. What does it mean to you if someone remembers your name—or does not remember it?

2 Memory Encoding

Explain how memories are encoded.

Encoding is the process by which information gets into memory storage. When you are listening to a lecture, watching a movie, enjoying music on your iPod, or talking with a friend, you are encoding information into memory. In everyday experiences, encoding has much in common with learning.

Some information gets into memory virtually automatically, whereas encoding other information takes effort. Let's examine some of the encoding processes that require effort. The issues that interest psychologists include how effectively we attend to information, how deeply we process it, how extensively we elaborate it with details, and how much we use mental imagery to encode it.

encoding The process by which information gets into memory storage.

Attention

Clearly, we cannot consciously remember something that we never saw, never heard, or never felt. To begin the process of memory encoding, we have to attend to information (Posner & Rothbart, 2007). As we saw in Chapter 5, attention plays an important role in perception. Recall that selective attention involves focusing on a specific aspect of experience while ignoring others. Attention is selective because the brain's resources are limited. Although our brains are remarkably efficient, they cannot attend to everything. Limitations mean that we have to attend selectively to some things in our environment and ignore others (Knudsen, 2007). So, on that special night, you never noticed the bus that roared past or the people who passed you while you strolled along the street with your significant other. Those aspects of that night will not make it into your enduring memory.

Divided attention also affects memory encoding. It occurs when a person must attend to several things simultaneously (Savage & others, 2006). Imagine that on some evening you are

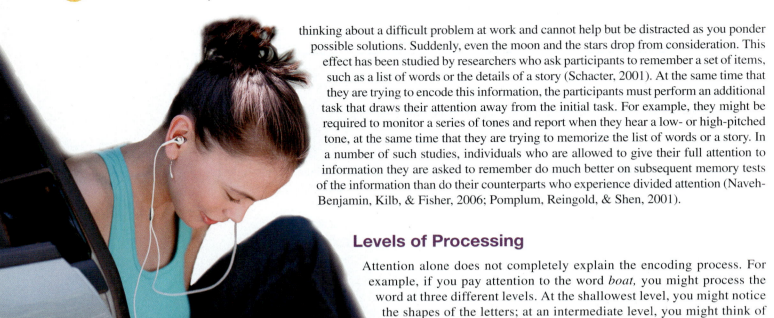

thinking about a difficult problem at work and cannot help but be distracted as you ponder possible solutions. Suddenly, even the moon and the stars drop from consideration. This effect has been studied by researchers who ask participants to remember a set of items, such as a list of words or the details of a story (Schacter, 2001). At the same time that they are trying to encode this information, the participants must perform an additional task that draws their attention away from the initial task. For example, they might be required to monitor a series of tones and report when they hear a low- or high-pitched tone, at the same time that they are trying to memorize the list of words or a story. In a number of such studies, individuals who are allowed to give their full attention to information they are asked to remember do much better on subsequent memory tests of the information than do their counterparts who experience divided attention (Naveh-Benjamin, Kilb, & Fisher, 2006; Pomplum, Reingold, & Shen, 2001).

Levels of Processing

Attention alone does not completely explain the encoding process. For example, if you pay attention to the word *boat,* you might process the word at three different levels. At the shallowest level, you might notice the shapes of the letters; at an intermediate level, you might think of characteristics of the word (such as that it rhymes with *coat*); and at the deepest level, you might think about the kind of boat you would like to own and the last time you went fishing.

This model of the encoding process was proposed by Fergus Craik and Robert Lockhart (1972). The concept of **levels of processing** refers to the idea that encoding occurs on a continuum from shallow to deep, with deeper processing producing better memory (Figure 8.2).

- *Shallow level:* The sensory or physical features of stimuli are analyzed. For instance, we might detect the lines, angles, and contours of a printed word's letters or detect a sound's frequency, duration, and loudness (recall the discussion of feature detection in Chapter 5).

Listening to music on your iPod involves encoding—processing those tunes for storage in your memory.

- *Intermediate level:* The stimulus is recognized and given a label. For example, we identify a four-legged barking object as a dog.
- *Deepest level:* Information is processed semantically, in terms of its meaning. At this deepest level, we make associations. We might associate the barking dog with a warning of danger or with good times, such as playing fetch with a pet. The more associations we make, the deeper the processing (Ragland & others, 2006).

A number of studies have shown that people's memories improve when they make associations to stimuli and use deep processing, as opposed to attending only to the physical

levels of processing The idea that encoding occurs on a continuum from shallow to deep, with deeper processing producing better memory.

FIGURE 8.2

Depth of Processing According to the levels of processing principle, deeper processing of stimuli produces better memory of them.

Depth of Processing

Shallow Processing	Physical and perceptual features are analyzed.	The lines, angles, and contour that make up the physical appearance of an object, such as a car, are detected.
Intermediate Processing	Stimulus is recognized and labeled.	The object is recognized as a car.
Deep Processing	Semantic, meaningful, symbolic characteristics are used.	Associations connected with *car* are brought to mind—you think about the Porsche or Ferrari you hope to buy or the fun you and friends had on spring break when you drove a car to the beach.

aspects of the stimuli and using shallow processing (Howes, 2006). For example, researchers have found that, if you encode something meaningful about a face and make associations with it, you are more likely to remember it (Harris & Kay, 1995). So, our server who strives to remember the face of the customer and to imagine her eating the food she has ordered is using deep processing. You might attach meaning to the face of a person in your introductory psychology class by noting that she reminds you of someone you have seen on TV, and you might associate her face with your psychology class.

Elaboration

Cognitive psychologists have recognized that good encoding of a memory depends on more than just depth of processing. Within deep processing, the more extensive the processing, the better the memory (Kellogg, 2007). **Elaboration** is the extensiveness of processing at any given level. For example, rather than memorizing the definition of *memory,* you would do better to learn the concept of memory by coming up with examples of how information enters your mind, how it is stored, and how you can retrieve it. Thinking of examples of a concept is a good way to understand it. Self-reference is another effective way to elaborate information (Czienskowski & Giljohann, 2002; Hunt & Ellis, 2004) (Figure 8.3). For example, if the word *win* is on a list of words to remember, you might think of the last time you won a bicycle race; or if the word *cook* appears, you might recall the last time you made dinner. In general, deep elaboration—elaborate processing of meaningful information—is an excellent way to remember.

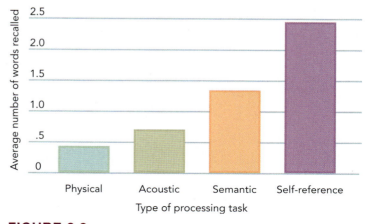

elaboration Extensiveness of processing at any given level of memory.

One reason that elaboration produces good memory is that it adds to the *distinctiveness* of "memory codes" (Ellis, 1987). By elaborating on an experience, we create a highly unique representation of it in memory. If we think of remembering as searching for a particular bit of information, the more distinctive an experience, the easier it will be to find in the mental storehouse of memory. To remember a piece of information such as a name, an experience, or a fact about geography, you need to search for the code that contains this information among the mass of codes contained in long-term memory.

The search process is easier if the memory code is somehow unique (Hunt & Kelly, 1996). The situation is not unlike searching for a friend at a crowded airport. If that friend is 6 feet tall and has flaming red hair, she will be easier to find than a friend who is 5 feet 5 inches tall with brown hair. Similarly, highly distinctive memory codes can be more easily differentiated. Importantly, while the value of distinctiveness here is most apparent during retrieval, the creation of a distinctive memory occurs at encoding. Also, as encoding becomes more elaborate, more information is stored. And as more information is stored, the more likely it is that the code will be distinctive—that is, easy to differentiate from other memory codes. For example, if you meet someone with whom you hope to become better friends someday, you will do a better job of remembering his name if you initially encode a lot of information about him, such as his appearance, occupation, and something he has said. You are more likely to remember him than someone who encodes him only as "blond."

The process of elaboration is also evident in the physical activity of the brain. Neuroscience research has shown a link between elaboration during encoding and brain activity (Kirchhoff & Buckner, 2006; Kirchhoff, Schapiro, & Buckner, 2005). In one study, individuals were placed in magnetic resonance imaging (MRI) machines (see Chapter 3), and one word was flashed every

FIGURE 8.3

Memory Improves When Self-Referencing Is Used In one study, researchers asked participants to remember lists of words according to the words' physical, acoustic (sound), semantic (meaning), or self-referent characteristics. As can be seen, when individuals generated self-references for the words, they remembered them better.

2 seconds on a screen inside (Wagner & others, 1998). Initially, the individuals simply noted whether the words were in uppercase or lowercase letters. As the study progressed, they were asked to determine whether each word was concrete, such as *chair* or *book,* or abstract, such as *love* or *democracy*. In this study, the participants showed more neural activity in the left frontal lobe of the brain during the "concrete/abstract" task than they did when they were asked merely to state whether the words were in uppercase or lowercase letters. And they demonstrated better memory in the concrete/abstract task. The researchers concluded that greater elaboration of information is linked with neural activity, especially in the brain's left frontal lobe, and with improved memory.

Imagery

One of the most powerful ways to make memories distinctive is to use mental imagery (Murray, 2007; Quinn & McConnell, 2006). Psychologist Alexander Luria (1968) chronicled the life of S., whose unique visual imagination allowed him to remember an extraordinary amount of detail. Luria had become acquainted with S. in the 1920s in Russia. Luria began with some simple research to test S.'s memory. For example, he asked S. to recall a series of words or numbers, a standard method of testing memory skills. Luria concluded that S. had no apparent limits to his ability to recall. In such tests, people remember at most five to nine numbers. Not only could S. remember as many as 70 numbers, but he could also recall them accurately in reverse order. S. moreover could report the sequence flawlessly with no warning or practice even as long as 15 years after his initial exposure to the sequence. In addition, after the 15-year interval, S. could describe what Luria had been wearing and where he had been sitting when S. learned the list. Similar feats of recall included accurately reproducing passages from languages he did not know—after hearing the passage only once! How could S. manage such tasks? As long as each number or word was spoken slowly, S. could represent it as a visual image that was meaningful to him. These images were durable—S. easily remembered the image he created for each sequence long after he learned the sequence. Imagery helped S. remember complicated lists of items and information. For example, S. once was asked to remember the following formula:

$$N \cdot \sqrt{d^2 \cdot \frac{85}{VX}} \cdot 3\sqrt{\frac{276^2 \cdot 86x}{n^2 V \cdot \pi 264}} \, n^2 b$$
$$= sv \frac{1624}{32^2} \cdot r^2 s$$

S. studied the formula for 7 minutes and then reported how he memorized it. Notice in his account of this process, which follows, how he used imagery:

> Neiman (*N*) came out and jabbed at the ground with his cane (·). He looked up at a tall tree, which resembled the square-root sign (√), and thought to himself: "No wonder this tree has withered and begun to expose its roots. After all, it was here when I built these two houses" (*d²*). Once again he poked his cane (·). Then he said: "The houses are old, I'll have to get rid of them; the sale will bring in far more money." He had originally invested 85,000 in them (85). . . . (Luria, 1968)

S.'s complete story was four times this length. But the imagery in the story he created must have been powerful, because S. remembered the formula perfectly 15 years later without any advance notice.

S. certainly represents an extreme case of amazing *mnemonic* ability—that is, skill in remembering. But imagery functions as a powerful tool for encoding. Recall that one of our student waiters mentioned imagining the person eating the food to remember the customer's order. Classic studies by Allan Paivio (1971, 1986, 2007) documented how imagery can improve memory. Paivio argues that memory is stored in one of two ways: as a verbal code (a word or a label) or as an image code. Paivio thinks that the image code, which is highly detailed and distinctive, produces better memory. His *dual-code hypothesis* claims that memory for pictures is better than memory for words because pictures—at least those that can be named—are stored both as image codes and as verbal codes. Thus we have two potential avenues by which information can be retrieved.

REVIEW, ASSESS, AND SHARPEN YOUR THINKING

Review

2 Explain how memories are encoded.

- Summarize how attention is involved in memory.
- Discuss elaboration.
- Describe the levels of processing involved in memory.
- Explain the role of imagery in memory.

Assess

1. Which of the following is an example of processing at the deepest level?
   A. remembering that your friend likes lavender
   B. recognizing solid lines
   C. identifying an object as a computer mouse
   D. detecting that a sound has a low frequency

2. Laura is trying to remember the five factors of personality (Openness to Experience, Conscientiousness, Extraversion, Agreeableness, and Neuroticism). To help her, she uses the first letters of each factor to spell out OCEAN. What technique has Laura used?
   A. elaboration
   B. a mnemonic
   C. declaration
   D. shallow processing

3. What does the dual-code hypothesis state?
   A. Memory is better for words than pictures.
   B. Memory is better for pictures than words.
   C. Memory is best when processed at the deepest level.
   D. Memory is unrelated to the level of processing.

4. Why is elaboration helpful in strengthening memory codes?
   A. Because it involves rehearsal.
   B. Because it makes the memory code less distinctive.
   C. Because it makes the memory code more unique.
   D. Because processing happens at a lower level.

5. Focusing on the physical features of an object is an example of what type of processing?
   A. shallow processing
   B. intermediate processing
   C. deep processing
   D. elaboration

Sharpen Your Thinking

Think of a common object or location that you see every day (for example, your backpack or a building you pass daily) but that is not currently in your sight. Draw the object or location. Later compare your results with the real thing. What differences do you notice? Does what you learned about encoding help to explain the differences?

3 Memory Storage

Discuss how memories are stored.

The quality of encoding does not alone determine the quality of memory. A memory also needs to be stored properly after it is encoded. **Storage** encompasses how information is retained over time and how it is represented in memory.

We remember some information for less than a second, some for half a minute, and some for minutes, hours, years, or even a lifetime. Richard Atkinson and Richard Shiffrin (1968) formulated an early popular theory of memory that acknowledged the varying life span of memories (Figure 8.4). The **Atkinson-Shiffrin theory** states that memory storage involves three separate systems:

- *Sensory memory:* time frames of a fraction of a second to several seconds
- *Short-term memory:* time frames up to 30 seconds
- *Long-term memory:* time frames up to a lifetime

storage Retention of information over time and the representation of information in memory.

Atkinson-Shiffrin theory The view that memory storage involves three separate systems: sensory memory, short-term memory, and long-term memory.

FIGURE 8.4

Atkinson and Shiffrin's Theory of Memory In this model, sensory input goes into sensory memory. Through the process of attention, information moves into short-term memory, where it remains for 30 seconds or less unless it is rehearsed. When the information goes into long-term memory storage, it can be retrieved over a lifetime.

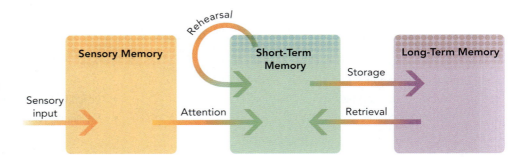

sensory memory Information from the world that is held in its original form only for an instant, not much longer than the brief time it is exposed to the visual, auditory, and other senses.

FIGURE 8.5

Auditory and Visual Sensory Memory
If you hear this bird's call while walking through the woods, your auditory sensory memory holds the information for several seconds. If you see the bird, your visual sensory memory holds the information for only about 1/4 of a second.

As you read about these three memory storage systems, you will find that time frame is not the only thing that makes them different from one another. Each type of memory operates in a distinctive way and has a special purpose.

Sensory Memory

Sensory memory holds information from the world in its original sensory form for only an instant, not much longer than the brief time it is exposed to the visual, auditory, and other senses (Deouell & others, 2006). Sensory memory is very rich and detailed, but the information in it is quickly lost unless we use certain strategies that transfer it into short-term or long-term memory.

Think about all the sights and sounds you encounter as you walk to class on a typical morning. Literally thousands of stimuli come into your field of vision and hearing—cracks in the sidewalk, chirping birds, a noisy motorcycle, the blue sky, faces of hundreds of people. You do not process all of these stimuli, but you do process a number of them. In general, you process many more stimuli at the sensory level than you consciously notice. Sensory memory retains this information from your senses, including a large portion of what you think you ignore.

But sensory memory does not retain the information very long. *Echoic memory* (from the word *echo*) is the name given to auditory sensory memory, which is retained for up to several seconds. Imagine standing in an elevator with a friend who suddenly asks, "What was that song?" about the music that was being piped in. If your friend has asked his question quickly enough, you just might have a trace of the tune left on your sensory registers. *Iconic memory* (from the word *icon*, which means "image") is the name given to visual sensory memory, which is retained only for about one-fourth of a second (Figure 8.5). Visual sensory memory is responsible for our ability to "write" in the air using a sparkler on the 4th of July—the residual iconic memory is what makes a moving point of light appear to be a line. The sensory memory for other senses, such as smell and touch, has received little attention in research studies.

The first scientific research on sensory memory focused on iconic memory. In George Sperling's (1960) classic study, participants were presented with patterns of stimuli such as those in Figure 8.6. As you look at the letters, you have no trouble recognizing them. But Sperling flashed the letters on a screen for very brief intervals, about 1/20 of a second. After a pattern was flashed on the screen, the participants could report only four or five letters. With such short exposure, reporting all nine letters was impossible.

Some of the participants in Sperling's study reported feeling that, for an instant, they could see all nine letters within a briefly flashed pattern. But they ran into trouble when they tried to name all the letters they had initially *seen*. One hypothesis to explain this experience is that all nine letters were initially processed as far as the iconic sensory memory level. This is why all nine letters were *seen*. However, forgetting from iconic memory was so rapid that the participants did not have time to transfer all the letters to short-term memory, where they could be named.

Sperling reasoned that, if all nine letters are actually processed in sensory memory, they should all be available for a brief time. To test this possibility, Sperling sounded a low, medium, or high tone just after a pattern of letters was shown. The participants were told that the tone was a signal to report only the letters from the bottom, middle, or top row. Under these conditions, the participants performed much better, and this outcome suggests a brief memory for most or all of the letters in the display.

Short-Term Memory

Much information goes no further than the stage of auditory and visual sensory memory. This information is retained for only a brief instant. However, some of the information, especially that to which we pay attention, is transferred to short-term memory. **Short-term memory** is a limited-capacity memory system in which information is usually retained for only as long as 30 seconds unless strategies are used to retain it longer. Compared with sensory memory, short-term memory is limited in capacity, but it can store information for a longer time.

The limited capacity of short-term memory was examined by George Miller (1956) in the classic paper "The Magical Number Seven, Plus or Minus Two." Miller pointed out that on many tasks individuals are limited in how much information they can keep track of without external aids. Usually the limit is in the range of 7 ± 2 items. The most widely cited example of the 7 ± 2 phenomenon involves *memory span,* which is the number of digits an individual can report back in order after a single presentation of them. Most college students can remember 8 or 9 digits without making errors (think about how easy it is to remember a phone number, for instance). Longer lists pose problems because they exceed short-term memory capacity. If you rely on simple short-term memory to retain longer lists, you probably will make errors.

Chunking and Rehearsal   Two ways to improve short-term memory are chunking and rehearsal. *Chunking* involves grouping or "packing" information that exceeds the 7 ± 2 memory span into higher-order units that can be remembered as single units. In essence, chunking is a form of memory encoding: specifically, elaboration. It works by making large amounts of information more manageable (Gobet & Clarkson, 2004).

For an example of chunking, consider this list: *hot, city, book, forget, tomorrow,* and *smile.* Try to hold these words in memory for a moment; then write them down. If you recalled the words, you succeeded in holding 30 letters, grouped into six chunks, in memory. Now hold the following in memory and then write it down:

O   LDH   ARO   LDAN   DYO   UNGB   EN

How did you do? Do not feel bad if you did poorly. This string of letters is very difficult to remember, even though it is arranged in chunks. However, if you chunk the letters to form the meaningful words "Old Harold and Young Ben," they become much easier to remember.

Another way to improve short-term memory involves *rehearsal,* the conscious repetition of information (Bunting, Cowan, & Scott Saults, 2006). Information stored in short-term memory lasts half a minute or less without rehearsal. However, if rehearsal is not interrupted, information can be retained indefinitely. Rehearsal is often verbal, giving the impression of an inner voice, but it can also be visual or spatial, giving the impression of a private inner eye (Pearson, 2006). One way to use your visualization skills is to retain the appearance of an object or a scene for a period of time after you have viewed it. People who are unusually good at this task are said to have *eidetic imagery,* or a photographic memory. All of us can retain images to some degree, but a small number of us may be so good at preserving an image that, for example, we literally "see" the page of a textbook as we try to remember information during a test. However, true eidetic imagery is so rare it has been difficult to study; some psychologists even doubt its existence (Gray & Gummerman, 1975).

Rehearsal works best when we must briefly remember a list of numbers or items such as orders on a menu. When we need to remember information for longer periods of time, as when we are studying for a test coming up next week or even an hour from

FIGURE 8.6

Sperling's Sensory Memory Experiment   This array of stimuli is similar to those flashed for about 1/20 of a second to the participants in Sperling's study.

---

short-term memory A limited-capacity memory system in which information is retained for only as long as 30 seconds unless strategies are used to retain it longer.

working memory A three-part system that temporarily holds information as people perform cognitive tasks. Working memory is a kind of mental "workbench" on which information is manipulated and assembled to help individuals perform other cognitive tasks.

now, other strategies usually work better. A main reason rehearsal does not work well for retaining information over the long term is that rehearsal often involves just mechanically repeating information, without imparting meaning to it. The fact that, over the long term, we remember information best when we add meaning to it demonstrates the importance of deep, semantic processing.

Working Memory   Some experts believe that Atkinson and Shiffrin's theory of the three time-linked memory systems is too simplistic (Baddeley, 2006, 2007). They believe that memory does not always work in a neatly packaged three-stage sequence, and they think that both short-term and long-term memory are far more complex and dynamic. For example, some experts think that short-term memory uses long-term memory's contents in more flexible ways than simply retrieving information from it (Murdock, 1999). And they believe that short-term memory involves far more than rehearsal and passive storage of information. We now examine the working-memory view of short-term memory.

British psychologist Alan Baddeley (1993, 1998, 2001, 2003, 2006, 2007) proposed the concept of **working memory,** a three-part system that temporarily holds information as people perform cognitive tasks. Working memory is a kind of mental "workbench" on which information is manipulated and assembled to help us comprehend written and spoken language, make decisions, and solve problems. If all of the information in your computer is like long-term memory, then working memory might be compared to what you have open on your computer desktop. Note that working memory is not like a passive storehouse with shelves to store information until it moves to long-term memory. Rather, it is an active memory system (Gathercole, 2007; Hitch, 2006).

Figure 8.7 shows Baddeley's view of the three components of working memory. Think of them as an executive (the central executive) who has two assistants (the phonological loop and visuospatial working memory) to help do the work.

1. The *phonological loop* is specialized to briefly store speech-based information about the sounds of language. The phonological loop contains two separate components: an acoustic code (the sounds of what you heard), which decays in a few seconds, and rehearsal, which allows individuals to repeat the words in the phonological store.

2. *Visuospatial working memory* stores visual and spatial information, including visual imagery (Repovs & Baddeley, 2006). Visuospatial working memory also has been called the *visuospatial scratch pad.* As in the case of the phonological loop, the capacity of visuospatial working memory is limited. For example, if you try to put too many items in visuospatial working memory, you cannot represent them accurately enough to retrieve them successfully. The phonological loop and visuospatial memory function independently. You could rehearse numbers in the phonological loop while making spatial arrangements of letters in visuospatial working memory.

3. The *central executive* integrates information not only from the phonological loop and visuospatial working memory but also from long-term memory. In Baddeley's (2006, 2007) view, the central executive plays important roles in attention, planning, and organizing. The central executive acts much like a supervisor who monitors which information and issues deserve attention and which should be ignored. It also selects which strategies to use to process information and solve problems. As with the other two components of working memory—phonological loop and visuospatial working memory—the central executive has a limited capacity.

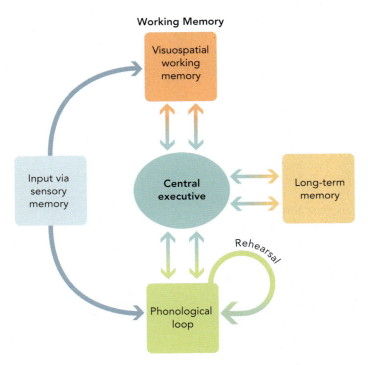

Working Memory

FIGURE 8.7

Working Memory In Baddeley's working-memory model, working memory consists of three main components: the phonological loop, visuospatial working memory, and the central executive. The phonological loop and visuospatial working memory serve as assistants, helping the central executive do its work. Input from sensory memory goes to the phonological loop, where information about speech is stored and rehearsal takes place, and to visuospatial working memory, where visual and spatial information, including imagery, is stored. Working memory is a limited-capacity system, and information is stored there for only a brief time. Working memory interacts with long-term memory, drawing information from long-term memory and transmitting information to long-term memory for longer storage.

The concept of working memory can help us understand how brain damage influences cognitive skills (Cicerone & others, 2006; Wood & Rutterford, 2006). For example, some types of amnesiacs (individuals with memory loss) perform well on working-memory tasks but not on long-term memory tasks. Another group of patients have normal long-term memory abilities yet do very poorly on working-memory tasks. One such patient has good long-term memory despite having a memory span of only two digits (Baddeley, 1992). The phonological loop was the source of this patient's memory problem. Because he could not maintain verbal codes in the loop, his memory span suffered. Working-memory deficits also are involved in Alzheimer disease—a progressive, irreversible brain disorder in older adults that we considered in Chapter 4 (Levinoff & others, 2006). Baddeley (2006, 2007) believes the central executive of the working-memory model is the culprit—Alzheimer patients have great difficulty coordinating different mental activities, one of the central executive's functions.

Long-Term Memory

Long-term memory is a relatively permanent type of memory that stores huge amounts of information for a long time. The capacity of long-term memory is indeed staggering. John von Neumann, a distinguished computer scientist, put the size at 2.8×10^{20} (280 quintillion) bits, which in practical terms means that our storage capacity is virtually unlimited. Von Neumann assumed that we never forget anything; but even considering that we do forget things, we can hold several billion times more information than a large computer.

Long-term memory is complex, as Figure 8.8 shows. At the top level, it is divided into substructures of explicit memory and implicit memory. Explicit memory can be further subdivided into episodic and semantic memory. Implicit memory includes the systems involved in procedural memory, classical conditioning, and priming.

In simple terms, explicit memory has to do with remembering who, what, where, when, and why; implicit memory has to do with remembering how. To explore the distinction, let's look at a person known as H. M. He had a severe case of epilepsy and underwent surgery in 1953 that involved removing the hippocampus and a portion of the temporal lobes of both hemispheres in his brain. (We examined the location and functions of these areas of the brain in Chapter 3.) His epilepsy improved, but something devastating happened to his memory. Most dramatically, he developed an inability to form new memories that outlive working memory. H. M.'s memory time frame is only a few minutes at most, so he lives, as he has done since 1953, in a perpetual present and cannot remember past events (explicit memory). In contrast, his memory of how to do things (implicit memory) was less affected. For example, he can learn new physical tasks. In one such task, H. M. was asked to trace the outline of a star-shaped figure while he was able to view the figure and his hand only through a mirror. This is a task that most people find difficult in the beginning. Over 3 days

FIGURE 8.8

Systems of Long-Term Memory
Long-term memory stores huge amounts of information for long periods of time, much like a computer's hard drive. The hierarchy in the figure shows the division of long-term memory at the top level into explicit memory and implicit memory. Explicit memory can be further divided into episodic and semantic memory; implicit memory includes procedural memory, priming, and classical conditioning.

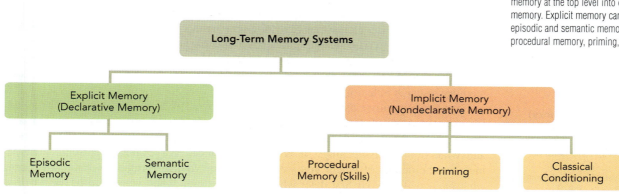

Long-Term Memory Systems

Explicit Memory (Declarative Memory) — Implicit Memory (Nondeclarative Memory)

Episodic Memory | Semantic Memory | Procedural Memory (Skills) | Priming | Classical Conditioning

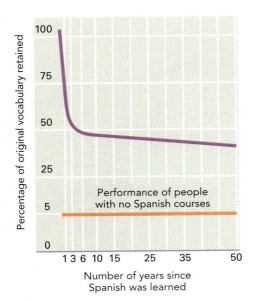

FIGURE 8.9

Memory for Spanish as a Function of Age Since Spanish Was Learned

An initial steep drop over about a 3-year period in remembering the vocabulary learned in Spanish classes occurred. However, there was little dropoff in memory for Spanish vocabulary from 3 years after taking Spanish classes to 50 years after taking them. Even 50 years after taking Spanish classes, individuals still remembered almost 50 percent of the vocabulary.

long-term memory A relatively permanent type of memory that stores huge amounts of information for a long time.

explicit memory (declarative memory) The conscious recollection of information, such as specific facts or events and, at least in humans, information that can be verbally communicated.

episodic memory The retention of information about the where, when, and what of life's happenings.

of training, H. M. learned this task as effectively and rapidly as normal individuals. On the second and third days, he began at the level he had achieved the previous day (a success in implicit memory), even though he was completely unaware that he had previously practiced the task (a failure in explicit memory). H. M.'s situation clearly demonstrates a distinction between explicit memory, which was dramatically impaired in his case, and implicit memory, which in his case was less influenced by his surgery.

We now explore the subsystems of explicit and implicit memory. After we examine these basic structures, we survey the theories developed to explain how they are organized. We also look at recent discoveries in neuroscience that shed light on where in the brain memory is stored.

Explicit Memory **Explicit memory (declarative memory)** is the conscious recollection of information, such as specific facts or events and, at least in humans, information that can be verbally communicated (Tulving, 1989, 2000). Examples of using explicit, or declarative, memory include recounting the events in a movie you have seen and describing a basic principle of psychology to someone.

How long does explicit memory last? Remember that explicit memory includes things you are learning in your classes even now. Will it stay with you? Research by Harry Bahrick has examined this very question. Ohio Wesleyan University, where Bahrick is a professor of psychology, is a small (about 1,800 students) liberal arts school that boasts very loyal alumni who faithfully return to campus for reunions and other events. Bahrick (1984) took advantage of this situation to undertake an ingenious study on the retention of course material over time. He gave vocabulary tests to individuals who had taken Spanish in college as well as to a control group of college students who had not taken Spanish in college. The individuals chosen for the study had used Spanish very little since their college courses. Some individuals were tested at the end of an academic year (just after having taken the courses), but others were tested years after graduation—as many as 50 years later. When how much had been forgotten was assessed, a striking pattern of results emerged (Figure 8.9). Essentially, forgetting tended to occur in the first 3 years after taking the classes and then leveled off, such that adults maintained considerable knowledge of Spanish vocabulary words up to 50 years later.

Bahrick (1984) assessed not only how long ago adults studied Spanish, but also how well they did in their Spanish courses during college. Those who got an *A* 50 years earlier remembered more Spanish than adults who got a *C* when taking Spanish only 1 year earlier! Thus, how well students initially learned the material was even more important than how long ago they studied it.

Bahrick (2000) suggests that such long-term retention of information might be characterized as *permastore* content. Permastore memory represents that portion of original learning that appears destined to be with the person virtually forever, even without rehearsal. In addition to focusing on course material, Bahrick and colleagues (1974) have probed adults' memories for the faces and names of their high school classmates. Thirty-five years after graduation, the participants visually recognized 90 percent of the portraits of their high school classmates, with name recognition being almost as high. These results held even in relatively large classes (the mean class size in the study was 294).

What might predict such astonishing long-term memory? At least part of the story lies in how this information is encoded. Bahrick has found that gradual learning is the key. That is, acquiring a language or any skill might be facilitated by learning over the course of several sessions spaced apart rather than all at once. These findings suggest the relevance of basic memory research to learning course material.

Canadian cognitive psychologist Endel Tulving (1972, 1989, 2000) has been the foremost advocate of distinguishing between two subtypes of explicit memory: episodic and semantic. **Episodic memory** is the retention of information about the where, when, and what of life's happenings. It is autobiographical. For example, episodic memory includes the details of where you were when your younger brother or sister was born; what happened on your first date; what you were doing when you heard of the terrorist attacks of September 11, 2001; and what you had for breakfast this morning.

Semantic memory is a person's knowledge about the world. It includes your areas of expertise, general knowledge of the sort you are learning in school, and everyday knowledge about the meanings of words, famous individuals, important places, and common things. For example, semantic memory is involved in a person's knowledge of chess, of geometry, and of who Martin Luther King, Jr., Laura Bush, and Russell Crowe are. An important aspect of semantic memory is that it appears to be independent of an individual's personal identity with the past. You can access a fact—such as that Lima is the capital of Peru—and not have the foggiest notion of when and where you learned it.

Some examples help to clarify the distinction between episodic and semantic memory. Your memory of your first day on campus involves episodic memory. If you take a history class, your memory of the information you need to know to do well on the next test involves semantic memory.

Consider also that, in a certain type of amnesiac state, a person might forget entirely who she is—her name, family, career, and all other information about herself—yet she can talk and demonstrate general knowledge about the world (Rosenbaum & others, 2005). Her episodic memory is impaired, but her semantic memory is functioning. Tulving (1989) reported an especially dramatic case of this type: a young man named K. C. After suffering a motorcycle accident, K. C. lost virtually all use of his episodic memory. The loss was so profound that he was unable to recollect consciously a single thing that had ever happened to him. At the same time, K. C.'s semantic memory was sufficiently preserved that he could learn about his past as a set of facts, just as he would learn about another person's life. He could report, for example, that the saddest day of his life was when his brother drowned about 10 years before. But further questioning revealed that K. C. had no conscious memory of the event. He simply knew about the drowning because he was able to recall—apparently through use of his semantic memory—what he had been told about his brother by other members of his family.

Figure 8.10 summarizes some aspects of the episodic/semantic distinction. The differences that are listed are controversial. One criticism is that many cases of explicit, or declarative, memory are neither purely episodic nor purely semantic but fall in a gray area in between. Consider your memory for what you studied last night. You probably added knowledge to your semantic memory—that was, after all, the reason you were studying. You probably remember where you were studying, as well as about when you started and when you stopped. You probably also can remember some minor occurrences, such as a burst of loud laughter from the room next door or the coffee you spilled on the desk. Is episodic or semantic memory involved here? Tulving (1983, 2000) argues that semantic and episodic systems often work together in forming new memories. In such cases, the memory that ultimately is formed might consist of an autobiographical episode *and* semantic information.

Implicit (Nondeclarative) Memory

In addition to explicit memory, there is a type of long-term memory that is related to nonconsciously remembering skills and sensory perceptions rather than consciously remembering facts. **Implicit memory (nondeclarative memory)** is memory in which behavior is affected by prior experience without a conscious recollection of that experience. Examples of implicit memory include the skills of playing tennis, snowboarding, and typing on a computer keyboard. Another example of implicit memory is the repetition in your mind of a song you heard playing in the supermarket, even though you did not notice that song playing.

Three subsystems of implicit memory are procedural memory, classical conditioning, and priming. All instances of these subsystems consist of memories that you are not aware of, although they predispose you to behave in certain ways (Slotnick & Schacter, 2006).

Procedural memory involves memory for skills. For example (assuming you are an expert typist), as you type a paper, you are not conscious of where the keys are for the various letters, but your well-learned, nonconscious skill of typing allows you to hit the

Characteristic	Episodic Memory	Semantic Memory
Units	Events, episodes	Facts, ideas, concepts
Organization	Time	Concepts
Emotion	More important	Less important
Retrieval process	Deliberate (effortful)	Automatic
Retrieval report	"I remember"	"I know"
Education	Irrelevant	Relevant
Intelligence	Irrelevant	Relevant
Legal testimony	Admissible in court	Inadmissible in court

FIGURE 8.10

Some Differences Between Episodic and Semantic Memory
These characteristics have been proposed as the main ways to differentiate episodic from semantic memory.

semantic memory A person's knowledge about the world.

implicit memory (nondeclarative memory) Memory in which behavior is affected by prior experience without that experience being consciously recollected.

procedural memory Memory for skills.

PSYCHOLOGY AND LIFE

Harnessing the Power of Priming

What does the power of priming mean for everyday life? One bit of advice is to be careful how you prime yourself. Look around at your environment. What stands out? What sorts of messages might you be encoding without realizing it?

If nothing else, studies indicate that a few Post-it notes of encouragement, perhaps featuring an inspiring quote or two, might not be a bad idea. Subtle reminders of what makes life worth living, things you enjoy, the people you love, and the reasons you are pursuing your goals may help keep you focused and able to harness the power of positive thinking in your daily life. Surrounding yourself with chronic reminders of your aspirations might just allow you to take advantage of the power of priming!

right keys. Once you have learned to drive a car, you remember how to do it: You do not have to remember consciously how to drive the car as you put the key in the ignition, turn the steering wheel, depress the gas pedal, and step on the brake pedal.

To illustrate the distinction between explicit memory and procedural memory, imagine you are at Wimbledon. Serena Williams moves gracefully for a wide forehand, finishes her follow-through, runs quickly back to the center of the court, pushes off for a short ball, and volleys the ball for a winner. If asked about this sequence, she probably would have difficulty explaining each move. In contrast, if we were to ask her who her toughest opponent is, she might quickly respond, "My sister." In the first instance, she would be unable verbally to describe exactly what she had done because her actions had been based on procedural memory. In the second case, she has no problem answering our question because it is based on explicit memory.

Another type of implicit memory involves *classical conditioning,* a form of learning discussed in Chapter 7 (Brignell & Curran, 2006). Recall that classical conditioning involves the automatic learning of associations between stimuli. For instance, an individual who is constantly criticized may develop high blood pressure or other physical problems. Classically conditioned associations such as this involve nonconscious, implicit memory.

A final type of implicit memory process is priming. **Priming** is the activation of information that people already have in storage to help them remember new information better and faster (Geraci, 2006). In a common demonstration of priming, individuals study a list of words (such as *hope, walk,* and *cake*). Then they are given a standard recognition task to assess explicit memory. They must select all of the words that appeared in the list—for example, "Did you see the word *hope*? Did you see the word *form*?" Then participants perform a "stem-completion" task, which assesses implicit memory. In this task, they view a list of incomplete words (for example, *ho__, wa__, ca__*), called word stems, and must fill in the blanks with whatever word comes to mind. The results show that individuals more often fill in the blanks with the previously studied words than would be expected if they were filling in the blanks randomly. For example, they are more likely to complete the stem *ho__* with *hope* than with *hole*. This result occurs even when individuals do not recognize the words on the earlier recognition task. Because priming takes place even when explicit memory for previous information is not required, it is assumed to be an involuntary and nonconscious process (Verfaellie & others, 2006).

In a sense, priming occurs when something in the environment evokes a response in memory—such as the activation of a particular concept or network of meaning. Priming a term or concept makes it more available in memory (Kahan, Sellinger, & Broman-Fulks, 2006;

priming A type of implicit memory process involving the activation of information that people already have in storage to help them remember new information better and faster.

Orfanidou, Marsien-Wilson, & Davis, 2006). John Bargh and other social psychologists have demonstrated that priming can have a surprising influence on social behavior as well (Bargh, 2005, 2006; Chartrand, Maddux, & Lakin, 2005; Pinel & others, 2006; Smith & others, 2006). For example, in one study, college students were asked to unscramble a series of words to make a sentence (Bargh, Chen, & Burrows, 1996). For some of the participants, the items in the series included such words as *rude, aggressively, intrude,* and *bluntly.* For other students, the words included *polite, cautious,* and *sensitively.* Upon completing the scrambled sentences, participants were to report to the experimenter, but each participant encountered the experimenter deep in conversation with another person. Who was more likely to interrupt the ongoing conversation? Among those who were primed with words connoting rudeness, 67 percent interrupted the experimenter. Among those in the "polite" condition, a full 84 percent of the participants waited the entire 10 minutes—never interrupting the ongoing conversation.

Bargh and his colleagues argue that primes have an automatic impact on behavior, and they call this effect *ideomotoring*—the way that automatic processes impact social behavior outside of awareness (Bargh, 2005, 2006; Ferguson, Bargh, & Nayak, 2005). Priming can also spur goal-directed behavior. For example, Bargh and colleagues (2001) asked students to perform a word-find puzzle. Embedded in the puzzle were either neutral words (*shampoo, robin*) or achievement-related words (*compete, win, achieve*). Participants who were exposed to the achievement-related words did better on a later puzzle task, finding 26 words in other puzzles, while those with the neutral primes found only 21.5. Other research has shown that individuals primed with words like *professor* and *intelligent* performed better at a game of Trivial Pursuit than those primed with words like *stupid* and *hooligan* (Dijksterhuis & Van Knippenberg, 1998). Significantly, these effects occur without awareness, with no participants reporting suspicion about the effects of the primes on their behavior. The influence of priming on everyday life is the focus of the Psychology and Life box.

How Memory Is Organized   Cognitive psychologists have been successful in classifying the types of long-term memory. But explaining the forms of long-term memory does not address the question of how the different types of memory are organized for storage. The word *organized* is important: Memories are not haphazardly stored but instead are carefully sorted.

Here is a demonstration. Recall the 12 months of the year as quickly as you can. How long did it take you? What was the order of your recall? Chances are, you listed them within a few seconds in "natural," chronological order (January, February, March, and so on). Now try to remember the months in alphabetical order. How long did it take you? Did you make any errors? It should be obvious that your memory for the months of the year is organized in a particular way. Indeed, one of memory's most distinctive features is its organization. Researchers have found that, if people are encouraged to organize material simply, their memories of the material improve even if they receive no warning that their memories will be tested (Mandler, 1980). Psychologists have developed four main theories of how long-term memory is organized: hierarchies, semantic networks, schemas, and connectionist networks.

Hierarchies   In many instances, we remember facts better when we organize them hierarchically (Alvarez-Lacalle & others, 2006; Colom & others, 2006). A *hierarchy* is a system in which items are organized from general to specific classes. One common example is the organizational chart showing the relationship of units in a business or a school, with the CEO or president at the top, the vice presidents or deans at the next level, and the managers or professors at a third level. This textbook also is organized hierarchically— with four levels of headings—to help you understand how the various bits of information in the book are related; the table of contents provides a visual representation of the hierarchy of the top two levels of headings.

In an early research study, Gordon Bower and his colleagues (1969) showed the importance of hierarchical organization in memory. Participants who were given words in hierarchies remembered them better than those who were given words in random groupings (Figure 8.11).

Semantic Networks   We often use semantic networks to organize material in episodic memory (a form of explicit memory). One of the first network theories claimed that

FIGURE 8.11

Example of Hierarchical Organization
A study by Gordon Bower and colleagues (1969) showed that when words are organized hierarchically, as in this example, individuals remember them better than they do when given the words in random groupings.

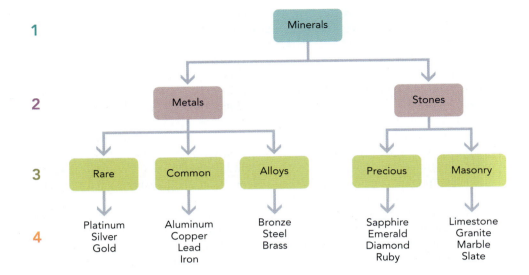

schema A preexisting mental concept or framework that helps people to organize and interpret information.

FIGURE 8.12

Revision of the Semantic Network View of Long-Term Memory In this model, a typical item is closer to the node (center) of its category than an atypical item. Thus the more typical canary is closer to the node *bird* than the atypical ostrich but farther from the node *bird* than more typical items such as wings and feathers.

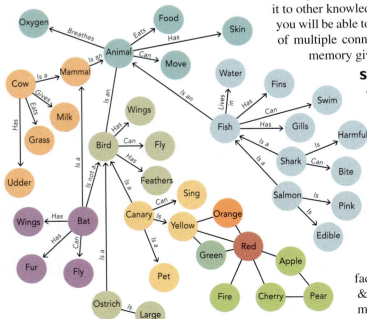

our memories can be envisioned as a complex network of nodes that stand for labels or concepts. The network was assumed to be hierarchically arranged, with more concrete concepts (robin, for example) nested under more abstract concepts (bird).

More recently, cognitive psychologists realized that such hierarchical networks are too simple to describe the way human cognition actually works (Shanks, 1991). For example, people take longer to answer the true-or-false statement "An ostrich is a bird" than they do to answer the statement "A robin is a bird." Memory researchers now see the semantic network as more irregular and distorted: A typical bird, such as a robin, is closer to the node, or center, of the category *bird* than is the atypical ostrich. Figure 8.12 presents an example of the revised model, which allows us to show how typical information is while still illustrating how it is linked together.

We add new material to a semantic network by placing it in the middle of the appropriate region of memory. The new material is gradually tied in to related nodes in the surrounding network. This model reveals why, if you cram for a test, you will not remember the information over the long term. The new material is not woven into the long-term web. In contrast, discussing the material or incorporating it into a research paper interweaves it and connects it to other knowledge you have. These multiple connections increase the probability that you will be able to retrieve the information many months or even years later. The concept of multiple connections fits with the description of the importance of elaboration in memory given earlier in the chapter.

Schemas   You and a friend have driven to a new town where neither of you has ever been before. It has been a long drive, and you are tired and hungry. You stop at a local diner, have a seat, and look over the menu. You have never been in this diner before, but you know exactly what is going to happen. Why? Because you have a schema for what happens in a restaurant. When we store information in memory, we often fit it into the collection of information that already exists, as you do even in a new experience with a diner. A **schema** is a preexisting mental concept or framework that helps people to organize and interpret information. Schemas from prior encounters with the environment influence the way we encode, make inferences about, and retrieve information (Morris, 2006).

Semantic network theories assume that memory involves specific facts with clear links from one to another (Passafiume, Di Giacomo, & Carolei, 2006). In contrast, schema theory claims that long-term memory is not very exact. We seldom find precisely the memory that we want, or at least not all of what we want; hence, we have to reconstruct

Shown here are representative scripts from a Japanese tea ceremony, a Western dinner, and an Ethiopian meal. With which script do you feel most comfortable?

the rest. Our schemas support the reconstruction process, helping us fill in gaps between our fragmented memories.

We have schemas for lots of situations and experiences—for scenes and spatial layouts (a beach, a bathroom), as well as for common events (playing football, writing a term paper). A **script** is a schema for an event (Schank & Abelson, 1977). Scripts often have information about physical features, people, and typical occurrences. This kind of information is helpful when people need to figure out what is happening around them. For example, if you are enjoying your after-dinner coffee in an upscale restaurant and a man in a tuxedo comes over and puts a piece of paper on the table, your script tells you that the man probably is a waiter who has just given you the check. Thus scripts help to organize our storage of memories about events.

Connectionist Networks   Theories of semantic networks and schemas have little or nothing to say about the role of the physical brain in memory. Thus a new theory based on brain research has generated a wave of excitement among psychologists. **Connectionism, or parallel distributed processing (PDP),** is the theory that memory is stored throughout the brain in connections among neurons, several of which may work together to process a single memory (Borowsky & Besner, 2006; Takashima & others, 2006). We initially considered the concept of neural networks in Chapter 3 and the idea of parallel processing pathways in Chapter 5. This section expands on those discussions and applies these concepts to memory.

In the connectionist view, memories are neither abstract concepts (as in semantic network theories) nor large knowledge structures (as in schema theories). Instead, memories are more like electrical impulses, organized only to the extent that neurons, the connections among them, and their activity are organized. Any piece of knowledge—such as your dog's name—is embedded in the strengths of hundreds or thousands of connections among neurons and is not limited to a single location. Figure 8.13 compares the semantic-network, schema, and connectionist-network theories of memories.

How does the connectionist process work? A neural activity involving memory, such as remembering your dog's name, is distributed across a number of areas of the cerebral cortex. The locations of neural activity, called *nodes,* are interconnected. When a node reaches a critical level of activation, it can affect another node, either by exciting it or by inhibiting it, across synapses. We know that the human cerebral cortex contains millions of neurons that are richly interconnected through hundreds of millions of synapses. Because of these synaptic connections, the activity of one neuron can be influenced by many other neurons. For example, if an excitatory connection exists between neurons A and B, activity

script A schema for an event.

connectionism (parallel distributed processing [PDP]) The theory that memory is stored throughout the brain in connections among neurons, several of which may work together to process a single memory.

FIGURE 8.13

Key Features of Semantic Network, Schema, and Connectionist Theories

The figure compares the main aspects of three key theories of memory.

	Theory		
	Semantic Network	**Schema**	**Connectionist**
Nature of memory units	Abstract concepts ("bird")	Large knowledge structures ("going to a restaurant")	Small units, connections among neurons
Number of units	Tens of thousands	Unknown	Tens of millions
Formation of new memories	Form new nodes	Form new schemas or modify old ones	Increased strength of excitatory connections among neurons
Attention to brain structure	Little	Little	Extensive

in neuron A will tend to increase activity in neuron B. If the connection is inhibitory, activity in neuron A will tend to reduce the activity in neuron B. Because of these simple reactions, the connectionist view argues that changes in the strength of synaptic connections are the fundamental bases of memory (de Zubicaray, 2006; Maia & Cleeremans, 2005).

Part of the appeal of the connectionist view is that it is consistent with what we know about brain function. Another part of its appeal is that, when programmed on a computer, the connectionist view has successfully predicted the results of some memory experiments (Marcus, 2001; McClelland & Rumelhart, 1986). Its insights into the organization of memory also support brain research undertaken to determine where memories are stored in the brain (Lin, Osan, & Tsien, 2006; Rogers & Kesner, 2006).

Thus far we have examined the many ways cognitive psychologists think about how information is stored. But the question remains, *where?* Is there a spot in your brain where that special evening with your significant other is waiting for retrieval?

The question of the physical location of memories has long fascinated psychologists. In the 1960s, researchers examined this question using planaria (worms) (Walker & Milton, 1966). In this study, worms first were trained to travel through a maze. Then the trained worms were sacrificed and fed to naive worms—worms that had not been trained. Remarkably, the worms that had eaten the trained worms picked up the maze more quickly than the worms that had not cannibalized their maze-skilled comrades. Clearly, human memory is not the same as worm memory—and cannibalism is not an effective means of gaining information. But this old research does highlight the notion that although memory may seem to be a mysterious phenomenon, it, like all psychological processes, must occur in a physical place: the brain.

Where Memories Are Stored Karl Lashley (1950) spent a lifetime looking for a location in the brain in which memories are stored. He trained rats to discover the correct pathway in a maze and then cut out various portions of the animals' brains and retested their memory of the maze pathway. After experimenting with thousands of rats, Lashley found that the loss of various cortical areas did not affect rats' ability to remember the pathway. Lashley concluded that memories are not stored in a specific location in the brain. Other researchers, continuing Lashley's quest, agreed that memory storage is diffuse, but they developed some other insights. Canadian psychologist Donald Hebb (1949, 1980) suggested that assemblies of cells, distributed over large areas of the cerebral cortex, work together to represent information. Hebb's idea of distributed memory was farsighted.

Neurons and Memory Today many neuroscientists believe that memory is located in specific sets or circuits of neurons (Aleksandrov, 2006; Wang, Hu, & Tsien, 2006). Brain researcher Larry Squire, for example, says that most memories are probably clustered in groups of about 1,000 neurons (1990, 2004, 2007). Single neurons, of course, are at work in memory (Squire, 2007). Researchers who measure the electrical activity of single cells have found that some respond to faces and others to eye or hair color, for example. But in

Memory and Sensation: Why Does Smell Share a Special Relationship with Memory?

You smell a turkey roasting in the oven, and suddenly you are once again 6 years old and eagerly anticipating your family's Thanksgiving dinner. Or the smell of the tamales your *abuela* (grandmother) used to make reminds you of so many Christmases past. Perhaps less pleasantly, you smell the cologne of a former romantic partner, and your last argument with your "ex" is vividly present to you. Of all of the senses, smell seems to bear the strongest relationship to memory, and a smell can trigger rich emotional memories. Indeed, Marcel Proust described this link so powerfully in his novel *Swann's Way* that the term the *Proust effect* was coined for the ability of smell to transport us into vivid memory.

A smell can trigger rich emotional memories.

Why does smell share such a special relationship with memory? At least part of the answer is anatomical. Recall from Chapter 5 that nerves in the nose send information about smells to the primary olfactory cortex in the brain. That cortex links directly to the amygdala and hippocampus. Thus, smells have a superhighway to the brain structures involved in emotion (the amygdala) and memory consolidation (the hippocampus) (Galan & others, 2006; Herz, Schlanker, & Beland, 2004). Rachel Herz (2004) found that autobiographical memories that were cued by odors (a campfire, fresh-cut grass, popcorn) were more emotional and more evocative than such memories cued by pictures or sounds. Indeed, smells can be powerful tools for memory. Herz and Gerald Cupchik (1995; Herz, 1998) found that individuals performed better on a surprise memory test if the same odor cue was present in the room during learning and recall. One implication of that study is that it might be a good idea to wear the same cologne to an exam that you typically wear to class.

But showing that smells indeed influence memory, and that the brain seems to have evolved to give smell a privileged place relative to other sensory input, does not help us understand why the special status of smell is adaptive. Why would it be adaptive to give smell a special link with emotion and memory? Many other animals detect important information about their environments from smell; that is why, for instance, dogs' noses are so close to the ground (and so sensitive). Animals use smells to navigate through the world—to detect what is good (the smell of a food) and what is bad (the scent of a predator). In humans, emotions play a similar role, in that they tell us how we are doing in the world in terms of what matters to us. Perhaps for humans, the special link between smells and emotions allows us quickly to learn associations between particular smells and stimuli that are good (morning coffee) or bad (spoiled milk) for us. As the examples above suggest, smells may have a special power in the positive emotional experience of nostalgia. The right smells alone can transport us powerfully to the good old days.

---

order for you to recognize your Uncle Albert, individual neurons that provide information about hair color, size, and other characteristics act together.

Researchers also believe that brain chemicals may be the ink with which memories are written. Ironically, some of the answers to complex questions about neural mechanics of memory come from studies on a very simple experimental animal—the inelegant sea slug. Eric Kandel and James Schwartz (1982) chose this large snail-without-a-shell because of the simple architecture of its nervous system, which consists of only about 10,000 neurons. (You might recall from Chapter 3 that the human brain has about 100 billion neurons.) The sea slug is hardly a quick learner or an animal with a good memory, but it is equipped with a reliable reflex. When anything touches the gill on its back, it quickly withdraws it. First the researchers accustomed the sea slug to having its gill prodded. After a while, the animal ignored the prod and stopped withdrawing its gill. Next the researchers applied an electric shock to its tail when they touched the gill. After many rounds of the shock-accompanied prod, the sea slug violently withdrew its gill at the slightest touch. The researchers found that the sea slug remembered this message for hours or even weeks. They also determined that shocking the sea slug's gill releases the neurotransmitter serotonin at the synapses of its nervous system, and this chemical release basically provides a reminder that the gill was shocked. This "memory" informs the nerve cell to send out chemical commands to retract

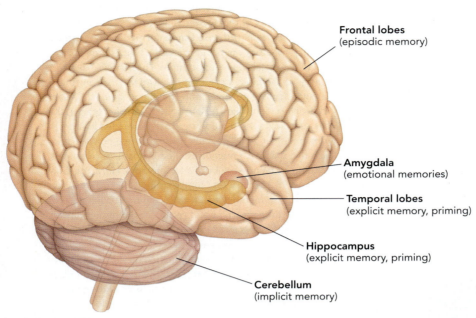

Frontal lobes
(episodic memory)

Amygdala
(emotional memories)

Temporal lobes
(explicit memory, priming)

Hippocampus
(explicit memory, priming)

Cerebellum
(implicit memory)

FIGURE 8.14

Structures of the Brain Involved in Different Aspects of Long-Term Memory Note that explicit memory and implicit memory appear to involve different locations in the brain.

the gill the next time it is touched. If nature builds complexity out of simplicity, then the mechanism used by the sea slug may work in the human brain as well.

Researchers have proposed the concept of *long-term potentiation* to explain how memory functions at the neuron level. In line with connectionist theory, this concept states that, if two neurons are activated at the same time, the connection between them— and thus the memory—may be strengthened (Kavushansky & others, 2006; Lee & Thompson, 2006). Long-term potentiation has been demonstrated experimentally by administering a drug that increases the flow of information from one neuron to another across the synapse (Shakesby, Anwyl, & Rowan, 2002). In one study, rats given the drug learned a maze with far fewer mistakes along the way than those not given the drug (Service, 1994). In another study, the genes of mice were altered to increase long-term potentiation in the hippocampus and other areas of the brain (Tang & others, 1999; Tsien, 2000). The mice with the enhanced genes remembered information better than mice whose genes had not been altered. These studies raise the possibility of someday improving memory through drugs or even gene enhancement to increase neural connections (Schacter, 2001).

Brain Structures and Memory Functions Whereas some neuroscientists are unveiling the cellular basis of memory, others are examining its broad-scale architecture in the brain. Many different parts of the brain and nervous system are involved in the rich, complex process that is memory (Rolls, 2007; Slotnick & Schacter, 2007). Although there is no one "memory" center in the brain, researchers have demonstrated that specific brain structures are involved in particular aspects of memory. For example, the amygdala plays an important role in emotional memories (Doyere & others, 2007; Paz & others, 2006).

Figure 8.14 shows the location of brain structures involved in different types of long-term memory. Note that implicit and explicit memory appear to involve different locations in the brain.

- *Explicit memory:* Neuroscientists have found that the hippocampus, the temporal lobes in the cerebral cortex, and other areas of the limbic system are involved in explicit memory (Lee & Thompson, 2006). In many aspects of explicit memory, information is transmitted from the hippocampus to the frontal lobes, which are involved in both retrospective and prospective memory (McDaniel & Einstein, 2007). The left frontal lobe is especially active when we encode new information into memory; the right frontal lobe is more active when we subsequently retrieve it (Babiloni & others, 2006; Woodward & others, 2006). However, as we saw in Chapter 4, researchers have found that older adults also begin to use the left frontal lobe in retrieval, a development that may be one way older adults compensate for memory problems (Cabeza, 2002; Kramer, Fabiani, & Colcombe, 2006). And as we mentioned earlier, the amygdala, which is part of the limbic system, is involved in emotional memories.
- *Implicit memory:* The cerebellum is involved in the implicit memory required to perform skills (Quintero-Gallego & others, 2006). Various areas of the cerebral cortex, such as the temporal lobes and hippocampus, function in priming (Kristjansson & others, 2006).

Neuroscientists studying memory have benefited greatly from the use of MRI scans, which allow the tracking of neural activity during cognitive tasks (Cabeza & St. Jacques, in press; Raichle & Mintun, 2006). In one research study, participants were shown color photographs of indoor and outdoor scenes while in an MRI machine (Brewer & others, 1998). They were not told that they would be given a memory test about the scenes. After the MRI scans, they were asked which pictures they remembered well, vaguely, or not at all. Their memories were compared with the brain scans. The greater the activation in both prefrontal lobes and a particular region of the hippocampus, the better the participants remembered the scenes. Pictures paired with weak brain activity in these areas were forgotten.

As can be seen in our discussion so far, there is currently extensive interest in studying links between memory and neuroscience. The Intersection on page 300 showcases another example of overlapping fields of psychology, this time involving memory and sensation.

 REVIEW, ASSESS, AND SHARPEN YOUR THINKING

Review

3 Discuss how memories are stored.

- Explain sensory memory.
- Summarize how short-term memory works.
- Describe how long-term memory functions and the role of the brain in memory storage.

Assess

1. Memory for auditory stimuli is known as
   - A. iconic memory.
   - B. echoic memory.
   - C. short-term memory.
   - D. long-term memory.

2. How many units of information can be kept in short-term memory at a time?
   - A. 2–4
   - B. 4–5
   - C. 5–9
   - D. 10–15

3. Knowing that George H. W. Bush was the 41st president of the United States of America is an example of which type of memory?
   - A. eidetic memory
   - B. implicit memory
   - C. explicit memory
   - D. episodic memory

4. Which structure of the brain is most associated with implicit memory for skills?
   - A. cerebellum
   - B. frontal lobe
   - C. hippocampus
   - D. amygdala

5. Which of the following theories of memory is focused on the interconnection between small nodes of information distributed throughout the brain?
   - A. schema
   - B. connectionist networks
   - C. semantic networks
   - D. hierarchies

Sharpen Your Thinking

How might semantic-network theory explain why cramming for a test is not a good way to acquire long-term memory?

4 Memory Retrieval

Summarize how memories are retrieved.

Remember that unforgettable night of shining stars with your romantic partner? Let's say the evening has indeed been encoded deeply and elaborately in your memory. Through the years you have thought about the night a great deal and maybe told your best friends about it. The story of that night has become part of the longer story of your life with your significant other. Fifty years later, your grandson asks, "How did you two end up together?" You share that story you have been saving for just such a question. What are the processes that allow you to do so? Memory **retrieval** takes place when information that was retained in memory is taken out of storage. You might think of long-term memory as a library. You retrieve information in a fashion similar to the process you use to locate and check out a book in an actual library. To retrieve something from your mental data bank, you search your store of memory to find the relevant information.

retrieval The memory process of taking information out of storage.

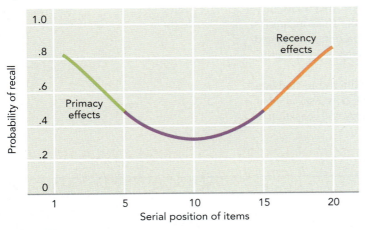

FIGURE 8.15

The Serial Position Effect When a person is asked to memorize a list of words, the words memorized last usually are recalled best, those at the beginning next best, and those in the middle least efficiently.

The efficiency with which you retrieve information from memory is impressive. It usually takes only a moment to search through a vast storehouse to find the information you want. When were you born? What was the name of your first date? Who developed the first psychology laboratory? You can, of course, answer these questions instantly. Yet retrieval of memory is a complex and sometimes imperfect process (Dodd, Castel, & Roberts, 2006; Spear, 2007).

Before examining ways that retrieval may fall short, let's turn to some basic concepts and variables that are known to affect the likelihood that information will be accurately encoded, stored, and ultimately retrieved. As we will see, retrieval is very much dependent on the circumstances under which a memory was encoded and the way it was retained (Gardiner, 2007; Radvansky, 2006).

Serial Position Effect

The **serial position effect** is the tendency to recall the items at the beginning and end of a list more readily than those in the middle. If you are a fan of reality TV, you might notice that you always seem to remember the first person to get "voted off" and the last few survivors. But all those people in the middle are just a blur. The *primacy effect* refers to better recall for items at the beginning of a list. The *recency effect* refers to better recall for items at the end of the list. Together with the relatively low recall of items from the middle of the list, this pattern makes up the *serial position effect* (Surprenant, 2001). See Figure 8.15 for a typical serial position effect that shows a weaker primacy effect and a stronger recency effect. One application of primacy and recency effects is the advice to job candidates to try to be the first or last candidate interviewed.

These effects are explained using principles of encoding that we have already examined. With respect to the primacy effect, the first few items in the list are easily remembered because they are rehearsed more or because they receive more elaborative processing than do words later in the list (Atkinson & Shiffrin, 1968; Craik & Tulving, 1975). Working memory is relatively empty when the items enter, so there is little competition for rehearsal time. And because the items get more rehearsal, they stay in working memory longer and are more likely to be encoded successfully into long-term memory. In contrast, many items from the middle of the list drop out of working memory before being encoded into long-term memory.

As for the recency effect, the last several items are remembered for different reasons. First, when these items are recalled, they might still be in working memory. Second, even if these items are not in working memory, their recency compared with other list items makes them easier to recall. For example, if you are a sports fan, try remembering a game you saw at the end of the season. You probably will find that more recent games are easier to remember than earlier games.

Retrieval Cues and the Retrieval Task

Two other factors involved in retrieval are (1) the nature of the cues that can prompt your memory and (2) the retrieval task that you set for yourself. If effective cues for what you are trying to remember do not seem to be available, you need to create them—a process that takes place in working memory (Carpenter & DeLosh, 2006). For example, if you have a block about remembering a new friend's name, you might go through the alphabet, generating names that begin with each letter. If you manage to stumble across the right name, you will probably recognize it.

We can learn to generate retrieval cues (Allan & others, 2001). One good strategy is to use different subcategories as retrieval cues. For example, write down the names of as many of your classmates from middle or junior high school as you can remember. When you run out of names, think about the activities you were involved in during those school years, such as math class, student council, lunch, drill team, and so on. Did this set of cues help you to remember more of your classmates?

serial position effect The tendency for items at the beginning and at the end of a list to be recalled more readily than those in the middle.

Although cues help, your success in retrieving information also depends on the task you set for yourself. For instance, if you are simply trying to decide if something seems familiar, retrieval is probably a snap. Let's say you see a short, dark-haired woman walking toward you. You quickly decide she is someone who lives in the next dorm or shops at the same supermarket as you do. But remembering her name or a precise detail, such as when you met her, can be harder. Such distinctions have implications for police investigations: A witness might be certain she has previously seen a face, yet she might have a hard time deciding if it was at the scene of the crime or in a mug shot.

Recall and Recognition   The presence or absence of good cues and the retrieval task required are factors in an important memory distinction: recall versus recognition (Nobel & Shiffrin, 2001). *Recall* is a memory task in which the individual has to retrieve previously learned information, as on essay tests. *Recognition* is a memory task in which the individual only has to identify (recognize) learned items, as on multiple-choice tests. Recall tests such as essay tests have poor retrieval cues. You are told to try to recall a certain class of information ("Discuss the factors that caused World War II"). In recognition tests such as multiple-choice tests, you merely judge whether a stimulus is familiar (whether it matches something you experienced in the past).

You probably have heard some people say that they are terrible at remembering names but that they never forget a face. What they likely are really saying is that they are better at recognition (realizing that they have seen a face before) than at recall (remembering a person's name in response to his or her face). If you have made that claim yourself, try to recall an actual face. It is not easy, as law enforcement officers know. In some cases, they bring in an artist to draw the suspect's face from witnesses' descriptions (Figure 8.16). But recalling faces is difficult, and artists' sketches of suspects are frequently not detailed or accurate enough to result in apprehension.

Encoding Specificity   Another consideration in understanding retrieval is the *encoding specificity principle,* which states that information present at the time of encoding or learning tends to be effective as a retrieval cue (Hannon & Craik, 2001; Zeelenberg, 2005). For example, you know your instructors in your classes—you see them all the time in class. But coming upon one of them in an unexpected setting (say, at a bar or in a doctor's office) or in more casual clothes, you might find the person's name escapes you. Memory might fail because the cues you encoded are not available for use. Encoding specificity is compatible with our earlier discussion of elaboration. Recall that the more elaboration you use in encoding information, the better your memory of the information will be. Encoding specificity and elaboration reveal how interdependent encoding and retrieval are.

Context and State at Encoding and Retrieval   An important consequence of encoding specificity is that a change in context between encoding and retrieval can cause memory to fail (Fanselow, 2007; Smith, 2007). In many instances, people remember better when they attempt to recall information in the same context in which they learned it—a process referred to as *context-dependent memory*. This better recollection is believed to occur because they have encoded features of the context in which they learned the information along with the actual information. Such features can later act as retrieval cues (Dobbins & Han, 2006; Eich, 2007).

In one study, scuba divers learned information on land and under water (Godden & Baddeley, 1975). Later they were asked to recall the information when they were either on land or under water. The divers' recall was much better when the encoding and retrieval contexts were the same (both on land or both under water).

Just as external contexts can influence memory, so can internal states (Duka, Weissenborn, & Dienes, 2001; Weissenborn & Duka, 2000). People tend to remember information better when their psychological state or mood is similar at encoding and retrieval, a process referred to as *state-dependent memory*. For example, when people are in sad moods, they are more likely to remember negative experiences such as failure and rejection. When they are in happy moods, they are inclined to remember positive experiences such as

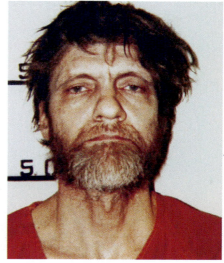

FIGURE 8.16

Remembering Faces (*Top*) The FBI artist's sketch of Ted Kaczynski. Kaczynski, also known as the Unabomber, is a serial killer who conducted a sequence of mail bombings targeting universities and airlines beginning in the late 1970s. (*Bottom*) A photograph of Kaczynski. The FBI widely circulated the artist's sketch, which was based on bits and pieces of observations people had made of the infamous Unabomber, in the hope that someone would recognize him. Would you have been able to recognize Kaczynski from the artist's sketch? Probably not. Although most people say they are good at remembering faces, they usually are not as good as they think they are.

success and acceptance (Mineka & Nugent, 1995). Unfortunately, when individuals who are depressed recall negative experiences, it tends to perpetuate their depression (Nolen-Hoeksema, 2007).

Priming   Retrieval also benefits from *priming*. Recall that priming means that people remember information better and faster when it is preceded by similar information. Priming is a form of implicit memory that is nonconscious (Goddard, Dritschel, & Burton, 2001).

Priming is likely involved in unintentional acts of plagiarism (Schacter, 1996). For example, let's say you propose an idea to a friend, who seems unimpressed by it or even rejects it outright. Weeks or months later, the friend excitedly describes your idea as if she had just come up with it herself. Her memory of having the idea has been primed by your explanation of the idea. When you call your friend's attention to the fact that her idea is really your idea, you likely will face either heated denial or a sheepish apology born of a sudden dose of explicit memory.

Special Cases of Retrieval

We began this discussion by likening the retrieval process to looking for and finding a book in the library. But the process of retrieving information from long-term memory is not as precise as the library analogy suggests. When we search through our long-term memory storehouse, we do not always find the exact "book" we want. Or we might find the book we want but discover that several pages are missing. We have to fill in these gaps somehow.

Our memories are affected by a number of things, including the pattern of facts we remember, schemas and scripts, the situations we associate with memories, and the personal or emotional context. Certainly, everyone has had the experience of remembering a shared situation with a particular individual, only to have him or her remind us, "Oh, that wasn't *me*!" Such moments (allegedly a common characteristic of James Frey's controversial "memoir" that was mentioned at the beginning of this chapter) have provided convincing evidence that memory may well be best understood as "reconstructive." This subjective quality of memory certainly has implications for important day-to-day procedures such as eyewitness testimony (Greene, 1999).

While the factors that we have discussed so far relate to the retrieval of generic information, various kinds of special memory retrieval also have generated a great deal of research. These memories have special significance because of their relevance to the self, to their emotional or traumatic character, or because they show unusually high levels of apparent accuracy (Piolino & others, 2006). We now turn to these special cases of memory. Researchers in cognitive psychology have debated whether these memories rely on processes that are different from those already described or are simply extreme cases of typical memory processes (Lane & Schooler, 2004; Schooler & Eich, 2000).

Retrieval of Autobiographical Memories   **Autobiographical memory,** a special form of episodic memory, is a person's recollections of his or her life experiences (Cabeza & St. Jacques, in press; Knez, 2006). Autobiographical memories are complex and seem to contain unending strings of stories and snapshots, but researchers have found that they can be categorized (Roediger & Marsh, 2003). For example, based on their research, Martin Conway and David Rubin (1993) sketched a structure of autobiographical memory that has three levels (Figure 8.17). The most abstract level consists of *life time periods;* for example, you might remember something about your life in high school. The middle level in the hierarchy is made up of *general events,* such as a trip you took with your friends after you graduated from high school. The most concrete level in the hierarchy is composed of *event-specific knowledge;* for example, from your postgraduation trip, you might remember the exhilarating time you had the very first time you jet-skied. When people tell their life stories, all three levels of information are usually present and intertwined.

autobiographical memory A special form of episodic memory consisting of a person's recollections of his or her life experiences.

Level	Label	Description
Level 1	Life time periods	Long segments of time measured in years and even decades
Level 2	General events	Extended composite episodes measured in days, weeks, or months
Level 3	Event-specific knowledge	Individual episodes measured in seconds, minutes, or hours

FIGURE 8.17

The Three-Level Hierarchical Structure of Autobiographical Memory When people relate their life stories, all three levels of information are typically present and intertwined.

Most autobiographical memories include some reality and some myth. Personality psychologist Dan McAdams argues that autobiographical memories are in fact less about facts and more about meanings (2001, 2006; McAdams & others, 2006). They provide a reconstructed, embellished telling of the past that connects the past to the present. According to McAdams, autobiographical memories form the core of our personal identity. A number of studies have now shown that the stories we tell about our lives have important implications (Kroger, 2007). For instance, McAdams and his colleagues have demonstrated that individuals who describe important life experiences that go from bad to better (redemptive stories) are more generative—that is, they are the kind of people who make a contribution to future generations, people who leave a legacy that will outlive them (Bauer, McAdams, & Sakaeda, 2005). These individuals are also better adjusted than those whose self-defining memories go from good to bad (labeled *contamination stories*).

Similar results have come from research on parents of children with Down syndrome. Parents whose autobiographical memories ended happily when recalling the experience of finding out about their child's diagnosis scored higher on measures of happiness, life meaning, and personal growth (King & others, 2000). Similarly, research on the coming-out stories of gay men and lesbians has shown that individuals whose autobiographical memory includes warm acceptance and the experience of falling in love are likely to score higher on measures of psychological well-being as well as personality development

Many people have flashbulb memories of where they were and what they were doing when terrorists attacked the World Trade Center towers in New York City on September 11, 2001.

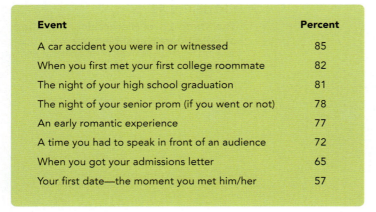

Event	Percent
A car accident you were in or witnessed	85
When you first met your first college roommate	82
The night of your high school graduation	81
The night of your senior prom (if you went or not)	78
An early romantic experience	77
A time you had to speak in front of an audience	72
When you got your admissions letter	65
Your first date—the moment you met him/her	57

FIGURE 8.18

College Students' Flashbulb Memories The numbers refer to the percent of college students who said these events triggered memories of flashbulb quality.

(King & Smith, 2005). Clearly, the construction and reconstruction of autobiographical memory may reveal important aspects of how individuals function, grow, and discover meaning in their lives (Crawley & Eacott, 2006; King & Hicks, 2006).

Retrieval of Emotional Memories When we remember our life experiences, the memories are often wrapped in emotion. Emotion affects the encoding and storage of memories and thus shapes the details that are retrieved. The role that emotion plays in memory is of considerable interest to contemporary researchers and has echoes in public life.

Flashbulb memory is the memory of emotionally significant events that people often recall with more accuracy and vivid imagery than everyday events (Curci & Luminet, 2006; Davidson, Cook, & Glisky, 2006). Perhaps you can remember where you were when you first heard of the terrorist attacks on the United States on September 11, 2001. An intriguing dimension of flashbulb memories is that several decades later, people often remember where they were and what was going on in their lives at the time of such an emotionally charged event. These memories seem to be part of an adaptive system that fixes in memory the details that accompany important events so that they can be interpreted at a later time.

The vast majority of flashbulb memories are of a personal nature rather than of nationally prominent events or circumstances. In one study, college students were asked to report the three most vivid memories in their lives (Rubin & Kozin, 1984). Virtually all of these memories were of a personal nature. They tended to center on an injury or accident, sports, members of the opposite sex, animals, deaths, the first week of college, and vacations. Students also answered questions about the kinds of events that were most likely to produce flashbulb memories. Figure 8.18 shows which types of events more than 50 percent of the students said were of flashbulb quality.

Most people express confidence about the accuracy of their flashbulb memories. However, most flashbulb memories probably are not as accurately etched in our brains as we think. One way to examine the accuracy of flashbulb memories is to examine how consistent the details of these memories remain over time. For instance, one study examined memories for the details of the attempted assassination of President Ronald Reagan (Pillemer, 1984). About 80 percent of the details that were remembered 1 month after the shooting were also remembered 7 months later. Other research has shown lower consistency over time; for example, one study found that 25 percent of participants included contradictory information in their memories of the *Challenger* space shuttle disaster (Neisser & Harsch, 1992).

Still, on the whole, flashbulb memories do seem more durable and accurate than memories of day-to-day happenings (Davidson, Cook, & Glisky, 2006). One reason that flashbulb memories might tend to be well preserved in memory is that they are quite likely to be rehearsed in the days following the event. However, it is not just the discussion and rehearsal of information that make flashbulb memories so long-lasting. The emotions triggered by flashbulb events also are involved in their durability. The emotional arousal you experienced when you heard about the terrorist attacks also likely contributed to the vividness of your memory.

Although we have focused on negative news events as typical of flashbulb memories, such memories can also occur for positive events. An individual's wedding day and the birth of a child are events that may become milestones in personal history and are always remembered.

Memory for Traumatic Events In 1890, the American psychologist and philosopher William James said that an experience can be so arousing emotionally as to almost leave a scar on the brain's tissue. Personal traumas are candidates for the type of emotionally arousing experience to which James was referring.

Some psychologists argue that memories of emotionally traumatic events are accurately retained, possibly forever, in considerable detail (Langer, 1991). There is good evidence that memory for traumatic events is usually more accurate than memory for ordinary events

flashbulb memory The memory of emotionally significant events that people often recall more accurately and vividly than everyday events.

(Berntsen & Rubin, 2006; Schooler & Eich, 2000). Consider the traumatic experience of the children who were kidnapped at gunpoint on a school bus in Chowchilla, California, in 1983 and then buried underground for 16 hours before escaping. The children had the classic signs of traumatic memory: detailed and vivid recollections.

However, when a child psychiatrist interviewed the children 4 to 5 years after the chilling episode, she noted striking errors and distortions in the memories of half of them (Terr, 1988). How can a traumatic memory be so vivid and detailed, yet at the same time have inaccuracies? A number of factors can be involved. Some children might have made perceptual errors while encoding information because the episode was so shocking. Others might have distorted the information and recalled the episode as being less traumatic than it actually was in order to reduce their anxiety about it. Other children, in discussing the traumatic event with others, might have incorporated bits and pieces of these people's recollections of what happened into their own version of the event.

Usually, memories of real-life traumas are more accurate and longer-lasting than memories of everyday events. Although memories of traumas are subject to deterioration and distortion, the central part of the memory is almost always effectively remembered. Where distortion often arises is in the details of the traumatic episode. Stress-related hormones likely play a role in memories that involve personal trauma. The release of stress-related hormones, signaled by the amygdala (see Figure 8.14), likely accounts for some of the extraordinary durability and vividness of traumatic memories (Bucherelli & others, 2006).

For rescuers as well as victims in natural and other disasters, memories are typically longer-lasting and more accurate than are recollections of ordinary events. Here Coast Guard Petty Officer 2nd Class Shawn Beaty of Long Island, New York, looks for survivors in the wake of Hurricane Katrina in New Orleans in August 2005.

Repressed Memories   To say that traumatic events are likely to be remembered hardly seems controversial. But a great deal more debate surrounds the question of whether such memories can be *forgotten and then recovered* (McNally, 2005). *Repression* refers to a defense mechanism by which a person is so traumatized by an event that he or she forgets it and then forgets the act of forgetting. According to psychodynamic theory, which we considered in Chapter 1, repression's main function is to protect the individual from threatening information. Repression does not erase a memory, but it makes conscious remembering extremely difficult (Anderson & Green, 2001).

Just how extensively repression occurs is a controversial issue. Most studies of traumatic memory indicate that a traumatic life event such as childhood sexual abuse is very likely to be remembered. However, there is at least some evidence that childhood sexual abuse may not be remembered. Linda Williams and her colleagues have conducted a number of investigations of memories of childhood abuse (Liang, Williams, & Siegel, 2006; Williams, 2003, 2004). One study involved 129 women for whom hospital records indicated an abuse experience (Williams, 1995). Seventeen years after the abuse incident, the women were contacted and asked (among other things) if they had ever been the victim of childhood sexual abuse. Of the 129 women, 80 reported remembering and never having forgotten the experience. Ten percent of the participants reported having forgotten about the abuse at least for some portion of their lives. Those who reported "recovering" these memories were younger at the time of the incident and were much less likely to have received support from their mothers after the abuse.

If it does exist, repression can be considered a special case of **motivated forgetting,** which occurs when individuals forget something because it is so painful or anxiety-laden that remembering is intolerable (Anderson & others, 2004; Joormann & others, 2005). This type of forgetting may be a consequence of the emotional trauma experienced by victims of rape or physical abuse, war veterans, or survivors of earthquakes, plane crashes, and other terrifying events. These emotional traumas may haunt people for many years unless they can put the details out of mind. Even when people have not experienced trauma, they may use motivated forgetting to protect themselves from memories of painful, stressful, or otherwise unpleasant circumstances.

Can so-called recovered memories be considered authentic? See the Critical Controversy on page 330 to explore this intriguing question further.

Eyewitness Testimony   By now, you should realize that memory is not a perfect reflection of reality. Understanding the distortions of memory is especially important when people are called on to report what they saw or heard in relation to a crime. Eyewitness testimonies, like other sorts of memories, may contain errors (Bruck, Ceci, & Principe, 2006; Wright &

motivated forgetting An act of forgetting something because it is so painful or anxiety-laden that remembering it is intolerable.

Critical Controversy

Memories: Recovered, Discovered, or False?

George Franklin, a California man, spent 6 years in prison for the 1969 murder of a young woman. His own daughter's testimony, based on her memory of the crime, was at the heart of the prosecution's case against him. What made this case unusual is that the daughter's memories were allegedly recovered in adulthood as a part of her own ongoing therapy (Loftus & Ketcham, 1991). In fact, Franklin became the first person in the United States to be convicted on the basis of repressed memory evidence. During the 1990s, memories allegedly recovered during therapy also served as the basis for many charges of physical and sexual abuse in various cases. George Franklin's conviction was eventually overturned when it came out that his daughter might have lied about having been hypnotized before the trial.

The idea that childhood abuse—and, in particular, sexual abuse—can be completely repressed yet lead to psychological disorders in adulthood was first expressed by Sigmund Freud (1917). Some therapists today continue to believe that adult disorders such as depression, thoughts of suicide, eating disorders, low self-esteem, sexual dysfunction, and trouble maintaining relationships may stem from sexual abuse in childhood. Treatment usually involves bringing these long-repressed childhood traumas back into consciousness, thus freeing the client from their unconscious effects.

Almost all accused parents vehemently deny having ever abused their offspring in childhood. In 1992, the False Memory Syndrome (FMS) Foundation was formed as a parents' support group. An extraordinary aspect of this organization is that its founders are the parents of a woman who is a cognitive psychologist and whose interest in repressed memory is both professional and personal (Freyd, 1996).

It was against this bitter backdrop that experimental psychology entered the fray. Led by the research of memory expert Elizabeth Loftus, study after study found that it is easy to create false memories, especially by using hypnosis (Loftus, 2005, 2006, 2007; Clark & Loftus, 2006; Garry & Loftus, 2007; Wright & Loftus, 2007). All that is required is to hypnotize someone and to suggest that he or she has had an experience. After hypnosis, that person may well "remember" the experience as vividly real. In one study, Loftus and Jacquie Pickrell (2001) persuaded people that they had met Bugs Bunny at Disneyland, even though Bugs is a Warner Bros. character that would never appear at a Disney theme park. The research procedure was quite simple. Four groups of participants read ads and then answered questionnaires about a trip to Disneyland. One group saw an ad that mentioned no cartoon characters, the second read the same ad and saw a 4-foot-tall cardboard figure of Bugs Bunny, the third read a fake ad for Disneyland with Bugs Bunny in it, and the fourth saw the same fake ad along with the cardboard bunny. Although less than 10 percent of the first two groups later reported having actually met Bugs Bunny on a trip to Disneyland, approximately 30 to 40 percent of the third and fourth groups reported remembering meeting Bugs at Disneyland.

Such research added to growing skepticism. There is no question that individuals can "remember," in extraordinary detail, events that are quite unlikely (for example, satanic ritual abuses and alien abductions—indeed, there has never been a proven case of satanic ritual abuse in the United States). Certainly therapeutic techniques such as visualization and hypnosis are prone to contribute to false memories (Schooler & Eich, 2000). Are so-called recovered memories ever authentic? Cognitive psychologist Jonathan Schooler (2002) has suggested that such memories are better termed "discovered" memories, because whether they are accurate or not, individuals certainly experience them as real. Schooler and his colleagues (1997) investigated a number of cases of discovered memories of abuse, in which they sought independent corroboration by others. They were able to identify cases in which a discovered memory could be verified by the perpetrator or some third party. Indeed, such cases do exist. For example, Frank Fitzpatrick's memory of previously "forgotten" abuse at the hands of a Catholic priest was corroborated by witnesses who had also been abused (*Commonwealth of Massachusetts v. Porter,* 1993). Schooler and colleagues found that, in cases of authentic discovered memories, the circumstances leading to the recollection of the memory were similar to the original abuse (for example, hearing about someone else being abused or seeing a movie about it) and did not include therapeutic interventions.

Thus, although some cases of recovered memories clearly have led to unjust treatment (as for George Franklin), it is inappropriate to reject all claims by adults that they were victims of childhood sexual abuse. Current consensus is well represented by the American Psychological Association's (1995) interim report of a working group investigating memories of childhood abuse, which offers these tentative conclusions: (1) Controversies regarding adult recollections should not be allowed to obscure the fact that child sexual abuse is a complex and pervasive problem in the United States that has historically gone unacknowledged; (2) most people who were sexually abused as children remember all or part of what happened to them; (3) it is possible for memories of abuse that have been forgotten for a long time to be remembered, although the mechanism by which such delayed recall occurs is not currently well understood; (4) it is also possible to construct convincing false memories for events that never occurred, although the mechanism by which these false memories occur is not currently well understood; (5) there are gaps in our knowledge about the processes that lead to accurate and inaccurate recollections of childhood abuse.

What Do You Think?

- How should courts of law deal with "discovered memories"?
- Suppose you meet someone who reports a recovered memory of childhood abuse. How can you tell whether that memory should be believed? How might the individual's revelation change your attitude about him or her?
- How does our perspective on discovered memories affect our view of childhood abuse in general? If we cannot trust the testimony of adult survivors of abuse, how can we determine the frequency of childhood abuse today?

Loftus, 2007). But faulty memory in criminal matters has especially serious consequences. When eyewitness testimony is inaccurate, the wrong person may go to jail or even be put to death, or the person who committed the crime might not be prosecuted. Estimates are that between 2,000 and 10,000 people are wrongfully convicted each year in the United States because of faulty eyewitness testimony (Cutler & Penrod, 1995). It is important to note that often witnessing a crime is a traumatic event for the individual, and so this type of memory typically fits in the larger category of memory for highly emotional events.

Much of the interest in eyewitness testimony focuses on distortion, bias, and inaccuracy in memory (Garry & Loftus, 2007; Loftus, 2006). One reason for distortion is that memory fades. In one study, people were able to identify pictures with 100 percent accuracy after a 2-hour time lapse. However, 4 months later they achieved an accuracy of only 57 percent; chance alone accounts for 50 percent accuracy (Shepard, 1967).

Unlike a videotape, memory can be altered by new information (Dysart & Lindsay, 2007). In one study, students were shown a film of an automobile accident and were asked how fast the white sports car was going when it passed a barn (Loftus, 1975). In fact, there was no barn in the film. However, 17 percent of the students who were asked the question mentioned the barn in their answer.

Bias is also a factor in faulty memory (Brigham & others, 2007). Studies have shown that people of one ethnic group are less likely to recognize individual differences among people of another ethnic group (Behrman & Davey, 2001). Latino eyewitnesses, for example, may have trouble distinguishing among several Asian suspects. In one experiment, a mugging was shown on a television news program (Loftus, 1993). Immediately after, a lineup of six suspects was broadcast, and viewers were asked to phone in and identify which one of the six individuals they thought committed the robbery. Of the 2,000 callers, more than 1,800 identified the wrong person. In addition, even though the robber was White, one-third of the viewers identified an African American or a Latino suspect as the criminal.

Hundreds of individuals have been harmed by witnesses who have made a mistake that they could have avoided (Loftus, 2006; Wright & Loftus, 2007). One estimate indicates that each year, approximately 7,500 people are arrested for and wrongly convicted of serious crimes in the United States (Huff, 2002). Faulty memory is not just about accusing the wrong person. For example, faulty memories were evident in descriptions of the suspects' vehicle in the sniper attacks that killed 10 people in the Washington, D.C., area in 2002. Witnesses reported seeing a white truck or van fleeing several of the crime scenes. It appears that the white van may have been near one of the first shootings and that media repetition of

Faulty memories complicated the search for the perpetrators in the sniper attacks that killed 10 people in the Washington, D.C., area in 2002. Police released photos of the type of white truck or van that witnesses said they saw fleeing some of the crime scenes (right). In the end, however, the suspects were driving a blue car when law enforcement officials apprehended them (above).

this information contaminated the memories of witnesses to later attacks, making them more likely to remember the white trucks. When caught, the sniper suspects were driving a blue car.

Before police even arrive at a crime scene, witnesses talk among themselves, and this dialogue can contaminate memories. In one situation, Elizabeth Loftus (2003) personally witnessed this effect when she entered a shop moments after a robbery had taken place and before police had arrived. In the immediate aftermath, customers and employees shared their memories, in the process influencing others' thoughts. This is why, during the Washington, D.C., sniper attacks in 2002, law enforcement officials advised any persons who might witness the next attack immediately to write down what they had seen—even on their hands if they did not have a piece of paper.

REVIEW, ASSESS, AND SHARPEN YOUR THINKING

Review

4 Summarize how memories are retrieved.
- Describe the serial position effect.
- Explain the role of retrieval cues and the retrieval task.
- Discuss the following special cases of retrieval: autobiographical memory, emotional memory, memory of traumatic events, repressed memory, and eyewitness testimony.

Assess

1. While watching television, Meenu sees a series of five advertisements. The first is for breakfast cereal, the second is for cat food, the third is for a car, the fourth is for a lawyer, and the fifth is for a new movie. Which advertisement will Meenu be most likely to remember?
   A. the lawyer advertisement
   B. the cat food advertisement
   C. the car advertisement
   D. the breakfast cereal advertisement

2. A fill-in-the-blank exam tests which type of memory task?
   A. recall
   B. recognition
   C. context-dependent memory
   D. encoding specificity

3. Which statement about eyewitness testimony is most accurate?
   A. Eyewitness testimony is most accurate when the race of the eyewitness differs from the race of the subject.

   B. Eyewitness memories for a crime are less prone to error than other types of memory.
   C. Distortions in eyewitness testimony rarely lead to wrongful convictions.
   D. Eyewitness memories can be subject to alteration by new information and bias.

4. Which level of autobiographical memory is least concrete?
   A. event-specific knowledge
   B. life time periods
   C. episodic memory
   D. general events

5. Events such as the assassination of President Kennedy, the space shuttle Challenger explosion, and September 11, 2001 can create
   A. motivated forgetting.
   B. repression.
   C. flashbulb memories.
   D. contamination stories.

Sharpen Your Thinking

Do you think that, on the whole, negative emotional events are likely to be more memorable than positive ones? How would you go about studying whether negative events are more memorable than positive ones?

5 Forgetting

Describe how the failure of encoding and retrieval are involved in forgetting.

Human memory also has its imperfections, as we have all experienced. It is not unusual for two people to argue about whether something did or did not happen, each supremely confident that his memory is accurate and the other person's is faulty. And we all have had the frustrating experience of trying to remember the name of some person or some place but not quite being able to retrieve it.

Imperfections of memory are also in evidence in the stunning, high-profile disagreements that erupt in our nation's legal and political arenas. The trials of Michael Jackson and others show how common it is in a court case for one person to remember events one way and for someone else to recall them differently. Those who played a significant role in highly publicized events such as the search-and-recovery efforts after 9/11, the run-up to the war in Iraq, and the delivery of emergency aid to the victims of Hurricane Katrina often paint different pictures of what happened from their memories. Missed appointments, misplaced eyeglasses, the failure to recall the name of a familiar face, and inability to recall your password for Internet access are everyday examples of forgetting. Why do we forget?

One of psychology's pioneers, Hermann Ebbinghaus (1850–1909), was the first person to conduct scientific research on forgetting. In 1885, he made up and memorized a list of 13 nonsense syllables and then assessed how many of them he could remember as time passed. (*Nonsense syllables* are meaningless combinations of letters that are unlikely to have been learned already, such as *zeq, xid, lek, vut,* and *riy*.) Even just an hour later, Ebbinghaus could recall only a few of the nonsense syllables he had memorized. Figure 8.19 shows Ebbinghaus's learning curve for nonsense syllables. Based on his research, Ebbinghaus concluded that the most forgetting takes place soon after we learn something.

If we forget so quickly, why put effort into learning something? Fortunately, researchers have demonstrated that forgetting is not as extensive as Ebbinghaus envisioned (Jarrold & Towse, 2006). Ebbinghaus studied meaningless nonsense syllables. When we memorize more meaningful material—such as poetry, history, or the content of this text—forgetting is neither so rapid nor so extensive. Following are some of the factors that influence how well we can retrieve information from long-term memory.

Hermann Ebbinghaus (1850–1909)
Ebbinghaus was the first psychologist to conduct scientific research on forgetting.

Encoding Failure

Sometimes when people say they have forgotten something, they have not really forgotten it; rather, they never encoded the information in the first place. *Encoding failure* occurs when the information was never entered into long-term memory.

As an example of encoding failure, think about what the U.S. penny looks like. In one study, researchers showed 15 versions of the penny to participants and asked them which was correct (Nickerson & Adams, 1979). Look at the pennies in Figure 8.20 (but do not read the caption yet) and see if you can tell which one is the real penny. Most people do not do well on this task. Unless you are a coin collector, you likely have not encoded a lot of specific details about pennies. You may have encoded just enough information to distinguish them from other coins (pennies are copper-colored, dimes and nickels are silver-colored; pennies fall between the sizes of dimes and quarters).

The penny exercise illustrates that we encode and enter into long-term memory only a small portion of our life experiences. In a sense, then, encoding failures really are not cases of forgetting; they are cases of not remembering.

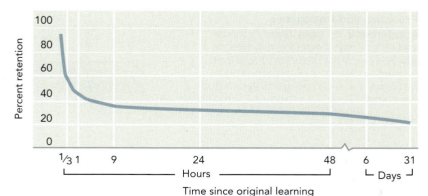

Time since original learning

FIGURE 8.19

Ebbinghaus's Forgetting Curve
The figure illustrates Ebbinghaus's conclusion that most forgetting occurs soon after we learn something.

FIGURE 8.20

Which Is a Real U.S. Penny? In the original experiment, 15 versions of pennies were shown to participants: only 1 was an actual U.S. penny. Included here are only 7 of the 15 versions, and as you likely can tell, this still is a very difficult task. Why? By the way, the actual U.S. penny is (c).

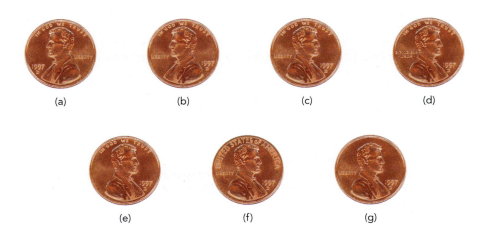

(a)   (b)   (c)   (d)

(e)   (f)   (g)

interference theory Theory stating that people forget not because memories are lost from storage but because other information gets in the way of what they want to remember.

proactive interference Situation in which material that was learned earlier disrupts the recall of material learned later.

retroactive interference Situation in which material learned later disrupts the retrieval of information learned earlier.

Retrieval Failure

Problems in retrieving information from memory are clearly examples of forgetting (Gardiner, 2007; Spear, 2007). Psychologists have theorized that the causes of retrieval failure include problems with the information in storage, the effects of time, personal reasons for remembering or forgetting, and the brain's condition (Miller & Matzel, 2006; Sweatt, 2007).

Interference   Interference has been proposed as one reason that people forget (Sangha & others, 2005). **Interference theory** states that people forget not because memories are lost from storage but because other information gets in the way of what they want to remember.

There are two kinds of interference: proactive and retroactive. **Proactive interference** occurs when material that was learned earlier disrupts the recall of material learned later (Hedden & Yoon, 2006). Remember that *pro-* means "forward in time." For example, suppose you had a good friend 10 years ago named Prudence and that last night you met someone named Patience. You might find yourself calling your new friend Prudence because the old information (Prudence) interferes with retrieval of new information (Patience). **Retroactive interference** occurs when material learned later disrupts the retrieval of information learned earlier (Delprato, 2005). Remember that *retro-* means "backward in time." Suppose you have lately become friends with Ralph. In sending a note to your old friend Raul, you might mistakenly address it to Ralph because the new information (Ralph) interferes with the old information (Raul). Figure 8.21 depicts another example of proactive and retroactive interference.

FIGURE 8.21

Proactive and Retroactive Interference *Pro-* means "forward"; in proactive interference, old information has a forward influence by getting in the way of new material learned. *Retro-* means "backward"; in retroactive interference, new information has a backward influence by getting in the way of material learned earlier.

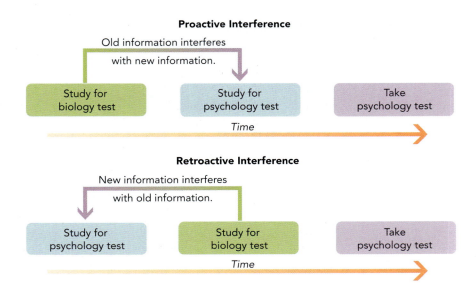

Proactive Interference

Old information interferes with new information.

| Study for biology test | Study for psychology test | Take psychology test |

Time

Retroactive Interference

New information interferes with old information.

| Study for psychology test | Study for biology test | Take psychology test |

Time

Proactive and retroactive interference might both be explained as problems with retrieval cues. The reason the name Prudence interferes with the name Patience and the name Ralph interferes with the name Raul might be that the cue you are using to remember the one name does not distinguish between the two memories. For example, if the cue you are using is "my good friend," it might evoke both names. The result might be retrieval of the wrong name or a kind of blocking in which each name interferes with the other and neither comes to mind. Retrieval cues (such as "friend" in our example) can become overloaded, and when that happens we are likely to forget or to retrieve incorrectly.

Decay and Transience Another possible reason for forgetting is the passage of time. **Decay theory** states that when something new is learned, a neurochemical "memory trace" is formed, but over time this trace tends to disintegrate. Decay theory suggests that the passage of time always increases forgetting.

Memory researcher Daniel Schacter (2001) refers to the forgetting that occurs with the passage of time as *transience*. As an example of transience, consider the dramatic conclusion, on October 3, 1995, to the most sensational criminal trial in recent times: A jury acquitted former football star O. J. Simpson of murdering his wife and her friend. The Simpson verdict seemed like just the kind of flashbulb memory that most people would retain vividly for years to come. In one research study, undergraduate students provided detailed accounts of how they learned about the Simpson verdict, shortly after it was announced (Schmolck, Buffalo, & Squire, 2000). However, 15 months later, only half remembered the details, and nearly 3 years after the verdict, less than 30 percent of the students' memories were accurate.

Memories often do fade with the passage of time, but decay or transience alone cannot explain forgetting. For example, under the right retrieval conditions, memories that seem to have been forgotten can be retrieved. You might have forgotten the face or name of someone in your high school class, but when you return to the setting in which you knew the person, you may remember.

Tip-of-the-Tongue Phenomenon One glitch in retrieving information that we are all familiar with is the **tip-of-the-tongue phenomenon,** or **TOT state.** It is a type of "effortful retrieval" that occurs when people are confident that they know something but they cannot quite pull it out of memory (James, 2006; Maril & others, 2005). People in a TOT state usually can successfully retrieve characteristics of the word, such as the first letter and the number of syllables, but cannot retrieve the word itself.

In one study of the TOT state, participants viewed photographs of famous people and were asked to say their names (Yarmey, 1973). The researcher found that people tended to use two strategies to try to retrieve the name of a person they thought they knew. One strategy was to pinpoint the person's profession. For example, one participant correctly identified the famous person as an artist, but the artist's name, Picasso, remained elusive. Another retrieval strategy was to repeat initial letters or syllables—such as *Monetti, Mona, Magett, Spaghetti,* and *Bogette* in the attempt to identify stage and screen star Liza Minnelli.

The TOT state arises because a person can retrieve some of the desired information but not all of it (Maril, Wagner, & Schacter, 2001; Schacter, 1996, 2001). For example, imagine that you are at a college social event and spot two people standing together. You easily recall that one of them is Barbara. You know that you have seen the other person before and are sure his name begins with a *B* (a good retrieval cue). You are certain that you know his name, although you cannot remember it at the moment. But maybe when you were introduced to him, you did not pay enough attention to his name to remember more than the first letter. Your confidence in the retrieval cue can induce a strong—sometimes spurious—feeling of knowing other information (in this case, the name) that you actually have not stored in memory.

Prospective Memory: Remembering (or Forgetting) When to Do Something The main focus of this chapter has been on **retrospective memory,** which is remembering the past. **Prospective memory** involves remembering information about doing something in the future; it includes memory for intentions (McDaniel & Einstein, 2007). Prospective memory includes both *timing*—when we have to do something—and *content*—what it is we have to do.

decay theory Theory stating that when something new is learned, a neurochemical "memory trace" is formed, but over time this trace tends to disintegrate.

tip-of-the-tongue phenomenon (TOT state) The "effortful retrieval" that occurs when people are confident that they know something but cannot pull it out of memory.

retrospective memory Remembering the past.

prospective memory Remembering information about doing something in the future, including memory for intentions.

A distinction can be made between time-based and event-based prospective memory. *Time-based* prospective memory is your intention to engage in a given behavior after a specified amount of time has gone by (such as an intention to make a phone call to someone in 1 hour). In *event-based* prospective memory, you engage in the intended behavior when it is elicited by some external event or cue (such as giving a message to your roommate when you see her). The cues available in event-based prospective memory make it more effective than time-based prospective memory (McDaniel & Einstein, 2007; Seifert & Patalano, 2001).

Some failures in prospective memory are referred to as "absentmindedness." We are more absentminded when we become preoccupied with something else, are distracted by something, or are under a lot of time pressure (Matlin, 2001). Absentmindedness often involves a breakdown between attention and memory storage (Schacter, 2001). Absentmindedness may especially be a problem when we have too little time or are too distracted to elaboratively encode something we need to remember. We spend a great deal of our lives on autopilot, a state that helps us to perform routine tasks effectively but also makes us vulnerable to absentminded errors. Fortunately, research has shown that our goals are encoded into memory along with the features of situations that would allow us to pursue them. Our memories, then, prepare us to recognize when a situation presents an opportunity to achieve those goals (Seifert & Patalano, 2001).

Continuing research on prospective memory is providing new clues that will help people improve their memories. In one study, individuals were given 4 minutes to recall what they did yesterday, last week, or last year (retrospective memories) and 4 minutes to recall what they intended to do tomorrow, next week, or next year (prospective memories) (Maylor, Chater, & Brown, 2001). More prospective memories were recalled than retrospective memories. Researchers also have found that older adults perform worse on prospective memory tasks than younger adults do, but typically these findings are true only for artificial lab tasks (West & Bowry, 2005). In real life, older adults generally perform as well as younger adults in terms of prospective memory (Rendell & Craik, 2000). Generally, prospective memory failure (forgetting to do something) occurs when retrieval is a conscious, effortful (rather than automatic) process (Henry & others, 2004).

Amnesia Recall the case of H. M. in the discussion of explicit and implicit memory. In H. M.'s surgery, the part of his brain that was responsible for laying down new memories

Alabama businesswoman Patsy Cannon was in a car crash in 1986. Her injury was so severe that it left her with retrograde amnesia, and she had to relearn virtually everything she used to know. Cannon did not even recognize her own daughter. (Left) Cannon in 1986 just prior to the car crash. (Right) Cannon in a recent photo. Referring to her life before the accident, she has said, "That person is dead; I am a new person."

was damaged beyond repair. The result was **amnesia,** the loss of memory. Although some types of amnesia clear up over time, H. M.'s amnesia endured.

H. M. suffered from **anterograde amnesia,** a memory disorder that affects the retention of new information and events (*antero-* indicates amnesia that moves forward in time) (Gilboa & others, 2006). What he learned before the surgery (and thus before the onset of amnesia) was not affected. For example, H. M. could identify his friends, recall their names, and even tell stories about them—*if* he had known them before surgery. People who met H. M. after surgery remained strangers, even if they spent thousands of hours with him. H. M.'s postsurgical experiences were rarely encoded in his long-term memory.

Amnesia also occurs in a form known as **retrograde amnesia,** which involves memory loss for a segment of the past but not for new events (*retro-* indicates amnesia that moves back in time) (Gold, 2006). Retrograde amnesia is much more common than anterograde amnesia and frequently occurs when the brain is assaulted by an electrical shock or a physical blow—such as a head injury to a football player. In contrast to anterograde amnesia, in retrograde amnesia the forgotten information is *old*—it occurred prior to the event that caused the amnesia—and the ability to acquire new memories is not affected. Sometimes individuals have both anterograde and retrograde amnesia.

amnesia The loss of memory.

anterograde amnesia A memory disorder that affects the retention of new information and events.

retrograde amnesia A memory disorder that involves memory loss for a segment of the past but not for new events.

 REVIEW, ASSESS, AND SHARPEN YOUR THINKING

Review

5 Describe how the failure of encoding and retrieval are involved in forgetting.
- Define encoding failure.
- Discuss four reasons for retrieval failure.

Assess

1. Who conducted the first research on forgetting?
   A. Daniel Schacter
   B. Sigmund Freud
   C. Hermann Ebbinghaus
   D. Alan Baddeley

2. When does most forgetting occur?
   A. in the first hour
   B. in the first day
   C. in the first month
   D. in the first year

3. Esperanza recently moved and got a new phone number. When she tries to remember her old phone number, she has problems because she keeps thinking of her new phone number. What has happened?
   A. encoding failure
   B. proactive inference

   C. transience
   D. retroactive interference

4. The experience of being confident that something is known but cannot be retrieved from memory is known as
   A. transience
   B. tip-of-the-tongue phenomenon
   C. anterograde amnesia
   D. retroactive interference

5. Being unable to make new memories is known as
   A. anterograde amnesia.
   B. tip-of-the-tongue phenomenon.
   C. retrograde amnesia.
   D. transcience.

Sharpen Your Thinking

Think about three or four instances recently in which you were unable to remember something. What principle of forgetting do you think best explains your failure to remember in each case?

6 Study Tips from the Science of Memory

Evaluate study strategies based on an understanding of memory.

Now that you are familiar with the basic processes of memory, how can you apply your knowledge to improving your academic performance? No matter what model of memory we use, the message is clear: We can improve our memory for material by thinking deeply about it and connecting the information to other things we know. Perhaps the one most well-connected node or most elaborate schema to which we can relate something is the self—what we know and think about ourselves. To make something more meaningful and to secure its place in memory, we must make it matter to ourselves.

If we think about memory as a physical event in the brain, we can see that memorizing material is like training a muscle. Repeated recruitment of sets of neurons creates the connection we want to have available at exam time and throughout our lives.

Encoding, Rehearsal, and Retrieval of Course Material

Before you engage the powerful process of memory, the first step in improving your academic performance is to make sure the information you are studying is accurate and well organized. You should review your course notes routinely and catch potential errors and ambiguities early. There is no sense in memorizing inaccurate or incomplete information. Second, organize the material in a way that will allow you to commit it to memory effectively. You will remember information better if you consciously organize it while trying to absorb it. Arrange information, rework material, and give it a structure that will help you to remember it. One organizational technique is to use a hierarchy such as an outline. You might also devise a concept map, which draws on semantic-network theory, or create analogies (such as the earlier comparison of retrieval from long-term memory to finding a book in the library) that take advantage of your preexisting schemas.

Once the material to be remembered is accurate and well organized, it is time to memorize. The first step in successfully memorizing material is to process it effectively so that it will be stored in long-term memory. Although some types of information are encoded automatically, the academic learning process usually requires considerable effort (Bruning & others, 2004). Recall that encoding involves paying attention, processing information at an appropriate level, elaborating, and using imagery. Learning and studying in a way that actively engages memory with the material is vital. Encoding material is not simply something that you should do before a test. Rather, during class, while reading, or in discussing issues, you are given—and should take advantage of—your first opportunity to create associations to course material.

While learning material initially, relate it to your life, and attend to examples that help you do just that. After class, rehearsal of the course material over time helps to solidify it in memory. Some students find that rewriting their notes is a good form of rehearsal. But rehearsal does not have to be a solitary exercise. Talking to people about what you have learned and how it is important to real life will help to reinforce memory. Keep in mind that you are more likely to remember information over the long term if you understand it rather than just mechanically rehearse and memorize it. Rehearsal works well for information in short-term memory, but when you need to encode, store, and then retrieve information from long-term memory, it is much less efficient. Thus, for most information, understand it, give it meaning, elaborate on it, and personalize it.

An important next step is to test yourself. It is not enough simply to look at your notes and think, "Oh, yes, I know this!" Remember, sometimes recognition instills a false sense of knowing. If you look at a definition and it seems so familiar that you are certain you know it, *test yourself*. What happens when you close the book and try to reconstruct the definition? Check your personal definition with the technical one in the book. How did you do? While reading and studying, ask yourself other questions as well, such as "What is the meaning of what I just read?" "Why is this important?" and "What is an example of the concept I just read about?" When you have made a concerted effort to ask yourself questions about what you have read or about an activity in class, you will expand the number of associations you make with the information you will need to retrieve later.

Mnemonic Strategies

Another tip for improving memory performance for course materials is to use mnemonic strategies. **Mnemonics** are specific visual and/or verbal memory aids. Following are three types of mnemonic devices:

- *Method of loci:* You develop an image of items to be remembered and then store them mentally in familiar locations (which is what *loci* means). Rooms of houses or stores on a street are common locations used in this memory strategy. For example, if you need to remember a list of brain structures, you can mentally place them in the rooms of a house you are familiar with, such as the entry hall, the living room, the dining room, and the kitchen. Then, when you need to retrieve the information, you imagine the house, mentally go through the rooms, and retrieve the concepts.
- *Keyword method:* You attach vivid imagery to important words. For example, to remember that the limbic system consists of two main regions—amygdala and hippocampus—you might imagine two legs (limbs) (limbic system) ambling (amygdala) like a hippo (hippocampus).
- *Acronyms:* To form an acronym, you create a word from the first letters of items to be remembered. For example, *HOMES* can be used to remember the Great Lakes: *H*uron, *O*ntario, *M*ichigan, *E*rie, and *S*uperior. An acronym commonly used to remember the sequence of colors in the light spectrum is the name of an imaginary man named *ROY G. BIV: R*ed, *O*range, *Y*ellow, *G*reen, *B*lue, *I*ndigo, and *V*iolet.

Many experts on memory and study skills recommend using mnemonics mainly when you need to memorize a list of items or specific facts. However, in most cases, techniques that promote memory by developing an understanding of the material are better than rote memorization.

If you are genuinely seeking to improve your memory performance, also keep in mind that the brain is a physical organ. Perhaps the best way to promote effective memory storage is to make sure that your brain is able to function at maximum capacity. For most of us, that means being well rested, well nourished, and free of mind-altering substances.

So, you have studied not just hard but deeply, elaborating on important concepts and committing lists to memory. You have slept well and eaten a nutritious breakfast, and now it is time to take the exam. How can you best retrieve the essential information? One way to improve the accuracy and efficiency of retrieval is through the use of retrieval cues. Of course, one potential retrieval cue is out of the question—your class notes have been put aside. But remember that the exam itself is full of questions about topics that you have thoughtfully encoded. Recall that research on long-term memory has shown that material that has been committed to memory is there for a very long time—even among those who may experience a moment of panic when the test is handed out. Focus on the concepts on the test. Use them to trigger your insights.

mnemonics Specific visual and/or verbal memory aids.

 REVIEW, ASSESS, AND SHARPEN YOUR THINKING

Review

6 Evaluate study strategies based on an understanding of memory.

- Describe effective encoding, rehearsal, and retrieval strategies for recalling course material.
- Explain what a mnemonic strategy is and give some examples.

Assess

1. What mnemonic strategy involves mentally putting concepts into a physical space, such as the rooms of a house?
   A. keyword method
   B. method of loci
   C. acronyms
   D. mnemonics

2. What should you do first when starting to study?
   A. organize your study material
   B. test yourself
   C. ensure your materials are accurate
   D. rehearse the material

3. A math student knows that she should first calculate what comes inside the parentheses, then calculate exponents, then multiply and divide, and finally add and subtract by remembering the phrase Please Excuse My Dear Aunt Sally. She is using which of the following mnemonic strategies?
   A. keyword method
   B. method of loci
   C. acronyms
   D. mnemonics

Sharpen Your Thinking

Get together with three or four students in this class and compare your note-taking and study strategies. How are your strategies similar to or different from those of the other students? What did you learn from the comparison and this chapter about how to study more effectively?

7 Memory and Health and Wellness

Discuss the multiple functions of memory in human life.

We began this chapter by recognizing that memory is essential to many aspects of human life, from waiting on tables to performing academic tasks. Acts of memory—remembering to take your vitamins and medication, or to stick to a diet—are also important for your good health. But memory is more than an internalized "to do" list, as we now consider.

The Vital Role of Autobiographical Memory

Memory serves multiple functions. Autobiographical memory, for example, may be one of the most important aspects of human life (Cabeza & St. Jacques, in press). For instance, one of the many functions that autobiographical memory serves is to allow us to learn from our experiences (Pillemer, 1998). In autobiographical memory, we store the lessons we have learned from life. These memories become a resource to which we can turn when faced with life's difficulties.

Autobiographical memory also allows us to understand ourselves and provides us with a source of identity (Alea & Bluck, 2003; Singer, 2004). In his studies of self-defining autobiographical memories, Jefferson Singer and his colleagues maintain that these internalized stories of personal experience serve as signs of the meaning we have created out of our life experience and give our lives coherence (Conway, Singer, & Tagini, 2004; Singer, 2004; Singer & Blagov, 2004). Autobiographical memories are one domain in which the notion that each human being is truly unique—"like a snowflake," as your kindergarten teacher may have noted—is supported. No matter how similar two people are, the storehouse of life experience that is represented in autobiographical memory is genuinely each person's own.

A final function of autobiographical memory is its role in social bonding. The social function of autobiographical memory may be its most vital (Alea & Bluck 2003; Bruce, 1989; Nelson, 1993). Our memories are valuable not just as indicators of lessons learned or identity, but also as a way to share a part of ourselves with others. Sharing personal experience is a way to foster intimacy, create bonds, and deepen existing ones. When we know a person's most cherished autobiographical memory, we know that she is no longer just an acquaintance but clearly a friend. To the extent that social bonds are necessary for survival, it makes sense that human beings can remember and share those memories with each other.

Memory and Aging

As a process that is rooted in the brain, memory is also an indicator of brain functioning. Preserving memory is of vital importance as we age. A strong message from research on aging and memory is that, as for many things in life, the phrase "Use or lose it!" applies to memory.

Consider the case of Richard Wetherill, a retired lecturer and an uncommonly good chess player (Melton, 2005). Wetherill was so skilled that he was able to think eight moves ahead in a chess match. At some point, he noticed that he was having trouble playing chess—he was able to think only five moves ahead. He was sure that something was seriously wrong with himself, despite his wife's assurances that she noticed no changes. A battery of cognitive tests revealed no abnormalities, and a brain scan was similarly reassuring. Two years later, Wetherill was dead, and the autopsy showed a brain ravaged by Alzheimer disease. Brain damage of this sort should indicate a person who was incapable of coherent thought. Yet Wetherill's symptoms had been limited to a small decline in his chess ability.

His case is surprising but also surprisingly typical. Individuals who lead active intellectual lives seem to be protected against the mental decline typically associated with age. Indeed, research has shown that individuals who are educated, have high IQs, and remain mentally engaged in complex tasks tend to cope better with a variety of assaults to the brain, including Alzheimer disease, stroke, head injury, and even poisoning with neurotoxins (Melton, 2005). Some research has suggested that an active mental life leads to the accumulation of a "cognitive store"—an emergency stash of mental capacity that allows individuals to avoid the negative effects of harm to the brain.

Yaakov Stern found that among a group of individuals with Alzheimer disease who appeared to be equal in terms of their outward symptoms, those who were more educated were actually suffering from much worse brain damage—yet they were functioning at a level similar to others with relatively less damage (Stern & others, 1992). Stern and his colleagues (2004) have also shown that intellectual pursuits such as playing chess and reading reduce the severity of Alzheimer symptoms. Apparently, a lifetime of mental activity and engagement produces this cognitive reserve that allows the brain to maintain its ability to recruit new neural networks that compensate for damage. These brains are better able to move to a backup plan to maintain the individual's level of functioning (Andel & others, 2005). The clear message from these studies is the importance of building up a cognitive reserve by staying mentally active throughout life. In addition to educational achievement, staying physically active also seems to play a role in maintaining a sharp mind (Kramer, Fabiani, & Colcombe, 2006; Sumic & others, 2007).

Our memories are an intimate way to share a part of ourselves with others, as a grandfather does with his grandchild.

Memory and Everyday Life

Before we leave the science of memory, let's consider the role of memory in shaping meaningful experiences in daily life. Think of the most meaningful event of your life. Clearly, that event is one that you remember, among *all* the things you have experienced in your life. We all have vivid autobiographical memories that stand out as indicators of meaning (such as those studied by Jefferson Singer that were discussed above).

But everyday life is filled with potentially remarkable moments—a beautiful sunrise, a delicious meal prepared just for you, an unexpected telephone call from a friend. Experiencing everyday life in its richness requires us to be available and engaged. Sometimes the daily chores and hassles of life lead us to feel that we are just going through the motions. This sort of mindless living may be a way to survive, but it is unlikely to be a way to thrive. The processes of attention and encoding that we have explored in this chapter suggest that actively engaging in life—investing ourselves in the events of the day (Cantor & Sanderson, 1999)—is the way we can be assured that our life stories are rich and nuanced. That way, when someone asks, "So, tell me about yourself," we have a story to tell.

REVIEW, ASSESS, AND SHARPEN YOUR THINKING

Review

7 **Discuss the multiple functions of memory in human life.**

- Describe the role of autobiographical memory in the experience of identity and social relationships.
- Discuss some strategies involved in maintaining healthy memory function throughout life.
- Explain the relationship among mindful living, memory, and the experience of meaning in life.

Assess

1. **Which of the following is most helpful in retaining memory as we age?**
   A. avoiding challenging tasks
   B. minimizing auditory and visual stimuli
   C. engaging in mentally stimulating tasks
   D. exercise

2. **Which of the following is not a function of autobiographical memory?**
   A. social bonding
   B. learning from experience
   C. identity
   D. structural encoding

3. **Which of the following will likely assist in creating meaningful memories?**
   A. avoiding stress
   B. engaging with the world around you
   C. isolating yourself from others
   D. "going through the motions" of life

Sharpen Your Thinking

Do you know someone who has been affected by Alzheimer disease? If so, how have memory changes influenced the person's life and the lives of his or her loved ones?

1 THE NATURE OF MEMORY

Identify the three processes of memory.

Memory is the retention of information over time through encoding, storage, and retrieval—the three processes involved in memory. Encoding involves getting information into storage, storage consists of retaining information over time, and retrieval involves taking information out of storage.

2 MEMORY ENCODING

Explain how memories are encoded.

Attention

To begin the process of memory encoding, we have to attend to information. Selective attention is a necessary part of encoding. Memory is often negatively influenced by divided attention.

Levels of Processing

Levels of processing theory states that information is processed on a continuum from shallow (sensory or physical features are encoded) to intermediate (labels are attached to stimuli) to deep (the meanings of stimuli and their associations with other stimuli are processed). Deeper processing produces better memory.

Elaboration

Elaboration, the extensiveness of processing at any given level of memory, improves memory.

Imagery

Using imagery, or mental pictures, as a context for information can improve memory.

3 MEMORY STORAGE

Discuss how memories are stored.

Sensory Memory

The Atkinson-Shiffrin theory describes memory as a three-stage process: sensory memory, short-term memory, and long-term memory. Sensory memory holds perceptions of the world for only an instant, not much longer than the brief time the person is exposed to visual, auditory, and other sensory input. Visual sensory memory (iconic memory) retains information about one-fourth of a second; auditory sensory memory (echoic memory), for several seconds.

Short-Term Memory

Short-term memory is a limited-capacity memory system in which information is usually retained for as long as 30 seconds. Short-term memory's limitation is 7 ± 2 bits of information. Chunking and rehearsal can benefit short-term memory. Baddeley's concept of working memory characterizes short-term memory as more active and complex than Atkinson and Shiffrin proposed. Baddeley's model of working memory has three components: a central executive and two assistants (phonological loop and visuospatial working memory).

Long-Term Memory

Long-term memory is a relatively permanent type of memory that holds huge amounts of information for a long period of time. Long-term memory can be divided into two main subtypes: explicit and implicit memory. Explicit memory is the conscious recollection of information, such as specific facts or events. Implicit memory affects behavior through prior experiences that are not consciously recollected. Explicit memory has two dimensions. One dimension includes episodic memory and semantic memory. The other dimension includes retrospective memory and prospective memory. Implicit memory is multidimensional, too. It includes systems for procedural memory, priming, and classical conditioning.

4 MEMORY RETRIEVAL

Summarize how memories are retrieved.

Serial Position Effect

The serial position effect is the tendency for items at the beginning and the end of a list to be remembered better than items in the middle of a list. The primacy effect refers to better recall for items at the beginning of the list. The recency effect refers to better memory for items at the end of a list.

Retrieval Cues and the Retrieval Task

Memory retrieval is easier when effective cues are present. Another factor in effective retrieval is the nature of the retrieval task. Simple recognition of previously remembered information in the presence of cues is generally easier than recall of the information. The encoding specificity principle states that information present at the time of encoding or learning tends to be effective as a retrieval cue. In many instances, people recall information better when they attempt to recall it in the same context or internal state in which they learned the information. These processes are referred to as context-dependent and state-dependent memory, respectively. Retrieval also benefits from priming, which activates particular connections or associations in memory. The tip-of-the-tongue phenomenon occurs when we cannot quite pull something out of memory.

Special Cases of Retrieval

Five special cases of retrieval are autobiographical memory, emotional memory, memory for trauma, repressed memory, and eyewitness testimony. Autobiographical memory is a person's recollections of his or her life experiences. Autobiographical memory has three levels: (1) life time periods, (2) general events, and (3) event-specific knowledge. Biographies of the self connect the past and the present to form our identity. Emotional memories may be especially vivid and enduring. Particularly significant emotional memories, known as flashbulb memories, capture emotionally significant events that people often recall with more accuracy and vivid imagery than they do everyday events. Memory for personal trauma also is usually more accurate than memory for ordinary events, but it, too, is subject to distortion and inaccuracy. People tend to remember the core information about a personal trauma but might distort some of the details. Personal trauma can cause individuals to repress emotionally laden information so that it is not accessible to consciousness. Repression does not erase a memory; it just makes it far more difficult to retrieve. Eyewitness testimony may contain errors due to memory decay or bias. Wording of questions and lineup instructions are examples of circumstances that influence eyewitness testimony.

5 FORGETTING

Describe how the failure of encoding and retrieval are involved in forgetting.

Encoding Failure

Encoding failure is forgetting information that was never entered into long-term memory.

SUMMARY

Retrieval Failure

Retrieval failure can occur for at least four reasons. Interference theory states that we forget not because memories are lost from storage but because other information gets in the way of what we want to remember. Interference can be proactive or retroactive. Decay theory states that when something new is learned, a neurochemical memory trace is formed, but over time this chemical trail tends to disintegrate; the term for the phenomenon of memories fading with the passage of time is *transience*. Motivated forgetting, which occurs when people want to forget something, is common when a memory becomes painful or anxiety-laden, as in the case of emotional traumas such as rape and physical abuse. Amnesia, the physiologically based loss of memory, can be anterograde, affecting the retention of new information or events; retrograde, affecting memories of the past but not new events; or both.

6 STUDY TIPS FROM THE SCIENCE OF MEMORY

Evaluate study strategies based on an understanding of memory.

Encoding, Rehearsal, and Retrieval of Course Material

Effective encoding strategies when studying include being a good time manager and planner, paying attention and minimizing distraction, understanding the material rather than relying on rote memorization, asking yourself questions, and taking good notes. Research on memory suggests that the best way to remember course material is to relate it to many different aspects of your life.

Mnemonic Strategies

Effective mnemonic strategies for remembering and retrieving course material include the method of loci, the keyword method, and the use of acronyms to remember lists.

7 MEMORY AND HEALTH AND WELLNESS

Discuss the multiple functions of memory in human life.

The Vital Role of Autobiographical Memory

Autobiographical memories, particularly self-defining memories, play a significant role in identity and social relationships. Our self-defining memories provide a unique source of identity, and sharing those memories with others plays a role in social bonding.

Memory and Aging

Engaging in challenging cognitive tasks throughout life can stave off the effects of age on memory and lessen the effects of Alzheimer disease.

Memory and Everyday Life

Engaging in everyday life means living memorably. Mindfulness to life events provides a rich resource of experiences upon which to build a storehouse of autobiographical memory.

Key Terms

memory, p. 304
encoding, p. 305
levels of processing, p. 306
elaboration, p. 307
storage, p. 309
Atkinson-Shiffrin theory, p. 309
sensory memory, p. 310
short-term memory, p. 311
working memory, p. 312
long-term memory, p. 313

explicit memory (declarative memory), p. 314
episodic memory, p. 314
semantic memory, p. 315
implicit memory (nondeclarative memory), p. 315
procedural memory, p. 315
priming, p. 316
schema, p. 318
script, p. 319

connectionism (parallel distributed processing [PDP]), p. 319
retrieval, p. 323
serial position effect, p. 324
autobiographical memory, p. 326
flashbulb memory, p. 328
motivated forgetting, p. 329
interference theory, p. 334
proactive interference, p. 334
retroactive interference, p. 334

decay theory, p. 335
tip-of-the-tongue phenomenon (TOT state), p. 335
retrospective memory, p. 335
prospective memory, p. 335
amnesia, p. 337
anterograde amnesia, p. 337
retrograde amnesia, p. 337
mnemonics, p. 339

Assess Your Knowledge

1. On average, what is the limit of memory span?
   A. 4–5 items
   B. 5–7 items
   C. 5–9 items
   D. 9–11 items

2. Which part of working memory stores information about speech?
   A. central executive
   B. phonological loop
   C. visuospatial working memory
   D. iconic memory

3. Atkinson and Shiffrin divide memory storage into three systems. Which of the following is not one of those systems?
   A. long-term memory
   B. sensory memory
   C. working memory
   D. short-term memory

4. Which of the following is an example of semantic memory?
   A. remembering how to ride a bike
   B. remembering your first kiss
   C. remembering how to type the letter "T" on a keyboard without looking
   D. remembering who Harriet Tubman was

5. To what does the term *permastore* refer?

   A. the seemingly endless capacity of memory
   B. problems with recall of information stored in long-term memory
   C. memories that will never be forgotten
   D. the movement of information from working memory to long-term memory

6. _____ is a type of explicit memory, whereas _____ is a type of implicit memory.

   A. Procedural memory, semantic memory
   B. Semantic memory, procedural memory
   C. Semantic memory, episodic memory
   D. Episodic memory, semantic memory

7. Which of the following statements is true?

   A. Recall is best for items presented at the beginning of a list.
   B. Recall is usually best for items presented at the end of a list.
   C. Recall is usually best for items presented in the middle of a list.
   D. Recall is best for items presented either at the beginning or end of a list.

8. Someone who has forgotten where they grew up is experiencing

   A. anterograde amnesia.
   B. retrograde amnesia.
   C. brain damage.
   D. the tip-of-the-tongue phenomenon.

9. Labeling an object is an example of

   A. processing at the shallow level.
   B. processing at the intermediate level.
   C. processing at the deepest level.
   D. elaboration.

10. Auditory memory is known as _____, whereas visual memory is known as _____.

    A. short-term memory, long-term memory
    B. long-term memory, short-term memory
    C. iconic memory, echoic memory
    D. echoic memory, iconic memory

11. Long-term potentiation refers to

    A. items in long-term memory being remembered better.
    B. the length of elaboration.
    C. the development of schemas.
    D. strengthened connections between neurons.

12. Answering a multiple-choice question on an exam requires what type of memory retrieval?

    A. autobiographical memory
    B. context-dependent memory
    C. recall
    D. recognition

13. Which of the following is true about decay theory?

    A. Memory becomes worse as we age because of cognitive decline.
    B. Memory lessens over time because the memory trace begins to disappear.
    C. Memory is worse for items learned at the beginning of a list.
    D. Memory problems occur because new learned information gets in the way of recall.

14. Taking the first letter of a list of items and making a word out of those first letters is an example of

    A. the mnemonic device of acronyms.
    B. the mnemonic device of keywords.
    C. the mnemonic device of transience.
    D. the mnemonic device of method of loci.

15. Which of the following is a function of autobiographic memory?

    A. transience
    B. identity
    C. motivated forgetting
    D. flashbulb memory

Go to Appendix B for answers to these questions.

Apply Your Knowledge

1. Some people believe that they have memories from past lives stored in their brain. Consider each of the ways the brain may store memory. Are any of these compatible with memories from past lives?

2. It is sometimes difficult to believe that our memories are not as accurate as we think. To test your ability to be a good eyewitness, visit one of the following websites:

   http://www.pbs.org/wgbh/pages/frontline/shows/dna/

   http://www.psychology.iastate.edu/faculty/gwells/ theeyewitnesstest.html

   Did this exercise change your opinion of the accuracy of eyewitness testimony?

3. Think about the serial position effect. What does it s about how you should organize your study time? When should you study information you think is most important?

4. For 1 week, keep a diary of the most memorable events of your day. Review the list at the end of the week. Do you still remember those events? Are they mostly negative or positive? What aspects of your life seem to be most memorable to you? What are some domains of life where you might work on being more "mindful"?

CHAPTER 9

THINKING, INTELLIGENCE, AND LANGUAGE

Experiencing Psychology

FROM ALARM CLOCKS TO TOILET PAPER

Going about our daily lives, we rarely think about how much our everyday existence depends on the great ideas of others. Yet in our morning routine alone, we are surrounded with evidence of other people's genius. How did you wake up this morning? If you used an alarm clock, you owe gratitude to Levi Hutchins, a 26-year-old clockmaker who in 1787 resolved to rise at 4 A.M. every morning. He invented the alarm clock (although he never bothered to patent or mass-produce it; rather, he was satisfied simply with never oversleeping). Did you make a cup of coffee? Then a moment of thanks to Melitta Bentz may be in order. She was the German housewife who patented the coffee filter in 1908. Did you turn on a light switch? Work on a computer? Make a phone call? Sit in an air-conditioned room? Use toilet paper?

If you answered yes to these questions, a host of famous and not-so-famous great minds played crucial roles in your life this morning (including Humphry Davy, Thomas Alva Edison, Stanley Mazor, Alexander Graham Bell, Willis Haviland Carrier, and Joseph Coyetty—who in 1857 invented toilet paper). These examples vividly show how human ingenuity touches us at almost every turn.

What we think of as the necessities of modern living started out as someone's idea—an individual's curiosity and questioning about how things work and how they could work better. Bill Bowerman, the inventor of Nike shoes, asked, "What happens if I pour rubber over a waffle iron?" Masaru Ibuka, Sony's founder and longtime chief advisor and the inspiration for the Walkman and the iPod, asked, "Why don't we remove the recording function and speaker from the portable music player and put the headphones directly on the player?" These questions and the ideas they spawned were ridiculed at first. Ibuka was told that the Walkman would never sell: "A player without speakers—you must be crazy!" The critics' skepticism aside, these dramatic inventions started with mental processes. They were physical expressions of critical thinking—of looking at the status quo, realizing that it could be improved, and devising creative solutions. Of course, seeing a project through also depends on the power of ideas, as well as on the confidence that even a very unusual dream could change the world.

PREVIEW

Cognitive psychology is the study of such mental processes—of forming ideas, solving problems, and making decisions. In this chapter we investigate the basic cognitive processes of thinking, problem solving, reasoning, and decision making. We review two capacities associated with superior problem solving: critical thinking and creativity. We examine what intelligence is and how differences in intelligence can influence the quality of thought processes. We then explore the unique contribution of language to our mental processes and end up with a look at the role that thinking and problem solving play in health and wellness.

1 The Cognitive Revolution in Psychology

Describe cognitive psychology and discuss the role of the computer in the development of the field.

Cognitive psychology is a relatively young field, scarcely more than a half-century old. After the first decade of the 1900s, behaviorism had a stranglehold on the thinking processes of experimental psychologists. Recall that behaviorists like B. F. Skinner believed that the human mind is a black box best left to philosophers and that observable behavior is the proper focus of psychology. From a behaviorist perspective, speaking of the mental processes occurring in that dark place between your ears is heresy.

In the 1950s the situation began to change. For one thing, the advent of computers provided a new way to think about the workings of the human mind. If we could "see" what computers were doing internally, maybe we could use our observations to study human mental processes. Indeed, computer science and the idea of artificial intelligence (see below) were key motivators in the birth of the study of human cognition. The first modern computer, developed by John von Neumann in the late 1940s, showed that machines could perform logical operations. In the 1950s, researchers speculated that some mental operations might be modeled by computers, and they believed that such modeling might shed light on how the human mind works (Marcus, 2001).

Cognitive psychologists often use the computer as an analogy to help explain the relation between cognition and the brain (Forsythe, Bernard, & Goldsmith, 2006). The physical brain is described as the computer's hardware; cognition, as its software. Herbert Simon (1969) was among the pioneers in comparing the human mind to computer processing systems. In this analogy, the sensory and perceptual systems provide an "input channel," similar to the way data are entered into the computer (Figure 9.1). As input (information) comes into the mind, mental processes, or operations, act on it, just as the computer's software acts on the data. The transformed input generates information that remains in memory much in the way a computer stores what it has worked on. Finally, the information is retrieved from memory and "printed out" or "displayed" (so to speak) as an overt, observable response.

Computers provide a logical and concrete model of how information is processed in the mind, but the model is perhaps oversimplified. Inanimate computers and human brains function quite differently in some respects (Auyang, 2001). For example, most computers receive information from a human who has already coded the information and removed much of its ambiguity. In contrast, each brain cell, or neuron, can respond to information, often ambiguous, transmitted through sensory receptors such as the eyes and ears.

Computers can do some things better than humans. Computers can perform complex numerical calculations much faster and more accurately than humans could ever hope to (Forouzan, 2007). Computers can also apply and follow rules more consistently and with fewer errors than humans and can represent complex mathematical patterns better than humans.

Mathematician John von Neumann (1903–1957) pioneered in the early development of computers. The fact that his computer could perform logical operations led researchers to imagine that some mental processes might be modeled by computers and that such modeling might shed light on how the human mind functions.

Human

Input

⬇

Brain, mind, cognition (memory, problem solving, reasoning, consciousness)

⬇

Output

Computers

Input

⬇

Hardware and software (memory, operations)

⬇

Output

FIGURE 9.1

Computers and Human Cognition An analogy is commonly drawn between human cognition and the way computers work. The physical brain is analogous to a computer's hardware, and cognition is analogous to a computer's software.

But the brain's extraordinary capabilities will probably not be mimicked completely by computers at any time in the near future. Attempts to use computers to process visual information or spoken language have achieved only limited success in highly specific situations. The human brain also has incredible ability to learn new rules, relationships, concepts, and patterns that it can generalize to novel situations. In comparison, computers are quite limited in their ability to learn and generalize. Although a computer can improve its ability to recognize patterns or use rules of thumb to make decisions, it does not have the means to develop new learning goals. Furthermore, the human mind is aware of itself; the computer is not. Indeed, no computer is likely to approach the richness of human consciousness (McGovern & Baars, 2007; Zelazo, Moscovitch, & Thompson, 2007).

Nonetheless, the computer's role in cognitive psychology continues to increase. An entire scientific field called **artificial intelligence (AI)** is dedicated to creating machines capable of performing activities that require intelligence when they are done by people. AI is especially helpful in tasks requiring speed, persistence, and a vast memory (McDermott, 2007). AI systems also assist in diagnosing medical illnesses and prescribing treatment, examining equipment failures, evaluating loan applicants, and advising students about which courses to take (Lopes & Santos-Victor, 2007; Soltesz & Cohn, 2007).

While new technologies have had a profound impact on cognitive psychology, fertile collaborations with researchers in other social sciences, such as linguistics and anthropology, have demonstrated important processes (such as language) that the behaviorist approach could not explain. It finally became acceptable for psychologists to talk about *thoughts* and *thinking* after all.

By the late 1950s the cognitive revolution was in full swing, and it reached its peak in the 1980s. The term *cognitive psychology* became a label for approaches that sought to explain observable behavior by investigating mental processes and structures that cannot be directly observed (Kellogg, 2007;

artificial intelligence (AI) The science of creating machines capable of performing activities that require intelligence when they are done by people.

Artificial intelligence systems have been used to assist in medical diagnosis and treatment.

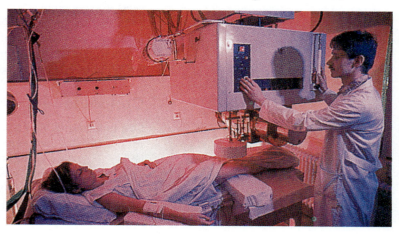

Sternberg, 2007a, 2007b, 2008). Cognitive psychologists study **cognition**—the way in which information is processed and manipulated in remembering, thinking, and knowing. In Chapter 8, we examined the processes involved in memory. We now build on that knowledge by exploring the processes of thinking, problem solving, and decision making.

REVIEW, ASSESS, AND SHARPEN YOUR THINKING

Review

① **Describe cognitive psychology and discuss the role of the computer in the development of the field.**

- Trace how the computer has provided cognitive psychologists a new way to study the human mind, and explain what is meant by artificial intelligence and the cognitive revolution.

Assess

1. **When did the cognitive revolution in psychology begin?**
   A. the 1900s   B. the 1950s
   C. the 1980s   D. the 2000s

2. **Which field of science is concerned with developing machines that mimic intelligent human behavior?**
   A. cognitive science
   B. cognitive neuroscience
   C. artificial intelligence
   D. computer science

3. **A human's _____ is to a computer's _____.**
   A. eye, memory
   B. brain, hardware
   C. cognition, keyboard
   D. memory, software

Sharpen Your Thinking

The advent of computer science and the notion of artificial intelligence helped propel the field of cognitive psychology. Do you think that computers think the way humans do? Why or why not?

2 Thinking

Explain the processes involved in thinking and describe capacities related to superior thinking.

Consider what happens when you finish a project on a computer. When you save the work you have completed, you might hear a little sound from inside the computer—and you know it is processing what you have just done. Unlike a computer, the brain does not make noise to let us know it is working. Rather, the processing that the brain engages is the silent process of thinking. **Thinking** involves manipulating information mentally, such as by forming concepts, solving problems, making decisions, and reflecting in a critical or creative manner.

In this section we probe into the nature of concepts, which are basic components of thinking, and we explore the cognitive processes of problem solving, reasoning, and decision making. We also examine three capacities related to enhanced problem solving: critical thinking, creativity, and expertise.

Concepts

One fundamental aspect of thinking is the notion of concepts. **Concepts** are mental categories that are used to group objects, events, and characteristics. Humans have a special ability for creating categories to help us make sense of information in our world (Grief & others, 2006; Hartman & Stratton-Salib, 2007). We know that apples and oranges are both fruits. We know that poodles and collies are both dogs and that cockroaches and ladybugs are both insects. These items differ from each other in various ways, and yet we recognize that they "belong together" because we have concepts for fruits, dogs, and insects.

cognition The way in which information is processed and manipulated in remembering, thinking, and knowing.

thinking Manipulating information mentally, as when we form concepts, solve problems, make decisions, and reflect in a creative or critical manner.

concepts Mental categories that are used to group objects, events, and characteristics.

Concepts are important for four reasons. First, concepts allow us to generalize. If we did not have concepts, each object and event in our world would be unique and brand new to us each time we encountered it. Second, concepts allow us to associate experiences and objects. Basketball, ice hockey, and track are sports. The concept *sport* gives us a way to compare these activities. Neoclassicism, impressionism, and expressionism are all schools of art. The concept *schools of art* lets us compare paintings by artists from these different schools (Figure 9.2). Third, concepts aid memory, making it more efficient so that we do not have to reinvent the wheel each time we come across a piece of information. Imagine having to think about how to sit in a chair every time you found yourself in front of one. Fourth, concepts provide clues about how to react to a particular object or experience. Perhaps you have had the experience of trying an exotic new cuisine and feeling a bit puzzled as you consider the contents of your plate. If a friend tells you reassuringly, "That's food!" you know that, given the concept *food,* it is okay to dig in.

Two models have been proposed to explain the structure of concepts: the classical model and the prototype model (Medin, Proffitt, & Schwartz, 2000). In the **classical model,** all instances of a concept share defining properties. For example, the concept of triangle requires that a geometric form have three sides, a square requires four equal sides, and so forth. This view of concepts describes the categories of geometric forms well, but it may not be complete. If a concept depends on its defining characteristics, then specifying these characteristics should be straightforward. However, it can be difficult to define the characteristics of even frequently used concepts. For example, "can fly" might seem to be an appropriate defining characteristic of the concept *bird.* However, ostriches and penguins are birds that do not fly.

Another drawback of the classical model is that it cannot explain how people are able to judge some instances of a concept as being more typical than others. For example, apples are considered more typical of the concept *fruit* than are plums, and robins are considered to be more typical of the concept *bird* than are penguins. From the classical perspective, membership in a category is all or nothing, yet these differences seem to imply that some members of a category are more typical than others.

A different theory, the prototype model, addresses this weakness in the classical model. The **prototype model** emphasizes that when people evaluate whether a given item reflects a certain concept, they compare the item with the most typical item(s) in that category and look for a "family resemblance." Birds generally fly, sing, and build nests, but there are exceptions to these properties—we know that a penguin is still a bird, even if it does not do these things. The prototype model maintains that characteristic properties are used to create a representation of the average or ideal member—the prototype—for each concept.

Membership in a concept can be graded rather than all or none (Rosch, 1973). Better members of the concept (such as robins for the concept of bird and apples for the concept of fruit) have more characteristic properties associated with the category than the poorer members of the category (such as penguins and plums and even tomatoes). Potential members of the concept are then compared with this prototype. In evaluating whether something (Jill) belongs in the category (high achievers), we ask ourselves how typical the item is of the category or how similar it is to the prototype. Typicality judgments are in turn related to other variables, such as speed with which an object is put into a category. The prototype model is able to explain these typicality effects (Minda & Smith, 2001).

These two models account for some but not all of the findings regarding the structure of concepts, and each has its proponents (Medin, Lynch, & Solomon, 2000).

Problem Solving

Concepts tell us what we think about but not why we think. Why do we engage in the mental effort of thinking? Consider Levi Hutchins, the ambitious young clockmaker. He wanted to beat the sun up every morning but was faced with a dilemma in accomplishing that goal. **Problem solving** is an attempt to find an appropriate way of attaining a goal when the goal is not readily available. Among the methods for doing so are following the steps required for problem solving, overcoming mental obstacles, and developing expertise.

classical model Model stating that all instances of a concept share defining properties.

prototype model Model emphasizing that when people evaluate whether a given item reflects a certain concept, they compare the item with the most typical item(s) in that category and look for a "family resemblance."

problem solving An attempt to find an appropriate way of attaining a goal when the goal is not readily available.

FIGURE 9.2

The Concept of Schools of Art The concept of schools of art lets us compare paintings by different artists. How do other neoclassicist paintings compare with the one by Michelangelo? How do other impressionist paintings compare with the one by Monet? How do other expressionist paintings compare with the one by Klee?

Monet's Palazzo Da Mula, Venice

Michelangelo's Libyan Sibyl, *Sistine Chapel*

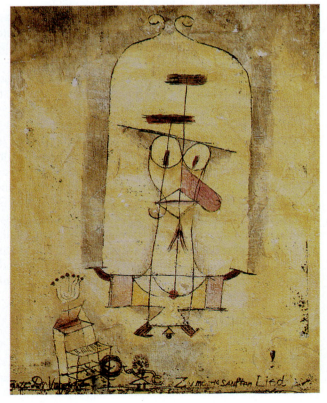

Klee's Dance You Monster to My Soft Song

Steps in Problem Solving Psychological research points to four steps in the problem-solving process:

1. Find and frame problems.
2. Develop good problem-solving strategies.
3. Evaluate solutions.
4. Rethink and redefine problems and solutions over time.

Let's examine how each of these steps contributes to solving problems.

1. Find and Frame Problems Recognizing a problem is the first step toward a solution (Mayer, 2000). Finding and framing problems often involves asking questions in creative ways and seeing what others do not. The positive psychology movement began because some psychologists noticed a lack of research on human strengths (Seligman, 2000).

This aspect of problem solving is difficult to learn. While learning to solve problems might involve doing exercises involving well-defined problems with well-defined steps for solving them, learning to recognize problems is no small accomplishment. Many real-world problems are ill defined or vague and have no clearly defined solutions (Schunk, 2008). The inventors described at the beginning of this chapter saw problems that everyone else was content to live with: Who needed a microcomputer? A telephone? A light bulb? Or toilet paper? The answer is, everyone (at least today), but only these visionaries were able to see a problem that might be solved, where others were simply satisfied with the status quo. Recognizing problems involves being aware of and open to one's experiences (two mental habits we will address later). It also means listening carefully to that voice in your head that occasionally sighs, "There must be a better way."

2. Develop Good Problem-Solving Strategies Once you find a problem and clearly define it, you need to develop strategies for solving it. Among the effective strategies are subgoals, algorithms, and heuristics.

Subgoaling involves setting intermediate goals or defining intermediate problems that put you in a better position for reaching the final goal or solution. Imagine you are writing a paper for a psychology class. What might be some subgoaling strategies for approaching this task? One might be locating the right books and research journals on your chosen topic. At the same time that you are searching for the right publications, you will likely benefit from establishing some subgoals within the time frame you have for completing the project. If the paper is due in 2 months, you might set a subgoal of a first draft of the paper 2 weeks before it is due, another subgoal of completing your reading for the paper 1 month before it is due, and yet another subgoal of starting library research tomorrow. Notice that, in establishing the subgoals for meeting the deadline, we worked backward. Working backward in establishing subgoals is a good strategy. You first create the subgoal that is closest to the final goal and then work backward to the subgoal that is closest to the beginning of the problem-solving effort.

Algorithms are strategies that guarantee a solution to a problem. Algorithms come in different forms, such as formulas, instructions, and the testing of all possible solutions (Allen, Pertea, & Salzberg, 2004; Kawato & Samejima, 2007). We often use algorithms in cooking (by following a recipe) and driving (by following directions to an address).

An algorithmic strategy might take a long time. Sitting in front of a rack of letters in a game of Scrabble, you might find yourself moving the tiles around and trying all possible combinations to make a high-scoring word. Trying every possible combination is one way to solve the problem. However, clearly, the algorithmic strategy of trying out all possible solutions should be applied to problems with a small number of possible solutions.

Instead of using an algorithm to solve this type of problem, you might rely on your basic knowledge of words and language—some rules of thumb about what goes with what. **Heuristics** are shortcut strategies or guidelines that suggest a solution to a problem but do not guarantee an answer (Kozhevnikov, 2007; Rossi & Rossi, 2007). In your Scrabble game, you know that if you have a *q*, you are going to need a *u*. If you have an *x* and a *t*, the

subgoaling Setting intermediate goals or defining intermediate problems in order to be in a better position to reach the final goal or solution.

algorithms Strategies that guarantee a solution to a problem.

heuristics Shortcut strategies or guidelines that suggest, but do not guarantee, a solution to a problem.

fixation Using a prior problem-solving strategy and failing to look at a problem from a fresh, new perspective.

functional fixedness A type of fixation in which individuals fail to solve a problem because they are fixated on a thing's usual functions.

t is probably not going to come right before the *x*. In this situation, heuristics allow us to be more efficient than algorithms would.

In the real world, the types of problems we face are likelier to be solved by heuristics than by algorithms. Heuristics help us narrow down the possible solutions to find the one that works (Moons & Mackie, 2007).

3. Evaluate Solutions Once we think we have solved a problem, we will not know how effective our solution is until we find out if it works. It helps to have in mind a clear criterion for the effectiveness of the solution. For example, what will your criterion be for judging the effectiveness of your solution to the psychology assignment, your psychology paper? Will you judge your solution effective if you simply complete the paper? If you get an *A*? If the instructor says that it is one of the best papers ever turned in on the topic?

4. Rethink and Redefine Problems and Solutions over Time An important final step in problem solving is to rethink and redefine problems continually (Bereiter & Scardamalia, 1993). People who are good problem solvers tend to be more motivated than the average person to improve on their past performances and to make original contributions. Can we make the computer faster and more powerful? Can we make the iPod smaller?

An Obstacle to Problem Solving: Becoming Fixated One of the key ingredients of being a good problem solver is to acknowledge that one does not know everything—that one's strategies and conclusions are always open to revision. In a sense, optimal problem solving may require that a person have a certain amount of humility, or the ability to admit that one is not perfect and that there may be better ways than one's tried and true methods to solve life's problems.

It is easy to fall into the trap of becoming fixated on a particular strategy for solving a problem. **Fixation** involves using a prior strategy and failing to look at a problem from a fresh, new perspective. For instance, **functional fixedness** occurs when individuals fail to solve a problem because they are fixated on a thing's usual functions. If you have ever used a shoe to hammer a nail, you have overcome functional fixedness to solve a problem.

An example of a problem that requires overcoming functional fixedness is the Maier string problem, which is depicted in Figure 9.3 (Maier, 1931). The problem is to figure out how to tie two strings together when you must stand in one spot and cannot reach both at the same time. It seems as though you are stuck, but there is a pair of pliers on a table. Can you solve the problem?

The solution is to use the pliers as a weight, tying them to the end of one string (Figure 9.4). Swing this string back and forth like a pendulum and grasp the stationary string.

FIGURE 9.3

Maier String Problem How can you tie the two strings together if you cannot reach them both at the same time?

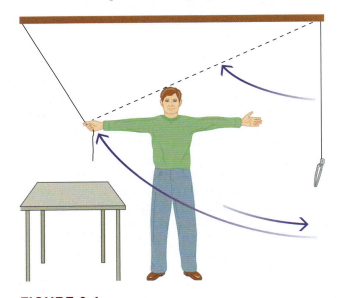

FIGURE 9.4

Solution to the Maier String Problem Use the pliers as a weight to create a pendulum motion that brings the second string closer.

The Candle Problem
How would you mount a candle on a wall so that it won't drip wax on a table or a floor while it is burning?

The Nine-Dot Problem
Take out a piece of paper and copy the arrangement of dots shown below. Without lifting your pencil, connect the dots using only four straight lines.

The Six-Matchstick Problem
Arrange six matchsticks of equal length to make four equilateral triangles, the sides of which are one matchstick long.

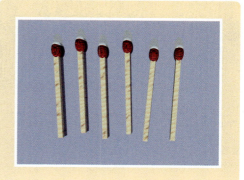

Solutions to the problems are presented at the end of the chapter on page 357.

FIGURE 9.5

Examples of How Fixation Impedes Problem Solving These tasks help psychologists measure creative problem solving.

Your past experience with pliers and fixation on their usual function makes this a difficult problem to solve. To solve the problem, you need to find an unusual use for the pliers—in this case, as a weight to create a pendulum.

Effective problem solving often necessitates trying something new or thinking outside the box. This might require admitting that one's past strategies were not ideal or do not readily translate to a particular situation. Students who are used to succeeding in high school by cramming for tests and relying on parental pressure to get homework done may find that in college these strategies are no longer viable ways to succeed.

To explore how fixation might be involved in your own problem solving, see Figure 9.5.

Reasoning and Decision Making

In addition to forming concepts and solving problems, thinking includes the higher-order mental processes of reasoning and decision making. These activities require rich connections among neurons and the ability to apply judgment. The end result of this type of thinking is an evaluation, a conclusion, or a decision.

Reasoning   **Reasoning** is the mental activity of transforming information to reach conclusions. Reasoning is involved in problem solving and decision making. It is a skill closely tied to critical thinking (Decker, Hill, & Dean, 2007; Risen & Gilovich, 2006). Reasoning can be either inductive or deductive (Figure 9.6). **Inductive reasoning,** which is driven by incoming data, involves reasoning from the specific to the general or from the bottom-up (Tenenbaum, Griffiths, & Kemp, 2006). That is, it consists of drawing conclusions (forming concepts) about all members of a category based on observing only some members. For example, in a literature class after reading a few of Shakespeare's plays, you might draw some likely conclusions about his general ways of using language. Psychological research is often inductive as well, studying a sample of participants in order to draw conclusions about the population from which the sample is drawn.

In contrast, **deductive reasoning** is reasoning from the general to the specific (Shynkaruk & Thompson, 2006; Witteman & others, 2007). The fictional British detective Sherlock Holmes was a master at deductive reasoning. When solving a case, he sorted through a number of clues to zero in on the one correct solution to a crime. When psychologists and other scientists use theories and intuitions to make predictions and then evaluate their predictions by making further observations, deductive reasoning is at work.

reasoning The mental activity of transforming information to reach conclusions.

inductive reasoning Reasoning from the specific to the general or from the bottom-up.

deductive reasoning Reasoning from the general to the specific.

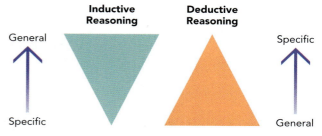

FIGURE 9.6

Inductive and Deductive Reasoning (*Left*) The upside-down pyramid represents inductive reasoning—going from specific to general. (*Right*) The right-side-up pyramid represents deductive reasoning—going from general to specific.

*"You take all the time you need, Larry—this certainly
is a big decision."*

Deductive reasoning is always certain in the sense that, if the initial rules or assumptions are true, the conclusion will follow directly as a matter of logic. When psychologists develop a hypothesis from a theory, they are using a form of deductive reasoning, because the hypothesis is a specific, logical extension of the general theory. And if the theory is true, then the hypothesis will be true as well.

Decision Making Think of all the decisions you have to make in your life. Should I major in biology, psychology, or business? Should I go to graduate school right after college or get a job first? Should I establish myself in a career before settling down to have a family? Should I buy a house or rent? Do I want fries with that? **Decision making** involves evaluating alternatives and choosing among them.

In inductive reasoning, people use established rules to draw conclusions. In contrast, when we make decisions, such rules are not established, and we do not know the consequences of the decisions (L. Cox, 2007; Edwards, Miles, & von Winterfeldt, 2007). Some of the information might be missing, and we might not trust all of the information we have.

New Directions in Research: Decision Making Without Awareness Cognitive psychology is about mental processes, and many of the ones we have considered so far are part of conscious awareness. But there is evidence that reasoning and decision making can occur outside of conscious awareness. That is, sometimes we can be thinking without knowing it (Dijksterhuis & Nordgren, 2006). Indeed, some very important information processing can be going on in your brain without your realizing it is happening.

No doubt you have had the experience of consciously grappling with a problem and spending a good deal of time trying to solve it, with no success. Then you take a break to chat with a friend, listen to music, or go running, and suddenly the solution just pops into your head. Recent research by Ap Dijksterhuis and colleagues might ring a bell for you (2006). In a series of studies, the researchers asked people to make decisions or approached people who were making decisions. In their laboratory studies, participants were given complex problems to solve after a few minutes of thought. But half of the participants were distracted during the thinking period and were not permitted to concentrate consciously on the problems. The results showed that those who were distracted performed better than those who were allowed to think the problems through consciously.

Approaching people who were facing important purchases, Dijksterhuis and colleagues found that when a person is making a complex decision, approaching the decision in a consciously deliberative rational fashion is not always wise. Indeed, when selecting among complex products (for example, expensive items such as cars and furniture), those who engaged in the least conscious thinking selected better products (based on objective measures) and were more satisfied with their purchases. Dijksterhuis and colleagues concluded that for small problems, conscious thought is fine, but in complex decision making, sometimes it just might be best to sleep on it.

Problems in Decision Making: Biases and Flawed Heuristics Another fruitful subject of decision-making research is the biases and flawed heuristics (rules of thumb) that affect the quality of decisions. In many cases, our decision-making strategies are well adapted to deal with a variety of problems (Nisbett & Ross, 1980). However, we are prone to make a number of mistakes in our thinking (Stanovich, 2007). Here we review some specific biases and heuristics that might lead to such mistakes.

Confirmation bias is the tendency to search for and use information that supports our ideas rather than refutes them (McKenzie, 2006). Our decisions can also become further biased because we tend to seek out and listen to people whose views confirm our own and tend to avoid those who have dissenting views.

decision making Evaluating alternatives and
making choices among them.

confirmation bias The tendency to search for
and use information that supports, rather than
refutes, our ideas.

It is easy to detect the confirmation bias in the way that many people think. Consider politicians. They often accept news that supports their views and dismiss evidence that runs counter to their views. Also consider physicians who misdiagnose a patient because one or two symptoms fit with previous successful diagnoses they have made. In their desire to confirm their diagnosis, they ignore symptoms that do not fit their diagnosis. Avoiding confirmation bias means applying the same rigorous analysis to both sides of an argument.

Hindsight bias is our tendency to report falsely, after the fact, that we accurately predicted an outcome. It is sometimes referred to as the "I knew it all along effect." With this type of bias, people tend to view events that have happened as more predictable than they were and to misremember themselves as being more accurate in their predictions than they actually were (Roese & others, 2006). Hindsight bias sometimes comes into play in critiques of psychological findings. For example, in reading the results of a study indicating that money is not strongly related to happiness, a person might say, "I always knew that!" (Myers & Diener, 1995).

Recall that heuristics are rules of thumb that suggest a solution but do not ensure that it will work. Sometimes heuristics can lead to mistakes. The **availability heuristic** refers to a prediction about the probability of an event based on the ease of recalling or imagining similar events (Keller, Siegrist, & Gutscher, 2006). An example of an error that involves this heuristic is the stereotype of the tortured creative genius. Examples of tortured creative geniuses tend to be vividly present in our memory. Artist Vincent van Gogh, writers Virginia Woolf and William Faulkner, and poet Sylvia Plath all had emotional problems. Yet despite the ease with which these individuals might come to mind, they are the exception rather than the rule; in general, researchers have found no relation between genius and mental disorder. Recent studies support the conclusion that gifted people tend to be more mature and have fewer emotional problems than others, and they are likely to have grown up in a positive family climate (Kaufman & Sternberg, 2007).

To be effective thinkers who solve problems efficiently and accurately and who make sound, satisfying decisions, we must think in particular ways. As the Intersection explores, our current mood is a variable that might potentially have a role in determining whether we think through problems and choices well or poorly.

Thinking Critically and Creatively

Problem solving and decision making are basic cognitive processes that we engage in multiple times each day. Certain strategies lead to better solutions and choices than others, and some people are particularly good at these cognitive exercises. Here we examine two skills associated with superior problem solving: critical thinking and creativity.

Critical Thinking   In Chapter 1, we defined *critical thinking* as thinking reflectively and productively and evaluating the evidence. People who think critically grasp the deeper meaning of ideas, keep an open mind about different approaches and perspectives, and decide for themselves what to believe or do (Sternberg, Roediger, & Halpern, 2007). Like effective problem solving, critical thinking requires that individuals maintain a sense of humility about what they know. It means being open to questioning long-held assumptions and being motivated to see past the obvious.

Critical thinking is vital to effective problem solving. However, few schools teach students to think critically and to develop a deep understanding of concepts (Brooks & Brooks, 2001). Instead, especially with the pressure to maximize students' scores on standardized tests, schools spend too much time on getting students to give a single correct answer in an imitative way rather than encouraging new ideas (Bransford & others, 2006). Too often, teachers ask students to recite, define, describe, state, and list rather than to analyze, infer, connect, synthesize, criticize, create, evaluate, think, and rethink. Too often in the culture at large, we are inclined to stay on the surface of problems rather than to stretch our minds. The cultivation of two mental habits is essential to critical thinking: mindfulness and open-mindedness.

hindsight bias The tendency to report falsely, after the fact, that we accurately predicted an outcome.

availability heuristic A prediction about the probability of an event based on the ease of recalling or imagining similar events.

Emotion and Cognition: How Are You Feeling and Thinking Today?

Do you have to get into a bad mood to be good at math? Studies on the relationship between mood and thinking might lead you to think so. Researchers have examined the ways that our moods influence the way we think (Blanchette & others, 2007; Chuang, 2007; Phelps, 2006). Negative moods and positive moods have been shown to relate to two different styles of problem solving and decision making.

Negative moods are associated with narrow, analytical thinking (Clore, Gasper, & Garvin, 2001). People who are feeling crabby are less likely to use the heuristic shortcuts we examined earlier in this chapter (Isbell, 2004) and are more likely instead to think problems through carefully, reaching conclusions based on logic. In contrast, historically, research has shown that positive moods are related to using heuristic shortcuts and to making errors such as those described in the chapter. Researchers have explained these results in two ways. First, it was suggested that positive moods set off a series of associations with diverse material in memory so that the person is unable to think about the problem at hand (Mackie & Worth, 1989). Second, it was proposed that happy people are simply too busy maintaining their positive mood to stop and think about the problem at hand (Wegener, Petty, & Smith, 1995). In a way, this research led to a portrait of the happy person as, well, a bit dim. Under the influence of positive mood, people just could not be expected to think very much or very clearly.

The problem with these generalizations is that they have trouble explaining why *most* people are, in fact, pretty happy (Diener & Diener, 1996). Why would humans have evolved to value and seek out an affective state that is associated with being mindless? Surely, positive moods must have some value.

Social psychologist Alice Isen pioneered in the study of the adaptive effects of positive mood on cognition. In the early 1970s, when no one else was interested in the potential cognitive and social benefits of positive moods, Isen began a program of research that changed the way psychologists think about the role of positive emotional experience in thinking and behaving. In her lab, she found ways to make people happy—by offering refreshments, cookies, money, and showing funny movies—and she probed into what the effects of positive mood would be on a variety of outcomes. At first she examined helping behavior (Isen & Levin, 1972), but eventually she turned to the effects of positive feelings on the way people think. Over the years, Isen has found strong evidence for the role of positive mood in creativity, originality, and efficient thinking. In a good mood, people are likely to be more cognitively flexible and to be more creative in their concept formations and structures (Compton & others, 2004; Isen, 2001, 2004). Positive moods are related to enhanced creative problem solving (Isen, 1984; Isen & Daubman, 1984; Gasper, 2004). Positive moods

allow us to be better brainstormers—to come up with more ideas in response to a task and to be more open to all of the fantastic or crazy possibilities we think of (Gasper, 2004).

In contrast to previous research showing positive moods to relate to mindlessness, Isen (2004) found that a positive mood makes people more likely to engage in thoughtful responsiveness to situations (by taking relevant information into account) and to learn from new experiences. A significant problem with past research was that it focused on activities that were generally meaningless to the participants. For people in a good mood, superior performance has been found for tasks that are personally relevant (Forgas, 2001). Given a personally relevant task, happy people are decidedly more efficient than their unhappy counterparts—they wisely use heuristics that speed them to the right answer (Lyubomirsky, King, & Diener, 2005). In one study, happy doctors were likelier to come to the appropriate diagnosis more quickly than unhappy doctors (Estrada, Isen, & Young, 1997). Happy people, compared to unhappy individuals, are better able to ignore unimportant information (Isen & Means, 1983).

Happy moods allow us to be more efficient at settling on a satisfying choice, while unhappy moods leave us lost in thought in the juice aisle.

The tendency for people to engage in narrow, analytical thinking when they are in a bad mood may be particularly

problematic in today's world, where we face a multitude of choices for just about every decision—from the kind of orange juice we buy to the kind of college we attend. Happy moods allow us to be more efficient at settling on a satisfying choice, while unhappy moods leave us lost in thought in the juice aisle (Schwartz & others, 2002). Although heuristics can sometimes lead us to mistakes, they also maximize efficiency; we are likely to reach the answer sooner. And efficiency matters in the fast-paced real world.

Research has also examined how moods influence what some psychologists refer to as our level of focus—the extent to which we focus on the details or on the "big picture." Negative moods foster a narrow or local mindset. Positive moods foster a global perspective—that is, when we are in a good mood, we are likelier to appreciate the big picture, to see the forest for the trees (Gasper & Clore, 2002).

When we face a problem, our moods may stimulate different kinds of thinking. It may be that a negative mood is required before we can fully tap into our analytical abilities and that a positive mood fosters creative association, unusual and unique thoughts, and a sense of the big picture. While a negative mood may facilitate the search for an answer, a positive mood allows us to take a break from trying, to enjoy the moment, and potentially to see the right answer staring us in the face.

Mindfulness means being alert and mentally present for one's everyday activities. The mindful person maintains an active awareness of the circumstances of his or her life. According to Ellen Langer (1997, 2000, 2005; Langer & Moldoveanu, 2000), mindfulness is a key to critical thinking. Langer distinguishes mindful behavior from mindless behaviors—the automatic activities we engage in without thought. In a classic study, Langer (Langer, Blank, & Chanowitz, 1978) found that people (as many as 90 percent) would mindlessly give up their place in line for a copy machine when someone asked, "Can I go first? I need to make copies" as compared to when the same person simply said, "Can I go first?" (just 60 percent) (Langer, Blank, & Chanowitz, 1978). For the mindless persons in the study, even a completely meaningless justification—after all, everyone in line was there to make copies—was reason enough to step aside.

A mindful person creates new ideas, is open to new information, and is aware of more than one perspective, whereas a mindless person is entrapped in old ideas, engages in automatic behavior, and operates from a single perspective.

Open-mindedness means being receptive to other ways of looking at things. People often do not even know that there is another side to an issue or evidence contrary to what they believe (Slife & Yanchar, 2000). Simple openness to other viewpoints can help to keep people from jumping to conclusions. As Socrates once said, such caution in thinking—that is, knowing what it is you do not know—is sometimes the first step to true wisdom. Sometimes humility is a requirement of truly effective problem solving.

Being mindful may take effort, and maintaining an open mind may be a challenge. Indeed, these two mental habits may at times be more difficult than the alternative of simply going through life on automatic pilot. Yet critical thinking is valuable because it allows us better to predict the future, to evaluate situations objectively, and to make appropriate changes. One might go so far as to say that critical thinking requires a certain amount of courage. When we expose ourselves to a broad range of perspectives, we risk finding out that our assumptions might be wrong. When we engage our critical minds, we may discover problems, but we are also more likely to have opportunities to make positive changes.

Creative Thinking　In addition to thinking critically, coming up with the best solution to a problem may involve thinking creatively. The word *creative* can apply to an activity or a person, and creativity as a process may be open to even those who do not think of themselves as creative. When we talk about **creativity** as a characteristic of a person, we are referring to the ability to think about something in novel and unusual ways and to come up with unconventional solutions to problems (Abraham & Windmann, 2007; Ward, 2007).

Creative people tend to be divergent thinkers (Guilford, 1967). **Divergent thinking** produces many answers to the same question. In contrast, the kind of thinking required on conventional intelligence tests is **convergent thinking.** For example, a typical item on an intelligence test is "How many quarters will you get in return for 60 dimes?" There is only one correct answer to this question. However, the following question has many possible answers: "What image comes to mind when you hear the phrase 'sitting alone in a dark room'?"

Along with being divergent thinkers, creative individuals have been described as showing the following characteristics (Perkins, 1994).

I want to learn to live in the moment... Just not *this* moment. Some other moment. Like a moment on the beach.

© CartoonStock.com

mindfulness Being alert and mentally present for one's everyday activities.

open-mindedness Being receptive to the possibility of other ways of looking at things.

creativity The ability to think about something in novel and unusual ways and come up with unconventional solutions to problems.

divergent thinking Thinking that produces many answers to the same question; characteristic of creativity.

convergent thinking Thinking that produces one correct answer; characteristic of the type of thinking required on traditional intelligence tests.

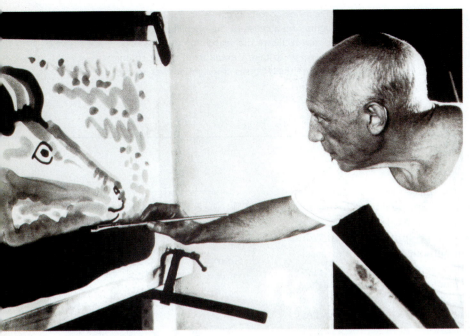

One characteristic of creative individuals such as the late artist Pablo Picasso is a willingness to take risks and to make mistakes.

- *Flexibility and playful thinking:* Creative thinkers are flexible and play with problems, and this trait gives rise to a paradox: Although creativity takes hard work, the work goes more smoothly if it is taken lightly. In a way, humor greases the wheels of creativity (Goleman, Kaufman, & Ray, 1993). When you are joking around, you are more likely to consider any possibility. Having fun helps to disarm the inner censor that can condemn your ideas as off base. *Brainstorming* is a technique in which members of a group are encouraged to come up with as many ideas as possible, play off one another's ideas, and say practically whatever comes to mind. Individuals usually avoid criticizing others' ideas until the end of the session.

- *Inner motivation:* Creative people often are motivated by the joy of creating. They tend to be less inspired than less creative people by grades, money, or favorable feedback from others. Thus, creative people are motivated more internally than externally.

- *Willingness to face risk:* Creative people make more mistakes than their less imaginative counterparts. It is not that they are less proficient but that they come up with more ideas and more possibilities. They win some; they lose some. For example, the twentieth-century Spanish artist Pablo Picasso created more than 20,000 paintings, but not all of them were masterpieces. Creative thinkers learn to cope with unsuccessful projects and see failure as an opportunity to learn.

- *Objective evaluation of work.* Despite the stereotype that creative people are eccentric and highly subjective, most creative thinkers strive to evaluate their work objectively. They may use an established set of criteria to make judgments or rely on the judgments of respected, trusted others. In this manner, they can determine whether further creative thinking will improve their work.

The word *creative* applies not only to people but also to activities. Even individuals who do not think of themselves as creative can engage in creative thinking. Just as problem solving itself is understood as occurring over a series of steps, so is the creative process. Coming up with a creative solution to a problem has been described as a five-step sequence:

1. *Preparation:* You become immersed in a problem or an issue that interests you and arouses your curiosity.

2. *Incubation:* You churn ideas around in your head. This is the point at which you are likely to make some unusual connections in your thinking.

3. *Insight:* At this point, you experience the "Aha!" moment, when all the pieces of the puzzle seem to fit together.

4. *Evaluation:* Now you must decide whether the idea is valuable and worth pursuing. Is the idea really novel, or is it obvious?

5. *Elaboration:* This final step often covers the longest span of time and the hardest work. This is what the famous twentieth-century American inventor Thomas Edison was talking about when he said that creativity is 1 percent inspiration and 99 percent perspiration. Elaboration may require a great deal of perspiration.

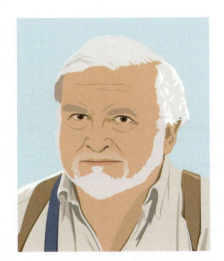

The research of Mihaly Csikszentmihalyi (1934–) focuses on areas such as creativity and innovation. He is perhaps best known for developing the concept of flow—a state of focused attention wherein an individual is completely immersed in and thus "at one with" an activity.

Mihaly Csikszentmihalyi (1996; his last name is pronounced chick-zent-mee-high, but if you ever meet him, you can call him "Mike") believes that this five-step sequence provides a helpful framework for thinking about how creative ideas are formed and developed. However, he argues that creative people do not always go through the steps in a linear

PSYCHOLOGY AND LIFE

Living a More Creative Life

Csikszentmihalyi (1996) interviewed 90 leading figures in art, business, government, education, and science to learn how creativity works. He discovered that creative people regularly take on challenges that absorb them. Based on his interviews with some of the most creative people in the world, he concluded that the first step toward a more creative life is to cultivate your curiosity and interest. Following are his recommendations for doing so:

• *Try to be surprised by something every day.* Maybe it is something you see, hear, or read about. Become absorbed in a lecture or a book. Be open to what the world is telling you. Life is a stream of experiences. Swim widely and deeply in it, and your life will be richer.

• *Try to surprise at least one person every day.* In many things you do, you have to be predictable and patterned. Do something different. Ask a question you normally would not ask. Invite someone to go to a show or to a museum you have never visited.

• *Write down each day what surprised you and how you surprised others.* Most creative people keep a diary, notes, or lab records to ensure that experiences are not fleeting or forgotten. Start with a specific task. Each evening, record the most surprising event that occurred that day and your most surprising action. After a few days, reread your notes and reflect on your past experiences. After a few weeks, you might see a pattern of interest emerging in your notes, one that might suggest an area you can explore in greater depth.

• *When something sparks your interest, follow it.* Usually when something captures our attention, it is short-lived—an idea, a song, a flower. Too often, we do not explore the idea, song, or flower further or we think these things are not our business because we are not experts on them. However, the world is our business. We cannot know which parts are most interesting until we make a serious effort to learn as much about as many aspects of it as possible.

• *Wake up in the morning with a specific goal to look forward to.* Creative people wake up eager to start the day. Why? Not necessarily because they are cheerful, enthusiastic types but because they know that there is something meaningful to accomplish each day, and they cannot wait to get started.

• *Take charge of your schedule.* Figure out which time of the day is your most creative time. Some of us are more creative late at night; others, early in the morning. Carve out time for yourself when your creative energy is at its best.

• *Spend time in settings that stimulate your creativity.* In Csikszentmihalyi's (1996) research, he gave people an electronic pager and beeped them randomly at different times of the day. When he asked them how they felt, they reported the highest levels of creativity when walking, driving, or swimming. These activities are semiautomatic in that they take only a certain amount of attention, leaving some attention capacity available so that the individual can make connections among ideas. Highly creative people also report coming up with novel ideas in the deeply relaxed state of being half-asleep and half-awake.

How many of the recommendations for living a more creative life do you currently practice? How might you benefit from these suggestions *beyond* becoming more creative?

sequence. For example, elaboration is often interrupted by periods of incubation. Fresh insights also may appear during incubation, evaluation, and elaboration. And in terms of a time frame, insight might last for years, or it might take only a few hours. Sometimes the creative idea consists of one deep insight, and other times a series of small ones. For further insight on Csikszentmihalyi's research and tips on living a more creative life, see the Psychology and Life box.

Stephen J. Hawking is a world-renowned expert in physics who has authored best-selling books such as A Brief History of Time *and* The Universe in a Nutshell. *Experts such as Hawking solve problems differently than novices do because they have a broader knowledge base, better domain-specific memory, and more effective strategies. They also practice more intentionally than novices.*

Expertise

Some people seem to have special skills to solve problems in a particular domain. From chess masters to math whizzes, from spelling bee champions to master chefs: The world is full of people who have a special talent for what they do. We call these individuals experts, and we give the name **expertise** to the particular talent—that "something special"—that characterizes their work.

Researchers are very interested in how experts and novices differ in the way they think and solve problems (Ericsson & others, 2006). Researchers have studied experts and novices in such diverse areas as chess, physics, mathematics, electronics, medicine, squash, and history (Gobet & Charness, 2006; Norman & others, 2006). They have found that experts have acquired extensive knowledge that affects what they pay attention to and how they organize, represent, and interpret information. The way they encode and store information in turn influences their ability to remember, reason, and solve problems (Bransford & others, 2006).

Experts solve problems differently than novices do because they have a broader knowledge base, better domain-specific memory, and more effective strategies (Ericsson & others, 2006). Experts also engage in more intentional practice than novices. Generally, expertise itself is understood as domain specific, meaning that the ability to solve specific kinds of problems effectively is often limited to a particular field. For example, a person might be a chess pro but a terrible budget keeper or party planner. When an individual shows a more general talent for problem solving in life, we might say that he or she is a person of intelligence, a characteristic to which we now turn.

REVIEW, ASSESS, AND SHARPEN YOUR THINKING

Review

2 **Explain the processes involved in thinking and describe capacities related to superior thinking.**

- Define what concepts are, including their four functions, and give two theories that explain concepts.
- List the steps in problem solving and cite two potential biases or problems in problem solving.
- Define reasoning and contrast inductive and deductive reasoning; define decision making and discuss research and problems in decision making.
- Describe critical thinking and creative thinking and their role in enhancing cognitive effectiveness.
- Define and discuss expertise.

Assess

1. Which of the following is an example of a concept?
   - A. basketball
   - B. daisy
   - C. automobiles
   - D. flamingo

2. Deductive reasoning starts at the _____ and goes to the _____.
   - A. general, specific
   - B. specific, general
   - C. fixation, functional
   - D. functional, fixation

3. A researcher believes that the treatment he developed is effective. When he tests the treatment, he finds that sometimes it is successful and sometimes it is not successful. He states that the unsuccessful tests are due to faults with the tests rather than faults with the treatment. However, he believes that the successful tests are due to the effectiveness of the treatment. Which of the following is occurring?
   - A. hindsight bias
   - B. availability heuristic
   - C. confirmation bias
   - D. critical thinking

4. Which of the following is not characteristic of creative thinkers?
   - A. inner motivation
   - B. functional fixedness
   - C. objectiveness
   - D. risk taking

5. **Which type of thinking is most appropriate when there is only one correct answer?**

A. divergent thinking   B. expert thinking

C. critical thinking   D. convergent thinking

Sharpen Your Thinking

Do you have a particular expertise? If so, what is it? Describe your abilities in an area in which you are particularly good. Now choose an ability you would like to improve. Can you apply your expertise in one area of life to another domain? Why or why not?

3 Intelligence

Describe intelligence and its measurement and discuss influences on and types of intelligence.

Like *creative,* the word *intelligent* can apply to a behavior or a person. We might say that someone who decides to quit smoking has made an intelligent choice. When applied to a person, **intelligence** refers to individual differences in problem-solving skills and in important abilities. That is, within psychology, intelligence is understood as something that is relatively stable and on which people can be compared.

Cultures vary in the way they define intelligence (Shiraev & Levy, 2007; Sternberg & Grigorenko, 2008). Most Euro-Americans, for example, think of intelligence in terms of reasoning and thinking skills, but people in Kenya consider responsible participation in family and social life an integral part of intelligence. An intelligent person in Uganda is someone who knows what to do and follows through with appropriate action. Intelligence to the Iatmul people of Papua New Guinea involves the ability to remember the names of 10,000 to 20,000 clans. The residents of the widely dispersed Caroline Islands incorporate the talent of navigating by the stars into their definition of intelligence (Figure 9.7). In the United States, we generally think of intelligence as an all-purpose ability to do well on cognitive tasks, to solve problems, and to learn from experience.

expertise The quality of having a particular talent—that "something special"—for the things that one does in a particular domain.

intelligence Problem-solving skills and the ability to adapt to and learn from life's everyday experiences.

FIGURE 9.7

Iatmul and Caroline Islander Intelligence The intelligence of the Iatmul people of Papua New Guinea involves the ability to remember the names of many clans. On the 680 Caroline Islands in the Pacific Ocean east of the Philippines, the intelligence of their inhabitants includes the ability to navigate by the stars.

Validity

Does the test measure what it purports to measure?

Reliability

Is test performance consistent?

Standardization

Are uniform procedures for administering and scoring the test used?

FIGURE 9.8

Test Construction and Evaluation
Tests can be a tool for measuring important abilities such as intelligence. Good tests show high reliability and validity and are standardized so that scores can be compared across people.

reliability The extent to which a test yields a consistent, reproducible measure of performance.

standardization Developing uniform procedures for administering and scoring a test, as well as creating norms for the test.

mental age (MA) An individual's level of mental development relative to that of others.

intelligence quotient (IQ) An individual's mental age divided by chronological age multiplied by 100.

Alfred Binet (1857–1911) *Alfred Binet constructed the first intelligence test after being asked to create a measure to determine which children would benefit from instruction in France's schools.*

Measuring Intelligence

In psychology, measuring intelligence has generally been accomplished through intelligence tests. Certainly, a person's intelligence quotient (IQ) can be a powerful measure. To understand how IQ is derived and what it means, let's first examine the criteria for a good intelligence test: validity, reliability, and standardization.

Validity, as discussed in Chapter 2, refers to the soundness of conclusions to be drawn from an experiment. In the realm of testing, *validity* specifically refers to the extent to which a test measures what it is intended to measure. If a test is supposed to measure intelligence, then it should measure intelligence, not some other characteristic of the person, such as anxiety. One of the most important measures of validity is the degree to which it predicts an individual's performance when assessed by other measures, or criteria, of the attribute (Gronlund, 2006). For example, a psychologist might validate an intelligence test by asking employers of the individuals who took the intelligence test how intelligent they are at work. The employers' perceptions would be a criterion for measuring intelligence. When the scores on a measure relate to important outcomes (like employers' evaluations), then we say the test has high *criterion validity.*

Reliability is the extent to which a test yields a consistent, reproducible measure of performance. Reliability and validity are related. If a test is valid, then it must be reliable, but a reliable test need not be valid. People can respond consistently on a test, but the test might not be measuring what it purports to measure.

Good tests are not only reliable and valid but also standardized (Gregory, 2007). **Standardization** involves developing uniform procedures for administering and scoring a test, as well as creating *norms,* or performance standards, for the test. Uniform testing procedures require that the testing environment be as similar as possible for all individuals.

Norms are created by giving the test to a large group of individuals representative of the population for whom the test is intended. Norms tell us which scores are considered high, low, or average. Many tests of intelligence are designed for individuals from diverse groups. So that the tests are applicable to such different groups, many of them have norms for individuals of different ages, socioeconomic statuses, and ethnic groups (Popham, 2002). Figure 9.8 summarizes the criteria for test construction and evaluation.

IQ Tests In 1904, the French Ministry of Education asked psychologist Alfred Binet to devise a method that would determine which students did not benefit from regular classroom instruction. School officials wanted to reduce overcrowding by placing students who did not benefit from regular education in special schools. Binet and his student Theophile Simon developed an intelligence test to meet this request. The test consisted of 30 items ranging from the ability to touch one's nose or ear when asked to the ability to draw designs from memory and to define abstract concepts.

Binet developed the concept of **mental age (MA),** which is an individual's level of mental development relative to that of others. Binet reasoned that a mentally retarded child would perform like a normal child of a younger age. He developed norms for intelligence by testing 50 non-retarded children from the ages of 3 to 11. Children suspected of mental retardation were given the test, and their performances were compared with those of children of the same chronological age in the normal sample. Average mental age (MA) corresponds to chronological age (CA), which is age from birth. A very bright child has an MA considerably above CA; a less bright child has an MA considerably below CA.

The term **intelligence quotient (IQ)** was devised in 1912 by William Stern. IQ consists of an individual's mental age divided by chronological age multiplied by 100:

$$IQ = (MA/CA) \times 100$$

If mental age is the same as chronological age, then the individual's IQ is 100 (average); if mental age is above chronological age, the IQ is more than 100 (above average); if mental age is below chronological age, the IQ is less than 100 (below average). For example, a 6-year-old child with a mental age of 8 has an IQ of 133, whereas a 6-year-old child with a mental age of 5 has an IQ of 83.

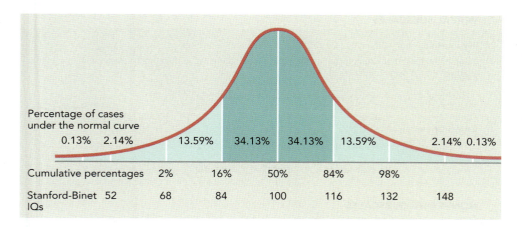

Percentage of cases
under the normal curve

| 0.13% | 2.14% | 13.59% | 34.13% | 34.13% | 13.59% | 2.14% | 0.13% |

| Cumulative percentages | 2% | | 16% | | 50% | | 84% | | 98% | | |
| Stanford-Binet IQs | 52 | | 68 | | 84 | | 100 | | 116 | | 132 | | 148 |

FIGURE 9.9

The Normal Curve and Stanford-Binet IQ Scores The distribution of IQ scores approximates a normal curve. Most of the population falls in the middle range of scores, between 84 and 116. Notice that extremely high and extremely low scores are rare. Only about 1 in 50 individuals has an IQ of more than 132 or less than 68.

The Binet test has been revised many times to incorporate advances in the understanding of intelligence and intelligence testing (Caruso, 2001). Many of the revisions were carried out by Lewis Terman, who applied Stern's IQ concept to the test, developed extensive norms, and provided detailed instructions for each problem on the test. In 1985, the test, now called the Stanford-Binet (because the revisions were done at Stanford University), was revised to analyze an individual's responses in four content areas: verbal reasoning, quantitative reasoning, abstract/visual reasoning, and short-term memory. A general composite score also is obtained to reflect overall intelligence.

The current Stanford-Binet is given to individuals from the age of 2 through adulthood. It includes a wide variety of items, some requiring verbal responses, others nonverbal responses. For example, items that characterize a 6-year-old's performance on the test include the verbal ability to define at least six words, such as *orange* and *envelope,* and the nonverbal ability to trace a path through a maze. Items that reflect the average adult's intelligence include defining such words as *disproportionate* and *regard,* explaining a proverb, and comparing idleness and laziness.

Over the years, the Binet test has been given to thousands of children and adults of different ages selected at random from different parts of the United States. Administering the test to large numbers of individuals and recording the results have revealed that intelligence measured by the Binet approximates a normal distribution (Figure 9.9). A **normal distribution** is a symmetrical, bell-shaped curve, with a majority of the scores falling in the middle of the possible range and few scores appearing toward the extremes of the range. The Stanford-Binet continues to be one of the most widely used individual tests of intelligence (Kamphaus & Kroncke, 2004).

Another set of widely used tests is the *Wechsler scales,* developed by David Wechsler. They include the Wechsler Preschool and Primary Scale of Intelligence–III (WPPSI-III) to test children 4 to 6½ years of age; the Wechsler Intelligence Scale for Children–IV Integrated (WISC-IV Integrated) for children and adolescents 6 to 16 years of age; and the Wechsler Adult Intelligence Scale–III (WAIS-III).

Not only do the Wechsler scales provide an overall IQ, but they also yield verbal and performance IQs. Verbal IQ is based on six verbal subscales; performance IQ, on five performance subscales. This setup allows the examiner quickly to see patterns of strengths and weaknesses in different areas of the student's intelligence. Figure 9.10 shows three of the Wechsler subscales.

Cultural Bias in Testing Many early intelligence tests were culturally biased, favoring people who were from urban rather than rural environments, of middle socioeconomic status rather than low socioeconomic status, and White rather than African American (Provenzo, 2002). For example, a question on an early test asked what one should do if one finds a 3-year-old child in the street. The correct answer was "call the police." But children from inner-city families who perceive the police as adversaries are unlikely to choose this answer. Similarly, children from rural areas might not choose this answer if there is

"The five candles represent his mental age."
© CartoonStock.com.

normal distribution A symmetrical, bell-shaped curve with a majority of the scores falling in the middle of the possible range and few scores appearing toward the extremes of the range.

FIGURE 9.10

Sample Subscales of the Wechsler Adult Intelligence Scale—Revised The Wechsler includes 11 subscales, 6 verbal and 5 nonverbal. Examples from four of the subscales are shown here. Simulated items similar to those found in the Wechsler Adult Intelligence Scale—Revised. Copyright © 1981, 1955 by Harcourt Assessment, Inc. Reproduced with permission. All rights reserved. "Wechsler Adult Intelligence Scale" and "WAIS" are trademarks of the Psychological Corporation, a Harcourt Assessment Company, registered in the United States of America and/or other jurisdictions.

VERBAL SUBSCALES

Similarities

An individual must think logically and abstractly to answer a number of questions about how things might be similar.

Example: "In what ways are boats and trains the same?"

Comprehension

This subscale is designed to measure an individual's judgment and common sense.

Example: "Why do individuals buy automobile insurance?"

NONVERBAL SUBSCALES

Picture Arrangement

A series of pictures out of sequence is shown to an individual, who is asked to place them in their proper order to tell an appropriate story. This subscale evaluates how individuals integrate information to make it logical and meaningful.

Example: "The pictures below need to be placed in an appropriate order to tell a story."

Block Design

An individual must assemble a set of multicolored blocks to match designs that the examiner shows. Visual-motor coordination, perceptual organization, and the ability to visualize spatially are assessed.

Example: "Use the four blocks on the left to make the pattern at the right."

no police force nearby. Such questions clearly do not measure the knowledge necessary to adapt to one's environment or to be "intelligent" in an inner-city or a rural neighborhood (Scarr, 1984). In addition, members of minority groups may not speak English or may speak nonstandard English. Consequently, they may be at a disadvantage in trying to understand verbal questions that are framed in standard English, even if the content of the test is appropriate (Cathers-Shiffman & Thompson, 2007).

The experience of Gregory Ochoa illustrates how cultural bias in intelligence tests can affect people. As a high school student, Gregory and his classmates took an IQ test. Looking at the test questions, Gregory understood only a few words because he did not speak English very well and spoke Spanish at home. Several weeks later, Gregory was placed in a special class for mentally retarded students. Many of the students in the class, it turns out, had last names such as Ramirez and Gonzales. Gregory lost interest in school, dropped out, and eventually joined the navy, where he took high school courses and earned enough credits to attend college later. He graduated from San Jose City College as an honor student, continued his education, and became a professor of social work at the University of Washington in Seattle.

As a result of cases such as Gregory's, researchers have sought to develop tests that accurately reflect a person's intelligence, regardless of cultural background (Reynolds, Livingston, & Willson, 2006). **Culture-fair tests** are intelligence tests that are intended to be culturally unbiased. Researchers have created two types of such tests. The first includes questions that are familiar to people from all socioeconomic and ethnic backgrounds. The second type of culture-fair test contains no verbal questions. Figure 9.11 shows a sample question from the Raven Progressive Matrices Test. Even though tests such as the Raven Progressive Matrices are designed to be culture-fair, people with more education still score higher than those with less education do.

Why is it so hard to create culture-fair tests? Just as the definition of intelligence may vary by culture, most tests of intelligence reflect what is important to the dominant culture. If tests have time limits, the test will be biased against groups not concerned with time. If languages differ, the same words might have different meanings for different language groups. Even pictures can produce bias, because some cultures have less experience with drawings and photographs (Anastasi & Urbina, 1996).

Within the same culture, different groups can have different attitudes, values, and motivation, and these variations can affect their performance on intelligence tests. Questions about railroads, furnaces, seasons of the year, distances between cities, and so on can be biased against groups who have less experience than others with these contexts. One explanation for the effects of education on IQ test scores is that education (and other environmental factors) may actually influence intelligence, a possibility to which we now turn.

Genetic and Environmental Influences on Intelligence

There is no doubt that genes influence intelligence (Plomin, De Fries, & Fulker, 2007). Researchers have found genetic markers (unique genetic locations) for intelligence on chromosomes 4, 6, and 22 (Plomin & Craig, 2001). In fact, the genetic marker on chromosome 6 was shown to be carried by approximately one-third of children with high IQs but by only one-sixth of children with average IQs (Chorney & others, 1998). As studies on the human genome continue, researchers will likely find and identify more markers, so the issue with respect to genetics and intelligence is the *degree* to which our genes make us smart (Petrill, 2003).

How strong is the correlation between parental IQ and children's IQ? Scientists often use the concept of **heritability**—the proportion of the IQ differences in a population that is attributed to genetic differences—to sort out the effects of heredity and environment. The *heritability index* is computed using correlational statistical techniques. Thus, the highest degree of heritability is 1.00, and correlations of .70 and above suggest a strong genetic influence. A committee of respected researchers convened by the American Psychological Association concluded that by late adolescence, the heritability of intelligence is about .75, which reflects a strong genetic influence (Neisser & others, 1996).

Interestingly, researchers have found that the heritability of intelligence increases from childhood to adulthood (from as low as 35 percent in childhood to as high as 75 percent in adulthood) (McGue & others, 1993). Why might hereditary influences on intelligence increase with age? Possibly, as we grow older, our interactions with the environment are shaped less by the influence of others and the environment on us and more by our ability to choose environments that allow the expression of genetic tendencies we have inherited (Neisser & others, 1996). For example, children's parents sometimes push them into environments that are not compatible with their genetic inheritance (wanting them to be doctors or engineers, for example), but as adults these individuals may choose to select their own career and intellectual interests (being sculptors or hardware store owners).

While genetic heritage makes a contribution to IQ, most researchers agree that for most people, modifications in environment can change their IQ scores considerably (Campbell, 2006; Ramey, Ramey, & Lanzi, 2006; Rutter, 2007a). Enriching an environment can improve school achievement and the skills needed for employment. Although genetic endowment may always influence intellectual ability, environmental factors and opportunities do make a difference (Sternberg & Grigorenko, 2008).

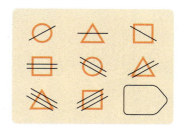
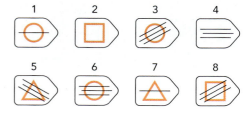

FIGURE 9.11

Sample Item from the Raven Progressive Matrices Test For this item, the respondent must choose which of the numbered figures would come next in the order. Can you explain why the right answer is number 6? Simulated item similar to those found in the Raven's Advanced Progressive Matrices. Copyright © 1998 by Harcourt Assessment, Inc. Reproduced with permission. All rights reserved.

"Mum, Dad, good news! My IQ test proved negative."

© CartoonStock.com.

culture-fair tests Intelligence tests that are intended to be culturally unbiased.

heritability The proportion of the IQ differences in a population that is attributed to genetic differences.

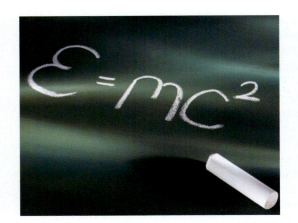

Environmental influences also have been found in adoption studies. For example, according to one study, moving children into families with better environments than the children had in the past increased the children's IQs by an average of 12 points (Lucurto, 1990). In another study, researchers went into homes and observed how extensively parents from welfare families and middle-income professional families talked and communicated with their young children (Hart & Risley, 1995). They found that middle-income professional parents were much likelier to talk and communicate with their young children than welfare parents were. And how much the parents talked and communicated with their children in the first 3 years of their lives was correlated with the children's Stanford-Binet IQ scores at age 3: The more the parents talked and communicated with their children, the higher the children's IQs were.

Researchers are increasingly interested in manipulating the early environment of children who are at risk for impoverished intelligence (Ramey, Ramey, & Lanzi, 2006). Many low-income parents have difficulty providing an intellectually stimulating environment for their children. Programs that educate parents to be more sensitive caregivers and that train them to be better teachers can make a difference in a child's intellectual development, as can support services such as high-quality child-care programs (Sameroff, 2006).

One effect of education on intelligence can be seen in rapidly increasing IQ test scores around the world, something called the *Flynn effect* (Flynn, 1999, 2006; Mingroni, 2004). Scores on these tests have been rising so fast that a high percentage of people regarded as having average intelligence at the turn of century would be regarded as having below-average intelligence today (Figure 9.12). Because the increase has taken place in a relatively short period of time, it cannot be due to heredity but rather may be due to rising levels of education attained by a much greater percentage of the world's population or to other environmental factors, such as the explosion of information to which people are exposed.

Of course, environmental influences are complex (Bronfenbrenner & Morris, 2006). Growing up with all the advantages does not necessarily guarantee success. Children from wealthy families may have easy access to excellent schools, books, travel, and tutoring, but they may take such opportunities for granted and not be motivated to learn and to achieve. And alternatively, poor or disadvantaged children may be highly motivated and successful.

Let's return for a moment to the notion that began our discussion of intelligence—the idea that the word *intelligent* describes not only people but also behaviors. Mastering skills, thinking about life actively, and making life decisions thoughtfully are intelligent behaviors that people can engage in regardless of the numerical intelligence quotient that is somewhere on their permanent record. Intelligent behavior is always an option, no matter one's IQ score. As described in Chapter 7, our beliefs about intelligence, specifically whether it is fixed or changeable, have important implications for the goals we set for learning new skills (Dweck, 2006). We never know what we might accomplish if we try, and no one is doomed because of a number, no matter how powerful it may seem.

FIGURE 9.12

The Increase in IQ Scores from 1932 to 1997 As measured by the Stanford-Binet intelligence test, American children seem to be getting smarter. Scores of a group tested in 1932 fell along a bell-shaped curve, with half below 100 and half above. Studies show that, if children took that same test today, using the 1932 scale, half would score above 120. Few of them would score in the "intellectually deficient" range, and about one-fourth would rank in the "very superior" range.

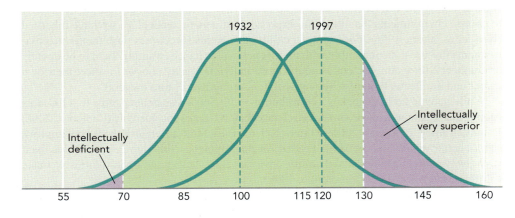

Extremes of Intelligence

Intelligence, then, appears to emerge from a synthesis of genetic heritage and environmental factors. As mentioned earlier, scores on IQ tests generally conform to the bell-shaped normal curve. We now examine the implications of falling on either of the tails of that curve.

Giftedness   There have always been people whose abilities and accomplishments outshine those of others—the whiz kid in class, the star athlete, the natural musician. People who are **gifted** have high intelligence (an IQ of 130 or higher) and/or superior talent in a particular area. Lewis Terman (1925) conducted a study of 1,500 children whose Stanford-Binet IQs averaged 150, placing them in the top 1 percent. A popular myth is that gifted children are maladjusted, but Terman found that his participants (sometimes called the Termites) were not only academically gifted but also socially well adjusted. Many of these gifted children went on to become successful doctors, lawyers, professors, and scientists. Do gifted children grow into gifted and highly creative adults? In Terman's research, gifted children typically did become experts in a well-established domain, such as medicine, law, or business. Although the Termites contributed innovative ideas in these domains, they did not become major creators (Winner, 2000, 2006). That is, they did not create a new domain or revolutionize an old domain.

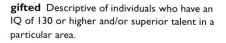

The results for the Terman study, however, may not be directly relevant to our world today. If we are indeed in the information age (Hunt, 1995), it may be that today's highly gifted individuals enjoy a better match between their skills and society's needs than gifted people of earlier times. For previous generations, society was less technologically oriented. In addition, for women and others, there were obstacles to accomplishments in many realms of life. In light of sweeping social and economic changes over recent decades, it might be that today's gifted children are better able to use their gifts in innovative and important ways in adulthood. Indeed, the results from a longitudinal study of profoundly gifted children begun by Julian Stanley at Johns Hopkins University in 1971 seem to indicate just that.

The Study of Mathematically Precocious Youth, or SMPY, includes 320 participants who were recruited based on IQ scores before the age of 13. The average IQ of the group has been estimated at 180. This is a group that is said to represent the top 1 in 10,000 (Lubinski & others, 2001). In a follow-up study of these individuals at age 23, David Lubinski and colleagues (2006) found these strikingly gifted young people to be doing remarkable things. At age 23, they were pursuing doctoral degrees at a rate 50 times higher than the average. One had completed a degree at MIT with perfect grades in 3 years and then completed Harvard Medical School by the age of 23. Others reported on achievements such as receiving creative writing awards, creating art and music, publishing in scholarly journals, and developing commercially viable software and video games. One had implemented a software library as part of a $10 million sale for her corporation. These individuals were generally normal 23-year-olds in other ways, expressing interest in finding a romantic partner, having a family, and so on. Thus, unlike the Termites of Terman's study, this group was quite creative (Wai, Lubinski, & Benbow, 2005).

Like intelligence itself, giftedness is likely a product of both heredity and environment. Experts who study giftedness point out that gifted individuals recall that they had signs of high ability in a particular area at a very young age, prior to or at the beginning of formal training (Howe & others, 1995), suggesting the importance of innate ability in giftedness. However, researchers also have found that the individuals who enjoy world-class status in the arts, mathematics, science, and sports all report strong family support and years of training and practice (Bloom, 1985). Recall that deliberate practice is an important characteristic of individuals who become experts in a domain. For example, in one study, the best musicians engaged in twice as much deliberate practice over their lives as the least successful ones did (Ericsson, Krampe, & Tesch-Römer, 1993).

More precise answers to the nature/nurture question may be forthcoming, as the SMPY participants are also part of the human genome project, as described in Chapter 3.

Mental Retardation   Just as some individuals are at the high extreme of intelligence, others are at the lower end. These individuals are sometimes referred to as mentally retarded. **Mental retardation** is a condition of limited mental ability in which an individual has a

gifted Descriptive of individuals who have an IQ of 130 or higher and/or superior talent in a particular area.

mental retardation A condition of limited mental ability in which the individual has a low IQ, usually below 70, has difficulty adapting to everyday life, and has an onset of these characteristics in the so-called developmental period.

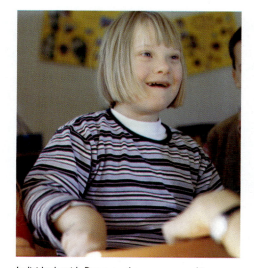

Individuals with Down syndrome may excel in sensitivity toward others. The possibility that other strengths or intelligences coexist with cognitive ability (or disability) has led some psychologists to propose the need for expanding the concept of intelligence.

"You're wise, but you lack tree smarts."

low IQ, usually below 70 on a traditional intelligence test, and has difficulty adapting to everyday life; he or she first exhibited these characteristics during the so-called developmental period—by age 18. The reason for including developmental period in the definition of mental retardation is that we do not usually think of a college student who suffers massive brain damage in a car accident, resulting in an IQ of 60, as mentally retarded. Low IQ and low adaptiveness are evident in childhood, not following a long period of normal functioning that is interrupted by an insult of some form. In the United States, about 5 million people fit this definition of mental retardation.

There are several classifications of mental retardation ranging from mild, to moderate, to severe or profound (Hallahan & Kauffman, 2006). The large majority of individuals diagnosed with mental retardation fit into the mild category. Most school systems still use these classifications. However, because these categories are based on IQ ranges, they are not perfect predictors of functioning. The American Association on Mental Retardation (1992) developed a different classification based on the degree of support required for a person with mental retardation to function at the highest level; these categories of support are *intermittment, limited, extensive,* and *pervasive.*

Mental retardation may have an organic cause, or it may be social and cultural in origin (Hodapp & Dykens, 2006). *Organic retardation* is mental retardation caused by a genetic disorder or by brain damage; *organic* refers to the tissues or organs of the body, so there is some physical damage in organic retardation. Down syndrome, one form of organic mental retardation, occurs when an extra chromosome is present in the individual's genetic makeup. Most people who suffer from organic retardation have IQs between 0 and 50.

Cultural-familial retardation is a mental deficit in which no evidence of organic brain damage can be found. Individuals with this type of retardation have IQs between 55 and 70. Psychologists suspect that such mental deficits result at least in part from growing up in a below-average intellectual environment. As children, those who are familially retarded can be identified in school, where they often fail, need tangible rewards (candy rather than praise), and are highly sensitive to what others—both peers and adults—expect of them (Vaughn, Bos, & Schumm, 2003). However, as adults, the familially retarded are usually invisible, perhaps because adult settings do not tax their cognitive skills as sorely. It may also be that the familially retarded increase their intelligence as they move toward adulthood.

Thus, the most distinctive feature of mental retardation is inadequate intellectual functioning. Yet it is not unusual to find clear functional differences between two people who have the same low IQ—for example, with one of them being married, employed, and involved in the community and the other requiring constant supervision in an institution. Such differences in social competence have led psychologists to include deficits in adaptive behavior in their definition of mental retardation (Hallahan & Kauffman, 2006). A person with Down syndrome may never be likely to accomplish the amazing academic feats of gifted individuals. But he or she may be capable of building close, warm relations with others, serving as an inspiration to loved ones, and bringing a smile into an otherwise gloomy day (Poehlmann & others, 2006; Robison, 2000; Van Riper, 2007). The possibility of other strengths or intelligences existing alongside cognitive ability (or disability) has inspired some psychologists to suggest that we need more than one concept of intelligence.

Theories of Multiple Intelligences

Is it more appropriate to think of an individual's intelligence as a general ability or as a number of specific abilities? Robert Sternberg and Howard Gardner have proposed influential theories oriented to the second viewpoint—that is, multiple intelligences.

Sternberg's Triarchic Theory   Robert J. Sternberg (1986, 2004, 2008) developed the **triarchic theory of intelligence,** which states that intelligence comes in multiple (specifically, three) forms. These forms are

- *Analytical intelligence:* The ability to analyze, judge, evaluate, compare, and contrast.
- *Creative intelligence:* The ability to create, design, invent, originate, and imagine.
- *Practical intelligence:* The ability to use, apply, implement, and put ideas into practice.

Gardner's Eight Frames of Mind   Howard Gardner (1983, 1993, 2002) suggests there are eight types of intelligence, or "frames of mind." These are described here, with examples of the types of vocations in which they are reflected as strengths (Campbell, Campbell, & Dickinson, 2004):

- *Verbal:* The ability to think in words and use language to express meaning. Occupations: author, journalist, speaker.
- *Mathematical:* The ability to carry out mathematical operations. Occupations: scientist, engineer, accountant.
- *Spatial:* The ability to think three-dimensionally. Occupations: architect, artist, sailor.
- *Bodily-kinesthetic:* The ability to manipulate objects and be physically adept. Occupations: surgeon, craftspeople, dancer, athlete.
- *Musical:* A sensitivity to pitch, melody, rhythm, and tone. Occupations: composer, musician, counselor.
- *Interpersonal:* The ability to understand and interact effectively with others. Occupations: teacher, mental health professional.
- *Intrapersonal:* The ability to understand oneself. Occupations: theologian, psychologist.
- *Naturalist:* The ability to observe patterns in nature and understand natural and humanmade systems. Occupations: farmer, botanist, ecologist, landscaper.

According to Gardner, everyone has all of these intelligences to varying degrees. As a result, we prefer to learn and process information in different ways. People learn best when they can do so in a way that uses their stronger intelligences.

Evaluating Multiple-Intelligences Approaches   Sternberg's and Gardner's approaches have much to offer. They have stimulated teachers to think more broadly about what makes up children's competencies. And they have motivated educators to develop programs that instruct students in multiple domains. These approaches have also contributed to interest in assessing intelligence and classroom learning in innovative ways, such as by evaluating student portfolios (May, 2006; Moran & Gardner, 2006; Robinson, Shore, & Enerson, 2007).

Still, doubts about multiple-intelligences approaches persist. A number of psychologists think that the multiple-intelligences views have taken the concept of specific intelligences too far (Johnson & others, 2004). Some argue that a research base to support the three intelligences of Sternberg or the eight intelligences of Gardner has not yet emerged. One expert on intelligence, Nathan Brody (2000, 2007), observes that people who excel at one type of intellectual task are likely to excel in others. Thus, individuals who do well at memorizing lists of digits are also likely to be good at solving verbal problems and spatial layout problems. If musical skill reflects a distinct type of intelligence, ask other critics, why not label the skills of outstanding chess players, prizefighters, painters, and poets as types of intelligence? Debate is ongoing over whether the multiple-intelligences view is the optimal approach for characterizing intelligence.

Our discussion of cognitive abilities has highlighted how individuals differ in terms of the quality of their thinking and how thoughts may differ from one another. Some thoughts reflect critical thinking, creative thinking, expertise, or intelligence. Other thoughts are perhaps less inspired. But one thing thoughts have in common is that they often involve language. Recall from Chapter 8 how strongly the words we put to our experiences influence our memories of those experiences. Even when we talk to ourselves, we do it with words. The central role of language in cognitive activity is the topic to which we now turn.

triarchic theory of intelligence Sternberg's theory that there are three main types of intelligence: analytical, creative, and practical.

 REVIEW, ASSESS, AND SHARPEN YOUR THINKING

Review

3 Describe intelligence and its measurement and discuss influences on and types of intelligence.

- Explain intelligence and its measurement and detail the role of bias in IQ testing.
- Relate how genetics and environment contribute to intelligence.
- Discuss the contrasting characteristics of gifted and mentally retarded individuals.
- Describe two approaches to multiple intelligences.

Assess

1. The reproducibility of a test's result is known as
   A. criterion validity.   B. validity.
   C. standardization.   D. reliability.

2. A 10-year-old child has a mental age of 8. What is the child's IQ?
   A. 60   B. 80
   C. 100   D. 125

3. What is the heritability index for intelligence?
   A. approximately .35   B. approximately .50
   C. approximately .75   D. approximately .90

4. Someone with an IQ at or above _____ is considered gifted.
   A. 100   B. 130
   C. 150   D. 200

5. According to Sternberg's triarchic theory, intelligence consists of analytical intelligence, creative intelligence, and
   A. verbal intelligence.
   B. spatial intelligence.
   C. interpersonal intelligence.
   D. practical intelligence.

Sharpen Your Thinking

A CD is being sold to parents for testing their child's IQ and performance in relation to his or her grade in school. The company that makes the CD says that the product helps parents get involved in their child's education. What might be some problems with parents' giving their children an IQ test and interpreting the results?

4 Language

Identify the possible connections between language and thought and summarize how language is acquired and develops.

Language is a form of communication, whether spoken, written, or signed, that is based on a system of symbols. We need language to speak with others, listen to others, read, and write (Hoff & Shatz, 2007). Language is not just how we talk to others but how we reason and solve problems. That little voice inside our head speaks to us in our mother tongue.

Before exploring the links between language and cognition, let's examine the way language is structured.

The Structure of Language

All human languages possess **infinite generativity,** the ability to produce an endless number of meaningful sentences. The beauty of language is that this superb flexibility comes from a relatively limited set of rules. In fact, all human languages are characterized by four main rule systems:

- **Phonology:** a language's sound system. Language is made up of basic sounds, or phonemes. Phonological rules ensure that certain sound sequences occur (for example,

---

language A form of communication, whether spoken, written, or signed, that is based on a system of symbols.

infinite generativity The ability to produce an infinite number of sentences using a relatively limited set of rules.

phonology A language's sound system.

sp, ba, or *ar*) and others do not (for example, *zx* or *qp*) (Kuhl & others, 2006; Stoel-Gammon & Sosa, 2007). A good example of a phoneme in the English language is /k/, the sound represented by the letter *k* in the word *ski* and the letter *c* in the word *cat.* Although the /k/ sound is slightly different in these two words, the /k/ sound is described as a single phoneme in English. In some languages, though, such as Arabic, this variation creates separate phonemes.

- **Morphology:** a language's rules for word formation. Every word in the English language is made up of one or more morphemes. A morpheme is the smallest unit of language that carries meaning. Some words consist of a single morpheme—for example, *help.* Others are made up of more than one: For example, *helper* has two morphemes, *help + er.* The morpheme *-er* means "one who"—in this case, "one who helps." As you can see, not all morphemes are words; for example, *pre-, -tion,* and *-ing* are morphemes. Just as the rules that govern phonemes ensure that certain sound sequences occur, the rules that govern morphemes ensure that certain strings of sounds occur in particular sequences.

- **Syntax:** a language's rules for combining words to form acceptable phrases and sentences (Chang, Dell, & Bock, 2006). If someone says, "John kissed Emily" or "Emily was kissed by John," you know who did the kissing and who was kissed in each case because you share that person's understanding of sentence structure. You also understand that the sentence "You didn't stay, did you?" is a grammatical sentence but that "You didn't stay, didn't you?" is unacceptable and ambiguous.

- **Semantics:** the meaning of words and sentences in a particular language. Every word has a unique set of semantic features (Waxman & Lidz, 2006). *Girl* and *woman,* for example, share many semantic features (for instance, both signify female human beings), but they differ semantically in regard to age. Words have semantic restrictions on how they can be used in sentences. The sentence "The bicycle talked the boy into buying a candy bar" is syntactically correct but semantically incorrect. The sentence violates our semantic knowledge that bicycles do not talk.

With this basic understanding of language and its structure in place, we can examine some connections between language and cognition.

Links Between Language and Cognition

As a vast system of symbols, language is capable of expressing most thoughts, and language is the vehicle for communicating most of our thoughts to each other. We do not always think in words, but our thinking would be greatly impoverished without words. This connection between language and thought has been of considerable interest to psychologists. Some have argued that we cannot think without language, a proposition that has produced heated controversy. Is thought dependent on language, or is language dependent on thought?

Language's Role in Cognition What role does language play in important cognitive activities? Recall from Chapter 8 that memory is stored not only in the form of sounds and images but also in words. Language helps us think, make inferences, tackle difficult decisions, and solve problems (Amsel & Byrnes, 2001). Language can be thought of as a tool for representing ideas (Gentner & Lowenstein, 2001).

Today, most psychologists would accept these points. However, linguist Benjamin Whorf (1956) went a step further. He argued that language actually determines the way we think. Whorf and his student Edward Sapir were specialists in Native American languages, and they were fascinated by the possibility that people might view the world differently as the result of the different languages they speak. The Inuit people in Alaska, for instance, have a dozen or more words to describe the various textures, colors, and physical states of snow. But English has relatively few words to describe snow, and thus, according to Whorf's view, English speakers cannot as easily talk or even think about it. The Hopi language has no words for past or future, so Whorf would argue that traditional Hopis focus mainly on the present.

morphology A language's rules for word formation.

syntax A language's rules for the way words are combined to form acceptable phrases and sentences.

semantics The meaning of words and sentences in a particular language.

Whorf's view is that our cultural experiences with a particular concept shape a catalog of names that can be either rich or poor. Consider how rich your mental library of names for "camel" might be if you had extensive experience with camels in a desert world and how poor your mental library of names for "snow" might be if you lived in a tropical world of palm trees and parrots. Despite its intriguing appeal, Whorf's view is controversial, and many psychologists do not believe it plays a pivotal role in shaping thought.

Critics of Whorf's ideas say that words merely reflect, rather than cause, the way we think. The Inuits' adaptability and livelihood in Alaska depend on their capacity to recognize various conditions of snow and ice. A skier or snowboarder who is not Inuit might also know numerous words for snow, far more than the average person, and a person who does not know the words for the different types of snow might still be able to perceive these differences.

Cognition's Role in Language   Researchers also study the possibility that cognition is an important foundation for language (Evans & Green, 2006; McNamara, de Vega, & O'Reilly, 2007). If language were a reflection of cognition in general, we would expect to find a close link between language ability and general intellectual ability. In particular, we would expect to find that problems in one domain (cognition) are paralleled by problems in the other domain (language). For example, we would anticipate that general mental retardation is accompanied by lowered language abilities.

That is often, but not always, the case. For instance, individuals with Williams syndrome (a genetic disorder that affects about 1 in 20,000 births) tend to show extraordinary verbal, social, and musical abilities while having an extremely low IQ and difficulty with motor tasks. Williams syndrome demonstrates that mental retardation is not always accompanied by poor language skills.

In sum, although thought influences language, and language influences thought, there is increasing evidence that language and thought are not part of a single system. Instead, they seem to have evolved as separate, modular, biologically prepared components of the mind.

Biological and Environmental Influences on Language

Everyone who uses language in some way "knows" its rules and has the ability to create an infinite number of words and sentences. Where does this knowledge come from? Is it the product of biology? Or is language learned and influenced by experiences?

Biological Influences   Estimates vary, but scientists believe that humans acquired language about 100,000 years ago. In evolutionary time, then, language is a very recent human ability. However, a number of experts believe biological evolution that took place long before language emerged undeniably shaped humans into linguistic creatures (Chomsky, 1975). The brain, nervous system, and vocal apparatus of our predecessors changed over hundreds of thousands of years. Physically equipped to do so, *Homo sapiens* went beyond grunting and shrieking to develop abstract speech. This sophisticated language ability gave humans an enormous edge over other animals and increased their chances of survival (Pinker, 1994).

Language Universals   The famous linguist Noam Chomsky (1975) is one of those who argue that humans are biologically prewired to learn language at a certain time and in a certain way. According to Chomsky and many other language experts, the strongest evidence for language's biological basis is the fact that children all over the world reach language milestones at about the same time developmentally and in about the same order, despite vast variations in the language input they receive from their environments. For example, in some cultures adults never talk to infants under 1 year of age, yet these infants still acquire language. Also, there is no convincing way other than biological factors to explain how quickly children learn language (Maratsos, 1999).

In Chomsky's view, children cannot possibly learn the full rules and structure of languages by only imitating what they hear. Rather, nature must provide children with a biological, prewired, universal grammar, allowing them to understand the basic rules of all languages and to apply these rules to the speech they hear. They learn language without awareness of the underlying logic involved.

Language and the Brain   There is strong evidence to back up those who believe language has a biological foundation. Neuroscience research has shown that the brain contains particular regions that are predisposed to be used for language (Schmalhofer & Perfetti, 2007). As we saw in Chapter 3, accumulating evidence further suggests that language processing, such as speech and grammar, mainly occurs in the brain's left hemisphere (Ferstl, 2007). Recall the importance of Broca's area, which contributes to speech production, and Wernicke's area, which is involved in language comprehension. Neuroscience research also has shown that the left hemisphere comprehends syntax and grammar but the right hemisphere does not (Nakano & Blumstein, 2004).

Using brain-imaging techniques such as PET scans, researchers have found that, when an infant is about 9 months old, the part of the brain that stores and indexes many kinds of memory becomes fully functional (Bauer, 2007). This is also the time at which infants appear to be able to attach meaning to words—a development suggesting a link among language, cognition, and the development of the brain.

MIT linguist Noam Chomsky (1928–) was one of the early architects of the view that children's language development cannot be explained by environmental input. In Chomsky's view, language has strong biological underpinnings, with children biologically prewired to learn language at a certain time and in a certain way.

Environmental Influences   Decades ago, behaviorists opposed Chomsky's hypothesis and argued that language represents nothing more than chains of responses acquired through reinforcement (Skinner, 1957). A baby happens to babble "ma-ma"; mama rewards the baby with hugs and smiles; the baby says "mama" more and more. Bit by bit, said the behaviorists, the baby's language is built up. According to behaviorists, language is a complex learned skill, much like playing the piano or dancing.

The behavioral view of language learning has several problems. First, it does not explain how people create novel sentences—sentences that people have never heard or spoken before. Second, children learn the syntax of their native language even if they are not reinforced for doing so. Social psychologist Roger Brown (1973) spent long hours observing parents and their young children. He found that parents did not directly or explicitly reward or correct the syntax of most children's utterances. That is, parents did not say "good," "correct," "right," "wrong," and so on. Also, parents did not offer direct corrections such as, "You should say two shoes, not two shoe." However, as we will see shortly, many parents do expand on their young children's grammatically incorrect utterances and recast many of those that have grammatical errors (Bonvillian, 2005).

The behavioral view is no longer considered a viable explanation of how children acquire language. But a great deal of research describes ways in which children's environmental experiences influence their language skills. Many language experts argue that a child's experiences, the particular language to be learned, and the context in which learning takes place can strongly influence language acquisition (Snow & Yang, 2006; Tomasello, 2006).

Language is not learned in a social vacuum. Most children are bathed in language from a very early age (Jaswal & Fernald, 2007; Tomasello, 2006). The support and involvement of caregivers and teachers greatly facilitate a child's language learning (Pan & others, 2005; Snow & Yang, 2006). For example, one recent study found that when mothers immediately smiled and touched their 8-month-old infants after they babbled, the infants subsequently

made more complex speechlike sounds than when mothers responded to their infants in a random manner (Goldstein, King, & West, 2003) (Figure 9.13).

In another study, researchers observed the language environments of children from two different backgrounds: middle-income professional families and welfare families (Hart & Risley, 1995). Then they examined the children's language development. All of the children developed normally in terms of learning to talk and acquiring the basic rules of English and a fundamental vocabulary. However, the researchers found enormous differences in the sheer amount of language the children were exposed to and the level of the children's language development. For example, in a typical hour, the middle-income professional parents spent almost twice as much time communicating with their children as the welfare parents did. The children from the middle-income professional families heard about 2,100 words an hour; their child counterparts in welfare families, only 600 words an hour. The researchers estimated that, by 4 years of age, the average welfare-family child would have 13 million fewer words of cumulative language experience than the child in the average middle-income professional family. Amazingly, some of the 3-year-old children from middle-class professional families had a recorded vocabulary that exceeded the recorded vocabulary of some of the welfare parents.

FIGURE 9.13

The Power of the Smile and Touch
Research has shown that when mothers immediately smiled and touched their 8-month-old infants after they babbled, the infants subsequently made more complex speechlike sounds than when mothers responded randomly to their infants.

In yet another study, researchers carefully assessed the level of maternal speech to infants (Huttenlocher & others, 1991). As indicated in Figure 9.14, mothers who regularly used a higher level of language when interacting with their infants had infants with markedly higher vocabularies. By the second birthday, vocabulary differences were substantial.

What are some good strategies for parents in talking to their babies? They include (Baron, 1992):

- *Be an active conversational partner.* Initiate conversation with the infant. If the infant is in a day-long child-care program, ensure that he or she gets adequate language stimulation from adults.

- *Talk as if the infant will understand what you are saying.* Adults can generate positive self-fulfilling prophecies by addressing their young children as if they will understand what is being said. The process may take 4 to 5 years, but children gradually rise to match the language model presented them.

- *Use a language style with which you feel comfortable.* Do not worry about how you sound to other adults when you talk with an infant. The mood and feeling you convey, not the content, is more important when talking with an infant. Use whatever type of baby talk you feel comfortable with in the first years of the child's life.

Research findings about environmental influences on language learning complicate the understanding of its foundations. In the real world of language learning, children appear to be neither exclusively biologically programmed linguists nor exclusively socially driven language experts (Ratner, 1993). We have to look at how biology and environment interact when children learn language. That is, children are biologically prepared to learn language but benefit enormously from being bathed in a competent language environment from an early age (Gathercole & Hoff, 2007; Snow, 2007; Tomasello, 2006).

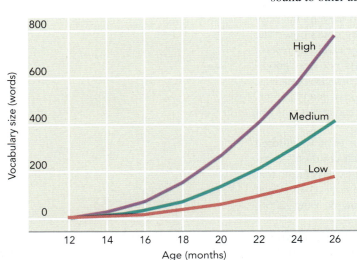

FIGURE 9.14

Level of Maternal Speech and Infant Vocabulary Even if babies sometimes seem pretty oblivious, moms who talk to their infants are building vocabulary in the little ones.

Early Development of Language

One of the most interesting things about the development of language is that the child's linguistic interactions with parents and others obey certain rules (Berko Gleason, 2005). Although children are learning vocabulary and concepts from an early age, they are also learning how their language is stitched together. In a classic study of this aspect of language learning, Jean Berko (1958) presented preschool and first-grade children with cards like the one shown in Figure 9.15. The children were asked to look at the card while the experimenter read the words on it aloud. Then the children were asked to supply the missing word. *Wugs* is the correct response for the card shown. Coming up with *wugs* might seem easy, but it requires an understanding of morphological rules (in this case, the proper word ending for plurals). Although the children's responses were not always completely accurate, they were much better than chance. What makes Berko's study so impressive is that the words were fictional, created solely for the purpose of the study. Thus, the children could not have based their answers on remembering past instances of hearing the words. Instead, they were forced to rely on rules.

Most individuals do develop a clear understanding of their language's structure during childhood, as well as a large vocabulary. Most adults in the United States have acquired a vocabulary of nearly 50,000 words. Researchers have taken a great interest in the process by which these aspects of language develop (Hollich & Huston, 2007). Through many studies, we now have an understanding of the important milestones of language development (Figure 9.16).

0–6 Months	Cooing Discrimination of vowels Babbling present by 6 months
6–12 Months	Babbling expands to include sounds of spoken language Gestures used to communicate about objects First words spoken 10–13 months
12–18 Months	Understands 50+ words on average
18–24 Months	Vocabulary increases to an average of 200 words Two-word combinations
2 Years	Vocabulary rapidly increases Correct use of plurals Use of past tense Use of some prepositions
3–4 Years	Mean length of utterances increases to 3–4 morphemes in a sentence Use of "yes" and "no" questions, wh- questions Use of negatives and imperatives Increased awareness of pragmatics
5–6 Years	Vocabulary reaches an average of about 10,000 words Coordination of simple sentences
6–8 Years	Vocabulary continues to increase rapidly More skilled use of syntactical rules Conversational skills improve
9–11 Years	Word definitions include synonyms Conversational strategies continue to improve
11–14 Years	Vocabulary increases with addition of more abstract words Understanding of complex grammar forms Increased understanding of function a word plays in a sentence Understands metaphor and satire
15–20 Years	Understands adult literary works

FIGURE 9.15

Stimuli in Berko's Classic Study of Children's Understanding of Morphological Rules In Jean Berko's study, young children were presented cards such as this one with a "wug" on it. Then the children were asked to supply the missing word and say it correctly.

Note: This list is meant not to be exhaustive but rather to highlight some of the main language milestones. Also keep in mind that there is a great deal of variation in the ages at which children can reach these milestones and still be considered within the normal range of language development.

FIGURE 9.16

Language Milestones All children are different and acquire language at varying rates, but these milestones provide a general sense of how language emerges in human life.

FIGURE 9.17

From Universal Linguist to Language-Specific Listener A baby is shown in Patricia Kuhl's research laboratory. In this research, babies listen to tape-recorded voices that repeat syllables. When the sounds of the syllables change, the babies quickly learn to look at the bear. Using this technique, Kuhl has demonstrated that babies are universal linguists until about 6 months of age but in the next 6 months become language-specific listeners.

Around the world, young children learn to speak in two-word utterances at 18 to 24 months of age.

whole-language approach An approach to learning to read that stresses that reading instruction should parallel a child's natural language learning; so reading materials should be whole and meaningful.

Language researchers are fascinated by babies' speech even before the little ones say their first words (Hollich & Huston, 2007). Babbling—endlessly repeating sounds and syllables, such as *bababa* or *dadada*—begins at the age of 3 to 6 months and is determined by biological readiness, not by the amount of reinforcement or the ability to hear (Locke, 1993). Even deaf babies babble for a time (Lenneberg, Rebelsky, & Nichols, 1965). Babbling probably allows the baby to exercise its vocal cords and helps develop the ability to articulate different sounds.

Patricia Kuhl's research reveals that, long before they begin to learn words, infants can sort through a number of spoken sounds in search of the ones that have meaning (Kuhl, 1993, 2000, 2007; Kuhl & others, 2005, 2006). Kuhl argues that, from birth to about 6 months of age, children are "universal linguists" who are capable of distinguishing each of the sounds that make up human speech. But by about 6 months of age, they have started to specialize in the speech sounds of their native language (Figure 9.17).

An important language task for infants is to fish out individual words from the nonstop stream of sound that makes up ordinary speech (Brownlee, 1998). But to do so, they have to find the boundaries between words, a very difficult task for infants because adults do not pause between words when they speak. Still, researchers have found that infants begin to detect word boundaries by 8 months of age. For example, in one study, 8-month-old infants listened at home to recorded stories that contained unusual words, such as *hornbill* and *python* (Jusczyk & Hohne, 1997). Two weeks later, the researchers tested the infants with two lists of words—one made up of words they had already heard in the stories and the other of new, unusual words that had not appeared in the stories. The infants listened to the familiar words for a second longer, on average, than to new words.

A child's first words, uttered at the age of 10 to 13 months, name important people *(dada),* familiar animals *(kitty),* vehicles *(car),* toys *(ball),* food *(milk),* body parts *(eye),* clothes *(hat),* household items *(clock),* and greetings *(bye).* These were babies' first words a century ago, and they are babies' first words still (Clark, 1983; Bloom, 2004).

By the time children reach the age of 18 to 24 months, they usually utter two-word statements. They quickly grasp the importance of expressing concepts and the role that language plays in communicating with others (Schafer, 1999). To convey meaning in two-word statements, the child relies heavily on gesture, tone, and context. Although these two-word sentences omit many parts of speech, they are remarkably succinct in conveying many messages. These utterances are called *telegraphic speech* because when people relied on telegrams for communication, they tried to be short and precise, excluding any unnecessary words. In every language, a child's first combination of words has this economical quality.

Language and Education

The early development of language skills through informal interaction with parents and other people in the family's social circle is an essential part of language acquisition. However, formal education in schools is also important. There children learn more sophisticated rules of language structure, increase their vocabularies, and apply language skills to learn about a wide variety of concepts. In fact, one of the main purposes of schooling is to increase language skills. The way that schools work toward this goal are controversial, however. One controversy swirls around the question of how children best learn to read. The reading debate focuses on two very different approaches to learning to read: the whole-language approach versus the phonics approach (Reutzel & Cooter, 2008).

The **whole-language approach** stresses that reading instruction should parallel children's natural language learning. In some whole-language classes, beginning readers are taught to recognize whole words or even entire sentences and to use the context of what they are reading to guess at the meaning of words. Reading materials that support the whole-language approach are whole and meaningful—that is, children are given material in its complete form, such as stories and poems, so that they learn to understand language's communicative function. Reading is connected with listening and writing skills. Although there are variations in whole-language programs, most share the premise that reading should be integrated with other skills and subjects, such as science and social studies, and that it should focus on real-world material. Thus, a class might read newspapers, magazines, or books and then write about and discuss them.

Critical Controversy   Is Bilingual Education a Good Thing?

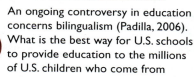

An ongoing controversy in education concerns bilingualism (Padilla, 2006). What is the best way for U.S. schools to provide education to the millions of U.S. children who come from homes in which English is not the primary language?

For the last two decades, the preferred strategy has been *bilingual education,* which teaches academic subjects to immigrant children in their native language while gradually teaching English (Diaz-Rico, 2008; Echevarria, Vogt, & Short, 2008; Ovando, Combs, & Collier, 2006). Supporters of bilingual education programs argue that if children who do not know English are taught only in English, they will fall behind in academic subjects. How, they ask, can 7-year-olds learn arithmetic or history taught only in English when they do not speak the language?

Many schools provide only 1 year of bilingual instruction (Hakuta, Butler, & Witt, 2000). Such short-term bilingual programs are the targets of criticism, because it generally takes immigrant children approximately 3 to 5 years to develop speaking proficiency and 7 years to develop reading proficiency in English. Furthermore, immigrant children vary in their ability to learn English (Diaz-Rico, 2008; Lessow-Hurley, 2005). Children who come from lower socioeconomic backgrounds tend to have more difficulty than those from higher socioeconomic backgrounds (Hakuta, 2001). Thus, especially for immigrant children from low socioeconomic backgrounds, more years of bilingual education may be needed than they currently are receiving.

On the other side of the debate are the opponents of bilingual education. They argue that, as a result of these programs, the children of immigrants are not learning English and are thus left at a permanent disadvantage in U.S. society. California, Arizona, and Massachusetts have significantly reduced their bilingual education programs. Some states continue to endorse bilingual education, but the mandate that test scores be reported separately for ELLs (English language learners—students whose main language is not English) in the No Child Left Behind state assessments has shifted attention to literacy in English (Rivera & Collum, 2006; Snow & Yang, 2006).

What have researchers found regarding outcomes of bilingual education programs? Drawing conclusions about the effectiveness of bilingual education programs is difficult because of variations across programs in the number of years they are in effect, type of instruction, qualities of schooling other than bilingual education, teachers, children, and other factors. Further, to date no experiments have been conducted that compare bilingual education with English-only education in the United States (Snow & Yang, 2006). Some experts have concluded that the quality of instruction is more important in determining outcomes than the language in which it is delivered (Lesaux & Siegel, 2003).

Research supports bilingual education in that (1) children have difficulty learning a subject when it is taught in a language they do not understand, and (2) when both languages are integrated in the classroom, children learn the second language more readily and participate more actively (Gonzales, Yawkey, & Minaya-Rowe, 2006; Hakuta, 2001, 2005). However, many of the research results report only modest rather than strong support for bilingual education, and some supporters of bilingual education now acknowledge that English-only instruction can produce positive outcomes for English language learners (Lesaux & Siegel, 2003; Snow & Yang, 2006).

What Do You Think?

- How important is it for new immigrants to the United States to learn to speak fluent English as soon as possible?

- Is bilingual education likely to be a divisive issue in American Society? Why or why not?

- Are you monolingual (a speaker of just one language) or bilingual? If you are monolingual, do you wish that, as a young child, you had learned one or more other languages in addition to your native language? Explain. If you are bilingual or multilingual, what positive or negative effects do you think your language fluency has had on your development?

In contrast, the **phonics approach** emphasizes that reading instruction should teach basic rules for translating written symbols into sounds. Early phonics-centered reading instruction involves simplified materials. Children are given complex reading materials, such as books and poems, only after they have learned correspondence rules that relate spoken phonemes to the alphabet letters that are used to represent them.

Which approach is better? Research suggests that children can benefit from both methods, but instruction in phonics needs to be emphasized (Vacca & others, 2006). An increasing number of experts in the field of reading now conclude that direct instruction in phonics is a key aspect of learning to read (Mayer, 2004; Mraz, Padak, & Rasinski, 2008).

To read about another issue related to children's education, see the Critical Controversy, which examines whether bilingual education is beneficial.

phonics approach An approach to learning to read that emphasizes basic rules for translating written symbols into sounds.

REVIEW, ASSESS, AND SHARPEN YOUR THINKING

Review

④ Identify the possible connections between language and thought and summarize how language is acquired and develops.
- Define language and describe the structure of language.
- Identify the possible connections between language and thought.
- Discuss biological and environmental influences on language.
- Describe the major milestones in early language development.
- Explain the opposing views of how schools should approach teaching reading.

Assess

1. The rules for combining words in a language are known as _____, whereas the meaning of words that have been combined is known as _____.
   A. phonology, morphology
   B. morphology, phonology
   C. semantics, syntax
   D. syntax, semantics

2. The smallest meaningful unit of language is
   A. a phoneme.
   B. a morpheme.
   C. syntax.
   D. semantics.

3. Which approach to teaching someone to read would be more likely to have students read magazine articles rather than learn rules about language?
   A. phonics approach
   B. phonemic approach
   C. whole-language approach
   D. developmental approach

4. Noam Chomsky's view of language acquisition centers on
   A. environmental factors.
   B. biological factors.
   C. social factors.
   D. person-specific factors.

5. What is telegraphic speech?
   A. speech that contains only the most important words
   B. speech that consists of declarative sentences
   C. speech that has multiple levels of meaning
   D. speech that is loud in its volume

Sharpen Your Thinking

How did you learn to read? Was it an effective approach? Explain.

5 Thinking, Problem Solving, and Health and Wellness

Discuss the importance of cognitive appraisal with respect to stress and describe various styles of coping.

What stresses you out? As described in Chapter 3, stress is that feeling we have when life's challenges seem beyond our control or ability to handle. Stressors are changes in our lives—environmental events that place demands on us. Stressors can be anything from losing irreplaceable notes from a class, to being yelled at by a friend, to failing a test, to being in a car wreck. But although everyone's body may have a similar response to stressors, not everyone perceives the same events as stressful. Indeed, whether an experience "stresses us out" depends a lot on how we think about that experience. For example, you may perceive an upcoming job interview as threatening, whereas your roommate may perceive it as a challenging opportunity. He or she might feel some anxiety but see the experience as a chance to shine. You might view a *D* on a paper as threatening; your roommate may view the same grade as an incentive to work harder. To some degree, then, what is stressful depends on how we think about events—what psychologists call cognitive appraisal (Maier, Waldstein, & Synowski, 2003).

Cognitive Appraisal and Coping

Cognitive appraisal is individuals' interpretation of the events in their lives as harmful, threatening, or challenging and their determination of whether they have the resources to

cognitive appraisal Individuals' interpretation of the events in their lives as harmful, threatening, or challenging and their determination of whether they have the resources to cope effectively with the events.

cope effectively with the events. When faced with stressful events, we cope with them as best we can. **Coping** is essentially a kind of problem solving. It involves managing taxing circumstances, expending effort to solve life's problems, and seeking to master or reduce stress.

The importance of cognitive appraisal to stress and coping was most clearly presented by Richard Lazarus (1993, 2000). In Lazarus's view, people appraise events in two steps: primary appraisal and secondary appraisal. In *primary appraisal,* individuals interpret whether an event involves *harm* or loss that has already occurred, a *threat* of some future danger, or a *challenge* to be overcome. Lazarus believed that perceiving a stressor as a challenge to be overcome, rather than as a threat, is a good strategy for reducing stress. To understand Lazarus's concept of primary appraisal, consider two students, each of whom has a failing grade in a psychology class at midterm. Student A is almost frozen by the stress of the low grade and looks at the rest of the term as a threatening circumstance. In contrast, student B does not become overwhelmed by the harm already done and the threat of future failures. She looks at the low grade as a challenge that she can address and overcome.

In *secondary appraisal,* individuals evaluate their resources and determine how effectively they can be used to cope with the event. This appraisal is *secondary* because it both comes after primary appraisal and depends on the degree to which the event is appraised as harmful, threatening, or challenging. For example, student A might have some helpful resources for coping with her low midterm grade, but she views the stressful circumstance as so harmful and threatening that she does not take stock of and use her resources. Student B, in contrast, evaluates the resources she can call on to improve her grade during the second half of the term. These include asking the instructor for suggestions about how to study better for the tests in the course, setting up a time management program to include more study hours, and consulting with several classmates who are doing well about their strategies.

Research has identified two types of coping. **Problem-focused coping** is the cognitive strategy of squarely facing one's troubles and trying to solve them. For example, if you are having trouble with a class, you might go to the campus study skills center and sign up for a training program to learn how to study more effectively. Having done so, you have faced your problem and attempted to do something about it. Problem-focused coping might involve the problem-solving steps we examined earlier in this chapter.

Emotion-focused coping involves responding to the stress that you are feeling—trying to manage your emotional reaction—rather than focusing on the problem itself. In emotion-focused coping, you might avoid the source of your stress, rationalize what has happened to you, deny the problem is occurring, laugh it off, or call on your religious faith for support. If you use emotion-focused coping, you might avoid going to a class that is a problem for you. You might say the class does not matter, deny that you are having difficulty with it, laugh and joke about it with your friends, or pray that you will do better. Such emotion-focused coping is not necessarily a good way to face a problem. For example, in one study, depressed individuals used coping strategies geared to avoiding their problems more than individuals who were not depressed (Ebata & Moos, 1989).

Yet sometimes emotion-focused coping can be beneficial in dealing with problems. Denial is one of the main protective psychological mechanisms for navigating the flood of feelings that occurs when the reality of death or dying becomes too great. For example, following the death of a loved one bereaved individuals who directed their attention away from their negative feelings had fewer health problems and were rated as better adjusted by their friends, compared to bereaved individuals who did not use this coping strategy (Coifman & others, 2007). Denial can be used to avoid the destructive impact of shock by postponing the time when we have to deal with stress. In other circumstances, however, emotion-focused coping can be a problem. Denying that the person we dated does not love us anymore when he or she has become engaged to someone else keeps us from getting on with our life.

Many individuals successfully use both problem-focused and emotion-focused coping when adjusting to a stressful circumstance. For example, in one study, individuals said they used both problem-focused and emotion-focused coping

NON SEQUITUR © 2002 Wiley Miller. Dist. By Universal Press Syndicate. Reprinted with permission. All rights reserved.

coping Managing taxing circumstances, expending effort to solve life's problems, and seeking to master or reduce stress.

problem-focused coping The cognitive strategy of squarely facing one's troubles and trying to solve them.

emotion-focused coping Responding to the emotional aspects of stress rather than focusing on the problem causing the stress.

approach coping Directly confronting a problem with active attempts to solve it.

avoidant coping Coping with a problem by trying to ignore it.

strategies in 98 percent of the stressful encounters they face (Folkman & Lazarus, 1980). Over the long term, though, problem-focused coping rather than emotion-focused coping usually works best (Folkman & Moskowitz, 2004; Heppner & Lee, 2001; Park & Adler, 2003).

Another distinction between coping styles is the difference between approach coping and avoidant coping. **Approach coping,** like problem-focused coping, means actively engaging with the problem. In some sense, approach coping is a specific example of critical thinking and mindfulness; it means allowing oneself to be aware of all sides of life's problems. **Avoidant coping** means coping with a problem by trying one's best to ignore it.

Strategies for Successful Coping

Perhaps not surprisingly, approach coping is generally more effective than avoidant coping. Positive emotional experiences and traits have been shown to relate to approach coping (Miller & Schnoll, 2000; Chen & others, 1996). Although we might think of happy people as tending to deny negative aspects of life, research reveals the opposite. For example, Lisa Aspinwall has found that optimistic people are likelier to attend to and remember potentially threatening health-related information than pessimists are (Aspinwall, 1998; Aspinwall & Brunhart, 1996). Aspinwall views optimism as a resource that allows individuals to engage constructively with potentially frightening information. Optimists engage with life from a place of strength, so when an optimist finds out, for example, that a favorite pastime, tanning, is bad for health, the information is important but not overwhelming. In contrast, pessimists are already living in a bleak world and prefer not to hear more bad news. A pessimistic sun lover is likely to view reports on the negative health effects from tanning as disturbing.

A stressful circumstance becomes considerably less stressful when a person successfully copes with it. Successful coping is associated with a number of factors, including a sense of personal control, a healthy immune system, personal resources, and positive emotions. Keep in mind that for stressful life events, as with any problem-solving challenge, multiple strategies often work better than a single strategy (Folkman & Moskowitz, 2004). People who have experienced a stressful life event or a cluster of life events (such as a parent's death, a divorce, and a significant reduction in income) might try to think in ways that will help solve life's problems by actively embracing problem solving and taking advantage of opportunities for positive experiences, even in the context of bad times. Remember that positive emotion can help you get a sense of the big picture, devise a variety of possible solutions, and allow you to make creative connections. These processes might help you carve meaning out of life's many experiences.

The Candle Problem
The solution requires a unique perception of the function of the box in which the matches came. It can become a candleholder when tacked to the wall.

The Nine-Dot Problem
Most people have difficulty with this problem because they try to draw the lines within the boundaries of the dots. Notice that by extending the lines beyond the dots, the problem can be solved.

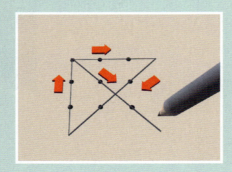

The Six-Matchstick Problem
Nothing in the instructions said that the solution had to be two-dimensional.

Solutions to problems from Figure 9.5

REVIEW, ASSESS, AND SHARPEN YOUR THINKING

Review

5 Discuss the importance of cognitive appraisal with respect to stress and describe various styles of coping.
- Explain the role of cognitive appraisal in coping with stress, including different types of appraisal.
- Outline effective strategies for coping.

Assess

1. A stressor is interpreted as a threat. During what stage of stress-and-coping does this interpretation happen?
   - A. problem-focused coping
   - B. emotion-focused coping
   - C. primary appraisal
   - D. secondary appraisal

2. Problem-focused coping is to _____ as emotion-focused coping is to _____.
   - A. avoidant coping, approach coping
   - B. approach coping, avoidant coping

   - C. primary appraisal, secondary appraisal
   - D. secondary appraisal, primary appraisal

3. In general, what type of coping strategy is usually best over the long term?
   - A. avoidant coping
   - B. problem-focused coping
   - C. emotion-focused coping
   - D. it depends

Sharpen Your Thinking

Do you think your emotional responses to life events are primarily under your control or not? Think of a time when you have felt stressed out by some event or experience. How did you appraise the situation? How might you have appraised it differently?

1 THE COGNITIVE REVOLUTION IN PSYCHOLOGY

Describe cognitive psychology and discuss the role of the computer in the development of the field.

Cognition is the way in which information is processed and manipulated in remembering, thinking, and knowing. The cognitive revolution of the past 50-plus years reveals a strong interest in the way the mind works to process and manipulate information. The computer has played an important role in this revolution, prompting the model of the mind as an information-processing system. A byproduct of the cognitive revolution is artificial intelligence (AI), the science of creating machines capable of performing activities that require intelligence when they are done by people.

2 THINKING

Explain the processes involved in thinking and describe capacities related to superior thinking.

Concepts

Concepts are mental categories used to group objects, events, and characteristics. Concepts are important because they help us to generalize, improve our memories, and keep us from constantly having to learn. Two models of concept structure are classical (all instances of a concept share defining properties) and prototypical (people decide whether an item reflects a concept by comparing it with the most typical item of the concept).

Problem Solving

Problem solving is an attempt to find an appropriate way of attaining a goal when the goal is not readily available. The four main steps in problem solving are to (1) find and frame the problem, (2) develop good problem-solving strategies, (3) evaluate solutions, and (4) rethink and redefine problems and solutions over time. Finding and framing problems is an often-overlooked dimension of problem solving. Among effective strategies for solving problems are subgoaling (setting intermediate goals that put you in a better position to reach your goal), using algorithms (strategies that guarantee a solution), and using heuristics (strategies or guidelines that suggest, but do not guarantee, a solution to a problem).

Reasoning and Decision Making

Reasoning is the mental activity of transforming information to reach conclusions. It is closely tied to critical thinking. Inductive reasoning is reasoning from the specific to the general. Analogies draw on inductive reasoning. Deductive reasoning is reasoning from the general to the specific. Decision making involves evaluating alternatives and making choices among them. One type of decision-making research investigates how people weigh costs and benefits of various outcomes. Another type studies people's biases and the flawed heuristics they use in making decisions. These biases and flaws include confirmation bias, hindsight bias, and the availability heuristic.

Thinking Critically and Creatively

Two skills that enhance problem solving are critical thinking and creativity. Critical thinking involves thinking reflectively and productively and evaluating the evidence. Critical thinking includes mindfulness

SUMMARY

and keeping an open mind. Creativity is the ability to think about something in novel and unusual ways and come up with unconventional solutions to problems. Creativity has often been described as occurring in a five-step process: preparation, incubation, insight, evaluation, and elaboration. Characteristics of creative thinkers include flexibility and playful thinking, inner motivation, willingness to face risk, and objective evaluation of work.

Expertise

There is considerable interest in the role of expertise in problem solving. Compared with novices, experts have a superior knowledge base, are better at remembering information in the domain in which they are experts, use better problem-solving strategies, and engage in deliberate practice to a far greater extent.

3 INTELLIGENCE

Describe intelligence and its measurement and discuss influences on and types of intelligence.

Measuring Intelligence

Intelligence consists of the ability to solve problems and to adapt to and learn from everyday experiences. A key aspect of intelligence involves individual variations. Traditionally, intelligence has been measured by tests designed to compare people's performance on cognitive tasks. Binet developed the first intelligence test and created the concept of mental age. A good test of intelligence meets three criteria: validity, reliability, and standardization. Validity is the extent to which a test measures what it is intended to measure. Validity can be assessed in terms of content validity and criterion validity. Criterion validity involves either concurrent or predictive validity. Reliability is how consistently an individual performs on a test. Standardization focuses on uniform procedures for administering and scoring a test; it also involves norms.

Two widely used intelligence tests are the Stanford-Binet and the Wechsler. A source of bias in intelligence testing is cultural bias. Culture-fair tests are intelligence tests that are intended to be culturally unbiased. Many psychologists believe that such culture-fair tests cannot replace traditional intelligence tests.

Genetic and Environmental Influences on Intelligence

Researchers have found genetic markers for intelligence on specific chromosomes. Many studies show that intelligence has a reasonably strong heritability component, although criticisms of the heritability concept have been made. Environmental influences on intelligence have been demonstrated in studies of the effects of parenting, intervention programs for children at risk for having low IQs and dropping out of school, and sociohistorical changes. Research has revealed the positive effects of educational child care on intelligence. The fact that intelligence test scores have risen considerably around the world in recent decades—called the Flynn effect—supports the role of environment in intelligence.

Extremes of Intelligence

At the extreme ends of intelligence are the gifted and the mentally retarded. People who are gifted have high intelligence (IQ of 130 or higher) and/or superior talent for a particular domain. Recent research has shown that individuals who are gifted are likely to make important and creative contributions.

Mental retardation is a condition of limited mental ability in which the individual has a low IQ, usually below 70; has difficulty adapting to everyday life; and has an onset of these characteristics during the so-called developmental period. Most affected individuals have IQs in the mild retardation category. Mental retardation can have an organic cause (called organic retardation) or can be social and cultural in origin (called cultural-familial retardation).

Theories of Multiple Intelligences

Instead of focusing on intelligence as a single broad cognitive ability, some psychologists have broken intelligence up into a variety of areas of life skills. Sternberg's triarchic theory states there are three main types of intelligence: analytical, creative, and practical. Gardner identifies eight types of intelligence: verbal skills, mathematical skills, spatial skills, bodily-kinesthetic skills, musical skills, interpersonal skills, intrapersonal skills, and naturalist skills. The multiple intelligences approaches have broadened the definition of intelligence and motivated educators to develop programs that instruct students in different domains. Critics maintain that the multiple-intelligences theories include factors that really are not part of intelligence, such as musical skills and creativity. Critics also say that there is not enough research to support the concept of multiple intelligences.

4 LANGUAGE

Identify the possible connections between language and thought and summarize how language is acquired and develops.

The Structure of Language

Language is a form of communication, whether spoken, written, or signed, that is based on a system of symbols. All human languages have some common characteristics, including infinite generativity and organizational rules about structure. Language has four sets of structural rules: phonology, the sound system of a language; morphology, the rules for combining morphemes, meaningful strings of sounds that contain no smaller meaningful parts; syntax, the ways words are combined to form acceptable phrases and sentences; and semantics, the meaning of words and sentences.

Links Between Language and Cognition

Thoughts and ideas are associated with words. Language does not completely determine thought but does influence it. For instance, different languages promote different ways of thinking. Language is also important in cognitive activities such as memory. Cognitive activities also can influence language. Although language and thought influence each other, there is increasing evidence that they are not part of a single, automated cognitive system but, rather, evolved as separate, modular, biologically prepared components of the mind.

Biological and Environmental Influences on Language

Evolution shaped humans into linguistic creatures. Chomsky said that humans are biologically prewired to learn language at a certain time and in a certain way. Chomsky and other experts believe that the strongest evidence for the biological foundations of language resides in the fact that children all over the world reach language milestones at about the same age and in the same order, despite vast variations in the language input they receive from the environment. In addition, there is strong evidence that particular regions in the brain, such as Broca's area and Wernicke's area, are predisposed to be used for language.

Behaviorists have advocated that language is primarily determined by environmental influences, especially reinforcement and imitation. However, evidence suggests that reinforcement and imitation are not responsible for children's acquisition of language's rule systems. Nonetheless, it is important for children to interact with language-skilled people. Evidence for the influence of the environment on language acquisition comes from studies comparing children in language-impoverished and language-enriched environments. Children are biologically prepared to learn language but benefit enormously from being in a competent language environment from early in development.

Early Development of Language

Children develop language through interactions with their social environment. A classic study revealed that preschool and first-grade children use linguistic rules in their language and can apply these results to novel (and even nonsense) words. Early language development is illustrated by infant babbling. Very young children show a special capacity for distinguishing the sounds that make up human speech. Research has shown that by 8 months, children are able to detect word units in the stream of language. By about 13 months of age, children are able to name important people, objects, and pets. By the age of 2 years, children are typically speaking two-word utterances. These utterances, sometimes called telegraphic speech because they are very short, allow the child to communicate desires effectively with language.

Language and Education

A critical issue for education is the optimal way to teach children to read. Two approaches include the whole-language approach and the phonics approach. The whole-language approach stresses that reading instruction should parallel children's natural language learning. The phonics approach emphasizes that reading instruction should teach basic rules for translating written symbols into sounds. Research suggests that children can benefit from both approaches but that instruction in phonics needs to be emphasized.

5 THINKING, PROBLEM SOLVING, AND HEALTH AND WELLNESS

Discuss the importance of cognitive appraisal with respect to stress and describe various styles of coping.

Cognitive Appraisal and Coping

The way individuals think about life events determines whether they experience them as stressful. Cognitive appraisal refers to individuals' interpretation of the events in their lives as either threatening (and therefore stressful) or challenging (and therefore not stressful). Coping refers to people's attempts to handle situations that they perceive as stressful. Coping can take the form of problem-focused coping, which centers on addressing a problem directly, or emotion-focused coping, which involves managing the emotions caused by a stressful event. In addition, coping is characterized as approach (directed at doing something about the problem) or avoidant (directed at distracting oneself from the problem).

Strategies for Successful Coping

Research has shown that active engagement is generally a more beneficial coping strategy than is avoidance, although avoidance may have its place in coping with traumatic events.

Key Terms

Assess Your Knowledge

1. In classifying items, the _____ model focuses on defining characteristics of an item, whereas the _____ model focuses on comparing the item to what is typical for items in that same category.
   A. algorithm, heuristic
   B. heuristic, algorithm
   C. prototype, classical
   D. classical, prototype

2. If a person's mental age is 20 and his or her chronological age is 20, what is his or her IQ?
   A. 20
   B. 80
   C. 100
   D. 200

3. Someone who has difficulty exploring more than one possible solution to a problem is demonstrating
   A. functional fixedness.
   B. deductive reasoning.
   C. inductive reasoning.
   D. subgoaling.

4. Looking for available information that is consistent with our viewpoint is an example of
   A. the availability heuristic.
   B. hindsight bias.
   C. functional fixedness.
   D. confirmation bias.

5. Which of the following is true about the normal distribution?
   A. Intelligence is not normally distributed.
   B. Most scores fall in the tails of the normal distribution.
   C. The normal distribution is bell-shaped.
   D. The normal distribution is positively skewed.

6. What is the relationship between reliability and validity?
   A. A reliable test is valid.
   B. A valid test is reliable.
   C. A reliable test is not valid.
   D. A valid test is not reliable.

7. What is the common criterion for IQ in determining mental retardation (in combination with a functional analysis)?
   A. an IQ below 100
   B. an IQ below 85
   C. an IQ below 70
   D. an IQ below 55

8. The sentence "the book ate the yellow house" is problematic because
   A. it has incorrect syntax.
   B. it has incorrect semantics.
   C. it has incorrect phonology.
   D. it has incorrect morphology.

9. What does the work of Benjamin Whorf say about the relationship between experience and thinking?
   A. People with more experience are smarter than those with less experience.
   B. People with more words to describe a topic can think about the topic in more depth.
   C. There is not a relationship between experience and thinking.
   D. People who cannot talk have difficulty with cognitive processes.

10. Noam Chomsky's work focuses on which of the following?
    A. the emotional aspect of language
    B. the cultural aspect of language
    C. the behavioral aspect of language
    D. the biological aspect of language

11. Antony is trying to find a job. Which of the following is an example of an avoidant coping strategy?
    A. sending out resumes
    B. watching television
    C. interviewing with employers
    D. searching job listings

12. Coming up with a list of coping strategies to deal with a specific stressor is a part of which stage of the stress and coping process?
    A. secondary appraisal
    B. primary appraisal
    C. approach coping
    D. avoidant coping

13. Approach coping is to _____ as avoidant coping is to _____.
    A. problem-focused coping, emotion-focused coping
    B. emotion-focused coping, problem-focused coping
    C. primary appraisal, secondary appraisal
    D. secondary appraisal, primary appraisal

14. At what age do children first begin saying words?
    A. 4 to 6 months
    B. 10 to 13 months
    C. 18 to 24 months
    D. after age 2

15. According to Sternberg's triarchic theory of intelligence, which type of intelligence is necessary for designing the layout of a room?
    A. analytical
    B. creative
    C. practical
    D. spatial

Go to Appendix B for answers to these questions.

Apply Your Knowledge

1. The computer is currently the dominant model psychologists use to think about how our brains process information. Could this model contribute to functional fixedness among psychologists? If so, how? Can you think of a model other than the computer to describe how the brain works? Think back to how the brain actually works—in what ways might it be similar to a computer, and in what ways does it differ?

2. Many different intelligence tests are available online. Do a web search for intelligence tests and take one. How reliable is the test you took, and how do you know if it is reliable? How well standardized is the test, and on what evidence do you base your answer? How valid is the test, and how do you know what its validity is?

3. Consider volunteering for a local Special Olympics event. How do you think personal experience with those considered mentally retarded influences one's view of intelligence? Explain.

4. Consider the characteristics of gifted people and creative people. Which would you rather be? Why? If you had children, which would you rather have—gifted children or creative children? Why? (Of course, we assume that you would not choose to be mentally retarded or to have children who are, but if this would be your choice, justify it.)

5. Are you, or is anyone you know, bilingual? If so, discuss the following issue: Does the language you use have an impact on the person you are, the topics you discuss, or the experiences you share? Explain in detail.

CHAPTER 10

CHAPTER OUTLINE

MOTIVATION AND EMOTION

Experiencing Psychology

THE MOTIVATION AND EMOTION OF LANCE ARMSTRONG

"Why did he do it?" So often when someone does something reprehensible, we ask why. In life, the intentions underlying behavior are often as important as the behavior itself. After all, we say, "It's the thought that counts," even when a loved one presents us with a sweater that is two sizes too big. In psychology, these "why" questions pertain to the realm of motivation. Motivation is the domain in which psychologists probe the basic questions of what is essential to, and about, human beings.

Motivation is not only of interest when someone does something horrible or gives us a disappointing birthday present. Motivation also matters deeply in the pursuit of excellence. Consider the 3-week, 2,000-mile Tour de France, the world's premier bicycle race, which is one of the great tests not only of personal endurance but also of human motivation in sports. American Lance Armstrong has won the Tour de France cycling event seven times, from 1999 to 2005. This accomplishment is all the more remarkable because Armstrong was diagnosed with testicular cancer in 1996. Coming back to cycling after chemotherapy was no easy task. In 1998, during his first bicycle race following the treatments, Armstrong pulled over and quit. But ultimately, he said, "I had the same emotions when I was sick as I have as a competitive athlete. At first I was angry, then I felt motivated and driven to get better. And then when I knew I was getting better, I knew I was winning." Armstrong realized that he needed to focus on the reasons he loved cycling. With this new perspective he tried again, and this time, with a vengeance.

Armstrong's experience with cancer also motivated him to think about his priorities in life. He says that the experience ultimately made him a happier and better person. He became a spokesperson for cancer and established the Lance Armstrong Foundation, which supports cancer awareness and research. You have probably seen those yellow LIVE**STRONG** wristbands, 58 million of which have been sold worldwide.

When you are motivated, you do something. The way you feel—your emotions—can either strengthen or weaken your motivation. For Lance Armstrong, motivation and emotion played a significant role in his recovery and accomplishments. We see motivation at work in his intense drive to make it through grueling practices, day after day; to battle cancer and defeat it; to set a goal of winning the Tour de France and then winning it; and to donate his time and effort to promoting cancer research and awareness. Emotion is in evidence in the anger that emerged when Armstrong found out that he had cancer; his fear that he would die; and his elation and joy of winning the Tour de France seven times.

Motivation and emotion are strongly connected. Our emotions are intimately tied with the pursuit of goals: We feel good or bad, depending on how we are tracking toward achieving the goals we value. The goals that we adopt reflect our feelings of frustration with current circumstances and our hope that things can get better. ▪

PREVIEW

In this chapter, we examine the way psychologists conceptualize and study motivation and emotion. We begin by reviewing some general approaches to motivation. We then consider two important physiological sources of motivation, hunger and sex, followed by an important positive psychological view of motivation—self-determination theory. Next we turn to the topic of emotion and examine biological, cognitive, and sociocultural influences on emotion. The chapter concludes with a survey of the role of emotions in health and wellness.

1 Theories of Motivation

Describe evolutionary, drive reduction, and optimum arousal theories of motivation.

Motivation is the force that moves people to behave, think, and feel the way they do. Motivated behavior is energized, directed, and sustained. Psychologists have proposed a variety of theories about why organisms are motivated to do what they do. In this section we explore some of the main approaches to motivation, beginning with the evolutionary approach, which emphasizes the biological basis of motivation.

The Evolutionary Approach

In the early history of psychology, the evolutionary approach emphasized the role of instincts in motivation. Ethology—the study of animal behavior—also has described motivation from an evolutionary perspective.

An **instinct** is an innate (unlearned), biological pattern of behavior that is assumed to be universal throughout a species. Generally, an instinct is set in motion by a "sign stimulus"— something in the environment that turns on a fixed pattern of behavior. A student of Darwin's evolutionary theory, American psychologist William McDougall (1908), argued that all behavior involves instincts. In particular, he said that we have instincts for acquisitiveness, curiosity, pugnacity, gregariousness, and self-assertion. It was not long before a number of psychologists had crafted laundry lists of instincts, some lists running to thousands of items. However, it soon became apparent that what the early instinct theorists were doing was naming a behavior rather than explaining it. If we say that people have an instinct for sex, for curiosity, or for acquisitiveness, we are merely naming these behaviors, not explaining them.

Although the approach of merely labeling behaviors as instincts landed in psychology's trash heap many years ago, the idea that some motivation is unlearned is still alive and well today. It is widely accepted that instinctive behavior is common in nonhuman species, and in Chapter 4 you learned that human infants come into the world equipped with some unlearned instincts, such as sucking. Most attachment theorists also believe that infants have an unlearned instinct for orienting toward a caregiver.

motivation The force that moves people to behave, think, and feel the way they do.

instinct An innate (unlearned), biological pattern of behavior that is assumed to be universal throughout a species.

Recently, evolutionary psychology, which we discussed in Chapter 1, has rekindled interest in the evolutionary basis of motivation. According to evolutionary psychologists, the motivation for sex, aggression, achievement, and other behaviors is rooted in our evolutionary past (Bjorklund, 2007; Buss, 2008; Geary, 2006). Because evolutionary approaches emphasize the passing on of one's genes, these theories focus on domains of life that are especially relevant to reproduction. We will explore these approaches in more detail in Chapter 12.

In general, however, most human behavior is far too complex to be explained on the basis of instinct. Indeed, it would hardly seem adaptive for humans to have a fixed action pattern that is invariably set in motion by a particular signal in the environment. To understand human behavior, psychologists have developed a variety of other approaches, to which we now turn.

Drive Reduction Theory

Another way to think about motivation is through the constructs of drive and need. A **drive** is an aroused state that occurs because of a physiological need. You can think of a drive as a psychological itch that requires scratching. A **need** is a deprivation that energizes the drive to eliminate or reduce the deprivation. Generally, psychologists think of needs as underlying our drives. You may have a need for water; the drive that accompanies that need is your feeling of being thirsty. Usually but not always, needs and drives are closely associated in time. For example, when your body needs food, your hunger drive will probably be aroused. An hour after you have eaten a hamburger, your body might still need essential nutrients (thus you need food), but your hunger drive might have subsided.

This example should reinforce for you that drive pertains to a psychological state, whereas need involves a physiological state. But drives do not always follow from needs. For example, if you are deprived of oxygen because of a gas leak, you may feel lightheaded but may not realize that your condition is the result of a gas leak that is creating a need for air. Moreover, drives sometimes seem to come out of nowhere. Imagine having eaten a fine meal and feeling full to the point of not wanting another single bite—until the waiter wheels over the dessert cart and suddenly you feel ready to tackle the double chocolate oblivion, despite your lack of hunger.

Drive reduction theory explains that, as a drive becomes stronger, we are motivated to reduce it. The goal of drive reduction is **homeostasis,** the body's tendency to maintain an equilibrium, or steady state. Literally hundreds of biological states in our bodies must be maintained within a certain range: temperature, blood sugar level, potassium and sodium levels, oxygenation, and so on. When you dive into an icy swimming pool, your body uses energy to maintain its normal temperature. When you walk out of an air-conditioned room into the heat of a summer day, your body releases excess heat by sweating. These physiological changes occur automatically to keep your body in an optimal state of functioning.

An analogy for homeostasis is the thermostat that keeps the temperature constant in a house. For example, assume that the thermostat in your house is set at 68 degrees during the winter. The furnace heats the house to 68 degrees, and then the furnace shuts off. Without a source of heat, the temperature in the house eventually falls below 68 degrees—if the outside temperature is colder. The thermostat detects this change and turns the furnace back on again. The cycle is repeated so that the temperature is maintained within narrow limits. Today, homeostasis is used to explain both physiological and psychological imbalances.

Most psychologists believe that drive reduction theory does not provide a comprehensive framework for understanding motivation because people often behave in ways that increase rather than reduce a drive. For example, when dieting, you might choose to skip meals, but this tactic can increase your hunger drive rather than reduce it. Similarly, many other things that you might opt to do involve increasing (not decreasing) tensions—for example, taking a challenging course in school, raising a family, and working at a difficult job.

drive An aroused state that occurs because of a physiological need.

need A deprivation that energizes the drive to eliminate or reduce the deprivation.

homeostasis The body's tendency to maintain an equilibrium, or steady state.

How did homeostasis come into play when these swimmers ran into the frigid ocean water in a traditional New Year's Day ritual?

According to the Yerkes-Dodson law, sport professionals such as golfer Tiger Woods and tennis champion Maria Sharapova perform best under conditions of moderate arousal—neither too high nor too low.

Optimum Arousal Theory

Rather than acting to decrease their drives, individuals sometimes seem to seek out stimulation—for example, by doing daring or fear-inducing things such as bungee jumping, racing cars, or watching scary movies. These behaviors suggest that individuals seek arousal (a state of alertness or activation) in their lives.

Is there an optimum level of arousal that motivates behavior? Early in the twentieth century, two psychologists described what optimum arousal might be. Their formulation, now known as the **Yerkes-Dodson law,** states that performance is best under conditions of moderate arousal, rather than either low or high arousal. At the low end of arousal, you may be too lethargic to perform tasks well; at the high end, you may not be able to concentrate. Think about how aroused you were the last time you took a test. If your arousal was too high, your performance probably suffered. If it was too low, you may not have worked fast enough to finish the test. Also, think about performance in sports. Being too aroused usually harms athletes' performance. For example, a thumping heart and rapid breathing have accompanied many golfers' missed putts and basketball players' failed freethrow attempts. However, if athletes' arousal is too low, they may not concentrate well on the task at hand.

Yerkes-Dodson law Principle stating that performance is best under conditions of moderate arousal rather than low or high arousal.

 REVIEW, ASSESS, AND SHARPEN YOUR THINKING

Review

1. Describe evolutionary, drive reduction, and optimum arousal theories of motivation.
   - Define motivation and instinct and explain the evolutionary approach to motivation.
   - Summarize drive reduction theory.
   - Discuss optimum arousal theory.

Assess

1. _____ is to feeling hungry as _____ is to a requirement for caloric intake.
   A. A drive, a need
   B. A need, a drive
   C. Homeostasis, heterostasis
   D. Heterostasis, homeostasis

2. Natalie will be taking an exam today. According to the Yerkes-Dodson law, which of the following would allow Natalie to score highest on the exam?
   A. no anxiety
   B. a moderate amount of anxiety
   C. high anxiety
   D. high relaxation

3. **Which of the following statements is correct?**
   A. Instincts have little to do with human behavior.
   B. Instincts are learned patterns of behavior.
   C. Instincts direct most aspects of human behavior.
   D. Instincts are innate and biological patterns.

4. **What is the goal according to drive-reduction theory?**
   A. spark motivation
   B. respond only to instinct
   C. achieve homeostasis
   D. limit arousal

Sharpen Your Thinking

Think about the relationship between arousal and performance in your own life. Have there been times when you knew that being a little nervous might be a good thing?

2 Hunger

Explain the physiological basis of hunger and the nature of eating behavior.

Some of the influence of motivation in our lives is tied to physiological needs. Two behaviors that are central to our personal survival and to the survival of our species are eating and sex. In this section we examine the basic motivational processes underlying eating. We have to eat to stay alive and hunger is a powerful motivator. Food is an important aspect of life in all cultures. What mechanisms cause us to feel hungry?

The Biology of Hunger

You are sitting in class and it is 2 P.M. You were so busy today that you skipped lunch. As the professor lectures, your stomach growls. What role, if any, do such gastric signals play in hunger?

Gastric Signals   In 1912, Walter Cannon and A. L. Washburn conducted an experiment that revealed a close association between stomach contractions and hunger (Figure 10.1). As part of the procedure, a partially inflated balloon was passed through a tube inserted in Washburn's mouth and pushed down into his stomach. A machine that measures air pressure was connected to the balloon to monitor Washburn's stomach contractions. Every time Washburn reported hunger pangs, his stomach was also contracting. This finding, which was confirmed in subsequent experiments with other volunteers, led the two researchers to believe that gastric activity was *the* basis for hunger.

Stomach signals are not the only factors that affect hunger, however. People whose stomachs have been surgically removed still get hunger pangs. And although the stomach may contract to signal hunger, it also can send signals that stop hunger. We all know that a full stomach can decrease our appetite. In fact, the stomach actually tells the brain not only how full it is but also how much nutrient is present. That is why rich food stops hunger

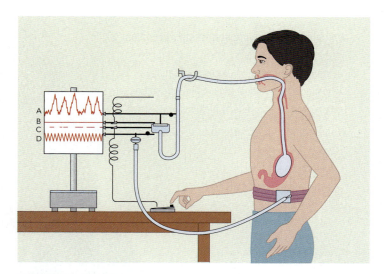

FIGURE 10.1

Cannon and Washburn's Classic Experiment on Hunger In this experiment, the researchers demonstrated that stomach contractions, which were detected by the stomach balloon, accompany a person's hunger feelings, which were indicated by pressing the key. Line A in the chart records increases and decreases in the volume of the balloon in the participant's stomach. Line B records the passage of time. Line C records the participant's manual signals of feelings of hunger. Line D records a reading from the belt around the participant's waist to detect movements of the abdominal wall and ensure that such movements are not the cause of changes in stomach volume.

faster than the same amount of water. The hormone *cholecystokinin (CCK)* helps start the digestion of food, travels to the brain through the bloodstream, and signals us to stop eating (Hayes & others, 2006). But hunger involves a lot more than an empty stomach.

Blood Chemistry Three important chemical substances play a role in hunger, eating, and satiety (the sense of being filled and not wanting to eat more): glucose, insulin, and leptin.

Glucose (blood sugar) is an important factor in hunger, probably because the brain is critically dependent on sugar for energy. One set of sugar receptors, located in the brain itself, triggers hunger when sugar levels fall too low. Another set of sugar receptors is in the liver, which stores excess sugar and releases it into the blood when needed. The sugar receptors in the liver signal the brain when its sugar supply falls, and this signal also can make you hungry.

Another important factor in blood sugar control is the hormone *insulin*, which causes excess sugar in the blood to be stored in cells as fats and carbohydrates (Pliquett & others, 2006). Insulin injections cause profound hunger because they lower blood sugar drastically. Judith Rodin (1984) has investigated the role of insulin and glucose in hunger and eating behavior. She has pointed out that, when we eat complex carbohydrates such as cereals, bread, and pasta, insulin levels go up but then fall off gradually. When we consume simple sugars such as candy bars and Coke, insulin levels rise and then fall sharply—the all-too-familiar "sugar low." Glucose levels in the blood are affected by complex carbohydrates and simple sugars in similar ways. The consequence is that we are more likely to eat within the next several hours after eating simple sugars than after eating complex carbohydrates. And the food we eat at one meal often influences how much we will eat at our next meal. Thus, consuming donuts and candy bars, which provide no nutritional value, sets up an ongoing sequence of what and how much we probably will crave the next time we eat.

Another chemical substance, called *leptin* (from the Greek word *leptos,* which means "thin"), is involved in satiety. Leptin, a protein that is released by fat cells, decreases food intake and increases energy expenditure (Klok, Jakobsdottir, & Drent, 2007; Wardlaw & Hampl, 2007). The role of leptin in long-term satiety was discovered in a strain of *ob mice,* genetically obese mice (Campfield & others, 1995). The ob mouse has a low metabolism, overeats, and gets extremely fat. A particular gene called *ob* normally produces leptin. However, because of a genetic mutation, the fat cells of ob mice cannot produce leptin. Leptin strongly affects metabolism and eating, acting as an antiobesity hormone (Correia & Haynes, 2007; Gunturu & Ten, 2007). If ob mice are given daily injections of leptin, their metabolic rate increases, they become more active, and they eat less. Consequently, their weight falls to a normal level. Figure 10.2 shows an untreated ob mouse and an ob mouse that has received injections of leptin.

In humans, leptin concentrations have been linked with weight, percentage of body fat, weight loss in a single diet episode, and cumulative percentage of weight loss in all diet episodes (Brennan & Mantzoros, 2006; Enriori & others, 2006). Today, scientists are interested in the possibility that disorders in the production and uptake of leptin may explain human obesity, and these new lines of inquiry suggest that this hormone may eventually help obese individuals lose weight (Yingzhong & others, 2006).

Brain Processes Chapter 3 described the central role of the hypothalamus in regulating important body functions, including hunger. More specifically, activity in two areas of the hypothalamus contributes to our understanding of hunger. The *lateral hypothalamus* is involved in stimulating eating. When it is electrically stimulated in a well-fed animal, the animal begins to eat. And if this area of the hypothalamus is destroyed, even a starving animal will show no interest in food. The *ventromedial hypothalamus* is involved in reducing hunger

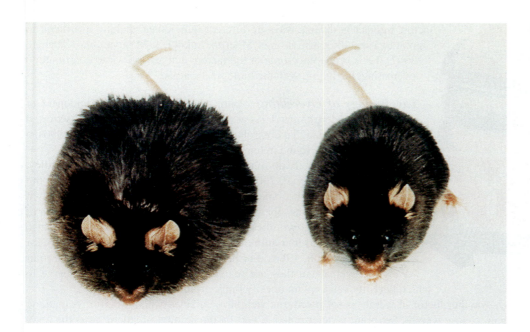

FIGURE 10.2

Leptin and Obesity The ob mouse on the left is untreated; the one on the right has been given injections of leptin.

and restricting eating. When this area of an animal's brain is stimulated, the animal stops eating. When the area is destroyed, the animal eats profusely and quickly becomes obese.

Today, neuroscientists believe that the lateral and ventromedial hypothalamuses play roles in hunger, but that there is much more to the brain's role in determining hunger than these on/off centers in the hypothalamus. They are exploring how neurotransmitters (the chemical messengers that convey information from neuron to neuron) and neural circuits (clusters of neurons that often involve different parts of the brain) function in hunger (Aja, 2006; Halford & others, 2007).

Leptin influences eating by inhibiting the production of a neuropeptide neurotransmitter in the hypothalamus that induces eating (Chen, Kent, & Morris, 2006). The neurotransmitter serotonin is partly responsible for the satiating effect of CCK, and serotonin antagonists have been used to treat obesity in humans (Hayes & others, 2006). Neural circuits involved in the action of such drugs may be in the brain stem, as well as the hypothalamus (Ahima, 2006). The neural circuitry also extends to the cerebral cortex, where humans make decisions about whether to eat or not. A recent study revealed that successful dieters had a greater activation in an area of the prefrontal cortex involved in controlling behavior than unsuccessful dieters (DelParigi & others, 2007).

Obesity and Eating Behavior

Obesity is a major public health problem in the United States. Sixty percent of Americans are overweight, and the percentage of the population that is considered obese (dangerously overweight) has nearly doubled since 1980. As shown in Figure 10.3, the prevalence of obesity in U.S. adults has increased from slightly less than 20 percent in 1997 to 25 percent in 2005 (National Center for Health Statistics, 2006). Being obese or overweight increases one's risk for a variety of health problems, including hypertension, cardiovascular disease, diabetes, and kidney disease (Hensrud & Klein, 2006; Lastra, Manrique, & Sowers, 2006). The healthcare costs linked to obesity were estimated to be $75 billion in 2003 alone.

Why do so many Americans overeat to the point of being obese? Overeating is a motivational puzzle, as it involves eating when one is not in need of nutrition. As is the case with much behavior, in eating, biological, cognitive, and sociocultural

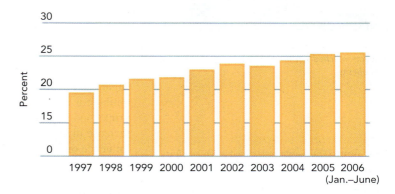

FIGURE 10.3

Prevalence of Obesity Among Adults Aged 20 Years and Over: United States, 1997–June 2006 Obesity has steadily grown as a health problem for U.S. adults.

factors interact in diverse ways in different individuals, making it difficult to point to a specific cause (Longo-Mbenza, Lukoki, & M'buyambia-Kabangu, 2007). Let's probe into some of the factors that are known to contribute to overeating, beginning with the biological causes.

The Biology of Overeating Until recently, the genetic component of obesity was underestimated. As we considered earlier, scientists discovered an ob gene in mice that controls the production of leptin. In the 1990s, a similar gene was found in humans.

Some individuals do inherit a tendency to be overweight (Walley, Blakemore, & Froguel, 2006). Only 10 percent of children who do not have obese parents become obese themselves, whereas 40 percent of children who have one obese parent become obese, and 70 percent of children who have two obese parents become obese. Researchers also have documented that animals can be inbred to have a propensity for obesity (Blundell, 1984). Further, identical human twins have similar weights, even when they are reared apart. Estimates of the degree to which heredity can explain obesity range from 25 to 70 percent.

Another factor in weight is **set point,** the weight maintained when no effort is made to gain or lose weight. Set point is determined in part by the amount of stored fat in the body (Fehm, Kern, & Peters, 2006). Fat is stored in *adipose cells,* or fat cells. When these cells are filled, you do not get hungry. When people gain weight—because of genetic predisposition, childhood eating patterns, or adult overeating—the number of their fat cells increases, and they might not be able to get rid of extra ones. A normal-weight individual has 30 to 40 billion fat cells. An obese individual has 80 to 120 billion fat cells. Consequently, an obese individual has to eat more to feel satisfied. Some scientists have proposed that fat cells may shrink but might not go away.

Americans' love of high-calorie, nutrient-poor fast foods and sugar-drenched soft drinks is contributing to a national epidemic of obesity.

Cognitive and Sociocultural Factors in Hunger and Obesity Not too long ago, psychologists believed that obesity stemmed from such factors as unhappiness and response to external food cues. These ideas make some sense; drowning one's sorrows in chocolate or eating some delicious cookies just because they are there seem like common enough occurrences to explain overeating. But a number of cognitive and sociocultural factors are more important than emotional state and external stimuli (Rodin, 1984).

Time and place, for example, affect our eating. Learned associations of food with a particular place and time are characteristic of organisms (Devine, 2005; Fiese, Foley, & Spagnola, 2006). For example, when it is noon we are likely to feel hungry even if we have had a big breakfast and snacked at midmorning. We also associate eating with certain places. Many people link watching television with eating and feel uncomfortable if they are not eating something while they are watching TV.

The human gustatory system and taste preferences developed at a time when reliable food sources were scarce. Our earliest ancestors probably developed a preference for sweets because ripe fruit, which is a concentrated source of sugar (and calories), was so accessible. Today many people still have a sweet tooth, but, unlike our ancestors' ripe fruit that contained sugar *plus* vitamins and minerals, the soft drinks and candy bars we snack on often fill us with nutrient-free calories. The alarming increase in obesity in the United States since 1900 is strong evidence of the environment's influence on weight.

set point The weight maintained when no effort is made to gain or lose weight.

anorexia nervosa An eating disorder that involves the relentless pursuit of thinness through starvation.

bulimia nervosa An eating disorder in which the individual consistently follows a binge-and-purge eating pattern.

Dieting

Ironically, even as obesity is on the rise, dieting is a continuing obsession in the United States. In Chapter 16 we will take up the question of how individuals successfully lose weight. Here, we explore other factors in dieting, including restrained eating, the potential hazards of dieting, and disordered eating.

Restrained Eaters Many people spend their lives on one long diet, interrupted by occasional hot fudge sundaes or fistfuls of chocolate chip cookies. They are *restrained eaters,* individuals who chronically restrict their food intake to control their weight (Rennie, Siervo, & Jebb, 2006). Restrained eaters are often on diets, are very conscious of what they eat, and tend to feel guilty after splurging on sweets (de Lauzon-Guillain & others, 2006). An interesting characteristic of restrained eaters is that when they stop dieting, they tend to binge-eat—that is, to consume large quantities of food in a short time (McFarlane, Polivy, & Herman, 1998). Restrained eaters let a minor dieting slip-up escalate to overindulgence: One donut can ruin an entire diet.

The Potential Hazards of Dieting The topic of dieting is of great interest to many diverse groups in the United States, including the public, health professionals, policymakers, the media, and the powerful diet and food industries. On one side are the societal norms that promote a lean, aesthetic body. This ideal is supported by $30 billion a year in sales of diet books, programs, videos, foods, and pills. On the other side are health professionals and a growing minority of the press, who, although they recognize that the rate of obesity is alarming, are frustrated by the widespread obsession with excessive thinness that can lead to chronic dieting and serious health risks.

© Mike Baldwin / Cornered

"Try to get more exercise."

© CartoonStock.com.

One concern is weight cycling (yo-yo dieting), in which the person is in a recurring cycle of dieting and weight gain (Goldbeter, 2006). Researchers have found a link between frequent changes in weight and chronic disease (Brownell & Rodin, 1994). Also, liquid diets and other very low-calorie strategies are related to gallbladder damage.

Disordered Eating Dieting is a pervasive concern in the United States, but many people who are on diets should not be. The motivation to be thin can be so strong that some individuals diet even when their bodies need food. Indeed, the pressure to be thin, and thus to diet, is greatest among young women, yet they do not have the highest risk for obesity. Two eating disorders that have been linked to the emphasis on the thin ideal for young women are anorexia nervosa and bulimia nervosa (Harrison & Hefner, 2006; Stice & others, 2007). **Anorexia nervosa** is an eating disorder that involves the relentless pursuit of thinness through starvation. Anorexia nervosa, which affects less than 1 percent of young women, is a relatively rare but serious health problem. It has been said that anorexia nervosa has the highest mortality rate (about 5.6 percent per decade) of any psychological disorder (Birmingham & others, 2005; Hoek, 2006; Keel & others, 2003; Sullivan, 1995). The main characteristics of anorexia nervosa are (Nolen-Hoeksema, 2007):

- Weighing less than 85 percent of what is considered normal for age and height.
- Having an intense fear of gaining weight that does not decrease with weight loss.
- Having a distorted body image (Dohm & others, 2001). Even when individuals with anorexia nervosa are extremely thin, they never think they are thin enough: They weigh themselves frequently, often take their body measurements, and gaze critically at themselves in mirrors.

Anorexia nervosa typically begins in the teenage years, often following an episode of dieting and some type of life stress (Lewinsohn, Striegel-Moore, & Seeley, 2000). Most anorexics are White female adolescents or young adults from well-educated, middle- and upper-income families that are competitive and high achieving. These young women are often perfectionists who set very high standards for themselves (Forbush, Heatherton, & Keel, 2007).

Bulimia nervosa is an eating disorder in which the individual consistently follows a binge-and-purge eating pattern. The bulimic goes on an eating binge and then purges by self-induced vomiting or use of laxatives. As with anorexics, most bulimics are preoccupied with food, have a strong fear of becoming overweight, and are depressed or anxious (Byrne & McLean, 2002; Cooley & Toray, 2001; Speranza & others, 2003). Bulimia nervosa differs from anorexia nervosa in that the binge-and-purge pattern in bulimia nervosa occurs within a normal weight range; thus, the disorder is often difficult to detect (Mizes & Miller, 2000).

Bulimia nervosa typically begins in late adolescence or early adulthood (Levine, 2002). The vast majority of cases are girls and women. Bulimia nervosa is thought to affect 1 percent of young women (Hoek, 2006), and rates of bulimia appear to be on the decline (Keel & others, 2006). Many young women who develop bulimia nervosa are characterized by a high degree of perfectionism (Forbush, Heatherton, & Keel, 2007) coupled with low levels of self-efficacy (Bardone Cone & others, 2006). These are young women with very high standards but little confidence that they can achieve their goals.

REVIEW, ASSESS, AND SHARPEN YOUR THINKING

Review

2 Explain the physiological basis of hunger and the nature of eating behavior.
- Discuss the biology of hunger.
- Describe the biological, cognitive, and sociocultural factors involved in overeating and obesity.
- Discuss the problems associated with dieting and eating disorders.

Assess

1. Which of the following is not a characteristic of bulimia nervosa?
   A. binging and purging
   B. fear of weight gain
   C. disordered mood
   D. weighing under normal limits

2. _____ is a protein released by fat cells that is involved in satiety.
   A. Leptin   B. Adipose
   C. Glucose   D. Cholecystokinin

3. A person who weighs less than 85% of his or her normal weight
   A. is potentially anorexic.
   B. is likely a restrained eater.
   C. is morbidly obese.
   D. is engaging in weight cycling.

4. Ob mice are missing genes that produce
   A. insulin.
   B. glucose.
   C. leptin.
   D. cholecystokinin.

5. Andre's weight is consistently 185 pounds. Andre's weight is
   A. obese.
   B. socioculturally-determined.
   C. his set point.
   D. maintained by dieting.

Sharpen Your Thinking

The "freshman 15" refers to the approximately 15 pounds that many students gain in their first year of college. What factors might explain this weight increase?

3 Sexuality

Discuss the motivations for sexual behavior.

Of course, we do not need sex for everyday survival, the way we need food and water, but we do need it for the survival of the species. Like hunger, sex has a strong physiological basis, as well as cognitive and sociocultural components. In this section, we review some of the key issues involved in the human need for sex. We first examine this fascinating topic from the perspective of its biological underpinnings.

The Biology of Sex

What brain areas are involved in sex? What role do hormones play in sexual motivation? What is the nature of the human sexual response pattern?

The Hypothalamus, Cerebral Cortex, and Limbic System   Motivation for sexual behavior is centered in the hypothalamus (Romero-Carbente, Camacho, & Paredes, 2006). However, like many other areas of motivation, brain functioning related to sex radiates outward to connect with a wide range of other brain areas in both the limbic system and the cerebral cortex.

The importance of the hypothalamus in sexual activity has been shown by electrically stimulating or surgically removing it. Electrical stimulation of certain hypothalamic areas increases sexual behavior; surgical removal of some hypothalamic areas produces sexual inhibition. Electrical stimulation of the hypothalamus in a male can lead to as many as 20 ejaculations in 1 hour. The limbic system, which runs through the hypothalamus, also seems to be involved in sexual behavior. Its electrical stimulation can produce penile erection in males and orgasm in females.

In humans, the temporal lobes of the neocortex play an important role in moderating sexual arousal and directing it to an appropriate goal object (Carroll, 2007). Temporal lobe damage in male cats has been shown to impair the animals' ability to select an appropriate partner. Male cats with temporal lobe damage try to copulate with everything in sight: teddy bears, chairs, and even researchers. Temporal lobe damage in humans also has been associated with changes in sexual activity (Mendez & others, 2000).

The brain tissues that produce sexual feelings and behaviors are activated by various neurotransmitters in conjunction with various sex hormones. Sexual motivation also is characterized by a basic urge-reward-relief neural circuit. The motivation for sex is generated by excitatory neurotransmitters (Hull & Dominguez, 2006). The intense reward of orgasm is caused by a massive rush of dopamine, and the deep feeling of relaxation that follows is linked with the hormone oxytocin, which we examined in Chapter 3 (Thackare, Nicholson, & Whittington, 2006).

Sex Hormones   Sex hormones are powerful chemicals that are controlled by the master gland in the brain, the pituitary. The two main classes of sex hormones are estrogens and androgens. **Estrogens,** the class of sex hormones that predominate in females, are produced mainly by the ovaries. **Androgens,** the class of sex hormones that predominate in males, are produced by the testes in males and by the adrenal glands in both males and females. Testosterone is an androgen. Estrogens and androgens can influence sexual motivation in both sexes.

The secretion of sex hormones is regulated by a feedback system. The pituitary gland, regulated by the hypothalamus, monitors hormone levels. The pituitary gland signals the testes or ovaries to manufacture the hormone. Then the pituitary gland, through interaction with the hypothalamus, detects the point at which an optimal hormone level is reached and stops production of the hormone.

The role of hormones in motivating human sexual behavior, especially for women, is not clear (Hyde & DeLamater, 2006). For men, higher androgen levels are associated with sexual motivation and orgasm frequency (Thiessen, 2002). Nonetheless, sexual behavior is so individualized in humans that it is difficult to specify the effects of hormones (Susman & Rogol, 2004).

The Human Sexual Response Pattern   What physiological changes do humans experience during sexual activity? To answer this question, William Masters and Virginia Johnson (1966) carefully observed and measured the physiological responses of 382 female and 312 male volunteers as they masturbated or had sexual intercourse. The **human sexual response pattern** consists of four phases—excitement, plateau, orgasm, and resolution— as identified by Masters and Johnson (Figure 10.4).

estrogens The main class of female sex hormones, produced principally by the ovaries.

androgens The class of sex hormones that predominate in males; they are produced by the testes in males and by the adrenal glands in both males and females.

human sexual response pattern Identified by Masters and Johnson, the four phases of physical reactions that occur in humans as a result of sexual stimulation. These phases are excitement, plateau, orgasm, and resolution.

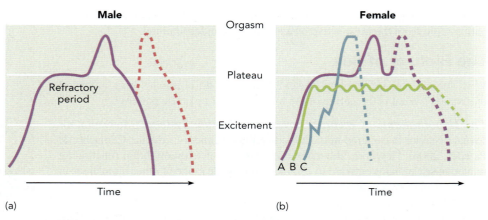

FIGURE 10.4

Male and Female Sexual Response Patterns Identified by Masters and Johnson
(a) The excitement, plateau, orgasm, and resolution phases of the human male sexual response pattern. Notice that males enter a refractory period, which lasts from several minutes up to a day, in which they cannot have another orgasm. (b) The excitement, plateau, orgasm, and resolution phases of the human female sexual response pattern. Notice that female sexual responses follow one of three basic patterns: Pattern A somewhat resembles the male pattern, except it includes the possibility of multiple orgasm (the second peak in pattern A) without falling below the plateau level. Pattern B represents nonorgasmic arousal. Pattern C represents intense female orgasm, which resembles the male pattern in its intensity and rapid resolution.

The *excitement phase* begins erotic responsiveness; it lasts from several minutes to several hours, depending on the nature of the sex play involved. Engorgement of blood vessels and increased blood flow in genital areas and muscle tension characterize the excitement phase. The most obvious signs of response in this phase are lubrication of the vagina and partial erection of the penis.

The second phase of the human sexual response, the *plateau phase,* is a continuation and heightening of the arousal begun in the excitement phase. The increases in breathing, pulse rate, and blood pressure that occurred during the excitement phase become more intense, penile erection and vaginal lubrication are more complete, and orgasm is closer.

The third phase of the human sexual response cycle is *orgasm.* How long does orgasm last? Some individuals sense that time is standing still when it takes place, but orgasm lasts for only about 3 to 15 seconds. Orgasm involves an explosive discharge of neuromuscular tension and an intense pleasurable feeling. However, orgasms are not all alike. For example, females show three different patterns in the orgasm phase: multiple orgasms; no orgasm; and excitement rapidly leading to orgasm, bypassing the plateau phase (this pattern most clearly corresponds to the male pattern in intensity and resolution; see Figure 10.4).

Following orgasm, the individual enters the *resolution phase,* in which blood vessels return to their normal state. One difference between males and females in this phase is that females may be stimulated to orgasm again without delay. Males enter a *refractory period,* lasting anywhere from several minutes to a day, in which they cannot have another orgasm. The length of the refractory period increases as men age.

Cognitive and Sensory/Perceptual Factors

From experience, we know that our cognitive world plays an important role in our sexuality (Kelly, 2006). We might be sexually attracted to someone but understand that it is important to inhibit our sexual urges until the relationship has time to develop and we get to know the person better. We have the cognitive capacity to think about the importance of not raping or inflicting sexual harm on others. We also have the cognitive capacity to generate sexual images—to become sexually aroused just by thinking about erotic images (Whipple, Ogden, & Komisaruk, 1992).

Sexual motivation is influenced by *sexual scripts,* stereotyped patterns of expectancies for how people should behave sexually (recall from the discussion of memory in Chapter 8 that *scripts* are schemas for events). We carry these scripts with us in our memories. Two well-known sexual scripts are the traditional religious script and the romantic script. In the *traditional religious script,* sex is accepted only within marriage. Extramarital sex is taboo, especially for women. Sex means reproduction and sometimes affection. In the *romantic script,* sex is equated with love. In this script, if we develop a relationship with someone and fall in love, it is acceptable to have sex with the person whether we are married or not.

Typically, women and men have different sexual scripts (Jones, 2006). Women tend to link sexual intercourse with love more than men do, and men are more likely to emphasize sexual conquest. Some sexual scripts involve a double standard: For example, it is okay for male but not female adolescents to have sex, and women bear the blame if they become pregnant.

Cognitive interpretation of sexual activity also involves our perception of the individual with whom we are having sex and his or her perception of us. We imbue our sexual acts with such perceptual questions as the following: Is he loyal to me? What is our future relationship going to be like? How important is sex to her? What if she gets pregnant? Amid the wash of hormones in sexual activity is the cognitive ability to control, reason about, and try to make sense of the activity.

Along with cognitive factors, sensory/perceptual factors are involved in sexual behavior. The sensory system of touch usually predominates during sexual intimacy, but vision also plays an important role for some individuals (Brown, Steele, & Walsh-Childers, 2002).

Men and women differ in how much touch and visual stimulation motivate them sexually. In general, women are more aroused by touch; men, by what they see. This difference might explain why erotic magazines and movies are directed more toward men than toward women (Money, 1986). Women are more aroused by tender, loving touches that are coupled with verbal expressions of love than men are. Moreover, men are likely to become sexually aroused quickly, whereas women's sexual arousal tends to build gradually.

Cultural Factors

Sexual motivation also is influenced by cultural factors (Shiraev & Levy, 2007; Strong & others, 2006). The range of sexual values across cultures is substantial. Some cultures consider sexual pleasures to be normal or desirable; other cultures view sexual pleasures as weird or abnormal.

Consider the people who live on the small island of Inis Beag off the coast of Ireland. They know nothing about tongue kissing or hand stimulation of the penis, and they detest nudity. For both females and males, premarital sex is out of the question. Men avoid most sexual experiences because they believe that sexual intercourse reduces their energy level and is bad for their health. Under these repressive conditions, sexual intercourse occurs only at night and takes place as quickly as possible as the husband opens his nightclothes under the covers and the wife raises her nightgown. As you might suspect, female orgasm is rare in this culture (Messinger, 1971).

In contrast, the Mangaian culture in the South Pacific might seem promiscuous to us. In Mangaia, young boys are taught about masturbation and are encouraged to engage in it as much as they like. At age 13, the boys undergo a ritual that initiates them into sexual manhood. First, their elders instruct them about sexual strategies, including how to aid their female partner in having orgasms. Then, 2 weeks later, the boy has intercourse with an experienced woman who helps him hold back from ejaculation until she can achieve orgasm with him. By the end of adolescence, Mangaians have sex pretty much every day. Mangaian women report a high frequency of orgasm.

Sexual Behavior and Orientation

Few cultures are as isolated and homogeneous as are Inis Beag and Mangaia. In the United States, sexual behaviors and attitudes reflect the country's diverse, multicultural population, and Americans fall somewhere in the middle of a continuum going from repressive to liberal. We are more conservative in our sexual habits than once thought but somewhat more open-minded regarding sexual orientation than a century ago.

Sexual Attitudes and Practices Describing sexual practices in the United States has always been challenging (Dunne, 2002). In 1948, Alfred Kinsey and his colleagues shocked the nation by reporting that his survey of U.S. sexual practices revealed that half of American men had engaged in extramarital affairs. However, Kinsey's results were not representative because he recruited volunteers wherever he could find them, including hitchhikers who passed through town, fraternity men, and even mental patients. Despite the study's flaws, the Kinsey data were widely circulated, and many people felt that they must be leading more conservative sexual lives than others.

Subsequent large-scale magazine surveys confirmed the trend toward permissive sexuality (for example, a *Playboy* magazine poll of its readers) (Hunt, 1974). In these surveys, Americans were portrayed as engaging in virtually unending copulation. However, surveys in *Playboy* and *Cosmopolitan* might appeal to subscribers who want to use the survey to brag about their sexual exploits.

Not until 1994 were more accurate data obtained from a well-designed, comprehensive study of U.S. sexual patterns. Robert Michael and his colleagues (1994) interviewed nearly 3,500 people from 18 to 50 years of age who were randomly selected, a sharp contrast from earlier samples that were based on unrepresentative groups of volunteers. Here are some of the key findings from that major survey:

- Americans tend to fall into three categories: One-third have sex twice a week or more, one-third a few times a month, and one-third a few times a year or not at all.

- Married couples have sex most often and are the most likely to have orgasms when they do. Figure 10.5 portrays the frequency of sex for married and noncohabiting individuals in the year before the survey was taken.

FIGURE 10.5

The 1994 *Sex in America* Survey

Percentages show noncohabiting and cohabiting (married) males' and females' responses to the question "How often have you had sex in the past year?"

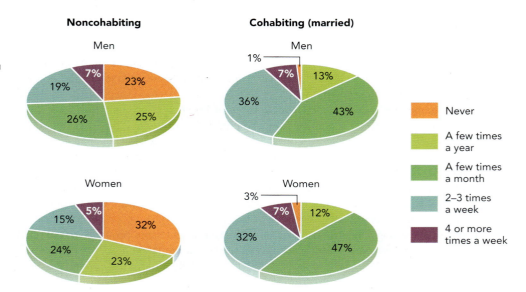

- Most Americans do not engage in kinky sexual acts. When asked about their favorite sexual acts, the vast majority (96 percent) said that vaginal sex was "very" or "somewhat" appealing. Oral sex was in third place, after an activity that many might not even label a sexual act—watching a partner undress.

- Adultery is clearly the exception rather than the rule. Nearly 75 percent of the married men and 85 percent of the married women indicated that they have never been unfaithful.

- Men think about sex far more often than women do—54 percent of the men said they think about it every day or several times a day, whereas 67 percent of the women said they think about it only a few times a week or a few times a month.

In sum, one of the most powerful messages in the 1994 survey was that Americans' sexual lives are more conservative than was previously believed. Although 17 percent of the men and 3 percent of the women said they have had sex with at least 21 partners, the overall impression from the survey was that for most Americans, marriage and monogamy rule sexual behavior.

More recent surveys have shown similar results. For instance, in 2004 ABC polled a nationally representative sample and found that, contrary to media portrayals like those in *Desperate Housewives* and *Grey's Anatomy,* individuals in committed relationships were more likely (74 percent) than singles (33 percent) to have sex once a week or more. In addition, 84 percent of Americans who were in a committed relationship reported being sexually faithful throughout the relationship.

Men and women differ in some ways sexually. As noted above, men think about sex more than women do and women link sexual behavior with love more than men do. A review of research also concluded that men report more frequent feelings of sexual arousal, have more frequent sexual fantasies, and rate the strength of their own sex drive higher than women do (Baumeister, Catanese, & Vohs, 2001). Men also are more likely to masturbate, have more permissive attitudes about casual premarital sex, and have a more difficult time adhering to their vows of sexual fidelity when they become married (Oliver & Hyde, 1993; Peplau, 2003).

Women appear to be more erotically flexible than men (Baumeister, 2000; Baumeister & Stillman, 2006; Diamond, 2008). That means that compared to men, women tend to show more changes in their sexual patterns and desires over their lifetime. Women are likelier than men, for instance, to have had sexual experiences with same- and opposite-sex partners, even if they identify themselves strongly as heterosexual or lesbian. A number of studies show that within a heterosexual relationship, women tend to be "gatekeepers" of sexual activity, setting the upper limit on sexual activity, and that men tend to set the lower limit. Roy Baumeister (2000) suggested that flexibility may be an inherent part of female sexuality because most sexual encounters involve a woman's changing her answer from no to yes.

Sex is a topic about which, as a society, we have had difficulty talking plainly. Former president Bill Clinton famously denied having sex with intern Monica Lewinsky and noted that whether he had sex with her depended on the definition of "sex." Although many people found his response less than satisfying, there is reason to believe that in general people are not quite sure what qualifies as sex and what does not. For example, as Figure 10.6 shows, there has been a dramatic increase in oral sex during adolescence (Brady & Halpern-Felsher, 2007; Cornell & Halpern-Felsher, 2006; Tillman & Brewster, 2006). Many adolescents report that having oral sex is not really sex. A recent study found that adolescents who practiced oral sex were older, had engaged in heavy drinking in the past month, perceived their peers to be sexually active, and thought their friends would approve of their sexual activity more than adolescents who had not engaged in oral sex (Bersamin & others, 2006a, 2006b). What is especially worrisome about the increase in oral sex during adolescence is how casually individuals engage in it. For many adolescents, oral sex appears to be a recreational activity, and because many adolescents do not view oral sex

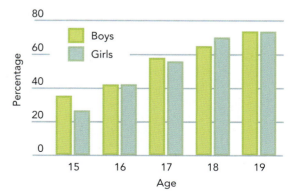

FIGURE 10.6

Percentage of U.S. 15- to 19-Year-Old Boys and Girls Who Report Engaging in Oral Sex But is it "really sex"? This figure shows the percentage of young people under the age of 20 who report having engaged in oral sex.

Source: National Center for Health Statistics (2002).

"as sex," they believe it is a safe alternative to intercourse (Cornell & Halpern-Felsher, 2006; Weill, 2005).

Many U.S. youth report learning about sex from television, movies, and music (Ashby, Arcari, & Edmonson, 2006). A recent research review found that frequent watching of soap operas and music videos was linked with greater acceptance of casual attitudes about sex and higher expectations of engaging in sexual activity (Ward, 2003). Although some people have expressed concern that educating children and young adolescents about sex might lead to early sexual experimentation, research suggests the opposite. Talking to children about sex, relationships, and birth control is a good predictor of delaying first sexual intercourse (Alford, 2003).

Public policy in the United States has swung away from giving youth information about sex toward abstinence-only programs. The United States has the highest rate of teen pregnancy in the developed world—at least twice the rate in Canada and many European countries and 10 times the rate in the Netherlands. No abstinence-only program has been shown to have an effect on delaying first sexual experience (Hauser, 2004; Santelli & others, 2006). Furthermore, a challenge to programs that do not provide any information about birth control or sexuality beyond abstinence is that students who have been exposed to abstinence-only programs may be less likely to use birth control and protection against sexually transmitted infections (STIs) when they do have sex (Brückner & Bearman, 2005). In contrast, students who are exposed to comprehensive sexuality education classes do not engage in sexual activity more often or earlier but do use contraception and practice safer sex more consistently when they become sexually active (Kirby, 2001).

Sexual Orientation   An individual's **sexual orientation** refers to the direction of the person's erotic interests. An individual who identifies himself or herself as homosexual is generally sexually attracted to members of the same sex.

Until the end of the nineteenth century, it was commonly believed that people were either heterosexual or homosexual. Today, it is more accepted to view sexual orientation not as an either-or proposition but as a continuum from exclusive male–female relations to exclusive same-sex relations (King, 2005). Some individuals moreover are *bisexual,* meaning that they are sexually attracted to people of both sexes. In addition, because a person's erotic attractions may be fluid, referring to such a thing as a fixed sexual orientation may be misleading because it ignores the potential flexibility of human sexual attraction and behavior (Diamond, 2008).

It is difficult to know with precision how many lesbians, gays, and bisexuals there are in the world, because fears of discrimination may prevent individuals from answering honestly on surveys. However, in 2000 the U.S. Bureau of the Census added the category "unmarried partners" to the options for respondents, and from the census data (combined with the information on the sex of respondents) experts estimate that at least 1.2 million Americans are living in same-sex households. Such households exist in 99 percent of counties throughout the United States, and approximately 1 in 4 of these households includes children (O'Barr, 2006).

Research shows that gay and lesbian individuals are similar to their heterosexual counterparts in many ways. Regardless of their sexual orientation, all people have similar physiological responses during sexual arousal and seem to be aroused by the same types of tactile stimulation. Investigators typically find no differences among lesbians, gays, bisexuals, and heterosexuals in a wide range of attitudes, behaviors, and psychological adjustment (Hyde & DeLamater, 2006).

Many gender differences that appear in heterosexual relationships occur in same-sex relationships (Savin-Williams & Diamond, 2004). For example, lesbians have fewer sexual partners than gay men, and lesbians have less permissive attitudes about casual sex outside a primary relationship than gay men (Peplau, 2002, 2003; Peplau & Fingerhut, 2007; Peplau, Fingerhut, & Beals, 2004). Indeed, the gist of much research on sexual

sexual orientation The direction of the person's erotic interests, whether heterosexual, homosexual, or bisexual.

attraction and behaviors is that gay men are, essentially, men, and that lesbians are, essentially, women.

Why are some individuals lesbian, gay, or bisexual, and others heterosexual? Speculation about this question has been extensive (Kelly, 2006; King, 2005). Researchers have explored the possible biological basis of same-sex attraction, especially in men (Quinsey, 2003). A very early prenatal critical period might influence sexual orientation (Swaab & others, 2002). In the second to fifth months after conception, exposure of the fetus to hormone levels characteristic of females might cause the individual (male or female) to become attracted to males (Ellis & Ames, 1987). But like most explanations for the origins of sexual orientation, this critical-period hypothesis is controversial (Gooren, 2006).

Like many other psychological characteristics, an individual's sexual orientation—whether same-sex, heterosexual, or bisexual—is most likely determined by a combination of genetic, hormonal, cognitive, and environmental factors (Baldwin & Baldwin, 1998). Most experts on sexual orientation believe that no one factor alone causes sexual orientation and that the relative weight of each factor can vary from one individual to the next. Moreover, no particular parenting style has been shown to relate to the development of children's sexual orientation.

Gay marriage and gay parenting have inspired strong controversy, especially in political election years. In addressing these issues, psychologists rely on scientific evidence. After reviewing that evidence, the American Psychological Association issued a press release supporting gay marriage and opposing discrimination against gay men and lesbians in matters such as parenting, adoption, and child custody (APA, 2004). The APA's stand was based on the considerable research supporting the central role of committed intimate relationships in human functioning (as will be discussed further in Chapter 12), as well as studies showing that children reared by gay men and lesbians tend to be as well adjusted as those from heterosexual households in cognitive, moral, social, and emotional measures (Chan, Raboy, & Patterson, 1998).

An individual's sexual preference is most likely determined by a combination of genetic, hormonal, cognitive, and environmental factors.

These endorsements represent a turn-around, as homosexuality was classified as a mental disorder by both the American Psychiatric Association and the American Psychological Association until the 1970s. Attitudes about gays and lesbians have become more positive in society in general (Kaiser Family Foundation, 2001). This increased acceptance likely stems in part from gay men's and lesbians' greater openness with others about their lives. In 2001, 73 percent of the general public reported knowing someone who is gay, compared to just 24 percent in 1984. Indeed, 70 percent or more of those surveyed in 2001 said that they believed there should be laws protecting gays and lesbians from discrimination at work and in housing. Younger Americans are particularly likely to support gay rights (Pew Research Center, 2007). Indeed, a recent survey of members of Generation Next (those born between 1981 and 1988) found that 58 percent believed that homosexuality ought to be accepted, and nearly half felt that same-sex marriage should be legal (Pew Research Center, 2007).

Still, there are those who oppose the social acceptance of gay people, particularly evangelical Christians. The intense national debate over whether gays should be allowed to marry has highlighted the fact that, despite progress in gaining acceptance, gay men and lesbians are still struggling for equal rights.

How can gays and lesbians adapt to a world in which they are an often debated minority? Accepting oneself as gay is an important aspect of psychological well-being for gay men and lesbians (Savin-Williams, 2006). A positive gay identity, rejection of negative gay stereotypes, and gay activism correlate with well-being (Luhtanen, 1996). When Ellen DeGeneres came out as a lesbian on the cover of *Time,* some people felt that it was inappropriate to disclose such highly personal information. However, being "out of the closet" correlates positively with well-being in gay men and lesbians and may be an important factor in physical health as well (King & Smith, 2004; Luhtanen, 1996). A large longitudinal study of HIV-positive gay men found that those who were "in the closet" were three times more likely to develop cancer and several infectious diseases compared to those who were more open about their sexual orientation (Cole & others, 1996).

REVIEW, ASSESS, AND SHARPEN YOUR THINKING

Review

3 Discuss the motivations for sexual behavior.
- Describe the biology of sex.
- Identify cognitive and sensory/perceptual factors that affect sexual behavior.
- Summarize the importance of culture in sexual motivation.
- Characterize sexual behavior and orientation in the United States.

Assess

1. Among lesbians and gay men, what is the relationship between being open about one's sexual orientation and well-being?

   A. Openness is related to increased depression.

   B. Openness always puts one at risk for victimization.

   C. There is not a clear link between openness and well-being.

   D. Openness is related to increased psychological and physical health.

2. In what brain structure is the motivation for sexual behavior centered?

   A. hypothalamus   B. temporal lobes

   C. hippocampus   D. medulla

3. Which stage of the sexual response pattern is characterized by a decrease in the activation of blood vessels?

   A. plateau phase

   B. resolution phase

   C. excitement phase

   D. orgasm

4. According to research led by Robert Michael, who reports having sex the most frequently?

   A. noncohabitating men

   B. cohabitating men

   C. noncohabitating women

   D. cohabitating women

5. What does the psychological research have to say about children raised by lesbian or gay parents?

   A. These children are more likely to grow up to be lesbian or gay.

   B. These children have more psychological problems than children raised by heterosexual parents.

   C. These children are similar in their overall adjustment to children raised by heterosexual parents.

   D. These children are more likely to be permissive in their moral codes than children raised by heterosexual parents.

Sharpen Your Thinking

What is your personal attitude toward homosexuality? Is it the same as your parents' views or different? If you are heterosexual, imagine what your life might be like if you were gay. If you are gay or bisexual, imagine your life as a straight person. How would your hopes and dreams for the future differ, if at all?

4 Beyond Hunger and Sex: Approaches to Motivation in Everyday Life

Characterize approaches to motivation in everyday life.

Food and sex are certainly crucial to our survival, individually and as a species. But surviving is not all we do. Think about the wide range of human actions and achievements reported in the news, such as a man's donation of his kidney to a best friend and the appointment of a woman who grew up in poverty as the CEO of a major corporation. Such individuals' behaviors are not easily explained by motivational approaches that focus on physiological needs or drive reduction. Furthermore, although early approaches to motivation, such as Freudian psychoanalysis (which we will discuss in Chapter 11), emphasized the role of unconscious drives as determinants of behavior, more recently psychologists have begun to appreciate the role of conscious experience in motivation. In this section, we explore the ways that psychologists have come to understand the processes that underlie everyday human behavior. We begin by considering the pioneering work of humanistic theorist Abraham Maslow.

Maslow's Hierarchy of Human Needs

Is getting an *A* in this class more important than eating? If the person of your dreams told you that you were marvelous, would that statement motivate you to throw yourself in front of a car for the person's safety? According to the humanistic theorist Abraham Maslow (1954, 1971), our basic needs must be satisfied before our higher needs can be. Maslow's **hierarchy of needs** states that individuals' main needs are satisfied in the following sequence: physiological, safety, love and belongingness, esteem, and self-actualization (Figure 10.7).

According to this hierarchy, people are motivated to satisfy their need for food first and to satisfy their need for safety before their need for love. If we think of our needs as calls for action, hunger and safety needs bellow loudly, while the need for self-actualization beckons with a whisper. Maslow asserted that the lower needs in the hierarchy come from deficiencies such as being hungry, lonely, or afraid and that we see the higher-level needs in a person who is relatively sated in these basic needs. Such an individual can turn his or her attention to the fulfillment of a higher calling.

Self-actualization, the highest and most elusive of Maslow's needs, is the motivation to develop one's full potential as a human being. According to Maslow, self-actualization is possible only after the other needs in the hierarchy are met. Maslow cautions that most people stop maturing after they have developed a high level of esteem and thus do not become self-actualized.

The idea that human motives are hierarchically arranged is an appealing one. Maslow's theory stimulates us to think about the ordering of motives in our own lives. However, Maslow's ordering of the needs is debatable. Some people might seek greatness in a career to achieve self-esteem, while putting on hold their needs for love and belongingness. Certainly history is full of examples of individuals who, in the direst of circumstances, still were able to engage in selfless acts of kindness. Research shows that it is the poorest individuals who are most likely to give generously.

Perhaps Maslow's greatest contribution to our understanding of motivation is that he asked the key question about motivation for modern people: How can we explain what humans do, once their bellies are chronically full? That is, how do we explain the "why" of human behavior when survival is not the most pressing need? This is the kind of questioning that inspired *self-determination theory* (Deci & Ryan, 2002).

Self-Determination Theory

Building from Maslow's humanistic perspective, Edward Deci and Richard Ryan (2000) have explored the role of motivation in optimal human functioning from a perspective that emphasizes particular kinds of needs as factors in psychological and physical well-being. **Self-determination theory** asserts that there are three basic organismic needs—competence, autonomy, and relatedness. These psychological needs are innate and exist in each person. These needs are basic to human growth and functioning, just as water, soil, and sunshine are necessary for plant growth. This metaphor is especially apt because once we plant a seed, all it requires to thrive and grow is a supportive environment. Similarly, self-determination theory holds that all of us have the capacity for growth and fulfillment in us, ready to emerge if given the right context.

Importantly, from the self-determination theory perspective, these organismic needs do not arise from deficits. Self-determination theory is not a drive reduction theory. Like Maslow, Deci and Ryan (2000) hold that these needs concern personal growth, not filling deficiencies. Let's examine each of these needs in depth.

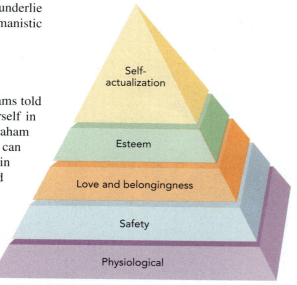

FIGURE 10.7

Maslow's Hierarchy of Needs Abraham Maslow developed the hierarchy of human needs to show that we have to satisfy basic physiological needs before we can satisfy other, higher needs.

hierarchy of needs Maslow's view that individuals' main needs are satisfied in the following sequence: physiological, safety, love and belongingness, esteem, and self-actualization.

self-actualization The highest and most elusive of Maslow's needs; the motivation to develop one's full potential as a human being.

self-determination theory A theory of motivation that proposes that three basic, organismic needs (competence, autonomy, and relatedness) characterize intrinsic motivation.

Asian students score considerably higher than U.S. students on math achievement tests.

Competence The first organismic need described by self-determination theory, competence, is met when we feel that we are able to bring about desired outcomes (Reis & others, 2000). Competence motivation involves self-efficacy (the feeling that you can accomplish your goals) and mastery (the sense that you can gain skills and overcome obstacles). Competence is also related to expectancies for success.

One domain in which competence needs may be met is in the realm of achievement. Some individuals are highly motivated to succeed and spend considerable effort striving to excel—for example, consider mountain climber Erik Weihenmayer, the first blind person to successfully climb the Seven Summits, the highest peaks in the world, including Mount Everest. Wiehenmayer decided to embark on the goal after reading about Mount Everest in braille. Although he certainly shattered stereotypes about what a blind person can accomplish, his tremendous efforts also allowed him to stand on the peak of Everest as "just another climber."

Relatedness The second organismic need described by self-determination theory is relatedness, the need to engage in warm relations with other people. Some psychologists have proposed that the need to belong is the strongest human motivator (Baumeister & Leary, 2000). The need for relatedness is reflected in the importance of parents' nurturing children's development, the intimate moments of sharing private thoughts in friendship, the uncomfortable feelings we have when we are lonely, and the powerful attraction we have for someone else when we are in love.

Dan McAdams (1989) has examined how one aspect of relatedness, the intimacy motive, is linked with a variety of aspects of human life. The intimacy motive is defined as an enduring concern for warm interpersonal encounters for their own sake. Intimacy motivation is revealed in the warm, positive interpersonal imagery in the stories people tell. Intimacy motive has been shown to relate to positive outcomes, such as heightened levels of happiness and lowered work strain (McAdams & Bryant, 1987). A study of the coming-out stories of gay men and lesbians demonstrated that intimacy-related imagery (for example, experiencing falling in love or warm acceptance from others) was associated with both measures of well-being and personality development (King & Smith, 2005).

Autonomy The final need proposed by self-determination theory is autonomy—our sense that we are in control of our own lives. Autonomy means being independent and self-reliant. Autonomy is a central aspect of feeling that one's behavior is self-motivated and emerging from genuine interest. Of course, many of the behaviors we engage in may feel like things we are forced to do, but the feeling of autonomy is strongly related to well-being (Sheldon & others, 2005).

Kennon Sheldon and colleagues (2005) have found that age relates to the experience of autonomy. For example, older Americans feel more autonomous than younger Americans when paying taxes, voting, and tipping.

Research on the role of motivation in well-being has supported the idea that progress on goals that serve the three organismic needs is strongly related to well-being (Sheldon & Elliot, 1998). Further, valuing more extrinsic qualities—such as money, prestige, and physical appearance—over these organismic concerns is associated with lowered well-being, lowered self-actualization, and physical illness (Kasser & Ryan, 1996; Kasser & others, 2004).

Issues in Self-Determination Theory Like any theory, self-determination theory has its controversies. One important issue is the extent to which the three needs are indeed universal. Cultures vary in how strongly they promote the needs for competence, relatedness, and autonomy. Many Western cultures—among them, the United States,

Canada, and western European countries—emphasize individual achieve-ment, independence, and self-reliance. In contrast, many Eastern cul-tures—such as China, Japan, and Korea—stress affiliation, cooperation, and interdependence (Triandis, 2000). However, cross-cultural evidence suggests that the needs emphasized by self-determination theory are likely to be valued in both Western and Eastern cultures.

© CartoonStock.com

Self-determination theory has implications for public policy in education. Recent programs such as No Child Left Behind have advocated high-stakes testing for students as the main criterion by which the quality of education is measured. These assessment tests focus on an external outcome, not the process of learning (Blumenfeld, Kempler, & Krajcik, 2006). Thus, from the perspective of self-determination theory, they are likely to undermine the healthier, more growth-oriented motivations of both students and educators. When teachers and students are in educational contexts that emphasize "teach-ing to the test," important aspects of education, such as critical thinking and creativity, are likely to be neglected. Research has shown, for example, that teachers who feel pressured to achieve the higher standards are less supportive and engage in controlling and instructing behaviors in their classrooms. And students in these situations perform more poorly on objective tests (Kohn, 2000; Ryan & Stiller, 1991).

Self-determination theory maintains that one of the most important aspects of healthy motivation is the sense that we do the things we do because we have freely chosen to do them. When we can choose our behaviors and feel ownership over those choices, we are likely to experience heightened fulfillment (Blumenfeld, Kempler, & Krajcik, 2006). Self-determination theory states that when our behaviors follow from the needs for compe-tence, autonomy and relatedness, we experience intrinsic motivation. When our behavior serves needs for other values, such as prestige, money, or approval, our behavior is extrinsi-cally motivated (Deci & Ryan, 1994; Ryan & Deci, 2000, 2001). We examine this impor-tant distinction between intrinsic and extrinsic motivation next.

Intrinsic Versus Extrinsic Motivation

One way psychologists understand the "why" of our goals is the distinction between intrin-sic and extrinsic motivation. **Intrinsic motivation** is based on internal factors such as organ-ismic needs (autonomy, competence, and relatedness), as well as curiosity, challenge, and effort. When we are intrinsically motivated, we engage in a behavior because we enjoy it. **Extrinsic motivation** involves external incentives such as rewards and punishments. When we are extrinsically motivated, we engage in a behavior for some external pay-off. Some students study hard because they are internally motivated to put forth considerable effort and achieve high quality in their work (intrinsic motivation). Other students study hard because they want to make good grades or avoid parental disapproval (extrinsic motivation).

"No, I didn't get a raise. He gave me another plaque."

© CartoonStock.com.

Almost every boss, parent, or teacher has wondered whether to offer a reward to someone who does well (extrinsic motivation) or whether to let the results of the individual's self-determined efforts be the reward (intrinsic motivation). If someone is producing shoddy work, seems bored, or has a negative attitude, offering incen-tives may improve motivation. But there are times when external rewards can diminish achievement motivation. One study showed that, among students who already had a strong interest in art, those who did not expect a reward spent more time drawing than did their counterparts who knew they would be rewarded for drawing (Lepper, Greene, & Nisbett, 1973). The problem with using a reward as an incentive is that individuals may perceive that the reward rather than their own motivation caused their achieve-ment behavior.

Many psychologists believe intrinsic motivation has more positive outcomes than extrinsic motivation (Blumenfeld, Kempler, & Krajcik, 2006; Brophy, 2004; Ryan & Deci, 2001). They argue that intrinsic motivation is more likely to produce competent behavior and mastery. Indeed, research comparisons often reveal that people whose motivation is intrinsic show more interest, excitement, and confidence in what they are doing than those

intrinsic motivation Motivation that is based on internal factors such as organismic needs (autonomy, competence, and relatedness), as well as curiosity, challenge, and effort.

extrinsic motivation Motivation that involves external incentives such as rewards and punishments.

The distinction between intrinsic and extrinsic motivation is well established in psychology. The basic idea is that we can be motivated by internal (intrinsic) factors, such as self-generated goals, or external (extrinsic) factors, such as praise and monetary rewards. It is commonly argued that intrinsic motivation is preferable to extrinsic motivation because it leads to more positive outcomes (Deci, Ryan, & Koestner, 2001). Also, extrinsic motivation is thought to reduce intrinsic motivation (Lepper, Greene, & Nisbett, 1973). A wide variety of social (extrinsic) events—such as deadlines, surveillance, and coercive rewards—can reduce the enjoyment (intrinsic motivation) associated with work, play, and study (Enzle & Anderson, 1993; Enzle, Roggeveen, & Look, 1991). These ideas have exerted a broad influence in educational and occupational settings, where teachers and employers seek to increase the intrinsic motivation of their students and employees, respectively (Blumenfeld, Kempler, & Krajcik, 2006; Wigfield & others, 2006).

However, two reviews of studies on intrinsic and extrinsic motivation reached opposite conclusions (Cameron, Banko, & Pierce, 2001; Deci, Koestner, & Ryan, 1999). Edward Deci and his colleagues (1999) analyzed 128 studies and concluded that the main negative effect of external rewards was to restrict self-determination and interfere with intrinsic motivation. In contrast, an analysis of 145 studies by Judy Cameron and her colleagues (Cameron, Banko, & Pierce, 2001) yielded mixed results. Cameron's group found that extrinsic rewards sometimes produced the expected negative effects on intrinsic motivation but that sometimes they had a positive effect or no effect at all. The true state of affairs, Cameron and colleagues suggest, is that extrinsic motivation has no overall effect on intrinsic motivation.

For example, some psychologists argue that tangible reinforcers such as money and prizes often undermine intrinsic motivation, whereas a verbal reinforcer such as praise can enhance intrinsic motivation (Carton, 1996). Thus, giving money to a beginning reader to read books may undermine that child's interest in reading, but praising that child for good reading may increase the child's interest. Similarly, Cameron (2001) believes that extrinsic motivation undermines intrinsic motivation when intrinsic motivation is high, but can be very helpful when intrinsic motivation is low. Thus, many beginning readers are motivated to read and may actually lose interest if they are reinforced for reading. In contrast, children who are not internally motivated to read may benefit from reinforcement and encouragement until their intrinsic motivation increases.

The problem, according to Cameron and her colleagues (Cameron, 2001; Cameron, Banko, & Pierce, 2001; Cameron & Pierce, 2002), lies in the rigid acceptance of general statements about motivation, such as "Extrinsic motivation reduces internal motivation." In the case of beginning readers, using this statement as a guiding principle may not damage the intrinsic motivation of motivated readers, but it may leave poorly motivated beginning readers with little reason to practice their reading. These researchers argue that people often do things that are not intrinsically motivating (such as mowing the lawn and studying mathematics) and that, without external rewards, they may simply lose interest in doing them. In such cases, extrinsic motivation may help foster intrinsic motivation in an activity. For example, a creative mathematics teacher might use rewards such as extra credit, math games, and verbal praise as a way to instill a lifelong love of mathematics.

Cameron's research (2001) suggests that psychologists need a better understanding of extrinsic rewards and intrinsic motivation so that they can distinguish between the effects of verbal and material reinforcement, for example, and between weak and strong intrinsic motivation. A richer understanding of intrinsic and extrinsic motivation might allow for more accurate predictions of when extrinsic motivation will reduce, increase, or not affect intrinsic motivation. It might then be possible for employers and teachers to help employees and students develop the deep intrinsic motivation that most people agree is indispensable to well-being.

What Do You Think?

- Can you think of examples in your own life when your intrinsic motivation was reduced by external rewards? Can you cite instances when your intrinsic motivation was increased by external rewards?
- What other factors might determine whether extrinsic motivation influences intrinsic motivation?
- If you were a classroom teacher and a child in your class was not motivated to learn, how would you use intrinsic and/or extrinsic motivation to help the child become more motivated to learn?

whose motivation is extrinsic. Intrinsic motivation often results in improved performance, persistence, creativity, and self-esteem (Ryan & Deci, 2001).

Some psychologists stress that many very successful individuals are both intrinsically motivated (have a high personal standard of achievement and emphasize personal effort) and extrinsically motivated (are highly competitive). Lance Armstrong, for example, had powerful intrinsic motivation to come back from testicular cancer to win the Tour de France. However, the extrinsic motivation of winning the trophy and the millions of dollars in endorsement contracts also likely played a role in his motivation. For the most part, though, psychologists believe that intrinsic motivation is the key to achievement

Motivation and Cognition: How Do We Resist Temptation?

It is bound to happen. You get up on Friday and commit to studying all weekend, and over lunch a friend invites you to a party on Saturday night. You commit to losing those last 10 pounds, and without fail the Girl Scouts show up peddling their delicious but forbidden cookies. You commit to a long-term romantic partner, and almost as if by magic, into your life walks an attractive, charming new acquaintance.

Motivation is about committing to the pursuit of valued goals, but often it seems the world conspires against you, dangling temptation at every turn (Mischel & Ayduk, 2004). How do you "stick with the program" when daily life so often tries to derail you from steadfastly pursuing your goals?

Psychologists from a variety of fields have been interested in the human capacity to resist temptation. Research on animal learning, social cognition, and self-control has significant implications for our ability to stay the course. One of the most important underlying problems in resisting temptation is delay of gratification—putting off a pleasurable experience in the interest of some larger but later reward. Successful delay of gratification can be seen in the student who does not go out with friends but instead stays in and studies for an upcoming test, perhaps thinking, "There will be plenty of time to party after this test is over." Delay of gratification is challenging for humans and other animals. Think about it—future pay-offs are simply much less certain than current rewards. If an organism is in a situation where rewards are few and far between, it might make sense to eat or drink whatever is around right now (Logue, 1995).

Eminent psychologist Walter Mischel and his colleagues (Mischel, Cantor, & Feldman, 1996; Mischel & Moore, 1980) examined how children managed to delay gratification successfully. He placed children in a difficult situation—alone in a room with a very tempting treat in their reach: a cookie. The children were told that if they wanted to at any time, they could simply ring a bell and eat the cookie. Otherwise, they could wait until the experimenter returned, and then they would get two cookies. The children were then left alone to face this self-control dilemma. In truth, the experimenter was not coming back. The researchers were interested in measuring how long the children could wait before giving in to temptation and eating the cookie.

The first set of results examined how the children who were able to resist temptation did so. There were a variety of responses to this unusual situation. Some children sat dead still, focused on the tempting cookie. Some stared the cookie down. Some smelled the cookie. Others turned away, sang songs, picked their noses, or did anything but pay attention to the cookie. Mischel and colleagues found that the kids who were able to distract themselves by focusing on "cool thoughts" (that is, non-cookie-related things) were better able to delay gratification. In contrast, children who remained focused on the cookie and all its delightful qualities—what Mischel called "hot thoughts"—were unable to wait and tended to eat the cookie sooner (Metcalfe & Mischel, 1999).

These findings have implications for self-control. Imagine that you are in a long-term romantic relationship that you wish to continue, and you meet an appealing new person to whom you are physically attracted. Should you cultivate a friendship with him or her? Maybe you should not, if you want to avoid temptation and preserve your current relationship. Think about all the current and potential "cookies" in your life—those things that have the power to distract you from achieving your long-term plans. Mischel's research with children demonstrates that avoiding these hot issues might be a good way to see a long-term plan through to its completion.

When facing a temptation, you might be inclined to concentrate simply on *not doing* the forbidden thing. Such a strategy might seem reasonable, but it is not likely to produce successful self-control. Dan Wegner (1989) demonstrated the difficulty involved in not thinking about a particular thing when he asked research participants to not think about a white bear. A white bear is probably not something that would come up very often in naturally occurring thought except perhaps for inhabitants of the Arctic. Yet just telling people not to think about white bears made thoughts of a white bear start to pop up in their minds.

Think about all the current and potential "cookies" in your life.

This "ironic effect" of thought suppression—the fact that when we try not to think about something, we are all the more likely to think about it—suggests that the approach of

(continued)

"just don't think about it" is likely to increase, not decrease, the frequency of forbidden thoughts. A lesson from the research laboratories of both Walter Mischel and Dan Wegner might be that rather than focusing on what you *do not* want, you should focus passionately on what you *do* want. Distraction is an option, but choosing a distraction that is consuming in its own right might be the best way to keep your mind off temptation. Instead of focusing on *not* eating that last chocolate chip cookie, how about getting into a great novel or taking a walk on a beautiful day?

Whereas concentrating your energy on not thinking about a temptation is particularly bad for self-control, staying focused on the goal of self-control may be crucial. Research by Andrew Ward and Traci Mann (2000) highlights the importance of such mindfulness, especially when one is trying to stay on track to reach a goal. They found that dieters who were distracted from their diet goals tended to eat more than those who were able to focus their attention. Ward and Mann sat dieters in front of bowls of M&Ms and Doritos and a plate of cookies. All of the participants were asked to at least try the snacks, but the dieters who were distracted by a mental task ate more. Apparently, distraction away from goals can lead to mindless consumption (Mann & Ward, 2004). Think about this effect the next time you buy an extra-large popcorn and a super-size sugary drink before sitting down to watch a movie.

Research on the underlying link between goals and the temptations that threaten their achievement provides surprisingly encouraging news. Ayelet Fishbach and her colleagues (2003) suggest that goals and temptations are linked to each other cognitively. They point out that to self-regulate effectively, individuals must be able to resist momentary enticements (the pleasure of a hot fudge sundae) in the pursuit of higher-priority goals (a healthy, fit body). Thus, the researchers hypothesized that goals and temptations are linked so that when exposed to temptation, an individual should put high-priority goals in the forefront.

In a set of provocative studies, they found that priming individuals with temptation actually led to the activation of the goals those temptations threaten. The good news is that the association runs in only one direction: When we think of a temptation, we are likely to remember our goals, but when we think about goals, we do not think immediately of a temptation. In one study, the researchers had dieters sit in rooms filled with either a variety of fitness magazines (a prime for their dietary goals), *Chocolatier* magazine and a variety of sweet foods (a prime for temptation), or magazines about the economy and geography (the control condition). Results showed that dieters who were surrounded by sweets and reminders of chocolate were more likely than dieters in the other two groups to rate themselves as committed to cutting down on French fries, pizza, chips, and so on. In addition, these individuals (as well as the participants exposed to the fitness magazines) were more likely to choose an apple over a Twix candy bar in return for participation.

Fishbach and colleagues maintain that one thing responsible for these effects is the habitual way that we defend our most cherished goals against derailing by temptation. The more we overcome temptation, the better able we will be to do so in the future. Indeed, Roy Baumeister has likened willpower to a muscle (Baumeister, 2002; Baumeister & Exline, 2000). The more we exercise that muscle, the better we become at accomplishing the sometimes challenging task of overcoming temptation and seeing our goals to fruition.

(Blumenfeld, Kempler, & Krajcik, 2006). Armstrong, like many other athletic champions, decided early on that he was training and racing for himself—not for his parents, coaches, or the medals. To read further about intrinsic and extrinsic motivation, see the Critical Controversy.

Self-Regulation: The Successful Pursuit of Goals

Many psychologists today approach motivation in the way that you yourself might—by asking about goals and values and seeking to understand how these motivational forces shape behavior. These approaches to motivation include the concept of self-regulation. **Self-regulation** is the process by which an organism pursues important objectives (Carver & Scheier, 2000). A key aspect of self-regulation is getting feedback about how we are doing in our goal pursuits. Our daily mood has been proposed as a way that we may receive this feedback—that is, we feel good or bad depending on how we are doing in the areas of life we value. Note that the role of mood in self-regulation means that we cannot be happy all the time. In order to effectively pursue our goals, we have to be open to the bad news that might occasionally come our way (King, 2007a).

Recruiting all of your willpower to pursue a goal you have consciously chosen can be difficult. To learn more about the ways motivation and cognition relate to sticking with a goal, see the Intersection.

One way to study self-regulation is to focus on self-generated goals, which, as we considered in Chapter 2, play a significant role in well-being (Franken, 2007). Psychologists have referred to goals by various names, including personal projects, best possible selves,

self-regulation The process by which an organism pursues important objectives, centrally involving getting feedback about how we are doing in our goal pursuits.

PSYCHOLOGY AND LIFE

How Goal-Directed Are You?

To evaluate how goal-directed you are, consider how much each of the following statements is like you or not like you:

- I set long-term and short-term goals.
- I set challenging goals that are neither too easy nor beyond my reach.
- I am good at managing my time and setting priorities to make sure I get the most important things done.
- I regularly make "to do" lists and successfully get most items done.
- I set deadlines and consistently meet them.
- I regularly monitor how well I'm progressing toward my goals and make changes in my behavior if necessary.
- When I am under pressure, I still plan my days and weeks in a clear, logical manner.
- I set task-involved, mastery goals rather than ego-involved or work-avoidant goals.

If most of these descriptions characterize you, then you likely are a goal-directed individual. If these statements do not characterize you, then consider ways that you can become more goal-directed.

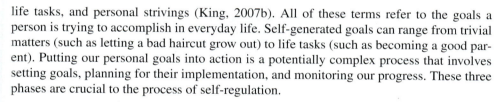

life tasks, and personal strivings (King, 2007b). All of these terms refer to the goals a person is trying to accomplish in everyday life. Self-generated goals can range from trivial matters (such as letting a bad haircut grow out) to life tasks (such as becoming a good parent). Putting our personal goals into action is a potentially complex process that involves setting goals, planning for their implementation, and monitoring our progress. These three phases are crucial to the process of self-regulation.

Goal Setting, Planning, and Monitoring   Individuals' success improves when they set goals that are specific, short term, and challenging (Bandura, 1997; Schunk & Zimmerman, 2006). A fuzzy, nonspecific goal is "I want to be successful." A concrete, specific goal is "I want to have a 3.5 average at the end of the semester." You can set both long-term (distal) and short-term (proximal) goals. It is okay to set long-term goals, such as "I want to be a clinical psychologist," but if you do, make sure that you also create short-term goals as steps along the way, such as "I want to get an *A* on the next psychology test," and "I will do all of my studying for this class by 4 P.M. on Sunday." Make commitments in bite-size chunks. A house is built one brick at a time; an artist paints one stroke at a time. You also should work in small increments.

Another good strategy is to set challenging goals (Anderman & Wolters, 2006). Strong interest and involvement in activities are sparked by challenges. Easy-to-reach goals generate little interest or effort. However, unrealistically high goals can bring failure and diminish self-confidence.

It is also important that your goals concern what you want to accomplish and not what you want to avoid. Researchers have found that the pursuit of avoidant goals is associated with poor performance and distress (Elliot & Sheldon, 1999).

Planning how to reach a goal and monitoring progress toward the goal are critical aspects of achievement (Wigfield & others, 2006). Researchers have found that high-achieving individuals monitor their own learning and systematically evaluate their progress toward their goals more than low-achieving individuals do (Anderman & Wolters, 2006; Wigfield & others, 2006). To evaluate how goal-directed you are, see the Psychology and Life box.

REVIEW, ASSESS, AND SHARPEN YOUR THINKING

Review

4 **Characterize approaches to motivation in everyday life.**
- Describe Maslow's approach to motivation.
- Define the self-determination theory perspective.
- Contrast intrinsic and extrinsic motivation.
- Discuss the concept of self-regulation and goal setting.

Assess

1. Rank order the following needs according to Maslow's hierarchy: love, hunger, self-esteem, shelter.
   A. Love must be fulfilled first, followed by hunger, safety, and finally self-esteem.
   B. Self-esteem must be fulfilled first, followed by love, safety, and hunger.
   C. Hunger must be fulfilled first, followed by safety, love, and finally self-esteem.
   D. Safety must be fulfilled first, followed by hunger, love, and finally self-esteem.

2. Which is the highest of needs, according to Maslow?
   A. love and belonging
   B. esteem
   C. safety
   D. self-actualization

3. Self-efficacy is most related to which of the needs outlined by self-determination theory?
   A. autonomy   B. relatedness
   C. competence   D. self-actualization

4. Of the following, who will likely perform best?
   A. someone with high extrinsic motivation
   B. someone with low extrinsic motivation
   C. someone with high intrinsic motivation
   D. someone with low intrinsic motivation

5. The goal "I want to avoid getting fat" is problematic because
   A. it is too specific.
   B. it focuses on something to be avoided.
   C. it is not challenging enough.
   D. it cannot be accomplished.

Sharpen Your Thinking

Make a list of your daily goals. How do they relate to the organismic needs you have read about in this chapter?

5 Emotion

Summarize views of emotion.

Anyone who has watched an awards show on television knows the link between motivation and emotion. Strolling in on the red carpet, the nominees stress how honored they are to be nominated; but behind the Hollywood smiles is the longing to win. When the announcement is made, "And the Oscar goes to . . . .," the cameras zoom in to catch a glimpse of real emotion: the winner's face lighting up with joy, and, of course, the moment of disappointment for the others.

In everyday life, motivation and emotion are closely linked. Think about sex, which often is associated with joy; about aggression, which usually is associated with anger; and about achievement, which is associated with pride, joy, and anxiety. The terms *motivation* and *emotion* both come from the Latin word *movere,* which means "to move." Both motivation and emotion spur us into action. In addition, the concept of self-regulation implies that our emotions give us feedback about how we are doing in the goals that motivate us.

Just as there are different kinds and intensities of motivation, so it is with emotions. A person can be more motivated to eat than to have sex and at different times can be more or less hungry or more or less interested in having sex. Similarly, a person can be happy (anywhere from fairly happy to ecstatic) or angry (anywhere from simply annoyed to fuming).

Defining emotion is difficult because it is not easy to tell when a person is in an emotional state. Are you in an emotional state when your heart beats fast, your palms sweat, and your stomach churns? Or are you in an emotional state when you think about how much you are in love with someone? Or when you smile or grimace? The body, the mind, and the face play important roles in emotion, although psychologists debate which of these components is the most important aspect of emotion and how they mix to produce emotional experiences (Davidson, Scherer, & Goldsmith, 2002). For our purposes, **emotion** is feeling, or affect, that can involve physiological arousal (such as a fast heartbeat), conscious experience (thinking about being in love with someone), and behavioral expression (a smile or grimace).

The Biology of Emotion

A friend you have been counseling about a life problem calls you to say, "We need to talk." As your friend's visit approaches, you might feel a bit nervous. What could be going on? You might feel burdened—you have a lot of work to do, and you do not have time for a talk session. You might worry that she is angry or disappointed about something you have done. But when she arrives with a gift-wrapped package and big smile, your nerves give way to relief. When she announces, "I wanted to give you this present to say thanks for all your help over the last few weeks," your heart warms, and you feel a strong sense of your enduring bond with her. As you moved through the emotions of worry, relief, and joy, your body changed. Indeed, the body is an important part of our emotional experience.

Arousal   Recall from Chapter 3 that the *autonomic nervous system (ANS)* takes messages to and from the body's internal organs, monitoring such processes as breathing, heart rate, and digestion. The ANS is divided into the sympathetic and the parasympathetic nervous systems (Figure 10.8). The *sympathetic nervous system (SNS)* is involved in the body's arousal; it is responsible for a rapid reaction to a stressor, sometimes referred to as the fight-or-flight response. The SNS immediately causes an increase in blood pressure, a faster heart rate, more rapid breathing for greater oxygen intake, and more efficient blood flow to the brain and major muscle groups. All of these changes prepare us for action. At the same time, the body stops digesting food, because it is not necessary for immediate action (which could explain why just before an exam, students usually are not hungry).

The *parasympathetic nervous system (PNS)* calms the body. Whereas the sympathetic nervous system prepares the individual for fighting or running away, the parasympathetic nervous system promotes relaxation and healing. When the PNS is activated, heart rate and blood pressure drop, stomach activity and food digestion increase, and breathing slows.

The sympathetic and parasympathetic nervous systems evolved to improve the human species' likelihood for survival, but it does not take a life-threatening situation to activate them. Emotions such as anger and fear are associated with elevated SNS activity as exemplified in heightened blood pressure and heart rate. But states of happiness and contentment also activate the SNS to a lesser extent.

Measuring Arousal   Because arousal includes a physiological response, researchers have been intrigued by how to measure it accurately. One aspect of emotional arousal is *galvanic skin response (GSR),* a rise in the skin's electrical conductivity when sweat gland activity increases. Measurement of this electrical activity provides an index of arousal that has been used in a number of studies of emotion.

emotion Feeling, or affect, that can involve physiological arousal, conscious experience, and behavioral expression.

FIGURE 10.8

The Autonomic Nervous System and Its Role in Arousing and Calming the Body Remember that the two sides of the autonomic nervous system work in different ways. The sympathetic nervous system acts in "sympathy" with you, so that when you are afraid or stressed, it responds by arousing you. The parasympathetic nervous system calms down your body and maintains its healthy functioning.

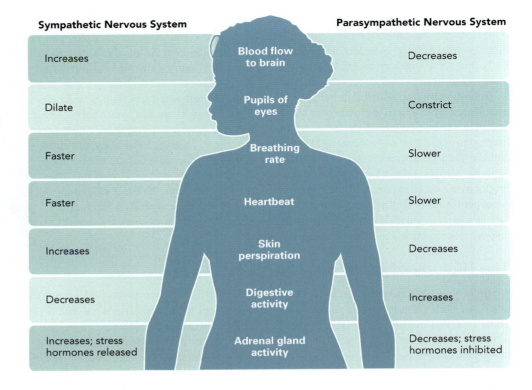

Sympathetic Nervous System		Parasympathetic Nervous System
Increases	Blood flow to brain	Decreases
Dilate	Pupils of eyes	Constrict
Faster	Breathing rate	Slower
Faster	Heartbeat	Slower
Increases	Skin perspiration	Decreases
Decreases	Digestive activity	Increases
Increases; stress hormones released	Adrenal gland activity	Decreases; stress hormones inhibited

polygraph A machine that monitors bodily changes thought to be influenced by emotional states; it is used by examiners to try to determine whether someone is lying.

Examiners use a polygraph to tell whether someone is lying. A polygraph monitors changes in the body believed to be influenced by emotional states. Controversy has swirled about the polygraph's use because it is unreliable.

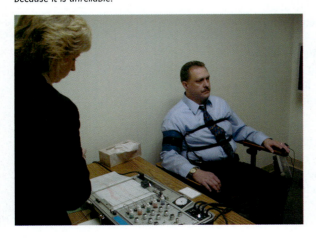

Another measure of arousal is the **polygraph,** a machine used by examiners to try to determine whether someone is lying. The polygraph monitors changes in the body—heart rate, breathing, and electrodermal response (an index detecting skin resistance to passage of a weak electric current)—thought to be influenced by emotional states.

In a typical polygraph test, the examiner asks the individual a number of neutral questions and several key, less neutral questions. If the individual's heart rate, breathing, and electrodermal responses increase substantially when the key questions are asked, the individual is assumed to be lying. (Lying also has been linked with certain emotional facial expressions.)

How accurate is the lie detector? Although it measures the degree of arousal to a series of questions, no one has found a unique physiological response to deception (Lykken, 1987, 2001; Seymour & others, 2000). Heart rate and breathing can increase for reasons other than lying, and this effect can make it difficult to interpret the physiological indicators of arousal.

Accurately identifying truth or deception is linked with the skill of the examiner and the skill of the individual being examined. Body movements and the presence of certain drugs in the person's system can interfere with the polygraph's accuracy. Sometimes the mere presence of the polygraph and the individual's belief that it is accurate in detecting deception trigger a confession of guilt. Police may use the polygraph in this way to get a suspect to confess. However, in too many instances it has been misused and misrepresented. Experts argue that the polygraph errs just under 50 percent of the time, especially as it cannot distinguish between such feelings as anxiety and guilt (Iacono & Lykken, 1997).

The Employee Polygraph Protection Act of 1988 restricts polygraph testing outside government agencies, and most courts do not accept the results of polygraph testing. However, some psychologists defend the polygraph's use, saying that polygraph results are as sound as other admissible forms of evidence, such as hair fiber analysis (Grubin & Madsen, 2006; Honts, 1998).

The majority of psychologists, though, argue against the polygraph's use because of its inability to tell who is lying and who is not (Iacono & Lykken, 1997; Lykken, 1998; Saxe, 1998; Steinbrook, 1992).

James-Lange and Cannon-Bard Theories

Imagine that you and your date are enjoying a picnic in the country. Suddenly, a bull runs across the field toward you. Why are you afraid? Two well-known theories of emotion that involve physiological processes provide answers to this question.

Common sense tells you that you are trembling and running away from the bull because you are afraid. But William James (1950) and Carl Lange (1922; his last name is pronounced "Long-uh") said emotion works in the opposite way. The **James-Lange theory** states that emotion results from physiological states triggered by stimuli in the environment: Emotion occurs *after* physiological reactions. Moreover, each emotion—from anger to rapture—has a distinct set of physiological changes, evident in changes in heart rate, breathing patterns, sweating, and other responses. Essentially, the James-Lange theory proposes that, after the initial perception, the experience of the emotion results from the perception of one's own physiological changes.

Let's see how the James-Lange theory would explain fear in the situation with the bull. You see the bull scratching its hoof on the ground, and you begin to run away. Your aroused body then sends sensory messages to your brain, at which point emotion is perceived. According to this theory, you do not run away because you are afraid; rather, you are afraid because you are running away. In other words, you perceive a stimulus in the environment, your body responds, and you interpret the body's reaction as emotion.

Walter Cannon (1927) objected to the assumption in the James-Lange theory that each emotional experience has its own particular set of physiological changes. He argued that different emotions could not be associated with specific physiological changes because autonomic nervous system responses are too diffuse and slow to account for rapid and differentiated emotional responses.

To understand Cannon's view, imagine the bull and the picnic once again. Seeing the bull scratching its hoof causes the thalamus of your brain to do two things simultaneously: First, it stimulates your autonomic nervous system to produce the physiological changes involved in emotion (increased heart rate, rapid breathing); second, it sends messages to your cerebral cortex, where the experience of emotion is perceived. Philip Bard (1934) supported this analysis, and so the theory became known as the **Cannon-Bard theory,** the theory that emotion and physiological reactions occur simultaneously. In the Cannon-Bard theory, the body plays a less important role than in the James-Lange theory. Figure 10.9 shows how the James-Lange and Cannon-Bard theories differ.

The question of whether emotions involve discrete autonomic nervous system responses continues to be debated (Keltner & Ekman, 2000). Recent studies have documented some emotion-specific autonomic nervous system responses (Christie & Friedman, 2004). For example, fear, anger, and sadness are associated with increased heart rate, but disgust is not (Bryant, 2006; Hamer & others, 2006). Also, anger is linked with increased blood flow to the hands, an effect that is not triggered by fear.

Neural Circuits and Neurotransmitters

Contemporary researchers are more interested in charting the neural circuitry of emotions and discovering the role of neurotransmitters in emotion than was the case in the early twentieth century (Kalat & Shiota, 2007). The focus of much of their work has been on the amygdala, the almond-shaped structure in the limbic system, discussed in Chapter 3. The amygdala houses circuits that are activated when we experience negative emotions.

Joseph LeDoux and his colleagues have conducted a number of research studies that focus on the neural circuitry of one emotion: fear (LeDoux, 1996, 2002; Phelps & LeDoux, 2005; Radley & others, 2006). The amygdala plays a central role in fear. When the amygdala determines that danger is present, it shifts into high gear, marshaling the resources of the brain in an effort to protect the organism from harm. This fear system was designed by evolution to detect and respond to predators and other types of natural dangers that threaten survival or territory.

James-Lange theory Theory stating that emotion results from physiological states triggered by stimuli in the environment.

Cannon-Bard theory Theory stating that emotion and physiological reactions occur simultaneously.

FIGURE 10.9

James-Lange and Cannon-Bard Theories From the James-Lange perspective, the experience of fear is an outcome of physiological arousal. In the Cannon-Bard view, fear occurs at the same time as the physiological response.

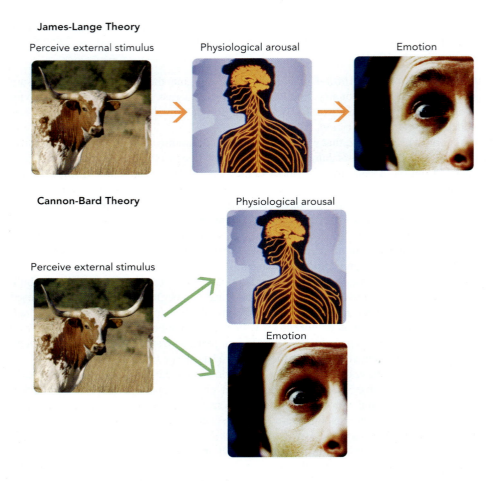

The amygdala receives neurons from the senses of sight, hearing, smell, and touch. If any of these neurons communicates a danger, the amygdala becomes activated and immediately sends out messages to various organs that respond in ways to prevent harm to the organism.

The brain circuitry that involves the emotion of fear can follow two pathways: a direct pathway from the thalamus to the amygdala or an indirect pathway from the thalamus through the sensory cortex to the amygdala (Figure 10.10). The direct pathway does not convey detailed information about the stimulus, but it has the advantage of speed. And speed clearly is an important characteristic of information available to an organism facing a threat to its survival. The indirect pathway carries nerve impulses from the sensory organs (eyes and ears, for example) to the thalamus (recall that the thalamus is a relay station for incoming sensory stimuli); from the thalamus, the nerve impulses travel to the sensory cortex, which then sends appropriate signals to the amygdala.

Recall from Chapter 8 that the amygdala is linked with emotional memories. LeDoux and his colleagues say that the amygdala hardly ever forgets (Debiec & LeDoux, 2006; LeDoux, 2000, 2001; Sigurdsson & others, 2006). This quality is useful, because once we learn that something is dangerous, we do not have to relearn it. However, we pay a penalty for this ability. Many people carry fears and anxieties around with them that they would like to get rid of but cannot seem to shake. Part of the reason for this dilemma is that the amygdala is well connected to the cerebral cortex, in which thinking and decision making primarily occur (Rauch, Shin, & Phelps, 2006). The amygdala is in a much better position to influence the cerebral cortex than the other way around, because it sends more connections to the cerebral cortex than it gets back. This may explain why it is so hard to control our emotions, and why, once fear is learned, it is so hard to erase.

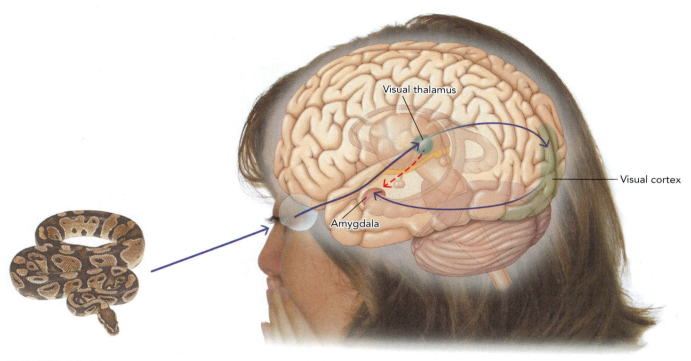

FIGURE 10.10

Direct and Indirect Brain Pathways in the Emotion of Fear Information about fear can follow two pathways in the brain when an individual sees a snake. The direct pathway (*broken arrow*) conveys information rapidly from the thalamus to the amygdala. The indirect pathway (*solid arrows*) transmits information more slowly from the thalamus to the sensory cortex (here, the visual cortex), then to the amygdala.

LeDoux (2000, 2002) says that it is unlikely that the amygdala mediates all emotions. However, there is some evidence that the amygdala participates in positive emotions as well as negative emotions. A recent research review concluded that various regions of the limbic system, including the amygdala, are involved in the experience of positive emotions (Burgdorf & Panksepp, 2006). In this review, the neurotransmitter dopamine was especially active in the limbic system during the experiencing of positive emotions. Different regions of the prefrontal cortex likely are more involved in happy emotions than sad emotions (Habel & others, 2005).

Researchers are also finding that the cerebral hemispheres may be involved in understanding emotion. Richard Davidson and his colleagues have shown that the cerebral hemispheres work differently in approach- and withdrawal-related emotions (Davidson, 2000; Davidson, Shackman, & Pizzagalli, 2002; Reuter-Lorenz & Davidson, 1981; Urry & others, 2004). Approach-related emotions, such as happiness, are linked more strongly with left hemisphere brain activity, whereas withdrawal-related emotions, such as disgust, show stronger activity in the right hemisphere. Recall that research we reviewed in Chapter 3 suggests that people who show relatively more left than right prefrontal activation tend to be happier.

Researchers are also intrigued by the roles that neurotransmitters play in the neural pathways of emotions. Endorphins and dopamine are involved in positive emotions such as happiness, and norepinephrine functions in regulating arousal (Berridge, 2006; Burgdorf & Panksepp, 2006).

Cognitive Factors

Does emotion depend on the tides of the mind? Are we happy only when we think we are happy? Cognitive theories of emotion center on the premise that emotion always has a cognitive component (Derryberry & Reed, 2002; Frijda, 2007; Johnson-Laird, Mancini, &

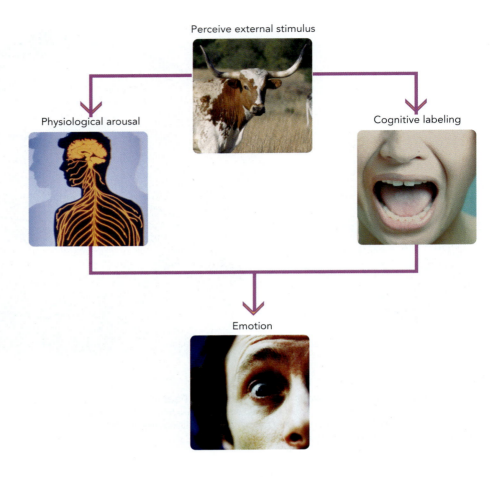

Perceive external stimulus

Physiological arousal

Cognitive labeling

Emotion

Gangemi, 2006). Thinking is said to be responsible for feelings of love and hate, joy and sadness. Cognitive theorists also recognize the role of the brain and body in emotion, but they give cognitive processes the main credit for emotion.

The Two-Factor Theory of Emotion In the **two-factor theory of emotion** developed by Stanley Schachter and Jerome Singer (1962), emotion is determined by two factors: physiological arousal and cognitive labeling (Figure 10.11). They argued that we look to the external world for an explanation of why we are aroused. We interpret external cues and label the emotion. For example, if you feel good after someone has made a pleasant comment to you, you might label the emotion "happy." If you feel bad after you have done something wrong, you may label the feeling "guilty."

To test their theory of emotion, Schachter and Singer (1962) injected volunteer participants with epinephrine, a drug that produces high arousal. After participants were given the drug, they observed someone else behave in either a euphoric way (shooting papers at a wastebasket) or an angry way (stomping out of the room). As predicted, the euphoric and angry behavior influenced the participants' cognitive interpretation of their own arousal. When they were with a happy person, they rated themselves as happy; when they were with an angry person, they said they were angry. But this effect occurred only when the participants were not told about the true effects of the injection. When they were told that the drug would increase their heart rate and make them jittery, they said the reason for their own arousal was the drug, not the other person's behavior.

Psychologists have had difficulty replicating the results of the Schachter and Singer experiment, but, in general, research supports the belief that misinterpreted arousal intensifies emotional experiences (Leventhal & Tomarken, 1986). An intriguing study by Donald Dutton and Arthur Aron (1974) substantiates this conclusion. In the study, an attractive woman approached men while they were walking across the Capilano River

Bridge in British Columbia. Only men without a female companion were approached. The woman asked the men to make up a brief story for a project she was doing on creativity. The Capilano River Bridge sways dangerously more than 200 feet above rapids and rocks (Figure 10.12). The female interviewer made the same request of other men crossing a much safer, lower bridge. The men on the Capilano River Bridge told more sexually oriented stories and rated the female interviewer more attractive than did men on the lower, less frightening bridge.

The Primacy Debate: Cognition or Emotion? Which comes first, thinking or feeling? Fans of the vintage version of TV's *Star Trek* may recognize this theme from the frequent arguments between Mr. Spock, the logical Vulcan, and Bones, the emotional doctor on the *Enterprise*. In the 1980s and 1990s, two eminent psychologists, Richard Lazarus (1922–2002) and Robert Zajonc (sounds like "science"), debated the question of which is central, cognition or emotion. Lazarus (1991) argued for the primacy of thinking—he believed cognitive activity to be a precondition for emotion. Lazarus said that we cognitively appraise ourselves and our social circumstances. These appraisals—which include values, goals, commitments, beliefs, and expectations—determine our emotions. People may feel happy because they have a deep religious commitment, angry because they did not get the raise they anticipated, or fearful because they expect to fail an exam.

Zajonc (1984) disagreed with Lazarus. Emotions are primary, he said, and our thoughts are a result of them. Zajonc famously argued that "preferences need no inferences," meaning that the way we feel about something on a "gut level" requires no thought. Which of the two psychologists is right? Both likely are correct. Lazarus talked mainly about a cluster of related events that occur over a period of time, whereas Zajonc described single events or a simple preference for one stimulus over another. Lazarus was concerned with love over the course of months and years, a sense of value to the community, and plans for retirement; Zajonc spoke about a car accident, an encounter with a snake, and a preference for ice cream rather than spinach.

Some of our emotional reactions are virtually instantaneous and probably do not involve cognitive appraisal, such as shrieking upon detecting a snake. Other emotional circumstances, especially long-term feelings such as a depressed mood or anger toward a friend, are likelier to involve cognitive appraisal. Indeed, the direct and indirect brain pathways described earlier support the idea that some of our emotional reactions do not involve deliberate thinking, whereas others do (LeDoux, 2001).

Behavioral Factors

Remember that our definition of emotion includes not only physiological and cognitive components but also a behavioral component. The behavioral component can be verbal or nonverbal. Verbally, a person might show love for someone by professing it verbally or might display anger by saying nasty things. Nonverbally, a person might smile, frown, show a fearful expression, look down, or slouch.

The most interest in the behavioral dimension of emotion has focused on the nonverbal behavior of facial expressions (Bimler & Paramei, 2006). Emotion researchers have been intrigued by people's ability to detect emotion from a person's facial expression (Schwaninger & others, 2006; Susskind & others, 2006). In a typical research study, participants, shown photographs like those in Figure 10.13, are usually able to identify these six emotions: happiness, anger, sadness, surprise, disgust, and fear (Ekman & O'Sullivan, 1991).

Might our facial expressions not only reflect our emotions but also influence them? According to the **facial feedback hypothesis,** facial expressions can influence emotions as well as reflect them. In this view, facial muscles send signals to the brain, which help individuals to recognize the emotion they are experiencing (Keillor & others, 2002). For example, we feel happier when we smile and sadder when we frown.

Support for the facial feedback hypothesis comes from an experiment by Paul Ekman and his colleagues (1983). In this study, professional actors moved their facial muscles in

FIGURE 10.12

Capilano River Bridge Experiment: Misinterpreted Arousal Intensifies Emotional Experiences (*Top*) The precarious Capilano River Bridge in British Columbia. (*Bottom*) The experiment in progress. An attractive woman approached men while they were crossing the bridge; she asked them to make up a story to help her with a creativity project. She also made the same request on a lower, much safer bridge. The men on the Capilano River Bridge told more sexually oriented stories, probably because they were aroused by the fear or excitement of being up so high on a swaying bridge and interpreted their arousal as sexual attraction for the female interviewer.

facial feedback hypothesis The idea that facial expressions can influence emotions as well as reflect them.

FIGURE 10.13

Recognizing Emotions in Facial Expressions Look at the six photographs and determine the emotion reflected in each of the six faces. (*Top*) happiness, anger, sadness (*bottom*) surprise, disgust, fear.

very precise ways, such as raising their eyebrows and pulling them together, raising their upper eyelids, and stretching their lips horizontally back to their ears (you might want to try this yourself). They were asked to hold their expression for 10 seconds, during which time the researchers measured their heart rate and body temperature. When they moved facial muscles in the ways described, they showed a rise in heart rate and a steady body temperature—physiological reactions that characterize fear. When the actors made an angry facial expression (with a penetrating stare, brows drawn together and downward, and lips pressed together or opened and pushed forward), their heart rate and body temperature both increased. The facial feedback hypothesis provides support for the James-Lange theory of emotion discussed earlier—namely, that emotional experiences can be generated by changes in and awareness of our own bodily states.

Sociocultural Factors

Are the facial expressions that are associated with different emotions largely innate, or do they vary across cultures? Are there gender variations in emotion?

Culture and the Expression of Emotion In *The Expression of the Emotions in Man and Animals,* Charles Darwin stated that the facial expressions of human beings are innate, not learned; are the same in all cultures around the world; and evolved from the emotions of animals (1965). Darwin compared the similarity of human snarls of anger with the growls of dogs and the hisses of cats. He compared the giggling of chimpanzees when they are tickled under their arms with human laughter.

Today psychologists still believe that emotions, especially facial expressions of emotion, have strong biological ties (Gelder & others, 2006; Peleg & others, 2006). For example, children who are blind from birth and have never observed the smile or frown on another person's face smile or frown in the same way that children with normal vision do.

FIGURE 10.14

Emotional Expressions in the United States and New Guinea (*Left*) Two women from the United States. (*Right*) Two men from the Fore tribe in New Guinea. Notice the similarity in their expressions of disgust and happiness. Psychologists believe that the facial expression of emotion is virtually the same in all cultures.

If emotions and facial expressions that go with them are unlearned, then they should be the same the world over.

Extensive research has examined the universality of facial expressions and the ability of people from different cultures accurately to label the emotion that lies behind facial expressions. Paul Ekman's careful observations reveal that the many faces of emotion do not differ significantly from one culture to another (Ekman, 1980, 1996, 2003). For example, Ekman and his colleague photographed people expressing emotions such as happiness, fear, surprise, disgust, and grief. When they showed the photographs to people from the United States, Chile, Japan, Brazil, and Borneo (an Indonesian island in the western Pacific Ocean), all tended to label the same faces with the same emotions (Ekman & Friesen, 1968). Another study focused on the way the Fore tribe, an isolated Stone Age culture in New Guinea, matched descriptions of emotions with facial expressions (Ekman & Friesen, 1971). Before Ekman's visit, most of the Fore had never seen a Caucasian face. Ekman showed them photographs of American faces expressing emotions such as fear, happiness, anger, and surprise. Then he read stories about people in emotional situations. The Fore were able to match the descriptions of emotions with the facial expressions in the photographs. The similarity of facial expressions of emotions by persons in New Guinea and the United States is shown in Figure 10.14.

Whereas facial expressions of basic emotions appear to be universal, display rules for emotion vary (Fischer, 2006; Fok & others, 2008). **Display rules** are sociocultural standards that determine when, where, and how emotions should be expressed. For example, although happiness is a universally expressed emotion, when, where, and how it is displayed may vary from one culture to another. The same is true for other emotions, such as fear, sadness, and anger. For example, members of the Utku culture in Alaska discourage anger by cultivating acceptance and by dissociating themselves from any display of anger. If a trip is hampered by an unexpected snowstorm, the Utku do not express frustration but accept the snowstorm and build an igloo. The importance of display rules is especially evident when we evaluate the emotional expression of another. Does that grieving husband on a morning talk show seem appropriately distraught over his wife's murder? Or might he be a suspect?

Like facial expressions, some other nonverbal signals appear to be universal indicators of certain emotions. For example, when people are depressed, it shows not only in their sad facial expressions but also in their slow body movements, downturned heads, and slumped posture.

Many nonverbal signals of emotion, though, vary from one culture to another (Mesquita, 2002). For example, male-to-male kissing is commonplace in Yemen but uncommon in the United States. And the "thumbs up" sign, which in most cultures means either everything is okay or the desire to hitch a ride, is an insult in Greece, similar to a raised third finger in the United States—something to keep in mind if you find yourself backpacking through Greece.

display rules Sociocultural standards that determine when, where, and how emotions should be expressed.

In the Middle Eastern country of Yemen, male-to-male kissing is commonplace, but in the United States it is less common.

Gender Influences Unless you have been isolated on a mountaintop, you probably know the stereotype about gender and emotion: She is emotional; he is not. This stereotype is a powerful and pervasive image in our culture (Shields, 1991).

Is this stereotype supported by research on emotional experiences? Researchers have found that females and males are often more alike in the way they experience emotion than the stereotype would lead us to believe. Women and men often use the same facial expressions, adopt the same language, and describe their emotional experiences similarly when they keep diaries about their experiences. For many emotional experiences, researchers do not find differences between females and males—both sexes are equally likely to experience love, jealousy, anxiety in new social situations, anger when they are insulted, grief when close relationships end, and embarrassment when they make mistakes in public (Tavris & Wade, 1984).

When we go beyond stereotypes and consider some specific emotional experiences, contexts in which emotion is displayed, and certain beliefs about emotion, gender does matter in understanding emotion (Brannon, 1999; Brody, 1999; Shields, 1991). Women have been found to be more accurate at recognizing the emotional content of faces, especially when the task is made challenging by showing the faces for a very short time (Hall & Matsumoto, 2004). Women also report themselves as experiencing emotions for a longer period than men (Birditt & Fingerman, 2003). It is important to keep in mind that both women and men are certainly aware of the gender-specific expectations for emotional behavior. Indeed, men who embrace a stereotypically masculine gender identity are more likely to report themselves as less emotional (Jakupcak & others, 2003). Gender differences in emotion are much more tied to social context than to biological sex (Brody, 1999).

Classifying Emotions

There are more than 200 words for emotions in the English language, indicating the complexity and variety of emotions. Not surprisingly, psychologists have created ways to classify emotions. One of these schemes is the wheel model. Another is a two-dimensional model.

The Wheel Model A number of psychologists have classified the emotions we experience by placing them on a wheel, or what psychologists call a *circumplex*. One such model was proposed by Robert Plutchik (1980) (Figure 10.15). He believes emotions have four dimensions: (1) They are positive or negative, (2) they are primary or mixed, (3) many are polar opposites, and (4) they vary in intensity. Ecstasy and enthusiasm are positive emotions; grief and anger are negative emotions.

Another wheellike model of emotion was proposed by Sylvan Tompkins (1962). Tompkins described the basic emotions as fear, anger, joy, distress, disgust, interest, surprise, contempt, and shame. Figure 10.16 shows that there is some consensus between Plutchik and Tompkins. Theorists such as Plutchik and Tompkins view emotions as essentially innate reactions that require little cognitive interpretation. As such, their views reflect an evolutionary perspective. In this perspective, the basic emotions evolved and were retained because of their adaptive survival value.

FIGURE 10.15

Plutchik's Classification of Emotions
Plutchik theorized that people experience the eight basic emotions represented in the colored sections of the drawing, as well as combinations of these emotions, shown outside the wheel.

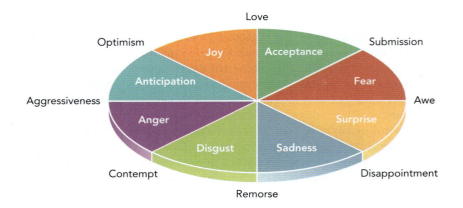

The Two-Dimensional Approach   The two-dimensional approach to classifying emotions argues that there are two broad dimensions of emotional experiences: negative affectivity and positive affectivity. *Negative affectivity (NA)* refers to negative emotions such as anxiety, anger, guilt, and sadness. *Positive affectivity (PA)* refers to positive emotions such as joy, happiness, love, and interest. Research has shown that emotions tend to go together based on their valence, so that if someone is sad, he or she is also likely to be angry or worried, while if a person is happy, he is or she is also likely to be feeling confident, joyful, and content (Watson, 2001).

In considering the functions of emotions in our lives, it is fairly easy to come up with a good reason for us to have emotions like fear and anger. Negative emotions carry direct and immediate adaptive benefits in situations that threaten survival. As noted in Chapter 9, negative emotions such as anxiety and depression often narrow attention (Basso & others, 1996). In a sense, negative emotions are easier to understand than positive feelings. Negative emotions clearly indicate that something is wrong and that action is needed. But it is more difficult to recognize an "action tendency" behind positive emotions. What function might positive emotions play in human life?

Confronting this challenge, Barbara Fredrickson has proposed the **broaden-and-build model** of positive emotion (Fredrickson, 1998, 2001, 2006). She argues that the function of positive emotions lies in their effects on our attention and our ability to build resources. The broaden-and-build model begins with the influence of positive emotions on cognitive processing.

As noted in Chapter 9, and in contrast to negative affect, positive moods broaden our attentional focus; they allow us to see the forest and not be blinded by the trees. As a result, when in a good mood, we may be more disposed to "think outside the box"—to see unusual possibilities that escaped us before. In addition, a good mood, Fredrickson says, gives us a chance to build resources—to make friends, exercise, branch out in new ways. These activities allow us to build up strengths that we can use when we encounter life's difficulties (Cohn & Fredrickson, 2006; Waugh & Fredrickson, 2006). For example, joy broadens people by creating the urge to play, push the limits, and be creative. Interest broadens people by creating the motivation to explore, absorb new information and experiences, and expand the self (Csikszentmihalyi, 1990; Ryan & Deci, 2000). Positive emotions facilitate approach behavior (Otake & others, 2006; Watson, 2001), meaning that when we are feeling good, we are more likely to go after the rewards we want and to face our problems "head on."

Positive emotions can serve as markers of well-being (Fredrickson, 2001). When people's lives are characterized by joy, happiness, love, and interest, it is likely that these override negative emotions such as sadness, anger, and despair (Diener, 1999). Positive emotions can also improve coping. In one study, individuals who experienced more positive emotions than others developed broader-based coping strategies, such as thinking about different ways to deal with a problem, stepping back from the situation, and being more objective (Fredrickson & Joiner, 2000, 2002).

In some cases, positive emotions can undo lingering negative emotions (Fredrickson, 2001). For example, mild joy and contentment have been found to undo the lingering cardiovascular effects of negative emotions such as sadness (Fredrickson & Levenson, 1998). In sum, positive emotions likely serve important functions in an individual's adaptation, growth, and social connection. By building personal and social resources, positive emotions improve people's well-being.

Before leaving the two-dimensional approach, let's focus on two specific examples of each of these types of emotion: anger and gratitude.

A Negative Emotion: Anger   Anger is a powerful emotion. It has strong effects not only on social relationships but also on the person experiencing the emotion. We can easily recount obvious examples of anger that causes such harm—unrestrained and recurrent violence toward others, verbal and physical abuse of children, perpetual bitterness, the tendency to carry a "chip on the shoulder" in which a person overinterprets others' actions as demeaning, and the inability to inhibit the expression of anger. Is there a healthy way to deal with this emotion?

Plutchik	Tompkins
Fear	Fear
Anger	Anger
Joy	Joy
Sadness	Distress
Acceptance	Interest
Surprise	Surprise
Disgust	Contempt
Anticipation	Shame

FIGURE 10.16
Comparison of Plutchik's and Tompkins's Classifications of Basic Emotions Notice the ways in which these two classification systems are similar and different.

broaden-and-build model A model emphasizing that the key to the adaptiveness of positive emotional states lies in their effects on our attention and our ability to build resources.

catharsis The release of anger or aggressive energy by directly or vicariously engaging in anger or aggression; the catharsis hypothesis states that behaving angrily or watching others behave angrily reduces subsequent anger.

Catharsis is the release of anger or aggressive energy by directly or vicariously engaging in anger or aggression; the *catharsis hypothesis* states that behaving angrily or watching others behave angrily reduces subsequent anger. Psychodynamic theory promotes catharsis as an important way to reduce anger, arguing that people have a natural, biological tendency to display anger. From this perspective, taking out your anger on a friend or a loved one should reduce your subsequent tendency to display anger; so should heavy doses of anger on television and the anger we see in professional sports and other aspects of our culture. Why? Such experiences release pent-up anger.

Social cognitive theory argues strongly against this view. This theory states that, by acting angrily, people often are rewarded for their anger and that, by watching others display anger, people learn how to be angry themselves. Which view is right? Research on catharsis suggests that acting angrily does not have any long-term power to reduce anger. Quite the contrary, venting anger often leads a person to feel even angrier. Expressing anger can escalate into an argument, shouted recriminations, screaming, or crying (Tavris, 1989).

Every person gets angry at one time or another. How can we control our anger so it does not become destructive? Mark Twain once remarked, "When angry, count four; when very angry, swear." Carol Tavris (1989), noted emotion researcher and author, makes the following recommendations:

1. When your anger starts to boil and your body is getting aroused, work on lowering the arousal by waiting. Emotional arousal will usually decrease if you just wait long enough.

2. Cope with the anger in ways that involve neither being chronically angry over every little annoyance nor passively sulking, which simply rehearses your reasons for being angry.

3. Form a self-help group with others who have been through similar experiences with anger. The other people will likely know what you are feeling, and together you might come up with some good solutions to anger problems.

4. Take action to help others. This strategy can put your own miseries in perspective, as exemplified by the actions of the women who organized Mothers Against Drunk Driving or any number of people who work to change conditions so that others will not suffer as they did.

5. Seek ways of breaking out of your usual perspective. Some people have been rehearsing their "story" for years, repeating over and over the reasons for their anger. Retelling the story from other participants' points of view often helps people to find routes to empathy.

A Positive Emotion: Gratitude A positive emotion that has recently sparked particular interest is gratitude (Bartlett & DeSteno, 2006; Miley & Spinella, 2006; Tangney, Stuewig, & Mashek, 2007). A complex positive emotion, gratitude comes from the experience of having something good in your life that you realize you have not earned or necessarily deserved. Gratitude may be defined as our awareness that something good has happened in our lives along with awareness that someone else is responsible for that good thing. Philosopher Robert Solomon suggested that gratitude is not only "the best answer to the tragedies of life. It is the best approach to life itself" (Solomon, 2002).

Gratitude is a universal experience: Every culture includes the idea of gratitude. Thanksgiving is a national holiday in the United States—the only holiday dedicated to the celebration of an emotion. Furthermore, the experience of exchange relationships in nonhuman primates suggests that our evolutionary forerunners might show the beginnings of gratitude (Bonnie & de Waal, 2004).

Robert Emmons and Michael McCullough (2004) have conducted a number of studies demonstrating the ways that being grateful can lead to enhanced happiness and psychological well-being. In one study, they asked participants to keep a diary in which they counted their blessings every day. Those who counted their blessings were better off on a variety of measures of well-being.

Other research has shown that experiences of gratitude lead to more helping behavior (Bartlett & DeSteno, 2006; Tsang, 2006). Although some individuals do seem to be more grateful than others, what is most encouraging about this

"Oh alright…. My gratitude blazes within me with the white hot intensity of a thousand burning suns…. Now can I please have my newspaper?"

© CartoonStock.com.

research is that experimental evidence indicates that even those who are not naturally grateful can benefit by taking a moment to count their blessings (Emmons & McCullough, 2003; McCullough, Emmons, & Tsang, 2002).

 REVIEW, ASSESS, AND SHARPEN YOUR THINKING

Review

5 Summarize views of emotion.

- Define emotion and explain the biology of emotion in terms of arousal and neural activity.
- Discuss cognitive theorists' two-factor theory and the primacy debate over cognition and emotion.
- Describe behavioral expressions of emotion.
- Identify sociocultural similarities and differences in the expression of emotion.
- Compare the wheel model and the two-dimensional model of classifying emotions and describe psychological approaches to anger and gratitude.

Assess

1. The James-Lange theory of emotion states that
   - A. emotion happens first, followed by physiological reactions.
   - B. physiological reactions happen first, followed by emotion.
   - C. physiological reactions and emotion happen simultaneously.
   - D. the body plays a minimal role in emotion.

2. Which of the following describes the indirect neural pathway involved in fearful stimuli?
   - A. Neural pathways go to the thalamus, then to the hypothalamus, and then to the amygdala.
   - B. Neural pathways go to the thalamus, then to the sensory cortex, and then to the amygdala.
   - C. Neural pathways go to the thalamus and then to the hippocampus.
   - D. Neural pathways go to the thalamus, then to the hypothalamus, then to the sensory cortex, and then to the hippocampus.

3. The facial feedback hypothesis is consistent with which theory of emotion?
   - A. James-Lange theory
   - B. Cannon-Bard theory
   - C. two-factor direct theory
   - D. indirect theory

4. The old saying "boys don't cry" is consistent with which of the following?
   - A. James-Lange theory
   - B. Cannon-Bard theory
   - C. display rules
   - D. the facial feedback hypothesis

5. The release of anger is known as
   - A. negative affectivity.
   - B. the broaden-and-build model.
   - C. display rules.
   - D. catharsis.

Sharpen Your Thinking

Describe the last time you felt gratitude. What prompted this feeling?

6 Emotion and Health and Wellness

Discuss the role of emotions in physical and psychological health and wellness.

A great deal of research has examined the relation between our emotional lives and our physical and psychological well-being. Just as emotions are deeply embedded in our physical bodies, they can have enormous impact on our physical functioning—and on our mental health as well.

Positive Emotions, Health, and Coping

Researchers have focused mainly on the role of negative factors, such as emotional stress and anger, in illness. However, the recent interest in positive psychology has sparked research on

Happy people are more likely than sad people to take part in health-promoting activities such as recreational sports.

the role that positive emotions might play in reducing illness and promoting health (Cloninger, 2006; Moskowitz, Folkman, & Acree, 2003; Vaughn & Roesch, 2003). Although research concerning the effects of negative states is more extensive, positive emotional states are thought to be associated with healthy patterns of physiological functioning in both the cardiovascular system and the immune system (Barak, 2006). Being characterized by positive affect also is linked to increased longevity (Pressman & Cohen, 2005).

Positive emotions have been linked with the release of secretory immunoglobulin A (S-IgA), the antibody that is believed to be the first line of defense against the common cold (Barak, 2006). In one study, S-IgA levels increased after healthy college women watched a funny, happy video but decreased after the women viewed a sad video (Labott & Martin, 1990). Indeed, levels of S-IgA are positively linked with frequent use of humor as a coping strategy (Dillon, Minchoff, & Baker, 1985/1986). In another study, increased frequency of desirable events predicted higher levels of immune response on subsequent days (Stone & others, 1994). Researchers also have found that when people can regain and maintain positive emotional states, they are less likely to get sick or to use medical services when faced with a stressful life experience (Goldman, Kraemer, & Salovey, 1996).

Moods also can influence people's beliefs regarding their ability to carry out health-promoting behaviors. For example, in one study, happy individuals were more likely to engage in health-promoting behaviors and had more confidence that these behaviors would relieve their illness than were sad individuals (Salovey & Birnbaum, 1989).

The Interplay of Positive Emotions and Resilience

Recent research on coping with stressful circumstances further illuminates the important role of positive emotional experiences in dealing with life's challenges. Resilience is a characteristic that has been associated with the capacity to thrive during difficult times (Masten, 2006). Resilience refers to the ability to bounce back from negative experiences, to be flexible and adaptable when things are not going well. Resilient individuals might be thought of as tall trees that have the ability to bend but not break in response to strong winds. In contrast, people who lack resilience might be characterized as more brittle—more likely to snap or break in the face of adversity (Block & Kremen, 1996).

Interestingly, resilient individuals are also distinguished by their tendency to experience positive emotion. These individuals are zestful, optimistic, and energetic in their approach to life (Block & Kremen, 1996; Klohnen, 1996). Resilient individuals cultivate positive emotion in their lives through the use of humor (Segerstrom, 2006).

Recently, research has begun to address the ways that the experience of positive emotions might enhance the ability of resilient individuals to cope as successfully as they do with life's challenges. Michelle Tugade, Barbara Fredrickson, and Lisa Feldman Barrett (2004) found that the superior coping of resilient individuals came from their ability to use positive emotions to bounce back from negative emotional experiences. Using measures of cardiovascular activity, they found that resilient individuals were better able to regulate their responses to stress (for instance, being told they were about to give an important speech) by strategically experiencing positive emotion. Resilient individuals seem to show a kind of emotional wisdom; they capitalize on the capacity of positive emotions to reverse the stress of negative feelings. This skill has also been demonstrated in response to a specific very stressful life event: the terrorist attacks of September 11, 2001.

Fredrickson, Tugade, and their colleagues (2003) had begun a study of resilience and positive emotion in early 2001. As part of that study, they had measured not only resilience but also a variety of other psychological characteristics. Following the 9/11 attacks, the researchers realized that they had an opportunity to examine how resilience might relate to coping with this horrific crisis. They followed up on the individuals whom they had studied earlier that year (none of whom had been directly affected by the attacks) and examined their experiences in the weeks following 9/11. The results were striking. Although all participants felt a broad range of negative emotions—including fear, anxiety, horror, anger, and sadness—they also experienced positive emotions such as gratitude, love, and an increased closeness to others.

Individuals who had previously scored high on resilience were particularly likely to demonstrate growth in psychological resources, such as optimism and feelings of well-being, through the difficult experience of 9/11. Resilient individuals were also less likely to respond to 9/11 with depressive symptoms. Importantly, the capacity of resilient individuals to grow through this difficult time and to avoid depression was explained by their capacity for the experience of positive emotions (alongside the negative ones). The experience of positive emotions even during a crisis was the key to the benefits of resilience. Resilient individuals were buffered from the negative effects of distress by the experience of positive emotions.

It may strike you as odd to focus on positive emotions in such a difficult situation as the post–9/11 crisis. In fact, the resilient people in the study did feel distress—it was not the case that they were simply inappropriately happy while everyone else was suffering. Rather, even as they felt profoundly saddened by the historic tragedy, resilient individuals were able to flourish because of their openness to the positive things in life—perhaps a smile from a friend, a warm hug, the reassurance of family. Thus, even during the most harrowing of times, positive emotional experiences may be an important ingredient in the human capacity to survive and even thrive.

 REVIEW, ASSESS, AND SHARPEN YOUR THINKING

Review

6 Discuss the role of emotions in physical and psychological health and wellness.

- Describe the relation of positive emotional experience to health and coping.
- Discuss the relationship between positive emotions and resilience in response to the 9/11 attacks.

Assess

1. **What is the relationship between emotions and immune functioning?**
   A. Positive emotions are related to release of secretory immunoglobulin A, which weakens the immune system.
   B. Positive emotions are related to release of secretory immunoglobulin A, which strengthens the immune system.
   C. Negative emotions are related to release of secretory immunoglobulin A, which weakens the immune system.
   D. Negative emotions are related to release of secretory immunoglobulin A, which strengthens the immune system.

2. **Prospering despite life's difficulties is termed**
   A. resilience.   B. active coping.
   C. emotion regulation. D. primary appraisal.

3. **How are resilient people able to regulate stress?**
   A. by engaging in active coping
   B. by using relaxation techniques
   C. by their increased immune functioning
   D. by experiencing positive affect

Sharpen Your Thinking

Research has shown that positive emotions can have value even during very difficult times. Think about a difficult experience in your own life. What were some positive moments that occurred even during that difficult time? How did they affect your ability to cope?

SUMMARY

1 THEORIES OF MOTIVATION

Describe evolutionary, drive reduction, and optimum arousal theories of motivation.

The Evolutionary Approach

Motivation gives our behavior, thoughts, and feelings a purpose. Motivated behavior is energized, directed, and sustained. Early evolutionary theorists considered motivation to be based on instinct: the innate biological pattern of behavior that is assumed to be universal throughout a species. The idea that some of our motivation is unlearned and involves physiological factors is still present today. The evolutionary view emphasizes that various aspects of motivation that provided evolutionary advantages were passed down through the genes from generation to generation.

Drive Reduction Theory

A drive is an aroused state that occurs because of a physiological need. A need is a deprivation that energizes the drive to eliminate or reduce the deprivation. Drive reduction theory was proposed as an explanation of motivation, with the goal of drive reduction being homeostasis, the body's tendency to maintain an equilibrium.

Optimum Arousal Theory

Optimum arousal theory focuses on the Yerkes-Dodson law, which states that performance is best under conditions of moderate rather than low or high arousal. Moderate arousal often serves us best when we tackle life's tasks, but there are times when low or high arousal is linked with better performance.

2 HUNGER

Explain the physiological basis of hunger and the nature of eating behavior.

The Biology of Hunger

Interest in the stomach's role was stimulated by Cannon's classic research, but stomach signals are not the only factors that affect hunger. Glucose (blood sugar) and insulin are both important factors in hunger. Glucose is needed for the brain to function, and low levels of glucose increase hunger. Insulin (which decreases glucose) can cause a rise in hunger. Leptin, a protein secreted by fat cells, decreases food intake and increases energy expenditure. The brain is also involved in the experience of hunger. The hypothalamus plays an important role in regulating hunger. The lateral hypothalamus is involved in stimulating eating; the ventromedial hypothalamus, in restricting eating. Neuroscientists are exploring the roles of neurotransmitters and neural circuits in hunger.

Obesity and Eating Behavior

Obesity is a serious and pervasive problem in the United States. Heredity, basal metabolism, set point, and fat cells are biological factors involved in obesity. Until recently, the strong genetic component in obesity has been underestimated. Time and place affect eating, as does the type of food available. Our early ancestors ate fruits to satisfy nutritional needs, but today we fill up on the empty calories in candy and soda. The dramatic increase in obesity beginning in the late twentieth century underscores the significance of environmental factors in obesity.

Dieting

Dieting for weight loss and restrained eating for weight control are common in U.S. society. Many people, especially in their teens and 20s, diet even if they do not need to lose weight. The pressure to be thin can be harmful for people who are not overweight. Anorexia nervosa and bulimia nervosa are two eating disorders that have been linked to perfectionism and cultural beliefs about the beauty of thinness.

3 SEXUALITY

Discuss the motivations for sexual behavior.

The Biology of Sex

Motivation for sexual behavior involves the hypothalamus. The pituitary gland controls the secretion of two classes of sex hormones: estrogens, which predominate in females, and androgens, which have stronger concentrations in males. The role of sex hormones in human sexual behavior, especially in women, is not clear. Masters and Johnson mapped out the human sexual response pattern, which consists of four physiological phases: excitement, plateau, orgasm, and resolution.

Cognitive and Sensory/Perceptual Factors

Thoughts and images are central in the sexual lives of humans. Sexual scripts influence sexual behavior, as do sensory/perceptual factors. Females tend to be more sexually aroused by touch; males, by visual stimulation.

Cultural Factors

Sexual values vary extensively across cultures. These values exert a significant effect on sexual behavior.

Sexual Behavior and Orientation

Describing sexual practices in the United States has always been challenging due to the difficulty of surveying a representative sample of the population. In general, research shows that people are less sexually active and less likely to cheat than popular beliefs may suggest. Sexuality education has sometimes been a controversial issue, but research shows that nations with comprehensive sex education have far lower rates of teen pregnancy and STIs than does the United States.

Sexual orientation refers to the direction of a person's erotic attraction. Sexual orientation—heterosexual, homosexual, or bisexual—is most likely determined by a combination of genetic, hormonal, cognitive, and environmental factors. Based on scientific evidence, the APA recently supported gay marriage and argued against discriminating against gay men and lesbians in parenting, custody, and adoption.

4 BEYOND HUNGER AND SEX: APPROACHES TO MOTIVATION IN EVERYDAY LIFE

Characterize approaches to motivation in everyday life.

Maslow's Hierarchy of Human Needs

According to Maslow's hierarchy of needs, our main needs are satisfied in this sequence: physiological, safety, love and belongingness, esteem, and self-actualization. Maslow gave the most attention to self-actualization, the motivation to develop to one's full potential.

Self-Determination Theory

Self-determination theory states that intrinsic motivation occurs when individuals are engaged in the pursuit of organismic needs that are innate and universal. These needs include competence, relatedness, and autonomy.

Intrinsic Versus Extrinsic Motivation

Intrinsic motivation—based on internal factors such as self-determination, curiosity, challenge, and effort—is one of the most widely studied aspects of achievement motivation. Extrinsic motivation is based on external incentives, such as rewards and punishments.

Most psychologists believe that intrinsic motivation is more positively related to achievement than is extrinsic motivation.

Self-Regulation: The Successful Pursuit of Goals

Self-regulation involves setting goals, monitoring progress, and making adjustments in our behavior to attain our desired outcomes. Research suggests that setting subgoals to reach a long-term goal is a good strategy.

5 EMOTION

Summarize views of emotion.

The Biology of Emotion

Emotion is feeling, or affect, that has three components: physiological arousal, conscious experience, and behavioral expression. The biology of emotion focuses on physiological arousal involving the autonomic nervous system and its two subsystems. The galvanic skin response and the polygraph have been used to measure emotional arousal.

The James-Lange theory states that emotion results from physiological states triggered by environmental stimuli: Emotion follows physiological reactions. The Cannon-Bard theory states that emotion and physiological reactions occur simultaneously. Contemporary biological views of emotion increasingly highlight neural circuitry and neurotransmitters. LeDoux has charted the neural circuitry of fear, which focuses on the amygdala and consists of two pathways, one direct and the other indirect. It is likely that positive and negative emotions use different neural circuitry and neurotransmitters.

Cognitive Factors

Schachter and Singer's two-factor theory states that emotion is the result of both physiological arousal and cognitive labeling. Lazarus believed that cognition always directs emotion, but Zajonc has argued that emotion directs cognition. Both probably are right.

Behavioral Factors

Research on the behavioral component of emotion focuses on facial expressions. The facial feedback hypothesis states that facial expressions can influence emotions, as well as reflect them.

Sociocultural Factors

Most psychologists believe that facial expressions of basic emotions are the same across cultures. However, display rules, which involve nonverbal signals of body movement, posture, and gesture, vary across cultures. The stereotype that women are emotional and men are not is just a stereotype. However, there are many contextual influences on the expression of emotion by males and females.

Classifying Emotions

Classifications of emotions have included wheel models and the two-dimensional approach. Plutchik's wheel model portrays emotions in terms of four dimensions: positive or negative, primary or mixed, polar opposites, and intensity. Both Plutchik's and Tompkins's lists of basic emotions reflect an evolutionary perspective. The two-dimensional approach to classifying emotions argues that there are just two broad dimensions of emotional experiences: positive affectivity and negative affectivity. Positive emotions likely play an important role in well-being through adaptation, growth, social connection, and the building of personal and social resources.

6 EMOTION AND HEALTH AND WELLNESS

Discuss the role of emotions in physical and psychological health and wellness.

Positive Emotions, Health, and Coping

Positive emotional experiences have been shown to relate to enhanced immune functioning, better health, and longevity. In addition, positive emotions are related to effective coping, such as attending to threatening health information.

The Interplay of Positive Emotions and Resilience

Resilience is an individual's capacity to thrive even during difficult times. Resilience is related to the experience of positive emotions. Research on coping in the aftermath of the 9/11 terrorist attacks has demonstrated that resilient individuals were more likely to experience positive emotions such as love and gratitude after 9/11, and these positive experiences allowed them to grow even from this very difficult event.

Key Terms

motivation, p. 390

instinct, p. 390

drive, p. 391

need, p. 391

homeostasis, p. 391

Yerkes-Dodson law, p. 392

set point, p. 396

anorexia nervosa, p. 396

bulimia nervosa, p. 397

estrogens, p. 399

androgens, p. 399

human sexual response pattern, p. 399

sexual orientation, p. 404

hierarchy of needs, p. 407

self-actualization, p. 407

self-determination theory, p. 407

intrinsic motivation, p. 409

extrinsic motivation, p. 409

self-regulation, p. 412

emotion, p. 415

polygraph, p. 416

James-Lange theory, p. 417

Cannon-Bard theory, p. 417

two-factor theory of emotion, p. 420

facial feedback hypothesis, p. 421

display rules, p. 423

broaden-and-build model, p. 425

catharsis, p. 426

Assess Your Knowledge

1. A physiological requirement is a(n) _____; the resulting arousal is a(n) _____.
   A. instinct, motivation
   B. motivation, instinct
   C. drive, need
   D. need, drive

2. Tamesha has an upcoming test. She is so nervous about the test that she develops a rash. What would the Yerkes-Dodson law predict about her performance on the test?
   A. Tamesha will do well because she has high arousal.
   B. Tamesha will do well because she has low arousal.
   C. Tamesha will do poorly because she has high arousal.
   D. Tamesha will do poorly because she has low arousal.

3. How are anorexia nervosa and bulimia nervosa different?
   A. Anorexia involves binging and purging, whereas bulimia does not.
   B. Individuals with bulimia are generally within normal weight limits, whereas individuals with anorexia are not.
   C. Bulimia involves fear of gaining weight, whereas anorexia does not.
   D. Individuals with anorexia are preoccupied with food, whereas individuals with anorexia are not.

4. Which of the following is at the base of Maslow's hierarchy of needs?
   A. safety needs
   B. love and belonging needs
   C. self-actualization needs
   D. physiological needs

5. Someone who has suffered an extreme trauma, but who has recovered fully is said to
   A. engage in active coping.
   B. be resilient.
   C. have positive emotions.
   D. be high in gratitude.

6. Fat cells are known as
   A. glucose cells.
   B. insulin cells.
   C. leptin cells.
   D. adipose cells.

7. Testosterone is a type of a _____ hormone.
   A. estrogen
   B. insulin
   C. pituitary
   D. androgen

8. Psychological research shows that lesbian women are most like
   A. heterosexual men.
   B. gay men.
   C. heterosexual women.
   D. transgender individuals.

9. The beginning of the human sexual response pattern is the
   A. orgasm.
   B. resolution phase.
   C. plateau phase.
   D. excitement phase.

10. Which of the following is not a component of self-determination theory?
    A. autonomy
    B. competition
    C. relatedness
    D. competence

11. The view that emotional responses and physiological reactions occur simultaneously is consistent with which of the following theories?
    A. the Cannon-Bard theory
    B. the broaden-and-build theory
    C. the facial feedback theory
    D. the James-Lange theory

12. Different cultural expectations about the expression of emotions are called
    A. the two-factor theory of emotion.
    B. self-regulation.
    C. set points.
    D. display rules.

13. Which of the following statements about the two-dimensional approach to emotion and the two-factor theory of emotions is true?
    A. The two-dimensional approach states that emotions are determined by physiological arousal and cognitive labeling.
    B. The two-dimensional approach states that emotions are either positive or negative.
    C. The two-factor theory states that emotions are based on behavior and cultural expectations.
    D. The two-factor theory states that emotions help us to avoid danger and find food.

14. Which of the following is an example of an extrinsic motivation?
    A. a feeling of fulfillment
    B. a sense of competence
    C. earning money
    D. satisfying your curiosity

15. The skin's resistance to conducting electricity is measured by
    A. electrodermal response.
    B. adipose cells.
    C. leptin.
    D. cholecystokinin

Go to Appendix B for answers to these questions.

Apply Your Knowledge

1. Ask your friends and your parents to define the word *motivation*. Think about the way your friends define motivation and the way psychologists approach motivation. What are the similarities? What are the differences? How do your friends differ from your parents? How do these individuals differ from psychologists? Why do you think these differences exist?

2. Do a web search for the word *hunger*. What kinds of sites are listed first? How do the topics that these sites cover compare with the discussion of hunger in the text? What insight do the sites give you into the role of environment in hunger?

3. How much of our interpretation of emotions depends on verbal or nonverbal cues? Try the following exercise: Watch a movie that you are not familiar with and find a scene featuring a number of people. First watch the scene with the sound off and try to guess what emotions are being experienced by each person; describe the nonverbal cues that led you to your conclusions. Find a different scene, and listen to it without watching to guess what emotions are being experienced; describe the verbal cues that you used. Then watch both scenes with the sound on. Were verbal or nonverbal cues more useful?

4. Take a moment to write down your deepest thoughts and feelings regarding a negative event in your life. When you have finished, look at what you have written for words indicating emotions. Count up the positive and negative emotion words. What type of emotion dominates? Think about that time in your life and try to remember any positive feelings you had. How may those positive feelings have helped you to cope with the negative event?

CHAPTER 11

PERSONALITY

Experiencing Psychology

WHAT MAKES YOU YOU?

You probably had a parent or grade-school teacher tell you that people are like snowflakes, with no two exactly alike. They might have said something like, "You're special just because you are you." What makes you a snowflake and not a boring ice cube? How are you unique?

Fans of procedural crime dramas such as *CSI* and *Law & Order* know that one thing that can unmistakably identify a person is fingerprints. Left at a crime scene, a fingerprint (if it is in the law enforcement database) can catch the criminal every time, because fingerprints are unique. In the 100 years that fingerprints have been collected and with nearly 100 million fingers printed, no two people have had the same fingerprints. Still, you may be surprised that identical twins, who are genetically identical, do not have the same fingerprints. The reason they do not is that fingerprints are determined not simply by genes but also by prenatal environmental factors, so that even individuals with the same DNA do not have identical fingerprints.

The irises of our eyes are another physical characteristic that distinguishes us from all other people. Unlike fingerprints, irises cannot be worn down (or filed off, if you are thinking like a hit man)—they are stable and unique throughout a person's life. And irises have six times the number of distinguishing characteristics that fingerprints have.

Of course, the person who told you that you are unique was not talking about your fingerprints or irises but rather about the person that you are, with all of your personal characteristics—traits, abilities, beliefs, goals, and experiences. And that is what personality psychology, the topic of this chapter, is all about. To paraphrase Henry Murray, a personality psychologist, "All of us are in some ways like all other people, in some ways like some other people, and in some ways like no other person." By that, Murray meant that although we share certain attributes with all other human beings (such as our physical anatomy), and we share certain attributes with some others (for example, our family members and people who are the same age as we are), in other ways we are truly unique. Personality psychology explores the psychological attributes that make us who we are—the unified and enduring core characteristics that account for our existence as the same person throughout our lives. In short, personality psychology is the scientific study of what makes you you.

Personality psychologists can be found in nearly every subdiscipline of psychology, including clinical, developmental, social, and cognitive. Because the main topic of personality psychology is the person, its concerns intersect with many of the key concerns for *all* of psychology, including human development; characteristics that are likely to remain stable or change over the life span; effects of the social context, including culture; differences from individual to individual with respect to coping; and mental and physical illness.

Preview

In this chapter, we survey the classic theories of personality as well as more contemporary research in the field. We examine the nature of the person–situation debate, briefly consider how personality is assessed, and finally take stock of the central role of personality in health and wellness.

personality A pattern of enduring, distinctive thoughts, emotions, and behaviors that characterize the way an individual adapts to the world.

psychodynamic perspectives Views of personality as primarily unconscious (that is, beyond awareness) and as developing in stages. Most psychoanalytic perspectives emphasize that early experiences with parents play a role in sculpting personality.

1 Psychodynamic Perspectives

Define personality and summarize the psychodynamic perspectives.

Personality is a concept that is familiar to everyone but difficult to define. In this chapter, we define **personality** as a pattern of enduring, distinctive thoughts, emotions, and behaviors that characterize the way an individual adapts to the world.

Have you ever had a friend rave about a movie to you—and then, while sitting in the theater, you thought, "Am I seeing the *same* film?" Personality theorists and researchers ask why individuals react to the same situation in different ways, and they come up with different answers. Just as you and your friend might have differing takes on a movie, personality psychologists answer the question of what personality is in differing ways. Some emphasize traits, others highlight motivation, and still others focus on patterns of beliefs and thoughts. One common question that is often addressed in personality research is when and if personality characteristics cause behavior.

Psychodynamic perspectives view personality as being primarily unconscious (that is, beyond awareness) and as developing in stages. Most psychodynamic perspectives emphasize that early experiences with parents play an important role in sculpting the individual's personality. Psychodynamic theorists believe that behavior is merely a surface characteristic and that to truly understand someone's personality we have to explore the symbolic meanings of behavior and the deep inner workings of the mind (Hergenhahn & Olson, 2007). These characteristics were sketched by the architect of psychoanalytic theory, Sigmund Freud. As you learned in Chapter 1, some psychodynamic theorists who followed Freud have diverged from his theory but still embrace his core ideas.

Freud's Psychoanalytic Theory

Sigmund Freud (1917), one of the most influential thinkers of the twentieth century, was born in Austria in 1856 and died in London at the age of 83. Freud spent most of his life in Vienna, but he left the city near the end of his career to escape the Holocaust. A medical doctor who specialized in neurology, Freud developed his ideas about personality from his work with psychiatric patients.

Freud was extremely ambitious and wanted to change the world. And we can see that he largely succeeded in that goal by imagining ourselves in the following situation. In a romantic moment when you are kissing your significant other, imagine hearing your partner say, "I love you so much, Chris." But there is a problem: Chris is not your name; it is the name of your partner's previous love interest. How might you respond? Despite your loved one's protestations that it was an honest mistake, a complete accident, you know it must "mean

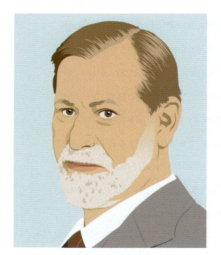

Sigmund Freud (1856–1939) *Freud's theories have strongly influenced how people in Western cultures view themselves and their world.*

something." *Freudian slips* are misstatements that Freud believed reveal unconscious thoughts. Freud is the only psychologist whose name has become a common part of our everyday language.

Freud has had such a phenomenal impact that just about everyone has an opinion about him, even those who have never studied his work. Most people assume that Freud thought everything was about sex. And that is true, except by *sex* Freud did not mean sexual activity in the usual sense. Freud defined sex as organ pleasure. Anything that was pleasurable was sex, according to Freud. So, if you have ever heard someone describe the joys of a double chocolate fudge cake as "better than sex," you might keep in mind that in Freud's view, eating that double chocolate fudge cake *is* sex.

Freud developed *psychoanalysis*, his approach to personality, out of his work with patients who were suffering from hysteria. *Hysteria* refers to physical symptoms that have no physical cause. For instance, a person might be unable to see, even with perfectly healthy eyes, or unable to walk, despite having no physical injury. During Freud's time, many young women suffered from physical problems that could not be explained through actual physical illness. Freud came to understand that hysterical symptoms were caused by unconscious psychological conflicts. These conflicts were generally centered on experiences in which the person wanted to do one thing but was forced to do another through the social pressures of Victorian society. One of Freud's patients, Fraulein Elisabeth Von R., suffered from horrible pains in her legs that prevented her from walking. Through analysis, Freud discovered that Fraulein Elisabeth had had a number of experiences in which she wanted nothing more than to take a walk, but she was prevented from doing so by her duty to her ill father.

TV and movie portrayals of hysterical symptoms typically culminate with a psychologist's unlocking the unconscious secret of the person's problem. On a soap opera, a young heroine's problems may be solved in one climactic episode: It turns out that she was hysterically blind because she saw her father cheating on her mother with another woman. Importantly, Freud believed that hysterical symptoms were *overdetermined*—that is, they had a multitude of causes in the unconscious. Unlocking one unconscious traumatic memory might work for Hollywood, but it does not represent Freud very well. Eventually, Freud came to use hysterical symptoms as his metaphor for understanding dreams, slips of the tongue, and ultimately all human behavior. Everything we do, according to Freud, has a multitude of unconscious causes.

On the basis of his work analyzing patients (as well as himself), Freud developed his model of the human personality. He described personality as being like an iceberg, existing mostly below the level of awareness, just as the massive part of an iceberg lies beneath the surface of the water. Figure 11.1 illustrates this analogy and how extensive the unconscious part of our mind is, in Freud's view.

Personality's Structures

Notice that Figure 11.1 shows the iceberg divided into three segments. The reason is that Freud (1917) believed that personality has three structures, which he called the id, the ego, and the superego. These Latin labels may not capture Freud's true meaning in naming the structures. The id is literally the "it," the ego is the "I," and the superego is the "above-I."

The **id,** that part of you that Freud called an "it," consists of unconscious drives and is the individual's reservoir of psychic energy. In Freud's view, the id has no contact with reality. The id works according to the *pleasure principle,* the Freudian concept that the id always seeks pleasure and avoids pain.

It would be a dangerous and scary world, however, if our personalities were all id. As young children mature, they learn they cannot slug other

"Good morning beheaded—uh, I mean beloved."
© The New Yorker Collection 1979 Dana Fradon from cartoonbank.com. All Rights Reserved.

id The Freudian structure of personality that consists of unconscious drives and is the individual's reservoir of psychic energy.

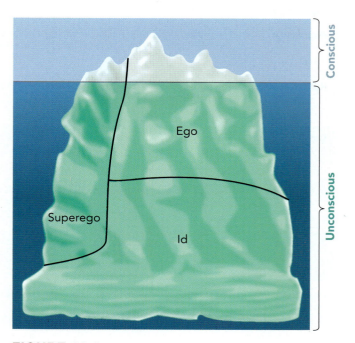

FIGURE 11.1

The Conscious and Unconscious Mind: The Iceberg Analogy The analogy of the conscious and unconscious mind to an iceberg is often used to illustrate how much of the mind is unconscious in Freud's theory. The conscious mind is the part of the iceberg above water; the unconscious mind, the part below water. Notice that the id is totally unconscious, whereas the ego and superego can operate at either the conscious or the unconscious level.

ego The Freudian structure of personality that deals with the demands of reality.

superego The Freudian structure of personality that harshly judges the morality of our behavior.

defense mechanisms The ego's protective methods for reducing anxiety by unconsciously distorting reality.

children in the face. They also learn that they have to use the toilet instead of their diaper. As children experience the demands and constraints of reality, a new structure of personality is formed—the **ego,** the Freudian structure of personality that deals with the demands of reality. According to Freud, the ego abides by the *reality principle.* It tries to bring the individual pleasure within the norms of society. Most of us accept the obstacles to satisfaction that exist in our world. We recognize that our sexual and aggressive impulses cannot go unrestrained. Few of us are voracious gluttons, sexual wantons, or cold-blooded killers. The ego helps us to test reality, to see how far we can go without getting into trouble and hurting ourselves. Whereas the id is completely unconscious, the ego is partly conscious. It houses our higher mental functions—reasoning, problem solving, and decision making, for example. For this reason, the ego is referred to as the executive branch of the personality; like an executive in a company, it makes the rational decisions that help the company succeed.

The id and ego do not consider whether something is right or wrong. The **superego** is the harsh internal judge of our behavior. The superego is reflected in what we often call "conscience" and evaluates the morality of our behavior. Like the id, the superego does not consider reality; it considers only whether the id's impulses can be satisfied in acceptable moral terms.

Both the id and the superego make life rough for the ego. Your ego might say, "I will have sex only occasionally and be sure to use an effective form of birth control." But your id says, "I want to be satisfied; sex feels so good." And your superego says, "I feel guilty about having sex at all."

Defense Mechanisms The ego calls on a number of strategies to resolve the conflict among its demands for reality, the wishes of the id, and the constraints of the superego. These **defense mechanisms** reduce anxiety by unconsciously distorting reality. For example, when the ego blocks the pleasurable pursuits of the id, a person feels anxiety, which the ego resolves by means of defense mechanisms. Figure 11.2 describes several defense

FIGURE 11.2

Defense Mechanisms Defense mechanisms reduce anxiety in various ways, in all instances by distorting reality.

Defense Mechanism	How It Works	Example
Repression	The master defense mechanism; the ego pushes unacceptable impulses out of awareness, back into the unconscious mind.	A young girl was sexually abused by her uncle. As an adult, she can't remember anything about the traumatic experience.
Rationalization	The ego replaces a less acceptable motive with a more acceptable one.	A college student does not get into the fraternity of his choice. He says that if he had tried harder he could have gotten in.
Displacement	The ego shifts feelings toward an unacceptable object to another, more acceptable object.	A woman can't take her anger out on her boss so she goes home and takes it out on her husband.
Sublimation	The ego replaces an unacceptable impulse with a socially acceptable one.	A man with strong sexual urges becomes an artist who paints nudes.
Projection	The ego attributes personal shortcomings, problems, and faults to others.	A man who has a strong desire to have an extramarital affair accuses his wife of flirting with other men.
Reaction Formation	The ego transforms an unacceptable motive into its opposite.	A woman who fears her sexual urges becomes a religious zealot.
Denial	The ego refuses to acknowledge anxiety-producing realities.	A man won't acknowledge that he has cancer even though a team of doctors has diagnosed his cancer.
Regression	The ego seeks the security of an earlier developmental period in the face of stress.	A woman returns home to mother every time she and her husband have a big argument.

mechanisms, many of which were introduced and developed by Freud's daughter Anna. All of them work to protect the ego and reduce anxiety.

Repression is the most powerful and pervasive defense mechanism, according to Freud; it pushes unacceptable id impulses out of awareness and back into the unconscious mind. Repression is the foundation for all of the psychological defense mechanisms, the goal of which is to push, or *repress,* threatening impulses out of awareness. Freud said that our early childhood experiences, many of which he believed were sexually laden, are too threatening and stressful for us to deal with consciously, so we reduce the anxiety of childhood conflict through repression.

Two final points about defense mechanisms need to be understood. First, they are unconscious; we are not aware that we are calling on them. Second, when used in moderation or on a temporary basis, defense mechanisms are not necessarily unhealthy. For example, the defense mechanism of *denial* can help a person cope with impending death, and the defense mechanism of *sublimation* means transforming our unconscious impulses into activities that benefit society. From Freud's perspective, defense mechanisms are a vital way for the ego to survive in a stressful world.

Psychosexual Stages of Personality Development

As Freud listened to his patients, he became convinced that their personalities were the result of experiences early in life. Freud believed that we go through universal stages of personality development and that at each stage of development we experience sex or pleasure in one part of the body more than in others. *Erogenous zones,* according to Freud, are parts of the body that have especially strong pleasure-giving qualities at particular stages of development. Freud thought that our adult personality is determined by the way we resolve conflicts between these early sources of pleasure—the mouth, the anus, and then the genitals—and the demands of reality.

- *Oral stage (first 18 months):* The infant's pleasure centers on the mouth. Chewing, sucking, and biting are chief sources of pleasure that reduce tension in the infant.

- *Anal stage (18 to 36 months):* During a time when most children are experiencing toilet training, the child's greatest pleasure involves the anus and urethra and the eliminative functions associated with them. Freud recognized that there is pleasure in "going" and "holding it" as well as in the experience of control over one's parents in deciding when to do either.

- *Phallic stage (3 to 6 years):* The name of Freud's third stage comes from the Latin word *phallus,* which means "penis." Pleasure focuses on the genitals as the child discovers that self-stimulation is enjoyable. In Freud's view, the phallic stage has a special importance in personality development because it triggers the Oedipus complex. This name comes from the Greek tragedy in which Oedipus unwittingly killed his father and married his mother. The **Oedipus complex** is the boy's intense desire to replace his father and enjoy the affections of his mother. Eventually, the boy recognizes that his father might punish him for these incestuous wishes, specifically by cutting off the boy's penis. *Castration anxiety* refers to the boy's intense fear of being mutilated by his father. To reduce this conflict, the boy identifies with his father, striving to be like him. The intense castration anxiety is repressed and serves as the foundation for the superego.

In the phallic stage, Freud recognized that there were differences between boys and girls. Freud believed that the lack of castration anxiety in girls explains why women never truly develop a superego in the same sense that men do. This physical fact explained why (in Freud's view) women are morally inferior to men and why women were "second-class citizens" in Victorian society. Freud's view of the phallic stage is where the notion that "anatomy is destiny" originates.

Freud believed that girls experience "castration completed," resulting in penis envy—the intense desire to obtain a penis by eventually marrying and bearing a son.

Oedipus complex In Freud's theory, a young boy's intense desire to replace his father and enjoy the affections of his mother.

Stage	Adult Extensions (Fixations)	Sublimations	Reaction Formations
Oral	Smoking, eating, kissing, oral hygiene, drinking, chewing gum	Seeking knowledge, humor, wit, sarcasm, being a food or wine expert	Speech purist, food faddist, prohibitionist, dislike of milk
Anal	Notable interest in one's bowel movements, love of bathroom humor, extreme messiness	Interest in painting or sculpture, being overly giving, great interest in statistics	Extreme disgust with feces, fear of dirt, prudishness, irritability
Phallic	Heavy reliance on masturbation, flirtatiousness, expressions of virility	Interest in poetry, love of love, interest in acting, striving for success	Puritanical attitude toward sex, excessive modesty

FIGURE 11.3

Defense Mechanisms and Freudian Stages If a person is fixated at a psychosexual stage, the fixation can color his or her personality in many ways, including the defense mechanisms the person might use to cope with anxiety.

Freud felt that women were somewhat childlike in their development and that it was good that fathers and eventually husbands would guide them throughout their lives. He asserted that the only hope for the moral development of women was education. Notably, Freud was never satisfied with his own approach to the development of girls and women. He always allowed women to pursue careers in psychoanalysis, and many of his earliest followers were women.

- *Latency period (6 years to puberty):* This phase is not a developmental stage but rather a kind of psychic time-out or intermission. After the drama of the phallic stage, the child represses all interest in sexuality. Although we now consider these years extremely important to development, Freud felt that this was a time in which no real development occurred.

- *Genital stage (adolescence and adulthood):* The genital stage is the time of sexual reawakening; the source of sexual pleasure now becomes someone outside of the family. Freud believed that unresolved conflicts with parents reemerge during adolescence. But once these conflicts are resolved, the individual becomes capable of developing a mature love relationship and functioning independently as an adult. Even in the best case, however, Freud felt that human beings were inevitably subject to intense conflict. Everyone, he believed, no matter how healthy or well adjusted, still has an id pressing for expression.

Freud argued that the individual may become fixated at any of these stages of development if he or she is underindulged or overindulged at a stage. For example, a parent might wean a child too early, be too strict in toilet training, punish the child for masturbation, or "smother" the child with too much attention. *Fixation* is the psychoanalytic defense mechanism that occurs when the individual remains locked in an earlier developmental stage. The issues from the psychosexual stage can color all aspects of the person's adult personality. The construct of fixation thus explains how, according to Freud's view, childhood experiences can have an enormous impact on adult personality. Figure 11.3 illustrates possible links between adult personality characteristics and fixation at the oral, anal, and phallic stages.

Psychodynamic Critics and Revisionists

Because Freud was among the first theorists to explore personality, over time some of his ideas have needed updating and revision, and some have been tossed out altogether. In particular, Freud's critics have said that his ideas about sexuality, early experience, social factors, and the unconscious mind were misguided (Adler, 1927; Erikson, 1968; Fromm, 1947; Horney, 1945; Jung, 1917; Kohut, 1977; Rapaport, 1967; Sullivan, 1953). His critics stress the following points:

- Sexuality is not the pervasive force behind personality that Freud believed it to be. Nor is the Oedipus complex as universal as Freud believed. Freud's concepts were heavily influenced by the setting in which he lived and worked—turn-of-the-century Vienna, a society that was, compared with contemporary society, sexually repressed and paternalistic.

collective unconscious Jung's term for the impersonal, deepest layer of the unconscious mind, shared by all human beings because of their common ancestral past.

archetypes The name Jung gave to the emotionally laden ideas and images that have rich and symbolic meaning for all people.

- The first 5 years of life are not as powerful in shaping adult personality as Freud thought; later experiences deserve more attention.

- The ego and conscious thought processes play more dominant roles in our personality than Freud gave them credit for; he claimed that we are forever captive to the instinctual, unconscious clutches of the id. Also, the ego has a separate line of development from the id, so achievement, thinking, and reasoning are not always tied to sexual impulses.

- Sociocultural factors are much more important than Freud believed. In stressing the id's dominance, Freud placed more emphasis on the biological basis of personality. More contemporary psychodynamic scholars have especially emphasized the interpersonal setting of the family and the role of early social relationships in personality development.

The theories of three dissenters and revisionists—Horney, Jung, and Adler—have been particularly influential in the development of psychodynamic theories, the successors to Freud's psychoanalytic theory.

Karen Horney (1885–1952) *Horney developed the first feminist criticism of Freud's theory. Horney's view emphasizes women's positive qualities and self-evaluation.*

Horney's Sociocultural Approach   Karen Horney (1885–1952) rejected the classical psychoanalytic concept that anatomy is destiny and cautioned that some of Freud's most popular ideas were only hypotheses. She insisted that these hypotheses be supported with observable data before being accepted as fact. She also argued that sociocultural influences on personality development should be considered.

Consider Freud's concept of penis envy, which attributed some of the behavior of his female patients to their repressed desire to have a penis. Horney pointed out that women might envy the penis not because of some neurotic tendencies, but because of the status in society that is bestowed on those who have one. Further, she suggested that both sexes envy the attributes of the other, with men coveting women's reproductive capacities (Gilman, 2001).

Horney also believed that the need for security, not for sex, is the prime motive in human existence. Horney reasoned that an individual whose needs for security are met should be able to develop his or her capacities to the fullest extent. She viewed psychological health as allowing the person to freely and spontaneously express his or her talents and abilities.

Jung's Analytical Theory   Freud's contemporary Carl Jung (1875–1961) had a different complaint about psychoanalytic theory. Jung shared Freud's interest in the unconscious, but he believed that Freud underplayed the unconscious mind's role in personality. In fact, Jung believed that the roots of personality go back to the dawn of human existence. The **collective unconscious** is the impersonal, deepest layer of the unconscious mind, shared by all human beings because of their common ancestral past. In Jung's theory, the experiences of a common past have made a deep, permanent impression on the human mind.

The collective unconscious is expressed through what Jung called **archetypes,** emotionally laden ideas and images that have rich and symbolic meaning for all

Carl Jung (1875–1961) *Swiss psychoanalytic theorist Carl Jung developed the concepts of the collective unconscious and archetypes.*

people. Jung believed that these archetypes emerge in art, literature, religion, and dreams (Merchant, 2006; Roesler, 2006). He used archetypes to help people understand themselves (Urban, 2005).

Two common archetypes are the anima (woman) and animus (man). Jung believed each of us has a passive "feminine" side and an assertive "masculine" side. Another archetype, the mandala, a figure within a circle, has been used so often in art that Jung took it to represent the self (Figure 11.4). The persona is still another archetype; Jung thought that the persona represented the public mask that we all wear during social

FIGURE 11.4

The Mandala as an Archetype of the Self In his exploration of mythology, Carl Jung found that the self is often symbolized by a mandala, from the Sanskrit word for "circle." Jung believed that the mandala represents the self's unity.

interactions. Jung believed that the persona was an essential archetype because it allows us always to keep some secret part of ourselves hidden from others.

Adler's Individual Psychology Alfred Adler (1870–1937) was another of Freud's contemporaries. In Adler's **individual psychology,** people are motivated by purposes and goals—perfection, not pleasure, is the key motivator in human life. Unlike Freud, who believed in the overwhelming power of the unconscious mind, Adler argued that people have the ability to consciously monitor their lives. He also considered social factors more important than sexual motivation in shaping personality (Silverman & Corsini, 1984).

Adler thought that everyone strives for superiority by seeking to adapt, improve, and master the environment. Striving for superiority is our response to the uncomfortable feelings of inferiority we experience as infants and young children when we interact with bigger and more powerful people. *Compensation* is Adler's term for the individual's attempt to overcome imagined or real inferiorities or weaknesses by developing one's own abilities. Adler believed that compensation is normal, and he said that we often make up for a weakness in one ability by excelling in a different ability. For example, a mediocre student might compensate by excelling in athletics.

Evaluating the Pychodynamic Perspectives

Although psychodynamic theories have diverged from Freud's original psychoanalytic version, they do share some core principles:

- Personality is determined both by current experiences and, as the original psychoanalytic theory proposed, by early life experiences.
- Personality can be better understood by examining it developmentally— as a series of stages that unfold with the individual's physical, cognitive, and socioemotional development.
- We mentally transform our experiences, giving them meaning that shapes our personality.
- The mind is not all consciousness; unconscious motives lie behind some of our puzzling behavior.
- The individual's inner world often conflicts with the outer demands of reality, creating anxiety that is not easy to resolve.
- Personality and adjustment—not just the experimental laboratory topics of sensation, perception, and learning—are rightful and important topics of psychological inquiry.

Some have criticized psychodynamic perspectives for presenting too negative and pessimistic a view of the person. For example, critics say, these perspectives place too much weight on early experiences within the family and their influence on personality and do not acknowledge that we retain the capacity for change and adaptation throughout our lives. Some psychologists believe moreover that Freud and Jung put too much faith in the unconscious mind's ability to control behavior. Others object that Freud overemphasized the importance of sexuality in understanding personality; we are not born into the world with only a bundle of sexual and aggressive instincts.

Some have argued, too, that psychoanalysis is not a theory that can be tested through empirical research. But in fact numerous empirical studies on concepts such as defense mechanisms and the unconscious have proved this criticism to be unfounded (Cramer, 2000; Jorgensen & Zachariae, 2006). Another version of this argument may be accurate, however. Although it is certainly possible to test hypotheses derived from psychoanalytic theory through research, the question remains whether psychoanalytically oriented individuals who believe strongly in Freud's ideas would be open to research results that call for serious changes in the theory.

In light of these criticisms, it may be hard to appreciate why Freud had and continues to have an impact on the field of personality and on psychology in general. It is useful to

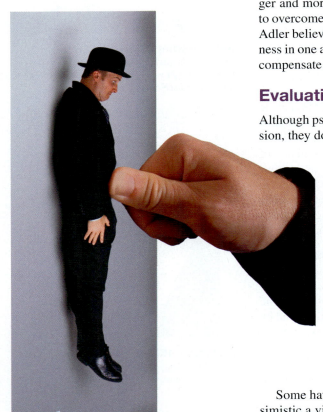

individual psychology The term for Adler's approach, which views people as motivated by purposes and goals and as striving for perfection over pleasure.

keep in mind that Freud made a number of important contributions to psychology, including being the first to propose that childhood is important to later functioning, that development might be understood in terms of stages, and that unconscious processes might play a significant role in human life.

 REVIEW, ASSESS, AND SHARPEN YOUR THINKING

Review

1 Define personality and summarize the psychodynamic perspectives.

- Define the concept of personality, describe the essence of the psychodynamic perspectives, and explain the key ideas in Freud's psychoanalytic theory.
- Discuss how the ideas of three psychodynamic critics and revisionists differed from Freud's.
- Identify the pros and cons of the psychodynamic perspectives.

Assess

1. According to Freud, our conscience resides in
   A. the ego.
   B. the collective unconscious.
   C. the id.
   D. the superego.

2. In what stage of Freud's psychosexual development does the Oedipus Complex occur?
   A. anal stage
   B. genital stage
   C. phallic stage
   D. oral stage

3. Which theorist focused on archetypes?
   A. Karen Horney
   B. Sigmund Freud
   C. Alfred Adler
   D. Carl Jung

4. Matt is romantically attracted to a coworker. However, he knows that he is not allowed to date coworkers, so he feels hatred toward her. What defense mechanism is Matt using?
   A. sublimation
   B. reaction formation
   C. projection
   D. denial

5. The anima and animus are examples of
   A. archetypes.
   B. defense mechanisms.
   C. the collective unconscious.
   D. penis envy.

Sharpen Your Thinking

What psychodynamic ideas may apply to all human beings? Which ones may not apply to everyone?

2 Humanistic Perspectives

Describe the humanistic perspectives.

Humanistic perspectives stress a person's capacity for personal growth, freedom to choose one's own destiny, and positive human qualities. Humanistic psychologists believe that each of us has the ability to cope with stress, to control our lives, and to achieve what we desire (Cain, 2001; Smith, 2001). Each of us has the capacity to break through and understand ourselves and our world; we can burst the cocoon and become a butterfly, say the humanists.

The humanistic perspectives provide clear contrasts to the psychodynamic perspectives, which often seem to be based on conflict, destructive drives, and a pessimistic view of human nature. The humanistic perspectives also contrast with behaviorism, discussed in Chapter 7, which at its extreme reduces human beings to puppets on the strings of rewards and punishments. Indeed, one of the motivational forces behind the development of humanistic psychology was to move beyond Freudian psychoanalysis and behaviorism to something that might capture the rich and potentially positive aspects of human nature.

humanistic perspectives Views of personality that stress the person's capacity for personal growth, freedom to choose a destiny, and positive qualities.

Maslow's Approach

A leading architect of the humanistic movement was Abraham Maslow (1908–1970). Maslow referred to humanistic psychology as "third force" psychology because it stressed neither Freudian drives nor the stimulus–response principles of behaviorism.

In Chapter 10 we looked at Maslow's approach to motivation, which conceived of motivation as a hierarchy of needs. You may recall that at the top of Maslow's (1954, 1971) hierarchy was the need for self-actualization. Self-actualization is the motivation to develop one's full potential as a human being. Maslow described self-actualizers as spontaneous, creative, and possessing a childlike capacity for awe. According to Maslow, a person at this optimal level of existence would be tolerant of others, have a gentle sense of humor, and be likely to pursue the greater good. Self-actualizers also maintain a capacity for "peak experiences," or breathtaking moments of spiritual insight. As examples of self-actualized individuals, Maslow included Pablo Casals (cellist), Albert Einstein (physicist), Ralph Waldo Emerson (writer), William James (psychologist), Thomas Jefferson (politician), Eleanor Roosevelt (humanitarian, diplomat), and Albert Schweitzer (humanitarian).

Created nearly 40 years ago, Maslow's list of self-actualized individuals is clearly biased in some ways. Maslow was most interested in focusing on highly successful individuals who, in his mind, represented the best of the human species. Because Maslow concentrated on people who were successful in a particular historical context, his self-actualizers were limited to those who had opportunities for success in that context. Maslow thus named considerably more men than women, and most of the individuals were from Western cultures and of European ancestry. Today, we might add to Maslow's list individuals such as the Dalai Lama (Tenzin Gyatso), Tibetan spiritual and political leader; Wangari Maathai, a Kenyan woman acclaimed for her work on behalf of democracy and the environment; and Muhammad Yunus, a Bangladeshi banker and crusader against poverty. All are recipients of the Nobel Peace Prize in recent years.

Rogers's Approach

The other key figure in the development of humanistic psychology, Carl Rogers (1902–1987), began his career as a psychotherapist struggling to understand the unhappiness of the individuals he encountered in therapy. Rogers's groundbreaking work provided the foundation for more contemporary studies of self-esteem, personal growth, and self-determination.

Like Freud, Rogers began his inquiry about human nature with people who were troubled. In the knotted, anxious, defensive verbal stream of his clients, Rogers (1961) noted the things that seemed to be keeping them from having positive self-concepts and reaching their full potential as human beings.

Rogers believed that most people have considerable difficulty accepting their own true, innately positive feelings. He emphasized that we are all born with an innate tendency toward growth and a gut instinct that will lead us to make good choices. In a sense, we are born with the seeds of a wonderful person inside us. However, as we grow up, people who are central to our lives condition us to move away from our genuine feelings. Too often, we hear our parents, siblings, teachers, and peers say things like "Don't do that," "You didn't do that right," and "How can you be so stupid?" When we do something wrong, we often get punished. Parents may even threaten to withhold their love unless we conform to their standards, which Rogers called conditions of worth. He felt that through exposure to such conditions, we become alienated from our genuine feelings in order to be the person we are expected to be. We might come to despise who we really are in favor of an idealized image of who we are "supposed" to be. The conditions of worth placed on us by others eventually become the standards by which we judge ourselves. Though very different in many ways, both Freud and Rogers recognized that the conflict between the self and one's duty was a key problem for their patients.

The Self Through the individual's experiences with the world, a self emerges—the "I" or "me" of our existence. Rogers did not believe that all aspects of the self are

Carl Rogers (1902–1987) *Carl Rogers was a pioneer in the development of the humanistic perspective.*

conscious, but he did believe they are all accessible to consciousness. The self is a whole, consisting of one's self-perceptions (how attractive I am, how well I get along with others, how good an athlete I am) and the values we attach to these perceptions (good/bad, worthy/unworthy).

Self-concept, a central theme in the views of Rogers and other humanists, is an individual's overall perceptions and assessments of his or her abilities, behavior, and personality. In Rogers's view, a person who has an inaccurate self-concept is likely to be maladjusted.

In discussing self-concept, Rogers distinguished between the real self, which is the self resulting from our experiences, and the ideal self, which is the self we would like to be. The greater the discrepancy between the real self and the ideal self, a condition Rogers called incongruence, the more maladjusted we will be. To improve our adjustment and become "congruent," we can develop more positive perceptions of our real self, worry less about what others want, and increase our positive experiences in the world.

Unconditional Positive Regard, Empathy, and Genuineness   Rogers proposed three methods to help a person develop a more positive self-concept: unconditional positive regard, empathy, and genuineness.

Rogers said that because people, regardless of what they do, need to be accepted by others, we must accept them without strings attached. **Unconditional positive regard** is Rogers's term for accepting, valuing, and being positive toward another person regardless of the person's behavior. When a person's behavior is inappropriate, obnoxious, or unacceptable, the person still needs the respect, comfort, and love of others (Assor, Roth, & Deci, 2004). Rogers strongly believed that unconditional positive regard elevates the person's self-worth. However, Rogers (1974) distinguished between unconditional positive regard directed at the individual as a person of worth and dignity, and directed at the individual's behavior. For example, a therapist who adopts Rogers's view might say, "I don't like your behavior, but I accept you, value you, and care about you as a person."

Rogers also said that we can help others develop a more positive self-concept if we are *empathic* and *genuine*. Being empathic means being a sensitive listener and understanding another's true feelings. Being genuine means being open with our feelings and dropping our pretenses and facades. The importance Rogers placed on the therapist's being a genuine person in the therapeutic relationship demonstrates his strong belief in the positive character of human nature. For Rogers, we can help others simply by being present for them as the authentic persons we are.

According to Rogers, unconditional positive regard, empathy, and genuineness are three essential ingredients of healthy human relations. We can use these techniques to help other people feel good about themselves and to help us get along better with others (Bozarth, Zimring, & Tausch, 2001).

Evaluating the Humanistic Perspectives

The humanistic perspectives made psychologists aware that the way we perceive ourselves and the world around us is a key element of personality. Humanistic psychologists also reminded us that we need to consider the whole person and the positive bent of human nature (Bohart & Greening, 2001). Their emphasis on conscious experience has given us the view that personality contains a well of potential that can be developed to its fullest (Hill, 2000).

Some critics believe that humanistic psychologists are too optimistic about human nature and overestimate the freedom and rationality of humans. And some say the humanists may promote excessive self-love and narcissism by encouraging people to think so positively about themselves. Self-determination theory, which we considered in Chapter 10, demonstrates the way that psychologists have tested humanistic ideas that might appear abstract and difficult to test.

self-concept A central theme in Rogers's and other humanists' views; self-concept refers to individuals' overall perceptions and assessments of their abilities, behavior, and personalities.

unconditional positive regard Rogers's term for accepting, valuing, and being positive toward another person regardless of the person's behavior.

REVIEW, ASSESS, AND SHARPEN YOUR THINKING

Review

2 Describe the humanistic perspectives.
- Define the main themes of the humanistic perspectives and explain the main elements of Rogers's theory.
- Evaluate the humanistic perspectives.

Assess

1. Feeling overwhelming happiness at the sight of a natural waterfall is an example of
   A. empathy.   B. unconditional positive regard.
   C. genuiness.   D. a peak experience.

2. A child who must consistently achieve in school in order to be provided affection by her parents is experiencing
   A. unconditional positive regard.   B. conditions of worth.
   C. self-actualization.   D. empathy.

3. Carl Rogers's approach focused on all of the following except:
   A. self-concept.
   B. empathy.
   C. self-actualization.
   D. unconditional positive regard.

4. Which of the following is true, according to Carl Rogers?
   A. When our ideal self is better than our actual self, the happier we are.
   B. When our actual self is better than our ideal self, the happier we are.
   C. When our ideal self and actual self are congruent, the happier we are.
   D. The ideal self and actual self are not involved in happiness.

5. Which of the following did Rogers say was involved in helping others?
   A. giving advice   B. being genuine
   C. challenging others   D. teaching them new skills

Sharpen Your Thinking

Is it possible both to be genuine and *to provide unconditional positive regard? How would a humanistic psychologist approach the treatment of someone who has committed a truly despicable act (rape or murder)? How would you feel if you were counseling someone who admitted to doing something you find morally wrong?*

3 Trait Perspectives

Discuss the trait perspectives.

Through the ages, people have described themselves and others in terms of basic traits. A **trait** is an enduring personality characteristic that tends to lead to certain behaviors. Around 400 B.C.E., Hippocrates, the "father of medicine," described human beings as having one of four basic personalities, determined by their physical makeup: choleric (quick-tempered), phlegmatic (placid), sanguine (optimistic), or melancholic (pessimistic). Others have proposed different sets of traits, but some descriptions of personality have remained remarkably constant. More than 2,000 years ago, for example, Theophrastus described the basic traits of the "stingy man," the "liar," and the "flatterer." If you are setting up a friend on a blind date, you are likely to describe the person in terms of traits rather than as having a "good personality." The trait perspectives on personality have been the dominant approach for the past two decades.

Trait Theories

Trait theories state that personality consists of broad, enduring dispositions (traits) that tend to lead to characteristic responses. In other words, people can be described in terms

trait An enduring personality characteristic that tends to lead to certain behaviors.

trait theories Theories stating that personality consists of broad, enduring dispositions (traits) that tend to lead to characteristic responses.

of the basic ways they behave, such as whether they are outgoing and friendly or dominant and assertive. People who have a strong tendency to behave in certain ways are described as high on the traits; those who have a weak tendency to behave in these ways are described as low on the traits. Although trait theorists differ about which traits make up personality, they agree that traits are the fundamental building blocks of personality (Friedman & Schustack, 2006).

Gordon Allport (1897–1967), who is sometimes referred to as the father of American personality psychology, was particularly bothered by the negative view of humanity that psychoanalysis portrayed. He rejected the notion that the unconscious was central to an understanding of personality. He further believed that to understand healthy people, we must focus on their lives in the present, not on their childhood experiences. Allport, who took a pragmatic approach to understanding the person, asserted that if you want to know something about someone, you should "just ask him" (or her). Allport believed that personality psychology should focus on understanding healthy, well-adjusted individuals, whom he described as showing a positive but objective sense of self and others, interest in issues beyond their own experience, a sense of humor, common sense, and a unifying philosophy of life—typically but not always provided by religious faith (Allport, 1961). Allport was dedicated to the idea that psychology should have relevance to social issues facing modern society, and his scholarship has influenced not only personality psychology but also the psychology of religion and prejudice.

In defining personality, Allport (1961) stressed the uniqueness of each person and his or her capacity to adapt to the environment. For Allport, the unit we should use to understand personality is the trait. He defined traits as mental structures that make different situations the same for the person. For instance, if Gabi is sociable, she is likely to behave in an outgoing, happy fashion whether she is at a party or in a group study session. Allport's definition implies that behavior should be consistent across different situations.

We get a sense of the down-to-earth quality of Allport's approach to studying personality by looking at his study of traits. In the late 1930s, Allport and his colleague H. S. Odbert (1936) sat down with two big unabridged dictionaries and pulled out all the words that could be used to describe a person—a method called the *lexical approach*. This approach is based on the idea that if a trait is important to people in real life, it ought to be represented in the natural language people use to talk about one another. Furthermore, the more important a trait is, the more likely it is that it should be represented by a single word. Allport and Odbert started with 18,000 words and then pared down that list to 4,500.

As you can appreciate, 4,500 traits would be a rather difficult inventory by which to define a personality. Imagine that you are asked to rate a person, Ignacio, on some traits. You use a scale from 1 to 5, with 1 meaning "not at all" and 5 meaning "very much." If you give Ignacio a 5 on "outgoing," what do you think you might give him on "shy"? Clearly, we may not need 4,500 traits to summarize the way we describe personality. But how might we whittle down these descriptors further, without losing something important?

With advances in statistical methods and the advent of computers, the lexical approach became considerably less unwieldy, as researchers began to analyze these many words to look for underlying structures that might account for their overlap. In 1946, Raymond Cattell applied the relatively new statistical procedure of *factor analysis* to the Allport and Odbert traits. Cattell concluded that 16 underlying factors would summarize the data well, and this work led to the development of the 16PF, a personality scale that is still used today.

Factor analysis essentially tells us what items on a scale people are responding to as if they mean the same thing. For example, if Ignacio got a 5 on "outgoing," he probably would get a 5 on "talkative" and a 1 or 2 on "shy." One important characteristic

Mother Goose & Grimm: © Grimmy, Inc. King Features Syndicate.

Critical Controversy   Can Personality Change?

As you talk on the phone with a friend, she tells you for what seems like the hundredth time about her boyfriend troubles. He never calls when he says he will. He always seems to have "forgotten" his wallet when they go out, and now she thinks he might be cheating on her *again*. As you count silently to 10, you are tempted to blurt it out: "Dump him already! He's never going to change!"

Of course, your friend might be banking on the notion that he *will* change. Can people really change? The answer to this question has implications for a variety of important life domains. For example, can criminals be rehabilitated? Can addicts truly recover from addictions? Do major life experiences such as marriage and parenthood cause personality changes? Can adults make changes to lead happier, healthier lives? Will all those self-help books ever help you to stop worrying and just enjoy life? And, of course, will that lousy boyfriend turn out to be suitable husband material after all?

Whether personality can change has been a topic of controversy throughout the history of the field of personality. Freud believed that personality was essentially fixed by the age of 6, with little development occurring over the rest of life. Jung split with Freud on this issue, believing that the most important development occurred during the middle years of life. One of psychology's most famous early thinkers, William James, once wrote that "it is well for the world that in most of us, by the age of thirty, the character has set like plaster, and will never soften again." Trait psychologists Paul Costa and Robert Mc-Crae concluded that, based on their work, James was on target: They suggested that most traits are indeed "essentially fixed" by age 30, with little meaningful change occurring throughout the rest of adulthood (Costa & McCrae, 1992, 2006; McCrae & Costa, 2006).

However, other research has provided evidence that meaningful personality change continues over time (Roberts, Wood, & Caspi, 2007). Sanjay Srivastava and his colleagues (2003) examined evidence from a sample of 132,515 respondents to a website, who completed measures of the big five personality traits. Participants ranged in age from 21 to 60. Comparing trait scores for those at different ages, the researchers found evidence suggesting change over the life course. Conscientiousness increased, especially in the 20s. Agreeableness increased dramatically in the 30s. Neuroticism declined for women, but not for men, over the life course. Young women were higher on neuroticism to start with, suggesting that men and women become more similar on this dimension of personality over time. The results of this large-scale study point to the possibility that with age, people may be increasingly better adapted to meet the challenges of life.

The study by Srivastava and his colleagues suggesting that personality traits may change was a cross-sectional study in which different individuals were assessed at the same time. However, this type of study is susceptible to what are called *cohort effects*—the possibility that people in the same generation (for instance, everyone born in the 1950s) share some common characteristics because of their similar history and differ systematically from other generations (such as people born in the 1990s) (Schaie, 2007). Individuals who lived through the Great Depression, for example, might have some things in common that set them apart from others.

Even stronger evidence is provided by longitudinal studies that follow the same individuals over a long period of time. Recently, Brent Roberts and his colleagues (Roberts, Walton, & Viechtbauer, 2006) analyzed 92 different longitudinal studies that included thousands of participants ranging from 12 to over 80 years old and that measured aspects of the big five across the life course. They concluded that there is indeed strong, consistent evidence for trait changes throughout life, even into adulthood. Social dominance (a facet of extraversion), conscientiousness, and emotional stability (the opposite of neuroticism) were found to increase especially between the ages of 20 and 40. Social vitality, another facet of extraversion, and openness to experience increased most during adolescence but then declined in old age. Agreeableness showed a steady increase over the life course. Over time, people were not just getting older—they were getting more responsible, kinder, and less worried.

Keep in mind that by definition, traits are considered to be stable. They might be the least likely aspect of personality to change, as compared, for example, to beliefs or goals. To find change in even these relatively stable dimensions is extraordinary and speaks to the important possibility that people can grow and change, especially in positive ways, over the life span. Other aspects of personality such as resilience, wisdom, complexity, and insight have also been shown to increase through life experience (Helson & Soto, 2005; Helson, Soto, & Cate, 2006).

What does this mean for your friend and her loser boyfriend? He just might shape up, but she might have to wait a very long time—and aren't there other, more agreeable and conscientious fish in the sea?

What Do You Think?

- Do you think personality can change throughout a person's life? Explain.
- Think about what you were like 5 years ago. Which aspects of your personality have changed? Which have stayed the same?
- If you have a friend who wants to be more outgoing, what would your advice be?

of factor analysis is that it relies on the scientist to interpret the meaning of the factors, and the researcher must make some decisions about how many factors are enough to explain the data (Goldberg & Digman, 1994). In 1963, W. T. Norman reanalyzed the data Cattell used and concluded that only five factors were needed to summarize these traits. Norman's research set the stage for the dominant approach in personality psychology today: the five-factor model (Digman, 1990).

The Five-Factor Model of Personality

Pick a friend and jot down 10 of that person's most notable personality traits. Did you perhaps list "reserved" or "a good leader"? "Responsible" or "unreliable"? "Sweet," "kind," or "friendly"? Maybe even "creative"? Researchers in personality psychology have found that there are essentially five broad personality dimensions that are represented in the natural language and that also summarize the various ways psychologists have studied traits (Costa & McCrae, 1998, 2006; Digman, 1990, 1996, 2002; Hogan, 1987, 2006; McCrae & Costa, 2006). The **big five factors of personality,** the "supertraits" that are thought to describe the main dimensions of personality, are neuroticism (emotional instability), extraversion, openness to experience, agreeableness, and conscientiousness. Although personality psychologists typically refer to the traits as N, E, O, A, and C on the basis of the order in which they emerged in a factor analysis, if you create an anagram from these first letters of the trait names, you get the word *OCEAN*. The traits are more fully defined in Figure 11.5.

Each of the five traits has been the topic of extensive research. Genetic factors have been shown to explain a substantial amount of variation in each of the big five traits. We consider a sampling of research findings on each trait here to give you a sense of the interesting work that has been inspired by the five-factor model:

- Neuroticism is related to feeling negative emotion more often than positive emotion in one's daily life and to experiencing more lingering negative states (Lucas & Fujita, 2000). Neuroticism has been shown to relate to more health complaints, although this association may not necessarily mean that neurotic individuals are actually more likely to be physically sick (Goodwin, Cox, & Clara, 2006).

- Extraverts are more likely than others to engage in social activities (Emmons & Diener, 1986).

- Openness is related to higher IQ, liberal values, open-mindedness, and tolerance. Openness to experience is related to creativity and creative accomplishments (King, McKee-Walker, & Broyles, 1996).

- Agreeableness is related to generosity, and when asked to make a wish for anything at all, agreeable people are more likely to make altruistic wishes such as "for world peace" (King & Broyles, 1997).

- Conscientiousness is linked to better-quality friendships (Jensen-Campbell & Malcolm, 2007) and has been shown to relate to healthy behaviors and longevity, an issue we return to at the end of this chapter (Mroczek, Spiro, & Griffin, 2006).

big five factors of personality The "supertraits" that are thought to describe the main dimensions of personality—specifically, neuroticism (emotional instability), extraversion, openness to experience, agreeableness, and conscientiousness.

"Henderson's got to go. His magnetic personality's not only disrupting the office, it's erasing all our software."

© CartoonStock.com.

FIGURE 11.5

The Big Five Factors of Personality
Each of the broad supertraits encompasses more narrow traits and characteristics. Use the acronym *OCEAN* to remember the big five personality factors (*o*penness, *c*onscientiousness, and so on).

Openness	**C**onscientiousness	**E**xtraversion	**A**greeableness	**N**euroticism (emotional stability)
• Imaginative or practical	• Organized or disorganized	• Sociable or retiring	• Softhearted or ruthless	• Calm or anxious
• Interested in variety or routine	• Careful or careless	• Fun-loving or somber	• Trusting or suspicious	• Secure or insecure
• Independent or conforming	• Disciplined or impulsive	• Affectionate or reserved	• Helpful or uncooperative	• Self-satisfied or self-pitying

Personality and Emotion: Are Some People Happier Than Others?

Some people seem to go through life having fun, while others appear to be prone to feeling distress at even the slightest problem. You might think that most of our daily emotional experience can be explained by the events that happen to us—of course, you reason, a person is going to be happy if she is doing well in school and has a loving romantic partner, but unhappy if she is doing poorly and has just experienced a romantic breakup. But interestingly, research has shown that life events explain relatively little about our daily mood. Rather, there is considerable stability in a person's mood over time (Watson & Walker, 1996). That means that someone who says she is pretty happy today is likely to say she is pretty happy on another day, even years later. On average, some people appear to be happier than others.

If we want to explain this stability, we might try to think of aspects of the person that are themselves relatively stable, such as personality traits. Indeed, one of the most consistent findings in personality research is the strong relationship between personality traits and emotional experience. Extraverts, who are outgoing and sociable, report higher levels of positive mood than do introverts. David Watson, a personality and clinical psychologist who specializes in the study of mood, has suggested that positive emotion is the "affective core" of the trait of extraversion (Watson & Clark, 1997).

Why are extraverts so happy? Two types of explanations aim to account for this strong link. So-called *instrumental explanations* state that personality has an *indirect* effect on emotional experience— that is, personality might influence the lifestyle choices a person makes, and those choices influence mood. Perhaps extraverts are more likely to favor activities that are themselves related to higher positive mood. For example, social activities are strongly related to positive mood. Maybe extraverts are happier because they choose to spend more time with others. However, this explanation, though logically sensible, does not appear to be the case. Research has shown that extraverts are happier than introverts even when they are alone (Argyle & Lu, 1990; Lucas, 2007).

Happy activities and happy thoughts are available for everyone.

Alternative explanations for the strong relation between extraversion and positive affect are called *temperamental explanations*. These explanations state that personality has a *direct* effect on emotional experience, so that extraversion can be thought of as a predisposition to experiencing positive mood (Larsen & Ketelaar, 1991). Such explanations take two forms. First, it may be that extraverts are more responsive to positive situations, so that when they encounter a pleasant situation they are more reactive to it. This explanation would predict that extraverts should be happier than introverts only when they are in a pleasant situation. For instance, an extravert at a great party would feel happier than an introvert at the same party, but these two people would not differ in happiness while sitting in a class listening to a lecture. A second temperamental explanation suggests that extraversion and positive affect are strongly linked even in neutral situations. This explanation asserts that extraverts just carry a hefty bundle of positive mood with them wherever they go and whatever they do (Lucas, 2007).

Richard Lucas and Brendan Baird (2004) conducted a series of studies to address these differing temperamental predictions. In six studies, they exposed students who differed on extraversion to a variety of positive or neutral stimuli. The positive mood conditions included writing about a dream vacation or winning the lottery, viewing pleasant film clips about gardening or a Bill Cosby comedy routine, or reading jokes and cartoons. The neutral mood conditions included writing about taking a drive or going grocery shopping or watching a financial news report from PBS. In all of the studies, the strong relation between extraversion and positive affect was found even in the neutral conditions. Extraverts were happier than introverts regardless of whether the researchers had tried to put them in a pleasant mood. Even when they had just read a financial news report, the extraverts were happier. Finally, Lucas and Baird examined a variety of studies that used daily diary methods (described in Chapter 2) in which individuals were "beeped" at various times during the day and asked to rate how they were feeling at the moment. Examining the connection between extraversion and mood at any given moment, Lucas and Baird found that regardless of the situation, when beeped at random times, extraverts reported higher levels of positive affect.

If you are an introvert, you may be feeling your mood deflating right about now. But it is important to keep a few things in mind. First, introverts were *not* found to be *un*happy in these studies. Introverts and extraverts alike responded with positive emotion toward the funny film clips. Second, introversion is not the same thing as shyness (Briggs, 1988). Introverts are not necessarily socially anxious or distressed. The introvert may be someone whose positive moods are more akin to contentment and quiet satisfaction than those of the outgoing extravert.

Indeed, for the introvert (and anyone else) who is interested in enhancing positive mood, research provides hints for effective strategies. First, introverts might take a lesson from extraverts and spend more time with the people they love. Second, extraverts have been found to be more likely than others to augment their positive moods so that happy moods persist longer and negative ones fade more rapidly (Hemenover, 2003). One way to capitalize on our positive moments in life is through savoring (Bryant & Veroff, 2007). Savoring—which means attending to our positive experiences and appreciating them— enhances our sense of well-being. Extraverts may have a shortcut to pleasurable experience, afforded to them by their basic personality. But even without the benefit of this disposition to happiness, happy activities and happy thoughts are available for everyone.

Keep in mind that because the five factors are theoretically independent of one another, a person can be any combination of them. Do you know a neurotic extravert or an agreeable introvert? Whether or not the big five traits are stable or can change has been an enduring debate in personality psychology. See the Critical Controversy to read about this debate.

Some research on the big five factors addresses the extent to which the factors appear in personality profiles in different cultures (Lingjaerde, Foreland, & Engvik, 2001; Miacic & Goldberg, 2007; Pukrop, Sass, & Steinmeyer, 2000). Do the five factors show up in the assessment of personality in cultures around the world? There is increasing evidence that they do (McCrae & Costa 2006; Ozer & Riese, 1994). Researchers have found that some version of the five factors appears in people in countries as diverse as Canada, Finland, Poland, China, and Japan (Paunonen & others, 1992). Research has generally supported the concept of the big five traits. Researchers have even begun to find evidence for the big five personality traits in animals, including domestic dogs (Gosling, Kwan, & John, 2003) and hyenas (Gosling & John, 1999). Despite this strong evidence, some personality researchers believe the big five might not end up being the final list of broad supertraits and that more specific traits are better predictors of behavior (Fung & Ng, 2006; Saucier, 2001; Simms, 2007).

In addition to studying change and stability in personality traits, psychologists also are interested in how such traits are linked to emotion. To read about this link, see the Intersection, which examines whether one of the big five traits—extraversion—might be involved in how happy individuals are.

Evaluating the Trait Perspectives

Studying people in terms of their personality traits has practical value. Identifying a person's traits allows us to know the person better. Also, the traits that we have influence our health, the way we think, our career success, and our relations with others (Levenson & Aldwin, 2006; Mroczek & Little, 2006; Roberts & others, 2007). Still, the trait approach has been critiqued for missing the importance of the situation in personality and behavior. Some have criticized the trait perspective for painting an individual's personality with very broad strokes. Dan McAdams (2001) has referred to the five-factor model as "the psychology of the stranger" because although it tells us much about what we might want to know about someone we have never met, it does not tell us very much about the nuances of each individual's personality. Personality psychologists who are interested in those nuances sometimes adopt the life story approach to personality, our next topic.

 REVIEW, ASSESS, AND SHARPEN YOUR THINKING

Review

3 Discuss the trait perspectives.
- Define traits and describe the views of Allport.
- Identify the big five factors in personality.
- Evaluate the trait perspectives.

Assess

1. Which of the following is not a big five factor of personality?
   A. openness to experience
   B. self-actualization
   C. conscientiousness
   D. extraversion

2. Which of the following statements is correct?
   A. A trait is a basic building block of personality.
   B. A trait is a behavior that occures outside a personality.
   C. A trait is the same size of component as a personality.
   D. A trait and a personality are the same thing.

3. Which of the following describes the lexical approach?

A. Personality can be described along five factors.

B. Traits are enduring characteristics that determine behavior.

C. Traits can be represented in language usage.

D. Personality can be described along 16 factors.

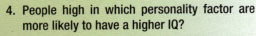

4. People high in which personality factor are more likely to have a higher IQ?

A. neuroticism   B. conscientiousness

C. agreeableness   D. openness to experience

5. What is the purpose of factor analysis?

A. to describe adaptive traits that make up personality

B. to describe commonalities in the way people respond to items on a scale

C. to compare's theories of personality

D. to determine whether personality changes over time

Sharpen Your Thinking

To what extent do you believe the big five factors capture your personality? Look at the characteristics of the five factors listed in Figure 11.5 and decide how you line up on each one. Then choose one of the factors, such as extraversion or openness, and give an example of how situation might influence the expression of this trait in your life.

4 Personological and Life Story Perspectives

Discuss the personological and life story perspectives.

personological and life story perspectives
Approaches to personality emphasizing that the way to understand the person is to focus on his or her life history and life story—aspects that distinguish that individual from all others.

Imagine giving a group of 1,000 people a questionnaire measuring them on each of the big five traits. In looking at their scores, you might conclude that people are *not* like snowflakes after all, but rather like Chips Ahoy cookies: They differ in small ways, but there are plenty that share very similar traits.

If two people have the same levels of the big five traits, do they essentially have the same personality? Researchers who approach personality from the personological and life story perspectives do not think so. Recall that we opened this chapter with the notion that each of us is unique and in some ways like no other human being on earth. **Personological and life story perspectives** stress that the way to understand the person is to focus on his or her life history and life story—aspects that distinguish that individual from all the other "snowflakes."

Murray's Personological Approach

Henry Murray's psychological profile of Adolf Hitler, developed in 1943 during World War II, continues to serve as a model for criminal profiling today.

Henry Murray (1893–1988) was a young biochemistry graduate student when he became interested in the psychology of personality after meeting Carl Jung and reading his work. Murray went on to become the director of the Psychological Clinic at Harvard at the same time that Gordon Allport was on the faculty there. Murray and Allport saw personality very differently. While Allport was most comfortable focusing on conscious experience and traits, Murray embraced the psychodynamic notion of unconscious motivation.

Murray coined the word *personology* to refer to the study of the whole person. He famously stated that "the history of the organism is the organism," meaning that in order to understand a person, we have to understand that person's history, including all aspects of the person's life. At the Harvard clinic, Murray assembled specialists of all sorts—including medical professionals, anthropologists, psychologists, and sociologists—who would analyze individuals from every possible perspective and seek to understand each person. The findings of this exercise were published in *Explorations in Personality* in 1938.

Murray applied his insights into personality during World War II, when he was called upon by the Office of Strategic Services (a precursor to the CIA) to develop a psychological profile of Adolf Hitler. That document, produced in 1943, accurately predicted that Hitler would commit suicide rather than be taken alive by the Allies. Murray's analysis of

Hitler was the first "offender profile," and it has served as a model for modern criminal profiling. Upon returning to Harvard after the war, Murray continued to do research in the field of personality. By chance, one of the participants in his studies was Theodore Kaczynski, who would later become infamous as the Unabomber, a mysterious terrorist who sent bomb-containing packages (which injured 29 people and killed 3 of them) to universities and airlines from the 1970s through the 1990s.

The aspect of Murray's research that has had the most impact on contemporary personality psychology is his approach to motivation. Murray believed that our motives are largely unknown to us, so that measures of motivation must be developed that do not just ask people to say what it is they want. Thus, along with Christiana Morgan, Murray developed the Thematic Apperception Test (or TAT), which we return to later in this chapter (Morgan & Murray, 1935). Moreover, a variety of scoring procedures have been developed for analyzing the unconscious motives that are revealed in imaginative stories (Smith, 1992).

Research by David Winter (2004) has analyzed presidential motives in inaugural addresses such as those delivered by Richard M. Nixon (left) and John F. Kennedy (right). Winter found that certain needs revealed in these speeches corresponded to later events during these individuals' terms in office.

Murray's approach to personality is reflected in current research on achievement, affiliation, and power motivation, as well as the intimacy motive, which we considered in Chapter 10. For example, David Winter (2005) analyzed the motives revealed in presidential inaugural addresses. He found that certain needs revealed in these speeches corresponded to later events during the person's tenure as president. For instance, presidents who scored high on need for achievement (such as Jimmy Carter) were less successful during their terms. Presidents who scored high on need for power tended to be judged as more successful (John F. Kennedy, Ronald Reagan), and presidents whose addresses included a great deal of warm, interpersonal imagery (suggesting high need for affiliation) tended to experience scandal during their presidencies (Richard M. Nixon).

The Life Story Approach and Identity

Following in the Murray tradition, Dan McAdams (2001, 2006) developed the *life story approach* to identity. Each of us has a unique life story, full of ups and downs. These stories represent our memories of what makes us who we are. McAdams found that the life story is a constantly changing narrative that serves to provide our lives with a sense of coherence. Just as Murray said that the history of the organism is the organism, McAdams suggested that our life stories are our identities.

McAdams has conducted research using large samples of individuals who have undergone "life story interviews." These interview responses are then coded for themes that are relevant to differing life stages and transitions. For example, McAdams and his colleagues found that kindergarten teachers (who are assumed to be high in generativity, which we considered in Chapter 4) are more likely to tell life stories characterized by a redemption pattern, with things going from bad to good. Other personality psychologists have relied on narrative accounts of life experiences as a means of understanding how individuals create meaning in life events (King & others, 2000). By using narratives, personal documents (such as diaries), and even letters and speeches, personality psychologists continue to look for the "deeper meaning" that cannot be addressed through self-report measures.

Finally, some personality psychologists take very seriously Murray's commitment to understanding the whole person, by focusing on just one case. *Psychobiography* is a means of inquiry in which the personality psychologist attempts to apply a personality theory to a single person's life (Runyon, 2007; Schultz, 2005). Freud himself wrote the first psychobiography in his analysis of Michelangelo. Some of the problems with his interpretations of Michelangelo's life have caused his work to become a road map for what a psychobiographer ought not to do (Elms, 2005).

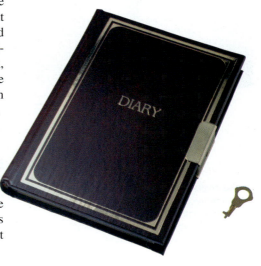

Evaluating the Life Story Approach and Similar Perspectives

Studying individuals through narratives and personal interviews provides an extraordinarily rich opportunity for the researcher. Imagine having the choice of reading someone's diary versus seeing that person's scores on a questionnaire measuring traits. Not many would pass up the chance to read the diary. However, life story studies are difficult and time-consuming; personologist Robert W. White (1992) referred to the study of narratives as exploring personality "the long way."

Collecting interviews and narratives is often just the first step. In order for these personal stories to become scientific data, they must be transformed into numbers, a process involving extensive coding and content analysis. Further, for narrative studies to be worthwhile, they must tell us something we could not have found out in a much easier way (King, 2003). Psychobiographical inquiries moreover are prone to the biases of the scholars who conduct them and may not serve the scientific goal of generalizability.

REVIEW, ASSESS, AND SHARPEN YOUR THINKING

Review

4 **Discuss the personological and life story perspectives.**
- Summarize the personological approach of Murray.
- Explain how the life story approach is involved in understanding identity.
- Describe the advantages and disadvantages of using narratives in research.

Assess

1. **Henry Murray's personology approach is consistent with which perspective?**
   A. humanistic perspective
   B. psychodynamic perspective
   C. trait perspective
   D. social cognitive perspective

2. **The in-depth study of someone's life conducted in order to validate a theory of personality is known as**
   A. psychobiography.
   B. personology.
   C. the life story approach.
   D. an offender profile.

3. **Which of the following is not true of psychobiography?**
   A. It provides rich data.
   B. It provides results that are widely generalizable.
   C. It is prone to bias.
   D. It focuses on a single person.

4. **Some of Murray's most important research on personology focuses on**
   A. objective tests.
   B. distinct features of personality.
   C. traits.
   D. unconscious motivations.

Sharpen Your Thinking

What might the work of Winter on presidents likely say about the motives of President George W. Bush?

5 Social Cognitive Perspectives

Explain the social cognitive perspectives.

social cognitive perspectives Approaches to personality emphasizing conscious awareness, beliefs, expectations, and goals. Social cognitive psychologists explore the person's ability to reason; to think about the past, present, and future; and to reflect on the self.

Social cognitive perspectives on personality emphasize conscious awareness, beliefs, expectations, and goals. While incorporating principles from behaviorism (see Chapter 7), social cognitive psychologists explore the person's ability to reason; to think about the past, present, and future; and to reflect on the self. They emphasize the person's individual interpretation of situations and thus focus on the uniqueness of each person by examining how behavior is tailored to the diversity of situations in which people find themselves. Social cognitive theorists are not interested in broad traits, but rather they investigate how more specific factors, such as beliefs, relate to behavior and performance. In this section we consider the two major social cognitive approaches, developed respectively by Albert Bandura and Walter Mischel.

Bandura's Social Cognitive Theory

B. F. Skinner, whose work we examined in Chapter 7, believed that there is no such thing as "personality"; rather, he emphasized behavior and felt that internal mental states were irrelevant to psychology. Albert Bandura (1986, 2001, 2006, 2007a, 2007b) found Skinner's approach to be far too simplistic for understanding human functioning. He took the basic tenets of behaviorism and added a recognition of the role of mental processes in determining behavior. While Skinner saw behavior as caused by the situation, Bandura pointed out that the person can cause situations, and sometimes the very definition of the situation itself depends on the person's beliefs about it. For example, is that upcoming exam an opportunity to show your stuff or a threat to your ability to achieve your goals? The test is the same either way, but a person's unique take on the test can influence a host of behaviors (studying, worrying, and so on).

Bandura's social cognitive theory states that behavior, environment, and person/cognitive factors are *all* important in understanding personality. Bandura coined the term *reciprocal determinism* to describe the way behavior, environment, and person/cognitive factors interact to create personality (Figure 11.6). The environment can determine a person's behavior, and the person can act to change the environment. Similarly, person/cognitive factors can both influence behavior and be influenced by behavior. From Bandura's perspective, then, behavior is a product of a variety of forces, some of which come from the situation and some of which the person brings to the situation. We now review the important processes and variables Bandura used to understand personality.

Observational Learning   Remember from Chapter 7 that Bandura believes that observational learning is a key aspect of how we learn. Through observational learning, we form ideas about the behavior of others and then possibly adopt this behavior ourselves. For example, a young boy might observe his father's aggressive outbursts and hostile exchanges with people; when the boy is with his peers, he interacts in a highly aggressive way, showing the same characteristics that his father's behavior does. Social cognitive theorists believe that we acquire a wide range of behaviors, thoughts, and feelings through observing others' behavior; these observations form an important part of our personalities.

Personal Control   Social cognitive theorists emphasize that we can regulate and control our own behavior, despite our changing environment (Bandura, 2006; Mischel, 2004). For example, another young executive who observes her boss behave in a dominant and sarcastic manner may find the behavior distasteful and go out of her way to be encouraging and supportive of her subordinates. Or imagine that someone tries to persuade you to join a particular social club on campus and makes you an enticing offer. You reflect on the offer, consider your interests and beliefs, and decide not to join. Your *cognition* (your thoughts) leads you to control your behavior and resist environmental influence in this instance. One important aspect of the experience of control is the belief that one has the ability to produce change in one's world, or self-efficacy.

Self-Efficacy   **Self-efficacy** is the belief that one can master a situation and produce positive outcomes. Bandura and others have shown that self-efficacy is related to a number of positive developments in people's lives, including solving problems, becoming more sociable, initiating a diet or an exercise program and maintaining it, and quitting smoking (Figure 11.7) (Bandura, 2001, 2006, 2007a, 2007b; Schunk, 2008; Schunk & Zimmerman, 2006). Self-efficacy influences whether people even try to develop healthy habits, as well as how much effort they expend in coping with stress, how long they persist in the face of obstacles, and how much stress and pain they experience (Brister & others, 2006;

Albert Bandura (1925–) *Bandura's practical, problem-solving–oriented social cognitive approach has made a lasting mark on personality theory and therapy.*

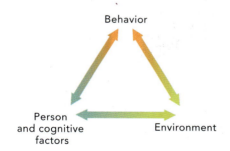

FIGURE 11.6

Bandura's Social Cognitive Theory
Bandura's social cognitive theory emphasizes reciprocal influences of behavior, environment, and person/cognitive factors.

self-efficacy The belief that one can master a situation and produce positive outcomes.

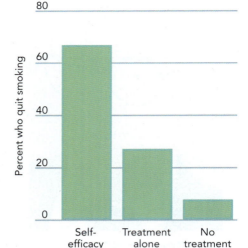

FIGURE 11.7

Self-Efficacy and Smoking Cessation In one study, smokers were randomly assigned to one of three conditions. In the self-efficacy condition, individuals were told they had been chosen for the study because they had great potential to quit smoking (Warnecke & others, 2001). Then, they participated in a 14-week program on smoking cessation. In the treatment-alone condition, individuals participated in the 14-week smoking cessation program but were told that they had been randomly selected for it. In the no-treatment control condition, individuals did not participate in the smoking cessation program. At the conclusion of the 14-week program, individuals in the self-efficacy condition were likelier to have quit smoking than their counterparts in the other two conditions.

Clark & Dodge, 1999; Sarkar, Fisher, & Schillinger, 2006). Self-efficacy is related, too, to whether people initiate psychotherapy to deal with their problems and whether it succeeds (Longo, Lent, & Brown, 1992). Researchers also have found that self-efficacy is linked with successful job interviewing and job performance (Judge & Bono, 2001; Tay, Ang, & Van Dyne, 2006).

Self-efficacy helps people in unsatisfactory situations by encouraging them to believe that they can succeed. In Chapter 16, we consider the role of self-efficacy in important life changes such as weight loss and smoking cessation. How can you increase your self-efficacy? The following strategies can help (Watson & Tharp, 2007):

- Select something you expect to be able to do, not something you expect to fail at accomplishing. As you develop self-efficacy, you can tackle more daunting projects.
- Distinguish between past performance and your present project. You might come to expect from past failures that you cannot do certain things. However, remind yourself that your past failures are in the past and that you now have a new sense of confidence and accomplishment.
- Pay close attention to your successes. Some individuals have a tendency to remember their failures but not their successes.
- Keep written records so that you will be concretely aware of your successes. A student who sticks to a study schedule for 4 days and then fails to stick to it on the 5th day should not think, "I'm a failure. I can't do this." This statement ignores the fact that the student was successful 80 percent of the time (keeping to the schedule 4 out of 5 days).
- Make a list of the specific kinds of situations in which you expect to have the most difficulty and the least difficulty. Begin with the easier tasks and cope with the harder ones after you have experienced some success.

Bandura's (2001, 2006) social cognitive approach to personality has been especially influential in shaping researchers' understanding of achievement behavior and has laid the groundwork for various approaches to clinical practice, as we will see in Chapter 15.

Mischel's Contributions

Like Bandura, Walter Mischel is a social cognitive psychologist who has been interested in exploring how personality influences behavior. Mischel has left his mark on the field of personality in two notable ways. First, his critique of the idea of consistency in behavior ignited a flurry of controversy that has become known as the person–situation debate. Second, he has proposed the CAPS model, a new way of thinking about personality. We discuss each of these contributions in turn.

Consistency and the Person–Situation Debate   Whether we are talking about unconscious sexual conflicts, traits, or motives, all of the approaches we have considered so far maintain that these various personality characteristics are enduring and influence behavior. These shared assumptions were attacked in 1968 with the publication of Walter Mischel's *Personality and Assessment,* a book that nearly ended the psychological study of personality.

To understand Mischel's argument, recall Gordon Allport's definition of a trait as a characteristic that ought to make different situations equivalent for a given person. This quality of traits suggests that a person should behave consistently in different situations—in other words, the individual should exhibit *cross-situational consistency.* For example, an outgoing person should act highly sociably whether she is at a party or in the library. However, Mischel looked at the research compiled on trait prediction of behavior and found it to be lacking. He concluded that there was no evidence for cross-situational consistency in behavior—and thus no evidence for the existence of personality as it had been previously assumed to exist.

Rather than understanding personality as consisting of broad, internal traits that make for consistent behavior across situations and time, Mischel said that personality often changes according to a given situation. Mischel asserted that behavior is discriminative—that is, a person looks at each situation and responds accordingly. Mischel's view is called *situationism,* the idea that personality and behavior often vary considerably from one context to another.

Personality psychologists responded to Mischel's situationist attack in a variety of ways, sparking what has become known as the *person–situation debate.* Researchers were able to show that it is not a matter of whether personality predicts behavior, but when and how it does so, often in combination with situational factors. The research findings were that (1) the narrower and more limited a trait is, the likelier it will predict behavior; (2) some people are consistent on some traits, and other people are consistent on other traits; and (3) personality traits exert a stronger influence on an individual's behavior when situational influences are less powerful. A very powerful situation is one that contains many clear cues about how a person is supposed to behave. For example, even a very talkative person typically sits quietly during a class lecture. But in weaker situations, such as during his or her leisure time, the person may spend most of the time talking. Moreover, individuals select the situations they are in, so that even if situations determine behavior, traits play a role in determining which situations they choose (such as going to a party or staying home to study) (Emmons & Diener, 1986).

Let's pause and consider what it means to be consistent. You might believe that being consistent is part of being a genuine, honest person and that tailoring behavior to different situations means being fake. On the other hand, consider that someone who never changes his or her behavior to fit a situation might be unpleasant—"a drag"—to have around. For example, think about someone who cannot put aside his competitive drive even when playing checkers with a 4-year-old. Clearly, adaptive behavior might involve sometimes being consistent and sometimes tailoring behavior to the situation.

Over time, Mischel (2004) has developed an approach to personality that he feels is better suited to capturing the nuances of the relationship between the individual and situations in producing behavior. Imagine trying to study personality without using traits or broad motives. What would you focus on? Mischel's answer to this dilemma is his CAPS theory.

CAPS Theory   Although his 1968 book nearly ended interest in the influence of personality on behavior, Mischel has continued to conduct research in the field. Indeed, Mischel's (2004) work on delay of gratification, discussed in Chapter 10, has demonstrated remarkable stability in behavior over time. Recall that in that work, children who had been able to delay eating a cookie in an experimental session were also able to perform better in academic work in college. Mischel's revised approach to personality is concerned with stability or coherence in the pattern of behavior *over time,* not with consistency across differing situations. That is, Mischel and his colleagues have studied how behaviors in very different situations have a coherent pattern, such as a child's waiting to eat the cookie versus that same individual's (as a grown college student) deciding to stay home and study instead of going out to party.

In keeping with the social cognitive emphasis on the person's cognitive abilities and mental states, Mischel conceptualizes personality as a set of interconnected **cognitive affective processing systems (CAPS)** (Mischel, 2004; Mischel & Shoda, 1999). This approach means that our thoughts and emotions about ourselves and the world affect our interactions with the environment and become linked in ways that matter to behavior. Personal control and self-efficacy can be thought of as connections that a person has made among situations, beliefs, and behaviors. For instance, someone who is excited by the challenge of a new assignment given by a boss may think about all the possible strategies to reach his or her goal and get to work immediately. Yet this go-getter may respond to other challenges differently, depending on who gives the assignment.

CAPS is called a "bottom-up" approach to personality. That means it is concerned with how personality works, not with what it is (Shoda & Mischel, 2006). From the CAPS perspective, it makes no sense to ask a person "How extraverted are you?" because the answer is always, "It depends." A person may be outgoing in one situation (on the first day of class) and not another (right before an exam), and that unique pattern of flexibility is what personality is all about.

Not surprisingly, the CAPS approach focuses on the way people behave in different situations and how they uniquely interpret situational features. From this perspective, knowing that Sasha is an extravert tells us little about how she will behave in a group discussion in her psychology class. We need to know about Sasha's beliefs and goals in the discussion

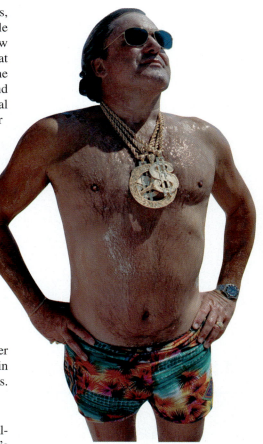

cognitive affective processing systems (CAPS) According to Mischel, a set of interconnected cognitive systems through which an individual's thoughts and emotions about self and the world become linked in ways that matter to behavior.

"Yes I'm a dog but I've got a great personality."
© CartoonStock.com.

(for example, does she want to impress the instructor? is she a psychology major? are the members of the class good friends of hers?), as well as her personal understanding of the situation itself (is this an opportunity to shine, or is she thinking about her test for the next class?). Research using this approach generally involves observing individuals behaving in a variety of contexts in order to identify the patterns of associations that exist among beliefs, emotions, and behavior for each individual person across different situations.

Evaluating the Social Cognitive Perspectives

Social cognitive theory focuses on the influence of environment on personality. The social cognitive approach has fostered a scientific climate for understanding personality that highlights the observation of behavior. Social cognitive theory emphasizes the influence of cognitive processes in explaining personality and suggests that people have the ability to control their environment.

Critics of the social cognitive perspective on personality take issue with one or more aspects of the approach, charging that:

- The social cognitive approach is too concerned with change and situational influences on personality and does not pay adequate tribute to the enduring qualities of personality.
- Social cognitive approaches ignore the role biology plays in personality.
- In its attempt to incorporate both the situation and the person into its view of personality, social cognitive psychology tends to lead to very specific predictions for each person in any given situation, making generalizations impossible.

REVIEW, ASSESS, AND SHARPEN YOUR THINKING

Review

5 Explain the social cognitive perspectives.
- Define the social cognitive perspectives and describe Bandura's social cognitive theory.
- Describe two of Mischel's contributions to personality psychology.
- Evaluate the social cognitive perspectives.

Assess

1. Which of the following is not a component of Bandura's social cognitive theory?
   A. self-efficacy
   B. unconscious motivations
   C. control
   D. observational learning

2. Roberta believes that she cannot successfully be admitted to graduate school. Roberta is
   A. high in self-efficacy.
   B. low in self-efficacy.
   C. high in personal control.
   D. low in personal control.

3. According to Walter Mischel's 1968 book, behavior is determined by
   A. traits.
   B. biology.
   C. situation.
   D. cognitive functions.

4. The cognitive affective processing systems (CAPS) approach conceptualizes behavior along all of the following dimensions except:
   A. biological dimensions.
   B. cognitive dimensions.
   C. contextual dimensions.
   D. affective dimensions.

5. Reciprocal determinism refers to
   A. cognitive, emotional, and biological factors impacting each other.
   B. behavior being determined by stable traits.
   C. the interplay of behavior, the environment, and personal characteristics.
   D. the person-situation debate.

Sharpen Your Thinking

How much does your personality depend on the situation? Give a specific example of how you are consistent or inconsistent from one situation to the next.

6 Personality Assessment

Characterize the main methods of personality assessment.

One of the great contributions of personality psychology to the science of psychology is its development of rigorous methods for measuring mental processes. Psychologists use a number of scientifically developed methods to evaluate personality (Gregory, 2007). They assess personality for different reasons, from clinical evaluation to career counseling and job selection (Hogan, 2006). Because personality psychology is primarily interested in the characteristics of the person, most personality tests are designed to assess stable, enduring characteristics, free of situational influence. The researcher's theoretical interest typically determines the method used to measure a particular psychological dimension. For example, a researcher interested in unconscious processes usually assesses personality by using a measure that does not rely on conscious knowledge.

Self-Report Tests

The most commonly used method of measuring personality characteristics is self-report. A **self-report test,** also called an *objective test* or *inventory,* directly asks people whether specific items describe their personality traits. For example, self-report personality tests include items such as:

- I am easily embarrassed.
- I love to go to parties.
- I like to watch cartoons on TV.

Self-report tests include many statements or questions such as these. Respondents choose from a limited number of answers (yes or no, true or false, agree or disagree). To get a sense of what a self-report personality test is like, see the Psychology and Life box.

Assessments of the Big Five Factors   Paul Costa and Robert McCrae (1992) constructed the Neuroticism Extraversion Openness Personality Inventory—Revised (or NEO-PI-R, for short), a self-report test geared to assessing the five-factor model: openness, conscientiousness, extraversion, agreeableness, and neuroticism (emotional instability). The test also evaluates six subdimensions that make up the five main factors. Other measures of the big five traits have relied on the lexical approach and offer the advantage of being available without a fee. Measures of the big five generally contain items that are quite straightforward; for instance, the trait "talkative" might show up on an extraversion scale. These items have what psychologists call **face validity,** meaning the extent to which a test item appears to be valid to those who are completing it. In other words, a test item has face validity if it seems on the surface to fit the trait in question.

Adherents of the trait perspectives such as the big five have strong faith in self-report tests, while acknowledging certain limitations. One problem with self-report tests centers on *social desirability*. To grasp the idea of social desirability, imagine answering the item "I am lazy at times." This statement is probably true for everyone, but would you feel comfortable admitting it? When motivated by social desirability, individuals say what they think the researcher wants to hear or what they think will make them look better. One way to measure the influence of social desirability is to give individuals a questionnaire designed to tap into this tendency. Such a scale typically contains many universally true but threatening items ("I like to gossip at times," "I have never said anything intentionally to hurt someone's feelings"). If scores on a trait measure correlate with this measure of social desirability, we know that the test takers were probably not being straightforward on the trait measure.

Another technique for getting around social desirability issues is to design scales so that it is virtually impossible for the respondent to know what the researcher is actually trying to measure. One means of accomplishing this goal is to use an **empirically keyed test,** a type of test that presents a host of questionnaire items to groups of people who are already known to differ in some central way (such as individuals with psychological disorders versus mentally healthy individuals). On the basis of the responses, the researcher can then select the items

self-report test Also called an objective test or inventory, a type of test that directly asks people whether specific items (usually true/false or agree/disagree) describe their personality traits.

face validity The extent to which a test item appears to be valid to those who are completing it.

empirically keyed test A type of test that presents a host of questionnaire items to groups of people who are already known to differ in some central way (such as individuals with a psychological disorder versus mentally healthy individuals).

PSYCHOLOGY AND LIFE

Are You a Nice Person?

In personality psychology, the term *agreeableness* describes someone who is kind and sympathetic to others. Agreeable people tend to trust others and assume that others are trustworthy. They are gentle, altruistic, and generous. In short, agreeable people are nice. How nice are you? Take the questionnaire below to find out.

These items were taken from the agreeableness scale on Lewis Goldberg's International Personality Item Pool website that allows you to test yourself on any number of personality characteristics (Goldberg & others, 2006). This site (http://ipip.ori.org/ipip/) is accessible to all and allows free access to the scale for research purposes.

© CartoonStock.com.

1 = very inaccurate (does not describe you at all)

2 = moderately inaccurate

3 = neither accurate nor inaccurate

4 = moderately accurate

5 = very accurate (describes you very well)

1. _____ I am interested in people.
2. _____ I sympathize with others' feelings.
3. _____ I feel little concern for others.
4. _____ I insult people.
5. _____ I make people feel at ease.
6. _____ I feel others' emotions.
7. _____ I am not interested in other people's problems.
8. _____ I have a soft heart.
9. _____ I take time out for others.
10. _____ I am not really interested in others.

To find out how you did on this assessment, first recode your responses to items 3, 4, 7, and 10—that is, give each rating its opposite. So, for a 5 you get a 1, for a 4 you get a 2, and so on. Add these scores to your answers for items 1, 2, 5, 6, 8, and 9 and divide by 10. Although there are no norms for this particular scale, you can get a sense of how nice you are by comparing your score to the midpoint of the 1 to 5 scale. If your score is higher than 3, you are probably pretty nice. If your score falls below 3, you might think about doing some volunteer work—or at least do something nice for someone in your life!

that best discriminate between the members of the differing groups (Segal & Coolidge, 2004). Items on an empirically keyed test rarely show a great deal of face validity.

MMPI The **Minnesota Multiphasic Personality Inventory (MMPI)** is the most widely used and researched empirically keyed self-report personality test. The MMPI was initially constructed in the 1940s to assess "abnormal" personality tendencies and to improve the diagnosis of individuals with psychological disorders. The most recent version of the inventory, the MMPI-2, is still widely used around the world to assess personality and predict outcomes (Butcher, 2004; Butcher & others, 2006; Exterkate, Bakker-Brehm, & de Jong, 2007; Sellbom & others, 2006). The scale features 550 items and provides information on a variety of personality characteristics.

Minnesota Multiphasic Personality Inventory (MMPI) The most widely used and researched empirically keyed self-report personality test.

The MMPI is not only used by clinical psychologists to assess a person's mental health; it is also used to predict which individuals will make the best job candidates and which career an individual should pursue. With computers now widely employed to score the MMPI-2 (Forbey & Ben-Porath, 2007), some critics warn that the availability of computer scoring has tempted some untrained individuals to use the test in ways for which it has not been validated.

An important consideration with respect to empirically keyed tests is that we do not always know why a given test item distinguishes between two groups. Imagine, for example, that an empirically keyed test of achievement motivation includes an item such as "I prefer to watch sports on TV instead of romantic movies," or an item to distinguish between higher-paid versus lower-paid managers in a work setting. Do these items measure achievement motivation or, instead, simply the respondents' gender? Although it might seem like a good idea for test constructors to hide what they are ultimately trying to measure from test takers, having the participants know what they are being asked about may help them to give their best, most honest responses. If the test takers know that a questionnaire is about extraversion, for example, they might have a better understanding of what each item means. In sum, self-report test items can be rather transparent (for example, as in the NEO-PI-R) or relatively vague and difficult (as in the MMPI).

It is likely that you would be able to give a reasonably good assessment of your own levels of traits such as neuroticism and extraversion. But what about the more mysterious aspects of yourself and others? If you are like most people, you think of psychological assessments as tools to find out things you do not already know about yourself. For that objective, psychologists might turn to projective tests.

Projective Tests

A **projective test** presents individuals with an ambiguous stimulus and then asks them to describe it or tell a story about it—in other words, to *project* their own meaning onto the stimulus. Projective tests are based on the assumption that the ambiguity of the stimulus allows individuals to invest it with their feelings, desires, needs, and attitudes. The test is especially designed to elicit the individual's unconscious feelings and conflicts, providing an assessment that goes deeper than the surface of personality (Aiken & Groth-Marnat, 2006; Leichtman, 2004). Projective tests attempt to get inside the mind to discover how the test taker really feels and thinks, going beyond the way the individual overtly presents himself or herself. Projective tests are theoretically aligned with the psychodynamic perspectives on personality, which give more weight than the other perspectives to the unconscious.

Perhaps the most famous projective test is the **Rorschach inkblot test,** developed in 1921 by the Swiss psychiatrist Hermann Rorschach. This test uses an individual's perception of the inkblots to determine his or her personality. The test consists of 10 cards, half in black and white and half in color, which the individual views one at a time (Figure 11.8). The person taking the Rorschach test is asked to describe what he or she sees in each of the inkblots. For example, an individual may say, "I see two fairies having a tea party" or "This is the rabbit's face from the movie *Donnie Darko*." These responses are scored for indicating various underlying psychological characteristics (Exner, 2003).

The Rorschach's usefulness in research is controversial. From a scientific perspective, researchers are skeptical about the Rorschach (Feshbach & Weiner, 1996; Garb & others, 2001; Hunsley & Bailey, 2001; Weiner, 2004). The test's reliability and validity have both been criticized. If the Rorschach were reliable, two different scorers would agree on the personality characteristics of the individual being tested. If the Rorschach were valid, it would predict behavior outside of the testing situation; that is, it would predict whether an individual will attempt suicide, become severely depressed, cope successfully with stress, or get along well with others. Conclusions based on research evidence suggest that the Rorschach does not meet these criteria of reliability and validity (Lilienfeld, Wood, & Garb, 2000). Thus, many psychologists have serious reservations about the Rorschach's use in diagnosis and clinical practice.

Although still administered in clinical circles, the Rorschach is not commonly used in personality research. However, the projective method itself remains a tool for studying personality, particularly the Thematic Apperception Test (TAT).

projective test Personality assessment tool that presents individuals with an ambiguous stimulus and then asks them to describe it or tell a story about it—in other words, to *project* their own meaning onto it.

Rorschach inkblot test A widely used projective test that uses an individual's perception of inkblots to determine his or her personality.

FIGURE 11.8

Type of Stimulus Used in the Rorschach Inkblot Test What do you see in this figure? Do you see two green seahorses? Or a pair of blue spiders? A psychologist who relies on the Rorschach test would examine your responses to find out who you really are.

FIGURE 11.9

Picture from the Thematic Apperception Test (TAT) What are these two women thinking and feeling? How did they come to this situation, and what will happen next? A psychologist who uses the TAT would analyze your story to find out your unconscious motives.

Thematic Apperception Test (TAT) A projective test designed to elicit stories that reveal something about an individual's personality.

FIGURE 11.10

Items from the Spouse Observation Checklist Couples are instructed to complete an extensive checklist for 15 consecutive evenings. Spouses record their partner's behavior and make daily ratings of their overall satisfaction with the spouse's behavior. The Spouse Observation Checklist is a behavioral assessment instrument. Reprinted by permission of the publishers from Thematic Apperception Test by Henry A. Murray, Card 12F, Cambridge, Mass.: Harvard University Press, Copyright © 1943 by the President and Fellows of Harvard College, Copyright © 1971 by Henry A. Murray.

The **Thematic Apperception Test (TAT),** which, as we earlier saw, was developed by Henry Murray and Christiana Morgan in the 1930s, is designed to elicit stories that reveal something about an individual's personality. The TAT consists of a series of pictures like the one in Figure 11.9, each on an individual card or shown to the person in a slide. The TAT test taker is asked to tell a story about each of the pictures, including events leading up to the situation described, the characters' thoughts and feelings, and the way the situation turns out. The tester assumes that the person projects his or her own unconscious feelings and thoughts into the story (Herzberg, 2000; Moretti & Rossini, 2004). In addition to being administered as a projective test in clinical practice, the TAT is used in research on people's need for achievement, affiliation, power, intimacy, and a variety of other needs (Brunstein & Maier, 2005; Schultheiss & Brunstein, 2005; Smith, 1992); unconscious defense mechanisms (Cramer, 2007; Cramer & Jones, 2007); and cognitive styles (Woike & Matic, 2004; Woike, Mcleod, & Goggin, 2003).

Other Assessment Methods

Unlike either projective tests or self-report tests, behavioral assessment of personality is based on observing the individual's behavior directly (Cooper, Heron, & Heward, 2007). Instead of removing situational influences, as projective tests and self-report measures do, behavioral assessment assumes that personality cannot be evaluated apart from the environment (Heiby & Haynes, 2004).

Behavioral assessment of personality emerged from the tradition of behavior modification, which we considered in Chapter 7 (Martin & Pear, 2007). Recall that often the first step in the process of changing an individual's maladaptive behavior is to make baseline observations of its frequency. The therapist then modifies some aspect of the environment, such as getting the parents and the child's teacher to stop giving the child attention when he or she engages in aggressive behavior. After a specified period of time, the therapist will observe the child again to determine if the changes in the environment were effective in reducing the child's maladaptive behavior.

What does a psychologist with a behavioral orientation do to assess personality? Direct observation may be desirable, but it is not always possible (Hartmann, Barrios, & Wood, 2004). When it is not, the psychologist might ask individuals to make their own assessments

Type of Behavior	Item
Shared activities	We sat and read together. We took a walk.
Pleasing interactive events	My spouse asked how my day was. We talked about personal feelings. My spouse showed interest in what I said by agreeing or asking relevant questions.
Displeasing interactive events	My spouse commanded me to do something. My spouse complained about something I did. My spouse interrupted me.
Pleasing affectionate behavior	We held each other. My spouse hugged and kissed me.
Displeasing affectionate behavior	My spouse rushed into intercourse without taking time for foreplay. My spouse rejected my sexual advances.
Pleasing events	My spouse did the dishes. My spouse picked up around the house.
Displeasing events	My spouse talked too much about work. My spouse yelled at the children.

of behavior, encouraging them to be sensitive to the circumstances that produced the behavior and the outcomes or consequences of the behavior. For example, a therapist might want to know the course of marital conflict in the everyday experiences of a couple. Figure 11.10 shows a Spouse Observation Checklist that couples can use to record their partners' behavior.

Owing to the influence of social cognitive theory, the use of cognitive assessment in personality evaluation has increased. The strategy is to discover what thoughts underlie the individual's behavior—that is, how individuals think about their problems (Watson & Tharp, 2007). What kinds of thoughts precede maladaptive behavior, occur during its manifestation, and follow it? Cognitive processes such as expectations, planning, and memory are assessed, possibly by interviewing the individual or asking him or her to complete a questionnaire. An interview might include questions that address whether the individual exaggerates his faults and condemns himself more than is warranted. A questionnaire might ask a person what her thoughts are after an upsetting event, or it might assess the way she thinks during tension-filled moments. Many personality psychologists incorporate friend or peer ratings of individuals' traits or other characteristics. Personality psychologists also employ a host of psychophysiological measures, such as heart rate and skin conductance.

Whether personality assessments are being used by clinical psychologists, psychological researchers, or other practitioners, the choice of assessment instrument depends greatly on the researcher's theoretical perspective. Figure 11.11 summarizes which methods are associated with each of the theoretical perspectives. The figure also summarizes each approach, including its major assumptions, and gives a sample research question addressed by each. Personality psychology is a diverse field, unified by a shared interest in understanding the person—that is, you.

FIGURE 11.11

Approaches to Personality Psychology
This figure summarizes the broad approaches to personality described in this chapter. Many researchers in personality do not stick with just one approach but apply the various theories and methods that are most relevant to their research questions.

Approach	Summary	Assumptions	Typical Methods	Sample Research Question
Psychodynamic	Personality is characterized by unconscious processes. Personality develops over stages, and childhood experiences are of great importance to adult personality.	The most important aspects of personality are unconscious.	Case studies, projective techniques.	How do unconscious conflicts lead to dysfunctional behavior?
Humanistic	Personality evolves out of the person's innate, organismic motives to grow and actualize the self. These healthy tendencies can be undermined by social pressure.	Human nature is basically good. By getting in touch with who we really are and what we really want, we can lead happier and healthier lives.	Questionnaires, interviews, observation.	Can situations be changed to support individuals' organismic values and enhance their well-being?
Social Cognitive	Personality is the pattern of coherence that characterizes a person's interactions with the situations he or she encounters in life. The individual's beliefs and expectations, rather than global traits, are the central variables of interest.	Behavior is best understood as changing across situations. To understand personality, we must understand what each situation means for a given person.	Multiple observations over different situations; videotaped behaviors rated by coders; questionnaires.	When and why do individuals respond to challenging tasks with fear vs. excitement?
Trait	Personality is characterized by a set of five general traits that are represented in the natural language that everyday people use to describe themselves and others.	Traits are relatively stable over time. Traits predict behavior.	Questionnaires, observer reports.	Are the five factors universal across cultures?
Personology and Life Story	To understand personality we must understand the whole person. Each person has a unique set of life experiences, and the stories we tell about those experiences make up our identities.	The life story provides a unique opportunity to examine the personality processes associated with behavior, development, and well-being.	Written narratives, TAT stories, autobiographical memories, interviews, and psychobiography.	How do narrative accounts of life experiences relate to happiness?

REVIEW, ASSESS, AND SHARPEN YOUR THINKING

Review

6 Characterize the main methods of personality assessment.
- Explain self-report tests.
- Discuss projective techniques.
- Describe some other methods of personality assessment in addition to self-report and projective measures.

Assess

1. **What assessment asks participants to tell a story about the stimuli they see?**
   A. Rorschach inkblot test
   B. Minnesota Multiphasic Personality Inventory
   C. NEO-P-I
   D. Thematic Apperception Test

2. **What is an empirically keyed test?**
   A. a test that has right and wrong answers
   B. a test that discriminates between different groups

   C. a test that has face validity
   D. a test that has both easy and difficult questions

3. **Which of the following is true about the Rorschach inkblot test?**
   A. It is often used in clinical settings.
   B. It is reliable.
   C. It is valid.
   D. It is often used in research settings.

4. **Which of the following assumptions is consistent with trait-based assessment?**
   A. Humans are innately altruistic.
   B. Life stories are key to understanding personality.
   C. Personality components are stable across the lifespan.
   D. Behavior is determined by the environmental context.

5. **Which of the following is a self-report assessment?**
   A. Thematic Apperception Test
   B. Minnesota Multiphasic Personality Inventory
   C. Rorschach inkblot test
   D. projective test

Sharpen Your Thinking

Think of a personality characteristic that you find interesting. How might you assess it?

7 Personality and Health and Wellness

Summarize how personality relates to health and wellness.

We regularly see headlines cautioning us that our personalities might be putting us at risk for heart disease, cancer, or some other illness. How exactly does personality relate to health and well-being?

Conscientiousness and Personal Control

Personality can matter to health directly and indirectly. Personality might affect health indirectly by leading to behaviors that are either good or bad for you. An example is the trait of conscientiousness. Recall that conscientious individuals are responsible and reliable; they like structure and seeing a task to its completion.

Conscientiousness is not the sexiest trait, but it might well be the most important trait of the big five when it comes to health. Brent Roberts and his colleagues (Roberts, Walton, & Bogg, 2005) have suggested that conscientiousness plays a significant role in health and longevity. Conscientious people tend to do all those things that they are told are good for their health, such as getting regular exercise, avoiding drinking and smoking, wearing seatbelts, and checking smoke detectors. This capacity to follow a sensible plan may be just what it takes to do the mundane tasks required to live a long, healthy life. Indeed, in one study, individuals who were low in conscientiousness were more likely to die earlier than their high-conscientious counterparts (Wilson & others, 2004).

Another personality characteristic associated with taking the right steps to lead a long, healthy life is a sense of personal control (Wrosch, Heckhausen, & Lachman, 2006). Feeling in control can reduce the experience of stress during difficult times (Taylor, 2006; Thompson, 2001). Feeling in control can lead to the development of problem-solving strategies to cope with the stress. An individual with a good sense of personal control might say, "If I stop smoking now, I will not develop lung cancer" or "If I exercise regularly, I won't develop cardiovascular disease." A recent study revealed that a sense of personal control was linked to a lower risk for common chronic diseases such as cancer and cardiovascular disease (Sturmer, Hasselbach, & Amelang, 2006).

Like conscientiousness, a sense of personal control might also help people avoid a risky lifestyle that involves health-compromising behaviors. Consider a study of East German migrants to West Germany who found themselves unemployed (Mittag & Schwarzer, 1993). They often turned to heavy drinking for solace unless they had a sense of personal control (as measured by such survey items as "When I'm in trouble, I can rely on my ability to deal with the problem effectively"). Across a wide range of studies, a sense of personal control over the stressful events that go on around people has been related to emotional well-being, successful coping with a stressful event, behavior change that can promote good health, and good health (Little, Snyder, & Wehmeyer, 2006; Stanton, Revenson, & Tennen, 2007; Taylor, 2006; Taylor & Stanton, 2007).

Other personality characteristics appear to relate to health through more direct routes. These traits may exacerbate stress so that the person's very personality leads him or her to stress out more than someone else would. Still other traits may help to buffer a person against the effects of stress (Ozer & Benet-Martinez, 2006).

Type A/Type B Behavior Patterns

In the late 1950s, a secretary for two California cardiologists, Meyer Friedman and Ray Rosenman, observed that the chairs in their waiting rooms were tattered and worn, but only on the front edges. The cardiologists had also noticed the impatience of their cardiac patients, who often arrived exactly on time and were in a great hurry to leave. Intrigued by this consistency, they conducted a study of 3,000 healthy men between the ages of 35 and 59 over 8 years to find out whether people with certain behavioral characteristics might be prone to heart problems (Friedman & Rosenman, 1974). During the 8 years, one group of men had twice as many heart attacks or other forms of heart disease as the other men. Further, autopsies of the men who died revealed that this same group had coronary arteries that were more obstructed than those of the other men.

Friedman and Rosenman described the common personality characteristics of the men who developed coronary disease as the **Type A behavior pattern.** They theorized that a cluster of characteristics—being excessively competitive, hard-driven, impatient, and hostile—is related to the incidence of heart disease. Rosenman and Friedman labeled the behavior of the healthier group, who were commonly relaxed and easygoing, the **Type B behavior pattern.**

Further research on the link between Type A behavior and coronary disease indicates that the association is not as strong as Friedman and Rosenman believed (Suls & Swain, 1998; R. Williams, 2001, 2002). However, researchers have found that certain components of Type A behavior are more precisely linked with coronary risk (Spielberger, 2004).

The Type A behavior component most consistently associated with coronary problems is hostility (Julkunen & Ahlstrom, 2006). People who are hostile outwardly or who turn anger inward are more likely to develop heart disease than their less angry counterparts (Eng & others, 2003; Matthews & others, 2004). Such people have been called "hot reactors"

Type A behavior pattern A cluster of characteristics—such as being excessively competitive, hard-driven, impatient, and hostile—related to the incidence of heart disease.

Type B behavior pattern A cluster of characteristics—such as being relaxed and easygoing—related to good health.

because of their intense physiological reactions to stress: Their hearts race, their breathing quickens, and their muscles tense up. One study found that hostility was a better predictor of coronary heart disease in older men than smoking, drinking, high caloric intake, or high levels of LDL cholesterol (Niaura & others, 2002).

A hostile personality may also affect the course of such diseases as AIDS. One study of 140 HIV-positive individuals found that the immune systems of those with hostile personalities who confronted distressing events weakened more than the immune systems of their counterparts who did not have hostile personalities (Ironson, 2001).

Optimism and Hardiness

One factor that is often related to positive functioning and adjustment is being optimistic (Peterson, 2006; Peterson & Seligman, 2003; Seligman & Pawelski, 2003; Smith & MacKenzie, 2006). Psychologists' interest in the concept of optimism has especially been fueled by Martin Seligman's (1990) theory and research on optimism. Seligman views optimism as a matter of how a person explains the causes of bad events. Optimists explain the causes of bad events as due to external, unstable, and specific causes. Pessimists explain bad events as due to internal, stable, and global causes.

Seligman's interest in optimism stemmed from his work on *learned helplessness,* which initially focused on animals who learned to become helpless (passive and unresponsive) after they experienced uncontrollable negative events (1975). In his view, pessimism is much like learned helplessness and the belief in an external source of control. Optimism is much like belief in self-efficacy and an internal source of control.

Other researchers have defined optimism as the expectancy that good things are more likely, and bad things less likely, to occur in the future (Carver & Scheier, 2004; Scheier & Carver, 1992; Srivastava & others, 2006). This view focuses on how people pursue their goals and values. In the face of adversity, optimists still believe that their goals and values can be attained. Their optimism keeps them working to reach their goals, whereas pessimism makes people give up.

Numerous research studies reveal that optimists generally function more effectively and are physically and mentally healthier than pessimists:

- *Physical health:* In one remarkable finding, people who were classified as optimistic at age 25 were healthier at ages 45 to 60 than those who had been classified as pessimistic (Peterson, Seligman, & Vaillant, 1988). In other studies, optimism has been linked to more effective immune system functioning and better health (Nes & Segerstrom, 2006; Segerstrom, 2003, 2005). Optimists also have been found to have lower blood pressure than pessimists (Räikkönen & others, 1999).
- *Mental health:* In one study, optimism was a better predictor than self-efficacy of the person's ability to avoid depression over time (Shnek & others, 2001). In another study, optimism was related to better mental health in cancer patients (Cohen, De Moor, & Amato, 2001). In a recent study, optimism was linked to decreased thoughts of suicide in college students (Hirsch, Conner, & Duberstein, 2007).

Another personality attribute that appears to allow a person to thrive during difficult times is **hardiness,** a trait characterized by a sense of commitment (rather than alienation) and of control (rather than powerlessness) and a perception of problems as challenges (rather than threats) (Maddi & others, 2006). The links among hardiness, stress, and illness were the focus of the Chicago Stress Project, which studied male business managers 32 to 65 years of age over a 5-year period (Kobasa, Maddi, & Kahn, 1982; Maddi, 1998). During the 5 years, most of the managers experienced stressful events such as divorce, job transfers, the death of a close friend, inferior performance evaluations at work, and work with an unpleasant boss.

In one aspect of the Chicago study, managers who developed an illness (ranging from the flu to a heart attack) were compared with those who did not (Kobasa, Maddi, & Kahn, 1982). Those who did not were likelier to have hardy personalities. Another aspect of the

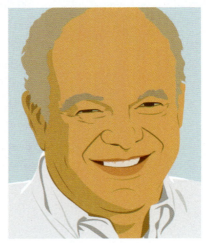

Martin Seligman (1942–) *Seligman went from pessimist to optimist and believes that others can, too. Seligman (1990) provided the details in his book* Learned Optimism. *Recall Seligman's interest in changing psychology from a discipline that focuses mainly on the negative aspects of life to one that spends more time charting the positive aspects of life.*

hardiness A trait characterized by a sense of commitment and control and a perception of problems as challenges rather than threats.

study investigated whether hardiness, along with exercise and social support, buffered stress and reduced illness in executives' lives (Kobasa & others, 1986). When all three factors were present in an executive's life, the level of illness dropped dramatically (Figure 11.12).

Other researchers also have found support for the role of hardiness in illness and health (Heckman & Clay, 2005; Matthews & Servaty-Seib, 2007). The results of hardiness research suggest the power of multiple factors, rather than any single factor, in buffering stress and maintaining health (Maddi, 1998; Maddi & others, 2006).

Traits and States

Thinking about the role of personality in health can sometimes be stressful itself. What if you know you are a touch on the hostile side? Or a pessimist? If personality is a stable aspect of a person, what good does it do you to find out that your personality is bad for physical health? Furthermore, does your discovery that you have traits that predispose you to illness mean that it is your own fault if you become ill?

One way to think about these issues is to focus on the difference between traits and states (Gupta & others, 2006; Marine & others, 2006). Traits are relatively enduring characteristics—the way a person generally is. States are more acute, time-limited experiences. A person's having a trait (such as hostility) that predisposes him or her to feelings of anger toward others does not mean that the individual is wired for a heart attack. We have to assume that the pathway from personality trait to disease goes through the state of anger. Thus, even someone who possesses the trait of hostility can take steps to avoid the state of anger—for example, by enrolling in an anger management class or seeking counseling. Knowing that one is prone to be pessimistic might be the first step toward learning to be more optimistic. After all, Seligman's best-seller was titled *Learned Optimism,* meaning that an optimistic style can be learned.

So, finding out that you have a personality style associated with stress or illness should not lead you to conclude that you are doomed. Rather, this information can allow you to take steps to improve your life, to foster good habits, and to make the most of your unique qualities.

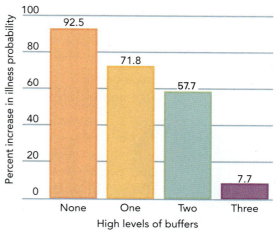

FIGURE 11.12

Illness in High-Stress Business Executives
In one study of high-stress business executives (all of whom were selected for this analysis because they were above the stress mean for the entire year of the study), a low level of all three buffers (hardiness, exercise, and social support) involved a high probability of at least one serious illness in that year. High levels of one, two, and all three buffers decreased the likelihood of at least one serious illness occurring in the year of the study.

 REVIEW, ASSESS, AND SHARPEN YOUR THINKING

Review

7 Summarize how personality relates to health and wellness.
- Describe how conscientiousness and personal control relate to physical health.
- Define the Type A behavior pattern and describe its relation to coronary heart disease.
- Identify two personality characteristics related to successful coping with stress.
- Explain how the distinction between traits and states relates to the role of personality in health and illness.

Assess

1. Relaxed individuals are known as
   A. Type A.
   B. Type B.
   C. Type C.
   D. Type Z.

2. Which personality trait is most linked to cardiac problems?
   A. impatience
   B. anxiety
   C. conscientiousness
   D. hostility

3. Which of the following are not characteristics of hardiness?
   A. feelings of commitment
   B. feelings of control
   C. viewing problems as challenges
   D. expecting that bad things will happen

4. _____ is long-lasting, whereas _____ is short-lived.
   A. A state, a trait
   B. A trait, a state
   C. Optimism, hardiness
   D. Hardiness, optimism

5. Why is there a link between conscientiousness and health?
   A. Conscientious people have adapted better genetic material.
   B. Conscientious people avoid experiencing new things.
   C. Conscientious people make healthier decisions.
   D. Conscientious people lack control in their lives.

Sharpen Your Thinking

Think of someone you know who seems to be especially good at handling life's challenges. What particular challenges has he or she faced? Would you describe this person as hardy? Optimistic? Hostile? Why?

SUMMARY

1 PSYCHODYNAMIC PERSPECTIVES

Define personality and summarize the psychodynamic perspectives.

Freud's Psychoanalytic Theory

Freud developed psychoanalysis through his work with hysterical patients. Hysterical symptoms are physical symptoms with no physical cause. Freud viewed these symptoms as representing conflicts between a person's desires and duty. Freud believed that most of the mind is unconscious, and he described the personality as having three structures: id, ego, and superego. The conflicting demands of these personality structures produce anxiety. Defense mechanisms protect the ego and reduce this anxiety. Freud was convinced that problems develop because of early childhood experiences. He said that we go through five psychosexual stages: oral, anal, phallic, latency, and genital. During the phallic stage, which occurs in early childhood, the Oedipus complex is a major source of conflict.

Psychodynamic Critics and Revisionists

A number of psychodynamic theorists criticized Freud for overemphasizing sexuality and the first 5 years of life. They argued that Freud gave too little credit to the ego, conscious thought, and sociocultural factors. Horney said that the need for security, not sex or aggression, is our most important need. Jung thought Freud underplayed the unconscious mind's role. He developed the concept of the collective unconscious and placed special emphasis on archetypes. Adler's theory, called individual psychology, stresses that people are striving toward perfection, not pleasure. Adler placed more emphasis on social motivation than Freud did.

Evaluating the Psychodynamic Perspectives

Weaknesses of the psychodynamic perspectives include overreliance on reports from the past, overemphasis of sexuality and the unconscious mind, a negative view of human nature, too much attention to early experience, and a male, Western bias. Strengths of the psychodynamic perspectives include recognizing the importance of childhood, conceptualizing development through stages, and calling attention to the potential role of unconscious processes in behavior. Psychodynamic perspectives have had a substantial influence on psychology as a discipline.

2 HUMANISTIC PERSPECTIVES

Describe the humanistic perspectives.

Maslow's Approach

Maslow called the humanistic movement the "third force" in psychology. Maslow developed the concept of a hierarchy of needs, with self-actualization being the highest human need.

Rogers's Approach

In Rogers's approach, each of us has a need for unconditional positive regard. As a result, the real self is not valued unless it meets the standards of other people. The self is the core of personality; it includes both the real and ideal selves. Rogers said that we can help others develop a more positive self-concept by treating them with unconditional positive regard, empathy, and genuineness. Rogers also stressed that each of us has the innate inner capacity to become a fully functioning person.

Evaluating the Humanistic Perspectives

The humanistic perspectives sensitize us to the importance of subjective experience, of consciousness, of self-conception, of consideration of the whole person, and of our innate positive nature. Humanistic psychology calls attention to the positive capacities of human beings. Its weaknesses are a tendency to be too optimistic and an inclination to encourage excessive self-love.

3 TRAIT PERSPECTIVES

Discuss the trait perspectives.

Trait Theories

A trait is an enduring personality characteristic that tends to produce certain behaviors. Trait theories emphasize that personality consists of broad, enduring dispositions that lead to characteristic responses. Trait theorists also are interested in how traits are organized within the individual. Traits are assumed to be essentially stable over time and across situations. Allport stated that traits render different situations functionally equivalent for the person. Allport used the lexical approach to personality traits, which involves using all the words in the natural language that could describe a person as a basis for understanding the underlying traits of personality.

The Five-Factor Model of Personality

The current dominant perspective in personality psychology is the five-factor model. The "big five" traits in this model include neuroticism, extraversion, openness to experience, agreeableness, and conscientiousness.

Evaluating the Trait Perspectives

Studying people in terms of their traits has practical value. Identifying a person's traits allows us better to predict the person's health, thinking, job success, and interpersonal skills. However, trait approaches have been criticized for focusing on broad dimensions and not attending to each person's uniqueness.

4 PERSONOLOGICAL AND LIFE STORY PERSPECTIVES

Discuss the personological and life story perspectives.

Murray's Personological Approach

Murray described personology as the study of the whole person, including all aspects of the person's life. Murray was interested in unconscious motivation and, with Morgan, developed the TAT, a projective measure of unconscious needs.

The Life Story Approach and Identity

Contemporary followers of Murray study personality through narrative accounts and interviews. McAdams introduced the life story approach to identity, which views identity as a constantly changing story with a beginning, a middle, and an end. Psychobiography is a form of personological inquiry that involves applying personality theory to one person's life.

Evaluating the Life Story Approach and Similar Perspectives

Life story approaches to personality reveal the richness of each person's unique life story. However, this work can be very difficult to carry out. Furthermore, psychobiography can be too subjective and may not be generalizable.

5 SOCIAL COGNITIVE PERSPECTIVES

Explain the social cognitive perspectives.

Bandura's Social Cognitive Theory

Social cognitive theory, created by Bandura and Mischel, states that behavior, environment, and person/cognitive factors are important in understanding personality. In Bandura's view, these factors reciprocally interact. Two important concepts in social cognitive theory are self-efficacy and personal control. Self-efficacy is the belief that one can master a situation and produce positive outcomes. Personal control refers to individuals' beliefs about whether the outcomes of their actions depend on their own

acts (internal) or on events outside of their control (external). Numerous research studies reveal that individuals characterized by self-efficacy and high levels of control generally show positive functioning and adjustment.

Mischel's Contributions

Mischel's (1968) *Personality and Assessment,* arguing that personality varies across situations, attacked some key ideas of personality psychology. Mischel's situationist attack stressed that people do not behave consistently across different situations but rather tailor their behavior to suit particular situations. Personality psychologists countered that personality does predict behavior for some people some of the time. Very specific personality characteristics predict behavior better than very general ones, and personality characteristics are more likely to predict behavior in weak versus strong situations. Mischel and his colleagues have developed an approach to personality emphasizing a cognitive affective processing system (CAPS). Mischel has suggested that personality is best understood as a person's habitual emotional and cognitive reactions to specific situations.

Evaluating the Social Cognitive Perspectives

A strength of social cognitive theory is its focus on cognitive processes and self-control. However, social cognitive approaches have not given adequate attention to enduring individual differences, to biological factors, and to personality as a whole.

6 PERSONALITY ASSESSMENT

Characterize the main methods of personality assessment.

Self-Report Tests

Self-report tests assess personality traits by asking test takers questions about their preferences and behaviors. The most popular test for measuring the big five is the NEO-PI-R, which uses self-report items to measure each of the big five traits. Even though a self-report test may have face validity, it may elicit invalid responses, as when people try to answer in a socially desirable way. Empirically keyed tests, which rely on items that are indirect questions about some criterion, were developed to overcome the problem of face validity. The Minnesota Multiphasic Personality Inventory (MMPI) is the most widely used and researched self-report personality test; its 10 clinical scales assist therapists in diagnosing psychological problems.

Projective Tests

Projective tests, designed to assess the unconscious aspects of personality, present individuals with an ambiguous stimulus and then ask them to describe it or to tell a story about it. Projective tests are based on the assumption that the ambiguity of the stimuli allows individuals to project their personalities onto them. The Rorschach inkblot test is a widely used projective test, although its effectiveness is controversial. The Thematic Apperception Test (TAT) is another projective test that has been used in personality research.

Other Assessment Methods

Behavioral assessment seeks to obtain objective information about personality through observation of behavior and its environmental ties. Cognitive assessment seeks to discover individual differences in processing and acting on information through interviews and questionnaires. Other assessment tools include obtaining peer reports and psychophysiological measures.

7 PERSONALITY AND HEALTH AND WELLNESS

Summarize how personality relates to health and wellness.

Conscientiousness and Personal Control

Conscientiousness and personal control relate to health and longevity through their association with healthy lifestyle choices.

Type A/Type B Behavior Patterns

The Type A behavior pattern is a set of characteristics that may put an individual at risk for the development of heart disease. Type A behavior includes hostility, time urgency, and competitiveness. Type B behavior, in contrast, refers to a more easygoing style.

Optimism and Hardiness

Optimism and hardiness are traits that are related to enhanced psychological and physical wellness and particularly to thriving during difficult times.

Traits and States

Personality traits that are related to health and wellness can also be thought of as states. Thus, even if a person is low on these traits, he or she can still benefit by seeking out states that foster positive attributes.

Key Terms

personality, p. 436

psychodynamic perspectives, p. 436

id, p. 437

ego, p. 438

superego, p. 438

defense mechanisms, p. 438

Oedipus complex, p. 438

collective unconscious, p. 441

archetypes, p. 441

individual psychology, p. 442

humanistic perspectives, p. 443

self-concept, p. 445

unconditional positive regard, p. 445

trait, p. 446

trait theories, p. 446

big five factors of personality, p. 449

personological and life story perspectives, p. 452

social cognitive perspectives, p. 454

self-efficacy, p. 455

cognitive affective processing systems (CAPS), p. 457

self-report test, p. 459

face validity, p. 459

empirically keyed test, p. 459

Minnesota Multiphasic Personality Inventory (MMPI), p. 460

projective test, p. 461

Rorschach inkblot test, p. 461

Thematic Apperception Test (TAT), p. 462

Type A behavior pattern, p. 465

Type B behavior pattern, p. 465

hardiness, p. 466

Assess Your Knowledge

1. Benjamin is very talkative and likes to be around others. Benjamin is high in which of the following?
   A. neuroticism
   B. extraversion
   C. agreeableness
   D. openness to experience

2. Who developed the first criminal psychological profile?
   A. Carl Rogers
   B. Gordon Allport
   C. Henry Murray
   D. Sigmund Freud

3. The Thematic Apperception Test grew out of which approach?
   A. personology
   B. humanistic
   C. social cognitive
   D. trait

4. According to Freud, hysteria refers to
   A. extreme display of emotion.
   B. problems brought on by inaccurate thought processes.
   C. symptoms relevant to menstruation and menopause.
   D. physical symptoms without physical causes.

5. What theorist placed emphasis on unconditional positive regard?
   A. Carl Jung
   B. Karen Horney
   C. Henry Murray
   D. Carl Rogers

6. According to Freud, which personality structure negotiates the pull between a person's baser needs and higher conscience?
   A. superego
   B. defense mechanisms
   C. ego
   D. id

7. Order Freud's psychosexual stages from earliest to latest.
   A. anal, phallic, oral, genital, latency period
   B. phallic, genital oral, latency period, anal
   C. oral, anal, phallic, latency period, genital
   D. oral, phallic, latency period, anal, genital

8. Someone who is altruistic, self-aware, and capable of experiencing wonder at the world is
   A. self-actualized.
   B. in the genital stage of psychosexual development.
   C. receiving unconditional positive regard.
   D. high in self-efficacy.

9. What theorist's work almost ended research interest into how personality impacts behavior?
   A. Karen Horney
   B. Walter Mischel
   C. Albert Bandura
   D. Henry Murray

10. The Minnesota Multiphasic Personality Inventory is
    A. a projective test.
    B. a reliable, but not valid test.
    C. a valid, but not reliable test.
    D. a self-report test.

11. How are optimism and self-efficacy different?
    A. Optimism is the belief that good things will happen, whereas self-efficacy is the belief that one's action will have the desired effect.
    B. Optimism focuses on positive expectations, whereas self-efficacy focuses on negative expectations.
    C. Optimism is a state, whereas self-efficacy is a trait.
    D. Optimism is passive, whereas self-efficacy is active.

12. Which approach to understanding personality focuses on situational factors?
    A. psychodynamic
    B. trait
    C. personology
    D. social cognitive

13. Someone who is punctual, hardworking, shy, and conservative is likely
    A. high in agreeableness, low in extraversion, and high in openness to experience.
    B. low in extraversion, high in conscientiousness, and low in openness to experience.

C. high in conscientiousness, low in neuroticism, and high in extraversion.
D. low in conscientiousness, low in openness to experience, and high in extraversion.

14. A person who is high in which of the following traits would likely be unhealthy?
    A. extraversion
    B. hostility
    C. competitiveness
    D. conscientiousness

15. On an assessment of depression, a question reads "I feel sad." This item
    A. has high reliability.
    B. has been empirically keyed.
    C. has high face validity.
    D. is projective.

Go to Appendix B for answers to these questions.

Apply Your Knowledge

1. Consider a facet of your personality that you might want to change. From the perspective of Freud's psychoanalytic theory, could you change this aspect of your personality? If so, how? From the perspective of the psychodynamic revisionists, would it be possible to make the desired change? If so, how?

2. How important has your childhood been to your adult personality? Choose an experience or series of experiences in childhood and describe how those experiences are represented in your current personality.

3. Mischel has argued that personality and behavior are discriminative across situations. Do the following speculative experiment to see just how easy (or difficult) it might be to change your personality. Choose some situation that you frequently encounter

and think about how you would change your behavior from your typical routine. What specifically would you change? What do you imagine the experience would be like?

4. Type "personality test" into an Internet search engine, and take two or more of the tests available online. Based on the results, which of the perspectives on personality that you studied in this chapter do the results seem to reflect most? How might the structure of the test have affected the outcome?

5. Now ask a friend to take the same tests as if he or she were you. How much did your friend's results reflect your own views of your personality?

CHAPTER 12

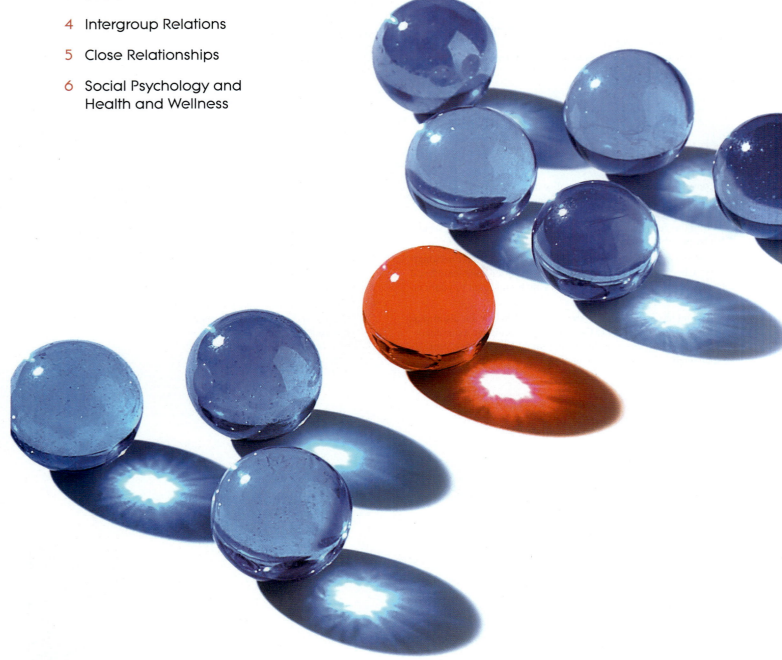

SOCIAL PSYCHOLOGY

Experiencing Psychology

ROSA PARKS: SPURRING SOCIAL ACTION

Humans are social animals. We are not evolved for solo living. We do not have a protective shell, and what "fur" we have is not particularly helpful in protecting us. Even the loneliest loner came into this world as a result of the actions of other people. Our very existence every day depends on being part of a social group. For example, it is highly unlikely that you have made all of your own clothes, built your own home, and hunted and gathered your own food. Rather, the influence of other people is evident in just about every aspect of our lives. Indeed, the very best and worst dimensions of our lives are often defined by those around us and our relationships with them (Parks, 2007; Spitzberg & Cupach, 2007).

Groups of people can do more than any individual acting alone, so it is no wonder that social progress has typically occurred through group action. Rosa Parks (1913–2005) was an African American seamstress in Montgomery, Alabama, who became a heroine of the civil rights movement when, on December 1, 1955, she refused to give up her seat on a bus to a White man. Ms. Parks is rightfully recognized as an individual who stood up (or, actually, sat down) for social equality, but she was also part of larger social groups—Americans, and specifically Americans of African heritage. Her defiant actions inspired Montgomery's African American leaders, who went on to organize a massive bus boycott that would spur many other such group protests and bring long overdue civil rights reforms to U.S. society.

Groups can also have powerful negative effects on people and society. Acting as part of a group, individuals may engage in abominable behavior that they would never do if acting alone. Indeed, the lynchings that occurred in the South as part of the struggle for racial equality exemplify the negative influence that group membership can have on behavior. More recently, the atrocities at Abu Ghraib prison in Iraq remind us of what people are capable of doing in the name of "following orders."

PREVIEW

This chapter is about social psychology—the study of how social situations affect people's thoughts, behaviors, influences on, and relations with others. We begin by formally defining social psychology and by examining humans' social cognitive nature. We then turn to how we influence others—followed by a survey of how they influence us. Next we explore the many faces of how we relate to others based on the groups to which we belong. We then probe into the fascinating world of our close relationships, including attraction, love, and factors associated with the success of long-term relationships. We conclude by considering the lessons of social psychology for our health and well-being.

1 Social Cognition

Describe how people think about the social world.

Social psychology is the study of how people think about, influence, and relate to other people. Human history is full of examples of the impact of social context on behavior, including events such as Rosa Parks's defiance and the subsequent bus boycott.

Social cognition is the area of social psychology that explores how people select, interpret, remember, and use social information (Augoustinos, Walker, & Donaghue, 2006). Each person may have a unique combination of expectations, memories, and attitudes based on his or her social history. Nevertheless, certain common principles apply to the way people process information in a social situation (Higgins & Molden, 2004; Roese & Sherman, 2007; Wyer, 2007), how we perceive others and come to understand their behaviors, and how our attitudes relate to our behavior and that of others (Johnson, 2007). Social cognition research takes the perspective of the cognitive psychologist but focuses on the ways we process the most important information we encounter—social information.

Person Perception

We may like to think that we never "judge a book by its cover." But research on the impact of facial appearance shows that often we do judge people on the basis of their looks, and that doing so has important implications. For example, Alexander Todorov and his colleagues (2005) examined the ways that our perceptions of faces can influence political campaign outcomes. These researchers asked people to rate the competence of people whose faces were pictured in photographs. The faces belonged to candidates in the 2000, 2002, and 2004 U.S. House and Senate elections. Respondents' ratings accurately predicted the outcome for about 70 percent of the races.

The face conveys a great deal of information about a person to a social perceiver (Becker & others, 2007; Ishai, 2007). Leslie Zebrowitz (1997) has studied the role of facial babyishness in person perception. A babyish face is defined as one that, like a baby's, is round and has large eyes, a small nose, a small chin, and a high forehead. Zebrowitz has found that when we look at adults with babyish faces, we assume that they possess babylike characteristics (Zebrowitz, Kikuchi, & Fellous, 2007). We think of baby-faced individuals as naive, weak, and less competent than persons with more mature faces. There is some good news for the baby-faced, however, because we also see individuals with babyish faces as more honest, warm, and caring. Indeed, judges are more likely to believe baby-faced individuals when they deny intentional transgressions, perhaps because their honest, guileless faces seem to indicate that they could not possibly be lying.

Physical Attractiveness and Other Perceptual Cues Within the area of person perception, physical attractiveness has been recognized as a powerful social cue. Attractive individuals are generally assumed to have a variety of other positive characteristics, including being better adjusted, socially skilled, friendly, likable, extraverted, and likely to achieve superior job performance (Langlois & others, 2000). Perhaps the most surprising research

social psychology The study of how people think about, influence, and relate to other people.

on this topic was conducted by Judith Langlois and her colleagues (Hoss & Langlois, 2003; Ramsey & others, 2004). In these studies, even infants as young as 3 to 6 months of age showed a preference for looking at attractive faces versus unattractive faces (as rated by adults). These positive expectations for physically attractive individuals have been referred to as the "beautiful is good" stereotype.

A **stereotype** is a generalization about a group's characteristics that does not consider any variations from one individual to another. Stereotypes are a natural extension of the limits on human cognitive processing and our reliance on concepts in cognitive processing (Wegener, Clark, & Petty, 2006). We simplify the task of understanding people by classifying them as members of groups or categories with which we are familiar. It takes more mental effort to consider a person's individual characteristics than it does to label him or her as a member of a particular group or category. Thus, when we categorize an individual, the categorization is often based on stereotypes.

Imagine, for example, that you meet a young man and find out that he is a college football player. You develop an impression of him based on the "football player" schema in your mind. Without seeking any additional information, you might perceive him as aggressive or insensitive. Importantly, stereotypes are social expectations based on characteristics that are often irrelevant to the question at hand; for example, you might be surprised to find out that the football player enjoys classical music and writes poetry.

So, is there any truth to the "beautiful is good" stereotype? Research has shown that attractive people may indeed possess a number of positive characteristics (Langlois & others, 2000). But does that mean that attractiveness is *naturally* related to, for example, enhanced social skills? Not necessarily, because stereotypes may be in play.

One way that stereotypes can influence individuals is through a phenomenon called *self-fulfilling prophecy*. In a self-fulfilling prophecy, our expectations cause us to act in ways that serve to make the expectations come true. The classic self-fulfilling prophecy study was conducted by Robert Rosenthal and Lenore Jacobsen in 1968. Teachers were told that 5 students were likely to be "late bloomers"—that these students had high levels of ability that would likely shine forth over time. In reality, the students had been randomly selected by the researchers. Sure enough, a year later, the researchers found that teachers' expectations for the late bloomers were actually reflected in student performance—these students showed increases in academic performance beyond those of students whom the researchers had not labeled. Self-fulfilling prophecy effects show the potential power of stereotypes and other sources of expectations on human behavior. If we think about how we ourselves interact with attractive versus unattractive people, we see that attractive people may encounter differential treatment from others throughout their lives as well, and that this special treatment increases the likelihood that they will develop enhanced social skills and be more self-confident than others.

Another obvious question might be "What makes a face attractive?" *People* magazine's "50 Most Beautiful People" issue might lead you to conclude that attractiveness is about being exceptional in some physical way: Consider Angelina Jolie's sensuous lips or George Clooney's dreamy eyes. For some time, researchers relied on ratings to tell them who was or was not attractive. They assumed that beauty was something about which social perceivers would agree, along the lines of the editors of *People* magazine. However, research has examined what it is about a face that makes it attractive. Using computer technology that allowed them to average together digitized photographs of a large group of individuals, Langlois and her colleagues (1994) created composite faces. A large sample of college students then rated the individual faces and the composites. The results showed that individual faces were less attractive than faces that were created by averaging 8, 16, or 32 other faces. These researchers concluded that attractive faces are actually "just average." While "averageness" is not the only predictor of attractiveness, Langlois and her colleagues suggest that being average is an essential component (along with variables such as symmetry and youthfulness) of attractiveness.

First Impressions   When we meet someone, it often takes very little time for the person to make an impression. Indeed, our first encounter can strongly influence his or her lasting

stereotype A generalization about a group's characteristics that does not consider any variations from one individual to another.

Look at the individual running. What are your impressions of her? Based on your impressions, would you categorize her as strong or weak? Active or passive? Good or bad?

impression on us (Bar, Neta, & Linz, 2006). Recall the *primacy effect,* described in Chapter 8, which refers to people's tendency to attend to and remember what they learned first (Anderson, 1965). The power of first impressions is likely due to just such an effect. How quickly do we make these initial impressions of others? In one recent study, judgments made after just a 100-millisecond exposure time to unfamiliar faces was sufficient for individuals to form an impression (Willis & Todorov, 2006).

When someone wants to impress you, a wise strategy is for the individual to put her best foot forward in your first encounter. Of course, once you become acquainted with her, you have a lot more information to use to form an opinion about her. You see her behaving in various ways and then come to a better understanding of who she really is. The process by which we come to understand the causes of others' behavior and form an impression of them as individuals is called *attribution.*

Attribution

There is probably nothing more interesting than other people. Trying to understand why they do the things they do, why they feel the way they feel—these puzzles fascinate not only psychologists but all of us. Finding causal explanations for the many things that people do is a complex task (Hilton, 2007). We can observe people's behavior and listen to what they say, but to determine the underlying cause of their behavior, we often have to make inferences from these observations. We have to take the information we have and come up with a good guess about who they are and what they are likely to do in the future.

Attribution theorists argue that we want to know why people do the things they do because the knowledge will enable us to cope more effectively with the situations that confront us (Gaunt & Trope, 2007; Krueger, 2007). **Attribution theory** views people as motivated to discover the underlying causes of behavior as part of their effort to make sense of the behavior. Thus, attributions are thoughts about why people behave the way they do. Attribution theorists say that people are a lot like detectives or scientists, seeking the reasons for human actions.

The Dimensions of Causality The attributions we make about behavior vary along three dimensions (Jones, 1998):

- *Internal/external causes: Internal attributions* include all causes internal to the person, such as his or her traits or abilities. *External attributions* include all causes external to the person, such as social pressure, aspects of the social situation, money, the weather, or luck. Did Beth get an *A* on the test because she is smart or because the test was easy?
- *Stable/unstable causes:* Is the cause relatively enduring and permanent or is it temporary? Did Jason blow up at his girlfriend because he is a hostile guy or because he was in a bad mood that day?
- *Controllable/uncontrollable causes:* We perceive that we can control some causes (for instance, by preparing delicious food for a picnic) but not others (if it rains that day).

Bernard Weiner (1986, 2006) argues that the various types of attributions have different emotional and motivational implications. When we believe that we have succeeded because of our internal characteristics, we can feel proud of our accomplishment. But if we believe that our success is due to external causes such as the ease of a task and luck, we do not get the same payoff.

Attributional Errors and Biases Researchers have identified some common errors and biases that infiltrate our attributions. The *fundamental attribution error* is important in understanding how people assign causes to their own behavior and the behavior they observe.

In attribution theory, the person who acts or produces the behavior to be explained is called the *actor.* The onlooker, or the person who offers a causal explanation of the actor's behavior or experience, is called the *observer.* Actors often explain their own behavior in terms of external causes. In contrast, observers frequently explain the actor's behavior in terms of internal causes. In committing the **fundamental attribution error,** observers

attribution theory Theory that views people as motivated to discover the underlying causes of behavior as part of their effort to make sense of the behavior.

fundamental attribution error The tendency for observers to overestimate the importance of internal traits and underestimate the importance of external situations when they seek explanations of an actor's behavior.

Actor

Tends to give external, situational explanations of own behavior

"I'm late with my report because other people keep asking me to help them with their projects."

Observer

Tends to give internal, trait explanations of actor's behavior

"She's late with her report because she can't concentrate on her own responsibilities."

FIGURE 12.1

The Fundamental Attribution Error In this situation, the supervisor is the observer and the employee is the actor.

overestimate the importance of internal traits and underestimate the importance of external situations when they seek explanations of an actor's behavior (Aronson, Wilson, & Akert, 2002) (Figure 12.1).

The fundamental attribution error suggests that most individuals have a tendency to explain social behavior in terms of the personalities of the people involved rather than the situation of the people (Aronson, Wilson, & Akert, 2002). For example, news coverage of Hurricane Katrina was replete with grim images of individuals who had not evacuated their Gulf Coast homes and were left homeless and helpless in the aftermath of the storm. Looking at those individuals, an observer might have concluded, "They were foolish not to get out in time." But in fact, situational factors such as the lack of financial resources or a means of transportation may have prevented many of them from leaving.

The Role of Heuristics in Social Information Processing Another source of bias in attribution and social information processing is the use of heuristics. Social cognition has long been interested in showing how the way we make social decisions can depend on heuristics (Chaiken & Ledgerwood, 2007; Reimer & Rieskamp, 2007). Heuristics (as described in Chapter 9) are cognitive shortcuts that allow us to make decisions rapidly. Given that heuristics are useful in information processing generally, they can play a role in social information processing. These heuristics might be seen as helpful tools that allow us to navigate the complex social landscape.

But heuristics can also lead to mistakes (Weaver & others, 2007), as in the case of the availability heuristic. Recall from Chapter 9 that the availability heuristic is the tendency to confuse the probability of an event's occurrence with the ease with which you can imagine it. For example, someone who has just witnessed an auto accident is likely to overestimate the chances that he or she will be in an accident sometime in the future. The availability heuristic leads to mistakes when we confuse the ease with which we can think of something with the actual likelihood of its occurrence. Figure 12.2 shows an example of the availability heuristic.

Another common heuristic is the false consensus effect. Ask yourself: "How many introductory psychology students want to be a psychology major?" Your answer is likely to depend on whether you yourself are or want to be a psychology major. The **false consensus effect** is an overestimation of the degree to which everybody else thinks or acts the way we do, and it results from the use of our own outlook or situation to predict that of others. False consensus effects can be important in social interactions, as in cases where individuals do not speak up even if they disagree with a speaker. Imagine that you hear someone in a group making a racially insensitive remark. The false consensus effect tells us that silence on the part of others in the group is very likely to be taken as agreement.

Stereotypes can be considered a type of heuristic in that they allow us to make quick judgments using very little information. As we will see shortly, stereotyping can have powerful, negative implications for the social world.

false consensus effect Overestimation of the degree to which everybody else thinks or acts the way we do, stemming from the use of our own outlook or situation to predict that of others.

List 1	List 2
Angelina Jolie	Josh Hartnett
Oprah Winfrey	Michael J. Fox
Meryl Streep	Chris Cooper
Julia Roberts	Alan Arkin
Kate Winslet	Ryan Gosling

FIGURE 12.2

The Availability Heuristic in Action Read the actors' names in List 1 out loud to a friend, one after the other. Then read aloud the names in List 2. Next ask your friend which list was longer—the one with men or the one with women. Chances are, your friend will think it was the list of women. A version of this activity was used by Stuart McKelvie (1997) to show that fame (which enhances the availability of a name) could lead to mistakes in the remembered frequency of male or female names. Because the women listed here are all more famous than the men listed, your friend might just fall prey to the availability heuristic.

The Self as a Social Object

Each of us carries around mental representations not only of others but also of ourselves. We can think of the self as our schema for who we are, what we are like (and not like), and how we feel about these perceptions.

One of the most important self-related variables is self-esteem, the degree to which we have a positive or negative attitude about ourselves (Harter, 2006). In general, research has shown that it is generally a good idea to feel good about yourself. Indeed, individuals with high self-esteem have been shown to have a variety of **positive illusions**—positive views of themselves that are not necessarily deeply rooted in reality. Constantine Sedikides and his colleagues have shown that many of us tend to think of ourselves as above average in a number of positive characteristics, including how trustworthy, moral, and attractive we are (Sedikides, 2007; Sedikides, Gaertner, & Toguchi, 2003; Sedikides, Gaertner, & Vevea, 2005; Sedikides & Gregg, 2006). Keep in mind that the very definition of *average* indicates that only some of us can be "above average."

Shelley Taylor and her colleagues (2003a, 2003b, 2007) have demonstrated that having positive illusions about the self is often related to heightened well-being in a variety of ways. Individuals who tend to have positive illusions about themselves are psychologically healthier and more likely to be judged positively by others. Self-esteem also affects our attributions about our own behavior. Individuals with high self-esteem, for instance, tend to give themselves breaks when it comes to judging their own behavior, an inclination that psychologists call self-serving bias.

Self-serving bias refers to the tendency to take credit for our successes and to deny responsibility for our failures. Think about taking a psychology exam. If you do well, you are likely to take credit for that success ("I'm smart" or "I knew that stuff")—that is, to make internal attributions. But if you do poorly, you are more likely to blame situational factors ("The test was too hard" or "I barely studied")—that is, to make external attributions.

Barbara Fredrickson and Tomi-Ann Roberts (1997) examined how another aspect of the self might relate to important outcomes. **Self-objectification** refers to the tendency to see oneself primarily as an object in the eyes of others. According to these researchers, women have been socialized to think of themselves and their physical bodies as objects in the social world. In a fascinating series of studies, researchers asked men and women first to try on some clothes—either a sweater or a swimsuit—and then to complete a math test. These researchers found that after trying on swimsuits, women performed much more poorly on the math test. They surmised that the experience of trying on the swimsuit heightened women's experience of self-objectification and body shame and reduced their mental resources for completing the math test (Fredrickson & others, 1998).

Stereotype Threat As we will see later in the chapter, stereotypes can have profound implications for group relations. They can also have an impact on the individuals who are members of stereotyped groups (Rosenthal & Crisp, 2006). A **stereotype threat** is an individual's fast-acting, self-fulfilling fear of being judged on the basis of a negative stereotype about his or her group. A person who feels a stereotype threat is well aware of stereotypical expectations for him or her as a member of the group. In stereotype-relevant situations, the individual experiences anxiety and apprehension about living "down" to expectations and consequently under-performs. Claude Steele and Eliot Aronson (Steele & Aronson, 1995, 2004) have shown that when a test is presented to African American and Euro-American students who have first simply checked a box indicating their ethnicity, the African Americans perform more poorly. Importantly, in situations where ethnicity was not made salient (even in this subtle way), no ethnic differences in performance emerged.

Stereotype threat has also been shown to affect the performance on math tests by women compared to men who have equally strong math training (Spencer, Steele, & Quinn, 1999). White men also can fall prey to stereotype threat. In a study of golf ability, Euro-American men performed more poorly than African American men when they were told the test measured "natural athletic ability" (Stone, 2002; Stone & others, 1999). The power of

positive illusions Positive views of oneself that are not necessarily deeply rooted in reality.

self-serving bias The tendency to take credit for one's successes and to deny responsibility for one's failures.

self-objectification The tendency to see oneself primarily as an object in the eyes of others.

stereotype threat An individual's fast-acting, self-fulfilling fear of being judged on the basis of a negative stereotype about his or her group.

stereotypes can be amazing. Asian women will perform better on a math test if asked first for their ethnicity, but more poorly if asked first about their gender (Shih & Sanchez, 2005; Shih & others, 2007). Yet some critics argue that the extent to which stereotype threat explains the testing gap between various groups has been exaggerated (Cullen, Hardison, & Sackett, 2004; Sackett, Hardison, & Cullen, 2005).

Social Comparison: Comparing Ourselves with Others   Have you ever felt a sense of accomplishment about getting a *B+* on a test, until you found out that your friend in the same class got an *A*? Or, having gotten the *A*, have you wanted to know just how many other people did as well? We gain self-knowledge from our own behavior, of course, but we also acquire it from others through **social comparison,** the process by which individuals evaluate their thoughts, feelings, behaviors, and abilities in relation to other people. Social comparison helps individuals to evaluate themselves, tells them what their distinctive characteristics are, and aids them in building an identity.

More than 50 years ago, Leon Festinger (1954) proposed a theory of social comparison. According to this theory, when no objective means are available to evaluate our opinions and abilities, we compare ourselves with others. Furthermore, to get an accurate appraisal of ourselves, we are most likely to compare ourselves with others who are similar to us, to people in communities like ours, to those with similar family backgrounds, and so on. Social comparison theory has been extended and modified over the years and continues to provide an important rationale for why we affiliate with others and how we come to know ourselves (Michinov & Michinov, 2001).

Festinger's social comparison concentrated on those who are similar to us; other researchers have focused on *downward social comparisons,* that is, comparisons with those whom we consider inferior to us. Individuals under threat (from negative feedback, low self-esteem, depression, or illness, for example) try to improve their mental well-being by comparing themselves with others who are less fortunate (Gibbons & McCoy, 1991). It can be comforting to tell ourselves, "Well, at least I'm not as bad off as that guy."

Attitudes

Social thinking involves not only perceptions and attributions but also attitudes. **Attitudes** are our opinions and beliefs about people, objects, and ideas—simply put, how we feel about things. We have attitudes about all sorts of things, as expressed in statements such as "People are basically good" and "Education is a key to improving society." Further, we live in a world in which people try to influence others' attitudes, as when politicians campaign to get our vote and advertisers try to convince us that their product is the best. Social psychologists are interested not only in how attitudes are changed but also in whether changing an individual's attitude will have an effect on his or her behavior—or whether changing an individual's behavior will lead to an attitude change (Crano & Prislin, 2006; Maio & Haddock, 2007).

Can Attitudes Predict Behavior?   People sometimes say one thing but do another. For example, they might respond in a poll that they prefer one candidate and then vote for another. But often, what people say is what they do. Studies over the past half-century indicate some of the conditions under which attitudes guide actions (McGuire, 2004; Smith & Fabrigar, 2000):

- *When the person's attitudes are strong* (Ajzen, 2001): For example, senators whose attitudes toward the president are "highly favorable" are more likely to vote for the president's policies than are senators who have only "moderately favorable" attitudes toward the chief executive.
- *When the person shows a strong awareness of his or her attitudes and when the person rehearses and practices them* (Fazio & Olsen, 2007; Fazio & others, 1982): For example, a person who has been asked to give a speech about the benefits of recycling is more likely to recycle than is an individual with the same attitude about recycling who has not put the idea into words or defined it in public.

social comparison The process by which individuals evaluate their thoughts, feelings, behaviors, and abilities in relation to other people.

attitudes Opinions and beliefs about people, objects, and ideas.

- *When the attitudes are relevant to the behavior:* For example, a survey of general liberal versus conservative political beliefs may be less likely to predict voting behavior than a survey that specifically asks individuals which candidate they are going to vote for.
- *When the person has a vested interest:* People are more likely to act on attitudes when the issue at stake is something that will affect them personally. For example, a classic study examined whether students would show up for a rally protesting a change that would raise the legal drinking age from 18 to 21 (Sivacek & Crano, 1982). Although students in general were against the change, only those in the critical age group (from 18 to 20) turned out to protest.

Can Behavior Predict Attitudes?

"The actions of men are the best interpreters of their thoughts," asserted seventeenth-century English philosopher John Locke. Does taking an action change attitudes?

Ample evidence exists that changes in behavior sometimes precede changes in attitudes (Bandura, 1989). Social psychologists offer two main explanations of why behavior influences attitudes. The first view, cognitive dissonance theory, is that we have a strong need for cognitive consistency; we change our attitudes to make them more consistent with our behavior (Carkenord & Bullington, 1995). The second view, self-perception theory, focuses on the idea that our attitudes are not completely clear even to us, so we observe our own behavior and make inferences about it to determine what our attitudes should be.

Cognitive Dissonance Theory Cognitive dissonance, a concept developed by Festinger (1957), is an individual's psychological discomfort (dissonance) caused by two inconsistent thoughts. According to the theory, we feel uneasy if we cannot justify to ourselves the difference between what we believe and what we do. Psychologists have used cognitive dissonance to explain practices such as initiation rites to get into Greek organizations, boot camp in the Marines, and the rigors of residency in medical school. From a cognitive dissonance perspective, individuals in these situations are likely to think, "If it's this hard to get into, it *must* be worth it!"

We can reduce cognitive dissonance in one of two general ways: change our attitudes to fit our behavior or change our behaviors to fit our attitudes.

Cognitive dissonance and dissonance reduction can be used to explain a variety of common human experiences. Cognitive dissonance may drive us to justify external things in our lives that are unpleasant (Aronson, 1995). As playwright George Bernard Shaw said of his father's alcoholism, "If you cannot get rid of the family skeleton, you may as well make it dance." "Making the family skeleton dance" helped Shaw to reduce the tension between his attitude about his father's drinking problem and its actual occurrence. Cognitive dissonance might also lead us to justify the negative things we do ourselves in order to maintain a feeling that we are decent, reasonable human beings. For example, when we have had a bad argument with someone, we often develop a negative attitude toward that person in an attempt to justify the nasty things we said.

Effort justification is one type of dissonance reduction, meaning we try to rationalize the amount of effort we put into something, so in general, goals that require considerable effort are the ones that we value most highly. If we expend considerable effort yet still do not reach the valued goal, we develop dissonance. We can reduce the dissonance by rationalizing it or making excuses. That is, we might try to convince ourselves that we did not work as hard as we actually did, or we could say that the goal was not all that important in the first place.

The temptation to rationalize is most intense when our self-esteem is involved (Aronson, 2000; Aronson, Cohen, & Nails, 1999). If you do something cruel, then it follows that you have to perform some mental gymnastics to keep yourself from thinking you are a cruel person. The clearest results in the hundreds of research studies on cognitive dissonance occur when self-esteem is involved, and the most dissonance results when individuals with the highest self-esteem act in cruel ways.

Not all of our thoughts and behaviors are aimed at reducing dissonance, of course. Sometimes we even learn from our mistakes. We catch ourselves doing something we do not approve of, look in the mirror, and say, "You blew it. Now what can you do to prevent that from happening again?"

cognitive dissonance A concept developed by Festinger; an individual's psychological discomfort (dissonance) caused by two inconsistent thoughts.

Self-Perception Theory   Not all social psychologists agree that cognitive dissonance explains the influence of behavior on attitudes. **Self-perception theory** reflects Daryl Bem's (1967) ideas about the connection between attitudes and behavior. According to self-perception theory, individuals make inferences about their attitudes by perceiving their behavior. That is, behaviors can cause attitudes because when we are questioned about our attitudes, we think back on our behaviors for information. When asked about your attitude toward exercise, for instance, you might think, "Well, I run every morning, so I must like it!" If you have ever played devil's advocate in an argument, meaning that you have defended a point just for the sake of argument, you might have found yourself realizing that maybe you do hold the views you have pretended to advocate. From Bem's perspective, your behavior has led you to recognize something about yourself that you had not noticed before. Bem believes that we are especially likely to look to our own behavior to determine our attitudes when our attitudes are not completely clear. Figure 12.3 compares cognitive dissonance theory and self-perception theory.

Which theory is right: cognitive dissonance or self-perception? The pattern of research on cognitive dissonance suggests that people do change their attitudes to avoid feeling cheap, stupid, or guilty about their behavior. But at the same time, Bem's self-perception theory is compelling. People who are not strongly committed to attitudes before acting on them do seem to analyze their behavior for hints about their true opinions (Aronson, Wilson, & Akert, 2002). Both cognitive dissonance theory and self-perception theory have merit in explaining the connection between attitudes and behavior, and these opposing views bring to light the complexity that may exist in this connection.

How Are People's Attitudes Changed?

You have probably tried to persuade your friends to go to a movie or to play the sport you passionately enjoy. If you are a parent, you have probably tried to persuade your children to eat their peas or to go to bed early. At some point in your life, you also likely have tried to convince someone to buy something from you. All of these examples involve persuasion or trying to change another person's attitudes.

Professional persuaders have similar goals, but they use more polished techniques based on extensive research on attitude change. What makes people decide to give up their original attitudes and to adopt new ones instead? What makes people decide to act on an attitude that they have not acted on before? Teachers, lawyers, and sales representatives study techniques that will help them sway their audiences (children, juries, and buyers). Politicians have arsenals of speechwriters and image consultants to ensure that their words are as persuasive as possible. Perhaps the most skilled persuaders of all are advertisers, who combine the full array of techniques in an effort to sell everything from cornflakes to cars to carpets.

A full review of the factors involved in persuasion and attitude change could fill volumes. Here are a few of social psychologists' findings, organized around the main elements of the communication process: who conveys the message (the communicator, or source), what the message is (the communication), how the message is conveyed (the medium), and who receives the message (the target, or audience).

The Communicator (Source)   Suppose you are running for president of the student body. You tell your fellow students that you are going to make life at your college better. Will they believe you? Most likely, that will depend on some of your characteristics as a communicator. Whether they believe you depends in large part on your *expertise* or *credibility*. If you have held other elective offices, the students would be likelier to believe you have the expertise to be their president. Trustworthiness, power, attractiveness, likeability, and similarity are all credibility characteristics that help a communicator change people's attitudes or convince them to act.

	Cognitive Dissonance Theory	Self-Perception Theory
Theorist	Festinger	Bem
Nature of Theory	We are motivated toward consistency between attitude and behavior and away from inconsistency.	We make inferences about our attitudes by perceiving and examining our behavior and the context in which it occurs, which might involve inducements to behave in certain ways.
Example	"I hate my job. I need to develop a better attitude toward it or else quit."	"I am spending all of my time thinking about how much I hate my job. I really must not like it."

FIGURE 12.3

Two Theories of the Connections Between Attitudes and Behavior Although we often think of attitudes as causing behavior, behavior can change attitudes, through either dissonance reduction or self-perception.

self-perception theory Bem's theory about the connection between attitudes and behavior; stresses that individuals make inferences about their attitudes by perceiving their behavior.

"All I'm saying is, giving a little something to the arts might help our image."

© The New Yorker Collection 1989. Peter Steiner from cartoonbank.com. All Rights Reserved.

The Message   What kind of message is persuasive? One line of research has focused on whether a rational or an emotional strategy is more effective. Is it better to use facts or logic to persuade someone? Or is it preferable to use basic emotional motivators such as love, sex, and fear?

Emotional appeals are very powerful (Visser & Cooper, 2007). How often, for example, have we seen swinging below the belt become a tactic in political campaigns? In the 2004 presidential race, the "Swift Boat Veterans" launched a scathing attack on Democratic candidate John Kerry that was widely condemned on both sides of the party fence. Such negative appeals play to the audience's emotions, whereas positive appeals are directed at the audience's logical, rational thinking. The less informed we are, the likelier it is that we will respond to an emotional appeal.

Another aspect of the message that has been of interest to social psychologists is the order in which arguments are presented. Should you wait until the end of your presentation to make your strongest points, or should you put your best foot forward at the beginning? The *foot-in-the-door strategy* involves presenting a weaker point at the beginning or making a small request with which the listeners will probably comply, saving the strongest point until the end—in other words, starting small and building (Cialdini, 1993). For example, a sales pitch for a health spa might offer you 4 weeks' use of the facility for $10 in the hope that, after the 4 weeks, you will pay $200 for a 1-year membership. In contrast, the *door-in-the-face strategy* involves a communicator's making the strongest point or demand in the beginning, which the listeners probably will reject. Then a weaker point or moderate "concessionary" demand is made toward the end. For example, the salesperson for the health spa might offer you the 1-year membership for $200, which you turn down, and then try to entice you with a "bargain" 4-weeks-for-$10 package.

The Medium   Another persuasion factor is which medium or technology to use to get the message across. Consider the difference between watching a presidential debate on television and reading about it in the newspaper. Television lets us see how the candidates deliver their messages, what their appearance and mannerisms are like, and so on. Because it presents live images, television is often considered to be a more powerful medium than print sources for changing attitudes.

The Target (Audience)   Age and attitude strength are two characteristics of the audience that determine whether a message will be effective. Younger people are likelier to change their attitudes than older ones. Weaker attitudes on the part of the audience make attitude change likelier than strong attitudes do.

As you think about the aspects of persuasion—including the source, message, medium, and target—you might wonder why all of these are necessary. If the message is a strong one, why would it matter that it was delivered by Brad Pitt instead of a noncelebrity? A strong argument should work, no matter who it comes from or how it is presented, right?

One model that has been proposed to explain how different aspects of appeals influence persuasion is the **elaboration likelihood model.** This theory identifies two ways to persuade: a central route and a peripheral route (DeMarree & Petty, 2007; Petty & Cacioppo, 1986; Petty, Wheeler, & Bizer, 2000). The central route to persuasion works by engaging someone thoughtfully with a sound, logical argument. The peripheral route involves non-message factors such as the source's credibility and attractiveness or emotional appeals. The peripheral route is effective when people are not paying close attention to what the communicator is saying. As you might guess, television commercials often involve the peripheral route to persuasion on the assumption that during the commercials you are probably not paying full attention to the screen. However, the central route is more persuasive when people have the ability, and the motivation, to pay attention to the facts (Lammers, 2000).

elaboration likelihood model Theory identifying two ways by which a communication can be persuasive—a central route and a peripheral route.

REVIEW, ASSESS, AND SHARPEN YOUR THINKING

Review

1 **Describe how people think about the social world.**

- Discuss some of the variables involved in person perception.
- Describe the three dimensions of attributions as well as various types of errors and biases in attributions and social judgment.
- Define the concepts of self-esteem, self-serving bias, self-objectification, and stereotype threat.
- Explain what attitudes are and describe the relationship between attitudes and behaviors.

Assess

1. **Stereotype threat refers to**
   A. the damage caused by stereotyping others.
   B. the ability to change someone's behavior by threatening to use a stereotype.
   C. humans' tendency to categorize people using broad generalizations.
   D. the fear of being judged by the negative stereotypes about one's group.

2. **Attribution theory states that causal attributions are based on all the following except:**
   A. internality-externality.
   B. consensus.
   C. controllability.
   D. stability.

3. **The fundamental attribution error is characterized by overemphasizing _____ and underemphasizing _____ when making attributions about others' behavior.**
   A. internal factors, external factors
   B. external factors, internal factors
   C. controllability, stability
   D. stability, controllability

4. **Which of the following is true about positive illusions?**
   A. Positive illusions are more common in people with low self-esteem.
   B. Positive illusions are always rooted in reality.
   C. Positive illusions have been linked to better well-being.
   D. Positive illusions are focused on actors rather than observers.

5. **Festinger's social comparison theory states that**
   A. when we are threatened we compare ourselves to others who are more fortunate.
   B. comparing ourselves to people who are similar to us allows us to more accurately appraise ourselves.
   C. we accurately judge ourselves only when we refuse to compare ourselves to others.
   D. we make external observations about our own behavior and internal observations about others behavior.

Sharpen Your Thinking

Think about a personal habit you would like to change. Using Bem's self-perception theory, devise a plan for changing that habit.

2 Social Behavior

Describe altruism and aggression.

Of course, we do not just think socially; we also behave in social ways that influence the people around us. Two types of behavior that have interested psychologists represent the extremes of human social activity: altruism and aggression.

Altruism

In 1998, Joyce Rush, a mother of five and a nurse, presented herself to the surgeons at Johns Hopkins transplant unit and offered to donate one of her kidneys to whoever might need it. Once news of her selfless act hit the media, the hospital received calls from numerous potential live organ donors.

Such selfless acts of kindness are certainly a part of our social experience—we have seen huge relief efforts following disasters, including those that helped the victims of the 9/11

altruism An unselfish interest in helping someone else.

egoism Giving to another person to ensure reciprocity; to gain self-esteem; to present oneself as powerful, competent, or caring; or to avoid social and self-censure for failing to live up to society's expectations.

attacks, the Indian Ocean tsunamis of 2004, the Gulf Coast hurricanes of 2005, and the crises in the Darfur region of Sudan. Even in history's darkest hours, individuals have stepped forward and acted with heroic kindness toward others. Oskar Schindler, whose story became famous in Steven Spielberg's movie *Schindler's List,* defied the Nazis during World War II and created a pipeline of survival and escape for many Jews.

In our everyday life, too, we witness and perform "random acts of kindness"—maybe adding a quarter to someone's expired parking meter or giving up our seat on a bus to a person in need. We may volunteer for the Special Olympics or act as a literacy tutor. We may give blood and donate to numerous worthy causes. What all of these acts have in common is **altruism,** an unselfish interest in helping someone else (Eisenberg, Fabes, & Spinrad, 2006).

Examining potentially altruistic behavior (also called *prosocial behavior*), psychologists commonly have questioned just how genuinely selfless it is, because "everyone knows" that people are naturally selfish. Dale Miller (1999, 2001) challenges this view of humanity, which he called *homo-economicus*—the assumption that each person is out for his or her own gain. Miller suggests that we are socialized to believe that humans are naturally selfish but that a great deal of research suggests that humans are not necessarily self-centered and do not engage in selfish acts as a knee-jerk response (Holmes, Miller, & Lerner, 2002). Recall from Chapter 1 that altruism has presented a puzzle for evolutionary psychologists (Van Vugt & Van Lange, 2006). How can a behavior that rewards others and not oneself be adaptive?

Interestingly, kindness is not exclusive to humans. Ethologists studying nonhuman primates have shown that altruistic acts of kindness also occur in other species (De Waal, 1996, 2006). As you read about research and theory on altruism, ask yourself whether you think altruism is a puzzle to be solved or a natural expression of human nature.

Psychological and Sociocultural Foundations of Altruism

How do psychologists account for acts of human altruism? One key aspect is the concept of *reciprocity,* which encourages us to do unto others as we would have them do unto us. Reciprocity is present in every widely practiced religion in the world, including Judaism, Christianity, Buddhism, and Islam. Complex human sentiments are involved in reciprocity: Trust in the people with whom we are interacting is probably the most important principle over the long run. But reciprocity can involve more negative sentiments, such as guilt, if we do not reciprocate a favor, and anger, if someone else does not reciprocate. One study found that college students were more likely to pledge to the charity of someone who had previously bought them candy (Webster & others, 1999). Altruistic reciprocity was more likely when the donor's name was made public to the recipient, but even when the recipient did not know who the donor was, altruistic reciprocity occurred, although at a lower level.

Not all seemingly altruistic behavior is unselfish. Some psychologists even argue that true altruism has never been demonstrated. Others assert that a distinction can be made between altruism and egoism in giving (Cialdini & others, 1987). **Egoism** involves giving to another person to ensure reciprocity; to gain self-esteem; to present oneself as powerful, competent, or caring; or to avoid social and self-censure for failing to live up to society's expectations. In contrast, altruism is giving to another person with the ultimate goal of benefiting that other person; any benefits that come to the giver are unintended.

Altruistic behavior is determined by the nature of both the person and the situation. Describing individuals as having altruistic or egoistic motives implies that psychological variables—a person's ability to empathize with the needy or to feel a sense of responsibility for another person's welfare—are important in understanding altruistic behavior. The stronger these personality dispositions are, the less we expect situational variables to influence whether giving, kindness, or helping occurs. But as with any human behavior, characteristics of the situation influence the strength of altruistic motivation (Hardy & Van Vugt, 2006). Some of these characteristics include the degree of need shown by the other individual, the needy person's responsibility for her plight, the cost of assisting the needy person, and the extent to which reciprocity is expected (Batson, 2003, 2006; Penner & others, 2005).

Emotions and Helping: Feeling Good and Doing Good Another psychological component of altruistic behavior is mood. A strong conclusion from the research literature on helping is that happy people are more likely to help (Snyder & Lopez, 2007). When people are in a good mood, they are more likely to pitch in. Does it then follow that when they are in a bad mood, people are less likely to help? Not necessarily, because adults (especially) generally understand that doing good for another person can be a mood booster. Thus, when in a bad mood, they might be likely to help if they think that doing so will improve their mood.

Empathy A key social emotion involved in altruism is empathy (Saarni & others, 2006). **Empathy** happens when we feel a oneness with the emotional state of another. Daniel Batson (2002, 2006; Batson & others, 2007) has spent the better part of his career searching for proof that truly altruistic behavior does exist. The key to such altruism is the extent to which we are able to put ourselves in another's shoes. When we are feeling empathy for someone else's plight, we are moved—not to make ourselves feel better but out of genuine concern for the other person. Empathy can produce altruistic behavior even toward members of rival groups and even when we believe no one will ever hear about our kind act (Fultz & others, 1986).

The Bystander Effect One of the most widely studied aspects of altruism is the question of why one person will help a stranger in distress, whereas another will not lift a finger (Abelson, Frey, & Gregg, 2004). Social psychologists have found that the response often depends on the circumstances.

Nearly 45 years ago, a young woman named Kitty Genovese was brutally murdered. She was attacked at about 3 A.M. in a respectable area of New York City. The murderer left and returned three times; he finally put an end to Kitty's life as she crawled to her apartment and screamed for help. It took the slayer about 30 minutes to kill Kitty. Thirty-eight neighbors watched the gory scene and heard Kitty Genovese's screams. No one helped or even called the police. This incident prompted social psychologists to study the **bystander effect,** the tendency for an individual who observes an emergency to help less when other people are present than when the observer is alone. Although the Genovese slaying occurred more than four decades ago, the bystander effect is evident today as well. In August 2007 a woman was physically assaulted and raped in the hallway of an apartment building in St. Paul. Security cameras captured the 30-minute attack, and as many as 10 witnesses walked past or opened their apartment doors (and then closed them) during the assault. No one called the police (KARE11.com, 2007).

Social psychologists John Darley and Bibb Latané (1968) documented the bystander effect in a number of emergencies. Most bystander intervention studies show that when alone, a person will help 75 percent of the time, but when another bystander is present, the figure drops to 50 percent. Apparently the difference is due to diffusion of responsibility among witnesses and the tendency to look to the behavior of others for clues about what to do. We may think that someone else will call the police or that, because no one else is helping, possibly the person does not need help.

Altruism and Gender Who are more helping and caring, men or women? The stereotype is women. However, as in most domains, it is a good idea to think about gender in context (Eisenberg, Fabes, & Spinrad, 2006; Renzetti & Curran, 2002). Researchers have found that women are more likely than men to help when the context involves nurturing, such as volunteering time to help a child with a personal problem. Men, on the other hand, are more likely to help in situations in which a perceived danger is present (for instance, picking up a hitchhiker), and they feel competent to help (as in helping someone fix a flat tire) (Eagly & Crowley, 1986).

Aggression

If altruism demonstrates the bright side of human nature, aggression may represent the dark side. Aggression seems to be an all-too-common occurrence in modern society. Murders

(Top) *An example of animal altruism—a baboon plucking bugs from another baboon. Most acts of animal altruism involve kin.* (Bottom) *Altruistic humans—research suggests that happy people are more likely to help other people.*

empathy A feeling of oneness with the emotional state of another person.

bystander effect The tendency of an individual who observes an emergency to help less when other people are present than when the observer is alone.

in the United States take place at the rate of 20,000 per year, and assaults at the rate of 700,000 per year; there are at least 200,000 reports of rape per year in the United States. In the twentieth century, 80 to 100 million people were violently killed. When social psychologists explore aggression, they ask questions such as, Is this dark side biologically based, or is it learned? How do aspects of the social context relate to aggression? Perhaps the greatest puzzle of aggression is that a species capable of incredible acts of kindness can also perpetrate horrifying acts of violence.

Biological Influences   There is nothing new about human aggression. The primate ancestors of human beings and the earliest humans are thought to have committed aggressive acts against others of their own kind. Shakespeare's King Lear asks, "Is there any cause in nature that makes these hard hearts?" In other words, is aggression an inborn characteristic of the human species? Researchers who approach aggression from a biological viewpoint examine the influence of evolutionary tendencies, genetics, and neurobiological factors in aggression.

Evolutionary Views   Ethologists say that certain stimuli release *innate* aggressive responses (Lorenz, 1965; Tinbergen, 1969). For example, a male robin will attack another male bird when it sees the red patch on the other bird's breast. When the patch is removed, no attack takes place. However, in the animal kingdom, most hostile encounters do not escalate to killing or even severe harm. Much of the fighting is ritualistic and involves threat displays. For example, elephant seals show approximately 65 threat displays for every fight that takes place (LeBoeuf & Peterson, 1969). The type of threat display varies from one species to the next: A cat arches its back, bares its teeth, and hisses; a chimpanzee stares, stomps the ground, and screams.

Evolutionary theorists believe that human beings are not much different from other animals (Freeman & Herron, 2007). A basic theme of their theory is the survival of the fittest (Kardong, 2008). Thus, they conclude that early in human evolution the survivors were probably aggressive individuals.

In the animal world, aggression often is ritualistic and typically involves threat displays such as a cat's arching its back, baring its teeth, and hissing.

Genetic Basis   Genes are important in understanding the biological basis of aggression (Lewis, 2007). The selective breeding of animals provides the evidence. After a number of breedings among only aggressive animals and among only docile animals, vicious and timid strains of animals emerge. The vicious strains attack nearly anything in sight; the timid strains rarely fight, even when attacked.

The genetic basis for aggression is more difficult to demonstrate with humans (Brennan, Mednick, & Kandel, 1991). Nonetheless, in one investigation of 573 sets of adult twins, identical twins had more similar aggressive tendencies than did fraternal twins (Rushton & others, 1986).

Neurobiological Factors   Studies by neuroscientists indicate how the brain is involved in the biological processes of aggression (Halasz & others, 2006; Wood & Liossi, 2006). In 1966, Charles Whitman climbed to the top of the campus tower at the University of Texas at Austin, from which vantage point he killed 15 people below with a high-powered rifle and then took his own life. An autopsy revealed a tumor in the limbic system of Whitman's brain, an area associated with emotion. In another instance, an electrode was implanted in the amygdala (which is part of the limbic system) of a meek female mental patient. Immediately after an electric current stimulated the amygdala, the mild-mannered woman became violent. She yelled, snarled, and flailed around the room (King, 1961). We do not appear to have a specific aggression center in the brain, but when the lower, more primitive areas of the brain (such as the limbic system) are stimulated by electric currents, aggressive behavior often results (Herbert, 1988).

Neurotransmitters have also been linked to highly aggressive behavior (Zalcman & Siegel, 2006). Individuals with depressive disorders who commit suicide by violent means (such as using a gun) have lower levels of the neurotransmitter serotonin than most people do (Van Winkle, 2000). In one study, young men whose serotonin levels were low relative to those of other men their age were far more likely to have committed a violent crime (Moffitt & others, 1998). Also, children who show high rates of aggression have lower levels of serotonin than children who display low rates of aggression (Blader, 2006).

Hormones are another biological factor that may play a role in aggression (Dorn & others, 2006). The hormone that is typically implicated in aggressive behavior is testosterone, commonly thought of as the male sex hormone (although both men and women have testosterone in their bodies). Research on rats and other animals has shown that testosterone relates to aggression (Cunningham & McGinnis, 2007). Results with humans have been less consistent (van Bokhoven & others, 2006), although higher testosterone levels have been found in incarcerated individuals convicted of ruthless murders—specifically, premeditated killing of a known victim (Dabbs, Riad, & Chance, 2001).

In addition, a recent longitudinal study of 96 adolescent boys followed from age 12 to age 21 found that those who developed a criminal record were higher in testosterone levels at age 16 (van Bokhoven & others, 2006). Higher levels of testosterone also were associated with higher levels of aggression and self-reported delinquent behavior. It is important to keep in mind, however, that testosterone levels are themselves influenced by behavior and experience; thus, behaving in an aggressive manner may increase a person's level of testosterone.

A fascinating study examined how testosterone is influenced by experience and how experience and testosterone together might help explain aggression (Klinesmith, Kasser, & McAndrew, 2006). In this study, college men interacted with either a gun or a children's toy. Testosterone was measured before and after this phase of the study. Men who interacted with the gun showed significantly higher increases in testosterone, compared to the control group. Furthermore, in a later part of the study, those men who had interacted with the gun were more aggressive (in this case, they put more hot sauce in a cup of water they thought someone else was going to drink). The fact that testosterone at least partially explains this increase in aggression suggests that testosterone changes may help shed light on why some people respond to violent cues with more violent behavior than others (Klinesmith, Kasser, & McAndrew, 2006).

Many of the studies of aggression that have been conducted in social psychology laboratories use experimental methods to examine aggressive behavior. These studies rely on a variety of behaviors that may be considered aggressive even if they do not involve, for example, actually punching someone in the face. In studies on aggression, participants might have an opportunity to "aggress" against another, for instance, by subjecting the individual to a blast of loud noise, dispensing a mild electrical shock, or even, as in the study described above, administering a large dose of Tabasco to swallow.

Psychological Factors Numerous psychological factors appear to be involved in aggression. They include individuals' responses to circumstances, as well as cognitive and learning factors.

Frustrating and Aversive Circumstances Many years ago, John Dollard and his colleagues (1939) proposed that frustration, the blocking of an individual's attempts to reach a goal, triggers aggression. Their *frustration-aggression hypothesis* states that frustration always leads to aggression. Not much later, however, psychologists found that aggression is not the only possible response to frustration. Some individuals who experience frustration become passive, for example (Miller, 1941).

Psychologists later recognized that a broad range of aversive experiences besides frustration can cause aggression. They include physical pain, personal insults, and unpleasant events such as divorce. Aversive circumstances also include the physical environment, including the weather. Murder, rape, and assault increase when temperatures are the hottest (during the third quarter of the year), as well as in the hottest years and in the hottest cities (Anderson & Bushman, 2002).

Cognitive Factors Aspects of the environment may prime us to behave aggressively (Englander, 2006). Recall from Chapter 8 that priming can involve making something salient to a person, even subliminally, or out of his or her awareness. Leonard Berkowitz (1993; Berkowitz & LePage, 1996) has shown how the mere presence of a weapon (such as a gun) may prime hostile thoughts and produce aggression (Anderson, Benjamin, & Bartholow, 1998). Indeed, in accordance with Berkowitz's ideas, a famous study in 1993 found that individuals who lived in a household with a gun were 2.7 times more likely to be murdered than those dwelling in a household without a gun (Kellerman & others, 1993).

Aversive circumstances that might stimulate aggression include factors in the physical environment such as noise, crowding, and heat waves.

A variety of other cognitive factors determine whether an individual responds aggressively to aversive situations (Baumeister, 1999; Berkowitz, 1990; Dodge, Coie, & Lynam, 2006). For instance, if a person perceives that another's actions are unfair or intentionally hurtful, aggression is more likely to occur.

Observational Learning Social cognitive theorists believe that aggression is learned through the processes of reinforcement and observational learning (Englander, 2006). Aggression can be learned by watching others engage in aggressive actions (Bandura, 1986). One of the most frequent opportunities people have to observe aggression in our culture is to watch violence on television, which we consider further in the discussion below on media violence.

Another psychological variable that has interested psychologists who study aggression is self-esteem. To read about this topic, see the Intersection.

Sociocultural Factors Aggression not only involves biological and cognitive factors but also is linked with factors in the wider social world. Among the sociocultural factors involved in aggression are variations in the "culture of honor" and the extent to which people watch violence in the media.

Cultural Variations and the Culture of Honor Aggression and violence are more common in some cultures than others (Kitayama & Cohen, 2007; Shiraev & Levy, 2007; Sorrentino & others, 2005). The U.S. homicide rate does not compare well with rates for other countries. For example, the U.S. homicide rate in 2004 was 5.5 per 100,000 (U.S. Bureau of Justice Statistics, 2006), five times the rate in Germany (BKA, 2006) and more than twice that of Canada's (Canadian Statistics, 2005). However, South Africa, Colombia, Mexico, and the Philippines have much higher homicide rates than the United States.

Crime rates tend to be higher in countries and communities with a considerable gap between the rich and poor (Messner, Raffalovich, & Shrock, 2002; Patterson, 1991; Popp, 2006). The *Gini index* is a measure of income disparities between the richest and poorest citizens of a nation. The lower the Gini index, the lower the income inequality. In the United States the Gini index for 2005 was 45, compared to 30 for Germany and 31 for Canada (CIA, 2005).

Dov Cohen has examined the ways that some cultural norms about masculine pride and family honor may foster aggressive behavior (Cohen, 2001; Vandello & Cohen, 2004). In cultures of honor, a person's (typically a man's) reputation is thought to be an essential aspect of his economic survival. Insults to a man's honor are seen as diminishing his reputation, and violence is accepted as a way to compensate for that loss. We find cultures of honor in

Social Psychology and Developmental Psychology: Does Self-Esteem Predict Aggression?

Low self-esteem is often implicated in society's ills. It is not uncommon to hear that an individual who has perpetrated some act of violence has led a difficult life and has low self-esteem. In the late 1990s, Roy Baumeister presented a provocative idea: He suggested that *high* self-esteem, not low self-esteem, is associated with aggression (Baumeister, 1999; Baumeister, Bushman, & Campbell, 2000; Baumeister & Butz, 2005; Baumeister & others, 2007; Bushman & Baumeister, 2002). In a variety of laboratory investigations, he showed that individuals who scored very high on a measure of self-esteem were more likely (not less likely) than their low self-esteem counterparts to aggress against others when their self-esteem was threatened. These findings stood counter to a long history of research in psychology promoting the idea that self-esteem was a central component of psychological health.

> *Baumeister presented a provocative idea: He suggested that high self-esteem, not low self-esteem, is associated with aggression.*

Following the publication of Baumeister's work, research conducted by developmental and personality psychologists challenged the notion that high self-esteem was bad. These researchers used longitudinal data collected from a large sample of individuals in Dunedin, New Zealand, to show that contrary to Baumeister's conclusions, low (not high) self-esteem was associated with a variety of negative outcomes, including aggression, delinquency, poor health, and limited economic prospects through the middle adulthood years (Donnellan & others, 2005; Trzesniewski & others, 2006).

How can we resolve this apparent conflict? One possibility is that Baumeister was talking about a particular kind of high self-esteem: inflated and unstable high self-esteem (Campbell & others, 2004; Konrath, Bushman, & Campbell, 2006). Individuals with unrealistically high self-esteem appear to be most prone to respond with aggression in response to a threat. Such individuals might be best described not as psychologically healthy but rather as narcissistic. For most people, though, it is more likely that low self-esteem rather than high self-esteem is linked to higher levels of aggression.

countries where family pride might lead to so-called honor killings in which, for example, a female rape victim is slain by her male family members to avoid their being contaminated by the rape.

Cohen has examined how, in the United States, southerners are more likely than northerners to be aggressive when honor is at stake. In one study, Cohen and his colleagues (1996) had White men who were from either the North or the South take part in an experiment that required them to walk down a hallway. A confederate passed all the men, bumping against them and quietly calling them a derogatory name. The southerners were more likely than the northerners to think their masculine reputation was threatened, to become physiologically aroused by the insult, and to engage in actual aggressive or dominant acts. In contrast the northerners were much less likely to perceive a vague random insult as "fightin' words."

Media Violence Images of violence pervade the U.S. popular media: newscasts, television shows, sports broadcasts, movies, video games, and song lyrics. Evildoers kill and get killed; police and detectives violently uphold or even break society's laws; sports announcers glorify players regardless of whether their behavior is sportsmanlike or contributes to their team's success.

One reason that violence seems so alluring on TV and in the movies is that it usually is portrayed unrealistically. Viewers rarely see its lasting effects. In real life, an injured person may not recover for weeks or months, or perhaps may not recover at all, but on television recovery is either assumed or takes only 30 to 60 minutes. It is easy to get the message that aggression and violence are the norm—in fact, are the preferred mode of behavior—in the United States.

Although some critics have argued against the conclusion that TV violence causes aggression (Freedman, 1984), many

Critical Controversy   Do Violent Video Games Lead to Violence?

On April 20, 1999, two teenagers, Eric Harris and Dylan Klebold, carried out a shooting rampage on their classmates and teachers at Columbine High School near Littleton, Colorado. Before killing themselves, they shot dead 12 students and a teacher and wounded 24 others. In the wake of the slayings, the media reported that Harris and Klebold were fans of violent video games, including *Doom* and *Wolfenstein*. Some people began to wonder if the boys had been so obsessively occupied with these violent games that they could no longer distinguish between fantasy and reality. Indeed, the parents of some of the victims filed several lawsuits against video game manufacturers, with no success. Is it possible that video games promote actual violence?

Video games are a relatively new media form, but they are extremely potent social contexts. It has been suggested that violent video games engage children and adolescents so intensely that they experience an altered state of consciousness in which "rational thought is suspended and highly arousing aggressive scripts are increasingly likely to be learned" (Roberts, Henriksen, & Foehr, 2004, p. 498). Unlike other media, such as TV shows, video games allow the individual to play an active role in perpetrating violence. Another difference from TV is that violent video games give players direct rewards ("winning points") for their behavior.

Psychologists have examined the role of violent video games in empathy, attitudes about violence, and violent behavior. Research has shown that video game exposure is related to lowered empathy (a key factor in prosocial behavior) as well as more pro-violent attitudes in middle schoolers (Funk, 2005). Correlational studies also indicate that children and adolescents who extensively play violent video games engage in more aggressive behavior and are more likely to perpetrate delinquent acts than their counterparts who spend less time playing the games or do not play them at all (Anderson & Bushman, 2001; Anderson & Dill, 2000). Chronic exposure to violent video games desensitizes individuals to violence (Bartholow, Bushman, & Sestir, 2006).

Social psychologist Craig Anderson has been a passionate and vocal critic of media violence, especially violent video games (Anderson, 2003; Anderson, Gentile, & Buckley, 2007; Anderson & Huesmann, 2007; Buckley & Anderson, 2006; Bushman & Anderson, 2007; Gentile & Anderson, 2006). Anderson and his colleagues (2004) have found that playing violent video games causes violent thoughts to become more accessible. For instance, those who play violent video games are more likely to complete the word *m---er* as *murder* rather than *mother*. In addition, it is notable that in video games, violence is rewarded, and the rewards are associated with

Youths' exposure to violent video games is related to lowered empathy, pro-violent attitudes, and a heightened likelihood of aggressive behavior and delinquent acts.

increasingly hostile thoughts and feelings (Carnagey & Anderson, 2005). Further, playing violent video games increases aggressive behavior in the laboratory. Most important, says Anderson, and contrary to industry claims, the most methodologically sophisticated studies are the ones that find these effects.

Of course, not everyone is interested in playing violent video games, and not every individual who does so becomes more aggressive. But Anderson's work suggests that those very individuals who enjoy playing such games and who play them often are likely to be affected by them. In addition, these individuals might be relatively unaware of the potential effects of pretending to hurt others on their later behavior.

What Do You Think?

- Do you or people whom you know play violent video games? What impact, if any, do you think this activity has on your or their thoughts and feelings?
- Would you allow your child to play violent video games? Why or why not?
- What would you say the characteristics are of people who enjoy playing violent video games? Do you think these characteristics influence the effects of the games themselves? Explain.
- What do you think policymakers should do with regard to the controversy over the effects of playing video games?

experts insist that TV violence can prompt aggressive or antisocial behavior in children (Anderson & Huesmann, 2007; Comstock & Scharrer, 2003, 2006; Dubow, Huesmann, & Greenwood, 2007). Of course, television violence is not the *only* cause of aggression in children or adults. There is no *one* cause of any social behavior. Aggression, like all other social behaviors, has multiple determinants (Donnerstein, 2001). The link between TV violence and aggression in children is influenced by children's aggressive tendencies, by their attitudes toward violence, and by the monitoring of children's exposure to it.

Another type of media violence that has interested social psychologists is violent pornography. Violent pornography refers to films, videos, and magazines portraying the degradation of women in a sexual context. The question most often posed about such media is whether they can foster violence toward women.

Based on several meta-analyses and on research of their own, Neil Malamuth and his colleagues concluded that pornography consumption does have a small effect on male sexual aggression, but they caution that it is only one of a number of factors that may lead to sexual violence against women (Malamuth, Addison, & Koss, 2000; Vega & Malamuth, 2007). They stress that the nature of pornographic material, the characteristics of the men viewing pornography, and the surrounding culture all combine to produce an effect. It is important to keep in mind that the consumption of erotica and even nonviolent pornography (sexually explicit materials that do not contain violence) is not associated with increases in sexual violence toward women (Malamuth, Addison, & Koss, 2000). Rather, the most problematic materials are those that depict women enjoying being the victims of male sexual violence. Such violent pornography reinforces the rape myth, the false belief that women actually desire coercive sex.

Researchers' major conclusions about human aggression and gender include the finding that men are more aggressive than women in all cultures. Similarly, aggression is more common in male animals, compared with females of the same species. These conclusions support the view that gender differences in aggression are biologically based.

Violent video games are yet another form of media that might influence aggressive behavior. To read further about this topic, see the Critical Controversy.

Aggression and Gender   Our stereotypes clearly tag boys and men as more aggressive than girls and women. In general, research has supported this view. As children, boys are more likely to engage in rough-and-tumble play and get in more fights in which they are physically aggressive toward each other (Bukowski, Brendgen, & Vitaro, 2007). As adolescents, males are more likely to be members of gangs and to commit violent acts (Dodge, Coie, & Lynam, 2006). Children and adolescents who are diagnosed with conduct disorder (a pattern of offensive behavior that violates the basic rights of others) are three times more likely to be boys than girls (Kjelsberg, 2005). As adults, men are more likely to be chronically hostile and to murder or rape than women are (White & Frabutt, 2006).

A classic analysis of research studies summarized the major conclusions about human aggression and gender, including that men are more aggressive than women in all cultures and that this difference emerges early in life (usually by age 2) (Maccoby & Jacklin, 1974). Despite strong evidence that gender is a factor in aggression, we need to remind ourselves of an important point about the conclusions drawn from psychological research. When we say that males are more aggressive than females, we cannot jump to the conclusion that all males are more aggressive than all females (Hyde, 2005, 2007). In any given culture, some females will be more aggressive than some males.

Ways to Reduce Aggression   Chapter 10 explored the powerful negative emotion of anger, which can generate aggression. We examined several strategies for reducing anger that apply to our evaluation of aggression. Specifically, social cognitive theorists believe that people who act aggressively often are rewarded for their aggression and that individuals learn to be aggressive by watching others behave aggressively. Research has supported this view (Bandura, 1986, 1997). Thus, promising strategies for reducing aggression are to decrease rewards for aggression and to allow people to observe fewer incidences of aggression.

Parents have been specially targeted to help children to reduce aggression. Because of their importance in children's lives, they often have considerable influence (Leaper & Friedman, 2007). Recommended parenting strategies include encouraging young children to develop empathy toward others and more closely monitoring adolescents' activities (Denham, Bassett, & Wyatt, 2007; Eisenberg, Fabes, & Spinrad, 2006).

REVIEW, ASSESS, AND SHARPEN YOUR THINKING

Review

2 Describe altruism and aggression.
- Identify the factors involved in altruism.
- Name the factors involved in aggression.

Assess

1. Kitty Genovese's murder, which was witnessed by over 35 of her neighbors, prompted research on which of the following phenomena?

   A. altruism
   B. the bystander effect
   C. aggression
   D. egoism

2. What does the psychological research have to say about homo-economicus?

   A. Human behavior can be predicted using economic theory.
   B. Humans are innately selfish.
   C. Human actions are based on supply of natural resources.
   D. Humans often engage in altruistic acts.

3. Which of the following is not a way to reduce aggression?

   A. minimizing the amount of violence witnessed
   B. increasing empathy
   C. rewarding aggression
   D. avoiding watching violent television or movies

4. Which neurotransmitter is associated with aggression?

   A. epinephrine
   B. dopamine
   C. serotonin
   D. oxytocin

5. Are men or women more aggressive?

   A. Men are more aggressive than women.
   B. Women are more aggressive than men.
   C. Men and women are equally aggressive.
   D. It depends on the context.

Sharpen Your Thinking

Which do you think is more characteristic of human nature—altruism or aggression? Why?

3 Social Influence

Identify how people are influenced in social settings.

Another topic of interest to social psychologists is how our behavior is influenced by other people and groups (Judd & Park, 2007; Monin, 2007). This section explores these aspects of social influence: conformity, obedience, and group influence.

Conformity and Obedience

Research on conformity and obedience started in earnest after World War II. Psychologists began to seek answers to the disturbing question of how ordinary people could be influenced to commit the sort of atrocities inflicted on Jews, Gypsies, and other minorities during the Holocaust. How extensively will people change their behavior to coincide more with what others are doing? How readily do people obey someone in authority? What factors influence whether people will resist such social influences? These questions are still relevant when we try to understand contemporary events such as vicious group attacks on ethnic minorities or gays. They also are relevant to understanding everyday human behavior.

Conformity **Conformity** is a change in a person's behavior to coincide more closely with a group standard. Conformity takes many forms and affects many aspects of people's lives. Conformity is at work, for example, when a person comes to college and starts to drink alcohol heavily at parties, even though he or she might have never been a drinker before.

conformity Change in a person's behavior to coincide more closely with a group standard.

Although conformity has some unpleasant or unattractive connotations, it is not an entirely negative behavior. Conforming to rules and regulations allows society to run smoothly. Consider how chaotic it would be if people did not conform to social norms such as stopping at a red light, driving on the correct side of the road, and not punching others in the face. In the United States, conformity is sometimes regarded negatively, because as a culture Americans value individuality. But not everyone views conformity in such a light. Some of the most dramatic and insightful work on conformity has examined how we sometimes act against our better judgment in order to conform.

Asch's Conformity Experiment Put yourself in this situation: You are taken into a room in which you see five other people seated around a table. A person in a white lab coat enters the room and announces that you are about to participate in an experiment on perceptual accuracy. The group is shown two cards, the first having only a single vertical line on it, the second card three vertical lines of varying length. You are told that the task is to determine which of the three lines on the second card is the same length as the line on the first card. You look at the cards and think, "What a snap. It's so obvious which is the same" (Figure 12.4).

What you do not know is that the other people in the room are confederates, which means that they are working with the experimenter. A **confederate** is a person who is given a role to play in a study so that social context can be manipulated. On the first several trials, everyone agrees about which line matches the standard. Then on the fourth trial, each of the others picks the same *incorrect* line. As the last person to make a choice, you have the dilemma of responding as your eyes tell you or conforming to what the others before you said. How do you think you would answer?

Solomon Asch conducted this classic experiment on conformity in 1951. He believed few of his volunteer participants would yield to group pressure. To test his hypothesis, Asch instructed the hired accomplices to give incorrect responses on 12 of the 18 trials. To his surprise, Asch (1951) found that the volunteer participants conformed to the incorrect answers 35 percent of the time.

In a more recent test of group pressure and conformity, college students watched the third George H. W. Bush–Bill Clinton presidential debate and then rated the candidates' performances (Fein & others, 1993). Students were randomly assigned to one of three groups: (1) a 30-student group that included 10 confederates of the experimenter who openly supported Bush and criticized Clinton, (2) a 30-student group that included 10 confederates who cheered Clinton and put down Bush, and (3) a 30-student group with no confederates of the experimenter. The effects of the group pressure exerted by the confederates were powerful; even Bush supporters rated Clinton's performance more favorably when their group included pro-Clinton confederates of the experimenter.

In sum, research has shown that the pressure to conform is strong (Pines & Maslach, 2002). The key question, of course, is Why? Why would we conform even when faced with clear-cut information such as the lines in the Asch experiment? Social psychologists have addressed this question as well.

Factors That Contribute to Conformity: Going Along to Be Right and Going Along to Be Liked Many factors influence whether an individual will conform (Griskevicius & others, 2006; Lonnqvist & others, 2006; Zimbardo, 2007). In general, two main factors have been identified as contributing to conformity: informational social influence or normative social influence.

Informational social influence refers to the influence other people have on us because we want to be right. The social group can provide us with information that we did not know,

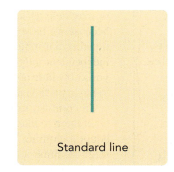
Standard line

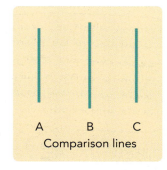
A B C
Comparison lines

FIGURE 12.4

Asch's Conformity Experiment The figures at the top show the stimulus materials for the Asch conformity experiment on group influence. The photograph shows the puzzlement of one subject after five confederates of the experimenter chose the incorrect line.

confederate A person who is given a role to play in a study so that social context can be manipulated.

informational social influence The influence other people have on us because we want to be right.

Honey, when you grow up I want you to be assertive, independent and strong-willed. But while you're a kid, I want you to be passive, pliable and obedient.

www.betsystreeter.com

Betsy Streeter. Used with permission.

or may help us see things in ways that had not occurred to us. As a result, we may conform because we have come to agree with the group. The tendency to conform based on informational social influence depends especially on two factors: how confident we are in our own independent judgment and how well informed we perceive the group to be. For example, if you know little about computers and three of your acquaintances who are IT geeks tell you not to buy a particular brand of computer, you are likely to conform to their recommendation.

In contrast, **normative social influence** is the influence others have on us because we want them to like and approve of us. Thus, if a particular group is important to us, we might adopt a clothing style that people in the group wear or use the same slang words, and we might assume a certain set of attitudes that characterizes the group's members (Chen & others, 2006). This influence is evident whether the group is an inner-city gang or members of a profession such as medicine or law.

Obedience   **Obedience** is behavior that complies with the explicit demands of the individual in authority. That is, we are obedient when an authority figure demands that we do something, and we do it. How is obedience different from conformity? In conformity, people change their thinking or behavior so that it will be more like that of others. In obedience, there is an explicit demand to conform (Blass, 2004, 2007).

Obedient behavior sometimes can be distressingly cruel. Perhaps the most infamous example of the destructive nature of obedience is the Nazi crimes against Jews and others during World War II. More recent examples include the obedience of radical Muslims who are instructed to participate in suicide attacks against Israelis and Westerners, as well as that of U.S. military personnel at Abu Ghraib prison in Iraq, who justified their abuse of detainees by asserting that they were just "following orders." Millions of people throughout history have obeyed commands to commit terrible acts such as these.

A classic experiment by Stanley Milgram (1965, 1974) provides insight into such obedience. Imagine that, as part of an experiment in psychology, you are asked to deliver a series of painful electric shocks to another person. You are told that the purpose of the study is to determine the effects of punishment on memory. Your role is to be the "teacher" and to punish the mistakes made by the "learner." Each time the learner makes a mistake, you are to increase the intensity of the shock by a certain amount.

You are introduced to the learner, a nice 50-year-old man who mumbles something about having a heart condition. He is strapped to a chair in the next room; he communicates with you through an intercom. The apparatus in front of you has 30 switches, ranging from 15 volts (light) to 450 volts (marked as dangerous, "severe shock XXX"). Before this part of the experiment, you were given a 75-volt shock to see how it felt.

As the trials proceed, the learner quickly runs into trouble and is unable to give the correct answers. Should you shock him? As you increase the intensity of the shock, the learner says that he is in pain. At 150 volts, he demands to have the experiment stopped. At 180 volts, he cries out that he cannot stand it anymore. At 300 volts, he yells about his heart condition and pleads to be released. But if you hesitate in shocking the learner, the experimenter tells you that you have no choice; the experiment must continue. How far will you go?

Prior to doing the study, Milgram asked 40 psychiatrists how they thought individuals would respond to this situation. The psychiatrists predicted that most teachers would go no farther than 150 volts, that fewer than 1 in 25 would go as far as 300 volts, and that only 1 in 1,000 would deliver the full 450 volts. The psychiatrists, it turns out, were way off the mark. The majority of the teachers obeyed the experimenter. In fact, almost two-thirds delivered the full 450 volts. Figure 12.5 shows the results of the Milgram study.

By the way, the 50-year-old man is in league with the experimenter, another confederate. In Milgram's study, the learner is not being shocked at all. Of course, the teachers are completely unaware that the learner is pretending to be shocked.

As you might imagine, the teachers in this experiment were uneasy about shocking the learner. At 240 volts, one teacher responded, "240 volts delivered; aw, no. You mean I've got to keep going with that scale? No sir, I'm not going to kill that man—I'm not going to give him 450 volts!" (Milgram, 1965). At the very strong voltage, the learner quit responding. When the teacher asked the experimenter what to do, the experimenter simply instructed the teacher to continue the experiment and told him that it was his obligation to complete the job.

normative social influence The influence that other people have on us because we want them to like and approve of us.

obedience Behavior that complies with the explicit demands of the individual in authority.

In variations of the experiment, Milgram discovered that more people would disobey in certain circumstances. Disobedience was more common when participants could see others disobey, when the authority figure was not perceived to be legitimate and was not close by, and when the victim was made to seem more human.

Recently, the ethics of Milgram's studies have been questioned. The volunteer teachers in Milgram's experiment clearly felt anguish, and some were very disturbed about "harming" another individual. After the experiment, they were told that the learner had not really been shocked. But even though they were told that they had not actually shocked or harmed anyone, was the anguish imposed on them ethical?

Milgram's studies certainly revealed a great deal about human nature. None of the volunteers expressed regret that they had taken part (responses that, you might note, could be attributed to cognitive dissonance). However, the ethical guidelines of the American Psychological Association stress that researchers should obtain informed consent from their volunteers. Individuals are supposed to feel as good about themselves when the experiment is over as they did when it began. Under today's guidelines, it is unlikely that the Milgram experiment would have been approved.

Resistance to Social Influence   "If a man does not keep pace with his companions, perhaps it is because he hears a different drummer. Let him step to the music which he hears, however measured or far away." American essayist and philosopher Henry David Thoreau's words suggest that some of us resist social influence, just as Rosa Parks did while riding a bus in Alabama in 1955. It is safe to say that as we go through life, we are both conformists and nonconformists. Sometimes we stand up and stand out, and sometimes we simply go with the flow.

Importantly, our relationship to the social world is reciprocal. Individuals may try to control us, but we can exert personal control over our actions and influence others in turn (Bandura, 2007a, 2007b; Knowles, Nolan, & Riner, 2007; Knowles & Riner, 2006). Although resisting authority may be difficult, living with the knowledge that you compromised your own moral integrity may be more difficult in the long run.

Group Influence

On February 2, 2005, Chico State University student Matthew Carrington died following a fraternity hazing in the basement of the Chi Tau house. He and another pledge were verbally taunted and forced to do pushups in raw sewage that had leaked onto the basement floor. They were also compelled to drink gallons and gallons of water. Both young men vomited and urinated on themselves. Eventually, Matthew Carrington suffered a seizure, and he died of water intoxication. Among those who were arrested and convicted in his death were four fraternity brothers who had never been in trouble before. Indeed, the group's ringleader was Gabriel Maestretti, a deeply religious former altar boy, high school homecoming king, and volunteer coach. Why and how do individuals who would never perform destructive acts, if acting on their own, perpetrate them when in a group? This is the central question that has driven research in the social psychology of group influence.

Deindividuation   One process that sheds light on the behavior of individuals in groups is **deindividuation,** which occurs when being part of a group reduces personal identity and erodes the sense of personal responsibility (Dietz-Uhler, Bishop-Clark, & Howard, 2005; Zimbardo, 2007). Examples of the effects of deindividuation include wild street celebrations after a team's victory in the World Series or Super Bowl and Ku Klux Klan violence.

One explanation for deindividuation is that groups give us anonymity. When we are part of a group, we may act in an uninhibited way because we believe that no one will be able to identify us. Moreover, being in a group is not the only way we might deindividuate—

Voltage range and description

Percent of subjects stopping at each voltage level

FIGURE 12.5

Milgram Obedience Study A 50-year-old man, the "learner," is strapped into a chair. The experimenter makes it look as if a shock generator is being connected to his body through several electrodes. The chart shows the percentage of "teachers" who stopped shocking the learner at each voltage level.

deindividuation The reduction of personal identity and erosion of the sense of personal responsibility that can arise when one is part of a group.

The effects of deindividuation are visible in fans' emotional support of the home team, intimidating rallies such as those carried out by the Ku Klux Klan, and mass patriotic observances such as the Fourth of July celebration pictured here.

darkness, costumes, and disguises can also allow us to conceal our identity. To get a sense of the way deindividuation works, you might try a version of the following study next Halloween (Diener & others, 1976). One Halloween night, researchers greeted trick-or-treaters in two different ways. All of the children were greeted with a smile, and half of the children were asked their names. Then all of the children were offered the bowl of candy and were told, "Now just take one!" The children who had given their names first were much more likely to "just take one" (Diener & Diener, 1974).

A less benign example of deindividuation may be seen in research on the behavior of onlookers observing a person perched on a building ledge, threatening suicide (Mann, 1981). What factors predicted whether the onlookers would taunt the person, daring him or her to jump? Onlookers were more likely to chant "jump" if a number of others were present and it was nighttime. In a crowd and under cover of darkness, individuals behave in ways that they would never even consider if alone or in broad daylight.

Social Contagion Have you ever noticed that a movie you watched in a crowded theater seemed funnier than it did when you watched the DVD alone at home? People laugh more when others are laughing. Babies cry when other babies are crying. The effects of others on our behavior can take the form of **social contagion,** imitative behavior involving the spread of behavior, emotions, and ideas (Cohen & Prinstein, 2006). One way to observe social contagion is to sit in a quiet but crowded library and start coughing. You will soon notice others doing the same thing. Similarly, imagine that you are walking down the sidewalk and come upon a group of people who are all looking up. How likely is it that you can avoid the temptation of looking up to see what is so interesting to them?

Group Performance Are two or three heads better than one? Some studies reveal that we do better in groups; others show that we are more productive when we work alone (Paulus, 1989). We can make sense out of these contradictory findings by looking closely at the circumstances in which performance is being analyzed.

Social Facilitation Imagine singing a show tune as part of a large chorus. Then imagine singing the same song alone on a stage. Most of us find that the quality of our singing is somehow better when we have a group around us (or a loud shower running). **Social facilitation** occurs when an individual's performance improves because of the presence of others (Mendes, 2007). Robert Zajonc (1965) argued that the presence of other individuals arouses us. The arousal produces energy and facilitates our performance in groups. If our arousal is too high, however, we are unable to learn new or difficult tasks efficiently. Social facilitation, then, improves our performance on well-learned tasks. For new or difficult tasks, we might be best advised to work things out on our own before trying them in a group.

social contagion Imitative behavior involving the spread of behavior, emotions, and ideas.

social facilitation Improvement in an individual's performance because of the presence of others.

Social Loafing   Another factor in group performance is how closely our behavior is monitored. **Social loafing** refers to each person's tendency to exert less effort in a group because of reduced accountability for individual effort. The effect of social loafing is lowered group performance (Latané, 1981). The larger the group, the likelier it is that an individual can loaf without detection. Among the ways to decrease social loafing are to increase the identifiability and uniqueness of individual contributions, to simplify the evaluation of these contributions, and to make the group's task more attractive (Karau & Williams, 1993).

Social loafing commonly occurs when a group of students is assigned a class project, and it is one reason that some students intensely dislike group assignments. These same individuals will not be surprised to learn that under certain conditions, working with others can increase individual effort (Levine, 2000). For example, a person who views the group's task as important (say, a student who strongly wants an *A* on the project) and who does not expect other group members to contribute adequately is likely to work harder than usual—and perhaps to do most of the work himself or herself.

Group Interaction and Decision Making   Many of the decisions we make take place in groups—juries, teams, families, clubs, school boards, and the U.S. Senate, for example (Bright & Goodman-Delahunty, 2006; Crampton, 2007; Levine & Moreland, 2006; Peláez & Dona, 2006). What happens when people put their minds to the task of making a group decision? How do they decide whether a criminal is guilty, whether a country should attack another, whether a family should stay home or go on vacation, or whether sex education should be part of a school curriculum? Three aspects of group decision making bear special mention: *risky shift* and *group polarization; groupthink;* and *majority/minority influence.*

Risky Shift and Group Polarization   Imagine that you have a friend, Lisa, who works as an accountant. All her life Lisa has longed to be a writer. In fact, she believes that she has the next great American novel in her head and that she just needs time and energy to devote to writing it. Would you advise Lisa to quit her job and go for it? What if you knew beforehand that her chances of success were 50-50? How about 60-40? How much risk would you advise her to take?

In one investigation, fictitious dilemmas like this one were presented, and participants were asked how much risk the characters in the dilemmas should take (Stoner, 1961). When the individuals discussed the dilemmas as a group, they were more willing to respond that the characters should make riskier decisions than when they were queried alone. The so-called **risky shift** is the tendency for a group decision to be riskier than the average decision made by the individual group members. Many studies have been conducted on this topic with similar results (Goethals & Demorest, 1995).

We do not always make riskier decisions in a group than when alone, however; hundreds of research studies show that being in a group moves us more strongly in the direction of the position we initially held (Moscovici, 1985). The **group polarization effect** is the solidification and further strengthening of a position as a consequence of a group discussion. For instance, imagine a committed pro-choice and an equally committed anti-abortion politician in the U.S. Senate who listen to the same endless hours of committee discussion about various abortion-related amendments. Research indicates that neither is likely to be converted to a different point of view. After two years on the committee, each will be even more strongly committed to his or her position than before the deliberations began. Initially held views often become more polarized because of group discussion.

Group polarization may occur because, during the discussion, people hear new, more persuasive arguments that strengthen their original position. Group polarization also might arise because of social comparison. We may find that our opinion is not as extreme as others' opinions, and we might be influenced to take a stand at least as strong as the most extreme advocate's position.

Groupthink: Getting Along but Being Very, Very Wrong   **Groupthink** refers to group members' impaired decision making and avoidance of realistic appraisal in order to maintain group harmony. Instead of engaging in an open discussion of all the available information, in groupthink, members of a group place the highest value on conformity and

The research of Norman Triplett of Indiana University, viewed by some to be the first North American sport psychologist, found that cyclists performed better when they raced in groups than when they rode by themselves, against the clock.

social loafing Each person's tendency to exert less effort in a group because of reduced accountability for individual effort.

risky shift The tendency for a group decision to be riskier than the average decision made by individual group members.

group polarization effect The solidification and further strengthening of an individual's position as a consequence of a group discussion.

groupthink Group members' impaired decision making and avoidance of realistic appraisal to maintain group harmony.

unanimity. Members are encouraged to "get with the program," and dissent meets with very strong disapproval. Groupthink involves many heads but only one group mind.

Groupthink can result in disastrous decisions. Irving Janis (1972) introduced the concept of groupthink to explain a number of enormous decision-making errors throughout history. Such errors include the lack of U.S. preparation for the Japanese bombing of Pearl Harbor during World War II, the escalation of the Vietnam War in the 1960s, the Watergate cover-up in 1974, and the *Challenger* space shuttle disaster in 1986. After the September 11, 2001, terrorist attacks, the possibility that groupthink interfered with the proper implementation of intelligence reared its head. Whistleblower Colleen Rowley, an FBI special agent, publicized the fact that the FBI power hierarchy was simply unresponsive to information that might have helped prevent the attacks. More recently, many have criticized President George W. Bush and his cabinet for not listening to dissenting voices in the days leading up to the war in Iraq.

Symptoms of groupthink include overestimating the power and morality of one's group, close-mindedness and lack of willingness to hear all sides of an argument, and pressure for uniformity. Groupthink can occur whenever groups value conformity over accuracy. Groupthink can be prevented if groups avoid isolation, allow all sides of an argument to be aired, have an impartial leader, and include outside experts in the debate.

Majority and Minority Influence Most groups make decisions by voting and, even in the absence of groupthink, the majority usually wins. The majority exerts influence on group decision making through both informational influence (they have greater opportunity to share their views) and normative influence (they set group norms). Those who do not go along may be ignored or even given the boot.

Prospects might seem dim for minority opinion holders, but they can make a difference. Because it is outnumbered, the minority cannot win through normative pressure. Instead, it must do its work through informational pressure. If the minority presents its views consistently and confidently, then the majority is likelier to listen to the minority's perspectives. A powerful way that minority opinion holders can have influence is by winning over former majority members to their points of view.

REVIEW, ASSESS, AND SHARPEN YOUR THINKING

Review

3 Identify how people are influenced in social settings.
- Define conformity and obedience and describe the classic studies on these topics.
- Discuss the influence of groups on behavior and decision making.

Assess

1. Which of the following is related to lessened deindividuation?
   - A. larger groups
   - B. saying someone's name
   - C. darkness
   - D. disguises

2. What is the difference between conformity and obedience?
   - A. Conformity has a stronger influence on behavior than obedience.
   - B. Conformity does not involve an explicit command from others.
   - C. Conformity happens in small groups, whereas obedience happens in large groups.
   - D. Conformity is based on wanting to be right; obedience is based on wanting to be liked.

3. Someone who conforms to be liked is altering her or his behavior because of
   - A. obedience.
   - B. informational social influence.
   - C. the effect of confederates.
   - D. normative social influence.

4. How are group polarization and risky shift different?
   - A. Group polarization involves the firmness of decisions, whereas risky shift involves the extremeness of decisions.
   - B. Group polarization happens in large groups, whereas risky shift happens in small groups.
   - C. Risky shift involves deindividuation, whereas group polarization does not.
   - D. Decisions made via risky shift are more dangerous than those made via group polarization.

5. Social contagion is
   A. the tendency of people to perform better when in the presence of others.
   B. the rapid spreading of bad ideas within a group.
   C. the spreading of behavior that imitates others' actions, thoughts, or emotions.
   D. the influence of minority groups on the majority group.

Sharpen Your Thinking

Think of a time when you held a minority opinion in a group you were in. Did you succeed in winning others over to your side? Using the research on majority/minority influence, discuss why you think you were successful or not.

4 Intergroup Relations

Discuss intergroup relations.

Conflicts between groups, especially ethnic and cultural groups, are rampant around the world today (Stevens & Gielen, 2007; Tyler & De Cremer, 2006). The Islamic terrorist organization al-Qaeda attacks the United States and other countries that its members perceive to be too secular and materialistic. And the wronged nations retaliate. Israelis and Palestinians fight over territory in the Middle East, each claiming religious and historical rights to the disputed land. In countries across Africa, tribal chiefs try to craft a new social order favorable to their own rule. Prejudice, stereotyping, ethnocentrism, and other concepts introduced by social psychologists can help us understand the intensity of such cultural and ethnic conflicts and can provide important insights into how to reduce the conflicts (Sanchez-Burks, 2007).

Group Identity: Us Versus Them

Think about the groups of which you are a member—possibly social organizations, your ethnic group, your nationality. When someone asks you to identify yourself, how often do you respond by mentioning these group memberships? And how much does it matter to you whether the people you associate with are members of the same groups as you?

Social Identity   **Social identity** refers to the way we define ourselves in terms of our group membership (Deaux, 2001). In contrast to personal identity, which can be highly individualized, social identity assumes some commonalities with others. A person's social identity might include identifying with a religious group, a country, a social organization, a political party, and many other groups (Carney & others, 2007; Haslam & Reicher, 2006). These diverse forms of social identity reflect the numerous ways people connect to groups and social categories (Abrams & Hogg, 2004; Hogg & Abrams, 2007; Postmes & Jetten, 2006). Social psychologist Kay Deaux (2001) identified five distinct types of social identity: ethnic and religious, political, vocations and avocations, personal relationships, and stigmatized groups (Figure 12.6).

Group conflict such as that between Israelis and Palestinians in the Middle East and between clashing tribal chiefs in Sudan is rampant in the world today.

Ethnicity and Religion

Asian American
Jewish
Southern Baptist
West Indian

Political Affiliation

Feminist
Republican
Environmentalist

Vocations and Avocations

Psychologist
Artist
Athlete
Military veteran

Relationships

Mother
Parent
Teenager
Widow

Stigmatized Identities

Person with AIDS
Homeless person
Overweight person
Alcoholic

FIGURE 12.6

Types of Identity When we identify ourselves, we draw on a host of different characteristics associated with the different social groups to which we belong.

social identity The way individuals define themselves in terms of their group membership.

social identity theory Tajfel's theory that social identities are a crucial part of individuals' self-image and a valuable source of positive feelings about themselves.

ethnocentrism The tendency to favor one's own ethnic group over other groups.

prejudice An unjustified negative attitude toward an individual based on the individual's membership in a group.

For many people, ethnic identity and religious identity are central aspects of their social identity (Kroger, 2007; Phinney, 2006). Ethnic identity can be a source of pride for individuals. In the United States, special events celebrate the rich cultural contributions of many different groups to the society. Examples include Black History Month, Chinese New Year, and various festivals enjoyed by Irish Americans, Italian Americans, Arab Americans, Polish Americans, and many others. In a sense, these celebrations reflect in-group pride. Also, these experiences may provide individuals with an important resource in coping with biases they may encounter in life. African Americans and Latinos, for example, as well as members of other groups such as women, gay men, and lesbians, often assert in-group pride to counter the negative messages transmitted by society about their group (Crocker, Major, & Steele, 1998). Indeed, ethnic identity may be a resource particularly for those in minority groups, so that feeling connected to one's ethnic group may buffer individuals from the stressful effects of injustice (Sellers & Shelton, 2003; Sellers & others, 2006).

Social psychologist Henry Tajfel (1978), himself a survivor of the Holocaust, wanted to explain the extreme violence and prejudice that his religious group (Jews) experienced. Tajfel's **social identity theory** states that our social identities are a crucial part of our self-image and a valuable source of positive feelings about ourselves. In order to feel good about ourselves, we need to feel good about the groups to which we belong. For this reason, when assigned to a group, individuals invariably think of that group as an *in-group,* a group that has special value, in comparison with other groups, called *out-groups*. To improve our self-image, we continually compare our in-groups with out-groups (Parks, 2007). In the process, we often focus more on the differences between the two groups than on their similarities.

Imagine two NBA fans: one a Phoenix Suns fan, the other a Dallas Mavericks fan. As these two fans talk, they are less likely to discuss how much they both like basketball than to argue about the virtues of their teams. As they strive to promote their social identities, they soon lapse into self-congratulatory remarks about their own team and nasty comments about the opposing team. In short order, the theme of the conversation becomes, "My team is good and I am good. Your team is bad and you are bad." And so it goes with the sexes, ethnic groups, nations, socioeconomic groups, religions, sororities, fraternities, and countless other groups. These comparisons often lead to competition and even discrimination against other groups. Thus, social identity theory helps explain prejudice and conflict between groups.

Research by Tajfel (1978) (along with a host of other researchers who have used his theory) showed how easy it is to lead people to think in terms of "us" and "them." In one experiment, he assigned those who overestimated the number of dots on a screen to one group and those who underestimated the number to another group. Such groups are referred to as *minimal groups,* because group assignment is completely arbitrary and meaningless. Once assigned to the two groups, the participants were asked to award money to the other participants. Invariably, individuals awarded money only to members of their own group. If we favor even the members of a group that was formed based on such trivial criteria, it is no wonder that we show intense in-group favoritism when differences are not so trivial.

Ethnocentrism The tendency to favor one's own ethnic group over other groups is called **ethnocentrism.** Ethnocentrism does not simply mean taking pride in one's group; it also involves asserting the group's superiority over other groups. As such, ethnocentrism encourages in-group/out-group, we/they thinking (Brewer, 2007; Smith, Bond, & Kagitcibasi, 2006). Consequently, ethnocentrism implies that ethnic out-groups are not simply different; they are worse than one's group. Hence ethnocentrism may underlie prejudice.

Prejudice

Prejudice is an unjustified negative attitude toward an individual based on the individual's membership in a group. The group can be made up of people of a particular ethnicity, sex,

Ethnic identity evokes pride in many people. Top (L–R): Here, Mexicans celebrate Cinco de Mayo; an African American man shops for ethnic clothing in Los Angeles; Bottom (L–R): Italian American soccer fans in Boston's North End rejoice at the Italian soccer team's World Cup win; and a Native American boy honors his heritage.

age, religion, or nationality, or it can consist of people who are different in some other way from a prejudiced person (Amodio & Devine, 2006; Diekman & Eagly, 2007; Sanchez-Burks, 2007). Prejudice as a worldwide phenomenon can be seen in many eruptions of hatred in human history. In the Balkan Peninsula of eastern Europe, Serbs were so prejudiced against Bosnians that they pursued a policy of "ethnic cleansing." Hutus in Rwanda were so prejudiced against Tutsis that they went on a murderous rampage, hacking off their arms and legs with machetes. Euro-Americans were so prejudiced against Native Americans that they systematically robbed them of their property and self-respect, killed them, and herded the survivors, like animals, onto reservations.

The most blatant instance of destructive prejudice in U.S. history is racial prejudice against African Americans. When Africans were brought to colonial America as slaves, they were considered property and treated inhumanely. In the first half of the twentieth century, most African Americans still lived in the South and remained largely segregated from White society by law; restaurants, movie theaters, and buses had separate areas for Whites and African Americans.

Racial prejudice may seem, at times, to be a thing of the past. Indeed, starting in the 1930s, polls taken over the years have shown that White Americans who once openly stated negative views about African Americans are now much less likely to admit to such views. But we have only to consider recent history to realize that there is still work to be done.

Racial prejudice was reflected in some news stories about Hurricane Katrina. Reports referred to African American victims who were looking for food as "looting," but described White victims who were doing the same thing as "finding" food.

In the aftermath of Hurricane Katrina in New Orleans, news reports referred to White victims as "finding" food but described African Americans who were doing the same things as "looting." Indeed, the apparent delay in getting aid to desperate hurricane survivors prompted rapper Kanye West to utter the highly controversial comment on a telethon that "George Bush doesn't care about Black people."

In the United States a person's views about race relations depend very much on that individual's own race and experience. A 2006 poll showed that nearly half (49 percent) of Blacks thought racial bias was a serious problem in the United States, compared to just 18 percent of Whites (CNN, 2006). In the same poll, fully 88 percent of individuals answered "no" to the question "Are you racist?"

In a striking study, Marianne Bertrand and Sendhil Mullainathan (2004) sent out 5,000 résumés in response to 1,200 job ads placed in newspapers in Chicago and Boston. They constructed résumés so that applicants were identical in qualifications but differed in how stereotypically White or Black their names sounded. "White" names included Meredith, Emily, Brad, and Greg. "Black" names included Tamika, Lakisha, Darnell, and Kareem. The researchers found that, even with identical qualifications, the White applicants were 50 percent more likely to be called for an interview.

Although few admit to being racist, racial bias still clearly exists in U.S. society. Even decades after legal segregation was abolished, a much higher percentage of African Americans than Whites live in impoverished neighborhoods and lack access to good schools, jobs, and healthcare. The potential role of race in perpetuating these disparities certainly came to the fore following Hurricane Katrina.

Because racial prejudice is socially unacceptable, few people today would readily admit to racist or prejudicial views (as shown in the poll mentioned above). It is not clear whether this situation is due to an actual change of heart or to a recognition of this changing social standard. Today, prejudiced individuals are more likely than before to appear unprejudiced on the surface while nevertheless holding racist views at a deeper level (Henry & Sears, 2007; Sears & Henry, 2007). Indeed, individuals may not be consciously aware of their own racial biases.

To confront this problem, social psychologists examine prejudicial attitudes on two levels—*explicit* or *overt racism* and *implicit* or *covert racism.* Explicit racism is a person's conscious and openly shared attitude. Implicit racism refers to attitudes that exist on a deeper, hidden level. Explicit and implicit attitudes predict different kinds of behavior. For instance, in one study a sample of White college students completed measures of explicit and implicit attitudes toward Black people (Dovidio, Kawakami, & Gaertner, 2002). Those students then interacted with a Black student partner. Explicit prejudice predicted what people said to a person of a different race—that is, White students who said they were not prejudiced were unlikely to say overtly racist things. Explicit prejudice also predicted how friendly *White individuals* felt they had behaved toward the person of a different race. However, implicit prejudice related to *nonverbal* aspects of the interaction, such as how close the White students sat to their partners as well as their facial expressions.

Implicit racism can be measured using the Implicit Associations Test, a computerized survey that assesses the ease with which a person can associate a Black or White person with good things (for example, flowers) or bad things (for example, misery) (Carney & others, 2007; Greenwald & Banaji, 1995; Nosek & Banaji, 2007; Nosek, Greenwald, & Banaji, 2006). This test is based on the idea that preexisting biases may make it easier to associate some social stimuli with positive rather than negative items.

How prejudiced are you? To find out, complete the Implicit Associations Test at **https://implicit.harvard.edu/implicit.**

Of course, African Americans are not the only ethnic minority groups that have been subjected to prejudice in the United States. Historically, Native Americans, as well as immigrants from Europe, Asia, and other parts of the world, have struggled against negative attitudes. Many Latinos, Vietnamese, and others also live in poverty and may have limited educational and employment opportunities.

Lesbians and gays also have been subjected to considerable prejudice by the heterosexual majority (Peplau & Fingerhut, 2007; Savin-Williams, 2006). This prejudice has been so intense that most homosexuals have stayed "in the closet" until relatively recently, hiding their sexual preferences for fear of losing their families, friends, jobs, or even their lives.

Why do people develop prejudice? Social psychologists have explored a number of possible reasons. Competition between groups, especially when resources are scarce, can contribute to prejudice. For example, immigrants often compete with established low-income members of a society for jobs—a situation that can lead to persistent conflict between the two groups. Cultural learning is also clearly involved. Children can adopt the prejudicial attitudes of their families and friends before they even meet a person from an outgroup. And when people are feeling bad about themselves, they might bolster their self-esteem by demeaning outgroup members.

A final factor that might underlie prejudice comes from the limits on our information-processing abilities. As already noted, human beings are limited in their capacity for effortful thought, but they face a social environment that is quite complex. To simplify the challenge of understanding others' behavior, people use categories or stereotypes. Stereotypes can be a powerful force in developing and maintaining prejudicial attitudes.

Stereotyping and Prejudice At the very root of prejudice is a *stereotype,* a generalization about a group. Stereotypes may lead to prejudice when they contain negative information, and may prevent individuals from noticing the variations that exist in any group (Wegener, Clark, & Petty, 2006). Researchers have found that we are less likely to detect variations among individuals who belong to "other" groups than among individuals who belong to "our" group. So, we might see the people in our in-group as varied, unique individuals while viewing the members of the out-groups as "all the same." Thinking that "they all look alike" can be a particular concern in the context of eyewitness identification (Brigham, 1986).

Discrimination Having a stereotype does not mean that you have to act on it. But if you do act on your prejudices, you may be guilty of **discrimination,** an unjustified negative or harmful action toward a member of a group simply because the person belongs to that group. Discrimination results when negative emotional reactions combine with prejudiced beliefs and are translated into behavior (Bretherton, 2007; Crosby & Ropp, 2002). Discrimination

discrimination An unjustified negative or harmful action toward a member of a group simply because he or she is a member of that group.

is the use of the power that comes from being a member of a particular group to treat others—for example, women or individuals from ethnic minority groups—unfairly.

Ways to Improve Interethnic Relations

Martin Luther King, Jr., said, "I have a dream that my four little children will one day live in a nation where they will not be judged by the color of their skin but by the content of their character." How might we attain the world without prejudice and discrimination that King envisioned? One pathway might be for people to come to know one another better so that they can all get along. Camps where Palestinian and Israeli children gather to "play for peace" (for example, in 2005 in Switzerland and 2000 in France) were established with the hope that such contact might lead to a more peaceful world. Yet in daily life people interact with individuals from other ethnic groups a great deal, and this contact does not necessarily lead to tolerance or warm relations.

Indeed, researchers have consistently found that contact itself—attending the same school, being next-door neighbors, or working in the same company—does not necessarily improve one's relations with people from other ethnic backgrounds (Brewer & Brown, 1998). Rather than focusing on contact per se, researchers have examined how various features of a contact situation may be optimal for reducing prejudice and promoting intergroup harmony. Studies have shown that contact is more effective if the people involved think that they are of equal status, feel that an authority figure sanctions their positive relationships, and believe that friendship might emerge from the interaction (Pettigrew & Tropp, 2006).

One important feature of optimal intergroup contact is *task-oriented cooperation*—working together on a shared goal. The significance of task-oriented cooperation to improving intergroup relations has been demonstrated in Sherif's Robbers Cave study and Aronson's jigsaw classroom.

Sherif's Robbers Cave Study It may be hard to imagine in our post-*Survivor* era, but even before Jeff Probst started handing out color-coded "buffs" on the TV show *Survivor* to contestants vying for a million dollars, Muzafer Sherif and his colleagues (1961) had the idea of exploring group processes by assigning 11-year-old boys to two competitive groups in a summer camp called Robbers Cave in Oklahoma. One group became known as the Rattlers, and the other was called the Eagles. If you have watched reality television, you have some idea how the experiment went.

Near the end of the first week of camp, each group learned of the other's existence. It took little time for "we/they" talk to surface ("They had better not be on our ball field." "Did you see the way one of them was sneaking around?"). Sherif, who disguised himself as a janitor so that he could unobtrusively observe the Rattlers and Eagles, arranged for the two groups to compete in baseball, touch football, and tug-of-war. Counselors manipulated and judged events so the teams were close. Each team perceived the other to be competing unfairly. Raiding the other group's area, burning the other group's flag, and fighting resulted. The Rattlers and Eagles also derided one another, holding their noses in the air as they crossed paths. Rattlers described all Rattlers as brave, tough, and friendly and called all Eagles sneaky and smart alecks. The Eagles reciprocated by calling the Rattlers crybabies.

After "we/they" conflict transformed the Rattlers and Eagles into opposing "armies," Sherif devised ways to reduce the hatred between the groups. He tried noncompetitive contact, but that did not work. Only when Sherif required both groups to work cooperatively to solve a problem did the Rattlers and Eagles develop a positive relationship. Sherif created tasks that required the efforts of both groups: working together to repair the only water supply to the camp, pooling their money to rent a movie, and cooperating to pull the camp truck out of a ditch. Figure 12.7 shows how competitive and cooperative activities changed perceptions of the out-group.

Aronson's Jigsaw Classroom Sherif's idea, creating cooperation between groups rather than competition, was later tested in the real world in Austin, Texas, when ethnic tensions increased and violence erupted among African Americans, Mexican Americans, and Whites in desegregated schools. Eliot Aronson, a prominent social psychologist,

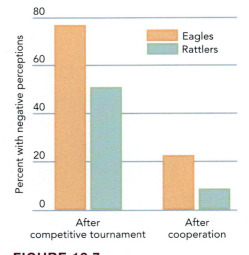

FIGURE 12.7

Attitudes Toward the Out-Group Following Competitive and Cooperative Activities In Sherif's research, hostility peaked after an athletic tournament, as reflected in the high percentage of Eagles and Rattlers who perceived the other group unfavorably following this event. However, after the groups worked together to reach a goal, their unfavorable attitudes toward each other dropped considerably.

was asked to help address the problem. Aronson (1986) thought it was more important to prevent ethnic hostility than to control it.

Aronson stressed that the reward structure of the classrooms needed to be changed from a setting of unequal competition to one of cooperation among equals, without making any curriculum changes. To accomplish this goal, he put together the *jigsaw classroom*. The jigsaw classroom works by creating a situation in which all of the students have to pull together to get the "big picture." Let's say we have a class of 30 students, some White, some African American, and some Latino. The academic goal is to learn about the life of the Indian political and spiritual leader Mahatma Gandhi. The class might be broken up into five study groups of six students each, with the groups being as equal as possible in ethnic composition and academic achievement level. Learning about Gandhi's life becomes a class project divided into six parts, with one part given to each member of the six-person group. The components might be different books about Gandhi or information about different aspects of his life. The parts are like the pieces of a jigsaw puzzle: They have to be put together to form the complete puzzle.

Aronson developed the concept of the jigsaw classroom to reduce ethnic conflict.

The strategy of emphasizing cooperation rather than competition and the jigsaw approach have been widely used in U.S. classrooms (Deutsch, 2006; Deutsch, Coleman, & Marcus, 2006). A number of studies reveal that this type of cooperative learning is associated with increased self-esteem, better academic performance, friendships among classmates, and improved interethnic perceptions (Slavin, 2006).

 REVIEW, ASSESS, AND SHARPEN YOUR THINKING

Review

4 Discuss intergroup relations.

- Describe Tajfel's social identity theory.
- Explain what prejudice is and discuss how social psychologists study it.
- Describe the role of cooperative tasks in improving intergroup relations.

Assess

1. **What does social identity theory have to say about groups?**
   A. Groups naturally cooperate with one another.
   B. Members of the in-group feel positively about members of the out-group.
   C. Groups will tend to highlight their differences rather than their similarities.
   D. Group membership has little to do with our sense of self.

2. **What is a minimal group?**
   A. an in-group
   B. an out-group
   C. a small group
   D. an arbitrarily formed group

3. **How is ethnocentrism different from social identity theory?**
   A. Ethnocentrism focuses on ethnic groups; social identity theory focuses on all groups to which one belongs.

   B. Ethnocentrism focuses on feeling pride in the group to which one belongs; social identity theory focuses on feeling envy of the group to which one does not belong.
   C. Ethnocentrism focuses on in-groups; social identity theory focuses on out-groups.
   D. Ethnocentrism focuses on arbitrary meaningful groups; social identity theory focuses on meaningful groups.

4. **A White woman says she is not racist but avoids sitting near Black individuals. She has**
   A. high explicit racism, low implicit racism.
   B. high explicit racism, high implicit racism.
   C. low explicit racism, low implicit racism.
   D. low explicit racism, high implicit racism.

5. **What did the Robbers Cave study reveal about reducing prejudice?**
   A. Prejudice is almost impossible to reduce.
   B. Prejudice can be reduced by working together toward a common goal.
   C. Prejudice can be reduced by competitive contact with members of other groups.
   D. Prejudice can be prevented by placing people into groups.

Sharpen Your Thinking

Describe the first time you realized that there was such a thing as race. Were you a child? How might that early experience explain your current attitudes?

5 Close Relationships

Explain the nature of close relationships.

If you are asked to make three wishes for anything at all, chances are one of those wishes will be for love, marriage, or a partner to share your life (King & Broyles, 1997). Along with good health and happiness, close relationships figure prominently in most notions of a good life. Every day we see commercials lauding the ability of this or that Internet dating service to link us up with the love of our life. One site even promises, "Find true love in 1 year or your money back." Indeed, U.S. consumers spent more than $245 million on Internet personals and dating services in the first 6 months of 2005 (Online Publishers Association, 2005).

Because close romantic relationships are so crucially important for most of us, it is no wonder that social psychologists should be interested in studying this fascinating aspect of human existence. Indeed, a vast literature has accumulated in social psychology, examining attraction, love, and intimacy.

Attraction

Research on interpersonal attraction has illuminated various factors that attempt to demystify the process of becoming attracted to someone.

Proximity, Acquaintance, and Similarity "If you can't be with the one you love, love the one you're with"—the song lyrics ring true at least with regard to one of the most important determinants of attraction. It is very unlikely that you are going to become attracted to someone without meeting the person. Proximity, or physical closeness, is a strong predictor of attraction. You are more likely to become attracted to an individual you pass in the hall every day than someone you rarely see. One potential mechanism for the role of proximity in attraction is the mere exposure effect (Zajonc, 1968, 2001). The **mere exposure effect** means that the more we encounter someone or something (a person, a word, an image), the more likely we are to start liking the person or thing even if we do not realize we have seen it before.

Rather surprisingly, we are not only more likely to be attracted to people whom we have seen before, but also more likely to like someone if we are led to believe we will be meeting that person. Let's say you are sitting in a room and an experimenter tells you there are two strangers next door, one of whom you will be meeting and the other not. Research shows that you are likely to begin to like the first person, in anticipation of your interaction (Insko & Wilson, 1977). In addition, if we find out that someone whom we do not know yet already likes us, that is a sure sign that we will find ourselves attracted to that person—in other words, we like those who like us. (For one thing, we know that they have excellent taste.) Potential matchmakers take note: If you want to join a pair of

"Can we log on together?"

© CartoonStock.com

---

mere exposure effect The outcome that the more we encounter someone or something (a person, a word, an image), the more likely we are to start liking the person or thing even if we do not realize we have seen it before.

friends up in a romantic relationship, tell each of them how much the other liked his or her picture!

In addition to proximity and the promise of acquaintanceship, similarity plays an important role in attraction. We have all heard that opposites attract, but what is true of magnets is not true of human beings, at least not typically. We like to associate with people who are similar to us (Berscheid, 2000). Our friends and lovers are much more like us than unlike us. We have similar attitudes, behavior patterns, taste in clothes, intelligence, personality, other friends, values, lifestyle, physical attractiveness, and so on. How does this finding explain those couples whom we all know who appear to be quite different from each other? One important distinction to consider is the difference between actual similarity and perceived similarity. Couples who like each other may overestimate their similarity, in a version of the false consensus effect. Perceived similarity may be more important than actual similarity in longer-term relationships.

The concept of *consensual validation* explains why people are attracted to others who are similar to them. Our own attitudes and behavior are supported when someone else's attitudes and behavior are similar to ours—their attitudes and behavior validate ours. Another reason that similarity matters is that we tend to shy away from the unknown. Similarity implies that we will enjoy doing things with another person who likes the same things and has similar attitudes. One study showed this sort of similarity to be especially important in successful marriages (Swann, De La Ronde, & Hixon, 1994).

Evolutionary Approaches to Attraction　Evolutionary psychologists focus on gender differences in the variables that account for attraction (Buss, 2008). From this perspective, the goal for both men and women is to procreate. For men, this evolutionary task is complicated by the fact that in the human species, paternity is somewhat more mysterious than motherhood. In order to be sure that a woman is not already pregnant with another man's child, the evolutionary approach states, men should be more attracted to younger women. For women, the task of producing offspring is an innately difficult one. Although a man might focus on quantity of sexual partners, a woman must focus on quality and search for a mate who will invest his resources in her and her offspring (Caporeal, 2007).

These ideas have been shown to be manifested in personal ads. When men seek women, they look for youth and beauty (a potential proxy for health and fertility), and they offer resources (for example, by describing themselves as "professional homeowner"). When women place ads seeking men, they are more likely to offer youth and beauty and to seek resources. The personal ads of gay men and lesbians have offered an intriguing context for consideration. In general, this research has supported the notion that gay men are indeed men, and lesbians are women. That is, gay men tend to seek youth and beauty, whereas lesbians seek personal qualities such as stability and a sense of humor.

Although evolutionary approaches tend to focus on the role of physical attractiveness in human mating (especially for men), research has shown that it is not the case that everyone wants a "10." Rather, many couples support a "matching hypothesis"—the 10's end up with the other 10's, and the 5's are happily coupled with the other 5's (Berscheid & others, 1971).

Love

Some relationships never progress much beyond the attraction stage. Other relationships deepen to friendship and perhaps even to love (Berscheid, 2006). Here we consider two types of love: romantic and affectionate.

Romantic and Affectionate Love　Poets, playwrights, and musicians through the ages have celebrated the fiery passion of romantic love—and lamented the searing pain when it fails. Think about songs and books that hit the top of the charts. Chances are, they are about romantic love.

Romantic love, also called *passionate love,* is love with strong components of sexuality and infatuation, and it often predominates in the early part of a love relationship (Hendrick

Friends often share similar attitudes, behavior, taste in clothing, personalities and lifestyles.

romantic love Also called passionate love; the type of love that has strong components of sexuality and infatuation and often predominates in the early part of a love relationship.

As love matures, passionate love tends to give way to affectionate love.

& Hendrick, 2006). Ellen Berscheid (1988) says that it is romantic love we mean when we say that we are "in love" with someone. It is romantic love she believes we need to understand if we are to learn what love is all about. Berscheid believes that sexual desire is the most important ingredient of romantic love.

Love is more than just passion. **Affectionate love,** also called companionate love, is the type of love that occurs when individuals desire to have the other person near and have a deep, caring affection for the person. There is a growing belief that the early stages of love have more romantic ingredients and that as love matures, passion tends to give way to affection (Berscheid & Regan, 2005).

Gender and Love   Of course, love is one of the central contexts where we ask questions about gender. We have all heard that women are from Venus and men are from Mars. Research on gender and love shows that men and women are both from planet earth. In general, men and women are much more similar than different when it comes to relationships (Hyde, 2005, 2007).

Still, there are some differences, although they are not always what you might expect. Do women and men hold different views of love? One study found that men conceptualize love in terms of passion, whereas women think of love more in terms of friendship (Fehr & Broughton, 2001). However, both women and men view love in affectionate terms. Although we often think of romantic love as a "chick thing," men, not women, are the ones who fall in love more quickly and easily (Dion & Dion, 2001). Men are also less likely than their female partners to break up premarital relationships.

Models of Close Relationships: Making Love Work

As if understanding attraction and love were not difficult enough, the question that truly plagues us in modern society is "How do we make love last?" The United States is the most divorce-prone nation in the world, with 50 percent of marriages in this country ending in divorce (Popenoe & Whitehead, 2006). Several factors predict whether a relationship will end in divorce. Couples who marry after age 20, who come from stable two-parent homes, and who are well- and similarly educated are less likely to divorce (Myers, 2000). Also, as the description of John Gottman's (2006) research in Chapter 4 indicates, successful marriage partners talk positively about their relationship, are friends, do not try to control their partner, and solve conflicts together.

Social psychologists have provided a number of theories and bodies of research to examine the processes by which couples stay together. Most of these findings have been shown to apply to heterosexual and homosexual couples alike (Peplau & Fingerhut, 2007).

Social Exchange Theory: The Importance of Equity   The social exchange approach to close relationships focuses on the costs and benefits of one's romantic partner. **Social exchange theory** is based on the notion of social relationships as involving an exchange of goods, the objective of which is to minimize costs and maximize benefits. This theory looks at human relations as an exchange of rewards between actors. According to social exchange theory, people's feelings about their relationships should be a function of how fair they feel the exchange has been. Essentially, social exchange theory asserts that we keep a mental balance sheet, tallying the plusses and minuses associated with our romantic partner—what we put in ("I paid for our last date") and what we get out ("He brought me flowers"). From this perspective, the most important predictor of relationship success is equity—that is, having both partners feel that each is doing his or her "fair share."

Early in relationships especially, equity (getting out what you put in) is a good predictor of satisfaction (DeMaris, 2007; Hendrick & Hendrick, 2006). However, as relationships progress, equity may no longer apply. In fact, research shows that over time, this kind of accounting not only is less likely to explain what happens in a relationship but also becomes distasteful to the partners. Happily married couples are less likely to

affectionate love Also called companionate love; the type of love that occurs when individuals desire to have the other person near and have a deep, caring affection for the person.

social exchange theory A theory based on the notion of social relationships as involving an exchange of goods, the objective of which is to minimize costs and maximize benefits.

keep track of "what I get versus what I give" and in fact will avoid thinking about the costs and benefits of their relationships (Buunk & Van Yperen, 1991; Clark & Chrisman, 1994). Surely we can all think of long-term relationships in which one partner remains committed even when the benefits are hard for the outsider to see—as in the case where the person's romantic partner is gravely ill for a long period of time.

Investment and Positive Illusions: How the Self Invests in Another Person Another way to think about long-term romantic relationships is to focus on the underlying factors that characterize stable, happy relationships compared to others. The **investment model** examines the ways that commitment, investment, and the availability of attractive alternative partners predict satisfaction and stability in relationships (Rusbult & others, 2004). From this perspective, long-term relationships are likely to continue when both partners are committed and invested in the relationship and when there are few attractive tempting alternatives around. Research in this tradition has shown that college students who are committed to their romantic partners are less likely to cheat on them sexually during spring break (Drigotas, Safstrom, & Gentilia, 1999). In addition, commitment predicts a willingness to sacrifice for a romantic partner. For example, in one study, individuals were given a chance to climb up and down a short staircase, over and over, to spare their partner from having to do so. Those who were more committed to their partner worked harder to climb up and down repeatedly, to spare their loved one the burden (Van Lange & others, 1997).

Research from the investment model perspective has also shown how being in a relationship can affect personal development. According to Caryl Rusbult and her colleagues, the "Michelangelo" phenomenon occurs when two people are in a healthy relationship (Drigotas & others, 1999; Kumashiro & others, 2006; Rusbult & others, 2005). Michelangelo said that he did not force a piece of marble into the form he wanted it to take; rather, he brought out the beautiful form that was embedded in the stone. Similarly, our close relationship partners help us to become the person we were meant to be, through their encouragement and support (Drigotas, 2002).

An alternative approach to studying successful relationships involves examining the role of positive illusions in stable, long-term relationships (Murray, Holmes, & Griffin, 2004). As you may recall, self-esteem is related to having a variety of overly positive views of the self. Research has shown that romantic partners tend to extend the same sorts of "breaks" to each other. Satisfied couples tend to view each other in overly positive ways. In addition, happy couples are more likely to link negative characteristics to more positive ones ("He works such long hours because he cares about our family so much") or to transform negative characteristics so that they become more positive ("Her sloppiness is kind of cute in such a capable, competent person").

© Mike Baldwin/Cornered

He gave her a big bear hug. The kind that says, I love you, I'll never leave you, I'm possessive, needy and insecure.

© CartoonStock.com

investment model A model emphasizing the ways that commitment, investment, and the availability of attractive alternative partners predict satisfaction and stability in relationships.

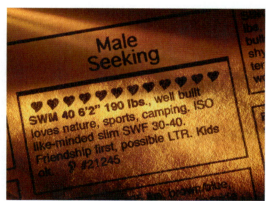

 REVIEW, ASSESS, AND SHARPEN YOUR THINKING

Review

5 Explain the nature of close relations.
- Describe the factors associated with attraction.
- Discuss how social psychologists think about love.
- Identify and summarize three approaches to adult romantic relationships.

Assess

1. **What does social exchange theory tell us about happiness in relationships?**
   A. We are happiest when we are giving in a relationship.
   B. We are happiest when we are receiving in a relationship.
   C. We are happiest when there is a balance between giving and receiving.
   D. Equity is only important to happiness in long-lasting relationships.

2. **Which of the following explains the finding that the more we are exposed to someone, the more we like that person?**
   A. consensual validation   B. mere exposure effect
   C. investment model   D. social exchange theory

3. **Consensual validation would predict**
   A. that opposites attract.
   B. that relationships with more give and take are best.

   C. that we are attracted to people who are similar to us.
   D. that romantic love is more important than affectionate love.

4. **Affectionate love is more common _____, whereas romantic love is more common _____.**
   A. in men, in women
   B. in women, in men
   C. early in a relationship, later in a relationship
   D. later in a relationship, early in a relationship

5. **Which of the following is not a component of the investment model?**
   A. availability of other romantic partners
   B. stability
   C. investment
   D. commitment

Sharpen Your Thinking

If you were a researcher interested in studying the process of falling in love, what type of research would you do? What variables do you think are most important in the experience of love?

6 Social Psychology and Health and Wellness

Describe social processes affecting health and wellness.

The principles of social psychology have provided a strong foundation for ongoing research in the areas of health and wellness (Kok & de Vries, 2006; Taylor & Stanton, 2007). For instance, social psychological research on persuasion has been applied to the task of creating messages to change attitudes and behaviors that have relevance to smoking and breast self-examinations (Fry & Prentice-Dunn, 2006; Kelly & others, 2006). Knowledge about social comparison has helped researchers in health and wellness to examine coping and illness (Buunk & others, 2006).

Research has also addressed the health implications of altruism. For example, a study of 423 older adult couples who were followed for 5 years revealed the benefits of altruism for physical health (Brown & others, 2003). At the beginning of the study, the couples were asked about the extent to which they had given or received emotional or practical help in the past year. Five years later, those who said they had helped others were half as likely to have died. One possible reason for this finding is that helping others may reduce the output of stress hormones, an effect that improves cardiovascular health and strengthens the immune system (Cacioppo & Berntson, 2007; Cacioppo, Tassinary, & Berntson, 2007).

In general, research on health and wellness has shown, again and again, that social ties are an important, if not the most important, variable in predicting health. A long list of studies supports this notion. In a landmark study, social isolation had six times the effect on mortality rates that cigarette smoking had (House, Landis, & Umberson, 1988). In another study involving 1,234 heart attack patients, those living alone were nearly twice as likely to have a second heart attack (Case & others, 1992). In a study of leukemia patients, of those who said that they had little support prior to undergoing a bone marrow transplant, only 20 percent were alive 2 years later, compared to 54 percent who reported that they felt strong support (Colón & others, 1991). Research shows, too, that widows die at a rate that is 3 to 13 times higher than that of married women for every known cause of death (Wortman & Boerner, 2007).

Having diverse social ties may be especially important in coping with stress (Cacioppo & others, 2007; Taylor, 2007; Taylor & Gonzaga, 2007; Taylor & Stanton, 2007). People who participate in more diverse social networks—for example, having a close relationship with a partner; interacting with family members, friends, neighbors, and fellow workers; and belonging to social and religious groups—live longer than people with fewer types of social relationships (Vogt & others, 1992). One study investigated the effects of diverse social ties on the susceptibility to getting a common cold (Cohen & others, 1997). Individuals reported the extent of their participation in 12 types of social ties. Then they were given nasal drops containing a cold virus and monitored for the appearance of a cold. Individuals with more diverse social ties were less likely to get a cold than their counterparts with less diverse social networks. One reason that these social ties are so important is that they indicate the level of social support a person is likely to receive.

Social Support and Health

Social support is information and feedback from others indicating that one is loved and cared for, esteemed and valued, and included in a network of communication and mutual obligation. Social support has three types of benefits: tangible assistance, information, and emotional support (Taylor, 2007):

- *Tangible assistance:* Family and friends can provide goods and services in stressful circumstances. For example, gifts of food are often given after a death in the family occurs, so that bereaved family members will not have to cook at a time when their energy and motivation are low.

- *Information:* Individuals who provide support can also recommend specific actions and plans to help the person under stress cope more successfully. Friends may notice that a co-worker is overloaded with work and suggest ways for him or her to manage time more efficiently or to delegate tasks more effectively.

- *Emotional support:* In stressful situations, individuals often suffer emotionally and may develop depression, anxiety, and loss of self-esteem. Friends and family can reassure the person under stress that he or she is a valuable individual who is loved by others. Knowing that others care allows a person to approach stress and to cope with stress with greater assurance.

One means by which people gain support during difficult times is through social sharing—turning to others who act as a sounding board or a willing ear. The importance of having people to talk with was demonstrated dramatically in a study of women with breast cancer: Being in a support group led to an increase in survival time (Spiegel & others, 1989).

Another way that some people try to find social support and make social connections is through the Internet. Sitting in front of a computer alone is not necessarily the optimal way to forge social connections, and recent studies indicate that extensive use of the Internet is related to loneliness (Carden & Rettew, 2006; Matsuba, 2006). However, some people use the Internet to form potentially strong new ties. Especially in the case of socially anxious and lonely individuals, the Internet may provide a positive way to make new contacts that eventually lead to face-to-face meetings and possibly even intimate relationships (Campbell, Cumming, & Hughes, 2006).

Sometimes, social sharing does not have to be very social to be helpful. As noted in Chapter 2, James Pennebaker and his colleagues have demonstrated

social support Information and feedback from others that one is loved and cared for, esteemed and valued, and included in a network of communication and mutual obligation.

Bob searched far and wide for his soul mate. It looked promising, aside from the language barrier and shipping costs.

© CartoonStock.com

PSYCHOLOGY AND LIFE

Harnessing the Healing Power of Writing

After reading about the benefits of writing for health, you may be interested in giving it a try. Here are tips for effectively harnessing the amazing power of writing:

- Find a quiet place to write and pick just one topic to explore through writing.

- Dedicate yourself to at least 20 minutes of writing about that topic.

- While writing, do not be concerned with grammar or spelling; just let yourself go and write about all of the emotions, thoughts, and feelings associated with the experience you are writing about.

- If you feel that writing about something negative is really not for you, try writing about your most positive life experiences, the people you care about, or all the things you feel grateful for in life.

Once you have written about a topic at convenient times for a couple of days, you might want to take a break. Research has shown that spacing writing out can lead to enhanced benefits. You might also set aside time to review what you have written. What sorts of emotions are you sharing? Are there aspects of an experience you have not really thought about before?

Keep in mind that it is not necessary to write every single day to enjoy the benefits of writing. You may find that it is helpful as an exercise to sit down and write whenever life starts bringing you down.

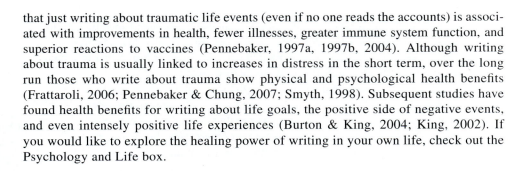

that just writing about traumatic life events (even if no one reads the accounts) is associated with improvements in health, fewer illnesses, greater immune system function, and superior reactions to vaccines (Pennebaker, 1997a, 1997b, 2004). Although writing about trauma is usually linked to increases in distress in the short term, over the long run those who write about trauma show physical and psychological health benefits (Frattaroli, 2006; Pennebaker & Chung, 2007; Smyth, 1998). Subsequent studies have found health benefits for writing about life goals, the positive side of negative events, and even intensely positive life experiences (Burton & King, 2004; King, 2002). If you would like to explore the healing power of writing in your own life, check out the Psychology and Life box.

Social Isolation and Life's Transitions

Clearly, social relationships are vital for survival, and loneliness can be debilitating. More than just an unwelcome social situation, chronic loneliness is linked with impaired physical and mental health (Cacioppo & others, 2002, 2006; Hawkley & others, 2006, 2007). Chronic loneliness can even lead to an early death (Cuijpers, 2001).

Each of us has times in our life when we feel lonely, particularly when we are going through major life transitions. For example, when individuals leave the familiar world of their hometown and family to begin college, they can feel especially lonely. Indeed, feeling lonely at the beginning of one's college career is quite common and normal (Cutrona, 1982). Many college freshmen feel anxious about meeting new people, and developing a new social life can create considerable anxiety. First-year students rarely take their popularity and social standing from high school into the college environment. There may be a dozen high school basketball stars, National Merit scholars, and former student council presidents in a single dormitory wing. Especially if students attend college away from home, they face the task of forming completely new social relationships.

If you are lonely, there are strategies you can use to become better connected with others. You might consider joining activities that involve others, such as volunteering your time for a cause you believe in. When interacting with others, you will improve your chances of developing enduring relationships if you are considerate, honest, trustworthy, and cooperative. Finally, if you cannot get rid of your loneliness on your own, you might want to contact the counseling services at your college.

 REVIEW, ASSESS, AND SHARPEN YOUR THINKING

Review

6 **Describe social processes affecting health and wellness.**

- Define social support and describe its role in health.
- Discuss how social isolation relates to health, and list positive steps toward relieving loneliness.

Assess

1. Providing someone with literature about successful treatments for cancer would be an example of what type of social support?
   A. emotional support
   B. informational support
   C. tangible assistance
   D. social sharing

2. Giving a sick friend a ride to the doctor's office is an example of what type of social support?
   A. social sharing
   B. emotional support
   C. tangible assistance
   D. informational support

3. Which of the following statements is correct?
   A. Receiving social support is more important to health than giving social support.
   B. Social isolation is a stronger predictor of death than cigarette smoking.
   C. People who live alone are healthier than those who live with others.
   D. It is more important to have friends that are all similar than to have friends that are diverse.

Sharpen Your Thinking

Think about your closest friends. How do you function as a source of social support for them?

SUMMARY

1 SOCIAL COGNITION

Describe how people think about the social world.

Person Perception

When we encounter another person, we perceive a variety of social cues that allow us to make an impression of the person. Facial features and physical attractiveness are two very potent sources of social information. We simplify our impressions by categorizing others. Self-fulfilling prophecy effects mean that our expectations of others can have a powerful impact on how they eventually behave. First impressions are important and influence later impressions.

Attribution

Attributions are our thoughts about why people behave the way they do and about who or what is responsible for the outcome of events. Attribution theory views people as motivated to discover the causes of behavior as part of their effort to make sense of it. The dimensions that we use to make sense of the causes of human behavior include internal/external, stable/unstable, and controllable/uncontrollable.

The fundamental attribution error is the tendency of observers to overestimate the importance of traits and underestimate the importance of situations when they seek explanations of an actor's behavior. When our self-esteem is threatened, we might depart from the fundamental attribution error and engage in a self-serving bias, attributing our successes to internal causes and our failures to external causes. In social situations, we call upon various heuristic shortcuts that allow us to make rapid decisions. One such heuristic is a stereotype—a generalization about a group's characteristics that does not consider any variations among individuals in the group.

The Self as a Social Object

In addition to developing schemas of other people, we also create a mental representation of the self. Self-esteem is an important aspect of the self and is related to holding unrealistically positive views of ourselves and our abilities. Self-objectification occurs when we become aware that others are viewing us as a social object. Stereotype threat is a type of fast-acting self-fulfilling prophecy about the self. In order to understand ourselves better, we might engage in social comparison, evaluating ourselves by comparison with others. Festinger stressed that social comparison is an important source of self-knowledge, especially when no other objective means is available. We tend to compare ourselves with similar others.

Attitudes

Attitudes are our opinions about people, objects, and ideas. We are better able to predict behavior on the basis of attitudes when the individual's attitudes are strong, when the person is very aware of his or her attitudes and expresses them often, and when the attitudes are specifically relevant to the behavior. Sometimes changes in behavior precede changes in attitude.

Cognitive dissonance theory, developed by Festinger, argues that we have a strong need for cognitive consistency. We change our attitudes to make them more consistent with our behavior in order to reduce dissonance. In many cases, we reduce dissonance by justifying our actions. Justification is the most intense when self-esteem is involved. Bem's self-perception theory stresses the importance of making inferences about attitudes by observing our own behavior, especially when our attitudes are not clear. Success in changing someone's attitudes may involve the communicator (source), the message, the medium, and the target (audience).

2 SOCIAL BEHAVIOR

Describe altruism and aggression.

Altruism

Altruism is an unselfish interest in helping someone else. Reciprocity often is involved in altruism. The motivation can be altruistic or egoistic. Psychologists have studied both person and situation variables in altruism. One important contributor to helping is emotion. Individuals who are in a good mood are more helpful. Guilt and empathy have also been linked to helping. The bystander effect is the concept that individuals who observe an emergency help less when someone else is present than when they are alone.

When examining the link between altruism and gender, context is important. Women are likelier to help in situations that are not dangerous and involve caregiving. Men are likelier to help in situations that involve danger or in which they feel competent.

Aggression

One view of the biological basis of aggression is that, early in human evolution, the most aggressive individuals were likely to be the survivors. Neurobiological factors involved in aggressive behavior include the amygdala, the neurotransmitter serotonin, alcohol's disinhibiting effects, and the hormone testosterone.

Psychological factors in aggression include frustrating and aversive circumstances. Sociocultural factors include cross-cultural variations, the culture of honor, and the violence in the media. Gender also is a factor. Males are consistently more physically aggressive than females, but gender differences in verbal aggression are not consistent.

3 SOCIAL INFLUENCE

Identify how people are influenced in social settings.

Conformity and Obedience

Conformity involves a change in a person's behavior to coincide with a group standard. Asch's classic study on judgments of line length illustrated the power of conformity. Many factors influence whether we will conform, including normative social influence and informational social influence.

Obedience is behavior that complies with the explicit demands of an individual in authority. Milgram's classic experiment demonstrated the power of obedience. Participants obeyed the experimenter's directions even though they thought they were hurting someone. As we go through life, we are both conformist and nonconformist; both obedient and not obedient. Sometimes we are overwhelmed by persuasion. At other times, we exert personal control and resist such influence.

Group Influence

People often change their behaviors when they are in a group. Deindividuation refers to the lack of inhibition and diffusion of responsibility that can occur in groups. Social contagion refers to imitative behaviors involving the spread of behavior, emotions, and ideas. Our performance in groups can be improved through social facilitation and lowered because of social loafing. Risky shift refers to the tendency for a group decision to be riskier than the average decision made by the individual group members. The group polarization effect is the solidification and further strengthening of a position as a consequence of group discussion. Groupthink involves impaired decision making and avoidance of realistic appraisal to maintain harmony in the group. The majority usually get their way in group influence, but occasionally the minority have their day.

4 INTERGROUP RELATIONS

Discuss intergroup relations.

Group Identity: Us Versus Them

Social identity is our definition of ourselves in terms of our group memberships. Tajfel's social identity theory states that when individuals are assigned to a group, they invariably think of it as the in-group, or "we." Identifying with the group allows them to have a positive self-image. Ethnocentrism is the tendency to favor one's own ethnic group over other groups. Ethnocentrism can have positive or negative outcomes.

Prejudice

Prejudice is an unjustified negative attitude toward an individual based on the individual's membership in a group. Among the reasons given for why an individual develops prejudice are the presence of competition between groups over scarce resources, the person's motivation to enhance his or her self-esteem, cognitive processes that contribute to a tendency to categorize and stereotype others, and cultural learning. Prejudice is based on stereotyping, a generalization about a group's characteristics that does not consider any variations from one individual to the next. The cognitive process of stereotyping can lead to discrimination, an unjustified negative or harmful action toward a member of a group simply because he or she belongs to that group. Discrimination results when negative emotional reactions combine with prejudicial beliefs and are translated into behavior.

Ways to Improve Interethnic Relations

Contact between ethnic groups by itself does not decrease conflict and improve relations. One effective strategy for enhancing the effects of intergroup contact is to set up task-oriented cooperation among individuals from different groups.

5 CLOSE RELATIONSHIPS

Explain the nature of close relationships.

Attraction

Factors associated with attraction include proximity, acquaintance, and similarity. We tend to be attracted to people whom we are likely to see often, whom we are likely to meet, and who are similar to us.

Love

Romantic love (passionate love) includes feelings of infatuation and sexual attraction. Affectionate love (companionate love) is more akin to friendship and includes deep, caring feelings for another.

Models of Close Relationships: Making Love Work

Social psychologists have introduced a number of models for understanding close relationships. Social exchange theory states that relationships are likely to be successful if individuals feel that they get out of the relationship what they put in. Other approaches to close relationships include the investment model and positive illusions.

6 SOCIAL PSYCHOLOGY AND HEALTH AND WELLNESS

Describe social processes affecting health and wellness.

Social Support and Health

Social support refers to the aid provided by others to a person in need. Support can take the form of tangible assistance, information, or emotional support. Social support has been found to correlate strongly with functioning under and coping with stress.

Social Isolation and Life's Transitions

Social isolation is a strong risk factor for physical illness and even death. Loneliness relates to a number of negative health outcomes, including sleep loss and susceptibility to illness. Loneliness often emerges when people make life transitions, so it is not surprising that loneliness is common among college freshmen. Strategies that can help to reduce loneliness include participating in activities with others and taking the initiative to meet new people.

Key Terms

social psychology, p. 474
stereotype, p. 475
attribution theory, p. 476
fundamental attribution error, p. 476
false consensus effect, p. 477
positive illusions, p. 478
self-serving bias, p. 478
self-objectification, p. 478
stereotype threat, p. 478
social comparison, p. 479

attitudes, p. 479
cognitive dissonance, p. 480
self-perception theory, p. 481
elaboration likelihood model, p. 482
altruism, p. 484
egoism, p. 484
empathy, p. 485
bystander effect, p. 485
conformity, p. 492
confederate, p. 493

informational social influence, p. 493
normative social influence, p. 494
obedience, p. 494
deindividuation, p. 495
social contagion, p. 496
social facilitation, p. 496
social loafing, p. 497
risky shift, p. 497
group polarization effect, p. 497
groupthink, p. 497

social identity, p. 500
social identity theory, p. 500
ethnocentrism, p. 500
prejudice, p. 500
discrimination, p. 503
mere exposure effect, p. 506
romantic love, p. 507
affectionate love, p. 508
social exchange theory, p. 508
investment model, p. 509
social support, p. 511

Assess Your Knowledge

1. Which of the following is true about stereotypes?
    A. Stereotypes take mental effort.
    B. Stereotypes are accurate.
    C. Stereotypes do not account for individual differences.
    D. Stereotypes are always negative.

2. Which of the following types of faces will be judged as most attractive?
    A. average faces
    B. faces with distinctive features
    C. faces with asymmetrical features
    D. older faces

3. Believing that everyone shares the same view as you is known as
    A. the availability heuristic.
    B. the false consensus effect.
    C. a stereotype.
    D. stereotype threat.

4. Marilyn smokes; however she is well aware of the negative health consequences of smoking. As a result, Marilyn feels guilty about smoking. Which of the following is Marilyn likely experiencing?
    A. effort justification
    B. self-objectification
    C. fundamental attribution error
    D. cognitive dissonance

5. Egoism refers to
    A. being altruistic to gain something in return.
    B. being self-centered.
    C. a lack of reciprocity.
    D. ignoring the needs of others.

6. Are men or women more altruistic?
    A. Men are more altruistic than women.
    B. Women are more altruistic than men.
    C. Men and women are equally altruistic.
    D. It depends on the context.

7. Having negative views of an out-group is _____. Acting in a hurtful manner to a member of an out-group is _____.
    A. explicit bias, implicit bias
    B. implicit bias, explicit bias
    C. prejudice, discrimination
    D. discrimination, prejudice

8. When a family member tells you how much he cares about you, he is providing you with
    A. tangible assistance.
    B. social sharing.
    C. emotional support.
    D. informational support.

9. Performing better when others are watching is known as
    A. social loafing.
    B. risky shift.
    C. social facilitation.
    D. social contagion.

10. What is a confederate?
    A. someone who causes conformity
    B. someone who is deindividuated
    C. someone who loafs
    D. someone who is given a role by an experimenter

11. Which of the following is a defining characteristic of group-think?
    A. accurate decision making
    B. decisions that are more extreme than normal
    C. minority viewpoints being discouraged
    D. group discord

12. Self-objectification refers to
    A. being overly critical of one's appearance.
    B. attributing personal success to internal factors.
    C. viewing oneself as an object for others.
    D. changing one's behavior because of fear of confirming a stereotype.

13. Social loafing is more likely to occur
    A. when groups are large.
    B. when groups are small.
    C. when the task is interesting.
    D. when people have distinct roles to play.

14. Which of the following is not a good indication that a person's attitude will be consistent with her or his behavior?
    A. The attitude is related to other people rather than to the self.
    B. The attitude has been thoroughly thought through.
    C. The attitude is strong.
    D. The attitude is related to the behavior.

15. Fundamental attribution error states that people make _____ attributions about the behavior others and _____ attributions about their own behavior.
    A. positive, negative
    B. negative, positive
    C. external, internal
    D. internal, external

Go to Appendix B for answers to these questions.

Apply Your Knowledge

1. We are often unaware of how many attributions we make about the behavior of others. To demonstrate this point to yourself, spend some time in a crowded area observing the interactions of others (or instead watch some scenes in television shows or movies). Take careful notes about the social behaviors that occur and then indicate your impression of why the people behaved as they did. What cues did you use to make your decision about their behavior? Did your knowledge of the fundamental attribution error influence your attributions? Why or why not?

2. Think about a movie or TV show you have recently seen that shows an example of altruism or aggression. Assess the influences that caused the characters to behave altruistically or aggressively. In what ways are these influences consistent with those discussed in the text, and in what ways do they differ?

3. Sit down with the personal ads from a local paper. Look at the ads placed by men and those placed by women. Does the content of the ads support the evolutionary predictions for what men and women look for and offer in their ads?

4. Many conclusions about the nature of relationships are based on correlational studies. Discuss the factors that contribute to the difficulty of carrying out experiments on relationships, and describe an experiment that you might conduct to test one of the factors described in the chapter as contributing to attraction or loneliness.

5. Interview the happiest couple you know. Ask them individually about the things that they think help make their relationship work. Then examine your notes. How do the characteristics of your "ideal" couple's relationship compare with the findings of research on close relationships?

6. Check out this website to see how averaging of faces works: **http://www.faceresearch.org/demos/average.** Pick some faces you think of as unattractive. What happens when you average them together? If you have a digital photograph of yourself and some friends, see what happens when you average those faces. Do you agree that average faces are more attractive than any single face?

CHAPTER 13

PSYCHOLOGICAL DISORDERS

Experiencing Psychology

MOE ARMSTRONG AND FREDERICK FRESE, LIVING PRETTY GOOD LIVES

What does it take to make a good life? If you imagine your best possible life in the future, what does it include? At first you might conjure up notions of wealth, fame, exotic travel, and luxury. But this type of life is probably not typical of the lives being lived around you. Consider how the "ordinary" people you know are living reasonably good lives every day. So maybe a good life includes the simple things—good health, a happy marriage, warm relationships, and a satisfying career (King & Napa, 1998; Scollon & King, 2004).

If you live in Cambridge, Massachusetts, you might recognize fellow city resident Moe Armstrong as leading a pretty good life. Armstrong is the 61-year-old director of consumer and family affairs for the Vinfen Corporation. In high school, he was an Eagle Scout and a star on the state championship football team, and he later served as a medical corpsman in the Marines during the Vietnam War. Armstrong is a sought-after public speaker and an award-winning activist who has appeared on *Larry King Live* and the *CBS Evening News*. He holds two master's degrees and enjoys writing poetry, cartooning, and photography. He and his wife have been married for 10 years. When considering his life experiences, Armstrong is grateful, noting that "I've had a pretty good life" (Bonfatti, 2005). His "pretty good life" is remarkable not only because of his accomplishments but also because Moe Armstrong has schizophrenia, a severe psychological disorder that is characterized by highly disordered thought processes.

Moe Armstrong's "pretty good life" is not an easy one. In fact, every day is a struggle. He takes antipsychotic medication, and, in his words, "I have many more limitations than other people, and that's very hard." Of course, his life is not perfect. But he tries to avoid relapse by cultivating "supportive, gentle, loving environments" (Boodman, 2002).

And there is Frederick J. Frese III, now age 68, who was diagnosed with schizophrenia when he was 27. A psychiatrist told him that he would probably spend the rest of his life in a state mental hospital. Defying that prediction, Frese earned a doctorate in psychology and spent 15 years as the director of psychology at Western Reserve Psychiatric Hospital in Ohio, the state's largest mental hospital. He has been married for 25 years and is the father of four children (Boodman, 2002).

The psychiatrist who first diagnosed Frese was mistaken, but his pessimistic prognosis is, perhaps, understandable. Schizophrenia is a profoundly devastating psychological disorder. A study of individuals with schizophrenia found that after 25 years, about 12 percent required long-term institutionalization (Harrison & others, 2001). Life with schizophrenia is so difficult that some individuals choose to end it. The risk for suicide for individuals with schizophrenia is eight times that for the general population (Harris & Barraclough, 1997; Harrison & others, 2001). The suicide rate among individuals with schizophrenia is as high as 13 percent (Pompili & others, 2005, 2007).

The remarkable stories of Moe Armstrong and Frederick Frese are exceptional but perhaps not as rare as you might think. In a 32-year longitudinal study on the long-term outcome of schizophrenia, one-half to two-thirds of individuals with the disorder showed improvement or even recovery (Harding & others, 1987). Although not all studies support the possibility of recovery (Mason & others, 1995), evidence has accumulated pointing to the potential of significant improvement in about 25 percent of cases (Drake, Levine, & Laska, 2007; Fleischhaker & others, 2005; Marshall & Rathbone, 2006). A 25-year international study found improvement in over half of the participants (Harrison & others, 2001). Whether their lives include psychiatric medication, therapy, or other treatment, many individuals are able to work and have relationships (Harrison & others, 2001). In short, they lead pretty good lives.

Armstrong, Frese, and John Nash, the mathematical genius who was the subject of the Academy Award–winning film *A Beautiful Mind,* all have schizophrenia. Even in the best of circumstances, concerns about relapse, medication, and the effects of the disorder on their daily existence may always be with them, affecting their lives in ways that few of us can truly grasp. None of these individuals has a perfect life. But then, who does? All of us face obstacles in creating a good life, and these obstacles can include not only schizophrenia but a range of psychological disorders, including depression and anxiety.

Psychological disorders are common in the United States and around the world. An estimated 26 percent of Americans over the age of 18 suffer from a diagnosable psychological disorder in a given year—an estimated 57.7 million U.S. adults (Kessler & others, 2005; National Institute of Mental Health [NIMH], 2006). Psychological disorders are the leading cause of disability in individuals aged 15 to 44 in the United States and Canada (World Health Organization, 2004). ■

PREVIEW

In this chapter we explore the meaning of the word *abnormal* as it relates to psychology, examine various theoretical approaches to understanding abnormal behavior, and survey the main psychological disorders. All humans have limitations—because of their characteristics, their experiences, or the environment in which they live—so it is appropriate that we examine a variety of imperfections that can have serious implications for the capacities of individuals to lead satisfying lives. At the chapter's conclusion, we look at the ways that psychological disorders can influence health and wellness, considering once again, as in the cases of Moe Armstrong and Frederick Frese, that a good life can be lived even within the limitations of a severe psychological disorder—and being reminded that imperfect lives remain valuable lives.

1 Defining and Explaining Abnormal Behavior

Discuss the characteristics, explanations, and classifications of abnormal behavior.

To understand psychological disorders, we need to pinpoint what is meant by abnormal behavior. Abnormal behavior is not easy to define (Oltmanns & Emery, 2007). The definition varies across academic disciplines and across social, medical, and legal institutions. For example, the federal courts define *insanity*—a legal term, not a psychological term—as the inability to appreciate the nature and quality or wrongfulness of one's acts (Redding, 2006). The American Psychiatric Association (2001, 2006) defines abnormal behavior in medical terms: a mental illness that affects or is manifested in a person's brain and can affect the way a person thinks, behaves, and interacts with people.

Keeping in mind that the line between what is normal and what is abnormal is not always clear-cut, we can use three criteria to help distinguish normal from abnormal behavior. **Abnormal behavior** is behavior that is deviant, maladaptive, or personally distressful over a long period of time. Only one of the three criteria listed needs to be met for the behavior to be classified as abnormal, but two or all three may be present.

Let's take a closer look at what each of the three criteria of abnormal behavior entails. First, abnormal behavior is *deviant*. One way that abnormal behavior has been described is as being *atypical*. People such as Oprah Winfrey, Brett Favre, and Steve Jobs are atypical, but we do not categorize them as abnormal. However, when atypical behavior deviates from what is acceptable in a culture, it often is considered abnormal. A woman who washes her hands three or four times an hour, takes seven showers a day, and cleans her apartment at least twice a day is abnormal because her behavior deviates from what we see as acceptable.

Second, abnormal behavior is *maladaptive*. Maladaptive behavior interferes with a person's ability to function effectively in the world. A man who believes that he can influence other people, even endanger them, through the way he breathes may go to great lengths to avoid people so that he will not put them in jeopardy. He might isolate himself from others, for their own good. His belief separates him from society and prevents his everyday functioning in the world; thus, his behavior is maladaptive.

Third, abnormal behavior involves *personal distress, over a long period of time.* Feeling distressed about aspects of our lives (work or school hassles or relationship problems) is certainly normal. Sadness is a natural part of life, in coping with loss and

abnormal behavior Behavior that is deviant, maladaptive, or personally distressful over a long period of time.

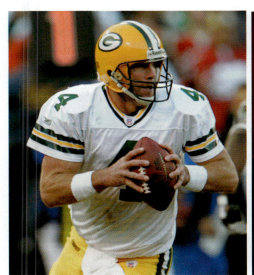

Accomplished people such as Green Bay Packers quarterback Brett Favre and Apple Computer co-founder Steve Jobs are atypical but not abnormal. However, when atypical behavior deviates from cultural norms, it often is considered abnormal.

personal tragedies. But distress becomes abnormal when it is unrelenting. When an individual feels intense sadness for a prolonged period or one who is unable to find pleasure even in activities he or she previously enjoyed may find the lack of pleasure in life to be distressing.

To appreciate why all three of these criteria are included in a definition of abnormal, consider someone who routinely wears six or seven layers of clothing, even when the temperature is a balmy 90 degrees. The person may prefer wearing all those clothes, but others notice that this is certainly atypical.

Theoretical Approaches to Psychological Disorders

What causes people to develop a psychological disorder, that is, to behave in deviant, maladaptive, and personally distressful ways? Theorists have suggested various approaches to getting at this question.

The Biological Approach   The *biological approach* to psychological disorders attributes them to organic, internal causes. Scientists who take a biological approach to psychological disorders primarily focus on the brain, genetic factors, and neurotransmitter functioning as the sources of the abnormality. The biological approach frequently uses drug therapy to treat abnormal behavior.

The biological approach is evident in the **medical model,** which describes psychological disorders as medical diseases with a biological origin. From the perspective of the medical model, abnormalities are called mental illnesses, the individuals afflicted are patients, and they are treated by doctors.

Biological views of psychological disorders fall into three main categories (Nolen-Hoeksema, 2007):

- *Structural views:* Abnormalities in the brain's structure cause psychological disorders.
- *Biochemical views:* Imbalances in neurotransmitters or hormones cause psychological disorders.
- *Genetic views:* Disordered genes cause psychological disorders.

We explore these biological factors later in the chapter.

The Psychological Approach   Chapter 11 described the psychodynamic, social cognitive, trait, and humanistic perspectives on personality. These perspectives serve as a foundation for understanding the psychological factors involved in psychological disorders:

- *Psychodynamic perspectives:* Psychodynamic perspectives stress that psychological disorders arise from unconscious conflicts that produce anxiety and result in maladaptive behavior. From the psychodynamic perspective, early childhood experiences and repressed sexual conflicts are the key to understanding abnormal behavior. Recall that these ideas stem from Freud's psychoanalytic theory but that some contemporary proponents of this approach place less emphasis on unconscious thought and sexuality (Novie, 2007).
- *Behavioral and social cognitive perspectives:* The behavioral perspective, described in Chapter 7, focuses on the rewards and punishments in the environment that determine abnormal behavior. This might involve examining how the person's abnormal behavior is rewarded by his or her social environment. Social cognitive theory accepts that environmental experiences are important determinants of psychological disorders but emphasizes that social cognitive factors also are involved (Bandura, 2007a, 2007b). In this way, observational learning, expectancies, self-efficacy, self-control, beliefs about oneself and the world, and many other cognitive processes are key aspects of psychological disorders.
- *Trait perspectives:* The five-factor model that summarizes the broad dimensions of personality characteristics (neuroticism, extraversion, openness to experience, agreeableness, and conscientiousness) has been used as a means of assessing psychological

medical model A biological approach that describes psychological disorders as medical diseases with a biological origin.

disorders, especially personality disorders (Durrett & Trull, 2005). Trait perspectives view abnormal behaviors and characteristics as variations on the normal personality characteristics seen in healthy populations (Widiger & Trull, 2007).

- *Humanistic perspectives:* These perspectives emphasize positive personal qualities, capacity for growth, and freedom to choose one's own destiny (Hazler, 2007). A psychological disorder reflects an inability to fulfill one's potential, likely arising from the pressures of society to conform to others' expectations and values. From this perspective the individual may feel alienated from his or her genuine goals and values or may find little joy even in the midst of a successful life. The humanistic perspective focuses less on diagnostic labels and more on the humanity of each individual in his or her life context.

These psychological approaches have played a large role in the development of ways to treat psychological disorders, as we will see in Chapter 14.

The Sociocultural Approach   Although the psychological approach mainly attributes psychological problems to unconscious conflicts, negative cognitions, low self-concept, and other factors within the individual, proponents of this approach nevertheless give environmental experiences a role in creating psychological disorders (Nolen-Hoeksema, 2007). The sociocultural approach, however, places *more* emphasis on the larger social contexts in which a person lives—including the individual's marriage or family, neighborhood, socioeconomic status, ethnicity, gender, and culture—than do the other approaches. For example, marital conflict might be the cause of psychological disorder in one individual. In this view, when a member of a family has a psychological problem, it may not be due to something within the individual but rather to ineffective family functioning (Appleton & Dykeman, 2007). Any number of psychological problems can develop because of family power struggles such as occur in sibling conflicts, the favoring of one child over another, and marital discord.

Individuals from low-income, minority neighborhoods have the highest rates of psychological disorders. In studies of the role of socioeconomic status and ethnicity in such disorders, socioeconomic status plays a much stronger role than does ethnicity: The living conditions of poverty create stressful circumstances that can contribute to the development of a psychological disorder (Dalton, Elias, & Wandersman, 2007; Koster & others, 2006).

Gender, another sociocultural factor, is associated with the presence of certain psychological disorders (Hyde, 2007; Nolen-Hoeksema, 2007). Women are more likely than men to develop anxiety disorders and depression. These disorders are sometimes called *internalizing disorders* because they involve turning negative feelings inward. Conversely, men are socialized to direct their energy toward the external world (to externalize their feelings), and they more often have *externalizing disorders,* those that involve "acting out" often aggressively toward others.

Many psychological disorders are universal (Al-Issa, 1982). However, the frequency and intensity of psychological disorders vary and depend on social, economic, technological, and religious aspects of cultures (Marsella & Yamada, 2007; Shiraev & Levy, 2007). Some disorders, though, are culture-related, as indicated in Figure 13.1.

An Interactionist Approach: The Biopsychosocial Model
Normal and abnormal behavior alike may involve biological, psychological, and sociocultural factors, such as those we have been

Women are more likely than men to develop internalizing disorders such as anxiety disorder and depression; men more often suffer from externalizing disorders such as aggression and substance abuse.

Disorder	Culture	Description/Characteristics
Amok	Malaysia, Philippines, Africa	This disorder involves sudden, uncontrolled outbursts of anger in which the person may injure or kill someone. Amok is often found in males who are emotionally withdrawn before the onset of the disorder. After the attack on someone, the individual feels exhausted and depressed and does not remember the rage and attack.
Anorexia Nervosa	Western cultures, especially the United States	This eating disorder involves a relentless pursuit of thinness through starvation and can eventually lead to death.
Windigo	Algonquin Indian hunters	This disorder involves a fear of being bewitched. The hunter becomes anxious and agitated, worrying he will be turned into a cannibal with a craving for human flesh.

FIGURE 13.1

Some Culture-Related Disorders Although many psychological disorders are universal, some are associated with specific cultures, as this figure illustrates.

considering, alone or in combination with other factors. Abnormal behavior can be influenced by biological factors (such as brain processes and heredity), psychological factors (such as distorted thoughts and low self-esteem), and sociocultural factors (such as ineffective family functioning and poverty).

Importantly though, in every case, there are exceptions to the rules associated with each of these approaches in its purest form. For example, not everyone with a genetic predisposition to schizophrenia develops the disorder. Similarly, not everyone who experiences childhood neglect develops depression; and even women who live in cultures that strongly discriminate against them do not always develop psychological disorders. Thus, to understand the development of psychological disorders, we must consider a variety of intersecting factors from each of the domains of experience.

Sometimes this interactionist approach is called *biopsychosocial*. From the biopsychosocial perspective, none of the factors considered is necessarily viewed as more important than another; rather, biological, psychological, and social factors are all significant ingredients in producing both normal and abnormal behavior. Furthermore, these ingredients may combine in unique ways, so that one depressed person might differ from another in terms of the key factors associated with the development of the disorder.

Whatever approach we use to understand psychological disorders, being diagnosed with such a disorder can have a profound impact on a person's life, not only because of the effects of the disorder itself, but because of what the diagnosis means to the person's family, friends, and acquaintances. To get a sense of your own views of people with mental illness, check out the Psychology and Life box.

Classifying Abnormal Behavior

The classification of psychological disorders goes back to the ancient Egyptians and Greeks and has its roots in biology and medicine. To this day, the classification of psychological disorders follows a medical model.

Classifying psychological disorders is difficult and controversial, but it does have some benefits. For one thing, a classification system provides a common basis for communicating. For example, if one psychologist says that her client is experiencing depression and another psychologist says that his client has a mood disorder, the two psychologists understand that the clients have exhibited certain behavior that has led to their diagnoses.

In addition, a classification system can help clinicians make predictions. It provides information about the likelihood that a disorder will occur, about which individuals are more susceptible to the disorder, about how the disorder progresses, and about the prognosis for treatment (Canino & others, 2004).

Finally, a classification system may benefit the person suffering from psychological symptoms such as persistent negative mood and lack of joy in life. The existence of a name for the disorder can be a comfort and a sign that something can be done to alleviate the suffering. Although having a name for a problem can be comforting, it can also have serious negative implications for the person, because of the power of labels and potential for stigma.

Labeling and Stigma One problem with classifying individuals according to psychological disorders is the issue of labeling, and the ways that labels can lead to stigma. A classic and controversial study illustrated that labels of psychological disorder can be very sticky—once a person has been given a label, it is hard to remove it. David Rosenhan

PSYCHOLOGY AND LIFE

Test Your Attitudes

Rate the following items using the scale of 1–5, with 1 indicating that you completely *disagree* with the statement and 5 indicating that you completely *agree* with the statement.

1	2	3	4	5
completely disagree	slightly agree	moderately agree	strongly agree	completely agree

_____ 1. I would rather not live next door to a person with a psychological disorder.

_____ 2. A person with a psychological disorder is unfit to raise children.

_____ 3. I would be afraid to be around a person with a psychological disorder.

_____ 4. I would not want to live in the same neighborhood as a group home for persons with psychological disorders.

_____ 5. A person with a psychological disorder cannot hold a job.

_____ 6. A person with a psychological disorder is dangerous or potentially violent.

Total: _____

Add up your score and divide by 6. If your score is 3 or higher, you may want to rethink your attitudes about individuals with psychological disorders.

It may be revealing to ask yourself how you would respond to these statements if the words "person with a psychological disorder" were replaced with "woman," "African American," or "gay man or lesbian." Sometimes even individuals who would not think of themselves as being prejudiced against other groups find themselves biased against the mentally ill. After reading this chapter, you might want to return to this exercise to see whether your attitudes have changed.

(1973) recruited eight college students, none with a psychological disorder, to see a psychiatrist at a hospital. They were instructed to act in a normal way except to complain about hearing voices that said such things as "empty" and "thud." All eight expressed an interest in leaving the hospital and behaved in a cooperative manner. Nonetheless, they were labeled with schizophrenia, a severe psychological disorder, and kept in the hospital from 3 to 52 days. Thus, the label of schizophrenia stuck to these individuals and caused the professionals they dealt with to interpret their quite normal behavior as abnormal.

Labels can be damaging when they draw attention to one aspect of a person and ignore others (Halgin & Whitbourne, 2007). For example, the labels "schizophrenic" or "person with anxiety disorder," often have negative connotations, such as "incompetent" or "dangerous." These sorts of connotations are stereotypes, which, as reviewed in Chapter 12, can have powerful negative implications for individuals. Even mental health professionals have been shown to fall prey to prejudicial attitudes toward those who are coping with psychological disorders (Nordt, Rossler, & Lauber, 2006).

Vivid cases of extremely harmful behavior by individuals with psychological disorders can perpetuate the stereotypes that individuals with psychological disorders are

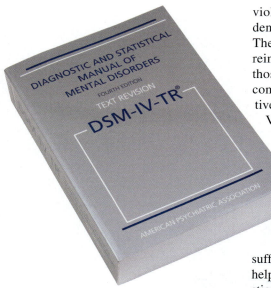

violent. For example, Cho Seung-Hui, a 23-year-old college student, murdered 32 students and faculty at Virginia Tech University on April 16, 2007, before killing himself. The fact that Cho suffered with psychological disorders throughout his life may have reinforced the notion that individuals with such disorders are dangerous people. Yet, those with psychological disorders (especially those in treatment) are no more likely to commit violent acts than the general population. Indeed, Cho was no more representative of people with psychological disorders than he was representative of students at Virginia Tech.

When an individual is given the label "mentally ill," a key concern is stigma. Stigma refers to a mark of shame that may promote avoidance or negative reactions from others. And feeling stigmatized can reduce individuals' self-esteem and promote negative reactions from others. Sadly, fear of being stigmatized may make individuals reluctant to seek help because they fear that they will be branded as "crazy."

In sum, though useful for a variety of reasons, classifying psychological disorders can have negative implications as well. Among those who study psychological disorders scientifically and those who dedicate themselves to treating individuals suffering from these disorders, the best compromise seems to be to use classifications to help understand, prevent, and treat disorders while also striving to prevent prejudice and stigma that negatively affect people's lives (Corrigan, 2007; Hinshaw, 2007).

The DSM-IV Classification System   In 1952, the American Psychiatric Association published the first major classification of psychological disorders in the United States, the *Diagnostic and Statistical Manual of Mental Disorders*. Its current version, the **DSM-IV** (American Psychiatric Association [APA], 1994), was introduced in 1994 and revised in 2000, producing the *DSM-IV-TR* (Text Revision) (APA, 2000). *DSM-V* is due in 2011. The *DSM-V* revision process began in 2007 with the appointment of workgroups that focus on various diagnostic categories. Up-to-date descriptions of the progress of the workgroups can be found at **www.dsm5.org.**

Throughout the development of the *DSM,* the number of diagnosable disorders has increased dramatically. The first *DSM* listed 112 disorders. In 1968, *DSM-II* listed 163. *DSM-IV-TR* includes 17 major classifications and describes 374 disorders.

Certainly, continuing changes in the *DSM* reflect advancements in knowledge about the classification of psychological disorders. On the basis of research and clinical experience, the *DSM-IV* added, dropped, or revised categories, and these changes have generated some controversy among the diagnosticians who rely on the classification system. Some have argued that the *DSM* has expanded to include behaviors that, while bothersome, do not qualify as psychological disorders.

A key feature of the *DSM-IV* is its *multiaxial system,* which classifies individuals on the basis of five dimensions, or axes, that take into account the individual's history and highest level of functioning in the previous year. This system ensures that the individual is not merely assigned to a psychological disorder category but instead is characterized in terms of a number of clinical factors.

The five axes of *DSM-IV* are

Axis I: All diagnostic categories except personality disorders and mental retardation

Axis II: Personality disorders and mental retardation

Axis III: General medical conditions

Axis IV: Psychosocial and environmental problems

Axis V: Current level of functioning

Axes I and II comprise the classification of psychological disorders. Figure 13.2 describes the major categories of these psychological disorders. Axes III through V may not be needed to diagnose a psychological disorder, but they are included so that the person's overall life situation is considered. Thus, a person might have a heart condition (Axis III), which has important implications for treatment because some antidepressant drugs can worsen heart disease. Axis IV includes occupational problems,

DSM-IV Abbreviation for the *Diagnostic and Statistical Manual of Mental Disorders,* Fourth Edition; the current version of the APA's major classification of psychological disorders.

Major Categories of Psychological Disorders   **Description**

Axis I Disorders

Major Categories of Psychological Disorders	Description
Disorders usually first diagnosed in infancy, childhood, or adolescence and communication disorders	Include disorders that appear before adolescence, such as attention deficit hyperactivity disorder, autism, and learning disorders (stuttering, for example).
Anxiety disorders	Characterized by motor tension, hyperactivity, and apprehensive expectations/thoughts. Include generalized anxiety disorder, panic disorder, phobic disorder, obsessive-compulsive disorder, and post-traumatic stress disorder.
Somatoform disorders	Occur when psychological symptoms take a physical form even though no physical causes can be found. Include hypochondriasis and conversion disorder.
Factitious disorders	Characterized by the individual's delibrate fabrication of a medical or mental disorder, but not for external gain (such as a disability claim).
Dissociative disorders	Involve a sudden loss of memory or change of identity. Include the disorders of dissociative amnesia, dissociative fugue, and dissociative identity disorder.
Delirium, dementia, amnestic, and other cognitive disorders	Consist of mental disorders involving problems in consciousness and cognition, such as substance-induced delirium or dementia related to Alzheimer disease.
Mood disorders	Disorders in which there is a primary disturbance in mood; include depressive disorders and bipolar disorder (which involves wide mood swings from deep depression to extreme euphoria and agitation).
Schizophrenia and other psychotic disorders	Disorders characterized by distorted thoughts and perceptions, odd communication, inappropriate emotion, and other unusual behaviors.
Substance-related disorders	Include alcohol-related disorders, cocaine-related disorders, hallucinogen-related disorders, and other drug-related disorders.
Sexual and gender-identity disorders	Consist of three main types of disorders: gender-identity disorders (person is not comfortable with identity as a female or male), paraphilias (person has a preference for unusual sexual acts to stimulate sexual arousal), and sexual dysfunctions (impairments in sexual functioning).
Eating disorders	Include anorexia nervosa and bulimia nervosa (see Chapter 10).
Sleep disorders	Consist of primary sleep disorders, such as insomnia and narcolepsy (see Chapter 6) and sleep disorders due to a general medical condition.
Impulse-control disorders not elsewhere classified	Include kleptomania, pyromania, and compulsive gambling.
Adjustment disorders	Characterized by distressing emotional or behavioral symptoms in response to an identifiable stressor.

Axis II Disorders

Major Categories of Psychological Disorders	Description
Mental retardation	Low intellectual functioning and an inability to adapt to everyday life (see Chapter 9).
Personality disorders	Develop when personality traits become inflexible and maladaptive.
Other conditions that may be a focus of clinical attention	Include relational problems (with a partner, sibling, and so on), problems related to abuse or neglect (physical abuse of a child, for example), or additional conditions (such as bereavement, academic problems, and religious or spiritual problems).

FIGURE 13.2

Main Categories of Psychological Disorders in the *DSM-IV* The *DSM-IV* provides a way for mental health professionals and researchers to communicate with each other about these well-defined psychological disorders.

economic problems, and family problems. On Axis V, the clinician makes a diagnosis about the highest level of adaptive functioning the person has attained in the preceding year in social, occupational, or school activities. This diagnosis ranges from a rating of 100 (superior functioning in a wide range of activities) to 10 (persistent danger of severely hurting self or others), with eight other ratings at 10-point increments. For example, a rating of 50 indicates serious symptoms or impairment in social, occupational, or school functioning.

The more than 200 mental health professionals who contributed to the development of the *DSM-IV* were a much more diverse group than their predecessors, who were mainly White male psychiatrists. More women, ethnic minorities, and non-psychiatrists, such as clinical psychologists, were involved in the construction of the *DSM-IV*, and greater attention was given to gender- and ethnicity-related diagnoses. For example, the *DSM-IV* contains an appendix titled "Guidelines for Cultural Formation and Glossary of Culture-Related Syndromes" (Nathan, 1994). Also, the *DSM-IV* is accompanied by a number of sourcebooks that present the empirical base of the *DSM-IV*. In previous versions of the *DSM*, the reasons for diagnostic changes were not always explicit, so the evidence that led to their formulation was never available for public evaluation.

The most controversial aspect of the *DSM-IV* is an issue that has existed since the publication of the *DSM-I* in 1952. Although more non-psychiatrists than ever were responsible for drafting the *DSM-IV*, it still classifies individuals based on their symptoms and uses medical terminology in the psychiatric tradition of thinking about mental disorders in terms of illness and disease (Nathan & Langenbucher, 2003; Oltmanns & Emery, 2007). This strategy implies an internal cause that is more or less independent of external or environmental factors (Kring & others, 2007). Thus, even though researchers have begun to shed light on the complex interaction of genetic, neurobiological, cognitive, and environmental factors in the *DSM* disorders, the *DSM-IV* continues to espouse the medical/disease model of psychological disorders (American Psychiatric Association, 2006).

***Critiques of the* DSM**   The *DSM-IV* has been criticized on a variety of grounds. For example, some have taken issue with the fact that the *DSM* labels what we might think of as everyday problems as "psychological disorders." For example, under learning or academic skills disorders, the *DSM-IV* includes the categories of reading disorder, mathematics disorder, and disorder of written expression. Under substance-related disorders, the *DSM-IV* includes the category of caffeine-use disorders. We do not usually consider these everyday problems to be psychological disorders, but including them implies that these "normal" behaviors should be treated as such. The developers of the *DSM* system argue that mental health providers have been treating many problems not included in earlier editions of *DSM* and that the classification system should be more comprehensive. One practical reason for including everyday problems in the *DSM-IV* is to encourage health insurance companies to support treatments, so that more people might seek professional help. Most health insurance companies reimburse their clients only for disorders listed in the *DSM-IV* system.

Another criticism of the *DSM-IV*, and indeed of this type of classification system in general, is that the system focuses strictly on pathology and problems, with a bias toward finding something wrong with anyone who becomes the object of diagnostic study. The critics say that because labels can become self-fulfilling prophecies (as described in Chapter 12), emphasizing strengths as well as weaknesses might help to destigmatize labels such as "paranoid schizophrenic" and "ex-mental patient." Focusing on strengths would also help to provide clues to treatments that promote mental competence rather than working only to reduce mental distress. Knowing the diagnostic label that is placed on a person may tell us a lot about what is going wrong, but it tells us nothing about what is going right. Knowing that Moe Armstrong has schizophrenia would not reveal that he is also capable of love and productive work. Identifying a person's strengths can be an important step toward maximizing his or her ability to contribute to society (Roten, 2007).

Of course, labels such as those described by the *DSM* are based on the notion that psychological disorders are real and often medically treatable. Some individuals from outside of psychology (and within it) have questioned this very assumption. To read about whether psychological disorders are real or a myth, see the Critical Controversy.

attention deficit hyperactivity disorder (ADHD) Psychological disorder in which the individual shows one or more of the following characteristics over a period of time: inattention, hyperactivity, and impulsivity.

Critical Controversy

Are Psychological Disorders a Myth?

On the June 24, 2005, broadcast of NBC's *Today Show,* Matt Lauer interviewed Tom Cruise, who was embroiled in a heated media debate with fellow actor Brooke Shields. Shields had published a book about her experience with postpartum depression following her daughter's birth and about her positive experience with the use of prescription antidepressants for her disorder. Cruise vehemently criticized the very idea of depression and especially scorned the use of prescription drugs to treat psychological disorders, dubbing psychiatry "a pseudo science." His words provoked a wide array of responses. The National Alliance for the Mentally Ill (NAMI), the American Psychiatric Association, and the National Mental Health Association (NMHA) issued a joint statement decrying Cruise's remarks and declaring, "While we respect the right of individuals to express their own points of view, they are not entitled to their own facts. Mental illnesses are real medical conditions that affect millions of Americans" (NAMI/APA/NMHA, 2005).

The reality of psychological disorders has sparked controversy outside the Hollywood community as well. Nearly 50 years ago, psychiatrist Thomas Szasz (1961) set off a bitter debate when he published *The Myth of Mental Illness.* Like Cruise, Szasz made the surprising claim that there is no such thing as "mental illness."

Szasz began his argument with a distinction between diseases of the brain and diseases of the mind. Although he accepted that there are diseases of the brain, such as epilepsy, he suggested that psychological disorders are not illnesses and are better labeled "problems of living." For Szasz, it was not just a question of semantics. Suppose that someone's "problems of living" stem from interacting with other people. In such instances, Szasz said, it is inconsistent to refer to that person's social problems as "mental illness" and to treat him or her through a medical model that prescribes drugs. Similarly, if a person believes that his body is already dead but does nothing more than offend or frighten other people with his bizarre thinking, what right do mental health professionals have to label him "mentally ill" and to administer drugs to him?

A more recent version of Szasz's critique is the *dimensional* approach. This perspective comes from psychologists who suggest that, rather than belonging in a different category from everyone else, individuals who suffer from psychological disorders should be understood as possessing extreme forms of the same characteristics and behaviors all people have (Maddux, Snyder, & Lopez, 2004). (The dimensional approach contrasts with a *categorical* approach, which views individuals who are diagnosed with a psychological disorder as qualitatively different from the norm.) An example of a dimensional approach is the use of the five-factor model of personality (described in Chapter 11) to understand personality disorders. From a dimensional perspective, personality disorders can be understood as extreme forms of the same traits that are observed in the normal population (Coker & Widiger, 2005; Maddux & Mundell, 2005).

In criticizing the medical model, advocates of dimensional views suggest that, like many other psychological constructs (such as self-esteem, prejudice, and stereotypes), psychological disorders are *socially constructed* (Lilienfeld & Marino, 1995). As such, they are influenced by social, political, historical, and economic factors. Does a young woman who refuses to marry have a psychological disorder, or is she simply independent? One of Freud's patients was first referred for treatment because of her disinterest in marriage. Does a gay male or lesbian have a psychological disorder? The psychological and psychiatric community thought so until the 1970s. If we acknowledge that the categories of psychological disorders may shift depending on the context, is it fair to stamp labels of various psychological disorders on individuals?

The controversy over attention deficit hyperactivity disorder provides a specific example. In **attention deficit hyperactivity disorder (ADHD),** individuals show one or more of the following characteristics over a period of time: inattention, hyperactivity, and impulsivity. ADHD is currently one of the most common psychological disorders of childhood, and the growth in diagnosis of this disorder in recent years is staggering (Jensen, 2006). In 1988, just 500,000 cases were diagnosed. In 2003, 4.4 million children were diagnosed with ADHD, and about half were put on a stimulant medication such as Adderall or Ritalin (Centers for Disease Control and Prevention, 2003). Currently, 5 to 7 million children are diagnosed with ADHD each year (National Center for Health

(continued)

In 2005 actor Tom Cruise denounced fellow actor Brooke Shields (left) after she publicized her experiences with postpartum depression. On the Today Show, *Cruise (right, with host Matt Lauer) attacked the very idea of depression and called psychiatry "a pseudo science." Cruise and Shields have since mended their very public differences.*

Statistics, 2006). Between 1990 and 1996, medication prescribed to treat children with ADHD increased by 500 percent (Drug Enforcement Administration, 1996).

There are certainly social factors related to ADHD diagnoses. Non-Latino White children living in affluent suburbs are more likely to be diagnosed than others—indeed, these children are twice as likely to be diagnosed as African American children. Non-Latino White boys are much more likely to be diagnosed than any other group (National Center for Health Statistics, 2006). In two school districts in Virginia, up to 17 percent of non-Latino White boys were diagnosed with ADHD (LeFever, Dawson, & Morrow, 1999). In contrast, in Utah, the diagnosis rate is as low as 3 percent. These differing rates suggest that either Utah is underdiagnosing or Virginia is overdiagnosing cases. This issue is of some importance, because animal research has shown that in the absence of ADHD, exposure to a stimulant such as Adderall or Ritalin can have long-lasting negative effects on the brain and predispose individuals to later addiction problems (Leo, 2005).

The sheer number of ADHD diagnoses has prompted some observers to wonder whether psychiatrists, parents, and teachers are simply pathologizing normal childhood behavior. The impulsivity, hyperactivity, and inattention that characterize ADHD are in fact typical of most children, especially boys. Indeed, some pediatricians have concluded that a diagnosis of ADHD is the equivalent of labeling a normal child whose personality is incompatible with his or her environment (Carey, 2002).

In response to the debate, the National Institute of Mental Health sponsored a conference that resulted in a "consensus statement" that ADHD is a real psychological disorder. Those who signed the statement (75 individuals) were psychiatrists and psychologists who reviewed the scientific basis for ADHD (Barkley & others, 2002). Furthermore, they concluded that children and youth with ADHD experience potentially harmful outcomes, including dropping out of school, having few or no friends, becoming pregnant as a teen, contracting sexually transmitted infections, and engaging in antisocial behaviors (Barkley & others,

2002). The statement's signers asserted that denying that ADHD is a real disorder amounts to believing that the world is flat.

In turn, critiques of the consensus statement argued that the biological basis of ADHD is not unique to that disorder but is a pattern shared with other childhood disorders (Timimi, 2004). Some of the critics conclude that 1 to 2 percent of children likely have a brain malfunction that warrants classification of something like ADHD, but that another 5 to 10 percent who are diagnosed with ADHD should not be (Carey, 2002). Furthermore, critics say that the use of prescription drugs removes responsibility from parents and teachers and leads society to ignore the environmental factors that may be involved in ADHD (Timimi, 2004). Finally, the critics point out that some of those signing the consensus statement were researchers funded by the pharmaceutical companies that produce Ritalin and other such drugs.

ADHD is not the only controversial diagnosis; indeed, some psychologists adopt a stance similar to Tom Cruise's—rejecting the very notion of mental illness (Eisenberg, 1988). In addition, ADHD is not alone in its link to pharmaceutical companies. It is not uncommon that such companies fund research that focuses on a disease model of psychological disorder. Those with a financial interest in promoting medication are likely to be interested in ways that medication can alleviate suffering.

To reach a resolution of this controversy, everyone agrees on the need for further research to clarify what "depression" and "schizophrenia" and "ADHD" really are. Nobody wants to label inappropriately, to misdiagnose, or to mistreat people who are already suffering.

What Do You Think?

- When do you think it is appropriate to label someone as having a psychological disorder?
- When do you think medical interventions for psychological disorders are appropriate?
- If a teacher suggested that your child be tested for ADHD, what would you do? Why?

 ## REVIEW, ASSESS, AND SHARPEN YOUR THINKING

Review

1 Discuss the characteristics, explanations, and classifications of abnormal behavior.

- Define abnormal behavior and summarize the biological, psychological, sociocultural, and interactionist approaches to psychological disorders.
- Describe the classification of psychological disorders and evaluate its advantages and disadvantages.

Assess

1. All of the following are characteristics of abnormal behavior except that
   A. it is typical.
   B. it causes distress.
   C. it is maladaptive.
   D. it is deviant.

2. Mental retardation is classified on which of the *DSM-IV* axes?
   A. Axis I
   B. Axis II
   C. Axis III
   D. Axis IV

3. How well someone is functioning day-to-day is coded on which *DSM-IV* axis?

A. Axis II   B. Axis III

C. Axis IV   D. Axis V

4. The finding that women are more likely to experience internalizing problems but men are more likely to exhibit externalizing behaviors is consistent with which theoretical approach?

A. psychodynamic   B. sociocultural

C. trait   D. social cognitive

5. Conceptualizing a psychological disorder as happening because of faulty thought processes, biological predispositions, and social stigma is consistent with which theoretical approach?

A. sociocultural

B. biological

C. biopsychosocial

D. psychodynamic

Sharpen Your Thinking

Think of someone you know whose personal habits make him or her different from the norm. Maybe you have a friend who has unusual food preferences or who dresses differently from others. Does this individual fit the definition of abnormal? Why or why not? Where do you draw the line between different and abnormal?

2 Anxiety Disorders

Distinguish among the various anxiety disorders.

Think about how you felt the morning of an important exam or just before a big presentation, or perhaps as you noticed the police lights flashing behind your speeding car. Did you feel jittery and nervous and experience tightness in your stomach? These are the feelings of normal anxiety. Anxiety is a diffuse, vague, highly unpleasant feeling of fear and dread.

Individuals with high levels of anxiety worry a lot, but their anxiety does not necessarily impair their ability to function in the world. In contrast, **anxiety disorders** are psychological disorders that feature motor tension (jumpiness, trembling, inability to relax); hyperactivity (dizziness, a racing heart, possible perspiration); and apprehensive expectations and thoughts. Anxiety disorders are different from the kind of everyday anxiety a person might experience: This anxiety is uncontrollable, is disproportionate to the actual danger the person might be in, and is disruptive of the person's ordinary life. Approximately 40 million American adults over the age of 18, or about 18.1 percent of people in this age group, are diagnosed with an anxiety disorder in any given year (Kessler & others, 2005; NIMH, 2006). The five types of anxiety disorders are generalized anxiety disorder, panic disorder, phobic disorders, obsessive-compulsive disorder, and post-traumatic stress disorder.

Generalized Anxiety Disorder

When you are worrying about a big test or feeling anxious about getting a speeding ticket, you know why you are anxious. **Generalized anxiety disorder** is different from such everyday feelings of anxiety because sufferers of this disorder experience persistent anxiety for at least 6 months, and an individual with generalized anxiety disorder is unable to specify the reasons for the anxiety (Kendler & others, 2007). People with generalized anxiety disorder are nervous most of the time. They may worry about their work, their relationships, or their health. They also may worry about minor things, such as being late for an appointment or whether their clothes fit just right. Their anxiety often shifts from one aspect of life to another. In the United States, approximately 6.8 million individuals over 18 years of age, or about 3.1 percent of this age group, have generalized anxiety disorder in any given year (NIMH, 2006).

What is the etiology of generalized anxiety disorder? (The term *etiology* here means the causes or significant antecedents of a psychological disorder.) Among the biological factors

anxiety disorders Psychological disorders that feature motor tension, hyperactivity, and apprehensive expectations and thoughts.

generalized anxiety disorder An anxiety disorder that consists of persistent anxiety for at least 6 months; the individual with this disorder cannot specify the reasons for the anxiety.

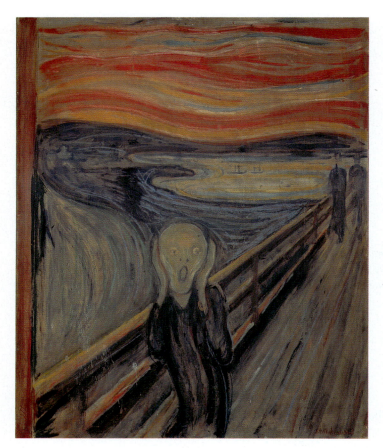

Many experts interpret Edvard Munch's painting The Scream *as an expression of the terror brought on by a panic attack.*

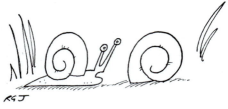

"...And how long have you been agoraphobic?"
© CartoonStock.com

panic disorder An anxiety disorder marked by recurrent sudden onsets of intense apprehension or terror.

agoraphobia A cluster of fears centered on public places and on an inability to escape or to find help should one become incapacitated.

involved in generalized anxiety disorder are a genetic predisposition, a deficiency in the neurotransmitter GABA, and respiratory system abnormalities (Hettema & others, 2006a, 2006b; Kendler & others, 2007). Among the psychological and sociocultural factors are having harsh self-standards that are virtually impossible to achieve or maintain; overly strict and critical parents (whose influence can produce low self-esteem and excessive self-criticism); automatic negative thoughts in the face of stress; and a history of uncontrollable stressors or traumas, such as an abusive parent.

Panic Disorder

Much like everyone else, you sometimes have a specific experience that sends you into a panic. For example, you work all night on a paper only to have your computer crash before you printed it out or saved your last changes. Or you are just about to dash across a street when you see a large truck coming right at you. Your heart races, your hands shake, and you might break out into a sweat.

In **panic disorder,** however, a person experiences recurrent, sudden onsets of intense apprehension or terror. The individual has frequent feelings of impending doom but may not feel anxious all the time. Panic attacks often strike without warning and can produce severe palpitations, extreme shortness of breath, chest pains, trembling, sweating, dizziness, and a feeling of helplessness (Dammen & others, 2006). Victims are seized by fear that they will die, go crazy, or do something they cannot control. They may feel that they are having a heart attack.

Charles Darwin, the scientist who proposed the theory of evolution, suffered from intense panic disorder (Barloon & Noyes, 1997). Actor Kim Basinger and former NFL running back Earl Campbell also have dealt with this disorder, along with approximately 6 million Americans over the age of 18 (about 2.7 percent of this age group) in any given year (Kessler & others, 2005; NIMH, 2006). In many instances, a stressful life event occurred in the 6 months prior to the onset of panic disorder, most often a threatened or an actual separation from a loved one or a change in job.

In the *DSM-IV,* panic disorder can be classified as with or without **agoraphobia,** a cluster of fears centered on public places and an inability to escape or find help if one should become incapacitated (Onur, Alkin, & Tural, 2006; Schmidt & Cromer, 2007). Being in crowded public places; traveling away from home, especially by public transportation; feeling confined or trapped; and being separated from a place or person all can produce agoraphobia, which leads some people to remain housebound. Agoraphobia usually first appears in early adulthood, with 0.8 percent of individuals in the United States classified as having the disorder in the absence of panic disorder (NIMH, 2006).

What is the etiology of panic disorder? In terms of biological factors, individuals may have a predisposition for the disorder, which runs in families and occurs more often in identical than in fraternal twins (Hettema & others, 2006a). One biological view is that individuals who experience panic disorder may have an autonomic nervous system that is predisposed to be overly active (Barlow, 1988). Another biological view is that panic disorder may be caused by problems involving either or both of two neurotransmitters: norepinephrine and GABA (Zwanzger & Rupprecht, 2005). In yet another biological link, panic attacks involve hyperventilation, or overbreathing (Freire & others, 2007; Nardi & others, 2006). Hormonal factors may also be important, helping to explain the tendency of women to be more likely than men to suffer from panic disorder (Altemus, 2006).

With respect to psychological factors, one view focuses on panic disorder with agoraphobia. It is called the *fear-of-fear hypothesis,* which means that agoraphobia may not represent fear of public places but fear of having a panic attack in public places. Another psychological interpretation of panic disorder is that individuals misinterpret harmless indicators of physiological arousal (for example, a slightly raised heartbeat) as an emergency (such as a heart attack). However, this model of panic disorder remains controversial (Austin & Richards, 2006).

In terms of sociocultural factors, American women are twice as likely as American men to have panic attacks with or without agoraphobia (Altemus, 2006). However, in India, men are far more likely to have panic disorders, probably because Indian women rarely leave home alone (McNally, 1994). The reasons that American women have a higher incidence of panic disorder, with or without agoraphobia, include gender socialization (boys are encouraged to be more independent; girls are more protected); traumatic experiences (girls are more often the targets of rape and child sexual abuse than boys); and biological differences in hormones as well as neurotransmitters, especially those associated with consolidating emotional memory (Altemus, 2006; Fodor & Epstein, 2002).

Phobic Disorder

Most people are afraid of spiders and snakes. Indeed, thinking about letting a tarantula crawl over one's face may give anyone the willies. It is not uncommon to be afraid of specific objects or experiences (such as extreme heights), but most of us do not experience these fears to the extent that they interfere with our lives. Some of us, however, have an irrational, overwhelming, persistent fear of a particular object or situation—an anxiety disorder called a **phobic disorder** or *phobia*. Whereas individuals with generalized anxiety disorder cannot pinpoint the cause of their nervous feelings, individuals with phobias can (Choy, Fyer, & Lipsitz, 2006).

A fear becomes a phobia when a situation is so dreaded that an individual goes to almost any length to avoid it. As with any anxiety disorder, phobias are fears that are uncontrollable, disproportionate, and disruptive. Snake phobia that keeps a city-dweller from leaving his apartment is clearly disproportionate to the actual chances of encountering a snake. Approximately 19.2 million people in the United States over 18, or about 8.7 percent, have a phobic disorder in any given year (NIMH, 2006). John Madden—former NFL coach, renowned football announcer, and successful video game consultant—has a famous fear of flying that has led him to take a bus to the various games that he is announcing.

Phobias come in many forms. Some of the most common phobias involve social situations, dogs, height, dirt, flying, and snakes. Figure 13.3 labels and describes a number of phobias.

Social phobia is an intense fear of being humiliated or embarrassed in social situations. Individuals with this phobia are afraid that they will say or do the wrong thing. As a consequence, they might avoid speaking up in a conversation, giving a speech, going out to eat, or attending a party. Their deep fear of such contexts can severely restrict their social

"Have you always had a fear of flying or did it start after the plane crash?"
© CartoonStock.com

phobic disorder Commonly called *phobia,* an anxiety disorder in which the individual has an irrational, overwhelming, persistent fear of a particular object or situation.

Acrophobia	Fear of high places	Arachnophobia	Fear of spiders	Mysophobia	Fear of dirt
Aerophobia	Fear of flying	Astrapophobia	Fear of lightning	Nyctophobia	Fear of darkness
Ailurophobia	Fear of cats	Cynophobia	Fear of dogs	Ophidiophobia	Fear of nonpoisonous
Algophobia	Fear of pain	Gamophobia	Fear of marriage		snakes
Amaxophobia	Fear of vehicles,	Hydrophobia	Fear of water	Thanatophobia	Fear of death
	driving	Melissophobia	Fear of bees	Xenophobia	Fear of strangers

FIGURE 13.3

Phobias This figure features some examples of phobic disorder, an anxiety disorder characterized by irrational and overwhelming fear of a particular object or experience.

Social Phobias	Percent Who Experience This Phobia in Their Lifetime
Public speaking	30.2
Talking in front of a small group	15.2
Talking with others	13.7
Using a toilet away from home	6.6
Writing while someone watches	6.4
Eating or drinking in public	2.7

FIGURE 13.4

Social Phobias in the United States In a national survey, the most common social phobia was public speaking (Kessler, Stein, & Bergland, 1998). Similar patterns have been identified in other cultures as well (Iancu & others, 2006).

© CartoonStock.com

obsessive-compulsive disorder (OCD)
An anxiety disorder in which the individual has anxiety-provoking thoughts that will not go away (obsession) and/or urges to perform repetitive, ritualistic behaviors to prevent or produce some future situation (compulsion).

life and increase their loneliness (Faytout & others, 2007). Successful singers Carly Simon and Barbra Streisand have dealt with social phobia. Figure 13.4 shows the percentage of people in the United States who say they have experienced a social phobia in their lifetime (Kessler, Stein, & Bergland, 1998).

What is the etiology of phobic disorders? In terms of biological factors, identical twins reared apart sometimes develop the same phobias; one pair independently became claustrophobic, for example (Eckert, Heston, & Bouchard, 1981). About 16 percent of first-degree relatives of individuals with social phobia have an increased risk of developing the phobia, compared with only 5 percent of the relatives of people without social phobia (Hettema & others, 2006a; Kessler, Olfson, & Bergland, 1998). A neural circuit has been proposed for social phobia that includes the thalamus, amygdala, and cerebral cortex (Larson & others, 2006). Also, a number of neurotransmitters may be involved in social phobia, especially serotonin (Nash & Nutt, 2005).

With regard to psychological factors, different theoretical perspectives provide different explanations (Prochaska & Norcross, 2007). Psychodynamic theorists say that phobias develop as defense mechanisms to ward off threatening or unacceptable impulses—for example, a person's fear that the id will take over and he or she will jump off the top of a tall building explains the individual's fear of heights. In contrast, learning theorists interpret phobias as learned fears (Clark & others, 2006). According to learning theorists, perhaps the individual with the fear of falling off a building experienced a fall from a high place earlier in life and therefore associates falling with pain—and consequently now fears high places (a classical conditioning explanation). Or he or she may have heard about or seen others who were afraid of high places (an observational-learning explanation). For instance, a little girl sitting next to her terrified mother who is clutching the handrails, white-knuckled, on a roller coaster that is slowly creeping uphill might develop a fear of heights.

Obsessive-Compulsive Disorder

Just before leaving on a long road trip, you might find yourself checking to be sure you locked the front door. You might pull away and be stricken with the thought that you forgot to turn off the coffeemaker. Or, upon going to bed the night before an early-morning flight, you might check your alarm clock a few times to be sure it will wake you for your 8 A.M. plane. This kind of checking behavior is a normal part of worrying. Obsessions are recurrent thoughts and compulsions are recurrent behaviors. **Obsessive-compulsive disorder (OCD)** is an anxiety disorder in which the individual has anxiety-provoking thoughts that will not go away (obsession) and/or urges to perform repetitive, ritualistic behaviors to prevent or produce some future situation (compulsion).

Individuals with OCD dwell on normal doubts and repeat their routines, sometimes hundreds of times a day (Torres & others, 2006). Approximately 2.2 million people in the United States over 18, or about 1 percent of this age group, have obsessive-compulsive disorder in any given year (NIMH, 2006). Among those who have coped with OCD are comedian and game show host Howie Mandel and radio shock jock Howard Stern.

The most common compulsions are excessive checking, cleansing, and counting. An individual with OCD might feel that she has to touch the doorway with her left hand whenever she enters a room, and count her steps as she walks across the room. If she does not complete this ritual, she may be overcome with a sense of fear that something terrible will happen. Indeed, most individuals do not enjoy their ritualistic behavior but feel extraordinarily anxious when they do not carry it out.

What is the etiology of obsessive-compulsive disorder? In terms of biological factors, there seems to be a genetic component, because OCD runs in families (Grabe & others, 2006; Steward & others, 2007). Also, brain-imaging studies have suggested neurological links for OCD (Cannistraro & others, 2006; Remijnse & others, 2006). One interpretation of these data is that the frontal cortex or basal ganglia are so active in OCD that numerous impulses reach the thalamus, generating obsessive thoughts or compulsive actions (Figure 13.5) (Rappaport, 1989). A study using fMRI examined the brain activity of individuals with OCD

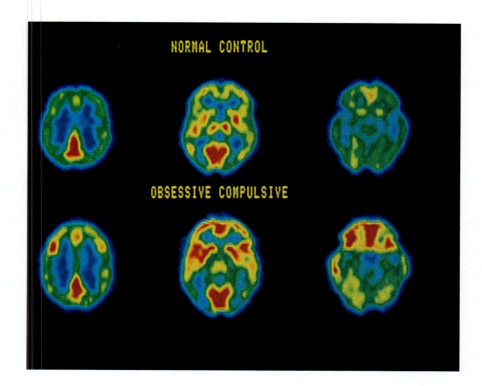

FIGURE 13.5

PET Scans of Individuals with Obsessive-Compulsive Disorder

(*Top*) Brain images of normal individuals. (*Bottom*) Brain images of individuals with obsessive-compulsive disorder (OCD). The brain images of the individuals with OCD show more activity in the frontal cortex, basal ganglia, and thalamus than the brain images of normal individuals.

before and after treatment. The results demonstrated that following effective treatment, a number of areas in the frontal cortex showed decreases in activation (Nakao & others, 2005). Interestingly, the amygdala, which is associated with the experience of anxiety, may be less rather than more active in individuals with OCD (Cannistraro & others, 2004). Depletion of the neurotransmitter serotonin likely is involved in the neural circuitry linked with OCD (Catapano & others, 2006; Fontenelle & others, 2007).

In terms of psychological factors, OCD often occurs during a period of life stress, such as the birth of a child, or a change in occupational or marital status (Ross & McClean, 2006; Uguz & others, 2007). According to the cognitive perspective, what differentiates individuals with OCD from those who do not have it is the ability to turn off negative, intrusive thoughts by ignoring or dismissing them (Park & others, 2006). Onset of the disorder frequently occurs in late adolescence or early adulthood, although it can also emerge in young children (O'Kearney, Anstey, & von Sanden, 2006).

Post-Traumatic Stress Disorder

If you have ever been in even a minor car accident, you may have found yourself having a nightmare or two about it. You might even find yourself needing to talk about it with your friends and reliving the experience for some time. After watching a particularly scary movie, you might worry about how you will sleep. This normal recovery process takes on a particularly devastating character in post-traumatic stress disorder. **Post-traumatic stress disorder (PTSD)** is an anxiety disorder that develops through exposure to a traumatic event, such as war; severely oppressive situations, such as the Holocaust; severe abuse, as in rape; natural disasters, such as floods and tornados; and unnatural disasters, such as plane crashes (Friedman, Keane, & Resick, 2007). In the United States, approximately 7.7 million people over the age of 18, or about 3.5 percent of this age group, have PTSD in any given year (NIMH, 2006).

PTSD Symptoms   The symptoms of PTSD vary but include the following:

- Flashbacks in which the individual relives the event
- Constricted ability to feel emotions, often reported as feeling numb, resulting in an inability to experience happiness, sexual desire, or enjoyable interpersonal relationships

post-traumatic stress disorder (PTSD) An anxiety disorder that develops through exposure to a traumatic event, severely oppressive situations, severe abuse, and natural and unnatural disasters.

- Excessive arousal, resulting in an exaggerated startle response or an inability to sleep
- Difficulties with memory and concentration
- Feelings of apprehension, including nervous tremors
- Impulsive outbursts of behavior, such as aggressiveness, or sudden changes in lifestyle

Not every individual exposed to the same event develops post-traumatic stress disorder, which overloads the individual's usual coping abilities (Gil & Caspi, 2006; Nemeroff & others, 2006). For example, it is estimated that 30 percent of Vietnam veterans experienced PTSD (Kulka & others, 1991).

Developmental Course of PTSD PTSD is characterized by anxiety symptoms that may either immediately follow the trauma or be delayed by months or even years (Breslau & Alvarado, 2007). Most individuals who are exposed to a traumatic, stressful event experience some of the symptoms in the days and weeks following exposure (National Center for Post-Traumatic Stress Disorder, 2006). Overall, approximately 8 percent of men and 20 percent of women go on to develop PTSD, and about 30 percent of these individuals develop a chronic form that persists throughout their life.

The course of PTSD typically involves periods of symptom increase followed by remission or decrease, although for some individuals the symptoms may be unremitting and severe (Bisson, 2007; Wilson, 2007). Ordinary events can serve as reminders of the trauma and trigger flashbacks or intrusive images.

A flashback can make the person lose touch with reality and reenact the event for a period of seconds, hours or, very rarely, days. A person having a flashback—which can come in the form of images, sounds, smells, and/or feelings—usually believes that the traumatic event is happening all over again (Speckens & others, 2007).

Combat and War-Related Traumas Much of what is known about PTSD comes from individuals who developed the disorder because of combat and war-related traumas (Johnson & Thompson, 2007). In one study of 124 survivors of the Holocaust, almost half were still suffering from PTSD 40 years later (Kuch & Cox, 1992). In another study, 10 percent of Vietnamese, Hmong, Laotian, and Cambodian refugees who left their war-torn countries to live in California had PTSD (Gong-Guy, 1986). A study of Bosnian refugees just after they had come to the United States indicated that 65 percent had PTSD (Weine & others, 1995). Many of these Bosnian refugees had been the victims of numerous atrocities, including mass rapes and murders of relatives and neighbors.

Rather than waiting years for the effects of the stress of combat to take its toll on those who have served in the military, branches of the U.S. armed forces now use military psychologists—those who specialize in research and application to military problems—and other mental health professionals in preventive efforts in combat zones around the world (Rabasca, 2000). The mental health units typically have a psychologist, a social worker, and several mental health technicians. Units also might have a psychiatrist, psychiatric nurses, and occupational therapists.

Recently, PTSD has been a concern for soldiers stationed in Iraq and Afghanistan (Seal & others, 2007). Nineteen percent of Marines and 17 percent of U.S. Army troops surveyed reported depression, anxiety, and PTSD symptoms (Greer, 2005). These statistics likely underestimate the true level of suffering, as the stigma associated with psychological disorders is particularly high in the military.

PTSD is a serious problem for U.S. troops serving today in Iraq and Afghanistan. For this reason, prior to deployment, U.S. troops receive stress-management training aimed at helping to prevent PTSD and other disorders that might be triggered by the unusually high-stress conditions they will face.

The Iraq War context is especially stressful, featuring surprise attacks, urban combat and street fighting, suicide bombers, and unrelenting fear of random violence. A survey of almost 3,000 soldiers who had just returned from the Iraq War revealed that 17 percent met the criteria for PTSD (Hoge & others, 2007). Because of concern over stigma, troops are being given stress-management training prior to being deployed, which is aimed at helping to prevent PTSD and other disorders (Greer, 2005; Ritchie & others, 2006). These troops are providing a valuable test for research on PTSD. Never before have researchers been able to assess combat troops before and after their tours of duty. Most research on PTSD in Vietnam War veterans did not even begin until the 1980s.

Abuse   Some experts consider sexual abuse and assault victims to be the single largest group of post-traumatic stress disorder sufferers (Hegadoren, Lasiuk, & Coupland, 2006). Abuse can come in many forms, including abuse of a spouse, the sexual abuse of rape or incest, and emotional abuse (as when parents harshly criticize and belittle their children) (Cicchetti & Toth, 2006). Researchers have found that approximately 95 percent of rape survivors experience PTSD symptoms in the first 2 weeks following the traumatic event. About 50 percent still have symptoms 3 months later, and as many as 25 percent have symptoms 4 to 5 years after the rape (Tolin & Foa, 2006).

Natural and Unnatural Disasters   Natural disasters such as tornados, hurricanes, earthquakes, and fires can cause the individuals who experience these traumatic events to develop PTSD (Mills, Edmondson, & Park, 2007). A recent study of Hurricane Katrina evacuees revealed that the majority of the evacuees experienced moderate (39 percent) to severe (24 percent) PTSD symptoms in the 2 weeks following the hurricane in 2005 (Coker & others, 2006). Fourteen years after a flood destroyed the community of Buffalo Creek in West Virginia, 25 percent of the survivors were still suffering from PTSD (Green & others, 1992, 1997). Among Australian children who had experienced a major brush fire, those who had been evacuated and who reported feeling very distressed by the trauma were more likely to show symptoms of PTSD 13 months later (Parslow, Jorm, & Christensen, 2006).

Unnatural disasters such as plane crashes and terrorist attacks also can cause individuals to develop post-traumatic stress disorder (Laugharne, Janca, & Widiger, 2007). The September 11th attacks were expected to produce PTSD in many of the survivors (Schein & others, 2006); research has supported this speculation, with many individuals in the New York City area experiencing symptoms of PTSD, as well as depression (Agronick & others, 2007; Stuber & others, 2006). But significantly, few individuals who were not receiving mental health treatment before the attacks sought or received help (Stuber & others, 2006). Thus, in the aftermath of disaster, individuals may not recognize their own need for therapeutic assistance.

 REVIEW, ASSESS, AND SHARPEN YOUR THINKING

Review

2 Distinguish among the various anxiety disorders.

- Define anxiety disorders and characterize generalized anxiety disorder.
- State the main features of panic disorder.
- Identify the sources of anxiety in phobic disorders.
- Explain obsessive-compulsive disorder.
- Describe post-traumatic stress disorder.

Assess

1. A discrete period of extreme anxiety that involves physical symptoms such as a pounding heart and sweating is a defining characteristic of which disorder?
   - A. generalized anxiety disorder
   - B. post-traumatic stress disorder
   - C. obsessive-compulsive disorder
   - D. panic disorder

2. Someone who fears going out in public because of concerns of losing control is likely experiencing
   - A. phobic disorder.
   - B. post-traumatic stress disorder.
   - C. agoraphobia.
   - D. obsessive-compulsive disorder.

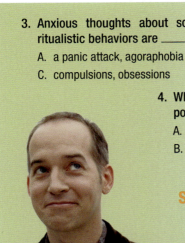

3. Anxious thoughts about something are _____, whereas ritualistic behaviors are _____.

A. a panic attack, agoraphobia
B. agoraphobia, a panic attack
C. compulsions, obsessions
D. an obsession, compulsions

4. Which of the following is true of post-traumatic stress disorder?

A. It is caused by panic attacks.
B. It is the natural outgrowth of experiencing trauma.
C. It may involve flashbacks.
D. The symptoms aways occur immediately following a trauma.

5. Intense fear of something that results in efforts to avoid the feared stimulus is a defining characteristic of

A. agoraphobia.
B. phobic disorder.
C. panic disorder.
D. generalized anxiety disorder.

Sharpen Your Thinking

Family and friends of individuals with obsessive-compulsive disorder frequently tell them to stop their obsessions and compulsions. However, just telling someone to stop these behaviors usually does not work. If you had a friend with this disorder, what would you try to do about it?

3 Mood Disorders

Compare the mood disorders and specify risk factors for depression and suicide.

mood disorders Psychological disorders in which there is a primary disturbance in mood (prolonged emotion that colors the individual's entire emotional state). Two main types are the depressive disorders and bipolar disorder.

depressive disorders Mood disorders in which the individual suffers from depression (an unrelenting lack of pleasure in life).

major depressive disorder (MDD) A mood disorder indicated by a major depressive episode and depressed characteristics, such as lethargy and hopelessness, lasting at least 2 weeks.

Mood disorders are psychological disorders in which there is a primary disturbance of mood (prolonged emotion that colors the individual's entire emotional state). The mood disturbance can include cognitive, behavioral, and somatic (physical) symptoms, as well as interpersonal difficulties.

Two main types of mood disorders are the depressive disorders and bipolar disorder. Depression can occur alone, as in the depressive disorders, or it can alternate with mania (an overexcited, unrealistically optimistic state), as in bipolar disorder. In the United States, approximately 20.9 million people over the age of 18, or about 9.5 percent of this age group, have a mood disorder in any given year (NIMH, 2006).

Depressive Disorders

Everyone feels blue sometimes. A romantic breakup, the death of a loved one, or a personal failure all can cast a dark cloud over life. Sometimes a person might feel unhappy and not really know why. **Depressive disorders** are mood disorders in which the individual suffers from depression (an unrelenting lack of pleasure in life). The severity of depressive disorders varies. Some individuals experience what is classified as *major depressive disorder (MDD),* whereas others are given the diagnosis of *dysthymic disorder (DD),* a more chronic depression with fewer symptoms than major depression (Benazzi, 2006; Klein, Shankman, & Rose, 2007). Both of these disorders involve a distinctive lack of pleasure in life.

Depressive disorders are rather common, and a number of successful individuals have been diagnosed with clinical depression. They include musicians Sheryl Crow, Eric Clapton, and Peter Gabriel; actors Drew Barrymore and Jim Carrey; and baseball player José Canseco, artist Pablo Picasso, photographer Diane Arbus, astronaut Buzz Aldrin (the second man to walk on the moon), and famed American architect Frank Lloyd Wright.

Major depressive disorder (MDD) involves a major depressive episode and depressed characteristics, such as lethargy and hopelessness, for at least 2 weeks. According to the National Institute of Mental Health, MDD is the leading cause of disability in the United States (NIMH, 2006). With MDD, the individual's daily functioning becomes impaired. A national study found that 16.2 percent of U.S. adults (about 34 million) had major depressive disorder in their lifetime, and 6.2 percent had MDD in the previous 12 months (NIMH, 2006).

This painting by Vincent Van Gogh, Portrait of Dr. Gachet, *reflects the extreme melancholy that characterizes the depressive disorders.*

Nine symptoms define a major depressive episode (of which, at least five must be present during a 2-week period):

1. Depressed mood most of the day
2. Reduced interest or pleasure in all or most activities
3. Significant weight loss or gain or significant decrease or interest in appetite
4. Trouble sleeping or sleeping too much
5. Psychomotor agitation or retardation
6. Fatigue or loss of energy
7. Feeling worthless or guilty in an excessive or inappropriate manner
8. Problems in thinking, concentrating, or making decisions
9. Recurrent thoughts of death and suicide

Dysthymic disorder is a depressive disorder that is generally more chronic and has fewer symptoms than major depressive disorder. The individual is in a depressed mood for most days for at least 2 years as an adult or at least 1 year as a child or adolescent. To be classified as having dysthymic disorder, the individual must not have experienced a major depressive episode, and the 2-year period of depression must not have been broken by a normal mood lasting more than 2 months. Two or more of these six symptoms must be present: poor appetite or overeating, sleep problems, low energy or fatigue, low self-esteem, poor concentration or difficulty making decisions, and feelings of hopelessness (Ryder, Schuller, & Bagby, 2006). Approximately 3.3 million people in the United States, or about 1.5 percent of the population, will have dysthymic disorder in any given year (NIMH, 2006).

Too often, depressed people (and those around them) may feel that they should be able to "snap out of it." But depression is a serious disorder. The inadequate care that results from a lack of understanding of depression is tragic. Given the range of treatments available, individuals who go untreated suffer needlessly.

Bipolar Disorder

Just as we all have our down times, there are times when things seem to be going phenomenally well. For individuals with bipolar disorder, the ups and downs of life take on an extreme and often harmful tone. **Bipolar disorder** is a mood disorder that is characterized by extreme mood swings that include one or more episodes of mania (an overexcited, unrealistically optimistic state).

Bipolar means that the person may experience both depression and mania. Most bipolar individuals experience multiple cycles of depression interspersed with mania. Less than 10 percent of bipolar individuals tend to experience manic-type episodes without depression. Approximately 5.7 million Americans, or about 2.6 percent of the U.S. population 18 years and older, have bipolar disorder in any given year (NIMH, 2006). Bipolar disorder does not prevent a person from being successful. Indeed, Tony Award–winning actor Patty Duke, famed American dancer and choreographer Alvin Ailey, and actor Carrie Fisher (Princess Leia) have been diagnosed as bipolar.

A manic episode is like the flip-side of a depressive episode (Gaudiano, Uebelacker, & Miller, 2007). Instead of feeling depressed, the individual feels euphoric and on top of the world. However, as the manic episode unfolds, the person can experience panic and eventually depression. Instead of feeling fatigued, as many depressed individuals do, an individual who experiences mania has tremendous energy and might sleep very little. A manic state also features an impulsivity that can get the individual in trouble in business and legal transactions. For example, the sufferer might spend his or her life savings on a foolish business venture.

According to the *DSM-IV*, manic episodes must last 1 week. They average 8 to 16 weeks. Individuals with bipolar disorder can have manic and depressive episodes four or more times a year, but they usually are separated by 6 months to a year.

Bipolar disorder is much less common than depressive disorders, but unlike depressive disorders (which are likelier to occur in women), bipolar disorder is equally common in women and men. About 1 or 2 in 100 people are estimated to experience bipolar disorder at some point in life (Kessler & others, 1994).

dysthymic disorder A depressive disorder that is generally more chronic and has fewer symptoms than major depressive disorder.

bipolar disorder A mood disorder characterized by extreme mood swings that include one or more episodes of mania (an overexcited, unrealistically optimistic state).

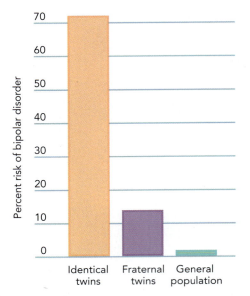

FIGURE 13.6

Risk of Bipolar Disorder in Identical and Fraternal Twins If One Twin Has the Disorder, and in the General Population Notice how much stronger the incidence of bipolar disorder is in identical twins, compared with fraternal twins and the general population. These statistics suggest a strong genetic role in the disorder.

Causes of Mood Disorders

Mood disorders can involve biological, psychological, and sociocultural factors. Although these disorders involve mood, there are some differences in factors thought to contribute to them and, below, we distinguish between depressive disorders and bipolar disorder as appropriate.

Biological Factors Biological explanations of mood disorders include heredity, neuro-physiological abnormalities, neurotransmitter deregulation, and hormonal factors (Nolen-Hoeksema, 2007). The links between biology and mood disorders are well established.

Heredity Depressive and bipolar disorders tend to run in families, although the family link is stronger for bipolar disorder than for depressive disorders (Craddock & Forty, 2006). One of the greatest risks for developing a mood disorder is having a biological parent who suffers from a mood disorder. In bipolar disorder, the rate of the disorder in first-degree relatives (parents, siblings) is 10 to 20 times higher than in the general population (MacKinnon, Jamison, & DePaulo, 1997). An individual with an identical twin who has bipolar disorder has a more than 60 percent probability of also having the disorder, and a fraternal twin more than 10 percent, whereas the rate of bipolar disorder in the general population is 1 to 2 percent (Figure 13.6). Researchers are zeroing in on the specific genetic location of bipolar disorder—with studies suggesting that it may be on chromosome 22 and in specific DNA locations (Hashimoto & others, 2005; Kuratomi & others, 2007).

Neurobiological Abnormalities One of the most consistent findings of neurobiological abnormalities in individuals with mood disorders is altered brain-wave activity during sleep. Depressed individuals experience less slow-wave sleep (which contributes to a feeling of being rested and restored) and go into rapid eye movement (REM) sleep earlier in the night than non-depressed individuals (Benca, 2001). These abnormalities correspond to reports by depressed individuals that they have difficulty going to sleep at night or remaining asleep, often wake up early and cannot get back to sleep, and do not feel rested after they sleep (Carney & others, 2006).

Neuroimaging studies also reveal decreased metabolic activity in the cerebral cortex of those with severe major depressive disorder (Ende, Demirakca, & Tost, 2006). Figure 13.7 shows the metabolic activity of an individual cycling through depressive and manic phases. Notice the decrease in metabolic activity in the brain during depression and the increase in metabolic activity during mania (Baxter & others, 1995).

Most areas of the brains of depressed individuals are underactive. For example, one section of the prefrontal cortex, which is involved in generating actions, is underactive in depressed individuals. However, certain brain areas are overactive. For instance, recent studies using brain-imaging techniques revealed that the amygdala is overactive in depression (Siegle, Carter, & Thase, 2006; Van Elst, Ebert, & Trimble, 2001). Some of depression's symptoms may be explained by this change in brain activity in the amygdala, which helps to store and recall emotionally charged memories and sends information to the prefrontal cortex at the sight of something fearful. In turn, the prefrontal cortex should signal the amygdala to slow down when the source of the fear is gone. But in depression, the prefrontal cortex may fail to send the all-clear signal. Thus, the amygdala may continue sending signals that keep triggering extended rumination about sad events.

Other recent research has revealed that activity in the brain region that is associated with the perception of rewards in the environment (the ventromedial prefrontal cortex) may differ for depressed and non-depressed individuals (Keedwell & others, 2005; Tye & Janak, 2007). This finding suggests that depressed

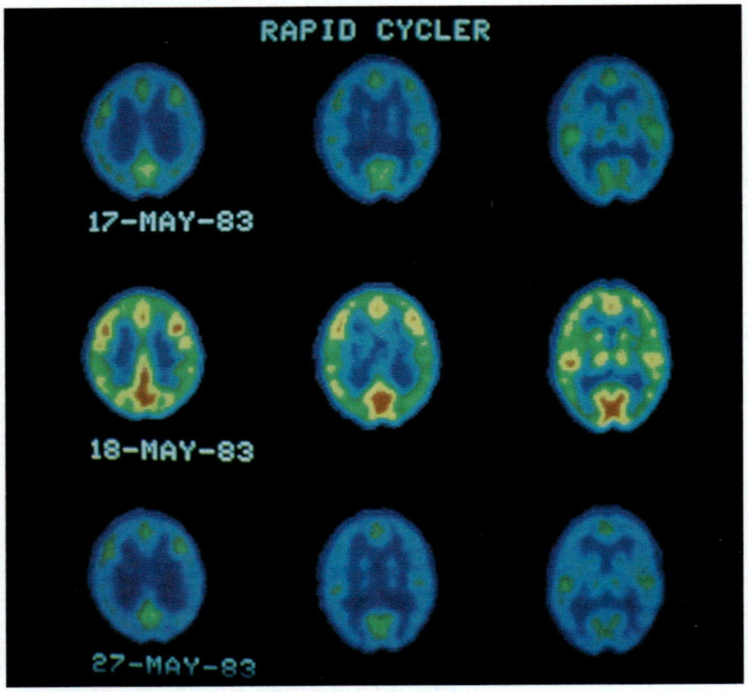

FIGURE 13.7

Brain Metabolism in Mania and Depression PET scans of an individual with bipolar disorder, who is described as a rapid-cycler because of how quickly severe mood changes occurred. (*Top, bottom*) The person's brain in a depressed state. (*Middle*) A manic state. The PET scans reveal how the brain's energy consumption falls in depression and rises in mania. The red areas in the middle row reflect rapid consumption of glucose.

individuals show disordered processing of rewards. In other words, the brain of a depressed person may not recognize opportunities for pleasurable experiences.

Another neurobiological abnormality in depression is neuron death or disability (Lucassen & others, 2006). Studies have shown that depressive disorders are linked to both neuron death and disability (Manji, 2001; Manji, Drevets, & Charney, 2001). Individuals with depression seem to have fewer neurons in some parts of their brains, including the prefrontal cortex, which should be sending the slowdown signals to the amygdala (Drevets, 2001). Research on mice has demonstrated that antidepressants may serve the function of protecting neurons (Haynes, Barber, & Mitchell, 2004) or even generating new neurons (neurogenesis) (Perera & others, 2007).

Problems in Neurotransmitter Regulation Depression likely involves problems in regulating a number of neurotransmitters. As you might recall from Chapter 3, neurotransmitters are the ways that impulses move from neuron to neuron. In order for the brain to function smoothly, these neurotransmitters must ebb and flow, often in harmony with one another. Abnormalities in the monoamine neurotransmitters—such as norepinephrine, serotonin, and dopamine—have been implicated in mood disorders (Mockett & others, 2007). An imbalance in the monoamine neurotransmitters in one direction is thought to be involved in depression; an imbalance in the other direction is implicated in mania. Researchers also have found abnormalities in the number of monoamine neurotransmitters in individuals with mood disorders (Stewart, 2007). For example, individuals with major depressive disorder appear to have too few receptors for serotonin and norepinephrine. Studies also have revealed that changes in the neurotransmitter glutamate occur in bipolar disorder (Pittenger, Sanacora, & Krystal, 2007). Still other research suggests that problems in regulating the amount of a neurotransmitter called substance P are involved in depression (Norman & Burrows, 2007).

Hormones Depressed individuals show chronic hyperactivity in the neuroendocrine glandular system and an inability to return to normal functioning following a stressful experience (Young & Korzun, 1998). In turn, the excess hormones produced by the neuroendocrine glands (such as the pituitary gland and adrenal cortex) may be linked to the problems in regulating the monoamine neurotransmitters just discussed (Schule, 2007).

Also with regard to the role of hormones in depression, some have argued that women's increased vulnerability to depression is linked to their ovarian hormones, estrogen and progesterone. However, evidence tying women's moods to their hormones is mixed at best (Nolen-Hoeksema, 2007). Some women do experience more depression during the postpartum period, menopause, and other times when their hormone levels are changing (Groer & Morgan, 2007). Nonetheless, the extent to which hormonal changes in women account for their higher rate of depression in comparison with men is less clear.

Psychological Factors Psychodynamic, behavioral, and cognitive theories have all proposed explanations for depression. These ideas are significant for their influence on treatment of disorders, as we consider in Chapter 14.

Psychodynamic Explanations Psychodynamic theories emphasize that depression stems from individuals' childhood experiences that prevented them from developing a strong, positive sense of self (Novie, 2007). In this view, depressed individuals become overly dependent on the evaluations and approval of others for their self-esteem mainly because of inadequate nurturing by parents.

Many modern psychodynamic theorists still rely on Freud's (1917) theory that depression is a turning-inward of aggressive instincts. Freud theorized that a child's early attachment to a love object (usually the mother) contains a mixture of love and hate. When the child loses the love object or when his or her dependency needs are frustrated, feelings of loss coexist with anger. Because the child cannot openly accept such angry feelings toward the individual he or she loves, the hostility is turned inward and experienced as depression. The unresolved mixture of anger and love is carried forward to adolescence and adulthood, when loss can bring back these early feelings of abandonment.

Behavioral Explanations Peter Lewinsohn and his colleagues proposed that life's stresses can lead to depression by reducing the positive reinforcers in a person's life (Lewinsohn & Gotlib, 1995; Lewinsohn, Joiner, & Rohde, 2001; Lewinsohn & others, 2006). The sequence goes like this. When people experience considerable stress in their lives, they may withdraw from the stress. The withdrawal produces a further reduction in positive reinforcers, which can lead to more withdrawal, which leads to even fewer positive reinforcers.

Another behavioral view of depression focuses on learned helplessness (see Chapter 7), which occurs when individuals are exposed to aversive stimulation, such as prolonged stress, over which they have no control. The inability to avoid such aversive stimulation produces an apathetic state of helplessness. Martin Seligman (1975) proposed that learned helplessness is one reason that some individuals become depressed. When individuals cannot control the stress they encounter, they eventually feel helpless and stop trying to change their situations. This helplessness spirals into a feeling of hopelessness.

Cognitive Explanations The cognitive approach provides another perspective on mood disorders (Alford & Beck, 2006; Williams & others, 2007). Depressed individuals rarely think positive thoughts. They interpret their lives in self-defeating ways and have negative expectations about the future (Gilbert, 2001). Psychiatrist Aaron Beck (1967) believes that such negative thoughts reflect schemas that shape depressed individuals' experiences. These habitual negative thoughts magnify and expand depressed persons' negative experiences (Kuyken & Beck, 2007). Depressed individuals might overgeneralize about a minor occurrence and think that they are worthless because, say, a work assignment was turned in late or their son was arrested for shoplifting. Or they might receive a work evaluation that shows a deficiency in one area and then magnify the significance of the evaluation. *Catastrophic thinking,* such as expecting to be fired and not being able to find another job, might ensue. The accumulation of such cognitive distortions can lead to depression (Butler & others, 2006).

Research on learned helplessness led Susan Nolen-Hoeksema (1995, 2000, 2003; Nolen-Hoeksema & others, 2007) to examine the ways that people cope when they are depressed. She found that some depressed individuals use a *ruminative coping style,* in which they focus intently on how they feel (their sadness and hopelessness) but do not try to do anything about the feelings: They just think repeatedly about their depression. In a series of research studies, Nolen-Hoeksema and her colleagues (Nolen-Hoeksema, Larson, & Grayson, 1999; Nolen-Hoeksema & Morrow, 1991; Nolen-Hoeksema, Parker, & Larson, 1994) revealed that individuals with depression remain depressed longer when they use a ruminative rather than an action-oriented coping style. Women are more likely than men to ruminate when they are depressed (Nolen-Hoeksema, 2007; Nolen-Hoeksema, Larson, & Grayson, 1999). In a recent study of almost 500 female adolescents, Nolen-Hoeksema and her colleagues (2007) found that rumination predicted future increases in major depression, binge eating, and substance abuse.

Another cognitive view of depression also involves a cognitive reformulation of the hopelessness involved in learned helplessness (Joiner & others, 2001; Northoff, 2007). It focuses on the attributions people make (see Chapter 12). When people make attributions, they attempt to explain what caused something to happen. Depression is thought to be related to what is called the pessimistic attributional style. In this style, individuals regularly explain negative events as having internal causes ("It is my fault I failed the exam"), stable causes ("I'm going to fail again and again"), and global causes ("Failing this exam shows how I won't do well in any of my courses"). Pessimistic attributional style means blaming oneself for negative events and expecting the negative events to recur in their lives in the future (Abramson, Seligman, & Teasdale, 1978) (Figure 13.8).

This pessimistic attributional style can be contrasted with an optimistic style, which is essentially its mirror opposite. Optimists make external attributions for bad things that happen ("I did badly on the test because it's hard to know what a professor wants on the first test"). They also recognize that these causes can change ("I'll do better on the next one").

Being either optimistic or pessimistic can have profound effects on a person's well-being, with optimistic individuals showing better physical and mental health (Taylor, 2006). In one study, researchers interviewed first-year college students at two universities and distinguished those with an optimistic style from those with a pessimistic style (Alloy, Abramson,

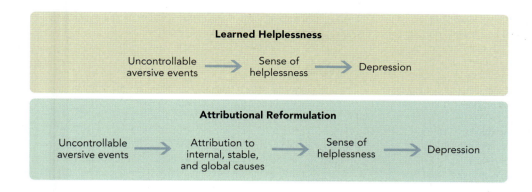

Learned Helplessness

Uncontrollable aversive events → Sense of helplessness → Depression

Attributional Reformulation

Uncontrollable aversive events → Attribution to internal, stable, and global causes → Sense of helplessness → Depression

FIGURE 13.8

Learned Helplessness and Attributional Reformulation of Learned Helplessness Learned helplessness and attributional styles are two ways of understanding the role of cognitive factors in depression.

& Francis, 1999). They interviewed the students on a regular basis over the next 2½ years. In this time frame, among students with no history of depression, 17 percent of the students with a pessimistic style developed major depression, whereas only 1 percent of those with an optimistic style did. Also, among students with a history of depression, 27 percent of those who had a pessimistic style relapsed into depression over the 2½ years, but only 6 percent of those with the optimistic style did. Further, at any age, optimism helps to ward off depression. In a recent study, an optimistic cognitive style was linked to a lower incidence of depression in elderly men over a 15-year period (Giltay, Zitman, & Kromhout, 2006).

Another cognitive explanation of depression focuses on what is called *depressive realism* (Allan, Siegel, & Hannah, 2007; McKendree-Smith & Scogin, 2000). Some individuals who are depressed may be seeing their world accurately and realistically. That is, there really are negative things going on in their lives that make them depressed. Researchers have found that when depressed individuals are asked to make judgments about how much control they have over situations that in fact cannot be controlled, they are accurate in saying that they do not have control (Alloy & Abramson, 1979). In contrast, nondepressed individuals often overestimate the amount of control they have in such situations, thus revealing an illusion of control over their world that depressed individuals do not have. According to this view, it may not be accurate, realistic thinking that prevents individuals from becoming depressed. Rather, optimism and a perceived but illusory sense of control over one's world may be responsible (Taylor & others, 2003b), although this view has its critics (Joiner & others, 2006). Also, it appears that the depressive realism explanation applies more to mild and moderate rather than severe depression (Ghaemi, 2007).

Mothers of young children are especially prone to stress and depression, and their vulnerability rises along with the number of children they have.

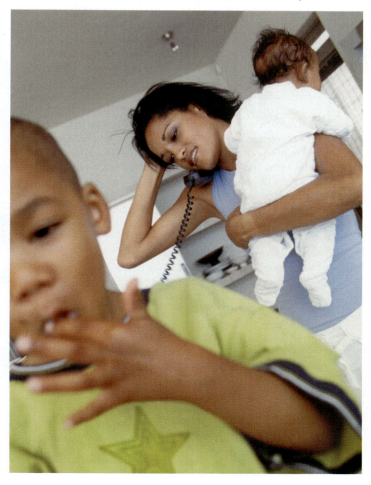

Sociocultural Factors Among the sociocultural factors involved in depression are relationships with other people, socioeconomic and ethnic variations, cultural variations, and gender.

Interpersonal Relationships One view of depression is that it may stem from problems that develop in relationships with other people (Constantine, 2006; Gladstone & others, 2007). Both proximal (recent) and distal (distant, earlier) interpersonal experiences might be involved in depression. In terms of proximal factors, recent marital conflict might trigger depression. With respect to distal factors, possibly inadequate early relationships with parents are carried forward to influence the occurrence of depression later in a person's life.

Socioeconomic and Ethnic Factors Individuals with a low socioeconomic status (SES), especially people living in poverty, are more likely to develop depression than their higher-SES counterparts (Boothroyd & others, 2006). A longitudinal study of adults revealed that depression increased as standard of living and

Clinical and Developmental Psychology: Can New Discoveries Bring Depressed Children a Happier Future?

Imagine once again living the life of a typical 3-year-old. Your daily routine would likely revolve around eating, playing, napping, and perhaps watching cartoons. For most 3-year-olds and even older children, life would seem to be a time of simple happiness. But for some children, childhood is clouded by depression. An estimated 1 to 2 percent of prepubertal children and 3 to 8 percent of adolescents experience depression (Lewinsohn & others, 1994). Children who develop depression are at a higher risk of a variety of problems, including substance abuse, academic problems, increased physical illness, and a 30-fold increase in suicide risk (Horowitz & Garber, 2006).

Childhood depression presents an array of challenging questions and problems that make it a most worthy topic of ongoing research. A unique issue in childhood depression is the question of whether the disorder is real or simply a developmental phase. Furthermore, depression in children raises the concern that, because childhood is a time of building skills and abilities that are essential to later development, a child who is experiencing depression may encounter difficulties with the normal course of development. In addition, childhood depression puts an individual at increased risk for depression in adulthood. Given these considerable issues, how can we come to understand this debilitating psychological disorder in the context of childhood—a time when individuals are faced with achieving a number of developmental milestones that lay the groundwork for future functioning? Developmental psychopathology provides promising pathways for discovery.

Developmental psychopathology emerged in the 1970s as the two established fields of developmental and clinical psychology merged (Masten, 2006; Masten, Burt, & Coatsworth, 2006). Developmental psychopathology is an example of the biopsychosocial approach we considered earlier. From this perspective, in order to understand childhood problems, we must employ an integrative framework that combines what we know about biological, psychological, and social factors in the emergence of normal and abnormal behavior. The goal of developmental psychopathology is to prevent and treat behavioral problems or disorders and to promote positive development (Masten, 2006). Rather than applying what is known about adult psychological disorders to children, developmental psychopathologists focus on the special developmental circumstances of children in seeking to understand what leads to negative outcomes.

Developmental psychopathology as a rule uses longitudinal studies that allow researchers to track the potentially causal relationships that exist in the unfolding of abnormal and normal behavior patterns (Braet & van Aken, 2006; Rudolph & Flynn, 2007). From this perspective, our understanding of abnormal behavior in children is embedded in our knowledge of normal development, and knowledge gained from studies of normal and abnormal patterns can shed light on each type of process (Phares, 2007).

Developmental psychopathology, then, acknowledges a variety of factors that may lead to depression in children, and it seeks to identify risk factors that might predispose a child to depression (Cicchetti & Toth, 2006).

Such risk factors might suggest avenues for intervention aimed at both prevention and treatment.

One longitudinal study that examined predictors of depression in children followed a sample of third-graders for 5 years (Nolen-Hoeksema, Girgus, & Seligman, 1992). Recall that research has shown that cognitive factors—especially a pessimistic attributional style—play a role in adult depressive disorders. But because cognitive development is a process that unfolds over time, such explanations perhaps cannot account for depression in very young children (Kaslow, Adamson, & Collins, 2000). Indeed, among third-graders, negative life events alone predicted depression. By the eighth grade, however, pessimistic style predicted depression, even without negative life events. It seems that once a style becomes a part of a person's psychological makeup, it can play a role in the maintenance of depression, even when the individual does not experience negative events. Acquiring cognitive skills is a normal developmental achievement, but at times these skills can take on a negative character.

For some children, childhood is clouded by depression.

Researchers have identified parental psychopathology as another risk factor for childhood depression. Parents who suffer from depression, an anxiety disorder, or substance abuse are more likely to have children who experience depression (Cicchetti & Toth, 2006). Clearly, if a parent suffers from a form of psychopathology, a genetic tendency may exist for the child also to develop such a disorder. However, not all children of parents with psychopathology develop problems. Family environmental factors may be crucial; indeed, maltreatment, neglect, and separation can predispose at-risk youth to the development of depression (Cicchetti & Toth, 2006). Such findings suggest that to promote healthy development, interventions might target parents whose children are at risk. In fact, a recent research review revealed that interventions aimed at youth who were at risk for depression did promote wellness in the targeted groups (Horowitz & Garber, 2006).

In addition to determining risk factors for depression, developmental psychopathology also is concerned with identifying protective factors—aspects of a child's psychological or social experience that may provide a buffer against the development of depression. An example of a protective factor is resilience, which we considered in Chapter 4. Resilient children are those who may seem at risk but who manage to thrive even in difficult circumstances (Masten, 2006).

Childhood is a time of extraordinary growth, development, and learning. Developmental psychopathologists are taking the problems of persistently sad and disengaged children seriously and are seeking to understand the sources of their suffering in order to give them a more promising future (Cicchetti and Toth, 2006; Phares, 2007).

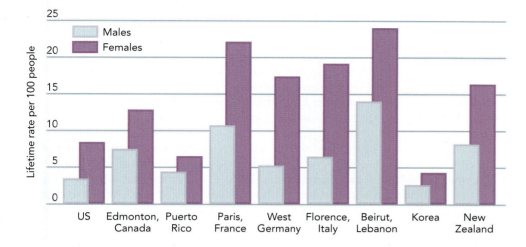

FIGURE 13.9
Gender Differences in Depression Across Cultures One study showed that women were more likely than men to have major depression in nine cultures (Weissman & Olfson, 1995).

employment circumstances worsened (Lorant & others, 2007). Studies also have found very high rates of depression in Native Americans, among whom poverty, hopelessness, and alcoholism are widespread (Teesson & Vogl, 2006).

Gender Bipolar disorder occurs about equally among women and men, but women are nearly twice as likely as men to develop depression. This gender difference occurs in many countries (Inaba & others, 2005) (Figure 13.9).

Studies have shown that depression is especially high among single women who are the heads of households and among young married women who work at unsatisfying, dead-end jobs (Whiffen & Demidenko, 2006). Marriage often confers a greater protective buffer against stress for men than for women (Brabeck & Brabeck, 2006). In unhappy marriages, women are three times as likely as men to be depressed. Mothers of young children are especially vulnerable to stress and depression (Rice & Else-Quest, 2006).

As noted above, poverty may be a pathway to depression, and three of every four people living in poverty in the United States are women and children (Belle & Dodson, 2006). Minority women also are a high-risk group for depression (Waite, 2006). A Canadian study of recent immigrants revealed that women had a higher rate of depression (17 percent) than men (11 percent) (Smith & others, 2007).

Careful diagnosis of depression in women is critical (Nolen-Hoeksema, 2007). According to the American Psychological Association's Task Force on Women and Depression, depression is misdiagnosed at least 30 to 50 percent of the time in women (McGrath & others, 1990). Approximately 70 percent of prescriptions for antidepressants are given to women, too often with improper diagnosis and monitoring.

To this point we have concentrated on depression in adults. However, there also is concern about the development of depression in children, as the Intersection makes clear.

Suicide

Severe depression and other psychological disorders can cause individuals to want to end their lives. Although attempting suicide is abnormal behavior, it is not uncommon for individuals to contemplate suicide at some point in life. For example, as many as two of every three college students have thought about suicide on at least one occasion. In 2004, 32,439 people in the United States committed suicide, making it the 11th leading cause of death (NIMH, 2006). It is thought that for every completed suicide, there are as many as 8 to 25 attempted suicides (NIMH, 2006a).

After about the age of 15, the suicide rate rises rapidly (Park & others, 2006). Suicide is the third-leading cause (after automobile accidents and homicides) of death today among adolescents 13 through 19 years of age (National Center for Health Statistics, 2005a).

Suicide tends to run in families. Five suicides occurred in different generations of the Hemingway family, including famous author Ernest (top) and his granddaughter Margaux (bottom).

Perhaps even more shocking, suicide is the third-leading cause of death among children age 10 to 14 (NIMH, 2006a).

Biological Factors   Genetic factors appear to play a role in suicide, which tends to run in families (Fu & others, 2002). One famous family that has been plagued by suicide is the Hemingway family. Five Hemingways, spread across generations, committed suicide. The best known of the five are the writer Ernest Hemingway (who took his own life at age 61) and his granddaughter Margaux (who committed suicide on the 35th anniversary of her father's suicide).

A number of studies have linked suicide with low levels of the neurotransmitter serotonin (Ryding & others, 2006). Postmortem analyses of the brains of individuals who have committed suicide show abnormally low levels of this transmitter. Also, individuals who attempt suicide and who have low levels of serotonin are 10 times likelier to attempt suicide again than are those attempters who have high levels of serotonin (Courtet & others, 2004).

Poor physical health, especially when it is long-standing and chronic, is another risk factor for suicide. For example, Ernest Hemingway had been in failing health for a number of years when he committed suicide.

Psychological Factors   Psychological factors that can contribute to suicide include mental disorders and traumas such as sexual abuse. Struggling with the stress of a psychological disorder can leave a person feeling hopeless, and the disorder itself may tax the person's ability to cope with the problems of life. Indeed, approximately 90 percent of individuals who commit suicide are estimated to have a diagnosable mental disorder (NIMH, 2006). The most common psychological disorders among individuals who commit suicide are depression and anxiety (Boden, Fergusson, & Horwood, 2006, 2007; Zonda, 2006).

Immediate and highly stressful circumstances—such as the loss of a job, flunking out of school, and an unwanted pregnancy—can lead people to threaten and/or to commit suicide (Westefeld & others, 2006). Also, substance abuse is linked with suicide more today than it was in the past (Galaif & others, 2007; Seguin & others, 2006).

In a fascinating set of studies, Thomas Joiner and his colleagues have focused on distinguishing between the suicide notes of suicide attempters and completers (Conner & others, 2007; Joiner, 2005; Joiner, Hollar, & Van Orden, 2006). They found that a sense of belongingness and burdensomeness separate those who attempt suicide from those who complete it. Essentially, individuals who feel that someone will miss them, and that someone still needs them, are less likely to complete the act of suicide.

Sociocultural Factors   The loss of a loved one through death, divorce, or separation can lead to a suicide attempt (Wortman & Boerner, 2007). There also is a link between suicide and a long-standing history of family instability and unhappiness. Chronic economic hardship, too, can be a factor in suicide (Foley & others, 2006).

In the United States, Native Americans have the highest suicide rate of all demographic groups, followed by Whites (Olson & Wahab, 2006). Worldwide, Hungary, Austria, Russia, Sri Lanka, and Japan are among the nations with the highest suicide rates, and Egypt, Guatemala, Iran, Peru, and the Dominican Republic are among those with the lowest rates (World Health Report, 2003). Suicide rates for the United States and Canada fall between the rates in these countries. The reasons for the variations include the degree to which there are cultural and religious norms against suicide.

There are gender differences in suicide as well (Fortuna & others, 2007). Women are three times more likely to attempt suicide than men. But men are four times more likely to complete suicide than women (Kochanek & others, 2004). The highest suicide rate is among non-Latino White men aged 85 and older. Men are more likely than women to use a firearm in a suicide attempt (Maris, 1998). Non-Latino White men account for 80 percent of all firearm-related suicides (NIMH, 2000).

Psychologists work with individuals to reduce the frequency and intensity of suicidal impulses. Figure 13.10 provides good advice on what to do and what not to do when someone is threatening suicide.

What to Do

1. Ask direct, straightforward questions in a calm manner. For example, "Are you thinking about hurting yourself?"

2. Be a good listener and be supportive. Emphasize that unbearable pain can be survived.

3. Take the suicide threat very seriously. Ask questions about the person's feelings, relationships, and thoughts about the type of method to be used. If a gun, pills, rope, or other means is mentioned and a specific plan has been developed, the situation is dangerous. Stay with the person until help arrives.

4. Encourage the person to get professional help and assist him or her in getting help. If the person is willing, take the person to a mental health facility or hospital.

What Not to Do

1. Don't ignore the warning signs.

2. Don't refuse to talk about suicide if the person wants to talk about it.

3. Don't react with horror, disapproval, or repulsion.

4. Don't offer false reassurances ("Everything will be all right") or make judgments ("You should be thankful for . . .").

5. Don't abandon the person after the crisis seems to have passed or after professional counseling has begun.

FIGURE 13.10

What to Do and What Not to Do When Someone Is Threatening Suicide Suspecting that someone you know may be thinking about suicide can be scary. Here are some suggestions for what to do. Most important, do not ignore the warning signs. Talk to a counselor on your campus if you feel too shy or afraid to say anything to the person yourself.

 REVIEW, ASSESS, AND SHARPEN YOUR THINKING

Review

3 Compare the mood disorders and specify risk factors for depression and suicide.

- Define mood disorders and depressive disorders, and distinguish among the different types of depressive disorders.

- Describe the mood disturbances that characterize bipolar disorder.

- Discuss the causes of mood disorders.

- Explain the factors that can lead to suicide.

Assess

1. Dysthymia differs from major depressive disorder in that
   A. dysthymia is more intense and longer-lasting.
   B. dysthymia is more intense and shorter-lasting.
   C. dysthymia is less intense and longer-lasting.
   D. dysthymia is less intense and shorter-lasting.

2. In order to be diagnosed with bipolar disorder, someone must experience
   A. a manic episode.
   B. a depressive episode.
   C. a manic episode and a depressive episode.
   D. a dysthymic episode.

3. Which of the following is not noted as a symptom of major depressive disorder in your text?
   A. fatigue   B. weight change
   C. thoughts of death   D. substance use

4. Which of the following is true about heredity and mood disorders?
   A. Heredity plays a small role in mood disorders.
   B. Heredity plays a larger role in bipolar disorder than in major depressive disorder.
   C. Heredity plays a larger role in major depressive disorder than in bipolar disorder.
   D. Heredity factors are equal in major depressive disorder and bipolar disorder.

5. Which of the following is true about suicide and gender?
   A. Women are more likely to attempt suicide than men.
   B. Men are more likely to attempt suicide than women.
   C. Men and women are equally likely to attempt suicide.
   D. Men and women are equally likely to complete suicide.

Sharpen Your Thinking

Do any of the theories about the causes of depression seem better at accounting for depression in college students? Explain.

4 Dissociative Disorders

Describe the dissociative disorders.

Have you ever been on a long car ride and completely lost track of time, so that you could not even remember a stretch of miles along the road? Or have you been so caught up in a day-dream that you were unaware of the passage of time? Such moments are examples of normal dissociation. *Dissociation* refers to a range of psychological experiences in which the person feels disconnected from immediate experience—unaware of central aspects of experience.

At the extreme end of dissociation are individuals who feel such a sense of disconnection persistently. **Dissociative disorders** are psychological disorders that involve a sudden loss of memory or change in identity. Under extreme stress or shock, the individual's conscious awareness becomes dissociated (separated or split) from previous memories and thoughts (Heim & Buhler, 2006; Serra & others, 2007). Individuals who develop dissociative disorders may have problems integrating different aspects of consciousness, so that experiences at different levels of awareness might be felt as if they are occurring to someone else (Dell & O'Neil, 2007). That is, in some individuals, facets of one person's consciousness itself are split and function independently of each other.

Dissociation is thought to be an individual's way of dealing with extreme stress by mentally protecting his or her conscious self from the traumatic event. Dissociative disorders often occur in individuals who also show signs of PTSD (Zucker & others, 2006). Both psychological disorders are thought to be rooted, in part, in extremely traumatic life events.

Three kinds of dissociative disorders are dissociative amnesia, dissociative fugue, and dissociative identity disorder.

Dissociative Amnesia and Fugue

Amnesia is the inability to recall important events (Cipolotti & Bird, 2006). Amnesia can result from a blow to the head, producing trauma in the brain. But **dissociative amnesia** is a dissociative disorder characterized by extreme memory loss that is caused by extensive psychological stress. For example, an individual showed up at a hospital and said he did not know who he was. After several days in the hospital, he awoke one morning and demanded to be released. Eventually he remembered that he had been involved in an automobile accident in which a pedestrian had been killed. The extreme stress of the accident and the fear that he might be held responsible triggered the amnesia.

Dissociative fugue (*fugue* means "flight") is a dissociative disorder in which the individual not only develops amnesia but also unexpectedly travels away from home and assumes a new identity. An alleged case of dissociative fugue was that of James Simmons/ Barre Cox. In 2000, the members of the White Rock Community Church, a predominantly gay and lesbian Christian church in Dallas, Texas, hired James Simmons to serve as their pastor. He had told members of his congregation that he had amnesia after being attacked and had been living on the road ever since. He presented himself as a celibate homosexual man. Nearly a year later, he was recognized as Barre Cox, a married father and San Antonio youth minister who had disappeared in 1984, just before taking on a new job as the pastor of a church (Yardley, 2001). While Simmons/Cox maintained that he had amnesia for his past life, others pointed out that he seemed to have left a life that did not satisfy him. Ultimately, he was voted out as pastor of the church.

Dissociative Identity Disorder

Dissociative identity disorder (DID), formerly called *multiple personality disorder,* is the most dramatic but least common dissociative disorder. Individuals suffering from this disorder have two or more distinct personalities or selves, like the fictional Dr. Jekyll and Mr. Hyde of Robert Louis Stevenson's short story. Each personality has its own memories, behaviors, and relationships. One personality dominates at one time, another personality takes over at another time, and the personalities are separated by a wall of amnesia. The shift between personalities usually occurs under distress (Sar & others, 2007).

dissociative disorders Psychological disorders that involve a sudden loss of memory or change in identity.

dissociative amnesia A dissociative disorder involving extreme memory loss caused by extensive psychological stress.

dissociative fugue A dissociative disorder in which the individual not only develops amnesia but also unexpectedly travels away from home and assumes a new identity.

dissociative identity disorder (DID) Formerly called *multiple personality disorder,* this is the most dramatic but least common dissociative disorder; individuals suffering from this disorder have two or more distinct personalities or selves.

FIGURE 13.11

The Three Faces of Eve Chris Sizemore, the subject of *The Three Faces of Eve*, is shown here with a work she painted, titled *Three Faces in One*.

One of the most famous cases of dissociative identity disorder involves the "three faces of Eve" (Thigpen & Cleckley, 1957) (Figure 13.11). Eve White was the original dominant personality. She had no knowledge of her second personality, Eve Black, although Eve Black had been alternating with Eve White for a number of years. Eve White was bland, quiet, and serious—a rather dull personality. By contrast, Eve Black was carefree, mischievous, and uninhibited. She would "come out" at the most inappropriate times, leaving Eve White with hangovers, bills, and a reputation in local bars that she could not explain. During treatment, a third personality, Jane, emerged. More mature than the other two, Jane seemed to have developed as a result of therapy. In some cases, therapists have been ascribed responsibility for creating a second or third personality. At one point, Eve said that her therapist had created one of her personalities.

A summary of research on dissociative identity disorder suggests that the disorder is characterized by an inordinately high rate of sexual or physical abuse during early childhood (Poythress, Skeem, & Lilienfeld, 2006; Sar, Akyuz, & Dogan, 2007). Sexual abuse has occurred in as many as 70 percent or more of dissociative identity disorder cases (Foote & others, 2006). Yet the majority of individuals who have been sexually abused do not develop dissociative identity disorder. Mothers of individuals who develop this disorder tend to be rejecting and depressed; fathers typically are distant, alcoholic, and abusive. The vast majority of individuals with dissociative identity disorder are women. When men develop the disorder, they show more aggression than women with the disorder (Ross & Norton, 1989). A genetic predisposition might exist, as the disorder tends to run in families (Dell & Eisenhower, 1990). And dissociative disorders may be related to lower volume in the hippocampus and amygdala, areas linked with emotional memory (Vermetten & others, 2006).

Fascinating as it is, dissociative identity disorder is rare. Until the 1980s, only about 300 cases had ever been reported (Suinn, 1984). In the past 25 years, hundreds more cases have been labeled as dissociative identity disorder, although some psychologists argue this increase represents a diagnostic fad. Others believe that the disorder is not so rare but has been frequently misdiagnosed as schizophrenia. Improved techniques for assessing physiological changes that occur when individuals change personalities increase the likelihood that more accurate rates of occurrence can be determined (Reinders & others, 2006).

REVIEW, ASSESS, AND SHARPEN YOUR THINKING

Review

4 **Describe the dissociative disorders.**
- Define dissociative disorders and characterize dissociative amnesia and dissociative fugue.
- Discuss dissociative identity disorder.

Assess

1. **Currently, multiple personality disorder is known as**
   - A. dissociative fugue.
   - B. dissociative amnesia.
   - C. dissociative identity disorder.
   - D. a dissociate disorder.

2. **People with dissociative identity disorder have unusually high rates of**
   - A. anxiety.
   - B. abuse as children.
   - C. depression.
   - D. divorce.

3. **Which of the following is true about dissociative identity disorder?**
   - A. Different personalities almost always have knowledge of the other personalities.
   - B. Dissociative identity disorder is the rarest of the dissociative disorders.
   - C. People with dissociative identity disorder do not have memory problems.
   - D. Dissociative identity disorder is a form of schizophrenia.

4. **Someone who suffers memory loss after of trauma is said to have**
   - A. dissociative identity disorder.
   - B. dissociative fugue.
   - C. dissociative amnesia.
   - D. schizophrenia.

Sharpen Your Thinking

Imagine that you are on a jury in which an individual who has been accused of killing someone claims that he suffers from dissociative identity disorder and does not remember committing the murder. How difficult would it be for you and the other jury members to determine whether he really has this disorder? What questions would you want answered before making your decision about the individual?

5 Schizophrenia

Characterize schizophrenia.

Walking along your usual route between classes, you come across a dead bird. Does it mean anything? Waiting to cross the street, a girl on a passing bus locks gazes with you. Does that mean anything? People with schizophrenia live in a world in which the meaning (or lack of meaning) of such events is no longer sensible. Recall from the stories at the beginning of the chapter that **schizophrenia** is a severe psychological disorder that is characterized by highly disordered thought processes. The term *schizophrenia* comes from the New Latin words *schizo,* meaning "split," and *phrenia,* meaning "mind." It signifies that the individual's mind is split from reality, and the person is cast into a frightening, chaotic world.

Schizophrenia is not the same as dissociative identity disorder. Schizophrenia involves the split of an individual's personality from reality, not the coexistence of several personalities within one individual. Approximately 2.2 million adults in the United States, or about 1.1 percent of the population 18 years and older, have schizophrenia in any given year (NIMH, 2006). Individuals with schizophrenia may show a broad array of symptoms, including disordered thought, odd communication, inappropriate emotion, abnormal motor behavior, and social withdrawal.

Schizophrenia is a serious, debilitating psychological disorder. About one-half of the patients in psychiatric hospitals are individuals with schizophrenia. As much as schizophrenia may

schizophrenia A severe psychological disorder that is characterized by highly disordered thought processes.

sound disturbing to an outsider, we can only imagine the ordeal of the persons living with it. Quite often the experience of schizophrenia is one of extraordinary terror (NIMH, 2006). For many with the disorder, controlling it means using powerful medications to combat symptoms. The most common cause of relapse in individuals is that they stop taking their medication. They might do so because they feel better or because they do not realize that their thoughts are disordered.

Seeking treatment for schizophrenia requires courage. It requires individuals with the disorder to accept that their perceptions of the world—their very sense of reality—is mistaken. This can be a difficult, threatening challenge: Having insight into the reality of schizophrenia means understanding just how devastating the disorder can be.

Symptoms of Schizophrenia

The symptoms of schizophrenia are generally classified as positive symptoms, negative symptoms, and cognitive deficits (NIMH, 2006).

Positive Symptoms   Schizophrenia's *positive symptoms* are the ones that you might already think of as characterizing the disorder, and these are generally not found in healthy people. Positive symptoms are marked by a distortion or an excess of normal function, and they are called "positive" because they reflect something added above and beyond normal behavior. Positive symptoms of schizophrenia include hallucinations, delusions, thought disorders, and disorders of movement.

Hallucinations are sensory experiences in the absence of real stimuli. These hallucinations are often auditory, and the person might complain of hearing voices, but hallucinations can be smells and tastes as well. Hallucinations can also involve seeing things that are not there. Viewers of the movie *A Beautiful Mind* might have been surprised to find out at the end of the film that John Nash's friend from college was in fact simply a hallucination.

Delusions are false, sometimes even preposterous, beliefs that are not part of the person's culture. One individual might think he is Jesus Christ; another, Napoleon. One individual might imagine that her thoughts are being broadcast over the radio; another might think that a double agent is controlling her every move. Delusions must be distinguished from beliefs based on cultural ideas—some religions believe that a person can have visions or that their god communicates with them personally, and generally psychology and psychiatry do not treat these as delusional. This distinction has come to the fore in recent cases involving evangelical Christian mothers with postpartum psychosis who believed that God was telling them to kill their children.

Psychologists use the term *thought disorder* to describe unusual, sometimes bizarre thought processes that are characteristic positive symptoms of schizophrenia. The thoughts of persons with schizophrenia can be disorganized and confused. Often these individuals do not make sense when they talk or write. For example, one individual with schizophrenia might say, "Well, Rocky, babe, help is out, happening, but where, when, up, top, side, over, you know, out of the way, that's it. Sign off." Such speech has no meaning for the listener. These incoherent, loose word associations are called *word salad*. The individual might also make up new words *(neologisms)* (Kerns & others, 1999). As well, schizophrenics can show **referential thinking,** which means ascribing personal meaning to completely random events, such as the girl catching a person's eye as a bus pulls away.

A final type of positive symptom is *disorders of movement.* A schizophrenic may seem especially clumsy and show unusual mannerisms and facial expressions such as grimacing. The individual may repeat certain motions over and over or, in extreme cases, may become catatonic. **Catatonia** is a state of immobility and unresponsiveness. The catatonic person remains motionless for long periods of time.

Negative Symptoms   Whereas schizophrenia's positive symptoms are characterized by a distortion or an excess of normal functions, schizophrenia's *negative symptoms* reflect behavioral deficits and the loss or decrease of normal functions. Thus, positive symptoms involve something added; negative symptoms reflect the absence of something.

Nobel Prize–winning mathematician John Forbes Nash, the subject of the film A Beautiful Mind, *suffers from schizophrenia, one symptom of which (as the movie reveals) is hallucinations.*

hallucinations Sensory experiences in the absence of real stimuli.

delusions False, sometimes even preposterous, beliefs that are not part of the person's culture.

referential thinking Ascribing personal meaning to completely random events.

catatonia A state of immobility and unresponsiveness.

FIGURE 13.12

A Person with Catatonic Schizophrenia
Unusual motor behaviors are prominent symptoms in catatonic schizophrenia. Individuals may cease to move altogether, sometimes holding bizarre postures.

flat affect A negative symptom in which the person shows little or no emotion, speaks without emotional inflection, and maintains an immobile facial expression.

disorganized schizophrenia A type of schizophrenia in which an individual has delusions and hallucinations that have little or no recognizable meaning.

catatonic schizophrenia A type of schizophrenia characterized by bizarre motor behavior that sometimes takes the form of a completely immobile stupor.

paranoid schizophrenia A type of schizophrenia that is characterized by delusions of reference, grandeur, and persecution.

undifferentiated schizophrenia A type of schizophrenia that is characterized by disorganized behavior, hallucinations, delusions, and incoherence.

One negative symptom is **flat affect,** which means that the person shows little or no emotion, speaks without emotional inflection, and maintains an immobile facial expression (Alvino & others, 2007). Schizophrenics also may be lacking in the ability to read the emotions of others (Chambon, Baudouin, & Franck, 2006; Kerns, 2005; Kring, Feldman-Barrett, & Gard, 2003). They may experience a lack of positive emotional experience in daily life and show a deficient ability to plan, initiate, and engage in goal-directed behavior. Unlike positive symptoms, negative symptoms do have a clear counterpart in healthy people—we all have times when we are "zoned out" or not particularly goal directed or engaged in the environment. Because it is not as obvious that negative symptoms are part of a psychiatric illness, people with schizophrenia are often perceived as lazy and unwilling to better their lives.

Cognitive Symptoms Cognitive symptoms of schizophrenia include difficulty sustaining attention, problems holding information in memory, and inability to interpret information and make decisions (Kerns, 2007; Kerns & Berenbaum, 2003). These cognitive symptoms may be quite subtle and are often detected only through neuropsychological tests.

Types of Schizophrenia

There are four main types of schizophrenia: disorganized, catatonic, paranoid, and undifferentiated. Their outward behavior patterns vary, but they have in common the characteristics of disordered thought processes.

Disorganized Schizophrenia In **disorganized schizophrenia,** an individual has delusions and hallucinations that have little or no recognizable meaning—hence the label "disorganized." An individual with disorganized schizophrenia may withdraw from human contact and may regress to silly, childlike gestures and behavior. Many of these individuals experienced isolation or maladjustment during adolescence.

Catatonic Schizophrenia **Catatonic schizophrenia** features bizarre motor behavior that sometimes takes the form of a completely immobile stupor (Figure 13.12). Even in this stupor, individuals with catatonic schizophrenia are completely conscious of what is happening around them. In a catatonic state, the individual sometimes shows *waxy flexibility;* for example, if the person's arm is raised and then allowed to fall, the arm stays in the new position.

Paranoid Schizophrenia **Paranoid schizophrenia** is characterized by delusions of reference, grandeur, and persecution. The delusions usually form an elaborate system based on a complete misinterpretation of events. It is not unusual for individuals with paranoid schizophrenia to develop all three delusions in the following order. First, they sense that they are special and misinterpret chance events as being directly relevant to their own lives (delusions of reference). A thunderstorm, for example, might be perceived as a personal message from God. Second, they believe that this special attention is the result of their special characteristics (delusions of grandeur). Individuals with delusions of grandeur think of themselves as exalted beings—as the pope or the president, for example. Third, they think that others are so jealous and threatened by these characteristics that they spy and plot against them (delusions of persecution). Individuals with delusions of persecution often feel that they are the target of a conspiracy.

Undifferentiated Schizophrenia **Undifferentiated schizophrenia** is characterized by disorganized behavior, hallucinations, delusions, and incoherence. This diagnosis is used when an individual's symptoms either do not meet the criteria for one of the other types or meet the criteria for more than one of the other types.

Causes of Schizophrenia

A great deal of research has been devoted to identifying the causes of schizophrenia. Here we consider the biological, psychological, and sociocultural factors involved in the disorder.

Relationship to person with schizophrenia

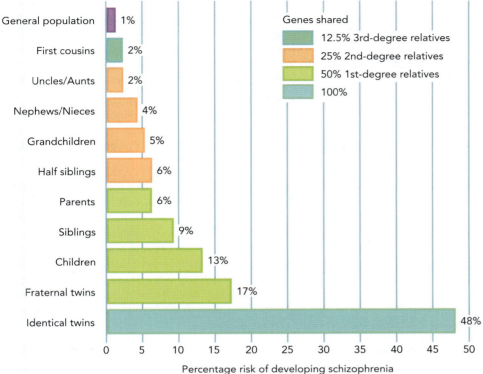

FIGURE 13.13

Lifetime Risk of Developing Schizophrenia, According to Genetic Relatedness
As genetic relatedness to an individual with schizophrenia increases, so does the risk of developing schizophrenia.

Biological Factors Research provides strong support for biological explanations of schizophrenia. Particularly compelling is the evidence for a genetic predisposition, but structural abnormalities and neurotransmitters also are linked to this severe psychological disorder (Picchioni & others, 2006; Ross & others, 2006).

Heredity Research supports the notion schizophrenia is at least partially due to genetic factors (Hall & others, 2007). As genetic similarity to a schizophrenic increases, so does a person's risk of becoming schizophrenic. As shown in Figure 13.13, an identical twin of an individual with schizophrenia has a 46 percent chance of developing the disorder, a fraternal twin 14 percent, a sibling 10 percent, a nephew or niece 3 percent, and an unrelated individual in the general population 1 percent (Cardno & Gottesman, 2000). Such data strongly suggest that genetic factors play a role in schizophrenia.

Researchers are seeking to pinpoint the chromosomal location of genes involved in susceptibility to schizophrenia (Harrison, 2007; Wood, Pickering, & Dechairo, 2007). They recently have found possible genetic markers for schizophrenia on chromosomes 10, 13, and 22 (Debanne & others, 2006; Faraone & others, 2006; Mulle & others, 2005).

Structural Brain Abnormalities Structural abnormalities in the brain have been found in individuals with schizophrenia. Imaging techniques such as MRI scans clearly show enlarged ventricles in the brains of these individuals (Pagsberg & others, 2006). Ventricles are fluid-filled spaces in the brain, and enlargement of the ventricles indicates atrophy, or deterioration, in other brain tissue. Individuals with schizophrenia also have a small frontal cortex (the area in which thinking, planning, and decision making take place) and show less activity than is seen in individuals who do not have schizophrenia (Cotter & others, 2002).

diathesis-stress model A model of schizophrenia that proposes a combination of biogenetic disposition and stress as the cause of the disorder.

It is important to keep in mind that brain differences between the brains of healthy individuals and those with schizophrenia are surprisingly small (NIMH, 2006). Microscopic studies of brain tissue after death reveal small changes in the distribution or characteristics of brain cells in schizophrenics. It appears that many of these changes occurred prenatally because they are not accompanied by glial cells, which are always present when a brain injury occurs after birth. It may be that problems in prenatal development predispose a brain to developing schizophrenic symptoms during puberty and young adulthood (Mueser & McGurk, 2004).

Problems in Neurotransmitter Regulation An early biological explanation for schizophrenia stated that individuals with schizophrenia produce higher than normal levels of the neurotransmitter dopamine and that the excess dopamine causes schizophrenia. That theory is probably too simple, although there is good evidence that dopamine does play a role in schizophrenia (Tamminga, 2006).

Psychological Factors Historically, psychologists often explained schizophrenia as rooted in childhood experiences with one's parents. Such theories have fallen by the wayside as the biological aspects of the disorder have been identified. But although contemporary theorists do not propose psychological factors as stand-alone causes of schizophrenia, stress may be a contributing factor. The **diathesis-stress model** argues that a combination of biogenetic disposition and stress causes schizophrenia (Meehl, 1962). The term *diathesis* means physical vulnerability or predisposition to a particular disorder. A defective gene makeup might produce schizophrenia only when the individual lives in a stressful environment. Advocates of the diathesis-stress view emphasize the importance of stress reduction and family support in treating schizophrenia.

Sociocultural Factors Disorders of thought and emotion are common to schizophrenia in all cultures, but the type and incidence of schizophrenic disorders may vary from culture to culture. Individuals living in poverty are likelier to have schizophrenia than people at higher socioeconomic levels. The link between schizophrenia and poverty is correlational, and contemporary theorists do not believe that poverty causes schizophrenia (Schiffman & Walker, 1998). Indeed, it is notable that across cultures, individuals with schizophrenia in developing, nonindustrialized nations tend to have better outcomes than those in developed, industrialized nations (Jablensky, 2000). This difference may be due to the fact that, in developing nations, family and friends are more accepting and supportive of individuals with schizophrenia.

Sociocultural factors are also implicated in the course of schizophrenia. At the opening of this chapter, we described Moe Armstrong, an accomplished man who happens to have schizophrenia. What factors predict better outcomes for individuals with this devastating disorder? Research findings are mixed, but some variables do seem to relate to longer-term improvements and functioning. Two factors that seem to make a difference are, quite simply, love and work. Marriage (Jablensky & others, 1992; Wiersma & others, 1998) and employment are related to better outcomes for individuals diagnosed with schizophrenia (Rosen & Garety, 2005). Also, warm supportive social relationships beyond marriage are also predictive of better prognosis (Jablensky & others, 1992). Individuals who experienced a particular trigger event before their first episode have been shown to have better outcomes as well (Rosen & Garety, 2005).

 REVIEW, ASSESS, AND SHARPEN YOUR THINKING

Review

5 Characterize schizophrenia.
- Discuss the various symptoms of schizophrenia.
- Describe the different types of schizophrenia.
- Explain the causes of schizophrenia.

Assess

1. Which of the following is a negative symptom of schizophrenia?

   A. hallucinations   B. flat affect

   C. delusions   D. word salad

2. Someone who believes that he has superhuman powers is suffering from

   A. hallucinations.   B. delusions.

   C. negative symptoms.   D. referential thinking.

3. A person with schizophrenia who displays abnormal lack of motor functioning is said to have

   A. undifferentiated schizophrenia.   B. paranoid schizophrenia.

   C. disorganized schizophrenia.   D. catatonic schizophrenia.

4. How is disorganized schizophrenia different from paranoid schizophrenia?

   A. In disorganized schizophrenia, the hallucinations and delusions are not meaningful, whereas in paranoid schizophrenia they are.

   B. Disorganized schizophrenia does not include hallucinations or delusions, but paranoid schizophrenia does.

   C. In disorganized schizophrenia, the person experiences delusions of reference, whereas in paranoid schizophrenia the person does not.

   D. Disorganized schizophrenia is a combination of other types of schizophrenia, including paranoid schizophrenia.

5. In the diathesis-stress model, diathesis refers to _____ and stress refers to _____.

   A. biological predisposition, environmental influences

   B. environmental influences, biological predisposition

   C. cognitive factors, sociocultural factors

   D. sociocultural factors, cognitive factors

Sharpen Your Thinking

Imagine that you are a clinical psychologist who has been given the opportunity to interview someone who has been diagnosed with paranoid schizophrenia. What questions would you want to ask the person?

6 Personality Disorders

Identify the behavior patterns typical of personality disorders.

Are there aspects of your personality that you would like to change? Maybe you worry too much or fall in love too easily. Imagine that your very personality—that thing about you that makes you *you*—was the core of your life difficulties. That is what happens with **personality disorders,** which are chronic, maladaptive cognitive-behavioral patterns that are thoroughly integrated into an individual's personality.

Individuals who have a personality disorder are troublesome to others, and their pleasure sources are either harmful or illegal (Hill & others, 2007). The patterns are often recognizable by adolescence or earlier. Personality disorders usually are not as bizarre as schizophrenia, and they do not produce the intense, diffuse feelings of fear and apprehension that characterize the anxiety disorders. Although in some sense these distinctions may make them sound less problematic, consider that by definition personality attributes are thought to be stable aspects of the person. Thus, personality disorders are very difficult to treat.

In the *DSM-IV,* the personality disorders are grouped into three clusters: odd/eccentric, dramatic/emotionally problematic, and chronic-fearfulness/avoidant.

Odd/Eccentric Cluster

The odd/eccentric cluster includes the paranoid, schizoid, and schizotypal disorders:

- *Paranoid:* These individuals have a lack of trust in others and are suspicious. They see themselves as morally correct yet vulnerable and envied.

personality disorders Chronic, maladaptive cognitive-behavioral patterns that are thoroughly integrated into the individual's personality.

- *Schizoid:* These individuals do not form adequate social relationships. They exhibit shy, withdrawn behavior and have difficulty expressing anger. Most are considered to be "cold" people.

- *Schizotypal:* These individuals show odd thinking patterns that reflect eccentric beliefs, overt suspicion, and overt hostility.

As you can see, some personality disorders have names that are similar to disorders described in other categories, such as schizotypal personality disorder and schizophrenic disorders. However, individuals with schizotypal disorder are not as clearly bizarre in their thinking and behavior as individuals with schizophrenia.

Dramatic/Emotionally Problematic Cluster

The dramatic and emotionally problematic cluster consists of the histrionic, narcissistic, borderline, and antisocial personality disorders:

- *Histrionic:* These individuals seek a lot of attention and tend to overreact. They respond more dramatically and intensely than is required by the situation—hence the term *histrionic*. The disorder is more common in women than men.

- *Narcissistic:* Narcissistic individuals have an unrealistic sense of self-importance, cannot take criticism, manipulate people, and lack empathy. These characteristics lead to substantial problems in relationships.

- *Borderline:* These individuals are often emotionally unstable, impulsive, unpredictable, irritable, and anxious. They have an unstable sense of identity and self. They also are prone to boredom. Their behavior is similar to that of individuals with schizotypal personality disorder, but they are not as consistently withdrawn and bizarre. Borderline personality disorder is related to childhood sexual abuse, but abuse may not be the primary cause of the disorder (Trull, 2001; Trull & Widiger, 2003).

- *Antisocial:* These individuals are guiltless, law-breaking, exploitive, self-indulgent, irresponsible, and intrusive. They often resort to a life of crime and violence. This disorder is far more common in men than in women.

Chronic-Fearfulness/Avoidant Cluster

The chronic-fearfulness/avoidant cluster includes the avoidant, dependent, passive-aggressive, and obsessive-compulsive personality disorders:

- *Avoidant:* These individuals are shy and inhibited yet desire interpersonal relationships, a distinguishing characteristic from the schizoid and schizotypal disorders. They often have low self-esteem and are extremely sensitive to rejection. This disorder is close to being an anxiety disorder but is not characterized by as much personal distress.

- *Dependent:* These individuals lack self-confidence and do not express their own personalities. They have a pervasive need to cling to stronger personalities, whom they allow to make decisions for them. The disorder is far more common in women than in men.

- *Passive-aggressive:* These individuals often pout and procrastinate; they are stubborn or are intentionally inefficient in an effort to frustrate others.

- *Obsessive-compulsive:* This personality disorder is often confused with obsessive-compulsive anxiety disorder. But this personality disorder does not refer to the kinds of thoughts and rituals found in OCD. Rather, the obsessive-compulsive personality refers to an individual who shows obsessive perfectionism, rigidity, and a need to apply a very strict moral code. A person who has obsessive-compulsive personality disorder is likely

to feel a great deal of anxiety if everything is not "just right." These individuals are obsessed with rules, are emotionally insensitive, and are oriented toward a lifestyle of productivity and efficiency; they exist in a world where there is only one right answer to every question and no room for the "gray" areas of life.

Some researchers have suggested that these personality disorders can be assessed and better understood as very extreme configurations of the five personality traits presented in Chapter 11. For instance, antisocial personality may be understood as a combination of high neuroticism, low agreeableness, and low conscientiousness (Reynolds & Clark, 2001). Schizotypal personality may be thought of as extremely high neuroticism, very low extraversion, and low agreeableness (Trull, 1992). Because these disorders are relatively rare but devastating, improving our ability to understand the processes involved in them in healthy participants might provide new clues for treatment.

 REVIEW, ASSESS, AND SHARPEN YOUR THINKING

Review

6 Identify the behavior patterns typical of personality disorders.
- Define personality disorders and discuss the odd/eccentric cluster.
- Explain the dramatic/emotionally problematic cluster.
- Describe the chronic-fearfulness/avoidant cluster.

Assess

1. Which of the following personality disorders is in the dramatic/emotionally-problematic cluster?
   A. schizoid
   B. antisocial
   C. passive-aggressive
   D. paranoid

2. Someone who engages in consistent illegal behavior and shows little remorse for hurting others has traits that are consistent with
   A. schizoid personality disorder.
   B. narcissistic personality disorder.
   C. antisocial personality disorder.
   D. passive-aggressive personality disorder.

3. How are schizoid and avoidant personality disorders different?
   A. Schizoid personality disorder involves odd, eccentric thinking, whereas avoidant personality disorder does not.
   B. Schizoid personality disorder involves a lack of desire for social relationships, whereas avoidant personality disorder involves a desire for social relationships.

   C. Schizoid personality disorder does not involve shyness, whereas avoidant personality disorder does.
   D. Schizoid personality disorder involves extreme sensitivity to rejection, whereas avoidant personality disorder does not.

4. Which of the following least belongs with other three?
   A. borderline personality disorder
   B. schizoid personality disorder
   C. schizotypal personality disorder
   D. paranoid personality disorder

5. Perfectionism is most associated with which of the following disorders?
   A. dependent personality disorder
   B. paranoid personality disorder
   C. narcissistic personality disorder
   D. obsessive-compulsive personality disorder

Sharpen Your Thinking

Do you think that personality disorders are best understood as qualitatively different from "normal" personality, or do you believe that they should be understood simply as extremes of the traits that describe us all? Why?

7 Psychological Disorders and Health and Wellness

Explain how psychological disorders affect health, and describe how individuals with disorders can improve their quality of life.

Psychological disorders are becoming more and more common. Chances are that you or someone you know will experience some sort of psychological disorder. What are the implications for health and wellness? To what kinds of programs and strategies can individuals with such disorders turn, to improve the quality of their health and lives?

Targeting Illness and Unhealthy Lifestyles

When a person is diagnosed with a psychological disorder, other aspects of health may be ignored. Individuals with psychological disorders thus are more likely to be physically ill and two times more likely to die than their psychologically healthy counterparts (Kumar, 2004; Phelan, Stradins, & Morrison, 2001). Individuals with psychological disorders are more likely to be obese, to smoke, to drink excessively, and to lead sedentary lives (Kim & others, 2007; Osborn, Nazareth, & King, 2006). They also are more likely than psychologically healthy people to suffer from risk factors for cardiovascular disease and from type II diabetes (Mykletun & others, 2007; Osborn, Nazareth, & King, 2006). Generally, they do not eat as well and exercise less than healthy individuals (Lindwall & others, 2007).

These findings are disturbing and perhaps surprising, because most of the individuals in the studies have had regular contact with mental health professionals. However, it may be that psychiatrists who are focused on psychological disorders are less likely to attend to the physical health needs of their patients (Robinson, 2005). In addition, primary care physicians who do not specialize in psychological disorders may be uncomfortable treating someone who has a psychological disorder. A further complication is that aspects of the disorders themselves may make it difficult for individuals to communicate their physical problems accurately and effectively.

You might be thinking that these physical health issues are perhaps less pressing than the psychological problems these individuals face. You might reason that if individuals who are struggling with schizophrenia want to smoke, why not just let them? Such thinking, however, sells short the capacity of psychological and psychiatric treatments to help the individual, and, most importantly, might compromise the ability of individuals with serious mental disorders to lead healthy, meaningful lives. Indeed, this type of thinking might reveal a subtle way that prejudice toward those with psychological disorders limits the treatment they receive. In fact, research has shown that health promotion programs can work well even with individuals who have a severe psychological disorder. For example, one study reported successful smoking cessation in individuals with schizophrenia who took part in a group therapy program (Addington & others, 1998).

Facing Up to and Overcoming Stigma

One important barrier, and an important stressor for individuals coping with a psychological disorder, as well as their families and loved ones, is stigma (Corrigan, 2005). As already described, feelings of stigma can prevent individuals from seeking treatment or from even talking about their problems with family and friends. Recall from Chapter 12 that stereotypes are generalizations about a group of people that have no bearing in reality. One especially harmful stereotype of individuals with psychological disorders is that such individuals are dangerous. As already noted, this stereotype is simply not reflected in the lives of the vast majority of individuals coping with psychological disorders.

Putting a label on a person can help us feel better about ourselves, by making psychological disorders something that only happens to other people. But the truth is that

Although Sheila Hollingsworth struggles with her schizophrenia, her story is one of success, not failure. She has refused to allow her disorder to rob her of a good life.

psychological disorders are not just about *other people.* They are about *people* and can happen to anyone. We may not be aware of the many good lives that are being lived by those who experience psychological disorders because their worries about stigma prevent them from "coming out." Thus, stigma leads to a catch-22: Positive examples of individuals coping with psychological disorders are often missing from our experience because those who are doing well shun public disclosure of their disorders (Jensen & Wadkins, 2007).

Sheila Hollingsworth is a 49-year-old African American woman and a divorced mother of two. She has a master's degree and works at the Baltic Street Mental Health Board. She is so beloved at work that everyone calls her "Sheila Love." She sings in her church choir, takes calligraphy classes, and is determined to lose 30 pounds (Bonfatti, 2005). Sheila has schizophrenia. But she has not allowed the stigma of this disorder to rob her of a good life. She works as a peer counselor and helps others by leading groups and modeling effective treatment. It can be enormously helpful for individuals coping with severe psychological disorders to see that someone is making it, one day at a time—struggling, to be sure, but creating a good life. Each of us can benefit from exposure to success stories such as Sheila's.

After reading this chapter, you know that many admired individuals have dealt with psychological disorders. These diagnoses do not detract from their accomplishments. Quite the contrary, the accomplishments are all the more remarkable in the context of the imperfect lives in which they have occurred. Each of our lives is imperfect in some ways. It takes courage to come forward and own a particular imperfection, but it also is an act that helps us recognize the hope that exists in every human context. We began this chapter by glimpsing a number of good but imperfect lives. It is fitting that we close with an excerpt from a poem by Moe Armstrong (2006):

My Name Is Moe Armstrong

There are no cures or miracles for mental illness.

I can improve my peace of mind.

I can feel better.

I can have a life with successes and joys.

At one time, mental illness constantly disrupted my life.

I have learned to live with my psychiatric condition and enjoy life.

REVIEW, ASSESS, AND SHARPEN YOUR THINKING

Review

7 Explain how psychological disorders affect health, and describe how individuals with disorders can improve their quality of life.

- Compare the physical health and fitness of individuals with psychological disorders to the bodily health and fitness of typical psychologically healthy individuals.
- Describe how stigma about psychological disorders may interfere with the ability of individuals to lead fulfilling lives.

Assess

1. Which of the following statements is not correct?

   A. Individuals with psychological disorders can benefit from health-promotion programs.

   B. Individuals with psychological disorders are less likely to smoke than those without psychological disorders.

   C. The physical health needs of individuals with psychological disorders may be ignored by physicians and psychiatrists.

   D. Individuals with psychological disorders exercise less than psychologically healthy individuals.

2. **Being open about having a psychological disorder**
   A. can lead to receiving treatment.
   B. makes people less likely to experience stigma.
   C. is unrelated to well-being.
   D. is very uncommon.

3. **Which of the following is not an explanation for why people with psychological disorders have more physical health problems?**

A. People with psychological disorders are more sedentary.
B. People with psychological disorders have problems learning healthy habits.
C. People with psychological disorders receive worse health care.
D. People with psychological disorders have problems talking with their physicians.

Sharpen Your Thinking

Imagine that someone you love is diagnosed with a psychological disorder. Given what you have read in this chapter, what sorts of expectations would you have for the person's future quality of life?

SUMMARY

1 DEFINING AND EXPLAINING ABNORMAL BEHAVIOR

Discuss the characteristics, explanations, and classifications of abnormal behavior.

Theoretical Approaches to Psychological Disorders

Psychologists define abnormal behavior as behavior that is deviant, maladaptive, or personally distressful. Theoretical perspectives on the causes of psychological disorders include biological, psychological, sociocultural, and biopsychosocial approaches.

With regard to biological factors, the medical model describes psychological disorders as diseases with a biological origin. Structural, biochemical, and genetic views also have been proposed. Psychological approaches include the psychodynamic perspective, the behavioral/social cognitive perspective, the trait approach, and the humanistic perspective. Sociocultural approaches place more emphasis on the larger social context in which a person lives than on psychological factors. Sociocultural contexts include the individual's marriage or family, neighborhood, socioeconomic status, ethnicity, gender, and culture. Biopsychosocial approaches are interactionist theories on understanding psychological disorders.

Classifying Abnormal Behavior

The classification of mental disorders gives mental health professionals a shorthand to use in their communications; it also allows clinicians to make predictions about disorders and to determine what kind of treatment is appropriate. The *Diagnostic and Statistical Manual of Mental Disorders (DSM)*, published by the American Psychiatric Association, is the classification system used by clinicians to diagnose and treat psychological disorders. The *DSM-IV* features a multiaxial diagnostic system that enables clinicians to characterize an individual on the basis of five dimensions. Some psychologists contend that the *DSM-IV* perpetuates the medical model of psychological disorders and labels some everyday problems that are not considered deviant or maladaptive as psychological disorders.

2 ANXIETY DISORDERS

Distinguish among the various anxiety disorders.

Generalized Anxiety Disorder

Anxiety is a diffuse, vague, highly unpleasant feeling of fear and apprehension. Generalized anxiety disorder is anxiety that persists for at least 1 month with no specific reason for the anxiety. Biological, psychological, and sociocultural factors may be involved.

Panic Disorder

Recurrent panic attacks marked by the sudden onset of intense apprehension or terror characterize panic disorder. Panic disorder can occur with or without agoraphobia. Biological and psychological factors may contribute to the development of panic disorder.

Phobic Disorder

Phobic disorders involve an irrational, overwhelming fear of a particular object, such as snakes, or a situation, such as flying. Biological and psychological factors have been proposed as causes of phobias.

Obsessive-Compulsive Disorder

Obsessive-compulsive disorder (OCD) is an anxiety disorder in which the individual has anxiety-provoking thoughts that will not go away (obsession) and/or urges to perform repetitive, ritualistic behaviors to prevent or produce some future situation (compulsion). Biological and psychological factors are likely involved in OCD.

Post-Traumatic Stress Disorder

Post-traumatic stress disorder (PTSD) is an anxiety disorder that develops through exposure to traumatic events, severely oppressive situations, severe abuse, and natural and unnatural disasters. Symptoms include flashbacks, which may appear immediately after the trauma or may be delayed.

3 MOOD DISORDERS

Compare the mood disorders and specify risk factors for depression and suicide.

Depressive Disorders

Mood disorders are psychological disorders in which there is a primary disturbance of mood. The mood disturbance can include cognitive, behavioral, and somatic (physical) symptoms, as well as interpersonal difficulties. Two main types of mood disorders are depressive disorders and bipolar disorder. The depressive disorders are mood disorders in which the individual suffers depression without experiencing mania. In major depressive disorder, the individual experiences a major depressive episode and depressed characteristics, such as lethargy and hopelessness, for 2 weeks or longer. Dysthymic disorder is generally more chronic and has fewer symptoms than major depressive disorder.

Bipolar Disorder

Bipolar disorder is characterized by extreme mood swings that include one or more episodes of mania (an overexcited, unrealistic, optimistic state). *Bipolar* means that the person may experience both depression and mania. Less than 10 percent of bipolar individuals experience mania without depression.

Causes of Mood Disorders

Biological explanations of mood disorders focus on heredity, neurophysiological abnormalities, neurotransmitter deregulation, and hormonal factors. Psychological explanations include psychoanalytic, behavioral, and cognitive perspectives. Sociocultural explanations emphasize interpersonal relationships, socioeconomic and ethnic factors, and gender.

Suicide

Severe depression and other psychological disorders can cause individuals to want to end their lives. Biological, psychological, and sociocultural explanations of suicide have been proposed.

4 DISSOCIATIVE DISORDERS

Describe the dissociative disorders.

Dissociative Amnesia and Fugue

Dissociative amnesia involves memory loss caused by extensive psychological stress. Dissociative fugue also involves a loss of memory, but individuals with this disorder also unexpectedly travel away from home or work, assume a new identity, and do not remember the old one.

Dissociative Identity Disorder

Dissociative identity disorder, formerly called multiple personality disorder, involves the presence of two or more distinct personalities in the same individual. This disorder is rare.

5 SCHIZOPHRENIA

Characterize schizophrenia.

Symptoms of Schizophrenia

Schizophrenia is a severe psychological disorder that is characterized by highly disordered thought processes. Individuals with schizophrenia may show odd communication, inappropriate emotion, abnormal motor behavior, and social withdrawal. Positive symptoms of schizophrenia refer to behaviors and experiences that are present in schizophrenics but lacking in healthy people, such as hallucinations and delusions. Negative symptoms of schizophrenia refer to behaviors and experiences that are part of healthy human life that are absent for those with this disorder.

Types of Schizophrenia

There are four main types of schizophrenia: disorganized, catatonic, paranoid, and undifferentiated. In disorganized schizophrenia, an individual has delusions and hallucinations that have little or no recognizable meaning. Catatonic schizophrenia is characterized by bizarre motor behavior, which may take the form of a completely immobile stupor. Paranoid schizophrenia is characterized by delusions of reference, grandeur, and persecution. Undifferentiated schizophrenia is characterized by disorganized behavior, hallucinations, delusions, and incoherence.

Causes of Schizophrenia

Biological factors (heredity, structural brain abnormalities, and neurotransmitter deregulation), psychological factors (diathesis-stress view), and sociocultural factors may be involved in schizophrenia. Psychological and sociocultural factors are not viewed as stand-alone causes of schizophrenia, but they are related to the course of the disorder.

6 PERSONALITY DISORDERS

Identify the behavior patterns typical of personality disorders.

Odd/Eccentric Cluster

Personality disorders are chronic, maladaptive cognitive-behavioral patterns that are thoroughly integrated into the individual's personality. The odd/eccentric cluster includes the paranoid, schizoid, and schizotypal personality disorders.

Dramatic/Emotionally Problematic Cluster

The dramatic/emotionally problematic cluster consists of the histrionic, narcissistic, borderline, and antisocial personality disorders. Biological, psychological, and sociocultural explanations of antisocial personality disorder have been proposed.

Chronic-Fearfulness/Avoidant Cluster

The chronic-fearfulness/avoidant cluster includes the avoidant, dependent, passive-aggressive, and obsessive-compulsive personality disorders.

7 PSYCHOLOGICAL DISORDERS AND HEALTH AND WELLNESS

Explain how psychological disorders affect health, and describe how individuals with disorders can improve their quality of life.

Targeting Illness and Unhealthy Lifestyles

Research has shown that individuals who suffer from psychological disorders often are at increased risk for unhealthy lifestyle practices such as inactivity, overeating, and smoking. Interventions to improve these physical habits can benefit these individuals in a broad way.

Facing Up to and Overcoming Stigma

Stigma is a key challenge for those with psychological disorders. Stigma is a source of stress in the lives of individuals who already suffer from debilitating disorders. Because negative examples of people with psychological disorders are more typically publicized than positive examples, we may be unaware of the fulfilling lives that many individuals who suffer from these disorders lead every day.

Key Terms

abnormal behavior, p. 521

medical model, p. 522

DSM-IV, p. 526

attention deficit hyperactivity disorder (ADHD), p. 529

anxiety disorders, p. 531

generalized anxiety disorder, p. 531

panic disorder, p. 532

agoraphobia, p. 532

phobic disorder, p. 533

obsessive-compulsive disorder (OCD), p. 534

post-traumatic stress disorder (PTSD), p. 535

mood disorders, p. 538

depressive disorders, p. 538

major depressive disorder (MDD), p. 538

dysthymic disorder, p. 539

bipolar disorder, p. 539

dissociative disorders, p. 548

dissociative amnesia, p. 548

dissociative fugue, p. 548

dissociative identity disorder (DID), p. 548

schizophrenia, p. 550

hallucinations, p. 551

delusions, p. 551

referential thinking, p. 551

catatonia, p. 551

flat affect, p. 552

disorganized schizophrenia, p. 552

catatonic schizophrenia, p. 552

paranoid schizophrenia, p. 552

undifferentiated schizophrenia, p. 552

diathesis-stress model, p. 554

personality disorders, p. 555

Assess Your Knowledge

1. How is obsessive-compulsive personality disorder different from obsessive-compulsive disorder (OCD)?
   A. Obsessive-compulsive personality disorder does not involve anxiety, whereas OCD does.
   B. Obsessive-compulsive personality disorder involves obsessive thoughts, whereas OCD involves ritualized behaviors.
   C. Obsessive-compulsive personality disorder is more debilitating than OCD.
   D. Obsessive-compulsive personality disorder does not involve ritualized behavior, whereas OCD does.

2. How many axes are included in the *DSM-IV* classification system?
   A. three   B. four
   C. five   D. six

3. How do phobic disorder and generalized anxiety differ?
   A. Phobic disorder is longer lasting that generalized anxiety disorder.
   B. Phobic disorder involves panic attacks, whereas generalized anxiety disorder does not.
   C. Phobic disorder involves agoraphobia, whereas generalized anxiety disorder does not.
   D. Phobic disorder focuses on a specific stimulus, whereas generalized anxiety disorder does not.

4. Which of the following is not a mood disorder?
   A. generalized anxiety disorder   B. dysthymic disorder
   C. major depressive disorder   D. bipolar disorder

5. Which disorder is accompanied by sudden travel and the assumption of a new identity?
   A. dissociate disorders
   B. dissociative amnesia
   C. dissociate identity disorder
   D. dissociative fugue

6. Someone who is experiencing increased energy, decreased need for sleep and euphoria
   A. has bipolar disorder.
   B. has major depressive disorder.
   C. is experiencing a manic episode.
   D. is dysthymic.

7. A person with schizophrenia who uses made-up words is displaying
   A. word salad.   B. hallucinations.
   C. neologisms.   D. delusions.

8. Which of the following is most characteristic of post-traumatic stress disorder?
   A. panic attacks
   B. an exaggerated startle response
   C. persistent nervousness about a variety of things
   D. extreme fear of an object or place

9. Continuously thinking about being depressed is known as
   A. catastrophic thinking.
   B. a ruminative coping style.
   C. dysthymic disorder.
   D. learned helplessness.

10. _____ symptoms of schizophrenia reflect a loss of normal functioning, while _____ symptoms reflect the addition functions that are of abnormal functioning.
    A. Cognitive, behavioral   B. Behavioral, cognitive
    C. Positive, negative   D. Negative, positive

11. Which of the following is not in the odd/eccentric cluster of personality disorder?
    A. paranoid   B. schizophrenia
    C. schizoid   D. schizotypal

12. Which of the following would not be coded on Axis I?
    A. paranoid personality disorder
    B. schizophrenia
    C. major depressive disorder
    D. panic disorder

13. A group of various neurotransmitters, known as _____, has been implicated in mood disorders.
    A. acetylcholine   B. monoamines
    C. adenosine deaminase   D. leptin

14. The diagnostic criteria for major depressive disorder states that a depressive episode must last at least
    A. one week.   B. two weeks.
    C. two months.   D. two years.

15. Which disorder is diagnosed with the labels of "with agoraphobia" or "without agoraphobia"?
    A. obsessive-compulsive disorder
    B. generalized anxiety disorder
    C. phobic disorder
    D. panic disorder

Go to Appendix B for answers to these questions.

Apply Your Knowledge

1. Spend 15 to 20 minutes observing an area with a large number of people (such as a mall, a cafeteria, or a stadium during a game) and identify behaviors that you would classify as abnormal. How does your list of behaviors compare with the definition of abnormal in the text? What would change on the list if you were in a different setting (such as a church, a bar, or a library)? What does this exercise tell you about defining abnormal behavior?

2. Imagine the following scenarios. For each, describe the kind of anxiety or dissociative disorder that the individual might be most likely to develop. Is it more likely that the person will or will not develop such a disorder?

   a. As a young child, Marcy is bitten by a dog.
   b. Alex is a New York City firefighter called to the World Trade Center to aid in the rescue efforts.
   c. Andy is involved in a serious automobile accident.
   d. Sam's parents are always critical about her behavior as she is growing up, and sometimes they lock her in a room for several days at a time.

3. Search the World Wide Web for support groups for some of the disorders described in this chapter. Which disorders seem to have a lot of support groups? Which have very few? What might account for the differences? How do the online discussions you find resonate with what you have read in this chapter? Are any of the experiences about which people chat online not represented in the psychological approach to disorders?

4. We often think of people who contend with psychological disorders as troubled and downtrodden. But like all people, these individuals have the capacity to be astonishingly creative. Check out the website maintained by the National Art Exhibitions of the Mentally Ill (NAEMI) to experience some of the amazing creations of artists who happen to suffer from mental illness. Just go to **http://www.naemi.org** and click on "Artists." How does your exploration of this artwork influence your feelings about mental illness?

CHAPTER 14

CHAPTER OUTLINE

THERAPIES

Experiencing Psychology

GETTING AND GIVING HELP: THE GLUE THAT BONDS US

No matter how strong or able we are, each of us needs help from others at some points in life. Imagine, for example, facing a move to a new apartment and being unable to afford professional movers. Unless you ask for the help of friends or family members, you know that you cannot possibly move that couch down three flights of stairs by yourself.

Sometimes the tables are turned, and we are called upon to help others. When the TV news broadcasts scenes of a natural disaster such as Hurricane Katrina, or of human violence such as the brutal conflict in the Darfur region of Sudan, we are moved by those images to wonder, "How can I help? What can I do?" In smaller ways we feel the urge to help others as we go about our daily routine. Perhaps we encounter someone struggling with a heavy load of books or files, and we stop to help. Or we see an elderly person taking a long time to cross a busy street and offer to walk along. Or maybe we assist someone else in moving that sofa down the stairs. Such helping is part of human nature and the glue that bonds us to one another.

Psychological burdens may be less visible than physical challenges, but they are no less real. When we are suffering because of a psychological problem, we may be reluctant to ask for help. For some reason, asking for help when faced with a couch and three flights of stairs is more acceptable than asking for help when faced with a psychological challenge such as coping with the loss of a loved one, getting through a romantic breakup, or just feeling lousy for no good reason. We might even think that asking for help is a sign of weakness or an admission that we are not as strong as we think we ought to be. Asking for help for a psychological problem itself requires strength and courage. Seeking such help is a sign that we are strong enough and brave enough to admit that we cannot go it alone any more than we could move that couch all alone. And knowing when and how to help someone else who is suffering with a psychological problem can also be difficult. There is a delicate balance between respecting the other person's abilities and sincerely desiring to intervene and make a difference.

PREVIEW

The science of psychology has led to the development of various treatment approaches to help relieve psychological suffering. These different forms of therapy are the focus of this chapter. As in Chapter 14, we take into account biological, psychological, and sociocultural factors, emphasizing here how they are used in various therapies to improve the lives of individuals with psychological disorders. We also examine the effectiveness of therapies and the wide range of mental health professionals who provide them. We close by exploring the implications of therapies for physical health and wellness.

1 Biological Therapies

Describe the biological therapies.

Biological therapies are treatments to reduce or eliminate the symptoms of psychological disorders by altering the way an individual's body functions. Drug therapy is the most common form of biomedical therapy. Much less widely used biomedical therapies are electroconvulsive therapy and psychosurgery. Recall from Chapter 1 that psychiatrists, who are medical doctors, can administer drugs as part of therapy. However, psychologists, who are not trained as medical doctors, cannot administer drugs as part of therapy in most states.

Psychologists and other mental health professionals may provide **psychotherapy,** a nonmedical process that helps individuals recognize and overcome their problems (Prochaska & Norcross, 2007). Their clients may be given psychotherapy only or in conjunction with biological therapy administered by psychiatrists and other medical doctors (Kazdin, 2007; Lister-Ford, 2007). Indeed, in many instances, a combination of psychotherapy and medication is a desirable course of treatment (de Maat & others, 2007; Furukawa, Watanabe, & Churchill, 2007).

Drug Therapy

Although medicine and herbs have long been used to alleviate symptoms of emotional distress, it was not until the twentieth century that drug treatments began to revolutionize mental healthcare. Psychotherapeutic drugs are used mainly in three diagnostic categories: anxiety disorders, mood disorders, and schizophrenia. This section discusses the effectiveness of drugs in these areas, beginning with drugs to treat anxiety.

Antianxiety Drugs **Antianxiety drugs** are commonly known as *tranquilizers.* These drugs reduce anxiety by making individuals calmer and less excitable. Benzodiazepines are the antianxiety drugs that most often offer the greatest relief for anxiety symptoms. They work by binding to the receptor sites of neurotransmitters that become overactive during anxiety. The most frequently prescribed benzodiazepines include Xanax, Valium, and Librium. A nonbenzodiazepine—buspirone, or BuSpar—is commonly used to treat generalized anxiety disorder.

Benzodiazepines are relatively fast-acting medications, taking effect even within hours. Buspirone must be taken daily for 2 to 3 weeks before it takes effect.

Benzodiazepines, like all drugs, have some side effects (Fields, 2007). They can be addicting. Also, drowsiness, loss of coordination, fatigue, and mental slowing can accompany their use. These effects can be hazardous when a person is driving or operating some types of machinery, especially when the individual first starts taking benzodiazepines.

biological therapies Treatments to reduce or eliminate the symptoms of psychological disorders by altering the way an individual's body functions.

psychotherapy The nonmedical process used by mental health professionals to help individuals recognize and overcome their problems.

antianxiety drugs Commonly known as tranquilizers; drugs that reduce anxiety by making individuals calmer and less excitable.

antidepressant drugs Drugs that regulate mood.

Benzodiazepines also have been linked to abnormalities in babies born to mothers who took them during pregnancy (Grover, Avasthi, & Sharma, 2006).

When benzodiazepines are combined with other medications, problems can result (Fidler & Kern, 2006). When combined with alcohol, anesthetics, antihistamines, sedatives, muscle relaxants, and some prescription pain medications, benzodiazepines can lead to depression.

Why are antianxiety drugs so widely used? Many individuals experience stress, anxiety, or both. Family physicians or psychiatrists prescribe these drugs to improve people's ability to cope with their problems effectively. The relaxed feelings brought on by antianxiety drugs bring welcome relief from high levels of anxiety and stress. Antianxiety medications are best used only temporarily for symptomatic relief. Too often, they are overused and can become addictive (Cook & others, 2007).

Antidepressant Drugs **Antidepressant drugs** regulate mood. The three main classes of antidepressant drugs are tricyclics, such as Elavil; monoamine oxidase (MAO) inhibitors, such as Nardil; and selective serotonin reuptake inhibitor (SSRI) drugs, such as Prozac. All of these antidepressants are thought to help depressed mood by their effects on the neurotransmitters in the brain. In different ways, they all allow the depressed person's brain to increase or maintain its level of important neurotransmitters, especially serotonin and norepinephrine. Let's take a look at each of these types of antidepressants.

The *tricyclics,* so-called because of their three-ringed molecular structure, are believed to work by increasing the level of certain neurotransmitters, especially norepinephrine and serotonin (Mico & others, 2006). The tricyclics reduce the symptoms of depression in approximately 60 to 70 percent of cases. The tricyclics usually take 2 to 4 weeks to improve mood. They sometimes have adverse side effects, such as restlessness, faintness, trembling, sleepiness, and memory difficulties.

The MAO inhibitors are thought to work because they block the enzyme monoamine oxidase. This enzyme breaks down the neurotransmitters serotonin and norepinephrine in the brain. The blocking action of MAO inhibitors is thought to allow these neurotransmitters to stick around and help regulate the person's mood. MAO inhibitors are not as widely used as the tricyclics because they are more toxic. However, some individuals who do not respond to the tricyclics do respond to the MAO inhibitors. The MAO inhibitors may be especially risky because of their potential interactions with certain foods and drugs (Nieuwstraten, Labiris, & Holbrook, 2006). Cheese and other fermented foods—as well as some alcoholic beverages, such as red wine—can interact with the inhibitors to raise blood pressure and, over time, to cause a stroke.

Psychiatrists increasingly are prescribing a type of drug called selective serotonin reuptake inhibitors (SSRIs) (Thase, 2006). SSRI drugs work mainly by interfering with the reabsorption of serotonin in the brain (Foley, DeSanty, & Kast, 2006). Figure 14.1 shows how this process works.

Three widely prescribed SSRI antidepressants are Prozac (fluoxetine), Paxil (paroxetine), and Zoloft (sertraline). Their increased prescription reflects their effectiveness in reducing the symptoms of depression with relatively fewer side effects than the other antidepressant drugs (Ksir, Hart, & Ray, 2008; Metzl & Angel, 2004). Nonetheless, they can have negative effects, including insomnia, anxiety, headache, and diarrhea. They also can impair sexual functioning and produce severe withdrawal symptoms if their use is ended too abruptly (Frohlich & Meston, 2005).

Beyond their usefulness in treating mood disorders, antidepressant drugs are often effective for a number of anxiety disorders, including generalized anxiety disorder, panic disorder, obsessive-compulsive disorder, social phobia, and post-traumatic stress disorder (Halgin & Whitbourne, 2007). In addition, eating disorders, especially bulimia nervosa, may be amenable to treatment with antidepressant drugs (Grilo, Masheb, & Wilson, 2006).

People have long used various herbal, nutritional, and other concoctions to help relieve emotional distress.

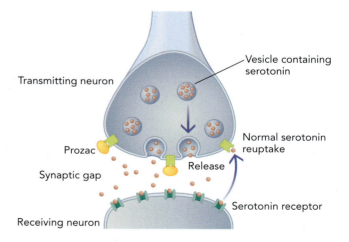

FIGURE 14.1

How the Antidepressant Prozac Works Serotonin is secreted by a transmitting neuron, moves across the synaptic gap, and then binds to receptors in a receiving neuron. Excess serotonin in the synaptic gap is normally reabsorbed by the transmitting neuron. However, Prozac blocks the reuptake of serotonin to the transmitting neuron, which leaves excess serotonin in the synaptic gap. The excess serotonin will be transmitted to the receiving neuron and circulated through the brain, thus reducing the serotonin deficit found in depressed individuals.

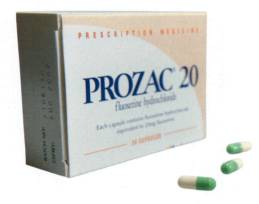

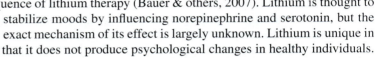

At least 25 percent of individuals with major depressive disorder do not respond to any antidepressant drug (Shelton & Hollon, 2000). Factors related to nonresponse include the presence of a personality disorder or psychotic symptoms.

Some antidepressant drugs are being developed to target neither norepinephrine nor serotonin but an amino acid called substance P. Studies are mixed on the ability of drugs that target substance P to reduce depression (Chahl, 2006; Norman & Burrows, 2007).

Lithium is widely used to treat bipolar disorder (Bourin & Prica, 2007). Lithium is the lightest of the solid elements in the periodic table of elements. If you have ever used a lithium battery (or are a fan of Nirvana or Evanescence), you know that lithium has uses beyond treating psychological disorders. The amount of lithium that circulates in the bloodstream must be carefully monitored because the effective dosage is precariously close to toxic levels. Kidney and thyroid gland complications can arise as a consequence of lithium therapy (Bauer & others, 2007). Lithium is thought to stabilize moods by influencing norepinephrine and serotonin, but the exact mechanism of its effect is largely unknown. Lithium is unique in that it does not produce psychological changes in healthy individuals. Indeed, the diagnosis of bipolar disorder may be made because the person is responsive to lithium.

The use of Prozac and other antidepressant drugs to treat depression is controversial. To read about issues involving the use of antidepressants with children, see the Critical Controversy.

Antipsychotic Drugs **Antipsychotic drugs** are powerful drugs that diminish agitated behavior, reduce tension, decrease hallucinations, improve social behavior, and produce better sleep patterns in individuals who have a severe psychological disorder, especially schizophrenia (Byrne, 2007; Green, 2007; Nasrallah & Lasser, 2006). Before antipsychotic drugs were developed in the 1950s, few, if any, interventions brought relief from the torment of psychotic symptoms. Once the effectiveness of these medications was apparent, the medical community significantly reduced more intrusive interventions, such as brain surgery, for schizophrenia (Grunberg, Klein, & Brown, 1998).

Neuroleptics are the most widely used class of antipsychotic drugs (Garver, 2006). The most widely accepted explanation for the effectiveness of neuroleptics is their ability to block the dopamine system's action in the brain (Lacasse, Perreault, & Williamson, 2006). People with schizophrenia may have too much of the neurochemical messenger dopamine. Numerous well-controlled investigations reveal that, when used in sufficient doses, neuroleptics reduce a variety of schizophrenic symptoms, at least in the short term (Turner & Stewart, 2006).

Neuroleptics do not cure schizophrenia; they treat only the symptoms of schizophrenia, not its causes. If an individual with schizophrenia stops taking the drug, the symptoms return. Neuroleptic drugs have substantially reduced the length of hospital stays for individuals with schizophrenia. However, although these individuals are able to return to the community because drug therapy keeps their symptoms from reappearing, many have difficulty coping with the demands of society. In the absence of symptoms, many struggle to justify continuing to take the very medications that have reduced the symptoms particularly because neuroleptic drugs can have severe side effects.

One potential side effect of neuroleptic drugs is *tardive dyskinesia*, a neurological disorder characterized by grotesque, involuntary movements of the facial muscles and mouth, as well as extensive twitching of the neck, arms, and legs (Soares-Weiser & Fernandez, 2007). As many as 20 percent of individuals with schizophrenia who take neuroleptics develop this disorder. As you may recall from Chapter 13, movement disorders are one of the symptoms of schizophrenia and tardive dyskinesia can also occur in individuals suffering from psychiatric disorders who have not taken neuroleptic drugs (Chouinard, 2006).

Newer drugs called *atypical antipsychotic medications* carry a much lower risk of this side effect (Remington, 2007). These medications were introduced in the 1990s. Like the SSRI drugs, atypical antipsychotic medications block the reuptake of the neurotransmitter serotonin. The two most widely used drugs in this group are clozapine (trade name Clozaril) and risperidone (Risperdal), which show promise for reducing schizophrenia's symptoms

lithium A drug that is widely used to treat bipolar disorder.

antipsychotic drugs Powerful drugs that diminish agitated behavior, reduce tension, decrease hallucinations, improve social behavior, and produce better sleep patterns in people who have a severe psychological disorder, especially schizophrenia.

Critical Controversy   Should Children Be Treated with Antidepressants?

In 1997, 13-year-old Matthew Miller hanged himself from a hook in his bedroom closet. The hook was barely higher than his height—to save his own life, he would have needed only to reach down to the floor with his feet. In 2000, Caitlin McIntosh, a 12-year-old straight-A student with artistic and musical talent, hanged herself with her shoelaces in the girls' room of her middle school. Both of these young people who ended their own lives so tragically had been struggling with depression. And both had been prescribed antidepressants shortly before their suicides. Matthew had started taking Zoloft 1 week before ending his life. Caitlin had been prescribed both Zoloft and Paxil 8 weeks before her death. Cases such as these call attention to the growing use of antidepressants in children and adolescents and to the potential risks involved. They raise the question, Do antidepressants elevate suicide risk in young people?

Professionals increasingly have used antidepressants such as Prozac, Paxil, and Zoloft to treat adult depression. This use has been both celebrated (Kramer, 1993) and criticized (Kirsch & Sapirstein, 1998; Kirsch & others, 2002). Given the apparent effectiveness of these drugs with adults, along with the rising rates of depression in children and adolescents (as described in Chapter 14), it is understandable that mental health professionals began to prescribe these drugs as treatment for mood disorders in younger individuals—even before official approval for such use.

It must be noted that antidepressants are powerful drugs, initially designed for adults. Although Matthew and Caitlin had been prescribed antidepressants in 1997 and 2000, it was not until 2003, based on two clinical trials, that the U.S. Food and Drug Administration (FDA, 2003) approved the use of Prozac for children aged 7 to 17 suffering from depression and obsessive-compulsive disorder. At the time, the listed side effects included dizziness, difficulty concentrating, nausea, tiredness, and slower growth compared to children not taking Prozac. Although Prozac was the only antidepressant specifically approved for use with children, prescriptions for a broad range of antidepressants for children increased dramatically in the next few years (Delate & others, 2004). The fastest-growing segment of users was preschoolers aged 5 and under.

The broad use of antidepressants for children and adolescents has been controversial (Andrade, Bhakta, & Singh, 2006; Giner & others, 2005). Researchers have found that among all the antidepressants, only Prozac has been effective in pediatric clinical trials (Jureidin & others, 2004). Some psychologists have pointed to the conflict of interest that arises when studies on antidepressant effectiveness among youth are funded by the pharmaceutical industry, as well as to the industry's tendency to downplay negative reactions to treatment (Whittington, Kendall, & Pilling, 2005). Added to generalized concerns over medicating children have been apprehensions that the very drugs prescribed to alleviate depression might be causing children to become suicidal.

In 2004, the FDA held hearings to address the concerns of parents and health professionals about the potential risk of suicide as an unexpected, tragic side effect of antidepressant treatment. Parents were called to tell their stories, many of which indicated no apparent previous risk of suicide and starkly illustrated the impulsiveness of the suicides. Some of the children had made plans for family activities for the very day after their suicides. Some had left sad evidence of the apparent randomness of their acts—a half-drunk glass of soda, an unfinished letter on the computer. Such real-life case studies can be emotionally engaging and persuasive, but are they generalizable to the population as a whole? What about the scientific evidence?

During the hearings, the FDA reviewed clinical trials of antidepressant use with children. The review looked at 23 clinical trials involving 4,300 children who were randomly assigned to receive either an antidepressant or a placebo (Hammad, 2004). None of the children in the studies committed or attempted suicide. Two main variables were the focus of this research. As one variable, some studies included participants' self-report ratings of their suicidal thoughts and behaviors. These ratings provided one source of information about the risk of suicide in the treatment and placebo groups. The second variable examined was adverse event reports—in this case, spontaneous statements of thoughts about suicide reported by the participants or their parents. The researchers found no differences between the treatment and placebo groups in self-reported suicidal thoughts or behaviors. However, the research did show an increase in adverse event reports in the participants in the treatment group. While the placebo participants showed 2 percent of such spontaneous reports of suicidal thoughts, those using antidepressants showed a 4 percent rate. This last finding, along with the dramatic personal cases presented by families, appears to have been the basis of the FDA's subsequent action.

In October 2004, the Food and Drug Administration required prescription antidepressants to carry the severest "black box" warning, describing the potential risk of antidepressants to be associated with suicidal thoughts and behaviors in children and adolescents (FDA, 2004). The black box warning has had at least two potential effects. First, because the FDA's ruling clearly recognized the need for closer monitoring of antidepressant use in adolescents—and for particular attention to potential behavioral changes that might suggest an increased risk of suicide—the warning ought to have made health professionals more sensitive to the importance of continuously monitoring children and adolescents using antidepressants. A second potential effect is that the warning might underlie a decrease in the prescription of antidepressants to youth, when in fact these drugs might be of real help to children with depression. Indeed, following the black box warning edict (and even before the box started appearing on the drug containers),

(continued)

prescriptions for antidepressants for children began to decline. Between March 2004 and June 2005, the number of prescriptions fell 20 percent compared to the same time frame the year before (Rosack, 2007).

Sorting out the possible connection between antidepressants and suicide in adolescents is complex for a variety of reasons. As many as 17 percent of adolescents think about suicide in any given year, and most teen suicides do not involve antidepressants (Centers for Disease Control and Prevention, 2004). As noted in Chapter 14, some 90 percent of individuals who attempt suicide are thought to suffer from a serious mental disorder, with depression being the most typical common factor. Would a depressed individual be just as likely to commit suicide with or without taking antidepressants? In addition, studies examining the effects of antidepressants generally exclude from participation individuals who are suicidal at the outset. As a result, positive effects of these drugs on reducing suicidal thoughts and behaviors are difficult to detect. Indeed, in a large-scale population study, the number of prescriptions for Prozac was negatively related to suicide rates over time (Milane & others, 2006).

Since the FDA called for the black box warning, a number of studies have found no link between antidepressants and suicide in either adults or children (Hammond, Laughren, & Racoosin, 2006; Markowitz & Cuellar, 2007). One study revealed that Prozac and cognitive-behavior therapy were both effective in reducing depression in children and adolescents, with a drop in suicidal thoughts from 29 percent to 10 percent in the treatment groups (March & others, 2004).

Despite the reputation of antidepressant medication as a quick fix for serious psychological disorders (Kramer, 1993), drug therapy may not be the treatment of first choice for children. Many children and adolescents have uncomplicated depression that can be treated effectively with psychotherapy alone (Melvin & others, 2006; Spielmans, Pasek, & McFall, 2007; Trowell & others, 2007). Indeed, in Great Britain, guidelines state that Prozac can be prescribed only in conjunction with ongoing psychotherapy (Boseley, 2006). In the United Kingdom and France, Paxil and Zoloft are not approved for pediatric use.

The controversy over the use of antidepressants with children and adolescents highlights many of the issues addressed throughout this book. How do we weigh dramatic case study evidence against less vivid scientific data that do not bear out those cases? Are special considerations required when professionals suggest the use of drug therapy in children? How can we best balance the potential benefits of drug treatment against the risks of that treatment? Throughout the debate, the profound tragedy of suicide has loomed, and certainly professionals have been moved to change their thinking and practices with regard to treating depression in youth.

What Do You Think?

- Have antidepressants helped anyone you know? If so, were you aware of negative side effects? Positive side effects? What was the nature of these effects?
- What do you think of the common practice of treating depression with medication first?
- Do you think occasional bouts of depression might play a normal role in psychological development? Why or why not?

without the side effects of neuroleptics (Kerwin, 2007; Olfson, Marcus, & Ascher-Svanum, 2007). Figure 14.2 shows the substantial reduction in negative symptoms when people with schizophrenia take risperidone (Marder, Davis, & Chouinard, 1997).

Strategies to increase the effectiveness of the antipsychotic drugs involve administering small dosages over time, rather than a large initial dose, and combining drug therapy with psychotherapy. Along with drug treatment, individuals with schizophrenia may need training in vocational, family, and social skills.

Figure 14.3 summarizes the drugs used to treat various psychological disorders, the disorders for which they are used, their effectiveness, and their side effects. Notice that, for some types of anxiety disorders, such as agoraphobia, MAO inhibitors (antidepressant drugs) might be used, rather than antianxiety drugs.

FIGURE 14.2

Effects of Risperidone (Risperdal) on Negative Symptoms of Individuals with Schizophrenia In one study, researchers found that, by just 1 week after starting treatment with risperidone, negative symptoms (such as disorganized thought and uncontrolled hostility/excitement) were substantially reduced in individuals with schizophrenia (Marder, Davis, & Chouinard, 1997). Negative symptoms in the placebo group actually increased slightly over the 8 weeks of the study.

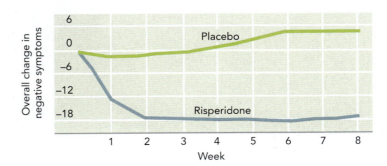

Psychological Disorder	Drug	Effectiveness	Side Effects
Everyday Anxiety and Anxiety Disorders			
Everyday anxiety	Antianxiety drugs; antidepressant drugs	Substantial improvement short-term	Antianxiety drugs: less powerful the longer people take them; may be addictive Antidepressant drugs: see below under depressive disorders
Generalized anxiety disorder	Antianxiety drugs	Not very effective	Less powerful the longer people take them; may be addictive
Panic disorder	Antianxiety drugs	About half show improvement	Less powerful the longer people take them; may be addictive
Agoraphobia	Tricyclic drugs and MAO inhibitors	Majority show improvement	Tricyclics: restlessness, fainting, and trembling MAO inhibitors: toxicity
Specific phobias	Antianxiety drugs	Not very effective	Less powerful the longer people take them; may be addictive
Mood Disorders			
Depressive disorders	Tricyclic drugs, MAO inhibitors, and SSRI drugs	Majority show moderate improvement	Tricyclics: cardiac problems, mania, confusion, memory loss, fatigue MAO inhibitors: toxicity SSRI drugs: nausea, nervousness, insomnia, and in a few cases, suicidal thoughts
Bipolar disorder	Lithium	Large majority show substantial improvement	Toxicity
Schizophrenic Disorders			
Schizophrenia	Neuroleptics; atypical antipsychotic medications	Majority show partial improvement	Neuroleptics: irregular heartbeat, low blood pressure, uncontrolled fidgeting, tardive dyskinesia, and immobility of face Atypical antipsychotic medications: less extensive side effects than with neuroleptics, but can have a toxic effect on white blood cells

FIGURE 14.3

Drug Therapy for Psychological Disorders The figure summarizes the types of drugs used to treat various psychological disorders.

Electroconvulsive Therapy

Electroconvulsive therapy (ECT), commonly called *shock therapy,* is used mainly to treat severely depressed individuals. The goal of ECT is to cause a seizure in the brain much like what happens spontaneously in some forms of epilepsy (Brown, 2007; Moss & Vaidya, 2006). A small electric current lasting for 1 second or less passes through two electrodes placed on the individual's head. The current excites neural tissue, stimulating a seizure that lasts for approximately 1 minute.

ECT has been used for more than 60 years. In earlier years, it often was used indiscriminately, sometimes even to punish patients. ECT is still used with as many as 100,000 individuals a year, primarily to treat major depressive disorder (Mayo Foundation, 2006). The contemporary use of ECT bears little resemblance to its earlier uses, as depicted in the now classic Jack Nicholson film *One Flew over the Cuckoo's Nest.* Today, ECT is given mainly to individuals who have not responded to drug therapy or psychotherapy, and its administration involves little discomfort. The patient is given anesthesia and muscle relaxants before the current is applied; this medication allows the individual to sleep through the procedure, minimizes convulsions, and reduces the risk of physical injury. Although in the past, electrical current was passed through the person's entire brain, increasingly ECT is applied only to the right side. The individual awakens shortly afterward with no conscious memory of the treatment.

How effective is electroconvulsive therapy? In one analysis of studies of the use of ECT, its effectiveness in treating depression was compared with that of cognitive therapy and antidepressant drugs (Seligman, 1994). ECT was as effective as cognitive therapy or

electroconvulsive therapy (ECT) Commonly called shock therapy; a treatment used for severely depressed individuals that causes a seizure to occur in the brain.

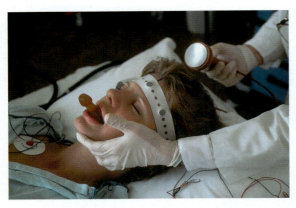

Electroconvulsive therapy (ECT), commonly called shock therapy, causes a seizure in the brain. ECT is still given to as many as 100,000 people a year, mainly to treat major depressive disorder.

drug therapy, with about four of five individuals showing marked improvement in all three therapies. However, as with the other therapies, the relapse rate for ECT is moderate to high. What sets ECT apart from other treatments is the rapid response that it can produce in a person's mood (Goforth & Holsinger, 2007). ECT may be especially effective as a treatment for acute depression in individuals who are at great risk of suicide (Kellner & others, 2006).

ECT is not without controversy. Its potential side effects remain a source of debate and contradictory findings (Cohen & others, 2000; Hihn & others, 2006). These potential side effects include memory loss and other cognitive impairments and are generally more severe than drug side effects (Hihn & others, 2006). Some individuals treated with ECT have reported prolonged and profound memory loss (Robertson & Pryor, 2006), with losses being most acute for impersonal rather than autobiographical memory (Lisanby & others, 2000). These side effects are typically lessened if only one side of the brain is stimulated. Despite these potential problems, some psychiatrists argue that for some individuals this invasive treatment can have life-enhancing and even life-saving benefits (Scott, 2006).

Psychosurgery

Psychosurgery is a biological therapy that involves removal or destruction of brain tissue to improve the individual's adjustment. The effects of psychosurgery are irreversible. In the 1930s, Portuguese physician Antonio Egas Moniz developed a procedure that became known as a *prefrontal lobotomy*. In this procedure, a surgical instrument is inserted into the brain and rotated, severing fibers that connect the frontal lobe, which is important in higher thought processes, and the thalamus, important in emotion. Moniz theorized that, by severing the connections between these brain structures, the surgeon could alleviate the symptoms of severe mental disorders. Although some patients may have benefited from these lobotomies, many were left in a vegetablelike state because of the massive assaults on their brains. Moniz himself felt that the procedure should be used with extreme caution, and only as a last resort. Incidentally, Moniz retired after being shot by a former patient, which left him a paraplegic.

After hearing about Moniz's procedure, American physician and neurologist Walter Freeman became the champion of *prefrontal lobotomies* (a term he coined). With his colleague James Watts, he performed the first lobotomy in the United States in 1936 (El-Hai, 2005). Freeman eventually developed his own technique, which he performed using a device similar to an ice pick, in surgeries that lasted mere minutes. Freeman was a dynamic and charismatic showman who argued strongly for the usefulness of the technique. In the 1950s and 60s, he traveled the country in a van he called the "lobotomobile," demonstrating the surgery in state-run mental institutions. In his career, Freeman performed over 3,000 lobotomies (El-Hai, 2005).

In 1949, when Moniz received the Nobel Prize for originally developing the lobotomy procedure, the legitimacy of the practice was further ensured. Indeed, prefrontal lobotomies were conducted on tens of thousands of patients from the 1930s through the 1960s. These numbers speak not only to Freeman's persuasive charm but also to the level of hopelessness and desperation many physicians felt in treating institutionalized patients with severe psychological disorders (Lerner, 2005).

Subsequently, research called into question the actual effectiveness of lobotomies in enhancing the lives of the many individuals who had undergone the procedure, pointing instead to the considerable damage that resulted (Landis & Erlick, 1950; Mettler, 1952). Many individuals who received lobotomies suffered permanent and profound brain damage (Whitaker, 2002). Ethical concerns were raised because, in many instances, giving consent for the lobotomy was a requirement for release from a mental hospital. Like ECT, lobotomies were being used as a form of punishment and control.

By the 1950s drug therapies had begun to emerge as alternatives to the invasive procedure of lobotomy. And by the late 1970s regulations were put into place that classified the procedure as experimental and that established safeguards for patients.

psychosurgery A biological therapy that involves removal or destruction of brain tissue to improve an individual's adjustment.

Fortunately, crude lobotomies are no longer performed, and the procedures used by Freeman are certainly not typical of the contemporary use of psychosurgery. Since the 1960s, psychosurgery has become more precise (Heller & others, 2006; Kopell, Machado, & Rezai, 2006). When psychosurgery is now performed, a small lesion is made in the amygdala or another part of the limbic system (Fountas & Smith, 2007). Today, only several hundred patients who have severely debilitating conditions undergo psychosurgery each year. Just as Moniz originally suggested, it is now used only as a last resort and with extreme caution (Ruck, 2003). Throughout this book, we have marveled at the amazing organ inside our head. Psychiatrists and psychologists have come to recognize that one should tamper with the brain only in the direst of cases (Pressman, 1998).

 REVIEW, ASSESS, AND SHARPEN YOUR THINKING

Review

1 **Describe the biological therapies.**
- Identify the types of drugs used to treat psychological disorders and evaluate their effects.
- Explain what electroconvulsive therapy is and when it is used.
- Discuss psychosurgery.

Assess

1. **Which type of antidepressant drug works by increasing levels of serotonin and norepinephrine?**
   A. selective serotonin reuptake inhibitors
   B. monoamine oxidase inhibitors
   C. benzodiazepines
   D. tricyclics

2. **Prefrontal lobotomy is a type of**
   A. psychosurgery.
   B. electroconvulsive therapy.
   C. neuroleptic.
   D. lithium.

3. **How do atypical antipsychotic medications work?**
   A. by increasing the release of presynaptic neurotransmitters
   B. by acting as an agonist to dopamine
   C. by stopping the reuptake of serotonin
   D. by inhibiting enzymes that break down norepinephrine

4. **What is tardive dyskinesia?**
   A. a side effect of antianxiety drugs
   B. involuntary movements of the face, neck, and extremities
   C. a type of psychosurgery
   D. the changes that occur in the synaptic gap as a result of medication

5. **Which of the following is true of electroconvulsive therapy?**
   A. It is less effective than medication.
   B. It takes several weeks to see results.
   C. Its side effects are generally considered more severe than medication.
   D. It is painful.

Sharpen Your Thinking

Is the use of biological therapies (such as medication) for the treatment of psychological disorders an easy way out? Why or why not? What, if any, are the implications of using biological treatments for the responsibility of the person undergoing treatment?

2 Psychotherapy

Define psychotherapy and characterize four types of psychotherapy.

Psychotherapy is the process that mental health professionals use to help individuals recognize, define, and overcome their psychological and interpersonal difficulties and improve their adjustment (Prochaska & Norcross, 2007). Psychotherapists employ a number of strategies to accomplish these goals: talking, interpreting, listening, rewarding, and modeling, for example. Both psychologists and psychiatrists use psychotherapy.

insight therapy A therapy that encourages insight and self-awareness; includes the psychodynamic and humanistic therapies.

psychodynamic therapies Therapies that stress the importance of the unconscious mind, extensive interpretation by the therapist, and the role of experiences in the early childhood years. The goal of the psychodynamic therapies is to help individuals recognize their maladaptive ways of coping and the sources of their unconscious conflicts.

psychoanalysis Freud's therapeutic technique for analyzing an individual's unconscious thoughts. Freud believed that clients' current problems could be traced to childhood experiences, many of which involved conflicts about sexuality.

free association The psychoanalytic technique of having individuals say aloud whatever comes to mind.

dream analysis The psychotherapeutic technique used to interpret a person's dream. Psychoanalysts believe that dreams contain information about the individual's unconscious thoughts and conflicts.

transference The psychoanalytic term for the client's relating to the analyst in ways that reproduce or relive important relationships in the client's life.

resistance The psychoanalytic term for the client's unconscious defense strategies that prevent the analyst from understanding the person's problems.

This section focuses on four main approaches to psychotherapy: psychodynamic, humanistic, behavior, and cognitive. The term **insight therapy** characterizes both psychodynamic and humanistic therapies, because they encourage insight and self-awareness. The psychodynamic therapies are the oldest of these approaches.

Psychodynamic Therapies

The **psychodynamic therapies** stress the importance of the unconscious mind, extensive interpretation by the therapist, and the role of early childhood experiences in the development of an individual's problems. The goal of the psychodynamic therapies is to help individuals recognize the maladaptive ways in which they have been coping with problems and the sources of their unconscious conflicts (Nolen-Hoeksema, 2007). Many psychodynamic approaches grew out of Freud's psychoanalytic theory of personality. Today some therapists with a psychodynamic perspective practice Freudian techniques, but others do not (Leffert, 2007; Midgley, 2006; Zerbe, 2007).

Freud's Psychoanalysis   **Psychoanalysis** is Freud's therapeutic technique for analyzing an individual's unconscious thoughts. Freud believed that clients' current problems could be traced to childhood experiences, many of which involved conflicts about sexuality. He also recognized that the early experiences were not readily available to the individual's conscious mind. Only through extensive questioning, probing, and analyzing was Freud able to put together the pieces of the person's personality and help the individual become aware of how these early experiences were affecting present adult behavior. The goal of psychoanalysis is to bring unconscious conflicts into conscious awareness, to free the person from influences on his or her current life.

To reach the shadowy world of the unconscious, psychoanalytic therapists often use the therapeutic techniques of free association, catharsis, interpretation, dream analysis, analysis of transference, and analysis of resistance; we survey each in turn.

Free association consists of encouraging individuals to say aloud whatever comes to mind, no matter how trivial or embarrassing (Hoffer, 2006). When Freud detected a person resisting the spontaneous flow of thoughts, he probed further. He believed that the crux of the person's emotional problem probably lurked below this point of resistance. Encouraging people to talk freely, Freud thought, would help emotional feelings to emerge. *Catharsis,* as we saw in a preceding chapter, is the release of emotional tension a person experiences when reliving an emotionally charged and conflicting experience.

To encourage his patients to relax, Freud had them recline on this couch while he sat in the chair on the left, out of their view.

Interpretation plays an important role in psychoanalysis. The person's statements and behavior are not taken at face value. To understand what is causing the person's conflicts, the therapist constantly searches for symbolic, hidden meanings in what the individual says and does. From time to time, the therapist suggests possible meanings of the person's statements and behavior.

Dream analysis is the technique used by psychoanalysts to interpret a person's dream. Psychoanalysts believe dreams contain information about unconscious thoughts, wishes, and conflicts (Andrade, 2007). From this perspective, dreams provide our unconscious with an outlet to express our unconscious wishes, a mental theater in which our deepest and most secret desires can be played out.

Freud distinguished between the dream's manifest and latent content. *Manifest content* is the psychoanalytic term for the conscious, remembered aspects of a dream. For instance, if you wake up in the morning remembering a dream about being back in second grade with your teacher scolding you for not turning in your homework, that is the manifest content of the dream. *Latent content* is the unconscious, unremembered parts of a dream, those hidden aspects of the unconscious that are symbolized by the manifest content. In order to understand the meaning of your dream, a psychoanalyst might ask you to free associate to each of the elements of the manifest content: What comes to your mind when you think of being in second grade? When you think of your teacher? According to Freud, the latent meaning of a dream is locked inside the unconscious mind of the dreamer. The goal of analysis is to unlock that secret meaning by probing into the deeper layers of the person's mind.

The psychoanalyst interprets the dream by analyzing the manifest content for disguised unconscious wishes and needs, especially those that are sexual and aggressive. Dream symbols can mean different things to different dreamers. For examples of the sexual symbols psychoanalysts might use to interpret dreams, see Figure 14.4. But caution is warranted here, because Freud recognized that the true meaning of any dream symbol depends on the individual dreamer. As he once quipped, "Sometimes a cigar is just a cigar."

Freud believed that transference was an inevitable and essential aspect of the analyst–patient relationship. **Transference** is the psychoanalytic term for the person's relating to the analyst in ways that reproduce or relive important relationships in the individual's life. A person might interact with an analyst as if the analyst were a parent or lover, for example. According to Freud, transference is a necessary part of the psychoanalytic relationship. Transference can be used therapeutically as a model of how individuals relate to important people in their lives (Corradi, 2006).

Resistance is the psychoanalytic term for the client's unconscious defense strategies that prevent the analyst from understanding the person's problems. Resistance occurs because it is painful for the client to bring conflicts into conscious awareness. By resisting therapy, the individual does not have to face the threatening truths that underlie his or her problems (Hoffman, 2006). Showing up late or missing sessions, arguing with the psychoanalyst, and faking free associations are examples of resistance. Some individuals talk on endlessly about a trivial matter to avoid facing their conflicts. A major goal of the analyst is to break through this resistance (Parsons, 2006).

Contemporary Psychodynamic Therapies   Although the face of psychodynamic therapy has changed extensively since its inception almost a century ago, many contemporary psychodynamic therapists still probe a person's unconscious thoughts about early childhood experiences to obtain clues to the person's current problems (Bovensiepen, 2006; Hamilton, 2006; Novie, 2007). Many contemporary psychodynamic therapists also try to help individuals gain insight into their emotionally laden, repressed conflicts (Hutterer & Liss, 2006). They also accord more power to the conscious mind and to a person's current relationships (Busch, 2007).

Sexual theme	Objects or activities in dreams that symbolize sexual themes
Male genitals, especially penis	Umbrellas, knives, poles, swords, airplanes, guns, serpents, neckties, tree trunks, hoses
Female genitals, especially vagina	Boxes, caves, pockets, pouches, the mouth, jewel cases, ovens, closets
Sexual intercourse	Climbing, swimming, flying, riding (a horse, an elevator, a roller coaster)
Parents	Kings, queens, emperors, empresses
Siblings	Little animals

FIGURE 14.4

Freudian Interpretation of Sexual Symbolism in Dreams Freud believed that dreams provide clues about our unconscious wishes. Remember that Freud thought that only the dreamer knows the true meaning of a dream symbol.

humanistic therapies Therapies that encourage clients to understand themselves and to grow personally. The humanistic therapies are unique in their emphasis on self-healing capacities.

client-centered therapy Rogers's humanistic therapy in which the therapist provides a warm, supportive atmosphere to improve the client's self-concept and encourage the client to gain insight about problems.

reflective speech A technique in which the therapist mirrors the client's own feelings back to the client.

Today individuals rarely lie on a couch or see their therapist several times a week. Instead, weekly appointments are typical, and people sit in a comfortable chair facing the therapist.

Only a small number of contemporary therapists rigorously practices Freudian psychoanalysis. Those who do use this therapy typically see an individual frequently. Some contemporary psychodynamic therapies also can be intensive and extensive, lasting for years. However, in some cases, contemporary psychodynamic therapy is brief, lasting only a few months.

Some contemporary psychodynamic therapists (Busch, 2007) focus on the self in social contexts, as was suggested by Erik Erikson (1968) and Heinz Kohut (1977). In Kohut's view, early social relationships with attachment figures, such as one's parents, are critical. As we develop, we internalize those relationships, and they provide the basis for our sense of self. Kohut (1977) believed that the job of the therapist is to replace unhealthy childhood relationships with the healthy relationship provided by the therapist. In Kohut's view, therapists need to interact with individuals in ways that are empathic and understanding (1977). Empathy and understanding are also cornerstones for humanistic therapies, our next topic.

Humanistic Therapies

The underlying philosophy of humanistic therapies is captured by the metaphor of how an acorn, if provided with appropriate conditions, will grow in positive ways, pushing naturally toward its actualization as an oak (Schneider, 2002). In the **humanistic therapies,** people are encouraged to understand themselves and to grow personally. The humanistic therapies are unique in their emphasis on the person's self-healing capacities (Feist & Feist, 2006). In contrast to the psychodynamic therapies, the humanistic therapies emphasize conscious rather than unconscious thoughts, the present rather than the past, and growth and self-fulfillment rather than illness.

Client-Centered Therapy **Client-centered therapy** is a form of humanistic therapy, developed by Carl Rogers (1961, 1980), in which the therapist provides a warm, supportive atmosphere to improve the client's self-concept and encourage the client to gain insight into problems. Compared with psychodynamic therapies, which emphasize analysis and interpretation by the therapist, client-centered therapy places far more emphasis on the client's self-reflection (Hill, 2000). In client-centered therapy, the goal of therapy is not to unlock the deep secrets of the unconscious but rather to help the client identify and understand his or her own genuine feelings (Hazler, 2007). One way to achieve this goal is through active listening and **reflective speech,** a technique in which the therapist mirrors the client's own feelings back to the client.

The relationship between the therapist and the person is an important aspect of Rogers's therapy. The therapist must enter into an intensely personal relationship with the client, not as a physician diagnosing a disease but as one human being to another. Rogers referred to the "client" and then to the "person" rather than the "patient."

Rogers believed each of us is born with the potential to be a fully functioning person, but we often live in a world in which we are valued only if we live up to conditions of worth. We are valued only if we meet certain standards, and we come to apply those standards to ourselves. Each of us needs to feel the positive regard of others, but this positive regard is often conditional—it comes with strings attached.

As noted in Chapter 11, Rogers believed that humans require three essential elements to grow: unconditional positive regard, empathy, and genuineness or authenticity. These three elements of personality development are reflected in his approach to therapy. To free a person from conditions of worth, the therapist engages in *unconditional positive regard,* which involves creating a warm and caring environment and never disapproving of the client, as a person. Rogers believed this unconditional positive regard provides a context for personal growth and self acceptance, just as soil, water, and sunshine provide a context for the acorn to become an oak.

Carl Rogers's client-centered therapy emphasized an unconditional positive regard that would provide a context for personal growth and self-acceptance—like the nurturing soil, water, and sunshine that allow an acorn to grow into a strong oak tree.

The therapist's role here is *nondirective*—that is, he or she does not lead the client to any particular revelation. The therapist is there to listen sympathetically to the client's problems and to encourage positive self-regard, independent self-appraisal, and decision making. Though client-centered therapists give approval of the person, they do not always approve of the person's behavior.

In addition to unconditional positive regard, Rogers advocated for the importance of *empathy* and *authenticity*. Through empathy the therapist strives to put himself or herself in the client's shoes, feeling the emotions the client is feeling. Authenticity involves letting the client know the therapist's feelings and not hiding behind a façade. Note that authenticity is meant to coexist with unconditional positive regard. The therapist must provide the client with positive regard no matter what, but at the same time that regard must be a genuine expression of the therapist's true feelings. The therapist may distinguish between the person's behavior and the person him- or herself. Although the client is always acknowledged as a valuable human being, his or her behavior can be evaluated negatively: "You are a good person but your actions are not." Rogers's positive view of humanity extended to his view of therapists. He believed that by being genuine with the client, the therapist could help the client improve.

Frederick (Fritz) Perls (1893–1970)
Perls was the founder of gestalt therapy.

Gestalt Therapy   **Gestalt therapy** is a humanistic therapy, developed by Fritz Perls (1893–1970), in which the therapist challenges clients in order to help them become more aware of their feelings and face their problems. Perls was trained in Europe as a Freudian psychoanalyst, but he developed his own ideas and eventually parted from some of Freud's teachings.

Perls (1969) agreed with Freud that psychological problems originate in unresolved past conflicts and that these conflicts need to be acknowledged and worked through. Also like Freud, Perls stressed that interpretation of dreams is an important aspect of therapy. But in other ways, Perls and Freud were miles apart. Perls believed that unresolved conflicts should be brought to bear on the here and now of the individual's life. The gestalt therapist *pushes* clients into deciding whether they will continue to allow the past to control their future or whether they will choose right now what they want to be in the future. To this end, Perls both confronted individuals and encouraged them to control their lives actively and to be open about their feelings (Garza, 1999).

The gestalt therapist uses a number of techniques to help clients to be open about their feelings, to develop self-awareness, and to take active control of their lives (Silverstein & Uhlhaas, 2004). The therapist sets examples, encourages congruence between verbal and nonverbal behavior, and uses role playing. To stimulate change, the therapist often openly confronts the client. To demonstrate an important point to a client, the gestalt therapist might exaggerate a client's characteristics.

In the following excerpt from a gestalt therapy session, the therapist (in this case, gestalt therapy founder Fritz Perls) exaggerates a phrase the client uses:

Perls: Now talk to your Top Dog! Stop nagging.

Jane: *[Loud, pained]* Leave me alone.

Perls: Yah, again.

Jane: Leave me alone.

Perls: Again.

Jane: *[Screaming it and crying]* Leave me alone!

Perls: Again.

Jane: *[She screams it, a real blast.]* Leave me alone! I don't have to do what you say! *[Still crying]* I don't have to be in this chair! I don't have to. You make me. You make me come here! *[Screams]* Aarhh. You make me pick my face *[crying]*, that's what you do. *[Screams and cries]* Aarhh! I'd like to kill you.

Perls: Say this again.

Jane: I'd like to kill you.

Perls: Again.

Jane: I'd like to kill you.

gestalt therapy Perls's humanistic therapy, in which the therapist challenges clients in order to help them become more aware of their feelings and face their problems.

behavior therapies Therapies that use principles of learning to reduce or eliminate maladaptive behavior.

systematic desensitization A method of behavior therapy based on classical conditioning that treats anxiety by getting the person to associate deep relaxation with increasingly intense anxiety-producing situations.

Another technique used in gestalt therapy is role playing by the client, the therapist, or both. For example, if an individual is bothered by conflict with her mother, the therapist might play the role of the mother and reopen the quarrel. The therapist might encourage the individual to act out her hostile feelings toward her mother by yelling, swearing, or kicking the couch, for example. In this way, gestalt therapists hope to help individuals better manage their feelings instead of letting their feelings control them.

The gestalt therapist is much more directive than the client-centered therapist. By being more directive, the gestalt therapist provides more interpretation and feedback (Haley, 2007; Zahm & Gold, 2002). Nonetheless, both of these humanistic therapies encourage individuals to take responsibility for their feelings and actions, to truly be themselves, to understand themselves, to develop a sense of freedom, and to look at what they are doing with their lives.

Behavior Therapies

Having explored the insight therapies—the psychodynamic and humanistic approaches—we turn to therapies that take a different approach to reducing people's problems and improving their adjustment: the behavior therapies. Behavior therapies offer action-oriented strategies to help people change what they are doing (Cooper, Heron, & Heward, 2007; Martin & Pear, 2007).

Behavior therapies use principles of learning to reduce or eliminate maladaptive behavior. Behavior therapies are based on the behavioral and social cognitive theories of learning and personality. Behavior therapists do not search for unconscious conflicts, as psychodynamic therapists do, or encourage individuals to develop accurate perceptions of their feelings and selves, as humanistic therapists do. Insight and self-awareness are not the keys to helping individuals develop more adaptive behavior patterns, say the behavior therapists.

Instead, behavior therapists assume that the overt symptoms are the problem. Individuals can become aware of why they are depressed and yet still be depressed, say the behavior therapists. Behavior therapists strive to eliminate the depressed symptoms or behaviors rather than trying to get individuals to gain insight into or awareness of why they are depressed (Kalodner, 2007; Miller, 2006).

The behavior therapies were initially based almost exclusively on the learning principles of classical and operant conditioning, but behavior therapies have become more diverse in recent years. As social cognitive theory grew in popularity, behavior therapists increasingly included observational learning, cognitive factors, and self-instruction in their efforts to help people with their problems (Watson & Tharp, 2007). In self-instruction, therapists try to get people to change what they say to themselves.

Systematic desensitization has a new format. Virtual reality technology is being used by some therapists to expose individuals to more vivid situations than their imagination might generate. Here, an individual with a fear of spiders is wearing a virtual reality headset and has become immersed in a vivid, three-dimensional world in which spiders appear very real.

Classical Conditioning Techniques Some behaviors, especially fears, can be acquired or learned through classical conditioning. If fears can be learned, possibly they can be unlearned as well (Stein & Matsunaga, 2006). If an individual has learned to fear snakes or heights through classical conditioning, perhaps the individual can unlearn the fear through counterconditioning (Tryon, 2005). Two types of counterconditioning are systematic desensitization and aversive conditioning.

Systematic Desensitization **Systematic desensitization** is a method of behavior therapy based on classical conditioning that treats anxiety by getting the person to associate deep relaxation with increasingly intense anxiety-producing situations (Wolpe, 1963). Consider the common fear of taking an exam. Using systematic desensitization, the behavior therapist first asks the person which aspects of the feared situation—in this case, taking an exam—are the most and least frightening. Then the behavior therapist arranges these circumstances in order from most to least frightening. An example of this type of desensitization hierarchy is shown in Figure 14.5.

The next step is to teach individuals to relax. Clients learn how to recognize the presence of muscular contractions or tensions in various parts of the

FIGURE 14.5

A Desensitization Hierarchy Involving Test Anxiety In this hierarchy, the individual begins with her least feared circumstance (a month before the exam) and moves through each of the circumstances until reaching her most feared circumstance (being in the process of answering the exam questions). At each step of the way, the person replaces fear with deep relaxation and successful visualizations.

1 A month before an examination	**8** One day before an examination
2 Two weeks before an examination	**9** The night before an examination
3 A week before an examination	**10** On the way to the university on the day of an examination
4 Five days before an examination	**11** Before the unopened doors of the examination room
5 Four days before an examination	**12** Awaiting distribution of examination papers
6 Three days before an examination	**13** The examination paper lies facedown before her
7 Two days before an examination	**14** In the process of answering the exam questions

body and then how to contract and relax different muscles. Once they are relaxed, the therapist asks them to imagine the least feared stimulus in the hierarchy. Subsequently, the therapist moves up the list of items, from least to most feared, while clients remain relaxed. Eventually, individuals are able to imagine the most fearsome situation without being afraid—in our example, answering exam questions. In this manner, instead of feeling anxious, individuals learn to relax while thinking about the exam.

Systematic desensitization is often used as an effective treatment for phobias, such as fear of giving a speech, fear of heights, fear of flying, fear of dogs, and fear of snakes. If you are afraid of snakes, for example, the therapist might initially have you watch someone handle a snake and then ask you to engage in increasingly more feared behaviors. You might first go into the same room with the snake, next approach the snake, then touch the snake; eventually, you might play with the snake. Figure 14.6 shows an example.

Desensitization involves exposing someone to a feared situation in a real or imagined way (Figueroa-Moseley & others, 2007). A more intense form of exposure involves *flooding,* which consists of exposing individuals to feared stimuli to an excessive degree while not allowing them to avoid the stimuli (Kneebone & Al-Daftary, 2006).

Aversive Conditioning   The other behavior therapy technique involving classical conditioning is **aversive conditioning,** which consists of repeated pairings of the undesirable behavior with aversive stimuli to decrease the behavior's rewards. Aversive conditioning is used to teach people to avoid such behaviors as smoking, overeating, and drinking alcohol. Electric shocks, nausea-inducing substances, and verbal insults are some of the noxious stimuli used in aversive conditioning (Sommer & others, 2006).

aversive conditioning A classical conditioning treatment that consists of repeated pairings of the undesirable behavior with aversive stimuli to decrease the behavior's rewards.

FIGURE 14.6

Systematic Desensitization Systematic desensitization is often used to help eliminate phobias. In this systematic desensitization treatment, the individual progresses from handling rubber snakes (*top left*), to peering at snakes in an aquarium (*top right*), to handling snakes with rubber gloves (*bottom left*), to handling live but harmless snakes (*bottom right*).

behavior modification The application of operant conditioning principles to change human behaviors; especially to replace unacceptable, maladaptive behaviors with acceptable, adaptive behaviors.

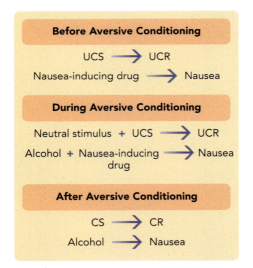

FIGURE 14.7

Classical Conditioning: The Backbone of Aversive Conditioning Classical conditioning can provide a conditional aversion to alcohol. After the association of the drug with alcohol, the alcohol becomes a conditioned stimulus for nausea. Recall the abbreviations UCS (unconditioned stimulus), UCR (unconditioned response), CS (conditioned stimulus), and CR (conditioned response).

If you have ever seen the film *A Clockwork Orange*, this sort of treatment may sound familiar. How could aversive conditioning be used to reduce a person's alcohol consumption? One way is that every time a person drank an alcoholic beverage, he or she also would consume a mixture that induced nausea. In classical conditioning terminology, the alcoholic beverage is the conditioned stimulus, and the nausea-inducing agent is the unconditioned stimulus. Through a repeated pairing of alcohol with the nausea-inducing agent, alcohol becomes the conditioned stimulus that elicits nausea, the conditioned response. As a consequence, alcohol no longer is associated with something pleasant but rather something highly unpleasant. Figure 14.7 illustrates how classical conditioning is the backbone of aversive conditioning.

Operant Conditioning Approaches The basic philosophy of using operant conditioning as a therapy approach is that, because maladaptive behavior patterns are learned, they can be unlearned. Therapy involves conducting a careful analysis of the person's environment to determine which factors need to be modified. Especially important is changing the consequences of the person's behavior to ensure that behavioral responses are followed by positive reinforcement.

Operant therapy's techniques focus on **behavior modification,** the application of operant conditioning principles to change human behavior; its main goal is to replace unacceptable, maladaptive behaviors with acceptable, adaptive ones. Consequences for behavior are established to ensure that acceptable actions are reinforced and unacceptable ones are not (Cooper, Heron, & Heward, 2007). Advocates of behavior modification believe that many emotional and behavior problems stem from inadequate (or inappropriate) response consequences (Martin & Pear, 2007).

A behavior modification system in which behaviors are reinforced with tokens (such as poker chips) that later can be exchanged for desired rewards (such as candy and money) is called a *token economy.* Token economies have been established in classrooms, institutions for individuals with mental or developmental disabilities, homes for delinquents, and psychiatric hospitals.

Behavior modification does not always work. One person may become so wedded to the tokens that, when they are no longer given, the positive behavior associated with them may disappear. Another person might continue the positive behavior without the tokens as rewards. Some critics object to behavior modification because they believe such extensive control of another person's behavior unethically infringes on the individual's rights. But as in the case of someone with an intense fear of exams, maladaptive responses can be turned into adaptive ones through behavior modification.

Cognitive Therapies

Cognitive therapies emphasize that individuals' cognitions, or thoughts, are the main source of abnormal behavior and psychological problems, and they attempt to change the individual's feelings and behaviors by changing cognitions. *Cognitive restructuring,* a general concept for changing a pattern of thought that is presumed to be causing maladaptive behavior or emotion, is central to cognitive therapies. Cognitive therapies differ from psychoanalytic therapies by focusing more on overt symptoms than on deep-seated unconscious thoughts, by providing more structure to the individual's thoughts, and by being less concerned about the origin of the problem. Unlike humanistic therapies, cognitive therapies provide more structure, more analysis, and more specific cognitive techniques.

Cognitive therapists guide individuals in identifying their irrational and self-defeating thoughts. Then they use various techniques to get clients to challenge these thoughts and consider different, more positive ways of thinking. These cognitive techniques often are implemented through a Socratic method of asking questions to help clients gain self-understanding about their negative thinking. As part of this process, a cognitive therapist usually asks clients what the worst thing is that could happen to them. Then clients must propose how they would cope with their ultimate worst situation. In this way, cognitive therapists help clients see that they will be able to cope even if the worst possible thing happens to them.

We next examine three main types of cognitive therapy: Albert Ellis's rational-emotive behavior therapy, Aaron Beck's cognitive therapy, and cognitive-behavior therapy.

Tony Soprano's psychiatrist, Jennifer Melfi, faced a tough job: how to make a killer feel better about himself.

Rational-Emotive Behavior Therapy   **Rational-emotive behavior therapy, or REBT,** is based on Albert Ellis's assertion that individuals develop a psychological disorder because of their beliefs, especially irrational and self-defeating beliefs. Ellis says that we usually talk to ourselves when we experience stress; too often, the statements are irrational, making them more harmful than helpful (1962, 1996, 2000, 2002, 2005).

Ellis (2000, 2002) believes that many individuals construct three basic demands: (1) I *absolutely must* perform well and win the approval of other people; (2) other people *have to* treat me kindly and fairly; and (3) my life conditions *should not* be frustrating but rather *should be* enjoyable. Once people convert their important desires into demands, they often create dysfunctional, exaggerated beliefs, such as "Because I'm not performing well, as I *absolutely must,* I'm an inadequate person."

The goal of REBT is to get the person to eliminate self-defeating beliefs by rationally examining them (Vernon, 2007). A client is shown how to dispute his or her dysfunctional beliefs—especially the absolute "musts"—and how to change them to realistic and logical thoughts. Homework assignments provide the client opportunities to engage in the new self-talk and experience the positive results of not viewing life in such a catastrophic way.

Beck's Cognitive Therapy   Aaron Beck developed a somewhat different form of cognitive therapy to treat psychological problems, especially depression (1976, 1993). A basic assumption Beck makes is that psychological problems, such as depression, result when people think illogically about themselves, the world they live in, and the future (2005, 2006). Beck's approach shares with Ellis's method the idea that the goal of therapy should be to help people to recognize and discard self-defeating cognitions.

In the initial phases of therapy, individuals are taught to make connections between their patterns of thinking and their emotional responses. The therapist helps them to identify their own automatic thoughts and to keep records of their thought content and emotional reactions. With the therapist's assistance, they learn to recognize logical errors in their thinking and to challenge the accuracy of these automatic thoughts. Logical errors in

cognitive therapies Therapies emphasizing that individuals' cognitions, or thoughts, are the main source of abnormal behavior and psychological problems.

rational-emotive behavior therapy (REBT) A therapy based on Ellis's assertion that individuals develop a psychological disorder because of their beliefs, especially those that are irrational and self-defeating; the goal of REBT is to get clients to eliminate self-defeating beliefs by rationally examining them.

Aaron Beck's method stresses that the goal of therapy should be to help people to recognize and eliminate illogical and self-defeating thinking.

thinking can lead an individual to the following erroneous beliefs (Carson, Butcher, & Mineka, 1996):

- Perceiving the world as harmful while ignoring evidence to the contrary—for example, a young woman's still feeling worthless even though a friend has just told her how much other people like her.
- Overgeneralizing on the basis of limited examples, such as a man's seeing himself as worthless because one individual stopped dating him.
- Magnifying the importance of undesirable events, such as seeing the loss of a dating partner as the end of the world.
- Engaging in absolutist thinking, such as exaggerating the importance of someone's mildly critical comment and perceiving it as proof of total inadequacy.

Figure 14.8 describes some of the most widely used cognitive therapy techniques.

The following case study involves a cognitive therapist's guidance of a depressed 26-year-old graduate student to understand the connection between how she interprets her experiences and how she feels, and to begin seeing the inaccuracy of her interpretations:

Student: I agree with the description of me but I guess I don't agree that the way I think makes me depressed.

Therapist: How do you understand it?

Student: I get depressed when things go wrong. Like when I fail a test.

Therapist: How can failing a test make you depressed?

Student: Well, if I fail I'll never get into law school.

Therapist: So failing the test means a lot to you. But if failing a test could drive people into clinical depression, wouldn't you expect everyone who failed the test to have depression? Did everyone who failed the test get depressed enough to require treatment?

Student: No, but it depends on how important the test was to the person.

Therapist: Right, and who decides the importance?

Student: I do.

Therapist: And so, what we have to examine is your way of viewing the test or the way that you think about the test and how it affects your chances of getting into law school. Do you agree?

Student: Right . . .

Therapist: Now what did failing mean?

Student: (Tearful) That I couldn't get into law school.

Therapist: And what does that mean to you?

Student: That I'm just not smart enough.

Therapist: Anything else?

Student: That I can never be happy.

Therapist: And how do these thoughts make you feel?

Student: Very unhappy.

Therapist: So it is the meaning of failing a test that makes you very unhappy. In fact, believing that you can never be happy is a powerful factor in producing unhappiness. So, you get yourself into a trap—by definition, failure to get into law school equals, "I can never be happy." (Beck & others, 1979, pp. 145–146)

Although Beck's and Ellis's cognitive therapies share some similarities, there also are differences. Rational-emotive behavior therapy is very directive, persuasive, and confrontational; in contrast, Beck's cognitive therapy involves more of an open-ended dialogue between the therapist and the individual. The aim of this dialogue in Beck's approach is to

Cognitive Therapy Technique	Description	Example
Challenge idiosyncratic meanings	Explore personal meaning attached to the client's words and ask the client to consider alternatives.	When a client says he will be "devastated" by his spouse's leaving, ask just how he would be devastated and ways he could avoid being devastated.
Question the evidence	Systematically examine the evidence for the client's beliefs or assertions.	When a client says she can't live without her spouse, explore how she lived without the spouse before she was married.
Reattribution	Help the client distribute responsibility for events appropriately.	When a client says that his son's failure in school must be his fault, explore other possibilities, such as the quality of the school.
Examine options and alternatives	Help the client generate alternative actions to maladaptive ones.	If a client considers leaving school, explore whether tutoring or going part-time to school are good alternatives.
Decatastrophize	Help the client evaluate whether he is overestimating the nature of a situation.	If a client states that failure in a course means he or she must give up the dream of medical school, question whether this is a necessary conclusion.
Fantasize consequences	Explore fantasies of a feared situation: if unrealistic, the client may recognize this; if realistic, work on effective coping strategies.	Help a client who fantasizes "falling apart" when asking the boss for a raise to role-play the situation and develop effective skills for making the request.
Examine advantages and disadvantages	Examine advantages and disadvantages of an issue, to instill a broader perspective.	If a client says he "was just born depressed and will always be that way," explore the advantages and disadvantages of holding that perspective versus other perspectives.
Turn adversity to advantage	Explore ways that difficult situations can be transformed to opportunities.	If a client has just been laid off, explore whether this is an opportunity for her to return to school.
Guided association	Help the client see connections between different thoughts or ideas.	Draw the connections between a client's anger at his wife for going on a business trip and his fear of being alone.
Scaling	Ask the client to rate her emotions or thoughts on scales to help gain perspective.	If a client says she was overwhelmed by an emotion, ask her to rate it on a scale from 0 (not at all present) to 100 (I fell down in a faint).
Thought stopping	Provide the client with ways of stopping a cascade of negative thoughts.	Teach an anxious client to picture a stop sign or hear a bell when anxious thoughts begin to snowball.
Distraction	Help the client find benign or positive distractions to take attention away from negative thoughts or emotions temporarily.	Have a client count to 200 by 13s when he feels himself becoming anxious.
Labeling of distortions	Provide labels for specific types of distorted thinking to help the client gain more distance and perspective.	Have a client keep a record of the number of times a day she engages in all-or-nothing thinking—seeing things as all bad or all good.

FIGURE 14.8

Cognitive Therapy Techniques Cognitive therapists develop strategies to help change the way people think.

get individuals to reflect on personal issues and discover their own misconceptions. Beck also encourages individuals to gather information about themselves and to try out unbiased experiments that reveal the inaccuracies of their beliefs.

Cognitive-Behavior Therapy   **Cognitive-behavior therapy** consists of a combination of cognitive therapy, with its emphasis on reducing self-defeating thoughts, and behavior therapy, with its emphasis on changing behavior (Watson & Tharp, 2007). An important aspect of cognitive-behavior therapy is *self-efficacy*, Albert Bandura's concept that one can master a situation and produce positive outcomes (1997, 2001, 2006, 2007a, 2007b). Bandura believes that self-efficacy is the key to successful therapy. At each step of the therapy process, people need to bolster their confidence by telling themselves, "I'm going to master my problem," "I can do it," "I'm improving," "I'm getting better,"

cognitive-behavior therapy Therapy consisting of a combination of cognitive therapy and behavior therapy; self-efficacy is an important goal of cognitive-behavior therapy.

and so on. As people gain confidence and engage in adaptive behavior, the successes become intrinsically motivating. Before long, individuals persist with considerable effort in their attempts to solve personal problems because of the positive outcomes that were set in motion by self-efficacy.

Self-instructional methods are cognitive-behavior techniques aimed at teaching individuals to modify their own behavior (Watson & Tharp, 2007). Using self-instructional methods, cognitive-behavior therapists try to get clients to change what they say to themselves. The therapist gives the client examples of constructive statements, known as reinforcing self-statements, that the client can repeat in order to take positive steps to cope with stress or meet a goal. The therapist also encourages the client to practice the statements through role playing and strengthens the client's newly acquired skills through reinforcements.

Following is a series of examples of self-instructional methods that individuals can use to cope with stressful situations (Meichenbaum, Turk, & Burstein, 1975):

Preparing for Anxiety or Stress

What do I have to do?

I'm going to map out a plan to deal with it.

I'll just think about what I have to do.

I won't worry. Worry doesn't help anything.

I have a lot of different strategies I can call on.

Confronting and Handling the Anxiety or Stress

I can meet the challenge.

I'll keep on taking one step at a time.

I can handle it. I'll just relax, breathe deeply, and use one of the strategies.

I won't think about the pain. I will think about what I have to do.

Coping with Feelings at Critical Moments

What is it I have to do?

I was supposed to expect the pain to increase. I just have to keep myself in control.

When the pain comes, I will just pause and keep focusing on what I have to do.

Reinforcing Self-Statements

Good, I did it.

I handled it well.

I knew I could do it.

Wait until I tell other people how I did it!

Using Cognitive Therapy to Treat Psychological Disorders Cognitive therapy has been used effectively in the treatment of some anxiety disorders, mood disorders, schizophrenia, and personality disorders (Beck, 2005; Parker & Fletcher, 2007). A recent review revealed that cognitive-behavior therapy was more effective than antidepressants in treating adult depression (Butler & others, 2006). In many instances, cognitive therapy used together with drug therapy is an effective treatment for psychological disorders (Starcevic, 2006).

Panic disorder is among the anxiety disorders to which cognitive therapy has been applied (Ayers & others, 2007; Labrecque & others, 2006). The central concept in the cognitive model of panic is that individuals catastrophically misinterpret relatively benign physical or psychological events. In cognitive therapy, the therapist encourages individuals to test the catastrophic misinterpretations by inducing an actual panic attack. The individuals then can test the notion that they will die or go crazy, which they find out is not the case. In one study, a combination of an SSRI drug and cognitive therapy effectively treated panic disorder (Azhar, 2001).

Cognitive therapy also shows considerable promise in the treatment of post-traumatic stress disorder, especially when therapists encourage clients to relive traumatic experiences so that they can come to grips with the threatening cognitions precipitated by those experiences (Vieweg & others, 2006). Cognitive therapy also has been successful in treating generalized anxiety disorder, certain phobias, and obsessive-compulsive disorder (Clark & others, 2006; Townsend & Grant, 2006).

In one study, cognitive-behavior therapy was given to children (as well as their parents) who were highly anxious about going to school (Dadds & others, 1999). As shown in Figure 14.9, the therapy (provided over a 10-week period) was considerably more effective in reducing anxiety than no therapy at all, and the positive effects of the therapy were still present 2 years later.

One of the earliest applications of cognitive therapy was in the treatment of depression. A number of studies have shown that cognitive therapy can be just as successful as, or in some cases superior to, drug therapy in the treatment of depressive disorders (Butler & others, 2006). Some studies also have demonstrated that individuals treated with cognitive therapy are less likely to relapse into depression than individuals treated with drug therapy (Jarrett & others, 2001).

Considerable strides have been made in recent years in applying cognitive therapy to the treatment of schizophrenia. Although not a substitute for drug therapy in the treatment of schizophrenia, cognitive therapy has been effective in reducing some symptoms such as belief in delusions and acting out impulsively (Naeem, Kingdon, & Turkington, 2006).

Cognitive therapy also has been used effectively in treating personality disorders (McMain & Pos, 2007; Palmer & others, 2006). The focus is on using cognitive therapy to change individuals' core beliefs and to reduce their automatic negative thoughts.

So far in this chapter, we have studied the biological therapies and psychotherapies. A comparison of the four psychotherapies—psychodynamic, humanistic, behavior, and cognitive—is presented in Figure 14.10.

The increasing interest in cognitive therapy and the dramatic advances in neuroscience have stimulated researchers to explore what is happening to the brain during cognitive therapy. To read about this fascinating new research frontier, see the Intersection.

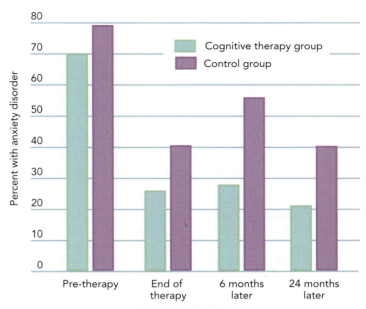

FIGURE 14.9

Effects of Cognitive-Behavior Therapy on Children's Anxiety About School Children and their parents participated in a 10-week cognitive-behavior therapy program. Compared with a control group of children, the children in the cognitive therapy program were less likely to have an anxiety disorder through 24 months after the therapy.

FIGURE 14.10

Therapy Comparisons Different therapies address the same problems in very different ways. Many therapists use the tools that seem right for any given client and his or her problems.

	Cause of Problem	Therapy Emphasis	Nature of Therapy and Techniques
Psychodynamic Therapies	Client's problems are symptoms of deep-seated, unresolved unconscious conflicts.	Discover underlying unconscious conflicts and work with client to develop insight.	Psychoanalysis, including free association, dream analysis, resistance, and transference: therapist interprets heavily, operant conditioning.
Humanistic Therapies	Client is not functioning at an optimal level of development.	Develop awareness of inherent potential for growth.	Person-centered therapy, including unconditional positive regard, genuineness, accurate empathy, and active listening; gestalt therapy including confrontation to encourage honest expression of feelings; self-appreciation emphasized.
Behavior Therapies	Client has learned maladaptive behavior patterns.	Learn adaptive behavior patterns through changes in the environment or cognitive processes.	Observation of behavior and its controlling conditions; specific advice given about what should be done; therapies based on classical conditioning, operant conditioning.
Cognitive Therapies	Client has developed inappropriate thoughts.	Change feelings and behaviors by changing cognitions.	Conversation with client designed to get him or her to change irrational and self-defeating beliefs.

Clinical Psychology and Neuroscience: Can Therapy Change the Brain?

Cognitively oriented therapies generally aim to change how people think, in order to help them overcome debilitating psychological disorders such as depression, anxiety, and post-traumatic stress disorder (PTSD). The cognitive approach to therapy assumes that how we think is an important part of how we feel, and that if we can change how we think about things—reinterpret events in more positive ways—we can feel better.

When we change our habitual patterns of thinking, we are also making physical changes in the brain.

Remember (from Chapter 3) that thinking is not only a mental event but also a physical event in the brain. A goal for cognitive-behavior therapy is to help us to alter our routine, automatic thinking habits. This way, for example, when we are faced with a bad grade, rather than dwelling on it we can think about how to do better in the future, what factors might have led to the failure, and how these circumstances can be adjusted (Butler & others, 2006; Kalodner, 2007). When we change our habitual patterns of thinking, we are also making physical changes in the brain. We might be activating brain areas we have not used. We might even be establishing new physical connections in the brain. Remarkably, recent advances in brain-imaging technology such as functional magnetic resonance imaging (or fMRI, discussed in Chapter 3) have allowed researchers to examine what actually happens in the brain when, through therapy, we change the way we think (Linden, 2006; Roffman & others, 2005).

Emotion regulation means bringing our automatic emotional reactions under our cognitive control, presumably so that we can accentuate the positive and eliminate the negative. Regulating emotion involves using cognitive strategies to change our emotional reactions, either heightening or lessening our feelings. By now, you will probably not be surprised to hear that automatic emotional responses involve activation in the amygdala, while the cognitive control of emotion is associated with activation in the prefrontal cortex (the very front of the brain—just behind the forehead) (Ochsner & Gross, 2005).

What happens to these areas of the brain when we actively try to control our emotional reactions? One study used fMRI to examine how these parts of the brain are activated during emotion regulation (Ray & others, 2005). Participants who were undergoing fMRI were asked to control their emotional responses to emotionally evocative pictures. The results indicated that controlling emotions involves activation in the left prefrontal cortex and that activation in this area is associated with changes in the amygdala, in line with a person's regulatory goals (that is, to be more or less responsive to a stimulus). The left prefrontal cortex can decrease activation in

the amygdala if the individual is trying to tone down the emotion, or it can increase the activation if the person is trying to intensify the emotion. One goal of cognitive therapy may be to help individuals gain control over automatic emotional reactions (in the amygdala) with control processes originating in the prefrontal cortex.

Brain imaging can also help to identify individuals who will be most responsive to therapeutic intervention. In one study, the brains of depressed individuals were scanned along with the brains of a control group of healthy individuals while they were shown different emotion-evoking words (Siegle, Carter, & Thase, 2006). Participants were then enrolled in 16 sessions of cognitive-behavior therapy. The researchers found that among depressed individuals, those who showed low levels of sustained brain activity in Brodmann's area 25 (a part of the brain's cerebral cortex associated with depression) during the pretherapy scan were most likely to improve with treatment. In addition, high sustained activity in the right amygdala prior to therapy was associated with decreased depression. This study shows that psychological disorders may be reflected in brain differences that can be used to identify which brain regions are most likely to change with therapy.

Another fMRI study examined brain processes and PTSD in individuals who had all been in automobile accidents (Farrow & others, 2005). Participants' brains were scanned before and after cognitive-behavior therapy. After therapy, individuals showed more activation in areas of the brain associated with social cognition and theory of mind, and these changes were related to feelings of forgiveness. Clearly, when the participants changed the way they were thinking, they literally changed the way their brains functioned.

Therapeutic interventions have also been shown to "wake up" parts of the brain that have been dormant. It is well established that schizophrenia, a severe psychological disorder described in Chapter 13, is associated with low levels of activity in the prefrontal cortex. This characteristic is sometimes referred to as *hypofrontality*, meaning that schizophrenia is characterized by low levels of activation in the brain area thought to be associated with high-order functions such as problem solving, judgment, and planning.

In one study, a therapeutic intervention called cognitive-remediation therapy (CRT) was given to a group of individuals who were profoundly disabled by schizophrenia for 10 years or more (Wykes & others, 2002). CRT is a psychological intervention that involves giving individuals practice in problem solving and information processing. The client essentially completes a variety of paper-and-pencil tasks that require skills such as cognitive flexibility, planning, and the use of working memory. Individuals with schizophrenia (who were on medication) and a control group of healthy individuals were scanned while engaging in a problem-solving task before and after those with schizophrenia completed CRT. Compared to healthy individuals, those with schizophrenia showed lower activation in the prefrontal cortex when solving such problems, but after CRT, those with schizophrenia showed increased activation during problem-solving tasks. Indeed, although participants with schizophrenia were significantly lower in activation prior to therapy compared to healthy participants, they were no longer different after therapy. This finding suggests that CRT had helped to normalize their brain function. This study is remarkable because it shows that a psychological intervention that focuses on engaging particular brain areas can lead to changes in the brain, even for patterns that were previously thought to be essentially stable, traitlike characteristics of the disorder.

The growing literature applying sophisticated scanning techniques to therapeutic interventions shows how knowledge about the brain can be used to track psychological processes such as emotion regulation, to identify brain areas that are particularly likely to respond to therapy, and to pinpoint brain changes associated with improvements in functioning. Because the brain is a physical organ in the body, we might assume that it is most sensitive to biological interventions. But research is showing that psychological interventions also can have a powerful influence on this amazing organ. In a sense, this dramatic research is revealing how, with the help of therapy, the brain is capable of changing itself.

 REVIEW, ASSESS, AND SHARPEN YOUR THINKING

Review

2 **Define psychotherapy and characterize four types of psychotherapy.**

- Explain what psychotherapy is and describe the psychodynamic therapies.
- Discuss the humanistic therapies.
- Summarize classical conditioning and operant conditioning approaches to behavior therapies.
- Distinguish among three cognitive therapies.

Assess

1. **Which psychotherapy is often used for treating phobic disorder?**
   A. aversive conditioning
   B. psychodynamic therapy
   C. systematic desensitization
   D. client-centered therapy

2. **Which psychotherapy approach would focus on the ways in which conflicts in early childhood relationships impact in current relationships?**
   A. client-centered therapy
   B. psychodynamic therapy
   C. cognitive therapy
   D. rational-emotive behavior therapy

3. **How are Ellis's rational-emotive behavior therapy and Beck's cognitive therapy different?**
   A. Ellis's approach seeks to eliminate self-defeating thoughts, whereas Beck's approach focuses on correcting logical errors and reducing thoughts.
   B. Ellis's approach is less directive than is Beck's.
   C. Ellis's approach focuses on helping clients understand the connections between their thoughts and their feelings; Beck's

approach focuses on helping people examine the demands they place on themselves.
   D. Ellis's approach is focused on behavioral concepts, whereas Beck's approach is focused on cognitive concepts.

4. **Which therapy has at its core unconditional positive regard?**
   A. psychodynamic therapy
   B. cognitive therapy
   C. gestalt therapy
   D. client-centered therapy

5. **The token economy is a(n) _____ technique; systematic desensitization is a(n) _____ technique.**
   A. cognitive, behavioral
   B. behavioral, cognitive
   C. classical conditioning, operant conditioning
   D. operant conditioning, classical conditioning

Sharpen Your Thinking

Imagine that you are a psychotherapist and that you diagnose an individual as having a depressive disorder. Which of the psychotherapies would you use to treat the individual? Explain your choice.

3 Sociocultural Approaches and Issues in Treatment

Explain the sociocultural approaches and issues in treatment.

In the treatment of psychological disorders, biological therapies change the person's body, behavior therapies modify the person's behavior, and cognitive therapies alter the person's thinking. This section focuses on sociocultural approaches to the treatment of psychological disorders. These methods view the individual as part of a social system of relationships that are influenced by various social and cultural factors (Nolen-Hoeksema, 2007). We first review sociocultural approaches, including group therapy, family and couples therapy, self-help support groups, and community mental health, and we then examine various cultural perspectives on therapy.

Because many psychological problems develop in the context of interpersonal relationships and group experiences—within family, marriage, work, or social groups—group therapy can be an important context for learning how to cope more effectively with these problems.

Group Therapy

A major issue in therapy is how to structure it to reach as many people in need as possible. One approach is for the therapist to see clients in a group (Yalom & Leszcz, 2006). Furthermore, there is good reason to believe that individuals who share a psychological problem may benefit from the empowering effect of observing others cope with a similar problem and that helping others cope can, in turn, improve individuals' feelings of competence and efficacy.

Advocates of group therapy stress that individual therapy is limited because it puts the client outside the normal context of relationships. But it is these very relationships, they argue, that may hold the key to successful therapy. Many psychological problems develop in the context of interpersonal relationships—within one's family, marriage, or peer group, for example. By taking into account the context of these important groups, therapy may be more successful.

Group therapy takes many diverse forms. Psychodynamic, humanistic, behavior, and cognitive therapy are all used in group therapy, in addition to approaches that are not based on the major psychotherapeutic perspectives (Rutan, Stone, & Shay, 2007). Six features make group therapy an attractive treatment format (Yalom, 1975, 1995; Yalom & Leszcz, 2006):

1. *Information:* Individuals receive information about their problems from either the group leader or other group members.

2. *Universality:* Many individuals develop the sense that no one else has frightening and unacceptable impulses. In the group, individuals observe that others feel anguish and suffering as well.

3. *Altruism:* Group members support one another with advice and sympathy and learn that they have something to offer others.

4. *Corrective recapitulation of the family group:* A therapy group often resembles a family (in family therapy, the group *is* a family), with the leaders representing parents and the other members siblings. In this new family, old wounds may be healed and new, more positive family ties made.

5. *Development of social skills:* Corrective feedback from peers may correct flaws in the individual's interpersonal skills. Self-centered individuals may see that they are self-centered if five other group members inform them about their self-centeredness; in individual therapy, the individuals might not believe the therapist.

6. *Interpersonal learning:* The group can serve as a training ground for practicing new behaviors and relationships. A hostile person may learn that he or she can get along better with others by behaving less aggressively, for example.

"I seem to respond best to group therapy."

Family and Couples Therapy

Family therapy is group therapy with family members. **Couples therapy** is group therapy with married or unmarried couples whose major problem lies within their relationship. These approaches stress that, although one person may have some abnormal symptoms, the symptoms are a function of the family or couple relationships (Appleton & Dykeman, 2007; Gladding, 2007; Simon, 2006). Psychodynamic, humanistic, and behavior therapies may be used in family and couples therapy (de Forster & Spivacow, 2006).

Four of the most widely used family therapy techniques are

1. *Validation:* The therapist expresses an understanding and acceptance of each family member's feelings and beliefs and thus validates the person. When the therapist talks with each family member, he or she finds something positive to say.

2. *Reframing:* The therapist helps families reframe problems as family problems, not an individual's problems. A delinquent adolescent boy's problems are reframed in terms of how each family member contributed to the situation. The father's lack of attention to his son and marital conflict may be involved, for example.

3. *Structural change:* The family therapist tries to restructure the coalitions in a family. In a mother–son coalition, the therapist might suggest that the father take a stronger disciplinarian role to relieve the mother of some of the burden. Restructuring might be as simple as suggesting that parents explore satisfying ways to be together; the therapist may recommend that once a week the parents go out for a quiet dinner together, for example.

4. *Detriangulation:* In some families, one member is the scapegoat for two other members who are in conflict but pretend not to be. For example, in the triangle of two parents and one child, the parents may insist that their marriage is fine but find themselves in subtle conflict over how to handle the child. The therapist tries to disentangle, or *detriangulate,* this situation by shifting attention away from the child to the conflict between the parents.

Couples therapy proceeds in much the same way as family therapy. Conflict in marriages and in relationships between unmarried individuals frequently involves poor communication. In some instances, communication has broken down entirely. The therapist tries to improve the communication between the partners (Snyder, Castellani, & Whisman, 2006). In some cases, the therapist will focus on the roles partners play: One may be strong, the other weak; one may be responsible, the other spoiled, for example. Couples therapy addresses diverse problems, such as alcohol abuse, jealousy, sexual messages, delayed childbearing, infidelity, gender roles, two-career families, divorce, and remarriage (Fals-Stewart, Birchler, & Kelley, 2006).

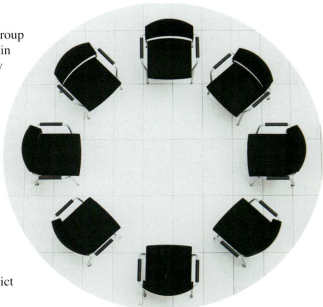

family therapy Group therapy with family members.

couples therapy Group therapy with married or unmarried couples whose major problem lies within their relationship.

In family therapy, the assumption is that particular patterns of interaction among the family members cause the observed abnormal symptoms.

Self-Help Support Groups

Self-help support groups are voluntary organizations of individuals who get together on a regular basis to discuss topics of common interest. The groups are not conducted by a professional therapist but by a paraprofessional or a member of the common interest group. A *paraprofessional* is someone who has been taught by a professional to provide

© CartoonStock.com

some mental health services but who does not have formal mental health training. The group leader and members provide support to help individuals with their problems.

Self-help support groups play an important role in our nation's mental health. A survey in 2002 revealed that for mental health support alone, nearly 7,500 such groups existed in the United States, with more than 1 million members (Goldstrom & others, 2006). In addition to reaching so many people in need of help, these groups are important because they use community resources and are relatively inexpensive. They also serve people who are less likely to receive help otherwise, such as less educated adults, individuals living in low-income circumstances, and homemakers.

Self-help support groups provide members with a sympathetic audience for confession, sharing, and emotional release. The social support, role modeling, and sharing of concrete strategies for solving problems that unfold in self-help groups add to their effectiveness. A woman who has been raped might not believe a male therapist who tells her that, with time, she will be able to put back together the pieces of her shattered life. But the same message from another rape survivor—someone who has had to work through the same feelings of rage, fear, and violation—might be more believable.

Alcoholics Anonymous (AA), founded in 1935 by a reformed alcoholic and a physician, is one of the best-known self-help groups. Mental health professionals often recommend AA for their alcoholic clients (Ferri, Amato, & Davoli, 2006; Suire & Bothwell, 2006).

Another self-help organization is Compeer, which matches community volunteers in supportive friendship relationships with children and adults receiving mental health treatment. In some cases, both partners in a Compeer relationship may have psychological disorders. There are myriad other self-help groups, such as Parents Without Partners, lesbian and gay support groups, cocaine abuse support groups, Weight Watchers and TOPS (Take Off Pounds Sensibly), child abuse support groups, and many medical (heart disease, cancer) support groups.

More recently, a multitude of online support groups has emerged (Andersson & others, 2006; Davison, Pennebaker, & Dickerson, 2000). Many individuals feel more comfortable sharing their intimate life experiences with a group of people they cannot actually see. Although it may seem as if an online support group exists for just about every problem imaginable, that is not necessarily the case. Research has shown that an online support group is more likely to emerge for problems that are potentially stigmatizing (such as depression and AIDS) and for problems that are more likely to be suffered by women rather than men (such as breast cancer) (Davison, Pennebaker, & Dickerson, 2000; Ussher & others, 2006; Thaxton, Emshoff, & Guessous, 2005). Online support groups have promise, but they also can be problematic. In the absence of guidance from a trained professional, online support group members may lack the expertise and knowledge to provide optimal advice. Indeed, the recent emergence of pro-anorexia (or "pro-ana") websites, which promote anorexia, exemplifies the potentially negative side of the online "support" phenomenon (Bardone-Cone & Cass, 2006; Mulveen & Hepworth, 2006).

For individuals who tend to cope by seeking information and affiliation with similar peers, self-help support groups can reduce stress and promote adjustment. However, as with any group therapy, there is a possibility that negative emotions will spread through the group, especially if the members face circumstances that deteriorate over time, as terminal cancer patients do. Group leaders who are sensitive to the spread of negative emotions can minimize such effects.

Community Mental Health

The community mental health movement was born in the 1960s, when essentially locking up individuals with psychological disorders and disabilities was recognized as inhumane and inappropriate. The deplorable conditions inside some psychiatric facilities at the time spurred movement as well. The central idea behind the community mental health movement was that individuals with disorders ought to remain within society and their families, receiving treatment in community mental health centers. This movement was also tied to economic issues, as it was thought that institutionalizing people was certainly more expensive than having them treated in the community at large. With the passage of the

Community Mental Health Act of 1963, large numbers of individuals with psychological disorders were transferred from mental institutions to community-based facilities, a process called *deinstitutionalization.* Although at least partially motivated by a desire to help individuals with psychological disorders more effectively, deinstitutionalization has also been implicated in rising rates of homelessness (Feldman, 1983). The success of community mental health services depends on the resources and commitment of the communities in which they occur.

Community mental health involves training teachers, ministers, family physicians, nurses, and others who directly interact with community members to offer lay counseling and workshops on such topics as coping with stress, reducing drug use, and assertiveness training (Benson, 2006). Advocates and providers of community mental health believe that the best way to treat a psychological disorder is to prevent it from happening in the first place (Dalton, Elias, & Wandersman, 2007). Prevention takes one of three courses: primary, secondary, or tertiary.

In the community mental health approach, ministers (along with others who directly interact with the community) offer counseling and workshops to help individuals cope with stress, eliminate drug dependence, and learn to assert themselves.

Primary prevention aims to reduce the number of new cases of psychological disorders. Some primary prevention programs target high-risk populations for prevention, such as children of alcoholics, children with chronic illnesses, and children in poverty.

In *secondary prevention,* screening for early detection of problems and early intervention may take place. Secondary prevention programs seek to reach large numbers of people. One way they do so is by educating paraprofessionals about preventing psychological problems and by teaming them up with psychologists. One type of early intervention involves screening schoolchildren to find those who show early signs of problems and then to provide them with psychological services.

Tertiary prevention focuses on treating psychological disorders that were not prevented or arrested early in the course of the disorders. Tertiary programs are often geared toward people who once required long-term care or hospitalization and who now are living in the community (Beeson & others, 2006). An example of a tertiary intervention is *halfway houses* (community residences for individuals who no longer require institutionalization but who still need support in readjusting to the community) for formerly hospitalized individuals with schizophrenia.

An explicit goal of community mental health is to help people who are disenfranchised from society, such as those living in poverty, to lead happier, more productive lives (Dalton, Elias, & Wandersman, 2007; Marshall & others, 2006). A key concept involved in this effort is *empowerment*—assisting individuals to develop the skills they need to control their own lives.

Cultural Perspectives

The psychotherapies discussed earlier in the chapter—psychodynamic, humanistic, behavior, and cognitive—focus mainly on the individual. This approach is compatible with the needs of many people in Western cultures, such as the United States, where the emphasis is on the individual rather than the group—family, community, ethnic group. However, these psychotherapies may not be as effective with people who live in cultures that place more importance on the group—called *collectivist* cultures. Some psychologists argue that family therapy is likely to be more effective with people in cultures that place a high value on the family, such as Latino and Asian cultures (Guo, 2005).

Ethnicity   Many ethnic minority individuals prefer discussing problems with parents, friends, and relatives rather than mental health professionals (Pedersen & others, 2007). Might therapy progress best, then, when the therapist and the client are from the same ethnic background? Researchers have found that, when there is an ethnic match between the therapist and the client and when ethnic-specific services are provided, clients are less likely to drop

out of therapy early and in many cases have better treatment outcomes (Jackson & Greene, 2000). Ethnic-specific services include culturally appropriate greetings and arrangements (for example, serving tea rather than coffee to Chinese American clients), providing flexible hours for treatment, and employing a bicultural/bilingual staff (Nystul, 1999).

Nonetheless, therapy can be effective when the therapist and client are from different ethnic backgrounds if the therapist has excellent clinical skills and is culturally sensitive (Akhtar, 2006; Gibson & Mitchell, 2003). Culturally skilled psychotherapists have good knowledge of their clients' cultural groups, understand sociopolitical influences, and have competence in working with culturally diverse groups (Abernathy & others, 2006; Matorin & others, 2006).

Gender   One byproduct of changing gender roles for women and men is evaluation of the goals of psychotherapy (Gilbert & Kearney, 2006; Nolen-Hoeksema, 2007). Traditionally, the goal of psychotherapy has been autonomy or self-determination for the client. However, autonomy and self-determination are often more central characteristics of life for men than for women, whose lives generally are more characterized by relatedness and connection with others. Thus, some psychologists believe that therapy goals should involve more emphasis on relatedness and connection with others, especially for women, or an emphasis on both autonomy/self-determination and relatedness/connection to others (Notman & Nadelson, 2002).

Because traditional therapy often has not adequately addressed the specific concerns of women in a sexist society, several nontraditional approaches have arisen. These nontraditional therapies emphasize the importance of helping people break free from traditional gender roles and stereotypes. Feminist therapists believe that traditional psychotherapy continues to carry considerable gender bias and that female clients cannot realize their full potential without becoming aware of society's sexism.

The goals of feminist therapists are no different from other therapists' goals, and feminist therapists make no effort to turn clients into feminists. However, they do want their female clients to be fully aware of how the nature of women's role in U.S. society can contribute to the development of a psychological disorder. Feminist therapists believe that women must become alert to the bias and discrimination in their own lives to achieve their mental health goals (Herlihy & McCollum, 2007).

REVIEW, ASSESS, AND SHARPEN YOUR THINKING

Review

3 Explain the sociocultural approaches and issues in treatment.

- Define group therapy.
- Describe family and couples therapy.
- Discuss the features of self-help support groups.
- Explain the community mental health approach.
- Identify cultural perspectives that can affect the success of treatment.

Assess

1. A family therapist who attempts to change the alliances among members of a family is using which of the following techniques?

   A. reframing   B. structural change

   C. detriangulation   D. validation

2. What is a paraprofessional?

   A. someone who helps a therapist to conduct therapy

   B. an unlicensed therapist

   C. the leader of a therapy group

   D. someone who has training in helping but lacks formal training as a therapist

3. **What is deinstitutionalization?**
   A. releasing a convict from the prison system
   B. the historic transfer of mental health clients from institutions to community agencies
   C. the process of having someone admitted to a treatment center against their will
   D. discharging someone with a psychological disorder from treatment

4. **Preventing the development of mental health problems before they begin is known as**
   A. tertiary prevention.
   B. primary prevention.

C. secondary prevention.
D. community prevention.

5. **Which of the following is not a goal of gender-oriented therapy?**
   A. developing closeness in relationships
   B. evaluating gender roles
   C. focusing exclusively on developing independence and autonomy
   D. conceptualizing psychological disorders within the context of women's roles

Sharpen Your Thinking

Which therapy setting do you think would benefit you the most—individual or group? Why?

4 The Effectiveness of Psychotherapy

Evaluate the effectiveness of psychotherapy.

Do individuals who go through therapy get better? Are some approaches more effective than others? Or is the situation similar to that of the Dodo bird in *Alice's Adventures in Wonderland*? Dodo was asked to judge the winner of a race. He decided, "Everybody has won and all must have prizes."

How should we evaluate the effectiveness of psychotherapy? Should we take the client's word? The therapist's word? What should be our criteria for effectiveness? Should we try to assess "good feelings," "adaptive behavior," "improved interpersonal relationships," "autonomous decision making," and "more positive self-concept"? During the past several decades, a huge amount of research has addressed these questions (Kazdin, 2007; Prochaska & Norcross, 2007).

Research on the Effectiveness of Psychotherapy

More than 50 years ago Hans Eysenck (1952) came to the shocking conclusion that psychotherapy was ineffective. A large body of recent research, however, points to the conclusion that psychotherapy does work (Beck, 2005; Butler & others, 2006; Lambert, 2001; Luborsky & others, 2002). Researchers have conducted literally hundreds of studies examining the effects of psychotherapy. The strategy used to analyze these diverse studies is meta-analysis, in which, as we have seen, the researcher statistically combines the results of many different studies (Rosenthal & DiMatteo, 2001). A number of persuasive meta-analyses have concluded that psychotherapy does work, and works well, for many psychological disorders (Lipsey & Wilson, 1993; Wampold, 2001).

Figure 14.11 provides a summary of numerous studies and reviews of research in which clients were randomly assigned to a no-treatment control group, a placebo control group, or a psychotherapy treatment (Lambert, 2001). As can be seen, individuals who did not get treatment improved, probably because they sought help from friends, family, clergy, or others. Individuals who were in a placebo control group fared better than non-treated individuals, probably because of having contact with a therapist, expectations of being

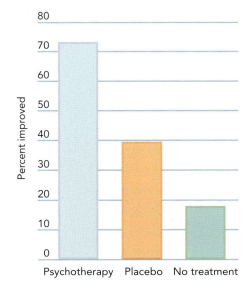

FIGURE 14.11

The Effects of Psychotherapy In a recent review of studies, more than 70 percent of individuals who saw a therapist improved, whereas less than 40 percent who received a placebo and less than 20 percent who received no treatment improved (Lambert, 2001).

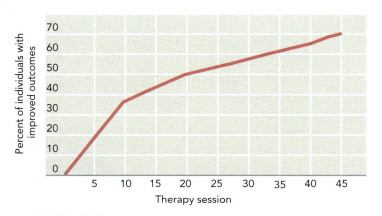

FIGURE 14.12

Number of Therapy Sessions and Improvement In one recent study, a large number of people undergoing therapy rated their well-being (based on symptoms, interpersonal relations, and quality of life) before each treatment session (Anderson & Lambert, 2001). The percentage of people who showed improved outcomes after each additional session of treatment indicated that about one-third of the individuals recovered by the 10th session, 50 percent by the 20th session, and 70 percent by the 45th session.

helped, or the reassurance and support that they got during the study. However, by far the best outcomes occurred for individuals who received psychotherapy.

Individuals who are thinking about seeing a psychotherapist want to know not only whether psychotherapy in general is effective but also (especially) which form of psychotherapy is most effective. Here, the Dodo bird hypothesis has often been shown to be correct—all win and all must have prizes. That is, although research strongly supports the notion that therapy works, no one therapy has been shown to be significantly better than the others (Hubble & Miller, 2004; Lambert, 2001; Luborsky & others, 2002; Wampold, 2001). These results suggest that it might make sense for consumers to find out about the types of available therapies and think about which might be best suited to their personality and problem.

Individuals who see a therapist also want to know how long it will take them to get better. In one study, individuals showed substantial improvement in therapy over the course of the first 6 months, with diminishing returns after that (Howard & others, 1996). In another study, individuals rated their symptoms, interpersonal relations, and quality of life on a weekly basis before each treatment session (Anderson & Lambert, 2001). Figure 14.12 shows that one-third of the individuals had improved outcomes by the 10th session, 50 percent by the 20th session, and 70 percent by the 45th session. In sum, therapy benefits most individuals with psychological problems at least through the first 6 months of therapy and possibly longer.

Common Themes in Psychotherapy

After carefully studying the nature of psychotherapy for more than 25 years, Jerome Frank concluded that effective psychotherapies have the common elements of expectations, mastery, and emotional arousal (1982; Frank & Frank, 1993). By inspiring expectations of help, the therapist motivates the client to continue going to therapy (Jennings & Skovholt, 1999). These expectations are powerful morale builders and symptom relievers in themselves (Arnkoff, Glass, & Shapiro, 2002). The therapist also increases the client's sense of mastery and competence (Brammer & MacDonald, 1999). For example, the client begins to feel that he or she can cope effectively with the world. Therapy also arouses the individual's emotions, an essential motivator for behavior change, according to Frank.

The **therapeutic alliance,** that is, the relationship between the therapist and client, is another important element of successful psychotherapy (Prochaska & Norcross, 2007; Strupp, 1995). A relationship in which the client has confidence and trust in the therapist is essential to effective psychotherapy (Knapp, 2007; McLeod, 2007). In one study, the most common ingredient in the success of different psychotherapies was the therapist's supportiveness of the client (Wallerstein, 1989). The client and therapist engage in a "healing ritual" that requires the active participation of both parties. As part of this ritual, the client becomes more hopeful and less alienated. It also is important for therapists to monitor the quality of their relationships with clients. Clients of therapists who did not assess the quality of the alliance were two times more likely to drop out of therapy (Hubble & Miller, 2004). Among those who completed therapy, clients of therapists who failed to assess their alliance were three to four times more likely to have a negative outcome (Hubble & Miller, 2004).

Therapy Integrations

In the single-therapy approach, the therapist believes that one particular kind of therapy works best. However, approximately 30 to 50 percent of practicing therapists do not identify themselves as adhering to one particular approach but rather refer to themselves as "integrative" or "eclectic" (Castonguay & others, 2003; Norcross & Prochaska, 1988).

therapeutic alliance The relationship between the therapist and client.

Integrative therapy is a combination of techniques from different therapies based on the therapist's judgment of which particular techniques will provide the greatest benefit for the client (Prochaska & Norcross, 2007).

Integrative therapy is characterized by openness to various ways of integrating diverse therapies. For example, a therapist might use a behavioral approach to treat an individual with panic disorder and a cognitive therapy approach to treat an individual with major depressive disorder. There is no single, well-defined integrative therapy that ties all of the therapy approaches together. For that reason, the term *therapy integration* probably best captures what is taking place in this field (Arkowitz, 1997).

In the past two decades, therapy integration has grown dramatically (Arkowitz, 1997; Santee, 2007). What has fostered the movement toward integrative therapy? The motivating factors include the proliferation of therapies, the inadequacy of a single therapy to be relevant to all clients and all problems, a lack of evidence that one therapy is better than others, and recognition that therapy commonalities play an important role in therapy outcomes (Norcross & Newman, 1992).

At their best, integrative therapies are effective, systematic uses of a variety of therapy approaches (Corey, 2001; Prochaska & Norcross, 2007). However, one worry about integrative therapies is that their increased use will result in an unsystematic, haphazard eclecticism, which some therapists say would be no better than a narrow, dogmatic approach to therapy (Lazarus, Beutler, & Norcross, 1992).

With the increased diversity of client problems and populations, future therapy integration is likely to include more attention to ethnic and cultural factors in treating clients (Santee, 2007; Sue, 2000). This increased ethnic and cultural diversity also will require therapists to integrate spiritual concerns into their therapy approach (Abernathy & others, 2006).

Integrative therapy also is at work when individuals are treated with both psychotherapy and drug therapy. For example, combined drug therapy and cognitive therapy has been effective in treating anxiety and depressive disorders (Dunner, 2001). And combined drug therapy and cognitive therapy holds promise in treating schizophrenia (Rector & Beck, 2001). This integrative therapy might be conducted by a mental health team that includes a psychiatrist and a clinical psychologist.

Therapy integrations are conceptually compatible with the biopsychosocial model of abnormal behavior described in Chapter 13. That is, many therapists believe that abnormal behavior involves biological, psychological, and social factors. Many single-therapy approaches concentrate on one aspect of the person more than others; for example, drug therapies focus on biological factors, and cognitive therapies probe psychological factors. Therapy integrations often take a broader look at individuals' problems.

Funding and Finding Therapy

Psychotherapy can be expensive. Even though reduced fees and, in some cases, free services can be arranged in public hospitals and community mental health centers, many people who most need psychotherapy do not get it. The challenge of paying for psychotherapy has led to substantial changes in mental healthcare delivery in recent years, especially the introduction of managed care. *Managed care* consists of strategies for controlling healthcare costs, including mental health treatment, and demand for accountability of treatment success. This goal typically is accomplished by interjecting a managed care organization between the mental health client and the providers of mental health services. Managed care providers attempt to offer services at lower costs by limiting traditional services, using stringent review procedures, and using lower-cost brief-treatment options (Brown & others, 2005). Managed care emerged in the early 1980s and has grown dramatically.

Criticisms of managed care abound and include the following (Boothroyd & others, 2006; Cohen, Marecek, & Gilham, 2006; Trivedi & others, 2006):

- Managed care organizations are reluctant to provide for more than a few therapy sessions for each patient.

integrative therapy A combination of techniques from different therapies based on the therapist's judgment of which particular techniques will provide the greatest benefit for the client.

Professional Type	Degree	Education Beyond Bachelor's Degree	Nature of Training
Clinical psychologist	PhD or PsyD	5–7 years	Requires both clinical and research training. Includes a 1-year internship in a psychiatric hospital or mental health facility. Some universities have developed PsyD programs, which have a stronger clinical than research emphasis. The PsyD training program takes as long as the clinical psychology PhD program and also requires the equivalent of a 1-year internship.
Psychiatrist	MD	7–9 years	Four years of medical school, plus an internship and residency in psychiatry are required. A psychiatry residency involves supervision in therapies, including psychotherapy and biomedical therapy.
Counseling psychologist	MA, PhD, PsyD, or EdD	3–7 years	Similar to clinical psychologist but with emphasis on counseling and therapy. Some counseling psychologists specialize in vocational counseling. Some counselors complete master's degree training, others PhD or EdD training, in graduate schools of psychology or education.
School psychologist	MA, PhD, PsyD, or EdD	3–7 years	Training in graduate programs of education or psychology. Emphasis on psychological assessment and counseling practices involving students' school-related problems. Training is at the master's or doctoral level.
Social worker	MSW/DSW or PhD	2–5 years	Graduate work in a school of social work that includes specialized clinical training in mental health facilities.
Psychiatric nurse	RN, MA, or PhD	0–5 years	Graduate work in a school of nursing with special emphasis on care of mentally disturbed individuals in hospital settings and mental health facilities.
Occupational therapist	BS, MA, or PhD	0–5 years	Emphasis on occupational training with focus on physically or psychologically handicapped individuals. Stresses getting individuals back into the mainstream of work.
Pastoral counselor	None to PhD or DD (Doctor of Divinity)	0–5 years	Requires ministerial background and training in psychology. An internship in a mental health facility as a chaplain is recommended.
Counselor	MA or MEd	2 years	Graduate work in a department of psychology or department of education with specialized training in counseling techniques.

FIGURE 14.13

Main Types of Mental Health Professionals A wide range of professionals with varying levels of training have taken on the challenge of helping people with psychological disorders.

- Long-term psychotherapy has been eliminated except for a relatively few wealthy clients who can pay their own way.
- Some managed care organizations are employing less-well-trained therapists because these individuals will work at lower fees.

Mental Health Professionals

Psychotherapy is practiced by a variety of mental health professionals, including clinical psychologists, psychiatrists, and counselors. Recall that psychiatrists have a medical degree. Clinical psychologists, in contrast, are trained in graduate programs in psychology. Figure 14.13 lists the main types of mental health professionals, their degrees, the years of education required, and the nature of their training.

Licensing and certification are two ways in which society retains control over individuals who practice psychotherapy (Harmatz, 1997). Laws at the state level are used to license or certify such professionals. These laws vary in toughness from one state to another, but invariably they specify the training the mental health professional must have and provide for some assessment of the applicant's skill through formal examination. Licensing boards exist to protect the public from unscrupulous individuals who might use the title "psychologist" to offer treatment, and collect payment, without sufficient training to do so.

Licensing and certification require mental health practitioners to engage in ethical practices. Laws typically address the importance of doing no harm to clients,

PSYCHOLOGY AND LIFE

Finding the Best Therapist for You

Remember that finding the best therapist for you may not be the same as finding a good plumber. Asking around for recommendations from your friends may not be an optimal strategy. What works for someone else might not work for you. Here are some suggestions to help you along the journey of finding the right professional for you.

1. *Identify the professional's credentials.* Regardless of the specific profession, some minimal credentials are important. All states have licensing regulations for professionals who provide public services. A therapist should be licensed or certified by the state in order to practice.

2. *Think about the kind of problem you are dealing with and the type of help you would prefer.* Psychologists, psychiatrists, and social workers differ in their approach to therapy based on differences in training. Psychologists tend to be focused on the person's emotions and behaviors; psychiatrists are trained as medical doctors, so their perspective is likely to involve physical aspects of psychological problems; and social workers are inclined to take a person's entire family and social situation into account. In addition, in some cases it may be important for a professional to have advanced, specialized training in a certain area. For example, for a person seeking help with a specific problem—such as drug abuse, alcohol abuse, or a sexual disorder—the therapist should have some training in that area.

3. *Be patient.* Because a large part of therapy involves the development of a relationship with the therapist, it may take several meetings to know for sure if things are going well. Give it between four and six weekly meetings. If it does not seem as if things are going the way you would like, discuss your progress with the therapist and ask what you should expect with regard to making progress.

4. *Be a thoughtful and careful consumer of mental health services.* Just as is true in seeking any services, the more informed you are about the services provided, the better the decision you can make about whether they are the right services for you. Calling around and asking specific questions about approaches and specializations is one way to become informed about the services offered by therapists. Consider how important it may be that the therapist is of your or the opposite sex, and whether it is important that he or she have experience with your specific difficulty, as well as other specific characteristics. You may also want to learn more about his or her theoretical orientation to therapy as described in this chapter. Another way to find out more about the therapist is to ask these kinds of questions during your first visit. Most professionals are quite comfortable talking about their background and training. Your confidence and trust in the professional is an important part of how well therapy will work for you.

5. *Keep an open mind.* Use these general guidelines when first looking for a therapist. Remember that people should continually evaluate their own progress throughout therapy, and, when they are dissatisfied with how it is going, they should discuss this feeling with their therapists. Therapy is like other services: When dissatisfied, you can always look for another therapist. Do not think that, just because one therapist has not been helpful, none will be. All therapists and therapeutic relationships are different. Finding the right therapist is one of the most important factors in therapy success.

protecting the privacy of clients, and avoiding inappropriate relationships with clients. Violations of ethical codes can result in a loss of the license to practice psychotherapy (Wierzbicki, 1999).

All of us have times when life's difficulties seem to catch up with us and begin to detract from our ability to reach our goals and fulfill our potential. If you are thinking about seeing a therapist, the Psychology and Life feature provides some guidelines to aid in finding the person who will help you overcome those difficulties and get things back on track.

REVIEW, ASSESS, AND SHARPEN YOUR THINKING

Review

4 **Evaluate the effectiveness of psychotherapy.**

- Discuss research on psychotherapy effectiveness.
- Describe common themes in psychotherapy.
- Explain therapy integrations.
- Summarize issues involved in finding and funding therapy.
- List the kinds of health professionals who are qualified to provide mental health treatment and state the effects of managed care on mental health treatment.

Assess

1. **Which of the following is a benefit of managed care?**
   A. short-term treatment
   B. consistently well-trained therapists
   C. availability of many therapy sessions
   D. reduced cost

2. **Which therapy is most effective?**
   A. psychodynamic   B. cognitive
   C. humanistic   D. they are equally effective

3. **Across different types of therapy, _____ is most related to successful outcomes.**
   A. theoretical orientation
   B. therapeutic relationship
   C. validation
   D. cognitive restructuring

4. **What is integrative therapy?**
   A. therapy that helps people to integrate various aspects of their lives
   B. therapy for persons with dissociative identity disorder
   C. therapy that uses techniques from various theories
   D. therapy that utilizes individual, family, and group techniques

5. **Which of the following professions would allow specialization in vocational counseling?**
   A. occupational therapist
   B. school psychologist
   C. counseling psychologist
   D. pastoral counselor

Sharpen Your Thinking

Explain why a control group is important in research on psychotherapy effectiveness.

5 Therapies and Health and Wellness

Discuss therapy's larger implications for health and wellness and characterize the client's role in therapeutic success.

Therapy is generally aimed at relieving psychological symptoms. A therapy is considered effective if it allows a person freedom from the negative effects of psychological disorders. Does therapy have larger implications for a person's physical health and psychological wellness? Researchers have examined this interesting question in a variety of ways.

Links Between Therapy and Physical and Psychological Health

There are many potential connections between psychotherapy and physical health. For example, receiving a cancer diagnosis can be a stressful experience for diagnosed individuals. Might psychotherapeutic help aimed at reducing this stress improve patients' ability to fight the disease? New research is indicating that therapy indeed is having such a positive effect. For instance, one recent study revealed that group-based cognitive therapy that focused on improving prostate cancer patients' stress management skills was effective in improving their quality of life (Penedo & others, 2006). Another recent study found that individual cognitive-behavior therapy reduced symptom severity in cancer patients undergoing chemotherapy (Sikorskii & others, 2006).

It might also be that psychotherapy that is directed at relieving psychological disorders such as depression can have important benefits for physical health. Recall from Chapter 13 that depression is associated with coronary heart disease (Strachowski & others, 2007; Wholley, 2006). Psychotherapy that reduces depression is likely, then, to reduce the risk of heart disease (Davidson & others, 2006). A research review revealed evidence of positive effects of psychotherapy on health behavior and physical illness, including habits and ailments such as smoking, chronic pain, chronic fatigue syndrome, and asthma (Eells, 2000).

Psychotherapy might also be a way to *prevent* psychological and physical problems. A recent study demonstrated the benefit of incorporating therapy into physical healthcare (Smit & others, 2006). Individuals who were waiting to see their primary healthcare provider were assigned to receive either physical health treatment as usual or that same treatment plus brief psychotherapy (a simple version of minimal contact cognitive-behavior therapy). The brief psychotherapy included a self-help manual, instructions in mood management, and six short telephone conversations with a prevention worker. The overall rate of depression was lowered significantly in the psychotherapy group, and this difference was cost effective. That is, the use of brief psychotherapy as a part of regular physical checkups was both psychologically and economically advantageous.

Elizabeth Edwards, the wife of Democratic presidential hopeful John Edwards, was diagnosed with breast cancer late in her husband's campaign for the White House in 2004. Psychotherapy can help individuals such as Edwards to achieve a reduction in stress, which in turn can improve their ability to fight their disease.

Psychotherapy, Wellness, and Personal Growth

Might psychotherapy also enhance psychological wellness? This question is important because the absence of psychological symptoms (the goal of most psychotherapy) is not the same thing as the presence of psychological wellness. Just as an individual who is without serious physical illness is not necessarily at the height of physical health, a person who is relatively free of psychological symptoms still might not show the qualities we associate with psychological thriving. Indeed, a lack of psychological wellness may predispose individuals to relapse or may make them vulnerable to problems (Ryff & Singer, 1998; Ryff, Singer, & Love, 2004; Thunedborg, Black, & Bech, 1995). Research has revealed that individuals who show not only a decrease in symptoms but also an increase in well-being are less prone to relapse (Fava, 2006; Ruini & Fava, 2004).

Recently, therapists have developed a new type of treatment, aimed at enhancing well-being. **Well-being therapy (WBT)** is a short-term (eight sessions), problem-focused, directive therapy that encourages clients to accentuate the positive (Fava, 2006; Fava & others, 2005; Ruini & Fava, 2004; Ruini & others, 2006). The first step in WBT is recognizing the positive in one's life when it happens. In WBT, the initial homework assignment asks clients to monitor their own happiness levels and keep track of moments of well-being. Clients are encouraged to note even small pleasures in their lives—a beautiful fall day, a relaxing chat with a friend, or the great taste of morning coffee. Clients then identify thoughts and feelings that are related to the premature ending of these moments. WBT is about learning to notice and savor positive experiences and coming up with ways to promote and celebrate life's good moments. WBT is effective in enhancing well-being, and it may also allow individuals to enjoy sustained recovery from mental disorders (Fava & others, 2005; Ruini & Fava, 2004; Ruini & others, 2006; Sonino & Fava, 2003).

Further, therapists have applied a positive approach to therapy by focusing on personal growth that might occur through the experience of difficulties in life (Cryder & others, 2006). **Post-traumatic growth** refers to the improvements individuals can see in themselves as the result of a struggle with negative life events. Richard Tedeschi and Lawrence Calhoun (2004) have examined post-traumatic growth in individuals who have experienced a life crisis such as rape, serious illness, or the loss of a child. Post-traumatic growth is

"Learn to enjoy the little things . . . for example, I'm delighted by all the pocket change I find under that couch!"

© CartoonStock.com

well-being therapy (WBT) A short-term, problem-focused, directive therapy that encourages clients to accentuate the positive.

post-traumatic growth Improvements individuals can see in themselves as a result of a struggle with negative life events.

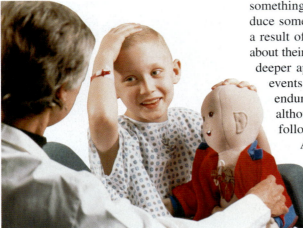

something of a paradox because this phenomenon acknowledges that real losses can produce something of value in a person's life. Individuals who say that they have grown as a result of devastating life circumstances report experiences such as heightened feelings about their ability to survive, enhanced capacity for intimacy and compassion for others, and deeper appreciation for the little things in life. Those who have survived negative life events may also develop a stronger, more sophisticated philosophy of life or a more enduring sense of spirituality or religious well-being (Tedeschi & Calhoun, 2004). So, although the traumatic event itself may always be viewed as regrettable, the struggle following the trauma can be valuable.

According to Tedeschi and Calhoun (2004), one way a therapist can promote growth is by listening without solving—that is, listening to an individual describe a personal experience of loss without jumping in and trying to fix the problem. Another avenue for promoting a client's growth is for the therapist to listen for and label themes of post-traumatic growth. Labeling post-traumatic growth does not mean spouting trite ideas such as "It's all good!" or "Every cloud has a silver lining." Rather, to facilitate growth, the therapist must allow clients to express their unique feelings and personal sense of positive change.

The Client's Role in Therapeutic Success

Although therapy clearly works, no one therapy is more successful than the others. What factors explain the mechanism by which a therapy works? In all of the meta-analyses of therapeutic outcome studies, one major factor in predicting therapeutic outcome is the client himself or herself. Indeed, the quality of the client's participation is the most important determinant of therapy outcome (McKay, Imel, & Wampold, 2006; Wampold, 2001). Even though the individual may seek therapy from a place of vulnerability, as we considered at the beginning of this chapter, it is that person's strengths, abilities, skills, and motivation that account for therapeutic success (Hubble & Miller, 2004; Wampold & Brown, 2005). In a review of the extensive evidence on therapeutic efficacy, it was noted that "the data make abundantly clear that therapy does not make clients work, but rather clients make therapy work" (Hubble & Miller, 2004, p. 347). Therapy can be viewed as a catalyst for bringing the person's own strengths back to the forefront of his or her life.

Life is complicated and filled with potential pitfalls. We all need help sometimes, and therapy is one way to improve oneself, physically and psychologically—to grow and become the best person we can be. Therapy is as complex as any other human relationship and potentially as magical, producing positive changes in one person's life through a meaningful relationship with another (Joseph & Linley, 2004).

 REVIEW, ASSESS, AND SHARPEN YOUR THINKING

Review

5 Discuss therapy's larger implications for health and wellness and characterize the client's role in therapeutic success.

- Describe the effects of psychotherapy on physical health.
- Summarize the effects of psychotherapy on wellness and personal growth.
- Discuss the client's role in therapeutic success.

Assess

1. For whom would psychotherapy be most appropriate?

A. someone living with schizophrenia

B. someone with a chronic illness

C. someone with few problems

D. all of the above

2. **Which of the following is not characteristic of well-being therapy?**
   A. continual therapy occurring over a long time period
   B. focusing on the positive
   C. celebrating happy moments
   D. sustaining recovery from mental illness

3. **Who is most responsible for success in therapy?**
   A. the therapist
   B. the client
   C. the community
   D. the managed care system

Sharpen Your Thinking

Think about the role therapy might play in improving health and wellness even for those who do not have psychological disorders. What sorts of life goals might a person seek to explore in an intervention such as well-being therapy, when life is going well?

1 BIOLOGICAL THERAPIES

Describe the biological therapies.

Drug Therapy

Psychotherapeutic drugs that are used to treat psychological disorders fall into three main categories: antianxiety drugs, antidepressant drugs, and antipsychotic drugs. Antianxiety drugs are commonly known as tranquilizers. Benzodiazepines are the most commonly used antianxiety drugs. Antidepressant drugs regulate mood; the three main classes are tricyclics, MAO inhibitors, and SSRI drugs. Lithium often is successful in treating bipolar disorder. The antidepressant drugs are increasingly being used to treat some anxiety disorders as well. Antipsychotic drugs are powerful drugs that are used to treat people with severe psychological disorders, especially schizophrenia. Psychotherapeutic drugs have varying effectiveness and side effects.

Electroconvulsive Therapy

Electroconvulsive therapy, commonly called shock therapy, is used to treat severe depression when other strategies have not worked. A potential side effect of this procedure is long-term memory loss.

Psychosurgery

Psychosurgery is an irreversible procedure in which brain tissue is destroyed in an attempt to improve adjustment. Today, psychosurgery is rarely used but is more precise than the early prefrontal lobotomies.

2 PSYCHOTHERAPY

Define psychotherapy and characterize four types of psychotherapy.

Psychodynamic Therapies

Psychotherapy is the process mental health professionals use to help individuals recognize, define, and overcome their psychological and interpersonal difficulties and improve their adjustment. Psychodynamic therapies stress the importance of the unconscious mind, early family experiences, and extensive interpretation by therapists.

In Freudian psychoanalysis, psychological disorders are caused by unresolved unconscious conflicts, believed to originate in early family experiences. A therapist's interpretation of free association, dreams, transference, and resistance provide tools for understanding the client's unconscious conflicts. Although psychodynamic therapy has changed, many contemporary psychodynamic therapists still probe the unconscious mind for early family experiences that might provide clues to clients' current problems. The development of the self in social contexts is an important theme in Kohut's contemporary approach.

Humanistic Therapies

In humanistic therapy, clients are encouraged to understand themselves and to grow personally. The humanistic therapies emphasize conscious thoughts, the present, and growth and fulfillment. Client-centered therapy was developed by Rogers. In this therapy, the therapist provides a warm, supportive atmosphere to improve the client's self-concept and to encourage the client to gain insight into problems. Client-centered techniques include active listening, reflective speech, unconditional positive regard, empathy, and authenticity.

Perls developed gestalt therapy, in which therapists question and challenge clients to help them become more aware of their feelings and face their problems. Gestalt psychologists use such therapeutic techniques as example setting and role playing. Gestalt therapy's techniques are more directive than Rogers's client-centered techniques.

Behavior Therapies

Behavior therapies use principles of learning to reduce or eliminate maladaptive behavior. They are based on the behavioral and social cognitive theories of personality. Behavior therapies seek to eliminate the symptoms of behaviors rather than to help individuals to gain insight into their problems. Behavior therapists increasingly use observational learning, cognitive factors, and self-instruction in their efforts to help people with their problems.

Classical conditioning and operant conditioning techniques are used in behavior therapies. The two main therapy techniques based on classical conditioning are systematic desensitization and aversive conditioning. In systematic desensitization, anxiety is treated by getting the individual to associate deep relaxation with increasingly intense anxiety-producing situations. A concentrated form of desensitization is flooding. In aversive conditioning, pairings of the undesirable behavior with aversive stimuli are repeated to decrease the behavior's rewards. In operant conditioning approaches to therapy, a careful analysis of the person's environment is conducted to determine which factors need to be modified. Behavior modification is the application of operant conditioning to change human behavior. Its main goal is to replace unacceptable, maladaptive behaviors with acceptable, adaptive ones. A token economy is a behavior modification system in which behaviors are reinforced with tokens that later can be exchanged for desired rewards.

Cognitive Therapies

Cognitive therapies emphasize that the individual's cognitions, or thoughts, are the main source of abnormal behavior. Cognitive therapies attempt to change the person's feelings and behaviors by changing cognitions. Three main forms of cognitive therapy are Ellis's rationale-emotive behavior therapy, Beck's cognitive therapy, and cognitive-behavior therapy.

Ellis's approach is based on the assertion that individuals develop psychological disorders because of their beliefs, especially those that are irrational and self-defeating. Beck's cognitive therapy has been especially effective in treating depression. In Beck's therapy, the therapist assists the client in learning about logical errors in thinking and then guides the client in challenging these thinking errors. Ellis's approach is more directive, persuasive, and confrontational than Beck's. Cognitive-behavior therapy combines cognitive therapy and behavior therapy techniques. Self-efficacy and self-instructional methods are used in this approach. Cognitive therapy has been demonstrated to be effective in treating a number of psychological problems.

3 SOCIOCULTURAL APPROACHES AND ISSUES IN TREATMENT

Explain the sociocultural approaches and issues in treatment.

Group Therapy

Group therapies emphasize that relationships can hold the key to successful therapy. Psychodynamic, humanistic, behavior, and cognitive therapies, as well as unique group approaches, are used in group therapy.

Family and Couples Therapy

Family therapy is group therapy with family members. Four widely used family therapy techniques are validation, reframing, structural change, and detriangulation. Couples therapy is group therapy with married or unmarried couples whose major problem is within their relationship.

Self-Help Support Groups

Self-help support groups are voluntary organizations of individuals who get together on a regular basis to discuss topics of common interest. They are conducted without a professional therapist. Recently, the Internet has emerged as a platform for self-help support groups.

Community Mental Health

The community mental health movement was born out of the belief that the mental healthcare system was not adequately reaching people in poverty and those who had been deinstitutionalized. Community mental health emphasizes primary, secondary, and tertiary prevention. Empowerment is often a goal of community mental health.

Cultural Perspectives

Psychotherapies' traditional focus on the individual may be successful in individualized cultures such as that of the United States. However, individual-centered psychotherapies may not work as well in collectivist cultures. Many ethnic minority individuals prefer to discuss problems with parents, friends, and relatives rather than with mental health professionals. Therapy is often more effective when there is an ethnic match between the therapist and the client, although culturally sensitive therapy can be provided by a therapist who is from a different ethnic background.

The emphasis on autonomy in psychotherapies may produce a problem for many women, who place a strong emphasis on connectedness in relationships. Some feminist-based therapies have emerged.

4 THE EFFECTIVENESS OF PSYCHOTHERAPY

Evaluate the effectiveness of psychotherapy.

Research on the Effectiveness of Psychotherapy

Psychotherapy is generally effective. Using meta-analysis, researchers have found that the cognitive and behavior therapies are successful in treating anxiety and depressive disorders. Relaxation therapy also has been effective in treating anxiety disorders.

Common Themes in Psychotherapy

Successful psychotherapy commonly includes positive expectations of help, increasing the client's sense of mastery, arousing the client's emotions, and developing the client's confidence and trust in the therapist.

Therapy Integrations

Approximately 30 to 50 percent of practicing therapists refer to themselves as "integrative" or "eclectic." Integrative therapy uses a combination of techniques from different therapies based on the therapist's judgment of which particular techniques will provide the greatest benefit for the client. In some instances, a combination of a particular type of psychotherapy and drug therapy is most effective in treating a psychological disorder.

Funding and Finding Therapy

Psychotherapy is not always available to those who need it. Managed care has led to substantial changes in the delivery of mental healthcare and has been criticized for eliminating long-term treatment for all but the wealthy and for using therapists who may not be as well qualified.

Mental Health Professionals

Mental health professionals include clinical and counseling psychologists, psychiatrists, school psychologists, social workers, psychiatric nurses, occupational therapists, pastoral counselors, and counselors. These professionals have different degrees, education, and training. Society retains control over individuals who practice psychotherapy through licensing and certification.

5 THERAPIES AND HEALTH AND WELLNESS

Discuss therapy's larger implications for health and wellness and characterize the client's role in therapeutic success.

Links Between Therapy and Physical and Psychological Health

Psychotherapy has been shown to help individuals cope with serious physical diseases. Psychotherapy can also aid in alleviating physical symptoms directly or by reducing psychological problems, such as depression, which are themselves related to physical illness. Research has also shown that brief psychotherapy may be a cost-effective way to prevent serious psychological disorders before they occur.

Psychotherapy, Wellness, and Personal Growth

Psychotherapy aims not only at reducing the presence of psychological illness but also at enhancing wellness and personal growth. Individuals who gain in wellness have been shown to be less likely to fall prey to recurrent psychological distress. A therapist can enhance the experience of personal growth by listening for and labeling signs of growth in individuals coping with difficult life circumstances. Interventions such as well-being therapy have been designed to promote wellness itself.

The Client's Role in Therapeutic Success

The key to successful therapy may lie not in a particular therapist or technique but in the person who is seeking treatment. Although an individual may come into the therapeutic situation in distress, it may be that his or her internal resources and strengths are brought forth by therapy, as a result of which the individual might expect a healthier, more satisfying life.

Key Terms

biological therapies, p. 566
psychotherapy, p. 566
antianxiety drugs, p. 566
antidepressant drugs, p. 567
lithium, p. 568
antipsychotic drugs, p. 568
electroconvulsive therapy (ECT), p. 571
psychosurgery, p. 572

insight therapy, p. 574
psychodynamic therapies, p. 574
psychoanalysis, p. 574
free association, p. 574
dream analysis, p. 575
transference, p. 575
resistance, p. 575
humanistic therapies, p. 576
client-centered therapy, p. 576

reflective speech, p. 576
gestalt therapy, p. 577
behavior therapies, p. 578
systematic desensitization, p. 578
aversive conditioning, p. 579
behavior modification, p. 580
cognitive therapies, p. 581
rational-emotive behavior therapy (REBT), p. 581

cognitive-behavior therapy, p. 583
family therapy, p. 589
couples therapy, p. 589
therapeutic alliance, p. 594
integrative therapy, p. 595
well-being therapy (WBT), p. 599
post-traumatic growth, p. 599

Assess Your Knowledge

1. A client who gives herself a painful pinch each time she has a craving for a cigarette is using which type of technique?
   A. token economy
   B. systematic desensitization
   C. aversive conditioning
   D. cognitive restructuring

2. What is post-traumatic growth?
   A. recovery from post-traumatic stress disorder
   B. becoming a stronger person because of negative events
   C. the outcome of well-being therapy
   D. a way to prevent mental disorders

3. Which of the following combinations will likely result in the best treatment outcome?
   A. a White male therapist and a Black female client
   B. a Black male therapist and a White male client
   C. a Latina female therapist and a Latina female client
   D. a White female therapist and an Asian male client

4. Prozac is an example of
   A. a benzodiazepine.
   B. a selective serotonin reuptake inhibitor.
   C. a neuroleptic.
   D. a tricyclic.

5. The greatest gains in therapy are usually made during the first
   A. week.   B. three months.
   C. six months.   D. year.

6. Treating an illness once it has already begun is known as
   A. tertiary prevention
   B. primary prevention
   C. secondary prevention
   D. community prevention

7. Helping a couple to understand that the problems in their relationship are not the fault of just one person is an example of
   A. reframing.   B. structural change.
   C. detriangulation.   D. validation.

8. Which of the following professionals has completed medical school?
   A. clinical psychologist
   B. counseling psychologist
   C. psychiatric nurse
   D. psychiatrist

9. Who is responsible for providing treatment within Alcoholics Anonymous?
   A. psychologists   B. psychiatrists
   C. community members   D. physicians

10. One way that group therapy may be better than individual therapy is that it
    A. is closer to real life because clients engage in multiple relationships in a group.
    B. is more effective than individual therapy.
    C. focuses one theoretical view rather than many.
    D. helps clients learn about themselves.

11. Who developed gestalt therapy?
    A. Albert Ellis   B. Fritz Perls
    C. Aaron Beck   D. Albert Bandura

12. Which therapy approach would be least directive?
    A. rational-emotive behavioral therapy
    B. client-centered therapy
    C. gestalt therapy
    D. behavior modification

13. The primary goal of community psychology is to help disenfranchised individuals. Which of the following is used to help accomplish this goal?
    A. assisting people to be admitted to mental institutions
    B. identifying mental disorders
    C. empowerment
    D. training clinical and counseling psychologists

14. _____ are used to treat schizophrenia, whereas _____ are used to treat anxiety.
    A. benzodiazepines, neuroleptics
    B. neuroleptics, benzodiazepines

    C. monoamine oxidase inhibitors, tricyclics
    D. tricyclics, monoamine oxidase inhibitors

15. Which of the following is frequently used to treat bipolar disorder?
    A. risperidone
    B. Prozac
    C. Xanax
    D. lithium

Go to Appendix B for answers to these questions.

Apply Your Knowledge

1. The chapter describes some types of psychosurgery previously performed on patients. Use the Internet to research the kinds of problems that are currently treated with psychosurgery. Do you think psychosurgery should still be used? Why or why not?

2. Think critically about the use of antidepressant and antipsychotic drugs. Using your library and online resources, do some research for evidence that drug therapy works. If you were diagnosed with a psychological disorder, would you take a drug? Why or why not?

3. Behavioral and cognitive approaches may be helpful to change behaviors that would not be considered abnormal but that you might want to change (for example, procrastinating, eating unhealthy food, or watching too much TV). Think about a behavior that you would like to do more or less frequently; then think like a behavior or cognitive therapist and describe the kinds of recommendations you might hear during a therapy session.

4. For which kinds of problems would you be most likely to choose one of the sociocultural approaches to therapy? Which approach would you choose? Do some research and see whether you can find a local group or therapist who would be helpful to someone with this kind of problem. Where would you turn if none were available in your area?

5. A recent development in the online world is e-therapy, also called cybertherapy, in which individuals can receive help from an online source. To explore this innovative approach, do an Internet search for e-therapy or locate a free e-therapist online. What do you think about this use of technology? Are there some disorders for which such a service would be particularly well or ill suited?

CHAPTER 15

HEALTH PSYCHOLOGY

Experiencing Psychology

DO NEW YEAR'S RESOLUTIONS WORK?

What are you doing this New Year's Eve? Your plans may include going to a party, watching the ball drop on Times Square in person or on TV, staying up late with friends, or viewing the fireworks at a local First Night celebration or from the beach in Rio. New Year's Eve is a night of ritual, champagne toasts, and midnight kisses.

Across various cultures, New Year's Eve is celebrated in different ways, all associated with good luck in the new year. In the southern United States, it is considered good luck to eat black-eyed peas, and in the Midwest folks enjoy sauerkraut and pork. In Spain, a lucky year is promised if you eat one grape with each stroke of the clock at midnight. The start of a new year is a good time to focus on new beginnings. And every December 31, millions of Americans resolve to change their lives in positive ways.

New Year's resolutions are a longstanding tradition dating back to ancient Rome. The month of January is named for Janus, the mythical Roman god of new beginnings and guardian of doors and entrances. Janus has two faces: one looking back on what has been and the other looking ahead to what is to come. Nearly half of all Americans make New Year's resolutions (ABC/AOL, 2006). The most common such resolutions concern positive changes in health. Indeed, the three most common New Year's resolutions are to stop smoking, to lose weight, and to exercise more (ABC/AOL, 2006). Maybe you have made such a resolution yourself—with the stroke of midnight, a solemn promise to lose those 10 pounds or to exercise every day.

Of course, everyone knows that New Year's resolutions do not work (Gollwitzer, 1999). Or do they? One study examined the success of individuals in pursuing New Year's resolutions (Norcross, Mrykalo, & Blagys, 2002). Participants in the study were contacted through random-digit dialing during the busy holiday season (between December 26 and December 31). Groups of individuals who were pursuing the same goals (mostly losing weight, exercising, and quitting smoking) were identified; but about half of these were planning to make a New Year's resolution and half were not. Then, the participants were contacted 6 months later and asked to rate their success at achieving their goals. How did making a New Year's resolution relate to actual success at the goals? At 6 months, 46 percent of the resolvers had succeeded in maintaining their resolutions, while only 4 percent of those who had the same goals but did not make a resolution attained the same level of success. Although adopting a healthier lifestyle can be difficult, success is possible if a person is ready to make a commitment. ▪

PREVIEW

In this chapter, we focus on health psychology, the field of psychology most directly devoted to promoting healthy practices and understanding the psychological processes that underlie healthy and unhealthy behaviors. In exploring the broad field of health psychology and the related area of behavioral medicine, we will discover how all of the various areas of psychology relate to physical health.

As the first section makes clear, you already know a great deal about health psychology from having read the preceding chapters in this book. In the second section, we turn attention to the contributions of health psychology to our understanding of how individuals can effect healthy changes in their lives.

Do you have any health-related resolutions? If so, you may find help in section 3, where we examine the process of making effective life changes and survey the tools available for assisting us. In the subsequent section, we target specific aspects of life that are potential areas for cultivating healthier habits. The chapter closes with a reconsideration of the major themes of this book.

1 What You Already Know About Health Psychology

Describe the scope of health psychology and behavioral medicine.

Health psychology emphasizes psychology's role in establishing and maintaining health and preventing and treating illness. Health psychology reflects the belief that lifestyle choices and psychological states can play important roles in health (Friedman & Silver, 2007; Taylor, 2006, 2007). A related discipline, **behavioral medicine,** is an interdisciplinary field that focuses on developing and integrating behavioral and biomedical knowledge to promote health and reduce illness. Behavioral medicine and health psychology are overlapping, and sometimes indistinguishable, fields. But when distinctions are made, behavioral medicine is viewed as a broader field that focuses on both behavioral and biomedical factors, whereas health psychology tends to focus on cognitive and behavioral factors.

Throughout this book, we have concluded each chapter by considering how the various topics of interest matter to physical health and wellness. In doing so, we have drawn links to a wide range of research in health psychology. Indeed, if you have read carefully, you are already an expert on many of the important concepts in health psychology.

The Biopsychosocial Model

Figure 15.1 reviews the topics we have covered in health psychology so far. The figure also shows that the interests of health psychologists and behavioral medicine researchers are broad (Carver, 2007; Kemeny, 2007; Stanton & Revenson, 2007).

An important point to bear in mind is that the biopsychosocial model that we discussed in Chapter 13 (in the context of psychological disorders) applies to health psychology as well,

health psychology A field that emphasizes psychology's role in establishing and maintaining health and in preventing and treating illness.

behavioral medicine An interdisciplinary field that focuses on developing and integrating behavioral and biomedical knowledge to promote health and reduce illness.

Area of Psychology	Major Concepts from Health Psychology
Biological Foundations of Psychology (Chapter 3)	*Stress* is the body's response to changes in the environment and is reflected in changes in the autonomic nervous system. *Acute stress* is the adaptive response to an immediate threat. *Chronic stress* represents the maladaptive persistent stress experience.
Developmental Psychology (Chapter 4)	Many aspects of healthy aging are within the individual's ability to control, including smoking, drinking alcohol, and physical activity. Stress and coping can be viewed as developmental processes and ways for individuals to grow through life experiences.
Sensation and Perception (Chapter 5)	*Healthy behaviors* can be seen as ways to take care of the precious gifts that are our senses.
Consciousness (Chapter 6)	The *mind* can affect the *body* in important ways. *Meditation* is one way to cope with stress and illness and may provide important health benefits.
Learning (Chapter 7)	The experience of stress is illuminated by animal research showing that the body's stress response is less likely to occur in contexts in which the following are present: an *outlet for frustration*, *predictable* events, a sense that conditions are *improving*, and a sense that the organism has *control* over negative outcomes. *Behavior modification programs* can be used to help change unhealthy behavior.
Memory (Chapter 8)	Maintaining an *active mind* can help stave off the effects of age on memory.
Thinking, Problem Solving, and Language (Chapter 9)	*Coping* is the specific term for problem-solving strategies, or changes in thoughts and behaviors, used to manage the emotions caused by stressful events (*emotion-focused coping*) or to solve the stressful problem itself (*problem-focused coping*). Coping can be either avoidant (trying not to think about the problem) or approach oriented (directly confronting the problem). *Appraisal* is the process by which we come to think of a life change as stressful or challenging.
Motivation and Emotion (Chapter 10)	Emotional experiences can have an impact on our health, including immune functioning and illness. Both negative and positive emotional states are associated with health outcomes. *Resilience* refers to the individual's capacity to avoid the negative impact of stressful life events.
Personality (Chapter 11)	Personality characteristics associated with enhanced physical well-being include *hardiness* and *optimism*. The anger dimension of *Type A behavior pattern* has been associated with the risk of cardiovascular disease.
Social Psychology (Chapter 12)	*Social support* refers to the comfort that we receive from our friends, family, and others during times of stress. The *social sharing* of emotionally upsetting events can have positive health benefits.
Psychological Disorders (Chapter 13)	Individuals who have a psychological disorder often show physical health deficits as well.
Therapies (Chapter 14)	Psychotherapy, though focused on psychological problems, can also have positive effects on physical health.
Industrial and Organizational Psychology (online)	*Work stress* can have a negative impact on health and wellness and at the extreme can lead to *burnout*.

FIGURE 15.1

Summary of Health Psychology Concepts Relevant to Psychology Subfields Many of the central concepts of health psychology draw from topics we have already covered. If you have read this entire book, you already know a great deal about health psychology.

because health psychology integrates biological, psychological, and social factors in health (Alford, 2007). For example, note from Figure 15.1 how the concept of stress is reflected in various areas of psychology. Biological psychology (Chapter 3), for instance, acknowledges the role of stress in the autonomic nervous system. One's state of consciousness (Chapter 6) and the process of thinking about events in particular ways (for example, through meditation) can reduce the experience of stress. Using problem-solving strategies (Chapter 9) to confront life's difficulties—that is, engaging in coping behavior—can have an impact on the body as well. Finally, the social context (Chapter 12), reflected in social support, can influence both an individual's experience of stress and his or her ability to cope with it.

The Relationship Between the Mind and Body

The fields of health psychology and behavioral medicine highlight the relationship between the mind and the body, a link we explored in Chapter 1. Although it is easy to think of ways

Shelley Taylor, a leading expert in health psychology, believes that recent trends in medicine, psychology, and healthcare have combined to make health psychology an important area of psychology. These trends include the rise of chronic or lifestyle-related illnesses, the expanding role of healthcare in the economy, the realization that psychological and social factors often play a significant role in health and illness, and the demonstrated importance of psychological interventions in improving healthcare. Health psychologists such as Taylor usually have a doctoral degree in psychology. At the graduate level, many doctoral programs in clinical, counseling, social, or experimental psychology have a specialized track in some area of health psychology.

the mind may influence health and wellness, it is important to appreciate that the body may influence the mind as well. That is, the way we feel physically may have implications for how we think. Health psychology and behavioral medicine are concerned not only with how psychological states influence health, but also with how health and illness may influence the person's psychological experience, including cognitive abilities, stress, and coping. For instance, one of the very first types of symptoms experienced by someone with AIDS may be cognitive changes that are not immediately recognized as part of the disease. A person who is feeling run-down may not realize that the level of fatigue is actually the beginning stage of an illness. In turn, being physically healthy can be a source of psychological wellness.

REVIEW, ASSESS, AND SHARPEN YOUR THINKING

Review

1. **Describe the scope of health psychology and behavioral medicine.**
   - Define health psychology and behavioral medicine and discuss how health psychology fits into the biopsychosocial model.
   - Discuss the relationship between the mind and body.

Assess

1. **How are behavioral medicine and health psychology different?**
   A. Behavioral medicine is a medical discipline, whereas health psychology is a social science discipline.
   B. Behavioral medicine focuses on how the body impacts the mind, whereas health psychology focuses on how the mind impacts the body.
   C. Behavioral medicine aims to treat illness, whereas health psychology aims to prevent illness.
   D. Behavioral medicine is a broader field with more focus on biomedical factors than is usually seen in health psychology.

2. **The health psychology topic of the relationship between feeling sad and having increasing health problems would fall under which of the other major topics in psychology?**
   A. developmental psychology   B. motivation and emotion
   C. social psychology   D. consciousness

3. **What is the relationship between the mind and the body?**
   A. The mind impacts the body.
   B. The body impacts the mind.
   C. There is not a relationship between the mind and the body.
   D. The mind and the body have a reciprocal relationship.

Sharpen Your Thinking

What has been your favorite topic covered in psychology so far? How is it relevant to your physical health?

2 Making Positive Life Changes

Describe the various theoretical models of change.

One of health psychology's missions is to help individuals identify and implement ways they can effectively change their behaviors for the better (Westmaas, Gil-Rivas, & Silver, 2007). **Health behaviors**—practices that have an impact on physical well-being—include adopting a healthy approach to stress, exercising, eating right, not smoking, drinking in moderation, and practicing safe sex. Before exploring what health psychologists have learned about the best ways to make these changes, we focus on the process of change itself.

Theoretical Models of Change

Changing behaviors, in many instances, begins by changing attitudes. As you might recall from Chapter 12, the relationship between attitudes and behaviors is not always straightforward. In understanding the process of making changes in behaviors, psychologists have sought to understand how changing attitudes can lead to changes in behavior.

A number of theoretical models have addressed the factors that likely play roles in effective health behavior changes. For example, the **theory of reasoned action** suggests that effective change requires individuals to have specific intentions about their behaviors, as well as positive attitudes about a new behavior, and to perceive that their social group looks on the new behavior positively as well (Ajzen & Albarracin, 2007; Ajzen & Fishbein, 2005). For instance, if a smoker wishes to quit smoking, she will be more successful if she devises an explicit intention of quitting, feels good about it, and believes that her friends support her.

Icek Ajzen (his last named is pronounced "I-zen") modified the theory of reasoned action to include the fact that not all of our behaviors are under our control. The **theory of planned behavior** includes the basic ideas of the theory of reasoned action but adds the person's perceptions of control over the outcome (Ajzen, 2002). These approaches to behavior change emphasize the ways that different aspects of the person's perception of his or her situation influence behavioral outcomes.

The theory of reasoned action and its extension, the theory of planned behavior, have been on target in predicting a wide range of health behaviors (Ajzen & Manstead, 2007), including cancer screening (Orbell & others, 2006; Ross & others, 2007), HIV prevention and risk (Kalichman, 2007), smoking prevention in youth (Guo & others, 2006, 2007), and exercise (Downs & others, 2006). Other theories have stressed the importance of awareness of the health threats posed by potentially harmful behaviors such as smoking and unprotected sex (Floyd, Prentice-Dunn, & Rogers, 2000; Fry & Prentice-Dunn, 2006). Social cognitive theories emphasize the importance of beliefs about one's ability to make healthy changes, as well as the individual's knowledge and skills (Bandura, 2007a, 2007b). All theoretical models of health behavior change make predictions about the type of intervention that should be successful in producing durable change.

The Stages of Change Model

The **stages of change model** describes the process by which individuals give up bad habits and adopt healthier lifestyles. The model breaks down behavioral changes into five steps, recognizing that real change does not occur overnight with one monumental decision (even if that night is New Year's Eve) (Prochaska, DiClemente, & Norcross, 1992; Prochaska, Norcross, & DiClemente, 1994) (Figure 15.2). Rather, change occurs over a series of progressive stages. Each stage is characterized by its own set of issues and challenges. Thinking of behavioral change in stages helps us identify the various processes that are involved in effective change and also allows for the development of interventions that target particular stages of change (Leamon, 2006; Lippke & Plotnikoff, 2006; Lippke & Ziegelmann, 2006).

Precontemplation The *precontemplation stage* occurs when individuals are not yet genuinely thinking about changing. They may be unaware that they have a problem behavior that needs to be changed. Individuals who drink a great deal but are not aware that their

health behaviors Practices that have an impact on physical well-being.

theory of reasoned action Model suggesting that effective change requires individuals to have specific intentions about their behaviors, as well as positive attitudes about a new behavior, and to perceive that their social group looks on the new behavior positively.

theory of planned behavior Model for effective change incorporating the theory of reasoned action but adding the person's perceptions of control over the outcome.

stages of change model Five-step model that describes the process by which individuals give up bad habits and adopt healthier lifestyles.

FIGURE 15.2

Stages of Change Model Applied to Losing Weight The stages of change model has been applied to many different health behaviors, including losing weight.

Stage	Description	Example
1. Precontemplation	Individuals are not yet ready to think about changing and may not be aware that they have a problem that needs to be changed.	Overweight individuals are not aware that they have a weight problem.
2. Contemplation	Individuals acknowledge that they have a problem but may not yet be ready to change.	Overweight individuals know they have a weight problem but aren't yet sure they want to commit to losing weight.
3. Preparation/ Determination	Individuals are preparing to take action.	Overweight individuals explore options they can pursue in losing weight.
4. Action/Willpower	Individuals commit to making a behavioral change and enact a plan.	Overweight individuals begin a diet and start an exercise program.
5. Maintenance	Individuals are successful in continuing their behavior change over time.	Overweight individuals are able to stick with their diet and exercise regimens for 6 months.

drinking is affecting their work may be in this precontemplation stage. At this stage, the key objective is *consciousness-raising*—that is, getting people to realize that their current behavior is a problem.

Individuals in the precontemplation stage likely need a wake-up call or reality check. A woman who smokes may find her consciousness raised by the experience of becoming pregnant. A man who is stopped for drunk driving may be forced to take a good look at his drinking. Similarly, overweight individuals may not realize their problem until they see photos of themselves taken at a family reunion. Here is a moment of consciousness-raising for those who like to eat fast food: Imagine ordering a Big Mac, large fries, and a large chocolate shake at McDonald's. Those who eat this meal will consume over 2,000 calories (the recommended adult caloric intake for an entire day).

Sometimes, consciousness-raising comes from the media. If you have seen Morgan Spurlock's Academy Award–nominated documentary *Super Size Me,* you know how devastating the consumption of fast food can be to health. Spurlock ate every meal at McDonald's for a month. By the end of filming he felt ill, had gained weight (from 185 to 210 pounds), and simply could not wait for the experience to end. His doctors were appalled by his increasingly fatty liver, and his (vegan) girlfriend noted the decline in his sexual prowess.

It is common for individuals in the precontemplation phase to deny that their current pattern of behavior is in fact a problem. The individual might defend such behaviors, claiming that "I don't drink/smoke/eat *that much!*" Overweight individuals may discover that they actually do eat "that much" when they start keeping track of calories.

Contemplation In the *contemplation stage,* individuals acknowledge the problem but may not be ready to commit to change. As the name of the stage suggests, at this point individuals are actively engaged in thinking about change. They might engage in a reevaluation of themselves and the place of this behavior in their life. They understandably may have mixed feelings about giving up a bad habit. For example, how will they deal with missing their friends on a smoke break? Or going out drinking? Or packing a healthy lunch instead of heading to the drive-thru? They may weigh the short-term gains of the harmful behavior against the long-term benefits of changing. Sure, they might reason, it would be nice to be thinner, but losing weight is going to take time, and that hot fudge sundae is right there, looking very delicious.

Preparation/Determination At the *preparation/determination stage,* individuals are getting ready to take action. At this point, self-belief and especially beliefs about one's ability to "see it through" are very important. A key consideration in this stage is whether individuals truly feel they are ready to change. In the study of New Year's resolutions described earlier, readiness to change predicted success at achieving New Year's resolutions (Norcross, Mrykalo, & Blagys, 2002).

During this stage, individuals start thinking concretely about how they might take on their new challenge. For example, they explore options of the best ways to quit smoking or drinking or to start an exercise program. Some smokers might consider trying out a nicotine patch or participating in a support group for people trying to quit. Individuals who are seeking to lose weight might think about joining a gym to get regular exercise or setting the alarm clock for a 6:00 A.M. run.

"It's not easy to quit smoking when they keep putting cigarettes in the cage!"

© CartoonStock.com

Action/Willpower At the *action/willpower stage,* individuals commit to making a real behavioral change and enact a plan for effective change. An important challenge at this stage is to find ways to support the new, healthy behavior pattern. One approach is to find reinforcements or rewards for the new behavior. Individuals who have quit smoking might focus on how much better food tastes after they have given up cigarettes. Successful dieters might treat themselves to a shopping run to buy new, smaller-size clothes. Acknowledging, enjoying, and even celebrating accomplishments can help to motivate consistent behavior.

Another source of support for new behaviors is the individual's social network (Taylor, 2007). Friends, family, and even members of a support group can help through their encouraging words and supportive behaviors. Members of a family might all quit smoking at the same time or join the individual in physical activities or healthier eating.

Finally, individuals may focus on alternative behaviors that replace the unhealthy ones. Perhaps, instead of bar hopping, they join a group dedicated to activities not associated with drinking alcohol, such as a dance club or community theater group. In other words, effective change also means avoiding tempting situations. Can you really quit smoking if you are spending your time with smokers? Can you avoid binge drinking if you regularly go to keg parties?

Maintenance In the *maintenance stage,* individuals succeed in avoiding temptation and consistently pursue healthy behaviors. One challenge during the maintenance stage is to avoid **relapse,** which means a return to the former unhealthy patterns. Individuals may become skilled at anticipating tempting situations and avoid them or actively prepare for them. If smokers know that after a big meal out with friends, they always enjoy a cigarette, they might mentally prepare themselves for that temptation before going out. Successful dieters might post a consciousness-raising photograph on the refrigerator.

At some point, individuals in maintenance may find that actively fighting the urge to indulge in unhealthy behaviors is no longer necessary. *Transcendence* means that they are no longer consciously engaged in maintaining their healthy lifestyle; rather, the lifestyle simply has become a part of who the individuals are. They are now nonsmokers, healthy eaters, or committed runners.

Relapse Contrary to popular belief, relapse is a common aspect of change. That is, for most people, real change takes many attempts. Relapse can be discouraging and can lead a person to feel like a failure. But the majority of people who eventually successfully change do not succeed on the first try. Rather, they try and fail and try again, cycling through the five stages several times before achieving a stable healthy lifestyle. Consequently, individuals who are experts in health behavior change consider relapse to be normal (Prochaska & Norcross, 2007; Prochaska, Norcross, & DiClemente, 1992).

If you have ever tried to adopt a healthier lifestyle by dieting, starting an exercise program, or quitting smoking, you might know how bad you feel when you experience relapse.

relapse A return to former unhealthy patterns.

But one slip does not mean you will never reach your goal. Rather, when a slip-up occurs, you have an opportunity to learn, to think about what led up to the relapse, and to devise a strategy for preventing it in the future. Successful dieters, for example, do not let one lapse ruin the week. Individuals who successfully keep weight off are those who do not get too down on themselves when they relapse (Phelan & others, 2003).

Evaluations of the Stages of Change Model   The stages of change model has been applied successfully to a broad range of behaviors, including cigarette smoking (Shumann & others, 2006), exercise (Lippke & Plotnikoff, 2006), safe-sex practices (Naar-King & others, 2006), marijuana use in teenagers (Walker & others, 2006), substance abuse more broadly (DiClemente, 2006; Migneault, Adams, & Read, 2005), and weight loss (MacQueen, Brynes, & Frost, 2002).

While the stages of change model has proven useful in studying a variety of behaviors, it is not without controversy (Brug & others, 2004; Joseph, Breslin, & Skinner, 1999). Little evidence has been found for the stages being mutually exclusive categories or for the sequential nature of the change process proposed (Littrell & Girvin, 2002). This means that some individuals might feel themselves to be in both action/willpower and maintenance at the same time, or may move from contemplation back to precontemplation.

Critics of the model also have pointed out that the it refers more to attitudes that change than to behaviors (West, 2005). Furthermore, all of the stages might be understood as promoting readiness to change, rather than change itself (West, 2005). Others have argued that despite these weaknesses, the stages of change model can be a tool for therapists who are trying to help clients institute healthy behavior patterns. Sometimes, sharing the model with those who are trying to change provides them with a useful language to use in understanding the change process, to reduce uncertainty, and to develop realistic expectations for the difficult journey (Hodgins, 2005).

REVIEW, ASSESS, AND SHARPEN YOUR THINKING

Review

2 Describe the various theoretical models of change.

- Discuss the theory of reasoned action and other theoretical models addressing factors that are important for successfully changing health behavior.
- Review the five stages of change and the challenges associated with each; discuss the role of relapse in changing behavior.

Assess

1. During what stage of the stages of change model is providing health information most appropriate?

   A. maintenance

   B. contemplation

   C. preparation/determination

   D. precontemplation

2. How are the theory of reasoned action and the theory of planned behavior different?

   A. The theory of reasoned action focuses on self-efficacy, whereas the theory of planned behavior does not.

   B. The theory of planned behavior focuses on perceptions of personal control, whereas the theory of reasoned action does not.

   C. The theory of reasoned action focuses on attitudes toward a health behavior, whereas the theory of planned behavior does not.

   D. The theory of planned behavior focuses on social norms, whereas the theory of reasoned action does not.

3. Someone who is in the process of determining the best way to go about making a change in health behaviors is in the

   A. contemplation stage.

   B. action/willpower stage.

   C. maintenance stage.

   D. preparation/determination stage.

4. **Which of the following is not a valid critique of the stages of change model?**
   A. People who complete the stages still relapse.
   B. People do not go through the stages in a sequential order.
   C. The model focuses more on attitudes than on behaviors.
   D. The model focuses on readiness to change, rather than actual change.

5. **Someone who maintains healthy behaviors without conscious effort is said to be in**
   A. contemplation.
   B. transcendence.
   C. maintenance.
   D. action/willpower.

Sharpen Your Thinking

Have you ever tried to make a change in your health behavior? Apply the stages of change model to your experience.

3   Tools for Effective Life Change

Discuss psychological and social tools that promote effective life change.

Making positive changes to promote our health can be a challenge. But fortunately, we all have a variety of psychological and social tools at our disposal to help us in the journey to a new, healthier life. In this section we consider three of these powerful tools: self-efficacy, motivation, and religious faith.

Self-Efficacy

Self-efficacy is the individual's belief that he or she can master a situation and produce positive outcomes. As we saw in Chapter 10, Albert Bandura (1997, 2001, 2006b, 2007a, 2007b) and others have shown that self-efficacy affects behavior in many areas of people's lives, ranging from solving personal problems to going on diets. Self-efficacy influences whether individuals try to develop healthy habits, how much effort they expend in coping with stress, how long they persist in the face of obstacles, and how much stress they experience.

Research has shown that self-efficacy is related to success in a wide variety of positive life changes, including sticking to a New Year's resolution (Norcross, Mrykalo, & Blagys, 2002), achieving weight loss (Annesi, 2007; Linde & others, 2006), engaging in regular exercise (Lippke & Plotnikoff, 2006), ceasing to smoke (Baldwin & others, 2006), quitting substance abuse (McPherson & others, 2006; Warren, Stein, & Grella, 2007), and practicing safe sex (Abbey & others, 2007). If there is a problem to be fixed, self-efficacy—that is, having a can-do attitude—is related to finding a solution.

Throughout this book, we have examined the placebo effect as a positive response to a treatment that has no medicinal power. Itself a powerful force, the placebo effect results from the individual's belief in the effectiveness of the treatment. Can you really lose those 10 pounds? Maybe or maybe not. But believing that you can allows you to harness the placebo effect. Self-efficacy is the power of belief in yourself.

Experiencing the emotional pay-off of small successes is important in achieving long-term goals. Being able to zip up "skinny jeans," for example, gives a dieter a sense of accomplishment.

Motivation

Recall from Chapter 10 that motivation refers to the "why" of behavior. Motivational tools for self-change involve changing for the right reasons. Change is most effective when you are doing it for you—because *you want to*. An analysis of intervention programs aimed at reducing childhood and adolescent obesity found that a strong predictor of program success (that is, weight loss in the children) was whether the children were required to join the program or did so voluntarily (Stice, Shaw, & Marti, 2006).

self-efficacy The belief that one can master a situation and produce positive outcomes.

Religious faith benefits health by providing social support, life meaning, mechanisms for coping with stressful events, a sense of hopefulness, and motivation for positive life changes. Here, U.S. Muslims worship at a mosque; Roman Catholics pray at a traditional Mexican-American service; and three generations of a Jewish family take part in a Passover Seder.

implementation intentions Specific strategies (such as setting specific plans and goals) for dealing with the challenges of making a life change.

Self-determination theory (SDT), presented in Chapter 10, distinguishes between *intrinsic motivation* (doing something because you want to) and *extrinsic motivation* (doing something for external rewards). Research has shown that creating a context in which people feel more in control, more autonomous, and more competent is associated with enhanced outcomes for a broad array of health behaviors, including controlling diabetes through diet (Williams & others, 2004), quitting smoking (Williams & others, 2006), and getting regular physical exercise (Hein & Hagger, 2007). Indeed, we are more likely to succeed in our New Year's resolutions if we approach them with a sense of both self-efficacy and autonomy—the latter meaning that we have chosen on our own to make a life change (Koestner & others, 2006).

Planning and goal setting are also crucial to making effective change. Researchers have found that individuals who are able to come up with specific strategies, or **implementation intentions,** for dealing with the challenges of making a life change are more successful than others at negotiating the road to change (Armitage, 2006; Koestner & others, 2006). Setting short-term, achievable goals also allows individuals to experience the emotional pay-off of small successes along the way to self-change (Kushner, 2007). The dieter who can take her "skinny jeans" out of the closet and zip them up is likely to feel a sense of accomplishment. The novice exerciser who catches a glimpse of his new biceps in the mirror gets a mood boost, as does the ex-smoker who can climb a flight of stairs without getting winded. These feelings of satisfaction can help to motivate continued effort toward achieving important health goals (Finch & others, 2005).

Enjoying the payoffs of our efforts to change also means that we must monitor our goal progress. As anyone who has watched *The Biggest Loser* will attest, stepping on a scale can be a scary prospect for someone who is trying to lose weight. But it is important to get feedback on progress in the pursuit of any goal. If an individual finds out that she is falling short, she can try to identify areas that need work. And if an individual finds that she is doing well, it is a potent motivator for future progress.

As we have seen, motivation is a powerful force in engaging in healthier behaviors. For further insight into its influence on health, see the Intersection, on why people do things that they know are bad for them.

Religious Faith

Not only are self-efficacy and various aspects of motivation related to initiating and maintaining a healthy lifestyle; religious faith is, too (Krause, 2006; Park, 2007). Many religions frown on excess and promote moderation. Indeed, weekly religious attendance relates to a host of healthy behaviors, including not smoking, taking vitamins, walking regularly, wearing seatbelts, engaging in strenuous exercise, enjoying sound sleep, and drinking moderately or not at all rather than heavily (Hill & others, 2006). A number of studies have definitively linked religious participation to a longer life (Hummer & others, 2004; Krause, 2006; McCullough & others, 2000).

Religious participation may also benefit health through its relation to social support (Taylor, 2007). Belonging to a faith community may give people access to a warm group of others who are available during times of need. This community is "there" to provide transportation to the doctor, to check in with the individual when things are going poorly, or simply to stand next to the individual during a worship service, as a fellow member of the community. The social connections promoted by religious activity can forestall anxiety and depression and can help to prevent isolation and loneliness (Koenig, 2007).

Religious faith and spirituality more generally may also be an important factor in good health because they provide a sense of meaning and a buffer against the effects of stressful life events (Batson & Stocks, 2004; Emmons, 2005; Silberman, 2005). Religious thoughts can play a role in maintaining hope and stimulating motivation for positive life changes. For example, studies have shown that some individuals with AIDS who lived much longer than expected had used religion as a coping strategy; specific benefits came from participating in religious activities such as praying and attending church services (Ironson & others, 2001) and that an increase in spirituality after testing positive for HIV is associated with

Health Psychology and Motivation: Why Do We Do the Things We Shouldn't Do?

Motivation can be a powerful force for positive life change. But what about behaviors that are not so positive—such as drinking too much, smoking, and having unsafe sex? Aren't these behaviors motivated as well? Health psychologists have come to recognize that understanding the motives that guide even unhealthy behavior can be important for understanding, changing, and preventing these behaviors.

> **Understanding the motives that guide even unhealthy behavior can be important for understanding, changing, and preventing these behaviors.**

Health psychologists have been especially interested in analyzing the reasons that individuals consume alcohol. Lynne Cooper and her colleagues have identified three motivations for drinking (Cooper, 1994; Cooper & others, 1992):

- *Social motives* include drinking alcohol because it is what your friends do or because you want to be sociable.
- *Coping motives* center on drinking alcohol to relax, to deal with stress, or to forget your worries.
- *Enhancement motives* include drinking because it is fun, because you like how it feels, or because it is exciting.

Research has shown that young adults most commonly drink for social reasons, with enhancement motives coming in a distant second (Kuntsche & others, 2006). Like enhancement motives, coping motives are not as common in young adults. Although all three motives for drinking are related to higher levels of drinking frequency (with enhancement motives being especially linked to drinking for men—Cooper & others, 1992), the motives that drive drinking can have implications for whether the behavior is harmful or harmless. Drinking to cope with life's negative events is typically associated with negative outcomes such as social and work problems or potential substance abuse.

Personality traits relate to drinking motives (Theakston & others, 2004). Research on the big five personality traits reveals that three of these traits are associated with drinking motives. Extraverts are more likely and conscientious individuals are less likely to drink for social and enhancement motives (Stewart & Devine, 2000). Neurotics are more likely to drink to cope (Stewart & Devine, 2000).

Drinking motives also are related to difficulties an individual might experience in reducing alcohol consumption. Individuals who drink because of coping or enhancement motives are more likely to experience preoccupation with drinking when they try to limit their alcohol consumption, suggesting that those who use alcohol for internal reasons may have difficulty when they try to decrease consumption (Stewart & Chambers, 2000).

In a 3-week study, researchers had college students log on to a secure website and report their drinking behavior, motives for drinking, and daily events in their life (Mohr & others, 2005). Some individuals were more likely to drink on a regular basis for a particular reason, such as to cope or to have fun. However, even within these stable tendencies, whether they drank at all and how much they drank depended on the immediate context, such as how they did on a test that day or whether friends were visiting from out of town.

Motivation has been studied with respect to a variety of other unhealthy behaviors. Even behavior that might seem patently self-defeating (smoking, unsafe sex) can be understood as the product of motivation (Cooper & others, 2006; Gynther & others, 1999). Although we have focused primarily on young adults, considering the motives that drive unhealthy behavior patterns can be useful for anyone, at any age or life stage.

Viewing maladaptive behavior from a motivational perspective helps us not only to understand the "why" behind those behaviors but also to think about how we might meet our needs for social interaction, coping, and enhancement without alcohol (or cigarettes or unsafe sex). If you recognize that you drink (and occasionally drink too much) because of a desire for positive social interactions, you might think about ways to enjoy your social network without putting your health at risk.

slower disease progression over 4 years (Ironson, Stuetzle, & Fletcher, 2006). Faith may help individuals to avoid burnout (Murray-Swank & others, 2006) and to negotiate life's difficulties without being overwhelmed (Mascaro & Rosen, 2006). Belief in the enduring meaningfulness of one's life can help one keep perspective and see life's hassles in the context of the big picture.

In sum, making positive life changes is a multistage process that can be complex and challenging. Fortunately, we have the tools to help us attain the goals of healthier life.

REVIEW, ASSESS, AND SHARPEN YOUR THINKING

Review

3 Discuss psychological and social tools that promote effective life change.

- Define self-efficacy and give examples of the variety of positive life changes with which it is associated.
- Recap what motivation is and discuss its role in bringing positive self-change.
- Describe the benefits of religious faith and practice to health and explain why religion is a key factor in good health.

Assess

1. Regular attendance at religious events is related to health because of all of the following except:
   - A. increased social support.
   - B. good moral fiber.
   - C. better ability to cope with stress.
   - D. a focus on meaningfulness of life.

2. Dan quits smoking because his partner wants him to. Leon quits smoking because he wants to be healthier. Who is expected to be more successful in quitting smoking?
   - A. Dan because he has high extrinsic motivation
   - B. Dan because he has high intrinsic motivation
   - C. Leon because he has high extrinsic motivation
   - D. Leon because he has high intrinsic motivation

3. To what does autonomy refer in relationship to health behaviors?
   - A. feeling able to successfully engage in health behaviors
   - B. expecting that engaging in health behaviors will have the intended outcome
   - C. choosing to engage in health behaviors on our own
   - D. receiving support from others for making health behavior changes

4. Someone who believes that he or she will be able to be successful at engaging in a health behavior has
   - A. self-efficacy.
   - B. implementation intentions.
   - C. faith.
   - D. extrinsic motivation.

Sharpen Your Thinking

Think about a change you would like to make in your life. How might self-efficacy, motivation, and religious faith contribute to accomplishing this goal, if at all?

4 Cultivating Good Habits

Describe strategies for cultivating good habits in five important realms of life.

Complete the following sentence: "I wish I could stop _____." If you could change one thing about your behavior, what would you choose? As we have already noted, many people build their New Year's resolutions around one or more aspects of their health. In this section, we explore five realms of life that, for you personally, might be due for some changes: stress management, physical activity, eating, smoking, and sexual interactions.

Maybe you wish you could "stop worrying so much" or "stop feeling so stressed out." Let's begin our look at cultivating good habits by examining the ways you might achieve this goal.

Controlling Stress

Although we have been discussing stress throughout this book, we pause and redefine *stress* here as the response of individuals to *stressors,* the circumstances and events that threaten them and tax their coping abilities. Hans Selye (1974, 1983), the founder of stress research, focused on the body's response to stressors, especially the wear and tear on the body due to the demands placed on it. After observing patients with different

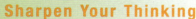

"Well of course I overeat when I'm under pressure. 'Stressed' spelled backwards is 'desserts'!"

© CartoonStock.com

problems—the death of someone close, loss of income, arrest for embezzlement—Selye concluded that any number of environmental events or stimuli will produce the same stress response. Regardless of which problem the patient had, similar symptoms appeared: loss of appetite, muscular weakness, and decreased interest in the world.

General adaptation syndrome (GAS) is Selye's term for the common effects on the body when demands are placed on it (Figure 15.3). The GAS consists of three stages: alarm, resistance, and exhaustion. Selye's model is especially useful in helping us understand the link between stress and health.

The body's first reaction to a stressor, in the *alarm stage,* is a temporary state of shock during which resistance to illness and stress falls below normal limits. In trying to cope with the initial effects of stress, the body quickly releases hormones that, in a short time, adversely affect the functioning of the immune system, our body's network of natural defenses. During this time the individual is prone to infections from illness and injury. Fortunately, the alarm stage passes rather quickly.

In the *resistance stage* of Selye's general adaptation syndrome, a number of glands throughout the body begin to manufacture different hormones that protect the individual in many ways. Endocrine and sympathetic nervous system activity are not as high as in the alarm stage, although they still are elevated. During the resistance stage, the body's immune system can fight off infection with remarkable efficiency. Similarly, hormones that reduce the inflammation normally associated with injury circulate at high levels.

If the body's all-out effort to combat stress fails and the stress persists, the individual moves into the *exhaustion stage.* At this point, the wear and tear on the body takes its toll— the person might collapse in a state of exhaustion, and vulnerability to disease increases. Serious, possibly irreversible damage to the body, such as a heart attack, or even death may occur in the exhaustion stage.

Stress and the Immune System Stress has important implications for physical health. Chronic stress can have negative implications for the functioning of the immune system. The interest in links between the immune system and stress spawned a new field of scientific inquiry, **psychoneuroimmunology,** which explores connections among psychological factors (such as attitudes and emotions), the nervous system, and the immune system (Ayers & others, 2007; Bachen, Cohen, & Marsland, 2007; Kemeny, 2007).

The immune system and the central nervous system are similar in their modes of receiving, recognizing, and integrating signals from the external environment (Sternberg & Gold, 1996). The central nervous system and the immune system both possess "sensory" elements, which receive information from the environment and other parts of the body, and "motor" elements, which carry out an appropriate response. Both systems also rely on chemical mediators for communication. A key hormone shared by the central nervous system and the immune system is corticotropin-releasing hormone (CRH), which is produced in the hypothalamus and unites the stress and immune responses.

A variety of research supports the idea that stress can profoundly influence the immune system. *Acute stressors* (sudden, one-time life events or stimuli) can produce immunological changes. For example, in relatively healthy HIV-infected individuals, as well as in individuals with cancer, acute stressors are associated with poorer immune system functioning (Gasser & Raulet, 2006). *Chronic stressors* (those that are long-lasting) are associated with an increasing downturn in immune system responsiveness rather than adaptation. This effect has been documented in a number of circumstances that include living next to a damaged nuclear reactor, failures in close relationships (divorce, separation, and marital distress), and burdensome caregiving for a family member with progressive illness (Glaser & Kiecolt-Glaser, 2005; Graham, Christian, & Kiecolt-Glaser, 2006).

Psychoneuroimmunology is a relatively young field whose findings need to be clarified, explained, and further verified. Researchers hope to determine the precise links among psychological factors, the brain, and the immune system (Besedovsky & Rey, 2007; Blalock &

FIGURE 15.3

Selye's General Adaptation Syndrome
The general adaptation syndrome (GAS) describes an individual's general response to stress in terms of three stages: (1) alarm, in which the body mobilizes its resources; (2) resistance, in which the body strives mightily to endure the stressor; and (3) exhaustion, in which resistance becomes depleted.

general adaptation syndrome (GAS) Selye's term for the common effects on the body when demands are placed on it. The GAS consists of three stages: alarm, resistance, and exhaustion.

psychoneuroimmunology The field that explores connections among psychological factors (such as attitudes and emotions), the nervous system, and the immune system.

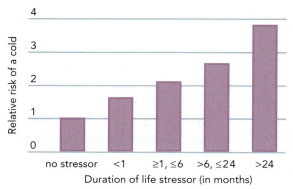

FIGURE 15.4

Stress and the Risk of Developing a Cold In the study by Cohen and others (1998), the longer individuals had a life stressor, the more likely they were to develop a cold. The four-point scale is based on the odds (0 = lower; 4 = higher) of getting a cold.

Smith, 2007; Marsland, Cohen, & Bachen, 2007). Preliminary hypotheses about the interaction that causes vulnerability to disease include the following:

1. Stressful experiences lower the efficiency of immune systems, making individuals more susceptible to disease.

2. Stress directly promotes disease-producing processes.

3. Stressful experiences may cause the activation of dormant viruses that diminish the individual's ability to cope with disease.

These hypotheses may lead to clues for more successful treatments for some of the most baffling diseases—cancer and AIDS among them (Jaffe, 2007; Letvin, 2007).

Sheldon Cohen and his colleagues have conducted a number of studies on the effects of stress, emotion, and social support on immunity and susceptibility to infectious disease (Cohen, Doyle, & Skoner, 1999; Cohen & others, 2003b; Cohen & others, 2006; Cohen & Lemay, 2007). Cohen and his colleagues (1998) found that adults who faced interpersonal or work-related stress for at least 1 month were more likely than counterparts who were less stressed to catch a cold after exposure to viruses. In the study, 276 adults were exposed to viruses and then quarantined for 5 days. The longer people had experienced major stress, the more likely they were to catch a cold. Individuals who reported high stress for the preceding 2 years tripled their risk of catching a cold (Figure 15.4). Those who experienced work-related stress for 1 month or longer were nearly five times more likely to develop colds than individuals without chronic stress. Those who experienced interpersonal stress for 1 month or more were twice as likely to catch a cold.

Cohen concluded that stress-triggered changes in the immune system and hormones might create greater vulnerability to infection. The findings suggest that when we know we are under stress, we need to take better care of ourselves than usual, although often we do just the opposite (Cohen & others, 2003a, 2006; Jackson & others, 2007).

Stress, Cardiovascular Disease, and Cancer There is also reason to believe that stress can increase an individual's risk for cardiovascular disease (Steptoe, Hamer, & Chida, 2007). Chronic emotional stress is associated with high blood pressure, heart disease, and early death (Schulz, 2007). Apparently, the surge in adrenaline caused by severe emotional stress causes the blood to clot more rapidly, and blood clotting is a major factor in heart attacks (Strike & others, 2006). Emotional stress also can contribute to cardiovascular disease in other ways (Khan & others, 2006). Individuals who have had major life changes (such as the loss of a spouse or another close relative and the loss of a job) have a higher incidence of cardiovascular disease and early death (Taylor, 2006). A longitudinal study of involuntary job loss among workers 50 years and older over a 10-year period revealed that displaced workers have a twofold increase in the risk of developing a stroke (Gallo & others, 2006b). In addition, people who are quick to anger or who display frequent hostility have an increased risk for cardiovascular disease (Al'absi & Bongard, 2006).

The body's internal reactions to stress are not the only risk. People who live in a chronically stressed condition are more likely to take up smoking, start overeating, and avoid exercising. All of these stress-related behaviors are linked with the development of cardiovascular disease (Khan & others, 2006).

Given the association of stress with poor health behaviors such as smoking, it is not surprising that stress has also been related to cancer risk. Stress sets in motion biological changes involving the autonomic, endocrine, and immune systems. If the immune system is not compromised, it appears to help provide resistance to cancer and slow its progression (Dunn, Koebel, & Schreiber, 2006; Yang & others, 2006). But researchers have found that the physiological effects of stress inhibit a number of cellular immune responses (Anderson & others, 2001). Cancer patients have diminished natural killer (NK)-cell activity in the blood (Ghiringhelli & others, 2006) (Figure 15.5). Low NK-cell activity is linked with the development of further malignancies, and the length of survival for the cancer patient is related to NK-cell activity (Boyiadzis & Foon, 2006).

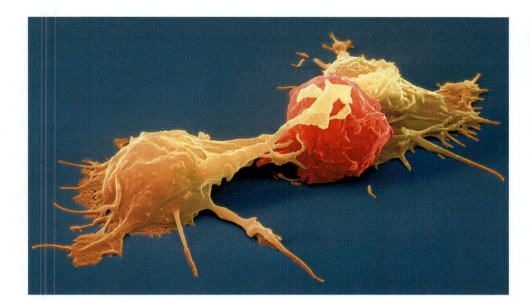

FIGURE 15.5

NK Cells and Cancer Two natural killer (NK) cells (*yellow*) are shown attacking a leukemia cell (*red*). Notice the blisters that the leukemia cell has developed to defend itself. Nonetheless, the NK cells are surrounding the leukemia cell and are about to destroy it.

Stress Management Programs   Nearly every day we are reminded that stress is bad for our health. "Avoid stress" may be a good prescription, but life is full of potentially stressful experiences, such as taking tests, dealing with conflicts at work, and having arguments with family and friends. Sometimes just checking your e-mail or answering your cell phone can be an invitation for stress.

Reducing stress may seem impossible or unrealistic. But remember that stress is not about what happens to us but rather how we think about what happens to us. As we considered in Chapter 9, the way we appraise life's changes determines whether those events are threatening (and thus stressful) or challenging (and perhaps even exciting). Research on stress and coping has demonstrated that taking a head-on approach to problems can lead to more effective problem solving and less stress (Carver, 2007). Of course, sometimes trying to manage stress on our own is still overwhelming. At such times, it makes sense to explore options for breaking the stress habit, such as enrolling in a stress management program.

Because many people have difficulty in regulating stress themselves, psychologists have developed various techniques that can be taught to individuals (Greenberg, 2008; Penedo & others, 2004). **Stress management programs** teach individuals how to appraise stressful events, how to develop skills for coping with stress, and how to put these skills into use in everyday life. Some stress management programs are broad in scope, teaching a range of techniques to handle stress; others teach a specific technique, such as relaxation or assertiveness training.

Stress management programs are often taught through workshops, which are being offered more often in the workplace (Blonna & Paterson, 2007; Taylor, 2006). Aware of the high cost in lost productivity due to stress-related disorders, many organizations have become increasingly motivated to help their workers identify and cope with the stressful circumstances in their lives.

Colleges are also developing stress management programs for students. If you are finding the experience of college extremely stressful and having difficulty coping with taxing circumstances in your life, you might want to consider enrolling in a stress management program at your college or in your community. Some stress management programs are also taught to individuals who are experiencing similar kinds of problems—such as migraine headache sufferers and individuals with chronically high blood pressure.

Do stress management programs work? In one study, men and women with hypertension (blood pressure greater than 140/90) were randomly assigned to one of three groups (Linden, Lenz, & Con, 2001). One group received 10 hours of individual stress management training; a second group was placed in a wait-list control group and eventually received stress management training; and a third group (a control group) received no stress management

stress management programs Programs that teach individuals to appraise stressful events, to develop skills for coping with stress, and to put these skills into use in everyday life.

exercise Structured activities whose goal is to improve health.

aerobic exercise Sustained exercise, such as jogging, swimming, or cycling, that stimulates heart and lung functioning.

FIGURE 15.6

The Jogging Hog Experiment Jogging hogs reveal the dramatic effects of exercise on health. In one investigation, a group of hogs was trained to run approximately 100 miles per week (Bloor & White, 1983). Then, the researchers narrowed the arteries that supplied blood to the hogs' hearts. The hearts of the jogging hogs developed extensive alternate pathways for blood supply, and 42 percent of the threatened heart tissue was salvaged compared with only 17 percent in a control group of nonjogging hogs.

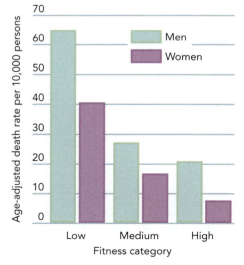

FIGURE 15.7

Physical Fitness and Mortality In this study of middle-aged and older adults, being moderately fit or highly fit meant that individuals were less likely to die over a period of 8 years than their low-fitness (sedentary) counterparts (Blair & others, 1989).

training (Linden, Lenz, & Con, 2001). Blood pressure was significantly reduced in the two groups that received the stress management training. The control group experienced no reduction in blood pressure. Also, the reduced blood pressure in the first two groups was linked to a reported reduction in psychological stress and improved ability to cope with anger.

Effectively coping with stress is essential for physical and mental health (Carver, 2007; Hales, 2007). But we can do a great deal more to promote better health. Healthful living—establishing healthy habits and evaluating and changing the behaviors that interfere with good health—helps us avoid the damaging effects of stress (Hahn, Payne, & Lucas, 2007; Robbins, Powers, & Burgess, 2008). Indeed, just as the biopsychosocial perspective predicts, healthy changes in one area of life can have benefits that overflow to other areas. One of the best ways to reduce stress is engaging in physical activity.

Becoming Physically Active

Imagine that there was a time when, to change a TV channel, people had to get up and walk a few feet to turn a knob. Consider the day when the individuals had to go physically to the library and hunt the card catalogs and shelves to find information rather than simply going online and Googling. As our daily tasks have become increasingly easy, we have become less active, and inactivity is now a serious health problem (Prentice, 2007). Sedentary lifestyles (that is, those that involve little if any physical activity) are associated with at least 17 different illnesses including diabetes, osteoporosis, heart disease, and colon, breast, and ovarian cancer (WHO, 2007).

Any activity that expends physical energy can be part of a healthy lifestyle. It can be as simple as taking the stairs instead of an elevator, walking or biking to class instead of driving, going ice skating instead of to a movie, or getting up and dancing instead of sitting at the bar. One recent study of older adults revealed that the more they expended energy in any daily activities, the longer they were likely to live (Manini & others, 2006).

Physical activity is a vital source of physical and psychological wellness. In addition to being related to how long people live (as we just saw), being physically active is related to a host of other positive outcomes, including a lower probability of developing cardiovascular disease (Matthews & others, 2007; Wilund, 2007), weight loss in overweight individuals (Shaw & others, 2006; Tate & others, 2007), improved cognitive functioning (Kramer, Erickson, & Colcombe, 2006; Kramer & Morrow, 2007), positive coping with stress (Hamer, 2006), increased self-esteem (Hallal & others, 2006), and less depression (Kirby, 2005). Even a real pig can benefit from exercise. Figure 15.6 shows the positive effects of physical activity, even in hogs.

Being physically active is like investing energy in a wellness bank account: Activity enhances physical well-being and gives us the ability to face life's potential stressors energetically (Fahey, Insel, & Roth, 2007).

Exercise is one special type of physical activity. **Exercise** formally refers to structured activities whose goal is to improve health. Although exercise designed to strengthen muscles and bones or to improve flexibility is important to fitness, many health experts stress the benefits of **aerobic exercise,** which is sustained activity—jogging, swimming, or cycling, for example—that stimulates heart and lung functioning. In one study, exercise literally meant a difference in life or death for middle-aged and older adults (Blair & others, 1989). More than 10,000 men and women were divided into categories of low fitness, medium fitness, and high fitness (Blair & others, 1989). Then they were studied over 8 years. As shown in Figure 15.7, sedentary participants (low fitness) were more than twice as likely to die during the study's 8-year time span than those who were moderately fit, and more than three times as likely to die as those who were highly fit. The positive effects of physical fitness occurred for both men and women.

Some health experts conclude that regardless of other risk factors—including smoking, high blood pressure, being overweight, and heredity—if you exercise enough to burn more than 2,000 calories a week, you can cut your risk of a heart attack by an impressive two-thirds (Sherwood, Light, & Blumenthal, 1989). To burn 300 calories a day through exercise, you would have to swim or run for about 25 minutes, walk for 45 minutes at about 4 miles an hour, or participate in aerobic dancing for 30 minutes.

Moderate	Vigorous
Walking briskly (3–4 mph)	Walking briskly uphill or with a load
Cycling for pleasure or transportation (≤10 mph)	Cycling, fast or racing (>10 mph)
Swimming, moderate effort	Swimming, fast treading crawl
Conditioning exercise, general calisthenics	Conditioning exercise, stair ergometer, ski machine
Racket sports, table tennis	Racket sports, singles tennis, racketball
Golf, pulling cart or carrying clubs	Golf, practice at driving range
Canoeing, leisurely (2.0–3.9 mph)	Canoeing, rapidly (≥4 mph)
Home care, general cleaning	Moving furniture
Mowing lawn, power mower	Mowing lawn, hand mower
Home repair, painting	Fix-up projects

FIGURE 15.8

Moderate and Vigorous Physical Activities At minimum, adults should strive for 30 minutes of moderate activity each day. That activity can become even more beneficial if we "pump it up" to vigorous.

Health experts recommend that adults engage in 30 minutes or more of moderate physical activity on most, preferably all, days of the week (for children, 60 minutes is recommended). Most advise that you should try to raise your heart rate to at least 60 percent of your maximum heart rate. However, only about one-fifth of adults are active at these recommended levels of physical activity. Figure 15.8 lists examples of the physical activities that qualify as moderate (and, for comparison, vigorous) activities.

Research suggests that both moderate and intense activities may produce important physical and psychological gains (Fahey, Insel, & Roth, 2007; Hamer, 2006). Some people enjoy intense exercise; others prefer moderate exercise. The enjoyment derived from exercise, added to its aerobic benefits, makes exercise one of life's most important activities.

One hint for becoming more physically active is not to limit yourself to only a few options. There are many activities that require physical exertion. Choose one you genuinely like. Important factors in sticking to an exercise plan include self-efficacy, making active choices, and experiencing positive reinforcement and social support (Cress & others, 2005). Finding a buddy who is interested in working out with you might be a powerful motivator.

A typical excuse for not exercising is "I just don't have enough time." You probably do have the time to make exercise a priority. How about swapping your TV time for a more active pursuit? Heavy TV viewing by college students is linked to their poor health (Astin, 1993).

Remember that effective goal pursuit requires monitoring yourself. A key to sticking to a program is charting your progress. Systematically recording your exercise workouts will help you keep track of how you are doing. This strategy is especially helpful for maintaining an exercise program over an extended period. One welcome payoff for increasing physical activity is weight loss. Researchers have found that the most effective component of weight-loss programs is regular exercise (Hoeger & Hoeger, 2008; Shaw & others, 2006). Another way to combat weight problems is through changes in diet, our next topic.

Eating Right

Like many people, your life change may revolve around losing weight. Weight, and particularly weight loss, seems to be an obsession in modern life. Recall from Chapter 10 that yo-yo dieting can have dire health implications. Furthermore, as noted in Chapter 10, for some people (particularly young women) weight concerns may be misplaced and may be a sign of harmful eating disorders such as anorexia nervosa or bulimia. Eating right does not mean dieting, nor does it always imply losing weight. Rather, eating right means eating sensible, nutritious foods that maximize health and wellness.

Moderate and intense exercise benefits physical and mental health.

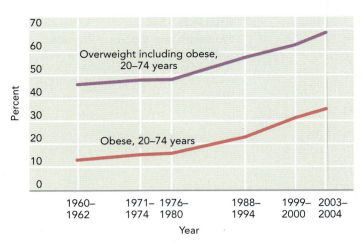

FIGURE 15.9

Changes in the Percentage of U.S. Adults 20 to 74 Years of Age Classified as Overweight or Obese, 1960–2004 Obesity and overweight continue to be major public health concerns in the United States.

Although eating disorders are a serious problem for some, the biggest health risk facing modern Americans is overweight and obesity. In recent years, the percentage of individuals who are overweight or obese has been increasing at an alarming rate. As indicated in Figure 15.9, the prevalence of being overweight or obese in the United States changed little from 1960 to 1980 (National Center for Health Statistics, 2006a). However, the percentage of overweight and obese 20- to 74-year-olds increased from less than 50 percent in 1960 to almost 70 percent in 2004. In that year, 30 percent of U.S. men and 34 percent of U.S. women were classified as obese. "Overweight" and "obese" are labels for ranges of weight that are greater than what is considered healthy for an individual's height (National Center for Health Statistics, 2006a).

Exercising regularly is one great way to lose weight. Making healthy dietary choices is another (Wardlaw & Hampl, 2007). Despite the growing variety of choices Americans can make in the grocery store, many of us are unhealthy eaters. We take in too much sugar and not enough foods high in vitamins, minerals, and fiber, such as fruits, vegetables, and grains. We eat too much fast food and too few well-balanced meals—choices that increase our fat and cholesterol intake, both of which are implicated in long-term health problems (Jeffery & others, 2006).

Changes in American nutritional standards over time have added to our confusion about which foods we should eat. Only a few decades ago, nutritionists promoted eggs and dairy foods as virtually ideal food sources. Now we hear that some dairy products, such as whole milk, butter, and eggs, should generally be avoided.

Today, nutritionists believe that proper nutrition involves more than merely taking in an appropriate number of calories (Insel & Roth, 2008). It depends on carefully selecting foods that provide appropriate nutrients along with their calories. A sound nutritional plan gives us the right amounts of all the nutrients we need—fat, carbohydrates, proteins, vitamins, minerals, and water.

Research on successful weight loss has found that self-efficacy and positive expectations predict greater weight loss (Finch & others, 2005; Linde & others, 2006). Healthy eating means becoming food conscious—aware of the caloric and nutritional properties of your diet. Successful weight loss, like physical activity, requires monitoring your progress, including counting calories and fat grams, but also stepping on the scale regularly to see how you are doing. Healthy eating does not mean trying out every fad diet that comes along but rather incorporating tasty, healthy foods into your everyday life. Healthy eating is not something that people should do just to lose weight—it is about incorporating lifelong healthy food habits. Several health goals can be accomplished through a sound nutritional plan. Not only does a well-balanced diet provide more energy, but it also can lower blood pressure and lessen the risk for cancer and tooth decay (Herder & Demmig-Adams, 2004).

Losing weight and opting for healthier foods can be difficult, especially when one is just starting out. Many weight-loss fads promise weight loss with no effort, no hunger, and no real change in one's food consumption. These promises are unrealistic. Making real, enduring changes in eating behavior is hard work. This does not mean individuals should adopt a pessimistic attitude. Rather, positive expectations and self-efficacy are important *because* the task at hand is a challenging one.

The National Weight Control Registry is an ongoing study of people who have lost at least 40 pounds and kept it off for at least 2 years. Research on these successful dieters gives us important tips on how people who keep the weight off achieve this goal (Raynor & others, 2005). One key practice is to be sure to have breakfast. Those who eat breakfast, especially whole-grain cereals, are more successful than others at weight control. Successful dieters also consume a limited range of foods chosen from all food groups and show consistency in what they eat, even on the weekends and the

"Run for your lives—it's Trans Fat!"

Can You Be Fat *and* Fit?

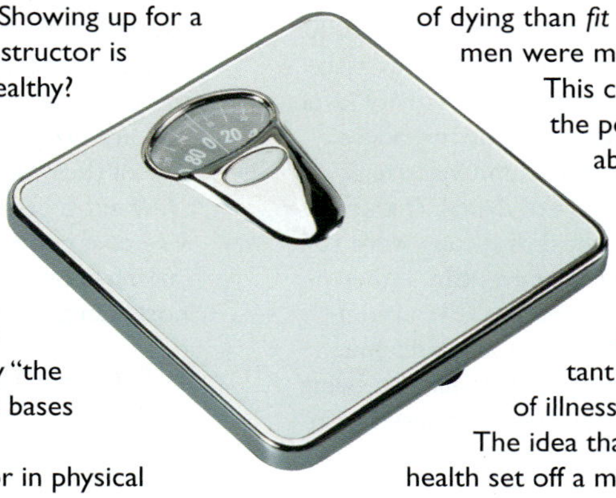

What does a healthy body look like? Showing up for a spinning class, you notice that your instructor is somewhat overweight. Is she really healthy? Or you check out the dugout while watching your favorite baseball team. How many of the players are actually thin? Even Babe Ruth, perhaps the greatest baseball player of all time, was a rotund guy known for his hearty appetite. One day at Coney Island, Ruth ate four steaks and eight hot dogs and drank eight sodas. The workout favored by "the Bambino" was generally limited to running the bases after hitting one of his many home runs.

Body weight is certainly an important factor in physical health. On the basis of longitudinal studies on large numbers of people, researchers have estimated that individuals who are obese at age 40 will live 6 to 7 years less than their thin counterparts, and individuals who are overweight at 40 lose 3 years of life on average (Peeters & others, 2003). An important question is, How do we know if someone is overweight or obese?

In considering what makes a body healthy, researchers focus on a variety of characteristics. One of the most commonly used measures is the *body mass index* (BMI), which is calculated by multiplying weight in pounds by 704.5 and then dividing by height in inches, squared:

$$\frac{\text{Weight (in pounds)} \times 704.5}{\text{Height (in inches)}^2}$$

Figure 15.10 shows a chart to determine BMI. Generally, body mass index gauges a person's weight in relation to his or her height. Measures of BMI may overestimate body fat in athletic individuals because muscle weighs more than fat. According to the Centers for Disease Control and Prevention (2006), a healthy BMI for an adult ranges between 18.5 and 24 (see Figure 15.10). Overweight refers to a BMI that is greater than or equal to 25, and obese is greater than or equal to 30. (Babe Ruth's BMI? A solidly overweight 28.) In terms of waist measurement, a waist circumference greater than 40 in men and 35 in women is also a risk for diabetes, cardiovascular disease, and early death.

Another important factor in physical health and the risk for serious illness is fitness. *Cardiorespiratory fitness* (CRF) refers to the ability of the body's circulatory and respiratory systems to supply fuel during sustained physical activity. CRF, usually measured with a treadmill test, is increased by engaging in aerobic exercise on a regular basis.

One study that compared BMI and CRF challenged the notion that BMI is an important risk factor for disease (Lee, Blair, & Jackson, 1999). The researchers measured leanness, obesity, and CRF in nearly 22,000 men 30 to 83 years of age. The men were followed over 8 years. During that time, 428 died. The researchers were interested in the contributions of weight and cardiorespiratory fitness to risk for death. Controlling for age, smoking, alcohol consumption, and parental history of heart disease, unfit lean men had double the risk of mortality of fit lean men, from all causes. Unfit lean men also had a higher risk

of dying than *fit obese* men. Regardless of body size, unfit men were more likely to die than fit men.

This controversial study set off a debate over the possibility that "fit and fat" might be a viable goal. It suggested that perhaps we have focused too much on weight and appearance and too little on cardiorespiratory fitness as the key to long, healthy living. Subsequent research has continued to support the notion that CRF is an important predictor of physical health and lower risk of illness such as diabetes (Gerson & Braun, 2006). The idea that fit and fat might translate into good health set off a media frenzy, spreading the happy news that it does not matter how fat people are, just whether they are active. Suddenly, it was safe to step on the scale again!

But within the scientific community, debate continued to rage. Controversy swirled around a fundamental question: Even if people can be fit and fat at the same time, does that make them *optimally* healthy? Is it possible to avoid the negative effects of overweight and obesity by being physically fit? A wide range of studies have examined whether being fit can compensate for

		Weight (pounds)												
	120	**130**	**140**	**150**	**160**	**170**	**180**	**190**	**200**	**210**	**220**	**230**	**240**	**250**
4'6"	29	31	34	36	39	41	43	46	48	51	53	56	58	60
4'8"	27	29	31	34	36	38	40	43	45	47	49	52	54	56
4'10"	25	27	29	31	34	36	38	40	42	44	46	48	50	52
5'0"	23	25	27	29	31	33	35	37	39	41	43	45	47	49
5'2"	22	24	26	27	29	31	33	35	37	38	40	42	44	46
5'4"	21	22	24	26	28	29	31	33	34	36	38	40	41	43
5'6"	19	21	23	24	26	27	29	31	32	34	36	37	39	40
5'8"	18	20	21	23	24	26	27	29	30	32	34	35	37	38
5'10"	17	19	20	22	23	24	26	27	29	30	32	33	35	36
6'0"	16	18	19	20	22	23	24	26	27	28	30	31	33	34
6'2"	15	17	18	19	21	22	23	24	26	27	28	30	31	32
6'4"	15	16	17	18	20	21	22	23	24	26	27	28	29	30
6'6"	14	15	16	17	19	20	21	22	23	24	25	27	28	29
6'8"	13	14	15	17	18	19	20	21	22	23	24	25	26	28

(Height listed vertically at left)

■ Underweight   ■ Healthy weight   ■ Overweight   ■ Obese

FIGURE 15.10

Determining Your Body Mass Index Body mass index is a measure of weight in relation to height. Anyone with a BMI of 25 or more is considered overweight, and people who have a body mass index of 30 or more (a BMI of 30 is roughly 30 pounds over a healthy weight) are considered obese. BMI has some limitations: It can overestimate body fat in people who are very muscular, and it can underestimate body fat in people who have lost muscle mass, such as the elderly.

being fat. Although most research has supported the importance of CRF, studies have not found support for the idea that fitness can compensate for being overweight. For example, in one study, more than 100,000 women were tracked over 24 years (Hu & others, 2004). Within the study period, slightly more than 10,000 participants died. Among these individuals, higher BMI was associated with all causes of death regardless of physical activity level. For the inactive lean, the risk of death was 1.55; for the obese but active, the risk was 1.91; and for the obese and inactive, it was 2.42 (higher numbers equal greater risk of dying). The active obese were better off than the inactive obese, but they were still at 91 percent greater risk of dying than the active lean. Other studies have similarly shown that both weight and CRF are important predictors of health and illness, but that being fit does not protect a person from the health risks of being fat, and being thin does not protect the person from the risks associated with being unfit (Christou & others, 2005; Church & others, 2005; Sullivan & others, 2005).

The conclusion drawn from these studies is that fitness and fatness are two independent predictors of health risk, and both have an impact on longevity. Can a person be both fat and fit? Yes, but fat and fit people are not as healthy as lean and fit people. Similarly, fat and fit people may be healthier than lean sedentary individuals. Essentially, research has shown that there are two avenues to pursue for optimal health: being physically active and maintaining a reasonable weight.

This controversy has highlighted the common tendency to equate a healthy body with a thin one. However, lean individuals who are inactive, smoke, drink to excess, or otherwise fail to take care of their bodies are not healthier than individuals who carry a few extra pounds but engage in vigorous exercise and otherwise take good care of themselves. A healthy body is more than a number on a scale or a slim silhouette in the mirror. As with most things in life, it is what's on the inside that counts.

What Do You Think?

- What is your BMI? What does it tell you about your health?
- If you had to work on one health goal, which would be easier—becoming fitter or losing weight? Why?
- Why do you think the media and the public were so excited by the idea that a fat fit person could also be healthy?

holiday season (Gorin & others, 2004). Also, a recent study of approximately 2,000 U.S. adults found that exercising 30 minutes a day, planning meals, and weighing themselves daily were the main strategies that successful dieters, compared to unsuccessful dieters, used (Kruger, Blanck, & Gillespie, 2006) (Figure 15.11).

In short, keeping weight off is an ongoing process. And the longer dieters keep the weight off, the less likely they are to gain it back (McGuire & others, 1999). Yes, the goal is difficult, but individuals' ability to accomplish it is a testament to the power of belief in themselves.

We have considered how exercise and nutrition can help individuals live healthily. In the above Critical Controversy, we explore an intriguing issue related to fitness, nutrition, and health—whether a person can be fat *and* fit.

Quitting Smoking

Another very challenging health-related goal is giving up smoking. Converging evidence from a number of studies underscores the dangers of smoking and being around those who smoke (Marsit & others, 2006; Ueda & others, 2006). For example, smoking is linked to 30 percent of cancer deaths, 21 percent of heart disease deaths, and 82 percent of chronic pulmonary disease deaths. Secondhand smoke is implicated in as many as 9,000 lung cancer deaths a year. Children of smokers are at special risk for respiratory and middle-ear diseases (Pattenden & others, 2006; Rees & Connolly, 2006).

Fewer people smoke today than in the past, and almost half of the living adults who ever smoked have quit. In 2004, 20.9 percent of all adults in the United States smoked (that is 44.5 million people), with men being more likely to smoke (23.8 percent) than women (18.5 percent) (National Center for Health Statistics, 2006). Although these numbers represent a substantial decline from 40 years ago, when 50 percent of men smoked, many people still smoke.

It is difficult to imagine that there is a person living today who is not aware that smoking causes cancer, and there is little doubt that most smokers would like to quit. But their addiction to nicotine makes quitting a challenge. Nicotine, the active drug in cigarettes, is a stimulant that increases the smoker's energy and alertness, a pleasurable and reinforcing experience. In addition, nicotine stimulates neurotransmitters that have a calming or

FIGURE 15.11

Comparison of Strategies in Successful and Unsuccessful Dieters
Losing weight and keeping it off can be challenging, but reaching these goals is not impossible. Successful dieters are those who engage in physical activity, plan their meals, and monitor their progress.

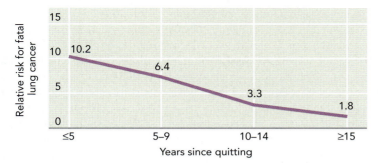

FIGURE 15.12

Fatal Lung Cancer and Years Since Quitting Smoking One study compared more than 43,000 former male smokers with almost 60,000 males who had never smoked (Enstrom, 1999). For comparison purposes, a zero level was assigned as the risk for fatal lung cancer for men who had never smoked. Over time, the relative risk for smokers who had quit declined, but even after 15 years it was still above that of nonsmokers.

pain-reducing effect (Johnstone & others, 2006). Smoking also works as a negative reinforcer by ending a smoker's painful craving for nicotine. The immediate gratification of smoking is hard to overcome even for those who recognize that smoking is "suicide in slow motion." Figure 15.12 shows that when individuals quit smoking, over time their risk for fatal lung cancer declines.

Research has confirmed that quitting smoking can be difficult. In a recent study, 70 smokers who were trying to kick the habit were given personal digital assistants (PDAs) and were beeped four times during the day every day for 10 weeks (McCarthy & others, 2006). Whenever they were beeped, the participants completed a 3-minute electronic assessment of their withdrawal symptoms, including cravings for a cigarette, negative mood, and feelings of hunger. During the 10-week period, each participant had an assigned "quit day"—the first day as a nonsmoker. This methodology allowed the researchers to track withdrawal symptoms and smoking behavior before and after quitting and on the very day of quitting as well. Finally, participants were followed up 3 months later to examine how successful they were in moving toward their goal of abstinence from cigarettes.

The researchers found that the first day without cigarettes can be especially hard, being a peak day for cravings. Also, cravings on that first day predicted whether individuals made it to 3 months without smoking—the stronger their cravings on the first day, the less likely they were to abstain from smoking across the 3 months (McCarthy & others, 2006). The experience of negative emotion during the weeks prior to quitting was also related to being less successful at maintaining abstinence at 3 months. One predictor of increased feeling of craving and distress was whether the individuals encountered another person smoking during the period just before quitting. Incidentally, these findings were true regardless of whether the individual was using a nicotine patch.

If you are trying to quit smoking (and if you do smoke, you should try to quit), the lesson from this study is that the early days of quitting will be the hardest—but the effort will get easier.

There are a variety of ways to quit smoking (Lam & others, 2006). Here we review some common methods:

- *Going cold turkey.* Some individuals succeed by simply stopping smoking without making any major changes in their lifestyle. They decide they are going to quit, and they do. Lighter smokers usually have more success with this approach than heavier smokers.
- *Using a substitute source of nicotine.* Nicotine gum, the nicotine patch, the nicotine inhaler, and nicotine spray work on the principle of supplying small amounts of nicotine to diminish the intensity of withdrawal (Frishman & others, 2006). Nicotine gum, available without a prescription, delivers nicotine orally when an individual gets

"I told you smoking was bad for you."

© CartoonStock.com

the urge to smoke. The nicotine patch is a nonprescription adhesive pad that releases a steady dose of nicotine to the individual. The dose is gradually reduced over an 8- to 12-week period. Nicotine spray delivers a half-milligram squirt of nicotine to each nostril. The usual dosage is one to two administrations per hour and then as needed to reduce cravings. The spray is typically used for 3 to 6 months. Success rates for nicotine substitutes have been encouraging. The percentage of study participants who are still not smoking after 5 months ranges from 18 percent for the nicotine patch to 30 percent for the nicotine spray (Centers for Disease Control and Prevention, 2001b).

- *Seeking therapeutic help.* Some smokers turn to a health professional for help kicking the habit. Two therapeutic strategies for quitting include medication such as antidepressant and therapeutic techniques based on behavioral principles. Bupropion SR, an antidepressant sold as Zyban, helps smokers control their cravings while they ease off nicotine. Zyban works at the neurotransmitter level in the brain by inhibiting the uptake of dopamine, serotonin, and norepinephrine. Smokers using Zyban to quit have had a 30 percent average success rate after 5 months of taking the antidepressant (Centers for Disease Control and Prevention, 2001b). More recently, varenicline (trade name Chantix) has been approved to help smokers quit. This drug partially blocks nicotinic receptors, reducing cravings and also decreasing the pleasurable sensations of smoking (FDA, 2006).

Two applications of behavioral therapy to smoking cessation use behavior modification techniques. In one form, the emphasis is on controlling stimuli associated with smoking. This behavior modification technique sensitizes the smoker to social cues associated with smoking. For example, the individual might associate a morning cup of coffee or a social drink with smoking. Stimulus control strategies help the smoker to avoid these cues or to learn to substitute other behaviors for smoking. This approach has met with mixed results.

A second behavioral technique is aversive conditioning. Chapters 7 and 13 discussed this behavior therapy technique, which involves repeated pairings of an undesirable behavior with aversive stimuli to decrease the behavior's rewards. Imagine smoking as many cigarettes as possible until the ashtray overflows, the smell of stale cigarettes seems permanently embedded in your fingertips, your throat is dry and scratchy, and you feel nauseated. The concept behind aversive conditioning is to make smoking so unpleasant that the individual does not want to smoke anymore. Sometimes this technique works; sometimes it does not.

No one method is foolproof for quitting smoking (Schnoll & Lerman, 2006). Often a combination of these methods is the best approach. And typically, truly quitting requires more than one try, as the stages of change model would suggest.

Practicing Safe Sex

Sexual behavior presents something of a paradox in U.S. society. Sex is everywhere—online, on TV, and in films; in songs and in music videos; in magazines and in newspapers. We are fascinated by sex. Yet talking about sex can be uncomfortable.

One thing that is certain is that satisfying sexual experience is part of a happy life (Strong & others, 2008). Sexual behavior also has important implications for physical health. Here we examine two aspects of physical health related to sexual behavior: preventing unwanted pregnancy and protecting oneself from sexually transmitted infections (STIs). Of course, both of these outcomes can be avoided by simply not having sex. However, even for individuals whose goal is abstinence, knowledge about protecting oneself from unwanted pregnancy and STIs can be important. As the stages of change model suggests, we sometimes fall short of our goals.

Preventing Unwanted Pregnancy   Most couples in the United States want to control whether and when they will conceive a child. These decisions require knowledge about sexuality and sexual behavior, as well as accurate information about contraception and skills to use the preferred method effectively. As we considered in Chapter 10, inadequate knowledge about contraception, coupled with inconsistent use of effective contraceptive methods, has given Americans the dubious distinction of having one of the highest adolescent pregnancy rates in the industrialized world. As one 17-year-old Los Angeles mother of a 1-year-old son said, "We are children having children."

In recent cross-cultural comparisons, the United States continued to have one of the highest rates of adolescent pregnancy and childbearing in the developed world, despite a considerable decline in the 1990s (Alan Guttmacher Institute, 2003; Centers for Disease Control and Prevention, 2003a). U.S. adolescent pregnancy rates are nearly twice those of Canada and Great Britain and at least four times the rates in France, Sweden, Germany, and Japan (Figure 15.13). Although U.S. adolescents are no more sexually active than their counterparts in countries such as France and Sweden, their adolescent pregnancy rate is much higher, perhaps because, compared to these other nations, the United States has less comprehensive sex education and less availability and use of condoms.

Despite the negative comparisons of the United States with many other developed countries, there are encouraging trends in U.S. adolescent pregnancy rates. In 2004, births to adolescent girls fell to a record low (Child Trends, 2006). The rate of births to adolescent girls has dropped a full 30 percent since 1991. Reasons for the decline include a decrease in sexual activity, increased contraceptive use, and fear of getting a sexually transmitted infection such as HIV.

Among adolescents in grades 9 to 12, the number reporting ever having sex was 47 percent in 2005, compared to 54 percent in 1991 (Centers for Disease Control and Prevention, 2005). The rates of sexual activity vary by ethnic group, with 68 percent of African American high school students reporting ever having sex compared to 43 percent of non-Latino White high school students.

Despite the decline in the overall rates, all of this sexual activity, of course, leads to high numbers of pregnancies. An estimated 750,000 U.S. adolescents get pregnant each year, with most of the pregnancies unintended (Alan Guttmacher Institute, 2006). Nearly 500,000 of those pregnancies result in live births. Adolescent pregnancy is estimated to cost the United States $7 billion annually because of the negative long-term outcomes for both adolescent mothers and their offspring.

Adolescent mothers are likely to underestimate the challenges of motherhood, with the youngest mothers often having the highest level of unrealistic expectations. Cynthia Rosengard and her colleagues (2006) interviewed nearly 250 pregnant girls ranging from 12 to 19 years of age. Among these adolescents, nearly one in four of the pregnancies was intended. Many of the pregnant adolescents expected that having a baby would bring them closer to the people around them, especially their boyfriends, and would not affect their ultimate life goals. Further, some young mothers believed that having a child would help to "keep them out of trouble." Some adolescent mothers also thought that because they were close in age, they likely could be friends with their children. Age was related to the ability to see the disadvantages of adolescent motherhood. Approximately 50 percent of the girls over the age of 18 felt unprepared for motherhood, whereas only 35 percent under the age of 16 felt similarly unprepared. The younger girls' positive expectations are especially troubling in light of the reality of adolescent pregnancy statistics.

Adolescent pregnancy is linked with a host of problems for the mother, such as less future education and lower socioeconomic status, and for the offspring as well (Bearinger

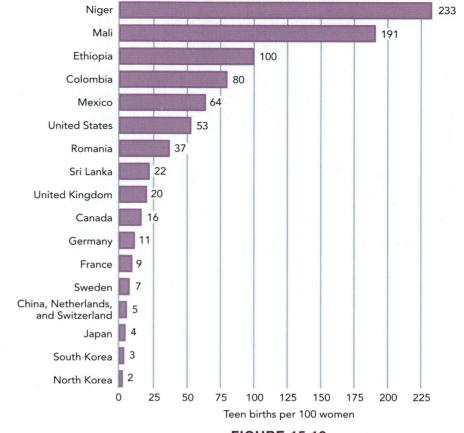

Teen births per 100 women

FIGURE 15.13

Adolescent Pregnancy Rates Across Several Countries, 2003 Adolescent pregnancies are extremely rare in countries where young people have access to comprehensive sex education and birth control.

When properly used, condoms not only prevent unintended pregnancy but also offer protection against sexually transmitted infections.

& others, 2007; Malamitsi-Puchner & Boutsikou, 2006). An estimated 80 percent of adolescent mothers rely on welfare at some point in time. Boys born to adolescent mothers are at higher risk for future incarceration, and girls born to adolescent mothers are themselves more likely to become pregnant during adolescence. Clearly, education and prevention are crucial to continued progress in reducing intended and unintended pregnancy among adolescents.

The good news is that adolescents are using contraceptives more frequently. For example, a recent study examined trends in U.S. ninth- to twelfth-graders' contraceptive use from 1991 to 2003 (Anderson, Santelli, & Morrow, 2006). Approximately one-third of the adolescents reported being sexually active in the previous 3 months. The use of condoms by males increased from 46 percent in 1991 to 63 percent in 2003. The percentage of adolescents who used either withdrawal or no method steadily declined from 33 percent in 1991 to 19 percent in 2003.

Although adolescent contraceptive use is increasing, many sexually active adolescents still do not use contraceptives, or they use them inconsistently (Davies & others, 2006). A national survey of U.S. 15- to 19-year-olds who have had sexual intercourse found that 47 percent of the boys said they always use a condom, but only 28 percent of the girls said they always use one (National Center for Health Statistics, 2004). Eleven percent of the boys and 18 percent of the girls said they never use a condom. Sexually active younger adolescents are less likely than older adolescents to take contraceptive precautions. Those who do are more likely to use a condom or withdrawal, whereas older adolescents are more likely to use the pill or a diaphragm. Incorporating information about contraception in secondary school curricula and building skills related to prevention can help youth take an active approach to preventing unwanted pregnancy.

In general, condoms are a key tool in the efforts to prevent teen pregnancy. As adolescents become young adults, their use of other contraceptive methods may become more common. One advantage of condoms is that, when properly used, they not only prevent unintended pregnancy but also protect the individual from sexually transmitted infections (STIs).

No method of contraception is best for everyone (Strong & others, 2008). When choosing a method of contraception, individuals need to consider such factors as their physical and emotional concerns, the method's effectiveness, the nature of their relationships, their values and beliefs, and the method's convenience. Calculations of the effectiveness of a contraceptive method often are based on the failure rates during the first year of use. It is estimated that if no contraceptive method were used, about 90 percent of women would become pregnant in their first year of being heterosexually active (Hatcher & others, 1988).

Protecting Against Sexually Transmitted Infections

A **sexually transmitted infection (STI)** is an infection that is contracted primarily through sexual activity—vaginal intercourse as well as oral-genital and anal-genital sex. STIs affect about one of every six adults (National Center for Health Statistics, 2005). STIs are often bacterial in origin, as in the case of gonorrhea and syphilis, or they can be caused by viruses, as in the case of genital herpes and HIV. STIs are an important health concern because they can have implications for a person's future fertility, risk of cancer, and life expectancy.

No single STI has had a greater impact on sexual behavior in the past decades than has HIV. **Acquired immune deficiency syndrome (AIDS)** is caused by the human immunodeficiency virus (HIV), a sexually transmitted infection that destroys the body's immune system. Without treatment, most people who contract HIV are vulnerable to germs that a normal immune system can destroy.

sexually transmitted infections (STIs)
Infections that are contracted primarily through sex—vaginal intercourse as well as oral-genital and anal-genital sex.

acquired immune deficiency syndrome (AIDS) A disease caused by the human immunodeficiency virus (HIV), a sexually transmitted infection that destroys the body's immune system.

Recent drug therapies have prompted some to begin thinking about HIV as a chronic rather than terminal condition. Responses to treatment vary among individuals, and keeping up with the "cocktail" of drugs necessary to continuously fight HIV can be challenging. The treatment known as highly active antiretroviral therapy (HAART) can involve taking between 6 and 22 pills each day, although recently the FDA approved the first one-pill-per-day treatment for HIV (Laurence, 2006). Side effects vary and include fatty deposits in the back and stomach.

Because of increased education and the development of more effective drug therapies, deaths due to AIDS have begun to decline in the United States (National Center for Health Statistics, 2006). There are no solid estimates for the life expectancy of someone who is HIV-positive because the existing treatments have been around for only about a decade. Even in this era of improved treatments, however, HIV remains an incurable infection that tragically can lead to early death.

Although the incidence of HIV/AIDS is relatively low in the United States, the disease has reached epidemic proportions in sub-Saharan Africa, where it is the leading cause of death (UNAIDS, 2006). An estimated 24.5 million people there were living with HIV in 2005. In 2005–2006, 2.7 million new infections occurred. In 2005 alone, an estimated 2 million people in sub-Saharan Africa died of AIDS. The cumulative death toll from AIDS has left more than 12 million children orphaned (UNAIDS, 2006). Adolescent girls in these countries, who are often sexually exploited by adult men, are the population most vulnerable to HIV infection. In Kenya, 25 percent of 15- to 19-year-old girls are HIV-positive, compared with only 4 percent of the boys in this age group. AIDS has become the leading cause of death in adolescents and young adults in sub-Saharan Africa (UNAIDS, 2006).

Protecting yourself from HIV and other STIs means taking steps to reduce risk in your sexual activity. It is not who you are but what you do that puts you at risk for HIV. Experts say that HIV can be transmitted only by:

- Sexual contact
- Other direct contact of cuts or mucous membranes with blood and sexual fluids
- Shared hypodermic needles
- Blood transfusions (which in the past few years have been tightly monitored) (Kalichman, 1996)

Anyone who is sexually active or uses intravenous drugs is at risk. No one is immune. The only 100 percent safe behavior is abstinence from sex, which is not perceived as an option by most individuals. Sensual activities such as kissing, French kissing, cuddling, massage, and mutual masturbation (that does not involve the exchange of bodily fluids) involve no risk of an STI. Sexual activities that involve penetration, including vaginal or anal intercourse as well as oral sex, are riskier behaviors that can be made less risky with the use of proper protection.

One of the best predictors of getting STIs is having sex with multiple partners. Having more than one sex partner increases the likelihood that you will encounter an infected partner. It is important to keep in mind that when you have sex with someone, you are being exposed not only to that person but also to his or her other sexual partners, past and present.

Just asking a sexual partner about his or her previous sexual behavior does not guarantee protection from HIV and other sexually transmitted infections. In one investigation, 655 college students were asked to answer questions about lying and sexual behavior (Cochran & Mays, 1990). Of the 422 respondents who said they were sexually active, 34 percent of the men and 10 percent of the women admitted they had lied so that their partner would have sex with them. Much higher percentages—47 percent of the men and 60 percent of the women—said they had been lied to by a potential sexual partner. When asked what aspects of their past they would be likeliest to lie about, more than 40 percent of the men and women said they would understate the number of their sexual partners. Twenty percent of the men, but only 4 percent of the women, said they would lie about their results from an HIV blood test.

Pat Hawkins is the associate executive director for policy and external affairs of the Whitman-Walker Clinic in Washington, D.C., helping HIV and AIDS patients. She came to the clinic as a volunteer in 1983, just after HIV/AIDS exploded into an epidemic. Hawkins says that she would not do anything else but community work. "Nothing gets you engaged so fast as getting involved," she comments. "We often keep the academic world separate from the real world, and we desperately need psychologists' skills in the real world." Hawkins was a double major in psychology and sociology as an undergraduate and then went on to obtain her PhD in community psychology.

In your own sexual experience, it may be difficult to gauge the accuracy of a partner's estimates of risk and his or her HIV status. Thus, the wisest course of action is always to protect yourself from infection by using a latex condom. When correctly used, latex condoms help to prevent the transmission of many STIs. Condoms are most effective in preventing gonorrhea, syphilis, chlamydia, and HIV. Recent research suggests that consistent condom use also significantly reduces the risk that males will transmit to their female partners the human papillomavirus (HPV), the virus that can cause cervical cancer in newly sexually active women (Winer & others, 2006). Recent research also supports the conclusion that although condoms are less effective against the spread of herpes than against other STIs, the consistent use of condoms significantly reduces the risk of herpes infection for both men and women (Wald, Langenberg, & Krantz, 2005).

Using a condom is sometimes perceived as ruining the mood or being inconvenient. Of course, the sobering question might be posed, "Which is more inconvenient: using a condom or contracting gonorrhea or AIDS?" Further, if a woman carries condoms, is she somehow communicating the message that she is too "easy"? The fact is that committed use of condoms is not a sign of being "easy" but one of responsibility, self-esteem, and maturity. If an individual is not ready to use condoms, he or she is not ready for sex. In general, condoms represent a great aid in preventing pregnancy and sexually transmitted infections.

Research has shown that programs to promote safe sex are especially effective if they include the eroticization of condom use—that is, making condoms a part of the sensual experience of foreplay (Harper & others, 2003; Scott-Sheldon & Johnson, 2006). Recent analyses of HIV prevention programs (including over 350 intervention groups and 100 control groups) by Delores Albarracin and her colleagues have produced important recommendations for the best ways to influence behavior (Albarracin, Durantini, & Earl, 2006; Albarracin & others, 2005; Durantini & others, 2006). The studies have found that fear tactics are relatively less effective and that programs emphasizing active skill building (for example, role playing the use of condoms), self-efficacy, and positive attitudes about condom use are effective with most groups. To evaluate your knowledge about condoms, take the quiz in the Psychology and Life box.

 ## REVIEW, ASSESS, AND SHARPEN YOUR THINKING

Review

4 Describe strategies for cultivating good habits in five important realms of life.

- Define stress, discuss its impact on the human body, and summarize strategies for reducing stress.
- Describe the benefits of physical activity and exercise.
- Evaluate what constitutes eating right and successful weight loss.
- Describe some methods for quitting smoking.
- Summarize the key information about preventing unwanted pregnancy and sexually transmitted infections.

Assess

1. During what stage of Selye's general adaptation syndrome are individuals most able to fight disease?

   A. illness stage   B. exhaustion stage

   C. alarm stage   D. resistance stage

2. Adults should get _____ or more minutes of moderate physical activity most days of the week.

   A. 15   B. 30

   C. 45   D. 60

PSYCHOLOGY AND LIFE

How Much Do You Know About Condoms?

Respond to the following items to test your knowledge of condom use, answering "true" or "false" for each.

Item	True	False
1. Individuals under the age of 25 who do not use condoms have a one in four chance of contracting a sexually transmitted infection.	_____	_____
2. Only latex or polyurethane condoms (not lambskin or novelty condoms) protect a person against STIs.	_____	_____
3. Using a lubricant with a condom is a good idea because it helps to prevent breakage.	_____	_____
4. Using Vaseline, baby oil, or massage oil as a lubricant can damage a condom.	_____	_____
5. Condoms are best stored in a dark, dry place at room temperature.	_____	_____
6. For full protection, a condom must be put on as soon as the penis is erect.	_____	_____
7. Used properly, condoms are 90 to 99 percent effective in preventing pregnancy.	_____	_____
8. To protect against STIs, condoms should be used for oral sex.	_____	_____
9. It is best to use a new condom for each act of intercourse, even if multiple acts occur in the same session.	_____	_____
10. Putting on a condom can be a sexy experience for both partners.	_____	_____

The right answer to all of these questions is *true*. Condoms are the only safer-sex aid that protects against both pregnancy and STIs.

Source: Adapted from http://www.ashastd.org/condom/condom_overview.cfm

---

3. A body mass index at or above _____ is considered obese.
   - A. 15
   - B. 20
   - C. 30
   - D. 45

4. HIV can be transmitted by all of the following except:
   - A. blood transfusions.
   - B. kissing.
   - C. sharing hypodermic needles.
   - D. sexual contact.

5. Having a person smoke enough cigarettes in one sitting to make them nauseated is an example of what type of quitting technique?
   - A. going cold turkey
   - B. behavioral therapy
   - C. using a nicotine substitute
   - D. antidepressant technique

Sharpen Your Thinking

How successful are you at maintaining a regular exercise program, eating nutritiously, not smoking, and making sound decisions about sex? Have your lifestyle and behavior in these areas affected your health? Might they affect your health in the future? Explain.

Even something as deceptively simple as perceiving a sunset (or a painting of a sunset) through our sense of vision becomes amazingly complex when we put it in the context of our life.

© CartoonStock.com

5 Integrating Psychology and Health and Wellness

Explain why positive psychology is the essence of psychology and how psychology applies to your physical health and well-being.

Many pages ago, we defined *psychology* as the scientific study of behavior and mental processes, broadly meaning the things we do, think, and feel. Reflect for a moment on the psychological approach to vision, which we explored in Chapter 5. When we studied the human visual system, we examined the process by which those amazing sense organs, our eyes, detect color, light, dark, shape, and depth. We probed the ways that the brain takes that information and turns it into perception—how a pattern of colors, shapes, and light come to be perceived as a flower, a fall day, a sunset. Visual systems, we discovered, are generally the same from one person to the next. Thus, you can memorize the different parts of the eye and know that your understanding is true for just about all the eyes you will encounter in life.

But even something as deceptively simple as perceiving a sunset through the sense of vision becomes amazingly complex when we put it in the context of a human life. Is that sunset the first you see while on your honeymoon? Or right after a painful romantic breakup? Or on the eve of the first day of your life as a new parent?

Placing even the most ordinary moment in the context of a human life renders it remarkably complex and undeniably fascinating. Indeed, this fascination is one of the primary motivations for the science of psychology itself. From time immemorial, individuals have pondered the mysteries of human behavior, emotion, and thought. Why do we do the things we do? And how do we think and feel? Throughout this book, we have explored the broad range of topics that have interested psychologists throughout the history of this young science.

As we come to the close of this introduction to psychology, it is useful to revisit two central themes that have been woven throughout this text: positive psychology and the importance of psychology to health and wellness. Reviewing these themes allows us (like the Roman god Janus) to look back but also ahead—to what psychology has come to mean to you and what it might continue to mean in the future.

Positive Psychology Is Plain Old Psychology

In Chapter 1, we discussed positive psychology, a movement in psychology toward an interest in health, functioning, and thriving. Positive psychology, focused as it is on the full range of human strengths and capacities, is sometimes viewed as an exception to "plain old psychology." Yet an approach to psychology that *begins* with healthy functioning makes sense. Recall the example of watchology from Chapter 1. If we want to understand how a watch works, we must begin with a working timepiece. Similarly, to understand how vision works, we begin by examining the way the healthy visual system functions. Taking it a step further, when we study other aspects of human life, psychology ought to begin with what works.

Throughout this book, we have noted all the ways that *you* work—your strengths, talents, abilities, and characteristics. We have highlighted how the science of psychology can contribute to human fulfillment and the identification of resources and capacities. Positive psychology *itself* is plain old psychology, for psychology is the study of human behavior, not just human dysfunction.

Psychology Is About *You*

A second theme of this book has concerned the applications of psychology to *your* physical health and well-being. We have examined how the mental and physical aspects of your existence intertwine and influence each other in dynamic and remarkable ways. At any given moment, as a human being, you are both a physical entity and a complex amalgam of mental processes, which are themselves reflected in the most complex organ ever discovered, the human brain. At every moment, both mind and body are present and influencing each other. Caring for your brain and mind—which have made it possible for you to read this book, study for tests, listen to lecture, fall in love, share with friends, help others, and make a difference in the world—is a life mission.

Throughout this book, we have paused to focus on moments of heroism, weakness, joy, and pain. In each of these moments of human experience, psychology has had a lesson to share. As we noted at the beginning of Chapter 1, learning about psychology is different from learning about any other science, because the science of psychology is so intimately about you. Making the most of psychology is, essentially, making the most of your life.

 REVIEW, ASSESS, AND SHARPEN YOUR THINKING

Review

5 Explain why positive psychology is the essence of psychology and how psychology applies to your physical health and well-being.
- Recap why an approach to psychology that begins with healthy functioning makes sense.
- Discuss the applications of psychology to your own physical health and mental well-being.

Assess

1. Which of the following is most consistent with the positive psychology approach?
   A. examining why people develop illnesses
   B. explaining why someone is obese
   C. determining what encourages regular exercise
   D. identifying the factors that lead to risky sexual behavior

2. Psychological processes affect which of the following?
   A. behavior
   B. the immune system
   C. coping processes
   D. all of the above

Sharpen Your Thinking

Before taking this course and reading this book, you may have had a variety of assumptions about psychology. Think back to your previous ideas about psychology. Which of these have proved to be accurate, and which inaccurate?

1 WHAT YOU ALREADY KNOW ABOUT HEALTH PSYCHOLOGY

Describe the scope of health psychology and behavioral medicine.

The Biopsychosocial Model

Health psychology is a multidimensional approach to health that emphasizes biological, psychological, and social factors. Closely aligned with health psychology is behavioral medicine, which combines medical and behavioral knowledge to reduce illness and promote health. These approaches demonstrate the biopsychosocial model by examining the interaction of the various levels of analysis. Stress is an example of a biological, psychological, and social construct.

The Relationship Between the Mind and Body

Health psychology and behavioral medicine bring the relationship of the mind and body to the forefront. These approaches examine the reciprocal relationships between the mind and body: how the body is influenced by psychological states and how mental life is influenced by physical health.

2 MAKING POSITIVE LIFE CHANGES

Describe the various theoretical models of change.

Theoretical Models of Change

The theory of reasoned action suggests that we can make changes by devising specific intentions for behavioral change. We are more likely to follow through on our intentions if we feel good about the change and if we feel that others around us also support the change. The theory of planned behavior incorporates these factors as well as our perceptions of control over the behavior.

The Stages of Change Model

The stages of change model posits that personal change occurs in a series of five steps: precontemplation, contemplation, preparation/determination, action/willpower, and maintenance. Each stage has its own challenges. Relapse is a natural part of the journey toward change.

SUMMARY

3 TOOLS FOR EFFECTIVE LIFE CHANGE

Discuss psychological and social tools that promote effective life change.

Self-Efficacy

Self-efficacy is the person's belief in his or her own ability to master a situation and produce positive outcomes. Self-efficacy has been shown to play an important role in a variety of health behaviors, including weight loss, smoking cessation, and practicing safe sex.

Motivation

Motivation is an important part of sustaining behavioral change. Change is more effective when the person does it for intrinsic reasons (because he or she really wants to) rather than extrinsic reasons (to gain rewards). Implementation intentions are the specific ways individuals plan to institute changes successfully.

Religious Faith

Religious faith is associated with enhanced health. One reason for this association is that religions often frown on excess and promote healthy behavior. Religious participation also allows individuals to benefit from a social group. Finally, religion provides a meaning system on which to rely in times of difficulty.

4 CULTIVATING GOOD HABITS

Describe strategies for cultivating good habits in five important realms of life.

Controlling Stress

Stress is the response of individuals when life circumstances threaten them and tax their ability to cope. Selye characterized the stress response with his concept of a general adaptation syndrome, which has three stages: alarm, resistance, and exhaustion. Chronic stress has been shown to take a toll on the body's natural disease-fighting abilities. Stress is also related to cardiovascular disease and cancer. To kick the stress habit means remembering that stress is a product of how we think about events in our lives. Taking control of our appraisals allows us to see potentially threatening events as challenges. When a person is unable to manage stress alone, stress management programs provide a viable source of help.

Becoming Physically Active

Exercise is associated with a multitude of positive psychological and physical benefits. Tips for increasing one's activity level include starting small by making changes in one's routine to incorporate physical activity (such as walking instead of driving to school); trying a variety of activities to find something one likes; finding an exercise partner; and swapping exercise for TV viewing. Keeping track of progress helps the individual to monitor his or her goal progress.

Eating Right

Eating right means selecting nutritious foods and maintaining healthy eating habits for a lifetime (not just while on a diet). Research has shown that eating breakfast (especially high-fiber cereal) is associated with successful weight loss and maintenance.

Quitting Smoking

Anyone who smokes should try to quit the habit, which poses serious threats to health. Methods of quitting include going cold turkey, using a substitute source of nicotine, and seeking therapy. While difficult at first, quitting smoking can be achieved.

Practicing Safe Sex

Practicing safe sex is another aspect of health behavior of interest to health psychologists. Condom use is one way to prevent both unwanted pregnancy and STIs.

5 INTEGRATING PSYCHOLOGY AND HEALTH AND WELLNESS

Explain why positive psychology is the essence of psychology and how psychology applies to your physical health and well-being.

Positive Psychology Is Plain Old Psychology

Although positive psychology is sometimes thought of as a relatively new idea, the notion that we should begin with function first, and study what works before tackling what does not, is the typical framework for most of psychology: We begin with working eyes and ears to study vision and hearing, for instance. As such, positive psychology is actually just "plain old psychology."

Psychology Is About *You*

More than any other science, psychology is about *you*—understanding how you work. This book has aimed to show the relevance of psychology to your health and wellness and to help you appreciate the many, and deep, connections between this relatively new science and your everyday life.

Key Terms

Assess Your Knowledge

1. Which of the following is a health-psychology-oriented topic within social psychology?
   A. Type A behavior patterns
   B. anxiety disorders
   C. receiving social support from friends in times of stress
   D. smoking in persons with schizophrenia

2. Which health theory focuses on intentions, attitudes, and social norms?
   A. social cognitive theory   B. theory of reasoned action
   C. self-determination theory   D. stages of change theory

3. During what stage of the stages of change does relapse occur?
   A. precontemplation   B. transcendence
   C. action/willpower   D. maintenance

4. Which discipline focuses on the relationship between psychological factors and the immune system?
   A. health psychology   B. immunology
   C. behavioral medicine   D. psychoneuroimmunology

5. In what stage of change is it most important to reward healthy behaviors?
   A. preparation/determination   B. maintenance
   C. action/willpower   D. contemplation

6. Which health theory focuses on intrinsic and extrinsic motivation?
   A. stages of change model   B. theory of reasoned action
   C. self-determination theory   D. social cognitive theory

7. Someone who has awareness of the benefits of a health behavior, but who is unsure about actually engaging in the behavior is in which stage of change?
   A. precontemplation   B. preparation/determination
   C. action/willpower   D. contemplation

8. All of the following help to explain the relationship between stress and health problems except:
   A. Stress puts people in closer contact to pathogens.
   B. Stress makes people more likely to engage in unhealthy coping strategies.

   C. Stress causes increased adrenaline, which causes more rapid blood clotting.
   D. Stress reduces the body's immune response.

9. Condoms are least effective at preventing the transmission of
   A. HIV.   B. gonorrhea.
   C. syphilis.   D. herpes.

10. The best way to prevent sexually transmitted infections is
    A. monogamy.   B. consistent use of condoms.
    C. marriage.   D. abstinence.

11. How are exercise and aerobic exercise different?
    A. Exercise specifically targets cardiovascular activity.
    B. Exercise is the most strenuous.
    C. Aerobic exercise is the most strenuous.
    D. Aerobic exercise specifically targets the strengthening of muscles and bones.

12. Which of the following would be an example of a chronic stressor?
    A. an upcoming test   B. a fight with a friend
    C. caring for an elderly parent   D. a flat tire

13. Which hormone is responsible for activating the immune system when faced with stress?
    A. androgen
    B. corticotropin-releasing hormone
    C. estrogen
    D. insulin

14. The approach that examines psychological, physiological and environmental influences on health and health behavior is the
    A. general adaptation approach.
    B. biopsychosocial approach.
    C. stages of change approach.
    D. self-determination approach.

15. Specific strategies for engaging in healthy behaviors are known as
    A. self-efficacy.   B. transcendence.
    C. implementation intentions.   D. autonomy.

Go to Appendix B for answers to these questions.

Apply Your Knowledge

1. Interview someone you know who has successfully lost weight, quit smoking, or started an exercise program. Ask the person about his or her experience of each of the stages of change. Does the theory fit your friend's experience? Why or why not?

2. Take one day and become a stress detective. Every time you hear someone mention how stressed out he or she is feeling, ask yourself questions: What is the stressful event? How is the person appraising the event? How might he or she appraise the situation in ways that would help decrease stress?

3. Select one bad habit you would like to break for 1 week—for example, smoking, eating sugary foods, or putting off getting aerobic exercise. Keep a journal of your progress each day in avoiding the bad habit. How easy or difficult did you find this little test in healthy life change?

4. Do an Internet search on the topic of stress management or coping with stress. Visit three or four sites and critically evaluate the suggestions made on the sites. How are they similar to the suggestions given in the text? How much information is available to evaluate the claims on the sites? Based on your critical evaluation, is the advice something you would follow or not? Explain.

5. One method that has helped to decrease unhealthy behaviors, such as smoking, is to make them more expensive. Currently, some people are calling for a tax on unhealthy foods. Would such a tax be useful? Would you be in favor of such a tax, or opposed? Why?

APPENDIX A: PRACTICE MID-TERM AND FINAL EXAMS

Practice Mid-Term Exam (Chapters 1–7)

1. Positive psychology is most consistent with which of the following approaches?
   A. evolutionary psychology
   B. psychodynamic psychology
   C. cognitive psychology
   D. humanistic psychology

2. What type of research design would best allow a researcher to determine whether students with higher SAT scores have higher GPAs in college?
   A. an experimental design
   B. a case-study design
   C. a correlational design
   D. a metaanalysis

3. Why is psychology considered a science?
   A. because psychologists have doctoral degrees
   B. because it focuses on unobservable concepts
   C. because it uses the scientific method
   D. because it is a social science

4. If a researcher discovers that her finding is significant at the .05 level, what does that mean?
   A. Her results are likely to have occurred because of chance.
   B. She has a 5 in 100 chance that her results occurred because of chance.
   C. She has nonsignificant findings.
   D. There is a 95% likelihood that her findings are not the result of chance.

5. Which part of the nervous system is responsible for mobilizing the body's resources when in danger?
   A. peripheral nervous system
   B. autonomic nervous system
   C. somatic nervous system
   D. sympathetic nervous system

6. Which of the following would be an expected outcome for someone whose corpus callosum was severed?
   A. speech problems, such as aphasia
   B. personality changes
   C. information not passing between the brain hemispheres
   D. seizures

7. A parent who gives a child a treat every 30 minutes that the child spends on homework is using what type of reinforcement schedule?
   A. fixed ratio
   B. variable ratio
   C. fixed interval
   D. variable interval

8. Monica has decided to become a physician. She feels very committed to this choice but made this choice before exploring other career options. In terms of career identity, Monica's identity status is
   A. identity moratorium.
   B. identity achievement.
   C. identity diffusion.
   D. identity foreclosure.

9. Someone who was just involved in a car accident and has a broken leg does not feel the pain until after arriving at the hospital and beginning to calm down. Which of the following likely happened at the time of the accident?
   A. there was an increase of endorphins in the brain
   B. the parasympathetic nervous system was activated
   C. dopamine receptors in the brain were blocked
   D. collateral sprouting began in the brain

10. Regina is studying hardiness. She is interested in determining how close most people are to the average level of hardiness. Which of the following would allow Regina to answer her question?
    A. the mean
    B. the range
    C. the standard deviation
    D. the median

11. Which of the following statements about the neural impulse is correct?
    A. When a neuron is activated, first, the inside of the neuron becomes positively charged; then, sodium ions enter the neuron.
    B. When a neuron is activated, first, the inside of the neuron becomes negatively charged; then sodium ions enter the neuron.
    C. When a neuron is activated, first, sodium ions enter the neuron; then the inside of the neuron becomes positively charged.
    D. When a neuron is activated, first, sodium ions enter the neuron; then the inside of the neuron becomes negatively charged.

12. Thomas does not believe in a god. Because he is atheist, Thomas's friend is concerned that he does not understand right and wrong. Thomas's views of right and wrong are not explicitly based on any religion. Rather, Thomas has come to his views through contemplation and by exposing himself to a variety of schools of thought. In what stage of moral development is Thomas?
    A. preconventional
    B. postconventional
    C. preoperational
    D. conventional

13. A researcher developed a study that examined the effects of writing down personal goals on physical health. He gave each participant a vaccine against Epstein-Barr virus and tested each participant's im-

mune reaction to the vaccine. Because he did not want participants to know that he was testing immune functioning, he told participants they were being given an injection of vitamins. Which of the following ethical issues is most relevant to this study?
A. confidentiality
B. deception
C. debriefing
D. informed consent

14. Which of the following would help to facilitate the developmental tasks associated with the identity versus identity confusion stage?
A. dating behavior, aimed at finding romantic fulfillment
B. exploring different career options
C. picking up an infant when it cries
D. memorizing state capitals

15. The reticular formation is located in which area of the brain?
A. hindbrain
B. midbrain
C. forebrain
D. cerebral cortex

16. A child who approaches a problem by making a hypothesis and then testing out that hypothesis is in the
A. concrete operational stage.
B. sensorimotor stage.
C. formal operational stage.
D. preoperational stage

17. Alzheimer disease involves all of the following except:
A. decline in memory.
B. decrease in brain plaques.
C. deficiency of acetylcholine.
D. language difficulties.

18. When light rays hit the eye, they are bent by two structures. The _____ does the majority of the bending and the _____ fine tunes it.
A. cornea, lens
B. lens, cornea
C. pupil, iris
D. iris, pupil

19. How are Weber's law and signal detection theory different?
A. Weber's law focuses on detecting differences between stimuli, whereas signal detection theory focuses on detecting the presence or absence of a stimuli.
B. Weber's law focuses on detecting the presence or absence of a stimuli, whereas signal detection theory focuses on detecting differences between stimuli.
C. Weber's law focuses on subliminal perception, whereas signal detection theory focuses on the absolute threshold.
D. Weber's law focuses on the absolute threshold, whereas signal detection theory focuses on subliminal perception.

20. Of the following brain waves, which are associated with the deepest level of sleep?
A. alpha
B. beta
C. delta
D. theta

21. Which of the following is an example of negative punishment?
A. activating a shock in a dog's collar when it barks
B. canceling a date when your partner drank the night before
C. a father discontinuing to nag at his son after his son cleans his room
D. taking a friend out to dinner after she completed a marathon

22. What does the suprachiasmatic nucleus do?
A. It is involved in the experience of emotions.
B. It acts as a relay station between sensory input and output to the body.
C. It is involved in synchronizing the body's day and night cycles.
D. It is involved in the perception of bodily motion.

23. Which of the following statements about substance use is correct?
A. Strong cravings are an example of physical dependence.
B. Both psychological and physical dependence must be present to be addicted.
C. Tolerance is an example of psychological dependence.
D. Withdrawal symptoms are an example of physical dependence.

24. Which theory of color perception accounts for afterimages?
A. trichromatic theory
B. gate control theory
C. parallel-processing theory
D. opponent-process theory

25. Khamla ate sea bass at a nice restaurant but contracted food poisoning and was sick all of the following night. Khamla now avoids sea bass. What is the conditioned stimulus?
A. the sea bass
B. the pathogen in the fish
C. the symptoms of sickness
D. the restaurant

26. Focusing on the structures of the mind is consistent with _____, whereas focusing on the purpose of cognitive processes is consistent with _____.
A. functionalism, structuralism
B. structuralism, functionalism
C. behavioral psychology, cognitive psychology
D. cognitive psychology, behavioral psychology

27. Which of the following is an example of a correlational study?
A. examining the impact of group therapy versus no therapy on people's anxiety levels
B. examining previously-published studies to determine the strength of the relationship between optimism and physical health
C. examining the behavior of a person with bipolar disorder
D. examining the relationship between self-reported frequency of exercise and coping strategies

28. Which of the following drugs least belongs with the others?
A. alcohol
B. MDMA (ecstasy)
C. heroin
D. barbiturates

29. A very loud bass guitar will produce sound waves that have _____ amplitude and _____ frequency.
A. high, high
B. low, low
C. high, low
D. low, high

30. Sound localization is possible because of
A. timing and intensity.
B. hair cells within the basilar membrane.
C. vibrations of the hammer.
D. the number of times a neuron fires.

Go to Appendix B for answers to these questions.

Practice Final Exam (Chapters 1–15)

1. Tameka is designing a study in which she will be examining the effects of therapy on depression. She is also interested in determining whether there are differences in depression based on race and sex. Tameka will randomly assign participants to either receive therapy or to be on a waiting list. She will then see whether people differ in their level of depression based on treatment group, race, and sex. What is the dependent variable?
   A. race
   B. depression
   C. treatment
   D. sex

2. Which of the following is true of norepinephrine?
   A. It slows down the heart.
   B. It is involved in love and bonding.
   C. It is released by both neurons and the adrenal gland.
   D. It is a natural opiate.

3. When you are listening to music, which lobe is most likely to be active?
   A. parietal
   B. temporal
   C. occipital
   D. frontal

4. Being able to develop a theory about something is an example of
   A. fluid intelligence.
   B. the concrete operational stage.
   C. crystallized intelligence.
   D. the preoperational stage.

5. _____ parenting is high in control and low in supportiveness, whereas _____ parenting is low in control and high in supportiveness.
   A. Authoritative, neglectful
   B. Authoritarian, indulgent
   C. Neglectful, authoritative
   D. Indulgent, authoritarian

6. The fovea contains _____, whereas the retina contains _____.
   A. cones, rods
   B. rods, cones
   C. cones, rods and cones
   D. rods and cones, cones

7. The mean IQ score is 100 and the standard deviation is 15. Giftedness is defined as _____ standard deviation(s) above the mean. Mental retardation is defined as _____ standard deviation(s) below the mean.
   A. 1, 2
   B. 2, 1
   C. 2, 2
   D. 3, 3

8. The *a* sound in the word cat is
   A. a phoneme.
   B. a morpheme.
   C. syntax.
   D. semantic.

9. Determining whether something is a car based on it having four wheels is an example of a(n)
   A. prototype model.
   B. schematic model.
   C. classical model.
   D. algorithmic model.

10. Which of the following is not a symptom of bulimia nervosa?
    A. binging
    B. purging
    C. weight less than normal
    D. preoccupation with food

11. Latoya is in her late 20s and has a lot of friends who are pregnant. Latoya believes that there has been an increase in the number of people in their late 20s having children. Latoya's belief is an example of
    A. a stereotype.
    B. the availability heuristic.
    C. self-serving bias.
    D. self-fulfilling prophecy.

12. How are men's and women's sexual response patterns different?
    A. Women rarely reach orgasm, whereas men do.
    B. Men have a refractory period, whereas women do not.
    C. The excitement phase lasts significantly longer for women than for men.
    D. Women have multiple orgasms, but men do not.

13. A photographer placed a model in a pose in which the model held her fists tight, her arm pulled back as if to punch, and her teeth clenched. What would the James-Lange theory predict about the model's emotions?
    A. she will feel angry after holding the pose
    B. she will feel angry before holding the pose
    C. she will not have an emotional reaction to the pose
    D. she will feel angry simultaneously with holding the pose

14. Which personality trait is most associated with altruism?
    A. openness to experience
    B. neuroticism
    C. conscientiousness
    D. agreeableness

15. The Thematic Apperception Test is most closely associated with which approach to personality?
    A. psychodynamic
    B. personological
    C. humanistic
    D. trait

16. Dr. Robbins notices that one of his students is late to class. Dr. Robbins decides that the student is lazy. Which of the following has happened?
    A. Dr. Robbins engaged in the self-fulfilling prophecy.
    B. Dr. Robbins made the fundamental attribution error.
    C. Dr. Robbins stereotyped the student.
    D. Dr. Robbins displayed self-serving bias.

17. Which of the following can help to explain riot behavior?
    A. deindividuation
    B. risky shift
    C. group polarization effect
    D. groupthink

18. A manager believes that people from the South are lazy. As such, he does not hire people from the South. Which of the following is true?
    A. Not hiring people from the South is an example of prejudice.
    B. Not hiring people from the South is an example of a stereotype.
    C. Not hiring people from the South is an example of discrimination.
    D. Not hiring people from the South is an example of bystander effect.

19. Consider the stressor of an upcoming test. Which of the following would be an avoidant coping technique?
    A. making an outline
    B. exercising
    C. reading the textbook
    D. creating flashcards

20. Mark is trying to quit smoking. He has not had a cigarette in four days. In what stage of change is Mark?
    A. maintenance
    B. contemplation
    C. action/willpower
    D. preparation/determination

21. Which therapy technique is most concerned with authenticity?
    A. cognitive behavioral
    B. humanistic
    C. psychodynamic
    D. behavioral

22. How do a clinical and counseling psychologist differ?
    A. A clinical psychologist attends medical school, whereas a counseling psychologist attends graduate school.
    B. A clinical psychologist has a doctoral degree, whereas a counseling psychologist has a masters degree.
    C. A clinical psychologist can prescribe medication, whereas a counseling psychologist cannot.
    D. A clinical psychologist does not focus on vocational issues, whereas a counseling psychologist does.

23. Which approach to therapy assumes that people's problems are a function of disordered thinking?
    A. behavioral
    B. cognitive
    C. psychodynamic
    D. humanistic

24. Which of the following treatments would be most in line with positive psychology?
    A. meditation
    B. psychodynamic psychotherapy
    C. selective serotonin reuptake inhibitors
    D. electroconvulsive therapy

25. Iris believes that human behavior can best be understood by examining the ways in which larger social forces influence people's actions. Iris's belief is most closely aligned with which of the following approaches?
    A. evolutionary psychology
    B. behavioral psychology
    C. sociocultural psychology
    D. psychodynamic psychology

26. Tamara is having a particularly stressful semester. In addition to having very hard coursework, she and her boyfriend just ended their relationship. According to the general adaptation syndrome, at what point in the semester would Tamara be most healthy?
    A. the beginning of the semester
    B. the middle of the semester
    C. the end of the semester
    D. after the semester is over

27. Which of the following is not an example of a behavioral therapy technique?
    A. free association
    B. systematic desensitization
    C. token economy
    D. aversive conditioning

28. Explaining depression via learned helplessness is consistent with the _____ approach.
    A. behavioral
    B. psychodynamic
    C. sociocultural
    D. cognitive

29. Which theory explains the effects of hypnosis as people acting in the way they believe people under hypnosis should act?
    A. cognitive theory
    B. behavioral theory
    C. social cognitive theory
    D. psychodynamic theory

30. How are schizotypal personality disorder and schizophrenia different?
    A. Schizotypal personality disorder does not include odd thought processes, whereas schizophrenia does.
    B. Schizotypal personality disorder is not as severe as schizophrenia.
    C. Schizotypal personality disorder is characterized by hallucinations, whereas schizophrenia is not.
    D. Schizotypal personality disorder is coded on Axis I, whereas schizophrenia is coded on Axis II.

31. Which neurotransmitter has been linked to suicide attempts?
    A. serotonin
    B. dopamine
    C. epinephrine
    D. norepinephrine

32. Waxy flexibility refers to
    A. extreme limberness of the arms and legs.
    B. body postures that remain in place without outside help.
    C. increased movement of the limbs.
    D. body movements that are abnormally slow.

33. Someone with schizoid personality disorder would most likely be
    A. high in extraversion.
    B. low in extraversion.
    C. high in conscientiousness.
    D. low in conscientiousness.

34. Benzodiazepines are an example of what type of drug?
    A. antidepressant
    B. antianxiety
    C. antipsychotic
    D. tricyclics

35. Mental processes include all of the following except:
    A. motives.
    B. behavior.
    C. thoughts.
    D. feelings.

36. Which type of design will allow a researcher to determine causality?
    A. correlational design
    B. case study design
    C. longitudinal design
    D. experimental design

37. A psychologist who is interested in preventing the development of a psychological disorder among persons in a neighborhood is likely a(n)
    A. health psychologist.
    B. community psychologist.
    C. clinical psychologist.
    D. environmental psychologist.

38. Prozac is an _____ for _____.
    A. agonist, serotonin
    B. antagonist, dopamine
    C. antagonist, serotonin
    D. agonist, dopamine

39. Which of the following structures is involved in kinesthetic perception?
    A. papillae
    B. semicircular canals
    C. basilar membrane
    D. cornea

40. Which of the following is an example of a conscious controlled process?
    A. daydreaming
    B. solving an algebraic equation
    C. watching television
    D. going under anesthesia

41. Pairing a neutral stimulus with a stimulus that naturally produces an effect is _____; the weakening of the effect of the conditioned stimulus is _____.
    A. discrimination, generalization
    B. generalization, discrimination
    C. acquisition, extinction
    D. extinction, acquisition

42. Being predisposed to make a connection between a conditioned stimulus and an unconditioned stimulus is known as
    A. instinctive drift.
    B. acquisition.
    C. expectancy learning.
    D. preparedness.

43. The law of effect states that behaviors followed by _____ will increase in frequency, whereas behaviors followed by _____ will decrease in frequency.
    A. conditioned stimuli, unconditioned stimuli
    B. unconditioned stimuli, conditioned stimuli
    C. negative outcomes, positive outcomes
    D. positive outcomes, negative outcomes

44. Speech is stored in which area of the working memory?
    A. iconic memory
    B. echoic memory
    C. phonological loop
    D. visuospatial working memory

45. Explicit memory is divided into
    A. implicit and nondeclarative memory.
    B. episodic and semantic memory.
    C. short-term and long-term memory.
    D. iconic and echoic memory.

46. Joel has been studying Carl Jung's theories. Prior to his focus on Jung's work, he studied Sigmund Freud's theories. When Joel is asked who developed the idea of the collective unconscious, he incorrectly remembers Freud. What has happened to Joel?
    A. decay
    B. transience
    C. proactive interference
    D. retroactive interference

47. Debra is very anxious. Keith is very focused on success. Megan is very hostile. Josh is lazy. Who would be expected to have coronary health problems?
    A. Debra
    B. Keith
    C. Megan
    D. Josh

48. According to self-determination theory, someone who feels that her actions will have a positive outcome is probably high in which of the following needs?
    A. relatedness
    B. self-actualization
    C. autonomy
    D. competence

49. A man who experiences same-sex sexual arousal becomes homophobic. According to Freud, what defense mechanism is the man using?
    A. projection
    B. denial
    C. reaction formation
    D. displacement

50. Marcia was given the following list of words to remember: apple, car, stereo. According to the serial position effect, what is a likely outcome when Marcia attempts to recall the words?
    A. Memory will be best for *apple*, then for *car*, then for *stereo*.
    B. Memory will be best for *car*, then for *stereo*, then for *apple*.
    C. Memory will be best for *apple*, then for *stereo*, then for *car*.
    D. Memory will be best for *stereo*, then for *apple*, then for *car*.

Go to Appendix B for answers to these questions.

APPENDIX B: ANSWERS TO *ASSESS YOUR KNOWLEDGE* CHAPTER QUIZZES AND THE PRACTICE MID-TERM AND FINAL EXAMS

Answers to the *Assess Your Knowledge* Chapter Quizzes

Chapter 1: What Is Psychology?

1. D
Why? The psychodynamic approach is concerned with unconscious thoughts and family relationships; the behavioral approach is concerned with behavior; and the structural approach is concerned with the structure of the mind. (Page 14)

2. C
Why? All the other types of psychologists are experimental and do not diagnose. (Page 19)

3. A
Why? Darwin is associated with natural selection; Wundt is associated with structuralism; and Buss is associated with evolutionary psychology. (Page 13)

4. B
Why? The psychodynamic approach is concerned with unconscious thoughts and family relationships; cognitive psychology is concerned with thoughts; and health psychology is concerned with the mind-body interaction. (Page 18)

5. D
Why? All the other options are observable behaviors. (Page 5)

6. C
Why? A and B are both true, but are not the reasons psychology is a science; psychology shares some similarities with the natural sciences, but also has many differences. (Page 5)

7. A
Why? The behavioral approach focuses on behaviors; the scientific method is a means of testing hypotheses; structuralism focuses on the structure of the mind. (Page 7)

8. B
Why? Structuralism and functionalism are early approaches to psychology that attempted to examine the structure and function of the mind. (Pages 10–11)

9. D
Why? The behavioral approach focuses on behavior, the cognitive approach on thoughts, and health psychology on the mind-body interaction. (Page 12)

10. C
Why? Industrial/organizational psychologists focus on factors within the workplace, while social psychologists focus on the influence of groups, and health psychologists focus on the mind-body interaction. Even though employment is of interest to industrial/organizational psychologists, the best answer is community psychologist. (Page 20)

11. A
Why? Groups are consistent with social psychology; stress is consistent with health psychology; and mental illness is consistent with clinical and counseling psychology. (Page 19)

12. A
Why? Wundt and Titchener are associated with structuralism and James is associated with functionalism. Descartes is associated with the field of philosophy. (Page 13)

13. A
Why? The psychodynamic approach is concerned with unconscious thoughts and family relationships; the evolutionary approach is concerned with adaptation; and the sociocultural approach is concerned with people's experiences in their cultures. (Page 14)

14. B

Why? Altruism is associated with the humanistic approach, adaptiveness with the evolutionary approach, and thoughts with the cognitive approach. (Page 13)

15. C

Why? Psychiatrists are medical doctors, who can prescribe medications and usually have MD degrees; psychologists are not medical doctors, but rather usually have Ph.D. degrees and usually cannot prescribe medications. (Page 19)

Chapter 2: Psychology's Scientific Methods

1. D

Why? Only an experimental design can test for causation because it is the only design in which the researcher manipulates variables and has control over extraneous variables through random assignment. (Pages 45–46)

2. D

Why? A negative correlation means that as scores on one variable go up, scores on the other go down. The larger the absolute value of the correlation, the stronger the relationship between two variables. A correlation between .51 and .75 (or −.51 and −.75) is considered strong. (Page 41)

3. C

Why? A meta-analysis involves examining a number of studies to determine the size of an effect. Though a meta-analysis could help to develop a theory, a theory could be developed many other ways. A random sample refers to a group of people chosen at random from a population. Finally, an operational definition is a way of objectively stating how a variable will be measured. (Page 34)

4. A

Why? A random sample gives every person in the population an equal chance of being selected. Choosing one classroom would not give everyone an equal chance of being selected (consider if the classroom was an honors class); sampling from soccer game attendees would preclude those who did not attend; choosing each 50th student who entered the building could result in problems if any students entered through a different door. (Page 36)

5. D

Why? A percentile refers to a ranking; the 47th percentile would indicate that the test taker scored higher than 47% of all persons taking the test. (Page 40)

6. A

Why? The mode is the number that occurs most frequently; in this dataset, 1 occurs most frequently. (Page 53)

7. D

Why? The .05 level of statistical significance means that a result only has a 5 percent or less rate of happening by chance. (Page 54)

8. C

Why? Both correlational and experimental statistics are used to test hypotheses. (Pages 52–54)

9. D

Why? Debriefing happens after the study has finished; confidentiality refers to keeping participants' data safe and secure; informed consent refers to informing participants of the risks and benefits of a study. Because the experimenter misrepresented the purpose of the study, deception is present, and could be ethically problematic. Deception should only be used if it will not harm the research participant; likewise, participants should be debriefed after. (Page 56)

10. C

Why? Ethnic gloss refers to overgeneralizing about an ethnic group and failing to examine the diversity within a group. The term Asian is too broad, as the study could have included participants from backgrounds such as Japanese, Thai, Lao, Vietnamese, Indian, and so forth. (Page 60)

11. B

Why? The mean reflects the average score. As such, it is a measure of control tendency. The standard deviation and range both reflect the spread of scores. (Pages 53–54)

12. B

Why? The placebo effect refers to individuals' expectations, rather than the actual experimental manipulation, accounts for the outcome. Experimenter bias refers to researchers' expectations affecting the outcome, whereas ecological and internal validity refer to the generalizability of the results and the degree to which the results are due to the independent variable, respectively. (Page 47)

13. D

Why? A control group does not receive any treatment, whereas an experimental group does receive treatment. (Page 46)

14. A

Why? Multivariate studies examine more than one variable; longitudinal studies measure at several time points; correlational studies do not manipulate variables; and experimental studies randomly assign participants. (Page 44)

15. D

Why? Correlation is expressed in either positive or negative numbers. The range of correlation falls within a range of −1.00 to +1.00. The greater the correlation, as expressed by the number within the range of 1.00 to +1.00, such as .88, the greater the relationship between variables. (Pages 43–45)

Chapter 3: Biological Foundations of Behavior

1. D

Why? The central nervous system is divided into the brain and spinal cord. The peripheral nervous system is divided into the somatic and autonomic nervous systems; the autonomic nervous system is divided into the sympathetic and parasympathetic nervous systems. (Pages 74–75)

2. B

Why? Efferent nerves send information from the brain to specific areas of the body; the sympathetic and parasympathetic nervous systems are involved in arousal and relaxation. (Page 74)

3. B

Why? Resting potential is a stable, negative charge on a neuron that is inactive. (Page 78)

4. D

Why? The axon carries the electrochemical charge down the neuron, whereas the cell body holds the nucleus. The terminal button initiates the release of neurotransmitters into the synaptic gap. The dendrite's receptor site receives the impulse. (Pages 76–77)

5. C

Why? Serotonin is involved in sleep, mood, attention, and learning; oxytocin is involved in love and bonding; acetylcholine is involved in the use of the muscles, as well as learning and memory. (Page 82)

6. D

Why? Endorphin receptors are activated by morphine and are responsible for the drugs' effects. Acetylcholine is involved in muscles, learning, and memory; GABA controls the signals being sent from neuron to neuron; and serotonin is associated with sleep, wakefulness, mood, attention, and learning. (Page 82)

7. D

Why? The pituitary gland is the master gland, regulating other glands; it is the adrenal gland that helps the body respond to stress by releasing epinephrine and norepinephrine. Meanwhile, the thyroid gland controls how quickly the body burns energy and makes protein. The parathyroid controls calcium within the blood. (Page 99)

8. B

Why? The association cortex is responsible for integrating information, as well as high-level thought processes; Broca's area plays a major role in the production of speech; the somatosensory cortex processes information from the senses. (Pages 94–95)

9. D

Why? The occipital lobe is involved in vision; the parietal lobe in spatial recognition, motor control, and attention; and the frontal lobe in intelligence and personality. (Page 91)

10. C

Why? Both MRI measures hydrogen atoms; fMRI measures changes in oxygen; and CT scans are three-dimensional X-rays. (Page 85)

11. D

Why? The synaptic gap is the space between two neurons; agonists facilitate the effects of a neurotransmitter; serotonin is a type of neurotransmitter. (Page 82)

12. A

Why? The medulla is located at the intersection of the brain and the spinal cord; it is located in the hindbrain with the cerebellum and pons. (Page 87)

13. C

Why? The cerebellum is involved in motor coordination; the hippocampus in memory; and the thalamus in relaying information between levels of the brain. (Page 87)

14. C

Why? An iron rod shot through Phineas Gage's frontal lobe, causing personality changes; the frontal lobe is involved in personality. The occipital lobe is involved with vision; the parietal lobe identifies spatial location, attention, and motor control; and the temporal lobe is dedicated to hearing, language processing, and memory. (Page 91)

15. B

Why? Aphasia refers to problems in producing or understanding language. (Page 94)

Chapter 4: Human Development

1. A

Why? Object permanence occurs during the sensorimotor stage, which is the first stage of development. Symbolic thinking begins to develop during the preoperational stage. The concrete operational stage is best demonstrated by the application of more logic and an ability to classify objects. Hypothetical thought and the use of logical processes occur during the formal operational stage. (Pages 125–26)

2. C

Why? The embryonic period is 3 weeks to 8 weeks; the germinal period is 1 week to 2 weeks; the fetal period is 2 months through 9 months. A zygote is a fertilized egg. (Page 120)

3. D

Why? Life themes refer to meaningful pursuits that take us beyond simple survival. Competition, wealth, and procreation are all consistent with survival strategies, but altruism is not necessary for survival; rather, it helps to make life meaningful. (Page 118)

4. A

Why? The preferential looking techniques allows researchers to determine at which image an infant prefers to look. This technique allows researchers to determine whether an infant can differentiate between two images or objects. Visual development refers to the development of the visual senses; habituation refers to a decrease in response to a stimuli over time; object permanence refers to the ability to realize that an object exists even if it cannot be seen. (Page 122)

5. B

Why? In the preoperational stage, children are egocentric and cannot take others' perspectives. (Page 126)

6. B

Why? Sucking is a reflex with which infants are born; because it is inborn it is not a skill that must develop over time. Habituation refers to a decrease in response to a stimuli over time; the preoperational stage is a stage of cognitive development. (Page 121)

7. D

Why? Identity versus identity confusion occurs in adolescence; trust versus mistrust occurs in infancy; intimacy versus isolation early adulthood. (Page 129)

8. D

Why? Erikson developed a theory of socioemotional development; Piaget developed a theory of cognitive development; Marcia developed a theory of identity. (Page 136)

9. D

Why? Ethnic identity is not the same for different people, though all races and ethnicities have ethnic identities. Moreover, research indicated there is a buffering effect against the stress of discrimination for those with strong ethnic identities. (Page 147)

10. C

Why? Telomeres protect the ends of chromosomes; life-expectancy refers to the life span of an average human in a given time and place; the free-radical theory focuses on damage to cells from free radicals. (Page 153)

11. A

Why? Cohort effects refer to effects based on group membership; crystallized intelligence consists of known facts and verbal skills; accommodation refers to adjustments in one's schemas. (Page 156)

12. A

Why? Authoritative parenting gives children freedom within limits; neglectful parenting ignores children; indulgent parenting provides children with few limits. (Page 133)

13. A

Why? The conventional stage is characterized by decisions based on laws and social mores; the postconventional stage is characterized by decisions based on generally-accepted as well as personal ethical codes. The formal operational stage is a stage of cognitive development. (Page 137)

14. C

Why? Kohlberg was the only other theorist who focused on moral development, but he does not give adequate attention to interpersonal relationships. (Pages 129–30)

15. B

Why? Assimilation refers to events being consistent with our expectations but trauma defies our expectations. While generativity can provide people with resources, those resources may or may not help them to overcome trauma. A midlife crisis refers to recognizing that one is aging and engaging in negative behaviors, which is not the norm for people in mid-life. (Pages 124–25)

Chapter 5: Sensation and Perception

1. D

Why? Weber's law states that two stimuli must differ by the same percentage, rather than the same amount, to be perceived as different, which is the case in a 1 dB change in volume at low and high levels of volume. (Page 178)

2. B

Why? Both the absolute threshold and subliminal perception refer to the amount of a stimulus needed to be perceived. Synaesthesia refers to a stimulus causing perception in another sense, such as a visual stimulus causing as an olfactory response. (Page 175)

3. B

Why? The absolute threshold refers to the point at which individuals can perceive a stimulus 50% of the time. (Pages 176–77)

4. A

Why? Purity determines richness; amplitude determines brightness; and wavelength determines hue. (Pages 183–84)

5. B

Why? The sclera is the white part of the eye; the iris is the colored part of the eye that controls the size of the pupil. After images are projected onto the retina, the information is sent to the visual cortex. (Page 185)

6. D

Why? Rods and cones are both sensitive to light, interpreting either black and white, or color; binding refers to the integration of various visual pathways. (Page 186)

7. C

Why? Trichromatic theory accounts for color blindness because people with color blindness have only two kinds of cones rather than three. (Pages 188–90)

8. B

Why? The pinna is a part of the outer ear; the others are part of the middle ear. (Page 200)

9. D

Why? The basilar membrane lines the wall of the cochlea; the eardrum vibrates in response to sound; and the oval window transmits sound to the cochlea. Only the tectorial membrane responds to hair cell movement. (Page 201)

10. D

Why? The back of the tongue is sensitive to bitter tastes, whereas the front of the tongue is sensitive to salty and sweet tastes. (Page 211)

11. B

Why? Propioceptive feedback is the information position of our body parts in relation to one another; it provides us information about the location of our body in space. (Page 212)

12. A

Why? The semicircular canals detect head motion; the olfactory bulb detects smell; and the basilar membrane helps detect sound. (Page 210)

13. A

Why? The gate-control theory of pain states that the spinal column controls a neural gate that can be opened or closed to allow the perception of pain. This theory has been revised somewhat based on new information about pain neurophysiology. (Page 209)

14. C

Why? The brain pathways for the vestibular senses begin in the auditory nerve, as structures of the ear play a key role in balance. (Page 213)

15. C

Why? The basilar membrane is involved in perception of sound. Frequency theory focuses on the number of times the auditory nerve fires; gate-control theory focuses on pain sensation; and trichromatic theory focuses on color vision. (Page 202)

Chapter 6: States of Consciousness

1. D

Why? Psychological dependence is characterized by an emotionally driven desire for the drug; tolerance is the need to take more of the drug to get the same effect; the nucleus accumbens is part of the reward pathway involved in the release of neurotransmitters when a drug is consumed. (Page 245)

2. D

Why? Alcohol is the second-most commonly-used drug in the United States. Of illegal drugs, marijuana is used most often by American high school students. Nicotine usage has been steadily decreasing in the United States. (Page 249)

3. B

Why? Marijuana is classified as a hallucinogen because it causes mild hallucinatory effects; it also has both stimulant and depressant effects. In almost all of the United States, marijuana is an illegal drug. (Pages 251–2)

4. C

Why? Both amphetamines and cocaine are addictive stimulants. They are made from different sources (amphetamines are made from chemicals such as cleaning products, cocaine is made from the coca leaf) and as such, amphetamines are not a form of cocaine. (Page 250)

5. C

Why? Daydreaming is a lower level of consciousness; Joseph is actively thinking about his thought processes. Likewise, stream-of-consciousness is the mind moving from one topic to the next. Subconscious awareness happens without active awareness. (Page 222)

6. D

Why? A controlled process is one that requires the most active form of attention. For experienced drivers, driving is "second nature." Subconscious awareness refers to awareness that occurs without our knowledge; altered consciousness is consciousness that is different than normal. (Page 224)

7. B

Why? The occipital lobe is involved in vision but is not responsible for circadian rhythms, or the cycle of fluctuations in our body. The limbic system is responsible for emotions, memory, and motivation. The thalamus integrates sensory input. (Page 228)

8. C

Why? Delta waves have the highest amplitude of brain waves involved in sleep and are present more than 50% of the time in stage 4 sleep. (Page 234)

9. D

Why? Alpha and beta waves predominate when people are awake. Delta waves predominate in stages 3 and 4, which are the deepest sleep stages. (Page 234)

10. B

Why? Somnambulism is sleepwalking; narcolepsy is uncontrollably falling asleep; night terrors are fearful awakening from sleep accompanied by physiological arousal. (Page 238)

11. B

Why? Unconsciousness is an idea developed by Freud and refers to our unacceptable thoughts and wishes. Hypnosedation is a method using hypnosis to reduce the amount of anesthesia used in surgery. The social cognitive behavior view of hypnosis states that hypnotized individuals act the way they expect someone would act under hypnosis. (Pages 242–43)

12. A

Why? An antagonist blocks the effect of a neurotransmitter. GABA is the main neurotransmitter affected by alcohol. (Page 246)

13. A

Why? Mindfulness meditation involves focusing one's thoughts, not avoiding them. (Pages 256–57)

14. A

Why? The cerebral cortex is involved in awareness; the hippocampus is involved in memory; the suprachiasmatic nucleus is involved in circadian rhythms. (Page 223)

15. B

Why? Social cognitive behavior is an explanation for the effects of hypnosis on behavior. Biological clocks are predictable cycles within the body, such as the sleep-waking cycle or the menstrual cycle. Stream-of-consciousness is the continuous flow of thoughts from one topic to the next. (Page 240)

Chapter 7: Learning

1. C

Why? Extinction refers to a weakening of a conditioned response; spontaneous recovery refers to a conditioned response reappearing after it had disappeared; counterconditioning refers to a process of minimizing a conditioned response. (Page 290)

2. A

Why? Something that naturally elicits a response without any pairing is an unconditioned stimulus. The conditioned stimulus is something that elicits a response only after it has been paired with a unconditioned stimulus. The unconditioned response is the response elicited from the unconditioned stimulus. The conditioned response is the response elicited from the conditioned stimulus. (Page 267)

3. C

Why? The drill is the unconditioned stimulus that elicits the unconditioned response of pain. The sound of the drill is the conditioned stimulus that elicits the conditioned response of sweating and Nikki's heart racing. (Page 267)

4. C

Why? The law of effect states that behaviors that are rewarded with increase and behaviors that are punished will decrease. Only option C is consistent with the law of effect. (Page 273)

5. A

Why? Positive punishment reduces a behavior by applying an unpleasant stimulus. Discrimination refers to responses made to only specific stimuli. Spontaneous recovery is the reemergence of a conditioned response. (Page 270)

6. D

Why? Classical conditioning involves pairing a neutral stimulus with a stimulus that naturally produces a reaction. Instinctive drift refers to an organism's natural instincts interfering with learning. Generalization refers to stimuli that are similar to the conditioned stimulus producing the same response. (Page 274)

7. C

Why? A variable-ratio schedule is one in which a reward is given after an average number of behaviors occurs, but is not predictable. A variable-interval schedule is one in which a reward is given after a variable amount of time has passed. A fixed-interval schedule is one in which a reward is given after a specific amount of time has passed. (Pages 276–77)

8. A

Why? Variable-ratio schedules produce high, steady behavior that is most resistant to extinction. Variable-interval schedules produce slow, steady behavior; fixed-ratio schedules produce increased behavior that drops off after the reward is given; fixed-interval schedules produce an increase in behavior just before the interval ends but a drop in behavior after the interval has ended. (Page 277)

9. A

Why? A negative punisher decreases behavior by taking away a valued stimulus; a positive reinforcer increases behavior by providing a valued stimulus; a positive punisher decreases behavior by providing an unwanted stimulus. (Page 275)

10. B

Why? A negative reinforcer increases behavior by taking away an unwanted stimulus; a positive reinforcer increases behavior by providing a

valued stimulus; a positive punishment decreases behavior by providing an unwanted stimulus. (Page 279)

11. D

Why? Negative reinforcement increases behavior by taking away an unwanted stimulus; classical conditioning involves pairing a neutral stimulus with a stimulus that naturally produces a reaction; operant learning involves behaviors being rewarded or punished. (Page 265)

12. C

Why? Entity theory states that intelligence is fixed and cannot be changed; learned helpless is the learned belief that outcomes in life are uncontrollable. Applied behavior analysis is a system for changing behavior. (Page 292)

13. B

Why? Instinctive drift refers to an organism's natural instincts interfering with learning; insight learning is learning that happens suddenly rather than gradually; contingency refers to the predictability of a two stimuli occurring together. (Page 290)

14. D

Why? Stressors that are both predictable and controllable make us feel less stressed than those that lack predictability or control. (Page 294)

15. A

Why? Contingency refers to the predictability of two stimuli occurring together, whereas continuity refers to the length of time between the presentation of the two stimuli. (Page 272)

Chapter 8: Memory

1. C

Why? The limit of memory span is usually 7 plus or minus 2. (Page 311)

2. B

Why? The central executive integrates memory information; the visuo-spatial working memory stores information that is visual and spatial; iconic memory is the name used for visual sensory memory. (Page 312)

3. C

Why? Working memory was not proposed by Atkinson and Shiffrin but rather by Alan Baddeley. (Page 309)

4. D

Why? Remembering how to ride a bike and to type specific letters on a keyboard are both examples of implicit memory; remembering your first kiss is an example of episodic memory. (Page 315)

5. C

Why? Permastore memories are memories that appear to stay with a person forever. (Page 314)

6. B

Why? Both semantic and episodic memory are types of explicit memory, whereas procedural memory is a type of implicit memory. (Page 315)

7. B

Why? Items at the beginning of a list will be remembered better than items in the middle; however, items at the end of a list will usually be remembered best. (Page 324)

8. B

Why? Anterograde amnesia is the inability to make new memories. Proactive interference is the disruption of newly learned knowledge. The

tip-of-the-tongue phenomenon is when someone feels that they know something but cannot easily recall it. (Page 337)

9. B

Why? Shallow processing involves recognition of physical characteristics of a stimulus; deepest processing involves focusing on the meaning of a stimulus; elaboration refers to the extent of processing. (Page 306)

10. D

Why? Short-term and long-term memories are not part of sensory memory. (Page 310)

11. D

Why? Long-term potentiation is the process of connections between neurons becoming stronger when two neurons close to one another fire at the same time. When long-term potentiation occurs, memory traces are strengthened. (Page 322)

12. D

Why? Autobiographical memory refers to memory for personal life events; context-dependent memory refers to increased recall when something is remembered in the same context in which it was learned. Recall memory involves retrieving previously learned information without the help of any cues. (Page 325)

13. B

Why? Decay theory describes a process of memory loss that is distinct from cognitive decline; answer C refers to the serial position effect and answer D refers to interference theory. (Page 335)

14. A

Why? Keywords refer to linking images to something to be remembered; method of loci refers to linking something to be remembered to specific locations, such as rooms in a house. Transience is not a mnemonic technique; it refers to forgetting over time. (Page 339)

15. B

Why? Transience refers to forgetting over time; motivated forgetting refers to forgetting something because it is painful or too emotionally-laden; a flashbulb memory is a vivid memory that forms because of extreme emotion. (Page 326)

Chapter 9: Thinking, Intelligence, and Language

1. D

Why? Algorithms are rules used to solve a problem; heuristics are cognitive shortcuts. (Page 351)

2. C

Why? A person's IQ is determined by dividing their mental age by their chronological age and multiplying by 100; thus 20 divided by 20 and multiplied by 100 is 100. (Page 364)

3. A

Why? Deductive and inductive reasoning involve reasoning from the general to the specific and vice versa. Subgoaling involves breaking down a goal into its separate components. (Page 354)

4. D

Why? The availability heuristic refers to overestimating the frequency of something's occurrence because it is readily available in our minds;

hindsight bias refers to incorrectly stating after the fact that we successfully predicted an outcome; functional fixedness refers to focusing on the usual function of an item and not seeing its alternate uses. (Pages 356–57)

5. C

Why? IQ, as measured by the Binet is normally distributed, which means that most scores fall in the middle of the bell-shaped curve. The normal distribution is not positively skewed, which would suggest that most scores occur in one tail. (Page 365)

6. B

Why? A valid test is reliable because it accurately measures what it says it measures, and time will not change accuracy. However, a reliable test may or may not be valid. Just because the scores are consistent over time does not mean the test is accurately measuring what it is designed to measure. (Page 364)

7. C

Why? IQ criterion for a diagnosis of mental retardation is usually defined as an IQ below 70. (Page 370)

8. B

Why? The sentence has correct syntax because a subject (*book*) is followed by a verb (*ate*) that refers to a direct object (*yellow house*, which is an adjective followed by a noun). However, it is not possible for a book to eat a house, so the sentence violates semantics. Phonology and morphology refer to the basic sounds and units of language. (Page 373)

9. B

Why? Whorf argued that the more words we have for something, the more we can think about it. (Page 373)

10. D

Why? Chomsky focuses on the biological aspect of language that predisposes infants to learn to talk. (Page 375)

11. B

Why? Avoidant coping involves strategies to avoid the stressor rather than change it. Each of the other strategies are aimed at actively confronting the stressor of being unemployed. (Page 382)

12. A

Why? Primary appraisal involves determining whether an event is a threat; both active and avoidant coping are coping strategies that happen after secondary appraisal, which involves determining what strategies can be used to cope with a stressor. (Page 381)

13. A

Why? Both problem-focused and approach coping focus on dealing directly with a stressor, while both emotion-focused and avoidant focus on avoiding a stressor. (Pages 381–82)

14. B

Why? By 6 months, children are babbling but by 18 to 24 months children have around 200 words; after age 2, children begin to implement syntactical rules correctly. (Page 378)

15. B

Why? Design is part of creative intelligence. Analytical intelligence includes analysis and evaluation and practical intelligence includes application and execution. Spatial intelligence is important in designing the layout of a room, but it is not part of Sternberg's triarchic theory. (Page 371)

Chapter 10: Motivation and Emotion

1. D

Why? Instincts are innnate patterns of behaviors and motivation is a force that directs people's behavior. (Page 391)

2. C

Why? The Yerkes-Dobson law says that performance is best at a moderate level of arousal. Tamesha's arousal is so high that she is having physical symptoms. As such, her arousal is too high for her to perform well. (Page 392)

3. B

Why? Both anorexia and bulimia can involve binging and purging, though it is more common in bulimia; both involve fear of gaining weight and a preoccupation with food. (Page 397)

4. D

Why? Physiological needs are at the base of the hierarchy, followed by safety needs, love and belonging needs, esteem needs, and finally self-actualization needs. (Page 407)

5. B

Why? Though active coping is related to better outcomes, it does not ensure recovery from trauma. Likewise, positive emotions generally and gratitude specifically are related to well-being but do not ensure recovery from trauma. (Page 428)

6. D

Why? Glucose is blood sugar and insulin is the hormone that stores glucose in cells. Leptin is a protein that is involved in satiety. (Page 394)

7. D

Why? Estrogen is a class of hormones that are mainly found in women; insulin is a hormone that stores glucose in cells; the pituitary gland monitors levels of testosterone. (Page 399)

8. C

Why? The research shows that lesbian women and heterosexual women show many gender similarities, just as do gay men and heterosexual men. (Page 404)

9. D

Why? The sexual response pattern starts with excitement, moves to plateau and then to orgasm, and ends with the resolution phase. (Page 400)

10. B

Why? Competition is not a component of self-determination theory. (Page 407)

11. A

Why? The broaden-and-build model states that positive emotions help us to build up resources; the facial feedback hypothesis states that our facial expressions can impact our mood, which is consistent with the James-Lange theory that physiological changes precede emotion. (Page 417)

12. D

Why? The two-factor theory of emotion states that emotion is determined by physiological arousal and cognitive labeling; self-regulation is the process of pursuing goals; set points are the natural weight of people when not trying to gain or lose weight. (Page 423)

13. B

Why? The two-dimensional approach states that emotions can be classified into positive affect and negative affect; the two-factor theory states

that emotions are determined by both physiological arousal and cognitive labeling. (Page 425)

14. C

Why? Fulfillment, competence, and curiosity are all needs that are internal to the person, whereas money is a reward for hard work. (Page 409)

15. A

Why? Adipose cells are fat cells; leptin is a protein involved in satiety; cholecystokinin is a hormone involved in digestion. (Page 415)

Chapter 11: Personality

1. B

Why? Neuroticism refers to anxiety and negative affect; agreeableness refers to trust, generosity, and altruism; openness to experience refers to open-mindedness and openness to engaging in novel tasks and situations. (Page 449)

2. C

Why? Murray's approach is called the personological approach and focuses on the study of the whole person. This approach posits that describing someone's personality requires understanding that person's history. Rogers focused on the humanistic approach; Allport focused on the trait approach; and Freud focused on the psychodynamic approach. (Page 452)

3. A

Why? The Thematic Apperception Test asks participants to tell a story about the pictures they see. This narrative approach is consistent with personology, which focuses on a person's life story. (Page 453)

4. D

Why? Emotional expression is known as catharsis; Freud was focused on unconscious, rather than conscious, processes; even though most of Freud's patients were women, both men and women can experience hysterical symptoms. (Page 437)

5. D

Why? Jung focused on the collective unconscious and archetypes; Horney focused on people's needs in relationship to society; Murray focused on the personological approach. (Page 445)

6. C

Why? Defense mechanisms are *created* by the ego to deal with the conflict between the id (baser needs) and superego (higher conscience). (Page 438)

7. C

Why? The oral stage happens during the first 18 months; the anal stage happens from 18 to 36 months; the phallic stage happens from 3 to 6 years; the latency period happens from 6 years to puberty; the genital stage happens in adolescence and adulthood. (Pages 439–40)

8. A

Why? The genital stage focuses on pleasure from interactions outside the family; unconditional positive regard heightens well-being; self-efficacy is the belief that one's actions will have the intended outcome. (Page 444)

9. B

Why? Mischel asserted that it is the situation, not personality factors that determine behavior; this belief was contrary to previous thinking about personality factors determining behavior. (Page 457)

10. D

Why? The MMPI asks participants to respond to questions about how they feel, think, or behave; it does not ask them to project onto a novel stimulus. The MMPI is both reliable and valid; reliability is a prerequisite to validity. (Page 460)

11. A

Why? Self-efficacy can focus on both positive and negative expectations; both optimism and self-efficacy can be learned, suggesting that they are more states than traits; both optimism and self-efficacy focus on expectations, so a passive/active distinction is not relevant. (Pages 455, 466)

12. D

Why? The psychodynamic focuses on unconscious urges; the trait approach focuses on broad, stable personality characteristics; personology focuses on life stories. (Page 463)

13. B

Why? Agreeableness refers to how easy going someone is; extraversion refers to how outgoing someone is; openness to experience refers to how open someone is to new experiences and is related to liberalness; neuroticism refers to how much someone worries; conscientiousness refers to how organized and disciplined someone is. (Page 449)

14. B

Why? Research on Type A behavior patterns reveals that hostility is the most toxic of personality characteristics. Both extraversion and conscientiousness have been linked to positive health outcomes. (Page 465)

15. C

Why? Face validity refers to how clearly the items on a test appear to be measuring the construct. Reliability refers to the extent to which a test gives consistent results; validity refers to how well the test measures what it is intended to measure. A test item can have face validity, but not be valid. Face validity is only one component of validity. A projective test asks participants to project onto a novel stimulus. (Page 459)

Chapter 12: Social Psychology

1. C

Why? Stereotypes are inaccurate generalizations about members of a group that are heuristic in nature. Stereotypes can be positive or negative. (Page 475)

2. A

Why? Research on attractiveness reveals that symmetrical, younger, and more average faces are judged as most attractive. (Page 506)

3. B

Why? The availability heuristic refers to overestimating something's frequency because of it being readily cognitively available; a stereotype is an overgeneralization about a group, whereas stereotype threat refers to behavior changing when group membership is made salient. (Page 477)

4. D

Why? Effort justification refers to feeling positively about something that took a great deal of effort; self-objectification refers to feeling like an object in the eyes of others; and the fundamental attribution error is overestimating internal traits and underestimating external conditions when explaining another person's behavior. (Page 480)

5. A

Why? Egoism ensures reciprocity in social exchanges; in other words, egoism is giving to another in order to gain something in return. (Page 484)

6. D

Why? Men are more altruistic in situations that involve danger or when men feel competent at completing a task; women are more altruistic in situations that involve nurturing. (Page 485)

7. C

Why? Explicit bias refers to prejudicial views about which people are open. Implicit bias refers to prejudicial views that are more hidden. (Page 503)

8. C

Why? Tangible assistance involves providing someone with needed goods or services; social sharing involves seeking social support by reaching out to others; informational support involves providing someone with needed information. (Page 511)

9. C

Why? Social loafing refers to people exerting less effort in the presence of larger groups; risky shift refers to groups making more extreme decisions than average; social contagion refers to imitative behavior in groups. (Page 496)

10. D

Why? A confederate plays a role in an experiment without the knowledge of the participants, as in Asch's conformity experiment. (Page 493)

11. C

Why? Groupthink involves flawed decision-making because of attempts to get along in the group; risky shift results in extreme decisions; group discord is discouraged in groupthink. (Pages 497–98)

12. C

Why? Criticalness of one's appearance in the extreme is known as body shame; internal attributions about success are known as self-serving bias; changing behavior because of fear of group generalizations is known as stereotype threat. (Page 478)

13. A

Why? Social loafing is lessened when groups are small, when the task is engaging and when people have unique contributions to make. (Page 497)

14. A

Why? Attitudes that are personally relevant, rehearsed, strong, and relevant to behavior are predictive of behaviors that are consistent with those attitudes. (Pages 480–81)

15. D

Why? The fundamental attribution error can be relevant to both positive and negative attributions about the self and others. (Page 476–77)

Chapter 13: Psychological Disorders

1. D

Why? Both obsessive-compulsive personality disorder and OCD involve anxiety, though OCD is worse. Obsessive-compulsive personality disorder does not include obsessive thoughts, though there is a preoccupation with orderliness and rules. (Page 556–57)

2. C

Why? The five axes of the *DSM-IV* classification system are: I. disorders other than personality disorders and mental retardation; II. personality disorders and mental retardation; III. medical conditions; IV. psychosocial factors; V. global assessment of functioning. (Page 526)

3. D

Why? Phobic disorder and generalized anxiety disorder can both vary in their duration; panic attacks and agoraphobia are associated most often with panic disorder rather than phobic disorder or generalized anxiety disorder. (Pages 531, 533)

4. A

Why? Generalized anxiety disorder is an anxiety disorder. (Page 531)

5. D

Why? Dissociative disorders is a category of disorders which includes dissociative fugure; dissociative amnesia involves loss of memory after a stressor; dissociative identity disorder involves multiple personalities or selves. (Page 548)

6. C

Why? The symptoms are consistent with a manic episode; in order to be diagnosed with bipolar disorder, the manic episode must last at least one week. Neither major depressive disorder nor dysthymic disorder involve manic episodes. (Page 539)

7. C

Why? Word salad refers to words strung together that do not make up a coherent thought; hallucinations refer to sensory experiences without attendant external stimuli; delusions refer to inaccurate and odd beliefs. (Page 551)

8. B

Why? Panic attacks are consistent with panic disorder; nervousness about a variety of things is consistent with generalized anxiety disorder; fear of a specific thing is consistent with phobic disorder. (Page 536)

9. B

Why? Catastrophic thinking is expecting that bad things will happen; dysthymic disorder is a disorder characterized by consistent low-grade depressive symptoms; learned helplessness is the belief that one's actions will be ineffective. (Page 542)

10. D

Why? Cognitive and behavioral symptoms of schizophrenia can be either positive or negative. (Page 551)

11. B

Why? Schizophrenia is not a personality disorder, it is an Axis I disorder. (Pages 555–56)

12. A

Why? Personality disorders are coded on Axis II. (Page 526)

13. B

Why? Adenosine deaminase and acetylcholine are neurotransmitters involved in sleep. Leptin is associated with obesity. (Page 541)

14. B

Why? Depressive episodes must last two weeks. (Page 538)

15. D

Why? Panic disorder is associated with agoraphobia because people may fear going out in public for fear of having another panic attack. (Page 532)

Chapter 14: Therapies

1. C

Why? Token economy refers to giving someone a token for engaging in desired behaviors; those tokens can then be exchanged for wanted rewards. Systematic desensitization involves teaching someone to relax in the presence of feared stimuli; cognitive restructuring refers to changing the way someone thinks about a problem. (Page 579)

2. B

Why? Recovery from PTSD may or may not result in post-traumatic growth; well-being therapy focuses on positive aspects of life rather than trauma; post-traumatic growth is about experiencing trauma and growing from it, rather than avoiding a disorder. (Page 599)

3. C

Why? Research on ethnicity and therapy indicates that a match between the therapist and the client is related to better outcomes; however, a therapist who differs from his or her client can still be effective if he or she is well-trained. (Page 591)

4. B

Why? Prozac is used to treat depression and does so by blocking reuptake of serotonin by the presynaptic neuron. (Page 567)

5. C

Why? After six months, therapy effectiveness tends to level off. (Page 594)

6. A

Why? Primary prevention is preventing an illness before it has developed; secondary prevention is focused on early intervention; community psychology focuses on all aspects of prevention, but hopes to prevent illness before it begins. (Page 591)

7. A

Why? Structural change is changing the coalitions families have formed; detriangulation is stopping scapegoating of one person by two others; validation is providing understanding and acceptance of families' problems and dynamics. (Page 589)

8. D

Why? Clinical and counseling psychologists attend graduate school in psychology; a psychiatric nurse attends graduate school in nursing. (Page 596)

9. C

Why? AA is conducted by and for persons struggling with alcoholism. (Page 590)

10. A

Why? Both individual and group therapy are effective, can use multiple theoretical approaches, and help clients learn about themselves. (Page 588)

11. B

Why? Ellis and Beck both developed cognitive therapies (Ellis's was called rational-emotive behavior therapy); Bandura developed the social cognitive approach. (Page 577)

12. B

Why? Client-centered therapy is by its nature non-directive. (Page 576)

13. C

Why? Community psychologists help people to live successfully in the community by empowering them, which means helping them develop the skills they need to take control of their own lives. (Page 591)

14. B

Why? Both monoamine oxidase inhibitors and tricyclics treat depression. (Page 571)

15. D

Why? Risperidone is used to treat schizophrenia; Prozac is used to treat depression; Xanax is used to treat anxiety. (Page 571)

Chapter 15: Health Psychology

1. C

Why? Type A is a personality topic; anxiety disorders and schizophrenia are psychological disorders topics. (Pages 608–9)

2. B

Why? Social cognitive theory focuses on the intersection of behavior, environment, and personal factors; self-determination theory focuses on internal and external motivation; stages of change model focuses on people's willingness and plans to change health behaviors. (Page 611)

3. D

Why? Precontemplation involves not being ready to change; transcendence is change that no longer requires conscious thought; action/willpower involves a commitment to change and actively working toward change. (Page 613)

4. D

Why? Health psychology focuses on the relationship between psychological factors and health; immunology is a branch of medicine that focuses on the immune system; behavioral medicine is an interdisciplinary field that focuses on the relationship between behavioral factors, biomedical factors, and health. (Page 619)

5. C

Why? In preparation/determination, people need help deciding in what type of action to engage; in maintenance, people need to avoid relapse; in contemplation, people need help evaluating the benefits of change. (Page 613)

6. C

Why? Stages of change model focuses on people's willingness and plans to change health behaviors; theory of reasoned action focuses on intentions, attitudes, and social norms; social cognitive theory focuses on the intersection of behavior, environment, and personal factors. (Page 616)

7. D

Why? Precontemplation involves not considering making a change; preparation/determination involves making concrete plans to change; action/willpower involves putting change plans into action. (Page 612)

8. A

Why? There is no evidence that stress makes people more or less likely to be near pathogens. (Pages 619–20)

9. D

Why? Condoms are very effective at preventing the spread of HIV, gonorrhea, and syphilis. Condom use helps to reduce the risk of transmitting herpes, but does not provide the same level of protection. (Page 632)

10. D

Why? Neither monogamy nor marriage ensures that someone's sexual partners are free of sexually transmitted infections, though both are preferable to having multiple sexual partners; condoms significantly reduce the transmission of sexually transmitted infections, but do not reduce the risk to zero. (Page 631)

11. C

Why? Exercise is designed to strengthen muscles and bones, and to increase flexibility. Aerobic exercise is sustained exercise that increases heart rate and respiration. (Page 622)

12. C

Why? Chronic stressors are long-lasting; a test, a fight, and a flat tire are discrete events and are known as acute stressors. (Page 619)

13. B

Why? Androgen and estrogen are sex hormones; insulin is responsible for storing sugar in cells. (Page 619)

14. B

Why? The general adaptation syndrome focuses on the body's response to stress; the stages of change model focuses on people's willingness and plans to change health behaviors; self-determination theory focuses on internal and external motivation. (Pages 608–9)

15. C

Why? Self-efficacy refers to people's views that they can successfully engage in a behavior; transcendence refers to change that no longer requires conscious thought; autonomy refers to engaging in behaviors of one's own free will. (Page 616)

Answers to the Practice Mid-term Exam

1. D

Why? Evolutionary psychology focuses on the adaptiveness of behavior; psychodynamic psychology focuses on unconscious processes and early relationships; cognitive psychology focuses on mental processes. The humanistic approach focuses on positive aspects of humans and is thus most closely associated with positive psychology. (Chapter 1, Page 7)

2. C

Why? An experimental design would require random assignment to groups and it would not be possible to assign people to have high or low SAT scores; a case-study design would only focus on one person and would only tell whether that one person demonstrated a relationship between SAT score and college GPA; a meta-analysis would examine already-completed studies to determine the size of a relationship, but would not answer new questions. (Chapter 2, Page 43)

3. C

Why? Many fields of study offer doctoral degrees, but that does not mean that every field with a doctoral degree is a science; psychology focuses on both observable behavior and unobservable mental processes; psychology is a social science but it is its use of the scientific method that makes it a science. (Chapter 2, Page 36)

4. D

Why? The .05 significance levels refers to the chances being 5% or less that the findings occurred by chance. Thus, there is a 95% chance that the findings did not occur by chance. (Chapter 2, Page 53)

5. D

Why? The peripheral nervous system takes information to and from the brain and spinal cord; the autonomic nervous system controls involuntary functioning of organs; the somatic nervous system conveys information about the skin and muscles. (Chapter 3, Page 75)

6. C

Why? The corpus callosum allows the two hemispheres of the brain to communicate; it is sometimes severed in people with severe seizure disorders. (Chapter 3, Page 94)

7. C

Why? A fixed-ratio schedule is one in which a reward is given after a certain number of behaviors occurs. A variable-ratio schedule is one in which a reward is given after an average number of behaviors occurs. A variable-interval schedule is one in which a reward is given after a variable amount of time has passed. A fixed-interval schedule is one in which a reward is given after a specific amount of time has passed. (Chapter 7, Page 277)

8. D

Why? Identity moratorium involves low commitment and high exploration; identity achievement involves high commitment and high exploration; identity diffusion involves low commitment and low exploration. (Chapter 4, Page 147)

9. A

Why? The parasympathetic nervous system calms the body; a car accident would activate the sympathetic nervous system; dopamine receptors are involved in experiencing pleasure as well as voluntary movement, attention, and mood; collateral sprouting refers to axons growing new branches. (Chapter 3, Page 82)

10. C

Why? The mean is the average score; the range is the highest and lowest scores; the median is the score that falls in the middle of the distribution. In order to see how close or far people are from average, one would need to examine a measure of dispersion, such as the standard deviation. (Chapter 2, Page 55)

11. A

Why? The inside of the neuron is negatively charged until it becomes activated, when it becomes positively charged; at that point, sodium ions, which are positively charged, enter the neuron. (Chapter 3, Pages 77–78)

12. B

Why? The postconventional stage is characterized by moral decisions being based on an evaluation of different moral codes; the preconventional stage is characterized by punishment and reward; the conventional stage is characterized by outside standards and laws. The preoperational stage is a stage of cognitive development. (Chapter 4, Page 137)

13. B

Why? Confidentiality involves keeping participant responses secret; debriefing involves telling participants of the purpose of the study after it has been completed; informed consent involves informing participants of their

role in the study and their rights; deception, on the other hand, involves not telling participants of the purpose of the study. (Chapter 2, Pages 58–59)

14. B

Why? Dating is a task associated with intimacy versus isolation; attending to an infant's needs is associated with trust versus mistrust; gaining knowledge is associated with industry versus inferiority. (Chapter 4, Page 146)

15. B

Why? The hindbrain includes the medulla, cerebellum, and pons; the forebrain includes the limbic system, thalamus, basal ganglia, and hypothalamus; the cerebral cortex contains the parietal, occipital, temporal, and frontal lobes. (Chapter 3, Page 87)

16. C

Why? The concrete operational stage involves logical, but concrete, reasoning; the sensorimotor stage involves coordination of sensory input; the preoperational stage involves using words and images to symbolize concrete objects. (Chapter 4, Page 127)

17. B

Why? Alzheimer's disease is characterized by an increase in brain plaques. (Chapter 4, Page 155)

18. A

Why? The pupil allows light into the eye; the iris controls the size of the pupil. (Chapter 5, Page 185)

19. A

Why? Weber's law states that in order for two stimuli to be detected as different, they must vary by a constant percentage; signal detection theory focuses on decisions about the presence of a stimulus in the absence of certainty. (Chapter 5, Page 178)

20. C

Why? Alpha and beta waves are present in waking; theta waves are present in light sleep. (Chapter 6, Page 234)

21. B

Why? Option A is an example of positive punishment; option C is an example of negative reinforcement; option D is an example of positive reinforcement. (Chapter 7, Page 279)

22. C

Why? The amygdala is involved in emotions; the thalamus acts as the relay station; the semicircular canals are involved in the perception of motion. (Chapter 6, Page 228)

23. D

Why? Cravings are an example of psychological dependence; someone with psychological dependence, physical dependence, or both is addicted; tolerance refers to the need to take larger amounts of the substance to achieve the same effect. (Chapter 6, Page 245)

24. D

Why? Trichromatic theory focuses on three separate receptors for color; gate control theory focuses on pain perception; parallel processing theory focuses on the processing of stimuli across different neural pathways. Opponent-process theory focuses on receptors for opposing colors, such as blue-yellow. Thus, when one receptor is activated by a color, an aftereffect of its opposite color will appear. (Chapter 5, Page 190)

25. A

Why? The pathogen is the unconditioned stimulus because it causes a reaction, in this case getting sick (the unconditioned response). If Khamla were to eat perfectly fine sea bass and feel sick, the subsequent sickness would be the conditioned response. (Chapter 7, Page 267)

26. B

Why? Focusing on cognitive processes is consistent with cognitive psychology; however, focusing on the structures of the mind is not an aspect of behavioral psychology, which focuses on observable behavior. (Chapter 1, Pages 10–11)

27. D

Why? Option A is an experimental design because it involves an experimenter assigning participants to groups; option B is a meta-analysis because it involves determining the strength of an effect in already-completed studies; option C is a case-study design because it examines one person. (Chapter 2, Page 43)

28. B

Why? Alcohol, heroin, and barbiturates are all depressants, while MDMA is a hallucinogen. (Chapter 6, Pages 246–52)

29. C

Why? High amplitude is related to loudness; low frequency is related to deeper pitch. (Chapter 6, Pages 199–200)

30. A

Why? Options B through D are related to the perception of sound, not the localization of sound. (Chapter 5, Page 204)

Answers to the Practice Final Exam

1. B

Why? The independent variable that is manipulated by the researcher is treatment. The purpose of the experiment is to determine whether the independent variable has an effect on the dependent variable of depression. In addition, the researcher is testing whether race and sex, which are also independent variables, are related to the dependent variable. (Chapter 2, Page 48)

2. C

Why? Norepinephrine increases heart rate; oxytocin is involved in love and bonding; endorphins are a natural opiate. (Chapter 3, Page 99)

3. B

Why? The parietal lobe is involved in spatial recognition and motor control; the occipital lobe is involved in vision; the frontal lobe is involved in intelligence and personality. (Chapter 3, Page 92)

4. A

Why? The concrete operational stage involves using logic to solve concrete problems; crystallized intelligence includes accumulated life experiences; the preoperational stage involves using words and symbols to represent objects. (Chapter 4, Page 156)

5. B

Why? Authoritative parenting is high in control and high in supportiveness; neglectful parenting is low in control and low in supportiveness. (Chapter 4, Page 133)

6. C

Why? The fovea only contains cones, but the retina contains both rods and cones. (Chapter 5, Page 186)

7. C

Why? Giftedness is defined as an IQ of 130 or higher, whereas mental retardation is defined as an IQ of 70 or lower. One standard deviation above the mean is 115 and two standard deviations above the mean is 130. (Chapter 9, Page 364)

8. A

Why? A morpheme is the smallest part of language that is meaningful; syntax is the rules for putting together words to make sentences; semantics is the meaning of words and sentences. (Chapter 9, Page 373)

9. C

Why? A prototype model compares something to an exemplar; schemas are structures for interpreting events; an algorithm is a strategy to solve an answerable problem. (Chapter 9, Page 351)

10. C

Why? Anorexia nervosa is associated with lower than normal weight. (Chapter 10, Page 397)

11. B

Why? A stereotype is a generalization about a group of people; self-serving bias is the tendency to attribute personal success to internal factors; the self-fulfilling prophecy is the change in behavior that occurs as a result of expectations. (Chapter 9, Page 357)

12. B

Why? Men and women show many similarities in their sexual response patterns, but men have a refractory period in which they must wait before reaching orgasm again. (Chapter 10, Page 400)

13. A

Why? The Cannon-Bard theory states that emotion and physiological arousal happen simultaneously. Neither theory states that emotion occurs before physiological arousal. (Chapter 10, Page 417)

14. D

Why? Agreeableness is related to being helpful toward and caring about others and is thus the trait most closely associated with altruism. (Chapter 11, Page 449)

15. B

Why? The TAT is a projective test that asks participants to tell a story about a novel stimulus and allows the tester to understand the stories someone tells to make sense of the world, a main tenet of personology. (Chapter 11, Page 462)

16. B

Why? The self-fulfilling prophecy refers to behavior changing based on expectation; stereotypes are generalizations about a group of people;

self-serving bias is the tendency to attribute personal success to internal factors. (Chapter 12, Pages 476–77)

17. A

Why? Risky shift is groups making more extreme decisions; group polarization is the will of the group becoming stronger concerning a decision; groupthink is going along with the group to quell conflict. (Chapter 12, Page 495)

18. C

Why? Prejudice is a negative view of someone from an other group; a stereotype is a generalization about a group; bystander effect is the tendency for people in groups to be less likely to engage in altruistic behavior than when alone. (Chapter 12, Page 503)

19. B

Why? Active coping strategies are aimed at tackling the stressor head-on; exercise, though a healthy activity, is not a way to actively approach a test. (Chapter 9, Page 382)

20. C

Why? Maintenance involves maintaining healthy behaviors once they are started; contemplation involves considering making a health change; preparation/determination involves making plans to start a health behavior. (Chapter 15, Page 613)

21. B

Why? Cognitive behavioral therapy is focused on changing behavioral and thought patterns; psychodynamic therapy is focused on unresolved unconscious conflicts or early childhood relationships; behavioral therapy is focused on changing behaviors. (Chapter 14, Page 577)

22. D

Why? Both counseling and clinical psychologists have doctoral degrees from graduate schools; in most cases, neither can prescribe medication. (Chapter 14, Page 596)

23. B

Why? Behavioral therapy assumes problems are the result of operant or classical learning; psychodynamic therapy assumes problems are the result of unconscious conflicts or early relationships; humanistic therapy assumes problems are the result of being inauthentic and lacking positive regard from others. (Chapter 14, Page 585)

24. A

Why? Meditation is a type of mindfulness that is related to increased well-being. Each of the other treatments focuses on fixing something that is wrong with the individual. Positive psychology has a focus on accentuating strengths rather than a focus on treating disorders. (Chapter 6, Page 257)

25. C

Why? The evolutionary approach focuses on the historical adaptiveness of behaviors; behavioral psychology focuses on observable behavior and the effects of pairing stimuli with outcomes; psychodynamic psychology focuses on unconscious thought processes and early childhood relationships. (Chapter 1, Page 15)

26. B

Why? The beginning of the semester would be the alarm stage, in which the body's resistance to illness is lessened; the middle of the semester would be in the resistance stage, in which the body's defenses are working well. At the end of the semester, exhaustion would begin and the body's defenses would weaken. When the stressor abruptly stops, the exhaustion phase will be in full swing. (Chapter 15, Page 619)

27. A

Why? Free association is a psychodynamic therapy technique. (Chapter 14, Page 574)

28. D

Why? Learned helplessness is a cognitive process; thus, the cognitive approach would be consistent with learned helplessness. (Chapter 13, Page 542)

29. C

Why? None of the other theories are discussed in the text in the context of hypnosis. Cognitive theory focuses on thought processes; behavioral theory focuses on operant and classical conditioning; psychodynamic theory focuses on unconscious drives and early relationships. (Chapter 6, Page 243)

30. B

Why? Schizotypal personality disorder is a personality disorder and, as such, does not imply as severe a disruption of functioning. (Chapter 13, Page 556)

31. A

Why? Research reveals that those who attempt and those who complete suicide have lower levels of serotonin. (Chapter 13, Page 546)

32. B

Why? Waxy flexibility is sometimes seen in persons with schizophrenia and refers to the phenomenon of moving a person's limb and the limb staying in that position. (Chapter 13, Page 552)

33. B

Why? Schizoid personality is associated with social withdrawal; therefore, persons with schizoid personality would be low in extraversion. (Chapter 13, Page 556)

34. B

Why? Benzodiazepines are used to treat anxiety. (Chapter 14, Page 566)

35. B

Why? Behavior is something that can be directly observed, whereas motives, thoughts, and feelings cannot. (Chapter 9, Page 350)

36. D

Why? Only an experimental design allows a researcher to determine causality because experimental designs involve random assignment to groups and manipulation of an independent variable. (Chapter 2, Page 48)

37. B

Why? Health psychologists focus on the intersection of the psychological and physical processes; a clinical psychologist focuses on treating mental disorders; an environmental psychologist focuses on the way in which physical environments affect people's mental processes. (Chapter 1, Page 20)

38. A

Why? Prozac is a selective serotonin reuptake inhibitor that increases the amount of serotonin in the brain; an antagonist blocks the action of a neurotransmitter. (Chapter 14, Page 567)

39. B

Why? Papillae are involved in taste perception; the basilar membrane is involved in auditory perception; the cornea is involved in visual perception. (Chapter 5, Page 213)

40. B

Why? Both daydreaming and watching television are examples of a lower-level of consciousness; being anesthetized is an example of no awareness. (Chapter 6, Page 224)

41. C

Why? Discrimination refers to responding to specific stimuli, but not to others; generalization refers to responding to similar stimuli in the same way as the conditioned stimulus. (Chapter 7, Pages 267–68)

42. D

Why? Instinctive drift refers to instincts interfering with learning; acquisition refers to initial learning; expectancy learning refers to the organism's expectancies influencing learning. (Chapter 7, Page 267)

43. D

Why? Conditioned and unconditioned stimuli are facets of classical conditioning; the law of effect refers to operant conditioning. (Chapter 7, Page 273)

44. C

Why? Iconic memory is sensory memory for images; echoic memory is sensory memory for auditory stimuli; the visuospatial working memory is the area of working memory that stores visual and spatial information. (Chapter 8, Page 312)

45. B

Why? Implicit memory, also known as nondeclarative memory, is memory for skills; explicit memory is a type of long-term memory; iconic and echoic memory is sensory memory. (Chapter 8, Pages 314–15)

46. C

Why? Decay refers to the diminishment of a memory trace; transience is forgetting over time; retroactive interference refers to information that was learned later interfering with recall of information that was learned earlier. (Chapter 8, Page 334)

47. C

Why? Hostility is associated with coronary heart disease and was found to be the carcinogenic aspect of Type A behavior patterns. (Chapter 11, Page 465)

48. D

Why? Relatedness refers to the need to connect to others. Self-actualization is not a need in self-determination theory; rather, it is part of Maslow's hierarchy of needs. Autonomy refers to the need to be independent. (Chapter 10, Page 407)

49. C

Why? Projection refers to attributing a personal need or shortcoming to others; denial refers to failing to acknowledge that something exists; displacement refers to taking feelings out on a more acceptable object. (Chapter 11, Page 438)

50. D

Why? Serial position effect refers to the tendency to have the best recall for items at the end of a list, followed by those at the beginning of a list, and then finally those in the middle of a list. (Chapter 8, Page 324)

A

abnormal behavior Behavior that is deviant, maladaptive, or personally distressful over a long period of time. p. 521

absolute threshold The minimum amount of stimulus energy that a person can detect. p. 176

accommodation An individual's adjustment of a schema to new information. p. 125

acquired immune deficiency syndrome (AIDS) A disease caused by the human immunodeficiency virus (HIV), a sexually transmitted infection that destroys the body's immune system. p. 630

acquisition (classical conditioning) The initial learning of the stimulus–response link, which involves a neutral stimulus being associated with an unconditioned stimulus and becoming the conditioned stimulus that elicits the conditioned response. p. 267

action potential The brief wave of electrical charge that sweeps down the axon during the transmission of a nerve impulse. p. 79

activation-synthesis theory Theory stating that dreaming occurs when the cerebral cortex synthesizes neural signals generated from activity in the lower part of the brain. p. 240

addiction Either a physical or a psychological dependence, or both, on a drug. p. 245

adrenal glands Important endocrine glands that are instrumental in regulating moods, energy level, and the ability to cope with stress. p. 99

aerobic exercise Sustained exercise, such as jogging, swimming, or cycling, that stimulates heart and lung functioning. p. 621

affectionate love Also called companionate love; the type of love that occurs when individuals desire to have the other person near and have a deep, caring affection for the person. p. 508

afferent nerves Sensory nerves that transport information to the brain. p. 74

agonist A drug that mimics or increases a neurotransmitter's effects. p. 82

agoraphobia A cluster of fears centered on public places and on an inability to escape or to find help should one become incapacitated. p. 533

alcoholism A disorder that involves long-term, repeated, uncontrolled, compulsive, and excessive use of alcoholic beverages and that impairs the drinker's health and social relationships. p. 248

algorithms Strategies that guarantee a solution to a problem. p. 353

all-or-none principle Once an electrical impulse reaches a certain level of intensity, it fires and moves all the way down the axon without losing any of its intensity. p. 79

altruism An unselfish interest in helping someone else. p. 484

amnesia The loss of memory. p. 337

androgens The class of sex hormones that predominate in males; they are produced by the testes in males and by the adrenal glands in both males and females. p. 139, 399

anorexia nervosa An eating disorder that involves the relentless pursuit of thinness through starvation. p. 396

antagonist A drug that blocks a neurotransmitter's effects. p. 82

anterograde amnesia A memory disorder that affects the retention of new information and events. p. 337

antianxiety drugs Commonly known as tranquilizers; drugs that reduce anxiety by making individuals calmer and less excitable. p. 566

antidepressant drugs Drugs that regulate mood. p. 566

antipsychotic drugs Powerful drugs that diminish agitated behavior, reduce tension, decrease hallucinations, improve social behavior, and produce better sleep patterns in people who have a severe psychological disorder, especially schizophrenia. p. 568

anxiety disorders Psychological disorders that feature motor tension, hyperactivity, and apprehensive expectations and thoughts. p. 531

apparent movement The perception that a stationary object is moving. p. 195

applied behavior analysis (behavior modification) The application of operant conditioning principles to change human behavior. p. 295

approach coping Directly confronting a problem with active attempts to solve it. p. 382

archetypes The name Jung gave to the emotionally laden ideas and images that have rich and symbolic meaning for all people. p. 440

artificial intelligence (AI) The science of creating machines capable of performing activities that require intelligence when they are done by people. p. 349

assimilation An individual's incorporation of new information into existing knowledge. p. 125

association cortex Region of the cerebral cortex in which the highest intellectual functions, including thinking and problem solving, occur; also called association areas. p. 94

associative learning Learning in which a connection, or an association, is made between two events. p. 264

Atkinson-Shiffrin theory The view that memory storage involves three separate systems: sensory memory, short-term memory, and long-term memory. p. 309

attachment The close emotional bond between an infant and its caregiver. p. 131

attention deficit hyperactivity disorder (ADHD) Psychological disorder in which the individual shows one or more of the following characteristics over a period of time: inattention, hyperactivity, and impulsivity. p. 528

attitudes Opinions and beliefs about people, objects, and ideas. p. 479

attribution theory Theory that views people as motivated to discover the underlying causes of behavior as part of their effort to make sense of the behavior. p. 476

auditory nerve Nerve that carries neural impulses to the brain's auditory areas. p. 204

authoritarian parenting A restrictive, punitive parenting style in which the parent exhorts the child to follow the parent's directions and to value hard work and effort. p. 133

authoritative parenting A parenting style that encourages children's independence (but still places limits and controls on their behavior); it includes extensive verbal give-and-take, and warm and nurturing interactions with the child. p. 133

autobiographical memory A special form of episodic memory consisting of a person's recollections of his or her life experiences. p. 326

automatic processes States of consciousness that require little attention and do not interfere with other ongoing activities. p. 224

autonomic nervous system The division of the peripheral nervous system that communicates with the body's internal organs. It consists of the sympathetic and parasympathetic nervous systems. p. 74

availability heuristic A prediction about the probability of an event based on the ease of recalling or imagining similar events. p. 357

aversive conditioning (classical conditioning) Treatment that consists of repeated pairings of the undesirable behavior with aversive stimuli to decrease the behavior's rewards. p. 579

avoidant coping   Coping with a problem by trying one's best to ignore it. p. 382

axon   The part of the neuron that carries information away from the cell body to other cells. p. 77

B

barbiturates   Depressant drugs that decrease the activity of the central nervous system. p. 248

basal ganglia   Large clusters of neurons, located above the thalamus and under the cerebral cortex, that work with the cerebellum and the cerebral cortex to control and coordinate voluntary movements. p. 89

behavior   Everything we do that can be directly observed. p. 5

behavior therapies   Therapies that use principles of learning to reduce or eliminate maladaptive behavior. p. 578

behavioral approach   A psychological perspective emphasizing the scientific study of observable behavioral responses and their environmental determinants. p. 13

behavioral medicine   An interdisciplinary field that focuses on developing and integrating behavioral and biomedical knowledge to promote health and reduce illness. p. 608

behaviorism   A theory of learning that focuses solely on observable behaviors, discounting the importance of such mental activity as thinking, wishing, and hoping. p. 264

big five factors of personality   The "supertraits" that are thought to describe the main dimensions of personality—specifically, neuroticism (emotional instability), extraversion, openness to experience, agreeableness, and conscientiousness. p. 449

binding   The bringing together and integration of what is processed through different pathways or cells. p. 188

binocular cues   Depth cues that are based on the combination of the images on the left and right eyes and on the way the two eyes work together. p. 192

biological approach   A psychological perspective that examines behavior and mental processes through a focus on the body, especially the brain and nervous system. p. 12

biological rhythms   Periodic physiological fluctuations in the body. p. 228

biological therapies   Treatments to reduce or eliminate the symptoms of psychological disorders by altering the way an individual's body functions. p. 566

bipolar disorder   A mood disorder characterized by extreme mood swings that include one or more episodes of mania (an overexcited, unrealistically optimistic state). p. 539

bottom-up processing   Processing that begins with sensory receptors registering environmental

information and sending it to the brain for analysis and interpretation. p. 173

brain stem   The region of the brain that includes most of the hindbrain (excluding the cerebellum) and the midbrain. p. 87

broaden-and-build model   A model emphasizing that the key to the adaptiveness of positive emotional states lies in their effects on our attention and our ability to build resources. p. 425

bulimia nervosa   An eating disorder in which the individual consistently follows a binge-and-purge eating pattern. p. 396

bystander effect   The tendency of an individual who observes an emergency to help less when other people are present than when the observer is alone. p. 485

C

Cannon-Bard theory   Theory stating that emotion and physiological reactions occur simultaneously. p. 417

case study   An in-depth look at a single individual; also known as a case history. p. 42

catatonia   A state of immobility and unresponsiveness. p. 551

catatonic schizophrenia   A type of schizophrenia characterized by bizarre motor behavior that sometimes takes the form of a completely immobile stupor. p. 552

catharsis   The release of anger or aggressive energy by directly or vicariously engaging in anger or aggression; the catharsis hypothesis states that behaving angrily or watching others behave angrily reduces subsequent anger. p. 426

cell body   The part of the neuron that contains the nucleus, which directs the manufacture of substances that the neuron needs for growth and maintenance. p. 76

central nervous system (CNS)   The brain and spinal cord. p. 74

cerebral cortex   Highest level of the forebrain, where the highest mental functions, such as thinking and planning, take place. p. 90

chromosomes   Threadlike structures that contain genes and DNA. Humans have 23 chromosome pairs in the nucleus of every cell. Each parent contributes one chromosome to each pair. p. 103

circadian rhythm   A daily behavioral or physiological cycle, such as the sleep/wake cycle. p. 228

classical conditioning   Learning by which a neutral stimulus becomes associated with a meaningful stimulus and acquires the capacity to elicit a similar response. p. 266

classical model   Model stating that all instances of a concept share defining properties. p. 351

client-centered therapy   Rogers's humanistic therapy in which the therapist provides a warm, supportive atmosphere to improve the client's

self-concept and encourage the client to gain insight about problems. p. 576

cognition   The way in which information is processed and manipulated in remembering, thinking, and knowing. p. 350

cognitive affective processing systems (CAPS)   According to Mischel, a set of interconnected cognitive systems through which an individual's thoughts and emotions about self and the world become linked in ways that matter to behavior. p. 457

cognitive appraisal   Individuals' interpretation of the events in their lives as harmful, threatening, or challenging and their determination of whether they have the resources to cope effectively with the events. p. 380

cognitive approach   A psychological perspective that focuses on the mental processes involved in knowing: how we direct our attention, perceive, remember, think, and solve problems. p. 14

cognitive dissonance   A concept developed by Festinger; an individual's psychological discomfort (dissonance) caused by two inconsistent thoughts. p. 480

cognitive theory of dreaming   Theory proposing that dreaming can be understood by applying the same cognitive concepts that are used in studying the waking mind. p. 239

cognitive therapies   Therapies emphasizing that individuals' cognitions, or thoughts, are the main source of abnormal behavior and psychological problems. p. 581

cognitive-behavior therapy   Therapy consisting of a combination of cognitive therapy and behavior therapy; self-efficacy is an important goal of cognitive-behavior therapy. p. 583

collective unconscious   Jung's term for the impersonal, deepest layer of the unconscious mind, shared by all human beings because of their common ancestral past. p. 440

concepts   Mental categories that are used to group objects, events, and characteristics. p. 350

concrete operational stage   The third Piagetian stage of cognitive development (approximately 7 to 11 years of age), in which thought becomes operational and intuitive reasoning is replaced by logical reasoning in concrete situations. p. 126

conditioned response (CR)   The learned response to the conditioned stimulus that occurs after the pairing of a conditioned stimulus and an unconditioned stimulus. p. 267

conditioned stimulus (CS)   A previously neutral stimulus that eventually elicits the conditioned response after being associated with the unconditioned stimulus. p. 267

cones   The receptors in the retina that process information about color. p. 186

confederate   A person who is given a role to play in a study so that social context can be manipulated. p. 493

confirmation bias   The tendency to search for and use information that supports, rather than refutes, our ideas. p. 356

conformity   Change in a person's behavior to coincide more closely with a group standard. p. 492

connectionism (parallel distributed processing—PDP)   The theory that memory is stored throughout the brain in connections between neurons, several of which may work together to process a single memory. p. 319

consciousness   Awareness of external events and internal sensations, including awareness of the self and thoughts about one's experiences; this awareness occurs under a condition of arousal. p. 222

control group   A comparison group that is as much like the experimental group as possible and is treated in every way like the experimental group except for the manipulated factor. p. 48

controlled processes   The most alert states of consciousness. p. 224

convergent thinking   Thinking that produces one correct answer; characteristic of the type of thinking required on traditional intelligence tests. p. 359

coping   Managing taxing circumstances, expending effort to solve life's problems, and seeking to master or reduce stress. p. 381

corpus callosum   The large bundle of axons that connects the brain's two hemispheres. p. 93

correlational research   A research strategy that identifies the relationships between two or more variables in order to describe how these variables change together. p. 43

counterconditioning   A classical conditioning procedure for weakening a conditioned response by associating the fear-provoking stimulus with a new response that is incompatible with the fear. p. 270

couples therapy   Group therapy with married or unmarried couples whose major problem lies within their relationship. p. 589

creativity   The ability to think about something in novel and unusual ways and come up with unconventional solutions to problems. p. 359

critical thinking   The process of thinking reflectively and productively, as well as evaluating evidence. p. 6

crystallized intelligence   An individual's accumulated information and verbal skills. p. 155

culture-fair tests   Intelligence tests that are intended to be culturally unbiased. p. 367

D

decay theory   Theory stating that when something new is learned, a neurochemical memory

trace is formed, but over time this trace tends to disintegrate. p. 335

decision making   Evaluating alternatives and making choices among them. p. 356

deductive reasoning   Reasoning from the general to the specific. p. 355

defense mechanisms   The ego's protective methods for reducing anxiety by unconsciously distorting reality. p. 438

deindividuation   The reduction of personal identity and erosion of the sense of personal responsibility that can arise when one is part of a group. p. 495

delusions   False, sometimes even preposterous, beliefs that are not part of the person's culture. p. 551

dendrites   Branches of a neuron that receive and orient information toward the cell body; most neurons have numerous dendrites. p. 76

deoxyribonucleic acid (DNA)   A complex molecule that contains genetic information; makes up chromosomes. p. 103

dependent variable   A factor that can change in an experiment in response to changes in the independent variable. p. 48

depressants   Psychoactive drugs that slow down mental and physical activity. p. 247

depressive disorders   Mood disorders in which the individual suffers from depression (an unrelenting lack of pleasure in life). p. 538

depth perception   The ability to perceive objects three dimensionally. p. 191

descriptive statistics   Mathematical procedures that are used to describe and summarize sets of data in a meaningful way. p. 54

development   The pattern of continuity and change in human capabilities that occurs throughout the course of life. p. 116

diathesis-stress model   A model of schizophrenia that proposes a combination of biogenetic disposition and stress as the cause of the disorder. p. 554

difference threshold   The smallest difference in stimulation required to discriminate one stimulus from another 50 percent of the time; also called just noticeable difference. p. 177

discrimination   In social psychology, an unjustified negative or harmful action toward a member of a group simply because he or she is a member of that group. p. 503

discrimination (classical conditioning)   The process of learning to respond to certain stimuli and not to others. p. 268

discrimination (operant conditioning)   The tendency to respond to stimuli that signal that a behavior will or will not be reinforced. p. 278

disorganized schizophrenia   A type of schizophrenia in which an individual has delusions and

hallucinations that have little or no recognizable meaning. p. 552

display rules   Sociocultural standards that determine when, where, and how emotions should be expressed. p. 423

dissociative amnesia   A dissociative disorder involving extreme memory loss caused by extensive psychological stress. p. 548

dissociative disorders   Psychological disorders that involve a sudden loss of memory or change in identity. p. 548

dissociative fugue   A dissociative disorder in which the individual not only develops amnesia but also unexpectedly travels away from home and assumes a new identity. p. 548

dissociative identity disorder (DID)   Formerly called multiple personality disorder, this is the most dramatic but least common dissociative disorder; individuals suffering from this disorder have two or more distinct personalities or selves. p. 548

distributional error   A common error in performance ratings, so called because it refers to ratings that fail to use the entire rating scale. p. 500

divergent thinking   Thinking that produces many answers to the same question; characteristic of creativity. p. 359

dominant-recessive genes principle   The principle that, if one gene of a pair governing a given characteristic (such as eye color) is dominant and one is recessive, the dominant gene overrides the recessive gene. A recessive gene exerts its influence only if both genes in a pair are recessive. p. 103

double-blind experiment   An experiment that is conducted so that neither the experimenter nor the participants are aware of which participants are in the experimental group and which are in the control group until after the results are calculated. p. 49

dream analysis   The psychotherapeutic technique used to interpret a person's dream. Psychoanalysts believe that dreams contain information about the individual's unconscious thoughts and conflicts. p. 574

drive   An aroused state that occurs because of a physiological need. p. 391

DSM-IV   Abbreviation for the *Diagnostic and Statistical Manual of Mental Disorders*, Fourth Edition; the current version of the APA's major classification of psychological disorders. p. 526

dysthymic disorder   A depressive disorder that is generally more chronic and has fewer symptoms than major depressive disorder. p. 539

E

ecological validity   The extent to which an experimental design is representative of the real-world issues it is supposed to address. p. 48

efferent nerves Motor nerves that carry the brain's output. p. 74

ego The Freudian structure of personality that deals with the demands of reality. p. 438

egoism Giving to another person to ensure reciprocity; to gain self-esteem; to present oneself as powerful, competent, or caring; or to avoid social and self-censure for failing to live up to society's expectations. p. 484

elaboration Extensiveness of processing at any given level of memory. p. 307

elaboration likelihood model Theory identifying two ways by which a communication can be persuasive—a central route and a peripheral route. p. 482

electroconvulsive therapy (ECT) Commonly called shock therapy; a treatment used for severely depressed individuals that causes a seizure to occur in the brain. p. 571

emerging adulthood The transition from adolescence to adulthood. p. 150

emotion Feeling, or affect, that can involve physiological arousal, conscious experience, and behavioral expression. p. 415

emotion-focused coping Responding to the emotional aspects of stress rather than focusing on the problem causing the stress. p. 381

empathy A feeling of oneness with the emotional state of another person. p. 485

empirically keyed test A type of test that presents a host of questionnaire items to groups of people who are already known to differ in some central way (such as individuals with a psychological disorder versus mentally healthy individuals). p. 459

encoding The process by which information gets into memory storage. p. 305

endocrine system A set of glands that regulate the activities of certain organs by releasing their chemical products (hormones) into the bloodstream. p. 98

episodic memory The retention of information about the where, when, and what of life's happenings. p. 314

estrogens The main class of female sex hormones, produced principally by the ovaries. p. 139, 399

ethnic gloss Using an ethnic label, such as "African American" or "Latino," in a superficial way that portrays the ethnic group as more homogeneous than it really is. p. 62

ethnocentrism The tendency to favor one's own ethnic group over other groups. p. 500

evolutionary approach A psychological perspective that uses evolutionary ideas such as adaptation, reproduction, and "survival of the fittest" as the basis for explaining specific human behaviors. p. 15

exercise Structured activities whose goal is to improve health. p. 621

experiment A carefully regulated procedure in which one or more variables believed to influence the behavior being studied are manipulated while all other variables are held constant. p. 48

experimental group A group in the research study whose experience is manipulated. p. 48

experimenter bias The influence of the experimenter's own expectations on the outcome of the research. p. 49

expertise The quality of having a particular talent—that "something special"—for the things that one does in a particular domain. p. 363

explicit memory (declarative memory) The conscious recollection of information, such as specific facts or events and, at least in humans, information that can be verbally communicated. p. 314

extinction (classical conditioning) The weakening of the conditioned response in the absence of the unconditioned stimulus. p. 268

extinction (operant conditioning) The situation where, because a previously reinforced behavior is no longer reinforced, there is a decreased tendency to perform the behavior. p. 279

extrinsic motivation Motivation that involves external incentives such as rewards and punishments. p. 409

F

face validity The extent to which a test item appears to be valid to those who are completing it. p. 459

facial feedback hypothesis The idea that facial expressions can influence emotions as well as reflect them. p. 421

false consensus effect Overestimation of the degree to which everybody else thinks or acts the way we do, stemming from the use of our own outlook or situation to predict that of others. p. 477

family therapy Group therapy with family members. p. 589

feature detectors Neurons in the brain's visual system that respond to particular features of a stimulus. p. 187

figure-ground relationship Principle by which individuals organize the perceptual field into stimuli that stand out (figure) and those that are left over (background, or ground). p. 191

fixation Using a prior problem-solving strategy and failing to look at a problem from a fresh, new perspective. p. 354

flashbulb memory The memory of emotionally significant events that people often recall more accurately and vividly than everyday events. p. 328

flat affect A negative symptom in which the person shows little or no emotion, speaks without

emotional inflection, and maintains an immobile facial expression. p. 552

fluid intelligence An individual's ability to reason abstractly. p. 155

forebrain The highest level of the brain. Key structures in the forebrain are the limbic system, thalamus, basal ganglia, hypothalamus, and cerebral cortex. p. 88

formal operational stage The fourth and final Piagetian stage of cognitive development (emerging from about 11 to 15 years of age), in which thinking becomes more abstract, idealistic, and logical. p. 127

free association The psychoanalytic technique of having individuals say aloud whatever comes to mind. p. 574

frequency theory Theory stating that perception of a sound's frequency depends on how often the auditory nerve fires. p. 203

frontal lobe The part of the cerebral cortex just behind the forehead that is involved in the control of voluntary muscles, intelligence, and personality. p. 92

functional fixedness A type of fixation in which individuals fail to solve a problem because they are fixated on a thing's usual functions. p. 354

functionalism An early school of psychology that was concerned with the functions and purposes of the mind and behavior in individuals' adaptation to the environment. p. 10

fundamental attribution error The tendency for observers to overestimate the importance of internal traits and underestimate the importance of external situations when they seek explanations of an actor's behavior. p. 476

G

gate-control theory of pain The spinal column contains a neural gate that can be open (allowing the perception of pain) or closed (blocking the perception of pain). p. 209

gender roles Expectations for how females and males should think, act, and feel. p. 140

general adaptation syndrome (GAS) Selye's term for the common effects on the body when demands are placed on it. The GAS consists of three stages: alarm, resistance, and exhaustion. p. 619

generalization (classical conditioning) The tendency of a new stimulus that is similar to the original conditioned stimulus to elicit a response that is similar to the conditioned response. p. 268

generalization (operant conditioning) The tendency to give the same response to similar stimuli. p. 278

generalized anxiety disorder An anxiety disorder that consists of persistent anxiety for at least 6 months; the individual with this disorder cannot specify the reasons for the anxiety. p. 531

genes   The units of hereditary information. They are short segments of chromosomes, composed of DNA. p. 103

genotype   An individual's genetic heritage; his or her actual genetic material. p. 107

gestalt psychology   School of psychology emphasizing that people naturally organize their perceptions according to certain patterns. p. 191

gestalt therapy   Perls's humanistic therapy in which the therapist challenges clients to help them become more aware of their feelings and face their problems. p. 577

gifted   Descriptive of individuals who have an IQ of 130 or higher and/or superior talent in a particular area. p. 369

glial cells   Cells that provide support and nutritional benefits in the nervous system. p. 76

group polarization effect   The solidification and further strengthening of an individual's position as a consequence of a group discussion. p. 497

groupthink   Group members' impaired decision making and avoidance of realistic appraisal to maintain group harmony. p. 497

H

habituation   Decreased responsiveness to a stimulus after repeated presentations. Habituation is used in infant research to examine if an infant can discriminate between an old stimulus and a new one. p. 123

hallucinations   Sensory experiences in the absence of real stimuli. p. 551

hallucinogens   Psychoactive drugs that modify a person's perceptual experiences and produce visual images that are not real. p. 251

hardiness   A trait characterized by a sense of commitment and control and a perception of problems as challenges rather than threats. p. 466

health behaviors   Practices that have an impact on physical well-being. p. 611

health psychology   A field that emphasizes psychology's role in establishing and maintaining health and in preventing and treating illness. p. 608

heritability   The proportion of the IQ differences in a population that is attributed to genetic differences. p. 367

heuristics   Shortcut strategies or guidelines that suggest, but do not guarantee, a solution to a problem. p. 353

hierarchy of needs   Maslow's view that individuals' main needs are satisfied in the following sequence: physiological, safety, love and belongingness, esteem, and self-actualization. p. 407

hindbrain   The lowest portion of the brain, consisting of the medulla, cerebellum, and pons. p. 87

hindsight bias   The tendency to report falsely, after the fact, that we accurately predicted an outcome. p. 357

homeostasis   The body's tendency to maintain an equilibrium, or a steady state. p. 391

hormones   Chemical messengers manufactured by the endocrine glands. p. 98

human sexual response pattern   Identified by Masters and Johnson, the four phases of physical reactions that occur in humans as a result of sexual stimulation. These phases are excitement, plateau, orgasm, and resolution. p. 399

humanistic approach   A psychological perspective that emphasizes a person's positive qualities, capacity for positive growth, and the freedom to choose any destiny. p. 14

humanistic perspectives   Views of personality that stress the person's capacity for personal growth, freedom to choose a destiny, and positive qualities. p. 443

humanistic therapies   Therapies that encourage clients to understand themselves and to grow personally. The humanistic therapies are unique in their emphasis on self-healing capacities. p. 576

hypnosis   An altered state of consciousness or simply a psychological state of altered attention and expectation, in which the individual is unusually receptive to suggestions. p. 241

hypothalamus   Small forebrain structure involved in regulating eating, drinking, and sex; directing the endocrine system; and monitoring emotion, stress, and reward. p. 89

hypothesis   An idea that is arrived at logically from a theory. It is a prediction that can be tested. p. 37

I

id   The Freudian structure of personality that consists of unconscious drives and is the individual's reservoir of psychic energy. p. 437

identity versus identity confusion   Erikson's fifth psychological stage in which adolescents face the challenge of finding out who they are, what they are all about, and where they are going in life. p. 146

implementation intentions   Specific strategies (such as setting specific plans and goals) for dealing with the challenges of making a life change. p. 616

implicit memory (nondeclarative memory)   Memory in which behavior is affected by prior experience without that experience being consciously recollected. p. 315

independent variable   The manipulated experimental factor in an experiment. p. 48

individual psychology   The term for Adler's approach, which views people as motivated by

purposes and goals and as striving for perfection over pleasure. p. 442

inductive reasoning   Reasoning from the specific to the general or from the bottom-up. p. 355

indulgent parenting   A parenting style in which parents are involved with their children but place few limits on them. p. 133

inferential statistics   Mathematical methods that are used to indicate whether data sufficiently support or confirm a research hypothesis. p. 56

infinite generativity   The ability to produce an infinite number of sentences using a relatively limited set of rules. p. 372

informational social influence   The influence other people have on us because we want to be right. p. 493

inner ear   Consists of oval window, cochlea, and basilar membrane. p. 201

insight learning   A form of problem solving in which the organism develops a sudden insight into or understanding of the problem's solution. p. 289

insight therapy   A therapy that encourages insight and self-awareness; includes the psychodynamic and humanistic therapies. p. 574

instinct   An innate (unlearned), biological pattern of behavior that is assumed to be universal throughout a species. p. 390

instinctive drift   The tendency of animals to revert to instinctive behavior that interferes with learning. p. 290

integrative therapy   A combination of techniques from different therapies based on the therapist's judgment of which particular techniques will provide the greatest benefit for the client. p. 595

intelligence   Problem-solving skills and the ability to adapt to and learn from life's everyday experiences. p. 363

intelligence quotient (IQ)   An individual's mental age divided by chronological age multiplied by 100. p. 364

interference theory   Theory stating that people forget not because memories are lost from storage but because other information gets in the way of what they want to remember. p. 334

internal validity   The extent to which changes in the dependent variable are due to the manipulation of the independent variable. p. 48

intrinsic motivation   Motivation that is based on internal factors such as organism needs (autonomy, competence, and relatedness), as well as curiosity, challenge, and effort. p. 409

investment model   A model emphasizing the ways that commitment, investment, and the availability of attractive alternative partners predict satisfaction and stability in relationships. p. 509

J

James-Lange theory   Theory stating that emotion results from physiological states triggered by stimuli in the environment. p. 417

K

kinesthetic senses   Senses that provide information about movement, posture, and orientation. p. 213

L

language   A form of communication, whether spoken, written, or signed, that is based on a system of symbols. p. 372

latent learning (implicit learning)   Unreinforced learning that is not immediately reflected in behavior. p. 288

law of effect   Thorndike's principle that behaviors followed by positive outcomes are strengthened, whereas behaviors followed by negative outcomes are weakened. p. 273

learned helplessness   The phenomenon of learning through experience that outcomes are not controllable. p. 292

learning   A relatively permanent change in behavior that occurs through experience. p. 264

levels of processing   The idea that coding occurs on a continuum from shallow to deep, with deeper processing producing better memory. p. 306

limbic system   Loosely connected network of structures—including the amygdala and hippocampus—that play important roles in memory and emotion. p. 89

lithium   A drug that is widely used to treat bipolar disorder. p. 568

longitudinal design   A special kind of systematic observation that involves obtaining measures of the variables of interest in multiple waves over time. p. 47

long-term memory   A relatively permanent type of memory that stores huge amounts of information for a long time. p. 314

M

major depressive disorder (MDD)   A mood disorder indicated by a major depressive episode and depressed characteristics, such as lethargy and hopelessness, lasting at least 2 weeks. p. 538

mean   A statistical measure of central tendency that is calculated by adding all the scores and then dividing by the number of scores. p. 54

median   A statistical measure of central tendency that falls exactly in the middle of a distribution of scores after they have been arranged (or ranked) from highest to lowest. p. 54

medical model   A biological approach that describes psychological disorders as medical diseases with a biological origin. p. 522

memory   The retention of information over time through the processes of encoding, storage, and retrieval. p. 304

mental age (MA)   An individual's level of mental development relative to that of others. p. 364

mental processes   The thoughts, feelings, and motives that each of us experiences privately but that cannot be observed directly. p. 5

mental retardation   A condition of limited mental ability in which the individual has a low IQ, usually below 70, has difficulty adapting to everyday life, and has an onset of these characteristics in the so-called developmental period. p. 369

mere exposure effect   The outcome that the more we encounter someone or something (a person, a word, an image), the more likely we are to start liking the person or thing even if we do not realize we have seen it before. p. 506

meta-analysis   A method that allows researchers to combine the results of several different studies on a similar topic in order to establish the strength of an effect. p. 36

midbrain   Located between the hindbrain and forebrain, a region in which many nerve-fiber systems ascend and descend to connect the higher and lower portions of the brain. p. 87

middle ear   Consists of eardrum, hammer, anvil, and stirrup. p. 201

mindfulness   Being alert and mentally present for one's everyday activities. p. 359

Minnesota Multiphasic Personality Inventory (MMPI)   The most widely used and researched empirically keyed self-report personality test. p. 460

mnemonics   Specific visual and/or visual memory aids. p. 339

mode   A statistical measure of central tendency; the score that occurs most often. p. 55

monocular cues   Depth cues that are available from the image in either eye. p. 194

mood disorders   Psychological disorders in which there is a primary disturbance in mood (prolonged emotion that colors the individual's entire emotional state). Two main types are the depressive disorders and bipolar disorder. p. 538

morphology   A language's rules for word formation. p. 373

motivated forgetting   An act of forgetting something because it is so painful or anxiety-laden that remembering it is intolerable. p. 329

motivation   The force that moves people to behave, think, and feel the way they do. p. 390

motor cortex   Area of the cerebral cortex that processes information about voluntary movement. p. 93

myelin sheath   The layer of fat cells that encases and insulates most axons. The myelin sheath speeds up the transmission of nerve impulses. p. 77

N

natural selection   An evolutionary process that favors organisms' traits or characteristics that are best adapted to reproduce and survive. p. 11

naturalistic observation   Observation of behavior in real-world settings with no effort made to manipulate or control the situation. p. 41

nature   An organism's biological inheritance. p. 117

need   A deprivation that energizes the drive to eliminate or reduce the deprivation. p. 391

negative punishment   A behavior decreases when a positive stimulus is removed from it. p. 279

negative reinforcement   Following a behavior with the removal of an aversive (unpleasant) stimulus to increase the frequency of the behavior. p. 275

neglectful parenting   A parenting style in which parents are uninvolved in their child's life. p. 133

nervous system   The body's electrochemical communication circuitry, made up of billions of neurons. p. 73

neural networks   Networks of nerve cells that integrate sensory input and motor output. p. 74

neurons   Nerve cells that are specialized for processing information. Neurons are the basic units of the nervous system. p. 76

neuroscience   The scientific study of the structure, function, development, genetics, and biochemistry of the nervous system. p. 12

neurotransmitters   Chemicals that carry information across the synaptic gap from one neuron to the next. p. 79

noise   Irrelevant and competing stimuli. p. 177

normal distribution   A symmetrical, bell-shaped curve with a majority of the scores falling in the middle of the possible range and few scores appearing toward the extremes of the range. p. 365

normative commitment   The sense of obligation an employee feels toward the organization because of the investment the organization has made in the person's personal and professional development. p. 494

normative social influence   The influence that other people have on us because we want them to like and approve of us. p. 494

nurture   An organism's environmental experience. p. 117

O

obedience　Behavior that complies with the explicit demands of the individual in authority. p. 494

observational learning　Learning that occurs when a person observes and imitates another's behavior; also called imitation or modeling. p. 265

obsessive-compulsive disorder (OCD)　An anxiety disorder in which the individual has anxiety-provoking thoughts that will not go away (obsession) and/or urges to perform repetitive, ritualistic behaviors to prevent or produce some future situation (compulsion). p. 534

occipital lobe　The part of the cerebral cortex at the back of the head that is involved in vision. p. 90

Oedipus complex　In Freud's theory, a young boy's intense desire to replace his father and enjoy the affections of his mother. p. 439

olfactory epithelium　A sheet of receptor cells for smell that lines the roof of the nasal cavity. p. 211

open-mindedness　Being receptive to the possibility of other ways of looking at things. p. 359

operant conditioning　Also called instrumental conditioning; a form of learning in which the consequences of behavior change the probability of the behavior's occurrence. p. 272

operational definition　An objective description of how a research variable is going to be measured and observed. p. 36

opiates　Opium and its derivatives; they depress the central nervous system's activity. p. 248

opponent-process theory　Theory stating that cells in the visual system respond to red-green and blue-yellow colors; a given cell might be excited by red and inhibited by green, whereas another might be excited by yellow and inhibited by blue. p. 190

outer ear　Consists of pinna and external auditory canal. p. 200

P

pain　The sensation that warns us that damage to our bodies is occurring. p. 208

panic disorder　An anxiety disorder marked by recurrent sudden onsets of intense apprehension or terror. p. 532

papillae　Bumps on the tongue that contain taste buds, the receptors for taste. p. 210

parallel processing　The simultaneous distribution of information across different neural pathways. p. 188

paranoid schizophrenia　A type of schizophrenia that is characterized by delusions of reference, grandeur, and persecution. p. 552

parasympathetic nervous system　The division of the autonomic nervous system that calms the body. p. 74

parietal lobe　Area of the cerebral cortex at the top of the head that is involved in registering spatial location, attention, and motor control. p. 92

perception　The brain's process of organizing and interpreting sensory information to give it meaning. p. 173

perceptual constancy　Recognition that objects are constant and unchanging even though sensory input about them is changing. p. 195

perceptual set　A predisposition, or readiness, to perceive something in a particular way. p. 180

performance appraisal　The evaluation of a person's success at his or her job. p. 499

peripheral nervous system (PNS)　The network of nerves that connects the brain and spinal cord to other parts of the body. It is divided into the somatic nervous system and the autonomic nervous system. p. 75

personality　A pattern of enduring, distinctive thoughts, emotions, and behaviors that characterize the way an individual adapts to the world. p. 436

personality disorders　Chronic, maladaptive cognitive-behavioral patterns that are thoroughly integrated into the individual's personality. p. 555

personological and life story perspectives　Approaches to personality emphasizing that the way to understand the person is to focus on his or her life history and life story—aspects that distinguish that individual from all others. p. 452

phenotype　The expression of an individual's genotype in observable, measurable characteristics. p. 107

phobic disorder　Commonly called *phobia*, an anxiety disorder in which the individual has an irrational, overwhelming, persistent fear of a particular object or situation. p. 533

phonics approach　An approach to learning to read that emphasizes basic rules for translating written symbols into sounds. p. 379

phonology　A language's sound system. p. 372

physical dependence　The physiological need for a drug, accompanied by unpleasant withdrawal symptoms, such as pain and craving, when the drug is discontinued. p. 245

pituitary gland　An important endocrine gland at the base of the skull that controls growth and regulates other glands. p. 98

place theory　The theory of hearing that states that each frequency produces vibrations at a particular spot on the basilar membrane. p. 202

placebo　A harmless, inert substance that may be given to participants instead of a presumed active agent, such as a drug, and that has no specific physiological effect. p. 49

placebo effect　The situation where participants' expectations, rather than the experimental treatment, produce an experimental outcome. p. 49

plasticity　The brain's special capacity for modification and change. p. 73

polygraph　A machine that monitors bodily changes thought to be influenced by emotional states; it is used by examiners to try to determine whether someone is lying. p. 416

population　The entire group about which the investigator wants to draw conclusions. p. 38

positive illusions　Positive views of oneself that are not necessarily deeply rooted in reality. p. 478

positive psychology movement　The push for a stronger emphasis on research involving the experiences that people value, the traits associated with optimal capacities for love and work, and positive group and civic values. p. 7

positive punishment　A behavior decreases when it is followed by an unpleasant stimulus. p. 279

positive reinforcement　Following a behavior with a rewarding stimulus to increase the frequency of the behavior. p. 275

post-traumatic growth　Improvements individuals can see in themselves as a result of a struggle with negative life events. p. 599

post-traumatic stress disorder (PTSD)　An anxiety disorder that develops through exposure to a traumatic event, severely oppressive situations, severe abuse, and natural and unnatural disasters. p. 535

preferential looking　A test of perception that involves giving an infant a choice of what object to look at and that is used to determine whether infants can distinguish between objects. p. 122

prejudice　An unjustified negative attitude toward an individual based on the individual's membership in a group. p. 500

preoperational stage　The second Piagetian stage of cognitive development (approximately 2 to 7 years of age), in which thought becomes more symbolic than in the sensorimotor stage but the child cannot yet perform operations. p. 126

preparedness　The species-specific biological predisposition to learn in certain ways but not others. p. 290

primary reinforcement　The use of reinforcers that are innately satisfying. p. 276

priming　A type of implicit memory process involving the activation of information that people already have in storage to help them remember new information better and faster. p. 316

proactive interference　Situation in which material that was learned earlier disrupts the recall of material learned later. p. 334

problem solving   An attempt to find an appropriate way of attaining a goal when the goal is not readily available. p. 351

problem-focused coping   The cognitive strategy of squarely facing one's troubles and trying to solve them. p. 381

procedural memory   Memory for skills. p. 315

projective test   Personality assessment tool that presents individuals with an ambiguous stimulus and then asks them to describe it or tell a story about it; in other words, to project their own meaning onto it. p. 461

prosocial behavior   Behavior that is intended to benefit other people. p. 138

prospective memory   Remembering information about doing something in the future. p. 335

prototype model   Model emphasizing that when people evaluate whether a given item reflects a certain concept, they compare the item with the most typical item(s) in that category and look for a "family resemblance." p. 351

psychoactive drugs   Substances that act on the nervous system to alter consciousness, modify perceptions, and change moods. p. 245

psychoanalysis   Freud's therapeutic technique for analyzing an individual's unconscious thoughts. Freud believed that clients' current problems could be traced to childhood experiences, many of which involved conflicts about sexuality. p. 574

psychodynamic approach   A psychological perspective emphasizing unconscious thought, the conflict between biological instincts and society's demands, and early family experiences. p. 13

psychodynamic perspectives   Views of personality as primarily unconscious (that is, beyond awareness) and as developing in stages. Most psychoanalytic perspectives emphasize that early experiences with parents play a role in sculpting personality. p. 436

psychodynamic therapies   Therapies that stress the importance of the unconscious mind, extensive interpretation by the therapist, and the role of experiences in the early childhood years. The goal of the psychodynamic therapies is to help individuals recognize their maladaptive ways of coping and the sources of their unconscious conflicts. p. 574

psychological dependence   The strong desire to repeat the use of a drug for emotional reasons, such as a feeling of well-being and stress reduction. p. 245

psychology   The scientific study of behavior and mental processes. p. 4

psychoneuroimmunology   The field that explores connections among psychological factors (such as attitudes and emotions), the nervous system, and the immune system. p. 619

psychopathology   The study of mental illness. p. 25

psychophysics   The field that studies links between the physical properties of stimuli and a person's experience of them. p. 176

psychosurgery   A biological therapy that involves removal or destruction of brain tissue to improve an individual's adjustment. p. 572

psychotherapy   The nonmedical process used by mental health professionals to help individuals recognize and overcome their problems. p. 566

puberty   A period of rapid skeletal and sexual maturation that occurs mainly in early adolescence. p. 143

punishment   A consequence that decreases the likelihood a behavior will occur. p. 279

R

random assignment   The assignment of participants to research groups by chance. p. 48

random sample   A sample that gives every member of the population an equal chance of being selected. p. 38

range   A statistical measure of variability that is the distance between the highest and lowest scores. p. 55

rational-emotive behavior therapy (REBT)   A therapy based on Ellis's assertion that individuals develop a psychological disorder because of their beliefs, especially those that are irrational and self-defeating; the goal of REBT is to get clients to eliminate self-defeating beliefs by rationally examining them. p. 581

reasoning   The mental activity of transforming information to reach conclusions. p. 355

referential thinking   Ascribing personal meaning to completely random events. p. 551

reflective speech   A technique in which the therapist mirrors the client's own feelings back to the client. p. 576

reinforcement   The process by which a stimulus or an event strengthens or increases the probability of a behavior or an event that it follows. p. 275

relapse   A return to former unhealthy patterns. p. 613

reliability   The extent to which a test yields a consistent, reproducible measure of performance. p. 364

REM sleep   Rapid eye movement sleep; stage 5 of sleep, in which dreaming occurs. p. 234

research participant bias   The influence of research participants' expectations on their behavior within an experiment. p. 49

resilience   A person's ability to recover from or adapt to difficult times. p. 141

resistance   The psychoanalytic term for the client's unconscious defense strategies that prevent the analyst from understanding the person's problems. p. 574

resting potential   The stable, negative charge of an inactive neuron. p. 78

reticular formation   A midbrain system that consists of a diffuse collection of neurons involved in stereotypical behaviors, such as walking, sleeping, or turning to attend to a sudden noise. p. 87

retina   The light-sensitive surface in the back of the eye that records what we see and converts it to neural impulses for processing in the brain. p. 185

retrieval   The memory process of taking information out of storage. p. 323

retroactive interference   Situation in which material learned later disrupts the retrieval of information learned earlier. p. 334

retrograde amnesia   A memory disorder that involves memory loss for a segment of the past but not for new events. p. 337

retrospective memory   Remembering the past. p. 335

risky shift   The tendency for a group decision to be riskier than the average decision made by individual group members. p. 497

rods   The receptors in the retina that are sensitive to light but are not very useful for color vision. p. 185

romantic love   Also called passionate love; the type of love that has strong components of sexuality and infatuation and often predominates in the early part of a love relationship. p. 507

Rorschach inkblot test   A widely used projective test that uses an individual's perception of inkblots to determine his or her personality. p. 461

S

sample   The subset of the population chosen by the investigator for study. p. 38

schedules of reinforcement   Timetables that determine when a behavior will be reinforced. p. 276

schema   A concept or framework that already exists at a given moment in a person's mind and that organizes information and provides a structure for interpreting it. p. 125, 318

schizophrenia   A severe psychological disorder that is characterized by highly disordered thought processes. p. 550

science   In psychology, the use of systematic methods to observe, describe, predict, and explain behavior. p. 5

script   A schema for an event. p. 319

secondary reinforcement   The use of reinforcers that are learned or conditioned. p. 276

secure attachment   An important aspect of socioemotional development in which infants use the caregiver, usually the mother, as a secure base from which to explore the environment. p. 132

selective attention   Focusing on a specific aspect of experience while ignoring others. p. 179

self-actualization   The highest and most elusive of Maslow's needs; the motivation to develop one's full potential as a human being. p. 407

self-concept   A central theme in Rogers's and other humanists' views; self-concept refers to individuals' overall perceptions and assessments of their abilities, behavior, and personalities. p. 445

self-determination theory   A theory of motivation that proposes that three basic, organismic needs (competence, autonomy, and relatedness) characterize intrinsic motivation. p. 407

self-efficacy   The belief that one can master a situation and produce positive outcomes. p. 455, 615

self-objectification   The tendency to see oneself primarily as an object in the eyes of others. p. 478

self-perception theory   Bem's theory about the connection between attitudes and behavior; stresses that individuals make inferences about their attitudes by perceiving their behavior. p. 481

self-regulation   The process by which an organism pursues important objectives, centrally involving getting feedback about how we are doing in our goal pursuits. p. 412

self-report test   Also called an objective test or inventory, a type of test that directly asks people whether specific items (usually true/false or agree/disagree) describe their personality traits. p. 459

self-serving bias   The tendency to take credit for one's successes and to deny responsibility for one's failures. p. 478

semantic memory   A person's knowledge about the world. p. 315

semantics   The meaning of words and sentences in a particular language. p. 373

semicircular canals   Structure in the inner ear containing the sensory receptors that detect head motion. p. 213

sensation   The process of receiving stimulus energies from the environment. p. 173

sensorimotor stage   The first Piagetian stage of cognitive development (birth to about 2 years of age), in which infants construct an understanding of the world by coordinating sensory experiences (such as seeing and hearing) with motor (physical) actions. p. 125

sensory adaptation   A change in the responsiveness of the sensory system based on the average level of surrounding stimulation. p. 182

sensory memory   Information from the world that is held in its original form only for an instant, not much longer than the brief time it is exposed to the visual, auditory, and other senses. p. 310

sensory receptors   Specialized cells that detect stimulus information and transmit it to sensory (afferent) nerves and the brain. p. 174

serial position effect   The tendency for items at the beginning and at the end of a list to be recalled more readily than those in the middle of the list. p. 324

set point   The weight maintained when no effort is made to gain or lose weight. p. 396

sexual orientation   The direction of the person's erotic interests, whether heterosexual, homosexual, or bisexual. p. 404

sexually transmitted infections (STIs)   Infections that are contracted primarily through sex—vaginal intercourse as well as oral-genital and anal-genital sex. p. 630

shaping   Rewarding approximations of a desired behavior. p. 274

short-term memory   A limited-capacity memory system in which information is retained for only as long as 30 seconds unless strategies are used to retain it longer. p. 311

signal detection theory   The theory about perception that focuses on decision making about stimuli in the presence of uncertainty; detection depends on a variety of factors besides the physical intensity of the stimulus and the sensory abilities of the observer. p. 178

social cognitive behavior view of hypnosis   Perspective that views hypnosis as a normal state in which the hypnotized person behaves the way he or she believes a hypnotized person should behave. p. 243

social cognitive perspectives   Approaches to personality emphasizing conscious awareness, beliefs, expectations, and goals; social cognitive psychologists explore the person's ability to reason; to think about the past, present, and future; and to reflect on the self. p. 454

social comparison   The process by which individuals evaluate their thoughts, feelings, behaviors, and abilities in relation to other people. p. 479

social contagion   Imitative behavior involving the spread of behavior, emotions, and ideas. p. 496

social exchange theory   A theory based on the notion of social relationships as involving an exchange of goods, the objective of which is to minimize costs and maximize benefits. p. 508

social facilitation   Improvement in an individual's performance because of the presence of others. p. 496

social identity   The way individuals define themselves in terms of their group membership. p. 500

social identity theory   Tajfel's theory that social identities are a crucial part of individuals' self-image and a valuable source of positive feelings about themselves. p. 500

social loafing   Each person's tendency to exert less effort in a group because of reduced accountability for individual effort. p. 497

social psychology   The study of how people think about, influence, and relate to other people. p. 474

social support   Information and feedback from others that one is loved and cared for, esteemed and valued, and included in a network of communication and mutual obligation. p. 511

sociocultural approach   A psychological perspective that examines the ways in which the social and cultural environments influence behavior. p. 15

somatic nervous system   The division of the PNS consisting of sensory nerves, whose function is to convey information to the CNS, and motor nerves, whose function is to transmit information to the muscles. p. 75

somatosensory cortex   Area of the cerebral cortex that processes information about body sensations. p. 93

spontaneous recovery   The process in classical conditioning by which a conditioned response can recur after a time delay without further conditioning. p. 268

stages of change model   Five-step model that describes the process by which individuals give up bad habits and adopt healthier lifestyles. p. 611

standard deviation   A statistical measure of variability that involves how much the scores vary on the average around the mean of the sample. p. 55

standardization   Developing uniform procedures for administering and scoring a test, as well as creating norms for the test. p. 364

standardized test   A test that requires people to answer a series of written or oral questions or sometimes both. p. 42

stereotype   A generalization about a group's characteristics that does not consider any variations from one individual to another. p. 475

stereotype threat   An individual's fast-acting, self-fulfilling fear of being judged on the basis of a negative stereotype about his or her group. p. 478

stimulants   Psychoactive drugs that increase the central nervous system's activity. p. 249

storage   Retention of information over time and the representation of information in memory. p. 309

stream of consciousness   James's concept that the mind is a continuous flow of changing sensations, images, thoughts, and feelings. p. 222

strengths-based management   A management style emphasizing that maximizing an employee's existing strengths is much easier than trying to build such attributes from the ground up. p. 503

stress The response of individuals to changes in circumstances and events that threaten their coping abilities. p. 108

stress management programs Programs that teach individuals to appraise stressful events, to develop skills for coping with stress, and to put these skills into use in everyday life. p. 621

stressors Circumstances and events that threaten individuals and tax their coping abilities. p. 108

structuralism An early school of psychology that attempted to identify the structures of the human mind. p. 10

subgoaling Setting intermediate goals or defining intermediate problems in order to be in a better position to reach the final goal or solution. p. 353

subliminal perception The detection of information below the level of conscious awareness. p. 177

superego The Freudian structure of personality that harshly judges the morality of our behavior. p. 438

suprachiasmatic nucleus (SCN) A small structure in the brain that synchronizes its own rhythm with the daily cycle of light and dark based on input from the retina. p. 228

sympathetic nervous system The division of the autonomic nervous system that arouses the body. p. 75

synapses Tiny junctions between two neurons, generally where the axon of one neuron meets the dendrites or cell body of another neuron. p. 79

syntax A language's rules for the way words are combined to form acceptable phrases and sentences. p. 373

systematic desensitization A method of behavior therapy based on classical conditioning that treats anxiety by getting the person to associate deep relaxation with increasingly intense anxiety-producing situations. p. 578

T

temperament An individual's behavioral style and characteristic way of responding. p. 132

temporal lobe The portion of the cerebral cortex just above the ears that is involved in hearing, language processing, and memory. p. 92

thalamus Forebrain structure that functions as a relay station to sort information and send it

to appropriate areas in the forebrain for further integration and interpretation. p. 89

Thematic Apperception Test (TAT) A projective test designed to elicit stories that reveal something about an individual's personality. p. 462

theory A broad idea or set of closely related ideas that attempts to explain certain observations. p. 36

theory of planned behavior Model for effective change incorporating the theory of reasoned action but adding the person's perceptions of control over the outcome. p. 611

theory of reasoned action Model suggesting that effective change requires individuals to have specific intentions about their behaviors, as well as positive attitudes about the new behavior, and to perceive that their social group looks on the behavior positively. p. 611

therapeutic alliance The relationship between the therapist and client. p. 594

thermoreceptors Sensory receptors, located under the skin, that respond to changes in temperature at or near the skin and provide input to keep the body's temperature at 98.6 degrees Fahrenheit. p. 208

thinking Manipulating information mentally, as when we form concepts, solve problems, make decisions, and reflect in a creative or critical manner. p. 350

third variable problem The situation where an extraneous variable that has not been measured accounts for the relationship between two others. p. 46

tip-of-the-tongue phenomenon (TOT state) The effortful retrieval that occurs when people are confident that they know something but cannot pull it out of memory. p. 335

tolerance The need to take increasing amounts of a drug to produce the same effect. p. 245

top-down processing Processing of perceptual information that starts out with cognitive processing at the higher levels of the brain. p. 173

training Teaching a new employee the essential requirements to do the job well. p. 498

trait An enduring personality characteristic that tends to lead to certain behaviors. p. 446

trait theories Theories stating that personality consists of broad, enduring dispositions (traits) that tend to lead to characteristic responses. p. 446

tranquilizers Depressant drugs that reduce anxiety and induce relaxation. p. 248

transduction The process of transforming physical energy into electrochemical energy. p. 173

transference The psychoanalytic term for the client's relating to the analyst in ways that reproduce or relive important relationships in the client's life. p. 574

triarchic theory of intelligence Sternberg's theory that there are three main types of intelligence: analytical, creative, and practical. p. 371

trichromatic theory Theory stating that color perception is produced by three types of receptors (cone cells in the retina) that are particularly sensitive to different, but overlapping, ranges of wavelengths. p. 189

two-factor theory of emotion Schachter and Singer's theory that emotion is determined by two main factors: physiological arousal and cognitive labeling. p. 420

Type A behavior pattern A cluster of characteristics—such as being excessively competitive, hard-driven, impatient, and hostile—related to the incidence of heart disease. p. 465

Type B behavior pattern A cluster of characteristics—such as being relaxed and easygoing—related to good health. p. 465

U

unconditional positive regard Rogers's term for accepting, valuing, and being positive toward another person regardless of the person's behavior. p. 445

unconditioned response (UCR) An unlearned response that is automatically elicited by an unconditioned stimulus. p. 267

unconditioned stimulus (UCS) A stimulus that produces a response without prior learning. p. 267

unconscious thought Freud's concept of a reservoir of unacceptable wishes, feelings, and thoughts that are beyond conscious awareness. p. 225

undifferentiated schizophrenia A type of schizophrenia that is characterized by disorganized behavior, hallucinations, delusions, and incoherence. p. 552

V

validity The soundness of the conclusions we draw from an experiment. In the realm of testing, validity specifically refers to the extent to which a test measures what it is intended to measure. p. 48

variable Anything that can change. p. 36

vestibular sense Senses that provide information about balance and movement. p. 213

visual illusion   A discrepancy between reality and the perceptual representation of it. p. 196

volley principle   Modification of frequency theory stating that a cluster of nerve cells can fire neural impulses in rapid succession, producing a volley of impulses. p. 203

W

Weber's law   The principle that two stimuli must differ by a constant minimum percentage (rather than a constant amount) to be perceived as different. p. 178

well-being therapy (WBT)   A short-term, problem-focused, directive therapy that encourages clients to accentuate the positive. p. 599

whole-language approach   An approach to learning to read that stresses that reading instruction should parallel a child's natural language learning; so reading materials should be whole and meaningful. p. 378

wisdom   Expert knowledge about the practical aspects of life. p. 158

working memory   A three-part system that temporarily holds information as people perform cognitive tasks. Working memory is a kind of mental "workbench" on which information is manipulated and assembled to help individuals perform other cognitive tasks. p. 312

Y

Yerkes-Dodson law   Principle stating that performance is best under conditions of moderate arousal rather than low or high arousal. p. 392

A

Aalsma, M. C., Lapsley, D. K., & Flannery, D. J. (2006). Personal fables, narcissism, and adolescent adjustment. *Psychology in the Schools, 43,* 481–491.

Aarts, H., Custers, R., & Holland, R. W. (2007). The nonconscious cessation of goal pursuit: When goals and negative affect are coactivated. *Journal of Personality and Social Psychology, 92,* 165–178.

Abbey, A., Parkhill, M. R., Buck, P. O., & Saenz, C. (2007). Condom use with a casual partner: What distinguishes college students' use when intoxicated? *Psychology of Addictive Behaviors, 21,* 76–83.

Abbott, B. B., Schoen L. S,, & Badia, P. (1984). Predictable and unpredictable shock: Behavioral measures of aversion and physiological measures of stress. *Psychological Bulletin, 96,* 45–71.

ABC/AOL. (2006, January 2). ABC News/AOL poll finds losing weight tops New Year's resolutions. American Online Press Release.

Abel, E. L. (2006). Fetal alcohol syndrome: A cautionary note. *Current Pharmaceutical Design, 12,* 1521–1529.

Abelson, R. P., Frey, K. P., & Gregg, A. P. (2004). *Experiments with people.* Mahwah, NJ: Erlbaum.

Abernathy, A. D., Houston, T. R., Mimms, T., & Boyd-Franklin, N. (2006). Using prayer in psychotherapy: Applying Sue's differential to enhance culturally competent care. *Cultural Diversity and Ethnic Minority Psychology, 12,* 101–114.

Abraham, A., & Windmann, S. (2007). Creative cognition: The diverse operations and the prospect of applying a cognitive neuroscience perspective. *Methods, 42,* 38–48.

Abrams, D., & Hogg, M. A. (2004). Metatheory: Lessons from social identity research. In A. W. Kruglanski & E. T. Higgins (Eds.), *Theory construction in social-personality psychology.* Mahwah, NJ: Erlbaum.

Abramson, L. Y., Seligman, M. E. P., & Teasdale, J. (1978). Learned helplessness in humans: Critique and reformulation. *Journal of Abnormal Psychology, 87,* 49–74.

Adamson, H. D. (2004). *Language minority students in American schools.* Mahwah, NJ: Erlbaum.

Addington, J., el-Guebaly, N., Campbell, W., Hodgkins, D. C., & Addington, D. (1998). Smoking cessation treatment for patients with schizophrenia. *American Journal of Psychiatry, 155,* 974–976.

Ader, R. (2000). On the development of psychoneuroimmunology. *European Journal of Pharmacology, 405,* 167–176.

Ader, R., & Cohen, N. (1975). Behaviorally conditioned immunosuppression. *Psychosomatic Medicine, 37,* 333–340.

Ader, R., & Cohen, N. (2000). Conditioning and immunity. In R. Ader, D. L. Felton, & N. Cohen (Eds.), *Psychoneuroimmunology* (3rd ed.). San Diego: Academic Press.

Adler, A. (1927). *The theory and practice of individual psychology.* Fort Worth: Harcourt Brace.

Adler, T. (1991, January). Seeing double? Controversial twins study is widely reported, debated. *APA Monitor, 22,* 1, 8.

Adolph, K. E., & Berger, S. E. (2006). Motor development. In W. Damon & R. Lerner (Eds.), *Handbook of child psychology* (6th ed.). New York: Wiley.

Adolph, K. E., & Joh, A. S. (2007). Motor development: How infants get into the act. In A. Slater & M. Lewis (Eds.), *Infant Development* (2nd ed.). New York: Oxford University Press.

Agargun, M. Y., Besiroglu, L., Cilli, A. S., Gulec, M., Aydin, A., Inci, R., & Selvi, Y. (2007). Nightmares, suicide attempts, and melancholic features in patients with unipolar depression. *Journal of Affective Disorders, 98,* 267–270.

Aggarwal, S., Carter, G.T., & Steinborn, J. J. (2005). Clearing the air: What the latest Supreme Court decision regarding medical marijuana really means. *American Journal of Hospice & Palliative Medicine, 22,* 327–329.

Agronick, G., Stueve, A., Vargo, S., & O'Donnell, L. (2007). New York City young adults' psychological reactions to 9/11: Findings from the Reach for Health longitudinal study. *American Journal of Community Psychology, 39,* 79–90.

Ahima, R. S. (2006). Adipose tissue as an endocrine organ. *Obesity, 14,* Suppl. 5, S242–S249.

Ahmed, N. U., Smith, G. L., Flores, A. M., Pamies, R. J., Mason, H. R., Woods, K. F., & Stain, S. C. (2005). Racial/ethnic disparity and predictors of leisure-time activity among U.S. men. *Ethnicity and Disease, 15,* 40–52.

Ahn, S., & Phillips, A. G. (2006). Dopamine efflux in the nucleus accumbens during within-session extinction, outcome-dependent, and habit-based instrumental responding for food reward. *Psychopharmacology.* (in press)

Ahola, K., Honkonen, T., Kivimaki, M., Virtanen, M., Isometsa, E., Aromaa, A., & Lonnqvist, J. (2006). Contribution of burnout to the association between job strain and depression: The Health 2000 Study. *Journal of Occupational and Environmental Medicine, 48,* 1023–1030.

Ahveninen, J., & others. (2006). Task-modulated "what" and "where" pathways in human auditory cortex. *Proceedings of the National Academy of Science USA, 103,* 14608–14613.

Aiken, L. R., & Groth-Marnat, G. (2006). *Psychological testing and assessment* (12th ed.). Boston: Allyn & Bacon.

Ainsworth, M. D. S. (1979). Infant–mother attachment. *American Psychologist, 34,* 932–937.

Ainsworth, M. S., Blehar, M. C., Waters, E., & Wall, S. (1978). *Patterns of attachment: A psychological study of the strange situation.* Oxford, England: Erlbaum.

Aja, S. (2006). Serotonin-3 receptors in gastric mechanisms of cholecystokinin-induced satiety. *American Journal of Physiology: Regulatory, Integrative, and Comparative Physiology, 291,* R112– R114.

Ajzen, I. (2001). Nature and operation of attitudes. *Annual Review of Psychology* (vol. 52). Palo Alto, CA: Annual Reviews.

Ajzen, I. (2002). Perceived behavioral control, self-efficacy, locus of control, and the theory of planned behavior. *Journal of Applied Social Psychology, 32,* 665–683.

Ajzen, I., & Albarracin, D. (2007). Predicting and changing behavior: A reasoned action approach. In I. Ajzen, D. Albarracin, & R. Hornik (Eds.), *Prediction and change in health behavior.* Mahwah, NJ: Erlbaum.

Ajzen, I., & Fishbein, M. (2005). The influence of attitudes on behavior. In. D. Albarracin, B. T. Johnson, & M. P. Zanna (Eds.), *The handbook of attitudes* (pp. 173–221). Mahwah, NJ: Erlbaum.

Ajzen, I., & Manstead, A. S. R. (2007). Changing health-related behaviours: An approach based on the theory of planned behaviour. In M. Hewstone, H. Schut, J. de Wit, K. van den Bos, & M. S. Stroebe (Eds.), *The scope of social psychology: Theory and applications* (pp. 43–63). New York: Psychology Press.

Akaike, A. (2006). Preclinical evidence of neuroprotection by cholinesterase inhibitors. *Alzheimer Disease and Associated Disorders, 20,* Suppl. 1, S8–S11.

Akhtar, S. (2006). Technical challenges faced by the immigrant psychoanalyst. *Psychoanalytic Quarterly, 75,* 21–43.

Al'absi, M., & Bongard, S. (2006). Neuroendocrine and behavioral mechanisms mediating the relationship between anger expression and cardiovascular risk: Assessment considerations and improvements. *Journal of Behavioral Medicine, 29,* 573–591.

Alan Guttmacher Institute. (2000, February 24). *United States and the Russian Federation lead the developed world in teenage pregnancy rates.* New York: Alan Guttmacher Institute.

Alan Guttmacher Institute. (2003). *Teen sex and pregnancy.* New York: Alan Guttmacher Institute.

Alan Guttmacher Institute. (2006). *Facts on American teens' sexual and reproductive health.* http://www.guttmacher.org/pubs/fb_ATSRH.html (accessed May 15, 2006).

Albarracin, D., Durantini, M. R., & Earl, A. (2006). Empirical and theoretical conclusions of an analysis of outcomes of HIV-prevention interventions. *Current Directions in Psychological Science, 15,* 73–78.

Albarracin, D., Gillette, J. C., Earl, A. N., Glasman, L. R., Durantini, M. R., & Ho, M. (2005). A test of major assumptions about behavior change: A comprehensive look at the effects of passive and active HIV-prevention interventions since the beginning of the epidemic. *Psychological Bulletin, 131,* 856–897.

Alberto, P., & Trautman, A. (2006). *Applied behavior analysis for teachers* (7th ed.). Upper Saddle River, NJ: Prentice-Hall.

Aldwin, C. M. (2007). *Stress, coping, and development* (2nd ed.). New York: Guilford.

Aldwin, C. M., Spiro, A., & Park, C. L. (2006). Health, behavior, and optimal aging. In J. E. Birren & K. W. Schaie (Eds.), *Handbook of the psychology of aging* (6th ed.). San Diego: Academic.

Aldwin, C. M., Yancura, L. A., & Boeninger, D. K. (2007). In C. M. Aldwin, C. L. Park, & A. Spiro (Eds.), *Handbook of health and aging.* New York: Guilford.

Alea, N., & Bluck, S. (2003). Why are you telling me that? A conceptual model of the social function of autobiographical memory. *Journal of Adult Development, 11,* 235–250.

Aleksandrov, Y. I. (2006). Learning and memory: Traditional and systems approaches. *Neuro-science and Behavioral Physiology, 36,* 969–985.

Alemdar, M., Kamaci, S., & Budak, F. (2006). Unilateral midbrain infarction causing downward gaze palsy. *Journal of Neuro-ophthalmology, 26,* 173–176.

Alexander, P. A., & Winne, P. H. (Eds.). (2006). *Handbook of educational psychology* (2nd ed.). Mahwah, NJ: Erlbaum.

Alford, B. A., & Beck, A. T. (2006). Psychotherapeutic treatment of depression and bipolar disorder. In D. L. Evans, D. S. Charney, & L. Lewis (Eds.), *The physician's guide to depression and bipolar disorders.* New York: McGraw-Hill.

Alford, L. (2007). Findings of interest from immunology and psychoneuroimmunology. *Manual Therapy, 12,* 176–180.

Alford, S. (2003). *Science and success: Sex education and other programs that work toprevent teen pregnancy, HIV & sexually transmitted infections.* Washington, DC: Advocates for Youth.

Allan, K., Wolf, H. A., Rosenthal, C. R., & Rugg, M. D. (2001). The effects of retrieval cues on post-retrieval monitoring in episodic memory: An electrophysiological study. *Brain Research, 12,* 289–299.

Allan, L. G., Siegel, S., & Hannah, S. (2007). The sad truth about depressive realism. *Quarterly Journal of Experimental Psychology, 60,* 482–495.

Allen, J. E., Pertea, M., & Salzberg, S. L. (2004). Computational gene prediction using multiple sources of evidence. *Genome Research, 14,* 142–148.

Allen, J. J. B., Harmon-Jones, E., & Cavender, J. H. (2001). Manipulation of frontal EEG asymmetry through biofeedback alters self-reported emotional responses and facial EMG. *Psychophysiology, 38,* 685–693.

Alloy, L. B., & Abramson, L. Y. (1979). Judgment of contingency in depressed and nondepressed students: Sadder but wiser? *Journal of Experimental Psychology: General, 108,* 441–485.

Alloy, L. B., Abramson, L. Y., & Francis, E. L. (1999). Do negative cognitive styles confer vulnerability to depression? *Current Directions in Psychological Science, 8,* 128–132.

Allport, G. W. (1961). *Pattern and growth in personality.* New York: Holt, Rinehart & Winston.

Allport, G. W., & Odbert, H. (1936). Trait-names: A psycho-lexical study. No. 211. Princeton, NJ: *Psychological Review Monographs.*

Alsop, B., & Porritt, M. (2006). Discriminability and sensitivity to reinforcer magnitude in a detection task. *Journal of the Experimental Analysis of Behavior, 85,* 41–56.

Altemus, M. (2006). Sex differences in depression and anxiety disorders: Potential biological determinants. *Hormones and Behavior, 50,* 534–538.

Altmann, C. F., Bledowski, C., Wibral, M., & Kaiser, J. (2007). Processing of location and pattern changes of natural sounds in the human auditory cortex. *NeuroImage, 35,* 1192–1200.

Alvarez-Lacalle, E., Dorow, B., Eckermann, J. P., & Moses, E. (2006). Hierarchical structures induce long-range dynamical correlations in written texts. *Proceedings of the National Academy of Science USA, 103,* 7956–7961.

Alvino, C., Kohlber, C., Barrett, F., Gur, R. E., Gur, R. C., & Verma, R. (2007). Computerized measurement of facial expression of emotions in schizophrenia. *Journal of Neuroscience Methods.* (in press)

Amato, P. R. (2006). Marital discord, divorce, and children's well-being: Results from a 20-year longitudinal study of two generations. In A. Clarke-Stewart & J. Dunn (Eds.), *Families count.* New York: Cambridge University Press.

Ambady, N., Bernieri, F. J., & Richeson, J. A. (2000). Toward a histology of social behavior: Judgmental accuracy from thin slices of the behavioral stream. In M. P. Zanna (Ed.), *Advances in experimental social psychology* (vol. 32, pp. 201–271). San Diego, CA: Academic.

Ambady, N., Krabbenhoft, M. A., & Hogan, D. (2006). The 30-sec sale: Using thin-slice judgments to evaluate sales effectiveness. *Journal of Consumer Psychology, 16,* 4–13.

American Academy of Ophthalmology. (2003). *Use of marijuana to treat glaucoma.* San Francisco: Author.

American Association of University Women. (2006). *Drawing the line: Sexual harassment on campus (2006).* Washington, DC: Author.

American Association on Mental Retardation, Ad Hoc Committee on Terminology and Classification. (1992). *Mental retardation* (9th ed.). Washington, DC: Author.

American Psychiatric Association. (1994). *Diagnostic and statistical manual of mental disorders* (4th ed.). Washington, DC: Author.

American Psychiatric Association. (2000). *Diagnostic and statistical manual of mental disorders, Fourth edition, Text revision.* Washington, DC: Author.

American Psychiatric Association. (2001). *Mental illness.* Washington, DC: Author.

American Psychiatric Association. (2006). *American Psychiatric Association practice guidelines for the treatment of psychiatric disorders.* Washington, DC: Author.

American Psychological Association. (1995). *Questions and answers about memories of child abuse.* Washington, DC: Author.

American Psychological Association. (2004, July 28). *APA supports legalization of same-sex civil marriages and opposes discrimination against lesbian and gay parents: Denying same-sex couples legal access to civil marriage is discriminatory and can adversely affect the psychological, physical, social, and economic well-being of gay and lesbian individuals.* Washington DC: Author.

American Sleep Apnea Association. (2006). *Get the facts about sleep apnea.* Washington, DC: Author.

Amiot, C. E., Terry, D. J., Jimmieson, N. L., & Callan, V. J. (2006). A longitudinal investigation of coping processes during a merger: Implications for job satisfaction and organizational identification. *Journal of Management, 32,* 552–574.

Amodio, D. M., & Devine, P. G. (2006). Stereotyping and evaluation in implicit race bias: Evidence for independent constructs and unique effects on behavior. *Journal of Personality and Social Psychology, 91,* 652–661.

Amsel, E., & Byrnes, J. (2001). Symbolic communication and cognitive development. In J. Byrnes & E. Amsel (Eds.), *Language, literacy, and cognitive development.* Mahwah, NJ: Erlbaum.

Amunts, K., Schlaug, G., Jancke, L., Steinmetz, H., Schleicher, A., Dabringhaus, A., & Zilles, K. (1997). Motor cortex and hand motor skills: Structural compliance in the human brain. *Human Brain Mapping, 5(3),* 206–215.

Anastasi, A., & Urbina, S. (1996). *Psychological testing* (7th ed.). Upper Saddle River, NJ: Prentice-Hall.

Ancoli-Israel, S. (2006). Sleep and aging: prevalence of disturbed sleep and treatment considerations in older adults. *Journal of Clinical Psychiatry, 66, Suppl. 9,* S24–S30.

Andel, R., Crowe, M., Pedersen, N. L., Mortimer, J., Crimmins, E., Johansson, B., & Gatz, M. (2005). Complexity of work and risk of Alzheimer's disease: A population-based study of Swedish twins. *Journals of Gerontology: Series B: Psychological Sciences and Social Sciences, 60B,* 251–258.

Anderman, E. M., & Wolters, C. A. (2006). Goals, values, and affect: Influences on student motivation. In P. A. Alexander & P. H. Winne (Eds.), *Handbook of educational psychology* (2nd ed.). Mahwah, NJ: Erlbaum.

Anderson, B. A., Golden-Kreutz, D. M., & DiLillo, V. (2001). Cancer. In A. Baum, T. A. Revenson, & J. E. Singer (Eds.), *Handbook of health psychology.* Mahwah, NJ: Erlbaum.

Anderson, C., & Huesmann, L. R. (2007). Human aggression. In M. A. Hogg & J. Cooper (Eds.), *The Sage handbook of social psychology* (concise 2nd ed.). Thousand Oaks, CA: Sage.

Anderson, C. A. (2003). Video games and aggressive behavior. In D. Ravitch and J. P. Viteritti (Eds.), *Kid stuff: Marketing sex and violence to America's children* (pp. 143–167). Baltimore: Johns Hopkins University Press.

Anderson, C. A., Benjamin, A. J., Jr., & Bartholow, B. D. (1998). Does the gun pull the trigger? Automatic priming effects of weapon pictures and weapon names. *Psychological Science, 9,* 308–314.

Anderson, C. A., & Bushman, B. J. (2001). Effects of violent video games on aggressive behavior, aggressive cognition, aggressive affect, physiological arousal, and prosocial behavior: A meta-analytic review of the scientific literature. *Psychological Science, 12,* 353–359.

Anderson, C. A., & Bushman, B. J. (2002). Human aggression. *Annual Review of Psychology* (vol. 53). Palo Alto, CA: Annual Reviews.

Anderson, C. A., Carnagey, N. L., Flanagan, M., Benjamin, A. J., Eubanks, J., & Valentine, J. C. (2004). Violent video games: Specific effects of violent content on aggressive thoughts and behavior. *Advances in Experimental Social Psychology, 36,* 199–249.

Anderson, C. A., & Dill, K. E. (2000). Video games and aggressive thoughts, feelings, and behavior in the laboratory and in life. *Journal of Personality and Social Psychology, 78,* 772–790.

Anderson, C. A., Gentile, D. A., & Buckley, K. E. (2007). *Violent video game effects on children and adolescents: Theory, research, and public policy.* New York: Oxford University Press.

Anderson, E. M., & Lambert, M. J. (2001). A survival analysis of clinically significant change in outpatient psychotherapy. *Journal of Clinical Psychology, 57,* 875–888.

Anderson, J. E., Santelli, J. S., & Morrow, B. (2006). Trends in adolescent contraceptive use, unprotected and poorly protected sex, 1991–2003. *Journal of Adolescent Health, 38,* 734–739.

Anderson, M. C., & Green, C. (2001, March 15). Suppressing unwanted memories by executive control. *Nature, 410,* 366–369.

Anderson, M. C., Ochsner, K. N., Kuhl, B., Cooper, J., Robertson, E., Gabrieli, S. W., Glover, G. H., & Gabrieli, J. D. (2004). Neural systems underlying the suppression of unwanted memories. *Science, 303,* 232–235.

Anderson, N. H. (1965). Primacy effects in personality impression formation using a generalized order effect paradigm. *Journal of Personality and Social Psychology, 2,* 1–9.

Andersson, G., Carlbring, P., Holmstrom, A., Sparthan, E., Furmark, T., Nilsson-Ihrfelt, E., Buhrman, M., & Ekselius, L. (2006). Internet-based self-help with therapist feedback and in vivo group exposure for social phobia: A randomized controlled trial. *Journal of Consulting and Clinical Psychology, 74,* 677–686.

Andrade, C., Bhakta, S. G., & Singh, N. M. (2006). Controversy revisited: Selective serotonin reuptake inhibitors in pediatric depression. *World Journal of Biological Psychiatry, 7,* 251–260.

Andrade, V. M. (2007). Dreaming as a primordial state of the mind: the clinical relevance of structural faults in the body ego as revealed in dreaming. *International Journal of Psychoanalysis, 88,* 55–74.

Annesi, J. J. (2007). Relations of changes in exercise self-efficacy, physical self-concept, and body satisfaction with weight changes in obese white and African American women initiating a physical activity program. *Ethnicity and Disease, 17,* 19–22.

Antecol, H., & Cobb-Clark, D. (2006). The sexual harassment of female active-duty personnel: Effects on job satisfaction and intentions to remain in the military. *Journal of Economic Behavior and Organization, 61,* 55–80.

Antonioni, D., & Park, J. (2001). The relationship between rater affect and three sources of 360-degree feedback ratings. *Journal of Management, 27,* 479–495.

Antonucci, T. C., Vandewater, E. A., & Lansford, J. E. (2000). Adult development and aging: Social processes and development. In A. Kazdin (Ed.), *Encyclopedia of psychology.* Washington, DC, & New York: American Psychological Association and Oxford University Press.

Appleton, V. E., & Dykeman, C. (2007). Family theory. In D. Capuzzi & D. Gross (Eds.), *Counseling and psychotherapy* (4th ed.). Upper Saddle River, NJ: Prentice-Hall.

Arana-Ward, M. (1997). As technology advances, a bitter debate divides the deaf. *Washington Post,* p. A1.

Archibald, A. B., Graber, J. A., & Brooks-Gunn, J. (2003). Pubertal processes and physical growth in adolescence. In G. R. Adams & M. Berzonsky (Eds.), *Handbook of adolescence.* Malden, MA: Blackwell.

Argyle, M., & Lu, L. (1990). The happiness of extraverts. *Personality and Individual Differences, 11,* 1011–1017.

Arias, A. J., Steinberg, K., Banga, A., & Trestman, R. L. (2006). Systematic review of the efficacy of meditation techniques as treatments for medical illness. *Journal of Alternative and Complementary Medicine, 12,* 817–832.

Arkowitz, H. (1997). Integrative theories of therapy. In P. L. Wachtel & S. B. Messer (Eds.), *Theories of psychotherapy.* Washington, DC: American Psychological Association.

Armitage, C. J. (2006). Evidence that implementation intentions promote transitions between the stages of change. *Journal of Consulting and Clinical Psychology, 74,* 141–151.

Armitage, R., Emslie, G. J., Hoffman, R. F., Rintelmann, J., & Rush, A. J. (2001). Delta sleep EEG in depressed adolescent females and healthy controls. *Journal of Affective Disorders, 63,* 139–148.

Armstrong, D. W., & Hatfield, B. D. (2006). Hormonal responses to opioid receptor blockade: During rest and exercise in cold and hot environments. *European Journal of Applied Physiology, 97,* 43–51.

Armstrong, M. (2006). *My name is Moe Armstrong.* http://209.58.132.78/moe/thoughts/name2.htm (accessed December 12, 2006).

Arndt, J., Routledge, C., Cox, C. R., & Goldenberg, J. L. (2005). The worm at the core: A terror management perspective on the roots of psychological dysfunction. *Applied and Preventative Psychology, 11,* 191–213.

Arnett, J. J. (2004). *Emerging adulthood.* New York: Oxford University Press.

Arnett, J. J. (2006). Emerging adulthood: Understanding the new way of coming of age. In J. J. Arnett & J. L. Tanner (Eds.), *Emerging adults in America.* Washington, DC: American Psychological Association.

Arnett, J. J. (2007). Socialization in emerging adulthood. In J. E. Grusec & P. D. Hastings (Eds.), *Handbook of socialization.* New York: Oxford University Press.

Arnkoff, D. B., Glass, C. R., & Shapiro, S. J. (2002). Expectations and preferences. In J. C. Norcross (Ed.), *Psychotherapy relationships that work.* New York: Oxford University Press.

Aron, A., & Aron, E. N. (2003). *Statistics for psychology* (3rd ed.). Upper Saddle River, NJ: Prentice-Hall.

Aron, A., Aron, E., & Coups, E. (2008). *Statistics for the behavioral and social sciences.* Upper Saddle River, NJ: Prentice-Hall.

Aronson, E. (1986, August). *Teaching students things they think they already know all about: The case of prejudice and desegregation.* Paper presented at the meeting of the American Psychological Association, Washington, DC.

Aronson, E. (1995). *The social animal* (7th ed.). New York: Freeman.

Aronson, E. (2000). *Nobody left to hate.* New York: Freeman.

Aronson, E., Wilson, T. D., & Akert, R. M. (2002). *Social psychology* (4th ed.). Upper Saddle River, NJ: Prentice-Hall.

Aronson, J. M., Cohen, G., & Nails, P. R. (1999). Unwanted consequences and the self: In search of the motivation for dissonance reduction. In E. Harmon-Jones & J. Mills (Eds.), *Cognitive dissonance.* Washington, DC: American Psychological Association.

Arshavsky, Y. I. (2006). "Scientific roots" of dualism in neuroscience. *Progress in Neurobiology, 79*, 190–204.

Arvey, R. D., Harpaz, I., & Liao, H. (2004). Work centrality and post-award work behavior of lottery winners. *Journal of Psychology: Interdisciplinary and Applied, 138*, 404–420.

Arvey, R. D., Rotundo, M., Johnson, W., Zhang, Z., & McGue, M. (2006). The determinants of leadership role occupancy: Genetic and personality factors. *Leadership Quarterly, 17*(1), 1–20.

Arvey, R. D., Zhang, Z., Avolio, B. J., & Krueger, R. F. (2007). Developmental and genetic determinants of leadership role occupancy among women. *Journal of Applied Psychology, 92*(3), 693–706.

Asch, S. E. (1951). Effects of group pressure on the modification and distortion of judgments. In H. S. Guetzkow (Ed.), *Groups, leadership, and men.* Pittsburgh: Carnegie University Press.

Ash, M., & Sturm, T. (Eds.). (2007). *Psychology's territories.* Mahwah, NJ: Erlbaum.

Ash, P. (2006). Adolescents in adult court: Does the punishment fit the criminal? *Journal of the American Academy of Psychiatry and the Law, 34*, 145–149.

Ashby, S. L., Arcari, C. M., & Edmonson, M. B. (2006). Television viewing and risk of sexual initiation by young adolescents. *Archives of Pediatric and Adolescent Medicine, 160*, 375–380.

Aspinwall, L. G. (1998). Rethinking the role of positive affect in self-regulation. *Motivation and Emotion, 22*, 1–32.

Aspinwall, L. G., & Brunhart, S. M. (1996). Distinguishing optimism from denial: Optimistic beliefs predict attention to health threats. *Personality and Social Psychology Bulletin, 22*, 993–1003.

Assor, A., Roth, G., & Deci, E. L. (2004). The emotional costs of parents' conditional regard: A self-determination theory analysis. *Journal of Personality, 72*, 47–88.

Astin, A. W. (1993). *What matters in college.* San Francisco: Jossey-Bass.

Atkinson, D. R. (2004). *Counseling American minorities* (6th ed.). New York: McGraw-Hill.

Atkinson, R. C., & Shiffrin, R. M. (1968). Human memory: A proposed system and its control processes. In K. W. Spence & J. T. Spence (Eds.), *The psychology of learning and motivation* (vol. 2). San Diego, CA: Academic.

Aucoin, K. J., Frick, P. J., & Bodin, S. D. (2006). Corporal punishment and child adjustment. *Journal of Applied Developmental Psychology, 27*, 527–541.

Augoustinos, M., Walker, I., & Donaghue, N. (2006). *Social cognition.* Thousand Oaks, CA: Sage.

Austin, D. W., & Richards, J. C. (2006). A test of core assumptions of the catastrophic misinterpretation model of panic disorder. *Cognitive Therapy and Research, 30*, 53–68.

Austin, J. T., & Crespin, T. R. (2006). Problems of criteria in industrial and organizational psychology. In W. Bennett, C. E. Lance, & D. J. Woehr (Eds.), *Performance measurement.* Mahwah, NJ: Erlbaum.

Avner, J. R. (2006). Altered states of consciousness. *Pediatric Review, 27*, 331–338.

Ayers, C. R., Sorrell, J. T., Thorp, S. R., & Wetherell, J. L. (2007). Evidence-based psychological treatments for late-life anxiety. *Psychology and Aging, 22*, 8–17.

Ayers, S., Baum, A., McManus, C., Newman, S., Wallston, K., Weinman, J., & West, R. (Eds.). (2007). *Cambridge handbook of psychology, health, and medicine.* New York: Cambridge University Press.

Azhar, M. Z. (2001). Comparison of Fluvoxamine alone, Fluvoxamine and cognitive psychotherapy and psychotherapy alone in the treatment of panic disorder in Kelantan: Implications for management by family doctors. *Medical Journal of Malaysia, 55*, 402–408.

Aziz, S., & Zickar, M. J. (2006). A cluster analysis investigation of workaholism as a syndrome. *Journal of Occupational Health Psychology, 11*, 52–62.

B

Babiloni, C., Vecchio, F., Cappa, S., Pasqualetti, P., Rossi, S., Miniussi, C., & Rossini, P. M. (2006). Functional frontoparietal connectivity during encoding and retrieval processes follows HERA model: A high resolution study. *Brain Research Bulletin, 68*, 203–212.

Bachen, E. A., Cohen, S., & Marsland, A. L. (2007). Psychoneuroimmunology. In S. Ayers, A. Baum, C. McManus, S. Newman, K. Wallston, J. Weinman, & R. West (Eds.), *Cambridge handbook of psychology, health, and medicine.* New York: Cambridge University Press.

Bachman, J. G., O'Malley, P. M., Schulenberg, J., Johnston, L. D., Bryant, A. L., & Merline, A. C. (2002). *The decline of substance abuse in young adulthood.* Mahwah, NJ: Erlbaum.

Baddeley, A. (1992). Working memory. *Science, 255*, 556–560.

Baddeley, A. (1993). Working memory and conscious awareness. In A. F. Collins, S. E. Gatherhole, M. A. Conway, & P. E. Morris (Eds.), *Theories of memory.* Mahwah, NJ: Erlbaum.

Baddeley, A. (1998). *Human memory* (rev. ed.). Boston: Allyn & Bacon.

Baddeley, A. (2001). *Is working memory still working?* Paper presented at the meeting of the American Psychological Association, San Francisco.

Baddeley, A. (2003). Working memory and language: An overview. *Journal of Communication Disorders, 36*, 189–208.

Baddeley, A. D. (2001). Is working memory still working? *American Psychologist, 56*, 851–864.

Baddeley, A. D. (2003). Working memory: Looking back and looking forward. *Nature Reviews: Neuroscience, 4*, 829–839.

Baddeley, A. D. (2006). Working memory: An overview. In S. Pickering (Ed.), *Working memory and education.* San Diego: Academic.

Baddeley, A. D. (2007). *Working memory, thought, and action.* New York: Oxford University Press.

Badler, J. B., & Heinen, S. J. (2006). Anticipatory movement timing using prediction and external cues. *Journal of Neuroscience, 26*, 4519–4525.

Baehr, E. K., Revelle, W., & Eastman, C. I. (2000). Individual differences in the phase and amplitude of the human circadian temperature rhythm with an emphasis on morningness-eveningness. *Journal of Sleep Research, 9*, 117–127.

Bahr, M., & Lingor, P. (2006). Brain repair: Experimental treatment strategies, neuroprotective and repair strategies in the lesioned adult CNS. *Advances in Experimental Medicine and Biology, 557*, 148–163.

Bahrick, H. P. (1984). Semantic memory content in permastore: Fifty years of memory for Spanish learned in school. *Journal of Experimental Psychology: General, 113*, 1–29.

Bahrick, H. P. (2000). Long-term maintenance of knowledge. In E. Tulving & F. I. M. Craik (Eds.), *The Oxford handbook of memory* (pp. 347–362). New York: Oxford University Press.

Bahrick, H. P., Bahrick, P. O., & Wittlinger, R. P. (1974). Long-term memory: Those unforgettable high-school days. *Psychology Today, 8*, 50–56.

Baillargeon, R. (1997). The object concept revisited. In C. E. Granrud (Ed.), *Visual perception and cognition in infancy.* Mahwah, NJ: Erlbaum.

Baldwin, A. S., Rothman, A. J., Hertel, A. W., Linde, J. A., Jeffery, R. W., Finch, E. A., & Lando, H. A. (2006). Specifying the determinants of the initiation and maintenance of behavior change: An examination of self-efficacy, satisfaction, and smoking cessation. *Health Psychology, 25*, 626–634.

Baldwin, J. D., & Baldwin, J. I. (1998). Sexual behavior. In H. S. Friedman (Ed.), *Encyclopedia of mental health* (vol. 3). San Diego: Academic.

Baldwin, T. T., & Padgett, M. Y. (1993). Management development: A review and commentary. In C. L. Cooper & I. T. Robertson (Eds.), *International review of industrial and organizational psychology* (pp. 35–38). Chichester, England: Wiley.

Baltes, P. B., Lindenberger, U., & Staudinger, U. M. (2006). Life-span theory in developmental psychology. In W. Damon & R. Lerner (Eds.), *Handbook of child psychology* (6th ed.). New York: Wiley.

Banaschewski, T., Ruppert, S., Tannock, R., Albrecht, B., Becker, A., Uebel, H., Sergeant, J. A., & Rothenberger, A. (2006). Color perception in ADHD. *Journal of Child Psychology and Psychiatry, 47*, 568–572.

Bandura, A. (1965). Influences of models' reinforcement contingencies on the acquisition of imitative responses. *Journal of Personality and Social Psychology, 1*, 589–596.

Bandura, A. (1986). *Social foundations of thought and action.* Englewood Cliffs, NJ: Prentice-Hall.

Bandura, A. (1989). Social cognitive theory. In R. Vasta (Ed.), *Six theories of child development.* Greenwich, CT: JAI Press.

Bandura, A. (1997). *Self-efficacy.* New York: Freeman.

Bandura, A. (2001). Social cognitive theory. *Annual Review of Psychology* (vol. 52). Palo Alto, CA: Annual Reviews.

Bandura, A. (2005). The primacy of self-regulation in health promotion. *Applied Psychology: An International Review, 54,* 245–254.

Bandura, A. (2006a). Going global with social cognitive theory: from prospect to paydirt. In D. E. Berger & K. Pezdek (Eds.), *The rise of applied psychology: New frontiers and rewarding careers.* Mahwah, NJ: Erlbaum.

Bandura, A. (2006b). Toward a psychology of human agency. *Perspectives on Psychological Science, 1,* 164–180.

Bandura, A. (2007a). Self-efficacy in health functioning. In S. Ayers & others (Eds.), *Cambridge handbook of psychology, health, and medicine.* New York: Cambridge University Press.

Bandura, A. (2007b). Social cognitive theory. In W. Donsbach (Ed.), *International handbook of communication.* Thousand Oaks, CA: Sage.

Bangasser, D. A., Waxler, D. E., Santoilo, J., & Shors, T. J. (2006). Trace conditioning and the hippocampus: The importance of contiguity. *Journal of Neuroscience, 26,* 8702–8706.

Banks, J. A. (2008). *Introduction to multicultural education* (4th ed.). Boston: Allyn & Bacon.

Bar, M., Neta, M., & Linz, H. (2006). Very first impressions. *Emotion, 6,* 269–278.

Barad, M., Gean, P. W., & Lutz, B. (2006). The role of the amygdala in the extinction of conditioned fear. *Biological Psychiatry, 60,* 322–328.

Barak, Y. (2006). The immune system and happiness. *Autoimmunity Reviews, 5,* 523–527.

Bard, P. (1934). Emotion. In C. Murchison (Ed.), *Handbook of general psychology.* Worcester, MA: Clark University Press.

Bardone-Cone, A. M., & Cass, K. M. (2006). Investigating the impact of pro-anorexia websites: A pilot study. *European Eating Disorders Review, 14,* 256–262.

Bargh, J. A. (2005). Bypassing the will: Towards demystifying the nonconscious control of social behavior. In R. Hassin, J. Uleman, & J. Bargh (Eds.), *The new unconscious.* New York: Oxford University Press.

Bargh, J. A. (2006). Agenda 2006: What have we been priming all these years? On the development, mechanisms, and ecology of nonconscious social behavior. *European Journal of Social Psychology, 36,* 147–168.

Bargh, J. A., Chen, M., & Burrows, L. (1996). The automaticity of social behavior: Direct effects of trait concept and stereotype activation on action. *Journal of Personality and Social Psychology, 71,* 230–244.

Bargh, J. A., Gollwitzer, P. M., Lee-Chai, A., Barndollar, K., & Trotschel, R. (2001). The automated will: Nonconscious activation and pursuit of behavioral goals. *Journal of Personality and Social Psychology, 81,* 1014–1027.

Barkley, R., & 74 others. (2002). International consensus statement on ADHD. *Clinical Child and Family Psychology, 5,* 89–111.

Barling, J., Weber, T., & Kelloway E. K. (1996). Effects of transformational leadership training on attitudinal and financial outcomes: A field experiment. *Journal of Applied Psychology, 81,* 827–832.

Barloon, T., & Noyes, R., Jr. (1997). Charles Darwin and panic disorder. *Journal of the American Medical Association, 277,* 138–141.

Barlow, D. H. (1988). *Anxiety and its disorders: The nature and treatment of anxiety and panic.* New York: Guilford.

Barnett, R. C., & Hyde, J. S. (2001). Women, men, work, and family: An expansionist theory. *American Psychologist, 56,* 781–796.

Baron, N. (1992). *Growing up with language.* Reading, MA: Addison-Wesley.

Baron-Cohen, S. (1995). *Mindblindness: An essay on autism and theory of mind.* Cambridge, MA: MIT Press.

Baron-Cohen, S. (2006). The hyper-systemizing, assortative mating theory of autism. *Progress in Neuro-Psychopharmacology & Biological Psychiatry, 30,* 865–872.

Barrett, G. V., & Kernan, M. G. (1987). Performance appraisal and terminations: A review of court decisions since Brito v. Zia with implications for personnel practices. *Personnel Psychology, 40,* 489–503.

Barrett, L. F., Mesquita, B., Ochsner, K. N., & Gross, J. J. (2007). The experience of emotion. *Annual Review of Psychology* (vol. 58). Palo Alto, CA: Annual Reviews.

Bartel, C. A., Blader, S., & Wrzesniewski, A. (Eds.). (2007). *Identity and the modern organization.* Mahwah, NJ: Erlbaum.

Bartel, C. A., Wrzesniewski, A., & Wiesenfeld, B. (2006). The struggle to establish organizational membership and identification in remote work contexts. In C. A. Bartel, S. Balder, & A. Wrzesniewski (Eds.), *Identity and the modern organization.* Mahwah, NJ: Erlbaum.

Bartel, C. A., Wrzesniewski, A., & Wiesenfeld, B. (2007). The struggle to establish organizational membership: Newcomer socialization in remote work contexts. In C. A. Bartel, S. Blader, & A. Wrzesniewski (Eds.), *Identity and the modern organization.* Mahwah, NJ: Erlbaum.

Bartholow, B. D., Bushman, B. J., & Sestir, M. A. (2006). Chronic violent video game exposure and desensitization to violence: Behavioral and event-related brain potential data. *Journal of Experimental Social Psychology, 42,* 532–539.

Bartlett, M. Y., & DeSteno, D. (2006). Gratitude and prosocial behavior: Helping when it costs you. *Psychological Science, 17,* 319–325.

Bardone Cone, A. M., Abramson, L. Y., Vohs, K. D., Heatherton, T. F., & Joiner, T. E., Jr. (2006). Predicting bulimic symptoms: An interactive model of self-efficacy, perfectionism, and perceived weight status. *Behaviour Research and Therapy, 44,* 27–42.

Bartolomeo, P. (2006). A parietofrontal network for spatial awareness in the right hemisphere of the human brain. *Archives of Neurology, 63,* 1238–1241.

Bartoshuk, L. (2008). Chemical senses: taste and smell. *Annual Review of Psychology (vol. 59).* Palo Alto, CA: Annual Reviews.

Bass, B. M. (1985). *Leadership and performance beyond expectations.* New York: Free Press.

Bass, B. M. (1998). *Transformational leadership: Industrial, military, and educational impact.* Mahwah, NJ: Erlbaum.

Basso, M. R., Schefft, B. K., Ris, M. D., & Dember, W. N. (1996). Mood and global-local visual processing. *Journal of the International Neuropsychological Society, 2,* 249–255.

Bateman, T. S., & Snell, S. A. (2007). *Management* (7th ed.). New York: McGraw-Hill.

Bates, J. E., & Pettit, G. S. (2007). Temperament, parenting, and socialization. In J. E. Grusec & P. D. Hastings (Eds.), *Handbook of socialization.* New York: Oxford University Press.

Batson, C. D. (2002). Addressing the altruism question experimentally. In S. G. Post, L. G. Underwood, J. P. Schloss, & W. B. Hurlbut (Eds.), *Altruism and altruistic love.* New York: Oxford University Press.

Batson, C. D. (2003). Altruism and prosocial behavior. In I. B. Weiner (Ed.), *Handbook of Psychology* (vol. 5). New York: Wiley.

Batson, C. D. (2006). "Not all self-interest after all": Economics of empathy-induced altruism. In D. DeCremer, M. Zeelenberg, & J. K. Murnigham (Eds.), *Social psychology and economics* (pp. 281–299). Mahwah, NJ: Erlbaum.

Batson, C. D., Duncan, B. D., Ackerman, P., Buckley, T., Birch, K., Cialdini, R. B., Schaller, M., Houlihan, D., Arps, K., Fultz, J., & Beaman, A. L. (2007). Issue 17: Does true altruism exist? In J. A. Nier (Ed.), *Taking sides: Clashing views in social psychology* (2nd ed., pp. 348–371). New York: McGraw-Hill.

Batson, C. D., & Stocks, E. L. (2004). Religion: Its core psychological functions. In J. Greenberg, S. L. Koole, & T. Pyszczynski (Eds.), *Handbook of experimental existential psychology* (pp. 141–155). New York: Guilford.

Bauer, J. J., McAdams, D. P., & Sakaeda, A. R. (2005). The crystallization of desire and the crystallization of discontent in narratives of life-changing decisions. *Journal of Personality, 73,* 1181–1213.

Bauer, M., & others. (2007). Using ultrasonography to determine thyroid size and prevalence of goiter in lithium-treated patients with affective disorders. *Journal of Affective Disorders.* (in press)

Bauer, P. (2008). Learning and memory: Like a horse and carriage. In A. Needham & A. Woodward (Eds.), *Learning and the infant mind.* New York: Oxford University Press. (in press)

Bauer, P. J. (2006). Event memory. In W. Damon & R. Lerner (Eds.), *Handbook of child psychology* (6th ed.). New York: Wiley.

Bauer, P. J. (2007). *Remembering the times of our lives.* Mahwah, NJ: Erlbaum.

Baumeister, R. F. (1999). *Evil: Inside human violence and cruelty.* New York: Freeman.

Baumeister, R. F. (2000). Gender differences in erotic plasticity: The female sex drive as socially flexible and responsive. *Psychological Bulletin, 126*(3), 347–374.

Baumeister, R. F. (2002). Yielding to temptation: Self-control failure, impulsive purchasing, and consumer behavior. *Journal of Consumer Research, 28,* 670–676.

Baumeister, R. F., Bushman, B. J., & Campbell, W. K. (2000). Self-esteem, narcissism, and aggression: Does violence result from low self-esteem or from threatened egotism? *Current Directions in Psychological Science, 9,* 26–29.

Baumeister, R. F., & Butz, D. A. (2005). Roots of hate, violence, and evil. In R. J. Sternberg (Ed.), *The psychology of hate* (pp. 87–102). Washington, DC: American Psychological Association.

Baumeister, R. F., Campbell, J. D., Krueger, J. I., Vohs, K. D., DuBois, D. L., & Tevendale, H. D. (2007). Issue 5: Applying social psychology: Are self-esteem programs misguided? In J. A. Nier (Ed.), *Taking sides: Clashing views in social psychology* (2nd ed., pp. 92–115). New York: McGraw-Hill.

Baumeister, R. F., Catanese, K. R., & Vohs, K. D. (2001). Is there a gender difference in strength of sex drive? *Personality and Social Psychology Review, 5,* 242–273.

Baumeister, R. F., & Exline, J. J. (2000). Self-control, morality, and human strength. *Journal of Social & Clinical Psychology, 19*(1), 29–42.

Baumeister, R. F., & Leary, M. R. (2000). The need to belong: Desire for interpersonal attachments as a fundamental human motivation. In E. T. Higgins & A . W. Kruglanski (Eds.). *Motivational science: Social and personality perspectives* (pp. 24–49). New York: Psychology Press.

Baumeister, R. F., & Stillman, T. (2006). Erotic plasticity: Nature, culture, gender, and sexuality. In R. D. McAnulty & M. M. Burnette (Eds.), *Sex and sexuality: Sexuality today: Trends and controversies* (vol. 1, pp. 343–359, 377).Westport, CT: Praeger/Greenwood Publishing Group.

Baumrind, D. (1991). Parenting styles and adolescent development. In J. Brooks-Gunn, R. Lerner, & A. C. Petersen (Eds.), *The encyclopedia of adolescence* (vol. 2). New York: Garland.

Baumrind, D. (1993). The average expectable environment is not good enough: A response to Scarr. *Child Development, 64,* 1299–1307.

Baumrind, D., Larzelere, R. E., & Cowan, P. A. (2002). Ordinary physical punishment: Is it harmful? Comment on Gershoff (2002). *Psychological Bulletin, 128,* 590–595.

Baxter, L. R., Jr., Phelps, M. E., Mazziotta, J. C., Schwartz, J. M., Gerner, R. H., Selin, C. E., & Sumida, R. M. (1995). Cerebral metabolic rates for glucose in mood disorders: Studies with positron emission tomography and fluorodeoxyglucose F 18. *Archives of General Psychiatry, 42,* 441–447.

Baylor, D. (2001). *Seeing, hearing, and smelling the world* [Commentary]. http://www.hhmi.org/senses (accessed October 2001).

BBC News. (2004, June 21). Creative side unlocked by stroke. http://news.bbc.co.uk/2/hi/health/3826857.stm (accessed July 25, 2006).

BBC News. (2005, July 5). Japanese breaks *pi* record. http://news.bbc.co.uk/2/hi/asia-pacific/4644103.stm (accessed October 10, 2006).

Bearinger, L. H., Sieving, R. E., Ferguson, J., & Sharma, V. (2007). Global perspectives on the sexual and reproductive health of adolescents: Patterns, prevention, and potential. *Lancet, 369,* 1220–1231.

Beck, A. (1967). *Depression.* New York: Harper & Row.

Beck, A. T. (1976). *Cognitive therapies and the emotional disorders.* New York: International Universities Press.

Beck, A. T. (1993). Cognitive therapy: Past, present, and future. *Journal of Consulting and Clinical Psychology, 61,* 194–198.

Beck, A. T. (2005). The current state of cognitive therapy: A 40-year retrospective. *Archives of General Psychiatry, 62,* 953–959.

Beck, A. T. (2006). How an anomalous finding led to a new system of psychotherapy. *Nature Medicine, 12,* 1139–1141.

Beck, A. T., Rush, A. J., Shaw, B. F., & Emery, G. (1979). *Cognitive therapy of depression.* New York: Guilford.

Becker, D. V., Kenrick, D. T., Neuberg, S. L., Blackwell, K. C., & Smith, D. M. (2007). The confounded nature of angry men and happy women. *Journal of Personality and Social Psychology, 92,* 179–190.

Becker, E. (1972) *Denial of death.* New York: Free Press.

Becker, J. L., Milad, M. P., & Klock, S. C. (2006). Burnout, depression, and career satisfaction: Cross-sectional study of obstetrics and gynecology residents. *American Journal of Obstetrics and Gynecology, 195,* 1444–1449.

Becker, P. M. (2005). Pharmacologic and nonpharmacologic treatments of insomnia. *Neurological Clinics, 23,* 1149–1163.

Beckers, T., Miller, R. R., De Houwer, J., & Urushihara, K. (2006). Reasoning rats: Forward blocking in Pavlovian animal conditioning is sensitive to constraints of causal inference. *Journal of Experimental Psychology: General, 135,* 92–102.

Beeli, G., Esslen, M., & Jancke, L. (2005). Synaesthesia: When coloured sounds taste sweet. *Nature, 434,* 38.

Beeson, M., Davison, I., Vostanis, P., & Windwo, S. (2006). Parenting programs for behavioral problems: Where do tertiary units fit in a comprehensive service? *Clinical Child Psychology and Psychiatry, 11,* 335–348.

Behrman, B. W., & Davey, S. L. (2001). Eyewitness identification in actual criminal cases:An archival analysis. *Law and Human Behavior, 25,* 475–491.

Bell, R. L., Rodd, Z. A., Lumeng, L., Murphy, J. M., & McBride, W. J. (2006). The alcohol-preferring P rat and animal models of excessive drinking. *Addiction Biology, 11,* 270–288.

Belle, D., & Dodson, L. (2006). Poor women and girls in a wealthy nation. In J. Worell & C. D. Goodheart (Eds.), *Handbook of girls' and women's health: Gender and well-being across the lifespan.* New York: Oxford University Press.

Bem, D. (1967). Self-perception: An alternative explanation of cognitive dissonance phenomena. *Psychological Review, 74,* 183–200.

Benazzi, F. (2006). Various forms of depression. *Dialogues in Clinical Neuroscience, 8,* 151–161.

Benca, R. M. (2001). Consequences of insomnia and its therapies. *Journal of Clinical Psychiatry, 62, Suppl. 10,* 33–38.

Bender, H. L., Allen, J. P., McElhaney, K. B., Antonishak, J., Moore, C. M., Kello, H. O., & Davis, S. M. (2007). Use of harsh physical discipline and developmental outcomes in adolescence. *Development and Psychopathology, 19,* 227–242.

Bendersky, M., & Sullivan, M. W. (2007). Basic methods in infant research. In A. Slater & M. Lewis (Eds.), *Introduction to infant development* (2nd ed.). New York: Oxford University Press obesity. *International Journal of Obesity and Related Metabolic Disorders, 25,* 721–726.

Bennett, C. I. (2007). *Comprehensive multicultural education* (6th ed.). Boston: Allyn & Bacon.

Bennett, P. A., & McDaniel, S. H. (2006). Coping in adolescent girls and women. In J. Worell & C. D. Goodheart (Eds.), *Handbook of girls' and women's psychological health: Gender and well-being across the lifespan.* New York: Oxford University Press.

Bennett, W., Lance, C. E., & Woehr, D. J. (Eds.). (2006). *Performance measurement.* Mahwah, NJ: Erlbaum.

Benson, P. (2007). Developmental assets. In R. K. Silbereisen & R. M. Lerner (Eds.), *Approaches to positive youth development.* Thousand Oaks, CA: Sage.

Benson, P. L., Scales, P. C., Hamilton, S. F., & Sesma, A. (2006). Positive youth development: Theory, research and applications. In W. Damon & R. Lerner (Eds.), *Handbook of child psychology* (6th ed.). New York: Wiley.

Benson, S. (2006). Community-based mental health care. *Creative Nursing, 12,* 14–16.

Bereiter, C., & Scardamalia, M. (1993). *Surpassing ourselves: An inquiry into the nature and implications of expertise.* Chicago: Open Court.

Bergman, M. E., Langhout, R. D., Palmieri, P. A., Cortina, L. M., & Fitzgerald, L. F. (2002). The (un)reasonableness of reporting: Antecedents and consequences of reporting sexual harassment. *Journal of Applied Psychology, 87,* 230–242.

Berko, J. (1958). The child's learning of English morphology. *World, 14,* 150–157.

Berko Gleason, J. (2005). *The development of language* (6th ed.). Boston: Allyn & Bacon.

Berkowitz, L. (1990). On the formation and regulation of anger and aggression: A cognitive neoassociationistic analysis. *American Psychologist, 45,* 494–503.

Berkowitz, L. (1993). *Aggression.* New York: McGraw-Hill.

Berkowitz, L., & LePage, A. (1996). Weapons as aggression-eliciting stimuli. In S. Fein & S. Spencer (Eds.), *Readings in social psychology: The art and science of research* (pp. 67–73). Boston: Houghton Mifflin.

Bernadin, H. J. (2007). *Human resource management* (4th ed.). New York: McGraw-Hill.

Bernhard, H., Fischbacher, U., & Fehr, E. (2006). Parochial altruism in humans. *Nature, 442,* 912–915.

Berntsen, D., & Rubin, D. C. (2006). Flashbulb memories and posttraumatic stress reactions across the life span: Age-related effects of the German occupation of Denmark during World War II. *Psychology of Aging, 21,* 127–139.

Berridge, C. W. (2006). Neural substrates of psychostimulant-induced arousal. *Neuropsychopharmacology, 31,* 2332–2340.

Berry, J. W. (2007). Acculturation. In J. E. Grusec & P. D. Hastings (Eds.), *Handbook of socialization.* New York: Guilford.

Berry, J. W., Phinney, J. S., Sam, D. L., & Vedder, P. (Eds.). (2006). *Immigrant youth in cultural transition.* Mahwah, NJ: Erlbaum.

Bersamin, M. M., Walker, S., Fisher, D. A., & Grube, J. W. (2006a). Correlates of oral sex and vaginal intercourse in early and middle adolescence. *Journal of Research on Adolescence, 16,* 59–68.

Bersamin, M. M., Walker, S., Waiters, E. D., Fisher, D. A., & Gruge, J. W. (2006b). Promising to wait: Virginity pledges and adolescent sexual behavior. *Journal of Adolescent Health, 36,* 428–436.

Berscheid, E. (1988). Some comments on love's anatomy. Or, whatever happened to an old-fashioned lust? In R. J. Sternberg & M. L. Barnes (Eds.), *Anatomy of love.* New Haven, CT: Yale University Press.

Berscheid, E. (2000). Attraction. In A. Kazdin (Ed.), *Encyclopedia of psychology.* Washington, DC, & New York: American Psychological Association and Oxford University Press.

Berscheid, E. (2006). Searching for the meaning of "love." In R. J. Sternberg & K. Weis (Eds.), *The new psychology of love* (pp. 171–183). New Haven, CT: Yale University Press.

Berscheid, E., Dion, K., Walster, E., & Walster, G. W. (1971). Physical attractiveness and dating choice: A test of the matching hypothesis. *Journal of Experimental Social Psychology, 7,* 173–189.

Berscheid, E., & Regan, P. C. (2005). *The psychology of interpersonal relationships.* New York: Prentice-Hall.

Bertrand, M., & Mullainathan, S. (2004). Are Emily and Greg more employable than Lakisha and Jamal? A field experiment on labor market discrimination. *American Economic Review, 94,* 991–1013.

Besedovsky, H. O., & Rey, A. D. (2007). Physiology of psychoneuroimmunology: A personal view. *Brain, Behavior, and Immunity, 21,* 34–44.

Bethmann, A., Tempelmann, C., De Bleser, R., Scheich, H., & Brechmann, A. (2007). Determining language laterality by fMRI and dichotic listening. *Brain Research, 1133,* 145–157.

Bettman, J. (2001). *Learning.* Unpublished manuscript, Fuqua School of Business, Duke University, Durham, NC.

Bhat, M. (2007). Role of glial neuronal intersections in forming blood-brain barrier. *Annual Review of Neuroscience* (vol. 30). Palo Alto, CA: Annual Reviews.

Bianchi, D. W., & Fisk, N. M. (2007). Fetomaternal cell trafficking and the stem cell debate: Gender matters. *Journal of the American Medical Association, 297,* 1489–1491.

Bimler, D. L., & Paramei, G. V. (2006). Facial-expression affective attributes and their configural correlates: Components and categories. *Spanish Journal of Psychology, 9,* 19–31.

Birditt, K. S., & Fingerman, K. L. (2003). Age and gender differences in adults' descriptions of emotional reactions to interpersonal problems. *Journals of Gerontology: Series B: Psychological Sciences and Social Sciences, 58B,* 237–245.

Birks, J. (2006). Cholinesterase inhibitors for Alzheimer's disease. *Cochrane Database System Review, 1,* DC005593.

Birmingham, C. L., Su, J., Hlynsky, J. A., Goldner, E. M., & Gao, M. (2005). The mortality rate from anorexia nervosa. *International Journal of Eating Disorders, 38,* 143–146.

Birren, J. E., & Schaie, K. W. (Eds.). (2006). *Handbook of the psychology of aging.* San Diego: Academic.

Birren, J. E., & Schaie, K. W. (Eds.) (2007). *Encyclopedia of gerontology.* Oxford, England: Elsevier.

Bishnoi, M., Chopra, K., & Kulkarni, S. K. (2006). Involvement of adenosinergic receptor system in an animal model of tardive dyskinesia and associated behavioral, biochemical, and neurochemical changes. *European Journal of Pharmacology, 552,* 55–66.

Bisson, J. I. (2007). Post-traumatic stress disorder. *British Medical Journal, 334,* 789–793.

Biswas-Diener, R., Vitterso, J., & Diener, E. (2005). Most people are pretty happy, but there is cultural variation: The Inughuit, the Amish, and the Maasai. *Journal of Happiness Studies, 6,* 205–226.

Bjorklund, D. F. (2007). *Why youth is not wasted on the young.* Malden, MA: Blackwell.

BKA. (2006). German federal crime statistics (German). http://www.bka.de/pks/pks2004/index2.html (accessed June 13, 2007).

Black, P. H. (2006). The inflammatory consequences of psychologic stress: Relationship to insulin resistance, obesity, atherosclerosis, and diabetes mellitus, type II. *Medical Hypotheses, 67,* 879–891.

Blader, J. C. (2006). Pharmacotherapy and postdischarge outcomes of child inpatients admitted for aggressive behavior. *Journal of Clinical Psychopharmacology, 26,* 419–425.

Blades, H. B. (2006). Killer coworker: The case of Michael McDermott, the Christmas killer. *The Forensic Examiner, 156,* 49–52.

Blair, S. N., Kohl, H. W., Paffenbarger, R. S., Clark, D. G., Cooper, K. H., & Gibbons, L. W. (1989). Physical fitness and all-cause mortality: A prospective study of healthy men and women. *Journal of the American Medical Association, 262,* 2395–2401.

Blake, R., & Sekuler, R. (2006). *Perception* (5th ed.). New York: McGraw-Hill.

Blalock, J. E., & Smith, E. M. (2007). Conceptual development of the immune system as a sixth sense. *Brain, Behavior, and Immunity, 21,* 23–33.

Blanchette, I., Richards, A., Melnyk, L., & Lavda, A. (2007). Reasoning about emotional contents following shocking terrorist attacks: A tale of three cities. *Journal of Experimental Psychology: Applied, 13,* 47–56.

Blass, T. (2004). *The man who shocked the world: The life and legacy of Stanley Milgram.* New York: Basic Books.

Blass, T. (2007). Unsupported allegations about a link between Milgram and the CIA: Tortured reasoning in *A Question of Torture. Journal of the History of the Behavioral Sciences, 43,* 199–203.

Bliese, P. D., & Jex, S. M. (2002). Incorporating a mulitilevel perspective into occupational stress research: Theoretical, methodological, and practical implications. *Journal of Occupational Health Psychology, 7,* 265–276.

Block, J. (1982). Assimilation, accommodation, and the dynamics of personality development. *Child Development, 53,* 281–295.

Block, J., & Kremen, A. M. (1996). IQ and ego-resiliency: Conceptual and empirical connections and separateness. *Journal of Personality and Social Psychology, 70,* 349–361.

Blonna, R. (2007). *Coping with stress in a changing world* (4th ed.). New York: McGraw-Hill.

Blonna, R., & Paterson, W. (2007). *Coping with stress in a changing world* (4th ed.). New York: McGraw-Hill.

Bloom, B. (1985). *Developing talent in young people.* New York: Ballantine.

Bloom, F., Nelson, C. A., & Lazerson, A. (2001). *Brain, mind, and behavior* (3rd ed.). New York: Worth.

Bloom, P. (2004). Myths of word learning. In D. G. Hall & S. R. Waxman (Eds), *Weaving a lexicon.* (pp. 205–224). Cambridge, MA: MIT Press.

Bloor, C., & White, F. (1983). Unpublished manuscript. LaJolla, CA: University of California, San Diego.

Blumenfeld, P. C., Kempler, T. M., & Krajcik, J. S. (2006). Motivation and cognitive engagement in learning environments. In R. K. Sawyer (Ed.), *The Cambridge handbook of learning sciences.* New York: Cambridge University Press.

Blundell, J. E. (1984). Systems and interactions: An approach to the pharmacology of feeding. In A. J. Stunkdard & E. Stellar (Eds.), *Eating and its disorders.* New York: Raven Press.

Blustein, D. L. (2006). *Psychology of working.* Mahwah, NJ: Erlbaum.

Boden, J. M., Fergusson, D. M., & Horwood, L. J. (2006, November). Anxiety disorders and suicidal behaviors in adolescence and young adulthood: Findings from a longitudinal study. *Psychological Medicine, 36,* 1–10.

Boden, J. M., Fergusson, D. M., & Horwood, L. J. (2007). Anxiety disorders and suicidal behaviours in adolescence and young adulthood: Findings from a longitudinal study. *Psychological Medicine, 37,* 431–440.

Bodrova, E., & Leong, D. J. (2007). *Tools of the mind* (2nd ed.). Geneva, Switzerland: International Bureau of Education, UNESCO.

Boekaerts, M. (2006). Self-regulation and effort investment. In K. A. Renninger. I. E Sigel, W. Damon, & R. M. Lerner (Eds.), *Handbook of child psychology* (6th ed., vol. 4, *Child psychology in practice,* pp. 345–377). Hoboken, NJ: Wiley.

Bogaert, A. F., Woodard, U., & Hafer, C. L. (1999). Intellectual ability and reactions to pornography. *Journal of Sex Research, 36,* 283–291.

Bohart, A. C., & Greening, T. (2001). Humanistic psychology and positive psychology. *American Psychologist, 56,* 81–82.

Bolte, S., Hubl, D., Feineis-Matthews, S., Prvulovic, D., Dierks, T., & Poustka, F. (2006). Facial affect recognition training in autism: Can we animate the fusiform gyrus? *Behavioral Neuroscience, 120,* 211–216.

Bonfatti, J. F. (2005). Hope holds the key: Finding inspiration. *Schizophrenia Digest, (Summer),* 31–34. www.schizophreniadigest.com

Bonnie, K. E., & de Waal, F. B. M. (2004). Primate social reciprocity and the origin of gratitude. In R. A. Emmons & M. E. McCullough (Eds.), *The psychology of gratitude* (pp. 213–229). Oxford, England: Oxford University Press.

Bono, G., & McCullough, M. E. (2006). Positive responses to benefit and harm: Bringing forgiveness and gratitude into cognitive psychotherapy. *Journal of Cognitive Psychotherapy, 20,* 147–158.

Bonvillian, J. (2005). Unpublished review of Santrock *Topical Life-Span Development,* 2nd ed. New York: McGraw-Hill.

Boodman, S. G. (2002, February 12). Beautiful but not rare recovery: John Nash's genius is extraordinary but recovery from schizophrenia is anything but. *Washington Post.*

Boothroyd, R. A., Best, K. A., Giard, J. A., Stiles, P. G., Suleski, J., Ort, R., & White, R. (2006). Poor and depressed, The tip of the iceberg: The unmet needs of enrollees in an indigent health care plan. *Adminstration and Policy in Mental Health and Mental Health Services Research, 33,* 172–181.

Borckardt, J. J. (2002). Case study examining the efficacy of a multi-modal psychotherapeutic intervention for hypertension. *International Journal of Clinical and Experimental Hypnosis, 50,* 189–201.

Born, J., Rasch, B., & Gais, S. (2006). Sleep to remember. *Neuroscientist, 12,* 410–424.

Bornstein, M. (2006). Parenting science and practice. In W. Damon & R. Lerner (Eds.), *Handbook of child psychology* (6th ed.). New York: Wiley.

Borowsky, R., & Besner, D. (2006). Parallel distributed processing and lexical-semantic effects in visual word recognition: Are a few stages necessary? *Psychological Review, 113,* 181–195.

Bosel, R. (2007). Brain imaging methods and the study of cognitive processes. In M. Ash & T. Sturm (Eds.), *Psychology's territories.* Mahwah, NJ: Erlbaum.

Boseley, S. (2006, June 12). Tough curbs on Prozac prescribed for children. *The Guardian.*

Bota, M., & Swanson, L. W. (2007). Online workbenches for neural network connections. *Journal of Comparative Neurology, 500,* 807–814.

Bouchard, T. J., Lykken, D. T., Tellegen, A., & McGue, M. (1996). Genes, drives, environment, and experience. In D. Lubinski & C. Benbow (Eds.), *Psychometrics and social issues concerning intellectual talent.* Baltimore: Johns Hopkins University Press.

Bourin, M., & Prica, C. (2007). The role of mood stabilizers in the treatment of the depressive facet of bipolar disorders. *Neuroscience and Biobehavioral Reviews.* (in press)

Bovensiepen, G. (2006). Attachment-dissociation network: Some thoughts about a modern complex theory. *Journal of Analytic Psychology, 51,* 451–466.

Bower, G. H., Clark, M., Winzenz, D., & Lesgold, A. (1969). Hierarchical retrieval schemes in recall of categorized word lists. *Journal of Verbal Learning and Verbal Behavior, 3,* 323–343.

Bowlby, J. (1969). *Attachment and loss* (vol. 1). London: Hogarth Press.

Bowlby, J. (1989). *Secure and insecure attachment.* New York: Basic Books.

Boyiadzis, M., & Foon, K. A. (2006). Natural killer cells: From bench to cancer therapy. *Expert Opinion on Biological Therapy, 6,* 967–970.

Brabeck, M. M., & Brabeck, K. M. (2006). Women and relationships. In J. Worell & C. D. Goodheart (Eds.), *Handbook of girls' and women's health: Gender and well-being across the lifespan.* New York: Oxford University Press.

Bradley, S. J., Oliver, G. D., Chernick, A. B., & Zucker, K. J. (1998). Experiments of nurture: Ablatio penis at 2 months, sex reassignment at 7 months, and a psychosexual follow-up in young adulthood. *Pediatrics, 102,* e9.

Brady, S. S., & Halpern-Felsher, B. L. (2007). Adolescents' reported consequences of having oral sex versus vaginal sex. *Pediatrics, 119,* 229–236.

Braet, C., & van Aken, M. A. G. (2006). Developmental psychopathology: Substantive, methodological and policy issues. *International Journal of Behavioral Development, 30,* 2–4.

Brammer, L. M., & MacDonald, G. (1999). *The helping relationship* (7th ed.). Boston: Allyn & Bacon.

Brandstadter, J. (2006). Action perspectives in human development. In W. Damon & R. Lerner (Eds.), *Handbook of child psychology* (6th ed.). New York: Wiley.

Brannick, M. T., & Levine, E. L. (2002). *Job analysis: Methods, research, and applications.* Thousand Oaks, CA: Sage.

Brannon, L. (1999). *Gender: Psychological perspectives* (2nd ed.). Boston: Allyn & Bacon.

Bransford, J., & others. (2006). Learning theories and education: Toward a decade of synergy. In P. A. Alexander & P.H. Winne (Eds.), *Handbook of educational psychology* (2nd ed.). Mahwah, NJ: Erlbaum.

Brasher, E. E., & Chen, P. Y. (1999). Evaluation of success criteria in job search: A process perspective. *Journal of Occupational and Organizational Psychology, 72,* 57–70.

Breer, H., Fleischer, J., & Strotmann, J. (2006). The sense of smell: Multiple olfactory subsystems. *Cellular and Molecular Life Sciences, 63,* 1465–1475.

Breitmeyer, B. G., Kafaligonul, H., Ogmen, H., Mardon, L., Todd, S., & Ziegler, R. (2006). Meta- and paracontrast reveal differences between contour- and brightness-processing mechanisms. *Vision Research, 46,* 2645–2658.

Breland, K., & Breland, M. (1961). The misbehavior of organisms. *American Psychologist, 16,* 681–684.

Brennan, A. M., & Mantzoros, C. S. (2006). Drug insight: The role of leptin in human pathophysiology—emerging clinical applications. *Nature Clinical Practice: Endocrinology and Metabolism, 2,* 318–327.

Brennan, P., Mednick, S., & Kandel, E. (1991). Congenital determinants of violent and property offencing. In D. Pepler & K. Rubin (Eds.), *The development and treatment of childhood aggression.* Mahwah, NJ: Erlbaum.

Breslau, N., & Alvarado, G. F. (2007). The clinical significance criterion in DSM-IV post-traumatic stress disorder. *Psychological Medicine, 37,* 1–8.

Brett, J. G., & Atwater, L. E. (2001). 360-degree feedback: Accuracy, reactions, and perceptions of usefulness. *Journal of Applied Psychology, 86,* 930–942.

Brewer, J. B., Zuo, Z., Desmond, J. E., Glover, G. H., & Gabrieli, J. D. E. (1998). Making memories: Brain activity that predicts how well visual experience will be remembered. *Science, 281,* 1185–1187.

Brewer, M. B. (2007). The social psychology of intergroup relations: Social categorization, ingroup bias, and outgroup prejudice. In A. W. Kruglanski & E. Tory Higgins (Eds.), *Social psychology: Handbook of basic principles* (2nd ed.). New York: Guilford.

Brewer, M. B., & Brown, R. J. (1998). Intergroup relations. In D. T. Gilbert, S. T. Fiske, & G. Lindzey (Eds.), *Handbook of social psychology* (4th ed., vol. 2). New York: McGraw-Hill.

Brickman, P., & Campbell, D. T. (1971). Hedonic relativism and planning the good society. In M. H. Appley (Ed.), *Adaptation-level theory* (pp. 287–302). New York: Academic.

Bridgman, T. (2007). Review of the three faces of leadership: Manager, artist, priest. *Personnel Review, 36,* 494–496.

Briggs, S. R. (1988). Shyness: Introversion or neuroticism? *Journal of Research in Personality, 22,* 290–307.

Brigham, J. C. (1986). Race and eyewitness identifications. In S. Worschel & W. G. Austin (Eds.), *Psychology of intergroup relations*. Chicago: Nelson-Hall.

Brigham, J. C., Bennett, L. B., Meissner, C. A., & Mitchell, T. L. (2007). The influence of race on eyewitness memory. In R.C. L. Lindsay, D. F. Ross, J. D. Read, & M. P. Toglia (Eds.), *The handbook of eyewitness memory: Vol II.* Mahwah, NJ: Erlbaum.

Bright, D., Cameron, K. S., & Caza, A. (2006). The ethos of virtuousness in downsized organizations. *Journal of Business Ethics.* (in press)

Bright, D., & Goodman-Delahunty, J. (2006). Gruesome evidence and emotion: Anger, blame, and jury decision-making. *Law and Human Behavior, 30,* 183–202.

Brignell, C. M., & Curran, H. V. (2006). Drugs, sweat, and fears: A comparison of the effects of diazepam and methylphenidate on fear conditioning. *Psychopharmacology, 186,* 504–516.

Brink, S. (2001, May 7). Your brain on alcohol. *U.S. News & World Report, 130*(18), 50–57.

Brinton, R. D., & Wang, J. M. (2006) Preclinical analyses of the therapeutic potential of allopregnanolone to promote neurogenesis in vitro and in vivo in transgenic mouse model of Alzheimer's disease. *Current Alzheimer's Research, 3,* 11–7.

Briones, T. L. (2006). Environment, physical activity, and neurogenesis: Implications for the treatment of Alzheimer's disease. *Current Alzheimer's Research, 3,* 49–54.

Brister, H., Turner, J. A., Aaron, L. A., & Manci, L. (2006). Self-efficacy is associated with pain, functioning, and coping in patients with chronic temporomandibular disorder pain. *Journal of Orofacial Pain, 20,* 115–124.

Broderick, R. (2003, July/August). A surgeon's saga. *Minnesota: The magazine of the University of Minnesota Alumni Association,* 26–31.

Brody, L. R. (1999). Gender emotion and the family. Cambridge, MA: Harvard University Press.

Brody, N. (2007). Does education influence intelligence? In P. C. Kyllonen, R. D. Roberts, & L. Stankov (Eds.), *Extending intelligence.* Mahwah, NJ: Erlbaum.

Bronfenbrenner, U., & Morris, P. A. (2006). The bioecological model of human development. In W. Damon & R. Lerner (Eds.), *Handbook of child psychology* (6th ed.). New York: Wiley.

Bronikowski, A. M., Morgan, T. J., Garland, T., & Carter, P. A. (2006). The evolution of aging and age-related physical decline in mice selectively bred for high voluntary exercise. *Evolution: International Journal of Organic Revolution, 60,* 1494–1508.

Brooks, D. J. (2006). Dopaminergic action beyond its effects on motor function: Imaging studies. *Journal of Neurology, 253,* 8–15.

Brooks, J. G., & Brooks, M. G. (2001). *In search of understanding: The case for the constructivist classroom.* Upper Saddle River, NJ: Prentice-Hall.

Brooks-Gunn, J., & Warren, M. P. (1989). The psychological significance of secondary sexual characteristics in 9- to 11-year-old girls. *Child Development, 59,* 161–169.

Brophy, J. (2004). *Motivating students to learn* (2nd ed.). Mahwah, NJ: Erlbaum.

Bretherton, C. (2007). The social psychology of stereotyping, discrimination and prejudice. *Journal of Community & Applied Social Psychology, 17,* 159–165.

Brown, F. C., Buboltz, W. C., & Soper, B. (2006). Development and evaluation of the Sleep Treatment and Education Program for Students (STEPS). *Journal of American College Health, 54,* 231–237.

Brown, G. S., Lambert, M. J., Jones, E. R., & Minami, T. (2005). Identifying highly effective psychotherapists in a managed care environment. *American Journal of Managed Care, 11,* 513–520.

Brown, R. (1973). *A first language: The early stages.* Cambridge, MA: Harvard University Press.

Brown, S., Martinez, M. J., & Parsons, L. M. (2006). Music and language side by side in the brain: A PET study of the generation of melodies and sentences. *European Journal of Neuroscience, 23,* 2791–2803.

Brown, S. L., Nesse, R. N., Vinokur, A. D., & Smith, D. M. (2003). Providing social support may be more beneficial than receiving it: Results from a prospective study of mortality. *Psychological Science, 14,* 320–327.

Brown, W. A. (2007). Treatment response in melancholia. *Acta Psychiatrica Scandinavica, 433,* 125–129.

Brownell, K. D., & Rodin, J. (1994). The dieting maelstrom: Is it possible to lose weight? *American Psychologist, 9,* 781–791.

Brownlee, S. (1998, June 15). Baby talk. *U.S. News & World Report,* 48–54.

Bruce, D. (1989). Functional explanations of memory. In L. W. Poon, D. C. Rubin, & B. A. Wilson (Eds.), *Everyday cognition in adulthood and late life* (pp. 44–58). Cambridge, England: Cambridge University Press.

Bruck, M., Ceci, S. J., & Principe, G. F. (2006). The child and the law. In K. A. Renninger, I. E. Sigel, W. Damon, & R. M. Lerner (Eds.), *Handbook of child psychology* (6th ed., vol. 4, *Child psychology in practice,* pp. 776–816). Hoboken, NJ: Wiley.

Brückner, H., & Bearman, P. (2005). After the promise: The STD consequences of adolescent virginity pledges. *Journal of Adolescent Health, 36,* 271–278.

Brug, J., Conner, M., Harré, N., Kremers, S., McKellar, S., & Whitelaw, S. (2004). The transtheoretical model and stages of change: A critique. Observations by five commentators on the paper by Adams, J. and White, M. (2004) Why don't stage-based activity promotion interventions work? *Health Education Research, 20,* 244–258.

Brugman, G. M. (2006). Wisdom and aging. In J. E. Birren & K. W. Schaie (Eds.), *Handbook of the psychology of aging* (6th ed.). San Diego: Academic.

Bruning, R. H., Schraw, G. J., Norby, M. M., & Ronning, R. R. (2004). *Cognitive psychology and instruction* (4th ed.). Upper Saddle River, NJ: Prentice-Hall.

Brunstein, J. (1993). Personal goals and subjective well-being: A longitudinal study. *Journal of Personality and Social Psychology, 65,* 1061–1070.

Brunstein, J., & Maier, G. W. (2005). Implicit and self-attributed motives to achieve: Two separate but interacting needs. *Journal of Personality and Social Psychology, 89,* 205–222.

Bryant, F. B., & Veroff, J. (2007). *Savoring: A new model of positive experience.* Mahwah, NJ: Erlbaum.

Bryant, R. A. (2006). Longitudinal psychophysiological studies of heart rate: Mediating effects and implications for treatment. *Annals of the New York Academy of Science, 1071,* 19–26.

Bucherelli, C., Baldi, E., Mariottini, C., Passani, M. B., & Blandina, P. (2006). Aversive memory reactivation engages in the amygdala only some neurotransmitters involved in consolidation. *Learning and Memory, 13,* 426–430.

Buckley, K. E., & Anderson, C. A. (2006). A theoretical model of the effects and consequences of playing video games. In P. Vorderer & J. Bryant (Eds.), *Playing video games—motives, responses, and consequences* (pp. 363–378). Mahwah, NJ: Erlbaum.

Buijs, R. M., Scheer, F. A., Kreier, F., Yi, C., Bos, N., Goncharuk, V. D., & Kalsbeek, A. (2006). Organization of circadian functions: Interaction with the body. *Progress in Brain Research, 153,* 341–360.

Bukach, C. M., Bub, D. N., Gauthier, I., & Tarr, M. J. (2006). *Journal of Cognitive Neuroscience, 18,* 48–63.

Bukowski, W. M., Brendgen, M., & Vitaro, F. (2007). Peers and socialization: Effects on externalizing and internalizing problems. In J. E. Grusec & P. D. Hastings (Eds.), *Handbook of socialization.* New York: Oxford University Press.

Bulakowski, P. F., Koldewyn, K., & Whitney, D. (2007). Independent coding of object
motion and position revealed by distinct contingent aftereffects. *Vision Research, 47,* 810–817.

Bunting, M., Cowan, N., & Scott Saults, J. (2006). How does running memory span work? *Quarterly Journal of Experimental Psychology, 59,* 1691–1700.

Bureau of Justice Statistics. (2006, December 21). *Teen drug use continues down in 2006, particularly among older teens; but use of prescription-type drugs remains high,* University of Michigan News and Information Services. http://www.ojp.usdoj.gov/bjs/dcf/du.htm (accessed May 25, 2007).

Burgdorf, J., & Panksepp, J. (2006). The neurobiology of positive emotions. *Neuroscience and Biobehavioral Reviews, 30,* 173–187.

Burger, J. M., & Caldwell, D. F. (2000). Personality, social activities, job-search behavior and interview success: Distinguishing between PANAS trait positive affect and NEO extraversion. *Motivation and Emotion, 24,* 51–62.

Burns, D. (1985). *Intimate connections.* New York: William Morrow.

Burton, C. M., & King, L. A. (2004). The health benefits of writing about peak experiences. *Journal of Research in Personality, 38,* 150–163.

Busch, F. (2007). "I noticed": The emergence of self-observation in relationship to pathological attractor sites. *International Journal of Psychoanalysis, 88,* 423–441.

Bushman, B. J., & Anderson, C. A. (2007). Measuring the strength of the effect of violent media on aggression. *American Psychologist, 62,* 253–254.

Bushman, B. J., & Baumeister, R. F. (2002). Does self-love or self-hate lead to violence? *Journal of Research in Personality, 36,* 543–545.

Buss, D. M. (2008). *Evolutionary psychology* (3rd ed.). Boston: Allyn & Bacon.

Buss, R. R., Sun, W., & Oppenheim, R. W. (2006). Adaptive roles of programmed cell death during nervous system development. *Annual Review of Neuroscience, 29,* 1–35.

Butcher, J. N. (2004). The Minnesota Multiphasic Personality Inventory (MMPI-2). In M. Hersen (Ed.), *Comprehensive handbook of psychological assessment* (vol. 2). New York: Wiley.

Butcher, J. N., Hamilton, C. K., Rouse, S. V., & Cumella, E. J. (2006). The desconstruction of the Hy Scale of MMPI-2: Failure of RC3 in measuring somatic symptom expression. *Journal of Personality Assessment, 87,* 186–192.

Butler, A. C., Chapman, J. E., Forman, E. M., & Beck, A. T. (2006). The empirical status of cognitive-behavioral therapy: A review of meta-analyses. *Clinical Psychology Review, 26,* 17–31.

Buunk, A. P., Zurriaga, R., Gonzales, P., Terol, C., & Roig, S. L. (2006). Targets and dimensions of social comparison among people with spinal cord injury and other health problems. *British Journal of Health Psychology, 11,* 677–693.

Buunk, B. P., & Van Yperen, N. W. (1991). Referential comparisons, relational comparisons, and exchange orientation: Their relation to marital satisfaction. *Personality and Social Psychology Bulletin, 17,* 709–717.

Byrne, P. (2007). Managing the acute psychotic episode. *British Medical Journal, 334,* 686–692.

C

Cabeza, R. (2002). Hemispheric asymmetry reduction in older adults: The HAROLD model. *Psychology and Aging, 17,* 85–100.

Cabeza, R., Nyberg, L., & Park, D. (Eds.). (2005). *Cognitive neuroscience of aging.* New York: Oxford University Press.

Cabeza, R., & St. Jacques, P. (2007). Functional neuroimaging of autobiographical memory. *Trends in Cognitive Science, 11,* 219–227.

Cacioppo, J. T., & Berntson, G. G. (2007). The brain, homeostasis, and health: Balancing demands of the internal and external milieu. In H. S. Friedman & R. C. Silver (Eds.), *Foundations of health psychology* (pp. 73–91). New York: Oxford University Press.

Cacioppo, J. T., Hawkley, L. C., Berntson, G. C., Ernst, J. M., Gibbs, A. C., Stickgold, R., & Hobson, J. A. (2002). Do lonely days invade the nights? Potential social modulation of sleep efficiency. *Psychological Science, 13*(4), 384–387.

Cacioppo, J. T., Hawkley, L. C., Kalil, A., Hughes, M. E., Waite, L., & Thisted, R. A. (2007). Happiness and the invisible threads of social connection: The Chicago Health, Aging, and Social Relations Study. In M. Eid & R. Larsen (Eds.), *The science of well-being.* New York: Guilford. (in press)

Cacioppo, J. T., Hughes, M. E., Waite, L. J., Hawkley, L. C. & Thisted, R. A. (2006). Loneliness as a specific risk factor for depressive symptoms: Cross-sectional and longitudinal analyses. *Psychology and Aging, 21,* 140–151.

Cacioppo, J. T., Tassinary, L., & Berntson, G. C. (Eds.). (2007). *Handbook of psychophysiology* (3rd ed.). New York: Cambridge University Press.

Caetano, R., & McGrath, C. (2005) Driving under the influence among U.S. ethnic groups. *Accident Analysis and Prevention, 37,* 217–224.

Cain, D. J. (2001). Defining characteristics, history, and evolution of humanistic psychotherapies. In D. J. Cain & J. Seeman (Eds.), *Humanistic psychotherapies.* Washington, DC: American Psychological Association.

Caldwell, S. (2004). *Statistics unplugged.* Belmont, CA: Wadsworth.

Cameron, J. (2001). Negative effects of reward on intrinsic motivation—A limited phenomenon: Comment on Deci, Koestner, and Ryan (2001). *Review of Educational Research, 71,* 29–42.

Cameron, J., Banko, K. M., & Pierce, W. D. (2001). Pervasive negative effects of rewards on intrinsic motivation: The myth continues. *Behavior Analyst, 24,* 1–44.

Cameron, J., & Pierce, W. D. (2002). Rewards and intrinsic motivation: Resolving the controversy. Westport, CT: Bergin & Garvey.

Cameron, K. S. (2003). Organizational virtuousness and performance. In K. S. Cameron, J. E. Dutton, & R. E. Quinn (Eds.), *Positive organizational scholarship: Foundations of a new discipline* (pp. 48–65). San Francisco: Berrett-Koehler Publishers.

Cameron, K. S. (2005). Organizational downsizing. In N. Nicholson, P. G. Audia, & M. M. Pilluta (Eds.), *The Blackwell encyclopedia of management.* Malden, MA: Blackwell.

Cameron, K. S. (2007). Positive organizational change. In S. Clegg & B. James (Eds.), *International encyclopedia of organizational studies.* Thousand Oaks, CA: Sage.

Cameron, K. S., & Caza, A. (2005). Developing strategies for responsible leadership. In J. P. Dohl & S. Stumph (Eds.), *Handbook of responsible leadership and governance in global business.* New York: Oxford University Press.

Cameron, K. S., Quinn, R. E., DeGraff, J., & Thakor, A. (2006). *Competing values leadership: Creating value in organizations.* New York: Edward Elgar.

Campbell, A. J., Cumming, S. R., & Hughes, I. (2006). Internet use by the socially fearful: Addiction or therapy? *Cyberpsychology and Behavior, 9,* 69–81.

Campbell, F. A. (2006). The malleability of the cognitive development of children of low income African-American families. In P. C. Kyllonen, R. D. Robers, & L. Stankov (Eds.), *Extending intelligence.* Mahwah, NJ: Erlbaum.

Campbell, L., Campbell, B., & Dickinson, D. (2004). *Teaching and learning through multiple intelligences.* Boston: Allyn & Bacon.

Campbell, W. K., Bonacci, A. M., Shelton, J., Exline, J. J., & Bushman, B. J. (2004). Psychological entitlement: Interpersonal consequences and validation of a self-report measure. *Journal of Personality Assessment, 83,* 29–45.

Campfield, L. A., Smith, F. J., Gulsez, Y., Devos, R., & Burn, P. (1995). Mouse OB protein: Evidence for a peripheral signal linking adiposity and central neural networks. *Science, 269,* 546–549.

Campion, M. A., Palmer, D. K., & Campion, J. E. (1997). A review of structure in the selection interview. *Personnel Psychology, 50,* 655–702.

Canadian Statistics. (2005). Crime in Canada. http://www.statcan.ca/Daily/English/050721/d050721a.htm|title=Crime in Canada. (accessed June 13, 2007).

Canino, G., & others. (2004). The DSM-IV rates of child and adolescent disorders in Puerto Rico. *Archives of General Psychiatry, 61,* 85–93.

Cannistraro, P. A., Makris, N., Howard, J. D., Wedig, M. M., Hodge, S. M., Wilhelm, S., Kennedy, D. N., & Rauch, S. L. (2006). A diffusion tensor imaging study of white matter in obsessive-compulsive disorder. *Depression and Anxiety.* (in press)

Cannistraro, P. A., Wright, C. I., Wedig, M. M., Martis, B., Shin, L. M., Wilhelm, S., & Rauch, S. L. (2004). Amygdala responses to human faces in obsessive-compulsive disorder. *Biological Psychiatry, 56,* 916–920.

Cantor, N., & Sanderson, C. A. (1999). Life task participation and well-being: The importance of taking part in daily life. In D. Kahneman, E. Diener, & N. Schwarz (Eds.), *Well-being: The foundations of hedonic psychology* (pp. 230–243). New York: Russell Sage Foundation.

Cantuti-Castelvetri, Shukitt-Hale, B., & Joseph, J. A. (2003). Dopamine neurotoxicity: Age-dependent behavioral and histological effects. *Neurobiology of Aging, 24,* 697–706.

Caporeal, L. R. (2007). Evolution. In A.W. Kruglanski & E. T. Higgins (Eds.), *Social psychology* (2nd ed.). New York: Guilford.

Carden, R., & Rettew, S. (2006). Internet chat room use, satisfaction with life, and loneliness. *Psychological Reports, 98,* 121–122.

Cardno, A. G., & Gottesman, I. I. (2000). Twin studies of schizophrenia: From bow-and-arrow concordances to Star Wars Mx and functional genomics. *American Journal of Medical Genetics, 97,* 12–17.

Carey, W. B. (2002). Is ADHD a valid disorder? In P. Jensen & J. Cooper (Eds.), *Attention deficit hyperactivity disorder: State of the science, best practices.* Kingston, NJ: Civic Research Institute.

Carkenord, D. M., & Bullington, J. (1995). Bringing cognitive dissonance to the classroom. In M. E. Ware & D. E. Johnson (Eds.), *Demonstrations and activities in teaching of psychology* (vol. 3). Mahwah, NJ: Erlbaum.

Carlo, G. (2006). Care-based and altruistically-based morality. In M. Killen & J. Smetana (Eds.), *Handbook of moral development.* Mahwah, NJ: Erlbaum.

Carlson, N. R. (2001). *Physiology of behavior* (7th ed.). Boston: Allyn & Bacon.

Carnagey, N. L., & Anderson, C. A. (2005). The effects of reward and punishment in violent video games on aggressive affect, cognition, and behavior. *Psychological Science,16*(11), 882–889.

Carney, C. E., Edinger, J. D., Meyer, B., Lindman, L., & Istre, T. (2006). Symptom-focused rumination and sleep disturbance. *Behavioral Sleep Medicine, 4,* 228–241.

Carney, D. R., Nosek, B. A., Greenwald, A. G., & Banaji, M. R. (2007). Implicit Association Test (IAT). In R. Baumeister & K. Vohs (Eds.), *Encyclopedia of social psychology.* Thousand Oaks, CA: Sage.

Carpenter, S. K., & DeLosh, E. L. (2006). Impoverished cue support enhances subsequent retention: Support for the elaborative retrieval explanation of the testing effect. *Memory and Cognition, 34,* 268–276.

Carroll, J. L. (2007). *Sexuality now* (2nd ed.). Belmont, CA: Thompson.

Carskadon, M. A. (2005). Sleep and circadian rhythms in children and adolescence: Relevance for athletic performance of young people. *Clinical Sports Medicine, 24,* 319–328.

Carskadon, M. A. (2006, March). *Too little, too late: Sleep bioregulatory processes across adolescence.* Paper presented at the meeting of the Society for Research on Adolescence, San Francisco.

Carskadon, M. A., Acebo, C., & Jenni, O. G. (2004). Regulation of adolescent sleep: Implications for behavior. *Annals of the New York Academy of Sciences, 102,* 276–291.

Carskadon, M. A., Mindell, J., & Drake, C. (2006, September). *Contemporary sleep patterns in the USA: Results of the 2006 National Sleep Foundation Poll.* Paper presented at the European Sleep Research Society, Innsbruck, Austria.

Carson, R. C., Butcher, J. N., & Mineka, S. (1996). *Abnormal psychology and life* (10th ed.). New York: HarperCollins.

Carstensen, L. L. (1995). Evidence for a life-span theory of socioemotional selectivity. *Current Directions in Psychological Science, 4,* 151–156.

Carstensen, L. L. (1998). A life-span approach to social motivation. In J. Heckhausen & C. Dweck (Eds.), *Motivation and self-regulation across the life span.* New York: Cambridge University Press.

Carstensen, L. L. (2006). The influence of a sense of time on human development. *Science, 312,* 1913–1915.

Carstensen, L. L., & Charles, S. T. (2003). Human aging: Why is even good news taken as bad? In L. A. Aspinall & U. M. Staudinger (Eds.), *A psychology of human strengths.* Washington, DC: American Psychological Association.

Carstensen, L. L., Charles, S. T., Isaacowitz, D., & Kennedy, Q. (2003). Life-span personality development and emotion. In R. J. Davidson, K. Scherer, & H. H. Goldsmith (Eds.), *Handbook of Affective Sciences.* Oxford: Oxford University Press.

Carstensen, L. L., Mikels, J. A., & Mather, M. (2006). Aging at the intersection of cognition, motivation, and emotion. In J. E. Birren & K. W. Schaie (Eds.), *Handbook of the psychology of aging* (6th ed.). San Diego: Academic.

Carter, C. S., Pournajafi-Nazarloo, H., Kramer, K. M., Ziegler, T. E., White-Traut, R., Bello, D., & Schwertz, D. (2007). Oxytocin: Behavioral associations and potential as a salivary biomarker. *Annals of the New York Academy of Sciences, 1098,* 312–322.

Carter, R. (1998). *Mapping the mind.* Berkeley: University of California Press.

Carton, J. S. (1996). The differential effects of tangible rewards and praise on intrinsic motivation: A comparison of cognitive evaluation theory and operant theory. *Behavior Analyst, 19,* 237–255.

Carver, C. S. (2007). Stress, coping, and health. In H. S. Friedman & R. C. Silver (Eds.), *Foundations of health psychology.* New York: Oxford University Press.

Carver, C. S., Pozo, C., Harris, S. D., Noriega, V., Scheier, M., Robinson, D., & others. (1993). How coping mediates the effect of optimism on distress: A study of women with early stage breast cancer. *Journal of Personality and Social Psychology, 65,* 375–390.

Carver, C. S., & Scheier, M. F. (2000). Origins and functions of positive and negative affect: A control process view. In E. T. Higgins & A .W. Kruglanski, (Eds.), *Motivational science: Social and personality perspectives* (pp. 256–272). New York: Psychology Press.

Carver, C. S., & Scheier, M. F. (2004). *Perspectives on personality* (5th ed.). Boston: Allyn & Bacon.

Case, R. B., Moss, A. J., Case, N., McDermott, M., & Eberly, S. (1992). Living alone after myocardial infarction. Impact on prognosis. *Journal of the American Medical Association, 267,* 515–519.

Cassidy, K. W., Werner, R. S., Rourke, M., Zubernis, L. S., & Balaraman, G. (2003). The relationship between psychological understanding and positive social behaviors. *Social Development, 12,* 198–221.

Castonguay, L. G., Gottfried, M. R., Halperin, G. S., & Reid, J. J. (2003). Psychotherapy integration. In I. B. Weiner (Ed.), *Handbook of psychology* (vol. 8). New York: Wiley.

Catapano, F., Perris, F., Masella, M., Rossano, F., Cigliano, M., Magliano, L., & Maj, M. (2006). Obsessive-compulsive disorder: A 3-year prospective follow-up study of patients treated with serotonin reuptake inhibitors: OCD follow-up study. *Journal of Psychiatric Research, 40,* 502–510.

Cathers-Schiffman, T. A., & Thompson, M. S. (2007). Assessment of English- and Spanish-speaking students with the WISC-III and Leiter-R. *Journal of Psychoeducational Assessment, 25,* 41–52.

Cattell, R. B. (1946). *The description and measurement of personality.* New York: Harcourt, Brace & World.

Cauller, L. (2001, May). *Review of Santrock, Psychology* (7th ed.). New York: McGraw-Hill.

Cawsey, T. F., & Deszca, G. (2007). *Toolkit for organizational change.* Thousand Oaks, CA: Sage.

CBS News. (2006, March 15). Ambien may prompt sleep eating. http://www.cbsnews.com/stories/2006/03/15/earlyshow/health/health_news/main1404632.shtml (accessed December 15, 2006).

Center for Family and Demographic Research. (2002). *Ohio population news: Marriage in U.S. and Ohio.* Bowling Green, Ohio: Author.

Centers for Disease Control and Prevention. (2001). *How to quit.* Atlanta: Author.

Centers for Disease Control and Prevention. (2003a). Births: Final data for 2002. *National Vital Statistics Reports, 52*(10), 1–5.

Centers for Disease Control and Prevention. (2003b). *HIV/AIDS.* Atlanta: Author.

Centers for Disease Control and Prevention. (2003c). *Morbidity and Mortality Weekly Report, 54,* 842–847.

Centers for Disease Control and Prevention, National Center for Injury Prevention and Control. (2004). *Web-based injury statistics query and reporting system* (WISQARS). http://www.cdc.gov/ncipc/wisqars/default. htm (accessed June 21, 2004).

Centers for Disease Control and Prevention. (2005). National Youth Risk Behavior Survey: 1991–2005. U.S. Department of Health and Human Services, Centers for Disease Control and Prevention.

Centers for Disease Control and Prevention. (2006). *2006 Surgeon General's Report 2006.* Washington, DC: Author.

Chai, W., Du., Q., Shay, J. W., & Wright, W. E. (2006). Human telomeres have different overhang sizes at leading versus lagging strands. *Molecular Cell, 21,* 427–435.

Chaiken, S., & Ledgerwood, A. (2007). Heuristic processing. In R. Baumeister & K. D. Vohs (Eds.), *Encyclopedia of social psychology.* Thousand Oaks, CA: Sage.

Chambon, V., Baudouin, J., & Franck, N. (2006). The role of configural information in facial emotion recognition in schizophrenia. *Neuropsychologia, 44,* 2437–2444.

Chan, R. W., Raboy, B., & Patterson, C. J. (1998). Psychosocial adjustment among children conceived via donor insemination by lesbian and heterosexual mothers. *Child Development, 69,* 326–332.

Chance, P. (2006). *Learning and behavior* (5th ed.). Belmont, CA: Wadsworth.

Chandel, N. S., & Budinger, G. R. (2007). The cellular basis for diverse responses to oxygen. *Free Radical Biology and Medicine, 42,* 165–174.

Chang, F., Dell, G. S., & Bock, K. (2006). Becoming syntactic. *Psychological Review, 113,* 234–272.

Chapman, D. S., & Webster, J. (2003). The use of technologies in the recruiting, screening, and selection processes for job candidates. *International Journal of Selection and Assessment, 11,* 113–120.

Charbonneau, D., Barling, J., & Kelloway, E. K. (2001). Transformational leadership behaviors, upward trust, and satisfaction in self-managed work teams. *Organizational Development Journal, 17,* 13–28.

Charles, S. T., & Carstensen, L. L. (2004). A life-span view of emotional functioning in adulthood and old age. In P. Costa (Ed.), *Advances in cell aging and gerontology.* New York: Elsevier.

Chartrand, T. L., Maddux, W. W., & Lakin, J. J. (2005). Beyond the perception–behavior link: Ubiquitous utility and motivational moderators of nonconscious mimicry. In R. Hassin, J. Uleman, & J. Baugh (Eds.), *The new unconscious.* New York: Oxford University Press.

Chaves, J. F. (2000). Hypnosis. In A. Kazdin (Ed.), *Encyclopedia of psychology.* Washington DC, and New York: American Psychological Association and Oxford University Press.

Chen, C. C., David, A., Thompson, K., Smith, C., Lea, S., & Fahy, T. (1996). Coping strategies and psychiatric morbidity in women attending breast assessment clinics. *Journal of Psychosomatic Research, 40,* 265–270.

Chen, H., Kent, S., & Morris, M. J. (2006). Is the CCCK2 receptor essential for normal regulation of body weight and adiposity? *European Journal of Neuroscience, 24,* 1427–1433.

Chess, S., & Thomas, A. (1977). Temperamental individuality from childhood to adolescence. *Journal of Child Psychiatry, 16,* 218–226.

Chester, J. A., Rausch, E. J., June, H. L., & Froehlich, J. C. (2006). Decreased reward during acute alcohol withdrawal in rats selectively bred for low alcohol drinking. *Alcoholism, 38,* 165–172.

Chichilnisky, E. J. (2007). Information processing in the retina. *Annual Review of Neuroscience* (vol. 30). Palo Alto, CA: Annual Reviews.

Child Trends. (2006, April). *Facts at a glance.* Washington, DC: Author.

Cho, Y. S., Lien, M. C., & Proctor, R. W. (2006). Stroop dilution depends on the nature of the color carrier but not on its location. *Journal of Experimental Psychology: Human Perception and Performance, 32,* 826–839.

Chomsky, N. (1975). *Reflections on language.* New York: Pantheon.

Chopp, M., Zhang, Z. G., & Jiang, Q. (2007). Neurogenesis, angiogenesis, and MRI indices of functional recovery from stroke. *Stroke, 38, Suppl. 2,* S827–S831.

Chorney, M. J., Chorney, K., Seese, N., Owen, M. J., Daniels, J., McGuffin, P., Thompson, L. A., Detterman, D. K., Benbow, C., Lubinski, D., Eley, T., & Plomin, R. (1998). A quantitative trait locus associated with cognitive ability in children. *Psychological Science, 9,* 159–166.

Chouinard, G. (2006). Interrelations between psychiatric symptoms and drug-induced movement disorder. *Journal of Psychiatry and Neuroscience, 31,* 177–180.

Choy, Y., Fyer, A. J., & Lipsitz, J. D. (2006). Treatment of specific phobia in adults. *Clinical Psychology Review.* (in press)

Christensen, L. B. (2007). *Experimental methodology* (10th ed.). Boston: Allyn & Bacon.

Christensen, M. S., Lundbye-Jensen, J., Geertsen, S. S., Petersen, T. H., Paulson, O. B., & Nielsen, J. B. (2007). Premotor cortex modulates somatosensory cortex during voluntary movements without proprioceptive feedback. *Nature Neuroscience, 10,* 417–419.

Christensen, P. N. (2007). Social relations model. In R. Baumeister & K. D. Vohs (Eds.), *Encyclopedia of social psychology.* Thousand Oaks, CA: Sage.

Christie, I. C., & Friedman, B. H. (2004). Autonomic specificity of discrete emotion and dimensions of affective space: A multivariate approach. *International Journal of Psychophysiology, 51,*143–153.

Christou, D. D., Gentile, G. L., DeSouza, C. A., & Seals, D. R. (2005). Fatness is a better predictor of cardiovascular disease risk factor profile than aerobic fitness in healthy men. *Circulation, 111,* 1904–1914.

Chuang, S. C. (2007). Sadder but wiser or happier and smarter? A demonstration of judgment and decision making. *Journal of Psychology, 141,* 63–76.

Church, R. M., & Kirkpatrick, K. (2001). Theories of conditioning and timing. In R. R. Mowrer & S. B. Klein (Eds.), *Handbook of contemporary learning theories.* Mahwah, NJ: Erlbaum.

Church, T. S., LaMonte, M. J., Barlow, C. E., & Blair, S. N. (2005). Cardiorespiratory fitness and body mass index as predictors of cardiovascular disease mortality among men with diabetes. *Archives of Internal Medicine, 165,* 2114–2120.

CIA (2005). *CIA world fact book.* https://www.cia.gov/library/publications/the-world-factbook/index.html

Cialdini, R. B., Schaller, M., Houlihan, D., Arps, K., Fultz, J., & Beaman, A. L. (1987). Empathy-based helping: Is it selflessly or selfishly motivated? *Journal of Personality and Social Psychology, 52,* 749–758.

Ciaramelli, E., Leo, F., Del Viva, M. M., Burr, D. C., & Ladavas, E. (2007). The contribution of the prefrontal cortex to global perception. *Experimental Brain Research, 181,* 427–434.

Cicchetti, D., & Toth, S. L. (2006). Developmental psychopathology and preventive intervention. In W. Damon & R. Lerner (Eds.), *Handbook of child psychology* (6th ed.). New York: Wiley.

Cicerone, K., Levin, H., Malec, J., Stuss, D., & Whyte, J. (2006). Cognitive rehabilitation interventions for executive function: Moving from bench to bedside in patients with traumatic brain injury. *Journal of Cognitive Neuroscience, 18,* 1212–1222.

Cipolli, C., Fagioli, I., Mazzetti, M., & Tuozzi, G. (2006). Consolidation effect of repeated processing of declarative knowledge in mental experiences during human sleep. *Brain Research Bulletin, 69,* 509–511.

Cipolotti, L., & Bird, C. M. (2006). Amnesia and the hippocampus. *Current Opinion in Neuroscience, 19,* 593–598.

Clark, D. M., Ehlers, A., Hackmann, A., McManus, F., Fennell, M., Grey, N., Waddington, L., & Wild, J. (2006). Cognitive therapy versus exposure and applied relaxation in social phobia: A randomized controlled trial. *Journal of Consulting and Clinical Psychology, 74,* 568–578.

Clark, M. S., & Chrisman, K. (1994). Resource allocation in intimate relationships: Trying to make sense of a confusing literature. In M. J. Lerner & G. Mikula (Eds.), *Entitlement and the affectional bond: Justice in close relationships* (pp. 65–88). New York: Plenum.

Clark, N. M., & Dodge, J. A. (1999). Exploring self-efficacy as a predictor of disease management. *Health Education & Behavior, 26,* 72–89.

Clarke, C. E., & Moore, A. P. (2007). Parkinson's disease. *American Family Physician, 75,* 1045–1048.

Clarke-Stewart, A. (2006). What have we learned: Proof that families matter, policies for parents and children, prospects for future work. In A. Clarke-Stewart & J. Dunn (Eds.), *Families count.* New York: Cambridge University Press.

Clarke-Stewart, A., & Brentano, C. (2006). *Divorce.* New Haven, CT: Yale University Press.

Cleeremans, A., & Sarrazin, J. C. (2007). Time, action, and consciousness. *Human Movement Science, 26,* 180–202.

Cleveland, J. N., Barnes-Farrell, J. L., & Ratz, J. M. (1997). Accommodation in the workplace. *Human Resource Management Review, 7,* 77–107.

Clifton, D. O., & Harter, J. K. (2003). Strengths investment. In K. S. Cameron, J. E. Dutton, & R. E. Quinn (Eds.), *Positive organizational scholarship* (pp. 111–121). San Francisco: Berrett & Koehler.

Clifton, D. O., & Nelson, P. (1992). Soar with your strengths. New York: Delacourt Press.

Cloninger, C. R. (2006). The science of well-being: An integrated approach to mental health and disorders. *World Psychiatry, 5,* 71–76.

Cloninger, S. (2008). *Theories of personality* (5th ed.). Upper Saddle River, NJ: Prentice-Hall.

Clore, G. L., Gasper, K., & Garvin, E. (2001). Affect as information. In J. P. Forgas (Ed.), *Handbook of affect and social cognition* (pp. 121–144). Mahwah, NJ: Erlbaum.

Close, C. E., Roberts, P. L., & Berger, R.E. (1990). Cigarettes, alcohol, and marijuana are related to pyospermia in infertile men. *Journal of Urology, 144,* 900–903.

CNN Poll. (2006, December 12). Most Americans see lingering racism—in others. http://www.cnn.com/2006/US/12/12/racism.poll/index.html (accessed June 13, 2007).

Coch, D., Fischer, K. W., & Dawson, G. (Eds.). (2007). *Human behavior, learning, and the developing brain.* New York: Guilford.

Cochran, S. D., & Mays, V. M. (1990). Sex, lies, and HIV. *New England Journal of Medicine, 322,* 774–775.

Cohen, A. B., Malka, A., Rozin, P., & Cherfas, L. (2006). Religion and unforgivable offenses. *Journal of Personality, 74,* 85–118.

Cohen, D. (2001). Cultural variation: Considerations and implications. *Psychological Bulletin, 127,* 451–471.

Cohen, D., Nisbett, R. E., Bowdle, B. F., & Schwarz, N. (1996). Insult, aggression, and the southern culture of honor: An "experimental ethnography." *Journal of Personality and Social Psychology, 70,* 945–960.

Cohen, D., Taieb, O., Flament, M., Benoit, N., Chevret, S., Corcos, M., Fossati, P., Jeammet, P., Allilaire, J., & Basquin, M. (2000). Absence of cognitive impairment at long-term follow-up in adolescents treated with ECT for severe mood disorder. *American Journal of Psychiatry, 157,* 460–462.

Cohen, G. L., & Prinstein, M. J. (2006). Peer contagion of aggression and health risk behavior among adolescent males: An experimental investigation of effects on public conduct and private attitudes. *Child Development, 77,* 967–983.

Cohen, J., Marecek, J., & Gillham, J. (2006). Is three a crowd? Clients, clinicians, and managed care. *American Journal of Orthopsychiatry, 76,* 251–259.

Cohen, K. R., & Henik, A. (2007). Can synaesthesia research inform cognitive science? *Trends in Cognitive Science, 11,* 177–184.

Cohen, L., De Moor, C., & Amato, R. J. (2001). The association between treatment-specific optimism and depressive symptomatology in patients enrolled in a Phase I cancer clinical trial. *Cancer, 91,* 1949–1953.

Cohen, L. B., & Cashon, C. H. (2006). Infant cognition. In W. Damon & R. Lerner (Eds.), *Handbook of child psychology* (6th ed.). New York: Wiley.

Cohen, S. (2002). Treatment of insomnia. *Lancet, 359,* 1433–1434.

Cohen, S., Alper, C. M., Doyle, W. J., Treanor, J. J., & Turner, R. B. (2006). Positive emotional style predicts resistance to illness after experimental exposure to rhinovirus or influenza a virus. *Psychosomatic Medicine, 68,* 809–815.

Cohen, S., Doyle, W. J., & Skoner, D. P. (1999). Psychological stress, cytokine production, and severity of upper respiratory illness. *Psychosomatic Medicine, 61,* 175–180.

Cohen, S., Doyle, W. J., Turner, R. B., Alper, C. M., & Skoner, D. P. (2003a). Emotional style and susceptibility to the common cold. *Psychosomatic Medicine, 65,* 652–657.

Cohen, S., Doyle, W. J., Turner, R. B., Alper, C. M., & Skoner, D. P. (2003b). Sociability and susceptibility to the common cold. *Psychological Science, 14,* 389–395.

Cohen, S., Frank, E., Doyle, W., Skoner, D. P., Rabin, B. S., & Gwaltney, J. M. (1998). Types of stressors that increase susceptibility to the common cold in healthy adults. *Health Psychology, 17,* 214–223.

Cohen, S., Glass, D. C., & Singer, J. E. (1973). Apartment noise, auditory discrimination, and reading ability in children. *Journal of Experimental Psychology, 9,* 407–422.

Cohen, S., & Lemay, E. (2007). Why would social networks be linked to affect and health practices? *Health Psychology.* (in press)

Cohen, S., Miller, G. E., & Rabin, B. S. (2001). Psychological stress and antibody response to immunization. *Psychosomatic Medicine, 63,* 7–18.

Cohen-Charash, Y., & Spector, P. E. (2001). The role of justice in organizations: A meta-analysis. *Organizational Behavior and Human Decision Processes, 86,* 278–321.

Cohn, M. A., & Fredrickson, B. L. (2006). Beyond the moment, Beyond the self: Shared ground between selective investment theory and the broaden-and-build theory of positive emotions. *Psychological Inquiry, 17*(1), 39–44.

Coifman, K. G., Bonanno, G. A., Ray, R. D., & Gross, J. J. (2007). Does repressing coping promote resilience? Affective-autonomic response discrepancy during bereavement. *Journal of Personality and Social Psychology, 92,* 745–758.

Coker, A. L., Hanks, J. S., Eggleston, K. S., Risser, J., Tee, P. G., Chronister, K. J., Troisi, C. L., Arafat, R., & Franzini, L. (2006). Social and mental health needs assessment of Katrina evacuees. *Disaster Management Response, 4,* 88–94.

Coker, A. L., & Widiger, T. A. (2005). Personality disorders. In J. E. Maddux & B. A. Winstead (Eds.), *Psychopathology: Foundations for a contemporary understanding* (pp. 201–227). Mahwah, NJ: Erlbaum.

Colapinto, J. (2000). *As nature made him.* New York: HarperAcademic.

Colby, A., Kohlberg, L., Gibbs, J., & Lieberman, M. (1983). A longitudinal study of moral judgment. *Monographs of the Society for Research in Child Development, 48* (21, serial no. 201).

Cole, M. (2006). Culture and cognitive development in phylogenetic, historical, and ontogenetic perspective. In W. Damon & R. Lerner (Eds.), *Handbook of child psychology* (6th ed.). New York: Wiley.

Cole, M., & Gajdamaschko, N. (2007). Vygotsky and culture. In H. Daniels, J. Wertsch, & M. Cole (Eds.), *The Cambridge companion to Vygotsky.* New York: Cambridge University Press.

Cole, P. M., & Tan, P. Z. (2007). Emotion socialization from a cultural perspective. In J. E. Grusec & P. D. Hastings (Eds.), *Handbook of socialization.* New York: Oxford University Press.

Cole, S. W., Kemeny, M. E., Taylor, S. E., & Visscher, B. R. (1996). Elevated physical health risk among gay men who conceal their homosexual identity. *Health Psychology, 15,* 243–251.

Coleman, P. D. (1986, August). *Regulation of dendritic extent: Human aging brain and Alzheimer's disease.* Paper presented at the meeting of the American Psychological Association, Washington, DC.

Collins, W. A., Maccoby, E. E., Steinberg, L., Hetherington , E. M., & Bornstein, M. H. (2000). Contemporary research on parenting: The case for nature and nurture. *American Psychologist, 55,* 218–232.

Collins, W. A., & Steinberg, L. (2006). Adolescent development in interpersonal context. In W. Damon & R. Lerner (Eds.), *Handbook of child psychology* (6th ed.). New York: Wiley.

Colom, R., Rebello, I., Abad, F. J., & Shin, P. C. (2006). Complex span tasks, simple span tasks, and cognitive abilities: A reanalysis of key studies. *Memory and Cognition, 34,* 158–171.

Colón, E. A., Callies, A. L., Popkin, M. K., & McGlave, P. B. (1991). Depressed mood and other variables related to bone marrow transplantation survival in acute leukemia. *Psychosomatics, 32,* 420–425.

Commoner, B. (2002). Unraveling the DNA myth: The spurious foundation of genetic engineering. *Harper's Magazine, 304,* 39–47.

Commonwealth of Massachusetts vs. Porter 31285-330. (Massachusetts, 1993).

Compton, R. J., Wirtz, D., Pajoumand, G., Claus, E., & Heller, W. (2004). Association between positive affect and attentional shifting. *Cognitive Therapy and Research, 28,* 733–744.

Comstock, G., & Scharrer, E. (2003). Meta-analyzing the controversy over television violence and aggression. In D. A. Gentile (Ed.), *Media violence and children: A complete guide for parents and professionals* (pp. 205–226). Westport, CT: Praeger/Greenwood Publishing Group.

Comstock, G., & Scharrer, E. (2006). Media and popular culture. In K. A. Renninger, I. E. Sigel, W. Damon, & R. M. Lerner (Eds.), *Handbook of child psychology* (6th ed., vol. 4, *Child psychology in practice,* pp. 817–863). Hoboken, NJ: Wiley.

Connell, A. M., & Dishion, T. J. (2006). The contribution of peers to monthly variation in adolescent depressed mood: A short-term longitudinal study with time-varying predictors. *Developmental Psychopathology, 18,* 139–154.

Conner, K. R., Britton, P. C., Sworts, L. M., & Joiner, T. E., Jr. (2007). Suicide attempts among individuals with opiate dependence: The critical role of belonging. *Addictive Behaviors, 32,* 1395–1404.

Connor, C. M., & Zwolan, T. A. (2004). Examining multiples sources of influence on the reading comprehension skills of children who use cochlear implants. *Journal of Speech, Language and Hearing Research, 47,* 509–526.

Constantine, M. G. (2006). Perceived family conflict, parental attachment, and depression in African American female adolescents. *Cultural Diversity and Ethnic Minority Psychology, 12,* 697–709.

Conway, M., & Rubin, D. (1993). The structure of autobiographical memory. In A. F. Collins, S. E. Gathercole, M. A. Conway, & P. E. Morris (Eds.), *Theories of memory.* Hillsdale, NJ: Erlbaum.

Conway, M. A., Singer, J. A., & Tagini, A. (2004). The self and autobiographical memory: Correspondence and coherence. *Social Cognition, 22,* 491–529.

Cook, J. M., Marshall, R., Masci, C., & Coyne, J. C. (2007). Physicians' perspectives on prescribing benzodiazepines for older adults: A qualitative study. *Journal of General Internal Medicine, 22,* 303–307.

Cooley, E., & Toray, T. (2001). Disordered eating in college freshmen women: A prospective study. *Journal of American College Health, 49,* 229–235.

Cooper, J. O., Heron, T. E., & Heward, W. L. (2007). *Applied behavior analysis* (2nd ed.). Upper Saddle River, NJ: Prentice-Hall.

Cooper, M. L. (1994). Motivations for alcohol use among adolescents: Development and validation of a four-factor model. *Psychological Assessment, 6,* 117–128.

Cooper, M. L., Pioli, M., Levitt, A., Talley, A. E., Micheas, L., & Collins, N. L. (2005). Attachment styles, sex motives, and sexual behavior: Evidence for gender-specific expressions of attachment dynamics. In M. Mikulincer & G. S. Goodman (Eds.), *Dynamics of romantic love: Attachment, caregiving, and sex* (pp. 243–274). New York: Guilford.

Cooper, M. L., Russell, M., Skinner, J. B., Windle, M. (1992). Development and validation of a three-dimensional measure of drinking motives. *Psychological Assessment, 4,* 123–132.

Cooper, R. M., & Zubek, J. P. (1958). Effects of enriched and restricted early environments on the learning ability of bright and dull rats. *Canadian Journal of Psychology, 12,* 159–164.

Cooper-Hakim, A., & Viswesvaran, C. (2005). The construct of work commitment: Testing an integrative framework. *Psychological Bulletin, 131,* 241–259.

Corballis, M. C. (2004, August). *The divided brain.* Paper presented at the 28th International Congress of Psychology, Beijing, China.

Corballis, P. M., Funnell, M. G., & Gazzaniga, M. S. (2002). Hemispheric asymmetries for simple visual judgments in the split brain. *Neuropsychologia, 40,* 401–410.

Coren, S., & Girus, J. S. (1972). Illusion decrement in intersecting figures. *Psychonomic Science, 26,* 108–110.

Corey, G. C. (2001). *Theory and practice of counseling and psychotherapy* (6th ed.). Belmont, CA: Wadsworth.

Cornell, J. L., & Halpern-Felsher, B. L. (2006). Adolescents tell us why teens have oral sex. *Journal of Adolescent Health, 38,* 299–301.

Corradi, R. B. (2006). A conceptual model of transference and its psychotherapeutic application. *Journal of the American Academy of Psychoanalysis and Dynamic Psychiatry, 34,* 415–439.

Correia, M. L., & Haynes, W. G. (2007). Lessons from leptin's molecular biology: Potential therapeutic actions of recombinant leptin and leptin-related compounds. *Mini Reviews in Medicinal Chemistry, 7,* 31–38.

Correll, J., Park, B., Judd, C. M., & Wittenbrink, B. (2002). The police officer's dilemma: Using ethnicity to disambiguate potentially threatening individuals. *Journal of Personality and Social Psychology, 83,* 1314–1329.

Corrigan, P. (Ed.). (2005). *On the stigma of mental illness: Practical strategies for research and social change.* Washington, DC: American Psychological Association.

Corrigan, P. W. (2007). How clinical diagnosis might exacerbate the stigma of mental illness. *Social Work, 52,* 31–39.

Costa, E., & Silva, J. A. (2006). Sleep disorders in psychiatry. *Metabolism, 55, Suppl. 2,* S40–S44.

Costa, P. T., & McCrae, R. R. (1992). *Revised NEO personality inventory.* Odessa, FL: Psychological Assessment Resources.

Costa, P. T., & McCrae, R. R. (1998). Personality assessment. In H. S. Friedman (Ed.), *Encyclopedia of mental health* (vol. 3). San Diego: Academic.

Costa, P. T., & McCrae, R. R. (2006). Age changes in personality and their origins: Comment on Roberts, Walter, and Viechtbauer (2006). *Psychological Bulletin, 132,* 26–28.

Coté, S. (1999). Affect and performance in organizational settings. *Current Directions in Psychological Science, 8,* 65–68.

Cotter, D., Mackay, D., Chana, G., Beasley, C., Landau, S., & Everall, I. P. (2002). Reduced neuronal size and glial density in area 9 of the dorsolateral prefrontal cortex in subjects with major depressive disorder. *Cerebral Cortex, 12,* 386–394.

Coulson, S., & Wu, Y. C. (2005). Right hemisphere activation of joke-related information: An event-related brain potential study. *Journal of Cognitive Neuroscience, 17,* 494–506.

Courtet, P., & others. (2004). Serotonin transporter gene may be involved in short-term risk of subsequent suicide attempts. *Biological Psychiatry, 55,* 46–51.

Cowan, P. A., & Cowan, C. P. (2001). What an intervention design reveals about how parents affect their children's academic achievement and social competence. In J. Borkowski, S. Landesman-Ramey, & M. Bristol (Eds.), *Parenting and the child's world: Multiple influences on intellectual and social-emotional development.* Mahwah, NJ: Erlbaum.

Cox, L. A. (2007). Health risk analysis for risk management decision-making. In W. Edwards, R. Miles, & D. von Winterfeldt (Eds.), *Advances in decision analysis.* New York: Cambridge University Press.

Cox, R. H. (2007). *Sport psychology* (6th ed.). New York: McGraw-Hill.

Craddock, N., & Forty, L. (2006). Genetics of affective (mood) disorders. *European Journal of Human Genetics, 14,* 660–668.

Craik, F. I., & Bialystok, E. (2006). Cognition through the lifespan: Mechanisms of change. *Trends in Cognitive Science, 10,* 131–138.

Craik, F. I. M., & Lockhart, R. S. (1972). Levels of processing; A framework for memory research. *Journal of Verbal Learning and Verbal Behavior, 11,* 671–684.

Craik, F. I. M., & Tulving, E. (1975). Depth of processing and retention of words in episodic memory. *Journal of Experimental Psychology: General, 104,* 268–294.

Cramer, P. (2000). Defense mechanisms in psychology today: Further processes for adaptation. *American Psychologist, 55,* 637–646.

Cramer, P. (2007). Longitudinal study of defense mechanisms: Late childhood to late adolescence. *Journal of Personality, 75,* 1–23.

Cramer, P., & Jones, C. J. (2007). Defense mechanisms predict differential lifespan change in self-control and self-acceptance. *Journal of Research in Personality, 41,* 841–855.

Crampton, D. (2007). Research review: Family group decision-making: A promising practice in need of more programme theory and research. *Child & Family Social Work, 12,* 202–209.

Crampton, S. M., & Wagner, J. A., III. (1994). Percept-percept inflation in microorganizational research: An investigation of prevalence and effect. *Journal of Applied Psychology, 79,* 67–76.

Crano, W. D., & Prislin, R. (2006). Attitudes and persuasion. *Annual Review of Psychology, 57,* 345–374.

Crawley, R. A., & Eacott, M. J. (2006). Memories of early childhood: Qualities of the experience of recollection. *Memory and Cognition, 34,* 287–294.

Cress, M. E., Buchner, D. M., Prohaska, T., Rimmer, J., Brown, M., Macera, C., DiPietro, L., & Chodzko-Zajko, W. (2005). Best practices for physical activity programs and behavior counseling in older adult populations. *Journal of Aging and Physical Activity, 13,* 61–74.

Crocker, J., Major, B., & Steele, C. (1998). Social stigma. In D. T. Gilbert, S. T. Fiske, & G. Lindzey (Eds.), *Handbook of social psychology* (4th ed., vol. 2). New York: McGraw-Hill.

Cromwell, H. C., Klein, A., & Mears, R. P. (2007). Single unit and population responses during inhibitory gating of striatal activity in freely moving rats. *Neuroscience, 146,* 69–85.

Crosby, F. J., & Ropp, S. A. (2002). Awakening to discrimination. In M. Ross & D. T. Miller (Eds.), *The justice motive in everyday life* (pp. 382–396). New York: Cambridge University Press.

Cross, S. E., Gore, J. S., & Morris, M. L. (2003). The relational-interdependent self-construal, self-concept consistency, and well-being. *Journal of Personality and Social Psychology, 85,* 933–944.

Crowley, K., Callahan, M. A., Tenenbaum, H. R., & Allen, E. (2001). Parents explain more to boys than to girls during shared scientific thinking. *Psychological Science, 12,* 258–261.

Crowley, S. J., Acebo, C., & Carskadon, M. A. (2007). Sleep, circadian rhythms and delayed phase in adolescence. *Sleep Medicine.* (in press)

Csikszentmihalyi, M. (1990). *Flow: The psychology of optimal experience.* New York: HarperPerennial.

Csikszentmihalyi, M. (1995). *Creativity.* New York: HarperCollins.

Csikszentmihalyi, M. (1996). *Creativity.* New York: HarperCollins.

Csikszentmihalyi, M., & Csikszentmihalyi, I. S. (Eds.). (2006). *A life worth living.* New York: Oxford University Press.

Csikszentmihalyi, M., & Rathunde, K. (1998). The development of the person: An experiential perspective on the ontogenesis of psychological complexity. In W. Damon (Ed.), *Handbook of child psychology* (5th ed., vol.1). New York: Wiley.

Cuijpers, P. (2001). Mortality and depressive symptoms in inhabitants of residential homes. *International Journal of Geriatric Psychiatry, 16,* 131–138.

Cullen, M. J., Hardison, C. M., & Sackett, P. R. (2004). Using SAT-grade and ability-job performance relationships to test predictions derived from stereotype threat theory. *Journal of Applied Psychology, 89,* 220–230.

Culp, M. C. (2005, December 25). The business case for compassion. *San Bernardino Sun.* http://www.sbsun.com/workwise/ci_3829431 (accessed June 15, 2006).

Culpepper, L. (2005). Insomnia: A primary care perspective. *Journal of Clinical Psychiatry, 66, Suppl. 9,* S14–S17.

Cunningham, R. L., & McGinnis, M. Y. (2007). Factors influencing aggression toward females by male rats exposed to anabolic androgenic steroids during puberty. *Hormones and Behavior, 51,* 135–141.

Curci, A., & Luminet, O. (2006). Follow-up of a cross-national comparison on flashbulb and event memory for the September 11th attacks. *Memory, 14,* 329–344.

Curran, K., DuCette, J., Eisenstein, J., & Hyman, I. A. (2001, August). *Statistical analysis of the cross-cultural data: The third year.* Paper presented at the meeting of the American Psychological Association, San Francisco.

Cutler, B. L., & Penrod, S. D. (1995). *Mistaken identities: The eyewitness, psychology, and the law.* New York: Cambridge University Press.

Cutrona, C. E. (1982). Transition to college: Loneliness and the process of social adjustment. In L. A. Peplau & D. Perlman (Eds.), *Loneliness.* New York: Wiley.

Czienskowski, U., & Giljohann, S. (2002). Intimacy, concreteness, and the "self-reference" effect. *Experimental Psychology, 49,* 73–79.

D

Dabbs, J. M., Jr., Riad, J. K., & Chance, S. E. (2001). Testosterone and ruthless homicide. *Personality and Individual Differences, 31,* 599–603.

Dadds, M. R., Holland, D. E., Barrett, P. M., & Spence, S. H. (1999). Early intervention and prevention of anxiety disorders in children: Results at 2-year follow-up. *Journal of Consulting & Clinical Psychology, 67,* 145–150.

Dafters, R. I. (2006). Chronic ecstasy (MDMA) use is associated with deficits in task-switching but not inhibition or memory updating executive functions. *Drug and Alcohol Dependence, 83*(2), 181–184.

Dahl, R. E. (2006). Sleeplessness and aggression in youth. *Journal of Adolescent Health, 38,* 641–642.

Dalton, J. H., Elias, M. J., & Wandersman, A. (2007). *Community psychology* (2nd ed.). Belmont, CA: Wadsworth.

Dammen, T., Bringager, C. B., Arnesen, H., Ekeberg, O., & Friis, S. (2006). A 1-year follow-up of chest-pain patients with and without panic disorder. *General Hospital Psychiatry, 28,* 516–524.

Dan, B., & Boyd, S. G. (2006). A neurophysiological perspective on sleep and its maturation. *Developmental Medicine and Child Neurology, 48,* 773–779.

Daniel, M. P., Mores, C., Carite, L., Boyer, P., & Denis, M. (2006). Dysfunctions of spatial cognition: The case of schizophrenic patients. *Cognitive Processes, 7, Suppl. 5,* S173.

Daniels, P., Noe, G. F., & Mayberry, R. (2006). Barriers to prenatal care among Black women of low socioeconomic status. *American Journal of Health Behavior, 30,* 188–198.

Danner, D. D., Snowdon, D. A., & Friesen, W. V. (2001). Positive emotions in early life and longevity: Findings from the Nun Study. *Journal of Personality and Social Psychology, 80,* 804–813.

Dao, T. K., Kerbs, J. J., Rollin, S. A., Potts, I., Gutierrez, R., Choi, K., Creason, A. H., Wolf, A., & Prevatt, F. (2006). The association of bullying dynamics and psychological stress. *Journal of Adolescent Health, 39,* 277–282.

Darley, J. M., & Latané, B. (1968). Bystander intervention in emergencies: Diffusion of responsibility. *Journal of Personality and Social Psychology, 8,* 377–383.

Darwin, C. (1965). *The expression of the emotions in man and animals.* Chicago: University of Chicago Press. (original work published 1872)

Darwin, C. (1979). *The origin of species.* New York: Avenal Books. (original work published 1859)

Dattilio, F. M. (Ed.). (2001). *Case studies in couple and family therapy.* New York: Guilford.

Davidson, K. W., & others. (2006). Assessment and treatment of depression in patients with cardiovascular disease: National Heart, Lung, and Blood Institute Working Group Report. *Psychosomatic Medicine, 68,* 645–650.

Davidson, P. S., Cook, S. P., & Glisky, E. L. (2006). Flashbulb memories for September 11th can be preserved in older adults. *Neuropsychology, Development, and Cognition B, 13,* 196–206.

Davidson, R. J. (1993). The neuropsychology of emotion and affective style. In M. Lewis & J. M. Haviland (Eds.), *Handbook of emotion.* New York: Guilford.

Davidson, R. J. (2000). Affective style, psychopathology, and resilience: Brain mechanisms and plasticity. *American Psychologist, 55,* 196–214.

Davidson, R. J., & Fox, N. A. (1982). Asymmetrical brain activity discriminates between positive and negative affective stimuli in human infants. *Science, 218,* 1235–1237.

Davidson, R. J., Kabat-Zinn, J., Schumacher, J., Rosenkranz, M. M., Daniel, S., Saki, F., Urbanowski, F., Harrington, A., Bonus, K., &

Sheridan, J. F. (2003). Alterations in brain and immune function produced by mindfulness meditation. *Psychosomatic Medicine, 65*(4), 564–570.

Davidson, R. J., Scherer, K. R., & Goldsmith, H. H. (Eds.). (2002). *Handbook of affective sciences.* New York: Oxford University Press.

Davidson, R. J., Shackman, A., & Pizzagalli, D. (2002). The functional neuroanatomy of emotion and affective style. In R. J. Davidson, K. R. Scherer, & H. H. Goldsmith (Eds.), *Handbook of affective sciences.* New York: Oxford University Press.

Davies, S. L., DeClemente, R. J., Wingood, G. M., Person, S. D., Dix, E. S., Harrington, K., Crosby, R. A., & Oh, K. (2006). Predictors of inconsistent contraceptive use among adolescent girls: Findings from a prospective study. *Journal of Adolescent Health, 38,* 734–739.

Davis, M. C., Zautra, A. J., Johnson, L. M., Murray, K. E., & Okvat, H. A. (2007). Psychosocial stress, emotion regulation, and resilience among older adults. In C. M. Aldwin, C. L. Park, & A. Spiro (Eds.), *Handbook of health and aging.* New York: Guilford.

Davison, K. P., Pennebaker, J. W., & Dickerson, S. S. (2000). Who talks? The social psychology of illness support groups. *American Psychologist, 55,* 205–217.

Dawson, D. A., Grant, B. F., Chou, S. P., & Stinson, F. S. (2007). The impact of partner alcohol problems on women's physical and mental health. *Journal of Studies on Alcohol and Drugs, 68,* 66–75.

Day, R., & Allen, T. D. (2004). The relationships between career motivation and self-efficacy with protégé career success. *Journal of Vocational Behavior, 64,* 72–91.

Deal, T. E., & Kennedy, A. A. (1982/2000). *Corporate cultures: The rites and rituals of corporate life.* New York: Penguin.

Dean, M. A., & Russell, C. J. (2005) An examination of biodata theory-based constructs in a field context. *International Journal of Selection and Assessment, 13,* 139–149.

Deaux, K. (2001). Social identity. In J. Worell (Ed.), *Encyclopedia of gender and women.* San Diego: Academic.

Debanne, M., Glaser, B., David, M. K., Feinstein, C., & Eliez, S. (2006). Psychotic symptoms in children and adolescents with 22q11.2 deletion syndrome: Neuropsychological and behavioral implications. *Schizophrenia Research, 84,* 187–193.

Debiec, J., & LeDoux, J. E. (2006). Noradrenergic signaling in the amygdale contributes to the reconsolidation of fear memory: Treatment implications for PTSD. *Annals of the New York Academy of Science, 1071,* 521–524.

Deci, E. L., Koestner, R., & Ryan, R. M. (1999). The undermining effect is a reality after all—Extrinsic rewards, task interest, and self-determination: Reply to Eisenberger, Pierce, and Cameron (1999) and Lepper, Henderlong, and Gingras (1999). *Psychological Bulletin, 125,* 692–700.

Deci, E., & Ryan, R. (1994). Promoting self-determined education. *Scandinavian Journal of Educational Research, 38,* 3–14.

Deci, E. L., & Ryan, R. M. (2000). The "what" and "why" of goal pursuits: Human needs and the self-determination of behavior. *Psychological Inquiry, 4,* 227–268.

Deci, E. L., & Ryan, R. M. (Eds.). (2002). *Handbook of self-determination research.* Rochester, NY: University of Rochester Press.

Deci, E. L., Ryan, R. M., & Koestner, R. (2001). The pervasive negative effects of rewards on intrinsic motivation: Response to Cameron (2001). *Review of Educational Research, 71,* 43–51.

Decker, S. L., Hill, S. K., & Dean, R. S. (2007). Evidence of construct similarity in executive functions and fluid reasoning abilities. *International Journal of Neuroscience, 117,* 735–748.

Deco, G., & Rolls, E. T. (2006). Decision making and Weber's law: A neurophysiological model. *European Journal of Neuroscience, 24,* 901–916.

Deeb, S. S. (2006). Genetics of variation in human color vision and the retinal cone mosaic. *Current Opinion in Genetics and Development, 16,* 301–307.

de Forster, Z. R., & Spivacow, M. A. (2006). Psychoanalytical psychotherapy for/with couples: Theoretical basis and clinical utility. *International Journal of Psychoanalysis, 87,* 255–257.

Delate, T., Greenberg, A. J., Simmons, V. A., & Motheral, B. R. (2004). Trends in the use of antidepressants in a national sample of commercially insured pediatric patients. *Psychiatric Services, 55,* 387–391.

de Lauzon-Guillain, B., Basdevant, A., Romon, M., Karlsson, J., Borys, J. M., Charles, M. A., & the FLVS Study Group. (2006). Is restrained eating a risk factor for weight gain in a general population? *American Journal of Clinical Nutrition, 83,* 132–138.

Dell, P. F., & Eisenhower, J. W. (1990). Adolescent multiple personality disorder: A preliminary study of eleven cases. *Journal of the American Academy of Child & Adolescent Psychiatry, 29,* 359–366.

Dell, P. F., & O'Neil, J. A. (Eds.). (2007). *Dissociation and the dissociative disorders: DSM-V and beyond.* New York: Routledge.

Deller, T., Haas, C. A., Freiman, T. M., Phinney, A., Jucker, M., & Frotscher, M. (2006). Lesion-induced axonal sprouting in the central nervous system. *Advances in Experimental Medicine and Biology, 557,* 101–121.

DelParigi, A., Chen, K., Salbe, A. D., Hill, J. O., Wing, R. R., Reiman, E. M., & Tataranni, P. A. (2007). Successful dieters have increased neural activity in cortical areas involved in the control of behavior. *International Journal of Obesity, 31,* 440–448.

Delprato, D. J. (2005). Retroactive interference as a function of degree of interpolated study without overt retrieval practice. *Psychonomic Bulletin and Review, 12,* 345–349.

DeLuga, R. J., & Mason, S. (2000). Relationship of resident assistant conscientiousness, extraversion, and positive affect with rated performance. *Journal of Research in Personality, 34,* 225–235.

de Maat, S. M., Dekker, J., Schoevers, R. A., & de Jonghe, F. (2007). Relative efficacy of psychotherapy and combined therapy in the treatment of depression: A meta-analysis. *European Psychiatry, 22,* 1–8.

DeMaris, A. (2007). The role of relationship inequity in marital disruption. *Journal of Social and Personal Relationships, 24,* 177–195.

DeMarree, K. G., & Petty, R. E. (2007). The elaboration likelihood model of persuasion. In R. F. Baumeister & K. D. Vohs (Eds.), *Encyclopedia of social psychology.* Thousand Oaks, CA: Sage.

Dement, W. C. (1999). *The promise of sleep.* New York: Delacorte Press.

Demeyer, M., Zaenen, P., & Wagemans, J. (2007). Low-level correlations between object properties and viewpoint can cause viewpoint-dependent object recognition. *Spatial Vision, 20,* 79–106.

Deming, W. E. (1986). *Out of the crisis.* Cambridge, MA: MIT Press.

Dempsey, R. J., & Kalluri, H. S. (2007). Ischemia-induced neurogenesis: Role of growth factors. *Neurosurgery Clinics of North America, 18,* 183–190.

Denham, S. A., Bassett, H. H., & Wyatt, T. (2007). The socialization of emotional competence. In J. E. Grusec & P. D. Hastings (Eds.), *Handbook of socialization.* New York: Guilford.

Dennis, C. L., & Ross, L. (2006). Women's perceptions of partner support and conflict in the development of postpartum symptom depression. *Journal of Advanced Nursing, 56,* 588–599.

Deouell, L. Y., Parnes, A., Pickard, N., & Knight, R. T. (2006). Spatial location is accurately tracked by human auditory sensory memory: Evidence from the mismatch negativity. *European Journal of Neuroscience, 24,* 1488–1494.

Derbyshire, E. (2007). The importance of adequate fluid and fiber intake during pregnancy. *Nursing Standard, 21,* 40–43.

DeRose, L. M., Wright, A. J., & Brooks-Gunn, J. (2006). Does puberty account for the differential in depression? In C. L. M. Keyes & S. H. Goodman (Eds.), *Women and depression.* New York: Cambridge University Press.

Derryberry, D., & Reed, M. (2002). Information processing approaches to individual differences in emotional reactivity. In R. J. Davidson, K. R. Scherer, & H. H. Goldsmith (Eds.), *Handbook of affective sciences.* New York: Oxford University Press.

DeSantis-Moniaci, D., & Altshuler, L. (2007). Comprehensive behavioral treatment of overweight and the pediatric practice. *Pediatric Annals, 36,* 102–108.

Deutsch, M. (2006). Cooperation and competition. In M. Deutsch, P. T. Coleman, & E. C. Marcus (Eds.), *Handbook of conflict resolution.* San Francisco: Jossey-Bass.

Deutsch, M., Coleman, P. T., & Marcus, E. C. (Eds.). (2006). *Handbook of conflict resolution* (2nd ed.). San Francisco: Jossey-Bass.

Devine, C. M. (2005). A life course perspective: Understanding food choices in time, social location, and history. *Journal of Nutritional Education and Behavior, 37,* 121–128.

Devlin, S., & Arneill, A. B. (2003). Health care environments and patient outcomes: A review of the literature. *Environment and Behavior, 35,* 665–694.

de Waal, F. (1996). *Good natured; The origins of right and wrong in humans and other animals.* Cambridge, MA: Harvard University Press.

de Waal, F. (2006). Primates and philosophers: How morality evolved. Princeton, NJ: Princeton University Press.

de Wit, S., Niry, D., Wariyar, R., Aitken, M. R., & Dickinson, A. (2007). Stimulus–outcome interactions during instrumental discrimination learning by rats and humans. *Journal of Experimental Psychology: Animal Behavioral Processes, 33,* 1–11.

de Zubicaray, G. I. (2006). Cognitive neuroimaging: Cognitive science out of the armchair. *Brain and Cognition, 60,* 272–281.

Diamond, L. (2008). *Sexual fluidity: Understanding women's love and desire.* Cambridge, MA: Harvard University Press.

Diamond, M., & Sigmundson, H. K. (1997). Sex reassignment at birth. *Archives of Pediatric and Adolescent Medicine, 151,* 298–304.

Diaz-Laplante, J. (2007). Humanistic psychology and social transformation: Path toward a likeable today and a just tomorrow. *Journal of Humanistic Psychology, 47,* 54–72.

Diaz-Rico, L. T. (2008). *A course for teaching English learners.* Boston: Allyn & Bacon.

Dick, D. M., & Bierut, L. J. (2006). The genetics of alcohol dependence. *Current Psychiatry Reports, 8,* 151–157.

DiClemente, C. C. (2006). Natural change and the troublesome use of substances: A life-course perspective. W. R. Miller & K. M. Carroll (Eds.), *Rethinking substance abuse: What the science shows, and what we should do about it* (pp. 81–96). New York: Guilford.

Diekman, A. B., & Eagly, A. H. (2007). Of women, men, and motivation: A role congruity account. In W. L. Gardner & J. Shah (Eds.), *Handbook of motivational science.* New York: Guilford.

Diener, E. (1999). Introduction to the special section on the structure of emotion. *Journal of Personality and Social Psychology, 76,* 803–804.

Diener, E. (2000). Subjective well-being: The science of happiness and a proposal for a national index. *American Psychologist, 55,* 34–43.

Diener, E., & Diener, C. (1996). Most people are happy. *Psychological Science, 7,* 181–185.

Diener, E., Diener, M., & Diener, C. (1995). Factors predicting the subjective well-being of nations. *Journal of Personality and Social Psychology, 69,* 851–864.

Diener, E., Emmons, R. A., Larsen, R. J., & Griffin, S. (1985). The Satisfaction with Life Scale. *Journal of Personality Assessment, 49,* 71–75.

Diener, E., Fraser, S. C., Beaman, A. L., & Kelem, R. T. (1976). Effects of deindividuation variables on stealing among Halloween trick-or-treaters. *Journal of Personality and Social Psychology, 33,* 178–183.

Diener, E., & Fujita, F. (1995). Resources, personal strivings, and subjective well-being: A nomothetic and idiographic approach. *Journal of Personality and Social Psychology, 68,* 926–935.

Dietz-Uhler, B., Bishop-Clark, C., Howard, E. (2005). Formation of and adherence to a self-disclosure norm in an online chat. *CyberPsychology & Behavior, 8,* 114–120.

Digman, J. M. (1990). Personality structure: Emergence of the five-factor model. *Annual Review of Psychology, 41,* 417–440.

Digman, J. M. (1996). The curious history of the five-factor model. In J. S. Wiggins (Ed.). *The five-factor model of personality: Theoretical perspectives* (pp. 1–20). New York: Guilford.

Digman, J. M. (2002). Historical antecedents of the five-factor model. In P. T. Costa & T. A. Widiger (Eds.), *Personality disorders and the five-factor model of personality* (2nd ed., pp. 17–22). Washington, DC: American Psychological Association.

Dijk, D. J. (2006). Sleep of aging women and men: Back to basics. *Sleep, 29,* 12–13.

Dijksterhuis, A., Bos, M. W., Nordgren, L. F., & van Baaren, R. B. (2006). On making the right choice: The deliberation-without-attention effect. *Science, 311,* 1005–1007.

Dijksterhuis, A., & Nordgren, L. F. (2006). A theory of unconscious thought. *Perspectives on Psychological Science, 1,* 95–109.

Dijksterhuis, A., & Van Knippenberg, A. (1998). The relation between perception and behavior or how to win a game of Trivial Pursuit. *Journal of Personality and Social Psychology, 74,* 865–877.

Dillon, K. M., Minchoff, B., & Baker, K. H. (1985/1986). Positive emotional states and enhancement of the immune system. *International Journal of Psychiatry in Medicine, 15,* 13–17.

Ding, J., & Sperling, G. (2006). A gain-control theory of binocular combination. *Proceedings of the National Academy of Science USA, 103,* 1141–1146.

Dion, K. K., & Dion, K. L. (2001). Gender and relationships. In R. K. Unger (Ed.), *Handbook of the psychology of women and gender* (pp. 256–271). Hoboken, NJ: Wiley.

Dobbins, I. G., & Han, S. (2006). Cue- versus probe-dependent prefrontal cortex activity during contextual remembering. *Journal of Cognitive Neuroscience, 18,* 1439–1452.

Dobkin, B. H., Curt, A., & Guest, J. (2006). Cellular transplants in China: Observational study from the largest human experiment in chronic spinal cord injury. *Neurorehabilitation and Neural Repair, 20,* 5–13.

Dodd, M. D., Castel, A. D., & Roberts, K. E. (2006). A strategy disruption component to retrieval-induced forgetting. *Memory and Cognition, 34,* 102–111.

Dodge, K. A., Coie, J. D., & Lynam, D. (2006). Aggression and antisocial behavior in youth. In W. Damon & R. Lerner (Eds.), *Handbook of child psychology* (6th ed.). New York: Wiley.

Doering-Silveira, E., Grob, C. S., de Rios, M. D., Lopez, E., Alonso, L. K., Tacla, C. D., & Dartiu X. (2005). Report on psychoactive drug use among adolescents using ayahuasca within a religious context. *Journal of Psychoactive Drugs, 37,* 141–144.

Dohm, F. A., Beattie, J. A., Aibel, C., & Striegel-Moore, R. H. (2001). Factors differentiating women and men who successfully maintain weight loss from women and men who do not. *Journal of Clinical Psychology, 57,* 105–117.

Dollard, J., Doob, L. W., Miller, N. E., Mowrer, O. H., & Sears, R. R. (1939). *Frustration and aggression.* New Haven, CT: Yale University Press.

Domjan, M. (2006). *The principles of learning and behavior* (6th ed.). Belmont, CA: Wadsworth.

Donnellan, M. B., Trzesniewski, K. H., Robins, R. W., Moffitt, T. E., & Caspi, A. (2005). Low self-esteem is related to aggression, antisocial behavior, and delinquency. *Psychological Science, 16,* 328–335.

Donovan, M. A. (2000). Cognitive, affective, and satisfaction variables as predictors of organizational behaviors: A structural equation modeling examination of alternative models. *Dissertation Abstracts International, 60* (9-B), 4943 (UMI No. AAI9944835).

Doran, S. M., Van Dongen, H. P., & Dinges, D. F. (2001). Sustained attention performance during sleep deprivation. *Archives of Italian Biology, 139,* 253–267.

Dorn, L., Dahl, R. E., Woodward, H. R., & Biro, F. (2006). Defining the boundaries of early adolescence: A user's guide to assessing pubertal status and pubertal timing in research with adolescents. *Applied Developmental Science, 10,* 30–56.

Dovidio, J. F., Kawakami, K., & Gaertner, S. L. (2002). Implicit and explicit prejudice and interracial interaction. *Journal of Personality and Social Psychology, 82,* 62–68.

Downs, D. S., Graham, G. M., Yang, S., Bargainnier, S., & Vasil, J. (2006). Youth exercise intention and past exercise behavior: Examining the moderating influences of sex and meeting exercise recommendations. *Research Quarterly for Exercise and Sport, 77,* 91–99.

Doyere, V., Debiec, J., Monfils, M. H., Schafe, G. E., & Ledoux, J. E. (2007). Synapse-specific reconsolidation of distinct fear memories in the lateral amygdala. *Nature Neuroscience, 10,* 414–416.

Drake, C., Levine, R., & Laska, E. A. (2007). Identifying prognostic factors that predict recovery in the presence of loss to follow-up. In K. Hopper, G. Harrison, A. Janca, & N. Sartorius (Eds.), *Recovery from schizophrenia: An international perspective: A report from the WHO Collaborative Project, the international study of schizophrenia* (pp. 69–72). New York: Oxford University Press.

Drevets, W. C. (2001). Neuroimaging and neuropathological studies of depression: Implications for the cognitive-emotional features of mood disorders. *Current Opinions in Neurobiology, 11,* 240–249.

Drigotas, S. M. (2002). The Michelangelo phenomenon and personal well-being. *Journal of Personality, 70,* 59–77.

Drigotas, S. M., Rusbult, C. E., Wieselquist, J., & Whitton, S. W. (1999). Close partner as sculptor of the ideal self: Behavioral affirmation and the Michelangelo phenomenon. *Journal of Personality and Social Psychology, 77,* 293–323.

Drigotas, S. M., Safstrom, C. A., & Gentilia, T. (1999). An investment model prediction of dating infidelity. *Journal of Personality and Social Psychology, 77,* 509–524.

Drug Enforcement Administration. (1996). *DEA report on Ritalin.* Washington DC: Author.

Drummond, S. P. A., Meloy, M. J., Yanagi, M. A., Orff, H. J., & Brown, G. G. (2005). Compensatory recruitment after sleep deprivation and the relationship to performance. *Psychiatry Research: Neuroimaging, 140,* 211–233.

Dryfoos, J. G., & Barkin, C. (2006). *Adolescence: Growing up in America today.* New York: Oxford University Press.

Dubno, J. R., Horwitz, A. R., & Ahlstrom, J. B. (2007). Estimates of basilar-membrane nonlinearity effects on masking of tones and speech. *Ear and Hearing, 28,* 2–17.

Dubow, E. F., Huesmann, L. R., & Greenwood, D. (2007). Media and youth socialization: Underlying processes and moderators of effects. In J. E. Grusec & P. D. Hastings (Eds.), *Handbook of socialization* (pp. 404–430). New York: Guilford.

Duffy, M. K., Ganster, D. C., & Pagon, M. (2002). Social undermining and social support in the workplace., *Academy of Management Journal, 45,* 331–351.

Duka, T., Weissenborn, R., & Dienes, Z. (2001). State-dependent effects of alcohol on recollective experiences, familiarity, and awareness of memory. *Psychopharmacology, 153,* 293–306.

Dunbar, R., & Barrett, L. (2007). *Oxford handbook of evolutionary psychology.* New York: Oxford University Press.

Duncan, A. E., Scherrer, J., Fu, Q., Bucholz, K. K., Heath, A. C., True, W. R., Haber, J. R., Howell, D., & Jacob, T. (2006). Exposure to paternal alcoholism does not predict development of alcohol-use disorders in offspring: Evidence from an offspring-of-twins study. *Journal of Studies on Alcohol, 67,* 649–656.

Dunifon, R., Duncan, G., & Brooks-Gunn, J. (2004). Long-term impact of parental organization and efficiency. In A. Kalil & T. DeLeiere (Eds.), *Family investments in children's potential.* Mahwah, NJ: Erlbaum.

Dunn, G. P., Koebel, C. M., & Schreiber, R. D. (2006). Interferons, immunity, and cancer immunoediting. *Nature Reviews: Immunology, 6,* 836–848.

Dunne, M. (2002). Sampling considerations. In M. W. Wiederman & B. E. Whitley (Eds.), *Handbook for conducting research on human sexuality.* Mahwah, NJ: Erlbaum.

Dunner, D. L. (2001). Acute and maintenance treatment of chronic depression. *Journal of Clinical Psychiatry, 62, Suppl. 6,* 10–16.

Dunnett, S. B. (1989). Neural transplantation: Normal brain function and repair after damage. *Psychologist, 1,* 4–8.

Dupre, K. E., & Barling, J. (2006). Predicting and preventing supervisory workplace aggression. *Journal of Occupational Health Psychology, 11,* 13–26.

Durgin, F. H., Evans, L., Dunphy, N., Klostermann, S., & Simmons, K. (2007). Rubber hands feel the touch of light. *Psychological Science, 18,* 152–157.

Durrett, C., & Trull, T. J. (2005). An evaluation of evaluative personality terms: A comparison of the big seven and five-factor model in predicting psychopathology. *Psychological Assessment, 17,* 359–368.

Dutton, D., & Aron, A. (1974). Some evidence for heightened sexual attraction under conditions of high anxiety. *Journal of Personality and Social Psychology, 30,* 510–517.

Dutton, R. C., Maurer, A. J., Sonner, J. M., Fanselow, M. S., Laster, M. J., & Eger, E. I. (2002). Isoflurane causes anterograde but not retrograde amnesia for Pavlovian fear conditioning. *Anesthesiology, 96,* 1223–1229.

Dweck, C. S. (2002a) Beliefs that make smart people dumb. In R. J. Sternberg (Ed.), *Why smart people can be so stupid* (pp. 24–41). New Haven, CT: Yale University Press.

Dweck, C. S. (2002b). The development of ability conceptions. In A. Wigfield & J. S. Eccles (Eds.), *Development of achievement motivation* (pp. 57–88). San Diego: Academic.

Dweck, C. S. (2006). *Mindset.* New York: Random House.

Dweck, C. S., & Leggett, E. L. (2000). A social-cognitive approach to motivation and personality. In E. T. Higgins & A. W. Kruglanski (Eds.), *Motivational science: Social and personality perspectives* (pp. 394–415). New York: Psychology Press.

Dysart, J. E., & Lindsay, R. C. L. (2007). The effects of delay on eyewitness identification witness accuracy: Should we be concerned? In R. C. L. Lindsay, D. F. Ross, J. D. Read, & M. P. Toglia (Eds.), *The handbook of eyewitness memory: Vol. II.* Mahwah, NJ: Erlbaum.

E

Eagleman, D. M., & Sejnowski, T. J. (2007). Motion signal bias localization judgments: A unified explanation for the flash-lag, flash-drag, flash-jump, and Frohlich illusions. *Journal of Vision, 7,* 3.

Eagly, A. H., & Crowley, M. (1986). Gender and helping behavior: A meta-analytic review of the social psychological literature. *Psychological Bulletin, 100,* 283–308.

Eagly, A. H., & Koenig, A. M. (2006). Social role theory of sex differences and similarities: Implications for prosocial behavior. In K. Dindia & D. J. Canary (Eds.), *Sex differences and similarities in communication.* Mahwah, NJ: Erlbaum.

Eastman, K. K. (1994). In the eyes of the beholder: An attributional approach to ingratiation and organizational citizenship behavior. *Academy of Management Journal, 37,* 1379–1391.

Eaton, D. K., Kann, L., Kinchen, S., Ross, J., Hawkins, J., Harris, W. A., Lowry, R., McManus, T., Chyen, D., Shanklin, S., Lim, C., Grunbaum, J. A., & Wechsler, H. (2006). Youth risk behavior surveillance—United States, 2005, *Morbidity and Morality Weekly Reports, 55,* 1–108.

Eccles, J. S. (2007). Families, schools, and developing achievement-related motivations and engagement. In J. E. Grusec & P. D. Hastings (Eds.), *Handbook of socialization.* New York: Guilford.

Echevarria, J., Vogt, M., & Short, D. J. (2008). *Making content comprehensible for English language learners* (3rd ed.). Boston: Allyn & Bacon.

Eckert, E. D., Heston, L. L., & Bouchard, T. J. (1981). MZ twins reared apart. In L. Gedda, P. Paris, & W. D. Nance (Eds.), *Twin research* (vol. 1). New York: Alan Liss.

Edenberg, H. J., & Foroud, T. (2006). The genetics of alcoholism: Identifying specific genes through family studies. *Addiction Biology, 11,* 386–396.

Edinger, J. D., Wohlgemuth, W. K., Radtke, R. A., Marsh, G. R., & Quillian, R. E. (2001). Cognitive behavioral therapy for treatment of chronic primary insomnia. *Journal of the American Medical Association, 285,* 1856–1864.

"Editorial: Heroes come in all ages." (2005, September 8). *USA Today.*

Edwards, B. (1979). *Drawing on the right side of the brain.* Los Angeles: Tarcher.

Eells, T. D. (2000). Can therapy affect physical health? *Journal of Psychotherapy Practice and Research, 9,* 100–104.

Eich, E. (2007). Mood, memory, and the concept of context. In H. L. Roediger, Y. Dubai, & S. Fitzpatrick (Eds.), *Science of memory: Concepts.* New York: Oxford University Press.

Eisenberg, L. (1988). The social construction of mental illness. *Psychological Medicine, 18*(1). 1–9.

Eisenberg, N., Fabes, R. A., & Spinrad, T. L. (2006). Prosocial development. In W. Damon & R. Lerner (Eds.), *Handbook of child psychology* (2nd ed.). New York: Wiley.

Eisenberg, N., & Murphy, B. (1995). Parenting and children's moral development. In M. H. Bornstein (Ed.), *Children and parenting* (vol. 4). Hillsdale, NJ: Erlbaum.

Eisenberg, N., Spinrad, T., & Sadovsky, A. (2006). Empathy-related responding in children. In M. Killen & J. Smetana (Eds.), *Handbook of moral development*. Mahwah, NJ: Erlbaum.

Eisenberg, N., & Valiente, C. (2002). Parenting and children's prosocial and moral development. In M. H. Bornstein (Ed.), *Handbook of parenting* (2nd ed.). Mahwah, NJ: Erlbaum.

Ekman, P. (1980). *The face of man*. New York: Garland.

Ekman, P. (1996). Lying and deception. In N. L. Stein, C. Brainerd, P. A. Ornstein, & B. Tversky (Eds.), *Memory for everyday emotional events*. Mahwah, NJ: Erlbaum.

Ekman, P. (2003). Emotions inside out: 130 years after Darwin's "The expression of emotions in man and animal." *Annals of the New York Academy of Science, 1000,* 1–6.

Ekman, P., Davidson, R. J., & Friesen, W. V. (1990). The Duchenne smile: Emotional expression and brain physiology: II. *Journal of Personality and Social Psychology, 58,* 342–353.

Ekman, P., Davidson, R. J., Ricard, M., & Wallace, B. A. (2005). Buddhist and psychological perspectives on emotions and well-being. *Current Directions in Psychological Science, 14,* 59–63.

Ekman, P., & Friesen, W. V. (1971). Constants across cultures in the face and emotion. *Journal of Personality and Social Psychology, 17,* 124–129.

Ekman, P., Levenson, R. W., & Friesen, W. V. (1983). Autonomic nervous system activity distinguishes among emotions. *Science, 223,* 1208–1210.

Ekman, P., & O'Sullivan, M. (1991). Facial expressions: Methods, means, and moues. In R. S. Feldman & B. Rime (Eds.), *Fundamentals of nonverbal behavior*. Cambridge, England: Cambridge University Press.

Ekstedt, M., Soderstrom, M., Akerstedt, T., Nilsson, J., Sondergaard, H. P., & Aleksander, P. (2006). Disturbed sleep and fatigue in occupational burnout. *Scandinavian Journal of Work and Environmental Health, 32,* 121–131.

Elder, G. A., De Gasperi, R., & Gama Sosa, M. A. (2006). Research update: Neurogenesis in adult brain and neuropsychiatric disorders. *Mt. Sinai Journal of Medicine, 73,* 931–940.

El-Hai, J. (2005). *The lobotomist: A maverick medical genius and his tragic quest to rid the world of mental illness*. Hoboken, NJ: Wiley.

Eliot, L. (2001). *What's going on in there? How the brain and mind develop in the first five years of life*. New York: Bantam Doubleday.

Elkind, D. (1978). Understanding the young adolescent. *Adolescence, 13,* 127–134.

Elliot, A. J., & Sheldon, K. M. (1999). Avoidance personal goals and the personality-illness relationship. *Journal of Personality and Social Psychology, 75,* 1282–1299.

Ellis, A. (1962). *Reason and emotion in psychotherapy*. New York: Lyle Stuart.

Ellis, A. (1996). A rational-emotive behavior therapist's perspective on Ruth. In G. Corey (Ed.), *Case approach to counseling and psychotherapy*. Pacific Grove, CA: Brooks/Cole.

Ellis, A. (2000). Rational emotive behavior therapy. In A. Kazdin (Ed.), *Encyclopedia of Psychology*. Washington, DC, and New York: American Psychological Association and Oxford University Press.

Ellis, A. (2002). Rational emotive behavior therapy. In M. Hersen & W. H. Sledge (Eds.), *Encyclopedia of psychotherapy*. San Diego: Academic.

Ellis, A. (2005). Why I (really) became a therapist. *Journal of Clinical Psychology, 61,* 945–948.

Ellis, H. C. (1987). Recent developments in human memory. In V. P. Makosky (Ed.), *The G. Stanley Hall Lecture Series*. Washington, DC: American Psychological Association.

Ellis, L., & Ames, M. A. (1987). Neurohormonal functioning and sexual orientation. *Psychological Bulletin, 101,* 233–258.

Elmes, D. G., Kantowitz, B. H., & Roediger, H. L. (2003). *Research methods in psychology* (7th ed.). Belmont, CA: Wadsworth.

Elms, A. C. (2005). Freud as Leonardo: Why the first psychobiography went wrong. In W. T. Schultz (Ed.), *The handbook of psychobiography* (pp. 210–222). New York: Oxford University Press.

Emmons, R. A. (2005). Striving for the sacred: Personal goals, life meaning, and religion. *Journal of Social Issues, 61,* 731–745.

Emmons, R. A. (2007). *THANKS! How the new science of gratitude can make you happier*. Boston: Houghton Mifflin.

Emmons, R. A., & Diener, E. (1986). Situation selection as a moderator of response consistency and stability. *Journal of Personality and Social Psychology, 51,* 1013–1019.

Emmons, R. A., & King, L. A. (1988). Conflict among personal strivings: Immediate and long-term implications for psychological and physical well-being. *Journal of Personality and Social Psychology, 48,* 1040–1048.

Emmons, R. A., & McCullough, M. E. (2003). Counting blessings versus burdens: An experimental investigation of gratitude and subjective well-being in daily life. *Journal of Personality and Social Psychology, 84,* 377–389.

Emmons, R. A., & McCullough, M. E. (Eds.). (2004). *The psychology of gratitude*. New York: Oxford University Press.

Ende, G., Demirakca, T., & Tost, H. (2006). The biochemistry of dysfunctional emotions: Proton MR spectroscopic findings in major depressive disorder. *Progress in Brain Research, 156,* 481–501.

Eng, P. M., Fitzmaurice, G., Kubzansky, L. D., Rimm, E. B., & Kawachi, I. (2003). Anger expression and risk of stroke and coronary heart disease among male health professionals. *Psychosomatic Medicine, 65,* 100–110.

Engel, A. K., & Singer, W. (2001). Temporal binding and the neural correlates of sensory awareness. *Trends in Cognitive Science, 5,* 16–25.

Engel, S. A., Remus, D. A., & Sainath, R. (2006). Motion from occlusion. *Journal of Vision, 6,* 649–652.

Englander, E. K. (2006). *Understanding violence* (3rd ed.). Mahwah, NJ: Erlbaum.

Enriori, P. J., Evans, A. E., Sinnayah, P., & Cowley, M. A. (2006). Leptin resistance and obesity. *Obesity, 14, Suppl. 5,* S254–S258.

Ensembl Human. (2007). *Explore the Homo sapiens genome*. www.ensembl. org/Homo_sapiens/index.html (accessed April 28, 2007).

Enstrom, J. E. (1999). Smoking cessation and mortality trends among two United States populations. *Journal of Clinical Epidemiology, 52,* 813–825.

Enzle, M. E., & Anderson, S. C. (1993). Surveillant intentions and intrinsic motivation. *Journal of Personality and Social Psychology, 64,* 257–266.

Enzle, M. E., Roggeveen, J. P., & Look, S. C. (1991). Self- versus other-reward administration and intrinsic motivation. *Journal of Experimental Social Psychology, 27,* 468–479.

Equal Employment Opportunity Commission. (2007). *Sexual harassment charges EEOC & FEPAs combined FY 1997–2006*. Washington, DC: Author. http://eeoc.gov/stats/harass/html

Ericsson, K. A., Charness, N., Feltovich, P. J., & Hoffman, R. R. (Eds.). (2006). *The Cambridge handbook of expertise and expert performance*. New York: Cambridge University Press.

Ericsson, K. A., Krampe, R. T., & Tesch-Römer, C. (1993). The role of deliberate practice in the acquisition of expert performance. *Psychological Review, 100,* 363–406.

Erikson, E. H. (1968). *Identity: Youth and crisis*. New York: Norton.

Erikson, E. H. (1969). *Gandhi's truth*. New York: Norton.

Eseards, W., Miles, R., & von Winterfeldt, D. (Eds.). (2007). *Advances in decision analysis*. New York: Cambridge University Press.

Estrada, C., Isen, A. M., & Young, M. J. (1997). Positive affect influences creative problem solving and reported source of practice satisfaction in physicians. *Motivation and Emotion, 18,* 285–299.

Evans, V., & Green, M. (2006). *Cognitive linguistics*. Mahwah, NJ: Erlbaum.

Eve, D. J., & Sanberg, P. R. (2007) The "current state of play" in transplantation and restoration research of the CNS. *Neurotoxicity Research, 11,* 145–150.

Exner, J. E., Jr. (2003). *The Rorschach: A comprehensive system* (4th ed.). Hoboken, NJ: Wiley.

Exterkate, C. C., Bakker-Brehm, D. T., & de Jong, C. A. (2007). MMPI-2 profiles of women with eating disorders in a Dutch day treatment sample. *Journal of Personality Assessment, 88,* 178–186.

Eysenck, H. J. (1952). The effects of psychotherapy: An evaluation. *Journal of Consulting Psychology, 16,* 319–324.

F

Fahey, T. D., Insel, P. M., & Roth, W. T. (2007). *Fit and well* (7th ed.). New York: McGraw-Hill.

Fals-Stewart, W., Birchler, G. R., & Kelly, M. L. (2006). Learning sobriety together: A randomized clinical trial examining behavioral couples therapy with alcoholic female patients. *Journal of Consulting and Clinical Psychology, 74,* 579–591.

Fancher, R. E. (1996). *Pioneers of psychology* (3rd ed.). New York: Norton.

Fanselow, M. S. (2007). What's so special about contexts? In H. L. Roediger, Y. Dubai, & S. Fitzpatrick (Eds.), *Science of memory: Concepts.* New York: Oxford University Press.

Faraone, S. V., & others. (2006). Genome scan of Han Chinese schizophrenia families from Taiwan: Confirmation of linkage to 10q22.3. *American Journal of Psychiatry, 163,* 1673–1675.

Farell, B. (2006). Orientation-specific computation in stereoscopic vision. *Journal of Neuroscience, 26,* 9098–9106.

Farrington, M., Wreghitt, T. G., Lever, A. M., Dunnett, S. B., Rosser, A. E., & Barker, R. A. (2006). Neural transplantation in Huntington's disease: The NEST-UK donor tissue microbiological screening program and review of the literature. *Cell Transplantation, 15,* 279–294.

Farrow, T. F. D., Hunter, M. D., Wilkinson, I. D., Gouneea, C., Fawbert, D., Smith, R., Lee, K., Mason, S., Spence, S. A., & Woodruff, P. W. R. (2005). Quantifiable change in functional brain response to empathic and forgivability judgments with resolution of posttraumatic stress disorder. *Psychiatry Research: Neuroimaging, 140,* 45–53.

Fassler, D. (2004, May 8). Commentary in B. Bower "Teen brains on trial." *Science News Online,* 1.

Fava, G. A. (2006). The intellectual crisis in psychiatric research. *Psychotherapy and Psychosomatics, 75,* 202–208.

Fava, G. A., Ruini, C., Rafanelli, C., Finos, L., Salmaso, L., Mangelli, L., & Sirigatti, S. (2005). Well-being therapy of generalized anxiety disorder. *Psychotherapy and Psychosomatics, 74,* 26–30.

Faymonville, M. E., Boly, M., & Laureys, S. (2006). Functional neuroanatomy of the hypnotic state. *Journal of Physiology, Paris, 99,* 463–469.

Faymonville, M. E., Meurisse, M., & Fissette, J. (1999). Hypnosedation: A valuable alternative to traditional anaesthetic techniques. *Acta Chirugica Belgium, 99,* 141–146.

Faytout, M., Tignol, J., Swndsen, J., Grabot, D., Aouizerate, B., & Lepine, J. P. (2007). Social phobia, fear of negative evaluation, and harm avoidance. *European Psychiatry, 22,* 75–79.

Fazio, R. H., Chen, J., McDonel, E. C., & Sherman, S. J. (1982). Attitude accessibility, attitude-behavior consistency, and the strength of the object-evaluation association. *Journal of Experimental Social Psychology, 18,* 339–357.

Fazio, R. H., & Olsen, A. (2007). Attitudes. In M.A. Hogg & J. Cooper (Eds.), *The Sage handbook of social psychology* (concise 2nd ed.). Thousand Oaks, CA: Sage.

Febo, M., Numan, M., & Ferris, C. F. (2005). Functional magnetic resonance imaging shows oxytocin activates brain regions associated with mother–pup bonding during suckling. *Journal of Neuroscience, 25,* 1163–1164.

Fehm, H. L., Kern, W., & Peters, A. (2006). The selfish brain: Competition for energy resources. *Progress in Brain Research, 153,* 129–140.

Fehr, B., & Broughton, R. (2001). Gender and personality differences in conceptions of love: An interpersonal theory analysis. *Personal Relationships, 8,* 115–136.

Fei-Fei, L., Iyer, A., Koch, C., & Perona, P. (2007). What do we perceive in a glance at a real-world scene? *Journal of Vision, 7,* 10.

Fein, S., Goethals, G. R., Kassin, S. M., & Cross, J. (1993, August). *Social influence and presidential debates.* Paper presented at the meeting of the American Psychological Association, Toronto.

Feist, J., & Feist, G. J. (2006). *Theories of personality* (6th ed.). New York: McGraw-Hill.

Fekkes, M., Pijpers, F. I., & Verllove-Vanhorick, S. P. (2006). Effects of an antibullying school program on bullying and health complaints. *Archives of Pediatric and Adolescent Medicine, 160,* 638–644.

Feldman, S. (1983). Out of the hospital, onto the streets: The overselling of benevolence. *Hastings Center Report, 13,* 5–7.

Ferguson, M. J., Bargh, J. A., & Nayak, D. A. (2005). After-affects: How automatic evaluations influence the interpretation of subsequent, unrelated stimuli. *Journal of Experimental Social Psychology, 41,* 182–191.

Fernandez Del Olmo, M., Cheeran, B., Koch, G., & Rothwell, J. C. (2007). Role of the cerebellum in externally paced rhythmic finger movements. *Journal of Neurophysiology, 98,* 145–152.

Ferreira, G., Ferry, B., Meurise, M., & Levy, F. (2006). Forebrain structures specifically activated by conditioned taste aversion. *Behavioral Neuroscience, 120,* 952–962.

Ferreira, J. G., Cruz, C. D., Neves, D., & Pignatelli, D. (2007). Increased extracellular signal regulated kinases phosphorylation in the adrenal gland in response to chronic ACTH treatment. *Journal of Endocrinology, 192,* 647–658.

Ferri, M., Amato, L., & Davoli, M. (2006). Alcoholics Anonymous and other 12-step programs for alcohol dependence. *Cochrance Database System Review, 3,* CD005032.

Ferris, G. R., Judge, T. A., Rowland, K. M., & Fitzgibbons, D. E. (1994). Subordinate influence and the performance evaluation process: Test of a model. *Organizational and Human Decision Processes, 58,* 101–135.

Ferstl, E. C. (2007). The functional neuroanatomy of text comprehension. In F. Schmalhofer & C. A. Perfetti (Eds.), *Higher level language processes in the brain.* Mahwah, NJ: Erlbaum.

Feshbach, S., & Weiner, B. (1996). *Personality* (4th ed.). Lexington, MA: Heath.

Festinger, L. (1954). A theory of social comparison processes. *Human Relations, 7,* 117–140.

Festinger, L. (1957). *A theory of cognitive dissonance.* Evanston, IL: Row Peterson.

Fidler, M., & Kern, S. E. (2006). Flexible interaction model for complex interactions of anesthetics. *Anesthesiology, 105,* 286–296.

Field, C. D., & Chichilnisky, E. J. (2007). Information processing in the primate retina: Circuitry and coding. *Annual Review of Neuroscience* (vol. 30). Palo Alto, CA: Annual Reviews.

Field, T. (2007). *The amazing infant.* Malden, MA: Blackwell.

Field, T., Diego, M., & Hernandez-Reif, M. (2007). Massage therapy research. *Developmental Review, 27,* 75–89.

Field, T. M. (1998). Massage therapy effects. *American Psychologist, 53,* 1270–1281.

Field, T. M. (2001). Massage therapy facilitates weight gain in preterm infants. *Current Directions in Psychological Science, 10,* 51–53.

Field, T. M. (2003). Stimulation of preterm infants. *Pediatrics Review, 24,* 4–11.

Field, T. M., Grizzle, N., Scafidi, F., & Schanberg, S. (1996). Massage and relaxation therapies' effects on depressed adolescent mothers. *Adolescence, 31,* 903–911.

Field, T. M., Hernandez-Reif, M., Feijo, L., & Freedman, J. (2006). Prenatal, perinatal, and neonatal stimulation. *Infant Behavior & Development, 29,* 24–31.

Field, T. M., Schanberg, S. M., Scafidi, F., Bauer, C. R., Vega-Lahr, N., Garcia, R., Nystrom, J., & Kuhn, C. M. (1986). Tactile/kinesthetic stimulation effects on preterm neonates. *Pediatrics, 77,* 654–658.

Fields, H. (2007). Physiology and pharmacology of mesolimbic dopamine neurons. *Annual Review of Neuroscience* (vol. 30). Palo Alto, CA: Annual Reviews.

Fields, R. (2007). *Drugs in perspective* (6th ed.). New York: McGraw-Hill.

Fiese, B. H., Foley, K. P., & Spagnola, M. (2006). Routine and ritual elements in family mealtimes: Contexts for child well-being and family identity. *New Directions in Child and Adolescent Development, 111,* 67–89.

Figueroa-Moseley, C., Jean-Pierre, P., Roscoe, J. A., Ryan, J. L., Kohli, S., Palesh, O. G., Ryan, E. P., Carroll, J., & Morrow, G. R. (2007). Behavioral interventions in treating anticipatory nausea and vomiting. *Journal of the National Comprehensive Cancer Network, 5,* 44–50.

Finch, E. A., Linde, J. A., Jeffery, R. W., Rothman, A. J., King, C. M., & Levy, R. L. (2005). The effects of outcome expectations and satisfaction on weight loss and maintenance: Correlational and experimental analyses—a randomized trial. *Health Psychology, 24*(6), 608–616.

Fine, M. A., & Harvey, J. H. (Eds.). (2006). *Divorce and relationship dissolution.* Mahwah, NJ: Erlbaum.

Fine, S. A., & Wiley, W. W. (1971). *An introduction to functional job analysis.* Kalamazoo, MI: W. E. Upjohn Institute.

Fischer, R. (2006). Congruence and functions of personal and cultural values: Do my values reflect my culture's values? *Personality and Social Psychology Bulletin, 32,* 1419–1431.

Fishbach, A., & Ferguson, M. J. (2007). The goal construct in social psychology. In A.W. Kruglanski & E. T. Higgins (Eds.), *Social psychology: Handbook of basic principles* (2nd ed.). New York: Guilford.

Fishbach, A., Friedman, R. S., & Kruglanski, A. W. (2003). Leading us not into temptation: Momentary allurements elicit overriding goal activation. *Journal of Personality and Social Psychology, 84,* 296–309.

Fitzgerald, L. F. (2003). Sexual harassment and social justice: Reflections on the distance yet to go. *American Psychologist, 58,* 915–924.

Fleischhaker, S., Schulz, E., Tepper, K., Martin, M., Hennighausen, K., & Remschmidt, H. (2005). Long-term course of adolescent schizophrenia. *Schizophrenia Bulletin, 31,* 769–780.

Fletcher, J. A., & Zwick, M. (2006). Unifying the theories of inclusive fitness and reciprocal altruism. *American Naturalist, 168,* 152–162.

Flint, M. S., Baum, A., Chambers, W. H., & Jenkins, F. J. (2007). Induction of DNA damage, alteration of DNA repair, and transcriptional activation by stress hormones. *Psychoneuroendocrinology. 32,* 470–479.

Floyd, D. L., Prentice-Dunn, S., & Rogers, R. W. (2000). A meta-analysis of research on protection motivation theory. *Journal of Applied Social Psychology, 30,* 407–429.

Flynn, J. R. (1999). Searching for justice: The discovery of IQ gains over time. *American Psychologist, 54,* 5–20.

Flynn, J. R. (2006). The history of the American mind in the 20th century: A scenario to explain gains over time and a case for the irrelevance of *g.* In P. C. Kyllonen, R. D. Roberts, & L. Stankov (Eds.), *Extending intelligence.* Mahwah, NJ: Erlbaum.

Fodor, I., & Epstein, J. (2002). Agoraphobia, panic disorder, and gender. In J. Worell (Ed.), *Encyclopedia of women and gender.* San Diego: Academic.

Fogel, S. M., & Smith, C. T. (2006). Learning-dependent changes in sleep spindles and Stage 2 sleep. *Journal of Sleep Research, 15,* 250–255.

Fok, M., Hui, C., Bond, M. H., Matsumoto, D., & Yoo, S. H. (2008). Integrating personality, context, relationship, and emotion type into a model of display rules. *Journal of Research in Personality.* (in press)

Foley, D. L., Goldston, D. B., Costello, E. J., & Angold, A. (2006). Proximal psychiatric risk factors for suicidality in youth: The Great Smoky Mountains Study. *Archives of General Psychiatry, 63,* 1017–1024.

Foley, K. F., DeSanty, K. P., & Kast, R. E. (2006). Burpropion: Pharmacology and therapeutic applications. *Expert Reviews in Neurotherapy, 6,* 1249–1265.

Folkman, S., & Lazarus, R. S. (1980). An analysis of coping in a middle-aged community sample. *Journal of Health and Social Behavior, 21,* 219–239.

Folkman, S., & Moskowitz, J. T. (2004). Coping: Pitfalls and promises. *Annual Review of Psychology* (vol. 54). Palo Alto, CA: Annual Reviews.

Fontenelle, L. F., Nascimento, A. L., Mendlowicz, M. V., Shavitt, R. G., & Versiani, M. (2007). An update on the pharmacological treatment of obsessive-compulsive disorder. *Expert Opinion in Pharmacotherapy, 8,* 563–583.

Foote, B., Smolin, Y., Kaplan, M., Legatt, M. E., & Lipschitz, D. (2006). Prevalence of dissociative disorders in psychiatric outpatients. *American Journal of Psychiatry, 163,* 566–568.

Forbey, J. D., & Ben-Porath, Y. S. (2007). Computerized adaptive personality testing: A review and illustration with the MMPI-2 computerized adaptive version. *Psychological Assessment, 19,* 14–24.

Forbush, K., Heatherton, T. F., & Keel, P. K. (2007). Relationships between perfectionism and specific disordered eating behaviors. *International Journal of Eating Disorders, 40,* 37–41.

Ford, J. K., & Kraiger, K. (1995). The application of cognitive constructs and principles to the instructional systems model of training: Implications for needs assessment, design, and transfer. In C. L. Cooper & I. T. Robertson (Eds.), *International Review of Industrial and Organizational Psychology* (pp. 1–48). Chichester, England: Wiley.

Forgas, J. P. (2001). *Feeling and thinking: The role of affect in social cognition.* New York: Cambridge University Press.

Forouzan, B. A. (2007). *Data communication networking* (4th ed.). New York: McGraw-Hill.

Forsythe, C., Bernard, M. L., & Goldsmith, T. E. (Eds.). (2006). *Cognitive systems.* Mahwah, NJ: Erlbaum.

Fortuna, L. R., Perez, D. J., Canino, G., Sribney, W., & Alegria, M. (2007). Prevalence and correlates of lifetime suicidal ideation and suicide attempts among Latino subgroups in the United States. *Journal of Clinical Psychiatry, 68,* 572–581.

Foster, R. G., Hankins, M. W., & Peirson, S. N. (2007). Light, photoreceptors, and circadian clocks. *Methods in Molecular Biology, 362,* 3–28.

Fouad, N. A. (2007). Work and vocational psychology. *Annual Review of Psychology* (vol. 58). Palo Alto, CA: Annual Reviews.

Foulkes, D. (1993). Cognitive dream theory. In M.A. Carskadon (Ed.), *Encyclopedia of sleep and dreams.* New York: Macmillan.

Foulkes, D. (1999). *Children's dreaming and the development of consciousness.* Cambridge, MA: Harvard University Press.

Fountas, K. N., & Smith, J. R. (2007). Historical evolution of stereotactic amygdalotomy for the management of severe aggression. *Journal of Neurosurgery, 106,* 710–713.

Fox, C. L., & Boulton, M. J. (2006). Friendship as a moderator of the relationship between social skills problems and peer victimisation. *Aggressive Behavior, 32,* 110–121.

Fox, S. I. (2008). *Human physiology* (10th ed.). New York: McGraw-Hill.

Fradella, H. F. (2006). *Forensic psychology: The use of behavioral sciences in civil and criminal justice.* Belmont, CA: Thomson.

Fraley, R. C. (2002). Attachment stability from infancy to adulthood: Meta-analysis and dynamic modeling of developmental mechanisms. *Personality and Social Psychology Review, 6,* 123–151.

Frank, J. D. (1982). Therapeutic components shared by all psychotherapies. In J. H. Harvey & M. M. Parks (Eds.), *Psychotherapy research and behavior change.* Washington, DC: American Psychological Association.

Frank, J. D., & Frank, J. B. (1993). *Persuasion and healing: A comparative study of psychotherapy.* Baltimore: Johns Hopkins University Press.

Franke, R. H., & Kaul, J. D. (1978). The Hawthorn experiments: First statistical interpretation. *American Sociological Review, 43,* 623–643.

Franken, R. E. (2007). *Human motivation* (6th ed.). Belmont, CA: Wadsworth.

Frattaroli, J. (2006). Experimental disclosure and its moderators: A meta-analysis. *Psychological Bulletin, 132,* 823–865.

Frederich, R. C., Hamann, A., Anderson, S., & others. (1995). Leptin levels reflect body lipid content in mice: Evidence for diet-induced resistance to leptin action. *Nature Medicine, 1,* 1311–1314.

Fredrick, S., & Loewenstein, G. (1999). Hedonic adaptation. In D. Kahneman, E. Diener, & N. Schwarz (Eds.), *Well-being: The foundations of hedonic psychology* (pp. 302–329). New York: Russell Sage Foundation.

Fredrickson, B. L. (1998). What good are positive emotions? *Review of General Psychology, 2,* 300–319.

Fredrickson, B. L. (2006). Unpacking positive emotions: Investigating the seeds of human flourishing. *Journal of Positive Psychology, 1,* 57–60.

Fredrickson, B. L., & Joiner, T. (2000). *Positive emotions trigger upward spirals toward emotional well-being.* Unpublished manuscript, University of Michigan, Ann Arbor, Department of Psychology.

Fredrickson, B. L., & Joiner, T. (2002). Positive emotions trigger upward spirals of well being. *Psychological Science, 13,* 172–176.

Fredrickson, B. L., & Cohn, M. A. (2007). Positive emotions. In M. Lewis, J. Haviland Jones, & L. F. Barrett (Eds.), *Handbook of emotions* (3rd ed.). New York: Guilford.

Fredrickson, B. L., & Levenson, R. W. (1998). Positive emotions speed recovery from the cardiovascular sequelae of negative emotions. *Cognition and Emotion, 12,* 191–220.

Fredrickson, B. L., & Roberts, T. (1997). Objectification theory: Toward understanding women's lived experiences and mental health risks. *Psychology of Women Quarterly, 21,* 173–206.

Fredrickson, B. L., Roberts, T., Noll, S. M., Quinn, D. M., & Twenge, J. M. (1998). That swimsuit becomes you: Sex differences in self-objectification, restrained eating, and math performance. *Journal of Personality and Social Psychology, 75,* 269–284.

Fredrickson, B. L., Tugade, M. M., Waugh, C. E., & Larkin, G. R. (2003). What good are positive emotions in crisis? A prospective study of resilience and emotions following the terrorist attacks on the United States on September 11th, 2001. *Journal of Personality and Social Psychology, 84,* 365–376.

Freedman, J. L. (1984). Effects of television violence on aggressiveness. *Psychological Bulletin, 96,* 227–246.

Freeman, S., & Herron, J. C. (2007). *Evolutionary analysis* (4th ed.). Upper Saddle River, NJ: Prentice-Hall.

Freire, R. C., Valenca, A. M., Nasciemento, I., Lopes, F. L., Mezzasalma, M. A., Zin, W. A., & Nardi, A. E. (2007). Clinical features of respiratory and nocturnal panic disorder subtypes. *Psychiatry Research.* (in press)

Freud, S. (1917). *A general introduction to psychoanalysis.* New York: Washington Square Press.

Freud, S. (1953). The interpretation of dreams. In J. Strachey (Ed.), *The standard edition of the complete psychological works of Sigmund Freud.* New York: Washington Square Press. (original work published 1900)

Freud, S. (1996). Number 23091. In R. Andrews, M. Biggs, & M. Seidel (Eds.), *Columbia world of quotations.* (original letter published 1918)

Freyd, J. J. (1996). *Betrayal trauma: The logic of forgetting childhood abuse.* Cambridge, MA: Harvard University Press.

Friedman, H. S., & Schustack, M. W. (2006). *Personality: Classic theories and modern research* (3rd ed.). Boston: Allyn & Bacon.

Friedman, H. S., & Silver, R. C. (Eds.). (2007). *Foundations of health psychology.* New York: Oxford University Press.

Friedman, M., & Rosenman, R. (1974). *Type A behavior and your heart.* New York: Knopf.

Friedman, M. J., Keane, T. M., & Resick, P. A. (Eds.). (2007). *Handbook of PTSD.* New York: Guilford.

Friedman, R., Myers, P., & Benson, H. (1998). Meditation and the relaxation response. In H. S. Friedman (Ed.), *Encyclopedia of mental health* (vol. 2). San Diego: Academic.

Friedrich, F. (2001). *Cognitive psychology 3120: Online notes.* ttp://www.psych.utah.edu/friedrich/friedrich.html.

Frijda, N. H. (2007). *The laws of emotion.* Mahwah, NJ: Erlbaum.

Frisch, M. B., Clark, M. P., Rouse, S. V., Rudd, M. D., Paweleck, J. K. Greenstone, A., & others. (2004). Predictive and treatment validity of life satisfaction and the Quality of Life Inventory. *Assessment, 10,* 1–13.

Frishman, W. H., Mitta, W., Kupersmith, A., & Ky, T. (2006). Nicotine and non-nicotine smoking cessation pharmacotherapies. *Cardiology in Review, 14,* 57–73.

Fritz, C., & Sonnentag, S. (2006). Recovery, well-being, and performance-related outcomes: The role of work overload and vacation experiences. *Journal of Applied Psychology, 91,* 936–945.

Frohlich, P., & Meston, C. M. (2005). Fluoxetine-induced changes in tactile sensation and sexual functioning among clinically depressed women. *Journal of Sex & Marital Therapy, 31*(2), 113–128.

Fromm, E. (1947). *Man for himself.* New York: Holt, Rinehart & Winston.

Fromme, K. (2006). Parenting and other influences on the alcohol use and emotional adjustment of children, adolescents, and emerging adults. *Psychology of Addictive Behaviors, 20,* 138–139.

Fry, R. B., & Prentice-Dunn, S. (2006). Effects of a psychosocial intervention on breast self-examination attitudes and behaviors. *Health Education Research, 21,* 287–295.

Fu, Q., Heath, A. C., Bucholz, K. K., Nelson, E. C., Glowinski, A. L., Goldberg, J., Lyons, M. J., Tsuang, M. T., Jacob, T., True, M. R., &

Eisen, M. A. (2002). A twin study of genetic and environmental influences on suicidality in men. *Psychological Medicine, 32,* 11–24.

Fuchs, P. A. (2006). Time and intensity coding at the hair cell's ribbon synapse. *Journal of Physiology, 566,* 7–12.

Fujino, Y. & others. (2006). A prospective cohort study of shift work and risk of ischemic heart disease in Japanese male workers. *American Journal of Epidemiology, 164,* 128–135.

Fuligni, A. J., & Fuligni, A. S. (2007). Immigrant families and the educational development of their children. In J. E. Lansford, K. Deater Deckhard, & M. H. Bornstein (Eds.), *Immigrant families in contemporary society.* New York: Guilford.

Fultz, J., Batson, C. D., Fortenbach, V. A., McCarthy, P. M., & Varney, L. L (1986). Social evaluation and the empathy-altruism hypothesis. *Journal of Personality and Social Psychology, 50.* 761–769.

Fung, H. H., & Ng, S. K. (2006). Age differences in the sixth personality factor: Age difference in interpersonal relatedness among Canadians and Hong Kong Chinese. *Psychology and Aging, 21,* 810–814.

Funk, J. B. (2005). Children's exposure to violent video games and desensitization to violence. *Child and Adolescent Psychiatric Clinics of North America, 14,* 387–404.

Furnham, A., & Stringfield, P. (1994). Congruence of self and subordinate ratings of managerial practices as a correlate of supervisor evaluation. *Journal of Occupational and Organizational Psychology, 67,* 57–67.

Furth, H. G., & Wachs, H. (1975). *Thinking goes to school.* New York: Oxford University Press.

Furukawa, T. A., Watanabe, N., & Churchill, R. (2007). Combined psychotherapy plus antidepressants for panic disorder with or without agoraphobia. *Cochrane Database of Systematic Reviews,* CD004364.

Fusar-Poli, P., & Broome, M. R. (2006). Conceptual issues in psychiatric neuroimaging. *Current Opinions in Psychiatry, 19,* 608–612.

 G

Gage, F. H. (2000). Mammalian neural stem cells. *Science, 287,* 1433–1438.

Gage, F. H., & Bjorklund, A. (1986). Cholinergic septal grafts into the hippocampal formation improve spatial learning and memory in aged rats by an atropine-sensitive mechanism. *Journal of Neuroscience, 6,* 2837–2847.

Gaillard, R., Del Cul, A., Naccache, L., Vinekier, F., Cohen, L., & Dehaene, S. (2006). Nonconscious semantic processing of emotional words modulates conscious access. *Proceedings of the National Academy of Science USA, 103,* 7524–7529.

Galaif, E. R., Sussman, S., Newcomb, M. D., & Locke, T. F. (2007). Suicidality, depression, and alcohol use among adolescents: A review of empirical findings. *International Journal of Adolescent Medicine and Health, 19,* 27–35.

Galambos, N. L. (2004). Gender and gender-role development in adolescence. In R. M. Lerner & L. Steinberg (Eds.), *Handbook of adolescent psychology.* New York: Wiley.

Galan, R. F., Weidert, M., Menzel, R., Herz, A. V., & Galizia, C. G. (2006). Sensory memory for odors is encoded in spontaneous correlated activity between olfactory glomeruli. *Neural Computation, 18,* 10–25.

Gale, J. T., Amirnovin, R., Williams, Z. M., Flaherty, A. W., & Eskandar, E. N. (2007). From symphony to cacophony: Pathophysiology of the human basal ganglia in Parkinson disease. *Neuroscience and Biobehavioral Reviews.* (in press)

Gallo, W. T., Bradley, E. H., Dubin, J. A., Jones, R. N. Falba, T. A., Teng, H. M., & Kasi, S. V. (2006a). The persistence of depressive symptoms in older workers who experience involuntary job loss: Results from the health and retirement survey. *Journals of Gerontology B: Psychological Sciences and Social Sciences, 61,* S221–S228.

Gallo, W. T., Teng, H. M., Falba, T. A., Kasl, S. V., Krumholz, H. M., & Bradley, E. H. (2006b). The impact of late career job loss on myocardial infarction and stroke: A 10-year follow-up using the health and retirement survey. *Occupational and Environmental Medicine, 63,* 683–687.

Gallup Organization. (1999). *The 31st annual Phi Delta Kappa/Gallup Poll.* Princeton, NJ: Author.

Gana, K., Alaphilippe, D., & Bailly, N. (2004). Positive illusions and mental and physical health in later life. *Aging and Mental Health, 8,* 58–64.

Garb, H. N., Wood, J. M., Nezworski, M. T., Grove, W. M., & Stejskal, W. J. (2001). Toward a resolution of the Rorschach controversy. *Psychological Assessment, 13,* 433–448.

Garbarino, S., Beelke, M., Costa, G., Violani, C., Lucidi, F., Ferrillo, F., & Sannita, G. (2002). Brain function and effects of shift work: Implications for clinical neuropharmacology. *Neuropsychobiology, 45,* 50–56.

Garcia, E. E., Bravo, M. A., Dickey, L. M., Cun, K., & Sun-Irminger, X. (2002). Rethinking school reform in the context of cultural and linguistic diversity. In L. Minaya-Rowe (Ed.), *Teaching training and effective pedagogy in the context of cultural diversity.* Greenwich, CT: IAP.

Garcia, J. (1989). Food for Tolman: Cognition and cathexis in concert. In T. Archer & L. Nilsson (Eds.), *Aversion, avoidance, and anxiety.* Mahwah, NJ: Erlbaum.

Garcia, J., Ervin, F. E., & Koelling, R. A. (1966). Learning with prolonged delay of reinforcement. *Psychonomic Science, 5,* 121–122.

Gardiner, J. M. (2007). Essence of retrieval and related concepts. In H. L. Roediger, Y. Dubai, & S. Fitzpatrick (Eds.), *Science of memory: Concepts.* New York: Oxford University Press.

Gardner, H. (1983). *Frames of mind.* New York: Basic Books.

Gardner, H. (1993). *Multiple intelligences.* New York: Basic Books.

Gardner, H. (2002). The pursuit of excellence through education. In M. Ferrari (Ed.), *Learning from extraordinary minds.* Mahwah, NJ: Erlbaum.

Garry, M., & Loftus, E. F. (2007). Repressed memory. In D. Clark (ed.), *Encyclopedia of law and society.* Thousand Oaks, CA: Sage.

Garver, D. L. (2006). Evolution of antipsychotic intervention in the schizophrenic psychosis. *Current Drug Targets, 7,* 1205–1215.

Garza, M. (1999). Review of Halonen/Santrock, *Psychology* (3rd ed.). New York: McGraw-Hill.

Gasper, K.. (2004). Permission to seek freely? The effect of happy and sad moods on generating old and new ideas. *Creativity Research Journal, 16*(2-3), 215–229.

Gasper, K., & Clore, G. L. (2002). Attending to the big picture: Mood and global versus local processing of visual information. *Psychological Science, 13,* 34–40.

Gasser, S., & Raulet, D. H. (2006). Activation and self-tolerance of natural killer cells. *Immunology Review, 214,* 130–142.

Gathercole, S. E. (2007). Working memory: What it is, and what it is not. In H. L. Roediger, Y. Dudai, & S. Fitzpatrick (Eds.), *Science of memory: Concepts.* New York: Oxford University Press.

Gathercole, V. C. M., & Hoff, E. (2007). Input and the acquisition of language: Three questions. In E. Hoff & M. Shatz (Eds.), *Blackwell handbook of language development.* Malden, MA: Blackwell.

Gaudiano, B. A., Uebelacker, L. A., & Miller, I. W. (2007). Course of illness in psychotic mania: Is mood congruence important? *Journal of Nervous and Mental Disease, 195,* 226–232.

Gaunt, R., & Trope, Y. (2007). Attribution and person perception. In M. A. Hogg & J. Cooper (Eds.), *The Sage handbook of social psychology* (concise 2nd ed.). Thousand Oaks, CA: Sage.

Gauthier, I., Behrmann, M., & Tarr, M. J. (2004). Are greebles like faces? Using the neuropsychological exception to test the rule. *Neuropsychologia, 42,* 1961–1970.

Gauthier, I., & Bukach, C. (2007). Should we reject the expertise hypothesis? *Cognition, 103,* 322–330.

Gauthier, I., Curran, T., Curby, K. M., & Collins, D. (2003). Perceptual inference supports a non-modular account of face processing. *Nature Neuroscience, 6,* 428–432.

Gauthier, I., Skudlarski, P., Gore, J. C., & Anderson, A. W. (2000). Expertise for cars and birds recruits brain areas involved in face recognition. *Nature Neuroscience, 3,* 191–197.

Geary, D. (2006). Evolutionary developmental psychology: Current status and future directions. *Developmental Review, 26,* 113–119.

Geers, A. E. (2002). Factors affecting the development of speech, language, and literacy in children with early cochlear implantation. *Language, Speech, and Hearing Services in Schools, 33,* 172–183.

Gelder, B. D., Meeren, H. K., Righart, R., Stock, J. V., van de Riet, W. A, & Tamietto, M. (2006). Beyond the face: Exploring rapid influences of context on face processing. *Progress in Brain Research, 155PB,* 37–48.

Geller, E. S. (2005). Behavior-based safety and occupational risk management. *Behavior Modification, 29,* 539–561.

Geller, E. S. (2006). Occupational injury prevention and applied behavior analysis. In A. C. Gielen, D. A. Sleet, & R. J. DiClemente (Eds.), *Injury and violence prevention: Behavioral science theories, methods, and applications.* (pp. 297–322). San Francisco: Jossey-Bass.

Gemignani, A., Sebastiani, L., Simoni, A., Santarcangelo, E. L., & Ghelarducci, B. (2006). Hypnotic trait and specific phobia: EEG and autonomic output during phobia stimulation. *Brain Research Bulletin, 69,* 197–203.

Gentile, D. A., & Anderson, C. A. (2006). Violent video games: Effects on youth and public policy implications. In N. Dowd, D. G. Singer, & R. F. Wilson (Eds.), *Handbook of children, culture, and violence* (pp. 225–246). Thousand Oaks, CA: Sage.

Gentner, D., & Lowenstein, J. (2001). Relational thinking and relational language. In J. Byrnes & E. Amsel (Eds.), *Language, literacy, and cognitive development.* Mahwah, NJ: Erlbaum.

George, J. M. (1995). Leader positive mood and group performance: The case of customer service. *Journal of Applied Social Psychology, 25,* 778–795.

George, J. M., & Brief, A. P. (1992). Feeling good—doing good: A conceptual analysis of the mood at work—organizational spontaneity. *Psychological Bulletin, 112,* 310–329.

George, L. K. (2006). Perceived quality of life. In R. H. Binstock & L. K. George (Eds.), *Handbook of aging and the social sciences* (6th ed.). San Diego: Academic.

Geraci, L. (2006). A test of the frontal lobe functioning hypothesis of age deficits in production priming. *Neuropsychology, 20,* 539–548.

Gershoff, E. T. (2002). Corporal punishment by parents and associated child behaviors and experiences: A meta-analysis and theoretical review. *Psychological Bulletin, 128,* 539–579.

Gerson, L. S., & Braun, B. (2006). Effect of high cardiorespiratory fitness and high body fat on insulin resistance. *Medicine and Science in Sports and Exercise, 38,* 1709–1715.

Gesell, A. (1934). *Infancy and human growth.* New York: Macmillan.

Ghaemi, S. N. (2007). Feeling and time: The phenomenology of mood disorders, depressive realism, and existential psychotherapy. *Schizophrenia Bulletin, 33,* 122–130.

Ghen, M. J., Roshan, R., Roshan, R. O., Blyweiss, D. J., Corso, N., Khalili, B., & Zenga, W. T. (2006). Potential clinical applications using stem cells derived from human umbilical cord blood. *Reproductive Biomedicine Online, 13,* 562–572.

Gheorghita, F., Kraftsik, R., Dubois, R., & Welker, E. (2006). Structural basis for map formation in the thalamocortical pathway of the barrelless mouse. *Journal of Neuroscience, 26,* 10057–10067.

Ghiringhelli, F., Menard, C., Martin, F., & Zitvogel, L. (2006). The role of regulatory T cells in the control of natural killer cells: Relevance during tumor progression. *Immunology Review, 214,* 229–238.

Gibbons, F. X., & McCoy, S. B. (1991). Self-esteem, similarity, and reactions to active versus passive downward comparison. *Journal of Personality and Social Psychology, 60,* 414–424.

Gibson, E. J. (2001). *Perceiving the affordances.* Mahwah, NJ: Erlbaum.

Gibson, R., & Mitchell, M. (2003). *Introduction to counseling and guidance* (6th ed.). Upper Saddle River, NJ:Prentice-Hall.

Giedd, J., & others. (2006). Puberty-related influences on brain development. *Molecular and Cellular Endocrinology, 25,* 154–162.

Giersch, A., Humphreys, G. W., Barthaud, J. C., & Landmann, C. (2006). A two-stage account of computing and binding occluded and visible contours: Evidence from visual agnosia and effects of lorazepam. *Cognitive Neuropsychology. 23,* 261–277.

Gil, S., & Caspi, Y. (2006). Personality traits, coping style, and perceived threat as predictors of posttraumatic stress disorder after exposure to a terrorist attack: A prospective study. *Psychosomatic Medicine, 68,* 904–909.

Gilbert, L. A., & Kearney, L. K. (2006). The psychotherapeutic relationship as a positive and powerful resource for girls and women. In J. Worell & C. D. Goodheart (Eds.), *Handbook of girls' and women's psychological health: Gender and well-being across the lifespan.* New York: Oxford University Press.

Gilbert, P. (2001). *Overcoming depression.* New York: Oxford University Press.

Gilboa, A., Winocur, G., Rosenbaum, R. S., Poreh, A., Gao, F., Black, S. E., Westmacott, R., & Moscovitch, M. (2006). Hippocampal contributions to recollection in retrograde and anterograde amnesia. *Hippocampus, 16,* 966–980.

Giles, L. C., Glonek, G. F. V., Luszcz, M. A., & Andrews, G. R. (2005). Effect of social networks on 10 year survival in very old Australians: The Australian longitudinal study of aging. *Journal of Epidemiology and Community Health, 59,* 574–579.

Gilligan, C. (1982). *In a different voice.* Cambridge, MA: Harvard University Press.

Gilligan, C. (1996). The centrality of relationships in psychological development. In G. Noam & K. W. Fischer (Eds.), *Development and vulnerability in close relationships.* Mahwah, NJ: Erlbaum.

Gilman, S. L. (2001). Karen Horney, M.D., 1885–1952. *American Journal of Psychoanalysis, 15,* 1205.

Giltay, E. J., Zitman, F. G., & Kromhout, D. (2006). Dispositional optimism and the risk of depressive symptoms during 15 years of follow-up: The Zutphen Elderly Study. *Journal of Affective Disorders, 91,* 45–52.

Giner, L., Nichols, C. M., Zalsman, G., & Oquendo, M. A. (2005). Selective serotonin reuptake inhibitors and the risk for suicidality in adolescents: An update. *International Journal of Adolescent Medicine and Health, 17,* 211–220.

Gladding, S. T. (2007). *Family therapy* (4th ed.). Upper Saddle River, NJ: Prentice-Hall.

Gladstone, G. L., Parker, G. B., & Malhi, G. S. (2006). Do bullied children become anxious and depressed adults? A cross-sectional investigation of the correlates of bullying and anxious depression. *Journal of Nervous and Mental Disorders, 194,* 201–208.

Gladstone, G. L., Parker, G. B., Malhi, G. S, & Wilhelm, K. A. (2007). Feeling unsupported? An investigation of depressed patients' perceptions. *Journal of Affective Disorders.* (in press)

Glasberg, B. R., & Moore, B. C. (2006). Prediction of absolute thresholds and equal-loudness contours using a modified loudness model. *Journal of the Acoustical Society of America, 120,* 585–588.

Glaser, R., & Kiecolt-Glaser, J. K. (2005). Stress-induced immune dysfunction: Implications for health. *Nature Reviews: Immunology, 5,* 243–251.

Gluck, M. A., & others. (Eds.). (2007). *Memory and mind.* Mahwah, NJ: Erlbaum.

Gobet, E., & Charness, N. (2006). Expertise in chess. In K. A. Ericsson, N. Charness, P. J. Feltovich, & R. R. Hoffman (Eds.), *The Cambridge handbook of expertise and expert performance.* New York: Cambridge University Press.

Gobet, F., & Clarkson, G. (2004). Chunks in expert memory: Evidence for the magical number four . . . or is it two? *Memory, 12,* 732–747.

Goddard, L., Dritschel, B., & Burton, A. (2001). The effects of specific retrieval instruction on social problem-solving in depression. *British Journal of Clinical Psychology, 40,* 297–308.

Godden, D. R., & Baddeley, A. D. (1975). Context-dependent memory in two natural environments: On land and under water. *British Journal of Psychology, 66,* 325–331.

Goethals, G. R., & Demorest, A. P. (1995). The risky shift is a sure bet. In M. E. Ware & D. E. Johnson (Eds.), *Demonstrations and activities in teaching of psychology* (vol. 3). Mahwah, NJ: Erlbaum.

Goforth, H. W., & Holsinger, T. (2007). Rapid relief of severe major depressive disorder by use of preoperative ketamine and electroconvulsive therapy. *Journal of ECT, 23,* 23–25.

Goh, V. H., Tong, T. Y., Lim, C. L., Low, E. C., & Lee, L. K. (2001). Effects of one night of sleep deprivation on hormone profiles and performance efficiency. *Military Medicine, 166,* 427–431.

Golan, O., & Baron-Cohen, S. (2006). Systemizing empathy: Teaching adults with Asperger syndrome or high-functioning autism to recognize complex emotions using interactive multimedia. *Development and Psychopathology, 18,* 591–617.

Gold, B. (2002). Integrative approaches to psychotherapy. In M. Hersen & W. H. Sledge (Eds.), *Encyclopedia of psychotherapy.* San Diego: Academic.

Gold, J. J., Hopkins, R. O., & Squire, L. R. (2006). Single-item memory, associative memory, and the human hippocampus. *Learning and Memory, 13,* 644–649.

Gold, P. E. (2006). The many faces of amnesia. *Learning and Memory, 13,* 506–514.

Goldberg, L. R., & Digman, J. M. (1994). Revealing structure in the data: Principles of exploratory factor analysis. In S. Strack & M. Lorr (Eds.), *Differentiating normal and abnormal personality* (pp. 216–242). New York: Springer.

Goldberg, L. R., Johnson, J. A., Eber, H. W., Hogan, R., Ashton, M. C., Cloninger, C. R., & Gough, H. G. (2006). The international personality item pool and the future of public-domain personality measures. *Journal of Research in Personality, 40,* 84–96.

Goldbeter, A. (2006). A model for the dynamics of human weight cycling. *Journal of Bioscience, 31,* 129–136.

Goldfarb, L., & Tzelgov, J. (2007). The cause of the within-language Stroop superiority effect and its implications. *Quarterly Journal of Experimental Psychology, 60,* 179–185.

Goldman, S. L., Kraemer, D. T., & Salovey, P. (1996). Beliefs about mood moderate the relationship of stress to illness and symptom reporting. *Journal of Psychosomatic Research, 41,* 115–128.

Goldstein, E. B. (2007). *Sensation and perception* (7th ed.). Pacific Grove, CA: Wadsworth.

Goldstein, M. H., King, A. P., & West, M. J. (2003). Social interaction shapes babbling: Testing parallels between birdsong and speech. *Proceedings of the National Academy of Sciences, 100*(13), 8030–8035.

Goldstrom, I. D., Campbell, J., Rogers, J. A., Lambert, D. B., Blacklow, B., Henderson, M. J., & Manderscheid, R. W. (2006). National estimates for mental health mutual support groups, self-help organizations, and consumer-operated services. *Administration and Policy in Mental Health, 33,* 92–103.

Goleman, D., Kaufman, P., & Ray, M. (1993). *The creative mind.* New York: Plume.

Gollwitzer, P. M. (1999). Implementation intentions: Strong effects of simple plans. *American Psychologist, 54,* 493–503.

Gollwitzer, P. M., & Oettingen, G. (2007). The role of goal setting and goal striving in medical adherence. In D. C. Park & L. L. Liu (Eds.), *Medical adherence and aging: Social and cognitive perspectives.* (pp. 23–47). Washington, DC: American Psychological Association.

Gomez-Mejia, L., Balkin, D. B., & Cardy, R. L. (2008). *Management* (3rd ed.). New York: McGraw-Hill.

Gong-Guy, E. (1986). *Depression in students of Chinese and Japanese ancestry: An acculturation, vulnerability and stress model.* Unpublished dissertation, University of California, Los Angeles.

Gonzales, V., Yawkey, T. D., & Minaya-Rowe, L. (2006). *English-as-a-second-language (ESL) teaching and learning.* Boston: Allyn & Bacon.

Goodwin, R. D., Cox, B. J., & Clara, I. (2006). Neuroticism and physical disorders among adults in the community: Results from the National Comorbidity Survey. *Journal of Behavioral Medicine, 29,* 229–238.

Gooren, L. (2006). The biology of human psychosexual differentiation. *Hormones and Behavior, 50*(4), 589–601.

Gordon, K. A., Valero, J., & Papsin, B. C. (2007). Binaural processing in children using bilateral cochlear implants. *Neuroreport, 18,* 613–617.

Gorin, A., Phelan, S., Wing, R. R., & Hill, J. O. (2004). Promoting long-term weight control: Does dieting consistency matter? *International Journal of Obesity Related Metabolic Disorder, 28,* 278–281.

Gosling, S. D., & John, O. P. (1999). Personality dimensions in nonhuman animals: A cross-species review. *Current Directions in Psychological Science, 8,* 69–75.

Gosling, S. D., Kwan, V. S. Y., & John, O. (2003). A dog's got personality: A cross-species comparison of personality judgments in dogs and humans. *Journal of Personality and Social Psychology, 85,* 1161–1169.

Gottlieb, G. (2007). Probabilistic epigenesis. *Developmental Science, 10,* 1–11.

Gottlieb, G., Wahlsten, D., & Lickliter, R. (2006). The significance of biology for human development. In W. Damon & R. Lerner (Eds.), *Handbook of child psychology* (6th ed.). New York: Wiley.

Gottman, J. (2006, April, 29). Secrets of long term love. *New Scientist, 2549,* 40.

Gottman, J. M. (1994). *What predicts divorce?* Mahwah, NJ: Erlbaum.

Gottman, J. M., Coan, J., Carrere, S., & Swanson, C. (1998). Predicting marital happiness and stability from newlywed interactions. *Journal of Marriage and the Family, 60,* 5–22.

Gottman, J. M., Gottman, J. S., & Declaire, J. (2006). *10 lessons to transform your marriage: America's love lab experts share their strategies for strengthening your relationship.* New York: Random House.

Gottman, J. M., Katz, L. F., & Hooven, C. (1997). *Meta-emotion: How families communicate.* Mahwah, NJ: Erlbaum.

Gottman, J. M., Ryan, K. D., Carrere, S., & Erley, A. M. (2002). Toward a scientifically based marital therapy. In H. A. Liddle & D. A. Santisteban (Eds.), *Family psychology.* Washington, DC: American Psychological Association.

Gottman, J. M., & Silver, N. (1999). *The seven principles for making marriages work.* New York: Crown.

Gould, E., Reeves, A. J., Graziano, M. S., & Gross, C. G. (1999). Neurogenesis in the neocortex of adult primates, *Science, 286*(1), 548–552.

Grabe, H. J., & others. (2006). Famiality of obsessive-compulsive disorder in nonclinical and clinical subjects. *American Journal of Psychiatry, 163,* 1986–1992.

Graber, J. A., Brooks-Gunn, J., & Warren, M. P.(2006). Pubertal effects on adjustment in girls: Moving from demonstrating effects to identifying pathways. *Journal of Youth and Adolescence, 35,* 391–401.

Graffin, N. F., Ray, W. J., & Lundy, R. (1995). EEG concomitants of hypnosis and hypnotic susceptibility. *Journal of Abnormal Psychology, 104,* 123–131.

Graham, J. E., Christian, L. M., & Kiecolt-Glaser, J. K. (2006). Stress, age, and immune function: Toward a lifespan approach. *Journal of Behavioral Medicine, 29,* 389–400.

Grandey, A. A., Kern, J. H., & Frone, M. R. (2007). Verbal abuse from outsiders versus insiders: Comparing frequency, impact on emotional exhaustion, and the role of emotional labor. *Journal of Occupational Health Psychology, 12,* 63–79.

Grandin, T. (1995/2006). *Thinking in pictures: My life with autism* (expanded ed.). New York: Random House.

Gray, C. R., & Gummerman, K. (1975). The enigmatic eidetic image: A critical examination of methods, data, and theories. *Psychological Bulletin, 82,* 383–407.

Green, B. L., Kramer, T. L., Grace, M. C., Gleser, G. C., Leonard, A. C., Vary, M. G., & Lindy, J. D. (1997). Traumatic events over the life span: Survivors of the Buffalo Creek disaster. In T. W. Miller (Ed.), *Clinical disorders and stressful life events* (pp. 283–305). Madison, CT: International Universities Press.

Green, B. L., Lindy, J. D., Grace, M. C., & Leonard, A. C. (1992). Chronic posttraumatic stress disorder and diagnostic comorbidity in a disaster sample. *Journal of Nervous & Mental Disease, 180,* 760–766.

Green, M. (2007). Stimulating the development of drug treatments to improve cognition in schizophrenia. *Annual Review of Clinical Psychology* (vol. 3). Palo Alto, CA: Annual Reviews.

Greenberg, D. A., & Jin, K. (2006). Growth factors and stroke. *NeuroRX, 3,* 458–465.

Greenberg, J., Solomon, S., & Pyszczynski, T. (1997). Terror management theory of self-esteem and cultural worldviews: Empirical assessments and conceptual refinements. In M. P. Zanna (Ed.), *Advances in experimental social psychology* (vol. 29, pp. 61–139). San Diego: Academic.

Greenberg, J. S. (2008). *Comprehensive stress management* (10th ed.). New York: McGraw-Hill.

Greene, R. L. (1999). Applied memory research: How far from bankruptcy? *Contemporary Psychology, 44,* 29–31.

Greenfield, P. M., Suzuki, L. K., & Rothstein-Fisch, C. (2006). Cultural pathways through human development. In W. Damon & R. Lerner (Eds.), *Handbook of child psychology* (6th ed.). New York: Wiley.

Greenfield, R. (2006). *Timothy Leary: A biography.* New York: Harcourt Books.

Greenough, W. T. (2001). *Commentary.* In J. W. Santrock, *Child Development* (9th ed.). Boston: McGraw-Hill.

Greenwald, A. G., & Banaji, M. R. (1995). Implicit social cognition: Attitudes, self-esteem, and stereotypes. *Psychological Review, 102,* 4–27.

Greenwald, H. P. (2007). *Management without control.* Thousand Oaks, CA: Sage.

Greer, M. (2005). A new kind of war. *APA Monitor, 36,* 40.

Gregory, R. J. (2007). *Psychological testing* (5th ed.). Boston: Allyn & Bacon.

Grief, M. L., Kemler Nelson, D. G., Keil, F. C., & Gutierrez, F. (2006). What do children know about animals and artifacts? Domain-specific requests for information. *Psychological Science, 17,* 455–459.

Griffin, R. W., & Lopez, Y. P. (2005). "Bad behavior" in organizations: A review and typology for future research. *Journal of Management, 31,* 988–1005.

Grilo, C. M., Masheb, R. M., & Wilson, G. T. (2006). Rapid response treatment to treatment for binge eating disorder. *Journal of Consulting and Clinical Psychology, 74,* 602–613.

Grinspoon, L. (1994). *Marihuana reconsidered.* Cambridge, MA: Harvard University Press.

Grinspoon, L. (2000, December 7). Why won't government let us use marijuana as medicine? *Boston Globe,* p. A23.

Griskevicius, V., Goldstein, N. J., Mortensen, C. R., Cialdini, R. B., & Kenrick, D. T. (2006). Going along versus going alone: When fundamental motives facilitate strategic (non)conformity. *Journal of Personality and Social Psychology, 91,* 281–294.

Groer, M. W., & Morgan, K. (2007). Immune, health, and endocrine characteristics of depressed postpartum mothers. *Psychoneuroendocrinolgy, 32,* 133–139.

Gronlund, N. E. (2006). *Assessment of student achievement* (8th ed.). Boston: Allyn & Bacon.

Grove, P. M., Brooks, K. R., Andrson, B. L., & Gillam, B. J. (2006). Monocular transparency and unpaired stereopsis. *Vision Research, 46,* 3042–3053.

Grover, S., Avasthi, A., & Sharma, Y. (2006). Psychotropics in pregnancy: Weighing the risks. *Indian Journal of Medical Research, 123,* 497–512.

Grubin, D., & Madsen, L. (2006). Accuracy and utility of post-conviction polygraph testing of sex offenders. *British Journal of Psychiatry, 188,* 479–483.

Grusec, J. E., & Davidov, M. (2007). Socialization in the family: The roles of parents. In J. E. Grusec & P. D. Hastings (Eds.), *Handbook of socialization.* New York: Oxford University Press.

Gueta, R., Barlam, D., Shneck, R. Z., & Rousso, I. (2006). Measurement of the mechanical properties of isolated tectorial membrane using atomic force microscopy. *Proceedings of the National Academy of Science USA, 103,* 14790–14795.

Guilford, J. P. (1967). *The structure of intellect.* New York: McGraw-Hill.

Guillot, C., & Greenway, D. (2006). Recreational ecstasy use and depression. *Journal of Psychopharmacology, 20,* 411–416.

Guilleminault, C., Kirisolglu, C., da Rosa, A. C., Lopes, C., & Chan, A. (2006). Sleepwalking, a disorder of REM sleep instability. *Sleep Medicine, 7,* 163–170.

Guion, R. M., & Highhouse, S. (2006). *Essentials of personnel assessment and selection.* Mahwah, NJ: Erlbaum.

Gulwadi, B. (2006). Seeking restorative experiences: Elementary school teachers' choices for places that enable coping with stress. *Environment and Behavior, 38,* 503–520.

Gump, B., & Matthews, K. (2000, March). Are vacations good for your health? The 9-year mortality experience after the multiple risk factor intervention trial. *Psychosomatic Medicine, 62,* 608–612.

Gunstad, J., Cohen, R. A., Paul, R. H., & Gordon, E. (2006). Dissociation of the component processes of attention in healthy adults. *Archives of Clinical Psychology, 21,* 645–650.

Gunturu, S. D., & Ten, S. (2007). Complications of obesity in childhood. *Pediatric Annals, 36,* 96–101.

Guo, Q., Johnson, C. A., Unger, J. B., Lee, L., Xie, B., Chou, C. P., Palmer, P. H., Sun, P., Gallaher, P., & Pentz, M. (2007). Utility of theory of reasoned action and theory of planned behavior for predicting Chinese adolescent smoking. *Addictive Behaviors, 32,* 1066–1081.

Guo, Y. (2005). Filial therapy for children's behavioral and emotional problems in mainland China. *Journal of Child and Adolescent Psychiatric Nursing, 18,* 171–180.

Gupta, N., Khera, S., Vempati, R. P., Sharma, R., & Bijlani, R. L. (2006). Effects of yoga on based lifestyle intervention on trait and state anxiety. *Indian Journal of Physiology and Pharmacology, 50,* 41–47.

Guttman, N., & Kalish, H. I. (1956). Discriminability and stimulus generalization. *Journal of Experimental Psychology, 51,* 79–88.

Gynther, L. M., Hewitt, J. K., Heath, A. C., & Eaves, L. J. (1999). Phenotypic and genetic factors in motives for smoking. *Behavior Genetics, 29,* 291–302.

H

Habeck, C., Rakitin, B. C., Moeller, J., Scarmeas, N., Zarahn, E., Brown, T., & Stern, Y. (2004). An event-related fMRI study of the neurobehavioral impact of sleep deprivation on performance of a delayed-match-to-sample task. *Brain Research, 18,* 306–321.

Habel, U., Klein, M., Kellermann, T., Shah, N. J., & Schneider, F. (2005). Same or different? Neural correlates of happy and sad mood in healthy males. *Neuroimage, 26,* 206–214.

Hagner, M. (2007). Mind reading, brain mirror, neuroimaging: Insight into the brain or the mind? In M. Ash & T. Sturm (Eds.), *Psychology's territories.* Mahwah, NJ: Erlbaum.

Hahn, D. B., Payne, W. A., & Lucas, E. B. (2007). *Focus on health* (8th ed.). New York: McGraw-Hill.

Hakuta, K. (2001). A critical period for second language acquisition? In D. Bailey, J. Bruer, F. Symons, & J. Lichtman (Eds.), *Critical thinking about critical periods* (pp. 193–205). Baltimore: Paul H. Brookes.

Hakuta, K. (2005, April). *Bilingualism at the intersection of research and public policy.* Paper presented at the meeting of the Society for Research in Child Development, Atlanta.

Hakuta, K., Butler, Y. G., & Witt, D. (2000). *How long does it take English learners to attain proficiency?* (Linguistic Minority Institute Policy Report 2000–2001). Berkeley: University of California.

Haladyna, T. M. (2002). *Essentials of standardized testing.* Boston: Allyn & Bacon.

Halasz, J., Toth, M., Kallo, I., Liposits, Z., & Haller, J. (2006). The activation of prefrontal cortical neurons in aggression—A double labeling study. *Behavioural Brain Research, 175,* 166–175.

Hales, D. (2007). *An invitation to health* (12th ed.). Belmont, CA: Wadsworth.

Haley, M. (2007). Gestalt theory. In D. Capuzzi & D. Gross (Eds.), *Counseling and psychotherapy* (4th ed.). Upper Saddle River, NJ: Prentice-Hall.

Halford, J. C., Harrold, J. A., Boyland, E. J., Lawton, C. L., & Blundell, J. E. (2007). Serotonergic drugs: Effects on appetite expression and use for the treatment of obesity. *Drugs, 67,* 27–55.

Halgin, R. P., & Whitbourne, S. K. (2007). *Abnormal psychology* (5th ed.). New York; McGraw-Hill.

Hall, H., Lawyer, G., Sillen, A., Jonsson, E. G., Agartz, I., Terenius, L., & Arnborg, S. (2007). Potential genetic variants in schizophrenia: A Bayesian analysis. *World Journal of Biological Psychiatry, 8,* 12–22.

Hall, J. A., & Matsumoto, D. (2004). Gender differences in judgments of multiple emotions from facial expressions. *Emotion, 14,* 201–206.

Hallahan, D. P., & Kauffman, J. M. (2006). *Exceptional learners* (10th ed.). Boston: Allyn & Bacon.

Hallal, P. C., Victora, C. G., Azevedo, M. R., & Wells, J. C. (2006). Adolescent physical activity and health: A systematic review. *Sports Medicine, 36,* 1019–1030.

Halpern, D. (2007). The nature and nurture of critical thinking. In R. J. Sternberg, H. Roediger, & D. Halpern (Eds.), *Critical thinking in psychology.* New York: Cambridge University Press.

Halpern, J. H. (1996). The use of hallucinogens in the treatment of addiction. *Addiction Research, 4,* 177–189.

Halpern, J. H. (2003). Hallucinogens: An update. *Current Psychiatry Reports, 5,* 347–354.

Halpern, J. H., & Sewell, R. A. (2005). Hallucinogenic botanicals of America: A growing need for focused drug education and research. *Life Sciences, 78,* 519–526.

Halpern, J. H., Sherwood, A. R., Hudson, J. I., Yurgelun-Todd, D., & Pope, H. G. (2005). Psychological and cognitive effects of long-term peyote use among Native Americans. *Biological Psychiatry, 58,* 624–631.

Hamer, M. (2006). Exercise and psychobiological processes: Implications for the primary prevention of coronary heart disease. *Sports Medicine, 36,* 829–838.

Hamer, M., Tanaka, G., Okamura, H., Tsuda, A., & Steptoe, A. (2007). The effects of depressive symptoms on cardiovascular and catecholamine responses to the induction of depressive mood. *Biological Psychology, 74,* 20–25.

Hamilton, B. E., Martin, J. A., Ventura, M. A., Sutton, P. D., & Mancker, F. (2005, December 29). Births: Preliminary data for 2004. *National Vital Statistics Reports, 54*(8), 1.

Hamilton, J. W. (2006). The critical effect of object loss in the development of episodic manic illness. *Journal of the American Academy of Psychoanalysis and Dynamic Psychiatry, 34,* 333–348.

Hammad, T. A. (2004, September 13). *Results of the analysis of suicidality in pediatric trials of newer antidepressants.* Presentation at the U.S. Food and Drug Administration, Psychopharmacologic Drugs Advisory Committee and the Pediatric Advisory Committee. www.fda.gov/ohrms/dockets/ac/04/slides/2004-4065S1 08 FDA-Hammad files/frame.htm (accessed July, 26, 2006).

Hammond, D. C. (2007). Review of the efficacy of clinical hypnosis with headaches and migraines. *International Journal of Clinical and Experimental Hypnosis, 55,* 207–219.

Hammond, T. A., Laughren, T., & Racoosin, J. (2006). Suicidality in pediatric patients treated with antidepressant drugs. *Archives of General Psychiatry, 63,* 332–339.

Handy, C. (1985) *Understanding organization.* Harmondsworth: Penguin.

Hankey, G. J. (2007). Clinical update: Management of stroke. *Lancet, 369,* 1330–1332.

Hannon, B., & Craik, F. I. (2001). Encoding specificity revisited: The role of semantics. *Canadian Journal of Experimental Psychology, 55,* 231–243.

Hansen, M., Janssen, I., Schiff, A., Zee, P. C., & Dubocovich, M. L. (2005). The impact of school daily schedule on adolescent sleep. *Pediatrics, 115,* 1555–1561.

Hanson, M. A., & Borman, W. C. (2006). Citizenship performance. In W. Bennett, C. E. Lance, & D. J. Woehr (Eds.), *Performance measurement.* Mahwah, NJ: Erlbaum.

Harden, S. P., Dey, C., & Gawne-Cain, M. L. (2007). Cranial CT of the unconscious adult patient. *Clinical Radiology, 62,* 404–415.

Harding, C. M., Books, G. W., Ashikaga, T., & others. (1987). The Vermont longitudinal study of persons with severe mental illness. *American Journal of Psychiatry, 144,* 718–726.

Hardy, C. L., & Van Vugt, M. (2006). Nice guys finish first: The competitive altruism hypothesis. *Personality and Social Psychology Bulletin, 32,* 1402–1413.

Harker, L. A., & Keltner, D. (2001). Expressions of positive emotion in women's college yearbook pictures and their relationship to personality and life outcomes across adulthood. *Journal of Personality and Social Psychology, 80,* 112–124.

Harkness, S., & Super, C. M. (1995). Culture and parenting. In M. H. Bornstein (Ed.), *Children and parenting* (vol. 2). Hillsdale, NJ: Erlbaum.

Harlow, H. F. (1958). The nature of love. *American Psychologist, 13,* 673–685.

Harman, D. (2006). Alzheimer's disease pathogenesis: Role of aging. *Annals of the New York Academy of Science, 1067,* 454–460.

Harmatz, M. (1997). Introduction to clinical psychology. In Santrock, J. W., *Psychology* (5th ed.). New York: McGraw-Hill.

Harms, P., Roberts, B. W., Woods, D. D. (2007). Who shall lead? An integrative personality approach to the study of the antecedents of status in informal social organizations. *Journal of Research in Personality, 41,* 689–699.

Harper, G. W., Hosek, S. G., Contreras, R., & Doll, M. (2003). Psychosocial factors impacting condom use among adolescents: A review and theoretical integration. *Journal of HIV/AIDS Prevention & Education for Adolescents & Children, 5,* 33–69.

Harris, D. M., & Kay, J. (1995). I recognize your face but I can't remember your name: Is it because names are unique? *British Journal of Psychology, 86,* 345–358.

Harris, E. C., & Barraclough, B. (1997). Suicide as an outcome for mental disorders: A meta-analysis. *British Journal of Psychiatry, 170,* 205–228.

Harris, J. A. (2006). Elemental representations of stimuli in associative learning. *Psychological Review, 113,* 584–605.

Harris, J. R. (1998). *The nurture assumption: Why children turn out the way they do?* New York: Free Press.

Harris, P. L. (2006). Social cognition. In W. Damon & R. Lerner (Eds.), *Handbook of child psychology* (6th ed.). New York: Wiley.

Harrison, G., Hopper, K., Craig, T., Laska, E., Siegle, C., Wanderling, J., Dube, K. S., & others. (2001). Recovery from psychotic illness: A 15- and 25-year international follow-up study. *British Journal of Psychiatry, 178,* 506–517.

Harrison, K., & Hefner, V. (2006). Media exposure, current and future body ideals, and disordered eating among preadolescent girls: A longitudinal panel study. *Journal of Youth and Adolescence, 35,* 153–163.

Harrison, P. J. (2007). Schizophrenia susceptibility genes and neurodevelopment. *Biological Psychiatry, 61,* 1119–1120.

Hart, B., & Risley, T. R. (1995). *Meaningful differences in the everyday experience of young Americans.* Baltimore: Paul H. Brookes.

Hartenbaum, N., & others. (2006). Sleep apnea and commercial motor vehicle operators. *Chest, 130,* 902–905.

Harter, J. K. (2000). Managerial talent, employee engagement, and business-unit performance. *Psychologist-Manager Journal, 4,* 215–224.

Harter, J. K., & Schmidt, F. L. (2002). *Employee engagement, satisfaction, and business unit level outcomes: Meta-analysis.* Princeton, NJ: Gallup Organization.

Harter, J. K., Schmidt, F. L., & Hayes, T. L. (2002). Business-unit-level relationship between employee satisfaction, employee engagement, and business outcomes: A meta-analysis. *Journal of Applied Psychology, 87*(2), 268–279.

Harter, S. (2006). The development of self-esteem. In M. H. Kernis (Ed.), *Self-esteem issues and answers: A sourcebook of current perspectives* (pp. 144–150). New York: Psychology Press.

Hartley, A. (2006). Changing role of the speed of processing construct in the cognitive psychology of aging. In J. E. Birren & K. W. Schaie (Eds.), *Handbook of the psychology of aging* (6th ed.). San Diego: Academic.

Hartman, M., & Stratton-Salib, B. C. (2007). Age differences in concept formation. *Journal of Clinical and Experimental Neuropsychology, 29,* 198–214.

Hartmann, E. (1993). Nightmares. In M. A. Carskadon (Ed.), *Encyclopedia of sleep and dreams.* New York: Macmillan.

Hartocollis, P. (2003). Time and the psychoanalytic situation. *Psychoanalysis Quarterly, 72,* 939–957.

Hartwell, L. (2008). *Genetics* (3rd ed.). New York: McGraw-Hill.

Harvey, J. L., Anderson, L. E., Baranowski, L. E., & Morath, R. (2007). Job analysis: Gathering job specific information. In D. L. Whetzel & G. R. Wheaton (Eds.), *Applied measurement.* Mahwah, NJ: Erlbaum.

Haselton, M. G. (2006, April 29). How to pick a perfect mate. *New Scientist, 2549,* 36.

Hashimoto, R., Okada, T., Kato, T., Kosuga, A., Tatsumi, M., Kamijima,K., & Kunugi, H. (2005). The breakpoint cluster region gene on chromosome 22q11 is associated with bipolar disorder. *Biological Psychiatry, 57,* 1097–1102.

Haslam, S. A., & Reicher, S. D. (2006). Debating the psychology of tyranny: Fundamental issues of theory, perspective and science. *British Journal of Social Psychology, 45,* 55–63.

Hatcher, R., & others. (1988). *Contraceptive technology, 1988–1989* (14th ed.). New York: Irvington.

Hauser D. (2004). *Five years of abstinence-only-until-marriage education: Assessing the impact.* Washington, DC: Advocates for Youth.

Haviland-Jones, J., Rosario, H. H., Wilson, P. & McGuire, T. R. (2005). An environmental approach to positive emotion: Flowers. *Evolutionary Psychology, 3,* 104–132.

Hawkley, L. C., Bosch, J. A., Engeland, C. G., Marucha, P. T., & Cacioppo, J. T. (2007). Loneliness, dysphoria, stress and immunity: A role of cytokines. In N. P. Plotnikoff, R. E. Faith, & A. J. Murgo (Eds.), *Cytokines: Stress and immunity* (2nd ed.). Boca Raton, FL: CRC Press.

Hayes, M. R., Chory, F. M., Gallagher, C. A., & Covasa, M. (2006). Serotonin type-3 receptors mediate cholecystokinin-induced satiation through gastric distension. *American Journal of Physiology: Regulatory, Integrative, and Comparative Physiology, 291,* R112–R114.

Haynes, L. E., Barber, D., & Mitchell, I. J. (2004). Chronic antidepressant medication attenuates dexamethasone-induced neuronal death and sublethal neuronal damage in the hippocampus and striatum. *Brain Research, 1026,* 157–167.

Hazler, R. J. (2007). Person-centered therapy. In D. Capuzzi & D. Gross (Eds.), *Counseling and psychotherapy* (4th ed.). Upper Saddle River, NJ: Prentice-Hall.

Hebb, D. O. (1949). *The organization of behavior: A neuropsychological theory.* New York: Wiley.

Hebb, D. O. (1980). *Essay on mind.* Mahwah, NJ: Erlbaum.

Hebb, D. O. (2002). *The organization of behavior.* Mahwah, NJ: Erlbaum.

Heckman, C. J., & Clay, D. L. (2005). Hardiness, history of abuse, and women's health. *Journal of Health Psychology, 10,* 767–777.

Hedden, T., & Yoon, C. (2006). Individual differences in executive processing predict susceptibility to interference in verbal working memory. *Neuropsychology, 20,* 511–528.

Hedge, J. W., & Kavanagh, M. J. (1988). Improving the accuracy of performance evaluations: Comparison of three methods of performance appraiser training. *Journal of Applied Psychology, 73,* 68–73.

Heeger, (1997). *Signal detection theory.* Unpublished handout. Stanford, CA: Stanford University, Department of Psychology.

Hegadoren, K. M., Lasiuk, G. C., & Coupland, N. J. (2006). Posttraumatic stress disorder Part III: Health effects of interpersonal violence among women. *Perspectives in Psychiatric Care, 42,* 163–173.

Heiby, E. M., & Haynes, S. (2004). Introduction to behavioral assessment. In M. Hersen (Ed.), *Comprehensive handbook of psychological assessment* (vol. 3). New York: Wiley.

Heim, G., & Buhler, K. E. (2006). Psychological trauma and fixed ideas in Pierre Janet's conception of dissociative disorders. *American Journal of Psychotherapy, 60,* 111–129.

Hein, V., & Hagger, M. S. (2007). Global self-esteem, goal achievement orientations, and self-determined behavioral regulations in a physical education setting. *Journal of Sports Science, 25,* 149–159.

Heine, S. J. (2005). Constructing good selves in Japan and North America. In R. M. Sorrentino, D. Cohen, J. M. Olson, & M. P. Zanna (Eds.), *Cultural and social behavior: The Ontario symposium* (vol. 10, pp. 95–116). Mahwah, NJ: Erlbaum.

Heller, A. C., Amar, A. P., Liu, C. Y., & Apuzzo, M. L. (2006). Surgery of the mind and mood: A mosaic of issues in time and evolution. *Neurosurgery, 59,* 720–733.

Helson, R. (1992). Women's difficult times and rewriting the life story. *Psychology of Women Quarterly, 16,* 331–347.

Helson, R., & Roberts, B. W. (1994). Ego development and personality change in adulthood. *Journal of Personality and Social Psychology, 66,* 911–920.

Helson, R., & Soto, C. J. (2005). Up and down in middle age: Monotonic and nonmonotonic changes in roles, status, and personality. *Journal of Personality and Social Psychology, 89,* 194–204.

Helson, R., Soto, C. J., & Cate, R. A. (2006). From young adulthood through the middle ages. In D. K. Mroczek & T. D. Little (Eds.), *Handbook of personality development.* Mahwah, NJ: Erlbaum.

Hemenover, S. H. (2003). Individual differences in rate of affect change: Studies in affective chronometry. *Journal of Personality and Social Psychology, 85,* 121–131.

Hendrick, C., & Hendrick, S. S. (2006). Styles of romantic love. In R. J. Sternberg & K. Weis (Eds.), *The new psychology of love* (pp. 149–170). New Haven, CT: Yale University Press.

Hendricks, J., & Hatch, L. R. (2006). Lifestyle and aging. In R. H. Binstock & L. K. George (Eds.), *Handbook of aging and the social sciences* (6th ed.). San Diego: Academic.

Henry, J. D., MacLeod, M. S., Phillips, L. H., & Crawford, J. R. (2004). A meta-analytic review of prospective memory and aging. *Psychology and Aging, 19,* 27–39.

Henry, P. J., & Sears, D. O. (2007). Symbolic and modern racism. In J. H. Moore (Ed.), *Encyclopedia of race and racism.* Farmington Hills, MI: Macmillan Reference.

Hensrud, D. D., & Klein, S. (2006). Extreme obesity: A new medical crisis in the United States. *Mayo Clinic Proceedings, 81, Suppl. 10,* S5–S10.

Heppner, P., & Lee, D. (2001). Problem-solving appraisal and psychological adjustment. In C. R. Snyder & S. J. Lopez (Eds.), *Handbook of positive psychology.* New York: Oxford University Press.

Herbert, J. (1988). The physiology of aggression. In J. Groebel & R. Hinde (Eds.), *Aggression and war: The biological and social bases.* New York: Cambridge University Press.

Herder, R., & Demmig-Adams, B. (2004). The power of a balanced diet and lifestyle in preventing cardiovascular disease. *Nutrition in Clinical Care, 7,* 46–55.

Hergenhahn, B. R., & Olson, M. H. (2001). *An introduction to theories of learning* (6th ed.). Upper Saddle River, NJ: Prentice-Hall.

Hergenhahn, B. R., & Olson, M. H. (2007). *Introduction to theories of personality* (7th ed.). Upper Saddle River, NJ: Prentice-Hall.

Hering, E. (1878). *Zur Lehre vom Lichtsinne* (illustration, 2nd ed.).Wien: C. Gerold's Sohn.

Herlihy, B., & McCollum, V. (2007). Feminist theory. In D. Capuzzi & D. Gross (Eds.), *Counseling and psychotherapy* (4th ed.). Upper Saddle River, NJ: Prentice-Hall.

Hermans, D., Craske, M. G., Mineka, S., & Lovibond, P. F. (2006). Extinction in human fear conditioning. *Biological Psychiatry, 60,* 361–368.

Hernandez, A., & Sachs-Ericsson, N. (2006). Ethnic differences in pain reports and the moderating role of depression in a community sample of Hispanic and Caucasian participants with serious health problems. *Psychosomatic Medicine, 68,* 121–128.

Herz, R. S. (1998). Are odors the best cues to memory? A cross-modal comparison of associative memory stimuli. *Annals of the New York Academy of Sciences, 855,* 670–674.

Herz, R. S. (2004). A naturalistic analysis of autobiographical memories triggered by olfactory, visual, and auditory stimuli. *Chemical Senses, 29,* 217–224.

Herz, R. S., & Cupchik, G. C. (1995). The emotional distinctiveness of odor-evoked memories. *Chemical Senses, 20,* 517–528.

Herz, R. S., Schankler, C., & Beland, S. (2004). Olfaction, emotion, and associative learning: Effects on motivated behavior. *Motivation and Emotion, 28,* 363–383.

Herzberg, E. (2000). Use of TAT in multicultural societies: Brazil and the United States. In R. H. Dana (Ed.), *Handbook of cross-cultural and multicultural personality assessment.* Mahwah, NJ: Erlbaum.

Herzog, H. A. (1995). Discussing animal rights and animal research in the classroom. In M. E. Ware & D. E. Johnson (Eds.), *Demonstrations and activities in teaching of psychology* (vol. 1). Mahwah, NJ: Erlbaum.

Hess, E., & Cameron, K. S. (2006). *Developing management skills* (6th ed.). Upper Saddle River, NJ: Prentice-Hall.

Hetherington, E. M. (2006). The influence of conflict, marital problem solving, and parenting on children's adjustment in nondivorced, divorced, and remarried families. In A. Clarke-Stewart & J. Dunn (Eds.), *Families count.* New York: Cambridge University Press.

Hetherington, E. M., & Stanley-Hagan, M. (2002). Parenting in divorced and remarried families. In M. Bornstein (Ed.), *Handbook of parenting* (2nd ed.). Mahwah, NJ: Erlbaum.

Hettema, J. M., An, S. S., Neale, M. C., Bukszar, J., van den Oord, E. J. C. G., Kendler, K. S., & Chen, X. (2006a).Association between glutamic acid decarboxylase genes and anxiety disorders, major depression, and neuroticism. *Molecular Psychiatry, 11*(8), 752–762.

Hettema, J. M., Neale, M. C., Myers, J. M., Prescott, C. A., & Kendler, K. S. A. (2006b). Population-based twin study of the relationship between neuroticism and internalizing disorders. *American Journal of Psychiatry, 163*(5), 857–864.

Higgins, E. T., & Molden, D. C. (2004). How strategies for making judgments and decisions affect cognition. In G. V. Bodenhausen & A. J. Lambert (Eds.), *Foundations of social cognition.* Mahwah, NJ: Erlbaum.

Hihn, H., Baune, B. T., Michael, N., Markowitsch, H., Aroit, V., & Pfleiderer, B. (2006). Memory performance in severely depressed patients treated by electroconvulsive therapy. *Journal of Electroconvulsive Therapy, 22,* 189–195.

Hilgard, E. R. (1977). *Divided consciousness: Multiple controls in human thought and action.* New York: Wiley.

Hilgard, E. R. (1992). Dissociation and theories of hypnosis. In E. Fromm & M. R. Nash (Eds.), *Contemporary hypnosis research.* New York: Guilford.

Hill, A., Habermann, N., Berner, W., & Briken, P. (2007). Psychiatric disorders in single and multiple sex murderers. *Psychopathology, 40,* 22–28.

Hill, C. E. (2000). Client-centered therapy. In A. Kazdin (Ed.), *Encyclopedia of psychology.* Washington, DC, & New York: American Psychological Association and Oxford University Press.

Hill, C. W. L., & Jones, G. R. (2001). *Strategic management* (5th ed.). Boston: Houghton Mifflin.

Hill, T. D., Burdette, A. M., Ellison, C. G., & Musick, M. A. (2006). Religious attendance and the health behaviors of Texas adults. *Preventive Medicine: An International Journal Devoted to Practice and Theory, 42,* 309–312.

Hilton, D. J. (2007). Causal explanation. In A. W. Kruglanski & E. T. Higgins (Eds.), *Social psychology* (2nd ed.). New York: Guilford.

Hingson, R. W., Heeren, T., & Winter, M. R. (2006). Age at drinking onset and alcohol dependence: Age of onset, duration, and severity. *Archives of Pediatric and Adolescent Medicine, 160,* 739–746.

Hinshaw, S. P. (2007). *The mark of shame: Stigma of mental illness and an agenda for change.* New York: Oxford University Press.

Hirsch, J. K., Conner, K. R., & Duberstein, P. R. (2007). Optimism and suicide ideation among young college students. *Archives of Suicide Research, 11,* 177–185.

Hitch, G. J. (2006). Working memory in children: A cognitive approach. In E. Bialystok & F. I. M. Craik (Eds.), *Lifespan cognition.* New York: Oxford University Press.

Hlushchuk, Y., & Hari, R. (2006). Transient suppression of ipsilateral primary somatosensory cortex during tactile finger stimulation. *Journal of Neuroscience, 26,* 5819–5824.

Hobfoll, S. E. (1989). Conservation of resources: A new attempt at conceptualizing stress. *American Psychologist, 44,* 513–524.

Hobson, A. (2000). Dreams: Physiology. In A. Kazdin (Ed.), *Encyclopedia of psychology.* Washington, DC, & New York: American Psychological Association and Oxford University Press.

Hobson, J. A. (1999). Dreams. In R. Conlan (Ed.), *States of mind.* New York: Wiley.

Hobson, J. A. (2004). Freud returns? Like a bad dream. *Scientific American, 290,* 89.

Hobson, J. A., Pace-Schott, E. F., & Stickgold, R. (2000). Dreaming and the brain. *Behavior and Brain Sciences, 23,* 793–842.

Hodapp, R. M., & Dykens, E. M. (2006). Mental retardation. In W. Damon & R. Lerner (Eds.), *Handbook of child psychology* (6th ed.). New York: Wiley.

Hodges, T. D., & Clifton, D. O. (2004). Strengths-based development in practice. In A. Linley & S. Joseph (Eds.), *Positive psychology in practice* (pp. 256–268). Hoboken, NJ: Wiley.

Hodgins, D. C. (2005). Weighing the pros and cons of changing change models: A comment on West (2005). *Addiction, 100,* 1042–1043.

Hoeger, W. W. K., & Hoeger, S. A. (2008). *Principles and labs for physical fitness* (6th ed.). New York: McGraw-Hill.

Hoek, H. W. (2006). Incidence, prevalence and mortality of anorexia nervosa and other eating disorders. *Current Opinion in Psychiatry, 19,* 389–394.

Hoff, E., & Shatz, M. (Eds.). (2007). *Blackwell handbook of language development.* Malden, MA: Blackwell.

Hoffer, A. (2006). What does the analyst want? Free association in relation to the analyst's activity, ambition, and technical innovation. *American Journal of Psychoanalysis, 66,* 1–23.

Hoffman, I. Z. (2006). The myths of free association and the potentials of the analytic relationship. *International Journal of Psychoanalysis, 87,* 43–61.

Hogan, E. H. Hornick, B. A., & Bouchoux, A. (2002). Focus on communications: Communicating the message: Clarifying the controversies about caffeine. *Nutrition Today, 37,* 28–35.

Hogan, R. (2006). *Personality and the fate of organizations.* Mahwah, NJ: Erlbaum.

Hoge, C. W., Terhakoian, A., Castro, C. A., Messer, S. C., & Engel, C. C. (2007). Association of posttraumatic stress disorder with somatic symptoms, health care visits, and absenteeism among Iraq War veterans. *American Journal of Psychiatry, 164,* 150–153.

Hogg, M. A., & Abrams, D. (2007). Intergroup behavior and social identity. In M. A. Hogg & J. Cooper (Eds.), *The Sage handbook of social psychology* (concise 2nd ed.). Thousand Oaks, CA: Sage.

Hogh, A., Henriksson, M. E., & Burr, H. (2005). A 5-year follow-up study of aggression at work and psychological health. *International Journal of Behavioral Medicine, 12,* 256–265.

Holden, C. (2007). Stem cell debate: Scientists protest "misrepresentation" as Senate vote looms. *Science, 315,* 315–316.

Holland, P. C. (1996). The effects of intertrial and feature-target intervals on operant serial feature-positive discrimination learning. *Animal Learning & Behavior, 24,* 411–428.

Hollich, G. J., & Huston, D. M. (2007). Language development: From speech to first words. In A. Slater & M. Lewis (Eds.), *Introduction to infant development* (2nd ed.). New York: Oxford University Press.

Holmes, J. G., Miller, D. T., & Lerner, M. J. (2002). Committing altruism under the cloak of self-interest: The exchange fiction. *Journal of Experimental Social Psychology, 38*(2), 144–151.

Holt, J., Warren, L., Wallance, R., Neher, J. O. (2006). Clinical inquiries: What behavioral interventions are safe for obesity? *Journal of Family Practice, 55,* 536–538.

Holtzheimer, P. E., & Nemeroff, C. B. (2006). Emerging treatments for depression. *Expert Opinions in Pharmacotherapy, 7,* 2323–2339.

Holzgrabe, U., Kapkova, P., Alptuzun, V., Scheiber, J., & Kugelmann, E. (2007). Targeting acetylcholinesterase to treat neurodegeneration. *Expert Opinion on Therapeutic Targets, 11,* 161–179.

Homayoun, H., Khavandgar, S., & Zarrindast, M. R. (2003). Morphine state-dependent learning: Interactions with alpha-sub-2-adrenoceptors and acute stess. *Behavioral Pharmacology, 14,* 41–48.

Honts, C. (1998, June). Commentary. *APA Monitor, 30.*

Hooper, J., & Teresi, D. (1993). *The 3-pound universe.* New York: Tarcher/Putnam.

Horgan, J. (2005, February 26). Psychedelic medicine: Mind bending, health giving. *New Scientist, 2488,* 36.

Horn, J. L., & Donaldson, G. (1980). Cognitive development II: Adulthood development of human abilities. In O. G. Brim & J. Kagan (Eds.), *Constancy and change in human development.* Cambridge, MA: Harvard University Press.

Horney, K. (1945). *Our inner conflicts.* New York: Norton.

Horowitz, J. L., & Garber, J. (2006). The prevention of depressive symptoms in children and adolescents: A meta-analytic review. *Journal of Consulting and Clinical Psychology, 74*(3), 401–415.

Horowitz, M. J. (1998). Psychoanalysis. In H. S. Friedman (Ed.), *Encyclopedia of mental health* (vol. 3). San Diego: Academic.

Horowitz, S. S., Tanyu, L. H., & Simmons, A. M. (2007). Multiple mechanosensory modalities influence development of auditory function. *Journal of Neuroscience, 27,* 782–790.

Horridge, A. (2006). Visual discrimination of spokes, sectors, and circles by the honeybee (*Apis mellifera*). *Journal of Insect Physiology, 52,* 984–1003.

Hoss, R. A., & Langlois, J. H. (2003). Infants prefer attractive faces. In O. Pascalis & A. Slater (Eds.), *The development of face processing in infancy and early childhood: Current perspectives* (pp. 27–38). Hauppauge, NY: Nova Science Publishers.

House, J. S., Landis, K. R., & Umberson, D. (1988). Social relationships and health. *Science, 241,* 540–545.

House, R. J. (2004). *Culture, leadership, and organizations: The GLOBE study of 62 societies.* Thousand Oaks, CA: Sage.

Houser, D. S., & Finneran, J. J. (2006). A comparison of underwater hearing sensitivity in bottlenose dolphins (*Tursiops truncatus*) determined by electrophysiological and behavioral methods. *Journal of the Acoustical Society of America, 120,* 1713–1722.

Howard, K. I., Moras, K., Brill, P. L., Martinovich, Z., & Lutz, W. (1996). Evaluation of psychotherapy: Efficacy, effectiveness, and patient progress. *American Psychologist, 51,* 1059–1064.

Howe, M. J. A., Davidson, J. W., Moore, D. G., & Sloboda, J. A. (1995). Are there early childhood signs of musical ability? *Psychology of Music, 23,* 162–176.

Howell, D. C. (2008). *Fundamental statistics for the behavioral sciences* (6th ed.). Belmont, CA: Wadsworth.

Howes, M. B. (2006). *Human memory.* Thousand Oaks, CA: Sage.

Hoyer, W. J., & Roodin, P. A. (2003). *Adult development and aging* (5th ed.). New York: McGraw-Hill.

Hoyer, W. J., & Verhaeghen, P. (2006). Memory aging. In J. E. Birren & K. W. Schaie (Eds.), *Handbook of the psychology of aging* (6th ed.). San Diego: Academic.

Hser, Y. I., Stark, M. E., Paredes, A., Huang, D., Anglin, M. D., & Rawson, R. (2006). A 12-year follow-up of a treated cocaine-dependent sample. *Journal of Substance Abuse and Treatment, 30,* 219–226.

Hu, F. B., Willett, W. C., Li, T., Stampfer, M. J., Colditz, G. A., & Manson, J. E. (2004). Adiposity as compared with physical activity in predicting mortaility among women. *New England Journal of Medicine, 351,* 2694–2703.

Hubble, M. A., & Miller, S. D. (2004). The client: Psychotherapy's missing link for promoting a positive psychology. In A. Linley & S. Joseph (Eds.), *Positive psychology in practice* (pp. 335–353). Hoboken, NJ: Wiley.

Hublin, C., Kaprio, J., Partinen, M., & Koskenvu, M. (2001). Parasomnias: Co-occurrence and genetics. *Psychiatric Genetics, 11,* 65–70.

Huff, C. R. (2002). What can we learn from other nations about the problem of wrongful conviction? *Judicature, 86,* 91–97.

Huffcutt, A. I., & Youngcourt, S. S. (2007). Employment interviews. In D. L. Whetzel & G. R. Wheaton (Eds.), *Applied measurement.* Mahwah, NJ: Erlbaum.

Hugdahl, K. (2001). *Psychophysiology: The mind–body perspective.* Cambridge, MA: Harvard University Press.

Hull, E. M., & Dominguez, J. M. (2006). Getting his act together: Roles of glutamate, nitric oxide, and dopamine in the medial preoptic area. *Brain Research, 1126,* 66–75.

Hummer, R. A., Ellison, C. G., Rogers, R. G., Moulton, B. C., & Romero, R. R. (2004). Religious involvement and adult mortality in the United States: Review and perspective. *Southern Medical Journal, 97,* 1223–1230.

Humphrey, N. (2006). S*eeing red: A study in consciousness.* Cambridge, MA: Belknap Press of Harvard University Press.

Hunsley, J., & Bailey, J. M. (2001). Whither the Rorschach? An analysis of the evidence. *Psychological Assessment, 13,* 472–485.

Hunt, E. (1995). *Will we be smart enough? A cognitive analysis of the coming work force.* New York: Russell Sage Foundation.

Hunt, M. (1974). *Sexual behavior in the 1970s.* Chicago: Playboy.

Hunt, R. R., & Ellis, H. C. (2004). *Fundamentals of cognitive psychology* (7th ed.). New York: McGraw-Hill.

Hunt, R. R., & Kelly, R. E. S. (1996). Accessing the particular from the general: The power of distinctiveness in the context of organization. *Memory and Cognition, 24,* 217–225.

Hunter, J. P., & Csikszentmihalyi, M. (2003). The positive psychology of interested adolescents. *Journal of Youth and Adolescence, 32,* 27–35.

Hurvich, L. M., & Jameson, D. (1969). Human color perception. *American Scientist, 57,* 143–166.

Huston, A. C., & Ripke, N. M. (2006). *Developmental contexts in middle childhood.* Mahwah, NJ: Erlbaum.

Huttenlocher, J., Haight, W., Bruk, A., Selzer, M., & Lyons, T. (1991). Early vocabulary growth: Relation to language input and gender. *Developmental Psychology, 27,* 236–248.

Huttenlocher, P. R., & Dabholkar, A. S. (1997). Regional differences in synaptogenesis in human cerebral cortex. *Journal of Comparative Neurology, 37*(2), 167–178.

Hutterer, J., & Liss, M. (2006). Cognitive development, memory, trauma, treatment: An integration of psychoanalytic and behavioral concepts in light of current neuroscience research. *Journal of the American Academy of Psychoanalytic and Dynamic Psychiatry, 34,* 287–302.

Hyde, J. S. (2005). The gender similarities hypothesis. *American Psychologist, 60,* 581–592.

Hyde, J. S. (2007). *Half the human experience* (7th ed.). Boston: Houghton Mifflin.

Hyde, J. S., & DeLamater, J. D. (2006). *Human sexuality* (9th ed.). New York: McGraw-Hill.

Hyde, M., & Power, D. (2006). Some ethical dimensions of cochlear implantation for deaf children and their families. *Journal of Deaf Studies and Deaf Education, 11,* 102–111.

Hyman, S. (2001, October 23). *Basic and clinical neuroscience in the post-genomic era.* Paper presented at the centennial symposium on the Celebration of Excellence in Neuroscience, the Rockefeller University, New York City.

Hyman, I., Kay, B., Tabori, A., Weber, M., Mahon, M., & Cohen, I. (2006). Bullying: Theory, research, and interventions. In C. M. Evertson & C. S. Weinstein (Eds.), *Handbook of classroom management.* Mahwah, NJ: Erlbaum.

Hyman, S. E., Malenka, R. C., & Nestler, E. J. (2006). Neural mechanisms of addiction. *Annual Review of Neuroscience* (vol. 29). Palo Alto, CA: Annual Reviews.

Hyson, M., Copple, C., & Jones, J. (2006). Early child development and education. In W. Damon & R. Lerner (Eds.), *Handbook of child psychology* (6th ed.). New York: Wiley.

I

Iacono, W. G., & Lykken, D. T. (1997). The validity of the lie detector: Two surveys of scientific opinion. *Journal of Applied Psychology, 82,* 426–433.

Ikegami, A., Olsen, C. M., D'Souza, M. S., & Duvauchelle, C. L. (2007). Experience-dependent effects of cocaine self-administration/conditioning on prefrontal and accumbens dopamine receptors. *Behavioral Neuroscience, 121,* 389–400.

Ilies, R., Arvey, R. D., & Bouchard T. J., Jr. (2006).Darwinism, behavioral genetics, and organizational behavior: A review and agenda for future research. *Journal of Organizational Behavior, 27*(2), 121–141.

Inaba, A., Thoits, P. A., Ueno, K., Gove, W. R., Evenson, R. J., & Sloan, M. (2005). Depression in the United States and Japan: Gender, marital status, and SES patterns. *Social Science & Medicine, 61,* 2280–2292.

Inglehart, R. (1990). *Culture shift in advanced industrial society.* Princeton, NJ: Princeton University Press.

Insel, P. M., & Roth, W. T. (2008). *Core concepts in health* (10th ed.). New York: McGraw-Hill.

Insko, C. A., & Wilson, M. (1977). Interpersonal attraction as a function of social interaction. *Journal of Personality and Social Psychology, 35,* 903–911.

Institute of Medicine. (2006, April). *Sleep disorders and sleep deprivation: An unmet public health problem.* Washington, DC: National Academies.

International Labor Organization. (2001). *World employment report, 2001.* Geneva: ILO Publications.

Ironson, G., Solomon, G., Balbin, E., O'Cleirigh, C., George, A., Schneiderman, N., & Woods, T. (2001, March). *Religious behavior, religious coping, and compassionate view of others is associated with long-term survival with AIDS.* Paper presented at the meeting of the American Psychosomatic Society, Monterey, CA.

Ironson, G., Stuetzle, R., & Fletcher, M. A. (2006). An increase in religiousness/spirituality occurs after HIV diagnosis and predicts slower disease progression over 4 years in people with HIV. *Journal of General Internal Medicine, 21,* S62–S68.

Irwin, M. R., Wang, M., Campomayor, C. O., Coliado-Hidalgo, A., & Cole, S. (2006). Sleep deprivation and activation of morning levels of cellular and genomic markers of inflammation. *Archives of Internal Medicine, 166,* 1756–1762.

Isbell, L. M. (2004). Not all people are lazy or stupid: Evidence of systematic processing in happy moods. *Journal of Experimental Social Psychology, 40,* 341–349.

Isen, A. M. (1984). Toward understanding the role of affect in cognition. In R. S. Wyer, Jr., & T. K. Srull (Eds.), *Handbook of social cognition* (vol. 3, pp. 179–236). Hillsdale, NJ: Erlbaum.

Isen, A. M. (2001). An influence of positive affect on decision making in complex situations: Theoretical issues with practical implications. *Journal of Consumer Psychology, 11,* 75–85.

Isen, A. M. (2004). Some perspectives on positive feelings and emotions: Positive affect facilitates thinking and problem solving. In A. S. R. Manstead, N. Frijda, & A. Fischer (Eds). *Feelings and emotions: The Amsterdam symposium* (pp. 263–281). New York, NY: Cambridge University Press.

Isen, A. M., & Daubman, K. (1984). The influence of affect on categorization. *Journal of Personality and Social Psychology, 47,* 1206–1217.

Isen, A. M., & Levin, P. F. (1972). Effect of feeling good on helping: Cookies and kindness. *Journal of Personality and Social Psychology, 21,* 384–388.

Isen, A. M., & Means, B. (1983). The influence of positive affect on decision-making strategy. *Social Cognition, 2,* 18–31.

Ishai, A. (2007). Sex, beauty, and the orbitofrontal cortex. *International Journal of Psychophysiology, 63,* 181–185.

Israel, B. A., Schulz, A.J., Estrada-Martinez, L., Zenk, S. N., Viruell-Fuentes, E., Villarruel, A. M., & Stokes, C. (2006). Engaging urban residents in assessing neighborhood environments and their implications for health. *Journal of Urban Health, 83,* 523–539.

J

Jablensky, E.. (2000). Epidemiology of schizophrenia: The global burden of disease and disability. *European Archives of Psychiatry and Clinical Neuroscience, 250,* 274–285.

Jablensky, E., Sartorius, N., Ernberg, G., & others. (1992). Schizophrenia: Manifestations, incidence and course in different cultures: A World Health Organization 10-country study. *Psychological Medicine, monograph suppl. 20,* 1–97.

Jackson, B., Kubzansky, L. D., Cohen, S., Jacobs, D. R., & Wright, R. (2007). Does harboring hostility hurt? Associations between hostility and pulmonary function in the CARDIA study. *Health Psychology, 26,* 333–340.

Jackson, J. F. (1993). Human behavioral genetics, Scarr's theory, and her views on interventions: A critical review and commentary on their implications for African American children. *Child Development, 64,* 1318–1332.

Jackson, L. C., & Greene, B. (2000). *Psychotherapy with African-American women.* New York: Guilford.

Jackson, S. L. (2006). *Research methods and statistics* (2nd ed.). Belmont, CA: Wadsworth.

Jackson, S. L. (2008). *Research methods.* Belmont, CA: Wadsworth.

Jaffe, E. S. (2007). Pathobiology of peripheral T-cell lymphomas. *Hematology, 26,* 317–322.

Jakupcak, M., Salters, K., Gratz, K. L., & Roemer, L. (2003). Masculinity and emotionality: An investigation of men's primary and secondary emotional responding. *Sex Roles, 49,* 111–120.

James, L. E. (2006). Specific effects of aging on proper name retrieval: Now you see them, now you don't. *Journals of Gerontology B: Psychological Sciences and Social Sciences, 61,* P180–P183.

James, W. (1904). The Chicago School. *Psychological Bulletin, 1,* 1–5.

James, W. (1950). *Principles of psychology.* New York: Dover. (original work published 1890)

Jameson, D., & Hurvich, L. M. (1989). Essay concerning color constancy. *Annual Review of Psychology* (vol. 40). Palo Alto, CA: Annual Reviews.

Janis, I. (1972). *Victims of groupthink: A psychological study of foreign-policy decisions and fiascos.* Boston: Houghton Mifflin.

Jansari, A. S., Spiller, M. J., & Redfern, S. (2006). Number synaesthesia: When hearing "four plus five" looks like gold. *Cortex, 42,* 253–258.

Jarrett, R. B., Kraft, D., Doyle, J., Foster, B. M., Eaves, G. G., & Silver, P. C. (2001). Preventing recurrent depression using cognitive therapy with and without a continuation phase: A randomized clinical trial. *Archives of General Psychiatry, 58,* 381–388.

Jarrold, C., & Towse, J. N. (2006). Individual differences in working memory. *Neuroscience, 139,* 39–50.

Jaswal, V. K., & Fernald, A. (2007). Learning to communicate. In A. Slater & M. Lewis (Eds.), *Introduction to infant development* (2nd ed.). New York: Oxford University Press.

Jazayeri, M., & Movshon, J. A. (2007). A new perceptual illusion reveals mechanisms of sensory decoding. *Nature, 446,* 912–915.

Jeffery, R. W., Baxter, J., McGuire, M., & Linde, J. (2006). Are fast food restaurants an environmental risk factor for obesity? *International Journal of Behavioral Nutrition and Physical Activity, 3,* 2.

Jenkins E. L., Layne L. A., & Kisner, S. M. (1992). Homicide in the workplace: The U.S. experience, 1980–1988. *American Association of Occupational Health Nurses, 40,* 215–221.

Jennings, L., & Skovholt, T. M. (1999). The cognitive, emotional, and relational characteristics of master therapists. *Journal of Counseling Psychology, 46,* 3–11.

Jensen, L. W., & Wadkins, T. A. (2007). Mental health success stories: Finding paths to recovery. *Issues in Mental Health Nursing, 28,* 325–340.

Jensen, M., & Patterson, D. R. (2006). Hypnotic treatment of chronic pain. *Journal of Behavioral Medicine, 29,* 95–124.

Jensen, P. S. (2006, October 24). *ADHD: A public health conference.* Atlanta: Centers for Disease Control and Prevention.

Jensen-Campbell, L. A., & Malcolm, K. T. (2007). The importance of conscientiousness in adolescent interpersonal relationships. *Personality and Social Psychology Bulletin, 33,* 368–383.

Jeong, J., Kim, D. J., Kim, S. Y., Chae, J. H., Go, H. J., & Kim, K. S. (2001). Effect of total sleep deprivation on the dimensional complexity of the waking EEG. *Sleep, 15,* 197–202.

Jia, S., Dallos, P., & He, D. Z. (2007). Mechanoelectric transduction of adult inner hair cells. *Journal of Neuroscience, 27,* 1006–1014.

Jiang, F., Blanz, V., & O'Toole, A. J. (2006). Probing the visual representation of faces with adaptation: A view from the other side of the mean. *Psychological Science, 17,* 493–500.

Johnson, A. M., Vernon, P. A., Harris, J. A., & Jang, K. L. (2004).Behavior genetic investigation of the relationship between leadership and personality. *Twin Research, 7*(1), 27–32.

Johnson, E. O., Roth, T., & Breslau, N. (2006). The association of insomnia with anxiety disorders and depression: Exploration of the direction of risk. *Journal of Psychiatric Research, 40,* 700–708.

Johnson, G. B. (2003). *The living world* (3rd ed.). New York: McGraw-Hill.

Johnson, G. B. (2008). *The living world* (5th ed.). New York: McGraw-Hill.

Johnson, G. B., & Losos, J. (2008). *Essentials of the living world* (2nd ed.). New York: McGraw-Hill.

Johnson, H., & Thompson, A. (2007). The development and maintenance of post-traumatic stress disorder (PTSD) in civilian adult survivors of war trauma and torture: A review. *Clinical Psychology Review.* (in press)

Johnson, M. H. (2007). Developing a social brain. *Acta Paediatrica, 96,* 3–5.

Johnson, R. E., & Chang, C. (2006). "I" is to continuance as "we" is to affective: The relevance of the self-concept for organizational commitment. *Journal of Organizational Behavior, 27*(5), 549–570.

Johnson, W., Bouchard, T. J., Krueger, R. F., McGue, M., & Gottesman, I. I. (2004). Just one g: Consistent results from three test batteries. *Intelligence, 32,* 95–107.

Johnson-Laird, P. N., Mancini, F., & Gangemi, A. (2006). A hyper-emotion theory of psychological illnesses. *Psychological Review, 113,* 822–841.

Johnston, L. D., O'Malley, P. M., Bachman, J. G., & Schulenberg, J. E. (2006). *Monitoring the future: National survey results on drug use: 1975–2005.* Bethesda, MD: National Institute on Drug Abuse.

Johnstone, E., Benowitz, N., Cargill, A., Jacob, R., Hinks, L., Day, I., Murphy, M., & Walton, R. (2006). Determinants of the rate of nicotine metabolism and the effects on smoking behavior. *Clinical Pharmacology and Therapeutics, 80,* 319–330.

Joiner, T. E., Jr. (2005). *Why people die by suicide.* Cambridge, MA: Harvard University Press.

Joiner, T. E., Jr., Hollar, D., & Van Orden, K. (2006). On Buckeyes, Gators, Super Bowl Sunday, and the miracle on ice: "Pulling together" is associated with lower suicide rates. *Journal of Social & Clinical Psychology, 25,* 179–195.

Joiner, T. E., Jr., Kistner, J. A., Stellrecht, N. E., & Merrill, K. A. (2006). On seeing clearly and thriving: Interpersonal perspicacity as adaptive (not depressive) realism (or where three theories meet). *Journal of Social & Clinical Psychology, 25,* 542–564.

Joiner, T. E., Steer, R. A., Abramson, L.Y., Mealsky, G. I., & Schmidt, N. B. (2001). Hopelessness depression as a distinct dimension of depressive symptoms among clinical and non-clinical samples. *Behavior Research and Therapy, 39,* 523–536.

Jonas, E., & Fischer, P. (2006). Terror management and religion: Evidence that intrinsic religiousness mitigates worldview defense following mortality salience. *Journal of Personality and Social Psychology, 91,* 553–567.

Jones, E. E. (1998). Major developments in five decades of social psychology. In D. T. Gilbert, S. T. Fiske, & G. Lindzey (Eds.), *Handbook of social psychology* (4th ed., vol. 1). New York: McGraw-Hill.

Jones, G. R., & George, J. M. (2007). *Essentials of contemporary management* (2nd ed.). New York: McGraw-Hill.

Jones, J. (2006, December 29). George W. Bush and Hillary Clinton most admired again. Gallup News Service, press release.

Jones, M. C. (1924). A laboratory study of fear: The case of Peter. *Journal of Genetic Psychology, 31,* 308–315.

Jones, R. (2006). Sex scripts and power: A framework to explain urban women's HIV sexual risk with male partners. *Nursing Clinics of North America, 41,* 425–436.

Joormann, J., Hertel, P. T., Brozovich, F., & Gotlib, J. H. (2005). Remembering the good, forgetting the bad: Intentional forgetting of emotional material in depression. *Journal of Abnormal Psychology, 114,* 640–648.

Jorgensen, M. M., & Zachariae, R. (2006). Repressive coping style and autonomic reactions to two experimental stressors in healthy men and women. *Scandinavian Journal of Psychology, 47,* 137–148.

Joscelyne, A., & Kehoe, E. J. (2007). Time and stimulus specificity in extinction of the conditioned nictitating membrane response in the rabbit (*Oryctolagus cuniculus*). *Behavioral Neuroscience, 121,* 50–62.

Joseph, J. (2006). *The missing gene.* New York: Algora.

Joseph, J., Breslin, C., & Skinner, H. (1999). Critical perspectives on the transtheoretical model and stages of change. In J. A. Tucker, D. M. Donovan, & G. A. Marlatt (Eds.), *Changing addictive behavior: Bridging clinical and public health strategies* (pp. 160–190). New York: Guilford.

Joseph, S., & Linley, P. A. (2004). Positive therapy: A positive psychological approach to therapeutic practice. In P. A. Linley & S. Joseph (Eds.), *Positive psychology in practice* (pp. 354–368). Hoboken, NJ: Wiley.

Joy, J. E., Watson, S. J., & Benson, J. A. (Eds.). (1999). *Institute of medicine. Marijuana and medicine: Assessing the science base.* Washington, DC: National Academy Press.

Judd, C. M., & Park, B. (2007). Diverging ideological viewpoints on pathways to more harmonious intergroup relations. In E. Borgida & others (Eds.), *The political psychology of democratic citizenship.* New York: Cambridge University Press. (in press)

Judge, T., Higgins, C., Thoresen, C., & Barrick, M. (1999). The big five personality traits, general mental ability, and career success across the life span. *Personnel Psychology, 52,* 621–652.

Judge, T. A., Thorson, C. J., Bono, J. E., & Patton, G. K. (2001). The job satisfaction–job performance relationship: A qualitative and quantitative review. *Psychological Bulletin, 127,* 376–407.

Juffer, F., Bakermans-Kranenburg, M. J., & van Ijzendoorn, M. H. (2007). *Promoting positive parenting.* Mahwah, NJ: Erlbaum.

Julkunen, J., & Ahlstrom, R. (2006). Hostility, anger, and sense of coherence as predictors of health-related quality of life: Results of an ASCOT substudy. *Journal of Psychosomatic Research, 61,* 33–39.

Jureidin, J. N., Doecke, C. J., Mansfield, P. R., Haby, M. M., Menkes, D. B., & Tonkin, A. L. (2004). Efficacy and safety of antidepressants for children and adolescents. *British Medical Journal, 328,* 879–883.

Jusczyk, P. W., & Hohne, E. A. (1997). Infants' memory for spoken words. *Science, 277,* 1984–1986.

K

Kabat-Zinn, J. (2006). *Coming to our senses: Healing ourselves and the world through mindfulness.* New York, NY: Hyperion.

Kabat-Zinn, J., Lipworth, L., & Burney, R. (1985). The clinical use of mindfulness meditation for the self-regulation of chronic pain. *Journal of Behavioral Medicine, 8,* 163–190.

Kabat-Zinn, J., Wheeler, E., Light, T., Skillings, A., Scharf, M. J., Cropley, T. G., Hosmer, D., & Bernhard, J. D. (1998). Influence of a mindfulness meditation-based stress reduction intervention on rates of skin clearing in patients with moderate to severe psoriasis undergoing phototherapy (UVB) and photochemotherapy (PUVA). *Psychosomatic Medicine, 60,* 625–632.

Kagan, J. (1992). Yesterday's premises, tomorrow's promises. *Developmental Psychology, 28,* 990–997.

Kagan, J. (2003). Biology, context, and developmental inquiry. *Annual Review of Psychology* (vol. 53). Palo Alto, CA: Annual Reviews.

Kagan, J. (2004, May 8). Commentary in B. Bower "Teen brains on trial." *Science News Online, 2.*

Kagan, J., & Fox, N. A. (2006). Biology, culture, and temperamental biases. In W. Damon & R. Lerner (Eds.), *Handbook of child psychology* (6th ed.). New York: Wiley.

Kagitcibasi, C. (2007). *Family, self, and human development across cultures.* Mahwah, NJ: Erlbaum.

Kahan, T. A., Sellinger, J. J., & Broman-Fulks, J. J. (2006). Associative priming and phonological priming after letter search on the prime. *American Journal of Psychology, 119,* 239–254.

Kaiser Family Foundation. (2001). *Inside-OUT: A report on the experiences of lesbians, gays, and bisexuals in America and the public's views on issues and policies related to sexual orientation.* Menlo Park, CA: Henry J. Kaiser Family Foundation.

Kalant, H. (2004). Adverse effects of cannabis on health: An update of the literature since 1996. *Progress in Neuropsychopharmacology, Biology, and Psychiatry, 28,* 849–863.

Kalat, J. W. (2007). *Biological psychology* (9th ed.). Belmont, CA: Wadsworth.

Kalat, J. W., & Shiota, M. N. (2007). *Emotion.* Belmont, CA: Wadsworth.

Kalia, M. (2006). Neurobiology of sleep. *Metabolism, 55S2,* S2–S6.

Kalichman, S. (1996). *Answering your questions about AIDS.* Washington, DC: American Psychological Association.

Kalichman, S. C. (2007). The theory of reasoned action and advances in HIV/AIDS prevention. In I. Ajzen, D. Albarracin, & R. Hornik (Eds.), *Prediction and change of health behavior.* Mahwah, NJ: Erlbuam.

Kalivas, P. W. (2007). Neurobiology of cocaine addiction: Implications for new pharmacotherapy. *American Journal of Addiction, 16,* 71–78.

Kalodner, C. R. (2007). Cognitive-behavioral theories. In D. Capuzzi & D. Gross (Eds.), *Counseling and psychotherapy* (4th ed.). Upper Saddle River, NJ: Prentice-Hall.

Kamel, N. S., & Gammack, J. K. (2006). Insomnia in the elderly: Cause, approach, and treatment. *American Journal of Medicine, 119,* 463–469.

Kamin, L. J. (1968). Attention-like processes in classical conditioning. In M. R. Jones (Ed.), *Miami symposium on the prediction of behavior: Aversive stimuli.* Coral Gables, FL: University of Miami Press.

Kamitani, Y., & Tong, F. (2006). Decoding seen and attended motion directions from activity in the human visual cortex. *Current Biology, 16,* 1096–1102.

Kamphaus, R. W., & Kroncke, A. P. (2004). "Back to the future" of the Stanford-Binet Intelligence Scales. In M. Herson (Ed.), *Comprehensive handbook of psychological assessment* (vol. 1). New York: Wiley.

Kanov, J. M., Maitlis, S., Worline, M. C., Dutton, J. E., Frost, P. J., & Lilius, J. M. (2006). Compassion in organizational life. In J. V. Gallos (Ed.), *Organization development: A Jossey-Bass reader* (pp. 793–812). San Francisco: Jossey-Bass.

Kanwisher, N. (2006). Neuroscience: What's in a face? *Science, 311,* 617–618.

Kanwisher, N., Livingstone, M. S., & Tsao, D. (2007). Face processing versus perceptual expertise: A debate. *Annual Review of Neuroscience* (vol. 30). Palo Alto, CA: Annual Reviews.

Kanwisher, N., Stanley, D., & Harris, A. (1999). The fusiform face area is selective for faces, not animals. *Neuroreport: For Rapid Communication of Neuroscience Research, 10,* 183–187.

Karam, E., Kypri, K., & Salamoun, M. (2007). Alcohol use among college students: An international perspective. *Current Opinion in Psychiatry, 20,* 213–221.

Karau, S. J., & Williams, K. D. (1993). Social loafing: A meta-analytic review and theoretical integration. *Journal of Personality and Social Psychology, 65,* 681–706.

Kardong, K. (2008). *Introduction to biological evolution* (2nd ed.). New York: McGraw-Hill.

Kaslow, N. J., Adamson, L. B., & Collins, M. H. (2000). A developmental psychopathology perspective on the cognitive components of child and adolescent depression. In A. Sameroff, M. Lewis, & S. M. Miller (Eds.), *Handbook of developmental psychopathology* (2nd ed., pp. 491–510). Dordrecht, Netherlands: Kluwer.

Kasser, T., & Ryan, R. M. (1993). A dark side of the American dream: Correlates of financial success as a central life aspiration. *Journal of Personality and Social Psychology, 65,* 410–422.

Kasser, T., & Ryan, R. M. (1996). Further examining the American dream: Differential correlates of intrinsic and extrinsic goals. *Personality and Social Psychology Bulletin, 22,* 280–287.

Kasser, T., Ryan, R. M., Couchman, C. E., & Sheldon, K. M. (2004). Materialistic values: Their causes and consequences. In T. Kasser & A. D. Kanner (Eds.), *Psychology and consumer culture: The struggle for a good life in a materialistic world* (pp. 11–28). Washington, DC: American Psychological Association.

Kasser, T., & Sharma, Y. S. (1999). Reproductive freedom, educational equality, and females' preference for resource-acquisition characteristics in mates. *Psychological Science, 10,* 374–377.

Katz, L. F. (1999, April). *Toward a family-based hypervigilance model of childhood aggression: The role of the mother's and the father's meta-emotion philosophy.* Paper presented at the meeting of the Society for Research in Child Development, Albuquerque.

Katzell, R. A., & Austin, J. T. (1992). From then to now: The development of industrial-organizational psychology in the United States. *Journal of Applied Psychology, 77,* 803–835.

Kauffman, J. M. (2005). *Characteristics of emotional and behavioral disorders of children and youth* (8th ed.). New York: Guilford.

Kaufman, J. C., & Sternberg, R. J. (2007). *The international handbook of creativity.* New York: Cambridge University Press.

Kaufman, L., Vassiliades, V., Noble, R., Alexander, R., Kaufman, J., & Edlund, S. (2007). Perceptual distance and the moon illusion. *Spatial Vision, 20,* 155–175.

Kavushansky, A., Vouimba, R., Cohen, H., & Richter-Levin, G. (2006). Activity and plasticity in the CA1, the dentate gyrus, and the amygdala following controllable vs. uncontrollable water stress. *Hippocampus, 16,* 35–42.

Kawato, M., & Samejima, K. (2007). Efficient reinforcement learning: Computational theories, neuroscience, and robotics. *Current Opinions in Neurobiology, 17,* 205–212.

Kazdin, A. E. (2007). Mediators and mechanisms of change in psychotherapy change. *Annual Review of Clinical Psychology* (vol. 3). Palo Alto, CA: Annual Reviews.

Kazdin, A. E., & Benjet, C. (2003). Spanking children: Evidence and issues. *Current Directions in Psychological Science, 12,* 99–103.

Keating, D. P. (2004). Cognitive and brain development. In R. Lerner & L. Steinberg (Eds.), *Handbook of adolescent psychology.* New York: Wiley.

Keedwell, P. A., Andrew, C., Williams, S. C. R., Brammer, M. J., & Phillips, M. L. (2005). A double dissociation of ventromedial prefrontal cortical responses to sad and happy stimuli in depressed and healthy individuals. *Biological Psychiatry, 58,* 495–503.

Keel, P. K., Dorer, D. J., Eddy, K. T., Franko, D., Charatan, D. L., & Herzog, D. B. (2003). Predictors of mortality in eating disorders. *Archives of General Psychiatry, 60,* 179–183.

Keel, P. K., Heatherton, T. F., Dorer, D. J., Joiner, T. E., & Zalta, A. K. (2006). Point prevalence of bulimia nervosa in 1982, 1992, and 2002. *Psychological Medicine, 36,* 119–127.

Keillor, J. M., Barrett, A. M., Crucian, G. P., Kortenkamp, S., & Heilman, K. M. (2002). Emotional experience and perception in the absence of facial feedback. *Journal of the International Neuropsychological Society, 8,* 130–135.

Keller, C., Siegrist, M., & Gutscher, H. (2006). The role of the affect and availability heuristics in risk communication. *Risk Analysis, 26,* 631–639.

Keller, M., & others. (2006). Lack of efficacy of substance P (neurokinin 1 receptor) antagonist aprepitant in the treatment of major depressive disorder. *Biological Psychiatry, 59,* 216–233.

Kellerman, A. L., and others. (1993). Gun ownership as a risk factor for homicide in the home. *New England Journal of Medicine, 329,* 1084–1091.

Kelley, E., & Mullen, J. (2006). Organizational response to workplace violence. In E. K. Kelloway, J. Barling, & J. J. Hurrell, Jr. (Eds.), *Handbook of workplace violence* (pp. 493–515). Thousand Oaks, CA: Sage.

Kellman, P. J., & Arterberry, M. E. (2006). Infant visual perception. In W. Damon & R. Lerner (Eds.), *Handbook of child psychology* (6th ed.). New York: Wiley.

Kellner, C. H., Knapp, R. G., Petrides, G., Rummans, T. A., Husain, M. M., Rasmussen, K., Mueller, M., Bernstein, H. J., O'Connor, K., Smith, G., Biggs, M., Bailine, S. H., Malur, C., Yim, E., McClintock, S., Sampson, S., & Fink, M. (2006). Continuation electroconvulsive therapy vs pharmacotherapy for relapse prevention in major depression: A multisite study from the Consortium for Research in Electroconvulsive Therapy (CORE). *Archives of General Psychiatry, 63,* 1337–1344.

Kellogg, R. T. (2007). *Fundamentals of cognitive psychology.* Thousand Oaks, CA: Sage.

Kelloway, E. K., Barling, J., & Hurrell, J. J., Jr. (Eds.). (2006). *Handbook of workplace violence.* Thousand Oaks, CA: Sage.

Kelly, G. F. (2006). *Sexuality today* (8th ed.). New York: McGraw-Hill.

Kelly, K. J., Stanley, L. R., Comello, M. L., & Gonzales, G. R. (2006). Tobacco counteradvertisements aimed at bicultural Mexican American youth: The impact of language and theme. *Journal of Health Communication, 11,* 455–476.

Keltner, D., & Ekman, P. (2000). Emotion: An overview. In A. Kazdin (Ed.), *Encyclopedia of psychology.* Washington, DC, & New York: American Psychological Association and Oxford University Press.

Kemeny, M. E. (2007). Psychoneuroimmunology. In H. S. Friedman & R. C. Silver (Eds.), *Foundations of health psychology.* New York: Oxford University Press.

Kendler, K. S., Gardner, C. O., Gatz, M., & Pedersen, N. L. (2007). The sources of co-morbidity between major depression and generalized anxiety disorder in a Swedish national twin sample. *Psychological Medicine, 37,* 453–462.

Kennedy, P. G. E., & Folk-Seang, J. F. (1986). Studies on the development, antigenic phenotype and function of human glial cells in tissue culture. *Brain, 109,* 1261–1277.

Kenrick, D. T., & MacFarlane, S. W. (1986). Ambient temperature and horn honking: A field study of the heat/aggression relationship. *Environment and Behavior, 18,* 179–191.

Kernis, M. H., Paradise, A. W., Whitaker, D. J., Wheatman, S. R., & Goldman, B. N. (2000). Master of one's psychological domain? Not likely if one's self-esteem is unstable. *Personality and Social Psychology Bulletin, 26,* 1297–1305.

Kerns, J. G. (2005). Positive schizotypy and emotion processing. *Journal of Abnormal Psychology, 114,* 392–401.

Kerns, J. G. (2007). Verbal communication impairments and cognitive control components in people with schizophrenia. *Journal of Abnormal Psychology, 116,* 279–289.

Kerns, J. G., & Berenbaum, H. (2003). The relationship between formal thought disorder and executive functioning component processes. *Journal of Abnormal Psychology, 112,* 339–352.

Kerns, J. G., Berenbaum, H., Barch, D. M., Banich, M. T., & Stolar, N. (1999). Word production in schizophrenia and its relationship to positive symptoms. *Psychiatry Research, 87,* 29–37.

Kerwin, R. (2007). When should clozapine be initiated in schizophrenia? Some arguments for and against earlier use of clozapine. *CNS Drugs, 21,* 267–278.

Kessler, R. C., Chiu, W. T., Demler, O., & Walters, E. E. (2005). Prevalence, severity, and comorbidity of twelve-month DSM-IV disorders in the National Comorbidity Survey Replication (NCS-R). *Archives of General Psychiatry, 62,* 617–627.

Kessler, R. C., McGonagle, K. A., Zhao, S., Nelson, C. B, Hughes, M., Eshleman, S., Wittchen, H., & Kendler, K. S. (1994). Lifetime and 12-month prevalence of DSM-III-R psychiatric disorders in the United States: Results from the National Comorbidity Study. *Archives of General Psychiatry, 51,* 8–19.

Kessler, R. C., Olfson, M., & Berglund, P. A. (1998). Patterns and predictors of treatment contact after first onset of psychiatric disorders. *American Journal of Psychiatry, 155,* 62–69.

Kessler, R. C., Stein, M. B., & Berglund, P. (1998). Social phobia subtypes in the National Comorbidity Survey. *American Journal of Psychiatry, 155,* 613–619.

Khan, N. A., & others. (2006). The 2006 Canadian hypertension education program recommendations for the management of hypertension: Part II—therapy. *Canadian Journal of Cardiology, 22,* 583–593.

Khatapoush, S., & Hallfors, D. (2004). "Sending the wrong message": Did medical marijuana legalization in California change attitudes about and use of marijuana? *Journal of Drug Issues, 34,* 751–770.

Kiernan, M., Civetta, J., Bartus, C., & Walsh, S. (2006). 24 hours on-call and acute fatigue no longer worsen resident mood under the 80-hour work week regulations. *Current Surgery, 63,* 237–241.

Kilicarslan, A., Isildak, M., Guven, G. S., Oz, S. G., Tannover, M. D., Duman, A. E., Saracbasi, O., & Sozen, T. (2006). Demographic, socio-economic, and educational aspects of obesity in an adult population. *Journal of the National Medical Association, 98,* 1313–1317.

Killen, M., & Smetana, J. (2006). *Handbook of moral development.* Mahwah, NJ: Erlbaum.

Killgore, W. D. S., Killgore, D. B., Day, L. M., Li, C., Kamimori, G. H., & Balkin, T. J. (2007). The effects of 53 hours of sleep deprivation on moral judgment. *SLEEP, 30,* 345–352.

Kim, J. N., & Lee, B. M. (2007). Risk factors, health risks, and risk management for aircraft personnel and frequent flyers. *Journal of Toxicology and Environmental Health B: Critical Reviews, 10,* 223–234.

Kim, J. Y., Oh, D. J., Yoon, T. Y., Choi, J. M., & Choe, B. K. (2007). The impacts of obesity on psychological well-being: A cross-sectional study about depressive mood and quality of life. *Journal of Preventive Medicine and Public Health, 40,* 191–195.

Kimble, G. A. (1961). *Hilgard and Marquis's conditioning and learning.* New York: Appleton-Century-Crofts.

Kimmell, E., & Crawford, M. C. (2002). Methods of studying gender. In J. Worell (Ed.), *Encyclopedia of women and gender.* New York: Oxford University Press.

King, B. M. (2005). *Human sexuality today* (5th ed.). Upper Saddle River, NJ: Prentice-Hall.

King, H. E. (1961). Psychological effects of excitement of the limbic system. In D. E. Sheer (Ed.), *Electrical stimulation of the brain*. Austin: University of Texas Press.

King, L. A. (2001). The health benefits of writing about life goals. *Personality and Social Psychology Bulletin, 27*, 798–807.

King, L. A. (2002). Gain without pain: Expressive writing and self regulation. In S. J. Lepore & J. Smyth (Eds.), *The writing cure*. Washington, DC: American Psychological Association.

King, L. A. (2003). Measures and meanings: The use of qualitative data in social and personality psychology. In C. Sansone, C. Morf, & A. Panter (Eds.), *Handbook of methods in social psychology* (pp.173–194). New York: Sage.

King, L. A. (2007a). Interventions for enhancing SWB: The pursuit of happiness. In R. J. Larsen & M. Eid (Eds.), *The science of subjective well-being*. New York: Guilford. (in press)

King, L. A. (2007b). Personal goals and life dreams: Positive psychology and motivation in daily life. In W. Gardner & J. Shah (Eds.), *Handbook of motivation science*. New York: Guilford. (in press)

King, L. A., & Broyles, S. (1997). Wishes, gender, personality, and well-being. *Journal of Personality, 65*, 50–75.

King, L. A., & Hicks, J. A. (2006). Narrating the self in the past and the future: Implications for maturity. *Research in Human Development, 3*, 121–138.

King, L. A., Hicks, J. A., Krull, J., & Del Gaiso, A. K. (2006). Positive affect and the experience of meaning in life. *Journal of Personality and Social Psychology, 90*, 179–196.

King, L. A., McKee-Walker, L., & Broyles, S. (1996). Creativity and the five factor model. *Journal of Research in Personality, 30*, 189–203.

King, L. A., & Miner, K. N. (2000). Writing about the perceived benefits of traumatic life events: Implications for physical health. *Personality and Social Psychology Bulletin, 26*, 220–230.

King, L. A., & Napa, C. (1998). What makes a life good? *Journal of Personality and Social Psychology, 75*, 156–165.

King, L. A., Richards, J., & Stemmerich, E. D. (1998). Daily goals, life goals, and worst fears: Means, ends, and subjective well-being. *Journal of Personality, 66*, 713–744.

King, L. A., Scollon, C. K., Ramsey, C. M., & Williams, T. (2000). Stories of life transition: Happy endings, subjective well-being, and ego development in parents of children with Down syndrome. *Journal of Research in Personality, 34*, 509–536.

King, L. A., & Smith, N. G. (2004). Gay and straight possible selves: Goals, identity, subjective well-being, and personality development. *Journal of Personality, 72*, 967–994.

King, L. A., & Smith, S. N. (2005). Happy, mature, and gay: Intimacy, power, and difficult times in coming out stories. *Journal of Research in Personality, 39*, 278–298.

Kirasic, K. C. (2004). *Midlife in context*. New York: McGraw-Hill.

Kirby, D. (2001). *Emerging answers: Research findings on programs to reduce teen pregnancy*. Washington, DC: National Campaign to Prevent Teen Pregnancy.

Kirby, S. (2005). The positive effect of exercise as therapy for clinical depression. *Nursing Times, 101*, 28–29.

Kirchhoff, B. A., & Buckner, R. L. (2006). Functional-anatomic correlates of individual differences in memory. *Neuron, 51*, 263–274.

Kirchhoff, B. A., Schapiro, M. L., & Buckner, R. L. (2005). Orthographic distinctiveness and semantic elaboration provide separate contributions to memory. *Journal of Cognitive Neuroscience, 17*, 1841–1854.

Kirsch, I., Moore, T. J., Scoboria, A., & Nicholls, S. S. (2002). The emperor's new drugs: An analysis of antidepressant medication data submitted to the U.S. Food and Drug Administration. *Prevention & Treatment, 5*(1).

Kirsch, I., & Sapirstein, G. (1998). Listening to Prozac but hearing placebo: A meta-analysis of antidepressant medication. *Prevention & Treatment, 1*(1) .

Kitayama, S., & Cohen, D. (Eds.). (2007). *Handbook of cultural psychology*. New York: Guilford.

Kitchener, K. S., & King, P. M. (1981). Reflective judgment: Concepts of justification and their relationship to age and education. *Journal of Applied Developmental Psychology, 2*, 89–111.

Kitchener, K. S., King, P. M., & DeLuca, S. (2006). The development of reflective judgment in adulthood. In C. Hoare (Ed.), *Handbook of adult development and learning*. New York: Oxford University Press.

Kjelsberg, E. (2005). Conduct disordered adolescents hospitalised 1963–1990. Secular trends in criminal activity. *European Journal of Child and Adolescent Psychiatry, 14*, 191-9.

Klatsky, R. L., & Lederman, S. J. (2003). Touch. In I. B. Weiner (Ed.), *Handbook of psychology* (vol. 4). New York: Wiley.

Klatzky, R. L., & Lederman, S. J. (2006). The perceived roughness of resistive virtual textures: Rendering by a force-feedback mouse. *TAP, 3*, 1–14.

Klein, D. N., Shankman, S. A., & Rose, S. (2007). Dysthymic disorder and double depression: Prediction of 10-year course trajectories and outcomes. *Journal of Psychiatric Research*. (in press)

Kline, W. B. (2003). *Interactive group work*. Upper Saddle River, NJ: Prentice-Hall.

Klinesmith, J., Kasser, T., & McAndrew, F. T. (2006). Guns, testosterone, and aggression: An experimental test of a mediational hypothesis. *Psychological Science, 17*, 568–571.

Klinger, E. (2000). Daydreams. In A. Kazdin (Ed.), *Encyclopedia of psychology*. Washington, DC, & New York: American Psychological Association and Oxford University Press.

Klohnen, E. C. (1996). Conceptual analysis and measurement of the construct of ego-resiliency. *Journal of Personality and Social Psychology, 70*, 1067–1079.

Klok, M. D., Jakobsdottir, S., & Drent, M. L. (2007). The role of leptin and ghrelin in the regulation of food intake and body weight in humans: A review. *Obesity Reviews, 8*, 21–34.

Klug, W. S., Cummings, M., & Spencer, C. (2007). *Essentials of genetics* (6th ed.). Upper Saddle River, NJ: Prentice-Hall.

Knapp, H. (2007). *Therapeutic communication*. Thousand Oaks, CA: Sage.

Kneebone, I. I., & Al-Daftary, S. (2006). Flooding treatment of phobia to having her feet touched by physiotherapists, in a young woman with Down's syndrome and a traumatic brain injury. *Neuropsychological Rehabilitation, 16*, 230–236.

Knez, I. (2006). Autobiographical memories for places. *Memory, 14*, 359–377.

Knott, V., McIntosh, J., Millar, A., Fisher, D., Villeneuve, C., Ilivitsky, V., & Horn, E. (2006). Nicotine and smoker status moderate brain and electric and mood activation induced by ketamine, an N-methyl-d-aspartate (NMDA) receptor antagonist. *Pharmacology, Biochemistry, and Behavior, 85*, 228–42.

Knowles, E. S., Nolan, J., & Riner, D. D. (2007). Resistance to persuasion. In R. Baumeister & K. Vohs (Eds), *Encyclopedia of social psychology*. Newbury Park, CA: Sage. (in press)

Knowles, E. S., & Riner, D. D. (2006). Omega approaches to persuasion: Overcoming resistance. In A. R. Pratkanis (Ed.), *Science of social influence*. New York: Psychology Press.

Knudsen, E. (2007). Mechanisms of attention. *Annual Review of Neuroscience* (vol. 30). Palo Alto, CA: Annual Reviews.

Kobasa, S., Maddi, S., & Kahn, S. (1982). Hardiness and health: A prospective study. *Journal of Personality and Social Psychology, 42*, 168–177.

Kobasa, S. C., Maddi, S. R., Puccetti, M. C., & Zola, M. (1986). Relative effectiveness of hardiness, exercise, and social support as resources against illness. *Journal of Psychosomatic Research, 29*, 525–533.

Kochanek, K. D., Murphy, S. L. Anderson, R. N, & Scott, C. (2004,October 12). Deaths: Final data for 2002. *National Vital Statistics Reports, 53*(5). Washington, DC: U.S. Department of Health and Human Services.

Kochanek, P. M. (2006). Pediatric trauma brain injury: quo vadis? *Developmental Neuroscience, 28*, 244–255.

Koenig, H. G. (2007). Religion and depression in older medical inpatients. *American Journal of Geriatric Psychiatry, 15*, 282–291.

Koestner, R., Horberg, E. J., Gaudreau, P., Powers, T., Di Dio, P., Bryan, C., Jochum, R., & Salter, N. (2006). Bolstering implementation plans for the long haul: The benefits of simultaneously boosting self-concordance or self-efficacy. *Personality and Social Psychology Bulletin, 32*, 1547–1558.

Kohlberg, L. (1969). Stage and sequence: The cognitive-developmental approach to socialization. In D. A. Goslin (Ed.), *Handbook of socialization theory and research*. Chicago: Rand McNally.

Kohlberg, L. (1976). Moral stages and moralization: The cognitive-developmental approach. In T. Lickona (Ed.), *Moral development and behavior*. New York: Holt, Rinehart & Winston.

Kohlberg, L. (1986). A current statement on some theoretical issues. In S. Modgil & C. Modgil (Eds.), *Lawrence Kohlberg*. Philadelphia: Falmer.

Köhler, W. (1925). *The mentality of apes*. New York: Harcourt Brace Jovanovich.

Kohn, A. (2000). *The case against standardized testing: Raising the scores, ruining the schools*. Portsmouth, NH: Heinemann.

Kohut, H. (1977). *Restoration of the self*. New York: International Universities Press.

Kok, G., & de Vries, N. K. (2006). Social psychology and health promotion. In P. A. M. Van Lange (Ed.), *Bridging social psychology*. Mahwah, NJ: Erlbaum.

Kolb, B., & Whishaw, I. Q. (2007). *Fundamentals of human neuropsychology* (5th ed.). New York: Worth.

Kondziolka D., Wechsler, L., Goldstein, S., Meltzer, C., Thulborn, K. R., Gebel, J., Jannetta, P., DeCesare, S., Elder, E. M., McGrogan, M., Reitman, M. A., & Bynum, L. (2000). Transplantation of cultured human neuronal cells for patients with stroke. *Journal of Neurology, 55,* 565–569.

Konrath, S., Bushman, B. J., & Campbell, W. K. (2006). Attenuating the link between threatened egotism and aggression. *Psychological Science, 17,* 995–1001.

Koob, G. F. (2006). The neurobiology of addiction: A neuroadaptational view. *Addiction, 101, Suppl. 1,* S23–S30.

Kopell, B. H., Machado, A. G., & Rezai, A. R. (2006). Not your father's lobotomy: Psychiatric surgery revisited. *Clinical Neurosurgery, 52,* 315–330.

Koppes, L. L. (2007). *Historical perspectives in industrial and organizational psychology*. Mahwah, NJ: Erlbaum.

Koppes, L. L., & Pickren, W. (2007). Industrial and organizational psychology: An evolving science. In L. L. Koppes (Ed.), *Historical perspectives in industrial and organizational psychology*. Mahwah, NJ: Erlbaum.

Kornbrot, D. E. (2006). Signal detection theory, the approach of choice: Model-based and distribution-free measures and evaluation. *Perception and Psychophysics, 68,* 393–414.

Kosslyn, S. M., Thompson, W. L., Kim, I. J., Rauch, S. L., & Alpert, N. M. (1996). Individual differences in cerebral blood flow in Area 17 predict the time to evaluate visualized letters. *Journal of Cognitive Neuroscience, 8,* 78–82.

Koster, A., Bosma, H., Kempen, G. I., Penninx, B. W., Beekman, A. T., Deeg, D. J., & van Eijk, J. T. (2006). Socioeconomic differences in incident depression in older adults: The role of psychosocial factors, physical health status, and behavioral factors. *Journal of Psychosomatic Research, 61,* 619–627.

Kotani, K., Saiga, K., Sakane, N., Mu, H., & Kurozawa, Y. (2007). Sleep status and blood pressure in a healthy normotensive female population. *International Journal of Cardiology.* (in press)

Kozhevnikov, M. (2007). Cognitive styles in the context of modern psychology: Toward an integrated framework of cognitive style. *Psychological Bulletin, 133,* 464–481.

Kraiger, K., & Ford, J. K. (2007). The expanding role of workplace training: Themes and trends influencing training practice and research. In L. L. Koppes (Ed.), *Perspectives in industrial and organizational psychology*. Mahwah, NJ: Erlbaum.

Kramer, A. F., Erickson, K. I., & Colcombe, S. J. (2006). Exercise, cognition, and the aging brain. *Journal of Applied Physiology, 101,* 1237–1242.

Kramer, A. F., Fabiani, M., & Colcombe, S. J. (2006). Contributions of cognitive neuroscience to the understanding of behavior and aging. In J. E. Birren & K. W. Schaie (Eds.), *Handbook of the psychology of aging* (6th ed.). San Diego: Academic.

Kramer, A. F., & Morrow, D. (2007). Cognitive training and expertise. In D. Park & N. Schwartz (Eds.), *Cognitive aging*. Philadelphia: Psychology Press.

Kramer, J. D. (1993) *Listening to Prozac.* New York: Penguin.

Krause, N. (2006). Religion and health in late life. In J. E. Birren & K. W. Schaie (Eds.), *Handbook of the psychology of aging* (6th ed.). San Diego: Academic.

Kreitner, R., & Kinicki, A. (2007). *Organizational behavior* (7th ed.). New York: McGraw-Hill.

Kring, A. M., Davison, G. C., Neale, J. M., & Johnson, S. L. (2007). *Abnormal psychology* (10th ed.). New York: Wiley.

Kring, A. M., Feldman-Barrett, L., & Gard, D. E. (2003). On the broad applicability of the affective circumplex: Representations of affective knowledge among schizophrenia patients. *Psychological Science, 14,* 207–214.

Kristjansson, A., Vuilleumier, P., Schwartz, S., Macaluso, E., & Driver, J. (2006). Neural basis for priming of pop-out during visual search revealed with fMRI. *Cerebral Cortex,* doi:10.1093/cercor/bhl072. (advance online publication)

Kroger, J. (2007). *Identity development* (2nd ed.). Thousand Oaks, CA: Sage.

Krogstad, U., Hofoss, D., Veenstra, M., & Hjortdahl, P. (2006). Predictors of job satisfaction among doctors, nurses and auxiliaries in Norwegian hospitals: Relevance for micro unit culture. *Human Resources for Health, 4,* 3.

Krueger, J. I. (2007). From social projection to social behaviour. *European Review of Social Psychology, 18,* 1–35.

Kruger, J., Blanck, H. M., & Gillespie, C. (2006). Dietary and physical activity behaviors among adults successful at weight loss maintenance. *The International Journal of Behavioral Nutrition and Physical Activity, 3,* 17.

Krystal, J. H., & others. (2006). Gamma-aminobutyric acid type A receptors and alcoholism: Intoxication, dependence, vulnerability, and treatment. *Archives of General Psychiatry, 63,* 957–968.

Ksir, C. J., Hart, C. L., & Ray, O. S. (2008). *Drugs, society, and human behavior* (12th ed.). New York: McGraw-Hill.

Kubzansky, L. D., Sparrow, D., Vokonas, P., & Kawachi, I. (2001). Is the glass half empty or half full? A prospective study of optimism and coronary heart disease in the normative aging study. *Psychosomatic Medicine, 63,* 910–916.

Kuch, K., & Cox, B. J. (1992). Symptoms of PTSD in 124 survivors of the Holocaust. *American Journal of Psychiatry, 149,* 337–340.

Kuhl, P. K. (1993). Infant speech perception: A window on psycholinguistic development. *International Journal of Psycholinguistics, 9,* 33–56.

Kuhl, P. K. (2000). A new view of language acquisition. *Proceedings of the National Academy of Science USA, 97,* 11850–11857.

Kuhl, P. K. (2007). Is speech learning "gated" by the social brain? *Developmental Science, 10,* 110–120.

Kuhl, P. K., Conboy, B. T., Padden, D., Nelson, T., & Pruitt, J. (2005). Early speech perception and later language development: Implications for the "critical period." *Language Learning and Development, 1,* 237–264.

Kuhl, P. K., Stevens, E., Hayashi, A., Deguchi, T., Kiritani, S., & Iverson, P. (2006). Infants show facilitation for native language phonetic perception between 6 and 12 months. *Developmental Science, 9,* 13–21.

Kuhn, P., & Franklin, S. (2006). The second decade of life: What develops (and how)? In W. Damon & R. Lerner (Eds.), *Handbook of child psychology* (6th ed.). New York: Wiley.

Kulka, R. A., Schlenger, W. E., Fairbank, J. A., Hough, R. L., Jordan, B. K., Marmar, C. R., & Weiss, D. S. (1990). *Trauma and the Vietnam war generation: Report of findings from the National Vietnam Veterans Readjustment Study*. Philadelphia: Brunner/Mazel.

Kulka, R. A., Schlenger, W. E., Fairbank, J. A., Jordan, B. K., & others. (1991). Assessment of posttraumatic stress disorder in the community: Prospects and pitfalls from recent studies of Vietnam veterans. *Psychological Assessment, 3,* 547–560.

Kumar, C. T. S. (2004). Physical illness and schizophrenia. *British Journal of Psychiatry, 184,* 541.

Kumashiro, M., Rusbult, C. E., Wolf, S. T., & Estrada, M. (2006). The Michelangelo phenomenon: Partner affirmation and self-movement toward one's ideal. In K. D. Vohs & E. J. Finkel (Eds.), *Self and relationships: Connecting intrapersonal and interpersonal processes* (pp. 317–341). New York: Guilford.

Kuntsche, E., Knibbe, R., Gmel, G., & Engels, R. (2006). Who drinks and why? A review of socio-demographic, personality, and contextual issues behind the drinking motives in young people. *Addictive Behaviors, 31,* 1844–1857.

Kuratomi, G., Iwamoto, K., Bundo, M., Kusumi, I., Kato, N., Iwata, N., Ozaki, N., & Kato, T. (2007). Aberrant DNA methylation associated with bipolar disorder identified from discordant monozygotic twins. *Molecular Psychiatry.* (in press)

Kurson, R. (2007). *Crashing through: A true story of risk, adventure, and the man who dared to see.* New York: Random House.

Kushner, M. G. (2007). The use of cognitive-behavioral therapy in the University of Minnesota's outpatient psychiatry clinic. *Minnesota Medicine, 90,* 31–33.

Kushner, R. F. (2007). Obesity management. *Gastroenterology Clinics of North America, 36,* 191–210.

Kuther, T. L., & Morgan, R. D. (2007). *Careers in psychology* (2nd ed.). Belmont, CA: Wadsworth.

Kuyken, W., & Beck, A. T. (2007). Cognitive therapy. In C. Freeman & M. J. Power (Eds.), *Handbook of evidence-based psychotherapy: A guide for research and practice.* New York: Wiley.

L

Labott, S. M., & Martin, R. B. (1990). Emotional coping, age, and physical disorder. *Behavioral Medicine, 16,* 53–61.

Labouvie-Vief, G. (1986, August). *Modes of knowing and life-span cognition.* Paper presented at the meeting of the American Psychological Association, Washington, DC.

Labouvie-Vief, G. (2006). Emerging structures of adult thought. In J. J. Arnett & J. L. Tanner (Eds.), *Emerging adults in America.* Washington, DC: American Psychological Association.

Labrecque, J., Dugas, M. J., Marchand, A., & Letarte, A. (2006). Cognitive-behavioral therapy for comorbid generalized anxiety disorder and panic disorder with agoraphobia. *Behavior Modification, 30,* 383–410.

Lacasse, H., Perreault, M. M., & Williamson, D. R. (2006). Systematic review of antipsychotics for the treatment of hospital-associated delirium in medically and surgically ill patients. *Annals of Pharmacotherapy, 40,* 1966–1973.

Lachman, M. E. (2004). Development in midlife. *Annual Review of Psychology* (vol. 54). Palo Alto, CA: Annual Reviews.

Lack, L. C., & Wright, H. R. (2007). Chronobiology of sleep in humans. *Cellular and Molecular Life Sciences.* (in press)

Laible, D. J., & Thompson, R. A. (2000). Mother–child discourse, attachment security, shared positive affect, and early conscience development. *Child Development, 71,* 1424–1440.

Laible, D. J., & Thompson, R. A. (2002). Mother–child conflict in the toddler years: Lessons in emotion, morality, and relationships. *Child Development, 73,* 1187–1203.

Laible, D. J., & Thompson, R. A. (2007). Early socialization: A relationship perspective. In J. E. Grusec & P. D. Hastings (Eds.), *Handbook of socialization.* New York: Guilford.

Laird, R. D., Pettit, G. S., Dodge, K. A., & Bates, J. E. (2005). Peer relationship antecedents of delinquent behavior in late adolescence: Is there evidence for demographic group differences in developmental processes? *Developmental Psychopathology, 17,* 127–144.

Lam, C. Y., Minnix, J. A., Robinson, J. D., & Cinciripini, P. M. (2006). A brief review of pharmacotherapies for smoking cessation. *Journal of the National Comprehensive Cancer Network, 4,* 583–589.

Lambert, M. J. (2001). The effectiveness of psychotherapy: What a century of research tells us about the effects of treatment. *Psychotherapeutically speaking–Updates from the Division of Psychotherapy* (29). Washington, DC: American Psychological Association.

Lamme, V. A. (2006). Toward a true neural stance on consciousness. *Trends in Cognitive Neuroscience. 10,* 494–501.

Lammers, H. B. (2000). Effects of deceptive packaging and product involvement on purchase intention: An elaboration likelihood model perspective. *Psychological Reports, 86,* 546–550.

Landau, M. J., Solomon, S., Greenberg, J., Cohen, F., Pyszczynski, T., Arndt, J., Miller, C. H., Ogilvie, D. M., & Cook, A. (2004). Deliver Us from evil: The effects of mortality salience and reminders of 9/11 on support for President George W. Bush. *Personality and Social Psychology Bulletin, 30,* 1136–1150.

Landis, C., & Erlick, D. (1950). An analysis of the Porteus Maze Test as affected by psychosurgery. *American Journal of Psychology, 63,* 557–566.

Landolt, H., Retey, J. V., Tonz, K., Gottselig, J. M., Khatami, R., Buckelmuller, I., & Achermann, P. (2004). Caffeine attenuates waking and sleep electroencephalographic markers of sleep homeostasis in humans. *Neuropsychopharmacology, 29,* 1933–1939.

Landrum, E., & Davis, S. F. (2007). *The psychology major* (3rd ed.). Upper Saddle River, NJ: Prentice-Hall.

Landrum, T. J., & Kauffman, J. M. (2006). Behavioral approaches to classroom management. In C. M. Evertson & C. S. Weinstein (Eds.), *Handbook of classroom management.* Mahwah, NJ: Erlbaum.

Lane, S. M., & Schooler, J. W. (2004). Skimming the surface: Verbal overshadowing of analogical retrieval. *Psychological Science, 15,* 715–719.

Lange, C. G. (1922). *The emotions.* Baltimore: Williams & Wilkins.

Lange, T., Dimitrov, S., Fehm, H. L., Westermann, J., & Born, J. (2006). Shift of monocyte function toward cellular immunity during sleep. *Archives of Internal Medicine, 166,* 1695–1700.

Langer, E. (2005). *On becoming an artist.* New York: Ballantine.

Langer, E., Blank, A., & Chanowitz, B. (1978). The mindlessness of ostensibly thoughtful action: The role of "placebic" information in interpersonal interaction. *Journal of Personality and Social Psychology, 36(6),* 635–642.

Langer, E., & Rodin, J. (1976). The effects of choice and enhanced personal responsibility for the aged: A field experiment in an institutional setting. *Journal of Personality and Social Psychology, 34,* 191–198.

Langer, E. J. (1997). *The power of mindful learning.* Reading, MA: Addison-Wesley.

Langer, E. J. (2000). Mindful learning. *Current Directions in Psychological Science, 9,* 220–223.

Langlois, J. H., Kalakanis, L., Rubenstein, A. J., Larson, A., Hallam, M., & Smoot, M. (2000). Maxims or myths of beauty? A meta-analytic and theoretical review. *Psychological Bulletin, 126,* 390–423.

Langlois, J. H., Roggman, L. A., & Musselman, L. (1994). What is average and what is not average about attractive faces? *Psychological Science, 5,* 214–220.

Lapierre, L. M., Spector, P. E., & Leck, J. D. (2005). Sexual versus nonsexual workplace aggression and victims' overall job satisfaction: A meta-analysis. *Journal of Occupational Health Psychology, 10,* 155–169.

Lapsley, D. K. (2006). Moral stage theory. In M. Killen & J. G. Smetana (Eds.), *Handbook of moral development* (pp. 37–66). Mahwah, NJ: Erlbaum.

Lapsley, D. K., & Narvaez, D. (2006). Moral education. In W. Damon & R. Lerner (Eds.), *Handbook of child psychology* (6th ed.). New York: Wiley.

Larsen, R. J., & Ketelaar, T. (1991). Personality and susceptibility to positive and negative emotional states. *Journal of Personality and Social Psychology, 61,* 132–140.

Larson, C. L., Schaefer, H. S., Siegle, G. J., Jackson, C. A. B., Anderle, M. J., & Davidson, R. J. (2006). Fear is fast in phobic individuals: Amygdale activation in response to fear-relevant stimuli. *Biological Psychiatry, 60,* 410–417.

Larson, R. (2000). Toward a psychology of positive youth development. *American Psychologist, 55,* 170–183.

Larson, R. (2007). From "I" to "we." In R. K. Silbereisen & R. M. Lerner (Eds.), *Approaches to positive youth development.* Thousand Oaks, CA: Sage.

Larson, R., & Wilson, S. (2004). Adolescence across place and time: Globalization and the changing pathways to adulthood. In R. Lerner & L. Steinberg (Eds.), *Handbook of adolescent psychology.* New York: Wiley.

Lashley, K. (1950). In search of the engram. In *Symposium of the Society for Experimental Biology* (vol. 4). New York: Cambridge University Press.

Lastra, G., Manrique, C., & Sowers, J. R. (2006). Obesity, cardiometabolic syndrome, and chronic kidney disease: The weight of the evidence. *Advances in Chronic Kidney Disease, 13,* 365–373.

Latané, B. (1981). The psychology of social impact. *American Psychologist, 36,* 343–356.

Latham, G. P., & Budworth, M. H. (2007). The study of work motivation in the 20th century. In L. L. Koppes (Ed.), *Perspectives in industrial and organizational psychology.* Mahwah, NJ: Erlbaum.

Laugharne, J., Janca, A., & Widiger, T. (2007). Posttraumatic stress disorder and terrorism: 5 years after 9/11. *Current Opinion in Psychiatry, 20,* 36–41.

Laurence, J. (2006). Editorial: Treating HIV infection with one pill per day. *AIDS Patient Care and STD, 20,* 601–603.

Lazarus, A. A., Beutler, L. E., & Norcross, J. C. (1992). The future of technical eclecticism. *Psychotherapy, 29,* 11–20.

Lazarus, R. S. (1991). On the primacy of cognition. *American Psychologist, 39,* 124–129.

Lazarus, R. S. (1993). Coping theory and research: Past, present, and future. *Psychosomatic Medicine, 55,* 234–247.

Lazarus, R. S. (2000). Toward better research on stress and coping. *American Psychologist 55,* 665–673.

Lazarus, R. S. (2003). Does the positive psychology movement have legs? *Psychological Inquiry, 14,* 93–109.

Leamon, M. H. (2006). When to refer patients for substance abuse assessment and treatment. *Primary Psychiatry, 13,* 46–51.

Leaper, C., & Friedman, C. K. (2007). The socialization of gender. In J. E. Grusec & P. D. Hastings (Eds.), *Handbook of socialization.* New York: Guilford.

Leary, M. R. (2008). *Introduction to behavioral research methods* (5th ed.). Boston: Allyn & Bacon.

LeBlanc, M. M., Dupre, K. E., & Barling, J. (2006). Public-initiated violence. In E. K. Kelloway, J. Barling, & J. J. Hurrell, Jr. (Eds.), *Handbook of workplace violence* (pp. 261–280). Thousand Oaks, CA: Sage.

Leblanc, N., Chen, S., Swank, P. R., Levin, H., & Schachar, R. (2006). Impairment and recovery in inhibitory control after traumatic brain injury in children: Effect of age at injury, injury severity, and lesion location. *Brain and Cognition, 60,* 208–209.

LeBoeuf, B. J., & Peterson, R. S. (1969). Social status and mating activity in elephant seals. *Science, 163,* 91–93.

Leckman, J. F., & Mayes, L. C. (2007). Nurturing resilient children. *Journal of Child Psychology and Psychiatry, 48,* 221–223.

Lederman, S., & Klatsky, R. (1998, June). Commentary in B. Azar's "From surgery to robotics, touch is the key." *APA Monitor,* 21.

LeDoux, J. E. (1996). *The emotional brain: The mysterious underpinnings of emotional life.* New York: Simon & Schuster.

LeDoux, J. E. (2000). Emotion circuits in the brain. *Annual Review of Neuroscience, 23,* 155–184.

LeDoux, J. E. (2001). *Emotion, memory, and the brain.* http://www.cns.nyu.edu/home/ledoux.html (accessed October 15, 2001).

LeDoux, J. E. (2002). *The synaptic self.* New York: Viking.

Lee, C., Smith, M. R., & Eastman, C. I. (2006). A compromise phase position for permanent night shift workers: Circadian phase after two night shifts with scheduled sleep and light/dark exposure. *Chronobiology International, 23,* 859–875.

Lee, C. D., Blair, S. N. & Jackson, A. S. (1999). Cardiorespiratory fitness, body composition, and all-cause and cardiovascular disease mortality in men. *American Journal of Clinical Nutrition, 69,* 373–380.

Lee, K. A. (2006). Sleep dysfunction in women and its management. *Current Treatment Options in Neurology, 8,* 376–386.

Lee, K. H., & Thompson, R. F. (2006). Multiple memory mechanisms in the cerebellum. *Neuron, 51,* 680–682.

LeFever, G. B., Dawson, K. V., & Morrow, A. L. (1999). The extent of drug therapy for attention deficit-hyperactivity disorder among children in public schools. *American Journal of Public Health, 89*(9), 1359–1364.

Leffert, M. (2007). A contemporary integration of modern and postmodern trends in psychoanalysis. *Journal of the American Psychoanalytic Association, 55,* 177–197.

Lefkowitz, J. (2000). The role of interpersonal affective regard in supervisory performance ratings: A literature review and proposed causal model. *Journal of Occupational and Organizational Psychology, 73,* 67–85.

Legaree, T. A., Turner, J., & Lollis, S. (2007). Forgiveness and therapy: A critical review of conceptualizations, practices, and values in the literature. *Journal of Marital and Family Therapy, 33,* 192–213.

Legerstee, M., Barna, J., & DiAdamo, C. (2000). Precursors to the development of intention at 6 months: Understanding people and their actions. *Developmental Psychology, 36,* 627–634.

Leibold, C., & Kempter, R. (2006). Memory capacity for sequences in a recurrent network with biological constraints. *Neural Computation, 18,* 904–941.

Leichtman, M. (2004). Projective tests. In M. Hersen (Ed.), *Comprehensive handbook of psychological assessment* (vol. 2). New York: Wiley.

Lejeune, H., Richelle, M., & Wearden, J. H. (2006). About Skinner and time: Behavior-analytic contributions to research on animal learning. *Journal of the Experimental Analysis of Behavior, 85,* 125–142.

Lenneberg, E. H., Rebelsky, F. G., & Nichols, I. A. (1965). The vocalization of infants born to deaf and hearing parents. *Human Development, 8,* 23–37.

Leo, J. L. (2005). Editorial: Methylphenidate-induced neuropathology in the developing rat brain: Implications for humans. *Ethical Human Psychology and Psychiatry. 7,* 107–110.

Lepore, S. J., & Smyth, J. (Eds.). (2002). *The writing cure.* Washington, DC: American Psychological Association

Lepper, M., Greene, D., & Nisbett, R. E. (1973). Undermining children's intrinsic interest with extrinsic rewards. *Journal of Personality and Social Psychology, 28,* 129–137.

Lerner, B. H. (2005). Last-ditch medical therapy—revisiting lobotomy. *New England Journal of Medicine, 353,* 119–121.

Lesaux, N. K., & Siegel, L. (2003). The development of reading in children who speak English as a second language. *Developmental Psychology, 39,* 1005–1019.

Leslie, A. M., German, T. P., & Polizzi, P. (2005). Belief-desire reasoning as a process of selection. *Cognitive Psychology, 50,* 45–85.

Leslie, A. M., & Thais, L. (1992). Domain specificity in conceptual development: Neuropsychological evidence from autism. *Cognition, 43,* 225–251.

Leslie, J. C., Shaw, D., Gregg, G., McCormick, N., Reynolds, D. S., & Dawson, G. R. (2006). Effects of reinforcement schedule on facilitation of operant extinction by chlordiazepoxide. *Journal of the Experimental Analysis of Behavior, 84,* 327–338.

Lessow-Hurley, J. (2005). *The foundation of dual language instruction* (4th ed.). Boston: Allyn & Bacon.

Letvin, N. L. (2007). Progress and obstacles in the development of an AIDS vaccine. *Nature Reviews: Immunology, 6,* 930–939.

Leung, J., Wang, N. Y., Yeagle, J. D., Chinnici, J., Bowditch, S., Francis, H. W., & Niparko, J. K. (2005). Predictive models for cochlear implantation in elderly candidates. *Archives of Otolaryngology Head and Neck Surgery, 131,* 1049–1054.

LeVay, S. (1994). *The sexual brain.* Cambridge, MA: MIT Press.

Levenson, M. R., & Aldwin, C. M. (2006). Change in personality processes and health outcomes. In D. K. Mroczek & T. D. Little (Eds.), *Handbook of personality development* (pp. 423–444). Mahwah, NJ: Erlbaum.

Levenson, M. R., & Crumpler, C. (1996). Three models of adult development. *Human Development, 39,* 135–149.

Levi, D. (2007). *Group dynamics for teams* (2nd ed.). Thousand Oaks, CA: Sage.

Levine, D. S. (2000). *Introduction to neural and cognitive modeling* (2nd ed.). Mahwah, NJ: Erlbaum.

Levine, J. M., & Moreland, R. L. (2006). *Small groups.* New York: Psychology Press.

Levine, R. L. (2002). Endocrine aspects of eating disorders in adolescents. *Adolescent Medicine, 13,* 129–144.

Levinoff, E. J., Phillips, N. A., Verret, L., Babins, L., Kelner, N., Akerib, V., & Chertkow, H. (2006). Cognitive estimation impairment in Alzheimer disease and mild cognitive impairment. *Neuropsychology, 20,* 123–132.

Levinson, D. J. (1978). *The seasons of a man's life.* New York: Knopf.

Levinson, D. J. (1996). *Seasons of a woman's life.* New York: Knopf.

Lewinsohn, P. M., Clarke, G. N., Seeley, J. R., & Rohde, P. (1994). Major depression in community adolescents: Age at onset, episode duration, and time to recurrence. *Journal of the American Academy of Child and Adolescent Psychiatry, 33,* 809–818.

Lewinsohn, P. M., & Gotlib, I. H. (1995). Behavioral therapy and treatment of depression. In E. E. Beckham & W. R. Leber (Eds.), *Handbook of depression* (2nd ed., pp. 352–375). New York: Guilford.

Lewinsohn, P. M., Joiner, T. E., & Rohde, P. (2001). Evaluation of cognitive diathesis-stress models in predicting major depressive disorder in adolescence. *Journal of Abnormal Psychology, 110,* 203–215.

Lewinsohn, P. M., Rohde, P., Seeley, J. R., Kline, D. N., & Gotlib, L. H. (2006). The psychological consequences of adolescent major depressive disorder on young adults. In T. E. Joiner, J. S., Brown, & J. Kistner (Eds.), *The interpersonal, cognitive, and social nature of depression.* Mahwah, NJ: Erlbaum.

Lewinsohn, P. M., Striegel-Moore, R. H., & Seeley, J. R. (2000). Epidemiology and natural course of eating disorders in young women from adolescence to young adulthood. *Journal of American Academy of Child and Adolescent Psychiatry, 39,* 1284–1292.

Lewis, R. (2007). *Human genetics* (7th ed.). New York: McGraw-Hill.

Lewis, R., Parker, B., Gaffin, D., & Hoefnagels, M. (2007). *Life* (6th ed.). New York: McGraw-Hill.

Leykin, Y., Amsterdam, J. D., DeRuets, R. J., Gallop, R., Shelton, R. C., & Hollon, S. D. (2007). Progressive resistance to a selective serotonin reuptake inhibitor but not to cognitive therapy in the treatment of major depression. *Journal of Consulting and Clinical Psychology, 75,* 267–276.

Liang, B., Williams, L. M., & Siegel, J. A. (2006). Relational outcomes of childhood sexual trauma in female survivors: A longitudinal study. *Journal of Interpersonal Violence, 21,* 42–57.

Lieberman, D. A. (2004). *Learning and memory.* Belmont, CA: Wadsworth.

Lieberman, M. D. (2007). Social cognitive neurosciences: A review of core processes. *Annual Review of Psychology* (vol. 58). Palo Alto, CA: Annual Reviews.

Liefbroer, A. C., & Dourleijn, E. (2006). Unmarried cohabitation and union stability: Testing the role of diffusion using data from 16 European countries. *Demography, 43,* 203–221.

Lilienfeld, S. O., & Marino, L. (1995). Mental disorder as a Roschian concept: A critique of Wakefield's "harmful dysfunction" analysis. *Journal of Abnormal Psychology, 104,* 411–420.

Lilienfeld, S. O., Wood, J. M., & Garb, H. N. (2000, November). The scientific status of projective techniques. *Psychological Science in the Public Interest, 1*(2).

Limke, T. L., & Rao, M. S. (2003). Neural stem cells in aging and disease. *Journal of Cellular and Molecular Medicine, 6,* 475–496.

Lin, L., Osan, R., & Tsien, J. Z. (2006). Organizing principles of real-time memory encoding: Neural clique assemblies and universal neural codes. *Trends in Neuroscience, 29,* 48–57.

Linde, J. A., Rothman, A. J., Baldwin, A. S., & Jeffery, R. W. (2006). The impact of self-efficacy on behavior change and weight change among overweight participants in a weight loss trial. *Health Psychology, 25,* 282–291.

Linden, D. E. (2006). How psychotherapy changes the brain—the contribution of functional neuroimaging. *Molecular Psychiatry, 11,* 528–538.

Linden, W., Lenz, J. W., & Con, A. H. (2001). Individualized stress management for primary hypertension: A randomized trial. *Archives of Internal Medicine, 161,* 1071–1080.

Lindgren, T., Andersson, K., & Norback, D. (2006). Perception of cockpit environment among pilots on commercial aircraft. *Aviation and Space Environment Medicine, 77,* 832–837.

Lindwall, M., Rennemark, M., Halling, A., Berglund, J., & Hassmen, P. (2007). Depression and exercise in elderly men and women: Findings from the Swedish national study on aging and care. *Journal of Aging and Physical Activity, 15,* 41–55.

Lingjaerde, O., Foreland, A. R., & Engvik, H. (2001). Personality structure in patients with winter depression, assessed in a depression-free state according to the five-factor model of personality. *Journal of Affective Disorders, 62,* 165–174.

Lippa, R. A. (2005). *Gender: Nature and nurture* (2nd ed.). Mahwah, NJ: Erlbaum.

Lippke, S., & Plotnikoff, R. C. (2006). Stages of change in physical exercise: A test of stage discrimination and nonlinearity. *American Journal of Health Behavior, 30,* 290–301.

Lippke, S., & Ziegelmann, J. P. (2006). Understanding and modeling health behavior: The multi-stage model of health behavior change. *Journal of Health Psychology, 11,* 37–50.

Lipsey, M. W., & Wilson, D. B. (1993). The efficacy of psychological, educational, and behavioral treatment: Confirmation from meta-analysis. *American Psychologist, 48,* 1181–1209.

Lisanby, S. H., Maddox, J. H., Prudic, J., Devanand, D. P., & Sackeim, H. A. (2000). The effects of electroconvulsive therapy on memory of autobiographical and public events. *Archives of General Psychiatry, 57,* 581–590.

Lister-Ford, C. (2007). *A short introduction to psychotherapy.* Thousand Oaks, CA: Sage.

Litt, J., Taylor, H. G., Klein, N., & Hack, M. (2005). Learning disabilities in children with very low birthweight: Prevalence, neuropsychological correlates, and educational interventions. *Journal of Learning Disabilities, 38,* 130–141.

Little, K. Y., Zhang, L., & Cook, E. (2006). Fluoxetine-induced alterations in human platelet serotonin transporter expression: Serotonin transporter polymorphism effects. *Psychiatry and Neuroscience, 31,* 333–339.

Little, T. D., Snyder, C. R., & Wehmeyer, M. (2006). The agentic self: On the nature and origins of personal agency across the life span. In D. K. Mroczek & T. D. Little (Eds.), *Handbook of personality development.* Mahwah, NJ: Erlbaum.

Littrell, J. H., & Girvin, H. (2002). Stages of change: A critique. *Behavior Modification, 26,* 223–273.

Liu, Q., Xie, F., Rolston, R., Moreira, P. I., Nunomura, A., Zhu, X., Smith, M. A., & Perry, G. (2007). Prevention and treatment of Alzheimer disease and aging: Antioxidants. *Mini Reviews in Medicinal Chemistry, 7,* 171–180.

Liu, S. J., & Lachamp, P. (2006). The activation of excitatory glutamate receptors evokes a long-lasting increase in the release of GABA from cerebellar stellate cells. *Journal of Neuroscience, 26,* 9332–9339.

Livaditis, M., & Tsatalmpasidou, E. (2007). A critical review of the physicalistic approaches of the mind and consciousness. *Cognitive Processing.* (in press)

Locke, J. L. (1993). *The child's path to spoken language.* Cambridge, MA: Harvard University Press.

Lockl, K., & Schneider, W. (2007). Knowledge about the mind: Links between theory of mind and later metamemory. *Child Development, 78,* 148–167.

Loftus, E. F. (1993). Psychologists in the eyewitness world. *American Psychologist, 48,* 550–552.

Loftus, E. F. (2003). Make-believe memories. *American Psychologist, 58,* 867–873.

Loftus, E. F. (2005). The malleability of memory. In H. Minkowich (Ed.), *Neuroscientific and psychoanalytic perspectives on memory.* London: International Neuro-Psychoanalysis Society.

Loftus, E. F. (2006). Memory distortions: Problems solved and unsolved. In M. Garry & H. Hayne (Eds.), *Do justice and let the skies fall.* Mahwah, NJ: Erlbaum.

Loftus, E. F. (2007). Memory distortions: Problems solved and unsolved. In M. Garry & H. Hayne (Eds.), *Do justice and let the sky fall.* Mahwah, NJ: Erlbaum.

Loftus, E. F., & Ketcham, K. (1991). *Witness for the defense: The accused, the eyewitness, and the expert who puts memory on trial.* New York: St. Martin's Press.

Loftus, E. F., & Pickrell, J. E. (2001, June). *Creating false memories.* Paper presented at the meeting of the American Psychological Society, Toronto.

Logue, A. W. (1995). *Self control: Waiting until tomorrow for what you want today.* Upper Saddle River, NJ: Pearson Education.

Lomber, S. G., Malhotra, S., & Hall, A. J. (2007). Functional specialization of non-primary auditory cortex of the cat: Areal and laminar contributions to sound localization. *Hearing Research.* (in press)

Longo, D. A., Lent, R. W., & Brown, S.D. (1992). Social cognitive variables in the prediction of client motivation and attribution. *Journal of Counseling Psychology, 39,* 447–452.

Longo-Mbenza, B., Lukoki, L. E., & M'buyambia-Kabangu, J. R. (2007). Nutritional status, socioeconomic status, heart rate, and blood pressure in African American school children and adolescents. *International Journal of Cardiology.* (in press)

Lonnqvist, J., Leikas, S, Paunonen, S., Nissinen, V., & Verkasalo, M. (2006). Conformism moderates the relations between values, anticipated regret, and behavior. *Personality and Social Psychology Bulletin, 32,* 1469–1481.

Lopes, M., & Santos-Victor, J. (2007). A developmental roadmap for learning by imitation in robots. *IEEE Transactions on Systems, Man, and Cybernetics B, 37,* 308–321.

Lorant, V., Croux, C., Weich, S., Deliege, D., Mackenbach, J., & Ansseau, M. (2007). Depression and socioeconomic risk factors: 7-year longitudinal population study. *British Journal of Psychiatry, 190,* 293–298.

Lorenz, K. Z. (1965). *Evolution and the modification of behavior.* Chicago: University of Chicago Press.

Low, C. A., Stanton, A., & Danoff-Burg, S. (2006). Expressive disclosure and benefit finding among breast cancer patients: Mechanisms for positive health effects. *Health Psychology, 25,* 181–189.

Lu, J., Sherman, D., Devor, M., & Saper, C. B. (2006). A putative flip-flop switch for control of REM sleep. *Nature, 441,* 589–594.

Lu, L. (2006). "Cultural fit": Individual and societal discrepancies in values, beliefs, and subjective well-being. *Journal of Social Psychology, 146,* 203–221.

Lu, Z. L., & Eskew, R. T. (2007). A special issue on application of od signal detection theory to visual perception. *Spatial Vision, 20,* 1–4.

Lubinski, D., Benbow, Camilla P., Webb, R. M., & Bleske-Rechek, A. (2006). Tracking exceptional human capital over two decades. *Psychological Science, 17,* 194–199.

Lubinski, D., Webb, R. M., Morelock, M. J., & Benbow, C. P. (2001). Top 1 in 10,000: A 10-year follow-up of the profoundly gifted. *Journal of Applied Psychology, 86,* 718–729.

Luborsky, L., Rosenthal, R., Diguer, L., Andrusyna, T. P., Berman, J. S., Levitt, J. T., Seligman, D. A., & Krause, E. D. (2002). The dodo bird verdict is alive and well—mostly. *Clinical Psychology: Science and Practice 9,* 2–12.

Lucas, R. E. (2007). Extraversion. In R. Baumeister & K. Vohs (Eds.), *The encyclopedia of social psychology.* Thousand Oaks, CA: Sage.

Lucas, R. E., & Baird, B. (2004). Extraversion and emotional reactivity. *Journal of Personality and Social Psychology, 86,* 473–485.

Lucas, R. E., Clark, A. E., Georgellis, Y., & Diener, E. (2003). Reexamining adaptation and the set point model of happiness: Reactions to changes in marital status. *Journal of Personality and Social Psychology, 84,* 527–539.

Lucas, R. E., Clark, A. E., Yannis, G., & Diener, E. (2004). Unemployment alters the setpoint for life satisfaction. *Psychological Science, 15,* 8–13.

Lucas, R. E., & Fujita, F. (2000). Factors influencing the relation between extraversion and pleasant affect. *Journal of Personality and Social Psychology, 79,* 1039–1056.

Lucassen, P. J., & others. (2006). Stress, depression, and hippocampal apoptosis. *CNS and Neurological Disorders Drug Targets, 5,* 531–546.

Lucurto, C. (1990). The malleability of IQ as judged from adoption studies. *Intelligence, 14,* 275–292.

Luhtanen, R. (1996, August). *Psychological well-being in lesbians and gay men.* Presented at the American Psychological Association Convention, Toronto, Canada.

Lumpkin, E. A., & Caterina, M. J. (2007). Mechanisms of sensory transduction in the skin. *Nature, 445,* 858–865.

Lund, I., & Lundeberg, T. (2006). Aspects of pain, its assessment and evaluation from an acupuncture perspective. *Acupuncture Medicine, 24,* 109–117.

Luo, Y., & Baillargeon, R. (2005). Can a self-propelled box have a goal? Psychological reasoning in 5-month-old infants. *Psychological Science, 16,* 601–608.

Luria, A. R. (1973). *The working brain.* New York: Penguin.

Lykken, D. T. (1987). The probity of the polygraph. In S. M. Kassin & L. S. Wrightsman (Eds.), *The psychology of evidence and trial procedures.* Newbury Park, CA: Sage.

Lykken, D. T. (1998). A tremor in the blood: Uses and abuses of the lie detector (2nd ed.). New York: Plenum Press.

Lykken, D. T. (2001). Lie detection. In W. E. Craighead & C. B. Nemeroff (Eds.), *The Corsini encyclopedia of psychology and behavioral science* (3rd ed.). New York: Wiley.

Lynn, S. J. (2007). Hypnosis reconsidered. *American Journal of Clinical Hypnosis, 49,* 195–197.

Lynn, S. J., & Cardena, E. (2007). Hypnosis and the treatment of posttraumatic conditions: An evidence-based approach. *International Journal of Clinical Hypnosis, 55,* 167–188.

Lynn, S. J., Das, L. S., Hallquist, M. N., & Williams, J. C. (2006). Mindfulness, acceptance, and hypnosis: Cognitive and clinical perspectives. *International Journal of Clinical and Experimental Hypnosis, 54,* 143–166.

Lythgoe, M. F., Pollak, T. A., Kalmas, M., de Haan, M., & Chong, W. (2005). Obsessive, prolific artistic output following subarachnoid hemorrhage. *Neurology, 64,* 397–398.

Lyubomirsky, S., King, L. A., & Diener, E. (2005). The benefits of frequent positive affect: Does happiness lead to success? *Psychological Bulletin, 131,* 803–855.

Lyubomirsky, S., & Ross, L. (1999). Changes in attractiveness of elected, rejected, and precluded alternatives: A comparison of happy and unhappy individuals. *Journal of Personality and Social Psychology, 76,* 988–1007.

M

Maas, J. (1998). *Power sleep.* New York: Villard.

Maccoby, E. E. (1998). *The two sexes: Growing up apart, coming together.* Cambridge, MA: Harvard University Press.

Maccoby, E. E. (2002). Gender and group processes. *Current Directions in Psychological Science, 11,* 54–58.

Maccoby, E. E. (2007). Historical overview of socialization research and theory. In J. E. Grusec & P. D. Hastings (Eds.), *Handbook of socialization.* New York: Oxford University Press.

Maccoby, E. E., & Jacklin, C. N. (1974). *The psychology of sex differences.* Palo Alto, CA: Stanford University Press.

MacKenzie, S. B., Podsakoff, P. M., & Ahearne, M. (1998). Some possible antecedents and consequences of in-role and extra-role salesperson performance. *Journal of Marketing, 62,* 87–98.

MacKenzie, S. B., Podsakoff, P. M., & Fetter, R. (1993). The impact of organizational citizenship behavior on evaluations of salesperson performance. *Journal of Marketing, 57,* 70–80.

Mackie, D. M., & Worth, L. T. (1989). Processing deficits and the mediation of positive affect in persuasion. *Journal of Personality and Social Psychology, 57,* 27–40.

MacKinnon, D., Jamison, K. R., & DePaulo, J. R. (1997). Genetics of manic depressive illness. *Annual Review of Neuroscience, 20,* 355–373.

Macknik, S. L. (2006). Visual masking approaches to visual awareness. *Progress in Brain Research, 155,* 177–215.

MacLeod, M. (2006, April 1). Mindless imitation teaches us how to be human. *New Scientist, 2545,* 42.

MacQueen, C. E., Brynes, A. E., & Frost, G. S. (2002).Treating obesity: A follow-up study. Can the stages of change model be used as a postal screening tool? *Journal of Human Nutrition and Dietetics, 15*(1), 3–7.

Madan, A., Palaniappan, L., Urizar, G., Wang, Y., Formann, S. P., & Gould, J. B. (2006). Sociocultural factors that affect pregnancy outcomes in two dissimilar immigrant groups in the United States. *Journal of Pediatrics, 148,* 341–346.

Madden, D. J., Gottlob, L. R., Denny, L. L., Turkington, T. G., Provenzale, J. M., Hawk, T. C., & others. (1999). Aging and recognition memory: Changes in regional cerebral blood flow associated with components of reaction time distributions. *Journal of Cognitive Neuroscience, 11,* 511–520.

Maddi, S. (1998). Hardiness. In H. S. Friedman (Ed.), *Encyclopedia of mental health* (vol. 3). San Diego: Academic.

Maddi, S. R., Harvey, R. H., Khoshaba, D. M., Lu, J. L., Persico, M., & Brow, M. (2006). The personality construct of hardiness, III: Relationships with repression, innovativeness, authoritarianism, and performance. *Journal of Personality, 74,* 575–597.

Maddux, J. E., & Mundell, C. E. (2005). Disorders of personality: Diseases or individual differences? In V. J. Derlega, B. A. Winstead, & W. H. Jones (Eds.), *Personality: Contemporary theory and research* (3rd ed.). Chicago: Nelson-Hall.

Maddux, J. E., Snyder, C. R., & Lopez, S. J. (2004). Toward a positive clinical psychology: Deconstructing the illness ideology and constructing an ideology of human strengths and potential. In A. Linley & S. Joseph (Eds.), *Positive psychology in practice* (pp. 320–334). Hoboken, NJ: Wiley.

Mader, S. S. (2008). *Inquiry into life* (12th ed.). New York: McGraw-Hill.

Mager, R. F. (1972). *Goals analysis.* Belmont, CA: Fearon.

Maguire, E. A., Gadian, G. D., Johnsrude, I. S., Good, C. D., Ashburner, J., Frackowiak, R. S. J., & Frith, C. D. (2000). Navigation-related structural change in the hippocampi of taxi drivers. *Proceedings of the National Academy of Science, 97,* 4398–4403.

Maia, T. V., & Cleeremans, A. (2005). Consciousness: Converging insights from connectionist modeling and neuroscience. *Trends in Cognitive Science, 9,* 397–404.

Maier, N. R. F. (1931). Reasoning in humans. *Journal of Comparative Psychology, 12,* 181–194.

Maio, G. R., & Haddock, G. (2007). Attitude change. In A. W. Kruglanski & E. T. Higgins (Eds.), *Social psychology: Handbook of basic principles* (2nd ed.). New York: Guilford.

Malamitsi-Puchner, A., & Boutsikou, T. (2006). Adolescent pregnancy and perinatal outcome. *Pediatric Endocrinology Review, 3, Suppl. 1,* S170–S171.

Malamuth, N. M., Addison, T., & Koss, M. (2000). Pornography and sexual aggression: Are there reliable effects and can we understand them? *Annual Review of Sex Research, 11,* 26–91.

Mandara, J. (2006). The impact of family functioning on African American males' academic achievement: A review and clarification of the empirical literature. *Teachers College Record, 108,* 206–233.

Mandler, G. (1980). Recognizing: The judgment of previous occurrence. *Psychological Review, 87,* 252–271.

Manini, T. M., & others. (2006). Daily activity energy expenditure and mortality among older adults. *Journal of the American Medical Association, 296,* 216–218.

Manji, H. K. (2001). Strategies for gene and protein expression studies in neuropsychopharmacology and biological psychiatry. *International Journal of Neuropsychopharmacology, 4,* 45.

Manji, H. K., Drevets, W. C., & Charney, D. S. (2001). The cellular neurobiology of depression. *Nature Medicine, 7,* 541–547.

Mann, L. (1981). The baiting crowd in episodes of threatened suicide. *Journal of Personality and Social Psychology, 41,* 703–709.

Mann, T., & Ward, A. (2004). To eat or not to eat: Implications of the attentional myopia model for restrained eaters. *Journal of Abnormal Psychology, 113,* 90–98.

Mantere, T., Tupala, E., Hall, H., Sarkoja, T., Rasanen, P., Bergstrom, K., Callaway, J., & Tihonen, J. (2002). Serotinin transporter distribution and density in the cerebral cortex of alcoholic and nonalcoholic comparison subjects:A whole-hemisphere autoradiograph study. *American Journal of Psychiatry, 159,* 599–606.

Maratsos, M. (1999). Some aspects of innateness and complexity in grammar acquisition. In M. Barrett (Ed.), *The development of language.* Philadelphia: Psychology Press.

March, J., Silva, S., Petrycki, S., Curry, J., Wells, K., Fairbank, J., Burns, B., Domino, M., McNulty, S., Vitiello, B., & Severe, J. (2004). Fluoxetine, cognitive-behavioral therapy, and their combination for adolescents with depression: Treatment for Adolescents with Depression Study (TADS) randomized controlled trial. *Journal of the American Medical Association, 292,* 807–820.

Marcia, J. E. (1980). Ego identity development. In J. Adelson (Ed.), *Handbook of adolescent psychology.* New York: Wiley.

Marcia, J. E. (2002). Identity and psychosocial development in adulthood. *Identity, 2,* 7–28.

Marcus, G. F. (2001). *The algebraic mind.* Cambridge, MA: MIT Books.

Marder, S. R., Davis, J. M., & Chouinard, G. (1997). The effects of risperidone on the five dimensions of schizophrenia derived by factor analysis: Combined results of the North American trials. *Journal of Clinical Psychiatry, 58,* 538–546.

Maril, A., Simons, J. S. Weaver, J. J., & Schacter, D. L. (2005). Graded recall success: An event-related fMRI comparison of tip of the tongue and feeling of knowing. *Neuroimage, 24,* 1130–1138.

Maril, A., Wagner, A. D., & Schacter, D. L. (2001). On the tip of the tongue: An event-related fMRI study of semantic retrieval failure and cognitive conflict. *Neuron, 31,* 653–660.

Marine, A., Rutosalainen, J., Serra, C., & Verbeek, J. (2006). Preventing occupational stress in healthcare workers. *Cochrane Database System Review, 18*(4), CD002892.

Maris, R. W. (1998). Suicide. In H. S. Friedman (Ed.), *Encyclopedia of mental health* (vol. 3). San Diego: Academic.

Marketdata Enterprises. (2006). *The US market for self-improvement products.* Tampa, FL: Marketdata Enterprises Inc.

Markides, K. S. (Ed.). (2007). *Encyclopedia of health and aging.* Thousand Oaks, CA: Sage.

Markowitz, S., & Cuellar, A. (2007). Antidepressants and youth: Healing or harmful? *Social Science Medicine, 64,* 2138–2151.

Marlow, A. (1999). *How to stop time: Heroin from A to Z.* New York: Basic Books.

Marr, D. (1982). *Vision.* New York: Freeman.

Marsella, A. J., & Yamada, A. M. (2007). Culture and psychopathology. In S. Kitayama & D. Cohen (Eds.), *Handbook of cultural psychology.* New York: Guilford.

Marsh, H. W. (1995). A Jamesian model of self-investment and self-esteem: Comment on Pelham (1995). *Journal of Personality and Social Psychology, 69,* 1151–1160.

Marshall, G. N., Berthold, S. M., Schell, T. L., Elliott, M. N., Chunn, C. A., & Hambarsoomians, K. (2006). Rates and correlates of seeking mental health services among Cambodian refugees. *American Journal of Public Health, 96,* 1829–1835.

Marshall, M., & Rathbone, J. (2006). Early intervention for psychosis. *Cochrance Database of Systematic Reviews, 4,* CD004718.

Marsiske, M., & Margrett, J. A. (2006). Everyday problem solving and decision making. In J.E. Birren & K.W. Schaie (Eds.), *Handbook of the psychology of aging* (6th ed.). San Diego: Academic.

Marsit, C. J., Karagas, M. R., Schned, A., & Kelsey, K. T. (2006). Carcinogen exposure and epigenetic silencing in bladder cancer. *Annals of the New York Academy of Sciences, 1076,* 810–821.

Marsland, A. L., Cohen, S., & Bachen, E. (2007). Common cold. In S. Ayers, A. Baum, C. McManus, S. Newman, K. Wallston, J. Weinman, & R. West (Eds.), *Cambridge handbook of psychology, health, and medicine.* New York: Cambridge University Press.

Martin, C. L., & Dinella, L. (2001). Gender development: Gender schema theory. In J. Worell (Ed.), *Encyclopedia of women and gender.* New York: Oxford University Press.

Martin, D. W. (2008). *Doing psychology experiments* (7th ed.). Belmont, CA: Wadsworth.

Martin, G. L., & Pear, J. (2007). *Behavior modification* (8th ed.). Upper Saddle River, NJ: Prentice-Hall.

Martin, S. J., & Clark, R. E. (2007). The rodent hippocampus and spatial memory: From synapses to systems. *Cellular and Molecular Life Sciences, 64,* 401–431.

Marvanova, M., & Nichols, C. D. (2007). Identification of neuroprotective compounds of Caenorhabditis elegans dopamine neurons aganist 6-OHDA. *Journal of Molecular Neuroscience, 31,* 127–138.

Masaki, T., & Nakajima, S. (2006). Taste aversion in rats induced by forced swimming, voluntary running, forced running, and lithium chloride injection treatments. *Physiology and Behavior, 88,* 411–416.

Mascaro, N., & Rosen, D. H. (2006). The role of existential meaning as a buffer against stress. *Journal of Humanistic Psychology, 46,* 168–190.

Mashour, G. A. (2006). Integrating the science of consciousness and anesthesia. *Anesthesia and Analgesia, 103,* 975–982.

Maslow, A. H. (1954). *Motivation and personality.* New York: Harper & Row.

Maslow, A. H. (1971). *The farther reaches of human nature.* New York: Viking.

Mason, P., Harrison, G., Glazebrook, C. & others. (1995). Characteristics of outcome in schizophrenia at 13 years. *British Journal of Psychiatry, 167,* 596–603.

Mason, R. A., & Adam Just, M. (2004). How the brain processes causal inferences in text. *Psychological Science, 15,* 1–7.

Mason, T. B., & Pack, A. I. (2005). Sleep terrors in childhood. *Journal of Pediatrics, 147,* 388–392.

Massimini, F., & Delle Fave, A. (2000). Individual development in bio-cultural perspective. *American Psychologist, 55,* 24–33.

Masten, A. S. (2001). Ordinary magic: Resilience processes in development. *American Psychologist, 56,* 227–238.

Masten, A. S. (2006). Developmental psychopathology: Pathways to the future. *International Journal of Behavioral Development, 31,* 46–53.

Masten, A. S., Burt, K. B., & Coatsworth, J. (2006). Competence and psychopathology in development. In D. Cicchetti & D. J. Cohen (Eds.), *Developmental psychopathology, Vol. 3: Risk, disorder, and adaptation* (2nd ed., pp. 696–738). Hoboken, NJ: Wiley.

Masten, A. S., & Coatsworth, J. D. (1998). The development of competence in favorable and unfavorable environments: Lessons from successful children. *American Psychologist, 53,* 205–220.

Masten, A. S., Obradovic, J., & Burt, K. B. (2006). Resilience in emerging adulthood. In J. J. Arnett & J. L. Tanner (Eds.), *Emerging adults in America.* Washington, DC: American Psychological Association.

Masten, A. S., & Shaffer, A. (2006). How families matter in child development: Reflections from research on risk and resilience. In A. Clarke-Stewart & J. Dunn (Eds.), *Families count.* New York: Cambridge University Press.

Masters, W. H., & Johnson, V. E. (1966). *Human sexual response.* Boston: Little, Brown.

Matlin, M. W. (2001). *Cognition* (5th ed.) Fort Worth, TX: Harcourt Brace.

Matlin, M. W. (2008). *Psychology of women* (6th ed.). Belmont, CA: Wadsworth.

Matorin, A. A., McCurtis, H., Jones, B. E., Varma, S., Nene, S., Ruiz, P., & Gorman, J. M. (2006). Psychotherapy with African American patients: A training perspective. *Journal of Psychiatric Practice, 12,* 187–194.

Matsuba, M. K. (2006). Searching for self and relationships online. *Cyberpsychology and Behavior, 9,* 275–284.

Matthews, C. E., Jurj, A. L., Shu, X. O., Li, H. L., Yang, G., Li, Q., Gao, Y. T., & Zheng, W. (2007). Influence of exercise, walking, cycling, and overall nonexercise physical activity on mortality in Chinese women. *American Journal of Epidemiology.* (in press)

Matthews, K. A., Schott, L. L., Bromberger, J., Cyranowski, J. Everson-Rose, S. A., & Sowers, M. F. (2007). Associations between depressive symptoms and inflammatory/hemostatic markers in women during the menopausal transition. *Psychosomatic Medicine, 69,* 124–130.

Matthews, L. L., & Servaty-Seib, H. L. (2007). Hardiness and grief in a sample of bereaved college students. *Death Studies, 31,* 183–204.

Maurer, T. J., Mitchell, D. R. D., & Barbeite, F. G. (2002). Predictors of attitudes toward a 360-degree feedback system and involvement in post-feedback management development activity. *Journal of Occupational and Organizational Psychology, 75,* 87–107.

May, F. B. (2006). *Teaching reading creatively* (7th ed.). Upper Saddle River, NJ: Prentice-Hall.

May, M. (2003). *Vision diary.* http://www.guardian.co.uk/g2/story/0,3604,1029268,00.html (accessed October 11, 2006).

Mayer, R. (2000). Problem solving. In M. A. Runco & S. Pritzker (Eds.), *Encyclopedia of psychology.* San Diego: Academic.

Mayer, R. E. (2004). Teaching and subject matter. *Annual Review of Psychology* (vol. 55). Palo Alto, CA: Annual Reviews.

Maylor, E. A., Chater, N., & Brown, G. D. (2001). Scale invariance in the retrieval of retrospective and prospective memories. *Psychonomic Bulletin Review, 8,* 162–167.

Mayo Foundation. (2006). *Electroconvulsive therapy (ECT):* Treating severe depression and mental illness. Rochester, MN: Author. http://www.mayo-clinic.com/health/electroconvulsive-therapy/MH00022

Mays, V. M., Cochran, S. D., & Barnes, N. W. (2007). Race, race-based discrimination, and health outcomes among African Americans. *Annual Review of Psychology* (vol. 58). Palo Alto, CA: Annual Reviews.

McAdams, D. P. (1989). Intimacy: The need to be close. New York: Doubleday.

McAdams, D. P. (2001). The psychology of life stories. *Review of General Psychology. 5,* 100–122.

McAdams, D. P. (2006). *The redemptive self: Stories Americans live by.* New York: Oxford University Press.

McAdams, D. P., Bauer, J. J., Sakaeda, A. R., Anyidoho, N. A., Machado, M. A., Magrino-Failla, K., White, K. W., & Pals, J. L. (2006). Continuity and change in life story: A longitudinal study of autobiographical memories in emerging adulthood. *Journal of Personality, 74,* 1371–1400.

McAdams, D. P., & Bryant, F. B. (1987). Intimacy motivation and subjective mental health in a nationwide sample. *Journal of Personality, 55,* 395–413.

McAllister, A. K. (2007). Dynamic aspects of synaptic maturation. *Annual Review of Neuroscience* (vol. 30). Palo Alto, CA: Annual Reviews.

McBurney, D. H., & White, T. L. (2007). *Research methods* (7th ed.). Belmont, CA: Wadsworth.

McCarley, R. W. (2007). Neurobiology of REM and NREM sleep. *SleepMedicine.* (in press)

McCarthy, D. E., Piasecki, T. M., Fiore, M. C., & Baker, T. B. (2006). Life before and after quitting smoking: An electronic diary study. *Journal of Abnormal Psychology, 115,* 454–466.

McClelland, J. L., & Rumelhart, D. E. (1986). *Parallel distributed processing: Explorations in the microstructure of cognition. Vol. 2: Psychological and biological models.* Cambridge, MA: MIT Press.

McCrae, R. R., & Costa, P. T. (2006). Cross-cultural perspectives on adult personality trait development. In D. K. Mroczek & T. D. Little (Eds.), *Handbook of personality development.* Mahwah, NJ: Erlbaum.

McCullough, J. L., & Kelly, K. M. (2006). Prevention and treatment of skin aging. *Annals of the New York Academy of Science, 1067,* 323–331.

McCullough, M. E., Bono, G., & Root, L. M. (2007). Rumination, emotion, and forgiveness: Three longitudinal studies. *Journal of Personality and Social Psychology, 92,* 490–505.

McCullough, M. E., Emmons, R. A., & Tsang, J. (2002). The grateful disposition: A conceptual and empirical topography. *Journal of Personality and Social Psychology, 82,* 112–127.

McCullough, M. E., Hoyt, W. T., Larson, D. B., Koenig, H. G., & Thoresen, C. (2000). Religious involvement and mortality: A meta-analytic review. *Health Psychology, 19,* 211–222.

McDaniel, M. A., & Einstein, G. O. (2007). *Prospective memory: An overview and synthesis of an emerging field.* Thousand Oaks, CA: Sage.

McDermott, D. (2007). Artificial intelligence and consciousness. In P. D. Zelazo, M. Moscovitch, & E. Thompson (Eds.), *The Cambridge handbook of consciousness.* New York: Cambridge University Press.

McEwen, B. S. (2006). Sleep deprivation as a neurobiologic and physiologic stressor: Allostasis and allostatic load. *Metabolism, 55, Suppl. 2,* S20–S23.

McFarlane, T., Polivy, J., & Herman, C. P. (1998). Dieting. In H. S. Friedman (Ed.), *Encyclopedia of mental health* (vol. 1). San Diego: Academic.

McGovern, K., & Baars, B. J. (2007). Cognitive theories of consciousness. In P. D. Zelazo, M. Moscovitch, & E. Thompson (Eds.), *The Cambridge handbook of consciousness.* New York: Cambridge University Press.

McGrath, E., Keita, G. P., Strickland, B., & Russo, N. F. (1990). *Women and depression: Risk factors and treatment issues.* Washington, DC: American Psychological Association.

McGregor, D. M. (1960). *The human side of enterprise.* New York: McGraw-Hill.

McGue, M., Bouchard, T. J., Iacono, W. G., & Lykken, D. T. (1993). Behavioral genetics of cognitive ability: A life-span perspective. In R. Plomin & G. E. McClearn (Eds.), *Nature, nurture, and psychology.* Washington, DC: American Psychological Association.

McGuire, M. T., Wing, R. R, Klem, M. L. Lang, W., & Hill, J. O. (1999). What predicts weight regain in a group of successful weight losers? *Journal of Consulting and Clinical Psychology, 67,* 177–185.

McGuire, W. J. (2004). The morphing of attitude-change into social-cognition. In G. V. Bodenhausen & A. J. Lambert (Eds.), *Foundations of social cognition.* Mahwah, NJ: Erlbaum.

McIntosh, W. D., Harlow, T. F., & Martin, L. L. (1995). Linkers and non-linkers: Goal beliefs as a moderator of the effects of everyday hassles on rumination, depression, and physical complaints. *Journal of Applied Social Psychology, 25,* 1231–1244.

McKelvie, S. (1997). The availability heuristic: Effects of fame and gender on the estimated frequency of male and female names. *Journal of Social Psychology, 137,* 63–78.

McKendree-Smith, N., & Scogin, F. (2000). Depressive realism: Effects of depression severity and interpretation time. *Journal of Clinical Psychology, 56,* 1601–1608.

McKenzie, C. R. (2006). Increased sensitivity to differentially diagnostic answers using familiar materials: Implications for confirmation bias. *Memory and Cognition, 34,* 577–588.

McKim, W. (2007). *Drugs and behavior* (6th ed.). Upper Saddle River, NJ: Prentice-Hall.

McKone, E., Kanwisher, N., & Duchaine, B. C. (2007). Can generic expertise explain special processing for faces? *Trends in Cognitive Sciences, 11,* 8-15.

McKone, E., & Robbins, R. (2007). The evidence rejects the expertise hypothesis: Reply to Gauthier & Bukach. *Cognition, 103,* 331–336.

McLeod, J. (2007). *Counseling skill.* New York: McGraw-Hill.

McLoyd, V. C., Aikens, N. L., & Burton, L. M. (2006). Childhood poverty, policy, and practice. In W. Damon & R. Lerner (Eds.), *Handbook of child psychology* (6th ed.). New York: Wiley.

McLoyd, V. C., & Smith, J. (2002). Physical discipline and behavior problems in African American, European American, and Hispanic children: Emotional support as a moderator. *Journal of Marriage and Family, 64,* 40–53.

McMain, S., & Pos, A. E. (2007). Advances in psychotherapy of personality disorders: A research update. *Current Psychiatry Reports, 9,* 46–52.

McManus, M. A., & Ferguson, M. W. (2003). Biodata, personality, and demographic differences of recruits from three sources. *International Journal of Selection and Assessment, 11,* 175–183.

McNally, D. (1990). *Even eagles need a push.* New York: Dell.

McNally, G. P., & Westbrook, R. F. (2006). A short intertribal facilitates acquisition of context-conditioned fear and a short retention interval facilitates its expression. *Journal of Experimental Psychology: Animal Behavior Processes, 32,* 164–172.

McNally, R. (1994). *Panic disorder: A critical analysis.* New York: Guilford.

McNally, R. J. (2005). Debunking myths about trauma and memory. *Canadian Journal of Psychiatry, 50,* 817–822.

McNamara, D. S., de Vega, M., & O'Reilly, T. (2007). Comprehension skill, inference making, and the role of knowledge. In F. Schmalhofer & C. A. Perfetti (Eds.), *Higher level language processes in the brain.* Mahwah, NJ: Erlbaum.

McNaughton, B. L., Battaglia, F. P., Jensen, O., Moser, E. I., & Moser, M. B. (2006). Path integration and the neural basis of the "cognitive map." *Nature Review: Neuroscience, 7,* 663–678.

McPherson, T. L., Cook, R. F., Back, A. S., Hersch, R. K., & Hendrickson, A. (2006). A field test of a web-based substance abuse prevention training program for health promotion professionals. *American Journal of Health Promotion, 20,* 396–400.

McReadie, R. G. (2003). Diet, smoking, and cardiovascular risk in people with schizophrenia: A descriptive study. *British Journal of Psychiatry, 183,* 534–539.

McShane, S., & von Glinow, M. A. (2007). *Organizational behavior.* New York: McGraw-Hill.

Meddis, R. (2006). Reply to comment on "Auditory-nerve first-spike latency and auditory absolute threshold: A computer model." *Journal of the Acoustical Society of America, 120,* 1192–1193.

Medin, D. L., Lynch, E. B., & Solomon, K. O. (2000). Are there kinds of concepts? *Annual Review of Psychology* (vol. 51). Palo Alto, CA: Annual Reviews.

Medin, D. L., Proffitt, J. B., & Schwartz, H. C. (2000). Concepts: Structure. In A. Kazdin (Ed.), *Encyclopedia of psychology.* Washington, DC, & New York: American Psychological Association and Oxford University Press.

Meehl, P. (1962). Schizotonia, schizotypy, schizophrenia. *American Psychologist, 17,* 827–838.

Meese, T. S., Summers, R. J., Holmes, D. J., & Wallis, S. A. (2007). Contextual modulation involves suppression and facilitation from the center and the surround. *Journal of Vision, 7,* 7.

Meichenbaum, D., Turk, D., & Burstein, S. (1975). The nature of coping with stress. In I. Sarason & C. Spielberger (Eds.), *Stress and anxiety.* Washington, DC: Hemisphere.

Mejia-Arauz, R., Rogoff, B., & Paradise, R. (2005). Cultural variation in children's observation during a demonstration. *International Journal of Behavioral Development. 29,* 282–291.

Melcher, T., & Gruber, O. (2006). Oddball and incongruity effects during Stroop task performance: A comparative fMRI study on selective attention. *Brain Research, 1121,* 136–149.

Melton, L. (2005, December 17). How brain power can help you cheat old age. *New Scientist, 2530,* 32.

Melvin, G. A., Tonge, B. J., King, N., Heyne, D., Gordon, M. S., & Klimkeit, E. (2006). A comparison of cognitive-behavioral therapy, sertaline, and their combination for adolescent depression. *Journal of the American Academy of Child and Adolescent Psychiatry, 45,* 1151–1161.

Melzack, R. (1973). *The puzzle of pain.* New York: Basic Books.

Melzack, R. & Katz, J. (2006). Pain in the 21st century: The neuromatrix and beyond. In G. Young, A. Kane, & K. Nicholson (Eds.), *Psychological knowledge in court: PTSD, pain, and TBI* (pp. 129–148). New York: Springer Science.

Melzack, R., & Wall, P. D. (1965). Pain mechanisms: A new theory. *Science, 150,* 971–979.

Mendes, W. B. (2007). Social facilitation. In R. Baumeister & K. Vohs (Eds.), *Encyclopedia of social psychology.* Thousand Oaks, CA: Sage.

Mendez, M. F., Chow, T., Ringman, J., Twitchell, G., &Hinkin, C. H. (2000). Pedophilia and temporal lobe disturbances. *Journal of Neuropsychiatry and Clinical Neurosciences, 12,* 71–76.

Merchant, J. (2006). The developmental/emergent model of archetype, its implications and its applications to shamanism. *Journal of Analytical Psychology, 51,* 125–144.

Mesquita, B. (2002). Emotions as dynamic cultural phenomena. In R. J. Davidson, K. R. Scherer, & H. H. Goldsmith (Eds.), *Handbook of affective sciences.* New York: Oxford University Press.

Messinger, J. C. (1971). Sex and repression in an Irish folk community. In D. S. Marshall & R. C. Suggs (Eds.), *Human sexual behavior.* New York: Basic Books.

Messner, S. F., Raffalovich, L. E., & Shrock, P. (2002). Reassessing the cross-national relationship between income inequality and homicide rates: Implications of data quality control in the measurement of income distribution. *Journal of Quantitative Criminology, 18,* 377–395.

Metcalfe, J., & Mischel, W. (1999). A hot/cool system analysis of delay of gratification: Dynamics of will power. *Psychological Review, 106,* 3–19.

Mettler, F. A. (Ed.). (1952). *Psychosurgical problems.* Oxford: Blakiston.

Metzl, J. M., & Angel, J. (2004). Assessing the impact of SSRI antidepressants on popular notions of women's depressive illness. *Social Science & Medicine, 58,* 577–584.

Meyer, J. P., & Allen, N. J. (1997). *Commitment in the workplace: Theory, research, and application.* Thousand Oaks, CA: Sage.

Meyer, J. P., Becker, T. E., & Vandenberghe, C. (2004). Employee commitment and motivation: A conceptual analysis and integrative model. *Journal of Applied Psychology, 89,* 991–1007.

Meyer, J. P., & Herscovitch, L. (2001). Commitment in the workplace: Toward a general model. *Human Resource Management Review, 11,* 299–326.

Meyer, J. P., Stanley, D. J., Herscovitch, L., & Topolnytsky, L. (2002). Affective, continuance, and normative commitment to the organization: A meta-analysis of antecedents, correlates, and consequences. *Journal of Vocational Behavior, 61,* 20–52.

Miacic, B., & Goldberg, L. R. (2007). An analysis of a cross-cultural personality inventory: The IPIP big five factors markers in Croatia. *Journal of Personality Assessment, 88,* 168–177.

Michel, S., Clark, J. P., Ding, J. M., & Colwell, C. S. (2006). Brain-derived neurotrophic factor and neurotrophin receptors modulate glutamate-induced phase shifts of the suprachiasmatic nucleus. *European Journal of Neuroscience, 24,* 1109–1116.

Michinov, E., & Michinov, N. (2001). The similarity hypothesis: A test of the moderating role of social comparison orientation. *European Journal of Social Psychology, 31,* 549–556.

Mico, J. A., Ardid, D., Berrocoso, E., & Eschalier, A. (2006). Antidepressants and pain. *Trends in Pharmacological Sciences, 27,* 348–354.

Midgley, N. (2006). Re-reading "Little Hans": Freud's case study and the question of competing paradigms in psychoanalysis. *Journal of the American Psychoanalytic Association, 54,* 537–539.

Migneault, J. P., Adams, T. B., & Read, J. P. (2005). Application of the transtheoretical model to substance abuse: Historical development and future directions. *Drug and Alcohol Review, 24,* 437–448.

Mikulincer, M., Florian, V., & Hirschberger, G. (2004). The terror of death and the quest for love: An existential perspective on close relationships. In J. Greenberg, S. L. Koole, & T. Pyszczynski (Eds.), *Handbook of experimental existential psychology* (pp. 287–304). New York: Guilford.

Milane, M. S., Suchard, M. A., Wong, M., & Licinio, J. (2006). Modeling of the temporal patterns of fluoxetine prescriptions and suicide rates in the United States. *PloS Medicine, 3,* e190 doi:10.1371/jo.

Miley, W. M., & Spinella, M. (2006). Correlations among measures of executive function and positive psychological attributes in college students. *Journal of General Psychology, 133,* 175–182.

Milgram, S. (1965). Some conditions of obedience and disobedience to authority. *Human Relations, 18,* 56–76.

Milgram, S. (1974). *Obedience to authority.* New York: Harper & Row.

Miller, D. B., & O'Callaghan, J. P. (2006). The pharmacology of wakefulness. *Metabolism, 55, Suppl. 2,* S13–S19.

Miller, D. T. (1999). The norm of self-interest. *American Psychologist, 54*(12), 1053–1060.

Miller, D. T. (2001).The norm of self-interest. In J. Dienhart, D. Moberg, & R. Duska (Eds.), *The next phase of business ethics: Integrating psychology and ethics (pp. 193–-210).* New York: Elsevier Science/JAI Press.

Miller, G. A. (1956). The magical number seven, plus or minus two: Some limits on our capacity for information processing. *Psychological Review, 48,* 337–442.

Miller, J. J., Fletcher, K., & Kabat-Zinn, J. (1995). Three-year follow-up and clinical implications of a mindfulness meditation-based stress reduction intervention in the treatment of anxiety disorders. *General Hospital Psychiatry, 17,* 192–200.

Miller, L. K. (2006). *Principles of everyday behavior analysis.* Belmont, CA: Wadsworth.

Miller, N. E. (1941). The frustration-aggression hypothesis. *Psychological Review, 48,* 337–442.

Miller, N. E. (1985). The value of behavioral research on animals. *American Psychologist, 40,* 432–440.

Miller, R. R., & Matzel, L. D. (2006). Retrieval failure versus memory loss in experimental amnesia: Definitions and processes. *Learning and Memory, 13,* 491–497.

Miller, S. M., & Schnoll, R. A. (2000). When seeing is feeling: A cognitive-emotional approach to coping with health stress. In M. Lewis & J. M. Haviland-Jones (Eds.), *Handbook of emotions* (2nd ed., pp. 538–557). New York: Guilford.

Mills, D. L., & Sheehan, E. A. (2007). Experience and developmental changes in the organization of language-relevant brain activity. In D. Coch, K. W. Fischer, & G. Dawson (Eds.), *Human behavior, learning, and the developing brain.* New York: Guilford.

Mills, M. A., Edmondson, D., & Park, C. L. (2007). Trauma and stress response among Katrina evacuees. *American Journal of Public Health, 97, Suppl. 1,* S116–S123.

Milner, A. D., & Goodale, M. A. (1995). *The visual brain in action.* New York: Oxford University Press.

Milton, J., Solodkin, A., Hlustik, P., & Small, S. L. (2007). The mind of expert motor performance is cool and focused. *Neuroimage, 35,* 804–813.

Mineka, S., & Nugent, K. (1995). Mood-congruent memory biases in anxiety and depression. In D. L. Schacter, J. T. Coyle, G. D. Fischbach, M. M. Mesulam, & L. E. Sullivan (Eds.), *Memory distortion: How minds, brains, and societies reconstruct the past.* Cambridge, MA: Harvard University Press.

Mingroni, M. A. (2004). The secular rise in IQ *Intelligence, 32,* 65–83.

Miniño, A. M., Heron, M., & Smith, B. I. (2004). *Deaths: Preliminary data for 2004.* Washington DC: National Center for Health Statistics.

Mirescu, C., Peters, J. D., Noiman, L., & Gould, E. (2006). Sleep deprivation inhibits adult neurogenesis in the hippocampus by elevating glucocorticoids. *Proceedings of the National Academy of Sciences, 103,* 19170–19175.

Mischel, W. (1968). *Personality and assessment.* New York: Wiley.

Mischel, W. (2004). Toward an integrative science of the person. *Annual Review of Psychology* (vol. 55). Palo Alto, CA: Annual Reviews.

Mischel, W., & Ayduk, O. (2004). Willpower in a cognitive-affective processing system: The dynamics of delay of gratification. In R. F. Baumeister & K. D. Vohs (Eds.), *Handbook of self-regulation: Research, theory, and applications* (pp. 99–129). New York: Guilford.

Mischel, W., Cantor, N., & Feldman, S. (1996). Principles of self-regulation: The nature of will power and self-control. In E. T. Higgins & A. W. Kruglanski (Eds.), *Social psychology: Handbook of basic principles.* New York: Guilford.

Mischel, W., & Moore, B. S. (1980). The role of ideation in voluntary delay for symbolically presented rewards. *Cognitive Therapy and Research, 4,* 211–221.

Mischel, W., & Shoda, Y. (1999). Integrating dispositions and processing dynamics within a unified theory of personality: The cognitive-affective personality system. In L. A. Pervin & O. P. John (Eds.), *Handbook of personality: Theory and research* (2nd ed., pp. 197–218). New York: Guilford.

Mitchell, D. G., Fine, C., Richell, R. A., Newman, C., Lumsden, J., Blair, K. S., & Blair, R. J. (2006). Instrumental learning and relearning in individuals with psychopathy and in patients with lesions involving the amygdala or orbitofrontal cortex. *Neuropsychology, 20,* 280–289.

Mitchell, K. E., Alliger, G. M., & Morfopoulos, R. (1997). Toward an ADA-appropriate job analysis. *Human Resource Management Review, 7,* 5–26.

Mitchell, M. L., & Jolley, J. M. (2007). *Research design explained* (6th ed.). Belmont, CA: Wadsworth.

Mittag, W., & Schwarzer, R. (1993). Interaction of employment status and self-efficacy on alcohol consumption: A two-wave study on stressful life transitions. *Psychology and Health, 8,* 77–87.

Mizes, J. S., & Miller, K. J. (2000). Eating disorders. In M. Herson & R. T. Ammerman (Eds.), *Advanced abnormal child psychology* (2nd ed.). Mahwah, NJ: Erlbaum.

Mockett, B. G., Guevremont, D., Williams, J. M., & Abraham, W. C. (2007). Dopamine D1/D5 receptor activation reverses NDMA receptor-dependent long-term depression in rat hippocampus. *Journal of Neuroscience, 27,* 2918–2926.

Moffitt, T. E., Brammer, G. L., Caspi, A., Fawcet, J. P., Raleigh, M., Yuwiler, A., & Silva, P. A. (1998). Whole blood serotonin relates to violence in an epidemiological study. *Biological Psychiatry, 43,* 446–457.

Mohr, C. D., Armeli, S., Tennen, H., Temple, M., Todd, M., Clark, J., & Carney, M. A. (2005). Moving beyond the keg party: A daily process study of college student drinking motivations. *Psychology of Addictive Behaviors, 19,* 392–403.

Mollet, G. A., & Harrison, D. W. (2006). Emotion and pain: A functional cerebral systems integration. *Neuropsychology Review, 16,* 99–121.

Money, J. (1986). *Lovemaps: Clinical concepts of sexual/erotic health and pathology, paraphilia, and gender transposition in childhood, adolescence, and maturity.* New York: Irvington.

Money, J., & Tucker P. (1975). *Sexual signatures: On being a man or woman.* Boston: Little Brown.

Monin, B. (2007). Normative influence. In R. Baumeister & K. D. Vohs (Eds.), *Encyclopedia of social psychology.* Thousand Oaks, CA: Sage.

Monti, J. M., & Monti, D. (2007). The involvement of dopamine in the modulation of sleep and waking. *Sleep Medicine Review, 11,* 113–133.

Moody, E. W., Sunsay, C., & Bouton, M. E. (2006). Priming and trial spacing in extinction: Effects on extinction performance, spontaneous recovery, and reinstatement in appetitive conditioning. *Quarterly Journal of Experimental Psychology, 59,* 809–829.

Moons, W. G., & Mackie, D. M. (2007). Thinking straight while seeing red: The influence of anger on information processing. *Personality and Social Psychology Bulletin.* (in press)

Moore-Ede, M. C., Sulzman, F. M., & Fuller, C. A. (1982). *The clocks that time us.* Cambridge, MA: Harvard University Press.

Moors, A., & De Houwer, J. (2006). Automaticity: A theoretical and conceptual analysis. *Psychological Bulletin, 132,* 297–326.

Moos, R. H. (1986). Work as a human context. In M. S. Pallack & R. Perloff (Eds.), *Psychology and work.* Washington, DC: American Psychological Association.

Moradi, F., Hipp, C., & Koch, C. (2007). Activity in the visual cortex is modulated by top-down attention locked to reaction time. *Journal of Cognitive Neuroscience, 19,* 331–340.

Moran, S., & Gardner, H. (2006). Extraordinary achievements. In W. Damon & R. Lerner (Eds.), *Handbook of child psychology* (6th ed.). New York: Wiley.

Morgan, B. L., & Korschgen, A. J. (2006). *Majoring in psych?: Career options for psychology undergraduates* (3rd ed.). Upper Saddle River, NJ: Prentice-Hall.

Morgan, C. D., & Murray, H. A. (1935). A method of investigating fantasies: The Thematic Apperception Test. *Archives of Neurology and Psychiatry, 34,* 289–306.

Morgeson, F. P., Campion, M. A., & Maertz, C. P. (2001). Understanding pay satisfaction: The limits of compensa6tion system implementation. *Journal of Business and Psychology, 16,* 133–149.

Morgeson, F. P., Reider, M. H., & Campion, M. A. (2005). Selecting individuals in team settings: The importance of social skills, personality characteristics, and teamwork knowledge. *Personnel Psychology, 58,* 583–611

Morris, B. (2006, January 6). Genentech: The best place to work now. CNN/MONEY. http://money.cnn.com/2006/01/06/news/companies/bestcos_genentech/index.htm

Morris, R. G. (2006). Elements of neurobiological theory of hippocampal function: The role of synaptic plasticity, synaptic tagging, and schemas. *European Journal of Neuroscience, 23,* 2829–2846.

Morrish, E., King, M. A., Smith, I. E., & Shneerson, J. M. (2004). Factors associated with a delay in the diagnosis of narcolepsy. *Sleep Medicine, 5,* 37–41.

Moscoso, S. (2000). A review of validity evidence, adverse impact and applicant reactions. *International Journal of Selection and Assessment, 8,* 237–247.

Moscovici, S. (1985). Social influence and conformity. In G. Lindzey & E. Aronson (Eds.), *Handbook of social psychology* (3rd ed., vol. 2). New York: Random House.

Moser, T., Brandt, A., & Lysakowski, A. (2006). Hair cell ribbon synapses. *Cell Tissue Research, 326,* 347–359.

Moskowitz, J. T., Folkman, S., & Acree, M. (2003). Do positive psychological states shed light on recovery from bereavement? Findings from a 3-year longitudinal study. *Death Studies, 27,* 471–500.

Moskowitz, M., & Levering, R. (2007). 2007 "100 Best Companies to Work For" in America. http://www.greatplacetowork.com/best/100best2007.php

Moss, L. E., & Vaidya, N. A. (2006). Electroconvulsive therapy as an alternative treatment for obese patients with mood disorders. *Journal of Electroconvulsive Therapy, 22,* 223–225.

Mott, M. (2004, February 11). Seizure-alert dogs save humans with early warnings. *National Geographic News.* http://news.nationalgeographic. com/news/2003/04/0416_030416_seizuredogs.html (accessed January 15, 2007).

Mraz, M., Padak, N. D., & Rasinski, T. V. (2008). *Evidence-based instruction in reading.* Boston: Allyn & Bacon.

Mroczek, D. K., & Little, T. D. (Eds.). (2006). *Handbook of personality development.* Mahwah, NJ: Erlbaum.

Mroczek, D. K., & Spiro, A. (2005). Change in life satisfaction during adulthood: Findings from the Veterans Affairs Normative Aging Study. *Journal of Personality and Social Psychology, 88,* 189–202.

Mroczek, D. K., Spiro, A., & Griffin, P. W. (2006). Personality and aging. In J. E. Birren & K. W. Schaie (Eds.), *Handbook of the psychology of aging* (6th ed.). San Diego: Academic.

Mueser, K. T., & McGurk, S. R. (2004). Schizophrenia. *Lancet, 363,* 2063–2072.

Mufti, P., Setna, F., & Nazir, K. (2006). Early neonatal mortality: Effects of interventions on the survival of low birth babies weighing 1000-2000g. *Journal of the Pakistan Medical Association, 56,* 174–176.

Muggleton, N., Tsakanikos, E., Walsh, V., & Ward, J. (2007). Disruption of synaesthesia following TMS of the right posterior parietal cortex. *Neuropsychologia, 45,* 1582–1585.

Mulle, J. G., McDonough, J. A., Chowdari, K. V., Nimgaonkar, V., & Chakravarti, A. (2005). Evidence for linkage to chromosome 13q32 n: An independent sample of schizophrenia families. *Molecular Psychiatry, 10,* 429–431.

Mulveen, R., & Hepworth, J. (2006). An interpretative phenomenological analysis of participation in a pro-anorexia internet site and its relationship with disordered eating. *Journal of Health Psychology, 11,* 283–296.

Mulvenna, C. M., & Walsh, V. (2006). Synaesthesia: Supernatural integration? *Trends in Cognitive Neuroscience, 10,* 350–352.

Mumford, M. D. (Ed.). (2006). *Pathways to outstanding leadership.* Mahwah, NJ: Erlbaum.

Mumford, M. D., Scott, G., & Hunter, S. T. (2006). Theory—charismatic, ideological, and pragmatic leaders: How do they lead, why do they lead, and who do they lead? In M. D. Mumford (Ed.), *Pathways to outstanding leadership.* Mahwah, NJ: Erlbaum.

Munakata, Y. (2006). Information processing approaches to development. In W. Damon & R. Lerner (Eds.), *Handbook of child psychology* (6th ed.). New York: Wiley.

Murakami, I. (2006). Fixational eye movements and motion perception. *Progress in Brain Research, 154,* 193–209.

Murdock, B. B. (1999). The buffer 30 years later: Working memory in a theory of distributed associative model (TODAM). In C. Izawa (Ed.), *On human memory.* Mahwah, NJ: Erlbaum.

Murphy, K. R., Cronin, B. E., & Tam, A. P. (2003). Controversy and consensus regarding the use of cognitive ability testing in organizations. *Journal of Applied Psychology, 88,* 660–671.

Murray, E. A. (2007). Visual memory. *Annual Review of Neuroscience* (vol. 29). Palo Alto, CA: Annual Reviews.

Murray, H. A. (1938). *Explorations in personality.* Cambridge, MA: Harvard University Press.

Murray, S. L., Holmes, J. G., & Griffin, D. W. (2004). The benefits of positive illusions: Idealization and the construction of satisfaction in close relationships. In H. T. Reis & C. E. Rusbult (Eds.), *Close relationships: Key readings* (pp. 317–338). Philadelphia: Taylor & Francis.

Murray-Swank, A. B., Lucksted, A., Medoff, D. R., Yang, Y., Wohlheiter, K., & Dixon, L. B. (2006). Religiosity, psychosocial adjustment, and subjective burden of persons who care for those with mental illness. *Psychiatric Services, 57,* 361–365.

Myers, D. G. (2000). *A quiet world.* Hartford, CT: Yale University Press.

Myers, D. G., & Diener, E. (1995). Who is happy? *Psychological Science, 6,* 10–19.

Myers, G. E. (1986). *William James: His life and thought.* New Haven, CT: Yale University Press.

Mykletun, A., Bjerkeset, O., Dewey, M., Prince, M., Overland, S., & Stewart, R. (2007). Anxiety, depression, and cause-specific mortality: The Hunt Study. *Psychosomatic Medicine.* (in press)

N

Naar-King, S., Wright, K., Parsons, J. T., Frey, M., Templin, T., & Ondersma, S. (2006). Transtheoretical model and condom use in HIV-positive youths. *Health Psychology, 25,* 648–652.

Nachev, P., & Husain, M. (2006). Disorders of visual attention and the posterior parietal cortex. *Cortes, 42,* 766–773.

Naeem, F., Kingdon, D., & Turkington, D. (2006). Cognitive behavior therapy for schizophrenia: Relationship between anxiety symptoms and therapy. *Psychology and Psychotherapy, 79,* 153–164.

Nakano, H., & Blumstein S. E. (2004). Deficits in thematic integration processes in Broca's and Wernicke's aphasia. *Brain and Language, 88,* 96–107.

Nakao, T., Nakagawa, A., Yoshiura, T., Nakatani, E., Nabeyama, M., Yoshizato, C., Kudoh, A., Tada, K., Yoshioka, K., & Kawamoto, M. (2005). A functional MRI comparison of patients with obsessive-compulsive disorder and normal controls during a Chinese character Stroop task. *Psychiatry Research: Neuroimaging,139*(2), 101–114.

Nansel, T. R., Overpeck, M., Pilla, R. S., Ruan, W. J., Simons-Morton, B., & Scheidt, P. (2001). Bullying behaviors among US youth: Prevalence and association with psychosocial adjustment. *Journal of the American Medical Association, 285,* 2094–2100.

Narayanan, L., Menon, S., & Spector, P. E. (1999). A cross-cultural comparison of job stressors and reactions among employees holding comparable jobs in two countries. *International Journal of Stress Management, 6,* 197–212.

Nardi, A. E., Valencia, A. M., Mezzasalama, M. A., Levy, S. P., Lopes, F. L., Nasciemento, I., Freire, R. C., Veras, A. B., & Zin, W. A. (2006). Comparison of hyperventilation and breath-holding in panic disorder: Patients responsive and non-responsive to both tests. *Psychiatry Research, 142,* 201–208.

Nardi, P. M. (2006). *Doing survey research* (2nd ed.). Boston: Allyn & Bacon.

Nash, J. R., & Nutt, D. J. (2005). Pharmacotherapy of anxiety. *Handbook of Experimental Pharmacology, 169,* 469–501.

Nash, M. R. (2001). The truth and the hype about hypnosis. *Scientific American, 285,* 46–49, 52–55.

Nasrallah, H. A., & Lasser, R. (2006). Improving patient outcomes in schizophrenia: Achieving remission. *Journal of Psychopharmacology, 20,* Suppl. 6, S57–S61.

Nathan, P., & Langerbucher, J. (2003). Diagnosis and classification. In I. B. Weiner (Ed.), *Handbook of Psychology* (vol. 8). New York: Wiley.

Nathan, P. E. (1994). DSM-IV. *Journal of Clinical Psychology, 50,* 103–109.

Nation, M., & Heflinger, C. A. (2006). Risk factors for serious alcohol and drug use: The role of psychosocial variables in predicting the frequency of substance abuse among adolescents. *American Journal of Alcohol Abuse, 32,* 415–433.

National Alliance for the Mentally Ill, American Psychiatric Association, National Mental Health Association. (2005, June 24). *Joint statement in response to Tom Cruise's* Today Show *interview.* Author.

National Center for Health Statistics. (1994). Advance report of final mortality statistics, 1991. *Monthly Vital Statistics Report, 42.*

National Center for Health Statistics. (2002). *America's families and living arrangements.* Atlanta: Centers for Disease Control and Prevention.

National Center for Health Statistics. (2003). *Health United States 2002.* Atlanta: Centers for Disease Control and Prevention.

National Center for Health Statistics. (2004, December 10). *Teens delaying sexual activity.* Atlanta: Centers for Disease Control and Prevention.

National Center for Health Statistics. (2005). *Early release of selected estimates from Jan–Mar 2005 National Health Interview Survey.* Washington, DC: Author.

National Center for Health Statistics. (2005a). *Death statistics.* Atlanta: Centers for Disease Control and Prevention.

National Center for Health Statistics. (2006). *Vital and health statistics.* Atlanta: Centers for Disease Control and Prevention.

National Center for Health Statistics. (2006a). *Health United States, 2006.* Atlanta: Centers for Disease Control and Prevention.

National Center for Post-Traumatic Stress Disorder (PTSD). (2006). *Facts about PTSD.* www.ncptsd.va.gov (accessed November 25, 2006).

National Highway Traffic Safety Administration (NHTSA). (2001). *Traffic safety facts.* Washington, DC: Author.

National Institute on Drug Abuse (NIDA). (2005). *Research report: Inhalant abuse.* Washington DC: Author.

National Institute of Mental Health. (2000). *Suicide facts.* Washington, DC: Author. http://www.nimh.nih.gov/genpop/su_fact.htm (accessed January 26, 2000).

National Institute of Mental Health. (2006). *The numbers count: Mental disorders in America.* Fact Sheet. Washington, DC: National Institutes of Health.

National Institute of Mental Health. (2006a). *Suicide in the U.S.: Statistics and prevention.* Washington, DC: Author. http://www.nimh.nih.gov/publicat/harmsway.cfm

National Sleep Foundation. (2001). *2001 Sleep in America Poll.* Washington, DC: Author.

National Sleep Foundation. (2006). *2006 Sleep in America Poll.* Washington, DC: Author.

National Sleep Foundation. (2007, March 6). *Stressed-out American women have no time for sleep.* Washington DC: Author.

Naveh-Benjamin, M., Kilb, A., & Fisher, T. (2006). Concurrent task effects on memory encoding and retrieval: Further support for an asymmetry. *Memory and Cognition, 34,* 90–91.

Nave, K. A. (2007). Molecular biology of myelination. *Annual Review of Neuroscience* (vol. 30). Palo Alto, CA: Annual Reviews.

Needham, A. (2008). Learning in infants' object perception, object-directed action, and tool use. In A. Needham & A. Woodward (Eds.), *Learning and the infant mind.* New York: Oxford University Press. (in press)

Needham, A., Barrett, T., & Peterman, K. (2002). A pick-me-up for infants' exploratory skills: Early simulated experiences reaching for objects using "sticky mittens" enhances young infants' object exploration skills. *Infant Behavior and Development, 25,* 279–295.

Neisser, U., Boodoo, G., Bouchard, T. J., Boykin, A. W., Brody, N., Ceci, S. J., Halpern, D. F., Loehlin, J. C., Perloff, R., Sternberg, R. J., & Urbina, S. (1996). Intelligence: Knowns & unknowns. *American Psychologist, 51,* 77–101.

Neisser, U., & Harsch, N. (1992). Phantom flashbulbs: False recollections of hearing the news about Challenger. In E. Winograd & U. Neisser (Eds.), *Affect and accuracy in recall: Studies of "flashbulb" memories* (pp. 9–31). New York: Cambridge University Press.

Nelson, C. A. (2007). A developmental cognitive neuroscience approach to the study of atypical development: A model involving infants of diabetic mothers. In G. Dawson, K. Fischer, & D. Coch (Eds.), *Human behavior and the developing brain* (2nd ed.). New York: Guilford.

Nelson, C. A., Thomas, K. M., & de Haan, M. (2006). Neural bases of cognitive development. In W. Damon & R. Lerner (Eds.), *Handbook of child psychology* (6th ed.). New York: Wiley.

Nelson, D. L, & Gehlert, D. R. (2006). Central nervous system biogenic amine targets for control of appetite and energy expenditure. *Endocrine, 29*(1), 49–60.

Nelson, K. (1993). The psychological and social origins of autobiographical memory. *Psychological Science, 4,* 7–14.

Nemeroff, C. B., Bremner, J. D., Foa, E. B., Mayberg, H. S., North, C. S., & Stein, M. B. (2006). Posttraumatic stress disorder: A state-of-the-science review. *Journal of Psychiatric Research, 40*(1), 1–21.

Nes, L. S., & Segerstrom, S. C. (2006). Dispositional optimism and coping: A meta-analytic review. *Personality and Social Psychology Review, 10,* 235–251.

Neuman, W. L. (2007). *Basics of social research* (2nd ed.). Boston: Allyn & Bacon.

Neumann, I. D. (2007). Oxytocin: The neuropeptide of love reveals some of its secrets. *Cell Metabolism, 5,* 231–233.

Neverlien, P. O., & Johnsen, T. B. (1991). Optimism-pessimism dimension and dental anxiety in children aged 10–12. *Community Dentistry and Oral Epidemiology, 19,* 342–346.

Newcomer, J. W. (2006). Medical risks in patients with bipolar disorder and schizophrenia. *Journal of Clinical Psychiatry, 67, Suppl. 9,* S25–S30.

Newman, B. M., & Newman, P. R. (2007). *Theories of human development.* Mahwah, NJ: Erlbaum.

Newson, L., Richerson, P. J., & Boyd, R. (2007). Cultural evolution and the shaping of cultural diversity. In S. Kitayama & D. Cohen (Eds.), *Handbook of cultural psychology.* New York: Guilford.

Niaura, R., Todaro, J. F., Strood, L., Spiro, A, Ward, K. D., & Weiss, S. (2002). Hostility, the metabolic syndrome, and incident coronary heart disease. *Health Psychology, 21,* 588–593.

Nichols, C. D., & Sanders-Bush, E. (2002). A single dose of lysergic acid diethylamide influences gene expression patterns with the mammalian brain. *Neuropsychopharmacology, 26k,* 634–642.

Nickerson, R. S., & Adams, M. J. (1979). Long-term memory for a common object. *Cognitive Psychology, 11,* 287–307.

Nieuwstraten, C., Labiris, N. R., & Holbrook, A. (2006). Systematic overview of drug interactions with antidepressant medications. *Canadian Journal of Psychiatry, 51,* 300–316.

Niparko, J. K. (2004). Speech, language, and reading skills after early cochlear implantation. *Journal of the American Medical Association, 291,* 2378–2380.

Nisbett, R. E. (1987). Lay trait theory: Its nature, origins, and utility. In N. E. Grunberg, R. E. Nisbett, J. Rodin, & J. E. Singer (Eds.), *A distinctive approach to psychological research: The influence of Stanley Schachter.* Hillsdale, NJ: Erlbaum.

Nisbett, R. E., & Ross, L. (1980). *Human inference.* Upper Saddle River, NJ: Prentice-Hall.

Nobel, P. A., & Shiffrin, R. M. (2001). Retrieval processes in recognition and cued recall. *Journal of Experimental Psychology: Learning, Memory, and Cognition, 27,* 384–413.

Noe, R. A., Hollenbeck, J. R., Gerhart, B., & Wright, P. M. (2007). *Fundamentals of human resource management* (2nd ed.). New York: McGraw-Hill.

Nolen-Hoeksema, S. (1995). Gender differences in coping with depression across the lifespan. *Depression, 3,* 81–90.

Nolen-Hoeksema, S. (2000). The role of rumination in depressive disorders and mixed anxiety/depressive symptoms. *Journal of Abnormal Psychology, 109,* 504–511.

Nolen-Hoeksema, S. (2003). *Women who think too much: How to break free from overthinking and reclaim your life.* New York: Holt.

Nolen-Hoeksema, S. (2007). *Abnormal psychology* (4th ed.). New York: McGraw-Hill.

Nolen-Hoeksema, S., Girgus, J. S., & Seligman, M. E. P. (1992). Predictors and consequences of childhood depressive symptoms: A 5-year longitudinal study. *Journal of Abnormal Psychology, 101,* 405–422.

Nolen-Hoeksema, S., Larson, J., & Grayson, C. (1999). Explaining the gender difference in depressive symptoms. *Journal of Personality & Social Psychology, 77,* 1061–1072.

Nolen-Hoeksema, S., & Morrow, J. (1991). A prospective study of depression and distress following a natural disaster: The 1989 Loma Prieta earthquake. *Journal of Personality & Social Psychology, 61,* 105–121.

Nolen-Hoeksema, S., Stice, E., Wade, E., & Bohon, C. (2007). Reciprocal relations between rumination and bulimic, substance abuse, and depressive symptoms in female adolescents. *Journal of Abnormal Psychology, 116,* 198–207.

Norcross, J. C., Mrykalo, M. S., & Blagys, M. D. (2002). Auld lang syne: Success predictors, change processes, and self-reported outcomes of New Year's resolvers and nonresolvers. *Journal of Clinical Psychology, 58,* 397–405.

Norcross, J. C., & Newman, C. F. (1992). Psychotherapy integration: Setting the context. In J. C. Norcross & M. R. Gottfried (Eds.), *Handbook of psychotherapy integration.* New York: Basic Books.

Norcross, J. C., & Prochaska, J. O. (1988). A study of eclectic (and integrative) views revisited. *Professional Psychology: Research and Practice, 19,* 170–174.

Nordt, C., Rossler, W., & Lauber, C. (2006). Attitudes of mental health professionals Toward people with schizophrenia and major depression. *Schizophrenia Bulletin, 32,* 709–714.

Norenzayan, A., & Heine, S. J. (2005). Psychological universals: What are they and how can we know? *Psychological Bulletin, 131,* 763–784.

Norman, G., Eva, K., Brooks, L., & Hamstra, S. (2006). Expertise in medicine and surgery. In K. A. Ericsson, N. Charness, P. H. Feltovich, & R. R. Hoffman (Eds.), *The Cambridge handbook of expertise and expert performance.* New York: Cambridge University Press.

Norman, T. R., & Burrows, G. D. (2007). Emerging treatments for major depression. *Expert Review of Neurotherapeutics, 7,* 203–213.

Norman, W. T. (1963). Toward an adequate taxonomy of personality attributes. *Journal of Abnormal and Social Psychology, 66,* 574–583.

Northoff, G. (2007). Psychopathology and pathophysiology of the self in depression—neuropsychiatric hypothesis. *Journal of Affective Disorders.* (in press)

Nosek, B. A., & Banaji, M. R. (2007). Implicit attitude. In P. Wilken, T. Bayne, & A. Cleeremans (Eds.), *Oxford companion to consciousness.* Oxford: Oxford University Press.

Nosek, B. A., Greenwald, A. G., & Banaji, M. R. (2006). The Implicit Association Test at age 7: A methodological and conceptual review. In J. A. Bargh (Ed.), *Social psychology and the unconscious: The automaticity of higher mental processes* (pp. 265–292). New York: Psychology Press.

Notman, M. T., & Nadelson, C. C. (2002). Women's issues. In M. Hersen & W. H. Sledge (Eds.), *Encyclopedia of psychotherapy.* San Diego: Academic.

Nottelmann, E. D., Susman, E. J., Blue, J. H., Inoff-Germain, G., Dorn, L. D., Loriaux, D. L., Cutler, G. B., & Chrousos, G. P. (1987). Gonadal and adrenal hormone correlates of adjustment in early adolescence. In R. M. Lerner & T. T. Foch (Eds.), *Biological-psychological interactions in early adolescence.* Hillsdale, NJ: Erlbaum.

NOVA. (2001, April 17). *Cracking the code of life.* http://www.pbs.org/wgbh/nova/genome (accessed November 17, 2003).

Novie, G. J. (2007). Psychoanalytic theory. In D. Capuzzi & D. Gross (Eds.), *Counseling and psychotherapy* (4th ed.). Upper Saddle River, NJ: Prentice-Hall.

Numan, M. (2006). Hypothalamic neural circuits regulating maternal responsiveness toward infants. *Behavioral and Cognitive Neuroscience Reviews, 5,* 163–190.

Nunez, P. L., & Srinivasan, R. (2006). A theoretical basis for standing and traveling brain waves measured with human EEG with implications for an integrated consciousness. *Clinical Neurophysiology, 117,* 2424–2435.

Nutt, D. J. (2001). Neurobiological mechanisms in generalized anxiety disorder. *Journal of Clinical Psychology, 62, Suppl. 11,* 22–27.

Nyberg, L. (2004, August). *Imaging Cognition.* Paper presented at the 28th International Congress of Psychology, Beijing, China.

Nystul, M. S. (1999). *Introduction to counseling.* Boston: Allyn & Bacon.

O

O'Barr, W. M. (2006). Multiculturalism in the marketplace: Targeting Latinas, African American women, and gay consumers. *Advertising and Society Review, 7*(4). http://muse.jhu.edu/journals/advertising_and_society_review/

O'Brien, C. P. (2006). Benzodiazepine use, abuse, and dependence. *Journal of Clinical Psychiatry, 66, Suppl. 2,* S28–S33.

Occupational Safety and Health Administration. (2002). *Fact sheet.* Washington, DC: Author. http://www.osha.gov/OshDoc/data_General_Facts/factsheet-workplace-violence.pdf

Ochsner, K. N., & Gross, J. J. (2005). Putting the "I" and the "Me" in emotion regulation. *Trends in Cognitive Sciences, 9,* 409–410.

Offer, D., Ostrov, E., Howard, K. I., & Atkinson, R. (1988). *The teenage world: Adolescents' self-image in ten countries.* New York: Plenum.

Ogawa, K., Nittono, H., & Hori, T. (2005). Brain potentials before and after eye movements: An electrophysiological approach to dreaming in REM sleep. *Sleep, 28,* 1077–1082.

Ogilvie, R. D., & Wilkinson, R. T. (1988). Behavioral versus EEG-based monitoring of all-night sleep/wake patterns. *Sleep, 11*(2), 139–155.

O'Kearney, R. T., Anstey, K. J., & von Sanden, C. (2006). Behavioral and cognitive behavioral therapy for obsessive-compulsive disorder in children and adolescents. *Cochrance Database of Systematic Reviews, 4,* CD004856.

Olds, J. M. (1958). Self-stimulation experiments and differential reward systems. In H. H. Jasper, L. D. Proctor, R. S. Knighton, W. C. Noshay, & R. T. Costello (Eds.), *Reticular formation of the brain.* Boston: Little, Brown.

Olds, J. M., & Milner, P. M. (1954). Positive reinforcement produced by electrical stimulation of the septal area and other areas of the rat brain. *Journal of Comparative and Physiological Psychology, 47,* 419–427.

Olfson, M., Marcus, S. C., & Ascher-Svanum, H. (2007). Treatment of schizophrenia with long-acting fluphenazine, haloperidol, or risperidone. *Schizophrenia Bulletin.* (in press)

Oliver, M. B., & Hyde, J. S. (1993). Gender differences in sexuality: A meta-analysis. *Psychological Bulletin, 114,* 29–51.

Olson, I. R., Page, K., Moore, K. S., Chatterjee, A., & Verfaellie, M. (2006). Working memory for conjunctions relies on the temporal lobe. *Journal of Neuroscience, 26,* 4596–4601.

Olson, L. M., & Wahab, S. (2006). American Indians and suicide: A neglected area of research. *Trauma, Violence, and Abuse, 7,* 19–33.

Oltmanns, T. F., & Emery, R. E. (2007). *Abnormal psychology* (5th ed.). Upper Saddle River, NJ: Prentice-Hall.

Olweus, D. (1993). Bully/victim problems among schoolchildren: Long-term consequences and an effective intervention program. In S. Hodgins (Ed.), *Mental disorder and crime* (pp. 317–349). Thousand Oaks, CA: Sage.

Ones, D. S., & Viswesvaran, C. (1998). Gender, age, and race differences in overt integrity tests: Results across four large-scale job applicant datasets. *Journal of Applied Psychology, 83,* 35–42.

Ones, D. S., & Viswesvaran, C., & Schmidt, F. L. (1993). Comprehensive meta-analysis of integrity test validities: Finding and implications for personnel selection and theories of job performance. *Journal of Applied Psychology, 78,* 679–703.

Online Publishers Association. (2005, October). *Online paid content U.S. market spending report.* New York: Online Publishers Association and Comscore Networks.

Onur, E., Alkin, T., & Tural, U. (2006). Panic disorder subtypes: Further clinical differences. *Depression and Anxiety.* (in press)

Opp, M. R. (2006). Sleep and psychoneuroimmunology. *Neurological Clinics, 24,* 493–506.

Orbell, S., Hagger, M., Brown, V., & Tidy, J. (2006). Comparing two theories of health behavior: A prospective study of noncompletion of treatment following cervical cancer screening. *Health Psychology, 25,* 604–615.

Oren, D. A., & Terman, M. (1998). Tweaking the human circadian clock with light. *Science, 279,* 333–334.

Orfanidou, E., Marslen-Wilson, W. D., & Davis, M. H. (2006). Neural response suppression predicts repetition priming of spoken words and pseudowords. *Journal of Cognitive Neuroscience, 18,* 1237–1252.

Organ, D. W., & Ryan, K. (1995). A meta-analytic review of attitudinal and dispositional predictors of organizational citizenship behavior. *Personnel Psychology, 48,* 775–802.

Osborn, D. P. J., Nazareth, I., & King, M. B. (2006). Risk of coronary heart disease in people with severe mental illness: Cross-sectional comparative study in primary care. *British Journal of Psychiatry, 188,* 271–277.

Oshiro, Y., Quevado, A. S., McHaffie, J. G., Kraft, R. A., & Coghill, R. C. (2007). Brain mechanisms supporting spatial discrimination of pain. *Journal of Neuroscience, 27,* 3388–3394.

Osipow, S. (2000). Work. In A. Kazdin (Ed.), *Encyclopedia of psychology.* Washington, DC, and New York: American Psychological Association and Oxford University Press.

Ost, L. (1991). Acquisition of blood and injection phobia and anxiety response patterns in clinical patients. *Behavior and Research Therapy, 23,* 263–282.

Ostir, G. V., Markides, K. S., Black, S. A., & Goodwin, J. S. (2000). Emotional well-being predicts subsequent functional independence and survival. *Journal of the American Geriatrics Society, 48,* 473–478.

Ostroff, C., & Judge, T. A. (Eds.). (2007). *Perspectives on organizational fit.* Mahwah, NJ: Erlbaum.

Otake, K., Shimai, S., Tanaka-Matsumi, J., Otsui, K., & Fredrickson, B. L. (2006). Happy people becoming happier through kindness: A counting kindnesses intervention. *Journal of Happiness Studies, 7,* 361–375.

Ovando, C. J., Combs, M. C., & Collier, V. P. (2006). *Bilingual education and ESL classrooms* (4th ed.). New York: McGraw-Hill.

Owen, A. M., Coleman, M. R., Boly, M., Davis, M. H., Laureys, S., & Pickard, J. D. (2006). Detecting awareness in the vegetative state. *Science, 313,* 1402.

Ozer, D. J., & Benet-Martinez, V. (2006). Personality and the prediction of consequential outcomes. *Annual Review of Psychology* (vol. 57). Palo Alto, CA: Annual Reviews.

Ozer, D. J., & Riese, S. P. (1994). Personality assessment. *Annual Review of Psychology* (vol. 45). Palo Alto, CA: Annual Reviews.

P

Padilla, A. M. (2006). Second language learning. In P. A. Alexander & P. H. Winne (Eds.), *Handbook of educational psychology* (2nd ed.). Mahwah, NJ: Erlbaum.

Pagsberg, A. K., & others. (2007). Structural brain abnormalities in early onset first-episode psychosis. *Journal of Neural Transmission, 114,* 489–498.

Paivio, A. (1971). *Imagery and verbal processes.* New York: Holt, Rinehart & Winston.

Paivio, A. (1986). *Mental representations: A dual coding approach.* New York: Oxford University Press.

Paivio, A. (2007). *Mind and its evolution.* Mahwah, NJ: Erlbaum.

Palmer, S., Davidson, K., Tyrer, P., Gumley, A., Tata, P., Norrie, J., Murray, H., & Seivewright, H. (2006). The cost-effectiveness of cognitive behavior therapy for borderline personality disorder: Results from the BOSCOT trial. *Journal of Personality Disorders, 20,* 466–481.

Palmieri, P. A., & Fitzgerald, L. F. (2005). Confirmatory factor analysis of posttraumatic stress symptoms in sexually harassed women. *Journal of Traumatic stress, 18,* 657–666.

Pan, B. A., Rowe, M. L., Singer, J. D., & Snow, C. E. (2005). Maternal correlates of growth in toddler vocabulary development in low-income families. *Child Development, 76,* 763–782.

Pan, F., & Massey, S. C. (2007). Rod and cone input to horizontal cells in the rabbit retina. *Journal of Comparative Neurology, 500,* 815–831.

Pandi-Perumal, S. R., Srinivasan, V., Poeggeler, B., Hardeland, R., & Cardinali, D. P. (2007). Drug insight: The use of melatonergic agonists for the treatment of insomnia-focus on ramelteon. *Nature Clinical Practice: Neurology, 3,* 221–228.

Park, C. L. (2004). Positive and negative consequences of alcohol consumption in college students. *Addictive Behaviors, 29,* 311–321.

Park, C. L. (2007). Religious and spiritual issues in health and aging. In C. M. Aldwin, C. L. Park, & A. Spiro (Eds.), *Handbook of health psychology and aging.* New York: Guilford.

Park, C. L., & Adler, N. E. (2003). Coping style as a predictor of health and well-being across the first year of medical school. *Health Psychology, 22,* 627–631.

Park, H. S., Shin, Y. W., Ha, T. H., Shin, M. S., Kim, Y. Y., Lee, Y. H., & Kwon, J. S. (2006). Effect of cognitive training focusing on organizational strategies in patients with obsessive-compulsive disorder. *Psychiatry and Clinical Neuroscience, 60,* 718–726.

Park, M. A. (2008). *Biological anthropology* (5th ed.). New York: McGraw-Hill.

Parke, R. D., & Buriel, R. (2006). Socialization in the family: Ethnic and ecological perspectives. In W. Damon & R. Lerner (Eds.), *Handbook of child psychology* (6th ed.). New York: Wiley.

Parker, G., & Fletcher, K. (2007). Treating depression with the evidence-based psychotherapies: A critique of the evidence. *Acta Psychiatrica Scandinavica, 115*(5), 352–359.

Parker, P. S. (2006). *Race, gender, and leadership.* Mahwah, NJ: Erlbaum.

Parks, M. R. (2007). *Personal relationships and personal networks.* Mahwah, NJ: Erlbaum.

Parra, L. C., & Pearlmutter, B. A. (2007). Illusory percepts from auditory adaptation. *Journal of the Acoustical Society of America, 121,* 1632–1641.

Parry, A., & Matthews, P. M. (2002). Functional magnetic resonance imaging: A window into the brain *Interdisciplinary Science Reviews, 27,* 50–60.

Parslow, R. A., Jorm, A. F., & Christensen, H. (2006). Associations of pre-trauma attributes and trauma exposure with screening positive for PTSD: Analysis of a community-based study of 2085 young adults. *Psychological Medicine, 36,* 387–395.

Parsons, H. M. (1974). What happened at Hawthorne? *Science, 183,* 922–932.

Parsons, M. (2006). The analyst's countertransference to the psychoanalytic process. *International Journal of Psychoanalysis, 87,* 1183–1198.

Partners for Life. (2007). *Partners for life: A service dog's tale.* http://cals. arizona.edu/agdiv/servicedog/ (accessed April 10, 2007).

Passafiume, D., Di Giacomo, & Carolei, A. (2006). Word-stem completion task to investigate semantic network in patients with Alzheimer's disease. *European Journal of Neurology, 13,* 460–464.

Pasupathy, A. (2006). Neural basis of shape representation in the primate brain. *Progress in Brain Research, 154,* 293–313.

Patten, S. B., Wang, J. L., Williams, J. V., Currie, S., Beck, C. A., Maxwell, C. A., & el-Guebaly, N. (2006). Descriptive epidemiology of major depression in Canada. *Canadian Journal of Psychology, 51,* 84–90.

Pattenden, S., & others. (2006). Parental smoking and children's respiratory health: Independent effects of prenatal and postnatal exposure. *Tobacco Control, 15,* 294–301.

Patterson, E. B. (1991). Poverty, income inequality, and community crime rates. *Criminology, 29,* 755–776.

Patterson, T. G., & Joseph, S. (2007). Person-centered personality theory: Support from self determination theory and positive psychology. *Journal of Humanistic Psychology, 47,* 117–139.

Paulus, P. B. (1989). An overview and evaluation of group influence. In P. B. Paulus (Ed.), *Psychology of group influence.* Mahwah, NJ: Erlbaum.

Paunonen, S., Jackson, D., Trzebinski, J., & Forserling, F. (1992). Personality structures across cultures: A multimethod evaluation. *Journal of Personality and Social Psychology, 62,* 447–456.

Pav, M., Kovru, H., Fiserova, A., & Lisa, V. (2007). Neurobiological aspects of depressive disorder and antidepressant treatment: Role of glia. *Physiological Research.* (in press)

Pavlov, I. P. (1927). *Conditioned reflexes* (G. V. Anrep, trans.). New York: Dover.

Payne, B. K. (2001). Prejudice and perception: The role of automatic and controlled processes in misperceiving a weapon. *Journal of Personality and Social Psychology, 81,* 181–192.

Paz, R., Pelletier, J. G., Bauer, E. P., & Pare, D. (2006). Emotional enhancement of memory via amygdala-driven facilitation of rhinal interactions. *Nature Neuroscience, 9,* 1321–1329.

PBS.org. (2007). *Sound and fury.* http://www.pbs.org/wnet/soundandfury/ (accessed November 12, 2006).

Pearce, J. M. (2007). Synaesthesia. *European Neuroscience, 57,* 120–124.

Pearson, C. M., Andersson, L. M., & Porath, C. L. (2005). Workplace incivility. In S. Fox & P. E. Spector (Eds.), *Counterproductive work behavior: Investigations of actors and targets* (pp. 177–200). Washington, DC: American Psychological Association.

Pearson, D. G. (2006). Rehearsal processes in visuo-spatial working memory. *Cognitive Processes, 7, Suppl. 5,* S163.

Pearson, N. J., Johnson, L. L., & Nahin, R. L. (2006). Insomnia, trouble sleeping, and complementary and alternative medicine: Analysis of the 2002 National Health Interview Survey data. *Archives of Internal Medicine, 166,* 1775–1782.

Pedersen, P. B., Lonner, W. J., Draguns, J. G., & Trimble, J. E. (Eds.). (2007). *Counseling across cultures* (6th ed.). Thousand Oaks, CA: Sage.

Peeters, A., Barendregt, J. J., Willekens, F., Mackenbach, J. P., Al Mamun, A., Bonneux, L. (2003). Obesity in adulthood and its consequences for life expectancy: A Life-Table analysis. *Annals of Internal Medicine, 138,* 24–32.

Peláez, J. I., & Dona, J. M. (2006). A majority model in group decision making using QMA-OWA operators. *International Journal of Intelligent Systems, 21,* 193–208.

Peleg, G., Katzier, G., Peleg, O., Kamara, M., Brodskey, L., Hel-Or, H., Keren, D., & Nevo, E. (2006). Hereditary family signature of facial expression. *Proceedings of the National Academy of Science USA, 103,* 15921–15926.

Penedo, F. J., & others. (2004). Cognitive-behavioral stress management improves stress management skills and quality of life in men recovering from treatment of prostate carcinoma. *Cancer, 100,* 192–200.

Penedo, F. J., Molton, I., Dahn, J. R., Shen, B. J., Kinsinger, D., Traeger, L., Siegel, S., Schneiderman, N., & Antoni, M. (2006). A randomized clinical trial of group-based cognitive-behavioral stress management in localized prostate cancer: Development of stress management skills improves quality of life and benefit finding. *Annals of Behavioral Medicine, 31,* 261–270.

Penfield, W. (1947). Some observations in the cerebral cortex of man. *Proceedings of the Royal Society, 134,* 349.

Pennebaker, J. W. (1997a). *Opening up: The healing power of expressing emotions* (rev. ed.). New York: Guilford.

Pennebaker, J. W. (1997b). Writing about emotional experiences as a therapeutic experience. *Psychological Science, 8,* 162–166.

Pennebaker, J. W. (2004). *Writing to heal: A guided journal for recovering from trauma emotional upheaval.* Oakland, CA: New Harbinger Press.

Pennebaker, J. W., & Chung, C. K. (2007). Expressive writing, emotional upheavals, and health. In H. S. Friedman & R. C. Silver (Eds.), *Foundations of health psychology* (pp. 263–284). New York: Oxford University Press.

Pennebaker, J. W., & Graybeal, A. (2001). Patterns of natural language use: Disclosure, personality, and social integration. *Current Directions in Psychological Science, 32,* 90–93.

Penner, L. A., Dovidio, J. F., Piliavin, J. A., & Schroeder, D. A. (2005). Prosocial behavior: Multilevel perspectives. *Annual Review of Psychology* (vol. 56). Palo Alto, CA: Annual Reviews.

Penney, L.M., & Spector, P. E. (2005). Job stress, incivility, and counterproductive work behavior (CWB): The moderating role of negative affectivity. *Journal of Organizational Behavior, 26,* 777–796.

Peplau, L. A. (2003). Human sexuality: How do men and women differ? *Current Directions in Psychological Science, 12,* 37–40.

Peplau, L. A., & Fingerhut, A. W. (2007). The close relationships of lesbians and gay men. *Annual Review of Psychology* (vol. 58). Palo Alto, CA: Annual Reviews.

Peplau, L. A., Fingerhut, A., & Beals, K. P. (2004). Sexuality in the relationships of lesbians and gay men. In J. H. Harvey & K. Wenzel (Eds.), *The handbook of sexuality in close relationships.* Mahwah, NJ: Erlbaum.

Perera, T. D., & others. (2007). Antidepressant-induced neuorogenesis in the hippocampus of adult nonhuman primates. *Journal of Neuroscience, 27,* 4894–4901.

Perkins, D. (1994, September). Creativity by design. *Educational Leadership,* 18–25.

Perkins, K. A., Marcus, M. D., Levine, M. D., D'Amico, D., Miller, A., Broge, M., Ashcom, J., & Shiffman, S. (2001). Cognitive-behavioral therapy to reduce weight concerns improves smoking cessation outcome in weight-concerned women. *Journal of Consulting and Clinical Psychology, 69,* 604–613.

Perls, F. (1969). *Gestalt therapy verbatim.* Lafayette, CA: Real People Press.

Perner, L. (2001). *The psychology of consumers.* Unpublished manuscript, George Washington University, Washington, DC.

Pert, A. B., & Snyder, S. H. (1973). Opiate receptor: Demonstration in a nervous tissue. *Science, 179,* 1011.

Pert, C. B. (1999). *Molecules of emotion.* New York: Simon & Schuster.

Peters, A., Conrad, M., Hubold, C., Schweiger, U., Fischer, B., & Fehm, H. L. (2007). The principle of homeostasis in the hypothalamus-pituitary-adrenal system: New insight from positive feedback. *American Journal of Physiology: Regulatory, Integrative, and Comparative Physiology.* (in press)

Petersen, T. J. (2006). Enhancing the efficacy of antidepressants with psychotherapy. *Journal of Psychopharmacology, 20, Suppl. 3,* S19–S28.

Peterson, C. (2006). *A primer in positive psychology.* New York: Oxford University Press.

Peterson, C., Park, N., & Seligman, M. E. P. (2006). Greater strengths of character and recovery from illness. *Journal of Positive Psychology, 1,* 17–26.

Peterson, C., & Seligman, M. E. P. (2003). Character strengths before and after September 11. *Psychological Science, 14,* 381–384.

Peterson, C., Seligman, M. E. P., & Vaillant, G. E. (1988). Pessimistic explanatory style is a risk factor for physical illness: A thirty-five year longitudinal study. *Journal of Personality and Social Psychology, 55,* 23–27.

Peterson, G. B. (2004). A day of great illumination: B. F. Skinner's discovery of shaping. *Journal of the Experimental Analysis of Behavior, 82,* 317–328.

Peterson, N. G., & Jeanneret, P. R. (2007). Job analysis: An overview and description of deductive methods. In D. L. Whetzel & G. R. Wheaton (Eds.), *Applied measurement.* Mahwah, NJ: Erlbaum.

Petrill, S. A. (2003). The development of intelligence: Behavioral genetic approaches. In R. J. Sternberg, J. Lautrey & T. I. Lubert (Eds.), *Models of intelligence: International perspectives.* Washington, DC: American Psychological Association.

Pettigrew, T. F., & Tropp, L. R. (2006). A meta-analytic test of intergroup contact theory. *Journal of Personality and Social Psychology, 90,* 751–783.

Petty, R. E., & Cacioppo, J. T. (1986). The elaboration likelihood of persuasion. In L. Berkowitz (Ed.), *Advances in experimental social psychology* (vol. 19). New York: Academic.

Petty, R. E., Wheeler, S. C., & Bizer, G. Y. (2000). Attitude functions and persuasion: An elaboration likelihood approach to matched versus mismatched messages. In G. R. Maio & J. M. Olson (Eds.), *Why we evaluate.* Mahwah, NJ: Erlbaum.

Pew Research Center. (2007, January 9). *A portrait of "Generation Next": How young people view their lives, futures and politics.* Washington, DC: Pew Research Center for the People and the Press.

Peyser, M. (2001, April 16). When "chains of love" becomes chains of fools. *Newsweek, 137,* 58–59.

Phares, V. (2007). *Understanding abnormal child psychology* (2nd ed.). New York: Wiley.

Phelan, M., Stradins, L., & Morrison, S. (2001). Physical health of people with severe mental illness. *British Medical Journal, 322,* 443–444.

Phelan, S., Hill, J. O., Lang, W., Dibello, J. R., Wing, R. R. (2003). Recovery from relapse among successful weight maintainers. *American Journal of Clinical Nutrition, 78,* 1079–1084.

Phelps, E. A. (2006). Emotion and cognition: Insights from studies of the human amygdala. *Annual Review of Psychology* (vol. 57). Palo Alto, CA: Annual Reviews.

Phelps, E. A., & LeDoux, J. E. (2005). Contributions of the amygdala to emotion processing: From animal models to human behavior. *Neuron, 48,* 175–187.

Phinney, J. S. (1989). Stages of ethnic identity development in minority group adolescents. *Journal of Early Adolescence, 9,* 34–49.

Phinney, J. S. (2003). Ethnic identity and acculturation. In K. M. Chun, P. B. Organista, & G. Marin (Eds.) *Acculturation.* Washington, DC: American Psychological Association.

Phinney, J. S. (2006). Ethnic identity exploration in emerging adulthood. In J. Arnett, J. Jensen, & J. L. Tanner (Eds.), *Emerging adults in America: Coming of age in the 21st century* (pp. 117–134). Washington, DC: American Psychological Association.

Phinney, J. S., Berry, J. W., Berry, D. L., & Vedder, S. P. (2006). Understanding immigrant youth: Conclusions and implications. In J. W. Berry, J. S. Phinney, D. L. Sam, & S. P. Vedder (Eds.), *Immigrant youth in cultural transmission.* Mahwah, NJ: Erlbaum.

Piaget, J. (1952). *The origins of intelligence in children.* New York: Oxford University Press.

Piaget, J., & Inhelder, B. (1969). *The child's conception of space* (F. J. Langdon & J. L. Lunzer, trans.). New York: Norton.

Picchioni, M. M., Toulopoulou, T., Landau, S., Davies, N., Ribchester, T., & Murray, R. M. (2006). Neurological abnormalities in schizophrenic twins. *Biological Psychiatry, 59,* 341–348.

Pillemer, D. B. (1984). Flashbulb memories of the assassination attempt on President Reagan. *Cognition, 16,* 63–80

Pillemer, D. B. (1998). *Momentous events: Vivid memories.* Cambridge, MA: Harvard University Press.

Pinel, E. C., Long, A. E., Landau, M. J., Alexander, K., & Pyszczynski, T. (2006). Seeing I to I: A pathway to interpersonal connectedness. *Journal of Personality and Social Psychology, 90,* 243–257.

Pines, A. M., & Maslach, C. (2002). *Experiencing social psychology* (4th ed.). New York: McGraw-Hill.

Pinker, S. (1994). *The language instinct.* New York: William Morrow.

Pinker, S. (2007). The mystery of consciousness. *Time, 169,* 58–62.

Piolino, P., Desgranges, B., Clarys, D., Guillery-Girard, B., Taconnat, L., Isingrini, M., & Eustache, F. (2006). Autobiographical memory, autonoetic consciousness, and self-perspective in aging. *Psychology and Aging, 21,* 510–525.

Pipes, M. E., Lamb, M. E., Orbach, Y., & Cederborg, A. C. (Eds.). (2007). *Child sexual abuse.* Mahwah, NJ: Erlbaum.

Pitkanen, T., Lyyra, A. L., & Pulkkinen, L. (2005). Age of onset of drinking and the use of alcohol in adulthood: A follow-up study for age 8–42 for females and males. *Addiction, 100,* 652–661.

Pittenger, C., Sanacora, G., & Krystal, J. H. (2007). The NDMA receptor as a therapeutic target in major depressive disorder. *CNS and Neurological Disorders: Drug Targets, 6,* 101–115.

Plant, E. A., & Peruche, B. M. (2005). The consequences of race for police officers' responses to criminal suspects. *Psychological Science, 16,* 180–183.

Plante, G. E. (2006). Sleep and vascular disorders. *Metabolism, 55, Suppl. 2,* S45–S49.

Plessner, H., Betsch, C., & Betsch, T. (Eds.). (2007). *Intuition and decision making.* Mahwah, NJ: Erlbaum.

Pliquett, R. U., Fuhrer, D., Falk, S., Zysset, S., von Carmon, D. Y., & Stumvoli, M. (2006). The effects of insulin on the central nervous system—focus on appetite regulation. *Hormone and Metabolic Research, 38,* 442–446.

Plomin, R., & Craig, I. (2001). Genetics, environment, and cognitive abilities: Review and work in progress toward a genome scan for quantitative trait locus associations using DNA pooling. *British Journal of Psychiatry, 40,* 41–48.

Plomin, R., DeFries, J. C., & Fulker, D. W. (2007). *Nature and nurture during infancy and early childhood.* New York: Cambridge University Press.

Poehlmann, J., Clements, M., Abbeduto, L., & Farsad, V. (2005). Family experiences associated with a child's diagnosis of Fragile X or Down syndrome: Evidence for disruption and resilience. *Mental Retardation, 43,* 255–267.

Pollard, I. (2007). Neuropharmacology of drugs and alcohol in mother and fetus. *Seminars in Fetal and Neonatal Medicine, 12,* 106–113.

Pomerantz, E. M., Saxon, J. L., & Oishi, S. (2000). The psychological trade-offs of goal investment. *Journal of Personality and Social Psychology, 79,* 617–630.

Pompili, M., Amador, X. F., Girardi, P., Harkavy-Friedman, J., & others. (2007). Suicide risk in schizophrenia: Learning from the past to change the future. *Annals of General Psychiatry, 6,* 10.

Pompili, M., Mancinelli, I., Kotzalidis, G. D., Girardi, P. & Tatrelli, R. (2005). Where schizophrenic patients commit suicide: A review of suicide among inpatients and former inpatients. *International Journal of Psychiatry and Medicine, 35,* 171–190.

Pomplum, M., Reingold, E. M., & Shen, J. (2001). Investigating the visual span in comparative search: The effects of task difficulty and divided attention. *Cognition, 81,* B57–67.

Popenoe, D., & Whitehead, B. D. (2005). *The state of our unions, 2005.* New Brunswick, NJ: Rutgers University Press.

Popenoe, D., & Whitehead, B. D. (2006). *The state of our unions: 2006.* New Brunswick, NJ: The National Marriage Project.

Popham, W. J. (2002). *Classroom assessment* (2nd ed.). Boston: Allyn & Bacon.

Popp, A. (2006, November). *Inequality and segregation as correlates of urban crime rates.* Paper presented at the annual meeting of the American Society of Criminology (ASC), Los Angeles.

Portnuff, C. D. F., & Fligor, B. J. (October, 2006). *Output levels of portable music players.* Presented at the American Auditory Society Conference, Cincinnati.

Posner, M. I., & Rothbart, M. K. (2007). Research on attention networks as a model for integration of psychological science. *Annual Review of Psychology* (vol. 58). Palo Alto, CA: Annual Reviews.

Postmes, T., & Jetten, J. (2006). Reconciling individuality and the group. In T. Potmes & J. Jetten (Eds.), *Individuality and the group: Advances in social identity* (pp. 258–269). Thousand Oaks, CA: Sage.

Powell, D. R. (2006). Families and early childhood interventions. In W. Damon & R. Lerner (Eds.), *Handbook of child psychology* (6th ed.). New York: Wiley.

Powell, H. W., & others. (2006). Hemispheric asymmetries in language-related pathways: A combined functional MRI and tractography study. *Neuroimage, 32,* 388–399.

Poythress, N. G., Skeem, J. L., & Lilienfeld, S. O. (2006). Associations among early abuse, dissociation, and psychopathy in an offender sample. *Journal of Abnormal Psychology, 115,* 288–297.

Prentice, W. E. (2007). *Get fit—stay fit* (4th ed.). New York: McGraw-Hill.

Prescott, T. J., & Humphries, M. D. (2007). Who dominates the dark basements of the brain? *Behavioral and Brain Sciences, 30,* 104–105.

Pressley, M., & Harris, K. R. (2006). Cognitive strategies instruction: From basic research to classroom instruction. In P. A. Alexander & P. H. Winne (Eds.), *Handbook of educational psychology* (2nd ed.). Mahwah, NJ: Erlbaum.

Pressley, M., & Hilden, K. (2006). Cognitive strategies. In W. Damon & R. Lerner (Eds.), *Handbook of child psychology* (6th ed.). New York: McGraw-Hill.

Pressman, J. (1998). *Last resort, Psychosurgery and the limits of medicine.* New York: Cambridge University Press.

Pressman, S. D., & Cohen, S. (2005). Does positive affect influence health? *Psychological Bulletin, 131,* 925–971.

Pritzker, M. A. (2002). The relationship among CEO dispositional attributes, transformational leadership behaviors and performance effectiveness. *Dissertation Abstracts International, 62*(12-B), 6008 (UMI No. AAI3035464).

Prochaska, J. O., DiClemente, C. C., & Norcross, J. C. (1992). In search of how people change: Applications to addictive behaviors. *American Psychologist, 47,* 1102–1114.

Prochaska, J. O., & Norcross, J. C. (2007). *Systems of psychotherapy* (6th ed.). Belmont, CA: Wadsworth.

Prochaska, J. O., Norcross, J. C., & DiClemente, C. C. (1994). *Changing for good: A revolutionary six-stage program for overcoming bad habits and moving your life positively forward.* New York: Avon Books.

Prouix, M. J. (2007). Bottom-up guidance in visual search for conjuctions. *Journal of Experimental Psychology: Human Perception and Performance, 33,* 48–56.

Provenzo, E. F. (2002). *Teaching, learning, and schooling in American culture: A critical perspective.* Boston: Allyn & Bacon.

Pukrop, R., Sass, H., & Steinmeyer, E. M. (2000). Circumplex models for the similarity relationships between higher-order factors of personality and personality disorders: An empirical analysis. *Contemporary Psychiatry, 41,* 438–445.

Putnam, S. P., Sanson, A. V., & Rothbart, M. K. (2002). Child temperament and parenting. In M. Bornstein (Ed.), *Handbook of parenting* (2nd ed.). Mahwah, NJ: Erlbaum.

Pyati, S., & Gan, T. J. (2007). Perioperative pain management. *CNS Drugs, 21,* 185–211.

Q

Quickfall, J., & el-Guebaly, N. (2006). Genetics and alcoholism: How close are we to potential applications? *Canadian Journal of Psychiatry, 51,* 461–467.

Quinn, J. G., & McConnell, J. (2006). The interval for interference in conscious visual imagery. *Memory, 14,* 241–252.

Quinsey, V. L. (2003). Etiology of anomalous sexual preferences in men. *Annals of the New York Academy of Sciences, 989,* 105–117.

Quintero-Gallego, E. A., Gomez, C. M., Casares, E. V., Marquez, J., & Perez-Santamaria, F. J. (2006). Declarative and procedural learning in children and adolescents with posterior fossa tumors. *Behavioral and Brain Functions, 15,* 9.

R

Raabe, B., & Beehr, T. A. (2003). Formal mentoring versus supervisor and co-worker relationships: Differences in perceptions and impact. *Journal of Organizational Behavior, 24,* 271–293.

Rabasca, L. (2000, June) More psychologists in the trenches. *Monitor on psychology, 31,* 50–51.

Radley, J. J., Johnson, L. R., Janssen, W. G., Martino, J., Lamprecht, R., Hof, P. R., LeDoux, J. E., & Morrison, J. H. (2006). Associative Pavlovian conditioning leads to an increase in spinophilin-immunoreactive dendritic spines in the lateral amygdale. *European Journal of Neuroscience, 24,* 876–884.

Radvansky, G. (2006). *Human memory.* Upper Saddle River, NJ: Prentice-Hall.

Ragins, B. R., Cotton, J. L., & Miller, J. S. (2000). Marginal mentoring: The effects of type of mentor, quality of relationship, and program design on work and career attitudes. *Academy of Management Journal, 43,* 1177–1194.

Ragland, J. D., McCarthy, E., Bilker, W. B., Brensinger, C. M., Valdez, J., Kohler, C., Gur, R. E., & Gur, R. C. (2006). Levels-of-processing effect on internal source monitoring in schizophrenia. *Psychological Medicine, 36,* 641–648.

Raichle, M. E., & Mintun, M. A. (2006). Brain work and brain imaging. *Annual Review of Neuroscience* (vol. 29). Palo Alto, CA: Annual Reviews.

Räikkönen, K., Matthews, K. A., Flory, J. D., Owens, J. F., & Gump, B. B. (1999). Effects of optimism, pessimism, and trait anxiety on ambulatory blood pressure and mood during everyday life. *Journal of Personality and Social Psychology, 76,* 104–113.

Rakic, P. (2002). Neurogenesis in adult primate neocortex: An evaluation of the evidence. *Nature Reviews: Neuroscience, 3,* 65–71.

Ramey, C. T., Ramey, S. L., & Lanzi, R. G. (2006). Children's health and education. In W. Damon & R. Lerner (Eds.), *Handbook of child psychology* (6th ed.). New York: Wiley.

Ramsey, J. L., Langlois, J. H., Hoss, R. A., Rubenstein, A. J., & Griffin, A. M. (2004) Origins of a stereotype: Categorization of facial attractiveness by 6-month-old infants. *Developmental Science. 7*(2), 201–211.

Rapaport, D. (1967). On the psychoanalytic theory of thinking. In M. M. Gill (Ed.), *The collected papers of David Rapaport.* New York: Basic Books.

Rapaport, S. (1994, November 28). Interview. *U.S. News and World Report,* 94.

Rappaport, J. L. (1989, March). The biology of obsessions and compulsions. *Scientific American,* 83–89.

Rathunde, K., & Csikszentmihalyi, M. (2006). The developing person: An experiential perspective. In W. Damon & R. Lerner (Eds.), *Handbook of child psychology* (6th ed.). New York: Wiley.

Ratner, N. B. (1993). Learning to speak. *Science, 262,* 260.

Rauch, S. L., Shin, L. M., & Phelps, E. A. (2006). Neurocircuitry models of posttraumatic stress disorder and extinction: Human neuroimaging research—past, present, and future. *Biological Psychiatry, 60,* 376–382.

Rawson, N. E., & Yee, K. K. (2006). Transduction and coding. *Advances in Otorhinolaryngology, 63,* 23–43.

Ray, R. D., Ochsner, K. N., Cooper, J. C., Robertson, E. R., Gabrieli, J. D. E., & Gross, J. J. (2005). Individual differences in trait rumination and the neural systems supporting cognitive reappraisal. *Cognitive, Affective & Behavioral Neuroscience, 5,* 156–168.

Raynor, H. A., Jeffrey, R. W., Phelan, S., Hill, J. O., & Wing, R. R. (2005). Amount of food groups variety consumed in the diet and long term weight loss maintenance. *Obesity Research, 13,* 883–890.

Raz, A. (2007). Suggestibility and hypnotizability: Mind the gap. *American Journal of Clinical Hypnosis, 49,* 205–210.

Recanzone, G. H., & Sutter, M. L. (2008). The biological basis of audition. *Annual Review of Psychology* (vol. 59). Palo Alto, CA: Annual Reviews.

Rector, N. A., & Beck, A. T. (2001). Cognitive behavioral therapy for schizophrenia: An empirical review. *Journal of Nervous and Mental Disorders, 189,* 278–287.

Redding, R. E. (2006). The brain-disordered defendant: Neuroscience and legal insanity in the twenty-first century. *American University Law Review, 56,* 51–127.

Ree, M. J., & Carretta, T. R. (2007). Tests of cognitive ability. In D. L. Whetzel & G. R. Wheaton (Eds.), *Applied measurement.* Mahwah, NJ: Erlbaum.

Rees, G. (2007). Neural correlates of the contents of visual awareness in humans. *Philosophical Transactions of the Royal Society of London. Series B. Biological Sciences, 261,* 877–886.

Rees, V. W., & Connolly, G. N. (2006). Measuring air quality to protect children from second-hand smoke in cars. *American Journal of Preventive Medicine, 31,* 363–368.

Reeve, C. (2000, May 1). Use the body's repair kit. *Time, 155,* 18,

Reid, P. T. (2002). Multicultural psychology: Bringing together gender and ethnicity. *Cultural Diversity & Ethnic Minority Psychology, 8*(2), 103–114.

Reid, P. T., & Zalk, S. R. (2001). Academic environments: Gender and ethnicity in U.S. higher education. In J. Worrell (Ed.), *Encyclopedia of women and gender.* New York: Oxford University Press.

Reiman, E. M. (2007). Linking brain imaging and genomics in the study of Alzheimer's disease and aging. *Annals of the New York Academy of Sciences, 1097,* 94–113.

Reimer, T., & Rieskamp, J. (2007). Fast and frugal heuristics. In R. F. Baumeister & K. D. Vohs (Eds.), *Encyclopedia of social psychology.* Thousand Oaks, CA: Sage.

Reinders, A. A., Nijenhuis, E. R., Quak, J., Koft, J., Haaksam, J., Paans, A. M., Willemsen, A. T., & den Boer, J. A. (2006). Psychobiological characteristics of dissociative identity disorder: A symptom provocation study. *Biological Psychiatry, 60,* 730–740.

Reis, H. T., Sheldon, K. M., Gable, S. L., Roscoe, J., & Ryan, R. M. (2000). Daily well-being: The role of autonomy, competence, and relatedness. *Personality and Social Psychology Bulletin, 26,* 419–435.

Reiss, S., & Wiltz, J. (2004). Why people watch reality TV. *Media Psychology, 6,* 363–378.

Remijnse, P. L., Neilen, M. M., van Balkom, A. J., Cath, D. C., van Oppen, P., Uylings, H. B., & Veltman, D. J. (2006). Reduced orbitofrontal-striatal activity on a reversal learning task I obsessive-compulsive disorder. *Archives of General Psychiatry, 63,* 1225–1236.

Remington, G. (2007). Tardive dyskinesia: Eliminated, forgotten or overshadowed? *Current Opinion in Psychiatry, 20,* 131–137.

Rendell, P. G., & Craik, F. I. M. (2000). Virtual week and actual week: Age-related differences in prospective memory. *Applied Cognitive Psychology, 14,* S43–S62.

Rennie, K. L., Siervo, M., & Jebb, S. A. (2006). Can self-reported dieting and dietary restraint identify underreporters of energy intake in dietary surveys? *Journal of the American Dietetic Association, 106,* 1667–1672.

Renzetti, C. M., & Curran, D. J. (2002). *Women, men, and society* (5th ed.). Boston: Allyn & Bacon.

Repacholi, B. M., & Gopnik, A. (1997). Early reasoning about desires: Evidence from 14- and 18-month-olds. *Developmental Psychology, 33,* 12–21.

Repovs, G., & Baddeley, A. D. (2006). Multi-component model of working memory: Explorations in experimental cognitive psychology. *Neuorscience, 139,* 5–21.

Rescorla, R. A. (1966). Predictability and number of pairings in Pavlovian fear conditioning. *Psychonomic Science, 4,* 383–384.

Rescorla, R. A. (1988). Pavlovian conditioning: It's not what you think it is. *American Psychologist, 43,* 151–160.

Rescorla, R. A. (2003). Contemporary study of Pavlovian conditioning. *Spanish Journal of Psychology, 6,* 185–195.

Rescorla, R. A. (2004). Spontaneous recovery varies inversely with the training-extinction interval. *Learning and Behavior, 32,* 401–408.

Rescorla, R. A. (2005). Spontaneous recovery of excitation but not inhibition. *Journal of Experimental Psychology: Animal Behavior Processes, 31,* 277–288.

Rescorla, R. A. (2006a). Stimulus generalization of excitation and inhibition. *Quarterly Journal of Experimental Psychology, 59,* 53–67.

Rescorla, R. A. (2006b). Spontaneous recovery from overexpectation. *Learning and Behavior, 34,* 13–20.

Reuter-Lorenz, P., & Davidson, R. J. (1981). Differential contributions of the two cerebral hemispheres to the perception of happy and sad faces. *Neuropsychologia, 19,* 609–613.

Reuters News Service. (2006, March 1). Bin Laden tape aided re-election, says Bush.

Reutzel, D. R., & Cooter, R. B. (2008). *Teaching children to read* (5th ed.). Upper Saddle River, NJ: Prentice-Hall.

Revell, V. L., & Eastman, C. I. (2005). How to trick mother nature into letting you fly around or stay up all night. *Journal of Biological Rhythms, 20,* 353–365.

Reynolds, C. R., Livingston, R., & Willson, V. (2006). *Measurement and assessment in education.* Boston: Allyn & Bacon.

Reynolds, S. K., & Clark, L. A. (2001) Predicting dimensions of personality disorder from domains and facets of the five factor model. *Journal of Personality, 69.* 199–222.

Rice, J. K., & Else-Quest, N. (2006). The mixed messages of motherhood. In J. Worell & C. D. Goodheart (Eds.), *Handbook of girls' and women's health: Gender and well-being across the lifespan.* New York: Oxford University Press.

Richards, A., French, C. C., Nash, G., Hadwin, J. A., & Donnelly, N. (2007). A comparison of selective attention and facial processing biases in typically developing children who are high and low in self-reported trait anxiety. *Development and Psychopathology, 19,* 481–495.

Riketta, M. (2002). Attitudinal organizational commitment and job performance: A meta-analysis. *Journal of Organizational Behavior, 23,* 257–266.

Riley, K. P., Snowdon, D. A., Derosiers, M. F., & Markesbery, W. R. (2005). Early linguistic ability, late life cognitive function, and neuropathology: Findings from the nun study. *Neurobiology of Aging, 26,* 341–347.

Risen, J., & Gilovich, T. (2006). Informal logical fallacies. In R. J. Sternberg, H. Roediger, & D. Halpern (Eds.), *Critical thinking in psychology.* Mahwah, NJ: Erlbaum.

Ritchie, E. C., Benedek, D., Malone, R., & Carr-Malone, R. (2006). Psychiatry and the military: An update. *Psychiatric Clinics of North America, 29,* 695–707.

Ritskes, R., Ritskes-Hoitinga, M., Stodkilde-Jorgensen, H., Baerentsen, K., & Hartman, T. (2003). MRI scanning during Zen meditation: The picture of enlightenment? *Constructivism in the Human Sciences, 8*(1), 85–90.

Rivera, C., & Collum, E. (Eds.). (2006). *State assessment of policy and practice for English language learners.* Mahwah, NJ: Erlbaum.

Robbins, G., Powers, D., & Burgess, S. (2008). *A wellness way of life.* New York: McGraw-Hill.

Robbins, T. L., & DeNisi, A. S. (1994). A closer look at interpersonal affect as a distinct influence on cognitive processing in performance evaluations. *Journal of Applied Psychology, 79,* 341–353.

Roberts, B., Walton, K. E., & Viechtbauer, W. (2006). Patterns of mean level change in personality traits across the life course: A meta-analysis of longitudinal studies. *Psychological Bulletin, 132,* 1–25.

Roberts, B. W., Caspi, A., & Moffitt, T. E. (2003). Work experiences and personality development in young adulthood. *Journal of Personality and Social Psychology, 84,* 582–593.

Roberts, B. W., Kuncel, N., Shiner, R. N., Caspi, A., & Goldberg, L. (2007). The power of personality: A comparative analysis of the predictive validity of personality traits, SES, and IQ. *Perspectives in Psychological Science.* (in press)

Roberts, B. W., Walton, K. E., & Bogg, T. (2005). Conscientiousness and health across the life course. *Review of General Psychology, 9*(2), 156–168.

Roberts, B. W., Wood, D., & Caspi, A. (2007). Personality development. In O. P. John, R. W. Robins, & L. A. Pervin (Eds.), *Handbook of personality: Theory and research* (3rd ed.). New York: Guilford.

Roberts, D. F., Henriksen, L., & Foehr, U. G. (2004). Adolescents and media. In R. M. Lerner & L. Steinberg (Eds.), *Handbook of adolescent psychology* (2nd ed., pp. 487–521). Hoboken, NJ: Wiley.

Robertson, H., & Pryor, R. (2006). Memory and cognitive effects of ECT: Informing and assessing patients. *Advances in Psychiatric Treatment, 12,* 228–237.

Robinson, A., Shore, B. M., & Enersen, D. L. (2007). Best practices in gifted education: An evidence-based guide. Waco, TX: Prufrock Press.

Robinson, L. (2005). Are psychiatrists real doctors? A survey of medical experience and training of psychiatric trainees in the west of Scotland. *Psychiatric Bulletin, 29,* 62–64.

Robison, R. J. (2000). Learning about happiness from persons with Down syndrome: Feeling the sense of joy and contentment. *American Journal on Mental Retardation, 105,* 372–376.

Rodin, J. (1984, December). Interview: A sense of control. *Psychology Today,* 38–45.

Roediger, H. L., & Marsh, E. J. (2003). Episodic and autobiographical memory. In I. B. Weiner (Ed.), *Handbook of psychology* (vol. 4). New York: Wiley.

Roehrs, T., & Roth, T. (1998). Reported in Maas, J. (1998). *Power sleep.* New York: Villard, p. 44.

Roese, N. J., Fessel, F., Summerville, A., Kruger, J., & Dilich, M. A. (2006). The propensity effect: When foresight trumps hindsight. *Psychological Science, 17,* 305–310.

Roese, N. J., & Sherman, J. W. (2007). Expectancy. In A. W. Kruglanski & E. T. Higgins (Eds.), *Social psychology: Handbook of basic principles* (2nd ed.). New York: Guilford.

Roese, N. J., & Summerville, A. (2005). What we regret most . . . and why. *Personality and Social Psychology Bulletin, 31,* 1273–1285.

Roesler, C. (2006). A narratological methodology for identifying archetypal story patterns in autobiographical narratives. *Journal of Analytical Psychology, 51,* 574–586.

Roethlisberger, F. J. (1941). *Management and morale.* Cambridge, MA: Harvard University Press.

Roethlisberger, F. J., & Dickson, W. J. (1939). *Management and the worker.* Cambridge, MA: Harvard University Press.

Roffman, J. L., Marci, C. D., Glick, D. M., Dougherty, D. D., & Rauch, S. L. (2005). Neuroimaging and the functional neuroanatomy of psychotherapy. *Psychological Medicine, 35,* 1385–1398.

Rogers, C. R. (1961). *On becoming a person.* Boston: Houghton Mifflin.

Rogers, C. R. (1974). In retrospect: Forty-six years. *American Psychologist, 29,* 115–123.

Rogers, C. R. (1980). *A way of being.* Boston: Houghton Mifflin.

Rogers, J. L., & Kesner, R. P. (2006). Lesions of the dorsal hippocampus or parietal cortex differentially affect spatial information processing. *Behavioral Neuroscience, 120,* 852–860.

Roll, J. M., & Shoptaw, S. (2006). Contingency management: Schedule effects. *Psychiatry Research, 144,* 91–93.

Rollenhagan, A., & Lubke, J. H. (2006). The morphology of excitatory central synapses: From structure to function. *Cell Tissue Research, 326,* 221–237.

Rolls, E. T. (2007). Memory systems in the brain. In H. L. Roediger, Y. Dubai, & S. Fitzpatrick (Eds.), *Science of memory: Concepts.* New York: Oxford University Press.

Romero-Carbente, J. C., Camacho, F. J., & Paredes, R. G. (2006). The role of the dorsolateral tegmentum in the control of male sexual behavior: A reevaluation. *Behavioral Brain Research, 170,* 262–270.

Rosack, J. (2007). Impact of FDA warning questioned in suicide rise. *Psychiatric News, 5,* 1.

Rose, A. J., & Asher, S. R. (2004). Children's strategies and goals in response to help-giving and help-seeking tasks within a friendship. *Child Development, 75,* 749–763.

Rose, R. J., Koskenvuo, M., Kaprio, J., Sarna, S., & Langinvainio, H. (1988). Shared genes, shared experiences, and similarity of personality: Data from 14,228 adult Finnish co-twins. *Journal of Personality and Social Psychology, 54,* 161–171.

Rosen, K., & Garety, P. (2005). Predicting recovery from schizophrenia: A retrospective comparison of characteristics at onset of people with single and multiple episodes. *Schizophrenia Bulletin, 31,* 735–750.

Rosenbaum, R. S., Kohler, S., Schacter, D. L., Moscovitch, M., Westmacott, R., Black, S. E., Gao, F., & Tulving, E. (2005). The case of K.C.: Contributions of a memory-impaired person to memory theory. *Neuropsychologia, 43,* 989–1021.

Rosenblatt, A., Greenberg, J., Solomon, S., Pyszczynski, T., & Lyon, D. (1989). Evidence for terror management theory: I. The effects of mortality salience on reactions to those who violate or uphold cultural values. *Journal of Personality and Social Psychology, 57,* 681–690.

Rosengard, C., Pollock, L., Weitzen, S., Meers, A., & Phipps, M. G. (2006). Concepts of the advantages and disadvantages of teenage childbearing among pregnant adolescents: A qualitative analysis. *Pediatrics, 118,* 503–510.

Rosenhan, D. L. (1973). On being sane in insane places. *Science, 179,* 250–258.

Rosenthal, H. E. S., & Crisp, R. J. (2006). Reducing stereotype threat by blurring intergroup boundaries. *Personality and Social Psychology Bulletin, 32,* 501–511.

Rosenthal, R. (1966). *Experimenter effects in behavioral research.* New York: Appleton-Century-Crofts.

Rosenthal, R. (1994). Interpersonal expectancy effects: A 30-year perspective. *Current Dimensions in Psychological Science, 3,* 176–179.

Rosenthal, R., & DiMatteo, M. R. (2001). Meta-analysis: Recent developments in quantitative methods for literature reviews. *Annual Review of Psychology, 52,* 59–62.

Rosenthal, R., & Jacobsen, L. (1968). *Pygmalion in the classroom.* Fort Worth: Harcourt Brace.

Rosnow, R. L., & Rosenthal, R. (2002). *Beginning behavioral research* (4th ed.). Upper Saddle River, NJ: Prentice-Hall.

Rosnow, R. L., & Rosenthal, R. (2008). *Beginning behavioral research* (6th ed.). Upper Saddle River, NJ: Prentice-Hall.

Ross, C. A., Margolis, R. L., Reading, S. A., Pletnikov, M., & Coyle, J. T. (2006). Neurobiology of schizophrenia. *Neuron, 52,* 139–153.

Ross, C. A., & Norton, G. R. (1989). Differences between men and women with multiple personality disorder. *Hospital & Community Psychiatry, 40,* 186–188.

Ross, L., Kohler, C. L., Grimley, D. M., & Anderson-Lewis, C. (2007). The theory of reasoned action and intention to seek cancer information. *American Journal of Health Behavior, 31,* 123–134.

Ross, L. E., & McClean, L. M. (2006). Anxiety disorders during pregnancy and the postpartum period: A systematic review. *Journal of Clinical Psychiatry, 67,* 1285–1298.

Ross, S. R., Hertenstein, M. J., & Wrobel, T. A. (2007). Maladaptive correlates of the failure to forgive self and others: Further evidence for the two-component model of forgiveness. *Journal of Personality Assessment, 88,* 158–167.

Rossi, E. L., & Rossi, K. L. (2007). What is a suggestion? The neuroscience of implicit processing of heuristics in therapeutic hypnosis and psychotherapy. *American Journal of Clinical Hypnosis, 49,* 267–281.

Rossi, S., Miniussi, C., Pasqualetti, P., Babiloni, C., Rossini, P. M., & Cappa, S. F. (2005). Age-related functional changes of prefrontal cortex in long-term memory: A repetitive transcranial magnetic stimulation study. *Journal of Neuroscience, 24,* 7939–7944.

Rothbart, M. K., & Bates, J. E. (2006). Temperament. In W. Damon & R. Lerner (Eds.), *Handbook of child psychology* (6th ed.). New York: Wiley.

Rothbaum, F., & Trommsdorff, G. (2007). Do roots and wings complement or oppose one another? The socialization of relatedness and autonomy in cultural context. In J. E. Grusec & P. D. Hastings (Eds.), *Handbook of socialization.* New York: Oxford University Press.

Routledge, C., Arndt, J., & Sheldon, K. M. (2004). Task engagement after mortality salience: The effects of creativity, conformity, and connectedness on worldview defense. *European Journal of Social Psychology, 34,* 477–487.

Rowe, J. W., & Kahn, R. L. (1997). *Successful aging.* New York: Pantheon.

Royzman, E. B., Cassidy, K. W., & Baron, J. (2003). "I know, you know": Epistemic egocentrism in children and adults. *Review of General Psychology, 7,* 38–65.

Rubin, D. C., & Kozin, M. (1984). Vivid memories. *Cognition, 16,* 81–95.

Rubin, K. H., Bukowski, W. M., & Parker, J. G. (2006). Peer interactions, relationships, and groups. In W. Damon & R. Lerner (Eds.), *Handbook of child psychology* (6th ed.). New York: Wiley.

Ruble, D. N., Martin, C. L., & Berenbaum, S. A. (2006). Gender development. In W. Damon & R. Lerner (Eds.), *Handbook of child psychology* (6th ed.). New York: Wiley.

Ruck, C. (2003). Psychosurgery. *Journal of Neurosurgery, 99,* 1113–1114.

Rudolf, K. I., Chang, S., Lee, H., Gottlieb, G. J., Greider, C., & DePinto, R. A. (1999). Longevity, stress, response, and cancer in aging telomerase-deficient mice. *Cell, 96,* 701–712.

Rudolph, K. D., & Flynn, M. (2007). Childhood adversity and youth depression: Influence of gender and pubertal status. *Development and Psychopathology, 19,* 497–521.

Ruini, C., Belaise, C., Brombin, C., Caffo, E., & Fava, G. A. (2006). Well-being therapy in school settings: A pilot study. *Psychotherapy and Psychosomatics, 75,* 331–336.

Ruini, C., & Fava, G. A. (2004). Clinical applications of well-being therapy. In A. Linley & S. Joseph (Eds.), *Positive psychology in practice* (pp. 371–387). Hoboken, NJ: Wiley.

Runyon, W. M. (2007). *Psychology and historical interpretation.* New York: Oxford University Press.

Rusbult, C. E., Kumashiro, M., Coolsen, M. K., & Kirchner, J. L. (2004). Interdependence, closeness, and relationships. In D. J. Mashek & A. P. Aaron (Eds.), *Handbook of closeness and intimacy.* (pp. 137–161). Mahwah, NJ: Erlbaum.

Rusbult, C. E., Kumashiro, M., Stocker, S. L., & Wolf, S. T. (2005). The Michelangelo phenomenon in close relationships. In A. Tesser, J. V. Wood, & D. A.Stapel (Eds.), *On building, defending, and regulating the self: A psychological perspective* (pp. 1–29). New York: Psychology Press.

Rushton, J. P., Fulker, D. W., Neal, M. C., Nias, D. K. B., & Eysenck, H. J. (1986). Altruism and aggression: The heritability of individual differences. *Journal of Personality and Social Psychology, 50,* 1192–1198.

Russo, D., Jones, G., & Arlettaz, R. (2007). Echolocation and passive listening by foraging mouse-eared bats *Myotis myotis* and *M. blythii. Journal of Experimental Biology, 210,* 166–176.

Rutan, J. S., Stone, W. N., & Shay, J. J. (2007). *Psychodynamic group therapy* (4th ed.). New York: Guilford.

Rutter, M. (2007). Gene-environment interdependence. *Developmental Science, 10,* 12–18.

Rutter, M. (2007a). Gene-environment interplay and developmental psychopathology. In A. S. Masten (Ed.), *Multilevel dynamics in developmental psychology.* Mahwah, NJ: Erlbaum.

Ryan, R. M., & Deci, E. L. (2000). Self-determination theory and the facilitation of intrinsic motivation, social development, and well-being. *American Psychologist, 55,* 68–78.

Ryan, R. M., & Deci, E. L. (2001). On happiness and human potentials: A review of research on hedonic and eudaimonic well-being. *Annual Review of Psychology* (vol. 52). Palo Alto, CA: Annual Reviews.

Ryan, R. M., & Stiller, J. (1991). The social contexts of internalization: Parent and teacher influences on autonomy, motivation and learning. In P. R. Pintrich & M. L. Maehr (Eds.), *Advances in motivation and achievement: Vol. 7. Goals and self-regulatory processes* (pp. 115–149). Greenwich, CT: JAI Press.

Ryder, A. G., Schuller, D. R., & Bagby, R. M. (2006). Depressive personality and dysthymia: Evaluating symptom and syndrome overlap. *Journal of Affective Disorders, 91,* 217–227.

Ryding, E., Ahnlide, J. A., Lindstrom, M., Rosen, I., & Traskman-Bendz, L. (2006). Regional brain serotonin and dopamine transport binding capacity in suicide attempters relate to impulsiveness and mental energy. *Psychiatry Research, 148,* 195–203.

Ryff, C. D., & Singer, B. (1998). Contours of positive human health. *Psychological Inquiry, 9,* 1–28.

Ryff, C. D., Singer, B. H., & Love, G. D. (2004). Positive health: Connecting well-being with biology. *Philosophical Transactions of the Royal Society of London, 359,* 1383–1394.

S

Saarni, C., Campos, J. J., Camras, L. A., & Witherington, D. (2006). Emotional development: Action, communication, and understanding. In W. Damon & R. Lerner (Eds.), *Handbook of child psychology* (6th ed.). New York: Wiley.

Sabatini, B. L. (2007). Anatomical and physiological plasticity of dendritic structures. *Annual Review of Neuroscience* (vol. 30). Palo Alto, CA: Annual Reviews.

Sabbagh, M. A., Moses, L. J., & Shiverick, S. (2006). Executive functioning and preschoolers' understanding of false beliefs, false photographs, and false signs. *Child Development, 77,* 1034–1049.

Sacchetti, B., Sacco, T., & Strata, P. (2007). Reversible inactivation of amygdala and cerebellum but not perihinal cortex impairs reactivated fear memories. *European Journal of Neuroscience.* (in press)

Sackett, P. R., Hardison, C. M., & Cullen, M. J. (2005). On interpreting research on stereotype threat and test performance. *American Psychologist, 60,* 271–272.

Sacks, O. (2006, June 19). Stereo Sue. *New Yorker,* 64–73.

Saladin, K. (2007). *Anatomy and physiology.* New York: McGraw-Hill.

Salas, E., DeRouin, & Gade, P. A. (2007). The military's contribution to our science and practice: People, places, and findings. In L. L. Koppes (Ed.), *Historical perspectives in industrial and organizational psychology.* Mahwah, NJ: Erlbaum.

Salin-Pascual, R. J., Valencia-Flores, M., Campos, R. M., Castano, A., & Shiromani, P. J. (2006). Caffeine challenge in insomniac patients after total sleep deprivation. *Sleep Medicine, 7,* 141–145.

Sallis, J. F., & Glanz, K. (2006). The role of built environments in physical activity, eating, and obesity in childhood. *The Future of Children, 16,* 89–108.

Salovey, P., & Birnbaum, D. (1989). Influence of mood on health-relevant cognitions. *Journal of Personality and Social Psychology, 57,* 539–551.

Salthouse, T. A. (1994). The nature of the influence of speed on adult age differences in cognition. *Developmental Psychology, 30,* 240–259.

Salva, Vanier, B., Laredo, J., Hartley, S., Chapotot, F., Moulin, C., Lofaso, F., & Guilleminault, C. (2007). Major depressive disorder, sleep EEG, and agomelatine: An open-label study. *International Journal of Neuropsychopharmacology.* (in press)

Salvador, R., Suckling, J., Coleman, M. R., Pickard, J. D., Menon, D., & Bullmore, E. (2005). Neurophysiological architecture of functional magnetic resonance images of the human brain. *Cerebral Cortex, 15,* 1332–1342.

Sameroff, A. (2006). Identifying risk and protective factors for healthy child development. In A. Clarke-Stewart & J. Dunn (Eds.), *Families count.* New York: Oxford University Press.

Sanchez-Burks, J. (2007). Cultural differences. In R. Baumeister & K. Vohs (Eds.), *Encyclopedia of social psychology.* Thousand Oaks: Sage.

Sandor, P. S., & Afra, J. (2005). Nonpharmacologic treatment of migraine. *Current Pain and Headache Reports, 9,* 202–205.

Sanford, S. D., Lichstein, K. L., Durrence, H. H., Riedel, B. W., Taylor, D. J., & Bush, A. J. (2006). The influence of age, gender, ethnicity, and insomnia on Epsworth sleepiness scores: A normative U.S. population. *Sleep Medicine, 7,* 319–326.

Sangha, S., Scheibenstock, A., Martens, K., Varshney, N., Cooke, R., & Lukowiak, K. (2005). Impairing forgetting by preventing new learning and memory. *Behavioral Neuroscience, 119,* 787–796.

Santelli J., Ott, M. A., Lyon, M., Rogers, J., Summers, D., & Schleifer, R. (2006). Abstinence and abstinence-only education: A review of U.S. policies and programs. *Journal of Adolescent Health, 38,* 72–81.

Santee, R. G. (2007). *An integrative approach to counseling.* Thousand Oaks, CA: Sage.

Santrock, J. W. (2007). *Life-span development* (10th ed.). New York: McGraw-Hill.

Santrock, J. W. (2008). *Educational psychology* (3rd ed.). New York: McGraw-Hill.

Sapolsky, R. M. (2004). *Why zebras don't get ulcers* (3rd ed.). New York: Henry Holt.

Sar, V., Akyuz, G., & Dogan, O. (2007). Prevalence of dissociative disorders among women in the general population. *Psychiatry Research, 149,* 169–176.

Sar, V., Koyuncu, A., Ozturk, E., Yargic, L. I., Kundakci, T., Yazici, A., Kuskonmaz, E., & Aksut, D. (2007). Dissociative disorders in the psychiatric emergency ward. *General Hospital Psychiatry, 29,* 45–50.

Sarkar, U., Fisher, L., & Schillinger, D. (2006). Is self-efficacy associated with diabetes self-management across race/ethnicity and health literacy? *Diabetes Care, 29,* 323–329.

Saucier, G. (2001, April). *Going beyond the big five.* Paper presented at the meeting of the Society for Research in Child Development, San Francisco.

Saul, S. (2006, March 8). Some sleeping pill users range far beyond bed. *New York Times.*

Savage, R., Cornish, K., Manly, T., & Hollis, C. (2006). Cognitive processes in children's reading and attention: The role of working memory, divided attention, and response inhibition. *British Journal of Psychology, 97,* 365–385.

Savin-Williams, R. (2006). *The new gay teenager.* Cambridge, MA: Harvard University Press.

Savin-Williams, R., & Diamond, L. (2004). Sex. In R. Lerner & L. Steinberg (Eds.). *Handbook of adolescent psychology* (2nd ed.). New York: Wiley.

Saxe, L. (1998, June). Commentary. *APA Monitor,* 30.

Sayal, K., Heron, J., Golding, J., & Emond, A. (2007). Prenatal alcohol exposure and gender differences in childhood mental health problems: A longitudinal population-based study. *Pediatrics, 119,* e426–e434.

Scarr, S. (1984, May). Interview. *Psychology Today,* 59–63.

Scarr, S. (1988). How genotypes and environments combine: Development and individual differences. In N. Bolger, A. Caspi, G. Downey, & M. Moorehouse (Eds.), *Persons in context: Developmental processes* (pp. 217–244). New York: Cambridge University Press.

Scarr, S. (1992). Keep our eyes on the prize: Family and child care policy in the United States, as it should be. In A. Booth (Ed.), *Child care in the 1990s: Trends and consequences* (pp. 215–222). Hillsdale, NJ: Erlbaum.

Scarr, S. (1993). Genes, experience, and development. In D. Magnusson & P. J. M. Caesar (Eds.), *Longitudinal research on individual development: Present status and future perspectives* (pp. 26–50). New York: Cambridge University Press.

Scarr, S. (2000). Toward voluntary parenthood. *Journal of Personality, 68,* 615–623.

Schacter, D. L. (2001). *The seven sins of memory.* Boston: Houghton Mifflin.

Schacter, D. L. (2007). Memory: Defining the core. In H. L. Roediger, Y. Dudai, & S. M. Fitzpatrick (Eds.), *Science of memory: Concepts.* New York: Oxford University Press.

Schacter, D. L., & Addis, D. R. (2007). Constructive memory: The ghosts of past and future. *Nature, 445,* 27.

Schachter, S., & Singer, J. E. (1962). Cognitive, social, and physiological determinants of emotional state. *Psychological Review, 69,* 379–399.

Schafer, G. (1999). Early speech perception and word learning. In M. Barrett (Ed.), *The development of language.* Philadelphia: Psychology Press.

Schaie, K. W. (1994). The life course of adult intellectual abilities. *American Psychologist, 49,* 304–313.

Schaie, K. W. (2006). Intelligence. In R. Schultz (Ed.), *Encyclopedia of aging* (4th ed.). New York: Springer.

Schaie, K. W. (2007). Generational differences: The age-cohort period model.. In J. E. Birren & K. W. Schaie (Eds.), *Encyclopedia of gerontology.* Oxford: Elsevier.

Schaie, K. W., & Zanjani, F. A. K. (2006). Intellectual development across adulthood. In C. Hoare (Ed.), *Handbook of adult development and learning.* New York: Oxford University Press.

Schank, R., & Abelson, R. (1977). *Scripts, plans, goals, and understanding.* Mahwah, NJ: Erlbaum.

Scheier, M. F., & Carver, C. S. (1992). Effects of optimism on psychological and physical well-being: Theoretical overview and empirical update. *Cognitive Therapy and Research, 16,* 201–228.

Schein, E. H. (2005). *Organizational culture and leadership* (3rd ed). San Francisco: Jossey-Bass.

Schein, L., Spitz, H. I., Burlingame, G. M., Muskin, P. R., & Vargo, S. (2006). Psychological effects of catastrophic disasters: Group approaches to treatment. New York: Haworth Press.

Schiffman, J., & Walker, E. (1998). Schizophrenia. In H. S. Friedman (Ed.), *Encyclopedia of mental health* (vol. 2). San Diego: Academic.

Schill, K., Zetzsche, C., & Wolter, J. (2006). Hybrid architecture for the sensorimotor representation of spatial configurations. *Cognitive Processes, 7,* Suppl. 5, S90–S92.

Schkade, D. A., & Kahneman, D. (1998). Does living in California make people happy? A focusing illusion in judgments of life satisfaction. *Psychological Science, 9,* 340–346.

Schlack, A., & Albright, T. D. (2007). Remembering visual motion: neural correlates of associative plasticity and motion recall in cortical area MT. *Neuron, 53,* 881–890.

Schmalhofer, F., & Perfetti, C. A. (Eds.). (2007). *Higher level language processes in the brain.* Mahwah, NJ: Erlbaum.

Schmidt, F. L., & Zimmerman, R. D. (2004). A counterintuitive hypothesis about employment interview validity and some supporting evidence. *Journal of Applied Psychology, 89,* 553–561.

Schmidt, N. B., & Cromer, K. R. (2007). Assessing the clinical utility of agoraphobia in the context of panic disorder. *Depression and Anxiety.* (in press)

Schmidt, P. J., Murphy, J. H., Haq, N., Rubinow, D. R., & Danaceau, M. A. (2004). Stressful life events, personal losses, and perimenopause-related depression. *Archives of Women's Mental Health, 17,* 19–26.

Schmolck, H., Buffalo, E. A., & Squire, L. R. (2000). Memory distortions develop over time: Recollections of the O. J. Simpson trial verdict after 15 and 32 months. *Psychological Science, 11,* 39–45.

Schneider, K. J. (2002). Humanistic psychotherapy. In M. Hersen & W. H. Sledge (Eds.), *Encyclopedia of psychotherapy.* San Diego: Academic.

Schnoll, R. A., & Lerman, C. (2006). Current and emerging pharmacotherapies for treating tobacco dependence. *Expert Opinion on Emerging Drugs, 11,* 429–444.

Schooler, J. W. (2002). Re-representing consciousness: Dissociations between experience and meta-consciousness. *Trends in Cognitive Sciences, 6,* 339–344.

Schooler, J. W., Ambadar, Z., & Bendiksen, M. (1997). A cognitive corroborative case study approach for investigating discovered memories of sexual abuse. In J. D. Read & D. S. Lindsay (Eds.), *Recollections of trauma: Scientific evidence and clinical practice* (pp. 379–387). New York: Plenum Press.

Schooler, J. W., Ariely, D., & Loewenstein, G. (2003). The explicit pursuit and assessment of happiness can be self-defeating. In I. Brocas & J. Carrillo (Eds.), *The psychology of economic decisions.* Oxford: Oxford University Press.

Schooler, J. W. & Eich, E. (2000). Memory for emotional events. In E. Tulving, E. & F. I. M. Craik (Eds.), *The Oxford handbook of memory* (pp. 379–392). New York: Oxford University Press.

Schule, C. (2007). Neuorendocrinological mechanisms of actions of antidepressant drugs. *Journal of Neuroendrocrinology, 19,* 213–226.

Schultheiss, O. C., & Brunstein, J. C. (2005). An implicit motive perspective on competence. In A. J. Elliot & C. S. Dweck (Eds.), *Handbook of competence and motivation* (pp. 31–51). New York: Guilford.

Schultz, R. (2007). Cardiovascular health study. In K. S. Markides (Ed.), *Encyclopedia of health and aging.* Thousand Oaks, CA: Sage.

Schultz, W. (2006). Behavioral theories and the neurophysiology of reward. *Annual Review of Psychology* (vol. 57). Palo Alto, CA: Annual Reviews.

Schultz, W., Dayan, P., & Montague, P. R. (1997). A neural substrate of prediction and reward. *Science, 275,* 1593–1599.

Schultz, W. T. (Ed). (2005). *The handbook of psychobiography.* New York: Oxford University Press.

Schulz-Stubner, S., Krings, T., Meister, I. G., Rex, S., Thron, A., & Rossaint, R. (2004). Clinical hypnosis modulates functional magnetic resonance imaging signal intensities and pain perception in a thermal stimulation paradigm. *Regional Anesthesia and Pain Medicine, 29,* 549–556.

Schumann, A., John, U., Rumpf, H., Hapke, U., & Meyer, C. (2006). Changes in the "stages of change" as outcome measures of a smoking cessation intervention: A randomized controlled trial. *Preventive Medicine: An International Journal Devoted to Practice and Theory, 43,* 101–106.

Schumann, C. M., & Amaral, D. G. (2006). Stereological analysis of amygdala neuron number in autism. *Journal of Neuroscience, 26,* 7674–7679.

Schunk, D. H. (2008). *Learning theories* (5th ed.). Upper Saddle River, NJ: Prentice-Hall.

Schunk, D. H., & Zimmerman, B. J. (2006). Competence and control beliefs: Distinguishing the means and the end. In P. A. Alexander & P. H. Winne (Eds.), *Handbook of educational psychology* (2nd ed.). Mahwah, NJ: Erlbaum.

Schwaninger, A., Wallraven, C., Cunningham, D. W., & Chiller-Glaus, S. D. (2006). Processing of facial identity and expression. *Progress in Brain Research, 156,* 321–343.

Schwartz, B., Ward, A. H., Monterosso, J., Lyubomirsky, S., White, K., & Lehman, D. (2002). Maximizing versus satisficing: Happiness is a matter of choice. *Journal of Personality and Social Psychology, 83,* 1178–1197.

Schwartz, R. H., Cooper, M. N., Oria, M., & Sheridan, M. J. (2003). Medical marijuana: A survey of teenagers and their parents. *Clinical Pediatrics, 42,* 547–551.

Schwela, D., Kephalopoulous, S., & Prasher, D. (2005). Confounding or aggravating factors in noise-induced health effects: Air pollutants and other stressors. *Noise Health, 7,* 41–50.

Scollon, C. N., & King, L. A. (2004). Is the good life the easy life? *Social Indicators Research, 68,* 127–162.

Scott, A. *(2006).* What I would say to a patient who asked me about this article. *Advances in Psychiatric Treatment, 12,* 237–238.

Scott, S. K., Rabito, F. A., Price, P. D., Butler, N. N., Schwartzbaum, J. A., Jackson, B. M., Love, R. L., & Harris, R. E. (2006). Comorbidity among the morbidly obese: A comparative study of 2002 U.S. hospital patient surcharges. *Surgery for Obesity and Related Disorders, 2,* 105–111.

Scott, T. R. (2000). Taste. In A. Kazdin (Ed.), *Encyclopedia of psychology.* Washington, DC, & New York: American Psychological Association and Oxford University Press.

Scott-Sheldon, L. A. J., & Johnson, B. T. (2006). Eroticizing creates safer sex: A research synthesis. *Journal of Primary Prevention, 27,* 619–640.

Seal, K. H., Bertenthal, D., Miner, C. R., Sen, S., & Marmar, C. (2007). Bringing war back home: Mental health disorders among 103,7888 U.S. veterans returning from Iraq and Afghanistan seen at Department of Veterans Affairs facilities. *Archives of Internal Medicine, 167,* 476–482.

Sears, D. O., & Henry, P. J. (2007). Symbolic racism. In R. Baumeister & K. Vohs (Eds.), *Encyclopedia of social psychology.* Newbury Park, CA: Sage.

Sedikides, C. (2007). Self-enhancement and self-protection: Powerful, pancultural, and functional. *Hellenic Journal of Psychology, 4,* 1–13.

Sedikides, C., Gaertner, L., & Toguchi, Y. (2003). Pancultural self-enhancement. *Journal of Personality and Social Psychology, 84,* 60–79.

Sedikides, C., Gaertner, L., & Vevea, J. L. (2005). Pancultural self-enhancement reloaded: A meta-analytic reply to Heine (2005). *Journal of Personality and Social Psychology, 89,* 539–551.

Sedikides, C., & Gregg, A. P. (2006). The self as a point of contact between social psychology and motivation. In P. A. M. Van Lange (Ed.), *Bridging social psychology: Benefits of transdisciplinary approaches* (pp. 233–238). Mahwah, NJ: Erlbaum.

Segal, D. L., & Coolidge, F. L. (2004). Objective assessment of personality and psychopathology. In M. Hersen (Ed.), *Comprehensive handbook of psychological assessment* (vol. 2). New York: Wiley.

Segerstrom, S. C. (2003). Individual differences, immunity, and cancer: Lessons from personality psychology. *Brain, Behavior and Immunity, 17, Suppl. 1,* S92–S97.

Segerstrom, S. C. (2005). Optimism and immunity: Do positive thoughts always lead to positive effects? *Brain, Behavior and Immunity, 19,* 195–200.

Segerstrom, S. C. (2006). Breaking Murphy's law: How optimists get what they want from life and pessimists can too. New York: Guilford.

Seguin, M., Lesage, A., Chawky, N., Guy, A., Daigle, F., Girard, G., & Turecki, G. (2006) Suicide cases in New Brunswick from April 2002 to May 2003: The importance of better recognizing substance and mood disorder comorbidity. *Canadian Journal of Psychiatry, 51,* 581–586.

Seifert, C. M., & Patalano, A. L. (2001). Opportunism in memory: Preparing for chance encounters. *Current Directions in Psychological Science, 10,* 198–201.

Seligman, M. E. P. (1970). On the generality of the laws of learning. *Psychological Review, 77,* 406–418.

Seligman, M. E. P. (1975). *Helplessness: On depression, development and death.* San Francisco: W. H. Freeman.

Seligman, M. E. P. (1990). *Learned optimism.* New York: Knopf.

Seligman, M. E. P. (1994). *What you can change and what you can't.* New York: Knopf.

Seligman, M. E. P. (2000). Positive psychology. In J. E. Gillham (Ed.), *The science of optimism and hope: Research essays in honor of Martin E. P. Seligman* (pp. 415–429). West Conshohocken, PA: Templeton Foundation Press.

Seligman, M. E. P., & Csikszentmihalyi, M. (2000). Positive psychology: An introduction. *American Psychologist, 55,* 5–14.

Seligman, M. E. P., & Pawelski, J. O. (2003). Positive psychology: FAQs. *Psychological Inquiry, 14,* 159–163.

Seligman, M. E. P., & Schulman, P. (1986). Explanatory style as a predictor of productivity and quitting among life insurance agents. *Journal of Personality and Social Psychology, 50,* 832–838.

Sellbom, M., Ben-Porath, Y. S., McNulty, J. L., Arbisi, P. A., & Graham, J. R. (2006). Elevation differences between MMPI-2 clinical and restructured clinical (RC) scales: Frequency, origins, and interpretive implications. *Assessment, 13,* 430–441.

Sellers, R. M., Copeland-Linder, N., Martin, P. P., & Lewis, R. L. (2006). Racial identity matters: The relationship between racial discrimination and psychological functioning in African American adolescents. *Journal of Research on Adolescence, 16,* 187–216.

Sellers, R. M., & Shelton, J. N. (2003). The role of racial identity in perceived racial discrimination. *Journal of Personality and Social Psychology, 84,* 1079–1092.

Seltzer, J. (2004). Cohabitation and family change. In M. Coleman & L. Ganong (Eds.), *Handbook of contemporary families.* Thousand Oaks, CA: Sage.

Selye, H. (1974). *Stress without distress.* Philadelphia: Saunders.

Selye, H. (1983). The stress concept: Past, present, and future. In C. I. Cooper (Ed.), *Stress research.* New York: Wiley.

Serra, L., Fadda, L., Buccione, I., Caltagirone, C., & Carlesimo, G. A. (2007). Psychogenic and organic amnesia: A multidimensional assessment of clinical, neuroradiological, neuropsychological, and psychopathological features. *Behavioral Neurology, 18,* 53–64.

Service, R. F. (1994). Will a new type of drug make memory-making easier? *Science, 266,* 218–219.

Sessa, B. (2007). Is there a case for MDMA-assisted psychotherapy in the UK? *Journal of Psychopharmacology, 21,* 220–224.

Sestieri, C., & others. (2006). "What" versus "where" in the audiovisual domain: An fMRI study. *Neuroimage,* doi:10.1016/j.neuroimage.2006.06.045.

Seth, A. K., Izhikevich, E., Reeke, G. N., & Edelman, G. M. (2006). Theories and measures of consciousness: An extended framework. *Proceedings of the National Academy of Science USA, 103,* 10799–10804.

Sewell, R. A., Halpern, J. H., & Pope, H. G. (2006). Response of cluster headache to psilocybin and LSD. *Neurology, 66,* 1920–1922.

Seymour, T. L., Seifert, C. M., Shafto, M. G., & Mosmann, A. L. (2000). Using response time measures to assess "guilty knowledge." *Journal of Applied Psychology, 85,* 30–37.

Shaban, H., & others. (2006). Generalization of amygdala LTP and conditioned fear in the absence of presynaptic inhibition. *Nature Neuroscience, 9,* 1028–1035.

Shakesby, A. C., Anwyl, R., & Rowan, M. J. (2002). Overcoming the effects of stress on synaptic plasticity in the intact hippocampus: rapid actions of serotonergic and antidepressant agents. *Journal of Neuroscience, 22,* 3638–3644.

Shankaran, S., Lester, B. M., Das, A., Bauer, C. R., Bada, H. S., Lagasse, L., & Higgins, R. (2007). Impact of maternal substance use during pregnancy on childhood outcome. *Seminars in Fetal and Neonatal Medicine, 12,* 143–150.

Shanks, D. R. (1991). Categorization by a connectionist network. *Journal of Experimental Psychology: Learning, Memory, and Cognition, 17,* 433–443.

Shanthly, N., Aruva, M. R., Zhang, K., Mathew, B., & Tahkur, M. L. (2006). Stem cells: A regenerative pharmaceutical. *Quarterly Journal of Nuclear Medicine and Molecular Imaging, 50,* 205–216.

Shaver, P. R., & Mikulincer, M. (2007). Attachment theory and research. In A. W. Kruglanski & E. T. Higgins (Eds.), *Social psychology* (2nd ed.). New York: Guilford.

Shaw, K., Gennat, H., O'Rourke, P., & Del Mar, C. (2006). Exercise for overweight or obesity. *Cochrane Database of Systematic Reviews, 4,* CD003817.

Shay, J. W., & Wright, J. E. (2005). Mechanism-based combination telomerase inhibition therapy. *Cancer Cell, 7,* 1–2.

Shay, J. W., & Wright, W. E. (2006). Telomerase therapeutics for cancer: Challenges and new directions. *Nature Reviews: Drug Discovery, 5,* 477–584.

Shay, J. W., & Wright, W. E. (2007). Hallmarks of telomere aging research. *Journal of Pathology, 211,* 114–123.

Sheldon, K. M. (2002). The self-concordance model of healthy goal-striving: When personal goals correctly represent the person. In E. L. Deci & R. M. Ryan (Eds.), *Handbook of self-determination research* (pp. 65–86). Rochester, NY: University of Rochester Press.

Sheldon, K. M., & Elliot, A. J. (1998). Not all personal goals are personal: Comparing autonomous and controlled reasons for goals as predictors of effort and attainment. *Personality and Social Psychology Bulletin, 24,* 546–557.

Sheldon, K. M., & Kasser, T. (2001) Getting older, getting better? Personal strivings and psychological maturity across the life span. *Developmental Psychology, 37,* 491–501.

Sheldon, K. M., Kasser, T., Houser-Marko, L., Jones, T., & Turban, D. (2005). Doing one's duty: Chronological age, felt autonomy, and subjective well-being. *European Journal of Personality, 19,* 97–115.

Shelton, R. C., & Hollon, S. D. (2000). Antidepressants. In A. Kazdin (Ed.), *Encyclopedia of psychology.* Washington, DC, & New York: American Psychological Association and Oxford University Press.

Shepard, R. N. (1967). Recognition memory for words, sentences, and pictures. *Journal of Verbal Learning and Verbal Behavior, 6,* 156–163.

Sherif, M., Harvey, O. J., White, B. J., Hood, W. R., & Sherif, C. W. (1961). *Intergroup cooperation and competition: The Robbers Cave experiment.* Norman: University of Oklahoma Press.

Sherman, A. M., Lansford, J. E., & Volling, B .L. (2006). Sibling relationships and best friendships in young adulthood: Warmth, conflict, and well-being. *Personal Relationships, 13*(2), 151–165.

Sherwood, A., Light, K. C., & Blumenthal, J. A. (1989). Effects of aerobic exercise training on hemodynamic responses during psychosocial stress in normotensive and borderline hypertensive Type A men: A preliminary report. *Psychosomatic Medicine, 51,* 123–136.

Shevelev, I. A., & Lazareva, N. A. (2007). Characteristics of the responses of visual cortex neurons with sensitivity to bars or cross-shaped figures in cats. *Neuroscience and Behavioral Physiology, 37,* 311–319.

Shields, S. A. (1991). Gender in the psychology of emotion. In K. T. Strongman (Ed.), *International Review of Studies of Emotion* (vol. 1). New York: Wiley.

Shier, D. N., Butler, J. L., & Lewis, R. (2007). *Hole's anatomy & physiology* (10th ed.). New York: McGraw-Hill.

Shih, M., Bonam, C., Sanchez, D., & Peck, C. (2007). The social construction of race: Biracial identity and vulnerability to stereotypes. *Cultural Diversity & Ethnic Minority Psychology, 13,* 125–133.

Shih, M., & Sanchez, D. T. (2005). Perspectives and research on the positive and negative of having multiple racial identities. *Psychological Bulletin, 131,* 569–591.

Shillington, A. M., & Clapp, J. D. (2006). Heavy alcohol use compared to acohol and marijuana use: Do college students experience a difference in substance use problems? *Journal of Drug Education, 36*(1), 91–103.

Shim, W. M., & Cavanaugh, P. (2006). Bi-directional illusory position shifts toward the end point of apparent motion. *Vision Research, 46,* 3214–3222.

Shiraev, E., & Levy, D. (2007). *Cross-cultural psychology* (3rd ed.). Boston: Allyn & Bacon.

Shnek, Z. M., Irvine, J., Stewart, D., & Abbey, S. (2001). Psychological factors and depressive symptoms in ischemic heart disease. *Health Psychology, 20,* 141–145.

Shoda, Y., & Mischel, W. (2006). Applying meta-theory to achieve generalisability and precision in personality science: Comment. *Applied Psychology: An International Review, 55,* 439–452.

Shotland, R. L. (1985, June). When bystanders just stand by. *Psychology Today,* 50–55.

Shull, R. L., & Grimes, J. A. (2006). Resistance to extinction following variable-interval reinforcement: Reinforcer rate and amount. *Journal of the Experimental Analysis of Behavior, 85,* 23–39.

Shynkaruk, J. M., & Thompson, V. A. (2006). Confidence and accuracy in deductive reasoning. *Memory and Cognition, 34,* 619–632.

Sieber, W. J., Rodin, J., Larson, L., Ortega, S., & Cummings, N. (1992). Modulation of human natural killer cell activity by exposure to uncontrollable stress. *Brain, Behavior, and Immunity, 6,* 141–156.

Siegel, S. (1988). State dependent learning and morphine tolerance. *Behavioral Neuroscience, 102,* 228–232.

Siegle, G. J., Carter, C. S., & Thase, M. E. (2006). Use of fMRI to predict recovery from unipolar depression with cognitive behavior therapy. *American Journal of Psychiatry, 163,* 735–738.

Siegler, R. S. (2006). Microgenetic analyses of learning. In W. Damon & R. Lerner (Eds.), *Handbook of child psychology* (6th ed.). New York: Wiley.

Sigurdsson, T., Doyere, V., Cain, C. K., & LeDoux, J. E. (2006). Long-term potentiation in the amygdale: A cellular mechanism of learning and memory. *Neuropharmacology.* (in press)

Sikorskii, A., Given, C., Given, B., Jeon, S., & McCorkle, R. (2006). Testing the effects of treatment complications on a cognitive-behavioral intervention for reducing symptom severity. *Journal of Pain and Symptom Management, 32,* 129–139.

Silbereisen, R. K., & Lerner, R. M. (Eds.). (2007). *Approaches to positive youth development.* Thousand Oaks, CA: Sage.

Silberman, I. (2005). Religion as a meaning system: Implications for the new millennium. *Journal of Social Issues, 61,* 641–663.

Silverman, N. N., & Corsini, R. J. (1984). Is it true what they say about Adler's individual psychology? *Teaching of Psychology, 11,* 188–189.

Silverstein, S. M., & Uhlhaas, P. J. (2004). Gestalt psychology: The forgotten paradigm in abnormal psychology. *American Journal of Psychology 117,* 259–277.

Sim, T. N., & Ong, L. P. (2005). Parent punishment and child aggression in a Singapore Chinese preschool sample. *Journal of Marriage and the Family, 67,* 85–99.

Simms, L. J. (2007). The big seven model of personality and its relevance to personality pathology. *Journal of Personality, 75,* 65–94.

Simon, G. M. (2006). The heart of the matter: A proposal for placing the self of the therapist at the center of family research and training. *Family Processes, 45,* 331–344.

Simon, H. A. (1969). *The sciences of the artificial.* Cambridge, MA: MIT Press.

Sims, C. S., Drasgow, F., & Fitzgerald, L. F. (2005). The effects of sexual harassment on turnover in the military: Time-dependent modeling. *Journal of Applied Psychology, 90,* 1141–1152.

Singer, J. A. (2004). Narrative identity and meaning making across the adult lifespan: An introduction. *Journal of Personality, 72,* 437–459.

Singer, J. A., & Blagov, P.(2004). The integrative function of narrative processing: Autobiographical memory, self-defining memories, and the life story of identity. In D. R. Beike, J. M. Lampinen, & D. A. Behrend (Eds.), *The self and memory* (pp. 117–138). New York: Psychology Press.

Sivacek, J., & Crano, W. D. (1982). Vested interest as a moderator of attitude-behavior consistency. *Journal of Personality and Social Psychology, 43*(2), 210–221.

Sivanathan, N., Arnold, K. A., Turner, N., & Barling, J. (2004). Leading well: Transformational leadership and well-being. In P. A. Linley & S. Joseph (Eds.), *Positive psychology in practice* (pp. 241–255). Hoboken, NJ: Wiley.

Skene, D. J., & Arendt, J. (2006). Human circadian rhythms: Physiological and therapeutic relevance of light and melatonin. *Annals of Clinical Biochemistry, 43,* 344–353.

Skinner, B. F. (1938). *The behavior of organisms: An experimental analysis.* New York: Appleton-Century-Crofts.

Skinner, B. F. (1948). *Walden Two.* New York: Macmillan.

Skinner, B. F. (1957). *Verbal behavior.* New York: Appleton-Century-Crofts.

Slade, E. P., & Wissow, L. S. (2004). Spanking in early childhood and later behavior problems: A prospective study of infants and young toddlers. *Pediatrics, 113,* 1321–1330.

Slater, A., Field, T., & Hernandez-Reif, M. (2007). The development of the senses. In A. Slater & M. Lewis (Eds.), *Introduction to infant development* (2nd ed.). New York: Oxford University Press.

Slavin, R. E. (2006). Translating research into widespread practice: The case of success for all. In M. A. Constas & R. J. Sternberg (Eds.), *Translating theory and research into educational practice: Developments in content domains, large-scale reform, and intellectual capacity* (pp. 113–126). Mahwah, NJ: Erlbaum.

Slotnick, S. D., & Schacter, D. L. (2006). The nature of memory related activity in early visual areas. *Neuropsychologia, 44,* 2874–2886.

Slotnick, S. D., & Schacter, D. L. (2007). The cognitive neuroscience of memory and consciousness. In P. D. Zelazo, M. Moscovitch, & E. Thompson (Eds.), *The Cambridge handbook of consciousness.* New York: Cambridge University Press.

Slutske, W. S. (2005). Alcohol use disorders among US college students and their non-college-attending peers. *Archives of General Psychiatry. 62,* 321–327.

Smit, F., Willemse, G., Koopmanschap, M., Onrust, S., Cuijpers, P., & Beekman, A. (2006). Cost-effectiveness of preventing depression in primary care patients: Randomized.trial. *British Journal of Psychiatry, 188,* 330–336.

Smith, B. (2007). *The psychology of sex and gender.* Belmont, CA: Wadsworth.

Smith, C. P. (Ed.), (1992). *Thematic content analysis for motivation and personality research.* New York: Cambridge University Press.

Smith, G. P. (1995) Dopamine and food reward. *Progress in Psychobiology and Physiological Psychology, 16,* 83–144.

Smith, K. L., Matheson, F. I., Moineddin, R., & Glazier, R. H. (2007). Gender, income, and immigration differences in depression in Canadian urban centers. *Canadian Journal of Public Health, 98,* 149–153.

Smith, M. B. (2001). Humanistic psychology. In W. E. Craighead & C. B. Nemeroff (Eds.), *The Corsini encyclopedia of psychology and behavioral science* (3rd ed.). New York: Wiley.

Smith, N. K., Larsen, J. T., Chartrand, T. L., Cacioppo, J. T., Katafiasz, H. A., & Moran, K. E. (2006). Being bad isn't always good: Affective context moderates the attention bias toward negative information. *Journal of Personality and Social Psychology, 90,* 210–220.

Smith, P. B., Bond, M. H., & Kagitcibasi, C. (2006). *Understanding social psychology across cultures: Living and working in a changing world.* Thousand Oaks, CA: Sage.

Smith, R. A., & Davis, S. (2007). *The psychologist as detective* (4th ed.). Upper Saddle River, NJ: Prentice-Hall.

Smith, S. (2007). Context and human memory. In H. L. Roediger, Y. Dubai, & S. Fitzpatrick (Eds.), *Science of memory: Concepts.* New York: Oxford University Press.

Smith, S. M., & Fabrigar, L. R. (2000). Attitudes: An overview. In A. Kazdin (Ed.), *Encyclopedia of psychology.* Washington, DC, & New York: American Psychological Association and Oxford University Press.

Smith, T. W., & MacKenzie, J. (2006). Personality and risk of physical illness. *Annual Review of Clinical Psychology* (vol. 2). Palo Alto, CA: Annual Reviews.

Smyth, J. (1998). Written emotional expression: Effect sizes, outcome types, and moderating variables. *Journal of Consulting and Clinical Psychology, 66,* 174–184.

Snarey, J. R. (1993). *How fathers care for the next generation: A four-decade study.* Cambridge, MA: Harvard University Press.

Snell, R. S., & Wong, Y. L. (2007). Differentiating good soldiers from good actors. *Journal of Management Studies* (online articles). doi:10.1111/ j.1467-6486.2007.00699.x

Snow, C. (2007, March). *Socializing children for academic success: The power and limits of language.* Paper presented at the meeting of the Society for Research in Child Development, Boston.

Snow, C. E., & Yang, J. Y. (2006). Becoming bilingual, biliterate, and bicultural. In W. Damon & R. Lerner (Eds.), *Handbook of child psychology* (6th ed.). New York: Wiley.

Snowdon, D. A. (1995). *An epidemiological study of aging in a select population and its relationship to Alzheimer's disease.* Unpublished manuscript, Sanders Brown Center on Aging, Lexington, KY.

Snowdon, D. A. (1997). Aging and Alzheimer's disease: Lessons from the nun study. *Gerontologist, 37,* 150–156.

Snowdon, D. A. (2001). *Aging with grace: What the nun study teaches us about longer, healthier, and more meaningful lives.* New York: Bantam.

Snowdon, D. A. (2003). Healthy aging and dementia: findings from the Nun study. *Annals of Internal Medicine, 139,* 450–454.

Snowdon, D. A. (2007, April). *Aging with grace: findings from the nun study.* Paper presented at the 22nd annual Alzheimer's regional conference, Seattle.

Snyder, C. R., & Lopez, S. J. (2006). *Positive psychology.* Thousand Oaks, CA: Sage.

Snyder, C. R., & Lopez, S. J. (Eds.). (2007). *Positive psychology: The scientific and practical explorations of human strengths.* Thousand Oaks, CA: Sage.

Snyder, D. K., Castellani, A. M., & Whisman, M. A. (2006). Current status and future directions in couple therapy. *Annual Review of Psychology* (vol. 57). Palo Alto, CA: Annual Reviews.

Soares-Weiser, K., & Fernandez-H. H. (2007). Tardive dyskinesia. *Seminars in Neurology, 27,* 159–169.

Sokolov, A., & Pavlova, M. (2006). Visual motion detection in hierarchical spatial frames of reference. *Experimental Brain Research, 174,* 477–486.

Solomon, R. C. (2002). *Spirituality for the skeptic.* New York: Oxford University Press.

Solomon, S., Greenberg, J., & Pyszczynski, T. (1991). Terror management theory of self-esteem. In C. R. Snyder & D. R. Forsyth (Eds.), *Handbook of social and clinical psychology: The health perspective* (pp. 21–40). Elmsford, NY: Pergamon Press.

Solomon, S. G., & Lennie, P. (2007). The machinery of color vision. *Nature Reviews: Neuroscience, 8,* 276–286.

Soltesz, E. G., & Cohn, L. H. (2007). Minimally invasive valve surgery. *Cardiology Review, 15,* 109–115.

Sommer, M., Hajak, G., Dohnel, K., Schwerdtner, J., Meinhardt, J., & Muller, J. L. (2006). Integration of emotion and cognition in patients with psychopathy. *Progress in Brain Research, 156C,* 457–466.

Song, S. (2006, March 27). Mind over medicine. *Time, 167,* 13.

Sonino, N., & Fava, G. A. (2003). Tolerance to antidepressant treatment may be overcome by ketoconazole. *Journal of Psychiatric Research, 37,* 171–173.

Sonnenfeld, J. A. (1985). Shedding light on the Hawthorne studies. *Journal of Occupational Behavior, 6,* 111–130.

Sorrentino, R., Cohen, D., Olson, J. M., & Zanna, M. P. (2005). *Cultural and social behavior: The Ontario symposium* (vol. 10). Mahwah, NJ: Erlbaum.

Sowell, E. (2004, May 8). Commentary in B. Bower "Teen brains on trial." *Science News Online,* 1.

Soyka, M., Preuss, U. W., Hesselbrock, V., Zill, P., Koller, G., & Bondy, B. (2007). GABA-A2 receptor subunit gene (GABRAA2) polymorphisms and risk for alcohol dependence. *Journal of Psychiatric Research.* (in press)

Spanos, N. P., & Chaves, J. F. (Eds.). (1989). *Hypnosis: The cognitive-behavior perspective.* Buffalo, NY: Prometheus.

Spear, N. E. (2007). Properties of memory retrieval. In H. L. Roediger, Y. Dubai, & S. Fitzpatrick (Eds.), *Science of memory: Concepts.* New York: Oxford University Press.

Speckens, A. E., Ehlers, A., Hackmann, A., Ruths, F. A, & Clark, D. M. (2007). Intrusive memories and rumination in patients with post-traumatic stress disorder: A phenomenological comparison. *Memory, 15,* 249–257.

Spector, P. E. (2006). *Industrial and organizational psychology: Research and practice* (4th ed.). Hoboken, NJ: Wiley.

Spector, P. E., Cooper, C. L., Sanchez, J. L., O'Driscoll, M., Sparks, K., Bernin, P., Bussing, A., Dewe, P. , & others. (2001). Do national levels of individualism and internal locus of control relate to well-being? An ecological level international study. *Journal of Organizational Behavior, 22,* 815–832.

Spellman, B. A. (2005). Could reality shows become reality experiments? *APS Observer, 18,* 34–35.

Spencer, M. B. (2006). Phenomenology and ecological systems theory: Development of diverse groups. In W. Damon & R. Lerner (Eds.), *Handbook of child psychology* (6th ed.). New York: Wiley.

Spencer, S. J., Steele, C. M., & Quinn, D. M. (1999). Stereotype threat and women's math performance. *Journal of Experimental Social Psychology, 35,* 4–28.

Speranza, M., Corcos, M., Atger, F., Paterniti, S., & Jeammet, P. (2003). Binge eating behaviours, depression and weight control strategies. *Eating and Weight Disorders, 8,* 201–206.

Sperry, R. W. (1968). Hemisphere deconnection and unity in conscious awareness. *American Psychologist, 23,* 723–733.

Sperry, R. W. (1974). Lateral specialization in surgically separated hemispheres. In F. O. Schmitt & F. G. Worden (Eds.), *The neurosciences: Third study program.* Cambridge, MA: MIT Press.

Spiegel, D., Bloom, J. R., Kraemer, H. C., & Gottheil, E. (1989, October 14). Effect of psychosocial treatment on survival of patients with metastatic breast cancer. *Lancet,* 888–891.

Spielberger, C. D. (2004, August). *Type A behavior, anger-hostility, and heart disease.* Paper presented at the 28th International Congress of Psychology, Beijing, China.

Spielmans, G. I., Pasek, L. F., & McFall, J. P. (2007). What are the active ingredients in cognitive and behavioral psychotherapy for anxious and depressed children? A meta-analytic review. *Clinical Psychology Review.* (in press)

Spitzberg, B. H., & Cupach, W. R. (Eds.). (2007). *The dark side of interpersonal communication* (2nd ed.). Mahwah, NJ: Erlbaum.

Spohr, H. L., Willms, J., & Steinhausen, H. C. (2007). Fetal alcohol spectrum disorders in young adulthood. *Journal of Pediatrics, 150,* 175–179.

Sprinthall, R. C. (2007). *Basic statistical analysis* (8th ed.). Boston: Allyn & Bacon.

Squire, L. (1990, June). *Memory and brain systems.* Paper presented at the meeting of the American Psychological Society, Dallas.

Squire, L. (2007). Memory systems as a biological concept. In H. L.Roediger, Y. Dudai, & S. Fitzpatrick (Eds.), *Science of memory: Concepts.* New York: Oxford University Press.

Squire, L. R. (2004). Memory systems of the brain: A brief history and current perspective. *Neurobiology of Learning and Memory, 82,* 171–177.

Srivastava, S., John, O. P., Gosling, S. D., & Potter, J. (2003). Development of personality in early and middle adulthood: Set like plaster or persistent change? *Journal of Personality and Social Psychology, 84,* 1041–1053.

Srivastava, S., McGonigal, K. M., Richards, J. M., Butler, E. A., & Gross, J. J. (2006). Optimism in close relationships: How seeing things in a positive light makes them so. *Journal of Personality and Social Psychology, 91,* 143–153.

Sroufe, L. A., Egeland, B., Carlson, E., & Collins, W. A. (2005). The place of early attachment in developmental context. In K. E. Grossmann, K. Grossmann, & E. Waters (Eds.), *The power of longitudinal research.* New York: Guilford.

Staddon, J. E., Chelaru, I. M., & Higa, J. J. (2002). A tune-trace theory of interval-timing dynamics. *Journal of the Experimental Analysis of Behavior, 77,* 105–124.

Stanovich, K. E. (2004). *How to think straight about psychology* (7th ed.). Boston: Allyn & Bacon.

Stanovich, K. E. (2007). *How to think straight about psychology* (8th ed.). Boston: Allyn & Bacon.

Stanton, A. L., & Revenson, T. A. (2007). Adjustment to chronic disease: Progress and promise in research. In H. S. Friedman & R. C. Silver (Eds.), *Foundations of health psychology.* New York: Oxford University Press.

Stanton, A. L., Revenson, T. A., & Tennen, H. (2007). Health psychology: Psychological adjustment to chronic disease. *Annual Review of Psychology* (vol. 58). Palo Alto, CA: Annual Reviews.

Starcevic, V. (2006). Anxiety states: A review of conceptual and treatment issues. *Current Opinions in Psychiatry, 19,* 79–83.

Staw, B. M., & Barsade, S. G. (1993). Affect and managerial performance: A test of the sadder-but-wiser vs. happier-and-smarter hypothesis. *Administrative Science Quarterly, 38,* 304–331.

Staw, B. M., Bell, N. E. & Clausen, J. A. (1986). The dispositional approach to job attitudes: A lifetime longitudinal test. *Administrative Science Quarterly, 31,* 56–77.

Staw, B. M., Sutton, R. I., & Pelled, L. H. (1994). Employee positive emotion and favorable outcomes at the workplace. *Organization Science, 5,* 51–71.

Stebbins, R. A. (2005). Choice and experienital definitions of leisure. *Leisure Sciences, 27,* 349–352.

Steele, C. M., & Aronson, J. (1995). Stereotype threat and the intellectual test performance of African-Americans. *Journal of Personality and Social Psychology, 69,* 797–811.

Steele, C. M., & Aronson, J. A. (2004). Stereotype threat does not live by Steele and Aronson (1995) alone. *American Psychologist, 59,* 47–48.

Steger, M. F., & Frazier, P. (2005). Meaning in life: One link in the chain from religion to well-being. *Journal of Counseling Psychology, 52,* 574–582.

Stein, D. J., & Matsunaga, H. (2006). Specific phobia: A disorder of fear and extinction. *CNS Spectrum, 11,* 248–251.

Stein, R. (2003). *Blinded by the light.* http://www.theage.com.au/articles/2003/09/01/1062403448264.html (accessed October 11, 2006).

Steinberg, L. (2005). Cognitive and affective development in adolescence. *Trends in Cognitive Science, 9,* 69–74.

Steinberg, L. (2006, March). *A new approach to the study of adolescent cognitive development.* Paper presented at the meeting of the Society for Research on Adolescence, San Francisco.

Steinberg, L. D. (2007). Risk-taking in adolescence. *Current Directions in Psychological Science.* (in press)

Steinbrook, R. (1992). The polygraph test: A flawed diagnostic method. *New England Journal of Medicine, 327,* 122–123.

Stenberg, D. (2007). Neuroanatomy and neurochemistry of sleep. *Cellular and Molecular Life Sciences.* (in press)

Stenfelt, S. (2006). Middle ear ossicles motion at hearing thresholds with air conduction and bone conduction stimulation. *Journal of the Acoustical Society of America, 119,* 2848–2858.

Stephan, K. E., Marshall, J. C., Friston, K. J., Rowe, J. B., Ritzl, A., Zilles, K., & Fink, G. R. (2003). Lateralized cognitive processes and lateralized task control in the human brain. *Science, 301,* 384–386.

Steptoe, A., Hamer, M., & Chida, Y. (2007). The effects of acute psychological stress on circulating inflammatory factors in humans: A review and meta-analysis. *Brain, Behavior, and Immunity.* (in press)

Stern, Y., Alexander, G. E., Prohovnik, I., & Mayeux, R. (1992). Inverse relationship between education and parietotemporal perfusion deficit in Alzheimer's disease. *Annals of Neurology, 32,* 371–375.

Stern, Y., Scarmeas, N., & Habeck, C. (2004). Imaging cognitive reserve. *International Journal of Psychology, 39* 18–26.

Sternberg, E. M., & Gold, P. W. (1996). The mind-body interaction in disease. *Mysteries of the mind.* New York: Scientific American.

Sternberg, R. J. (1986). *Intelligence applied.* Fort Worth: Harcourt Brace.

Sternberg, R. J. (Ed.). (2004). Definitions and conceptions of giftedness. Thousand Oaks, CA: Corwin Press.

Sternberg, R. J. (2006). *Cognitive psychology* (4th ed.). Belmont, CA: Wadsworth.

Sternberg, R. J. (2007). Critical thinking in psychology: It really is critical. In R. J. Sternberg, H. Roediger, & D. Halpern (Eds.), *Critical thinking in psychology.* New York: Cambridge University Press.

Sternberg, R. J. (2007a). *G, g's, or Jeez:* Which is the best model for developing abilities, competencies, and expertise? In P. C. Kyllonen, R. D. Roberts, & L. Stankov (Eds.), *Extending intelligence.* Mahwah, NJ: Erlbaum.

Sternberg, R. J. (2007b). Developing successful intelligence in all children: A potential solution to underachievement in ethnic minority children. In M. C. Wang & R. D. Taylor (Eds.), *Closing the achievement gap.* Philadelphia: Laboratory for Student Success at Temple University.

Sternberg, R. J. (2008). The triarchic theory of human intelligence. In N. Salkind (Ed.), *Encyclopedia of educational psychology.* Thousand Oaks, CA: Sage.

Sternberg, R. J., & Grigorenko, E. L. (2008). Ability testing across cultures. In L. Suzuki (Ed.), *Handbook of multicultural assessment* (3rd ed.). New York: Jossey-Bass. (in press)

Sternberg, R. J., Roediger, H., & Halpern, D. (Eds.). (2007). *Critical thinking in psychology.* New York: Cambridge University Press.

Steur, F. B., Applefield, J. M., & Smith, R. (1971). Televised aggression and the interpersonal aggression of preschool children. *Journal of Experimental Child Psychology, 11,* 442–447.

Stevens, M. J., & Gielen, U. P. (Eds.). (2007). Toward a global psychology: Theory, research, intervention, and pedagogy. Mahwah, NJ: Erlbaum.

Stevenson, B., & Wolfers, J. (2007). *Marriage and divorce: Changes and their driving forces.* Population Studies Center, Working Paper Series: University of Pennsylvania. Posted at ScholarlyCommons@Penn: http://repository.upenn.edu/psc working papers/8 (accessed May 10, 2007).

Steward, S. E., & others. (2007). A genetic family-based association study of OLIG2 in obsessive compulsive disorder. *Archives of General Psychiatry, 64,* 209–214.

Stewart, S. H., & Chambers, L. (2000). Relationships between drinking motives and drinking restraint. *Addictive Behaviors, 25,* 269–274.

Stewart, S. H., & Devine, H. (2000). Relations between personality and drinking motives in young people. *Personality and Individual Differences, 29,* 495–511.

Stewart, J. W. (2007). Treating depression with atypical features. *Journal of Clinical Psychiatry, 68, Suppl. 3,* S25–S29.

Stice, E., Presnell, K., Gau, J., & Shaw, H. (2007). Testing mediators of intervention effects in randomized controlled trials: An evaluation of two eating disorder prevention programs. *Journal of Consulting and Clinical Psychology, 75,* 20–32.

Stice, E., Shaw, H., & Marti, C. N. (2006). A meta-analytic review of obesity prevention programs for children and adolescents: The skinny on interventions that work. *Psychological Bulletin, 132,* 667–691.

Stickgold, R. (2001). Watching the sleeping brain watch us: Sensory processing during sleep. *Trends in Neuroscience, 24,* 307–309.

Stickgold, R., & Hobson, J. A. (2000). Visual discrimination learning requires sleep after training. *Nature Neuroscience, 3,* 1237–1238.

Stickgold, R., & Walker, M. P. (2005). Sleep and memory: An ongoing debate. *Sleep, 28,* 1225–1227.

Stoel-Gammon, C., & Sosa, A. V. (2007). Phonological development. In E. Hoff & M. Shatz (Eds.), *Blackwell handbook of language development.* Malden, MA: Blackwell.

Stokes, G. D., & Cooper, L. A. (2001) Content/construct approaches in life history form development for selection. *International Journal of Selection and Assessment, 9,* 138–151.

Stone, A. A., Neale, J. M., Cox, D. S., Napoli, A., Valdimarsdottir, H., & Kennedy-Moore, E. (1994). Daily events are associated with secretory immune response to an oral antigen in men. *Health Psychology, 13,* 440–446.

Stone, J. (2002). Battling doubt by avoiding practice: The effects of stereotype threat on self-handicapping in white athletes. *Personality and Social Psychology Bulletin, 28,* 1667–1678.

Stone, J., Lynch, C. I., Sjomeling, M., & Darley, J. M. (1999). Stereotype threat effects on Black and White athletic performance. *Journal of Personality and Social Psychology, 77,* 1213–1227.

Stores, G., Montgomery, P., & Wiggs, L. (2006). The psychosocial problems of children with narcolepsy and those with excessive daytime sleepiness of unknown origin. *Pediatrics, 118,* e1116–e1123.

Strachowski, D., Khaylis, A., Conrad, A., Neri, E., Spegel, D.,& Taylor, C. B. (2007). The effects of cognitive behavior therapy on depression in older patients with cardiovascular risk. *Depression and Anxiety.* (in press)

Strack, F., & Schwarz, N. (2007). Asking questions: Measurement in the social sciences. In M. Ash & T. Sturm (Rds.), *Psychology's territories.* Mahwah, NJ: Erlbaum.

Straus, M. A. (1991). Discipline and deviance: Physical punishment of children and violence and other crimes in adulthood. *Social Problems, 38,* 133–154.

Straus, M. A., Sugarman, D. B., & Giles-Sims, J. (1997). Spanking by parents and subsequent antisocial behavior of children. *Archives of Pediatric and Adolescent Medicine, 151,* 761–767.

Strawn, J. R., & Geracioti, T. D. (2007). Noradrenergic dysfunction and the psychopharmacology of posttraumatic stress disorder. *Depression and Anxiety.* (in press)

Stricker, J. L., Brown, G. G., Wetherell, L. A., & Drummond, S. P. A. (2006). The impact of sleep deprivation and task difficulty on networks of fMRI brain response. *Journal of the Neuropsychological Society, 12,* 591–597.

Stricker, L. J. (2005). The biographical inventory in naval aviation selection: inside the black box. *Military Psychology, 17,* 55–67.

Strike, P. C., Magid, K., Whitehead, D. L., Brydon, L., Bhattacharyya, M. R., & Steptoe, A. (2006). Pathophysiological processes underlying emotional triggering of acute cardiac events. *Proceedings of the National Academy of Science USA, 103,* 4322–4327.

Strong, B., Yarber, W., Sayad, B., & DeVault, C. (2008). *Human sexuality* (6th ed.). New York: McGraw-Hill.

Strupp, H. H. (1995). The psychotherapist's skills revised. *Clinical Psychology: Science and Practice, 2,* 70–74.

Stuber, J., Galea, S., Boscarino, J., & Schlesinger, M. (2006). Was there unmet mental health need after the September 11, 2001 terrorist attacks? *Social Psychiatry and Psychiatric Epidemiology, 41,* 230–234.

Sturmer, T., Hasselbach, P., & Amelang, M. (2006). Personality, lifestyle, and risk of cardiovascular disease and cancer: Follow-up of population-based cohort. *British Medical Journal, 332,* 1359.

Stuss, D. T. (2006). Frontal lobes and attention: Processes and networks, fractionation and integration. *Journal of the International Neuropsychological Society, 12,* 261–271.

Substance Abuse and Mental Health Services Administration (SAMHSA). (2005). *National survey on drug use and health.* Washington, DC: Author.

Substance Abuse and Mental Health Services Administration (SAMHSA). (2006). *National survey on drug use and health report, 11.* Washingon DC: Author.

Sue, S. (2000). Ethnocultural psychotherapy. In A. Kazdin (Ed.), *Encyclopedia of psychology.* Washington, DC, & New York: American Psychological Association and Oxford University Press.

Suh, E. M. (2002). Culture, identity consistency, and subjective well-being. *Journal of Personality and Social Psychology, 83,* 1378–1391.

Suinn, R. M. (1976, July). Body thinking: Psychology for Olympic champions. *Psychology Today, 10,* 38–41.

Suinn, R. M. (1984). *Fundamentals of abnormal psychology*. Chicago: Nelson-Hall.

Suire, J. G., & Bothwell, R. K. (2006). The psychosocial benefits of Alcoholics Anonymous. *American Journal of Addiction, 15*, 252–255.

Sullivan, P. F. (1995). Mortality in anorexia nervosa. *American Journal of Psychiatry, 152*, 1073–1074.

Sullivan, P. W., Morrato, E. H., Ghushchyan, V., Wyatt, H. R., & Hill, J. O. (2005). Obesity, inactivity, and the prevalence of diabetes and diabetes-related cardiovascular comorbidities in the U.S., 2000–2002. *Diabetes Care 28*, 1599–1603.

Suls, J., & Swain, A. (1998). Type A–Type B personalities. In H. S. Friedman (Ed.), *Encyclopedia of mental health* (vol. 3). San Diego: Academic.

Sumic, A., Michael, Y. L., Carlson, N. E., Howieson, D. B., & Kaye, J. A. (2007). Physical activity and the risk of dementia in the oldest old. *Journal of Aging and Health, 19*, 242–259.

Sun, T., Collura, R. V., Ruvolo, M., & Walsh, C. A. (2006). Genomic and evolutionary analyses of asymmetrically expressed genes in human fetal left and right cerebral cortex. *Cerebral Cortex, 16, Suppl. 1*, i18–i25.

Surprenant, A. M. (2001). Distinctiveness and serial position effects in tonal sequences. *Perception and Psychophysics, 63*, 737–745.

Susman, E. J., & Rogol, A. (2004). Puberty and psychological development. In R. Lerner & L. Steinberg (Eds.), *Handbook of adolescent psychology*. New York: Wiley.

Susskind, J. M., Littlewort, G., Bartlett, M. S., Movellan, J., & Anderson, A. K. (2007). Human and computer recognition of facial expressions of emotion. *Neuropsychologia, 45*, 152–162.

Sutherland, N. S. (1989). *MacMillan dictionary of psychology*. Houndmills/Basingstoke/Hampshire, England: Palgrave-MacMillan.

Swaab, D. F., Chung, W. C., Kruijver, F. P., Hofman, M. A., & Ishunina, T. A. (2002). Sexual differentiation of the human hypothalamus. *Advances in Experimental Medical Biology, 511*, 75–100.

Swann, W. B., De La Ronde, C., & Hixon, J. G. (1994). Authenticity and positive strivings in marriage and courtship. *Journal of Personality and Social Psychology, 66*, 857–869.

Swanson, J. (Ed.). (1999). *Sleep disorders sourcebook*. New York: Omnigraphics.

Swartz-Kulstad, J. L., & Martin, W. E. (2000). Culture as an essential aspect of person–environment fit. In W. E. Martin & J. L. Swartz-Kulstad (Eds.), *Person–environment psychology and mental health*. Mahwah, NJ: Erlbaum.

Sweatt, J. D. (2007). Molecular mechanisms of memory retrieval. In H. L. Roediger, Y. Dudai, & S. Fitzpatrick (Eds.), *Science of memory: Concepts*. New York: Oxford University Press.

Szasz, T. S. (1961). *The myth of mental illness: Foundations of a theory of personal conduct*. New York: Hoeber-Harper.

T

Taga, K. A., Markey, C. N., & Friedman, H. S. (2006). A longitudinal investigation of associations between boys' pubertal timing and adult behavioral health and well-being. *Journal of Youth and Adolescence, 35*, 380–390.

Tajfel, H. (1978). The achievement of group differentiation. In H. Tajfel (Ed.), *Differentiation between social groups*. London: Academic.

Takahashi, M., Shimizu, H., Saito, S., & Tomoyori, H. (2006). One percent ability and ninety-nine percent perspiration: A study of a Japanese memorist. *Journal of Experimental Psychology: Learning, Memory, and Cognition, 32*, 1195–1200.

Takashima, A., Jensen, O., Oostenveld, R., Maris, E., van de Coevering, M., & Fernandez, G. (2006). Successful declarative memory formation is associated with ongoing activity during encoding in a distributed neocortical network related to working memory: A magnetoencephalography study. *Neuroscience, 139*, 291–297.

Takeuchi, T., Miyasia, A., Inugami, M., & Yamamoto, Y. (2001). Intrinsic dreams are not produced without REM sleep mechanisms. *Journal of Sleep Research, 10*, 43–52.

Tamminga, C. A. (2006). The neurobiology of cognition in schizophrenia. *Journal of Clinical Psychology, 67*, e11.

Tang, Y. P., Shimizu, E., Dube, G. R., Rampon, C., Kerchner, G. A., Zhuo, M., Liu, G., & Tsien, J. Z. (1999). Genetic enhancement of learning and memory in mice. *Nature, 401*, 63–69.

Tangney, J. P., Stuewig, J., & Mashek, D. J. (2007). Moral emotions and moral behavior. *Annual Review of Psychology* (vol. 58). Palo Alto, CA: Annual Reviews.

Tangney, J. P., Stuewig, J., & Mashek, D. J. (2006). Moral emotions and moral behavior. *Annual Review of Psychology* (vol. 57). Palo Alto, CA: Annual Reviews.

Tanida, K., & Poppel, E. (2006). A hierarchical model of operational anticipation windows in driving an automobile. *Cognitive Processes, 7*, 275–287.

Tannenbaum, S. I. (2006). Applied measurement: Practical issues and challenges. In W. Bennett, C. E. Lance, & D. J. Woehr (Eds.), *Performance measurement*. Mahwah, NJ: Erlbaum.

Tarr, M. J., & Gauthier, I. (2000). FFA: A flexible fusiform area for subordinate-level visual processing automatized by expertise. *Nature Neuroscience, 3*, 764–769.

Tate, D. F., Jeffery, R. W., Sherwood, N. E., & Wing, R. R. (2007). Long-term weight losses associated with prescription of higher physical activity goals. Are higher levels of physical activity protective against weight gain? *American Journal of Clinical Nutrition, 85*, 954–959.

Tavris, C. (1989). *Anger: The misunderstood emotion* (2nd ed.). New York: Touchstone.

Tavris, C., & Wade, C. (1984). *The longest war: Sex differences in perspective* (2nd ed.). Fort Worth: Harcourt Brace.

Tay, C., Ang, S., & Van Dyne, L. (2006). Personality, biographical characteristics, and job interview success: A longitudinal study of the mediating effects of self-efficacy and the moderating effects of internal locus of causality. *Journal of Applied Psychology, 91*, 446–454.

Taylor, F. W. (1911). *Scientific management*. New York: Harper & Row.

Taylor, K. I., Moss, H. E., Stamatakis, E. A., & Tyler, L. K. (2006). Binding crossmodal object features in perirhinal cortex. *Proceedings of the National Academy of Science, USA, 103*, 8239–8244.

Taylor, M. S., Tracy, K. B., Renard, M. K., Harrison, J. K., & Carroll, S. J. (1995). Due process in performance appraisal: A quasi-experiment in procedural justice. *Administrative Science Quarterly, 40*, 495–523.

Taylor, S. E. (2001). Toward a biology of social support. In C. R. Snyder & S. J. Lopez (Eds.), *Handbook of positive psychology*. New York: Oxford University Press.

Taylor, S. E. (2006). *Health psychology* (6th ed.). New York: McGraw-Hill.

Taylor, S. E. (2007). Social support. In H. S. Friedman & R. C. Silver (Eds.), *Foundations of health psychology*. New York: Oxford University Press.

Taylor, S. E., Brown, J. D., Colvin, C. R., Block, J., & Funder, D. C. (2007). Issue 6: Do positive illusions lead to healthy behavior? In J. A. Nier (Ed.). *Taking sides: Clashing views in social psychology* (2nd ed., pp. 116–137). New York: McGraw-Hill.

Taylor, S. E., Lerner, J. S., Sherman, D. K., Sage, R. M., & McDowell, N. K. (2003a). Are self-enhancing cognitions associated with healthy or unhealthy biological profiles? *Journal of Personality and Social Psychology, 85*, 605–615.

Taylor, S. E., & Gonzaga, G. C. (2007). Affiliative response to stress: A social neuroscience model. In E. Harmon-Jones & P. Winkielman (Eds.), *Social neuroscience*. New York: Guilford.

Taylor, S. E., Lerner, J. S., Sherman, D. K., Sage, R. M., & McDowell, N. K. (2003b). Portrait of the self-enhancer: Well adjusted and well liked or maladjusted and friendless? *Journal of Personality and Social Psychology, 84*, 165–176.

Taylor, S. E., Peplau, L. A., & Sears, D. O. (2003). *Social psychology* (11th ed.). Upper Saddle River, NJ: Prentice-Hall.

Taylor, S. E., & Stanton, A. L. (2007). Coping resources, coping processes, and mental health. *Annual Review of Clinical Psychology* (vol. 3). Palo Alto, CA: Annual Reviews.

Tedeschi, W. G., & Calhoun, L. G. (2004). A clinical approach to posttraumatic growth. In A. Linley & S. Joseph, (Eds.), *Positive psychology in practice* (pp. 405–419). Hoboken, NJ: Wiley.

Teesson, M., & Vogl, L. (2006). Major depressive disorder is common among Native Americans, women, the middle aged, the poor, the widowed, separated, or divorced people. *Evidence-Based Mental Health, 9,* 59.

Tenenbaum, H. R., Callahan, M., Alba-Speyer, C., & Sandoval, L. (2002). Parent–child science conversations in Mexican descent families: Educational background, activity, and past experience as moderators. *Hispanic Journal of Behavioral Sciences, 24,* 225–248.

Tenenbaum, J. B., Griffiths, T. L., & Kemp, C. (2006). Theory-based Bayesian models of inductive learning and reasoning. *Trends in Cognitive Science, 10,* 309–318.

Teodorescu, M., & others. (2006). Correlates of daytime sleepiness in patients with asthma. *Sleep Medicine, 7,* 607–613,

Tepper, B. J., Duffy, M. K., Hoobler, J., & Ensley, M. D. (2004). Moderators of the relationships between coworkers' organizational citizenship behavior and fellow employees' attitudes. *Journal of Applied Psychology, 89,* 455–465.

Terman, L. (1925). *Genetic studies of genius. Vol. 1: Mental and physical traits of a thousand gifted children.* Stanford, CA: Stanford University Press.

Terr, L. C. (1988). What happens to early memories of trauma? *Journal of the American Academy of Child and Adolescent Psychiatry, 27,* 96–104.

Tetreault, M. K. T. (1997). Classrooms for diversity: Rethinking curriculum and pedagogy. In J. A. Banks & C. A. Banks (Eds.), *Multicultural education* (3rd ed.). Boston: Allyn & Bacon.

Thackare, H., Nicholson, H. D., & Whittington, K. (2006). Oxytocin—its role in male reproduction and new potential therapeutic uses. *Human Reproduction Update, 12,* 437–438.

Thase, M. E. (2006). Bipolar depression: Diagnostic and treatment considerations. *Developmental Psychopathology, 18,* 1213–1230.

Thaxton, L., Emshoff, J. G., & Guessous, O. (2005). Prostate cancer support groups: A literature review. *Journal of Psychosocial Oncology, 23*(1), 25–40.

Theakston, J. A., Stewart, S. H., Dawson, M. Y., Knowlden-Loewen, S. A. B., & Lehman, D. R. (2004). Big-five personality domains predict drinking motives. *Personality and Individual Differences, 37,* 971–984.

Thelen, E., & Smith, L. B. (2006). Dynamic development of action and thought. In W. Damon & R. Lerner (Eds.), *Handbook of child psychology* (6th ed.). New York: Wiley.

Thiessen, J. H. (2002). Relations of androgens and selected aspects of human behavior. *Maturitas, 41,* Suppl., 47–54.

Thigpen, C. H., & Cleckley, H. M. (1957). *Three faces of Eve.* New York. McGraw-Hill.

Thomas, M., Sing, H., Belenky, G., Holcomb, H., Mayberg, H., Dannals, R., Wagner, H., Thorne, D., Popp, K., Rowland, L., Welsh, A., Balwinksi, S., & Redmond, D. (2001). Neural basis of alertness and cognitive performance impairments during sleepiness: I. Effects of 24 hours of sleep deprivation on waking human regional brain activity. *Journal of Sleep Research, 9,* 335–352.

Thompson, L. L., & Choi, H-S. (Eds.). (2006). *Creativity and innovation in organizational teams.* Mahwah, NJ: Erlbaum.

Thompson, P. M., Giedd, J. N., MacDonald, D., Evans, A. C., & Toga, A. W. (2000). Growth patterns in the developing brain by using continuum sensor maps. *Nature, 404,* 190–193.

Thompson, P. M., & others. (2007). Tracking Alzheimer's disease. *Annals of the New York Academy of Sciences, 1097,* 183–214.

Thompson, R. A. (2006). The development of the person: Social understanding, relationships, conscience, self. In W. Damon & R. Lerner (Eds.), *Handbook of child psychology* (6th ed.). New York: Wiley.

Thoresen, C. J., Kaplan, S. A., Barsky, A. P., Warren, C. R., & de Chermont, K. (2003). The affective underpinnings of job perceptions and attitudes: A meta-analytic review and integration. *Psychological Bulletin, 129,* 914–945.

Thorndike, E. L. (1898). *Animal intelligence: An experimental study of the associative processes in animals* (Psychological Review, monograph supplements, no. 8). New York: Macmillan.

Thunedborg, K., Black, C. H., & Bech, P. (1995). Beyond the Hamilton depression scores in long-term treatment of manic-melancholic patients: Prediction of recurrence of depression by quality of life measurements. *Psychotherapy and Psychosomatics, 64,* 131–140.

Tillman, K. H., & Brewster, K. L. (2006, August). *Who's doing "it"? Oral sex among teens and young adults in the United States.* Paper presented at the annual meeting of the American Sociological Association, Montreal Convention Center, Montreal, Quebec, Canada.

Timimi, S. (2004). A critique of the international consensus statement on ADHD. *Clinical Child and Family Psychology Review, 7*(1), 59–63.

Tinbergen, N. (1969). *The study of instinct.* New York: Oxford University Press.

Todorov, A., Mandisodza, A. N., Goren, A., & Hall, C. C. (2005). Inferences of competence from faces predict election outcomes. *Science, 308*(5728), 1623–1626.

Toga, A. W., Thompson, P. M., & Sowell, E. R. (2006). Mapping brain maturation. *Trends in Neuroscience, 29,* 148–159.

Tolin, D. F., & Foa, E. B. (2006).Sex differences in trauma and posttraumatic stress disorder: A quantitative review of 25 years of research. *Psychological Bulletin, 132*(6), 959–992.

Tolman, E. C. (1932). *Purposive behavior in animals and man.* New York: Appleton-Century-Crofts.

Tolman, E. C. (1948). Cognitive maps in rats and men. *Psychological Review, 55,* 189–208.

Tolman, E. C., & Honzik, C. H. (1930). Degrees of hunger, reward and non-reward, and maze performance in rats. *University of California Publications in Psychology, 4,* 21–256.

Tomasello, M. (2006). Acquiring linguistic constructions. In W. Damon & R. Lerner (Eds.), *Handbook of child psychology* (6th ed.). New York: Wiley.

tom Dieck, S., & Brandstatter, J. H. (2006). Ribbon synapses in the retina. *Cell Tissue Research, 326,* 339–346.

Tompkins, S. S. (1962). *Affect, imagery, and consciousness* (vol. 1). New York: Springer.

Tong, F., Nakayama, K., Moscovitch, M., Weinrib, O., & Kanwisher, N. (2000). Response properties of the human fusiform face area. *Cognitive Neuropsychology, 17,* 257–279.

Torres, A. R., Prince, M. J., Bebbington, P. E., Bhurgra, D., Brugha, T. S., Farrell, M., Jenkins, R., Lewis, G., Meltzer, H., & Singleton, N. (2006). Obsessive-compulsive disorder: Prevalence, comorbidity, impact, and help-seeking in the British National Psychiatric Morbidity Survey of 2000. *American Journal of Psychiatry, 163,* 1978–1985.

Tov, W., & Diener, E. (2007). Cultural and subjective well-being. In S. Kitayama & D. Cohen (Eds.), *Handbook of cultural psychology.* New York: Guilford.

Townsend, M., & Grant, A. (2006). Integrating science, practice, and reflexivity—cognitive therapy with driving phobia. *Journal of Psychiatric Mental Health Nursing, 13,* 554–561.

Treasure, D. C., & Roberts, G. C. (2001). Students' perceptions of the motivational climate, achievement beliefs, and satisfaction in physical education. *Research Quarterly on Exercise and Sport, 72,* 165–175.

Triandis, H. C. (1994). *Culture and social behavior.* New York: McGraw-Hill.

Triandis, H. C. (2000). Cross-cultural psychology: History of the field. In A. Kazdin (Ed.), *Encyclopedia of psychology.* Washington, DC, and New York: American Psychological Association and Oxford University Press.

Triandis, H. C. (2007). Culture and psychology: A history of the study of their relationship. In S. Kitayama & D. Cohen (Eds.), *Handbook of cultural psychology.* New York: Guilford.

Tribukait, A. (2006). Subjective visual horizontal in the upright posture and asymmetry in roll-tilt perception: Independent measures of vestibular function. *Journal of Vestibular Research, 16,* 35–43.

Trivedi, A. N., Zaslavsky, A. M., Schneider, E. C., & Ayanian, J. Z. (2006). Relationship between quality of care and racial disparities in Medicare health plans. *Journal of the American Medical Association, 296,* 1998–2004.

Trowell, J., & others. (2007). Childhood depression: A place for psychotherapy. An outcome study comparing individual psychodynamic psychotherapy and family therapy. *European Child and Adolescent Psychiatry, 16,* 157–167.

Trull, T. J. (1992). DSM-III-R personality disorders and the five-factor model of personality: An empirical comparison. *Journal of Abnormal Psychology, 101,* 553–560.

Trull, T. J. (2001). Relationships of borderline features to parental mental illness, childhood abuse, Axis I disorder, and current functioning. *Journal of Personality Disorders, 15,* 19–32.

Trull, T. J., & Widiger, T. A. (2003). Personality disorders. In I. B. Weiner (Ed.), *Handbook of Psychology* (vol. 8). New York: Wiley.

Tryon, R. C. (1940). Genetic differences in maze-learning ability in rats. In *39th Yearbook, National Society for the Study of Education.* Chicago: University of Chicago Press.

Tryon, W. W. (2005). Possible mechanisms for why desensitization and exposure therapy work. *Clinical Psychology Review, 25,* 67–95.

Trzesniewski, K. H., Donnellan, M. B., Moffitt, T. E., Robins, R. W., Poulton, R., & Caspi, A. (2006). Low self-esteem during adolescence predicts poor health, criminal behavior, and limited economic prospects during adulthood. *Developmental Psychology, 42,* 381–390.

Tsai, W., Chen, C., & Chiu, S. (2005). Exploring boundaries of the effects of applicant impression management tactics in job interviews. *Journal of Management, 31,* 108–125.

Tsang, J. (2006). Gratitude and prosocial behaviour: An experimental test of gratitude. *Cognition & Emotion, 20,* 138–148.

Tsang, J., McCullough, M. E., & Hoyt, W. T. (2005). Psychometric and rationalization accounts of the religion-forgiveness discrepancy. *Journal of Social Issues, 61,* 785–805.

Tsien, J. Z. (2000). Linking Hebb's coincidence-detection to memory formation. *Current Opinions in Neurobiology, 10,* 266–273.

Tugade, M. M., Fredrickson, B. L., & Feldman Barrett, L. (2004). Psychological resilience and positive emotional granularity: Examining the benefits of positive emotions on coping and health. *Journal of Personality, 72,* 1161–1190.

Tulving, E. (1972). Episodic and semantic memory. In E. Tulving & W. Donaldson (Eds.), *Origins of memory.* San Diego: Academic.

Tulving, E. (1983). *Elements of episodic memory.* New York: Oxford University Press.

Tulving, E. (1989). Remembering and knowing the past. *American Scientist, 77,* 361–367.

Tulving, E. (2000). Concepts of memory. In E. Tulving & F. I. M. Craik (Eds.), *The Oxford handbook of memory.* New York: Oxford University Press.

Turiel, E. (2006). The development of morality. In W. Damon & R. Lerner (Eds.), *Handbook of child psychology* (6th ed.). New York: Wiley.

Turner, M. S., & Stewart, D. W. (2006). Review of the evidence of long-term efficacy of atypical antipsychotic agents in the treatment of patients with schizophrenia and related psychoses. *Journal of Psychopharmacology, 20,* Suppl. 6, S20–S27.

Turnipseed, D. L. (2002). Are good soldiers good? Exploring the link between organization citizenship behavior and personal ethics. *Journal of Business Research, 55,* 1–15.

Tyas, S. L., Salazar, J. C., Snowdon, D. A., Desrosier, M. F., Riley, K. P., Mendiondo, M. S., & Kryscio, R. J. (2007). Transitions to mild cognitive impairments, dementia, and death: Findings from the Nun Study. *American Journal of Epidemiology.* (in press)

Tye, K. M., & Janak, P. H. (2007). Amygdala neurons differentially encode motivation and reinforcement. *Journal of Neuroscience, 27,* 3937–3945.

Tyler, T. R., & De Cremer, D. (2006). Social psychology and economics. In P. A. M. Van Lange (Ed.), *Bridging social psychology.* Mahwah, NJ: Erlbaum.

U

Ueda, K., Jinbo, M., Li, T. S., Yagi, T., Suga, K., & Hamano, K. (2006). Computed tomography-diagnosed emphysema, not airway obstruction, is associated with the prognostic outcome of early-stage lung cancer. *Clinical Cancer Research, 12,* 6730–6736.

Uguz, F., Akman, C., Kaya, N., & Cilli, A. S. (2007). Postpartum-onset obsessive-compulsive disorder: Incidence, clinical features, and related factors. *Journal of Clinical Psychiatry, 68,* 132–138.

Ulrich, R. S. (1991). Stress recovery during exposure to natural and urban environments. *Journal of Environmental Psychology, 11,* 201–230.

Umbreit, J., Ferro, J., Liaupsin, C. J., & Lane, K. L. (2007). *Functional behavioral assessment and function-based intervention.* Upper Saddle River, NJ: Prentice-Hall.

UNAIDS. (2006). *Report on the global AIDS epidemic.* New York: Author.

Ungerleider, L. G., and Mishkin, M. (1982). Two cortical visual systems. In D. J. Engle, M. A. Goodale, & R. J. Mansfield (Eds.), *Analysis of visual behavior.* Cambridge, MA: MIT Press.

United Nations. (1999). *Demographic yearbook.* Geneva, Switzerland: United Nations.

United Nations. (2002). *Demographic yearbook.* Geneva, Switzerland: Author.

United Nations World Youth Report. (2005). *World youth report 2005: Young people today and in 2015.* Geneva, Switzerland: United Nations.

University of Michigan. (2006, February 6). *New cochlear implant could improve hearing.* Press release.

Urban, E. (2005). Fordham, Jung, and the self: A re-examination of Fordham's contributions to Jung's conceptualization of the self. *Journal of Analytical Psychology, 50,* 571–594.

Urry, H. L., Nitschke, J. B., Dolski, I., Jackson, D. C., Dalton, K. M., Mueller, C. J., Rosenkranz, M. A., Ryff, C. D., Singer, B. H., & Davidson, R. J. (2004). Making a life worth living: Neural correlates of well-being. *Psychological Science, 15,* 367–372.

U.S. Bureau of Justice Statistics. (2006). All crimes in the US in 2004. Washington, DC: Author.

U.S. Bureau of Labor Statistics. (2006, October 27). *Survey of workplace violence prevention, 2005.* Washington, DC: Author. http://www.bls.gov/iif/oshwc/osnr0026.pdf (accessed June 13, 2007).

U.S. Department of Justice. (2006). The *DOJ's efforts to combat methamphetamine.* Washington DC: Author. http://www.usdoj.gov/dea/pubs/press-rel/pr061606.html (accessed December 15, 2006).

U.S. Department of Labor. (1992). *Dictionary of occupational titles* (4th ed.). New York: McGraw-Hill.

U.S. Department of Labor. (2006–2007). *Occupational outlook handbook.* Washington, DC: Author.

U.S. Department of Transportation. (2005). *2005 data summary.* Washington, DC: National Center for Statistics and Analysis.

U.S. Food and Drug Administration. (2003, January 3). FDA approves Prozac for pediatric use to treat depression and OCD. *FDA Talk Paper.* Washington DC: Author.

U.S. Food and Drug Administration. (2004, October 15). *FDA launches a multi-pronged strategy to strengthen safeguards for children treated with antidepressant medications.* News release. Washington DC: Author.

U.S. Food and Drug Administration. (2005). *Office of Device Evaluation annual report fiscal year 2005.* Washington, DC: Center for Devices and Radiological Health.

U.S. Food and Drug Administration. (2006, May 11). *FDA approves novel medication for smoking cessation.* Washington, DC: Author.

Ussher, J., Kirsten, L., Butow, P., & Sandoval, M. (2006). What do cancer support groups provide which other supportive relationships do not? The experience of peer support groups for people with cancer. *Social Science & Medicine, 62,* 2565–2576.

V

Vacca, J. A. L., Vacca, R. T., Gove, M. K., Burkey, L. C., Lenhart, L. A., & McKeon, C. A. (2006). *Reading and learning to read* (6th ed.). Boston: Allyn & Bacon.

Vadum, A. E., & Rankin, N. O. (1998). *Psychological research.* New York: McGraw-Hill.

Vaillant, G. E. (1977). *Adaptation to life.* Boston: Little, Brown.

Vaillant, G. E. (1983). *The natural history of alcoholism.* Cambridge, MA: Harvard University Press.

Vaillant, G. E. (1992). Is there a natural history of addiction? In C. P. O'Brien & J. H. Jaffe (Eds.), *Addictive states.* Cambridge, MA: Harvard University Press.

Vaillant, G. E. (2002). *Aging well.* Boston: Little, Brown.

Vaillant, G. E., & Mukamal, K. (2001). Successful aging. *American Journal of Psychiatry, 158,* 839–847.

Valentine, V., & Curl, W. W. (2006). Concussions in adolescent athletes. *Instructional Course Lectures, 55,* 703–709.

Van Ameringen, M., Lane, R. M., Walker, J. R., Rudaredo, C., Chooka, P. R., Goldner, E., Johnston, E., Lavallee, Y., Saibal, N., Pecknold, J. C., Hadrava, V., & Swinson, R. P. (2001). Sertaline treatment of generalized social phobia: 20-week, double-blind, placebo-controlled study. *American Journal of Psychiatry, 158,* 275–281.

van Bokhoven, I., van Goozen, S. H. M., van Engeland, H., Schaal, B., Arseneault, L., Seguin, J. R., Assaad, J., Nagin, D. S., Vitaro, F., & Tremblay, R. E. (2006). Salivary testosterone and aggression, delinquency, and social dominance in a population-based longitudinal study of adolescent males. *Hormones and Behavior, 50,* 118–125.

Vandello, J. A., & Cohen, D. (2004). When believing is seeing: Sustaining norms of violence in cultures of honor. In M. Schaller & C. S. Crandall (Eds.). *The psychological foundations of culture* (pp. 281–304). Mahwah, NJ: Erlbaum.

Van den Boom, D. C. (1994). The influence of temperament and mothering on attachment and exploration: An experimental manipulation of sensitive responsiveness among lower-class mothers with irritable infants. *Child Development, 65,* 1457–1477.

Van Dick, R., Becker, T. E., & Meyer, J. P. (2006). Commitment and identification: Forms, foci, and future. *Journal of Organizational Behavior, 27,* 545–548.

Van Elst, L. T., Ebert, D., & Trimble, M. R. (2001). Hippocampus and amygdala pathology in depression. *American Journal of Psychiatry, 158,* 652–653.

Van Es, J. J., Vladusich, T., & Cornelissen, F. W. (2007). Local and relational judgments of surface color: Constancy indices and discrimination performance. *Spatial Vision, 20,* 139–154.

van Hateren, J. H. (2007). A model of spatiotemporal signal processing by primate cones and horizontal cells. *Journal of Vision, 7,* 3.

Van Katwyk, P. T., Fox, S., Spector, P. E., & Kelloway, E. K. (2000). Using the job-related affective well-being scale (JAWS) to investigate affective responses to work stressors. *Journal of Occupational Health Psychology, 52,* 219–230.

Van Lange, P. A. M., De Cremer, D., Van Dijk, E., & Van Vugt, M. (2007). Self-interest and beyond: Basic principles of social interaction. In A. W. Kruglanski & E. T. Higgins (Eds.), *Social psychology: Handbook of basic principles* (2nd ed.). New York: Guilford.

Van Lange, P. A. M., Rusbult, C. E., Drigotas, S. M., & Arriaga, X. B. (1997). Willingness to sacrifice in close relationships. *Journal of Personality and Social Psychology, 72,* 1373–1395.

van Marie, K., & Wynn, K. (2006). Six-month-old infants use analog magnitudes to represent duration. *Developmental Science, 9,* F41–F49.

Vanni, S., Henriksson, L., Viikari, M., & James, A. C. (2006).Retinotopic distribution of chromatic responses in human primary visual cortex. *European Journal of Neuroscience, 24,* 1821–1831.

van Reekum, C. M., Urry, H. L., Johnstone, T., Thurow, M. E., Frye, C. J., Jackson, J., Schaefer, H. S., Alexander, A. L. & Davidson R. J. (2007). Individual differences in amygdala and ventromedial prefrontal cortex activity are associated with evaluation speed and psychological well-being. *Journal of Cognitive Neuroscience, 19,* 237–248.

Van Riper, M. (2007). Families of children with Down syndrome: Responding to "a change in plans" with resilience. *Journal of Pediatric Nursing, 22,* 116–128.

Van Vugt, M., & Van Lange, P. A. M. (2006). The altruism puzzle: Psychological adaptations for prosocial behavior. In M. Schaller, J. S. Simpson, & D. T. Kenrick (Eds.), *Evolution and social psychology: Frontiers of social psychology* (pp. 237–261). Madison, CT: Psychosocial Press.

Van Winkle, E. (2000). The toxic mind: The biology of mental illness and violence. *Medical Hypotheses, 55,* 356–368.

Vaughn, A. A., & Roesch, S. C. (2003). Psychological and physical health correlates of coping in minority adolescents. *Journal of Health Psychology, 8,* 671–683.

Vaughn, S., Bos, C. S., & Schumm, J. S. (2003). *Teaching exceptional, diverse, and at-risk students in the general education classroom* (3rd ed.). Boston: Allyn & Bacon.

Vega, V., & Malamuth, N. M. (2007). Predicting sexual aggression: The role of pornography in the context of general and specific risk factors. *Aggressive Behavior, 33,* 104–117.

Verfaellie, M., Martin, E., Page, K., Parks, E., & Keane, N. M. (2006). Implicit memory for novel conceptual associations in amnesia. *Cognitive, Affective, and Behavioral Neuroscience, 6,* 91–101.

Verhagen, J. V., & Engelen, L. (2006). The neurocognitive bases of human multimodal food perception: Sensory integration. *Neuroscience and Biobehavioral Reviews, 30,* 613–650.

Vermetten, E., Schmahl, C., Lindner, S., Loewenstein, R. J., & Bremner, J. D. (2006). Hippocampal and amygdalar volumes in dissociative identity disorder. *American Journal of Psychiatry, 163,* 630–636.

Vernon, A. (2007). Rational emotive behavior therapy. In D. Capuzzi & D. Gross (Eds.), *Counseling and psychotherapy* (4th ed.). Upper Saddle River, NJ: Prentice-Hall.

Verquer, M. L., Beehr, T. A., & Wagner, S. H. (2003). A meta-analysis of relations between person–organization fit and work attitudes. *Journal of Vocational Behavior, 63,* 473–489.

Vetter, I., Kapitzke, D., Hermanussen, S., Moneith, G. R., & Cabot, P. J. (2006). The effects of pH on beta-endorphin and morphine inhibition of calcium transients in dorsal root ganglion neurons. *Journal of Pain, 7,* 488–499.

Vieweg, W. V., Julius, D. A., Fernandez, A., Beatty-Brooks, M., Hettema, J. M., & Pandurangi, A. K. (2006). Posttraumatic stress disorder: Clinical features, pathophysiology, and treatment. *American Journal of Medicine, 119,* 383–390.

Viney, W., & King, D. B. (2003). *History of psychology* (3rd ed.). Boston: Allyn & Bacon.

Visser, P. S., & Cooper, J. (2007). Attitude change. In M. A. Hogg & J. Cooper (Eds.), *The Sage handbook of social psychology* (concise 2nd ed.). Thousand Oaks, CA: Sage.

Vogt, T. M., Mullooly, J. P., Ernst, D., Pople, C. R., & Hollis, J. F. (1992). Social networks as predictors of ischemic heart disease, cancer, stroke, and hypertension. *Journal of Clinical Epidemiology, 45,* 659–666.

Vogt, W. P. (2007). *Quantitative research methods for professionals in education and other fields.* Boston: Allyn & Bacon.

Volim, B. A., Taylor, A. N., Richardson, P., Corcoran, R., Stirling, J., McKie, S., Deakin, J. F., & Elliott, R. (2006). Neuronal correlates of theory of mind and empathy: A functional magnetic resonance imaging study in a nonverbal task. *NeuroImage, 29,* 90–98.

Vollrath, M. A., Kwan, K. Y., & Corey, D. P. (2007). The micromachinery of mechanotransduction in hair cells. *Annual Review of Neuroscience* (vol. 30). Palo Alto, CA: Annual Reviews.

von Békésy, G. (1960). Vibratory patterns of the basilar membrane. In E. G. Wever (Ed.), *Experiments in hearing.* New York: McGraw-Hill.

von Bolhen und Halbach, O., & Dermietzel, R. (2006). *Neurotransmitters and Neuromodulators: Handbook of receptors and biological effects* (2nd ed.). Weinheim, Germany: Wiley-VCH.

von Helmholtz, H. (1852). On the theory of compound colors. *Philosophical Magazine, 4,* 519–534.

Voshaar, R. C., & others. (2006). Predictors of long-term benzodiazepine abstinence in participants of a randomized controlled benzodiazepine withdrawal program. *Canadian Journal of Psychiatry, 51,* 445–452.

Voss, H. U., Uluc, A. M., Dyke, J. P., Watts, R., Kobylarz, E. J., McCandliss, B. D., Heier, L. A., Beattie, B. J., Hamacher, K. A., Vallabhajosula, S., Goldsmith, S. J., Ballon, D., Giacino, J. T., & Schiff, N. D. (2006). Possible axonal regrowth in late recovery from the minimally conscious state. *Journal of Clinical Investigation, 116,* 2005–2011.

Voudouris, N. J., Peck, C. L., & Coleman, G. (1985). Conditioned placebo responses. *Journal of Personality and Social Psychology, 48,* 7–53.

Vygotsky, L. S. (1962). *Thought and language.* Cambridge, MA: MIT Press.

W

Wagner, A. D., Schacter, D. L., Rotte, M., Koutstaal, B., Maril, A., Dale, A. M., Rosen, B. R., & Buckner, R. L. (1998). Building memories: Remembering and forgetting of verbal experiences as predicted by brain activity. *Science, 281,* 1185–1187.

Wagner, U., Gais, S., & Born, J. (2001). Emotional memory formation is enhanced across sleep intervals with high amounts of rapid eye movement sleep. *Learning and Memory, 8,* 112–119.

Wai, J., Lubinski, D., & Benbow, C. P. (2005) Creativity and occupational accomplishments among intellectually precocious youths: An age 13 to age 33 longitudinal study. *Journal of Educational Psychology, 97,* 484–492.

Waite, R.vL. (2006). Variations in the experiences and expressions of depression among ethnic minorities. *Journal of the National Black Nurses Association, 17,* 29–35.

Wald, A., Langenberg, A. G., & Krantz, E. (2005). The relationship between condom use and herpes simplex virus acquisition. *Annals of Internal Medicine, 143,* 707–713.

Walker, D. D., Roffman, R. A., Stephens, R. S., Wakana, K., & Berghuis, J. (2006). Motivational enhancement therapy for adolescent marijuana users: A preliminary randomized controlled trial. *Journal of Consulting and Clinical Psychology, 74,* 628–632.

Walker, D. R., & Milton, G. A. (1966). Memory transfer vs. sensitization in cannibal planarians. *Psychonomic Science, 5,* 293–294.

Walker, M. P., & Stickgold, R. (2006). Sleep, memory, and plasticity. *Annual Review of Psychology* (vol. 57). Palo Alto, CA: Annual Reviews.

Wall, P. D., & Melzack, R. (1999). *Textbook of pain* (4th ed.). Philadelphia: Saunders.

Wallerstein, R. S. (1989). The psychotherapy research project of the Menninger Foundation: An overview. *Journal of Consulting and Clinical Psychology, 57,* 195–205.

Walley, A. J., Blakemore, A. I., & Froguel, P. (2006). Genetics of obesity and the prediction of risk for health. *Human Molecular Genetics, 15,* Suppl. 2, R124–R130.

Wampold, B. E. (2001). *The great psychotherapy debate: Models, methods, and findings.* Mahwah, NJ: Erlbaum.

Wampold, B. E., & Brown, G. S. (2005). Estimating variability in outcomes attributable to therapists: A naturalistic study of outcomes of managed care. *Journal of Consulting and Clinical Psychology, 73,* 914–923.

Wang, H., Hu, Y., & Tsien, J. Z. (2006). Molecular and systems mechanisms of memory consolidation and storage. *Progress in Neurobiology, 79,* 123–135.

Ward, A., & Mann, T. (2000). Don't mind if I do: Disinhibited eating under cognitive load. *Journal of Personality and Social Psychology, 78,* 753–763.

Ward, J., Hall, K., & Haslam, C. (2006). Patterns of memory dysfunction in current and 2-year abstinent MDMA users. *Journal of Clinical and Experimental Neuropsychology, 28,* 306–324.

Ward, L. M. (2003). Understanding the role of entertainment media in the sexual socialization of American youth: A review of empirical research. *Developmental Review, 23,* 347–388.

Ward, T. B. (2007). Creative cognition as a window on creativity. *Methods, 42,* 28–37.

Wardlaw, G. M., & Hampl, J. (2007). *Perspectives in nutrition* (7th ed.). New York: McGraw-Hill.

Warr, P. (2007). *Work, happiness, and unhappiness.* Mahwah, NJ: Erlbaum.

Warren, J. I., Stein, J. A., & Grella, C. E. (2007). Role of social support and self-efficacy in treatment outcomes among clients with co-occurring disorders. *Drug and Alcohol Dependence.* (in press)

Waterhouse, J., Reilly, T., Atkinson, G., & Edwards, B. (2007). Jet lag: Trends and coping strategies. *Lancet, 369,* 1117–1129.

Watkins, L. R., & Maier, S. F. (2000). The pain of being sick. *Annual Review of Psychology* (vol. 51). Palo Alto, CA: Annual Reviews.

Watson, A., El-Deredy, W., Bentley, D. E., Vogt, B. A., & Jones, A. K. (2006). Categories of placebo response in the absence of site-specific stimulation of analgesia. *Pain, 126,* 115–122.

Watson, D. (2001). Positive affectivity: The disposition to experience pleasurable emotional states. In C. R. Snyder & S. J. Lopez (Eds.), *Handbook of positive psychology.* New York: Oxford University Press.

Watson, D., & Clark, L. A. (1997). Extraversion and its positive emotional core. In R. Hogan, J. A. Johnson, & S. R., Briggs (Eds.), *Handbook of personality psychology* (pp. 767–793). San Diego: Academic.

Watson, D., & Walker, L. M. (1996). The long-term stability and predictive validity of trait measures of affect. *Journal of Personality and Social Psychology, 70*(3), 567–577.

Watson, D. L., & Tharp, R. G. (2007). *Self-directed behavior* (9th ed.). Belmont, CA: Wadsworth.

Watson, J. B. (1928). *Psychological care of the infant and child.* Philadelphia: Lippincott.

Watson, J. B., & Rayner, R. (1920). Conditioned emotional reactions. *Journal of Experimental Psychology, 3,* 1–14.

Waugh, C. E., & Fredrickson, B. L. (2006). Nice to know you: Positive emotions, self–other overlap, and complex understanding in the formation of a new relationship. *Journal of Positive Psychology, 1,* 93–106.

Waxman, S. R., & Lidz, J. L. (2006). Early word learning. In D. Kuhn & R. Siegler (Eds.), *Handbook of child psychology* (6th ed., vol. 2, pp. 299–335). Hoboken, NJ: Wiley.

Weaver, K., Garcia, S. M., Schwarz, N., & Miller, D. T. (2007). Inferring the popularity of an opinion from its familiarity: A repetitive voice can sound like a chorus. *Journal of Personality and Social Psychology, 92,* 821–833.

Webb, B. (2007). Insect behavior: Controlling flight altitude with optic flow. *Current Biology, 17,* R124–R125.

Webb, W. B. (2000). Sleep. In A. Kazdin (Ed.), *Encyclopedia of psychology.* Washington, DC, & New York: American Psychological Association and Oxford University Press.

Webster, J. M., Smith, R. H., Rhodes, A., & Whatley, M. A. (1999). The effect of a favor on public and private compliance: How internalized is the norm of reciprocity? *Basic and Applied Social Psychology, 21,* 251–260.

Webster, M. J., Herman, M. M., Kleinman, J. E., & Shannon Weikert, C. (2006). BDNF and trkB expression in the hippocampus and temporal cortex during the human life span. *Gene Expression Patterns, 6,* 941–951.

Wechsler, H., Davenport, A., Sowdall, G., Moetykens, B., & Castillo, S. (1994). Health and behavioral consequences of binge drinking in college. *Journal of the American Medical Association, 272,* 1672–1677.

Wechsler, H., Lee, J. E., Kuo, M., & Lee, H. (2000). College binge drinking in the 1990s—A continuing health problem: Results of the Harvard University School of Public Health 1999 College Alcohol Study. *Journal of American College Health, 48,* 199–210.

Wechsler, H., Lee, J. E., Kuo, M., Seibring, M., Nelson, T. F., & Lee, H. (2002). Trends in college binge drinking during a period of increased prevention efforts: Findings from 4 Harvard School of Public Health college alcohol study surveys: 1993–2001. *Journal of American College Health, 50,* 203–217.

Wegener, D. T., Clark, J. K., & Petty, R. E. (2006). Not all stereotyping is created equal: Differential consequences of thoughtful versus non-thoughtful stereotyping. *Journal of Personality and Social Psychology, 90,* 42–59.

Wegener, D. T., Petty, R. E., & Smith, S. M. (1995). Positive mood can increase or decrease message scrutiny: The hedonic contingency view of mood and message processing. *Journal of Personality and Social Psychology, 69,* 5–15.

Wegner, D. M. (1989/1990). *White bears and other unwanted thoughts: Suppression, obsession, and the psychology of mental control.* New York: Penguin.

Wei, P., & Zhou, X. (2006). Processing multidimensional objects under different perceptual loads: The priority of bottom-up perceptual saliency. *Brain Research, 1114,* 113–124.

Weill, S. S. (2005). *The real truth about teens and sex: From hooking up to friends with benefits—what teens are thinking, doing, and talking about, and how to help them make smart choices.* New York: Penguin.

Weineke, J. K., Thurston, S. W., Kelsey, K. T., Varkonyi, A., Wain, J. C., Mark, E. J., & Christiani, D. C. (1999). Early age at smoking initiation and tobacco carcinogen DNA damage in the lung. *Journal of the National Cancer Institute, 91,* 614–619.

Weiner, B. (1986). *An attributional theory of motivation and emotion.* New York: Springer-Verlag.

Weiner, B. (2006). Social motivation, justice, and the moral emotions: An attributional approach. Mahwah, NJ: Erlbaum.

Weiner, I. B. (2004). Rorschach assessment: Current status. In M. Hersen (Ed.), *Comprehensive handbook of psychological assessment* (vol. 2). New York: Wiley.

Weinstein, C. S. (2007). *Middle and secondary classroom management: Lessons from research and practice.* New York: McGraw-Hill.

Weiss, B., & Feldman, R. S. (2006). Looking good and lying to do it: Deception as an impression management strategy in job interviews. *Journal of Applied Social Psychology, 36,* 1070–1086.

Weissenborn, R., & Duka, T. (2000). State-dependent effects of alcohol on explicit memory: The role of semantic associations. *Psychopharmacology, 149,* 98–106.

Weissman, M., & Olfson, M. (1995). Depression in women: Implications for health care research. *Science, 269,* 799–801.

Wellman, H. M., Phillips, A. T., & Rodriguez, T. (2000). Young children's understanding of perception, desire, and emotion. *Child Development, 71,* 895–912.

Wellman, H. M., & Woolley, J. D. (1990). From simple desires to ordinary beliefs: The early development of everyday psychology. *Cognition, 35,* 245–275.

Wells, N. M., & Evans, G. W. (2003). Nearby nature: A buffer of life stress among rural children. *Environment and Behavior*, 35, 311–330.

Wen, T. C., Rogido, M., Genetta, T., & Sola, A. (2004). Permanent focal cerebral ischemia activates erythropoietin receptor in the neonatal rat brain. *Neuroscience Letters, 355,* 165–168.

Wenseleers, T., & Ratnieks, F. L. W. (2006). Enforced altruism in insect societies. *Nature, 444,* 50.

Wenzlaff, R. M., & Prohaska, M. L. (1989). When misery loves company: Depression, attributions, and responses to others' moods. *Journal of Experimental Social Psychology, 25,* 220–223.

Werner, J. M., & Bolino, M. C. (1997). Explaining U.S. courts of appeals decisions involving performance appraisal: Accuracy, fairness, and validation. *Personnel Psychology, 50,* 1–24.

Wesson, M. J., & Gogus, C. I. (2005). Shaking hands with a computer: An examination of two methods of organizational newcomer orientation. *Journal of Applied Psychology, 90,* 1018–1026.

West, R. (2005). Time for a change: Putting the transtheoretical (stages of change) model to rest. *Addiction, 100,* 1036–1039.

West, R., & Bowry, R. (2005). Effects of aging and working memory demands on prospective memory. *Psychophysiology, 42,* 698–712.

Westefeld, J. S., Button, C., Haley, J. T., Kettmann, J. J., MacConnell, J., Sandil, R., & Tallman, B. (2006). College student suicide: A call to action. *Death Studies, 30,* 931–956.

Westmaas, J. E., Gil-Rivas, V., & Silver, R. C. (2007). Designing and implementing: Interventions to promote health and prevent illness. In H. S. Friedman & R. C. Silver (Eds.), *Foundations of health psychology.* New York: Oxford University Press.

Wheeler, R., E., Davidson, R. J., & Tomarken, A. J. (1993). Frontal brain asymmetry and emotional reactivity: A biological substrate of affective style. *Psychophysiology, 30*(1), 82–89.

Whiffen, V. E., & Demidenko, N. (2006). Mood disturbances across the lifespan. In J. Worell, & C. D. Goodheart (Eds.), *Handbook of girls' and women's health: Gender and well-being across the lifespan.* New York: Oxford University Press.

Whipple, B., Ogden, G., & Komisaruk, B. (1992). Analgesia produced in women by genital self-stimulation. *Archives of Sexual Behavior, 9,* 87–99.

Whitaker, R. (2002). Mad in America: Bad science, bad medicine, and the mistreatment of the mentally ill. Cambridge, MA: Perseus.

White, J. W., & Frabutt, J. M. (2006). Violence against girls and women: An integrative developmental perspective. In J. Worell & C. D. Goodheart (Eds.), *Handbook of girls' and women's psychological health: Gender and well-being across the lifespan* (pp. 85–93). New York: Oxford University Press.

White, R. W. (1992). Exploring personality the long way: The study of lives. R. A. Zucker, A. I. Rabin, J. Aronoff, & S. J. Frank (Eds.), *Personality structure in the life course: Essays on personology in the Murray tradition* (pp. 3–21). New York: Springer.

Whitfield, K. E., King, G., Moller, S., Edwards, C. L., Nelson, T., & Vandenbergh, D. (2007). Concordance rates for smoking among African-American twins. *Journal of the American Medical Association, 99,* 213–217.

Whitford, T. J., Rennie, C. J., Grieve, S. M., Clark, C. R., Gordon, E., & Williams, L. M. (2006). Brain maturation in adolescence. *Human Brain Mapping, 28,* 228–237.

Whittington, C. J., Kendall, T., & Pilling, S. (2005). Are the SSRIs and atypical antidepressants safe and effective for children and adolescents? *Current Opinions in Psychiatry, 18,* 21–25.

Wholley, M. A. (2006). Depression and cardiovascular disease: Healing the broken-hearted. *Journal of the American Medical Association, 295,* 2874–2881.

Wickens, A. (2005). *Foundations of biopsychology* (2nd ed.). Upper Saddle River, NJ: Prentice-Hall.

Widiger, T. A., & Trull, T. J. (2007). Plate tectonics in the classification of personality disorder: Shifting to a dimensional model. *American Psychologist, 62,* 71–83.

Wiegand, D. M., & Geller, E. S. (2004). Connecting positive psychology and organizational behavior management: Achievement motivation and the power of positive reinforcement. *Journal of Organizational Behavior Management, 24,* 3–24.

Wiens, S. (2006). Subliminal emotion perception in brain imaging: Findings, issues, and recommendations. *Progress in Brain Research, 156,* 105–121.

Wiersma, D., Nienhuis, F. J., Slooff, C. J., & Giel, R. (1998). Natural course of schizophrenic disorders: A 15-year follow up of a Dutch incidence cohort. *Schizophrenia Bulletin, 24,* 75–85.

Wierzbicki, M. (1999). *Introduction to clinical psychology.* Boston: Allyn & Bacon.

Wigfield, A., Byrnes, J. P., & Eccles, J. S. (2006). Development during early and middle adolescence. In P. Alexander & P. Winne (Eds.), *Handbook of educational psychology* (2nd ed., pp. 87–113). New York: Macmillan.

Wigfield, A., Eccles, J. S., Schiefele, U., Roeser, R. W., & Davis-Kean, P. (2006). Development of achievement motivation. In W. Damon & R. Lerner (Eds.), *Handbook of child psychology* (6th ed.). New York: Wiley.

Williams, G. C., McGregor, H. A., Zeldman, A., Freedman, Z. R., & Deci, E. L. (2004). Testing a self-determination theory process model for promoting glycemic control through diabetes self-management. *Health Psychology, 23,* 58–66.

Williams, G. C., McGregor, H., Sharp, D., Kouides, R. W., Levesque, C. S., Ryan, R. M., & Deci, E. L. (2006). A self-determination multiple risk intervention trial to improve smokers' health. *Journal of General Internal Medicine, 21,* 1288–1294.

Williams, J. D., & Gruzelier, J. H. (2001). Differentiation of hypnosis and relaxation by analysis of narrow band theta and alpha frequencies. *International Journal of Clinical and Experimental Hypnosis, 49,* 185–206.

Williams, J. M. (2006). *Applied sport psychology* (5th ed.). New York: McGraw-Hill.

Williams, J. M. G., Teasdale, J. D., Segal, Z. V., & Kabat-Zinn, J. (2007). *The mindful way through depression.* New York: Guilford.

Williams, L. M. (1995). Recovered memories of abuse in women with documented child sexual victimization histories. *Journal of Traumatic Stress, 19,* 257–267.

Williams, L. M. (2003). Understanding child abuse and violence against women: A life-course perspective. *Journal of Interpersonal Violence, 18,* 441–451.

Williams, L. M. (2004). Researcher-advocate collaborations to end violence against women. *Journal of Interpersonal Violence, 19,* 1350–1357.

Williams, R. B. (2001). Hostility (and other psychosocial risk factors): Effects on health and the potential for successful behavioral approaches to prevention and treatment. In A. Baum, T. A. Revenson, & J. E. Singer (Eds.), *Handbook of health psychology.* Mahwah, NJ: Erlbaum.

Williams, R. B. (2002). Hostility, neuroendocrine changes, and health outcomes. In H. G. Koenig & H. J. Cohen (Eds.), *The link betgween religion and health.* New York: Oxford University Press.

Willis, J., & Todorov, A. (2006). First impressions: Making up your mind after a 100-ms exposure to a face. *Psychological Science, 17,* 592–598.

Willis, S. L., & Schaie, K. W. (2005). Cognitive trajectories in midlife and cognitive functioning in old age. In S. L. Willis & M. Martin (Eds.), *Middle adulthood.* Thousand Oaks, CA: Sage.

Wilson, J. F. (2007). Posttraumatic stress disorder needs to be recognized in primary care. *Annals of Internal Medicine, 146,* 617–620.

Wilson, M., & Daly, M. (2004). Marital cooperation and conflict. In C. B. Crawford & C. A. Salmon (Eds.), *Evolutionary psychology, public policy, and private decisions.* Mahwah, NJ: Erlbaum.

Wilson, M. A. (2007). A history of job analysis. In L.L. Koppes (Ed.), *Historical perspectives in industrial and organizational psychology.* Mahwah, NJ: Erlbaum.

Wilson, R. S., Mendes de Leon, D. F., Bienias, J. L., Evans, D. A., & Bennett, D. A. (2004). Personality and mortality in old age. *Journals of Gerontology: Psychological Sciences and Social Sciences, 59B,* 110–116.

Wilund, K. R. (2007). Is the anti-inflammatory effect of regular exercise responsible for r reduced cardiovascular disease? *Clinical Science, 112,* 543–555.

Windholz, G., & Lamal, P. A. (2002). Kohler's insight revisited. In R. A. Griggs (Ed.), *Handbook for teaching introductory psychology: Vol. 3: With an emphasis on assessment* (pp. 80–81). Mahwah, NJ: Erlbaum.

Winer, R. L., Hughes, J. P., Feng, O., O'Reilly, S., Kiviat, N. B., Holmes, K. K., & Koutsky, L. A. (2006). Condom use and the risk of genital human papillomavirus infection in young women. *New England Journal of Medicine, 354,* 2645–2654.

Winner, E. (2000). The origins and ends of giftedness. *American Psychologist, 55,* 159–169.

Winner, E. (2006). Development in the arts. In W. Damon & R. Lerner (Eds.), *Handbook of child psychology* (6th ed.). New York: Wiley.

Winter, D. G. (2005). Measuring the motives of political actors at a distance. In J. M. Post (Ed.), *The psychological assessment of political leaders: With profiles of Saddam Hussein and Bill Clinton* (pp. 153–177). Ann Arbor: University of Michigan Press.

Wise, P. M. (2006). Aging of the female reproductive system. In E. J. Masor & S. N. Austed (Eds.), *Handbook of the biology of aging* (6th ed.). San Diego: Academic.

Witelson, S. F., Kigar, D. L., & Harvey, T. (1999). The exceptional brain of Albert Einstein. *Lancet, 353,* 2149–2153.

Witteman, C. L., Harries, C., Bekker, H. L., & Van Aarle, E. J. (2007). Evaluating psychodiagnostic decisions. *Journal of Evaluation in Clinical Practice, 13,* 10–15.

Wobst, A. H. (2007). Hypnosis and surgery: Past, present, and future. *Anesthesia and Analgesia, 104,* 1199–1208.

Wocadlo, C., & Rieger, I. (2006). Educational and therapeutic resource dependency at early school age in children who were born very preterm. *Early Human Development, 82,* 29–37.

Woike, B., & Matic, D. (2004). Cognitive complexity in response to traumatic experiences. *Journal of Personality, 72,* 633–657.

Woike, B., Mcleod, S., & Goggin, M. (2003). Implicit and explicit motives influence accessibility to different autobiographical knowledge. *Personality and Social Psychology Bulletin, 29,* 1046–1055.

Wolbers, T., Schoell, E. D., Verleger, R., Kraft, S., McNamara, A., Jaskowski, P., & Buchel, C. (2006). Changes in connectivity profiles as a mechanism for strategic control over interfering subliminal information. *Cerebral Cortex, 16,* 857–864.

Wolkove, N., Elkholy, O., Baltzan, M., & Palayew, M. (2007). Sleep and aging: 1. Sleep disorders commonly found in older people. *Canadian Medical Association Journal, 176,* 1299–1304.

Wolpe, J. (1963). Behavior therapy in complex neurotic states. *British Journal of Psychiatry, 110,* 28–34.

Womelsdorf, T., Anton-Erxleben, K., Pieper, F., & Treue, S. (2006). Dynamic shifts of visual receptive fields in cortical area MT by spatial attention. *Nature Neuroscience, 9,* 1156–1160.

Wood, L. S., Pickering, E. H., & Dechairo, B. M. (2007). Significant support for DAO as a schizophrenia susceptibility locus: Examination of five genes putatively associated with schizophrenia. *Biological Psychiatry, 61,* 1195–1199.

Wood, R. L., & Liossi, C. (2006). Neuropsychological and neurobehavioral correlates of aggression following traumatic brain injury. *Journal of Neuropsychiatry & Clinical Neurosciences, 18,* 333–341.

Wood, R. L., & Rutterford, N.A. (2006). Demographic and cognitive predictors of long-term psychosocial outcome following traumatic brain injury. *Journal of the International Neuropsychological Society, 12,* 350–358.

Wood, S. C., Fay, J., Sage, J. R., & Anagnostaras, S. G. (2007). Cocaine and Pavlovian fear conditioning: Dose–effect analysis. *Behavioral Brain Research, 176,* 244–250.

Wood, W., & Eagly, A. H. (2002). A cross-cultural analysis of the behavior of women and men: Implications for the origins of sex differences. *Psychological Bulletin, 128*(5), 699–727.

Wood, W., & Eagly, A. H. (2007). Social structural origins of sex differences in human mating. In S. W. Gangestad & J. A. Simpson (Eds.), *The evolution of mind: Fundamental questions and controversies.* (pp. 383–390). New York: Guilford.

Woodward, T. S, Meier, B., Cairo, T. A., & Ngan, E. T. (2006). Temporo-prefrontal coordination increases when semantic associations are strongly encoded. *Neuropsychologia, 44,* 2308–2314.

Woodward, W. A., Lucci, A., & Cristofanilli, M. (2007). A gene signature in breast cancer. *New England Journal of Medicine, 356,* 1887–1888.

Workman, L., Chilvers, L., Yeomans, H., & Taylor, S. (2006). Development of cerebral lateralization for recognition of emotions in chimeric faces in children aged 5 to 11. *Laterality, 11,* 493–507.

World Health Organization. (2000). *The World Health Report.* Geneva, Switzerland: World Health Organization.

World Health Organization. (2003). *Suicide Rates.* http://www.who. int/mental_health/prevention/suicide/suiciderates/en/ (accessed June 18, 2007).

World Health Organization. (2004). *The world health report: Changing history.* Geneva, Switzerland: Author.

World Health Organization. (2007). *Sedentary lifestyle: A global public health problem.* http://www.who.int/moveforhealth/advocacy/information_sheets/sedentary/en/index.html (accessed June 30, 2007).

Wortman, C. B., & Boerner, K. (2007). Reactions to death of a loved one: Beyond the myths of coping with loss. In H. S. Friedman & R. C. Silver (Eds.), *Foundations of health psychology.* New York: Oxford University Press.

Wright, B. A., & Zhang, Y. (2006). A review of learning with normal and altered sound-localization cues in human adults. *International Journal of Audiology, 45, Suppl.,* S92–S98.

Wright, D., & Loftus, E. F. (2007). Eyewitness memory. In G. Cohen & M. A. Conway (Eds.), *Memory in the real world* (3rd ed.). New York: Psychology Press.

Wright, T. A., & Cropanzano, R. (1998). Emotional exhaustion as a predictor of job performance and voluntary turnover. *Journal of Applied Psychology, 83,* 486–493.

Wright, T. A., & Cropanzano, R. (2000). Psychological well-being and job satisfaction as predictors of job performance. *Journal of Occupational Health Psychology, 5,* 84–94.

Wright, T. A., & Staw, B. M. (1999). Affect and favorable work outcomes: Two longitudinal tests of the happy–productive worker thesis. *Journal of Organizational Behavior, 20,* 1–23.

Wrosch, C., Heckhausen, J., & Lachman, M. E. (2006). Goal management across adulthood and old age: The adaptive value of primary and secondary control. In D. K. Mroczek & T. D. Little (Eds.), *Handbook of personality development* (pp. 399–421). Mahwah, NJ: Erlbaum.

Wrzesniewski, A. (2003). Finding positive meaning in work. In K. S. Cameron, J. E. Dutton, & R. E. Quinn (Eds.), *Positive organizational scholarship: Foundations of a new discipline* (pp. 296–308). San Francisco: Berrett-Koehler.

Wrzesniewski, A., Dutton, J. E., & Debebe, G. (2003). Interpersonal sense-making and the meaning of work. In R. M. Kramer, M. Roderick, & B. M.

Staw (Eds.). *Research in organizational behavior: An annual series of analytical essays and critical reviews* (vol. 25, pp. 93–135). Oxford: Elsevier.

Wrzesniewski, A., McCauley, C. I., Rozin, P., & Schwartz, B. (1997). Jobs, careers, and callings: People's relations to their work. *Journal of Research in Personality, 31,* 21–33.

Wu, Y. H., & Swaab, D. F. (2007). Disturbance and strategies for reactivation of the circadian rhythm system in aging and Alzheimer's disease. *Sleep Medicine.* (in press)

Wyer, N. (2004). Value conflicts in intergroup perception: A social-cognitive perspective. In G. V. Bodenhausen & A. J. Lambert (Eds.), *Foundations of social cognition.* Mahwah, NJ: Erlbaum.

Wyer, R. S. (2007). Principles of mental representation. In A.W. Kruglanski & E. T. Higgins (Eds.), *Social psychology: Handbook of basic principles* (2nd ed.). New York: Guilford.

Wykes, T., Brammer, M., Mellers, J., Bray, P., Reeder, C., Williams, C., & Corner, J. (2002). Effects on the brain of a psychological treatment: Cognitive remediation therapy: Functional magnetic resonance imaging in schizophrenia. *British Journal of Psychiatry, 181,* 144–152.

Y

Yalom, I. D. (1975). *The theory and practice of group psychotherapy.* New York: Basic Books.

Yalom, I. D. (1995). *The theory and practice of group psychotherapy* (4th ed.). New York: Basic Books.

Yalom, I. D., & Leszcz, M. (2006). *Theory and practice of group psychotherapy* (5th ed.). New York: Basic Books.

Yang, M. Y., Zetler, P. M., Prins, R. M., Khan-Farooqi, H., & Liau, L. M. (2006). Immunotherapy for patients with malignant glioma: From theoretical principles to clinical applications. *Expert Review of Neurotherapeutics, 6,* 1481–1494.

Yardley, J. (2001, January 22). Dallas pastor resurrects fragments of his lost life. *New York Times.*

Yarmey, A. D. (1973). I recognize your face but I can't remember your name: Further evidence for the tip-of-the-tongue phenomenon. *Memory and Cognition, 1,* 287–290.

Yingzhong, Y., Dorma, Y., Rili, G., & Kubo, K. (2006). Regulation of body weight by leptin, with special reference to hypoxia-induced regulation. *Internal Medicine, 45,* 941–946.

Young, E., & Korzun, A. (1998). Psychoneuroendocrinology of depression: Hypothalamic-pituitary-gonadal axis. *Psychiatric Clinics of North America, 21,* 309–323.

Young, T. (1802). On the theory of light and colors. *Philosophical Transactions of the Royal Society of London, 92,* 12–48.

Yukl, G., & Lepsinger, R. (2005). Why integrating the leading and managing roles is essential for organizational effectiveness. *Organizational Dynamics, 34,* 361–375.

Yurgelun-Todd, D. (2007). Emotional and cognitive changes during adolescence. *Current Opinion in Neurobiology, 17,* 251–257.

Z

Zadra, A., Pilon, M., & Donderi, D. C. (2006). Variety and intensity of emotions in nightmares and bad dreams. *Journal of Nervous and Mental Disorders, 194,* 249–254.

Zahm, S., & Gold, E. (2002). Gestalt therapy. In M. Hersen & W. H. Sledge (Eds.), *Encyclopedia of psychotherapy.* San Diego: Academic.

Zaitchik, D. (1990). When representations conflict with reality: The preschooler's problem with false beliefs and "false" photographs. *Cognition, 35,* 41–68.

Zajonc, R. B. (1965). Social facilitation. *Science, 149,* 269–274.

Zajonc, R. B. (1968). Attitudinal effects of mere exposure. *Journal of Personality and Social Psychology, 9,* 1–27.

Zajonc, R. B. (1984). On the primacy of affect. *American Psychologist, 39,* 117–123.

Zajonc, R. B. (2001). Mere exposure: A gateway to the subliminal. *Current Directions in Psychological Science, 10,* 224–228.

Zalcman, S. S., & Siegel, A. (2006). The neurobiology of aggression and rage: Role of cytokines. *Brain, Behavior and Immunity, 20,* 507–514.

Zebrowitz, L. A. (1997). *Reading faces: Window to the soul?* Boulder, CO: Westview.

Zebrowitz, L. A., Kikuchi, M., & Fellous, J. (2007). Are effects of emotion expression on trait impressions mediated by babyfaceness? Evidence from connectionist modeling. *Personality and Social Psychology Bulletin, 33,* 648–662.

Zeelenberg, R. (2005). Encoding specificity manipulations do affect retrieval from memory. *Acta Psychologica, 119,* 107–121.

Zeitler, M., Fries, P., & Gielen, S. (2006). Assessing neuronal coherence with single-unit, multi-unit, and local field potentials. *Neural Computation, 18,* 2256–2281.

Zeki, S. (1991). Cerebral akinetopsia (visual motion blindness). A review. *Brain, 114,* 811–824.

Zelazo, P. D., Moscovitch, M., & Thompson, E. (Eds.). (2007). *The Cambridge handbook of consciousness.* New York: Cambridge University Press.

Zeman, A. (2006). What do we mean by "conscious" and "aware"? *Neuropsychological Rehabilitation, 16,* 356–376.

Zerbe, K. J. (2007). Psychotherapy and psychoanalysis: Fifty years later. *Journal of the American Psychoanalytic Association, 55,* 229–238.

Zhao, M., Ko, S. W., Wu, L., Toyoda, H., Xu, H., Quan, J., Li, J., Jia, Y., Ren, M., Xu, Z. C., & Zhuo, M. (2006). Enhanced presynaptic neurotransmitter release in the anterior cingulate cortex of mice with chronic pain. *Journal of Neuroscience, 26,* 8923–8930.

Zhaoping, L., & Guyader, N. (2007). Interference with bottom-up feature detection by higher-level object recognition. *Current Biology, 17,* 26–31.

Zheng, H., Patel, M., Hryniewicz, K., & Katz, S. D. (2006). Association of extended work shifts, vascular function, and inflammatory markers in internal medicine residents: A randomized crossover trial. *Journal of the American Medical Association, 296,* 1049–1050.

Zheng, X. S., Yang, X. F., Liu, W. G., Pan, D. S., Hu, W. W., & Li, G. (2007). Transplanation of neural stem cells into the traumatized brain induces lymphocyte infiltration. *Brain Injury, 21,* 275–278.

Zhou, F. C., Anthony, B., Dunn, K. W., Lindquist, W. B., Xu, Z. C., & Deng, P. (2007). Chronic alcohol drinking alters neuronal dendritic spines in the brain reward center nucleus accumbens. *Brain Research, 1134,* 148–161.

Zhu, Z., Disbrow, E. A., Zumer, J. M., McGonigle, D. J., & Nagarajan, S. S. (2007). Spatiotemporal integration of tactile information in human somatosensory cortex. *BMC Neuroscience, 14,* 21.

Zimbardo, P. (2007). *The Lucifer effect: Understanding how good people turn evil.* New York: Random House.

Zimmerman, B. J., & Schunk, D. H. (Eds.). (2001). *Self-regulated learning and academic achievement.* Mahwah, NJ: Erlbaum.

Zimmerman, B. J., & Schunk, D. H. (Eds.). (2003). *Educational psychology: A century of contributions.* Mahwah, NJ: Erlbaum.

Zonda, T. (2006). One-hundred cases of suicide in Budapest: A case-controlled autopsy study. *Crisis, 27,* 125–129.

Zou, Y., Zheng, J., Ren, T., & Nuttall, A. (2006). Cochlear transducer operating point adaptation. *Journal of the Acoustical Society of America, 119,* 2232–2241.

Zucker, M., Spinazzola, J., Blaustein, M., & van der Kolk, B. A. (2006). Dissociative symptomatology in posttraumatic stress disorder and disorders of extreme stress. *Journal of Trauma & Dissociation, 7,* 19–31

Zwanzger, P., & Rupprecht, R. (2005). Selective GABAergic treatment for panic? Investigations in experimental panic induction and panic disorder. *Journal of Psychiatry and Neuroscience, 30,* 167–175.

Text and Line Art Credits

CHAPTER THREE

Figure 3.3: From R. Lewis, *Life, 3rd Ed.* Copyright © 1998 The McGraw-Hill Companies, Inc. Reproduced with permission of The McGraw-Hill Companies. **Figure 3.4:** From R. Lewis, *Life, 3rd Ed.* Copyright © 1998 The McGraw-Hill Companies, Inc. Reproduced with permission of The McGraw-Hill Companies. **Figure 3.6:** From *Mapping the Mind* by Rita Carter, 1998. Reprinted by permission of Weidenfeld & Nicholson Ltd., a division of The Orion Publishing Group (London). **Figure 3.11:** From *Brain, Mind, and Behavior* by Floyd Bloom, et al. © 1985, 1988, 2001 by Educational Broadcasting Corp. Used with permission of Worth Publishers. **Figure 3.17:** From *Brain, Mind, and Behavior* by Floyd Bloom, et al. © 1985, 1988, 2001 by Educational Broadcasting Corp. Used with permission of Worth Publishers.

CHAPTER FOUR

Figure 4.3: From Tiffany M. Field, Saul M. Schanberg, Frank Scafidi, Charles R. Bauer, Nitza Vega-Lahr, Robert Garcia, Jerome Nystrom, and Cynthia M. Kuhn, "Tactile/Kinesthetic Stimulation Effects on Preterm Neonates," *Pediatrics,* May 1986; 77: 654–658. Used with permission. **Figure 4.6:** From John Santrock, *Topical Life-Span Development.* Copyright © 2002 The McGraw-Hill Companies, Inc. Reproduced with permission of The McGraw-Hill Companies. **Figure 4.9** (art): From John Santrock, *Life-Span Development, 9th Ed.* Copyright © The McGraw-Hill Companies, Inc. Reproduced with permission of The McGraw-Hill Companies. **Figure 4.15:** From John Santrock, *Life-Span Development, 8th Ed.* Copyright © 2002 The McGraw-Hill Companies, Inc. Reproduced with permission of The McGraw-Hill Companies. **Figure 4.20:** From John Santrock, *Child Development, 10th Ed.* Copyright © The McGraw-Hill Companies, Inc. Reproduced with permission of The McGraw-Hill Companies. **Figure 4.21:** From John Santrock, *Life-Span Development, 8th Ed.* Copyright © 2002 The McGraw-Hill Companies, Inc. Reproduced with permission of The McGraw-Hill Companies. **Figure 4.23:** From John Santrock, *Life-Span Development, 11th Ed.* Copyright © 2008 The McGraw-Hill Companies, Inc. Reproduced with permission of The McGraw-Hill Companies. **Figure 4.24:** From John Santrock, *Life-Span Development, 8th Ed.* Copyright © 2002 The McGraw-Hill Companies, Inc. Reproduced with permission of The McGraw-Hill Companies. **Figure 4.25:** From J.E. Schulenberg and N.R. Zarretti. In J.J. Arnett and J.L. Tanner (Eds.), *Emerging Adults in America: Coming of Age in the 21st Century,* Figure 6.1, p. 136. American Psychological Association. Used with permission. **Figure 4.26:** From J.E. Schulenberg and N.R. Zarretti. In J.J. Arnett and J.L. Tanner (Eds.), *Emerging Adults in America: Coming of Age in the 21st Century,* Figure 6.4, p. 139. American Psychological Association. Used with permission. **Figure 4.29:** From Grant Jarding, *USA Today,* January 5, 1999. Reprinted with permission. **Figure 4.33:** From John Santrock, *Life-Span Development, 8th Ed.* Copyright © 2002 The McGraw-Hill Companies, Inc. Reproduced with permission of The McGraw-Hill Companies. **Figure 4.34:** From John Santrock, *Life-Span Development, 8th Ed.* Copyright © 2002 The McGraw-Hill Companies, Inc. Reproduced with permission of The McGraw-Hill Companies. **Figure 4.35:** From John Santrock, *Life-Span Development, 8th Ed.* Copyright © 2002 The McGraw-Hill Companies, Inc. Reproduced with permission of The McGraw-Hill Companies. **Figure 4.36:** From "The Nature of the Influence of Speed on Adult Age Differences in Cognition," *Developmental Psychology,* 1994, 30, 240–259. Copyright © 1994 by the American Psychological Association. Adapted with permission. **Figure 4.37:** From L.L. Carstensen and S. Turk-Charles, *Psychology and Aging,* 9, 262. Copyright © 1994 by the American Psychological Association. Adapted with permission. **Figure 4.38:** From *Aging Well* by George Vaillant, M.D. Copyright © 2002 by George E. Vaillant, M.D. By permission of Little, Brown and Co.

CHAPTER FIVE

Figure 5.17: From Ishihara's Tests for Colour Deficiency. Published by Kanehara Trading, Inc. Tokyo, Japan. Used with permission. **Figure 5.18:** From Atkinson and Hilgard's *Introduction to Psychology 14th edition* by Atkins/Hilgard/Smith/Hoeksema/Fredrickson. 2003. Reprinted with permission of Wadsworth, a division of Thomson Learning: www.thomsonrights.com. Fax 800-730-2215. **Figure 5.27:** From Wathen-Dunn, Weiant, *Models for the Perceptions of Speech and Visual Form,* 1 figure "Movement Aftereffects." © 1967 Massachusetts Institute of Technology, published by The MIT Press. Used with permission. **Figure 5.29:** From James J. Gibson, *The Perception of the Visual World.* Copyright © 1950 by Houghton Mifflin Company. Reprinted with permission. **Figure 5.36:** From *Brain, Mind, and Behavior* by Floyd Bloom, et al. © 1985, 1988, 2001 by Educational Broadcasting Corp. Used with permission of Worth Publishers.

CHAPTER SIX

Figure 6.6: From Roffwarg et al., *Science* 152:604–609, Figure 1 (1966). Copyright © 1966 American Association for the Advancement of Science. Used with permission. **Figure 6.7:** From *Brain, Mind, and Behavior* by Floyd Bloom, et al. © 1985, 1988, 2001 by Educational Broadcasting Corp. Used with permission of Worth Publishers. **Figure 6.10:** From John Santrock, *Adolescence, 8th Ed.* Copyright © 2001 The McGraw-Hill Companies, Inc. Reproduced with permission of The McGraw-Hill Companies. **Figure 6.11:** National Institute of Drug Abuse 2001, Teaching Packet for Psychoactive Drugs, Slide 9. **Figure 6.13:** From *Journal of the American Medical Association,* 272, 1672–1677, 1994, data presented by H. Wechsler, Davenport, et al. *Journal of American Medical Association,* 272, 1672–1677. With permission from the American Medical Association. **Figure 6.14:** National Institute of Drug Abuse 2001, Teaching Packet for Psychoactive Drugs, Slides 12 and 13.

CHAPTER EIGHT

Figure 8.9: From John Santrock, *Life-Span Development, 11th Ed.* Copyright © 2008 The McGraw-Hill Companies, Inc. Reproduced with permission of The McGraw-Hill Companies. **Figure 8.11:** This figure was published in *Journal of Verbal Learning and Verbal Behavior* 3, A.M. Collins and M.R. Quillan, "Retrieval Time for Semantic Memory," 240–248. Copyright Elsevier 1969. **Figure 8.12:** Copyright © 1979. From *Cognitive Psychology and Information Processing* by R. Lachman et al. Reproduced by permission of Lawrence Erlbaum Associates, Inc., a division of Taylor & Francis Group. **Figure 8.15:** Copyright © 1974. From *Human Memory: Theory and Data* by B. Murdock, Jr. Reproduced by permission of Lawrence Erlbaum Associates, Inc., a division of Taylor & Francis Group. **Figure 8.18:** Reprinted from *Cognition,* 16, D.C. Rubin and M. Kozin, "College Students' Flashbulb Memories," pp. 81–95. Copyright 1984, with permission from Elsevier. **Figure 8.20:** © Exploratorium, www.exploratorium.edu. Used with permission.

CHAPTER NINE

Figure 9.9: From John Santrock, *Children, 7th Ed.* Copyright © 2003 The McGraw-Hill Companies, Inc. Reproduced with permission of The McGraw-Hill Companies. **Figure 9.12:** From "The Increase in IQ Scores from 1932–1997," by Ulric Neisser. Used with permission. **Figure 9.14:** From John Santrock, *Children, 8th Ed.* Copyright © The McGraw-Hill Companies, Inc. Reproduced with permission of The McGraw-Hill Companies. **Figure 9.15:** Reprinted courtesy of Jean Berko Gleason. **Figure 9.16:** From John Santrock, *Educational Psychology.* Copyright © 2001 The McGraw-Hill Companies, Inc. Reproduced with permission of The McGraw-Hill Companies.

CHAPTER TEN

Figure 10.3: NHIS, 1997–June 2006. Data are based on household interviews of a sample of the civilian noninstitionalized population. **Figure 10.4:** From W. Masters and V. E. Johnson, *Human Sexual Response.* Reprinted by permission of Lippincott Williams & Wilkins. **Figure 10.5:** From *Sex in America* by Robert T. Michael et al. © 1994 by CSG Enterprises, Edward O. Laumann, Robert T. Michael, and Gina Kolata. By permission of Little, Brown and Co. and Brockman, Inc.

CHAPTER ELEVEN

Figure 11.1: From *Psychology: A Scientific Study of Human Behavior* 5th edition by Wrightsman/Sigelman/Sanford. 1979. Reprinted with permission of Wadsworth, a division of Thomson Learning: www.thomsonrights. com. Fax 800-730-2215. **Figure 11.10:** From R. L. Weiss and B. A. Perry, *Assessment and Treatment of Marital Dysfunction,* Eugene: Oregon Marital Studies Program, 1979. Used with permission by R. L. Weiss. **Figure 11.12:** This article was published in *Journal of Psychosomatic Research,* Vol. 29, S. C. Kobasa, S. R. Maddi, M. C. Puccette, and M. Zola, pp. 525–533. Copyright Elsevier, 1986. Used with permission.

CHAPTER TWELVE

Figure 12.5: Adapted from Stanley Milgram, "Behavioral Study of Obedience," in *Journal of Abnormal and Social Psychology,* 67:371–378, 1963. **Figure 12.6:** The figure by K. Deaux was published in *Encyclopedia of Women and Gender: Sex Similarities and Differences and the Impact of Society of Gender,* 2, Volume Set, edited by Judith Worell, "Types of Identity." Copyright Elsevier 1969. **Figure 12.7:** From M. Sherif, O. J. Harvey, B. J. White, W. E. Hood, C. W. Sherif, *Intergroup Conflict and Cooperation: The Robber's Cave Experiment* (Wesleyan University Press, 1988). © 1988 by M. Sherif, O. J. Harvey, B. J. White, W. E. Hood, C. W. Sherif. Reprinted by permission of Wesleyan University Press. www.wesleyan.edu/wespress.

CHAPTER THIRTEEN

Figure 13.3: From the U.S. Department of Labor, *Dictionary of Occupational Titles,* 4th edition. Available online at www.occupationalinfo.org/. **Figure 13.4:** *Occupational Outlook Handbook* (2006–2007). Tomorrow's jobs. Washington, DC: U.S. Department of Labor. Chart 7. **Figure 13.10:** Data presented after Fritz, C., and Sonnentag, S. (2006). "Recovery, Well-Being, and Performance-Related Outcomes: The Role of Workload and Vacation Experiences." *Journal of Applied Psychology,* 91, 936–946. Data for graph from Table 2, p. 941.

CHAPTER FOURTEEN

Figure 14.6: Reprinted with permission form the *Annual Review of Neuroscience,* Volume 20 © 1997 by Annual Reviews. www.annualreviews. org. **Figure 14.9:** From Weissman and Olfson, *Science* 269:779, Figure 1 (1995). Copyright © 1995 American Association for the Advancement of Science. Used with permission. **Figure 14.13:** © Irving I. Gottesman 2004. Used by permission. **p. 559:** "My Name is Moe Armstrong." Courtesy of Moe Armstrong.

CHAPTER FIFTEEN

Figure 15.2: From Stephen R. Marder, M.D., et al., "The Effects of Risperidone on the Five Dimensions of Schizophrenia Derived by Factor Analysis: Combined Results of the North American Trials," *The Journal of Clinical Psychiatry* 58, pp. 538–546, 1997. Copyright 1997, Physicians Postgraduate Press. Reprinted by permission. **Figure 15.8:** Adapted from A. Freeman and M. A. Reinecke, "Cognitive Therapy" in A. S. Gurman, ed., *Essential Psychotherapies.* Adapted with permission of The Guilford Press. **Figure 15.9:** From *Journal of Consulting and Clinical Psychology,* 1999, 67, 145–150. Copyright © 1999 by the American Psychological Association. Adapted with permission. **Figure 15.11:** Reprinted with permission of Michael J. Lambert, Brigham Young University. **Figure 15.12:** From "A Survival Analysis of Clinically Significant Change in Outpatient Psychotherapy" by Anderson & Lambert, from *Journal of Clinical Psychology,* 57, 875–888, copyright © 2001. Reprinted with permission of John Wiley & Sons, Inc. **p. 577:** From F. Perls, 1969 Gestalt Therapy Verbatim. Gestalt Journal Press. Used with permission. **p. 582:** From A. T. Beck, A. J. Rush, B. F. Shaw, and G. Emery, *Cognitive Therapy of Depression,* 1979, pp. 145–146. Used with permission of The Guilford Press. **p. 584:** "Examples of Self-Instructional Methods" by Meichenbaum, Turk, and Burstein, 1975. From "The Nature of Coping with Stress" in I. Sarason and C. Spielberger, eds., *Stress and Anxiety.* Hemisphere Publishing. Used with permission by I. Sarason.

CHAPTER SIXTEEN

Figure 16.3: From H. Seyle, et al., *The Stress of Life.* Copyright © 1976 The McGraw-Hill Companies, Inc. Reproduced with permission of The McGraw-Hill Companies. **Figure 16.4:** From S. Cohen, E. Frank, W. J. Doyle, D. P. Skoner, B. S. Rabin, and J. M. Gwaltney (1998). "Types of Stressors that Increase Susceptibility to the Common Cold in Adults." *Health Psychology,* 17, 214–233. Copyright © 1998 by the American Psychological Association. Used with permission. **Figure 16.7:** From John Santrock, *Life-Span Development, 11th Ed.* Copyright © 2008 The McGraw-Hill Companies, Inc. Reproduced with permission of The McGraw-Hill Companies. **Figure 16.9:** National Center for Health Statistics (2006), Fig. 13. **Figure 16.10:** From John Santrock, *Life-Span Development, 11th Ed.* Copyright © 2008 The McGraw-Hill Companies, Inc. Reproduced with permission of The McGraw-Hill Companies.

Photo Credits

p. xvi: © Digital Vision/Getty Images; **p. xvii:** © Phil Schermeister/CORBIS; **p. xviii:** © Stockbyte/Getty Images; **p. xx:** © S.Kirchner/photocuisine/Corbis; **p. xxi:** © Burke/Triolo Productions/Brand X/Corbis; **p. xxii:** The McGraw-Hill Companies, Inc.; **p. xxiii:** © Stockbyte/PunchStock; **p. xxiv (top):** © Tetra Images/Corbis; **p. xxiv (bottom):** © RCWW, Inc./Corbis; **p. xxv (top):** © Steve Allen/Brand X; **p. xxv (middle):** © Burke/Triolo/Brand X Pictures; **p. xxv (middle):** The McGraw-Hill Companies, Inc. / Ken Karp photographer; **p. xxv (bottom):** © MM Productions/Corbis; **p. xxviii (collage):** © Photodisc/ Getty Images, © Stockdisc/PunchStock, © Comstock Images/Alamy; **p. xxix (top):** © Stockdisc/PunchStock; **p. xxix (bottom):** © Jim Craigmyle/Corbis; **p. xxxii (top):** © Peter M. Fisher/Corbis; **p. xxxii (middle top):** © Fly Fernandez/zefa/Corbis; **p. xxxii (middle bottom):** © Greg Vote/Corbis; **p. xxxii (bottom):** The McGraw-Hill Companies, Inc.; **p. xxxiii (top):** © Colin Anderson/Brand X/Corbis; **p. xxxiii (bottom):** © Bloomimage/Corbis.

Chapter 1 Opener: © Anne-Marie Weber/Taxi/Getty Images; **p. 5 (top, both):** © AGE Fotostock/SuperStock; **p. 5 (bottom):** © Michael Newman/ PhotoEdit, Inc.; **p. 6:** © artpartner-images.com/Alamy; **p. 7:** © Brand X Pictures/PunchStock; **p. 8 (top):** © William Thomas Cain/Stringer/ Getty Images; **p. 8 (bottom):** © Amos Morgan/Getty Images; **p. 9:** © Tom Grill/Corbis; **p. 11 (top):** © James Warwick/The Image Bank/Getty Images; **p. 12:** © Amos Morgan/Getty Images; **p. 13:** © Corbis; **p. 14:** © George Shelley/Corbis; **p. 16 (top):** © Reuters New Media, Inc./Corbis; **p. 16 (bottom):** © Warren Zinn/Army Times Publishing Company/Corbis; **p. 17:** © Amos Morgan/Getty Images; **p. 18 (top):** Courtesy of Richard Davidson, University of Wisconsin, Madison. Photo by Jeff Miller.; **p. 18 (bottom):** Courtesy of Carol S. Dweck, Stanford University; **p. 19:** Courtesy of James W. Pennebaker, University of Texas. Photo by Marsha Miller; **p. 20 (top left):** © Atlantide Phototravel/Corbis; **p. 20 (top middle):** © Chip Somodevilla/Getty Images; **p. 20 (top right):** © Peter Foley/Reuters/Corbis; **p. 20 (bottom left):** © Dennis MacDonald/PhotoEdit, Inc.; **p. 20 (bottom right):** © David McNew/Getty Images; **p. 21 (top):** © Pat Dessen; **p. 21 (bottom):** Courtesy of Barbara Fredrickson, University of North Carolina; **p. 22:** © Ray Hendley/ Index Stock Imagery, Inc.; **p. 25:** © Tomi/PhotoLink/Getty Images; **p. 26:** © Ryan McVay/Getty Images; **p. 27:** © Amos Morgan/Getty Images

Chapter 2 Opener: © Rose Mueller/Stock4B/Getty Images; **p. 33 (top):** © Creatas/Punchstock; **p. 33 (bottom):** © Donna Day/Getty Images; **p. 34:** © Editorial Image, LLC/Alamy; **p. 35:** © Peter Ciresa Cires/Index Stock; **p. 36:** © The McGraw-Hill Companies, Inc./John Flournoy, photographer; **p. 37:** © Amos Morgan/Getty Images; **p. 38 (top):** © Michael Newman/ PhotoEdit, Inc.; **p. 38 (bottom):** © Ken Regan Pictures; **p. 40:** © Richard T. Nowitz/Corbis; **p. 41:** © Bettmann/Corbis; **p. 43:** © D. Hurst/Alamy; **p. 44:** © Photographers Choice RF/SuperStock; **p. 47:** Image courtesy of The Advertising Archives; **p. 50:** © Steve Cole/Getty Images; **p. 50 (top):**

© David Gonzales/Icon SMI/Corbis; **p. 51:** © Amos Morgan/Getty Images; **p. 53:** © RF@PPS/Alamy; **p. 55:** © Medioimages/Photodisc/Getty Images; **p. 56:** © Amos Morgan/Getty Images; **p. 52:** © AGE Fotostock/SuperStock; **p. 58:** © Frank Micelotta/Getty Images for FOX; **p. 59:** © Royalty-Free/Corbis; **p. 60 (left):** © AFP/Corbis; **p. 60 (right):** © Bob Daemmrich/Stock Boston; **p. 63:** © Tomi/PhotoLink/Getty Images; **p. 64:** © Reuters/Corbis; **p. 65:** © Brand X Pictures; **p. 66:** © Amos Morgan/Getty Images

Chapter 3 Opener: © JGI /Royalty Free; **p. 73 (top left):** © Amana Productions, Inc./Getty Images; **p. 73 (top right):** © Heide Benser/zefa/Corbis; **p. 73 (bottom):** © David P. Hall/Corbis; **p. 76:** © Amos Morgan/Getty Images; **p. 81:** Centers for Disease Control; **p. 83 (top):** © Patrik Giardino/Corbis; **p. 83 (bottom):** © Amos Morgan/Getty Images; **p. 84:** © Jonathan Nourok/PhotoEdit, Inc.; **p. 85:** © Steven Peterson; **p. 86:** © Tetra Images/Alamy; **p. 87:** © Lennart Nilsson/Albert Bonniers Forlag AB; **p. 90 (top):** © John Whiley, California Institute of Technology, estate of James Olds; **p. 90 (bottom):** © A. Glauberman/Photo Researchers, Inc; **p. 91:** From: Damasio, H., Grabowski, T., Frank, R., Galaburda, A.M., Damasio, A.R.: The return of Phineas Gage: Clues about the brain from the skull of a famous patient. *Science,* 264:1102–1105, 1994. Departments of Neurology and Image Analysis Facility, University of Iowa; **p. 92:** Courtesy of Michael J. Tarr, Ph.D.; **p. 94:** © Richard Hamilton Smith/Corbis; **p. 96:** © Amos Morgan/Getty Images; **p. 98:** © Yann Arthus-Bertrand/Corbis; **p. 99:** © Lennart Nilsson/Albert Bonniers Forlag AB; **p. 100 (top):** © Tomi/PhotoLink/Getty Images; **p. 100 (bottom):** © Rex USA Ltd.; **p. 101:** © Arnaldo Magnani/Getty Images; **p. 102:** © Amos Morgan/Getty Images; **p. 104 (top):** © Nick Koudis/Getty Images; **p. 104 (bottom):** © Rick Rickman/Matrix; **p. 106 (top):** © Laura Dwight/PhotoEdit, Inc.; **p. 106 (bottom):** © Enrico Ferorelli; **p. 107:** © Joe Murphy/NBAE via Getty Images; **p. 108:** © Plush Studios/Digital Vision/Getty Images; **p. 110 (top):** © IT Stock Free/SuperStock; **p. 110 (bottom):** © Thinkstock/Jupiterimages

Chapter 4 Opener: © Stockbyte/Getty Images; **p. 116 (left):** © Angela Hampton/Alamy; **p. 116 (middle):** © First Light/Getty Images; **p. 116 (right):** © George Shelley/Corbis; **p. 117:** © Don Farrall/Getty Images; **p. 118 (top):** © Naashon Zalk/Corbis; **p. 118 (bottom):** © Kim Ludbrook/epa/Corbis; **p. 119:** © Amos Morgan/Getty Images; **p. 120 (all):** © Lennart Nilsson, *A Child Is Born*/Dell Publishing Company/Albert Bonniers Forlag AB; **p. 121:** Courtesy of Dr. Tiffany Fields/Touch Research Institutes; **p. 122:** Courtesy of Amy Needham, Duke University; **p. 126 (both):** © D. Goodman/Photo Researchers; **p. 127:** © Paul Fusco/Magnum Photos, Inc.; **p. 131:** © Martin Rogers/Stock Boston; **p. 132:** © Penny Tweedie/Getty Images; **p. 134:** © Joel Gordon; **p. 139 (both):** © Custom Medical Stock Photo; **p. 141:** © Ty Allison/Photographer's Choice/Getty Images; **p. 142:** © AGE Fotostock/SuperStock; **p. 143:** © Amos Morgan/Getty Images; **p. 147:** © USA Today Photo Library, Photo by Robert Deutsch; **p. 148:** © Nancy Richmond/The Image Works; **p. 149:** © Comstock Images/Alamy; **p. 150:** © Amos Morgan/Getty Images; **p. 152:** © Donna Day/Getty Images; **p. 153:** © Pascal Parrot/Sygma/Corbis; **p. 154:** Courtesy of Dr. Jerry W. Shay, PhD. UT Southwestern Medical Center; **p. 155 (margin):** From R. Cabeza, et al., "Age-related differences in neural activity during memory encoding and retrieval: A positron emission tomography study" in *Journal of Neuroscience,* 17, 391–400, 1997; **p. 155 (both):** From Charles Carroll and Dean Miller, *Health: The Science of Human Adaptation,* 5/e. © 1991 Wm. C. Brown Communications, Inc. Dubuque, IA. All rights reserved. Reprinted by permission; **p. 156:** Courtesy Office of Development, School Sisters of Notre Dame, Mankato, MN; **p. 156 (inset):** Steve Liss/Time Life Pictures/Getty Images; **p. 159:** © Design Pics Inc./Alamy; **p. 161:** © Mike Greenlar/The Image Works; **p. 163:** © Tomi/PhotoLink/Getty Images; **p. 164 (top):** © Marmaduke St. John/Alamy; **p. 164 (bottom):** © Reuters/Corbis; **p. 165:** © Amos Morgan/Getty Images

Chapter 5 Opener: © Bridget Webber/Photonica/Getty Images; **173:** © Ryan McVay/Getty Images; **p. 174 (top left):** © Ron Austing; Frank Lane Picture Agency/Corbis; **p. 174 (top right):** © Zig Leszczynski/Animals Animals; **p. 174 (bottom):** © Image Source/Punchstock; **p. 178:** © Doug Plummer/Photo Researchers, Inc.; **p. 179:** Photo by Robert G. Price, USDA Natural

Resources Conservation Service; **p. 181:** © Stockbyte/Getty Images; **p. 183:** © Amos Morgan/Getty Images; **p. 185:** Courtesy of X-Rite, Inc.; **p. 186:** © Frank S. Werblin; **p. 187:** Used with permission from "ABC's of the Human Body" 1987 by The Reader's Digest Association, Inc., Pleasantville, Ney York, www.rd.com. Photography by Morris Karo; **p. 188:** © RubberBall Productions/Getty Images; **p. 192:** "Relativity" by M. C. Escher. © 2002 Cordon Art — Baarn-Holland. All rights reserved.; **p. 193:** © 1994 Jun Oi; **p. 194:** © Erich Lessing/Art Resource, NY; **p. 196:** © Steve Allen/Getty Images; **p. 197 (bottom left):** © Radius Images/Alamy; **p. 197 (bottom right):** © TOMONARI TSUJI/amana images/Getty Images; **p. 186:** © Brooks Kraft/Corbis; **p. 199:** © Amos Morgan/Getty Images; **p. 203:** © Krista Kennell/ZUMA/Corbis; **p. 204:** © Barry Bland/Alamy; **p. 205:** © Mary Kate Denny/PhotoEdit, Inc.; **p. 207 (top):** © Amos Morgan/Getty Images; **P. 207 (bottom):** © Don Farrall/Photodisc/Getty Images; **p. 209 (top):** © Royalty Free/Corbis; **p. 209 (bottom):** © JIMIN LAI/AFP/Getty Images; **p. 211:** © Chip Simmons; **p. 213 (top):** © Dominic Rouse/The Image Bank/Getty Images; **p. 213 (bottom):** © Lennart Nilsson/Albert Bonniers Forlag AB; **p. 214:** © Tomi/PhotoLink/Getty Images; **p. 215:** © StockTrek/Getty Image; **p. 216:** © Amos Morgan/Getty Images

Chapter 6 Opener: © Red Chopsticks/Getty Images; **p. 222:** © Creatas/SuperStock; **p. 223:** © Comstock/Alamy; **p. 225:** © Erin Koran/McGraw-Hill; **p. 226:** © Blend Images/SuperStock; **p. 227:** © Amos Morgan/Getty Images; **p. 229 (left):** © Sean Murphy/Stone/Getty Images; **p. 229 (right):** © Philip Lee Harvey/Getty Images; **p. 230 (top):** © Frank Greenaway/Getty Images; **p. 230 (bottom):** © Royalty Free/Corbis; **p. 231:** Courtesy of San Diego Historical Society Union Tribune Collection; **p. 232 (top):** © Stockbyte/Getty Images; **p. 232 (bottom):** © Will and Deni McIntyre/Photo Researchers, Inc.; **p. 233:** © Moodboard/Corbis; **p. 234:** © Rubberball/Alamy; **p. 235:** © J. Allan Hobson & Hoffman La Roche, Inc.; **p. 238:** © Stockdisc/Getty Images; **p. 239 (left):** © Eric Lessing/Art Resource; **p. 239 (right):** © The Museum of Modern Art/Licensed by SCALA/Art Resource, NY; **p. 241 (top):** © Amos Morgan/Getty Images; **p. 241 (bottom):** © James Wilson/Woodfin Camp & Associates; **p. 242:** © Stanford News Service; **p. 243:** Courtesy of Etzel Cardena; **p. 244:** © Amos Morgan/Getty Images; **p. 245:** © Jupiter Images/Dynamic Graphics; **p. 248:** © Ingram Publishing/Alamy; **p. 249:** © Jonelle Weaver/Getty Images; **p. 252:** "Positron emission tomographic evidence of toxic effect of MDMA ("Ecstasy") on brain serotonin neurons in human beings" by UD McCann, Z Szabo, U Scheffel, RF Dannals, GA Ricaurte. *The Lancet,* 1998, Vol. 352, issue 9138, pages 1433–1437. Reprinted with permission form Elsevier Science; **p. 254:** © David McNew/Getty Images; **p. 256:** © Tomi/PhotoLink/Getty Images; **p. 257:** © Royalty-Free/Corbis; **p. 258:** © Goodshoot/Corbis; **p. 259:** © Amos Morgan/Getty Images

Chapter 7 Opener: © David Allan Brandt/Stone/Getty Images; **p. 266 (top):** © Amos Morgan/Getty Images; **p. 266 (bottom):** The Granger Collection, New York; **p. 269:** Courtesy of Professor Benjamin Harris; **p. 270 (top):** © Jim West/The Image Works; **p. 270 (bottom):** © Asia Images Group/Getty Images; **p. 271:** © Amos Morgan/Getty Images; **p. 272 (bottom left):** © Photofusion Picture Library/Alamy; **p. 272 (bottom right):** © Chris Ware/The Image Works; **p. 274:** © Nina Leen/Time & Life Pictures/Getty Images; **p. 275:** © Richard Cummins/Corbis; **p. 277:** © PictureQuest; **p. 278:** © Michael Dwyer/Alamy; **p. 280:** © Bob Daemmrich/The Image Works; **p. 282 (top):** © Kevin Mackintosh/Getty Images; **p. 282 (middle):** © Image 100/Royalty Free/Corbis; **p. 282 (bottom):** © Spencer Grant/PhotoEdit, Inc.; **p. 283:** © 3D4Medical.com/Getty Images; **p. 284:** © Amos Morgan/Getty Images; **p. 285:** © Tomi/PhotoLink/Getty Images; **p. 288 (all):** © SuperStock; **p. 289:** © Amos Morgan/Getty Images; **p. 290:** Courtesy of Animal Behavior Enterprises, Inc; **p. 291:** © Ingram Publishing/Alamy; **p. 292:** © Jacky Chapman/Alamy; **p. 293:** © Plush Studios/Digital Vision/Getty Images; **p. 297:** © Thinkstock/Jupiterimages

Chapter 8 Opener: © Laurence Dutton/The Image Bank/Getty; **p. 305:** © Amos Morgan/Getty Images; **p. 306:** © Anthony Redpath/Corbis; **p. 307:** © Plush Studios/Getty Images/Digital Vision; **p. 309:** © Amos Morgan/Getty Images; **p. 310:** © Danita Delimont/Alamy; **p. 313:** © Ingram Publishing/Alamy; **p. 315:** © Ingram Publishing/Alamy; **p. 316:** © David Muir/Getty Images/DigitalVision; **p. 316:** © Comstock/PunchStock; **p. 319 (left):** © James L. Shaffer; **p. 319 (middle):** © G. Aschendorf/Photo Researchers,

Page numbers in *italics* indicate illustrations.

Tannock, R., 179
Tanyu, L. H., 176
Tarr, M. J., 92
Tassinary, L., 510
Tata, P., 585
Tataranni, P. A., 395
Tate, D. F., 622
Tatrelli, R., 520
Tatsumi, M., 540
Tavris, C., 424, 426
Tay, C., 456
Taylor, A. N., 226
Taylor, C. B., 599
Taylor, D. J., 237
Taylor, H. G., 121
Taylor, K. I., 188
Taylor, S., 95, 119, 610
Taylor, S. E., 19, 405, 465, 478, 509, 511, 542, 543, 608, 613, 616, 620, 621
Teasdale, J. D., 542
Tedeschi, R., 599, 600
Tee, P. G., 537
Teesson, M., 545
Tellegen, A., 106
Tempelmann, C., 95
Temple, M., 617
Templin, T., 614
Ten, S., 394
Tenenbaum, H. R., 38, 39
Tenenbaum, J. B., 355
Teng, H. M., 620
Tennen, H., 19, 45, 617
Teodorescu, M., 237
Tepper, K., 520
Terenius, L., 553
Teresi, D., 91, 240
Terhakoian, A., 537
Terman, L., 364, 369
Terman, M., 229
Terol, C., 510
Terr, L. C., 329
Tesch-Römer, C., 369
Tetreault, M. K. T., 59
Tevendale, H. D., 489
Thackare, H., 399
Thais, L., 227
Thakor, A., 4, 96
Tharp, R. G., 109, 296, 456, 463, 578, 583, 584
Thase, M. E., 540, 567, 586
Thatcher, M., 3
Thaxton, L., 590
Theakston, J. A., 617
Thelen, E., 122
Thiessen, J. H., 399
Thigpen, C. H., 550
Thisted, R. A., 511, 512
Thoits, P. A., 545
Thomas, K. M., 100, 123, 124, 144
Thomas, M., 231
Thomas, S., 132, 241
Thompson, A., 536
Thompson, E., 349
Thompson, K., 382
Thompson, M. S., 366
Thompson, P. M., 123, 124, 154

Thompson, R., 138
Thompson, R. A., 118, 131, 138
Thompson, R. F., 322
Thompson, V. A., 355
Thompson, W. L., 85
Thoreau, H. D., 494
Thoresen, C., 616
Thorndike, E. L., 273
Thorne, D., 231
Thorp, S. R., 584, 619
Thorson, C. J., 456
Thron, A., 243
Thulborn, K. R., 101
Thurow, M. E., 96
Thurston, S. W., 249
Tidy, J., 611
Tignol, J., 534
Tihonen, J., 246
Tillman, K. H., 403
Timimi, S., 530
Tinbergen, N., 486
Titchener, E. B., 9–10
Todaro, J. F., 466
Todd, M., 617
Todd, S., 191
Todorov, A., 474, 476
Toga, A, W., 123, 124
Toguchi, Y., 478
Tolin, D. F., 537
Tolman, E. C., 286, 287, 288
tom Dieck, S., 186
Tomarken, A. J., 96
Tomasello, M., 118, 226, 375, 376
Tompkins, S., 424
Tompkins, S. S., 424
Tong, F., 92, 195
Tong, T. Y., 231
Tonge, B. J., 570
Tonkin, A. L., 569
Tonz, K., 236
Toray, T., 397
Torres, A. R., 534
Tost, H., 540
Toth, M., 486
Toth, S. L., 134, 537, 544
Toulopoulou, T., 553
Tov, W., 23, 32
Townsend, M., 585
Towse, J. N., 333
Toyoda, H., 79
Traeger, L., 599
Traskman-Bendz, L., 546
Trautman, A., 274, 280, 296
Treanor, J. J., 8, 572, 620
Tremblay, R. E., 487
Treue, S., 179
Triandis, H. C., 409, 570
Tribukait, A., 213
Trimble, J. E., 591
Trimble, M. R., 540
Trivedi, A. N., 595
Troisi, C. L., 537
Trommsdorff, G., 136
Trope, Y., 476
Tropp, L. R., 504
Trotschel, R., 317
Trowell, J., 570

True, M. R., 546
True, W. R., 248
Trull, T. J., 523, 556, 557
Tryon, R., 104
Tryon, W. W., 578
Trzebinski, J., 451
Trzesniewski, K. H., 489
Tsakanikos, E., 175
Tsang, J., 8, 426, 427
Tsao, D., 92
Tsatalmpasidou, E., 223
Tsien, J. Z., 320, 322
Tsuang, M. T., 546
Tsuda, A., 254
Tucker, P., 141
Tugade, M. M., 428, 429
Tulving, E., 158, 314, 315, 324
Tuozzi, G., 235
Tupala, E., 246
Tural, U., 532
Turban, D., 408
Turecki, G., 546
Turiel, E., 136
Turk, D., 584
Turkington, D., 585
Turkington, T. G., 154
Turner, J., 8
Turner, J. A., 455
Turner, J. M. W., 194f
Turner, M. S., 568
Turner, R. B., 8, 572, 620
Twain, M., 426
Twitchell, G., 399
Tyas, S. L., 45
Tye, K. M., 541
Tyler, L. K., 188
Tyler, T. R., 499
Tyrer, P., 585
Tzelgov, J., 179

U

Uebel, H., 179
Uebelacker, L. A., 539
Ueda, K., 626
Ueno, K., 545
Uguz, F., 535
Uhlhaas, P. J., 577
Ulrich, L., 215
Ulrich, R. S., 215
Uluc, A. M., 221
Umberson, D., 510
Unger, J. B., 611
Ungerleider, L. G., 187
Urban, E., 441
Urbanowski, F., 96, 257
Urbina, S., 367
Urizar, G., 121
Urry, H. L., 96, 419
Urushihara, K., 287
Ussher, J., 590
Uylings, H. B., 534

V

Vacca, J. A. L., 379
Vaccca, R. T., 379
Vaidya, N. A., 571

Vaillant, G., 164, 248
Vaillant, G. E., 160, 161, 164, 248, 466
Valdez, J., 306
Valdimarsdottir, H., 428
Valenca, A. M., 532
Valencia, A. M., 532
Valencia-Flores, M., 236
Valentine, J. C., 329
Valentine, V., 225
Valero, J., 205
Valiente, C., 135
Vallabhajosula, S., 221
Van Aarle, E. J., 355
van Aken, M. A. G., 544
Van Ameringen, M., 49
van Baaren, R. B., 356
van Balkom, A. J., 534
van Bokhoven, I., 487
van de Coevering, M., 319
van de Riet, W. A., 422
Van den Boom, D. C., 134
van den Oord, E. J. C. G., 532, 534
van der Kolk, B. A., 549
Van Dijk, E., 508
Van Dongen, H. P., 231
Van Dyne, L., 456
van Eijk, J. T., 523
Van Elst, L. T., 540
van Engeland, H., 487
Van Es, J. J., 191
van Gogh, V., 357, *538*
van Goozen, S. H. M., 487
van Hateren, J. H., 185
van Ijzendoorn, M. H., 131, 134
Van Knippenberg, A., 317
Van Lange, P. A. M., 16, 484, 509
van Marie, K., 178
van Oppen, P., 534
Van Orden, K., 546
van Reekum, C. M., 96
Van Riper, M., 370
Van Vugt, M., 484, 508
Van Winkle, E., 486
Van Yperen, N. W., 509
Vandello, J. A., 488
Vandenbergh, D., 105
Vanni, S., 188
Vargo, S., 537
Varkonyi, A., 249
Varma, S., 592
Varney, L. L., 486
Varshney, N., 334
Vary, M. G., 536, 537
Vasil, J., 611
Vassiliades, V., 197
Vaughn, A. A., 428
Vaughn, S., 370
Vecchio, F., 322
Vedder, P., 59
Vedder, S. P., 147
Vega, V., 489
Vega-Lahr, N., 121
Veltman, D. J., 534
Vempati, R. P., 467
Veras, A. B., 532
Verbeek, J., 467

Page numbers in **boldface** indicate terms defined in the margin; *t* indicates a table; *f* indicates an illustration.

Assess Section Quiz Answer Key

Chapter 1: What is Psychology? (p. 2)

Defining Psychology (p. 4)

1. B, p. 5   4. B, p. 5
2. A, p. 7   5. B, p. 5
3. B, p. 7

The Roots and Early Scientific Approaches of Psychology (p. 9)

1. C, p. 10   4. B, p. 10
2. D, p. 10   5. B, p. 11
3. A, p. 11

Contemporary Approaches to Psychology (p. 12)

1. C, p. 13   4. D, p. 14
2. D, p. 14   5. D, p. 12
3. C, p. 15

Areas of Specialization and Careers in Psychology (p. 18)

1. A, p. 19   4. D, p. 19
2. D, p. 18   5. B, p. 20
3. A, p. 19

Psychology and Health and Wellness (p. 25)

1. D, p. 25   3. D, p. 26
2. D, p. 26   4. C, p. 26

Chapter 2: Psychology's Scientific Methods (p. 30)

Psychology's Scientific Method (p. 33)

1. C, p. 33   4. B, p. 37
2. D, p. 35   5. A, p. 34
3. B, p. 36

Research Settings and Types of Research (p. 37)

1. B, p. 41   4. D, p. 46
2. B, p. 46   5. B, p. 44
3. C, p. 46

Analyzing and Interpreting Data (p. 51)

1. A, p. 53   4. A, p. 52
2. B, pp. 52, 54   5. C, p. 53
3. B, p. 52

The Challenges of Conducting and Evaluating Psychological Research (p. 55)

1. C, p. 56   4. A, p. 62
2. D, p. 56   5. B, p. 56
3. C, p. 60

The Scientific Method and Health and Wellness (p. 63)

1. B, p. 64   3. D, p. 65
2. D, p. 63   4. C, p. 64

Chapter 3: Biological Foundations of Behavior (p. 70)

The Nervous System (p. 73)

1. C, p. 75   4. B, p. 73
2. C, p. 75   5. A, p. 73
3. B, p. 74

Neurons (p. 76)

1. D, p. 76   4. A, p. 81
2. C, pp. 76–77   5. B, p. 82
3. B, p. 78

Structures of the Brain and Their Functions (p. 84)

1. A, p. 91   4. A, p. 94
2. A, p. 85   5. B, p. 91
3. D, p. 89

The Endocrine System (p. 98)

1. B, pp. 98–99
2. A, p. 99
3. B, p. 99

Brain Damage, Plasticity, and Repair (p. 100)

1. D, p. 101   4. B, p. 101
2. D, p. 101   5. B, p. 100
3. A, p. 101

Genetics and Behavior (p. 103)

1. A, p. 107   4. C, p. 103
2. C, p. 105   5. B, p. 103
3. D, p. 104

Psychology's Biological Foundations and Health and Wellness (p. 108)

1. C, p. 109   3. B, p. 108
2. C, p. 109   4. B, p. 109

Chapter 4: Human Development (p. 114)

Exploring Human Development (p. 116)

1. A, p. 117   3. A, p. 118
2. C, p. 118   4. C, p. 118

Child Development (p. 119)

1. D, p. 133   4. B, p. 119
2. B, p. 130   5. C, p. 122
3. D, p. 125

Adolescence (p. 143)

1. C, p. 147   4. A, p. 144
2. D, p. 145   5. C, p. 147
3. B, p. 144

Adult Development and Aging (p. 150)

1. D, p. 156   4. C, p. 153
2. C, p. 150   5. D, p. 153
3. D, p. 152

Developmental Psychology and Health and Wellness (p. 163)

1. D, p. 163
2. B, p. 164
3. A, p. 164

Chapter 5: Sensation and Perception (p. 170)

How We Sense and Perceive the World (p. 172)

1. C, p. 173   4. C, p. 177
2. B, p. 173   5. B, p. 182
3. B, p. 179

The Visual System (p. 183)

1. C, pp. 183–84   4. C, p. 194
2. D, pp. 185–86   5. A, p. 190
3. B, p. 184

The Auditory System (p. 199)

1. A, p. 201   4. D, p. 207
2. D, p. 200   5. C, p. 204
3. B, p. 200

Other Senses (p. 207)

1. C, p. 207   4. C, p. 211
2. B, p. 209   5. A, p. 213
3. B, p. 211

Sensation, Perception, and Health and Wellness (p. 214)

1. A, p. 214   2. C, p. 215

Chapter 6: States of Consciousness (p. 220)

The Nature of Consciousness (p. 222)

1. B, p. 222   4. C, p. 225
2. A, p. 224   5. A, p. 225
3. D, p. 224

Sleep and Dreams (p. 228)

1. D, p. 228   4. B, p. 232
2. D, p. 229   5. B, p. 234
3. B, p. 238

Hypnosis (p. 241)

1. A, p. 242   3. C, p. 243
2. B, p. 242   4. D, p. 243

Psychoactive Drugs (p. 244)

1. C, p. 248   4. D, p. 245
2. C, p. 251   5. A, p. 249
3. D, p. 248

Consciousness and Health and Wellness (p. 256)

1. B, p. 257   3. C, p. 257
2. D, p. 257